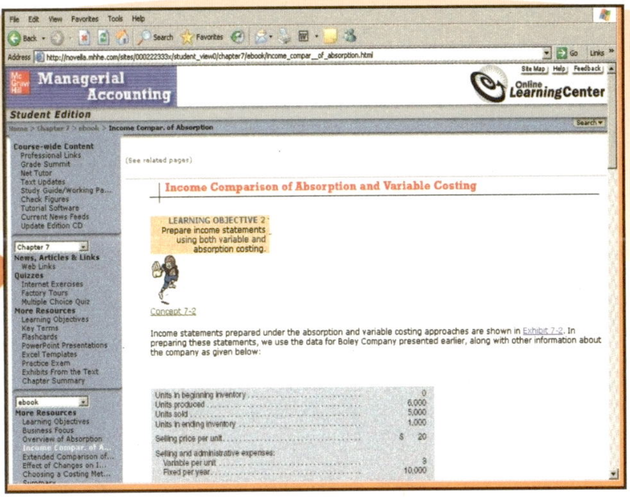

Interactive Online Version of the Textbook

In addition to the textbook, students can rely on this online version of the text for a convenient way to study. The interactive content is integrated with Homework Manager to give students quick access to relevant content as they work through problems, exercises, and practice quizzes.

Features:

- online version of the text is integrated with Homework Manager
- students referred to sections of the online book as they tackle an assignment or take a practice quiz

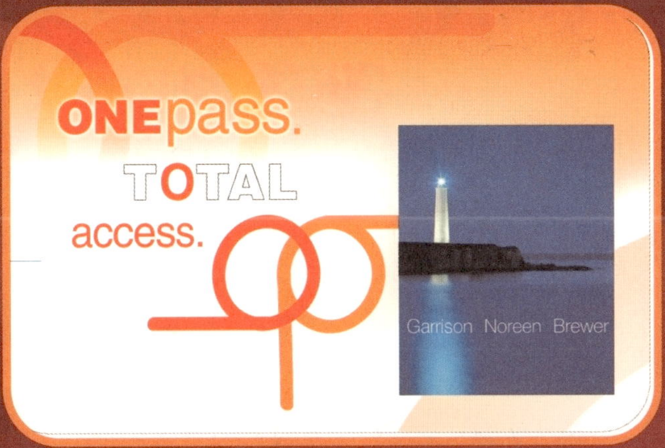

McGraw-Hill's OnePass eliminates the frustration of remembering multiple access codes for different online resources. Now students can use the access code found on their OnePass card to register and create one password for access to their book's online resources. By having just one access code for everything, students can go back and forth between tutorials as they study. And instructors can use OnePass to integrate these supplements into a learning path that fits a specific teaching style.

ONEpass

Homework Manager helps you

McGraw-Hill's
Homework
Manager

Assign coursework online

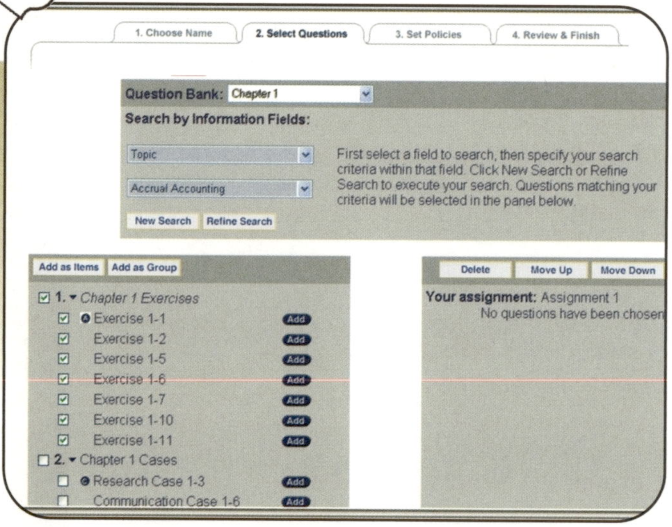

Problems and exercises from the book as well as questions from the testbank have been integrated into Homework Manager to give you many options as you deliver assignments and quizzes to students online. You can choose from static or algorithmic questions and have graded results automatically stored in your gradebook.

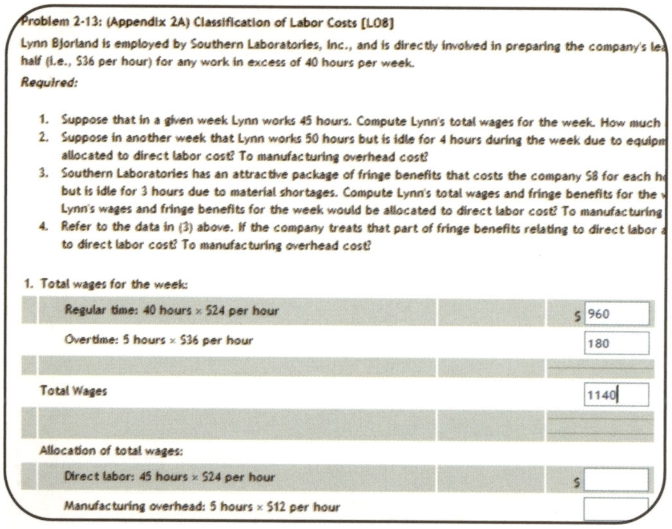

efficiently manage your class.

Control how content is presented.

Homework Manager gives you a flexible and easy way to present coursework to students. You determine which questions to ask and how much help students will receive as they work through assignments. For example, you can determine the number of attempts a student can make with each problem; provide hints and feedback with each question, including references to the online version of the text; and much more.

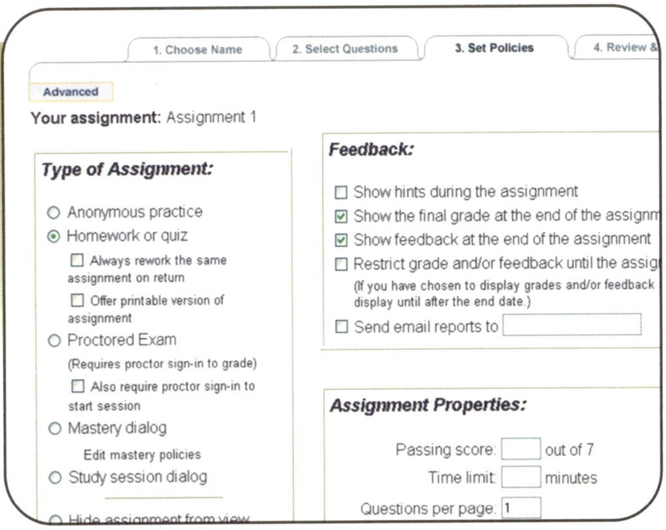

Track student progress.

Assignments are graded automatically, with the results stored in your private gradebook. Detailed results let you see at a glance how each student does on an assignment or an individual problem. You can even see how many attempts it took them to solve it. You can monitor how the whole class does on each problem, and even exactly where individual students might need extra help.

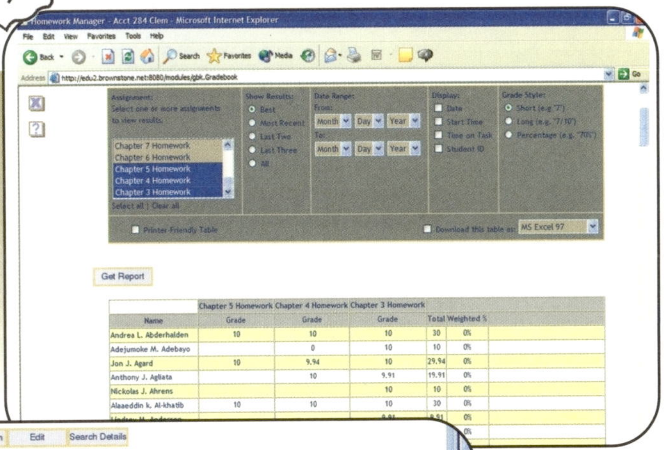

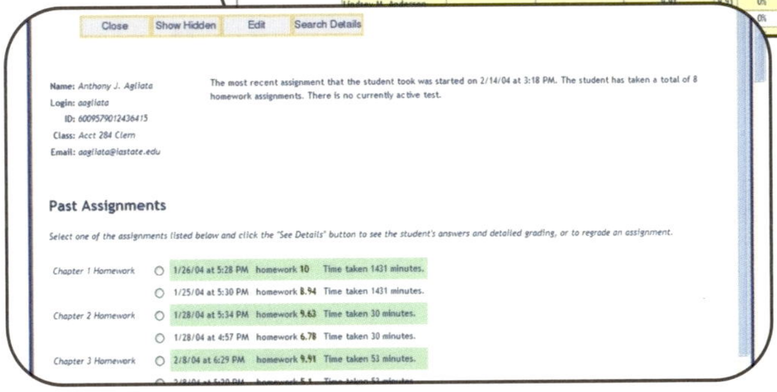

Professors can allow Homework Manager to give students helpful feedback.

Auto-grading and feedback.

Question 1: *Score 6.5/8*

Your response

Exercise 2-1: Using Cost Terms [LO2, LO5, LO7]

Following are a number of cost terms introduced in the chapter:

Period cost	Fixed cost
Variable cost	Prime cost
Opportunity cost	Conversion cost
Product cost	Sunk cost

Choose the cost term or terms above that most appropriately describe the costs identified in each of the following situations. A cost term can be used more than once.

1. Crestline Books, Inc., prints a small book titled *The Pocket Speller* . The paper going into the manufacture of the book would be called direct materials and classified as a Product cost (6%). In terms of cost behavior, the paper could also be described as a Product cost (0%) with respect to the number of books printed.
2. Instead of compiling the words in the book, the author hired by the company could have earned considerable fees consulting with business organizations. The consulting fees forgone by the author would be called Opportunity cost (6%).
3. The paper and other materials used in the manufacture of the book, combined with the direct labor cost involved, would be called Prime cost (6%).
4. The salary of Crestline Books' president would be classified as a Product cost (0%), and the salary will appear on the income statement as an expense in the time period in which it is incurred.
5. Depreciation on the equipment used to print the book would be classified by Crestline Books as a Product cost (6%). However, depreciation on any equipment used by the company in selling and administrative activities would be classified as a Period cost (6%). In terms of cost behavior, depreciation would probably be classified as a Fixed cost (6%) with respect to the number of books printed.
6. A Product cost (6%) is also known as an inventoriable cost,

Correct response

Exercise 2-1: Using Cost Terms [LO2, LO5, LO7]

Following are a number of cost terms introduced in the chapter:

Period cost	Fixed cost
Variable cost	Prime cost
Opportunity cost	Conversion cost
Product cost	Sunk cost

Choose the cost term or terms above that most appropriately describe the costs identified in each of the following situations. A cost term can be used more than once.

1. Crestline Books, Inc., prints a small book titled *The Pocket Speller* . The paper going into the manufacture of the book would be called direct materials and classified as a Product cost. In terms of cost behavior, the paper could also be described as a variable cost with respect to the number of books printed.
2. Instead of compiling the words in the book, the author hired by the company could have earned considerable fees consulting with business organizations. The consulting fees forgone by the author would be called Opportunity cost.
3. The paper and other materials used in the manufacture of the book, combined with the direct labor cost involved, would be called Prime cost.
4. The salary of Crestline Books' president would be classified as a Period cost, and the salary will appear on the income statement as an expense in the time period in which it is incurred.
5. Depreciation on the equipment used to print the book would be classified by Crestline Books as a Product cost. However, depreciation on any equipment used by the company in selling and administrative activities would be classified as a Period cost. In terms of cost behavior, depreciation would probably be classified as a Fixed cost with respect to the number of books printed.

INCORR

Immediately after finishing an assignment or quiz, students can compare their answers side by side with the detailed solutions. Students can try again with new numbers to see if they have mastered the concept.

Managerial Accounting

Eleventh Edition

Ray H. Garrison, D.B.A., CPA
Professor Emeritus
Brigham Young University

Eric W. Noreen, Ph.D., CMA
Professor Emeritus
University of Washington

Peter C. Brewer, Ph.D., CPA
Miami University—Oxford, Ohio

McGraw-Hill Irwin

Boston Burr Ridge, IL Dubuque, IA Madison, WI New York San Francisco St. Louis
Bangkok Bogotá Caracas Kuala Lumpur Lisbon London Madrid Mexico City
Milan Montreal New Delhi Santiago Seoul Singapore Sydney Taipei Toronto

Dedication

To our families and
to our many colleagues who use this book.

McGraw-Hill Irwin

MANAGERIAL ACCOUNTING

Published by McGraw-Hill/Irwin, a business unit of The McGraw-Hill Companies, Inc., 1221 Avenue of the Americas, New York, NY, 10020.

Some ancillaries, including electronic and print components, may not be available to customers outside the United States.

This book is printed on acid-free paper.

1 2 3 4 5 6 7 8 9 0 DOW/DOW 0 9 8 7 6 5 4

ISBN 0-07-283494-3 (student edition)

Editorial director: *Brent Gordon*
Publisher: *Stewart Mattson*
Executive editor: *Tim Vertovec*
Developmental editor I: *Sarah Wood*
Marketing manager: *Marc Chernoff*
Media producer: *Elizabeth Mavetz*
Lead project manager: *Pat Frederickson*
Production supervisor: *Debra R. Sylvester*
Lead designer: *Pam Verros*
Photo research coordinator: *Kathy Shive*
Photo researcher: *Charlotte Goldman*
Senior supplement producer: *Carol Loreth*
Senior digital content specialist: *Brian Nacik*
Cover photograph: © *Daryl Benson/Masterfile*
Typeface: *10.5/12 Times Roman*
Compositor: *Cenveo Indianapolis*
Printer: *R. R. Donnelley*

Library of Congress Cataloging-in-Publication Data

Garrison, Ray H.
Managerial accounting / Ray H. Garrison, Eric W. Noreen.—11th ed. / Ray H. Garrison, Eric W. Noreen, Peter C. Brewer.
p. cm.
Various multi-media instructional materials are available to supplement the text.
Includes index.
ISBN 0-07-283494-3 (alk. paper) — ISBN 0-07-298617-4 (aie : alk. paper)
1. Managerial accounting. I. Noreen, Eric W. II Brewer, Peter C. III. Title.
HF5657.4G37 2006
658.15'11—dc22

2004056942

www.mhhe.com

Garrison—Leading Textbook, Leading Technology

The wide array of technology assets that come with Managerial Accounting aren't add-ons thrown in at the last minute: They're extensions of the textbook itself, that work in unison to make managerial accounting as easy as possible to learn.

You may be tempted to put aside your CD and registration cards, planning to "get to them later"; you may even want to discard them outright. **Don't do it**! These supplements can offer you tremendous help as you go through the course; the sooner you become familiar with them, the sooner you can enjoy the immense benefits they have to offer.

Here's what you need to know to get the most out of *Managerial Accounting's* technology package.

Topic Tackler Plus

Topic Tackler provides focused help on the two most challenging topics in every chapter. How do you use Topic Tackler? Take your pick:

- Watch a short, high-quality video presentation.
- Review the topic highlights with a graphical slide show.
- Practice on numerous interactive exercises.
- Follow the links to more information on the World Wide Web.

However you want to use it, Topic Tackler is the perfect tool for review sessions, or just for some quick reinforcement as you read. Look for the Topic Tackler icon while you read—that means you'll find Topic Tackler ready to help you on that particular subject.

Turn to the inside front cover to learn how to get started using Topic Tackler!

OnePass eliminates the frustration of remembering multiple access codes for different online resources. Now students can use the access code found on their OnePass card to register and create one password for access to their book's online resources. By having just one access code for everything, students can go back and forth between tutorials as they study.

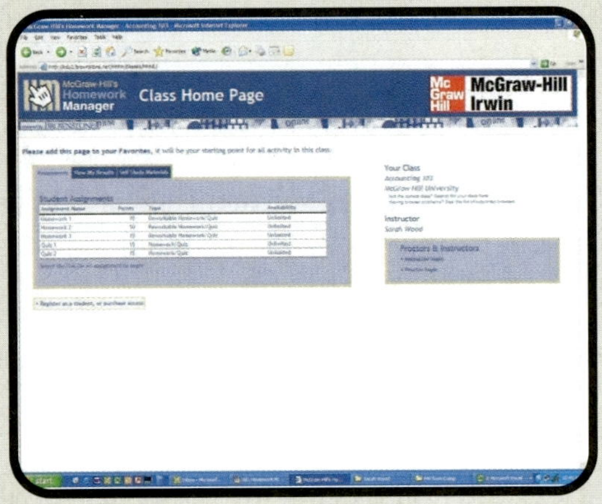

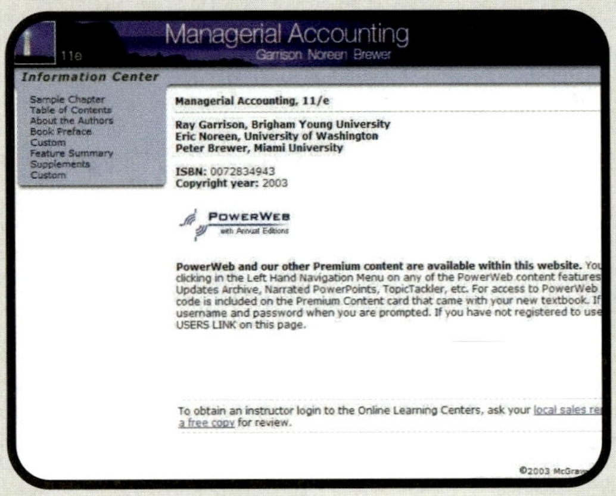

McGraw-Hill's Homework Manager

Practice makes perfect, and when it comes to managerial accounting, there's often no better practice than working with the numbers yourself. *Managerial Accounting* provides a great many problems for your instructor to assign or for you to do on your own, but there are only so many problems you can fit into a textbook. That's where McGraw-Hill's Homework Manager comes in.

McGraw-Hill's Homework Manager duplicates problems from the textbook in a convenient, online format. You can work problems and receive instant feedback on your answers, taking as many tries as you want. Because McGraw-Hill's Homework Manager uses specialized algorithms to generate values for each problem, it can produce infinite variations of certain text problems just by changing the values—you can practice on the same problem as many times as you need to, with fresh figures to work with every time.

Your instructor will have already decided whether to make McGraw-Hill's Homework Manager a part of your course, and he or she will create a course account and generate the assignments for you to do. Your McGraw-Hill's Homework Manager user guide will include an access code enabling you to enroll; refer to the guide for help in creating your account. Talk to your instructor to be sure McGraw-Hill's Homework Manager is available for you as you begin the course.

Online Learning Center (OLC)

When it comes to getting the most out of your textbook, the Online Learning Center is the place to start. The OLC follows *Managerial Accounting* chapter by chapter, offering all kinds of supplementary help for you as you read. OLC features include:

- Learning objectives
- Chapter overviews
- Internet-based activities
- Self-grading quizzes
- Links to text references
- Links to professional resources on the Web
- Job opportunity information
- Internet factory tours

Before you even start reading Chapter 1, go to this address and bookmark it:

www.mhhe.com/garrison11e

Remember, your Online Learning Center was created specifically to accompany Managerial Accounting—so don't let this great resource pass you by!

Student Supplements

Topic Tackler Plus CD-ROM

ISBN 0072986166

Free with the text, the Topic Tackler CD-ROM helps students master difficult concepts in managerial accounting through a creative, interactive learning process. Designed for study outside the classroom, this multimedia CD delves into chapter concepts with graphical slides and diagrams, Web links, video clips, and animations, all centered around engaging exercises designed to put students in control of their learning of managerial accounting topics.

Workbook/Study Guide

ISBN 0072986131

This study aid provides suggestions for studying chapter material, summarizes essential points in each chapter, and tests students' knowledge using self-test questions and exercises.

Ready Notes

ISBN 0073080667

This booklet provides Ready Slide exhibits in a workbook format for efficient note taking.

Student Lecture Aid

ISBN 007298614X

Much like the Ready Notes, this booklet offers a hard-copy version of all the Teaching Transparencies. Students can annotate the material during the lecture and take notes in the space provided.

Working Papers

ISBN 0072986123

This study aid contains forms that help students organize their solutions to homework problems.

Excel Templates

Prepared by Jack Terry of ComSource Associates, Inc., this spreadsheet-based software uses Excel to solve selected problems and cases in the text. These selected problems and cases are identified in the margin of the text with an appropriate icon. The Student Excel Templates are only available on the text's Web site.

Telecourse Guide

ISBN 0072986115

This study guide ties the Dallas County Community College Telecourse directly to this text.

Acknowledgments

Suggestions have been received from many of our colleagues throughout the world who have used the prior edition of Managerial Accounting. This is vital feedback that we rely on in each edition. Each of those who have offered comments and suggestions has our thanks.

The efforts of many people are needed to develop and improve a text. Among these people are the reviewers and consultants who point out areas of concern, cite areas of strength, and make recommendations for change. In this regard, the following professors provided feedback that was enormously helpful in preparing the eleventh edition of Managerial Accounting:

Noel Addy, Mississippi State University
Jack Bailes, Oregon State University
Mohamed Bayou, University of Michigan - Dearborn
Linda Benz, Jefferson Community College
Karen Bird, University of Michigan
Phillip A. Blanchard, University of Arizona
Lisa Bonitati Church, Rhode Island College
Arthur Braza, Three Rivers Community College
Sarah Brown, University of North Alabama
George R. Cash, Alabama A&M University
Kimberly Charron, University of Nevada Las Vegas
Julie Chenier, Louisiana State University - Baton Rouge
Richard Claire, Cañada College
Antoinette Clegg, Palm Beach Community College
Nolan Clemens, Jr., University of Dallas
Deb Cosgrove, University of Nebraska - Lincoln
Rita Counts, Radford University
Kraeg Danvers, Wayne State University
Betty David, Francis Marion University
Charles Davis, Baylor University
Dr. Henry Day, Mount Olive College
Patricia A. Doherty, Boston University
Carleton Donchess, Bridgewater State College
Roger Doost, Clemson University
Robert Deutsch, Campbell University
Barbara Eide, University of Wisconsin - La Crosse
Dennis Elam, Southwest Texas University
Jack R. Fay, Pittsburgh State University
Richard Fleischman, John Carroll University
Karen M. Foust, Tulane University
Susan Coomer Galbreath, Lipscomb University
Les Heitger, Indiana University - Bloomington
Sharon J. Huxley, Teikyo Post University
Wayne Ingalls, University of Maine
Gene Johnson, Clark College
Celina Jozsi, University of South Florida
Carl Keller, Indiana University - Purdue University at Ft. Wayne
Zafar Khan, Eastern Michigan University
Mike Klickman, University of Dallas
Frank Kopczynski, Plymouth State University
Barbara Kren, Marquette University
Kip Krumwiede, Brigham Young University
Sandra S. Lang, McKendree College
Chor T. Lau, California State University - Los Angeles
Keith Leeseberg, Manatee Community College
C. Angela Letourneau, Winthrop University
Robert Lin, California State University - Hayward
Larry Logan, University of Massachusetts - Dartmouth
Dr. Tim Lowder, Francis Marion University
Suzanne Lowensohn, Colorado State University
Gina Lord, Santa Rosa Junior College
Dorinda Lynn, Pensacola Jr. College

Lois Mahoney, University of Central Florida
Robert McConkie, Bethany College
Helga M. Mervine, Mercyhurst College
Betty K. Mullins, Hesser College
Kevin Nathan, Oakland University
Marguerite Nagy, Cuyahoga Community College
Kevin Nathan, Oakland University
Emeka T. Nwaeze, Rutgers University
Margaret O'Reilly-Allen, Rider University
Janet L. O'Tousa, University of Notre Dame
Emil A. Radosevich, Alberquerque Technical Vocational Institute
Judy Ann Ramage, Christian Brothers University
Martha Rassi, Glendale Community College
Dr. David Remmele, University of Wisconsin-Whitewater
Kimberley A. Richardson, James Madison University
John C. Roberts, St. Johns River Community College
Marilyn Salter, University of Central Florida
Angela Sandberg, Jacksonville State University
George Schmelzle, Indiana Purdue Fort Wayne
James A. Schweikart, Boston University
Ann Selk, University of Wisconsin, Green Bay
Lewis Shaw, Suffolk University
Jeff Shields, University of Southern Maine
John W. Shishoff, University of Dayton
Khim L. Sim, Western New England College
Bonnie Simmons, Elmhurst College
Kenneth Sinclair, Lehigh University
Douglas L. Smith, Samford University
Toni Smith, University of New Hampshire
Beverly Soriano, Framingham State College
Philip Stickney, Cochise College
Jeffrey M. Storm, Lincoln Land Community College
Suzy Summers, Furman University
Lateef Syed, Dominican University
Rita N. Taylor, University of Cincinnati
Gerald Thalman, North Central College
Ralph Tower, Wake Forest University
Michael Tyler, Barry University
Sankaran Venkateswar, Trinity University
Ron Vogel, College of Eastern Utah
Frank Walker, Lee University
Dan Ward, University of Louisiana at Lafayette
Marcia Weidenmier, Texas Christian University
Charles Wellens, Fitchburg State College
Micheline West, New Hampshire Community Technical College - Manchester
Jack Wiehler, San Joaquin Delta College
Priscilla Wisner, American Graduate School of International Business
Dr. Rahnl Wood, Northwest Missouri State University
Eric Yap, Ohlone College
Jennifer Yin, Rutgers University

We are grateful for the outstanding support from McGraw-Hill/Irwin. In particular, we would like to thank Brent Gordon, Editorial Director; Stewart Mattson, Publisher; Tim Vertovec, Executive Editor; Sarah Wood, Developmental Editor; Marc Chernoff, Marketing Manager; Pat Frederickson, Lead Project Manager; Debra Sylvester, Production Supervisor; Pam Verros, Lead Designer; Carol Loreth, Senior Supplement Producer; Kathy Shive, Photo Research Coordinator, Elizabeth Mavetz, Media Producer; Dan Wiencek, Advertising Manager; and Erwin Llereza, Advertising Manager.

Finally, we would like to thank Beth Woods and Barbara Schnathorst for working so hard to ensure an error-free eleventh edition.

We are grateful to the Institute of Certified Management Accountants for permission to use questions and/or unofficial answers from past Certificate in Management Accounting (CMA) examinations. Likewise, we thank the American Institute of Certified Public Accountants, the Society of Management Accountants of Canada, and the Chartered Institute of Management Accountants (United Kingdom) for permission to use (or to adapt) selected problems from their examinations. These problems bear the notations CPA, SMA, and CIMA respectively.

Ray H. Garrison • Eric Noreen • Peter Brewer

CONTENTS

Chapter 1

Managerial Accounting and the Business Environment 2

The Work of Management and the Need for Managerial Accounting Information 4

Planning 5

Directing and Motivating 5

Controlling 5

The End Results of Managers' Activities 6

The Planning and Control Cycle 6

Comparison of Financial and Managerial Accounting 6

Emphasis on the Future 6

Relevance of Data 8

Less Emphasis on Precision 8

Segments of an Organization 8

Generally Accepted Accounting Principles (GAAP) 9

Managerial Accounting—Not Mandatory 9

Organizational Structure 9

Decentralization 9

Line and Staff Relationships 10

The Chief Financial Officer 11

The Changing Business Environment 12

Just-In-Time (JIT) 12

JIT Consequences 14

Benefits of a JIT System 15

Total Quality Management (TQM) 15

Process Reengineering 16

The Theory of Constraints (TOC) 17

International Competition 18

E-Commerce 19

Professional Ethics 20

Code of Conduct for Management Accountants 22

Company Codes of Conduct 24

Codes of Conduct on the International Level 26

The Certified Management Accountant (CMA) 27

Summary 27

Glossary 28

Questions 29

Exercises 30

Problems 31

Group and Internet Exercises 33

Chapter 2

Cost Terms, Concepts, and Classifications 34

General Cost Classifications 36

Manufacturing Costs 36

Direct Materials 36

Direct Labor 36

Manufacturing Overhead 37

Nonmanufacturing Costs 38

Product Costs versus Period Costs 38

Product Costs 38

Period Costs 39

Cost Classifications on Financial Statements 41

The Balance Sheet 41

The Income Statement 42

Schedule of Cost of Goods Manufactured 43

Product Cost Flows 45

Inventoriable Costs 45

An Example of Cost Flows 46

Cost Classifications for Predicting Cost Behavior 48

Variable Cost 48

Fixed Cost 49

Cost Classifications for Assigning Costs to Cost Objects 50

Direct Cost 50

Indirect Cost 50

Cost Classifications for Decision Making 51

Differential Cost and Revenue 51

Opportunity Cost 52

Example 1 52

Example 2 52

Example 3 52

Sunk Cost 53

Summary 53

Review Problem 1: Cost Terms 54

Review Problem 2: Schedule of Cost of Goods Manufactured and Income Statement 55

Glossary *57*
Appendix 2A: Further Classification of Labor Costs *58*
Appendix 2B: Cost of Quality *59*
Questions *68*
Exercises *69*
Problems *73*
Cases *82*
Group and Internet Exercises *84*

Chapter 3

Systems Design: Job-Order Costing 86

Process and Job-Order Costing 88
Process Costing 88
Job-Order Costing 89
Job-Order Costing—An Overview 89
Measuring Direct Materials Cost 90
Job Cost Sheet 91
Measuring Direct Labor Cost 91
Application of Manufacturing Overhead 93
Using the Predetermined Overhead Rate *94*
The Need for a Predetermined Rate *94*
Choice of an Allocation Base for Overhead Cost 96
Computation of Unit Costs 96
Summary of Document Flows 96
Job-Order Costing—The Flow of Costs 98
The Purchase and Issue of Materials 98
Issue of Direct and Indirect Materials *98*
Issue of Direct Materials Only *99*
Labor Cost 99
Manufacturing Overhead Costs 100
The Application of Manufacturing Overhead 101
The Concept of a Clearing Account *101*
Nonmanufacturing Costs 102
Cost of Goods Manufactured 103
Cost of Goods Sold 103
Summary of Cost Flows 104
Problems of Overhead Application 104
Underapplied and Overapplied Overhead 104
Disposition of Under- or Overapplied Overhead Balances 109
Closed Out to Cost of Goods Sold *109*
Allocated between Accounts *110*
A General Model of Product Cost Flows 110
Multiple Predetermined Overhead Rates 110
Job-Order Costing in Service Companies 111
Use of Information Technology 112
Summary *113*
Review Problem: Job-Order Costing *114*
Glossary *116*
Appendix 3A: The Predetermined Overhead Rate and Capacity *117*
Questions *118*
Exercises *119*
Problems *126*
Cases *138*
Group and Internet Exercises *142*

Chapter 4

Systems Design: Process Costing 144

Comparison of Job-Order and Process Costing 146
Similarities between Job-Order and Process Costing 146
Differences between Job-Order and Process Costing 146
A Perspective of Process Cost Flows 147
Processing Departments 147
The Flow of Materials, Labor, and Overhead Costs 148
Materials, Labor, and Overhead Cost Entries 148
Materials Costs *149*
Labor Costs *149*
Overhead Costs *150*
Completing the Cost Flows *150*
Equivalent Units of Production 152
Weighted-Average Method 152
Production Report—Weighted-Average Method 153
Step 1: Prepare a Quantity Schedule and Compute the Equivalent Units 155
Step 2: Compute Costs per Equivalent Unit 156
Step 3: Prepare a Cost Reconciliation 156
Example of a Cost Reconciliation *156*
Operation Costing 159
Summary *159*
Review Problem: Process Cost Flows and Reports *160*
Glossary *162*
Appendix 4A: FIFO Method *162*
Questions *168*
Exercises *169*
Problems *174*
Cases *180*
Group and Internet Exercises *181*

Chapter 5

Cost Behavior: Analysis and Use 182

Types of Cost Behavior Patterns 184
Variable Costs 184
The Activity Base 185
Extent of Variable Costs 186
True Variable versus Step-Variable Costs 187
True Variable Costs 187
Step-Variable Costs 187
The Linearity Assumption and the Relevant Range 188
Fixed Costs 188
Types of Fixed Costs 190
Committed Fixed Costs 190
Discretionary Fixed Costs 191
The Trend toward Fixed Costs 192
Is Labor a Variable or a Fixed Cost? 192
Fixed Costs and the Relevant Range 193
Mixed Costs 194

The Analysis of Mixed Costs 196
Diagnosing Cost Behavior with a Scattergraph Plot 198
The High-Low Method 201
The Least-Squares Regression Method 204
Multiple Regression Analysis 206

The Contribution Format Income Statement 206
Why a New Income Statement Format? 206
The Contribution Approach 207

Summary 207
Review Problem 1: Cost Behavior 208
Review Problem 2: High-Low Method 209
Glossary 210
Appendix 5A: Least-Squares Regression Using Microsoft® Excel 210
Questions 212
Exercises 213
Problems 217
Cases 223
Group and Internet Exercises 227

Chapter 6

Cost-Volume-Profit Relationships 228

The Basics of Cost-Volume-Profit (CVP) Analysis 231
Contribution Margin 231
CVP Relationships in Graphic Form 233
Preparing the CVP Graph 233
Contribution Margin Ratio (CM Ratio) 235
Some Applications of CVP Concepts 236
Change in Fixed Cost and Sales Volume 236
Change in Variable Costs and Sales Volume 237
Change in Fixed Cost, Sales Price, and Sales Volume 237
Change in Variable Cost, Fixed Cost, and Sales Volume 238
Change in Regular Sales Price 239

Break-Even Analysis 239
Break-Even Computations 239
The Equation Method 239
The Contribution Margin Method 240
Target Profit Analysis 241
The CVP Equation 241
The Contribution Margin Approach 242
The Margin of Safety 242

CVP Considerations in Choosing a Cost Structure 244
Cost Structure and Profit Stability 244
Operating Leverage 246

Structuring Sales Commissions 247

The Concept of Sales Mix 248
The Definition of Sales Mix 248
Sales Mix and Break-Even Analysis 248

Assumptions of CVP Analysis 250

Summary 251
Review Problem: CVP Relationships 251
Glossary 254
Questions 254
Exercises 255
Problems 260
Cases 268
Group and Internet Exercises 272

Chapter 7

Variable Costing: A Tool for Management 274

Overview of Absorption and Variable Costing 276
Absorption Costing 276
Variable Costing 276
Unit Cost Computations 277

Income Comparison of Absorption and Variable Costing 278

Extended Comparison of Income Data 280

Effect of Changes in Production on Net Operating Income 284
Variable Costing 285
Absorption Costing 285
Choosing a Costing Method 288
The Impact on the Manager 288
CVP Analysis and Absorption Costing 289
Decision Making 290
External Reporting and Income Taxes 290
Advantages of Variable Costing and the Contribution Approach 291
Variable Costing and the Theory of Constraints 292
Impact of JIT Inventory Methods 292

Summary 293
Review Problem: Contrasting Variable and Absorption Costing 293
Glossary 295
Questions 295
Exercises 296
Problems 300
Cases 306
Group and Internet Exercises 310

Chapter 8

Activity-Based Costing: A Tool to Aid Decision Making 312

How Costs Are Treated under Activity-Based Costing 315
Nonmanufacturing Costs and Activity-Based Costing 315
Manufacturing Costs and Activity-Based Costing 315
Plantwide Overhead Rate 315
Departmental Overhead Rates 316
The Costs of Idle Capacity in Activity-Based Costing 317
Designing an Activity-Based Costing (ABC) System 317
Step 1: Identify and Define Activities and Activity Cost Pools 320
The Mechanics of Activity-Based Costing 323
Step 2: Whenever Possible, Directly Trace Overhead Costs to Activities and Cost Objects 323
Step 3: Assign Costs to Activity Cost Pools 324
Step 4: Calculate Activity Rates 327
Step 5: Assign Costs to Cost Objects 328
Step 6: Prepare Management Reports 330
Comparison of Traditional and ABC Product Costs 330
Product Margins Computed Using the Traditional Cost System 330
The Differences between ABC and Traditional Product Costs 331
Targeting Process Improvements 335
Activity-Based Costing and External Reports 337
The Limitations of Activity-Based Costing 338

Summary 339
Review Problem: Activity-Based Costing 340
Glossary 341
Appendix 8A: ABC Action Analysis 342
Questions 350
Exercises 351
Problems 361
Cases 369
Group and Internet Exercises 375

Chapter 9

Profit Planning 376

The Basic Framework of Budgeting 378
Personal Budgets 378
Difference between Planning and Control 378
Advantages of Budgeting 378
Responsibility Accounting 379
Choosing a Budget Period 380
The Self-Imposed Budget 381
Human Factors in Budgeting 382
Zero-Based Budgeting 382
The Budget Committee 384
The Master Budget: An Overview 385
The Sales Budget 385
The Cash Budget 385
Sales Forecasting—A Critical Step 385
Preparing the Master Budget 387
The Sales Budget 389
The Production Budget 390
Inventory Purchases—Merchandising Company 391
The Direct Materials Budget 391
The Direct Labor Budget 393
The Manufacturing Overhead Budget 394
The Ending Finished Goods Inventory Budget 395
The Selling and Administrative Expense Budget 395
The Cash Budget 396

The Budgeted Income Statement 399
The Budgeted Balance Sheet 400
International Aspects of Budgeting 402
Summary 403
Review Problem: Budget Schedules 403
Glossary 405
Questions 406
Exercises 406
Problems 408
Cases 421
Group and Internet Exercises 425

Chapter 10

Standard Costs and the Balanced Scorecard 426

Standard Costs—Management by Exception 429
Who Uses Standard Costs? 430
Setting Standard Costs 431
Ideal versus Practical Standards 431
Setting Direct Materials Standards 432
Setting Direct Labor Standards 432
Setting Variable Manufacturing Overhead Standards 434
Are Standards the Same as Budgets? 435
A General Model for Variance Analysis 435
Price and Quantity Variances 435
Using Standard Costs—Direct Materials Variances 436
Materials Price Variance—A Closer Look 438
Isolation of Variances 439
Responsibility for the Variance 439
Materials Quantity Variance—A Closer Look 440
Using Standard Costs—Direct Labor Variances 441
Labor Rate Variance—A Closer Look 441
Labor Efficiency Variance—A Closer Look 442
Using Standard Costs—Variable Manufacturing Overhead Variances 443
Manufacturing Overhead Variances—A Closer Look 443
Variance Analysis and Management by Exception 445
International Uses of Standard Costs 447
Evaluation of Controls Based on Standard Costs 447
Advantages of Standard Costs 447
Potential Problems with the Use of Standard Costs 448
Balanced Scorecard 449
Common Characteristics of Balanced Scorecards 450
A Company's Strategy and the Balanced Scorecard 452
Tying Compensation to the Balanced Scorecard 454
Advantages of Timely and Graphic Feedback 454
Some Measures of Internal Business Process Performance 456
Delivery Cycle Time 456
Throughput (Manufacturing Cycle) Time 456
Manufacturing Cycle Efficiency (MCE) 457
Some Final Observations Concerning the Balanced Scorecard 458
Summary 459
Review Problem: Standard Costs 459
Glossary 461
Appendix 10A: General Ledger Entries to Record Variances 462
Questions 464
Exercises 465
Problems 471
Cases 484
Group and Internet Exercises 488

Chapter 11

Flexible Budgets and Overhead Analysis 490

Flexible Budgets 492
Characteristics of a Flexible Budget 492
Deficiencies of the Static Budget 493
How a Flexible Budget Works 494
Using the Flexible Budgeting Concept in Performance Evaluation 495
The Measure of Activity—A Critical Choice 498
Variable Overhead Variances—A Closer Look 498
Actual versus Standard Hours 498
Spending Variance Alone 499
Interpreting the Spending Variance 500
Both Spending and Efficiency Variances 500
Interpreting the Efficiency Variance 500
Control of the Efficiency Variance 501
Activity-Based Costing and the Flexible Budget 502
Overhead Rates and Fixed Overhead Analysis 502
Flexible Budgets and Overhead Rates 502
Denominator Activity 503
Computing the Overhead Rate 504
Overhead Application in a Standard Cost System 505
The Fixed Overhead Variances 505

The Budget Variance—A Closer Look 506
The Volume Variance—A Closer Look 507
Graphic Analysis of Fixed Overhead Variances 508
Cautions in Fixed Overhead Analysis 509
Overhead Variances and Under- or Overapplied Overhead Cost 509

Summary 509
Review Problem: Overhead Analysis 510
Glossary 512
Questions 513
Exercises 513
Problems 519
Cases 531
Group and Internet Exercises 535

Chapter 12

Segment Reporting and Decentralization 538

Decentralization in Organizations 540
Advantages and Disadvantages of Decentralization 540

Responsibility Accounting 541
Cost, Profit, and Investment Centers 541
Cost Center 541
Profit Center 541
Investment Center 542
An Organizational View of Responsibility Centers 542

Decentralization and Segment Reporting 543
Building a Segmented Income Statement 543
Levels of Segmented Statements 546
Sales and Contribution Margin 546
Traceable and Common Fixed Costs 548
Identifying Traceable Fixed Costs 548
Activity-Based Costing 548
Traceable Costs Can Become Common Costs 550
Segment Margin 550
Segmented Financial Information on External Reports 552

Hindrances to Proper Cost Assignment 553
Omission of Costs 553
Inappropriate Methods for Assigning Traceable Costs among Segments 554
Failure to Trace Costs Directly 554
Inappropriate Allocation Base 554
Arbitrarily Dividing Common Costs among Segments 554

Evaluating Investment Center Performance—Return on Investment 555
The Return on Investment (ROI) Formula 556
Net Operating Income and Operating Assets Defined 556
Understanding ROI—The DuPont Perspective 556
Example 1: Increased Sales without Any Increase in Operating Assets 558
Example 2: Decreased Operating Expenses with No Change in Sales or Operating Assets 559
Example 3: Decreased Operating Assets with No Change in Sales or Operating Expenses 559
Example 4: Invest in Operating Assets to Increase Sales 560
ROI and the Balanced Scorecard 560
Criticisms of ROI 561

Residual Income 561
Motivation and Residual Income 563
Divisional Comparison and Residual Income 563

Summary 565
Review Problem 1: Segmented Statements 565
Review Problem 2: Return on Investment (ROI) and Residual Income 565
Glossary 567
Appendix 12A: Transfer Pricing 568
Review Problem 3: Transfer Pricing 574
Questions 576
Exercises 576
Problems 582
Cases 594
Group and Internet Exercises 597

Chapter 13

Relevant Costs for Decision Making 600

Cost Concepts for Decision Making 601
Identifying Relevant Costs and Benefits 601
Different Costs for Different Purposes 602
An Example of Identifying Relevant Costs and Benefits 602
Reconciling the Total and Differential Approaches 606
Why Isolate Relevant Costs? 608

Adding and Dropping Product Lines and Other Segments 609
An Illustration of Cost Analysis 609
A Comparative Format 611

Beware of Allocated Fixed Costs 611
The Make or Buy Decision 613
Strategic Aspects of the Make or Buy Decision 613
An Example of Make or Buy 614
Opportunity Cost 615
Special Orders 616
Utilization of a Constrained Resource 618
Contribution in Relation to a Constrained Resource 618
Managing Constraints 620
The Problem of Multiple Constraints 621
Joint Product Costs and the Contribution Approach 622
The Pitfalls of Allocation 622
Sell or Process Further Decisions 622
Activity-Based Costing and Relevant Costs 625
Summary 626
Review Problem: Relevant Costs 626
Glossary 627
Questions 628
Exercises 628
Problems 634
Cases 642
Group and Internet Exercises 650

Chapter 14

Capital Budgeting Decisions 652

Capital Budgeting—Planning Investments 654
Typical Capital Budgeting Decisions 654
The Time Value of Money 654
Discounted Cash Flows—The Net Present Value Method 655
The Net Present Value Method Illustrated 655
Emphasis on Cash Flows 657
Typical Cash Outflows 657
Typical Cash Inflows 657
Recovery of the Original Investment 658
Simplifying Assumptions 658
Choosing a Discount Rate 659
An Extended Example of the Net Present Value Method 659
Discounted Cash Flows—The Internal Rate of Return Method 661
The Internal Rate of Return Method Illustrated 661
Salvage Value and Other Cash Flows 661
Using the Internal Rate of Return 662
The Cost of Capital as a Screening Tool 662
Comparison of the Net Present Value and the Internal Rate of Return Methods 662
Expanding the Net Present Value Method 663
The Total-Cost Approach 663
The Incremental-Cost Approach 665
Least-Cost Decisions 666
Uncertain Cash Flows 667
An Example 668
Real Options 668
Preference Decisions—The Ranking of Investment Projects 669
Internal Rate of Return Method 669
Net Present Value Method 670
Other Approaches to Capital Budgeting Decisions 670
The Payback Method 671
Evaluation of the Payback Method 671
An Extended Example of Payback 673
Payback and Uneven Cash Flows 674
The Simple Rate of Return Method 674
Criticisms of the Simple Rate of Return 676
Postaudit of Investment Projects 676
Summary 677
Review Problem 1: Basic Present Value Computations 678
Review Problem 2: Comparison of Capital Budgeting Methods 679
Glossary 680
Appendix 14A: The Concept of Present Value 681
Appendix 14B: Inflation and Capital Budgeting 684
Appendix 14C: Future Value and Present Value Tables 687
Appendix 14D: Income Taxes in Capital Budgeting Decisions 691
Questions 695
Exercises 696
Problems 702
Cases 710
Group and Internet Exercises 714

Chapter 15

Service Department Costing: An Activity Approach 716

Allocations Using the Direct and Step Methods 718
Selecting Allocation Bases 718

Interdepartmental Services 719
Direct Method 720
Step Method 721
Reciprocal Method 722
Revenue Producing Departments 723
Allocating Costs by Behavior 723
Variable Costs 723
Fixed Costs 723
Should Actual or Budgeted Costs Be Allocated? 724
A Summary of Cost Allocation Guidelines 725
Implementing the Allocation Guidelines 725
Base Allocation Techniques 725
Effect of Allocations on Operating Departments 727
An Extended Example 728
Some Cautions in Allocating Service Department Costs 729
Pitfalls in Allocating Fixed Costs 729
Beware of Sales Dollars as an Allocation Base 731
Summary 732
Review Problem: Direct and Step Methods 733
Glossary 734
Questions 734
Exercises 734
Problems 738
Cases 743
Group and Internet Exercises 746

Chapter 16

"How Well Am I Doing?" Statement of Cash Flows 748

The Basic Approach to a Statement of Cash Flows 750
Definition of Cash 750
Constructing the Statement of Cash Flows Using Changes in Noncash Balance Sheet Accounts 751
An Example of a Simplified Statement of Cash Flows 753
Constructing a Simplified Statement of Cash Flows 753
The Need for a More Detailed Statement 755
Organization of the Full-Fledged Statement of Cash Flows 756
Operating Activities 756
Investing Activities 757
Financing Activities 757
Other Issues in Preparing the Statement of Cash Flows 758
Cash Flows: Gross or Net? 758
Operating Activities: Direct or Indirect Method? 758
Direct Exchange Transactions 759
An Example of a Full-Fledged Statement of Cash Flows 759
Eight Basic Steps to Preparing the Statement of Cash Flows 759
Setting Up the Worksheet (Steps 1–4) 761
Adjustments to Reflect Gross, Rather than Net, Amounts (Step 5) 762
Classifying Entries as Operating, Investing, or Financing Activities (Step 6) 764
The Completed Statement of Cash Flows (Steps 7 and 8) 765
Interpretation of the Statement of Cash Flows 765
Depreciation, Depletion, and Amortization 766
Summary 767
Review Problem 768
Glossary 770
Appendix 16A: The Direct Method of Determining the Net Cash Provided by Operating Activities 771
Questions 772
Exercises 773
Problems 776
Group and Internet Exercises 783

Chapter 17

"How Well Am I Doing?" Financial Statement Analysis 786

Limitations of Financial Statement Analysis 788
Comparison of Financial Data 788
The Need to Look beyond Ratios 788
Statement in Comparative and Common-Size Form 789
Dollar and Percentage Changes on Statements 789
Common-Size Statements 789
Ratio Analysis—The Common Stockholder 794
Earnings per Share 794
Price-Earnings Ratio 794
Dividend Payout and Yield Ratios 795
The Dividend Payout Ratio 795
The Dividend Yield Ratio 795
Return on Total Assets 795
Return on Common Stockholders' Equity 796
Financial Leverage 796
Book Value per Share 797

Ratio Analysis—The Short-Term Creditor 798
Working Capital 798
Current Ratio 798
Acid-Test (Quick) Ratio 799
Accounts Receivable Turnover 800
Inventory Turnover 800
Ratio Analysis—The Long-Term Creditor 801
Times Interest Earned Ratio 801
Debt-to-Equity Ratio 802
Summary of Ratios and Sources of Comparative Ratio Data 802
Summary 802
Review Problem: Selected Ratios and Financial Leverage 804
Glossary 807
Questions 807
Exercises 807
Problems 812

Appendix A
Pricing Products and Services 824
Introduction 825
The Economists' Approach to Pricing 825
Elasticity of Demand 826
The Profit-Maximizing Price 827
The Absorption Costing Approach to Cost-Plus Pricing 830
Setting a Target Selling Price Using the Absorption Costing Approach 830
Determining the Markup Percentage 831
Problems with the Absorption Costing Approach 832
Target Costing 833
Reasons for Using Target Costing 833
An Example of Target Costing 834
Summary 834
Glossary 835
Questions 835
Exercises 835
Problems 836

Appendix B
Profitability Analysis 840
Introduction 841
Absolute Profitability 841
Relative Profitability 841
Volume Trade-Off Decisions 844
Managerial Implications 846
Summary 847
Glossary 848
Questions 848
Exercises 848
Problems 849
Cases 852

Photo Credits 853
Index 854

Chapter

1

Managerial Accounting and the Business Environment

LEARNING OBJECTIVES

After studying Chapter 1, you should be able to:

LO1 Identify the major differences and similarities between financial and managerial accounting.

LO2 Understand the role of management accountants in an organization.

LO3 Understand the basic concepts underlying Just-In-Time (JIT), Total Quality Management (TQM), Process Reengineering, and the Theory of Constraints (TOC).

LO4 Understand the importance of upholding ethical standards.

Making Fact-Based Decisions in Real Time

BUSINESS FOCUS

Cisco Systems and Alcoa are on the leading edge of their industries and real-time management accounting is one of the keys to their success. Managers at these companies can drill down into the company's management accounting system to find the latest data on revenues, margins, order backlogs, expenses, and other data, by region, by business unit, by distribution channel, by salesperson, and so on. The Chief Financial Officer of Cisco, Larry Carter, says that with this kind of live information "you can empower all your management team to improve decision making." Richard Kelson, the Chief Financial Officer of Alcoa, says: "The earlier you get information, the easier it is to fix a problem." For example, with up-to-date data, managers at Alcoa saw a downturn in aerospace markets early enough to shift production from hard alloys that are used in aircraft to other products. John Chambers, the CEO of Cisco, says: "At any time in the quarter, first-line managers can look at margins and products and know exactly what the effect of their decisions will be." ■

Source: Thomas A. Stewart, "Making Decisions in Real Time," *Fortune*, June 26, 2000, pp. 332–333.

Managerial accounting is concerned with providing information to managers—that is, people *inside* an organization who direct and control its operations. In contrast, **financial accounting** is concerned with providing information to stockholders, creditors, and others who are *outside* an organization. Managerial accounting provides the essential data that are needed to run organizations. Financial accounting provides the essential data that are used by outsiders to judge a company's past financial performance.

Managerial accountants prepare a variety of reports. Some reports focus on how well managers or business units have performed—comparing actual results to plans and to benchmarks. Some reports provide timely, frequent updates on key indicators such as orders received, order backlog, capacity utilization, and sales. Other analytical reports are prepared as needed to investigate specific problems such as a decline in the profitability of a product line. And yet other reports analyze a developing business situation or opportunity. In contrast, financial accounting is oriented toward producing a limited set of specific prescribed annual and quarterly financial statements in accordance with generally accepted accounting principles (GAAP).

Because it is manager oriented, any study of managerial accounting must be preceded by some understanding of what managers do, the information managers need, and the general business environment. Accordingly, the purpose of this chapter is to briefly examine these subjects.

The Work of Management and the Need for Managerial Accounting Information

Every organization—large and small—has managers. Someone must be responsible for making plans, organizing resources, directing personnel, and controlling operations. This is true of the Bank of America, the Peace Corps, the University of Illinois, the Red Cross, and the Coca-Cola Corporation, as well as the local 7-Eleven convenience store. In this chapter, we will use a particular organization—Good Vibrations, Inc.—to illustrate the work of management. What we have to say about the management of Good Vibrations, however, is very general and can be applied to virtually any organization.

Good Vibrations runs a chain of retail outlets that sells a full range of music CDs. The chain's stores are concentrated in Pacific Rim cities such as Sydney, Singapore, Hong Kong, Beijing, Tokyo, and Vancouver. The company has found that the best way to generate sales, and profits, is to create an exciting shopping environment. Consequently, the company puts a great deal of effort into planning the layout and decor of its stores—which are often quite large and extend over several floors in key downtown locations. Management knows that different types of clientele are attracted to different kinds of music. The international rock section is generally decorated with bold, brightly colored graphics, and the aisles are purposely narrow to create a crowded feeling much like one would experience at a popular nightclub on Friday night. In contrast, the classical music section is wood-paneled and fully sound insulated, with the rich, spacious feeling of a country club meeting room.

Managers at Good Vibrations like managers everywhere, carry out three major activities—*planning, directing and motivating,* and *controlling.* **Planning** involves selecting a course of action and specifying how the action will be implemented. **Directing and motivating** involves mobilizing people to carry out plans and run routine operations. **Controlling** involves ensuring that the plan is actually carried out and is appropriately modified as circumstances change. Management accounting information plays a vital role in these basic management activities—but most particularly in the planning and control functions.

Planning

The first step in planning is to identify alternatives and then to select from among the alternatives the one that does the best job of furthering the organization's objectives. The basic objective of Good Vibrations is to earn profits for the owners of the company by providing superior service at competitive prices in as many markets as possible. To further this objective, every year top management carefully considers a range of options, or alternatives, for expanding into new geographic markets. This year management is considering opening new stores in Shanghai, Los Angeles, and Auckland.

When making this and other choices, management must balance the opportunities against the demands made on the company's resources. Management knows from bitter experience that opening a store in a major new market is a big step that cannot be taken lightly. It requires enormous amounts of time and energy from the company's most experienced, talented, and busy professionals. When the company attempted to open stores in both Beijing and Vancouver in the same year, resources were stretched too thinly. The result was that neither store opened on schedule, and operations in the rest of the company suffered. Therefore, entering new markets is planned very, very carefully.

Among other data, top management looks at the sales volumes, profit margins, and costs of the company's established stores in similar markets. These data, supplied by the management accountant, are combined with projected sales volume data at the proposed new locations to estimate the profits that would be generated by the new stores. In general, virtually all important alternatives considered by management in the planning process have some effect on revenues or costs, and management accounting data are essential in estimating those effects.

After considering all of the alternatives, Good Vibrations' top management decided to open a store in the booming Shanghai market in the third quarter of the year, but to defer opening any other new stores to another year. As soon as this decision was made, detailed plans were drawn up for all parts of the company that would be involved in the Shanghai opening. For example, the Personnel Department's travel budget was increased, since it would be providing extensive on-site training to the new personnel hired in Shanghai.

As in the Personnel Department example, the plans of management are often expressed formally in **budgets,** and the term *budgeting* is applied to generally describe this part of the planning process. Budgets are usually prepared under the direction of the **controller,** who is the manager in charge of the Accounting Department. Typically, budgets are prepared annually and represent management's plans in specific, quantitative terms. In addition to a travel budget, the Personnel Department will be given goals in terms of new hires, courses taught, and detailed breakdowns of expected expenses. Similarly, the manager of each store will be given a target for sales volume, profit, expenses, pilferage losses, and employee training. These data will be collected, analyzed, and summarized for management use in the form of budgets prepared by management accountants.

Directing and Motivating

In addition to planning for the future, managers must oversee day-to-day activities and keep the organization functioning smoothly. This requires the ability to motivate and effectively direct people. Managers assign tasks to employees, arbitrate disputes, answer questions, solve on-the-spot problems, and make many small decisions that affect customers and employees. In effect, directing is that part of the managers' work that deals with the routine and the here and now. Managerial accounting data, such as daily sales reports, are often used in this type of day-to-day decision making.

Controlling

In carrying out the **control** function, managers seek to ensure that the plan is being followed. **Feedback,** which signals whether operations are on track, is the key to effective control. In sophisticated organizations, this feedback is provided by detailed reports of various types. One of these reports, which compares budgeted to actual results, is called a **performance report.** Performance reports suggest where operations are not proceeding as planned and where some parts of the organization may require additional attention. For example, before opening the new Shanghai store in the third quarter of the year, the store's manager will be given sales volume, profit, and expense targets for the fourth quarter of the year. As the fourth quarter progresses, periodic reports will be made in which the actual sales volume, profit, and expenses are compared to the targets. If the actual results fall below the targets, top management will be alerted that the Shanghai store requires more attention. Experienced personnel can be flown in to help the new manager, or top management may conclude that its plans need to be revised. As we shall see in following chapters, providing this kind of feedback to managers is one of the central purposes of managerial accounting.

The End Results of Managers' Activities

As a customer enters one of the Good Vibrations stores, the results of management's planning, directing and motivating, and controlling activities will be evident in the many details that make the difference between a pleasant and an irritating shopping experience. The store will be clean, fashionably decorated, and logically laid out. Featured artists' videos will be displayed on TV monitors throughout the store, and the background rock music will be loud enough to send older patrons scurrying for the classical music section. Popular CDs will be in stock, and the latest hits will be available for private listening on earphones. Specific titles will be easy to find. Regional music, such as CantoPop in Hong Kong, will be prominently featured. Checkout clerks will be alert, friendly, and efficient. In short, what the customer experiences doesn't simply happen; it is the result of the efforts of managers who must visualize and then fit together the processes that are needed to get the job done.

The Planning and Control Cycle

The work of management can be summarized in a model such as the one shown in Exhibit 1–1. The model, which depicts the **planning and control cycle,** illustrates the smooth flow of management activities from planning through directing and motivating, controlling, and then back to planning again. All of these activities involve decision making, so it is depicted as the hub around which the other activities revolve.

Comparison of Financial and Managerial Accounting

LEARNING OBJECTIVE 1
Identify the major differences and similarities between financial and managerial accounting.

Financial accounting reports are prepared for external parties such as shareholders and creditors, whereas managerial accounting reports are prepared for managers inside the organization. This contrast in orientation results in a number of major differences between financial and managerial accounting, even though both disciplines often rely on the same underlying financial data. These differences are summarized in Exhibit 1–2.

As shown in Exhibit 1–2, financial and managerial accounting differ not only in their user orientation but also in their emphasis on the past and the future, in the type of data provided to users, and in several other ways. These differences are discussed in the following paragraphs.

Topic Tackler PLUS
1–1

Emphasis on the Future

Since *planning* is such an important part of the manager's job, managerial accounting has a strong future orientation. In contrast, financial accounting primarily provides summaries of past financial transactions. These summaries may be useful in planning, but only to a

EXHIBIT 1–1
The Planning and Control Cycle

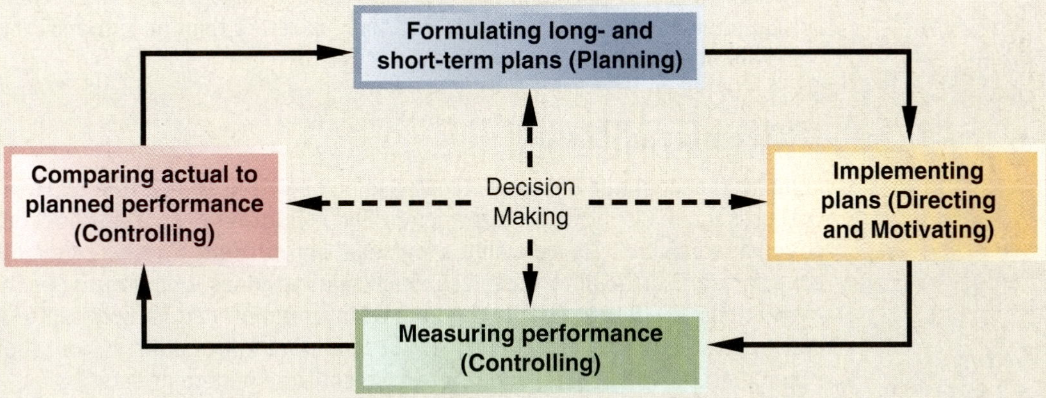

EXHIBIT 1–2
Comparison of Financial and Managerial Accounting

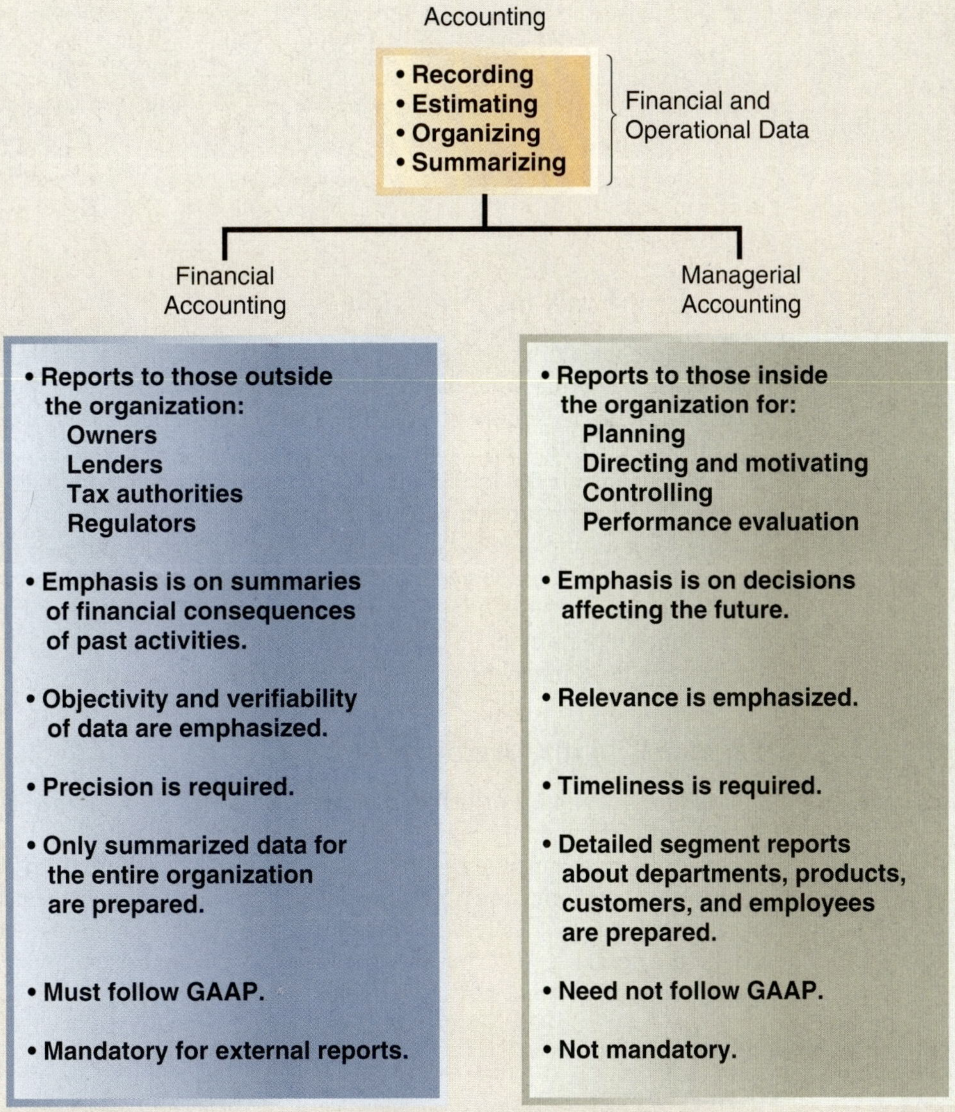

point. The future is not simply a reflection of what has happened in the past. Changes are constantly taking place in economic conditions, customer needs and desires, competitive conditions, and so on. All of these changes demand that the manager's planning be based in large part on estimates of what will happen rather than on summaries of what has already happened.

Relevance of Data

Financial accounting data are expected to be objective and verifiable. However, for internal uses the manager wants information that is relevant even if it is not completely objective or verifiable. By relevant, we mean *appropriate for the problem at hand.* For example, it is difficult to verify estimated sales volumes for a proposed new store at Good Vibrations, but this is exactly the type of information that is most useful to managers in their decision making. The managerial accounting information system should be flexible enough to provide whatever data are relevant for a particular decision.

IN BUSINESS

WHY DO YOU ASK?

Caterpillar has long been at the forefront of management accounting practice. When asked by a manager for the cost of something, accountants at Caterpillar have been trained to ask "What are you going to use the cost for?" One management accountant at Caterpillar explains: "We want to make sure the information is formatted and the right elements are included. Do you need a variable cost, do you need a fully burdened cost, do you need overhead applied, are you just talking about discretionary cost? The cost that they really need depends on the decision they are making."

Source: Gary Siegel, "Practice Analysis: Adding Value," *Strategic Finance,* November 2000, pp. 89–90.

Less Emphasis on Precision

Making sure that dollar amounts are accurate down to the last dollar or penny takes time and effort. While that kind of accuracy is required for external reports, most managers would rather have a good estimate immediately than wait for a more precise answer later. For this reason, managerial accountants often place less emphasis on precision than financial accountants do. In fact, one authoritative source recommends that, as a general rule, no one needs more than three significant digits in the data that are used in decision-making.[1] For example, in a decision involving hundreds of millions of dollars, estimates that are rounded off to the nearest million dollars are probably good enough. In addition to placing less emphasis on precision than financial accounting, managerial accounting places much more weight on nonmonetary data. For example, data about customer satisfaction may be routinely used in managerial accounting reports.

Segments of an Organization

Financial accounting is primarily concerned with reporting for the company as a whole. By contrast, managerial accounting focuses much more on the parts, or **segments,** of a company. These segments may be product lines, sales territories, divisions, departments, or any other categorization of the company's activities that management finds useful. Financial accounting does require some breakdowns of revenues and costs by major segments in external reports, but this is a secondary emphasis. In managerial accounting, segment reporting is the primary emphasis.

---

[1] *Statements on Management Accounting, Statement Number 5B, Fundamentals of Reporting Information to Managers,* Institute of Management Accountants, Montvale, NJ, p. 6.

Generally Accepted Accounting Principles (GAAP)

Financial accounting statements prepared for external users must be prepared in accordance with generally accepted accounting principles (GAAP). External users must have some assurance that the reports have been prepared in accordance with some common set of ground rules. These common ground rules enhance comparability and help reduce fraud and misrepresentation, but they do not necessarily lead to the type of reports that would be most useful in internal decision making. For example, GAAP requires that land be stated at its historical cost on financial reports. However, if management is considering moving a store to a new location and then selling the land that the store currently sits on, management would like to know the current market value of the land—a vital piece of information that is ignored under GAAP.

Managerial accounting is not bound by GAAP. Managers set their own rules concerning the content and form of internal reports. The only constraint is that the expected benefits from using the information should outweigh the costs of collecting, analyzing, and summarizing the data. Nevertheless, as we shall see in subsequent chapters, it is undeniably true that financial reporting requirements have heavily influenced management accounting practice.

Managerial Accounting—Not Mandatory

Financial accounting is mandatory; that is, it must be done. Various outside parties such as the Securities and Exchange Commission (SEC) and the tax authorities require periodic financial statements. Managerial accounting, on the other hand, is not mandatory. A company is completely free to do as much or as little as it wishes. No regulatory bodies or other outside agencies specify what is to be done, or, for that matter, whether anything is to be done at all. Since managerial accounting is completely optional, the important question is always, "Is the information useful?" rather than, "Is the information required?"

Organizational Structure

LEARNING OBJECTIVE 2
Understand the role of management accountants in an organization.

Management must accomplish its objectives by working through people. Presidents of companies like Good Vibrations could not possibly execute all of their company's strategies alone; they must rely on other people. This is done by creating an organizational structure that permits effective *decentralization.*

Decentralization

Decentralization is the delegation of decision-making authority throughout an organization by providing managers with the authority to make decisions relating to their area of responsibility. Some organizations are more decentralized than others. Because of Good Vibrations' geographic dispersion and the peculiarities of local markets, the company is highly decentralized.

Good Vibrations' president (also called chief executive officer or CEO) sets the broad strategy for the company and makes major strategic decisions such as opening stores in new markets, but much of the remaining decision-making authority is delegated to managers on various levels throughout the organization. These levels are as follows: The company has a number of retail stores, each of which has a store manager as well as a separate manager for each section such as international rock and classical/jazz. In addition, the company has support departments such as a central Purchasing Department and a Personnel Department. The organizational structure of the company is depicted in Exhibit 1–3 (page 10).

The arrangement of boxes shown in Exhibit 1–3 is called an **organization chart.** The purpose of an organization chart is to show how responsibility is divided among managers and to show formal lines of reporting and communication, or *chain of command.* Each box depicts an area of management responsibility, and the lines between the boxes show

EXHIBIT 1–3
Organization Chart, Good Vibrations, Inc.

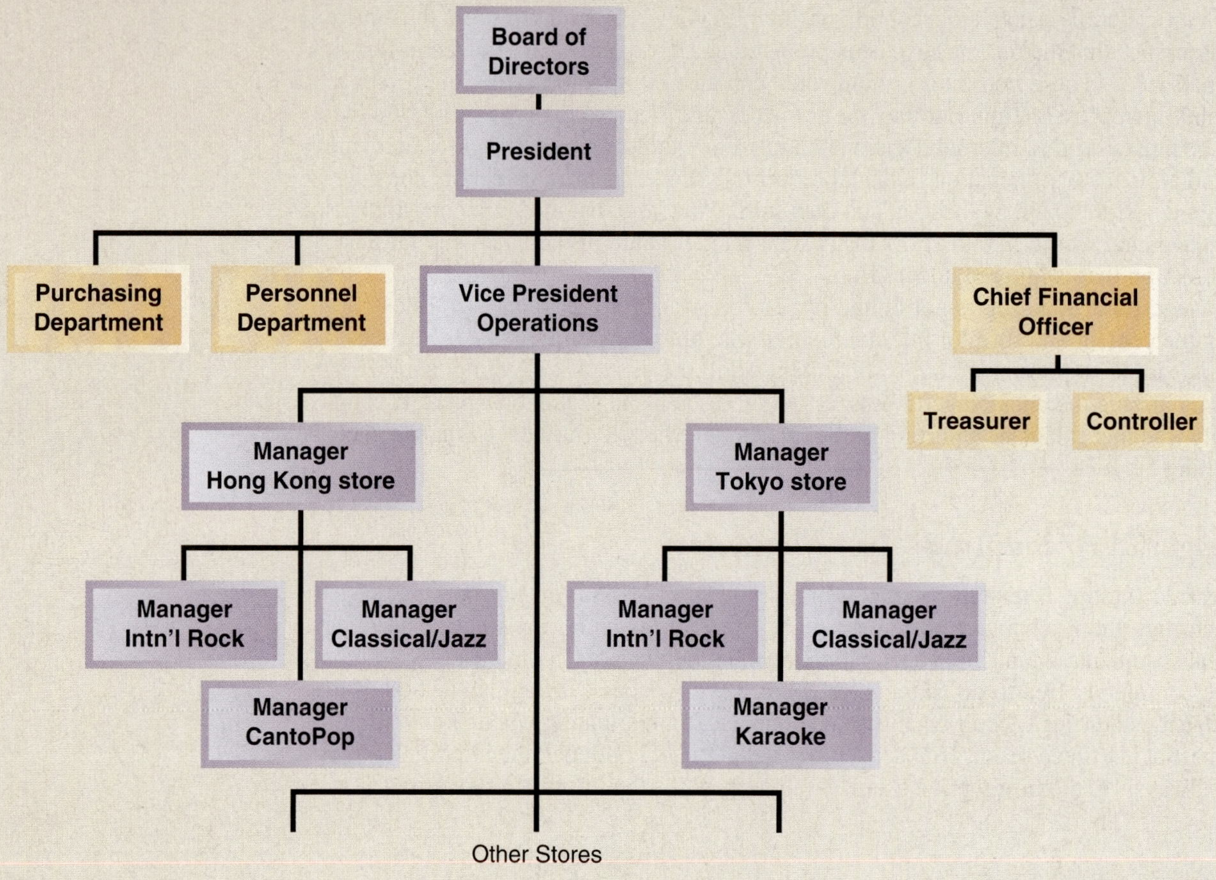

the lines of formal authority between managers. The chart tells us, for example, that the store managers are responsible to the operations vice president. In turn, the latter is responsible to the company president, who in turn is responsible to the board of directors. Following the lines of authority and communication on the organization chart, we can see that the manager of the Hong Kong store would ordinarily report to the operations vice president rather than directly to the president of the company.

Informal relationships and channels of communication often develop outside the formal reporting relationships on the organization chart as a result of personal contacts between managers. The informal structure does not appear on the organization chart, but it is often vital to effective operations.

Line and Staff Relationships

An organization chart also depicts *line* and *staff* positions in an organization. A person in a **line** position is *directly* involved in achieving the basic objectives of the organization. A person in a **staff** position, by contrast, is only *indirectly* involved in achieving those basic objectives. Staff positions support or provide assistance to line positions or other parts of the organization, but they do not have direct authority over line positions. Refer again to the organization chart in Exhibit 1–3. Since the basic objective of Good Vibrations is to sell recorded music at a profit, those managers whose areas of responsibility are directly related to the sales effort occupy line positions. These positions, which are shown in a darker color in the exhibit, include the managers of the various music departments in each store, the store managers, the operations vice president, and members of top management.

By contrast, the manager of the central Purchasing Department occupies a staff position, since the only function of the Purchasing Department is to support and serve the line departments by doing their purchasing for them. However, both line and staff managers have authority over the employees in their own departments.

The Chief Financial Officer

As previously mentioned, in the United States the manager of the accounting department is often known as the *controller*. The controller in turn reports to the *Chief Financial Officer (CFO)*. The **Chief Financial Officer** is the member of the top management team who is responsible for providing timely and relevant data to support planning and control activities and for preparing financial statements for external users. An effective CFO is considered a key member of the top management team whose advice is sought in all major decisions. The CFO is a highly paid professional who has command over the technical details of accounting and finance, who can provide leadership to other professionals in his or her department, who can analyze new and evolving situations, who can communicate technical data to others in a simple and clear manner, and who is able to work well with top managers from other disciplines.

It should be noted that few of the people who are trained as accountants and who work under the Chief Financial Officer in either the treasurer's office or the controller's office think of themselves as accountants. If asked, they are likely to identify themselves as working in finance. Management accounting is not about debits and credits or recording journal entries, although some knowledge of that is necessary. Management accounting is about helping managers to pursue the organization's goals. A recent report states that:

> Growing numbers of management accountants spend the bulk of their time as internal consultants or business analysts within their companies. Technological advances have liberated them from the mechanical aspects of accounting. They spend less time preparing standardized reports and more time analyzing and interpreting information. Many have moved from the isolation of accounting departments to be physically positioned in the operating departments with which they work. Management accountants work on cross-functional teams, have extensive face-to-face communications with people throughout their organizations, and are actively involved in decision making. . . . They are trusted advisors.[2]

IN BUSINESS

BEYOND THE NUMBERS

Judy C. Lewent is the Chief Financial Officer (CFO) of Merck, a major pharmaceutical company. She is in charge of 750 people and is intimately involved in the company's most important strategic decisions. Cynthia Beach, vice president of global investment research at Goldman Sachs & Co., says this about Lewent: "From my standpoint, Merck is one of the best-managed [pharmaceutical] companies, and Judy is a key reason why." Merck's chairman, CEO, and president Raymond Gilmartin adds this about Lewent: "Many CFOs take as their prime directive the timely, accurate delivery of detailed financial data and analysis to top management. While the importance of these services cannot be overestimated, with Judy they are simply one of the many ways she contributes to the business. [Lewent and her organization] make decisions about which developmental-product projects to fund and how to structure our product franchises, acquisition possibilities, and licensing arrangements."

Source: Russ Banham, "Merck Grows from the Inside Out, Powered by the CFO's Joint Ventures," *CFO*, October 2000, pp. 69–70.

[2] Gary Siegel Organization, *Counting More, Counting Less: Transformations in the Management Accounting Profession, The 1999 Practice Analysis of Management Accounting,* Institute of Management Accountants, Montvale, NJ, August 1999, p. 3.

IN BUSINESS

WHAT DOES IT TAKE?

A controller at McDonald's describes the characteristics needed by its most successful management accountants as follows:

> [I]t's a given that you know your accounting cold. You're expected to know the tax implications of proposed courses of action. You need to understand cost flows and information flows. You have to be very comfortable with technology and be an expert in the company's business and accounting software. You have to be a generalist. You need a working knowledge of what people do in marketing, engineering, human resources, and other departments. You need to understand how the processes, departments, and functions work together to run the business. You'll be expected to contribute ideas at planning meetings, so you have to see the big picture, keep a focus on the bottom line, and think strategically.

Source: Gary Siegel, James E. Sorensen, and Sandra B. Richtermeyer, "Becoming a Business Partner: Part 2," *Strategic Finance*, October 2003, pp. 37–41. Used with permission from the Institute of Management Accountants (IMA), Montvale, N.J., USA, www.imanet.org.

The Changing Business Environment

LEARNING OBJECTIVE 3
Understand the basic concepts underlying Just-In-Time (JIT), Total Quality Management (TQM), Process Reengineering, and the Theory of Constraints (TOC).

The last two decades have been a period of tremendous turmoil and change in the business environment. Competition in many industries has become worldwide in scope, and the pace of innovation in products and services has accelerated. This has been good news for consumers, since intensified competition has generally led to lower prices, higher quality, and more choices. However, the last two decades have been a period of wrenching change for many businesses and their employees. Many managers have learned that cherished ways of doing business don't work anymore and that major changes must be made in how organizations are managed and in how work gets done. And to add even more dynamism, the Internet has been changing ways of doing business in more and more industries since the mid 1990s.

Topic Tackler PLUS 1–2

These changes in the business environment have affected managerial accounting—as we will see throughout the rest of the text. First, however, it is necessary to have an appreciation of the ways in which organizations are transforming themselves to become more competitive. Since the early 1980s, many companies have gone through several waves of improvement programs, starting with *Just-In-Time (JIT)* and passing on to *Total Quality Management (TQM), Process Reengineering, Lean Production, Six Sigma,* and various other management programs—including in some companies the *Theory of Constraints (TOC).* When properly implemented, these improvement programs can enhance quality, reduce cost, increase output, eliminate delays in responding to customers, and ultimately increase profits. However, they have not always been wisely implemented, and considerable controversy remains concerning the ultimate value of each of these programs. Nevertheless, the current business environment cannot be properly understood without some appreciation of what these programs attempt to accomplish. Each is worthy of extended study, but we will discuss only those aspects of the programs that are essential for understanding managerial accounting. The details of improvement programs are best handled in operations management courses.

This section on the changing business environment will close with a discussion of the role of international competition and the impact of the Internet on business.

Just-In-Time (JIT)

Traditionally, manufacturers have forecasted demand for their products into the future and then have attempted to smooth out production to meet that forecasted demand. At the same time, they have also attempted to keep everyone and everything as busy as possible producing output so as to maximize "efficiency" and (hopefully) reduce costs. Unfortunately, this approach has a number of major drawbacks including large inventories, long production times, high defect rates, product obsolescence, an inability to meet delivery schedules, and (ironically) high costs. None of this is obvious—if it were, companies would long ago have abandoned this approach. Managers at Toyota are credited with the insight that an entirely new approach, called *Just-In-Time,* was needed.

When companies use the **Just-In-Time (JIT)** production and inventory control system, they purchase materials and produce units only as needed to meet actual customer demand. In a JIT system, inventories are reduced to the minimum and in some cases are zero. For example, the Memory Products Division of Stolle Corporation in Sidney, Ohio, slashed its work in process inventory from 10,000 units to 250 units by using JIT techniques.[3]

The JIT approach can be used in both merchandising and manufacturing companies. It has the most profound effects, however, on the operations of manufacturing companies, which maintain three classes of inventories—*raw materials, work in process,* and *finished goods.* **Raw materials** are the materials that are used to make a product. **Work in process** inventories consist of units of product that are only partially complete and will require further work before they are ready for sale to a customer. **Finished goods** inventories consist of units of product that have been completed but have not yet been sold to customers.

Traditionally, manufacturing companies have maintained large amounts of all three kinds of inventories to act as *buffers* so that operations can proceed smoothly even if there are unanticipated disruptions. Raw materials inventories provide insurance in case suppliers are late with deliveries. Work in process inventories are maintained in case a workstation is unable to operate due to a breakdown or other reason. Finished goods inventories are maintained to accommodate unanticipated fluctuations in customer demand.

While these inventories provide buffers against unforeseen events, they have a cost. In addition to the money tied up in the inventory, experts argue that the presence of inventories encourages inefficient and sloppy work, results in too many defects, and dramatically increases the amount of time required to complete a product.

IN BUSINESS

CHOPPING INVENTORIES AT PORSCHE

Industry insiders were writing off Porsche as an independent carmaker in the earlier 1990s. Sales in 1992 were down to less than 15,000 cars, one-fourth their 1986 peak, and losses had mounted to $133 million. That's when Wendelin Wiedeking became the top manager at the revered, but ailing, company.

Wiedeking hired two Japanese efficiency experts to help overcome Porsche's stubborn traditionalism. "They immediately tackled a wasteful inventory of parts stacked on shelves all over the three-story Stuttgart factory. One of the experts handed Wiedeking a circular saw. While astounded assembly workers watched, he moved down an aisle and chopped the top half off a row of shelves."

They proceeded to overhaul the assembly process, slashing the time required to build the new 911 Carrera model from 120 hours down to just 60 hours. They cut the time required to develop a new model from seven years to just three years. And a quality-control program has helped reduce the number of defective parts by a factor of 10. As a consequence of these, and other actions, the company's sales have more than doubled to about 34,000 cars, and earnings were about $55 million in the latest fiscal year.

Source: David Woodruff, "Porsche Is Back—And Then Some," *Business Week,* September 15, 1997, p. 57.

Under ideal conditions, a company operating a Just-In-Time system would purchase *only* enough materials each day to meet that day's needs. Moreover, the company would have no goods still in process at the end of the day, and all goods completed during the day would have been shipped immediately to customers. As this sequence suggests, "just-in-time" means that raw materials are received *just in time* to go into production, manufactured

[3] Nabil Hassan, Herbert E. Brown, Paula M. Sanders, and Nick Koumoutzis, "Stolle Puts World Class into Memory," *Management Accounting,* January 1993, pp. 22–25.

parts are completed *just in time* to be assembled into products, and products are completed *just in time* to be shipped to customers.

Although few companies have been able to reach this ideal, many companies have been able to reduce inventories to only a fraction of their previous levels. The result has been a substantial reduction in ordering and warehousing costs, and much more efficient and effective operations. In JIT, the traditional emphasis on keeping everyone busy is abandoned in favor of producing only what customers actually want—even if that means some workers are idle.

JIT Consequences Managers who attempted to implement the JIT approach found that it was necessary to make other major improvements in operations if inventories were to be significantly reduced. First, production would be held up and a deadline for shipping a product would be missed if a key part was missing or was found to be defective. So suppliers had to be able to deliver defect-free goods in just the right quantity and just when needed. This typically meant that the company would have to rely on a few, ultra-reliable suppliers that would be willing to make frequent deliveries in small lots just before the parts and materials would be needed in production. Second, the typical plant layout needed to be improved. Traditionally, similar machines were grouped together in a single location. All of the drill presses would be in one place, all of the lathes in another place, and so on. As a result, work in process had to be moved frequently over long distances—creating delays, difficulties in locating orders, and sometimes damage. In a JIT system, all of the machines required to make a single product or product line are typically brought together in one location—creating what is called a *focused factory* or a *manufacturing cell.* This improved plant layout allows workers to focus all of their efforts on one product from start to finish—creating a sense of ownership and pride in the product and minimizing handling and moving. One company was able to reduce the distance traveled by one product from three *miles* to just 300 feet. An improved plant layout can dramatically increase *throughput,* which is the total volume of production through a facility during a period, and it can dramatically reduce **throughput time** (also known as **cycle time**), which is the time required to make a product.

IN BUSINESS

CANON GOES CELLULAR

Canon has completely revamped its production processes in its photocopier plants, ripping out the conveyor belts and heavy equipment that used to be the core of its assembly lines. Instead, Canon has adopted cell production with small teams of about six workers concentrating on building a single type of copying machine. Instead of being bolted to the floor, the production equipment is lighter and more modular, and can be more easily moved into new configurations. Workers are "encouraged to come up with their own solutions. For example, one worker rigged a lid that comes down over photosensitive drums she is installing into copiers to prevent dust and light from harming them." As a result, assembly costs have been cut in half and productivity has been boosted by 20%.

Source: William J. Holstein, "Canon Takes Aim at Xerox," *Fortune,* October 14, 2002, pp. 215–220.

Changing over production from one product to another, which involves *setups,* also creates problems for JIT. **Setups** require activities—such as moving materials, changing machine settings, setting up equipment, and running tests—that must be performed whenever production is switched over to making a different product. For example, a company that makes side panels for DaimlerChrysler's PT Cruiser must prime and paint the steel panels with the color specified by DaimlerChrysler. Every time the color is changed, the spray paint reservoirs must be completely purged and cleaned. This may take hours and results in wasted paint. Because of the time and expense involved in such setups, many managers believe setups should be avoided and therefore items should be produced only in large batches. Think of this in terms of scheduling your classes. If you have to commute to school and pay for parking, would you rather have two classes back-to-back on the same day or on different days? By scheduling your classes back-to-back on the same day, you will only have to commute and pay for parking once.

Managers follow the same reasoning when they schedule production. If the customer has ordered 400 units, most managers would rather produce all of them in one big batch and incur the setup costs once rather than in two batches of 200 units each, which incurs the setup costs twice. Indeed, because of setup costs, most companies have rules about the minimum batch size that can be run. If the customer orders just 25 units, managers will still run the order in a batch of 400 units and keep the other 375 units in inventory in case someone orders the item later. The problem with this line of reasoning is that big batches result in large amounts of inventory—the exact opposite of what JIT attempts to accomplish. In JIT, this problem is attacked directly by reducing setup time so that it becomes insignificant. Simple techniques, such as doing as much setup work as possible in advance off-line rather than waiting until production is shut down, are often very effective in reducing setup time and costs. Reduced setup times make smaller batches more economical, which in turn makes it easier to respond quickly to the market with exactly the items that customers want.

Defective units create big problems in a JIT environment. If a completed order contains a defective unit, the company must ship the order with less than the promised quantity or it must restart the whole production process to make just one unit. At minimum, this creates a delay in shipping the order and may generate a ripple effect that delays other orders. For this and other reasons, defects cannot be tolerated in a JIT system. Companies that are deeply involved in JIT tend to become zealously committed to a goal of *zero defects.* Even though it may be next to impossible to attain the zero defect goal, companies have found that they can come very close. For example, Motorola, Allied Signal, and many other companies now measure defects in terms of the number of defects per *million* units of product.

Benefits of a JIT System Many companies—large and small—have employed JIT with great success. Among the major companies using JIT are Bose, Goodyear, Westinghouse, General Motors, Hughes Aircraft, Ford Motor Company, Black and Decker, Chrysler, Borg-Warner, John Deere, Xerox, Tektronix, and Intel. The main benefits of JIT include:

1. Funds that were tied up in inventories can be used elsewhere.
2. Areas previously used to store inventories are made available for other, more productive uses.
3. Throughput time is reduced, resulting in greater potential output and quicker response to customers.
4. Defect rates are reduced, resulting in less waste and greater customer satisfaction.

As a result of benefits such as those cited above, more companies are embracing JIT each year. Most companies find, however, that simply reducing inventories is not enough. To remain competitive in an ever changing and increasingly competitive business environment, companies must strive for *continuous improvement.*

IN BUSINESS

THE DOWNSIDE OF JIT

Just-In-Time (JIT) systems have many advantages, but they *are* vulnerable to unexpected disruptions in supply. A production line can quickly come to a halt if essential parts are unavailable. Toyota, the developer of JIT, found this out the hard way. One Saturday, a fire at Aisin Seiki Company's plant in Aichi Prefecture stopped the delivery of all brake parts to Toyota. By Tuesday, Toyota had to close down all of its Japanese assembly lines. By the time the supply of brake parts had been restored, Toyota had lost an estimated $15 billion in sales.

Source: "Toyota to Recalibrate 'Just-in-Time,'" *International Herald Tribune*, February 8, 1997, p. 9.

Total Quality Management (TQM)

Perhaps the most popular approach to continuous improvement is known as *Total Quality Management.* There are two major characteristics of **Total Quality Management (TQM):** (1) a focus on serving customers and (2) systematic problem solving using teams made up of front-line workers. A variety of specific tools are available to aid teams in their problem solving. One of these tools, **benchmarking,** involves studying organizations that are among the best in the world at performing a particular task. For example, General Mills studied NASCAR pit crews in action to figure out how to cut the time to change a production line from one product to another from 4.5 hours to just 12 minutes.[4]

Perhaps the most important feature of TQM is that "it improves productivity by encouraging the use of science in decision-making and discouraging counter-productive defensive behavior."[5]

Thousands of organizations have been involved in TQM and similar programs. Some of the more well-known companies are American Express, AT&T, Cadillac Motor Car, Corning, Dun & Bradstreet, Ericsson of Sweden, Federal Express, GTE Directories, First National Bank of Chicago, Florida Power and Light, General Electric, Hospital Corporation of America, IBM, Johnson & Johnson, KLM Royal Dutch Airlines, LTV, 3M, Milliken & Company, Motorola, Northern Telecom of Canada, Phillips of the Netherlands, Ritz Carlton Hotel, Texas Instruments, Westinghouse Electric, and Xerox. As this list illustrates, TQM is international in scope and is not confined to manufacturing. Indeed, a survey by the American Hospital Association of 3,300 hospitals found that 69% have launched quality-improvement programs. For example, Intermountain Healthcare's LDS Hospital in Salt Lake City is using TQM techniques to reduce infection rates among surgery patients and the toxic side effects of chemotherapy.[6]

In sum, TQM provides tools and techniques for continuous improvement based on facts and analysis; and if properly implemented, it avoids counterproductive organizational infighting.

Process Reengineering

Process Reengineering is a more radical approach to improvement than TQM. Instead of tweaking the existing system in a series of incremental improvements, in **Process Reengineering** a *business process* is diagrammed in detail, questioned, and then completely redesigned to eliminate unnecessary steps, to reduce opportunities for errors, and to reduce costs. A **business process** is any series of steps that are followed to carry out some task in a business. For example, the steps followed to make a large pineapple and Canadian bacon pizza at Godfather's Pizza are a business process. The steps followed by your bank when you deposit a check are a business process. While Process Reengineering is similar in some respects to TQM, its proponents view it as a more sweeping approach to change. One difference is that while TQM emphasizes a team approach involving people who work directly in the processes, Process Reengineering is more likely to be imposed from above and to use outside consultants.

Process Reengineering focuses on *simplification* and *elimination of wasted effort.* A central idea of Process Reengineering is that *all activities that do not add value to a product or service should be eliminated.* Activities that do not add value to a product or service that customers are not willing to pay for are known as **non-value-added activities.** For example, moving large batches of work in process from one workstation to another is a non-value-added activity. To some degree, JIT involves Process Reengineering as does TQM. These management approaches often overlap.[7]

Managers must be very careful when trying to convert business process improvements into more profits. There are only two ways to increase profits—decrease costs or increase sales. Cutting costs may seem easy—lay off workers who are no longer needed

---

[4] Pallavi Gogoi, "Thinking Outside the Cereal Box," *Business Week,* July 28, 2003, pp. 74–75.

[5] Karen Hopper Wruck and Michael C. Jensen, "Science, Specific Knowledge, and Total Quality Management," *Journal of Accounting and Economics* 18 (1994), pp. 247–287.

[6] Ron Wilson, "Excising Waste: Health-Care Providers Try Industrial Tactics in U.S. to Cut Costs," *The Wall Street Journal Europe,* November 10, 1993, pp. 1 & 8.

[7] Activity-based costing and activity-based management, both of which are discussed in Chapter 8, can be helpful in identifying areas in the company that could benefit from process reengineering.

because of the elimination of non-value-added activities. However, employees quickly get the message that process improvements lead to job losses and they will understandably resist further improvement efforts. If improvement is to be ongoing, employees must be convinced that the end result of improvement will be more secure rather than less secure jobs. This can only happen if management uses business process improvements to generate more business rather than to cut the workforce.

The Theory of Constraints (TOC)

A **constraint** is anything that prevents you from getting more of what you want. Every individual and every organization faces at least one constraint, so it is not difficult to find examples of constraints. You may not have enough time to study thoroughly for every subject *and* to go out with your friends on the weekend, so time is your constraint. United Airlines has only a limited number of loading gates available at its busy O'Hare hub, so its constraint is loading gates. Vail Resorts has only a limited amount of land to develop as homesites and commercial lots at its ski areas, so its constraint is land.

The **Theory of Constraints (TOC)** is based on the insight that effectively managing the constraint is a key to success. As an example, long waiting periods for surgery are a chronic problem in the National Health Service (NHS), the government-funded provider of health care in the United Kingdom. The diagram in Exhibit 1–4 illustrates a simplified version of the steps followed by a patient who is identified for surgery and eventually treated. The number of patients who can be processed through each step in a day is indicated in the exhibit. For example, appointments for outpatient visits can be made for up to 100 referrals from general practitioners in a day.

The constraint, or *bottleneck,* in the system is determined by the step that has the smallest capacity—in this case surgery. The total number of patients processed through the entire system cannot exceed 15 per day—the maximum number of patients who can be treated in surgery. No matter how hard managers, doctors, and nurses try to improve the processing rate elsewhere in the system, they will never succeed in driving down wait lists until the capacity of surgery is increased. In fact, improvements elsewhere in the system—particularly before the constraint—are likely to result in even longer waiting times and more frustrated patients and health care providers. Thus, improvement efforts must be focused on the constraint to be effective. A business process, such as the process for serving surgery patients, is like a chain. If you want to increase the strength of a chain, what is the most effective way to do this? Should you concentrate your efforts on strengthening the strongest link, all the links, or the weakest link? Clearly, focusing your effort on the weakest link will bring the biggest benefit.

Continuing with this analogy, the procedure to follow to strengthen the chain is clear. First, identify the weakest link, which is the constraint. Second, don't place a greater strain on the system than the weakest link can handle—if you do, the chain will break. In the case of the NHS, waiting lists become unacceptably long. Third, concentrate improvement efforts on strengthening the weakest link. Find ways to increase the number of surgeries that can be performed in a day. Fourth, if the improvement efforts are successful, eventually the

EXHIBIT 1–4
Processing Surgery Patients at an NHS Facility (simplified)*

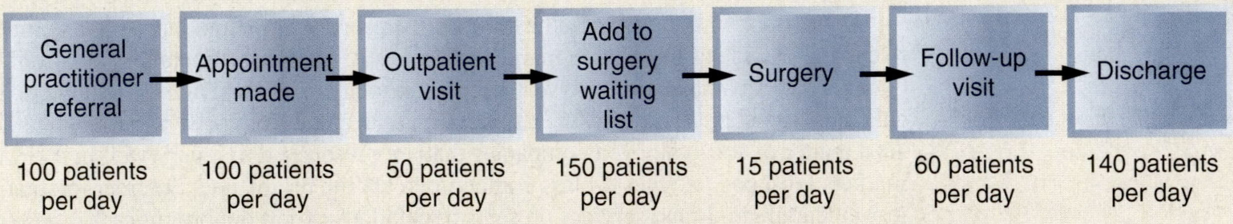

*This diagram originally appeared in the February 1999 issue of the U.K. magazine *Health Management.*

weakest link will improve to the point where it is no longer the weakest link. At that point, the new weakest link (i.e., the new constraint) must be identified, and improvement efforts must be shifted over to that link. This simple sequential process provides a powerful strategy for continuous improvement. The TOC approach is a perfect complement to other improvement tools such as TQM and process reengineering—it focuses improvement efforts where they are likely to be most effective.

IN BUSINESS

WATCH WHERE YOU CUT COSTS

At one hospital, the emergency room became so backlogged that its doors were closed to the public and patients were turned away for over 36 hours in the course of a single month. It turned out, after investigation, that the constraint was not the emergency room itself; it was the housekeeping staff. To cut costs, managers at the hospital had laid off housekeeping workers. This created a bottleneck in the emergency room because rooms were not being cleaned as quickly as the emergency room staff could process new patients. Thus, laying off some of the lowest paid workers at the hospital had the effect of forcing the hospital to idle some of its most highly paid staff and most expensive equipment!

Source: Tracey Burton-Houle, "AGI Continues to Steadily Make Advances with the Adaptation of TOC into Healthcare," www.goldratt.com/toctquarterly/august2002.htm.

IN BUSINESS

THE CONSTRAINT IS THE KEY

The Lessines plant of Baxter International makes medical products such as sterile bags. Management of the plant is acutely aware of the necessity to actively manage its constraints. For example, when materials are a constraint, management may go to a secondary vendor and purchase materials at a higher cost than normal. When a machine is the constraint, a weekend shift is often added on the machine. If a particular machine is chronically the constraint and management has exhausted the possibilities of using it more effectively, then additional capacity is purchased. For example, when the constraint was the plastic extruding machines, a new extruding machine was ordered. However, even before the machine arrived, management had determined that the constraint would shift to the blenders once the new extruding capacity was added. Therefore, a new blender was already being planned. By thinking ahead and focusing on the constraints, management is able to increase the plant's real capacity at the lowest possible cost.

Source: Eric Noreen, Debra Smith, and James Mackey, *The Theory of Constraints and Its Implications for Management Accounting* (Montvale, NJ: The IMA Foundation for Applied Research, Inc.), p. 67.

International Competition

Over the last several decades, competition has become worldwide in many industries. This has been caused by reductions in tariffs, quotas, and other barriers to free trade; improvements in global transportation systems; and increasing sophistication in international markets. These factors work together to reduce the costs of conducting international trade and make it possible for foreign companies to compete on a more equal footing with local companies.

Reductions in trade barriers have made it easier for agile and aggressive companies to expand outside of their home markets. As a result, very few companies can afford to be complacent. A company may be very successful today in its local market relative to its local competitors, but tomorrow the competition may come from halfway around the globe. As a matter of survival, even companies that are presently doing very well in their home markets must become world-class competitors. On the bright side, the freer international movement of goods and services presents tremendous export opportunities for those companies that can transform themselves into world-class competitors. And, from the standpoint of consumers, heightened competition promises an even greater variety of goods, at higher quality and lower prices.

What does increased global competition imply for managerial accounting? It would be very difficult for a company to become world-class if it plans, directs, and controls its operations and makes decisions using a second-class management accounting system. An excellent management accounting system will not by itself guarantee success, but a poor management accounting system can stymie the best efforts of people in an organization to make the company truly competitive.

Throughout this text we will highlight the differences between obsolete management accounting systems that get in the way of success and well-designed management accounting systems that can enhance a company's performance. It is noteworthy that elements of well-designed management accounting systems have originated in many countries. More and more, managerial accounting has become a worldwide discipline.

IN BUSINESS

GLOBAL FORCES

Traditionally, management accounting practices have differed significantly from one country to another. For example, Spain, Italy, and Greece have relied on less formal management accounting systems than other European countries. According to Professor Norman B. Macintosh, "In Greece and Italy the predominance of close-knit, private, family firms motivated by secrecy, tax avoidance, and largesse for family members along with lack of market competition (price fixing?) mitigated the development of management accounting and control systems. Spain also followed this pattern and relied more on personal relationships and oral inquisitions than on hard data for control." At the same time, other Western European countries such as Germany, France, and the Netherlands developed relatively sophisticated formal management accounting systems emphasizing efficient operations. In the case of France, these were codified in law. In England, management accounting practice was influenced by economists, who emphasized the use of accounting data in decision making. The Nordic countries tended to import management accounting ideas from both Germany and England.

A number of factors have been acting in recent years to make management accounting practices more similar within Europe and around the world. These forces include: intensified global competition, which makes it more difficult to continue sloppy practices; standardized information system software sold throughout the world by vendors such as SAP, PeopleSoft, Oracle, and Baan; the increasing significance and authority of multinational corporations; the global consultancy industry; the diffusion of information throughout academia; and the global use of market-leading textbooks.

Sources: Markus Granlund and Kari Lukka, "It's a Small World of Management Accounting Practices," *Journal of Management Accounting Research* 10, 1998, pp. 153–171; and Norman B. Macintosh, "Management Accounting in Europe: A View from Canada," *Management Accounting Research* 9, 1998, pp. 495–500.

E-Commerce

Widespread use of the Internet is a fairly new phenomenon, and the impact it will eventually have on business is far from settled. For a few brief months, it looked like dot.com startups would take over the business world—their stock market valuations reached astonishing heights. But, of course, the bubble burst and few of the startups are now in business. With the benefit of hindsight, it is now clear that the managers of the dot.com startups would have benefited from the use of many of the tools covered in this book, including cost concepts (Chapter 2), cost estimation (Chapter 5), cost-volume-profit analysis (Chapter 6), activity-based costing (Chapter 8), budgeting (Chapter 9), decision making (Chapter 13), and capital budgeting (Chapter 14). While applying these tools to a new company with little operational history would be difficult, it needs to be done. And the investors who plowed billions into dot.com startups only to see their money vanish would have been wise to pay attention to the tools covered in the chapters on the statement of cash flows (Chapter 16) and financial statement analysis (Chapter 17).

At the time of this writing, it is still not clear if a successful business model will emerge for Internet-based companies. It is generally believed that Amazon.com and eBay may have the best chances of building sustainable e-commerce businesses, but even Amazon.com has its detractors who believe it will never break even on a cash flow basis. If a successful e-commerce business model does emerge, it will be based on attracting enough profitable customers to cover the fixed expenses of the company as discussed in Chapter 6.

Established brick-and-mortar companies like General Electric, Wells Fargo, American Airlines, and Wal-Mart will undoubtedly continue to expand into cyberspace—both for business-to-business transactions and for retailing. The Internet has important advantages over more conventional marketplaces for some kinds of transactions such as mortgage banking. The financial institution does not have to tie up staff filling out forms—that can be done directly by the consumer over the Internet. And data and funds can be sent back and forth electronically—no UPS delivery truck needs to drop by the consumer's home to deliver a check. However, it is unlikely that a successful blockbuster business will ever be built around the concept of selling low-value, low-margin, and bulky items like groceries over the Internet.

Professional Ethics

LEARNING OBJECTIVE 4
Understand the importance of upholding ethical standards.

A series of major financial scandals involving Enron, Tyco International, HealthSouth, Adelphia Communications, WorldCom, Global Crossing, Arthur Andersen, Rite Aid, and other companies have raised deep concerns about ethics in business. The managers and companies involved in these scandals have suffered mightily—from huge fines to jail terms and financial collapse. And the recognition that ethical behavior is absolutely essential for the functioning of our economy has led to numerous regulatory changes and calls for new legislation. But why is ethical behavior so important? This is not a matter of just being "nice." Ethical behavior is the lubricant that keeps the economy running. Without that lubricant, the economy would operate much less efficiently—less would be available to consumers, quality would be lower, and prices would be higher. As James Surowiecki writes:

> [F]lourishing economies require a healthy level of trust in the reliability and fairness of everyday transactions. If you assumed every potential deal was a rip-off or that the products you were buying were probably going to be lemons, then very little business would get done. More important, the costs of the transactions that did take place would be exorbitant, since you'd have to do enormous work to investigate each deal and you'd have to rely on the threat of legal action to enforce every contract. For an economy to prosper, what's needed is not a Pollyanish faith that everyone else has your best interests at heart—"caveat emptor" [buyer beware] remains an important truth—but a basic confidence in the promises and commitments that people make about their products and services.[8]

Take a very simple example. Suppose that unethical farmers, distributors, and grocers knowingly tried to sell wormy apples as good apples and that grocers refused to take back wormy apples. What would you do? Go to another grocer? But what if all grocers acted in this way? What would you do then? You would probably either stop buying apples or you would spend a lot of time inspecting apples before buying them. So would everyone else. Now notice what has happened. Because farmers, distributors, and grocers cannot be trusted, sales of apples would plummet and those who did buy apples would waste a lot of time meticulously inspecting them. Everyone loses. Farmers, distributors, and groceries make less money, consumers enjoy fewer apples, and consumers waste time looking for worms.

One commentator argues that integrity is particularly critical in companies whose assets are largely intangible:

> [U]ntil quite recently, most corporate assets were tangible. . . . We still had plenty of business fraud, but in the end someone could go to the rail yard and see if the goods

[8] James Surowiecki, "A Virtuous Cycle," *Forbes,* December 23, 2002, pp. 248–256.

were there. In many of today's high-profile disasters, by contrast, the assets at the heart of the trouble are purely digital [such as Enron's bewildering partnerships] and digits are a lot easier to hide than boxcars.

In the new, digital, trust-based economy, the stakes are extraordinarily high. A company's trustworthiness, embodied in brand and reputation, is increasingly all that customers, employees, and investors have to rely on. . . . Experience shows that this asset is built slowly and painfully but can be lost in an eye blink, and in losing it, you lose everything.[9]

Thus, for the good of everyone—including profit-making companies—it is vitally important that business be conducted within an ethical framework that builds and sustains trust.

IN BUSINESS

NO TRUST—NO ENRON

Jonathan Karpoff reports on a particularly important, but often overlooked, aspect of the Enron debacle:

> As we know, some of Enron's reported profits in the late 1990s were pure accounting fiction. But the firm also had legitimate businesses and actual assets. Enron's most important businesses involved buying and selling electricity and other forms of energy. [Using Enron as an intermediary, utilities that needed power bought energy from producers with surplus generating capacity.] Now when an electric utility contracts to buy electricity, the managers of the utility want to make darned sure that the seller will deliver the electrons exactly as agreed, at the contracted price. There is no room for fudging on this because the consequences of not having the electricity when consumers switch on their lights are dire. . . .
>
> This means that the firms with whom Enron was trading electricity . . . had to trust Enron. And trust Enron they did, to the tune of billions of dollars of trades every year. But in October 2001, when Enron announced that its previous financial statements overstated the firm's profits, it undermined such trust. As everyone recognizes, the announcement caused investors to lower their valuations of the firm. Less understood, however, was the more important impact of the announcement; by revealing some of its reported earnings to be a house of cards, Enron sabotaged its reputation. The effect was to undermine even its legitimate and (previously) profitable operations that relied on its trustworthiness.
>
> This is why Enron melted down so fast. Its core businesses relied on the firm's reputation. When that reputation was wounded, energy traders took their business elsewhere. . . .

Energy traders lost their faith in Enron, but what if no other company could be trusted to deliver on its commitments to provide electricity as contracted? In that case, energy traders would have nowhere to turn. As a direct result, energy producers with surplus generating capacity would be unable to sell their surplus power. As a consequence, their existing customers would have to pay higher prices. And utilities that did not have sufficient capacity to meet demand on their own would have to build more capacity, which would also mean higher prices for their consumers. So a general lack of trust in companies such as Enron would ultimately result in overinvestment in energy-generating capacity and higher energy prices for consumers.

Source: Jonathan M. Karpoff, "Regulation vs. Reputation in Preventing Corporate Fraud," *UW Business*, Spring 2002, pp. 28–30

The Institute of Management Accountants (IMA) of the United States has adopted an ethical code called the *Standards of Ethical Conduct for Practitioners of Management Accounting and Financial Management* that describes in some detail the ethical responsibilities of management accountants. Even though the standards were specifically developed for management accountants, they have much broader application.

---

[9] Geoffrey Colvin, "Tapping the Trust Fund," *Fortune*, April 29, 2002, p. 44, © 2002, Time Inc. All rights reserved.

Code of Conduct for Management Accountants

The IMA's Standards of Ethical Conduct for Practitioners of Management Accounting and Financial Management is presented in full in Exhibit 1–5. The standards have two parts. The first part provides general guidelines for ethical behavior. In a nutshell, a management accountant has ethical responsibilities in four broad areas: First, to maintain a high level of professional competence; second, to treat sensitive matters with confidentiality; third, to maintain personal integrity; and fourth, to be objective in all disclosures. The second part of the standards specifies what should be done if an individual finds evidence of ethical misconduct. We recommend that you stop at this point and read the standards in Exhibit 1–5.

EXHIBIT 1–5
Standards of Ethical Conduct for Practitioners of Management Accounting and Financial Management

Practitioners of management accounting and financial management have an obligation to the public, their profession, the organization they serve, and themselves, to maintain the highest standards of ethical conduct. In recognition of this obligation, the Institute of Management Accountants has promulgated the following standards of ethical conduct for practitioners of management accounting and financial management. Adherence to these standards, both domestically and internationally, is integral to achieving the Objectives of Management Accounting. Practitioners of management accounting and financial management shall not commit acts contrary to these standards nor shall they condone the commission of such acts by others within their organizations.

Competence. Practitioners of management accounting and financial management have a responsibility to:

- Maintain an appropriate level of professional competence by ongoing development of their knowledge and skills.
- Perform their professional duties in accordance with relevant laws, regulations, and technical standards.
- Prepare complete and clear reports and recommendations after appropriate analysis of relevant and reliable information.

Confidentiality. Practitioners of management accounting and financial management have a responsibility to:

- Refrain from disclosing confidential information acquired in the course of their work except when authorized, unless legally obligated to do so.
- Inform subordinates as appropriate regarding the confidentiality of information acquired in the course of their work and monitor their activities to assure the maintenance of that confidentiality.
- Refrain from using or appearing to use confidential information acquired in the course of their work for unethical or illegal advantage either personally or through third parties.

Integrity. Practitioners of management accounting and financial management have a responsibility to:

- Avoid actual or apparent conflicts of interest and advise all appropriate parties of any potential conflict.
- Refrain from engaging in any activity that would prejudice their ability to carry out their duties ethically.
- Refuse any gift, favor, or hospitality that would influence or would appear to influence their actions.
- Refrain from either actively or passively subverting the attainment of the organization's legitimate and ethical objectives.
- Recognize and communicate professional limitations or other constraints that would preclude responsible judgment or successful performance of an activity.
- Communicate unfavorable as well as favorable information and professional judgments or opinions.
- Refrain from engaging in or supporting any activity that would discredit the profession.

EXHIBIT 1–5
(concluded)

Objectivity. Practitioners of management accounting and financial management have a responsibility to:

- Communicate information fairly and objectively.
- Disclose fully all relevant information that could reasonably be expected to influence an intended user's understanding of the reports, comments, and recommendations presented.

Resolution of Ethical Conflict. In applying the standards of ethical conduct, practitioners of management accounting and financial management may encounter problems in identifying unethical behavior or in resolving an ethical conflict. When faced with significant ethical issues, practitioners of management accounting and financial management should follow the established policies of the organization bearing on the resolution of such conflict. If these policies do not resolve the ethical conflict, such practitioner should consider the following courses of action:

- Discuss such problems with the immediate superior except when it appears that the superior is involved, in which case the problem should be presented initially to the next higher managerial level. If a satisfactory resolution cannot be achieved when the problem is initially presented, submit the issues to the next higher managerial level.
- If the immediate superior is the chief executive officer, or equivalent, the acceptable reviewing authority may be a group such as the audit committee, executive committee, board of directors, board of trustees, or owners. Contact with levels above the immediate superior should be initiated only with the superior's knowledge, assuming the superior is not involved. Except where legally prescribed, communication of such problems to authorities or individuals not employed or engaged by the organization is not considered appropriate.
- Clarify relevant ethical issues by confidential discussion with an objective advisor (e.g., IMA Ethics Counseling Service) to obtain a better understanding of possible courses of action.
- Consult your own attorney as to legal obligations and rights concerning the ethical conflict.
- If the ethical conflict still exists after exhausting all levels of internal review, there may be no other recourse on significant matters than to resign from the organization and to submit an informative memorandum to an appropriate representative of the organization. After resignation, depending on the nature of the ethical conflict, it may also be appropriate to notify other parties.

*Institute of Management Accountants, formerly National Association of Accountants, *Statements on Management Accounting: Objectives of Management Accounting*, Statement No. 1B, New York, NY, June 17, 1982 as revised in 1997.

The ethical standards provide sound, practical advice for management accountants and managers. Most of the rules in the ethical standards are motivated by a very practical consideration—if these rules were not generally followed in business, then the economy and all of us would suffer. Consider the following specific examples of the consequences of not abiding by the standards:

- Suppose employees could not be trusted with confidential information. Then top managers would be reluctant to distribute such information within the company and, as a result, decisions would be based on incomplete information and operations would deteriorate.
- Suppose employees accepted bribes from suppliers. Then contracts would tend to go to suppliers who pay the highest bribes rather than to the most competent suppliers. Would you like to fly in aircraft whose wings were made by the subcontractor who paid the highest bribe? Would you fly as often? What would happen to the airline industry if its safety record deteriorated due to shoddy workmanship on contracted parts and assemblies?

- Suppose the presidents of companies routinely lied in their annual reports and financial statements. If investors could not rely on the basic integrity of a company's financial statements, they would have little basis for making informed decisions. Suspecting the worst, rational investors would pay less for securities issued by companies and may not be willing to invest at all. As a consequence, companies would have less money for productive investments—leading to slower economic growth, fewer goods and services, and higher prices.

As these examples suggest, if ethical standards were not generally adhered to, everyone would suffer—businesses as well as consumers. Essentially, abandoning ethical standards would lead to a lower standard of living with lower-quality goods and services, less to choose from, and higher prices. In short, following ethical rules such as those in the Standards of Ethical Conduct for Practitioners of Management Accounting and Financial Management is absolutely essential for the smooth functioning of an advanced market economy.

The Standards of Ethical Conduct for Practitioners of Management Accounting and Financial Management call, in some cases, for individuals to go outside the chain of command to report wrongdoing. In the past, "whistle blowers" who have gone outside the chain of command have often been fired or have been retaliated against in other ways. The Sarbanes-Oxley Act, which was passed in 2002 in response to the wave of corporate scandals, gives new legal protections to those who report corporate misconduct. A manager who retaliates against an employee who reports misconduct can be imprisoned for up to 10 years.

IN BUSINESS

LOSING THEIR BEARINGS

Some would argue that changes in the roles of the management accountant and the Chief Financial Officer have gone too far in recent years. Don Keough, a retired Coca-Cola executive, recalls that, "In my time, CFOs were basically tough, smart, and mean. Bringing good news wasn't their function. They were the truth-tellers." But that had changed by the late 1990s in some companies. Instead, CFOs became corporate spokesmen, guiding stock analysts in their quarterly earnings estimates—and then making sure that those earnings estimates were beaten using whatever was necessary, including accounting tricks and in some cases outright fraud. CFOs at companies like Enron who allegedly became entangled in such corrupt practices found themselves under arrest and in handcuffs. What is needed? Greater personal integrity and less emphasis on meeting quarterly earnings estimates.

Source: Jeremy Kahn, "The Chief Freaked Out Officer," *Fortune*, December 9, 2002, pp. 197–202.

Company Codes of Conduct

"Those who engage in unethical behavior often justify their actions with one or more of the following reasons: (1) the organization expects unethical behavior, (2) everyone else is unethical, and/or (3) behaving unethically is the only way to get ahead."[10]

To counter the first justification for unethical behavior, many companies have adopted formal ethical codes of conduct. These codes are generally broad-based statements of a company's responsibilities to its employees, its customers, its suppliers, and the communities in which the company operates. Codes rarely spell out specific do's and don'ts or suggest proper behavior in a specific situation. Instead, they give broad guidelines.

Unfortunately, the single-minded emphasis placed on short-term profits in some companies may make it seem like the only way to get ahead is to act unethically. When top managers say, in effect, that they will only be satisfied with bottom-line results and will

[10] Michael K. McCuddy, Karl E. Reichardt, and David Schroeder, "Ethical Pressures: Fact or Fiction?" *Management Accounting*, April 1993, pp. 57–61.

accept no excuses, they are asking for trouble. See the accompanying In Business box "Taking a Chainsaw to Ethics" for a vivid example.

IN BUSINESS

TAKING A CHAINSAW TO ETHICS

"Chainsaw" Al Dunlap earned a reputation as a no-nonsense executive specializing in turning around struggling companies. He is known to have proudly declared: "If you want a friend, buy a dog. I've got two." The dark side of his tactics came to light after the debacle at Sunbeam, which he took over as CEO and then left in disgrace two years later. For a while, Dunlap was able to show consistent improvements in quarterly earnings at Sunbeam, but only later did his methods for achieving this record come to light. John A. Byrne describes what happened:

> By the fourth quarter, as it became more difficult to meet the numbers, a new and rather menacing management technique was invented. It was called "tasking." Kersh [Sunbeam's CFO] and Dunlap would gather the top executives in the boardroom and ask each to run through the numbers for their businesses. If one area was lagging, someone else would be asked to make up the difference so Dunlap's forecasts to Wall Street would be met.
>
> "They would say, 'I don't care what your plan was. I don't care what you delivered last month," recalls Dixon Thayer, head of international sales. "We are going to task you with this number.' Russ [Kersh] would give you a revenue and profit number and say, . . . Your life depends on hitting that number.' These numbers got to be so outrageous they were ridiculous."
>
> In an effort to hang on to their jobs and their options, some Sunbeam managers began all sorts of game playing. Commissions were withheld from independent sales reps. Bills went unpaid. . . . As Sunbeam moved toward the holiday season, its struggle to make its numbers became more desperate. . . . [T]he company offered retailers major discounts to buy grills nearly six months before they were needed. The retailers did not have to pay for the grills or accept delivery of them for six months.
>
> In the often esoteric interpretations that are made in accounting, Kersh was rarely conservative or bashful about his creative competence during his tenure as Sunbeam's CFO. In a self-congratulatory tone, he would point to his chest and boast to fellow executives that he was "the biggest profit center" the company had. . . . At meetings, executives recalled, Dunlap would say: "If it weren't for Russ and the accounting team, we'd be nowhere." Several executives heard Dunlap shout to subordinates: "Make the [?@!] number. And Russ, you cover it with your ditty bag."

Deirdra DenDanto, then 26, a recently hired member of the company's internal audit department, challenged the company's questionable practices from the start, but there was little follow-up to her recommendations. She finally resigned after unsuccessfully attempting to send a warning memo to the board of directors. A few months later, the accounting ploys Dunlap had been using to bolster earnings came unraveled, leading to a dramatic boardroom ouster. The company's losses in that year totaled almost $1 billion and its stock crashed to $6, from an earlier price of $53. The company and its employees still suffer from the aftermath.

Source: John A. Byrne, "Chainsaw: He Anointed Himself America's Best CEO. But Al Dunlap Drove Sunbeam into the Ground," *Business Week*, October 18, 1999, pp. 128–149.

IN BUSINESS

WHERE WOULD YOU LIKE TO WORK?

Nearly all executives claim that their companies maintain high ethical standards; however, not all executives walk the talk. Employees usually know when top executives are saying one thing and doing another and they also know that these attitudes spill over into other areas. Working in companies where top managers pay little attention to their own ethical rules can be extremely unpleasant. Several thousand employees in many different organizations were asked if they would recommend their company to prospective employees. Overall, 66% said that they would. Among those employees who believed that their top management strives to live by the company's stated ethical standards, the number of recommenders jumped to 81%. But among those who believed top management did not follow the company's stated ethical standards, the number was just 21%.

Source: Jeffrey L. Seglin, "Good for Goodness' Sake," *CFO*, October 2002, pp. 75–78.

Codes of Conduct on the International Level

The *Guideline on Ethics for Professional Accountants,* issued in July 1990 by the International Federation of Accountants (IFAC), governs the activities of *all* professional accountants throughout the world, regardless of whether they are practicing as independent CPAs, employed in government service, or employed as internal accountants.[11] In addition to outlining ethical requirements in matters dealing with competence, objectivity, independence, and confidentiality, the IFAC's code also outlines the accountant's ethical responsibilities in matters relating to taxes, fees and commissions, advertising and solicitation, the handling of monies, and cross-border activities. Where cross-border activities are involved, the IFAC ethical requirements must be followed if they are stricter than the ethical requirements of the country in which the work is being performed.[12]

In addition to professional and company codes of ethical conduct, accountants and managers in the United States are subject to the legal requirements of *The Foreign Corrupt Practices Act of 1977.* The Act requires that companies devise and maintain a system of internal controls sufficient to ensure that all transactions are properly executed and recorded. The Act specifically prohibits giving bribes, even if giving bribes is a common practice in the country in which the company is doing business.

IN BUSINESS

CAPITALISM AND GREED

Capitalism is often associated with ruthless, self-centered behavior, but is that a bum rap? Researchers have run many variations of the following experiment. Two randomly selected players who do not know each other are placed in different rooms. The individuals cannot see or hear each other and are never introduced to each other. The first player is given $100 and told to split the money any way he or she chooses with the second player. The first player could propose a $100/$0 split, a $80/$20 split, a $50/$50 split, or any other combination that adds up to $100. However, under the rules of the experiment, the second player is allowed to refuse the offer and in that case, neither player gets anything. The game is played only once for each pair of players.

What would a greedy person do? A greedy and ruthless first player would reason that the second player would accept a very low offer of perhaps $10 since $10 is better than nothing. However, in repeated experiments of this sort, people cast as player one were usually far more generous than this and people cast as player two often rejected small offers, even though that left them with nothing. Even more interestingly, responses differed across cultures. When the experiment was run with farmers from Hamilton, Missouri, player one offered on average $48—very close to a 50/50 split. In contrast, the average offer by player one among the Quichua Indians in Peru was only $25. The Quichua Indians subsist in a slash-and-burn agricultural society with little trading, whereas farmers from Hamilton, Missouri, live in a fully developed capitalist market economy. This experiment has been repeated in many communities around the world and the consistent result is that greed (i.e., a low average offer by player one) is associated with nonmarket, precapitalist societies, and in general, the more developed the local economy, the closer the offer by player one is to a 50/50 split.

It is not clear what is the cause and what is the effect. Do markets make people act less greedily or is suppression of greed a prerequisite to a fully developed market economy? At any rate, ruthless greed seems to be much more a hallmark of people who live in undeveloped, precapitalist societies than of those who live in fully developed market economies.

Source: David Wessel, "Capital: The Civilizing Effect of the Market," *The Wall Street Journal,* January 24, 2002, p. A1.

---

[11] A copy of this code can be obtained on the International Federation of Accountants' web site www.ifac.org.

[12] *Guideline on Ethics for Professional Accountants* (New York: International Federation of Accountants, July 1990), p. 23.

The Certified Management Accountant (CMA)

A management accountant who possesses the necessary qualifications and who passes a rigorous professional exam earns the right to be known as a *Certified Management Accountant (CMA)*. In addition to the prestige that accompanies a professional designation, CMAs are often given greater responsibilities and higher compensation than those who do not have such a designation. Information about becoming a CMA and the CMA program can be accessed on the Institute of Management Accountants' (IMA) web site www.imanet.org or by calling 1-800-638-4427.

To become a Certified Management Accountant, the following four steps must be completed:

1. File an Application for Admission and register for the CMA examination.
2. Pass all four parts of the CMA examination within a three-year period.
3. Satisfy the experience requirement of two continuous years of professional experience in management and/or financial accounting prior to or within seven years of passing the CMA examination.
4. Comply with the Standards of Ethical Conduct for Practitioners of Management Accounting and Financial Management.

IN BUSINESS

HOW'S THE PAY?

The Institute of Management Accountants has developed the following table that gives you an estimate of how much you would earn as a management accountant. (The table applies specifically to men. A similar table exists for women, who constitute about 31% of all IMA members.)

			Your Calculation
Start with this base amount		$64,625	
If you are TOP-level management	Add	$22,970	
OR, If you are ENTRY-level management	Subtract	$20,725	
Number of years in the field ______	Times	$521	
If you have an advanced degree	Add	$13,737	
If you hold the CMA	Add	$8,786	
If you hold the CPA	Add	$8,619	
Your estimated salary level			

For example, if you make it to top-level management in 10 years and have an advanced degree and a CMA, your estimated annual salary would be $115,328 ($64,625 + $22,970 + 10 × $521 + $13,737 + $8,786).

Source: Karl E. Reichardt and David Schroeder, *Strategic Finance*, "Members' Salaries Are Still Going Up," June 2003, pp. 27–40. Used with permission from the Institute of Management Accountants (IMA), Montvale, N.J., USA, www.imanet.org.

Summary

Managerial accounting assists managers in carrying out their responsibilities, which include planning, directing and motivating, and controlling.

Since managerial accounting is geared to the needs of managers rather than to the needs of outsiders, it differs substantially from financial accounting. Managerial accounting is oriented more toward the future, places less emphasis on precision, emphasizes segments of an organization (rather than the organization as a whole), is not governed by generally accepted accounting principles, and is not mandatory.

Most organizations are decentralized to some degree. The organization chart depicts who works for whom in the organization and which units perform staff functions rather than line functions. Accountants perform a staff function—they support and provide assistance to others inside the organization.

The business environment in recent years has been characterized by increasing competition and a relentless drive for continuous improvement. Several approaches have been developed to assist organizations in meeting these challenges—including Just-In-Time (JIT), Total Quality Management (TQM), Process Reengineering, and the Theory of Constraints (TOC).

JIT emphasizes the importance of reducing inventories to the barest minimum possible. This reduces working capital requirements, frees up space, reduces throughput time, reduces defects, and eliminates waste.

TQM involves focusing on the customer, and it employs systematic problem solving using teams made up of front-line workers. By emphasizing teamwork, a focus on the customer, and facts, TQM can avoid the organizational infighting that might otherwise block improvement.

Process Reengineering involves completely redesigning a business process in order to eliminate non-value-added activities and to reduce opportunities for errors. Process Reengineering relies more on outside specialists than TQM and is more likely to be imposed by top management.

The Theory of Constraints emphasizes the importance of managing the organization's constraints. Since the constraint is whatever is holding back the organization, improvement efforts usually must be focused on the constraint in order to be really effective.

Ethical standards serve a very important practical function in an advanced market economy. Without widespread adherence to ethical standards, material living standards would fall. Ethics are the lubrication that keep a market economy functioning smoothly. The Standards of Ethical Conduct for Practitioners of Management Accounting and Financial Management provide sound, practical guidelines for resolving ethical problems that might arise in an organization.

Glossary

At the end of each chapter, a list of key terms and their definitions is provided for your review. (These terms are printed in boldface where they are defined in the chapter.) Carefully study each term to be sure you understand its meaning. The list for Chapter 1 follows.

Benchmarking A study of organizations that are among the best in the world at performing a particular task. (p. 16)

Budget A detailed plan for the future, usually expressed in formal quantitative terms. (p. 5)

Business process A series of steps that are followed in order to carry out some task in a business. (p. 16)

Chief Financial Officer The member of the top management team who is responsible for providing timely and relevant data to support planning and control activities and for preparing financial statements for external users. An effective CFO is a key member of the top management team whose advice is sought in all major decisions. (p. 11)

Constraint Anything that prevents an organization or individual from getting more of what it wants. (p. 17)

Control The process of instituting procedures and then obtaining feedback to ensure that all parts of the organization are functioning effectively and moving toward overall company goals. (p. 5)

Controller The manager in charge of the accounting department in an organization. (p. 5)

Controlling Ensuring that the plan is actually carried out and is appropriately modified as circumstances change. (p. 4)

Cycle time See *Throughput time.* (p. 14)

Decentralization The delegation of decision-making authority throughout an organization by providing managers at various operating levels with the authority to make key decisions relating to their area of responsibility. (p. 9)

Directing and motivating Mobilizing people to carry out plans and run routine operations. (p. 4)

Feedback Accounting and other reports that help managers monitor performance and focus on problems and/or opportunities that might otherwise go unnoticed. (p. 5)

Financial accounting The phase of accounting concerned with providing information to stockholders, creditors, and others outside the organization. (p. 4)

Finished goods Units of product that have been completed but have not yet been sold to customers. (p. 13)

Just-In-Time (JIT) A production and inventory control system in which materials are purchased and units are produced only as needed to meet actual customer demand. (p. 13)

Line A position in an organization that is directly related to the achievement of the organization's basic objectives. (p. 10)

Managerial accounting The phase of accounting concerned with providing information to managers for use in planning and controlling operations and in decision making. (p. 4)

Non-value-added activity An activity that consumes resources or takes time but that does not add value for which customers are willing to pay. (p. 16)

Organization chart A visual diagram of a company's organizational structure that depicts formal lines of reporting, communication, and responsibility between managers. (p. 9)

Performance report A detailed report comparing budgeted data to actual data. (p. 6)

Planning Selecting a course of action and specifying how the action will be implemented. (p. 4)

Planning and control cycle The flow of management activities through planning, directing and motivating, and controlling, and then back to planning again. (p. 6)

Process Reengineering An approach to improvement that involves completely redesigning business processes in order to eliminate unnecessary steps, reduce errors, and reduce costs. (p. 16)

Raw materials Materials that are used to make a product. (p. 13)

Segment Any part of an organization that can be evaluated independently of other parts and about which the manager seeks financial data. Examples include a product line, a sales territory, a division, or a department. (p. 8)

Setup Activities that must be performed whenever production is switched over from making one type of item to another. (p. 14)

Staff A position in an organization that is only indirectly related to the achievement of the organization's basic objectives. Such positions provide service or assistance to line positions or to other staff positions. (p. 10)

Theory of Constraints (TOC) A management approach that emphasizes the importance of managing constraints. (p. 17)

Throughput time The time required to manufacture a unit of product. Throughput time is also known as cycle time. (p. 14)

Total Quality Management (TQM) An approach to continuous improvement that focuses on customers and using teams of front-line workers to systematically identify and solve problems. (p. 15)

Work in process Units of product that are only partially complete and will require further work before they are ready for sale to a customer. (p. 13)

Questions

1–1 What is the basic difference in orientation between financial and managerial accounting?

1–2 What are the three major activities of a manager?

1–3 Describe the four steps in the planning and control cycle.

1–4 Distinguish between line and staff positions in an organization.

1–5 What are the major differences between financial and managerial accounting?

1–6 Identify the benefits that can result from reducing the setup time for a product.

1–7 What are the major benefits of a JIT system?

1–8 Why is Process Reengineering a more radical approach to improvement than Total Quality Management?

1–9 How can Process Reengineering undermine employee morale?

1–10 Where does the Theory of Constraints recommend that improvement efforts be focused?

1–11 Why is adherence to ethical standards important for the smooth functioning of an advanced market economy?

Exercises

EXERCISE 1–1 The Roles of Managers and Management Accountants [LO1, LO2]

A number of terms that relate to organizations, the work of management, and the role of managerial accounting are listed below:

Budgets	Controller
Decentralization	Directing and motivating
Feedback	Financial accounting
Line	Managerial accounting
Nonmonetary data	Performance report
Planning	Precision
Staff	Chief Financial Officer

Choose the term or terms above that most appropriately complete the following statements:

1. A position on the organization chart that is directly related to achieving the basic objectives of an organization is called a ________ position.
2. When ________, managers oversee day-to-day activities and keep the organization functioning smoothly.
3. The plans of management are expressed formally in ________.
4. ________ consists of identifying alternatives, selecting from among the alternatives the one that is best for the organization, and specifying what actions will be taken to implement the chosen alternative.
5. A ________ position provides service or assistance to other parts of the organization and does not directly achieve the basic objectives of the organization.
6. The delegation of decision-making authority throughout an organization by allowing managers at various operating levels to make key decisions relating to their area of responsibility is called ________.
7. Managerial accounting places less emphasis on ________ and more emphasis on ________ than financial accounting.
8. ________ is concerned with providing information for the use of those who are inside the organization, whereas ________ is concerned with providing information for the use of those who are outside the organization.
9. The accounting and other reports coming to management that are used in controlling the organization are called ________.
10. The manager in charge of the accounting department is generally known as the ________.
11. A detailed report to management comparing budgeted data with actual data for a specific time period is called a ________.
12. The ________ is the member of the top management team who is responsible for providing timely and relevant data to support planning and control activities and for preparing financial statements for external users.

EXERCISE 1–2 The Business Environment [LO3]

A number of terms that relate to Just-In-Time, Total Quality Management, Process Reengineering, and Theory of Constraints are listed below:

Benchmarking	Setup
Constraint	Business process
Just-In-Time	Frequent
Non-value-added activities	Nonconstraint
Process Reengineering	Total Quality Management

Choose the term or terms above that most appropriately complete the following statements:

1. ________ is an incremental approach to improvement, whereas ________ tends to be a more radical approach that involves completely redesigning business processes.
2. A production system in which units are produced and materials are purchased only as needed to meet actual customer demand is called ________.
3. Increasing the rate of output of a ________ as the result of an improvement effort is unlikely to have much effect on profits.
4. ________ involves studying the business processes of companies that are considered among the best in the world at performing a particular task.
5. The activities involved in getting equipment ready to produce a different product are called a ________.

6. The Theory of Constraints suggests that improvement efforts should be focused on the company's ________.
7. In Process Reengineering, two objectives are to simplify and to eliminate ________.
8. A ________ is any series of steps that are followed in order to carry out some task in a business.

EXERCISE 1–3 Ethics in Business [LO4]

Mary Karston was hired by a popular fast-food restaurant as an order-taker and cashier. Shortly after taking the job, she was shocked to overhear an employee bragging to a friend about shortchanging customers. She confronted the employee who then snapped back: "Mind your own business. Besides, everyone does it and the customers never miss the money." Mary didn't know how to respond to this aggressive stance.

Required:

What would be the practical consequences on the fast-food industry and on consumers if cashiers generally shortchanged customers at every opportunity?

Problems

PROBLEM 1–4 Preparing an Organization Chart [LO2]

Bristow University is a large private school located in the Midwest. The university is headed by a president who has five vice presidents reporting to him. These vice presidents are responsible for, respectively, auxiliary services, admissions and records, academics, financial services (controller), and the physical plant.

In addition, the university has managers over several areas who report to these vice presidents. These include managers over central purchasing, the university press, and the university bookstore, all of whom report to the vice president for auxiliary services; managers over computer services and over accounting and finance, who report to the vice president for financial services; and managers over grounds and custodial services and over plant and maintenance, who report to the vice president for physical plant.

The university has four colleges—business, humanities, fine arts, and engineering and quantitative methods—and a law school. Each of these units has a dean who is responsible to the academic vice president. Each college has several departments.

Required:

1. Prepare an organization chart for Bristow University.
2. Which of the positions on your chart would be line positions? Why would they be line positions? Which would be staff positions? Why?
3. Which of the positions on your chart would have need for accounting information? Explain.

PROBLEM 1–5 Ethics and the Manager [LO4]

Richmond, Inc., operates a chain of department stores located in the northwest that has steadily grown to its present size of 44 stores. Two years ago, the board of directors of Richmond approved a large-scale remodeling of its stores to attract a more upscale clientele.

Before finalizing these plans, two stores were remodeled as a test. Linda Perlman, assistant controller, was asked to oversee the financial reporting for these test stores, and she and other management personnel were offered bonuses based on the sales growth and profitability of these stores. While completing the financial reports, Perlman discovered a sizable inventory of outdated goods that should have been discounted for sale or returned to the manufacturer. She discussed the situation with her management colleagues; the consensus was to ignore reporting this inventory as obsolete, since reporting it would diminish the financial results and their bonuses.

Required:

1. According to the Standards of Ethical Conduct for Practitioners of Management Accounting and Financial Management, would it be ethical for Perlman *not* to report the inventory as obsolete?
2. Would it be easy for Perlman to take the ethical action in this situation?

(CMA, adapted)

PROBLEM 1–6 Line and Staff Positions [LO2]

Special Alloys Corporation manufactures a variety of specialized metal products for industrial use. Most of the revenues are generated by large contracts with companies that have government defense contracts. The company also develops and markets parts to the major automobile companies. It employs many metallurgists and skilled technicians because most of its products are made from highly sophisticated alloys.

The company recently signed two large contracts; as a result, the workload of Wayne Washburn, the general manager, has become overwhelming. To relieve some of this overload, Mark Johnson was transferred from the Research Planning Department to the general manager's office. Johnson, who has been a senior metallurgist and supervisor in the Research Planning Department, was given the title "assistant to the general manager."

Washburn assigned several responsibilities to Johnson in their first meeting. Johnson will oversee the testing of new alloys in the Product Planning Department and be given the authority to make decisions as to the use of these alloys in product development; he will also be responsible for maintaining the production schedules for one of the new contracts. In addition to these duties, he will be required to meet with the supervisors of the production departments regularly to consult with them about production problems they may be experiencing. Washburn expects to be able to manage the company much more efficiently with Johnson's help.

Required:

1. Positions within organizations are often described as having (a) line authority or (b) staff authority. Describe what is meant by these two terms.
2. Of the responsibilities assigned to Mark Johnson as assistant to the general manager, which tasks have line authority and which have staff authority?
3. Identify and discuss the conflicts Mark Johnson may experience in the production departments as a result of his new responsibilities.

(CMA, adapted)

PROBLEM 1–7 Ethics in Business [LO4]

Consumers and attorney generals in more than 40 states accused a prominent nationwide chain of auto repair shops of misleading customers and selling them unnecessary parts and services, from brake jobs to front-end alignments. Lynn Sharpe Paine reported the situation as follows in "Managing for Organizational Integrity," *Harvard Business Review,* March-April, 1994:

> In the face of declining revenues, shrinking market share, and an increasingly competitive market . . . management attempted to spur performance of its auto centers. . . . The automotive service advisers were given product-specific sales quotas—sell so many springs, shock absorbers, alignments, or brake jobs per shift—and paid a commission based on sales. . . . [F]ailure to meet quotas could lead to a transfer or a reduction in work hours. Some employees spoke of the "pressure, pressure, pressure" to bring in sales.
>
> This pressure-cooker atmosphere created conditions under which employees felt that the only way to satisfy top management was by selling products and services to customers that they didn't really need.

Suppose all automotive repair businesses routinely followed the practice of attempting to sell customers unnecessary parts and services.

Required:

1. How would this behavior affect customers? How might customers attempt to protect themselves against this behavior?
2. How would this behavior probably affect profits and employment in the automotive service industry?

PROBLEM 1–8 Ethics; Just-In-Time (JIT) Purchasing [LO3, LO4]

(The situation described below was adapted from a case published by the Institute of Management Accountants' Committee on Ethics.*)

WIW is a publicly owned corporation that makes various control devices used in manufacturing mechanical equipment. J.B. is the president of WIW, Tony is the purchasing agent, and Diane is J.B.'s executive assistant. All three have been with WIW for about five years. Charlie is WIW's controller and has been with the company for two years.

J.B.: Hi, Charlie, come on in. Diane said you had a confidential matter to discuss. What's on your mind?

Charlie: J.B., I was reviewing our increased purchases from A-1 Warehouse Sales last week and wondered why our volume has tripled in the past year. When I discussed this with Tony he

---

*Neil Holmes, ed., "Ethics," *Management Accounting* 73, no. 8 (February 1992), p. 16. Used with permission from the Institute of Management Accountants (IMA), Montvale, N.J., USA, www.imanet.org.

seemed a bit evasive and tried to dismiss the issue by stating that A-1 can give us one-day delivery on our orders.

J.B.: Well, Tony is right. You know we have been trying to implement just-in-time and have been trying to get our inventory down.

Charlie: We still have to look at the overall cost. A-1 is more of a jobber than a warehouse. After investigating orders placed with them, I found that only 10% are delivered from their warehouse and the other 90% are drop-shipped from the manufacturers. The average markup by A-1 is 30%, which amounted to about $600,000 on our orders for the past year. If we had ordered directly from the manufacturers when A-1 didn't have an item in stock, we could have saved about $540,000 ($600,000 × 90%). In addition, some of the orders were late and not complete.

J.B.: Now look, Charlie, we get quick delivery on most items, and who knows how much we are saving by not having to stock this stuff in advance or worry about it becoming obsolete. Is there anything else on your mind?

Charlie: Well, J.B., as a matter of fact, there is. I ordered a Dun & Bradstreet credit report on A-1 and discovered that Mike Bell is the principal owner. Isn't he your brother-in-law?

J.B.: Sure he is. But don't worry about Mike. He understands this JIT approach. Besides, he's looking out for our interests.

Charlie (to himself): This conversation has been enlightening, but it doesn't really respond to my concerns. Can I legally or ethically ignore this apparent conflict of interests?

Required:

1. Would Charlie be justified in ignoring this situation, particularly since he is not the purchasing agent? In preparing your answer, consider the IMA's Standards of Ethical Conduct.
2. State the specific steps Charlie should follow to resolve this matter.

Group and Internet Exercises

GROUP EXERCISE 1–9 Ethics on the Job

Ethical standards are very important in business, but they are not always followed. If you have ever held a job—even a summer job—describe the ethical climate in the organization where you worked. Did employees work a full day or did they arrive late and leave early? Did employees honestly report the hours they worked? Did employees use their employer's resources for their own purposes? Did managers set a good example? Did the organization have a code of ethics and were employees made aware of its existence? If the ethical climate in the organization you worked for was poor, what problems, if any, did it create?

INTERNET EXERCISE 1–10

As you know, the World Wide Web is a medium that is constantly evolving. Sites come and go, and change without notice. To enable periodic updating of site addresses, this problem has been posted to the textbook website (www.mhhe.com/garrison11e). After accessing the site, enter the Student Center and select this chapter. Select and complete the Internet Exercise.

Chapter

2

Cost Terms, Concepts, and Classifications

LEARNING OBJECTIVES

After studying Chapter 2, you should be able to:

LO1 Identify and give examples of each of the three basic manufacturing cost categories.

LO2 Distinguish between product costs and period costs and give examples of each.

LO3 Prepare an income statement including calculation of the cost of goods sold.

LO4 Prepare a schedule of cost of goods manufactured.

LO5 Understand the differences between variable costs and fixed costs.

LO6 Understand the differences between direct and indirect costs.

LO7 Define and give examples of cost classifications used in making decisions: differential costs, opportunity costs, and sunk costs.

LO8 (Appendix 2A) Properly account for labor costs associated with idle time, overtime, and fringe benefits.

LO9 (Appendix 2B) Identify the four types of quality costs and explain how they interact.

LO10 (Appendix 2B) Prepare and interpret a quality cost report.

Costs Add Up

BUSINESS FOCUS

Understanding costs and how they behave is critical in business. Labor Ready is a company based in Tacoma, Washington, that was started in 1989 with an investment of $50,000. The company fills temporary manual labor jobs throughout the United States, Canada, and the UK—issuing over 6 million paychecks each year to more than half a million laborers. For example, the food vendors at the new Seattle Mariners' Safeco Field hire Labor Ready workers to serve soft drinks and food at baseball games. Employers are charged about $11 per hour for this service. Since Labor Ready pays its workers only about $6.50 per hour and offers no fringe benefits and has no national competitors, this business would appear to be a gold mine generating about $4.50 per hour in profit. However, the company must maintain 687 hiring offices, each employing a permanent staff of four to five persons. Those costs, together with payroll taxes, workmen's compensation insurance, and other administrative costs, result in a margin of only about 5%, or a little over 50¢ per hour. ■

Source: Catie Golding, "Short-Term Work, Long-Term Profits," *Washington CEO*, January 2000, pp. 10–12.

As explained in Chapter 1, the work of management focuses on (1) planning, which includes setting objectives and outlining how to attain these objectives; and (2) control, which includes the steps to take to ensure that objectives are realized. To carry out these planning and control responsibilities, managers need *information* about the organization. This information often relates to the *costs* of the organization.

In managerial accounting, the term *cost* is used in many different ways. The reason is that there are many types of costs, and these costs are classified differently according to the immediate needs of management. For example, managers may want cost data to prepare external financial reports, to prepare planning budgets, or to make decisions. Each different use of cost data demands a different classification and definition of costs. For example, the preparation of external financial reports requires the use of historical cost data, whereas decision making may require predictions about future costs.

In this chapter, we discuss many of the possible uses of cost data and how costs are defined and classified for each use. Our first task is to explain how costs are classified for the purpose of preparing external financial reports—particularly in manufacturing companies. To set the stage for this discussion, we begin the chapter by defining some terms commonly used in manufacturing.

General Cost Classifications

All types of organizations incur costs—business, nonbusiness, manufacturing, retail, and service. Generally, the kinds of costs that are incurred and the way in which these costs are classified depends on the type of organization. For this reason, we will consider in our discussion the cost characteristics of a variety of organizations—manufacturing, merchandising, and service.

Our initial focus in this chapter is on manufacturing companies, since their basic activities include most of the activities found in other types of business organizations. Manufacturing companies such as Texas Instruments, Ford, and DuPont are involved in acquiring raw materials, producing finished goods, marketing, distributing, billing, and almost every other business activity. Therefore, an understanding of costs in a manufacturing company can be very helpful in understanding costs in other types of organizations.

2–1

In this chapter, we develop cost concepts that apply to diverse organizations. For example, these cost concepts apply to fast-food outlets such as Kentucky Fried Chicken, Pizza Hut, and Taco Bell; movie studios such as Disney, Paramount, and United Artists; consulting firms such as Accenture and McKinsey; and your local hospital. The exact terms used in these industries may not be the same as those used in manufacturing, but the same basic concepts apply. With some slight modifications, these basic concepts also apply to merchandising companies such as Wal-Mart, The Gap, 7-Eleven, Nordstrom, and Tower Records that resell finished goods acquired from manufacturers and other sources. With that in mind, let us begin our discussion of manufacturing costs.

Manufacturing Costs

LEARNING OBJECTIVE 1
Identify and give examples of each of the three basic manufacturing cost categories.

Most manufacturing companies divide manufacturing costs into three broad categories: direct materials, direct labor, and manufacturing overhead. A discussion of each of these categories follows.

Direct Materials The materials that go into the final product are called **raw materials.** This term is somewhat misleading, since it seems to imply unprocessed natural resources like wood pulp or iron ore. Actually, raw materials refer to any materials that are used in the final product; and the finished product of one company can become the raw materials of another company. For example, the plastics produced by Du Pont are a raw material used by Compaq Computer in its personal computers. One study of 37 manufacturing industries found that materials costs averaged about 55% of sales revenues.[1]

Direct materials are those materials that become an integral part of the finished product and that can be physically and conveniently traced to it. This would include, for example, the seats Airbus purchases from subcontractors to install in its commercial aircraft. Also included is the tiny electric motor Panasonic uses in its CD players to make the CD spin.

Sometimes it isn't worth the effort to trace the costs of relatively insignificant materials to the end products. Such minor items would include the solder used to make electrical connections in a Sony TV or the glue used to assemble an Ethan Allen chair. Materials such as solder and glue are called **indirect materials** and are included as part of manufacturing overhead, which is discussed later in this section.

Direct Labor The term **direct labor** is reserved for those labor costs that can be easily (i.e., physically and conveniently) traced to individual units of product. Direct labor is sometimes called *touch labor,* since direct labor workers typically touch the product while it is being made. The labor costs of assembly-line workers, for example, would be direct labor costs, as would the labor costs of carpenters, bricklayers, and machine operators.

Labor costs that cannot be physically traced to the creation of products, or that can be traced only at great cost and inconvenience, are termed **indirect labor** and treated as part of manufacturing overhead, along with indirect materials. Indirect labor includes the labor costs of janitors, supervisors, materials handlers, and night security guards. Although the efforts of these workers are essential to production, it would be either impractical or impossible to accurately trace their costs to specific units of product. Hence, such labor costs are treated as indirect labor.

In some industries, major shifts are taking place in the structure of labor costs. Sophisticated automated equipment, run and maintained by skilled indirect workers, is increasingly replacing direct labor. Indeed, in the study cited above of 37 manufacturing industries, direct labor averaged only about 10% of sales revenues. In a few companies, direct labor has become such a minor element of cost that it has disappeared altogether as a separate cost category. More is said in later chapters about this trend and about the impact it is having on cost systems. However, the vast majority of manufacturing and service companies throughout the world continue to recognize direct labor as a separate cost category.

Manufacturing Overhead **Manufacturing overhead,** the third element of manufacturing cost, includes all costs of manufacturing except direct materials and direct labor. Manufacturing overhead includes items such as indirect materials; indirect labor; maintenance and repairs on production equipment; and heat and light, property taxes, depreciation, and insurance on manufacturing facilities. A company also incurs costs for heat and light, property taxes, insurance, depreciation, and so forth, associated with its selling and administrative functions, but these costs are not included as part of manufacturing overhead. Only those costs associated with *operating the factory* are included in the manufacturing overhead category. Several studies have found that manufacturing overhead averages about 16% of sales revenues.[2]

Various names are used for manufacturing overhead, such as *indirect manufacturing cost, factory overhead,* and *factory burden.* All of these terms are synonyms for *manufacturing overhead.*

Manufacturing overhead combined with direct labor is called **conversion cost** (or sometimes *value-added cost*). This term stems from the fact that direct labor costs and

---

[1] Germain Boer and Debra Jeter, "What's New About Modern Manufacturing? Empirical Evidence on Manufacturing Cost Changes," *Journal of Management Accounting Research,* Fall 1993, pp. 61–83.

[2] J. Miller, A. DeMeyer, and J. Nakane, *Benchmarking Global Manufacturing* (Homewood, IL: Richard D. Irwin, 1992), Chapter 2. The Boer and Jeter article cited above contains a similar finding concerning the magnitude of manufacturing overhead.

overhead costs are incurred to convert materials into finished products. Direct labor combined with direct materials is called **prime cost.**

Nonmanufacturing Costs

Generally, nonmanufacturing costs are subclassified into two categories:

1. Marketing or selling costs.
2. Administrative costs.

Marketing or selling costs include all costs necessary to secure customer orders and get the finished product into the hands of the customer. These costs are often called *order-getting and order-filling costs.* Examples of marketing costs include advertising, shipping, sales travel, sales commissions, sales salaries, and costs of finished goods warehouses.

Administrative costs include all executive, organizational, and clerical costs associated with the *general management* of an organization rather than with manufacturing, marketing, or selling. Examples of administrative costs include executive compensation, general accounting, secretarial, public relations, and similar costs involved in the overall, general administration of the organization *as a whole.*

Nonmanufacturing costs are also called selling, general, and administrative (SG&A) costs.

IN BUSINESS

WHY IS TUITION SO HIGH?

Do you ever wonder why tuition costs are so high? Administrative costs can be crushing. *Forbes* magazine reports that an average of 2.5 administrators are employed for each faculty member in public colleges and 1.9 in private colleges. The worst case is Mississippi, which has four administrators for every teacher. The best case is Colorado, which "manages to get by with just under two administrators per teacher." Much of the administrative work results from "the mandates that accompany federal money, such as affirmative action, and the personnel needed to monitor compliance with those mandates."

Source: Peter Brimelow, "The Paper Chase," *Forbes*, May 17, 1999, pp. 78–79.

Product Costs versus Period Costs

LEARNING OBJECTIVE 2
Distinguish between product costs and period costs and give examples of each.

In addition to the distinction between manufacturing and nonmanufacturing costs, there are other ways to look at costs. For instance, they can also be classified as either *product costs* or *period costs.* To understand the difference between product costs and period costs, we must first refresh our understanding of the matching principle from financial accounting.

Generally, costs are recognized as expenses on the income statement in the period that benefits from the cost. For example, if a company pays for liability insurance in advance for two years, the entire amount is not considered an expense of the year in which the payment is made. Instead, one-half of the cost would be recognized as an expense each year. The reason is that both years—not just the first year—benefit from the insurance payment. The unexpensed portion of the insurance payment is carried on the balance sheet as an asset called prepaid insurance. You should be familiar with this type of *accrual* from your financial accounting coursework.

The *matching principle* is based on the accrual concept and states that *costs incurred to generate a particular revenue should be recognized as expenses in the same period that the revenue is recognized.* This means that if a cost is incurred to acquire or make something that will eventually be sold, then the cost should be recognized as an expense only when the sale takes place—that is, when the benefit occurs. Such costs are called *product costs.*

Product Costs

For financial accounting purposes, **product costs** include all the costs that are involved in acquiring or making a product. In the case of manufactured goods, these costs consist of direct materials, direct labor, and manufacturing overhead. Product costs are viewed as "attaching" to units of product as the goods are purchased or manufactured, and they remain attached as the goods go into inventory awaiting sale. So initially, product costs are assigned to an inventory account on the balance sheet. When the goods are sold, the costs are released from inventory as expenses (typically called cost of goods sold) and matched against sales revenue. Since product costs are initially assigned to inventories, they are also known as **inventoriable costs.**

We want to emphasize that product costs are not necessarily treated as expenses in the period in which they are incurred. Rather, as explained above, they are treated as expenses in the period in which the related products *are sold.* This means that a product cost such as direct materials or direct labor might be incurred during one period but not treated as an expense until a following period when the completed product is sold.

Period Costs

Period costs are all the costs that are not included in product costs. These costs are expensed on the income statement in the period in which they are incurred, using the usual rules of accrual accounting you have already learned in financial accounting. Period costs are not included as part of the cost of either purchased or manufactured goods. Sales commissions and office rent are good examples of period costs. Neither commissions nor office rent are included as part of the cost of purchased or manufactured goods. Rather, both items are treated as expenses on the income statement in the period in which they are incurred. Thus, they are said to be period costs.

As suggested above, *all selling and administrative expenses are considered to be period costs.* Advertising, executive salaries, sales commissions, public relations, and other nonmanufacturing costs discussed earlier would all be period costs. They will appear on the income statement as expenses in the period in which they are incurred.

Exhibit 2–1 (page 40) contains a summary of the cost terms that we have introduced so far.

IN BUSINESS

DISSECTING THE VALUE CHAIN

United Colors of Benetton, an Italian apparel company headquartered in Ponzano, is unusual in that it is involved in all activities in the "value chain" from clothing design through manufacturing, distribution, and ultimate sale to customers in Benetton retail outlets. Most companies are involved in only one or two of these activities. Looking at this company allows us to see how costs are distributed across the entire value chain. A recent income statement from the company contained the following data:

	Millions of Euros	Percent of Revenues
Revenue	2,125	100.0%
Cost of sales	1,199	56.4
Selling, general, and administrative expenses:		
Payroll and related cost	126	5.9
Distribution and transport	45	2.1
Sales commissions	102	4.8
Advertising and promotion	125	5.9
Depreciation and amortization	62	2.9
Other expenses	141	6.6
Total selling, general, and administrative expenses	601	28.3%

Even though this company spends large sums on advertising and runs its own shops, the cost of sales is still quite high in relation to the revenue—56.4% of revenue. And despite the company's lavish advertising campaigns, advertising and promotion costs amounted to only 5.9% of revenue. (Note: One U.S. dollar was worth about 1.1218 euros at the time of this financial report.)

EXHIBIT 2–1
Summary of Cost Terms

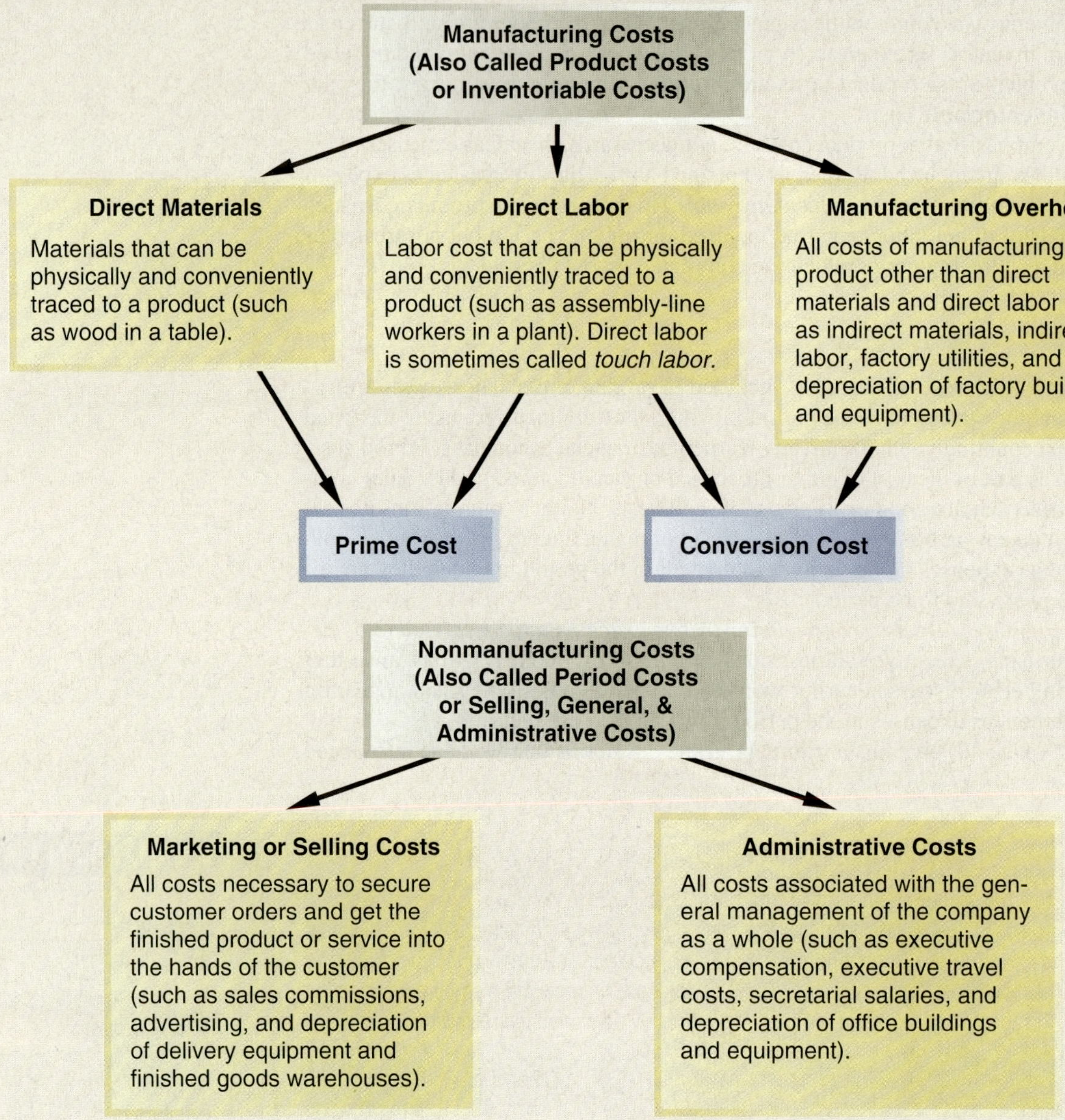

IN BUSINESS

BLOATED SALES AND ADMINISTRATIVE EXPENSES

Selling and administrative expenses tend to creep up during economic booms—creating problems when the economy falls into recession. Ron Nicol, a partner at the Boston Consulting Group, found that selling and administrative expenses at America's 1000 largest companies grew at an average rate of 1.7% per year between 1985 and 1996 and then exploded to an average of 10% growth per year between 1997 and 2000. If companies had maintained their historical balance between sales revenues on the one hand and selling and administrative expenses on the other hand, Nicol calculates that selling and administrative expenses would have been about $500 million lower in the year 2000 for the average company on his list.

Source: Jon E. Hilsenrath, "The Outlook: Corporate Dieting Is Far from Over," *The Wall Street Journal,* July 9, 2001, p. A1.

Cost Classifications on Financial Statements

Topic Tackler PLUS 2–2

In your prior accounting training, you learned that companies prepare periodic financial reports for creditors, stockholders, and others to show the financial condition of the company and the company's earnings performance over some specified time interval. The reports you studied were probably those of merchandising companies, such as retail stores, which simply purchase goods from suppliers for resale to customers.

The financial statements prepared by a *manufacturing* company are more complex than the statements prepared by a merchandising company because a manufacturing company must produce its goods as well as market them. The production process involves many costs that do not exist in a merchandising company, and these costs must be accounted for on the manufacturing company's financial statements. In this section, we focus our attention on how this accounting is carried out in the balance sheet and income statement.

The Balance Sheet

The balance sheet, or statement of financial position, of a manufacturing company is similar to that of a merchandising company. However, the inventory accounts differ between the two types of companies. A merchandising company has only one class of inventory—goods purchased from suppliers that are awaiting resale to customers. In contrast, manufacturing companies have three classes of inventories—*raw materials*, *work in process*, and *finished goods*. **Raw materials** are the materials that are used to make a product. **Work in process** consists of units of product that are only partially complete and will require further work before they are ready for sale to a customer. **Finished goods** consist of units of product that have been completed but have not yet been sold to customers. The overall inventory figure is usually broken down into these three classes of inventories in a footnote to the financial statements.

We will use two companies—Graham Manufacturing and Reston Bookstore—to illustrate the concepts discussed in this section. Graham Manufacturing is located in Portsmouth, New Hampshire, and makes precision brass fittings for yachts. Reston Bookstore is a small bookstore in Reston, Virginia, specializing in books about the Civil War.

The footnotes to Graham Manufacturing's Annual Report reveal the following information concerning its inventories:

GRAHAM MANUFACTURING CORPORATION
Inventory Accounts

	Beginning Balance	Ending Balance
Raw Materials	$ 60,000	$ 50,000
Work in Process	90,000	60,000
Finished Goods	125,000	175,000
Total inventory accounts	$275,000	$285,000

Graham Manufacturing's raw materials inventory consists largely of brass rods and brass blocks. The work in process inventory consists of partially completed brass fittings. The finished goods inventory consists of brass fittings that are ready to be sold to customers.

In contrast, the inventory account at Reston Bookstore consists entirely of the costs of books the company has purchased from publishers for resale to the public. In merchandising companies like Reston, these inventories may be called *merchandise inventory*. The beginning and ending balances in this account appear as follows:

RESTON BOOKSTORE Inventory Account	Beginning Balance	Ending Balance
Merchandise Inventory	$100,000	$150,000

LEARNING OBJECTIVE 3
Prepare an income statement including calculation of the cost of goods sold.

The Income Statement

Exhibit 2–2 compares the income statements of Reston Bookstore and Graham Manufacturing. For purposes of illustration, these statements contain more detail about cost of goods sold than you will generally find in published financial statements.

At first glance, the income statements of merchandising and manufacturing companies like Reston Bookstore and Graham Manufacturing are very similar. The only apparent difference is in the labels of some of the entries in the computation of the cost of goods sold. In the exhibit, the computation of cost of goods sold relies on the following basic equation for inventory accounts:

Basic Equation for Inventory Accounts

$$\text{Beginning balance} + \text{Additions to inventory} = \text{Ending balance} + \text{Withdrawals from inventory}$$

The logic underlying this equation, which applies to any inventory account, is illustrated in Exhibit 2–3. At the beginning of the period, the inventory contains a beginning

EXHIBIT 2–2
Comparative Income Statements: Merchandising and Manufacturing Companies

MERCHANDISING COMPANY
Reston Bookstore

The cost of merchandise inventory purchased from outside suppliers during the period. → (Add: Purchases)

Sales		$1,000,000
Cost of goods sold:		
Beginning merchandise inventory	$100,000	
Add: Purchases	650,000	
Goods available for sale	750,000	
Deduct: Ending merchandise inventory	150,000	600,000
Gross margin		400,000
Less operating expenses:		
Selling expense	100,000	
Administrative expense	200,000	300,000
Net operating income		$ 100,000

MANUFACTURING COMPANY
Graham Manufacturing

The manufacturing costs associated with the goods that were finished during the period. (See Exhibit 2–4 for details.) → (Add: Cost of goods manufactured)

Sales		$1,500,000
Cost of goods sold:		
Beginning finished goods inventory	$125,000	
Add: Cost of goods manufactured	850,000	
Goods available for sale	975,000	
Deduct: Ending finished goods inventory	175,000	800,000
Gross margin		700,000
Less operating expenses:		
Selling expense	250,000	
Administrative expense	300,000	550,000
Net operating income		$ 150,000

balance. During the period, additions are made to the inventory through purchases or other means. The sum of the beginning balance and the additions to the account is the total amount of inventory available. During the period, withdrawals are made from inventory. Whatever is left at the end of the period after these withdrawals is the ending balance.

These concepts are applied to determine the cost of goods sold for a merchandising company like Reston Bookstore as follows:

Cost of Goods Sold in a Merchandising Company

Beginning merchandise inventory + Purchases = Ending merchandise inventory + Cost of goods sold

or

Cost of goods sold = Beginning merchandise inventory + Purchases − Ending merchandise inventory

To determine the cost of goods sold in a merchandising company like Reston Bookstore, we only need to know the beginning and ending balances in the Merchandise Inventory account and the purchases. Total purchases can be easily determined in a merchandising company by simply adding together all purchases from suppliers.

The cost of goods sold for a manufacturing company like Graham Manufacturing is determined as follows:

Cost of Goods Sold in a Manufacturing Company

Beginning finished goods inventory + Cost of goods manufactured = Ending finished goods inventory + Cost of goods sold

or

Cost of goods sold = Beginning finished goods inventory + Cost of goods manufactured − Ending finished goods inventory

To determine the cost of goods sold in a manufacturing company like Graham Manufacturing, we need to know the *cost of goods manufactured* and the beginning and ending balances in the Finished Goods inventory account. The **cost of goods manufactured** consists of the manufacturing costs associated with goods that were *finished* during the period. The cost of goods manufactured figure for Graham Manufacturing is derived in Exhibit 2–4, which contains a *schedule of cost of goods manufactured.*

Schedule of Cost of Goods Manufactured

LEARNING OBJECTIVE 4
Prepare a schedule of cost of goods manufactured.

At first glance, the **schedule of cost of goods manufactured** in Exhibit 2–4 (page 44) appears complex and perhaps even intimidating. However, it is all quite logical. The schedule

EXHIBIT 2–3
Inventory Flows

Beginning balance + Additions = Total available − Withdrawals = Ending balance

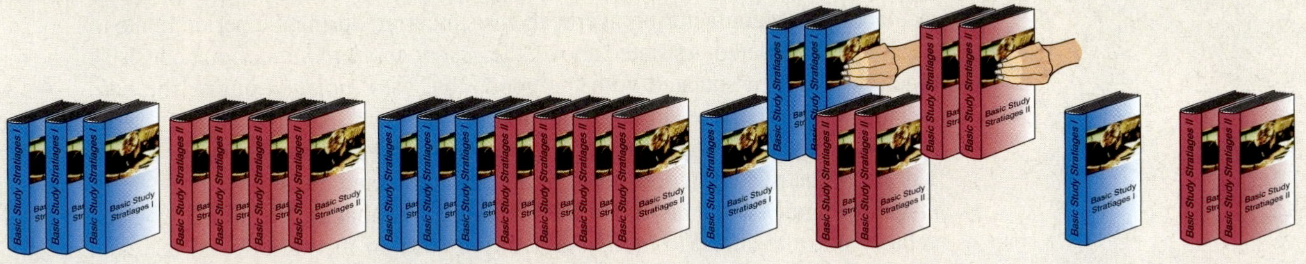

EXHIBIT 2–4
Schedule of Cost of Goods Manufactured

Direct materials:			Direct materials
Beginning raw materials inventory*	$ 60,000		
Add: Purchases of raw materials	400,000		
Raw materials available for use	460,000		
Deduct: Ending raw materials inventory	50,000		
Raw materials used in production		$410,000	
Direct labor		60,000	Direct labor
Manufacturing overhead:*			Manufacturing overhead
Insurance, factory	6,000		
Indirect labor	100,000		
Machine rental	50,000		
Utilities, factory	75,000		
Supplies	21,000		
Depreciation, factory	90,000		
Property taxes, factory	8,000		
Total overhead costs		350,000	
Total manufacturing costs:		820,000	Cost of goods manufactured
Add: Beginning work in process inventory		90,000	
		910,000	
Deduct: Ending work in process inventory		60,000	
Cost of goods manufactured (see Exhibit 2–2).		$850,000	

*We assume in this example that the Raw Materials inventory account contains only direct materials and that indirect materials are carried in a separate Supplies account. Using a Supplies account for indirect materials is a common practice among companies. In Chapter 3, we discuss the procedure to be followed if *both* direct and indirect materials are carried in a single account.

†In Chapter 3 we will see that the manufacturing overhead section of the schedule of cost of goods manufactured can be considerably simplified by using what is called a *predetermined manufacturing overhead rate.*

of cost of goods manufactured contains the three elements of product costs that we discussed earlier—direct materials, direct labor, and manufacturing overhead. The direct materials cost is not simply the cost of materials purchased during the period—rather it is the cost of materials *used* during the period. The purchases of raw materials are added to the beginning balance to determine the cost of the materials available for use. The ending materials inventory is deducted from this amount to arrive at the cost of the materials used in production. The sum of the three cost elements—materials, direct labor, and manufacturing overhead—is the total manufacturing cost. This is *not* the same thing, however, as the cost of goods manufactured for the period. The subtle distinction between the total manufacturing cost and the cost of goods manufactured is very easy to miss. Some of the materials, direct labor, and manufacturing overhead costs incurred during the period relate to goods that are not yet completed. As stated above, the *cost of goods manufactured* consists of the manufacturing costs associated with the goods that were *finished* during the period. Consequently, adjustments need to be made to the total manufacturing cost of the period for the partially completed goods that were in process at the beginning and at the end of the period. The costs that relate to goods that are not yet completed are shown in the work in process inventory figures at the bottom of the schedule. Note that the beginning work in process inventory must be added to the manufacturing costs of the period, and the ending work in process inventory must be deducted, to arrive at the cost of goods manufactured.

EXHIBIT 2–5
Cost Flows and Classifications in a Manufacturing Company

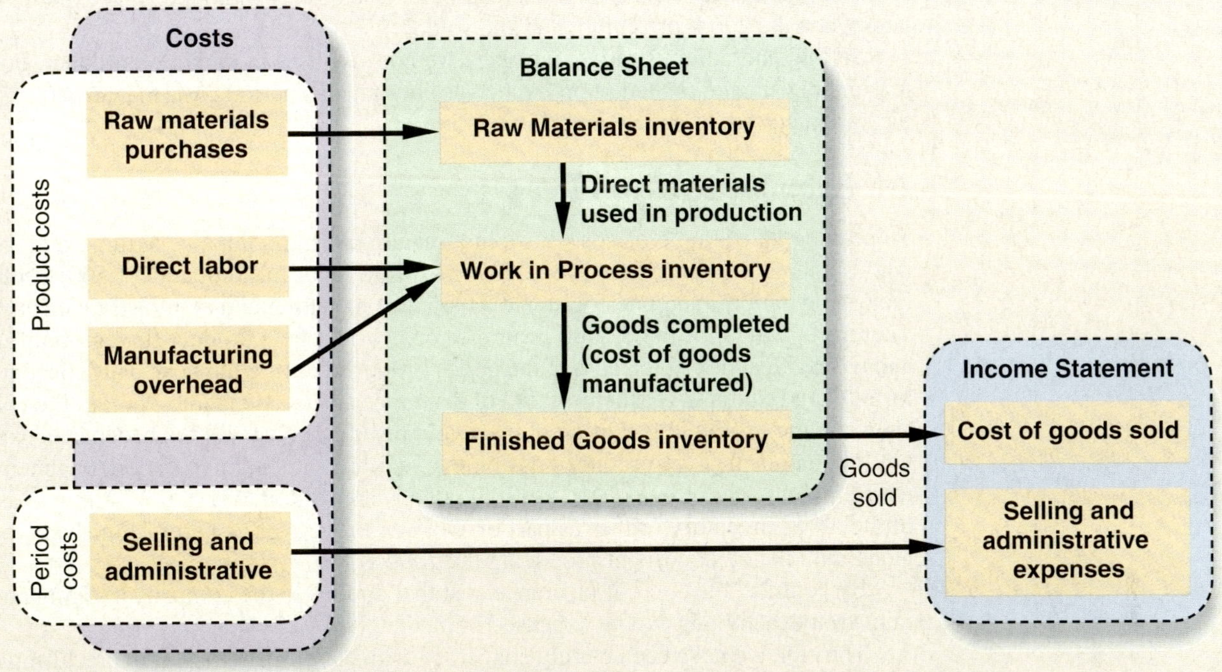

Product Cost Flows

Earlier in the chapter, we defined product costs as those costs that are incurred to either purchase or manufacture goods. For manufactured goods, these costs consist of direct materials, direct labor, and manufacturing overhead. It will be helpful at this point to look briefly at the flow of costs in a manufacturing company. This will help us understand how product costs move through the various accounts and how they affect the balance sheet and the income statement.

Exhibit 2–5 illustrates the flow of costs in a manufacturing company. Raw materials purchases are recorded in the Raw Materials inventory account. When raw materials are used in production, their costs are transferred to the Work in Process inventory account as direct materials. Notice that direct labor cost and manufacturing overhead cost are added directly to Work in Process. Work in Process can be viewed most simply as products on an assembly line. The direct materials, direct labor, and manufacturing overhead costs added to Work in Process in Exhibit 2–5 are the costs needed to complete these products as they move along this assembly line.

Notice from the exhibit that as goods are completed, their costs are transferred from Work in Process to Finished Goods. Here the goods await sale to customers. As goods are sold, their costs are transferred from Finished Goods to Cost of Goods Sold. At this point the various material, labor, and overhead costs required to make the product are finally recorded as expenses. Until that point, these costs are in inventory accounts on the balance sheet.

Inventoriable Costs

As stated earlier, product costs are often called inventoriable costs. The reason is that these costs go directly into inventory accounts as they are incurred (first into Work in Process and then into Finished Goods), rather than going into expense accounts. Thus, they are termed *inventoriable costs. This is a key concept since such costs can end up on the balance sheet as assets if goods are only partially completed or are unsold at the end of a period.* To illustrate this point, refer again to Exhibit 2–5. At the end of the period, the materials, labor, and overhead costs that are associated with the units in the Work in Process and Finished Goods inventory accounts will appear on the balance sheet as part of the company's assets. As explained earlier, these costs will not become expenses until later when the goods are completed and sold.

Selling and administrative expenses are not involved in making a product. For this reason, they are not treated as product costs but rather as period costs that are expensed as they are incurred, as shown in Exhibit 2–5.

An Example of Cost Flows

To provide an example of cost flows in a manufacturing company, assume that a company's annual insurance cost is $2,000. Three-fourths of this amount ($1,500) applies to factory operations, and one-fourth ($500) applies to selling and administrative activities. Therefore, $1,500 of the $2,000 insurance cost would be a product (inventoriable) cost and would be added to the cost of the goods produced during the year. This concept is illustrated in Exhibit 2–6, where $1,500 of insurance cost is added into Work in Process. As shown in the exhibit, this portion of the year's insurance cost will not become an expense until the goods that are produced during the year are sold—which may not happen until the following year or even later. Until the goods are sold, the $1,500 will remain as part of the asset, inventory (either as part of Work in Process or as part of Finished Goods), along with the other costs of producing the goods.

By contrast, the $500 of insurance cost that applies to the company's selling and administrative activities will be expensed immediately.

Thus far, we have been mainly concerned with classifications of manufacturing costs for the purpose of determining inventory valuations on the balance sheet and cost of goods sold on the income statement of external financial reports. However, costs are used for many other purposes, and each purpose requires a different classification of costs. We

EXHIBIT 2–6
An Example of Cost Flows in a Manufacturing Company

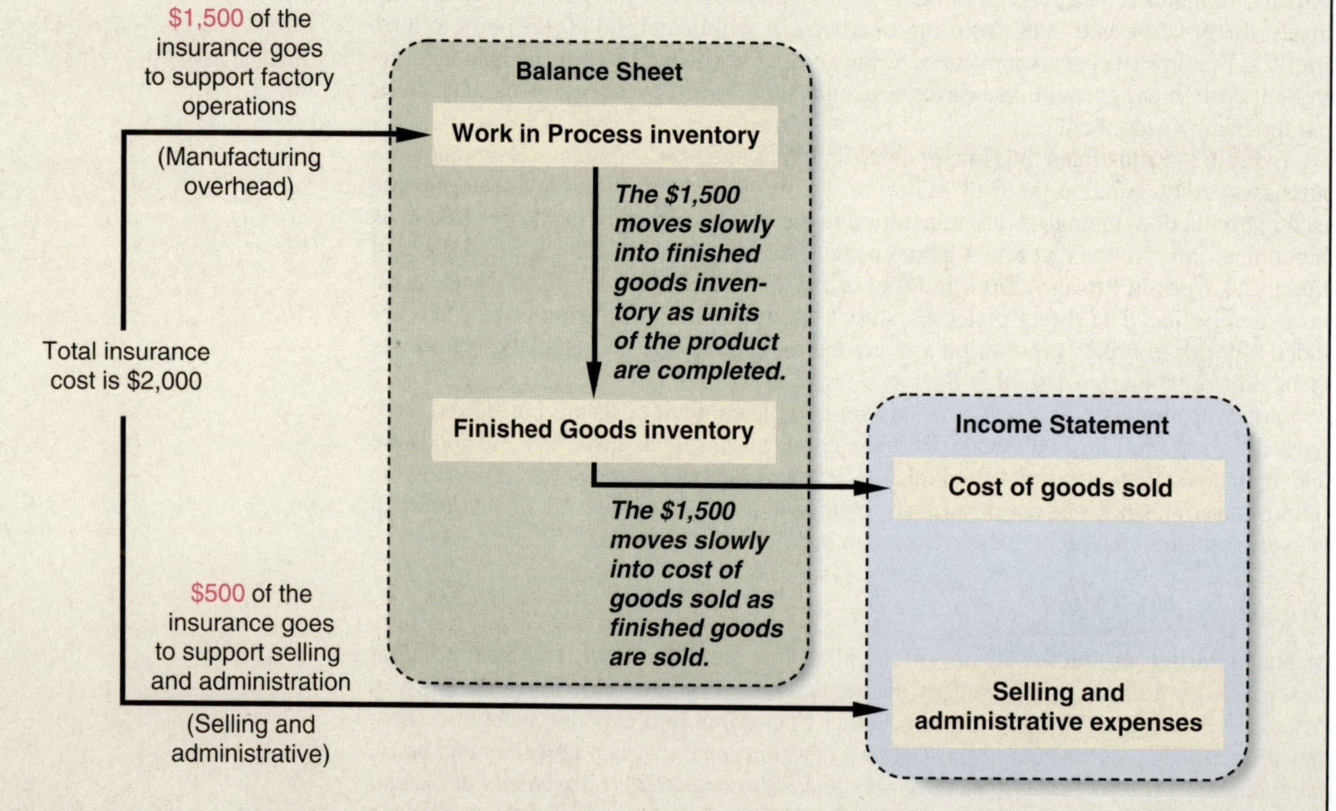

EXHIBIT 2–7
Summary of Cost Classifications

Purpose of Cost Classification	Cost Classifications

Preparing external financial statements	• Product costs (inventoriable)
	  • Direct materials
	  • Direct labor
	  • Manufacturing overhead
	• Period costs (expensed)
	  • Nonmanufacturing costs
	    • Marketing or selling costs
	    • Administrative costs

Predicting cost behavior in response to changes in activity	• Variable cost (proportional to activity) • Fixed cost (constant in total)
Assigning costs to cost objects such as departments or products	• Direct cost (can be easily traced) • Indirect cost (cannot be easily traced; must be allocated)
Making decisions	• Differential cost (differs between alternatives) • Sunk cost (past cost not affected by a decision) • Opportunity cost (forgone benefit)
Cost of quality (Appendix)	• Prevention costs • Appraisal costs • Internal failure costs • External failure costs

will consider several different purposes for cost classifications in the remaining sections of this chapter. These purposes and the corresponding cost classifications are summarized in Exhibit 2–7. To help keep the big picture in mind, we suggest that you refer back to this exhibit frequently as you progress through the rest of this chapter.

IN BUSINESS

PRODUCT OR PERIOD EXPENSE—WHO CARES?

Whether a cost is considered a product or period cost can have an important impact on a company's financial statements. Consider the following excerpts from a conversation recorded on the Institute of Management Accountant's Ethics Hot-Line:

Caller: My problem basically is that my boss, the division general manager, wants me to put costs into inventory that I know should be expensed. . . .
Counselor: Have you expressed your doubts to your boss?
Caller: Yes, but he is basically a salesman and claims he knows nothing about GAAP. He just wants the "numbers" to back up the good news he keeps telling corporate [headquarters], which is what corporate demands. Also, he asks if I am ready to make the entries that I think are improper. It seems he wants to make it look like my idea all along. Our company had legal problems a few years ago with some government contracts, and it was the lower level people who were "hung out to dry" rather than the higher-ups who were really at fault.
Counselor: . . . What does he say when you tell him these matters need resolution?
Caller: He just says we need a meeting, but the meetings never solve anything. . . .
Counselor: Does your company have an ethics hot-line?
Caller: Yes, but my boss would view use of the hot-line as snitching or even whistle-blowing. . . .
Counselor: . . . If you might face reprisals for using the hot-line, perhaps you should evaluate whether or not you really want to work for a company whose ethical climate is one you are uncomfortable in.

Source: Curtis C. Verschoor, "Using a Hot-Line Isn't Whistle-Blowing," *Strategic Finance*, April 1999, pp. 27–28. Reprinted with permission from the IMA, Montvale, NJ, USA www.imanet.org.

Cost Classifications for Predicting Cost Behavior

LEARNING OBJECTIVE 5
Understand the differences between variable costs and fixed costs.

Quite frequently, it is necessary to predict how a certain cost will behave in response to a change in activity. For example, a manager at AT&T may want to estimate the impact a 5% increase in long-distance calls would have on the company's total electric bill or on the total wages the company pays its long-distance operators. **Cost behavior** refers to how a cost will react to changes in the level of activity. As the activity level rises and falls, a particular cost may rise and fall as well—or it may remain constant. For planning purposes, a manager must be able to anticipate which of these will happen; and if a cost can be expected to change, the manager must be able to estimate how much it will change. To help make such distinctions, costs are often categorized as variable or fixed.

Variable Cost

A **variable cost** is a cost that varies, in total, in direct proportion to changes in the level of activity. The activity can be expressed in many ways, such as units produced, units sold, miles driven, beds occupied, lines of print, hours worked, and so forth. A good example of a variable cost is direct materials. The cost of direct materials used during a period will vary, in total, in direct proportion to the number of units that are produced. To illustrate this idea, consider the Saturn Division of GM. Each auto requires one battery. As the output of autos increases and decreases, the number of batteries used will increase and decrease proportionately. If auto production goes up 10%, then the number of batteries used will also go up 10%. The concept of a variable cost is shown in graphic form in Exhibit 2–8.

It is important to note that when we speak of a cost as being variable, we mean the *total* cost rises and falls as the activity level rises and falls. This idea is presented below, assuming that a Saturn's battery costs $24:

Number of Autos Produced	Cost per Battery	Total Variable Cost—Batteries
1	$24	$24
500	$24	$12,000
1,000	$24	$24,000

EXHIBIT 2–8
Variable and Fixed Cost Behavior

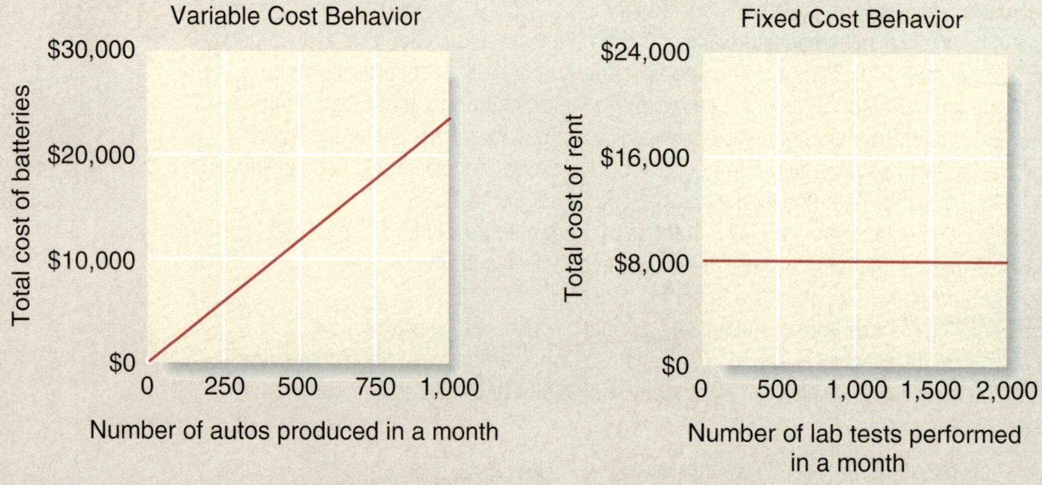

One interesting aspect of variable cost behavior is that a variable cost is constant if expressed on a *per unit* basis. Observe from the tabulation above that the per unit cost of batteries remains constant at $24 even though the total cost of the batteries increases and decreases with activity.

There are many examples of costs that are variable with respect to the products and services provided by a company. In a manufacturing company, variable costs include items such as direct materials and some elements of manufacturing overhead such as lubricants, shipping costs, and sales commissions. For the present, we will also assume that direct labor is a variable cost, although as we shall see in Chapter 5, direct labor may act more like a fixed cost in many situations. In a merchandising company, variable costs include items such as cost of goods sold, commissions to salespersons, and billing costs. In a hospital, the variable costs of providing health care services to patients would include the costs of the supplies, drugs, meals, and perhaps nursing services.

When we say that a cost is variable, we ordinarily mean that it is variable with respect to the amount of goods or services the organization produces. However, costs can be variable with respect to other things. For example, the wages paid to employees at a Blockbuster Video outlet will depend on the number of hours the store is open and not strictly on the number of videos rented. In this case, we would say that wage costs are variable with respect to the hours of operation. Nevertheless, when we say that a cost is variable, we ordinarily mean it is variable with respect to the amount of goods and services produced. This could be how many Jeep Cherokees are produced, how many videos are rented, how many patients are treated, and so on.

Fixed Cost

A **fixed cost** is a cost that remains constant, in total, regardless of changes in the level of activity. Unlike variable costs, fixed costs are not affected by changes in activity. Consequently, as the activity level rises and falls, total fixed costs remain constant unless influenced by some outside force, such as a price change. Rent is a good example of a fixed cost. Suppose the Mayo Clinic rents a machine for $8,000 per month that tests blood samples for the presence of leukemia cells. The $8,000 monthly rental cost will be sustained regardless of the number of tests that may be performed during the month. The concept of a fixed cost is shown in graphic form in Exhibit 2–8.

Very few costs are completely fixed. Most will change if there is a large enough change in activity. For example, suppose that the capacity of the leukemia diagnostic machine at the Mayo Clinic is 2,000 tests per month. If the clinic wishes to perform more than 2,000 tests in a month, it would be necessary to rent an additional machine, which would cause a jump in the fixed costs. When we say a cost is fixed, we mean it is fixed within some *relevant range*. The **relevant range** is the range of activity within which the assumptions about variable and fixed costs are valid. For example, the assumption that the rent for diagnostic machines is $8,000 per month is valid within the relevant range of 0 to 2,000 tests per month.

Fixed costs can create confusion if they are expressed on a per unit basis. This is because the average fixed cost per unit increases and decreases *inversely* with changes in activity. In the Mayo Clinic, for example, the average cost per test will fall as the number of tests performed increases. This is because the $8,000 rental cost will be spread over more tests. Conversely, as the number of tests performed in the clinic declines, the average cost per test will rise as the $8,000 rental cost is spread over fewer tests. This concept is illustrated in the table below:

Monthly Rental Cost	Number of Tests Performed	Average Cost per Test
$8,000	10	$800
8,000	500	$16
8,000	2,000	$4

EXHIBIT 2–9
Summary of Variable and Fixed Cost Behavior

	Behavior of the Cost (within the relevant range)	
Cost	In Total	Per Unit
Variable cost	Total variable cost increases and decreases in proportion to changes in the activity level.	Variable cost per unit remains constant.
Fixed cost	Total fixed cost is not affected by changes in the activity level within the relevant range.	Fixed cost per unit decreases as the activity level rises and increases as the activity level falls.

Note that if the Mayo Clinic performs only 10 tests each month, the rental cost of the equipment will average $800 per test. But if 2,000 tests are performed each month, the average cost will drop to only $4 per test. More will be said later about the problems created for both the accountant and the manager by this variation in unit costs.

Examples of fixed costs include straight-line depreciation, insurance, property taxes, rent, supervisory salaries, administrative salaries, and advertising.

A summary of both variable and fixed cost behavior is presented in Exhibit 2–9.

IN BUSINESS

THE COST OF A CALL

On average, the variable cost of physically transporting a telephone call is about 7% of the price a customer pays for the call. It now costs more to bill for the call than to provide it. Then why aren't telephone companies fabulously profitable? In short, they have extremely high fixed costs for equipment, buildings, and personnel. The prices the telephone companies charge to consumers must cover these fixed costs as well as the relatively small variable costs of completing a particular call for a customer.

Source: Scott Woolley, "Meltdown," *Forbes*, July 3, 2000, pp. 70–71.

Cost Classifications for Assigning Costs to Cost Objects

LEARNING OBJECTIVE 6
Understand the differences between direct and indirect costs.

Costs are assigned to cost objects for a variety of purposes including pricing, profitability studies, and control of spending. A **cost object** is anything for which cost data are desired—including products, product lines, customers, jobs, and organizational subunits. For purposes of assigning costs to cost objects, costs are classified as either *direct* or *indirect.*

Direct Cost

A **direct cost** is a cost that can be easily and conveniently traced to the particular cost object under consideration. The concept of direct cost extends beyond just direct materials and direct labor. For example, if Reebok is assigning costs to its various regional and national sales offices, then the salary of the sales manager in its Tokyo office would be a direct cost of that office.

Indirect Cost

An **indirect cost** is a cost that cannot be easily and conveniently traced to the particular cost object under consideration. For example, a Campbell Soup factory may produce dozens of varieties of canned soups. The factory manager's salary would be an indirect cost of a particular variety such as chicken noodle soup. The reason is that the factory manager's salary is not caused by any one variety of soup but rather is incurred as a consequence of running the entire factory. *To be traced to a cost object such as a particular product, the cost must be caused by the cost object.* The factory manager's salary is called a *common cost* of producing the various products of the factory. A **common cost** is a cost that is incurred to support a number of costing objects but cannot be traced to them individually. A common cost is a type of indirect cost.

A particular cost may be direct or indirect, depending on the cost object. While the Campbell Soup factory manager's salary is an *indirect* cost of manufacturing chicken noodle soup, it is a *direct* cost of the manufacturing division. In the first case, the cost object is the chicken noodle soup product. In the second case, the cost object is the entire manufacturing division.

Cost Classifications for Decision Making

LEARNING OBJECTIVE 7
Define and give examples of cost classifications used in making decisions: differential costs, opportunity costs, and sunk costs.

Costs are an important feature of many business decisions. In making decisions, it is essential to have a firm grasp of the concepts *differential cost, opportunity cost,* and *sunk cost.*

Differential Cost and Revenue

Decisions involve choosing between alternatives. In business decisions, each alternative will have costs and benefits that must be compared to the costs and benefits of the other available alternatives. A difference in costs between any two alternatives is known as a **differential cost.** A difference in revenues between any two alternatives is known as **differential revenue.**

A differential cost is also known as an **incremental cost,** although technically an incremental cost should refer only to an increase in cost from one alternative to another; decreases in cost should be referred to as *decremental costs.* Differential cost is a broader term, encompassing both cost increases (incremental costs) and cost decreases (decremental costs) between alternatives.

The accountant's differential cost concept can be compared to the economist's marginal cost concept. In speaking of changes in cost and revenue, the economist employs the terms *marginal cost* and *marginal revenue.* The revenue that can be obtained from selling one more unit of product is called marginal revenue, and the cost involved in producing one more unit of product is called marginal cost. The economist's marginal concept is basically the same as the accountant's differential concept applied to a single unit of output.

Differential costs can be either fixed or variable. To illustrate, assume that Nature Way Cosmetics, Inc., is thinking about changing its marketing method from distribution through retailers to distribution by door-to-door direct sale. Present costs and revenues are compared to projected costs and revenues in the following table:

	Retailer Distribution (present)	Direct Sale Distribution (proposed)	Differential Costs and Revenues
Revenues (Variable)	$700,000	$800,000	$100,000
Cost of goods sold (Variable)	350,000	400,000	50,000
Advertising (Fixed)	80,000	45,000	(35,000)
Commissions (Variable)	0	40,000	40,000
Warehouse depreciation (Fixed)	50,000	80,000	30,000
Other expenses (Fixed)	60,000	60,000	0
Total	540,000	625,000	85,000
Net operating income	$160,000	$175,000	$ 15,000

According to the above analysis, the differential revenue is $100,000 and the differential costs total $85,000, leaving a positive differential net operating income of $15,000 under the proposed marketing plan.

The decision of whether Nature Way Cosmetics should stay with the present retail distribution or switch to door-to-door direct selling could be made on the basis of the net operating incomes of the two alternatives. As we see in the above analysis, the net operating income under the present distribution method is $160,000, whereas the net operating income under door-to-door direct selling is estimated to be $175,000. Therefore, the door-to-door direct distribution method is preferred, since it would result in $15,000 higher net operating income. Note that we would have arrived at exactly the same conclusion by simply focusing on the differential revenues, differential costs, and differential net operating income, which also show a $15,000 advantage for the direct selling method.

In general, only the differences between alternatives are relevant in decisions. Those items that are the same under all alternatives and that are not affected by the decision can be ignored. For example, in the Nature Way Cosmetics example above, the "Other expenses" category, which is $60,000 under both alternatives, can be ignored, since it has no effect on the decision. If it were removed from the calculations, the door-to-door direct selling method would still be preferred by $15,000. This is an extremely important principle in management accounting that we will return to in later chapters.

IN BUSINESS

USING THOSE EMPTY SEATS

Cancer patients who seek specialized or experimental treatments must often travel far from home. Flying on a commercial airline can be an expensive and grueling experience for these patients. Priscilla Blum noted that many corporate jets fly with empty seats and she wondered why these seats couldn't be used for cancer patients. Taking the initiative, she founded Corporate Angel Network (www.corpangelnetwork.org), an organization that arranges free flights on some 1,500 jets from over 500 companies. There are no tax breaks for putting cancer patients in empty corporate jet seats, but filling an empty seat with a cancer patient doesn't involve any significant incremental cost. Since its founding, Corporate Angel Network has provided over 16,000 free flights.

Sources: Scott McCormack, "Waste Not, Want Not," *Forbes*, July 26, 1999, p. 118. Roger McCaffrey, "A True Tale of Angels in the Sky," *The Wall Street Journal*, February, 2002, p. A14. Helen Gibbs, Communication Director, Corporate Angel Network, private communication.

Opportunity Cost

Opportunity cost is the potential benefit that is given up when one alternative is selected over another. To illustrate this important concept, consider the following examples:

Example 1 Vicki has a part-time job that pays $200 per week while attending college. She would like to spend a week at the beach during spring break, and her employer has agreed to give her the time off, but without pay. The $200 in lost wages would be an opportunity cost of taking the week off to be at the beach.

Example 2 Suppose that Neiman Marcus is considering investing a large sum of money in land that may be a site for a future store. Rather than invest the funds in land, the company could invest the funds in high-grade securities. If the land is acquired, the opportunity cost will be the investment income that could have been realized if the securities had been purchased instead.

Example 3 Steve is employed with a company that pays him a salary of $30,000 per year. He is thinking about leaving the company and returning to school. Since returning to school would require that he give up his $30,000 salary, the forgone salary would be an opportunity cost of seeking further education.

Opportunity costs are not usually entered in the accounting records of an organization, but they are costs that must be explicitly considered in every decision a manager makes. Virtually every alternative has some opportunity cost attached to it. In example 3 above, for instance, if Steve decides to stay at his job, the higher income that could be realized in future years as a result of returning to school is an opportunity cost.

Sunk Cost

A **sunk cost** is a cost *that has already been incurred* and that cannot be changed by any decision made now or in the future. Since sunk costs cannot be changed by any decision, they are not differential costs. Therefore, sunk costs can and should be ignored when making a decision.

To illustrate a sunk cost, assume that a company paid $50,000 several years ago for a special-purpose machine. The machine was used to make a product that is now obsolete and is no longer being sold. Even though in hindsight the purchase of the machine may have been unwise, the $50,000 cost has already been incurred and cannot be undone. And it would be folly to continue making the obsolete product in a misguided attempt to "recover" the original cost of the machine. In short, the $50,000 originally paid for the machine is a sunk cost that should be ignored in decisions.

IN BUSINESS

THE SUNK COST TRAP

Hal Arkes, a psychologist at Ohio University, asked 61 college students to assume they had mistakenly purchased tickets for both a $50 and a $100 ski trip for the same weekend. They could go on only one of the ski trips and would have to throw away the unused ticket. He further asked them to assume that they would actually have more fun on the $50 trip. Most of the students reported that they would go on the less enjoyable $100 trip. The larger cost mattered more to the students than having more fun. However, the sunk costs of the tickets should have been totally irrelevant in this decision. No matter which trip was selected, the actual total cost was $150—the cost of both tickets. And since this cost does not differ between the alternatives, it should be ignored. Like these students, most people have a great deal of difficulty ignoring sunk costs when making decisions.

Source: John Gourville and Dilip Soman, "Pricing and the Psychology of Consumption," *Harvard Business Review*, September 2002, pp. 92–93.

Summary

In this chapter, we have looked at some of the ways in which managers classify costs. How the costs will be used—for preparing external reports, predicting cost behavior, assigning costs to cost objects, or decision making—will dictate how the costs are classified.

For purposes of valuing inventories and determining expenses for the balance sheet and income statement, costs are classified as either product costs or period costs. Product costs are assigned to inventories and are considered assets until the products are sold. At the point of sale, product costs become cost of goods sold on the income statement. In contrast, following the usual accrual practices, period costs are taken directly to the income statement as expenses in the period in which they are incurred.

In a merchandising company, product cost is whatever the company paid for its merchandise. For external financial reports in a manufacturing company, product costs consist of all manufacturing costs. In both kinds of companies, selling and administrative costs are considered to be period costs and are expensed as incurred.

For purposes of predicting cost behavior—how costs will react to changes in activity—managers commonly classify costs into two categories—variable and fixed. Variable costs, in total, are strictly proportional to activity. The variable cost per unit is constant. Fixed costs, in total, remain at the same level for changes in activity that occur within the relevant range. The average fixed cost per unit decreases as the number of units increases.

For purposes of assigning costs to cost objects such as products or departments, costs are classified as direct or indirect. Direct costs can be conveniently traced to cost objects. Indirect costs cannot be conveniently traced to cost objects.

For purposes of making decisions, the concepts of differential cost and revenue, opportunity cost, and sunk cost are of vital importance. Differential costs and revenues are the costs and revenues that differ between alternatives. Opportunity cost is the benefit that is forgone when one alternative is selected over another. Sunk cost is a cost that occurred in the past and cannot be altered. Differential costs and opportunity costs should be carefully considered in decisions. Sunk costs are always irrelevant in decisions and should be ignored.

These various cost classifications are *different* ways of looking at costs. A particular cost, such as the cost of cheese in a taco served at Taco Bell, could be a manufacturing cost, a product cost, a variable cost, a direct cost, and a differential cost—all at the same time. Taco Bell can be considered to be a manufacturer of fast food. The cost of the cheese in a taco would be considered a manufacturing cost and, as such, it would be a product cost as well. In addition, the cost of cheese would be considered variable with respect to the number of tacos served and would be a direct cost of serving tacos. Finally, the cost of the cheese in a taco would be considered a differential cost of making and serving the taco.

Review Problem 1: Cost Terms

Many new cost terms have been introduced in this chapter. It will take you some time to learn what each term means and how to properly classify costs in an organization. Consider the following example: Porter Company manufactures furniture, including tables. Selected costs are given below:

1. The tables are made of wood that costs $100 per table.
2. The tables are made by workers, at a wage cost of $40 per table.
3. Workers making the tables are supervised by a factory supervisor who is paid $38,000 per year.
4. Electrical costs are $2 per machine-hour. Four machine-hours are required to produce a table.
5. The depreciation on the machines used to make the tables totals $10,000 per year. The machines have no resale value and do not wear out through use.
6. The salary of the president of Porter Company is $100,000 per year.
7. Porter Company spends $250,000 per year to advertise its products.
8. Salespersons are paid a commission of $30 for each table sold.
9. Instead of producing the tables, Porter Company could rent its factory space for $50,000 per year.

Required:

Classify these costs according to the various cost terms used in the chapter. *Carefully study the classification of each cost.* If you don't understand why a particular cost is classified the way it is, reread the section of the chapter discussing the particular cost term. The terms *variable cost* and *fixed cost* refer to how costs behave with respect to the number of tables produced in a year.

Solution to Review Problem 1

	Variable Cost	Fixed Cost	Period (selling and administrative) Cost	Product Cost: Direct Materials	Product Cost: Direct Labor	Product Cost: Manufacturing Overhead	Sunk Cost	Opportunity Cost
1. Wood used in a table ($100 per table)	X			X				
2. Labor cost to assemble a table ($40 per table)	X				X			
3. Salary of the factory supervisor ($38,000 per year)		X				X		

	Variable Cost	Fixed Cost	Period (selling and administrative) Cost	Product Cost: Direct Materials	Product Cost: Direct Labor	Product Cost: Manufacturing Overhead	Sunk Cost	Opportunity Cost
4. Cost of electricity to produce tables ($2 per machine-hour)	X					X		
5. Depreciation of machines used to produce tables ($10,000 per year)		X				X	X*	
6. Salary of the company president ($100,000 per year)		X	X					
7. Advertising expense ($250,000 per year)		X	X					
8. Commissions paid to salespersons ($30 per table sold)	X		X					
9. Rental income forgone on factory space								X†

*This is a sunk cost, since the outlay for the equipment was made in a previous period.
†This is an opportunity cost, since it represents the potential benefit that is lost or sacrificed as a result of using the factory space to produce tables. Opportunity cost is a special category of cost that is not ordinarily recorded in an organization's accounting books. To avoid possible confusion with other costs, we will not attempt to classify this cost in any other way except as an opportunity cost.

Review Problem 2: Schedule of Cost of Goods Manufactured and Income Statement

The following information has been taken from the accounting records of Klear-Seal Company for last year:

Selling expenses	$140,000
Raw materials inventory, January 1	$90,000
Raw materials inventory, December 31	$60,000
Utilities, factory	$36,000
Direct labor cost	$150,000
Depreciation, factory	$162,000
Purchases of raw materials	$750,000
Sales	$2,500,000
Insurance, factory	$40,000
Supplies, factory	$15,000
Administrative expenses	$270,000
Indirect labor	$300,000
Maintenance, factory	$87,000
Work in process inventory, January 1	$180,000
Work in process inventory, December 31	$100,000
Finished goods inventory, January 1	$260,000
Finished goods inventory, December 31	$210,000

Management wants these data organized in a better format so that financial statements can be prepared for the year.

Required:

1. Prepare a schedule of cost of goods manufactured as in Exhibit 2–4.
2. Compute the cost of goods sold.
3. Using data as needed from (1) and (2) above, prepare an income statement.

Solution to Review Problem 2

1.

KLEAR-SEAL COMPANY
Schedule of Cost of Goods Manufactured
For the Year Ended December 31

Direct materials:		
Raw materials inventory, January 1	$ 90,000	
Add: Purchases of raw materials	750,000	
Raw materials available for use	840,000	
Deduct: Raw materials inventory, December 31	60,000	
Raw materials used in production		$ 780,000
Direct labor		150,000
Manufacturing overhead:		
Utilities, factory	36,000	
Depreciation, factory	162,000	
Insurance, factory	40,000	
Supplies, factory	15,000	
Indirect labor	300,000	
Maintenance, factory	87,000	
Total manufacturing overhead costs		640,000
Total manufacturing costs		1,570,000
Add: Work in process inventory, January 1		180,000
		1,750,000
Deduct: Work in process inventory, December 31		100,000
Cost of goods manufactured		$1,650,000

2. The cost of goods sold would be computed as follows:

Finished goods inventory, January 1	$ 260,000
Add: Cost of goods manufactured	1,650,000
Goods available for sale	1,910,000
Deduct: Finished goods inventory, December 31	210,000
Cost of goods sold	$1,700,000

3.

KLEAR-SEAL COMPANY
Income Statement
For the Year Ended December 31

Sales		$2,500,000
Less cost of goods sold (above)		1,700,000
Gross margin		800,000
Less selling and administrative expenses:		
Selling expenses	$140,000	
Administrative expenses	270,000	
Total selling and administrative expenses		410,000
Net operating income		$ 390,000

Glossary

Administrative costs All executive, organizational, and clerical costs associated with the general management of an organization rather than with manufacturing, marketing, or selling. (p. 38)

Common costs A common cost is incurred to support a number of cost objects but cannot be traced to them individually. For example, the wage cost of the pilot of a 747 airliner is a common cost of all of the passengers on the aircraft. Without the pilot, there would be no flight and no passengers. But no part of the pilot's wage is caused by any one passenger taking the flight. (p. 51)

Conversion cost Direct labor cost plus manufacturing overhead cost. (p. 37)

Cost behavior The way in which a cost reacts to changes in the level of activity. (p. 48)

Cost object Anything for which cost data are desired. Examples of possible cost objects are products, product lines, customers, jobs, and organizational subunits such as departments or divisions of a company. (p. 50)

Cost of goods manufactured The manufacturing costs associated with the goods that were finished during the period. (p. 43)

Differential cost A difference in cost between two alternatives. Also see *Incremental cost.* (p. 51)

Differential revenue The difference in revenue between two alternatives. (p. 51)

Direct cost A cost that can be easily and conveniently traced to a specified cost object. (p. 50)

Direct labor Factory labor costs that can be easily traced to individual units of product. Also called *touch labor.* (p. 37)

Direct materials Materials that become an integral part of a finished product and whose costs can be conveniently traced to it. (p. 37)

Finished goods Units of product that have been completed but not yet sold to customers. (p. 41)

Fixed cost A cost that remains constant, in total, regardless of changes in the level of activity within the relevant range. If a fixed cost is expressed on a per unit basis, it varies inversely with the level of activity. (p. 49)

Incremental cost An increase in cost between two alternatives. Also see *Differential cost.* (p. 51)

Indirect cost A cost that cannot be easily and conveniently traced to a specified cost object. (p. 50)

Indirect labor The labor costs of janitors, supervisors, materials handlers, and other factory workers that cannot be conveniently traced directly to particular products. (p. 37)

Indirect materials Small items of material such as glue and nails. These items may become an integral part of a finished product, but their costs cannot be easily or conveniently traced to it. (p. 37)

Inventoriable costs Synonym for *product costs.* (p. 39)

Manufacturing overhead All costs associated with manufacturing except direct materials and direct labor. (p. 37)

Marketing or selling costs All costs necessary to secure customer orders and get the finished product or service into the hands of the customer. (p. 38)

Opportunity cost The potential benefit that is given up when one alternative is selected over another. (p. 52)

Period costs Costs that are taken directly to the income statement as expenses in the period in which they are incurred or accrued. (p. 39)

Prime cost Direct materials cost plus direct labor cost. (p. 38)

Product costs All costs that are involved in the purchase or manufacture of goods. In the case of manufactured goods, these costs consist of direct materials, direct labor, and manufacturing overhead. Also see *Inventoriable costs.* (p. 38)

Raw materials Any materials that go into the final product. (p. 36)

Relevant range The range of activity within which assumptions about variable and fixed cost behavior are valid. (p. 49)

Schedule of cost of goods manufactured A schedule showing the direct materials, direct labor, and manufacturing overhead costs incurred for a period and that are assigned to Work in Process and completed goods. (p. 43)

Sunk cost Any cost that has already been incurred and that cannot be changed by any decision made now or in the future. (p. 53)

Variable cost A cost that varies, in total, in direct proportion to changes in the level of activity. A variable cost is constant per unit. (p. 48)

Appendix 2A: Further Classification of Labor Costs

LEARNING OBJECTIVE 8
Properly account for labor costs associated with idle time, overtime, and fringe benefits.

Idle time, overtime, and fringe benefits associated with direct labor workers pose particular problems in accounting for labor costs. Are these costs a part of the costs of direct labor or are they something else?

Idle Time

Machine breakdowns, materials shortages, power failures, and the like result in idle time. The labor costs incurred during idle time may be treated as a manufacturing overhead cost rather than as a direct labor cost. This approach spreads such costs over all the production of a period rather than just the jobs that happen to be in process when breakdowns or other disruptions occur.

To give an example of how the cost of idle time may be handled, assume that a press operator earns $12 per hour. If the press operator is paid for a normal 40-hour workweek but is idle for 3 hours during a given week due to breakdowns, labor cost would be allocated as follows:

Direct labor ($12 per hour × 37 hours)	$444
Manufacturing overhead (idle time: $12 per hour × 3 hours)	36
Total cost for the week	$480

Overtime Premium

The overtime premium paid to *all* factory workers (direct labor as well as indirect labor) is usually considered to be part of manufacturing overhead and is not assigned to any particular order. At first glance this may seem strange, since overtime is always spent working on some particular order. Why not charge that order for the overtime cost? The reason is that it would be considered unfair and arbitrary to charge an overtime premium against a particular order simply because the order *happened* to fall on the tail end of the daily production schedule.

To illustrate, assume that two batches of goods, order A and order B, each take three hours to complete. The production run on order A is scheduled early in the day, but the production run on order B isn't scheduled until late in the afternoon. By the time the run on order B is completed, two hours of overtime have been logged. The necessity to work overtime was a result of the fact that total production exceeded the regular time available. Order B was no more responsible for the overtime than was order A. Therefore, managers feel that all production should share in the premium charge that resulted. This is considered a more equitable way of handling overtime premium in that it doesn't penalize one run simply because it happens to occur late in the day.

Let us again assume that a press operator in a plant earns $12 per hour. She is paid time and a half for overtime (time in excess of 40 hours a week). During a given week, she works 45 hours and has no idle time. Her labor cost for the week would be allocated as follows:

Direct labor ($12 per hour × 45 hours)	$540
Manufacturing overhead (overtime premium: $6 per hour × 5 hours)	30
Total cost for the week	$570

Observe from this computation that only the overtime premium of $6 per hour is charged to the overhead account—*not* the entire $18 earned for each hour of overtime work ($12 regular rate × 1.5 = $18).

Labor Fringe Benefits

Labor fringe benefits are made up of employment-related costs paid by the employer and include the costs of insurance programs, retirement plans, various supplemental unemployment benefits, and hospitalization plans. The employer also pays the employer's share of Social Security, Medicare, workers' compensation, federal employment tax, and state unemployment insurance. These costs often add up to as much as 30% to 40% of base pay.

Many companies treat all such costs as indirect labor by adding them to manufacturing overhead. Other companies treat the portion of fringe benefits that relates to direct labor as additional direct labor cost. This approach is conceptually superior, since the fringe benefits provided to direct labor workers clearly represent an added cost of their services.

Appendix 2B: Cost of Quality

A company may have a product with a high-quality design that uses high-quality components, but if the product is poorly assembled or has other defects, the company will have high warranty repair costs and dissatisfied customers. People who are dissatisfied with a product are unlikely to buy the product again. They are also likely to tell others about their bad experiences. One study found that "[c]ustomers who have bad experiences tell approximately 11 people about it."[1] This is the worst possible sort of advertising. To prevent such problems, companies have been expending a great deal of effort to reduce defects. The objective is to have high *quality of conformance.*

Quality of Conformance

LEARNING OBJECTIVE 9
Identify the four types of quality costs and explain how they interact.

A product that meets or exceeds its design specifications and is free of defects that mar its appearance or degrade its performance is said to have high **quality of conformance.** Note that if an economy car is free of defects, it can have a quality of conformance that is just as high as a defect-free luxury car. The purchasers of economy cars cannot expect their cars to be as opulently equipped as luxury cars, but they can and do expect them to be free of defects.

Preventing, detecting, and dealing with defects causes costs that are called *quality costs* or the *cost of quality.* The use of the term *quality cost* is confusing to some people. It does not refer to costs such as using a higher-grade leather to make a wallet or using 14K gold instead of gold-plating in jewelry. Instead, the term **quality cost** refers to all of the costs that are incurred to prevent defects or that result from defects in products.

IN BUSINESS

THE QUALITY BLACK BELT

General Electric (GE) has adopted the "Black Belt" quality control program developed by Motorola, Inc. Individuals selected to be Black Belts undergo intensive training for four months in statistical process control and other quality-control techniques. GE's CEO has made it clear to young managers that "they haven't much future at GE unless they are selected to be Black Belts. [With this program,] your customers are happy with you, you are not firefighting, you are not running in a reactive mode." GE hopes to save $7 to $10 billion over ten years as a result of its Black Belt program.

Source: William M. Carley, "Charging Ahead: To Keep GE's Profits Rising, Welch Pushes Quality-Control Plan," *The Wall Street Journal*, January 13, 1997, pp. A1 and A6.

[1] Christopher W. L. Hart, James L. Heskett, and W. Earl Sasser, Jr., "The Profitable Art of Service Recovery," *Harvard Business Review,* July–August 1990, p. 153.

EXHIBIT 2B–1
Typical Quality Costs

Prevention Costs	Internal Failure Costs
Systems development Quality engineering Quality training Quality circles Statistical process control activities Supervision of prevention activities Quality data gathering, analysis, and reporting Quality improvement projects Technical support provided to suppliers Audits of the effectiveness of the quality system	Net cost of scrap Net cost of spoilage Rework labor and overhead Reinspection of reworked products Retesting of reworked products Downtime caused by quality problems Disposal of defective products Analysis of the cause of defects in production Re-entering data because of keying errors Debugging software errors
Appraisal Costs	**External Failure Costs**
Test and inspection of incoming materials Test and inspection of in-process goods Final product testing and inspection Supplies used in testing and inspection Supervision of testing and inspection activities Depreciation of test equipment Maintenance of test equipment Plant utilities in the inspection area Field testing and appraisal at customer site	Cost of field servicing and handling complaints Warranty repairs and replacements Repairs and replacements beyond the warranty period Product recalls Liability arising from defective products Returns and allowances arising from quality problems Lost sales arising from a reputation for poor quality

Quality costs can be broken down into four broad groups. Two of these groups—known as *prevention costs* and *appraisal costs*—are incurred in an effort to keep defective products from falling into the hands of customers. The other two groups of costs—known as *internal failure costs* and *external failure costs*—are incurred because defects are produced despite efforts to prevent them. Examples of specific costs involved in each of these four groups are given in Exhibit 2B–1.

Several things should be noted about the quality costs shown in the exhibit. First, quality costs don't relate to just manufacturing; rather, they relate to all the activities in a company from initial research and development (R&D) through customer service. Second, the number of costs associated with quality is very large; total quality cost can be quite high unless management gives this area special attention. Finally, the costs in the four groupings are quite different. We will now look at each of these groupings more closely.

Prevention Costs

Generally, the most effective way to manage quality costs is to avoid having defects in the first place. It is much less costly to prevent a problem from ever happening than it is to find and correct the problem after it has occurred. **Prevention costs** support activities whose purpose is to reduce the number of defects. Companies employ many techniques to prevent defects including statistical process control, quality engineering, training, and a variety of tools from Total Quality Management.

Note from Exhibit 2B–1 that prevention costs include activities relating to quality circles and statistical process control. **Quality circles** consist of small groups of employees that meet on a regular basis to discuss ways to improve quality. Both management and workers are included in these circles. Quality circles are widely used and can be found in manufacturing companies, utilities, health care organizations, banks, and many other organizations.

Statistical process control is a technique that is used to detect whether a process is in or out of control. An out-of-control process results in defective units and may be caused by a miscalibrated machine or some other factor. In statistical process control, workers use charts to monitor the quality of units that pass through their workstations. With these charts, workers can quickly spot processes that are out of control and that are creating defects. Problems can be immediately corrected and further defects prevented rather than waiting for an inspector to catch the defects later.

Note also from the list of prevention costs in Exhibit 2B–1 that some companies provide technical support to their suppliers as a way of preventing defects. Particularly in just-in-time (JIT) systems, such support to suppliers is vital. In a JIT system, parts are delivered from suppliers just in time and in just the correct quantity to fill customer orders. There are no stockpiles of parts. If a defective part is received from a supplier, the part cannot be used and the order for the ultimate customer cannot be filled on time. Hence, every part received from a supplier must be free of defects. Consequently, companies that use JIT often require that their suppliers use sophisticated quality control programs such as statistical process control and that their suppliers certify that they will deliver parts and materials that are free of defects.

IN BUSINESS

SIMPLE SOLUTIONS

Very simple and inexpensive procedures can be used to prevent defects. Yamada Electric had a persistent problem assembling a simple push-button switch. The switch has two buttons, an on button and an off button, with a small spring under each button. Assembly is very simple. A worker inserts the small springs in the device and then installs the buttons. However, the worker sometimes forgets to put in one of the springs. When the customer discovers such a defective switch in a shipment from Yamada, an inspector has to be sent to the customer's plant to check every switch in the shipment. After each such incident, workers are urged to be more careful, and for a while quality improves. But eventually, someone forgets to put in a spring, and Yamada gets into trouble with the customer again. This chronic problem was very embarrassing to Yamada.

Shigeo Shingo, an expert on quality control, suggested a very simple solution. A small dish was placed next to the assembly station. At the beginning of each operation, two of the small springs are taken out of a parts box containing hundreds of springs and placed in the dish. The worker then assembles the switch. If a spring remains on the dish after assembling the switch, the worker immediately realizes a spring has been left out, and the switch is reassembled. This simple change in procedures completely eliminated the problem.

Source: Shigeo Shingo and Dr. Alan Robinson, editor-in-chief, *Modern Approaches to Manufacturing Improvement: The Shingo System*, (Cambridge, MA: Productivity Press), pp. 214–216.

Appraisal Costs

Any defective parts and products should be caught as early as possible in the production process. **Appraisal costs,** which are sometimes called *inspection costs,* are incurred to identify defective products *before* the products are shipped to customers. Unfortunately, performing appraisal activities doesn't keep defects from happening again, and most managers now realize that maintaining an army of inspectors is a costly (and ineffective) approach to quality control.

Professor John K. Shank of Dartmouth College has aptly stated, "The old-style approach was to say, 'We've got great quality. We have 40 quality control inspectors in the factory.' Then somebody realized that if you need 40 inspectors, it must be a lousy factory. So now the trick is to run a factory without any quality control inspectors; each employee is his or her own quality control person."[2]

[2] Robert W. Casey, "The Changing World of the CEO," *PPM World* 24, no. 2, p. 31.

Employees are increasingly being asked to be responsible for their own quality control. This approach, along with designing products to be easy to manufacture properly, allows quality to be built into products rather than relying on inspection to get the defects out.

Internal Failure Costs

Failure costs are incurred when a product fails to conform to its design specifications. Failure costs can be either internal or external. **Internal failure costs** result from identifying defects before they are shipped to customers. These costs include scrap, rejected products, reworking of defective units, and downtime caused by quality problems. In some companies, as little as 10% of the company's products make it through the production process without rework of some kind. Of course, the more effective a company's appraisal activities, the greater the chance of catching defects internally and the greater the level of internal failure costs. This is the price that is paid to avoid incurring external failure costs, which can be devastating.

External Failure Costs

External failure costs result when a defective product is delivered to a customer. As shown in Exhibit 2B–1, external failure costs include warranty repairs and replacements, product recalls, liability arising from legal action against a company, and lost sales arising from a reputation for poor quality. Such costs can decimate profits.

In the past, some managers have taken the attitude, "Let's go ahead and ship everything to customers, and we'll take care of any problems under the warranty." This attitude generally results in high external failure costs, customer ill will, and declining market share and profits.

Distribution of Quality Costs

A company's total quality cost is likely to be very high unless management gives this area special attention. Quality costs for U.S. companies range between 10% and 20% of total sales, whereas experts say that these costs should be more in the 2% to 4% range. How does a company reduce its total quality cost? The answer lies in how the quality costs are distributed. Refer to the graph in Exhibit 2B–2, which shows total quality costs as a function of the quality of conformance.

The graph shows that when the quality of conformance is low, total quality cost is high and that most of this cost consists of costs of internal and external failure. A low quality of conformance means that a high percentage of units are defective and hence the company must incur high failure costs. However, as a company spends more and more on prevention and appraisal, the percentage of defective units drops (the percentage of defect-free units increases). This results in lower internal and external failure costs. Ordinarily, total quality cost drops rapidly as the quality of conformance increases. Thus, a company can reduce its total quality cost by focusing its efforts on prevention and appraisal. The cost savings from reduced defects usually swamp the costs of the additional prevention and appraisal efforts.

The graph in Exhibit 2B–2 has been drawn so that the total quality cost is minimized when the quality of conformance is less than 100%. However, some experts contend that the total quality cost is not minimized until the quality of conformance is 100% and there are no defects. Indeed, many companies have found that the total quality costs seem to keep dropping even when the quality of conformance approaches 100% and defect rates get as low as 1 in a million units. Others argue that total quality cost eventually increases as the quality of conformance increases. However, in most companies this does not seem to happen until the quality of conformance is very close to 100% and defect rates are very close to zero.

EXHIBIT 2B–2
Effect of Quality Costs on Quality of Conformance

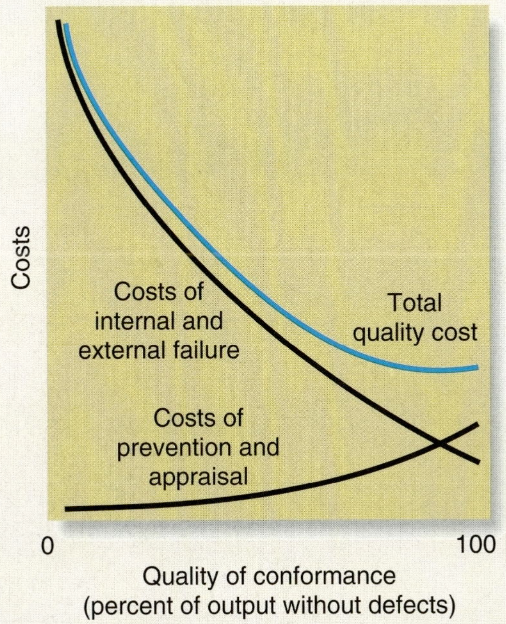

As a company's quality program becomes more refined and as its failure costs begin to fall, prevention activities usually become more effective than appraisal activities. Appraisal can only find defects, whereas prevention can eliminate them. The best way to prevent defects from happening is to design processes that reduce the likelihood of defects and to continually monitor processes using statistical process control methods.

Quality Cost Reports

LEARNING OBJECTIVE 10
Prepare and interpret a quality cost report.

As an initial step in quality improvement programs, companies often construct a *quality cost report* that provides an estimate of the financial consequences of the company's current level of defects. A **quality cost report** details the prevention costs, appraisal costs, and costs of internal and external failures that arise from the company's current quality control efforts. Managers are often shocked by the magnitude of these costs. A typical quality cost report is shown in Exhibit 2B–3 (page 64).

Several things should be noted from the data in the exhibit. First, Ventura Company's quality costs are poorly distributed in both years, with most of the costs being traceable to either internal failure or external failure. The external failure costs are particularly high in Year 1 in comparison to other costs.

Second, note that the company increased its spending on prevention and appraisal activities in Year 2. As a result, internal failure costs went up in that year (from $2 million in Year 1 to $3 million in Year 2), but external failure costs dropped sharply (from $5.15 million in Year 1 to only $2 million in Year 2). Because of the increase in appraisal activity in Year 2, more defects were caught inside the company before they were shipped to customers. This resulted in more cost for scrap, rework, and so forth, but saved huge amounts in warranty repairs, warranty replacements, and other external failure costs.

Third, note that as a result of greater emphasis on prevention and appraisal, *total* quality cost decreased in Year 2. As continued emphasis is placed on prevention and appraisal in future years, total quality cost should continue to decrease. That is, future

EXHIBIT 2B–3
Quality Cost Report

VENTURA COMPANY
Quality Cost Report
For Years 1 and 2

	Year 2		Year 1	
	Amount	Percent*	Amount	Percent*
Prevention costs:				
Systems development	$ 400,000	0.80%	$ 270,000	0.54%
Quality training	210,000	0.42%	130,000	0.26%
Supervision of prevention activities	70,000	0.14%	40,000	0.08%
Quality improvement projects	320,000	0.64%	210,000	0.42%
Total prevention cost	1,000,000	2.00%	650,000	1.30%
Appraisal costs:				
Inspection	600,000	1.20%	560,000	1.12%
Reliability testing	580,000	1.16%	420,000	0.84%
Supervision of testing and inspection	120,000	0.24%	80,000	0.16%
Depreciation of test equipment	200,000	0.40%	140,000	0.28%
Total appraisal cost	1,500,000	3.00%	1,200,000	2.40%
Internal failure costs:				
Net cost of scrap	900,000	1.80%	750,000	1.50%
Rework labor and overhead	1,430,000	2.86%	810,000	1.62%
Downtime due to defects in quality	170,000	0.34%	100,000	0.20%
Disposal of defective products	500,000	1.00%	340,000	0.68%
Total internal failure cost	3,000,000	6.00%	2,000,000	4.00%
External failure costs:				
Warranty repairs	400,000	0.80%	900,000	1.80%
Warranty replacements	870,000	1.74%	2,300,000	4.60%
Allowances	130,000	0.26%	630,000	1.26%
Cost of field servicing	600,000	1.20%	1,320,000	2.64%
Total external failure cost	2,000,000	4.00%	5,150,000	10.30%
Total quality cost	$7,500,000	15.00%	$9,000,000	18.00%

*As a percentage of total sales. In each year sales totaled $50,000,000.

increases in prevention and appraisal costs should be more than offset by decreases in failure costs. Moreover, appraisal costs should also decrease as more effort is placed in prevention.

IN BUSINESS

FIGHTING BUGS

Software bugs can have catastrophic consequences. Companies that sell products that rely on software know this, and fighting these particular defects can consume enormous resources. For example, it was once estimated that the cost of quality (i.e., the costs of preventing, detecting, and fixing bugs) at Raytheon Electronics Systems was almost 60% of the total cost of producing software for its products. That percentage has fallen to 15% due to new software management tools designed to prevent bugs from being written into the computer code in the first place.

Source: Otis Port, "Will Bugs Eat Up the U.S. Lead in Software?" *Business Week*, December 6, 1999, p. 118.

EXHIBIT 2B–4
Quality Cost Reports in Graphic Form

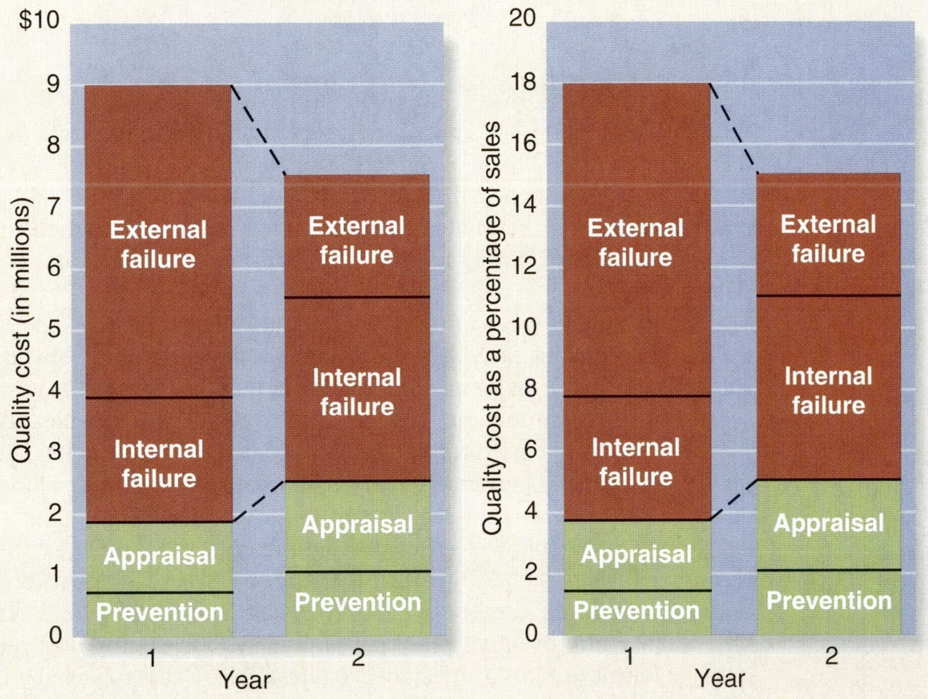

IN BUSINESS

EXTERNAL FAILURE; IT'S WORSE THAN YOU THINK

Venky Nagar and Madhav Rajan investigated quality costs at 11 manufacturing plants of a large U.S. company. They found that total quality costs were about 7% of sales. Moreover, they found that external failure costs as usually measured grossly understate the true impact of external failures on the company's profits. In addition to the obvious costs of repairing defective products that are under warranty, defective products sold to customers negatively impact the company's reputation and hence future sales. Statistical analysis of the data from the manufacturing plants indicated that a $1 increase in external failure costs such as warranty repairs was associated with a $26 decrease in cumulative future sales and a $10.40 cumulative decrease in future profits.

Source: Venky Nagar and Madhav V. Rajan, "The Revenue Implications of Financial and Operational Measures of Product Quality," *The Accounting Review* 76, no. 4, October 2001, pp. 495–513.

Quality Cost Reports in Graphic Form

As a supplement to the quality cost report shown in Exhibit 2B–3, companies frequently prepare quality cost information in graphic form. Graphic presentations include pie charts, bar graphs, trend lines, and so forth. The data for Ventura Company from Exhibit 2B–3 are presented in bar graph form in Exhibit 2B–4.

The first bar graph in Exhibit 2B–4 is scaled in terms of dollars of quality cost, and the second is scaled in terms of quality cost as a percentage of sales. In both graphs, the data are "stacked" upward. That is, appraisal costs are stacked on top of prevention costs, internal failure costs are stacked on top of the sum of prevention costs plus appraisal costs, and so forth. The percentage figures in the second graph show that total quality cost equals 18% of sales in Year 1 and 15% of sales in Year 2, the same as reported earlier in Exhibit 2B–3.

Data in graphic form help managers to see trends more clearly and to see the magnitude of the various costs in relation to each other. Such graphs are easily prepared using computer graphics and spreadsheet applications.

Uses of Quality Cost Information

A quality cost report has several uses. First, quality cost information helps managers see the financial significance of defects. Managers usually are not aware of the magnitude of their quality costs because these costs cut across departmental lines and are not normally tracked and accumulated by the cost system. Thus, when first presented with a quality cost report, managers often are surprised by the amount of cost attributable to poor quality.

Second, quality cost information helps managers identify the relative importance of the quality problems faced by their companies. For example, the quality cost report may show that scrap is a major quality problem or that the company is incurring huge warranty costs. With this information, managers have a better idea of where to focus their efforts.

Third, quality cost information helps managers see whether their quality costs are poorly distributed. In general, quality costs should be distributed more toward prevention and appraisal activities and less toward failures.

Counterbalancing these uses, three limitations of quality cost information should be recognized. First, simply measuring and reporting quality costs does not solve quality problems. Problems can be solved only by taking action. Second, results usually lag behind quality improvement programs. Initially, total quality cost may even increase as quality control systems are designed and installed. Decreases in quality costs may not begin to occur until the quality program has been in effect for a year or more. And third, the most important quality cost, lost sales arising from customer ill will, is usually omitted from the quality cost report because it is difficult to estimate.

Typically, during the initial years of a quality improvement program, the benefits of compiling a quality cost report outweigh the costs and limitations of the reports. As managers gain experience in balancing prevention and appraisal activities, the need for quality cost reports often diminishes.

IN BUSINESS

TRADING OFF QUALITY COSTS IN INDIA

The quality costs at tanneries operated by two leather companies in India are quite different. Company X spends about 5% of its quality costs on prevention, whereas Company Y spends over 14% of its quality costs on prevention. Consequently, the total quality cost at Company X is about 10% higher than at Company Y. By spending more on prevention, Company X should be able to lower its total quality cost.

Source: P. K. Bandyopadhyay and K. K. Ghosh, "An Indepth Analysis in Quality Costing—A Case," *The Management Accountant (India)*, March 1999, pp. 167–171.

International Aspects of Quality

Many of the tools used in quality management today were developed in Japan after World War II. In statistical process control, Japanese companies borrowed heavily from the work of W. Edwards Deming. However, Japanese companies are largely responsible for quality circles, JIT, the idea that quality is everyone's responsibility, and the emphasis on prevention rather than on inspection.

In the 1980s, quality reemerged as a pivotal factor in the market. Many companies now find that it is impossible to effectively compete without a very strong quality program in place. This is particularly true of companies that wish to compete in the European market.

The ISO 9000 Standards

The International Organization for Standardization (ISO), based in Geneva, Switzerland, has established quality control guidelines known as the **ISO 9000 standards.** Many companies and organizations in Europe will buy only from ISO 9000-certified suppliers. This means that the suppliers must demonstrate to a certifying agency that:

1. A quality control system is in use, and the system clearly defines an expected level of quality.
2. The system is fully operational and is backed up with detailed documentation of quality control procedures.
3. The intended level of quality is being achieved on a sustained, consistent basis.

The key to receiving certification under the ISO 9000 standards is documentation. It's one thing for a company to say that it has a quality control system in operation, but it's quite a different thing to be able to document the steps in that system. Under ISO 9000, this documentation must be so detailed and precise that if all the employees in a company were suddenly replaced, the new employees could use the documentation to make the product exactly as it was made by the old employees. Even companies with good quality control systems find that it takes up to two years of painstaking work to develop this detailed documentation. But companies often find that compiling this documentation results in improvements in their quality systems.

The ISO 9000 standards have become an international measure of quality. Although the standards were developed to control the quality of goods sold in European countries, they have become widely accepted elsewhere as well. Companies in the United States that export to Europe often expect their own suppliers to comply with the ISO 9000 standards, since these exporters must document the quality of the materials going into their products as part of their own ISO 9000 certification.

The ISO program for certification of quality management programs is not limited to manufacturing companies. The American Institute of Certified Public Accountants was the first professional membership organization in the United States to win recognition under an ISO certification program.[3]

Summary

Defects cause costs, which can be classified into prevention costs, appraisal costs, internal failure costs, and external failure costs. Prevention costs are incurred to keep defects from happening. Appraisal costs are incurred to ensure that defective products, once made, are not shipped to customers. Internal failure costs are incurred as a consequence of detecting defective products before they are shipped to customers. External failure costs are the consequences (in terms of repairs, servicing, and lost future business) of delivering defective products to customers. Most experts agree that management effort should be focused on preventing defects. Small investments in prevention can lead to dramatic reductions in appraisal costs and costs of internal and external failure.

Quality costs are summarized on a quality cost report. This report shows the type of quality costs being incurred and their significance and trends. The report helps managers understand the importance of quality costs, spot problem areas, and assess the way in which the quality costs are distributed.

[3] *The CPA Letter,* May 1998, p. 1.

Glossary

Appraisal costs Costs that are incurred to identify defective products before the products are shipped to customers. (p. 61)

External failure costs Costs that are incurred when a product or service that is defective is delivered to a customer. (p. 62)

Internal failure costs Costs that are incurred as a result of identifying defective products before they are shipped to customers. (p. 62)

ISO 9000 standards Quality control requirements issued by the International Organization for Standardization that relate to products sold in European countries. (p. 67)

Prevention costs Costs that are incurred to keep defects from occurring. (p. 60)

Quality circles Small groups of employees that meet on a regular basis to discuss ways of improving quality. (p. 60)

Quality cost Costs that are incurred to prevent defective products from falling into the hands of customers or that are incurred as a result of defective units. (p. 59)

Quality cost report A report that details prevention costs, appraisal costs, and the costs of internal and external failures. (p. 63)

Quality of conformance The degree to which a product or service meets or exceeds its design specifications and is free of defects or other problems that mar its appearance or degrade its performance. (p. 59)

Statistical process control A charting technique used to monitor the quality of work being done in a workstation for the purpose of immediately correcting any problems. (p. 61)

Questions

2–1 What are the three major elements of product costs in a manufacturing company?

2–2 Distinguish between the following: (a) direct materials, (b) indirect materials, (c) direct labor, (d) indirect labor, and (e) manufacturing overhead.

2–3 Explain the difference between a product cost and a period cost.

2–4 Describe how the income statement of a manufacturing company differs from the income statement of a merchandising company.

2–5 Of what value is the schedule of cost of goods manufactured? How does it tie into the income statement?

2–6 Describe how the inventory accounts of a manufacturing company differ from the inventory account of a merchandising company.

2–7 Why are product costs sometimes called inventoriable costs? Describe the flow of such costs in a manufacturing company from the point of incurrence until they finally become expenses on the income statement.

2–8 Is it possible for costs such as salaries or depreciation to end up as assets on the balance sheet? Explain.

2–9 What is meant by the term *cost behavior?*

2–10 "A variable cost is a cost that varies per unit of product, whereas a fixed cost is constant per unit of product." Do you agree? Explain.

2–11 How do fixed costs create difficulties in costing units of product?

2–12 Why is manufacturing overhead considered an indirect cost of a unit of product?

2–13 Define the following terms: differential cost, opportunity cost, and sunk cost.

2–14 Only variable costs can be differential costs. Do you agree? Explain.

2–15 (Appendix 2A) Mary Adams is employed by Acme Company. Last week she worked 34 hours assembling one of the company's products and was idle 6 hours due to material shortages. Acme's employees are engaged at their workstations for a normal 40-hour week. Ms. Adams is paid $15 per hour. Allocate her earnings between direct labor cost and manufacturing overhead cost.

2–16 (Appendix 2A) John Olsen operates a stamping machine on the assembly line of Drake Manufacturing Company. Last week Mr. Olsen worked 45 hours. His basic wage rate is $14 per hour, with time and a half for overtime (time worked in excess of 40 hours per week). Allocate Mr. Olsen's wages for the week between direct labor cost and manufacturing overhead cost.

2–17 (Appendix 2B) Costs associated with the quality of conformance can be broken down into four broad groups. What are these four groups and how do they differ?

2–18 (Appendix 2B) In their efforts to reduce the total cost of quality, should companies generally focus on decreasing prevention costs and appraisal costs?

2–19 (Appendix 2B) What is probably the most effective way to reduce a company's total quality costs?

2–20 (Appendix 2B) What are the main uses of quality cost reports?

2–21 (Appendix 2B) Why are managers often unaware of the magnitude of quality costs?

Exercises

EXERCISE 2–1 Classifying Manufacturing Costs [LO1]

The PC Works assembles custom computers from components supplied by various manufacturers. The company is very small and its assembly shop and retail sales store are housed in a single facility in a Redmond, Washington, industrial park. Listed below are some of the costs that are incurred at the company.

Required:

For each cost, indicate whether it would most likely be classified as direct labor, direct materials, manufacturing overhead, marketing and selling, or an administrative cost.

1. The cost of a hard drive installed in a computer.
2. The cost of advertising in the *Puget Sound Computer User* newspaper.
3. The wages of employees who assemble computers from components.
4. Sales commissions paid to the company's salespeople.
5. The wages of the assembly shop's supervisor.
6. The wages of the company's accountant.
7. Depreciation on equipment used to test assembled computers before release to customers.
8. Rent on the facility in the industrial park.

EXERCISE 2–2 Classification of Costs as Period or Product Cost [LO2]

A product cost is also known as an inventoriable cost. Classify the following costs as either product (inventoriable) costs or period (noninventoriable) costs in a manufacturing company:

1. Depreciation on salespersons' cars.
2. Rent on equipment used in the factory.
3. Lubricants used for maintenance of machines.
4. Salaries of finished goods warehouse personnel.
5. Soap and paper towels used by factory workers at the end of a shift.
6. Factory supervisors' salaries.
7. Heat, water, and power consumed in the factory.
8. Materials used for boxing products for shipment overseas. (Units are not normally boxed.)
9. Advertising costs.
10. Workers' compensation insurance on factory employees.
11. Depreciation on chairs and tables in the factory lunchroom.
12. The wages of the receptionist in the administrative offices.
13. Lease cost of the corporate jet used by the company's executives.
14. Rent on rooms at a Florida resort for holding of the annual sales conference.
15. Attractively designed box for packaging the company's product—breakfast cereal.

EXERCISE 2–3 Constructing an Income Statement [LO3]

Last month CyberGames, a computer game retailer, had total sales of $1,450,000, selling expenses of $210,000, and administrative expenses of $180,000. The company had beginning merchandise inventory of $240,000, purchased additional merchandise inventory for $950,000, and had ending merchandise inventory of $170,000.

Required:

Prepare an income statement for the company for the month.

EXERCISE 2–4 Prepare a Schedule of Cost of Goods Manufactured [LO4]

Lompac Products manufactures a variety of products in its factory. Data for the most recent month's operations appear below:

Beginning raw materials inventory	$ 60,000
Purchases of raw materials	$690,000
Ending raw materials inventory	$ 45,000
Direct labor	$135,000
Manufacturing overhead	$370,000
Beginning work in process inventory	$120,000
Ending work in process inventory	$130,000

Required:
Prepare a schedule of cost of goods manufactured for the company for the month.

EXERCISE 2–5 Classification of Costs as Fixed or Variable [LO5]
Below are a number of costs that are incurred in a variety of organizations.

Required:
Classify each cost as being variable or fixed with respect to the number of units of product or services sold by the organization by placing an *X* in the appropriate column.

	Cost Behavior	
Cost Item	Variable	Fixed
1. X-ray film used in the radiology lab at Virginia Mason Hospital in Seattle.		
2. The costs of advertising a Madonna rock concert in New York City.		
3. Rental cost of a McDonald's restaurant building in Hong Kong.		
4. The electrical costs of running a roller coaster at Magic Mountain.		
5. Property taxes on your local cinema.		
6. Commissions paid to salespersons at Nordstrom.		
7. Property insurance on a Coca-Cola bottling plant.		
8. The costs of synthetic materials used to make Nike running shoes.		
9. The costs of shipping Panasonic televisions to retail stores.		
10. The cost of leasing an ultra-scan diagnostic machine at the American Hospital in Paris.		

EXERCISE 2–6 Identifying Direct and Indirect Costs [LO6]
Northwest Hospital is a full-service hospital that provides everything from major surgery and emergency room care to outpatient clinics.

Required:
For each cost incurred at Northwest Hospital, indicate whether it would most likely be a direct cost or an indirect cost of the specified cost object by placing an *X* in the appropriate column.

Cost	Cost object	Direct Cost	Indirect Cost
Ex. Catered food served to patients	A particular patient	X	
1. The wages of pediatric nurses	The pediatric department		
2. Prescription drugs	A particular patient		
3. Heating the hospital	The pediatric department		
4. The salary of the head of pediatrics	The pediatric department		
5. The salary of the head of pediatrics	A particular pediatric patient		
6. Hospital chaplain's salary	A particular patient		
7. Lab tests by outside contractor	A particular patient		
8. Lab tests by outside contractor	A particular department		

EXERCISE 2–7 Differential, Opportunity, and Sunk Costs [LO7]
Northwest Hospital is a full-service hospital that provides everything from major surgery and emergency room care to outpatient clinics. The hospital's Radiology Department is considering replacing an old inefficient X-ray machine with a state-of-the-art digital X-ray machine. The new machine would provide higher quality X-rays in less time and at a lower cost per X-ray. It would

also require less power and would use a color laser printer to produce easily readable X-ray images. Instead of investing the funds in the new X-ray machine, the Laboratory Department is lobbying the hospital's management to buy a new DNA analyzer.

Required:
For each of the items below, indicate by placing an *X* in the appropriate column whether it should be considered a differential cost, an opportunity cost, or a sunk cost in the decision to replace the old X-ray machine with a new machine. If none of the categories apply for a particular item, leave all columns blank.

Item	Differential Cost	Opportunity Cost	Sunk Cost
Ex. Cost of X-ray film used in the old machine	X		
1. Cost of the old X-ray machine			
2. The salary of the head of the Radiology Department ...			
3. The salary of the head of the Pediatrics Department ...			
4. Cost of the new color laser printer			
5. Rent on the space occupied by Radiology			
6. The cost of maintaining the old machine			
7. Benefits from a new DNA analyzer			
8. Cost of electricity to run the X-ray machines			

EXERCISE 2–8 (Appendix 2A) Classification of Overtime Cost [LO8]

Several days ago you took your TV set into a shop to have some repair work done. When you later picked up the set, the bill showed a $75 charge for labor. This charge represented two hours of service time—$30 for the first hour and $45 for the second.

When questioned about the difference in hourly rates, the shop manager explained that work on your set was started at 4 o'clock in the afternoon. By the time work was completed two hours later at 6 o'clock, an hour of overtime had been put in by the repair technician. The second hour therefore contained a charge for an "overtime premium," since the company had to pay the repair technician time and a half for any work in excess of eight hours per day. The shop manager further explained that the shop was working overtime to "catch up a little" on its backlog of repairs, but it still needed to maintain a "decent" profit margin on the technicians' time.

Required:
1. Do you agree with the shop's computation of the service charge on your job?
2. Assume that the shop pays its technicians $14 per hour for the first eight hours worked in a day and $21 per hour for any additional time worked in a day. Prepare computations to show how the cost of the repair technician's time for the day (nine hours) should be allocated between direct labor cost and general overhead cost on the shop's books.
3. Under what circumstances might the shop be justified in charging an overtime premium for repair work on your set?

EXERCISE 2–9 (Appendix 2B) Classification of Quality Costs [LO9]
Listed below are a number of costs that are incurred in connection with a company's quality control system.

a. Product testing.
b. Product recalls.
c. Rework labor and overhead.
d. Quality circles.
e. Downtime caused by defects.
f. Cost of field servicing.
g. Inspection of goods.
h. Quality engineering.
i. Warranty repairs.
j. Statistical process control.
k. Net cost of scrap.
l. Depreciation of test equipment.
m. Returns and allowances arising from poor quality.
n. Disposal of defective products.
o. Technical support to suppliers.
p. Systems development.
q. Warranty replacements.
r. Field testing at customer site.
s. Product design.

Required:
1. Classify each of the costs above into one of the following categories: prevention cost, appraisal cost, internal failure cost, or external failure cost.
2. Which of the costs in (1) above are incurred in an effort to keep poor quality of conformance from occurring? Which of the costs in (1) above are incurred because poor quality of conformance has occurred?

EXERCISE 2–10 Preparation of Schedule of Costs of Goods Manufactured and Cost of Goods Sold [LO1, LO3, LO4]

The following cost and inventory data are taken from the accounting records of Mason Company for the year just completed:

Costs incurred:	
Direct labor cost	$70,000
Purchases of raw materials	$118,000
Indirect labor	$30,000
Maintenance, factory equipment	$6,000
Advertising expense	$90,000
Insurance, factory equipment	$800
Sales salaries	$50,000
Rent, factory facilities	$20,000
Supplies	$4,200
Depreciation, office equipment	$3,000
Depreciation, factory equipment	$19,000

	Beginning of the Year	End of the Year
Inventories:		
Raw materials	$7,000	$15,000
Work in process	$10,000	$5,000
Finished goods	$20,000	$35,000

Required:

1. Prepare a schedule of cost of goods manufactured in good form.
2. Prepare the cost of goods sold section of Mason Company's income statement for the year.

EXERCISE 2–11 Classification of Costs as Variable or Fixed and as Selling and Administrative or Product [LO2, LO5]

Below are listed various costs that are found in organizations.

1. Hamburger buns in a Wendy's outlet.
2. Advertising by a dental office.
3. Apples processed and canned by Del Monte.
4. Shipping canned apples from a Del Monte plant to customers.
5. Insurance on a Bausch & Lomb factory producing contact lenses.
6. Insurance on IBM's corporate headquarters.
7. Salary of a supervisor overseeing production of printers at Hewlett-Packard.
8. Commissions paid to Encyclopedia Britannica salespersons.
9. Depreciation of factory lunchroom facilities at a General Electric plant.
10. Steering wheels installed in BMWs.

Required:

Classify each cost as being either variable or fixed with respect to the number of units produced and sold. Also classify each cost as either a selling and administrative cost or a product cost. Prepare your answer sheet as shown below. Place an *X* in the appropriate columns to show the proper classification of each cost.

	Cost Behavior		Selling and Administrative	Product
Cost Item	Variable	Fixed	Cost	Cost

EXERCISE 2–12 Product Cost Flows; Product versus Period Costs [LO2, LO3]

The Devon Motor Company produces motorcycles. During April, the company purchased 8,000 batteries at a cost of $10 per battery. Devon withdrew 7,600 batteries from the storeroom during the month. Of these, 100 were used to replace batteries in motorcycles used by the company's traveling sales staff. The remaining 7,500 batteries withdrawn from the storeroom were placed in motorcycles being produced by the company. Of the motorcycles in production during April, 90% were completed and transferred from work in process to finished goods. Of the motorcycles completed during the month, 30% were unsold at April 30.

There were no inventories of any type on April 1.

Required:

1. Determine the cost of batteries that would appear in each of the following accounts at April 30:
   a. Raw Materials.
   b. Work in Process.
   c. Finished Goods.
   d. Cost of Goods Sold.
   e. Selling Expense.
2. Specify whether each of the above accounts would appear on the balance sheet or on the income statement at April 30.

EXERCISE 2–13 (Appendix 2A) Classification of Labor Costs [LO8]

Paul Clark is employed by Aerotech Products and assembles a component part for one of the company's product lines. He is paid $14 per hour for regular time and time and a half (i.e., $21 per hour) for all work in excess of 40 hours per week.

Required:

1. Assume that during a given week Paul is idle for five hours due to machine breakdowns and that he is idle for four more hours due to material shortages. No overtime is recorded for the week. Allocate Paul's wages for the week between direct labor cost and manufacturing overhead cost.
2. Assume that during the following week Paul works a total of 48 hours. He has no idle time for the week. Allocate Paul's wages for the week between direct labor cost and manufacturing overhead cost.
3. Paul's company provides an attractive package of fringe benefits for its employees. This package includes a retirement program and a health insurance program. Explain two ways that the company could handle the costs of its direct laborers' fringe benefits in its cost records.

Problems

PROBLEM 2–14 Classification of Costs [LO1, LO2, LO5, LO7]

Wollogong Group Ltd. of New South Wales, Australia, acquired its factory building about 10 years ago. For several years the company has rented out a small annex attached to the rear of the building. The company has received a rental income of $30,000 per year on this space. The renter's lease will expire soon, and rather than renewing the lease, the company has decided to use the space itself to manufacture a new product.

Direct materials cost for the new product will total $80 per unit. To have a place to store finished units of product, the company will rent a small warehouse nearby. The rental cost will be $500 per month. In addition, the company must rent equipment for use in producing the new product; the rental cost will be $4,000 per month. Workers will be hired to manufacture the new product, with direct labor cost amounting to $60 per unit. The space in the annex will continue to be depreciated on a straight-line basis, as in prior years. This depreciation is $8,000 per year.

Advertising costs for the new product will total $50,000 per year. A supervisor will be hired to oversee production; her salary will be $1,500 per month. Electricity for operating machines will be $1.20 per unit. Costs of shipping the new product to customers will be $9 per unit.

To provide funds to purchase materials, meet payrolls, and so forth, the company will have to liquidate some temporary investments. These investments are presently yielding a return of about $3,000 per year.

Required:

Prepare an answer sheet with the following column headings:

			Product Cost					
Name of the Cost	Variable Cost	Fixed Cost	Direct Materials	Direct Labor	Manufacturing Overhead	Period (selling and administrative) Cost	Opportunity Cost	Sunk Cost

List the different costs associated with the new product decision down the extreme left column (under Name of the Cost). Then place an *X* under each heading that helps to describe the type of cost involved. There may be *X*'s under several column headings for a single cost. (For example, a cost may be a fixed cost, a period cost, and a sunk cost; you would place an *X* under each of these column headings opposite the cost.)

PROBLEM 2–15 Cost Classification [LO2, LO5, LO6]
Listed below are a number of costs typically found in organizations.

1. Property taxes, factory.
2. Boxes used for packaging detergent produced by the company.
3. Salespersons' commissions.
4. Supervisor's salary, factory.
5. Depreciation, executive autos.
6. Wages of workers assembling computers.
7. Insurance, finished goods warehouses.
8. Lubricants for machines.
9. Advertising costs.
10. Microchips used in producing calculators.
11. Shipping costs on merchandise sold.
12. Magazine subscriptions, factory lunchroom.
13. Thread in a garment factory.
14. Billing costs.
15. Executive life insurance.
16. Ink used in textbook production.
17. Fringe benefits, assembly-line workers.
18. Yarn used in sweater production.
19. Wages of receptionist, executive offices.

Required:
Prepare an answer sheet with column headings as shown below. For each cost item, indicate whether it would be variable or fixed with respect to the number of units produced and sold; and then whether it would be a selling cost, an administrative cost, or a manufacturing cost. If it is a manufacturing cost, indicate whether it would typically be treated as a direct cost or an indirect cost with respect to units of product. Three sample answers are provided for illustration.

				Manufacturing (Product) Cost	
Cost Item	Variable or Fixed	Selling Cost	Administrative Cost	Direct	Indirect
Direct labor	V			X	
Executive salaries	F		X		
Factory rent	F				X

PROBLEM 2–16 Cost Classification [LO5, LO6]
Various costs associated with the operation of factories are given below:

1. Electricity used in operating machines.
2. Rent on a factory building.
3. Cloth used in drapery production.
4. Production superintendent's salary.
5. Wages of laborers assembling a product.
6. Depreciation of air purification equipment used in furniture production.
7. Janitorial salaries.
8. Peaches used in canning fruit.
9. Lubricants needed for machines.
10. Sugar used in soft-drink production.
11. Property taxes on the factory.
12. Wages of workers painting a product.
13. Depreciation on cafeteria equipment.
14. Insurance on a building used in producing helicopters.
15. Cost of rotor blades used in producing helicopters.

Required:
Classify each cost as either variable or fixed with respect to the number of units produced and sold. Also indicate whether each cost would typically be treated as a direct cost or an indirect cost with respect to units of product. Prepare your answer sheet as shown below:

	Cost Behavior		To Units of Product	
Cost Item	Variable	Fixed	Direct	Indirect
Example: Factory insurance		X		X

PROBLEM 2–17 (Appendix 2A) Allocating Labor Costs [LO8]

Mark Hansen is employed by Eastern Products, Inc., and works on the company's assembly line. Mark's basic wage rate is $20 per hour. The company's union contract states that employees are to be paid time and a half (i.e., $30 per hour) for any work in excess of 40 hours per week.

Required:

1. Suppose that in a given week Mark works 46 hours. Compute Mark's total wages for the week. How much of this amount would be allocated to direct labor cost? To manufacturing overhead cost?
2. Suppose in another week that Mark works 48 hours but is idle for 3 hours during the week due to machine breakdowns. Compute Mark's total wages for the week. How much of this amount would be allocated to direct labor cost? To manufacturing overhead cost?
3. Eastern Products, Inc., has an attractive package of fringe benefits that costs the company $6 for each hour of employee time (either regular time or overtime). During a particular week, Mark works 50 hours but is idle for 2 hours due to material shortages. Compute Mark's total wages and fringe benefits for the week. If the company treats all fringe benefits as part of manufacturing overhead cost, how much of Mark's wages and fringe benefits for the week would be allocated to direct labor cost? To manufacturing overhead cost?
4. Refer to the data in (3) above. If the company treats that part of fringe benefits relating to direct labor as added direct labor cost, how much of Mark's wages and fringe benefits for the week will be allocated to direct labor cost? To manufacturing overhead cost?

PROBLEM 2–18 (Appendix 2B) Quality Cost Report [LO9, LO10]

In response to intensive foreign competition, the management of Florex Company has attempted over the past year to improve the quality of its products. A statistical process control system has been installed and other steps have been taken to decrease the amount of warranty and other field costs, which have been trending upward over the past several years. Costs relating to quality and quality control over the last two years are given below:

	Costs (in thousands)	
	This Year	Last Year
Inspection	$900	$750
Quality engineering	$570	$420
Depreciation of test equipment	$240	$210
Rework labor	$1,500	$1,050
Statistical process control	$180	$0
Cost of field servicing	$900	$1,200
Supplies used in testing	$60	$30
Systems development	$750	$480
Warranty repairs	$1,050	$3,600
Net cost of scrap	$1,125	$630
Product testing	$1,200	$810
Product recalls	$750	$2,100
Disposal of defective products	$975	$720

Sales have been flat over the past few years, at $75,000,000 per year. A great deal of money has been spent in the effort to upgrade quality, and management is anxious to see whether or not the effort has been effective.

Required:

1. Prepare a quality cost report that contains data for both this year and last year. Carry percentage computations to two decimal places.
2. Prepare a bar graph showing the distribution of the various quality costs by category.
3. Prepare a written evaluation to accompany the reports you have prepared in (1) and (2) above. This evaluation should discuss the distribution of quality costs in the company, changes in this distribution that you see taking place, the reasons for changes in costs in the various categories, and any other information that would be of value to management.

PROBLEM 2–19 Classification of Various Costs [LO1, LO2, LO5, LO7]

Staci Valek began dabbling in pottery several years ago as a hobby. Her work is quite creative, and it has been so popular with friends and others that she has decided to quit her job with an aerospace firm and manufacture pottery full time. The salary from Staci's aerospace job is $3,800 per month.

Staci will rent a small building near her home to use as a place for manufacturing the pottery. The rent will be $500 per month. She estimates that the cost of clay and glaze will be $2 for each finished piece of pottery. She will hire workers to produce the pottery at a labor rate of $8 per pot. To sell her pots, Staci feels that she must advertise heavily in the local area. An advertising agency states that it will handle all advertising for a fee of $600 per month. Staci's brother will sell the pots; he will be paid a commission of $4 for each pot sold. Equipment needed to manufacture the pots will be rented at a cost of $300 per month.

Staci has already paid the legal and filing fees associated with incorporating her business in the state. These fees amounted to $500. A small room has been located in a tourist area that Staci will use as a sales office. The rent will be $250 per month. A phone installed in the room for taking orders will cost $40 per month. In addition, a recording device will be attached to the phone for taking after-hours messages.

Staci has some money in savings that is earning interest of $1,200 per year. These savings will be withdrawn and used to get the business going. For the time being, Staci does not intend to draw any salary from the new company.

Required:

1. Prepare an answer sheet with the following column headings:

			Product Cost					
Name of the Cost	Variable Cost	Fixed Cost	Direct Materials	Direct Labor	Manufacturing Overhead	Period (selling and administrative) Cost	Opportunity Cost	Sunk Cost

   List the different costs associated with the new company down the extreme left column (under Name of Cost). Then place an *X* under each heading that helps to describe the type of cost involved. There may be *X*'s under several column headings for a single cost. (That is, a cost may be a fixed cost, a period cost, and a sunk cost; you would place an *X* under each of these column headings opposite the cost.)

   Under the Variable Cost column, list only those costs that would be variable with respect to the number of units of pottery that are produced and sold.

2. All of the costs you have listed above, except one, would be differential costs between the alternatives of Staci producing pottery or staying with the aerospace firm. Which cost is *not* differential? Explain.

PROBLEM 2–20 Classification of Salary Cost as a Period or Product Cost [LO2]

You have just been hired by Ogden Company to fill a new position that was created in response to rapid growth in sales. It is your responsibility to coordinate shipments of finished goods from the factory to distribution warehouses located in various parts of the United States so that goods will be available as orders are received from customers.

The company is unsure how to classify your annual salary in its cost records. The company's cost analyst says that your salary should be classified as a manufacturing (product) cost; the controller says that it should be classified as a selling expense; and the president says that it doesn't matter which way your salary cost is classified.

Required:

1. Which viewpoint is correct? Why?
2. From the point of view of the reported net operating income for the year, is the president correct in his statement that it doesn't matter which way your salary cost is classified? Explain.

PROBLEM 2–21 Variable and Fixed Costs; Subtleties of Direct and Indirect Costs [LO5, LO6]

Madison Seniors Care Center is a nonprofit organization that provides a variety of health services to the elderly. The center is organized into a number of departments, one of which is the meals-on-wheels program that delivers hot meals to seniors in their homes on a daily basis. Below are listed a number of costs of the center and the meals-on-wheels program.

example The cost of groceries used in meal preparation.

a. The cost of leasing the meals-on-wheels van.
b. The cost of incidental supplies such as salt, pepper, napkins, and so on.
c. The cost of gasoline consumed by the meals-on-wheels van.

d. The rent on the facility that houses Madison Seniors Care Center, including the meals-on-wheels program.
e. The salary of the part-time manager of the meals-on-wheels program.
f. Depreciation on the kitchen equipment used in the meals-on-wheels program.
g. The hourly wages of the caregiver who drives the van and delivers the meals.
h. The costs of complying with health safety regulations in the kitchen.
i. The costs of mailing letters soliciting donations to the meals-on-wheels program.

Required:
For each cost listed above, indicate whether it is a direct or indirect cost of the meals-on-wheels program, whether it is a direct or indirect cost of particular seniors served by the program, and whether it is variable or fixed with respect to the number of seniors served. Use the below form for your answer.

		Direct or Indirect Cost of the Meals-on-Wheels Program		Direct or Indirect Cost of Particular Seniors Served by the Meals-on-Wheels Program		Variable or Fixed with Respect to the Number of Seniors Served by the Meals-on-Wheels Program	
Item	Description	Direct	Indirect	Direct	Indirect	Variable	Fixed
example	The cost of groceries used in meal preparation	X		X		X	

PROBLEM 2–22 (Appendix 2B) Analyzing a Quality Cost Report [LO10]

Mercury, Inc., produces pagers at its plant in Texas. In recent years, the company's market share has been eroded by stiff competition from overseas. Price and product quality are the two key areas in which companies compete in this market.

A year ago, the company's pagers had been ranked low in product quality in a consumer survey. Shocked by this result, Jorge Gomez, Mercury's president, initiated a crash effort to improve product quality. Gomez set up a task force to implement a formal quality improvement program. Included on this task force were representatives from the Engineering, Marketing, Customer Service, Production, and Accounting departments. The broad representation was needed because Gomez believed that this was a companywide program and that all employees should share the responsibility for its success.

After the first meeting of the task force, Holly Elsoe, manager of the Marketing Department, asked John Tran, production manager, what he thought of the proposed program. Tran replied, "I have reservations. Quality is too abstract to be attaching costs to it and then to be holding you and me responsible for cost improvements. I like to work with goals that I can see and count! I'm nervous about having my annual bonus based on a decrease in quality costs; there are too many variables that we have no control over."

Mercury's quality improvement program has now been in operation for one year. The company's most recent quality cost report is shown below.

MERCURY, INC.
Quality Cost Report
(in thousands)

	This Year	Last Year
Prevention costs:		
Machine maintenance	$ 120	$ 70
Training suppliers	10	0
Quality circles	20	0
Total prevention costs	150	70
Appraisal costs:		
Incoming inspection	40	20
Final testing	90	80
Total appraisal costs	130	100

continued

Internal failure costs:		
Rework	130	50
Scrap	70	40
Total internal failure costs	200	90
External failure costs:		
Warranty repairs	30	90
Customer returns	80	320
Total external failure costs	110	410
Total quality cost	$ 590	$ 670
Total production cost	$4,800	$4,200

As they were reviewing the report, Elsoe asked Tran what he now thought of the quality improvement program. Tran replied. "I'm relieved that the new quality improvement program hasn't hurt our bonuses, but the program has increased the workload in the Production Department. It is true that customer returns are way down, but the pagers that were returned by customers to retail outlets were rarely sent back to us for rework."

Required:

1. Expand the company's quality cost report by showing the costs in both years as percentages of both total production cost and total quality cost. Carry all computations to one decimal place. By analyzing the report, determine if Mercury, Inc.'s quality improvement program has been successful. *List specific evidence to support your answer.*
2. Do you expect the improvement program as it progresses to continue to increase the workload in the Production Department?
3. Jorge Gomez believed that the quality improvement program was essential and that Mercury, Inc., could no longer afford to ignore the importance of product quality. Discuss how Mercury, Inc., could measure the cost of *not* implementing the quality improvement program.

(CMA, adapted)

PROBLEM 2–23 Ethics and the Manager [LO2]

M. K. Gallant is president of Kranbrack Corporation, a company whose stock is traded on a national exchange. In a meeting with investment analysts at the beginning of the year, Gallant had predicted that the company's earnings would grow by 20% this year. Unfortunately, sales have been less than expected for the year, and Gallant concluded within two weeks of the end of the fiscal year that it would be impossible to ultimately report an increase in earnings as large as predicted unless some drastic action was taken. Accordingly, Gallant has ordered that wherever possible, expenditures should be postponed to the new year—including canceling or postponing orders with suppliers, delaying planned maintenance and training, and cutting back on end-of-year advertising and travel. Additionally, Gallant ordered the company's controller to carefully scrutinize all costs that are currently classified as period costs and reclassify as many as possible as product costs. The company is expected to have substantial inventories of work in process and finished goods at the end of the year.

Required:

1. Why would reclassifying period costs as product costs increase this period's reported earnings?
2. Do you believe Gallant's actions are ethical? Why or why not?

eXcel

PROBLEM 2–24 Schedule of Cost of Goods Manufactured; Income Statement; Cost Behavior [LO1, LO2, LO3, LO4, LO5]

Various cost and sales data for Meriwell Company for the just completed year appear in the worksheet below:

Required:

1. Prepare a schedule of cost of goods manufactured.
2. Prepare an income statement.
3. Assume that the company produced the equivalent of 10,000 units of product during the year just completed. What was the average cost per unit for direct materials? What was the average cost per unit for factory depreciation?
4. Assume that the company expects to produce 15,000 units of product during the coming year. What average cost per unit and what total cost would you expect the company to incur for

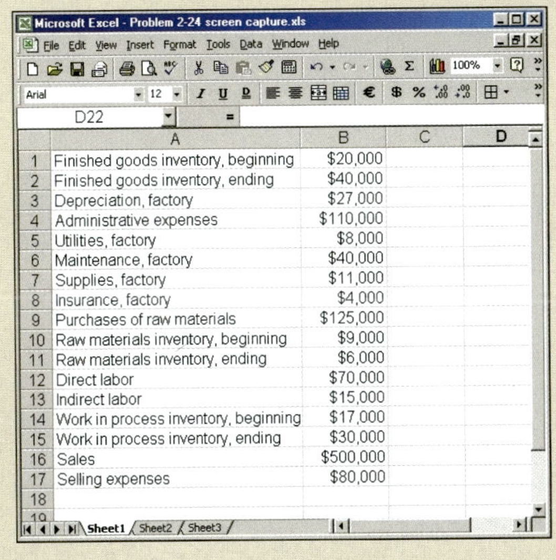

	A	B	C	D
1	Finished goods inventory, beginning	$20,000		
2	Finished goods inventory, ending	$40,000		
3	Depreciation, factory	$27,000		
4	Administrative expenses	$110,000		
5	Utilities, factory	$8,000		
6	Maintenance, factory	$40,000		
7	Supplies, factory	$11,000		
8	Insurance, factory	$4,000		
9	Purchases of raw materials	$125,000		
10	Raw materials inventory, beginning	$9,000		
11	Raw materials inventory, ending	$6,000		
12	Direct labor	$70,000		
13	Indirect labor	$15,000		
14	Work in process inventory, beginning	$17,000		
15	Work in process inventory, ending	$30,000		
16	Sales	$500,000		
17	Selling expenses	$80,000		
18				

direct materials at this level of activity? For factory depreciation? (In preparing your answer, assume that direct materials is a variable cost and that depreciation is a fixed cost; also assume that depreciation is computed on a straight-line basis.)

5. As the manager responsible for production costs, explain to the president any difference in the average costs per unit between (3) and (4) above.

PROBLEM 2–25 Cost Classification and Cost Behavior [LO2, LO5, LO6]

The Dorilane Company specializes in producing a set of wood patio furniture consisting of a table and four chairs. The set enjoys great popularity, and the company has ample orders to keep production going at its full capacity of 2,000 sets per year. Annual cost data at full capacity follow:

Factory labor, direct	$118,000
Advertising	$50,000
Factory supervision	$40,000
Property taxes, factory building	$3,500
Sales commissions	$80,000
Insurance, factory	$2,500
Depreciation, office equipment	$4,000
Lease cost, factory equipment	$12,000
Indirect materials, factory	$6,000
Depreciation, factory building	$10,000
General office supplies (billing)	$3,000
General office salaries	$60,000
Direct materials used (wood, bolts, etc.)	$94,000
Utilities, factory	$20,000

Required:

1. Prepare an answer sheet with the column headings shown below. Enter each cost item on your answer sheet, placing the dollar amount under the appropriate headings. As examples, this has been done already for the first two items in the list above. Note that each cost item is classified in two ways: first, as variable or fixed with respect to the number of units produced and sold; and second, as a selling and administrative cost or a product cost. (If the item is a product cost, it should also be classified as either direct or indirect as shown.)

	Cost Behavior		Selling or Administrative	Product Cost	
Cost Item	Variable	Fixed	Cost	Direct	Indirect*
Factory labor, direct	$118,000			$118,000	
Advertising		$50,000	$50,000		

*To units of product.

2. Total the dollar amounts in each of the columns in (1) above. Compute the average product cost of one patio set.
3. Assume that production drops to only 1,000 sets annually. Would you expect the average product cost of one set to increase, decrease, or remain unchanged? Explain. No computations are necessary.
4. Refer to the original data. The president's brother-in-law has considered making himself a patio set and has priced the necessary materials at a building supply store. The brother-in-law has asked the president if he could purchase a patio set from the Dorilane Company "at cost," and the president agreed to let him do so.
   a. Would you expect any disagreement between the two men over the price the brother-in-law should pay? Explain. What price does the president probably have in mind? The brother-in-law?
   b. Since the company is operating at full capacity, what cost term used in the chapter might be justification for the president to charge the full, regular price to the brother-in-law and still be selling "at cost"?

PROBLEM 2–26 Schedule of Cost of Goods Manufactured; Income Statement [LO1, LO2, LO3, LO4]
Swift Company was organized on March 1 of the current year. After five months of start-up losses, management had expected to earn a profit during August. Management was disappointed, however, when the income statement for August also showed a loss. August's income statement follows:

SWIFT COMPANY
Income Statement
For the Month Ended August 31

Sales		$450,000
Less operating expenses:		
Indirect labor cost	$ 12,000	
Utilities	15,000	
Direct labor cost	70,000	
Depreciation, factory equipment	21,000	
Raw materials purchased	165,000	
Depreciation, sales equipment	18,000	
Insurance	4,000	
Rent on facilities	50,000	
Selling and administrative salaries	32,000	
Advertising	75,000	462,000
Net operating loss		$ (12,000)

After seeing the $12,000 loss for August, Swift's president stated, "I was sure we'd be profitable within six months, but our six months are up and this loss for August is even worse than July's. I think it's time to start looking for someone to buy out the company's assets—if we don't, within a few months there won't be any assets to sell. By the way, I don't see any reason to look for a new controller. We'll just limp along with Sam for the time being."

The company's controller resigned a month ago. Sam, a new assistant in the controller's office, prepared the income statement above. Sam has had little experience in manufacturing operations. Additional information about the company follows:

a. Some 60% of the utilities cost and 75% of the insurance apply to factory operations. The remaining amounts apply to selling and administrative activities.
b. Inventory balances at the beginning and end of August were:

	August 1	August 31
Raw materials	$8,000	$13,000
Work in process	$16,000	$21,000
Finished goods	$40,000	$60,000

c. Only 80% of the rent on facilities applies to factory operations; the remainder applies to selling and administrative activities.

The president has asked you to check over the income statement and make a recommendation as to whether the company should look for a buyer for its assets.

Required:

1. As one step in gathering data for a recommendation to the president, prepare a schedule of cost of goods manufactured for August.
2. As a second step, prepare a new income statement for August.
3. Based on your statements prepared in (1) and (2) above, would you recommend that the company look for a buyer?

PROBLEM 2–27 Schedule of Cost of Goods Manufactured; Income Statement; Cost Behavior [LO1, LO2, LO3, LO4, LO5]

Selected account balances for the year ended December 31 are provided below for Superior Company:

Selling and administrative salaries	$110,000
Insurance, factory	$8,000
Utilities, factory	$45,000
Purchases of raw materials	$290,000
Indirect labor	$60,000
Direct labor	?
Advertising expense	$80,000
Cleaning supplies, factory	$7,000
Sales commissions	$50,000
Rent, factory building	$120,000
Maintenance, factory	$30,000

Inventory balances at the beginning and end of the year were as follows:

	Beginning of the Year	End of the Year
Raw materials	$40,000	$10,000
Work in process	?	$35,000
Finished goods	$50,000	?

The total manufacturing costs for the year were $683,000; the goods available for sale totaled $740,000; and the cost of goods sold totaled $660,000.

Required:

1. Prepare a schedule of cost of goods manufactured and the cost of goods sold section of the company's income statement for the year.
2. Assume that the dollar amounts given above are for the equivalent of 40,000 units produced during the year. Compute the average cost per unit for direct materials used and the average cost per unit for rent on the factory building.
3. Assume that in the following year the company expects to produce 50,000 units. What average cost per unit and total cost would you expect to be incurred for direct materials? For rent on the factory building? (Assume that direct materials is a variable cost and that rent is a fixed cost.)
4. As the manager in charge of production costs, explain to the president the reason for any difference in average cost per unit between (2) and (3) above.

PROBLEM 2–28 Income Statement; Schedule of Cost of Goods Manufactured [LO1, LO2, LO3, LO4]

Visic Corporation, a manufacturing company, produces a single product. The following information has been taken from the company's production, sales, and cost records for the just completed year.

eXcel

Production in units	29,000
Sales in units	?
Ending finished goods inventory in units	?
Sales in dollars	$1,300,000
Costs:	
Advertising	$105,000
Entertainment and travel	$40,000
Direct labor	$90,000
Indirect labor	$85,000
Raw materials purchased	$480,000
	continued

Building rent (production uses 80% of the space; administrative and sales offices use the rest)	$40,000
Utilities, factory	$108,000
Royalty paid for use of production patent, $1.50 per unit produced	?
Maintenance, factory	$9,000
Rent for special production equipment, $7,000 per year plus $0.30 per unit produced	?
Selling and administrative salaries	$210,000
Other factory overhead costs	$6,800
Other selling and administrative expenses	$17,000

	Beginning of the Year	End of the Year
Inventories:		
Raw materials	$20,000	$30,000
Work in process	$50,000	$40,000
Finished goods	$0	?

The finished goods inventory is being carried at the average unit production cost for the year. The selling price of the product is $50 per unit.

Required:

1. Prepare a schedule of cost of goods manufactured for the year.
2. Compute the following:
   a. The number of units in the finished goods inventory at the end of the year.
   b. The cost of the units in the finished goods inventory at the end of the year.
3. Prepare an income statement for the year.

PROBLEM 2–29 Working with Incomplete Data from the Income Statement and Schedule of Cost of Goods Manufactured [LO3, LO4]

Supply the missing data in the following cases. Each case is independent of the others.

	Case			
	1	2	3	4
Direct materials	$4,500	$6,000	$5,000	$3,000
Direct labor	?	$3,000	$7,000	$4,000
Manufacturing overhead	$5,000	$4,000	?	$9,000
Total manufacturing costs	$18,500	?	$20,000	?
Beginning work in process inventory	$2,500	?	$3,000	?
Ending work in process inventory	?	$1,000	$4,000	$3,000
Sales	$30,000	$21,000	$36,000	$40,000
Beginning finished goods inventory	$1,000	$2,500	?	$2,000
Cost of goods manufactured	$18,000	$14,000	?	$17,500
Goods available for sale	?	?	?	?
Ending finished goods inventory	?	$1,500	$4,000	$3,500
Cost of goods sold	$17,000	?	$18,500	?
Gross margin	$13,000	?	$17,500	?
Operating expenses	?	$3,500	?	?
Net operating income	$4,000	?	$5,000	$9,000

Cases

CASE 2–30 Inventory Computations from Incomplete Data [LO3, LO4]

Hector P. Wastrel, a careless employee, left some combustible materials near an open flame in Salter Company's plant. The resulting explosion and fire destroyed the entire plant and administrative offices. Justin Quick, the company's controller, and Constance Trueheart, the operations manager, were able to save only a few bits of information as they escaped from the roaring blaze.

"What a disaster," cried Justin. "And the worst part is that we have no records to use in filing an insurance claim."

"I know," replied Constance. "I was in the plant when the explosion occurred, and I managed to grab only this brief summary sheet that contains information on one or two of our costs. It says that our direct labor cost this year has totaled $180,000 and that we have purchased $290,000 in raw materials. But I'm afraid that doesn't help much; the rest of our records are just ashes."

"Well, not completely," said Justin. "I was working on the year-to-date income statement when the explosion knocked me out of my chair. I instinctively held onto the page I was working on, and from what I can make out, our sales to date this year have totaled $1,200,000 and our gross margin rate has been 40% of sales. Also, I can see that our goods available for sale to customers has totaled $810,000 at cost."

"Maybe we're not so bad off after all," exclaimed Constance. "My sheet says that prime cost has totaled $410,000 so far this year and that manufacturing overhead is 70% of conversion cost. Now if we just had some information on our beginning inventories."

"Hey, look at this," cried Justin. "It's a copy of last year's annual report, and it shows what our inventories were when this year started. Let's see, raw materials was $18,000, work in process was $65,000, and finished goods was $45,000.

"Super," yelled Constance. "Let's go to work."

To file an insurance claim, the company must determine the amount of cost in its inventories as of the date of the fire. You may assume that all materials used in production during the year were direct materials.

Required:

Determine the amount of cost in the Raw Materials, Work in Process, and Finished Goods inventory accounts as of the date of the fire. (Hint: One way to proceed would be to reconstruct the various schedules and statements that would have been affected by the company's inventory accounts during the period.)

CASE 2–31 Missing Data; Income Statement; Schedule of Cost of Goods Manufactured [LO1, LO2, LO3, LO4]

"I was sure that when our battery hit the market it would be an instant success," said Roger Strong, founder and president of Solar Technology, Inc. "But just look at the gusher of red ink for the first quarter. It's obvious that we're better scientists than we are businesspeople." The data to which Roger was referring follow:

SOLAR TECHNOLOGY, INC.
Income Statement
For the Quarter Ended March 31

Sales (32,000 batteries)		$ 960,000
Less operating expenses:		
Selling and administrative salaries	$110,000	
Advertising	90,000	
Maintenance, factory	43,000	
Indirect labor cost	120,000	
Cleaning supplies, factory	7,000	
Purchases of raw materials	360,000	
Rental cost, facilities	75,000	
Insurance, factory	8,000	
Depreciation, office equipment	27,000	
Utilities	80,000	
Depreciation, factory equipment	100,000	
Direct labor cost	70,000	
Travel, salespersons	40,000	1,130,000
Net operating loss		$ (170,000)

"At this rate we'll be out of business within a year," said Cindy Zhang, the company's accountant. "But I've double-checked these figures, so I know they're right."

Solar Technology was organized at the beginning of the current year to produce and market a revolutionary new solar battery. The company's accounting system was set up by Margie Wallace, an experienced accountant who recently left the company to do independent consulting work. The statement above was prepared by Zhang, her assistant.

"We may not last a year if the insurance company doesn't pay the $226,000 it owes us for the 8,000 batteries lost in the warehouse fire last week," said Roger. "The insurance adjuster says our claim is inflated, but he's just trying to pressure us into a lower figure. We have the data to back up our claim, and it will stand up in any court."

On April 3, just after the end of the first quarter, the company's finished goods storage area was swept by fire and all 8,000 unsold batteries were destroyed. (These batteries were part of the 40,000 units completed during the first quarter.) The company's insurance policy states that the company will be reimbursed for the "cost" of any finished batteries destroyed or stolen. Zhang has determined this cost as follows:

$$\frac{\text{Total costs for the quarter}}{\text{Batteries produced during the quarter}} = \frac{\$1{,}130{,}000}{40{,}000 \text{ units}}$$

$$= \$28.25 \text{ per unit}$$

$$8{,}000 \text{ batteries} \times \$28.25 \text{ per unit} = \$226{,}000$$

The following additional information is available on the company's activities during the quarter ended March 31:

a. Inventories at the beginning and end of the quarter were as follows:

	Beginning of the Quarter	End of the Quarter
Raw materials	$0	$10,000
Work in process	$0	$50,000
Finished goods	$0	?

b. Eighty percent of the rental cost for facilities and 90% of the utilities cost relate to manufacturing operations. The remaining amounts relate to selling and administrative activities.

Required:

1. What conceptual errors, if any, were made in preparing the income statement above?
2. Prepare a schedule of cost of goods manufactured for the first quarter.
3. Prepare a corrected income statement for the first quarter. Your statement should show in detail how the cost of goods sold is computed.
4. Do you agree that the insurance company owes Solar Technology, Inc., $226,000? Explain your answer.

Group and Internet Exercises

GROUP EXERCISE 2–32 Implications of Mass Production

Management accounting systems tend to parallel the manufacturing systems they support and control. Traditional manufacturing systems emphasized productivity (average output per hour or per employee) and cost. This was the result of a competitive philosophy that was based on mass producing a few standard products and "meeting or beating competitors on price." If a company is going to compete on price, it had better be a low-cost producer.

Companies achieved low unit cost for a fixed set of resources by maximizing the utilization of those resources. That is, traditional production strategies were based on the economies of mass production and maximizing output for a given productive capacity. The United States has experienced over 100 years of unprecedented economic prosperity in large part because innovators like Henry Ford applied these economic principles with a vengeance.

Competitors, never being completely satisfied with their present condition, were always looking for ways to lower the cost of a product or service even further to gain some temporary cost advantage. Additional productivity gains were achieved by standardizing work procedures, specializing work, and using machines to enhance the productivity of individual workers.

Required:

1. Henry Ford made a now-famous statement that the Model T "could be had in any color as long as it was black." Explain what he meant by this statement.
2. How would Henry Ford or any other manufacturer with a narrow product line gain even further efficiencies based on the traditional production model described above?
3. Are there any limits to lowering the cost of black Model Ts, black Bic pens, or any high-volume, commodity product? Explain.
4. Once understood, the economies of mass production were applied to most sectors of the American economy. Universities, hospitals, and airlines are prime examples. Describe how the concepts of mass production, standardization, and specialization have been applied to lower the costs of a university education. Of a stay in the hospital.

GROUP EXERCISE 2–33 If Big Is Good, Bigger Must Be Better

Steel production involves a large amount of fixed costs. Since competition is defined primarily in terms of price, American steel manufacturers (and many of their manufacturing and service industry counterparts) try to gain a competitive advantage by using economies of scale and investment in technology to increase productivity and drive unit costs lower. Their substantial fixed costs are the result of their size.

Required:

1. How are fixed costs and variable costs normally defined?
2. Give examples of fixed costs and variable costs for a steel company. What is the relevant measure of production activity?
3. Give examples of fixed and variable costs for a hospital, university, and auto manufacturer. What is the relevant measure of production or service activity for each of these organizations?
4. Using the examples of fixed and variable costs for steel companies from (2) above, explain the relationship between production output at a steel company and each of the following: total fixed costs, fixed cost per unit, total variable costs, variable cost per unit, total costs, and average unit cost.
5. With an *X* axis (horizontal axis) of tons produced and a *Y* axis (vertical axis) of total costs, graph total fixed costs, total variable costs, and total costs against tons produced.
6. With an *X* axis of tons produced and a *Y* axis of unit costs, graph fixed cost per unit, variable cost per unit, and total (or average) cost per unit against tons produced.
7. Explain how costs (total and per unit) behave with changes in demand once capacity has been set.

INTERNET EXERCISE 2–34

As you know, the World Wide Web is constantly evolving. Sites come and go, and change without notice. To enable periodic updating of site addresses, this problem has been posted to the textbook website (www.mhhe.com/garrision11e). After accessing the site, enter the Student Center and select this chapter. Select and complete the Internet Exercise.

Chapter

3

Systems Design: Job-Order Costing

LEARNING OBJECTIVES

After studying Chapter 3, you should be able to:

LO1 Distinguish between process costing and job-order costing and identify companies that would use each costing method.

LO2 Identify the documents used in a job-order costing system.

LO3 Compute predetermined overhead rates and explain why estimated overhead costs (rather than actual overhead costs) are used in the costing process.

LO4 Understand the flow of costs in a job-order costing system and prepare appropriate journal entries to record costs.

LO5 Apply overhead cost to Work in Process using a predetermined overhead rate.

LO6 Prepare schedules of cost of goods manufactured and cost of goods sold.

LO7 Use T-accounts to show the flow of costs in a job-order costing system.

LO8 Compute under- or overapplied overhead cost and prepare the journal entry to close the balance in Manufacturing Overhead to the appropriate accounts.

LO9 (Appendix 3A) Understand the implications of basing the predetermined overhead rate on activity at capacity rather than on estimated activity for the period.

BUSINESS FOCUS

Where's the Profit?

"Net profit participation" contracts in which writers, actors, and directors share in the net profits of movies are common in Hollywood. For example, Winston Groom, the author of the novel *Forrest Gump,* has a contract with Paramount Pictures Corp. that calls for him to receive 3% of the net profits on the movie. However, Paramount claims that *Forrest Gump* has yet to show any profits even though its gross receipts are among the highest of any film in history. How can this be?

Movie studios assess a variety of overhead charges including a charge of about 15% on production costs for production overhead, a charge of about 30% of gross rentals for distribution overhead, and a charge for marketing overhead that amounts to about 10% of advertising costs. After all of these overhead charges and other hotly contested accounting practices, it is a rare film that shows a profit. Fewer than 5% of released films show a profit for net profit participation purposes. Examples of "money-losing" films include *Rain Man, Batman,* and *Who Framed Roger Rabbit?* as well as *Forrest Gump.* Disgruntled writers and actors are increasingly suing studios, claiming unreasonable accounting practices that are designed to cheat them of their share of profits. How do companies ordinarily assign overhead costs to their products since overhead costs consist of those costs that cannot be easily traced to products? We will answer that question in this chapter. ■

Source: Ross Engel and Bruce Ikawa, "Where's the Profit?" *Management Accounting,* January 1997, pp. 40–47.

As discussed in Chapter 2, product costing is the process of assigning costs to the products and services provided by a company. An understanding of this costing process is vital to managers, since the way in which a product or service is costed can have a substantial impact on reported profits, as well as on key management decisions.

The essential purpose of any managerial costing system should be to provide cost data to help managers plan, control, direct, and make decisions. Nevertheless, external financial reporting and tax reporting requirements often heavily influence how costs are accumulated and summarized on managerial reports. This is true of product costing.

In this chapter and in Chapter 4, we use an *absorption costing* approach to determine product costs. This was also the method that was used in Chapter 2. In **absorption costing,** *all* manufacturing costs, fixed and variable, are assigned to units of product—units are said to *fully absorb manufacturing costs.* The absorption costing approach is also known as the **full cost** approach. Later, in Chapter 7, we look at product costing from a different point of view called *variable costing,* which is often advocated as an alternative to absorption costing. Chapter 7 also discusses the strengths and weaknesses of the two approaches.

In one form or another, most countries—including the United States—require absorption costing for both external financial reporting and for tax reporting. In addition, the vast majority of companies throughout the world also use absorption costing for managerial accounting purposes. Since absorption costing is the most common approach to product costing, we discuss it first and then deal with alternatives in subsequent chapters.

Process and Job-Order Costing

LEARNING OBJECTIVE 1
Distinguish between process costing and job-order costing and identify companies that would use each costing method.

In computing the cost of a product or a service, managers are faced with a difficult problem. Many costs (such as rent) do not change much from month to month, whereas production may change frequently, with production going up in one month and then down in another. In addition to variations in the level of production, several different products or services may be produced in a given period in the same facility. Under these conditions, how is it possible to accurately determine the cost of a product or service? In practice, assigning costs to products and services involves averaging across time and across products. The way in which this averaging is carried out depends heavily on the type of production process. Two costing systems are commonly used in manufacturing and in many service companies; these two systems are known as *process costing* and *job-order costing.*

Process Costing

A **process costing system** is used in situations where the company produces many units of a single product for long periods. Examples include producing paper at Weyerhaeuser, refining aluminum ingots at Reynolds Aluminum, mixing and bottling beverages at Coca-Cola, and making wieners at Oscar Meyer. All of these industries are characterized by an essentially homogeneous product that flows through the production process on a continuous basis.

The basic approach in process costing is to accumulate costs in a particular operation or department for an entire period (month, quarter, year) and then to divide this total cost by the number of units produced during the period. The basic formula for process costing is:

$$\begin{array}{c}\text{Unit product cost}\\\text{(per gallon, pound, bottle)}\end{array} = \frac{\text{Total manufacturing cost}}{\text{Total units produced (gallons, pounds, bottles)}}$$

Since one unit of product (gallon, pound, bottle) is indistinguishable from any other unit of product, each unit is assigned the same average cost as any other unit produced during the period. This costing technique results in a broad, average unit cost figure that applies to homogeneous units flowing in a continuous stream out of the production process.

Job-Order Costing

A **job-order costing system** is used in situations where many *different* products are produced each period. For example, a Levi Strauss clothing factory would typically make many different types of jeans for both men and women during a month. A particular order might consist of 1,000 stonewashed men's blue denim jeans, style number A312. This order of 1,000 jeans is called a *batch* or a *job*. In a job-order costing system, costs are traced and allocated to jobs and then the costs of the job are divided by the number of units in the job to arrive at an average cost per unit.

Other examples of situations where job-order costing would be used include large-scale construction projects managed by Bechtel International, commercial aircraft produced by Boeing, greeting cards designed and printed by Hallmark, and airline meals prepared by LSG SkyChefs. All of these examples are characterized by diverse outputs. Each Bechtel project is unique and different from every other—the company may be simultaneously constructing a dam in Zaire and a bridge in Indonesia. Likewise, each airline orders a different type of meal from LSG SkyChefs' catering service.

Job-order costing is also used extensively in service industries. Hospitals, law firms, movie studios, accounting firms, advertising agencies, and repair shops, for example, all use a variation of job-order costing to accumulate costs for accounting and billing purposes. Although the detailed example of job-order costing provided in the following section deals with a manufacturing company, the same basic concepts and procedures are used by many service organizations.

The record-keeping and cost assignment problems are more complex when a company sells many different products and services than when it has only a single product. Since the products are different, the costs are typically different. Consequently, cost records must be maintained for each distinct product or job. For example, an attorney in a large criminal law practice would ordinarily keep separate records of the costs of advising and defending each client. And the Levi Strauss factory mentioned above would keep separate track of the costs of filling orders for particular styles of jeans. Thus, a job-order costing system requires more effort than a process-costing system. Nevertheless, job-order costing is used by more than half the manufacturers in the United States

In this chapter, we focus on the design of a job-order costing system. In the following chapter, we focus on process costing and also look more closely at the similarities and differences between the two costing methods.

Job-Order Costing—An Overview

LEARNING OBJECTIVE 2
Identify the documents used in a job-order costing system.

To introduce job-order costing, we will follow a specific job as it progresses through the manufacturing process. This job consists of two experimental couplings that Yost Precision Machining has agreed to produce for Loops Unlimited, a manufacturer of roller coasters. Couplings connect the cars on the roller coaster and are a critical component in the performance and safety of the ride. Before we begin our discussion, recall from the previous chapter that companies generally classify manufacturing costs into three broad categories: (1) direct materials, (2) direct labor, and (3) manufacturing overhead. As we study the operation of a job-order costing system, we will see how each of these three types of costs is recorded and accumulated.

MANAGERIAL ACCOUNTING IN ACTION
The Issue

YOST PRECISION MACHINING

Yost Precision Machining is a small company in Michigan that specializes in fabricating precision metal parts that are used in a variety of applications ranging from deep-sea exploration vehicles to the inertial triggers in automobile air bags. The company's top managers gather every morning at 8:00 A.M. in the company's conference room for the daily planning meeting. Attending the meeting this morning are: Jean Yost, the company's president; David Cheung, the marketing manager; Debbie Turner, the production manager; and Marcus White, the company controller. The president opened the meeting:

Jean: The production schedule indicates we'll be starting job 2B47 today. Isn't that the special order for experimental couplings, David?

David: That's right, Jean. That's the order from Loops Unlimited for two couplings for their new roller coaster ride for Magic Mountain.

Debbie: Why only two couplings? Don't they need a coupling for every car?

David: That's right. But this is a completely new roller coaster. The cars will go faster and will be subjected to more twists, turns, drops, and loops than on any other existing roller coaster. To hold up under these stresses, Loops Unlimited's engineers had to completely redesign the cars and couplings. They want to thoroughly test the design before proceeding to large-scale production. So they want us to make just two of these new couplings for testing purposes. If the design works, then we'll have the inside track on the order to supply couplings for the whole ride.

Jean: We agreed to take on this initial order at our cost just to get our foot in the door. Marcus, will there be any problem documenting our cost so we can get paid?

Marcus: No problem. The contract with Loops stipulates that they will pay us an amount equal to our cost of goods sold. With our job-order costing system, I can tell you that number on the day the job is completed.

Jean: Good. Is there anything else we should discuss about this job at this time? No? Well then let's move on to the next item of business.

Measuring Direct Materials Cost

Topic Tackler PLUS 3–1

Yost Precision Machining will require four G7 Connectors and two M46 Housings to make the two experimental couplings for Loops Unlimited. If this were a standard product, there would be a *bill of materials* for the product. A **bill of materials** is a document that lists the type and quantity of each item of materials needed to complete a unit of product. In this case, there is no established bill of materials, so Yost's production staff determined the materials requirements from the blueprints submitted by the customer. Each coupling requires two connectors and one housing, so to make two couplings, four connectors and two housings are required.

When an agreement has been reached with the customer concerning the quantities, prices, and shipment date for the order, a *production order* is issued. The Production Department then prepares a *materials requisition form* similar to the form in Exhibit 3–1. The **materials requisition form** is a detailed source document that (1) specifies the type and quantity of materials to be drawn from the storeroom, and (2) identifies the job to which the costs of the materials are to be charged. The form is used to control the flow of materials into production and also for making entries in the accounting records.

EXHIBIT 3–1
Materials Requisition Form

Materials Requistion Number 14873 Date March 2
Job Number to Be Charged 2B47
Department Milling

Description	Quantity	Unit Cost	Total Cost
M46 Housing	2	$124	$248
G7 Connector	4	103	412
			$660

Authorized Signature *Bill White*

The Yost Precision Machining materials requisition form in Exhibit 3–1 shows that the company's Milling Department has requisitioned two M46 Housings and four G7 Connectors for job 2B47. This completed form is presented to the storeroom clerk who then issues the necessary raw materials. The storeroom clerk is not allowed to release materials without an authorized signature on the form.

Job Cost Sheet

After being notified that the production order has been issued, the Accounting Department prepares a *job cost sheet* similar to the one presented in Exhibit 3–2. A **job cost sheet** is a form prepared for each separate job that records the materials, labor, and overhead costs charged to the job.

After direct materials are issued, the Accounting Department records their costs directly on the job cost sheet. Note from Exhibit 3–2, for example, that the $660 cost for direct materials shown earlier on the materials requisition form has been charged to job 2B47 on its job cost sheet. The requisition number 14873 from the materials requisition form is also recorded on the job cost sheet to make it easier to identify the source document for the direct materials charge.

In addition to serving as a means for charging costs to jobs, the job cost sheet also serves as a key part of a company's accounting records. The job cost sheets form a subsidiary ledger to the Work in Process account. They are detailed records for the jobs in process that add up to the balance in Work in Process.

Measuring Direct Labor Cost

Direct labor cost is handled in much the same way as direct materials cost. Direct labor consists of labor charges that are easily traced to a particular job. Labor charges that cannot

EXHIBIT 3–2
Job Cost Sheet

JOB COST SHEET

Job Number 2B47 — Date Initiated March 2
Date Completed
Department Milling — Units Completed
Item Special order coupling
For Stock

Direct Materials		Direct Labor			Manufacturing Overhead		
Req. No.	Amount	Ticket	Hours	Amount	Hours	Rate	Amount
14873	$660	843	5	$45			

Cost Summary		Units Shipped		
		Date	Number	Balance
Direct Materials	$			
Direct Labor	$			
Manufacturing Overhead	$			
Total Cost	$			
Unit Product Cost	$			

be easily traced directly to any job are treated as part of manufacturing overhead. As discussed in the previous chapter, this latter category of labor costs is called *indirect labor* and includes tasks such as maintenance, supervision, and cleanup.

IN BUSINESS

RELATION OF DIRECT LABOR TO PRODUCT COST

How much direct labor is in the products you buy? Sometimes not very much. During a visit to the Massachusetts Institute of Technology, Chinese Prime Minister Zhu Rongji claimed that, of the $120 retail cost of a pair of athletic shoes made in China, only $2 goes to the Chinese workers who assemble them. The National Labor Committee based in New York estimates that the labor cost to assemble a $90 pair of Nike sneakers is only $1.20.

Source: Robert A. Senser, letter to the editor, *Business Week*, May 24, 1999, pp. 11–12.

Workers use *time tickets* to record the time they spend on each job and task. A completed **time ticket** is an hour-by-hour summary of the employee's activities throughout the day. An example of an employee time ticket is shown in Exhibit 3–3. When working on a specific job, the employee enters the job number on the time ticket and notes the amount of time spent on that job. When not assigned to a particular job, the employee records the nature of the indirect labor task (such as cleanup and maintenance) and the amount of time spent on the task.

At the end of the day, the time tickets are gathered and the Accounting Department enters the direct labor-hours and costs on individual job cost sheets. (See Exhibit 3–2 for an example of how direct labor costs are entered on the job cost sheet.) The daily time tickets are source documents that are used as the basis for labor cost entries into the accounting records.

IN BUSINESS

A MORE PRODUCTIVE USE OF TIME

Is it always worth the trouble to fill out labor time tickets? In a word, no. United Electric Controls, Inc., located in Waterton, Massachusetts, makes temperature and pressure sensors and controls. The manufacturing vice president decided he wanted employees to spend their time focusing on making products rather than on filling out labor time tickets. The company converted everyone into salaried workers and stopped producing labor reports.

Source: Richard L. Jenson, James W. Brackner, and Clifford Skousen, *Management Accounting in Support of Manufacturing Excellence*, 1996, The IMA Foundation for Applied Research, Inc., Montvale, New Jersey, p. 12.

EXHIBIT 3–3
Employee Time Ticket

Time Ticket No. 843 Date March 3
Employee Mary Holden Station 4

Started	Ended	Time Completed	Rate	Amount	Job Number
7:00	12:00	5.0	$9	$45	2B47
12:30	2:30	2.0	9	18	2B50
2:30	3:30	1.0	9	9	Maintenance
Totals		8.0		$72	

Supervisor R.W. Pace

The system we have just described is a manual method for recording and posting labor costs. Many companies now rely on computerized systems and no longer record labor time by hand on sheets of paper. One computerized approach uses bar codes to enter the basic data into the computer. Each employee and each job has a unique bar code. When an employee begins work on a job, he or she scans three bar codes using a handheld device much like the bar code readers at grocery store check-out stands. The first bar code indicates that a job is being started; the second is the unique bar code on his or her identity badge; and the third is the unique bar code of the job itself. This information is fed automatically via an electronic network to a computer that notes the time and then records all of the data. When the employee completes the task, he or she scans a bar code indicating the task is complete, the bar code on his or her identity badge, and the bar code attached to the job. This information is relayed to the computer that again notes the time, and a time ticket is automatically prepared. Since all of the source data is already in computer files, the labor costs can be automatically posted to job cost sheets (or their electronic equivalents). Computers, coupled with technology such as bar codes, can eliminate much of the drudgery involved in routine bookkeeping activities while at the same time increasing timeliness and accuracy.

IN BUSINESS

CLEANING UP WITH BAR CODES

Bradford Soap Works is a manufacturer of private label bar soap. Employees at the company wear identification badges on which a bar code is printed that reveals their identity, their functions, and their relevant personal data. The bar codes are used to keep track of the hours a worker is on the job and to charge a worker's time directly to specific orders. By automating the process of recording, collecting, and processing this information, the company has converted three full-time clerical positions to one part-time position. In addition, accuracy has improved dramatically—from 500 errors per 10,000 transactions to just one error per 10,000 transactions. The increased accuracy and timeliness of real-time data has improved shop-floor control and scheduling and the quality of data that are available for management decisions.

Source: Institute of Management Accountants and the Society of Management Accountants of Canada, *Redesigning the Finance Function, Statement Number 5E*, March 31, 1997, p. 20.

Application of Manufacturing Overhead

Topic Tackler PLUS 3–2

LEARNING OBJECTIVE 3
Compute predetermined overhead rates and explain why estimated overhead costs (rather than actual overhead costs) are used in the costing process.

Manufacturing overhead must be included with direct materials and direct labor on the job cost sheet since manufacturing overhead is also a product cost. However, assigning manufacturing overhead to units of product can be a difficult task. There are three reasons for this.

1. Manufacturing overhead is an *indirect cost*. This means that it is either impossible or difficult to trace these costs to a particular product or job.
2. Manufacturing overhead consists of many different items ranging from the grease used in machines to the annual salary of the production manager.
3. Even though output may fluctuate due to seasonal or other factors, total manufacturing overhead costs tend to remain relatively constant due to the presence of fixed costs.

Given these problems, about the only way to assign overhead costs to products is to use an allocation process. This allocation of overhead costs is accomplished by selecting an *allocation base* that is common to all of the company's products and services. An **allocation base** is a measure such as direct labor-hours (DLH) or machine-hours (MH) that is used to assign overhead costs to products and services.

The most widely used allocation bases are direct labor-hours and direct labor cost, with machine-hours and even units of product (where a company has only a single product) also used to some extent.

The allocation base is used to compute the **predetermined overhead rate** as follows:

$$\text{Predetermined overhead rate} = \frac{\text{Estimated total manufacturing overhead cost}}{\text{Estimated total units in the allocation base}}$$

Note that the predetermined overhead rate is based on estimates rather than actual results. This is because the *predetermined* overhead rate is computed *before* the period begins and is used to *apply* overhead cost to jobs throughout the period. The process of assigning overhead cost to jobs is called **overhead application.** The formula for determining the amount of overhead cost to apply to a particular job is:

$$\begin{array}{c}\text{Overhead applied to}\\ \text{a particular job}\end{array} = \begin{array}{c}\text{Predetermined}\\ \text{overhead rate}\end{array} \times \begin{array}{c}\text{Amount of the allocation}\\ \text{base incurred by the job}\end{array}$$

For example, if the predetermined overhead rate is \$8 per direct labor-hour, then \$8 of overhead cost is *applied* to a job for each direct labor-hour incurred by the job. When the allocation base is direct labor-hours, the formula becomes:

$$\begin{array}{c}\text{Overhead applied to}\\ \text{a particular job}\end{array} = \begin{array}{c}\text{Predetermined}\\ \text{overhead rate}\end{array} \times \begin{array}{c}\text{Actual direct labor-hours}\\ \text{charged to the job}\end{array}$$

Using the Predetermined Overhead Rate To illustrate the steps involved in computing and using a predetermined overhead rate, let's return to Yost Precision Machining. The company has estimated its total manufacturing overhead costs will be \$320,000 for the year and its total direct labor-hours will be 40,000. Its predetermined overhead rate for the year would be \$8 per direct labor-hour, as shown below:

$$\begin{aligned}\text{Predetermined overhead rate} &= \frac{\text{Estimated total manufacturing overhead cost}}{\text{Estimated total units in the allocation base}}\\ &= \frac{\$320{,}000}{40{,}000\text{ direct labor-hours}}\\ &= \$8\text{ per direct labor-hour}\end{aligned}$$

The job cost sheet in Exhibit 3–4 indicates that 27 direct labor-hours (i.e., DLHs) were charged to job 2B47. Therefore, a total of \$216 of manufacturing overhead cost would be applied to the job:

$$\begin{aligned}\begin{array}{c}\text{Overhead applied to}\\ \text{job 2B47}\end{array} &= \begin{array}{c}\text{Predetermined}\\ \text{overhead rate}\end{array} \times \begin{array}{c}\text{Actual direct labor-hours}\\ \text{charged to job 2B47}\end{array}\\ &= \$8\text{ per DLH} \times 27\text{ DLHs}\\ &= \$216\text{ of overhead applied to job 2B47}\end{aligned}$$

This amount of overhead has been entered on the job cost sheet in Exhibit 3–4. Note that this is *not* the actual amount of overhead caused by the job. Actual overhead costs are *not* assigned to jobs—if that could be done, the costs would be direct costs, not overhead. The overhead assigned to the job is simply a share of the total overhead that was estimated at the beginning of the year. When a company applies overhead cost to jobs as we have done—that is, by multiplying actual activity times the predetermined overhead rate—it is called a **normal cost system.**

The overhead may be applied as direct labor-hours are charged to jobs, or all of the overhead can be applied at once when the job is completed. The choice is up to the company. If a job is not completed at the end of the accounting period, however, overhead should be applied to value the work in process inventory.

The Need for a Predetermined Rate Instead of using a predetermined rate, a company could wait until the end of the accounting period to compute an actual overhead rate based on the *actual* total manufacturing costs and the *actual* total units in the allocation base for the period. However, managers cite several reasons for using predetermined overhead rates instead of actual overhead rates:

EXHIBIT 3–4
A Completed Job Cost Sheet

JOB COST SHEET

Job Number 2B47 | Date Initiated March 2
Date Completed March 8

Department Milling
Item Special order coupling | Units Completed 2
For Stock

Direct Materials		Direct Labor			Manufacturing Overhead		
Req. No.	Amount	Ticket	Hours	Amount	Hours	Rate	Amount
14873	$ 660	843	5	$ 45	27	$8/DLH	$216
14875	506	846	8	60			
14912	238	850	4	21			
	$1,404	851	10	54			
			27	$180			

Cost Summary	
Direct Materials	$1,404
Direct Labor	$ 180
Manufacturing Overhead	$ 216
Total Cost	$1,800
Unit Product Cost	$ 900*

Units Shipped		
Date	Number	Balance
March 8	—	2

*$1,800 ÷ 2 units = $900 per unit.

1. Managers would like to know the accounting system's valuation of completed jobs *before* the end of the accounting period. Suppose, for example, that Yost Precision Machining waits until the end of the year to compute its overhead rate. Then the cost of goods sold for job 2B47 would not be known until the close of the year, even though the job was completed and shipped to the customer in March. The seriousness of this problem can be reduced to some extent by computing the actual overhead more frequently, but that immediately leads to another problem as discussed below.
2. If actual overhead rates are computed frequently, seasonal factors in overhead costs or in the allocation base can produce fluctuations in the overhead rates. For example, the costs of heating and cooling a production facility in Illinois will be highest in the winter and summer months and lowest in the spring and fall. If an overhead rate were computed each month or each quarter, the predetermined overhead rate would go up in the winter and summer and down in the spring and fall. Two identical jobs, one completed in the winter and one completed in the spring, would be assigned different costs if the overhead rate were computed on a monthly or quarterly basis. Managers generally feel that such fluctuations in overhead rates and costs serve no useful purpose and are misleading.
3. The use of a predetermined overhead rate simplifies record keeping. To determine the overhead cost to apply to a job, the accounting staff at Yost Precision Machining simply multiplies the direct labor-hours recorded for the job by the predetermined overhead rate of $8 per direct labor-hour.

For these reasons, most companies use predetermined overhead rates rather than actual overhead rates in their cost accounting systems.

Choice of an Allocation Base for Overhead Cost

Ideally, the allocation base used in the predetermined overhead rate should be the *cost driver* of overhead cost. A **cost driver** is a factor, such as machine-hours, beds occupied, computer time, or flight-hours, that causes overhead costs. If a base is used to compute overhead rates that does not "drive" overhead costs, then the result will be inaccurate overhead rates and distorted product costs. For example, if direct labor-hours is used to allocate overhead, but in reality overhead has little to do with direct labor-hours, then products with high direct labor-hour requirements will be overcosted.

Most companies use direct labor-hours or direct labor cost as the allocation base for manufacturing overhead. However, as discussed in earlier chapters, major shifts are taking place in the structure of costs in many industries. In the past, direct labor accounted for up to 60% of the cost of many products, with overhead cost making up only a portion of the remainder. This situation has been changing—for two reasons. First, sophisticated automated equipment has taken over functions that used to be performed by direct labor workers. Since the costs of acquiring and maintaining such equipment are classified as overhead, this increases overhead while decreasing direct labor. Second, products are becoming more sophisticated and complex and are changed more frequently. This increases the need for highly skilled indirect workers such as engineers. As a result of these two trends, direct labor constitutes a smaller portion of product costs and overhead constitutes a larger portion in many industries.

In companies where direct labor and overhead costs have been moving in opposite directions, it would be difficult to argue that direct labor "drives" overhead costs. Accordingly, in recent years, managers in some companies have used *activity-based costing* principles to redesign their cost accounting systems. Activity-based costing is a costing technique that is designed to more accurately reflect the demands that products, customers, and other cost objects make on overhead resources. The activity-based approach is discussed in more detail in Chapter 8.

We hasten to add that although direct labor may not be an appropriate allocation base in some industries, in others it continues to be a significant driver of manufacturing overhead. Indeed, most manufacturing companies in the United States continue to use direct labor as the primary or secondary allocation base for manufacturing overhead. The key point is that the allocation base used by the company should really drive, or cause, overhead costs, and direct labor is not always an appropriate allocation base.

Computation of Unit Costs

With the application of Yost Precision Machining's $216 of manufacturing overhead to the job cost sheet in Exhibit 3–4, the job cost sheet is complete except for two final steps. First, the totals for direct materials, direct labor, and manufacturing overhead are transferred to the Cost Summary section of the job cost sheet and added together to obtain the total cost for the job. Then the total cost ($1,800) is divided by the number of units (2) to obtain the unit product cost ($900). As indicated earlier, *this unit product cost is an average cost and should not be interpreted as the cost that would actually be incurred if another unit were produced.* Much of the actual overhead costs would not change if another unit were produced, so the incremental cost of an additional unit is something less than the average unit cost of $900.

The completed job cost sheet is now ready to be transferred to the Finished Goods inventory account, where it will serve as the basis for valuing unsold units in ending inventory and for determining cost of goods sold.

Summary of Document Flows

The sequence of events discussed above is summarized in Exhibit 3–5. A careful study of the flow of documents in this exhibit will provide a good overview of the overall operation of a job-order costing system.

EXHIBIT 3–5
The Flow of Documents in a Job-Order Costing System

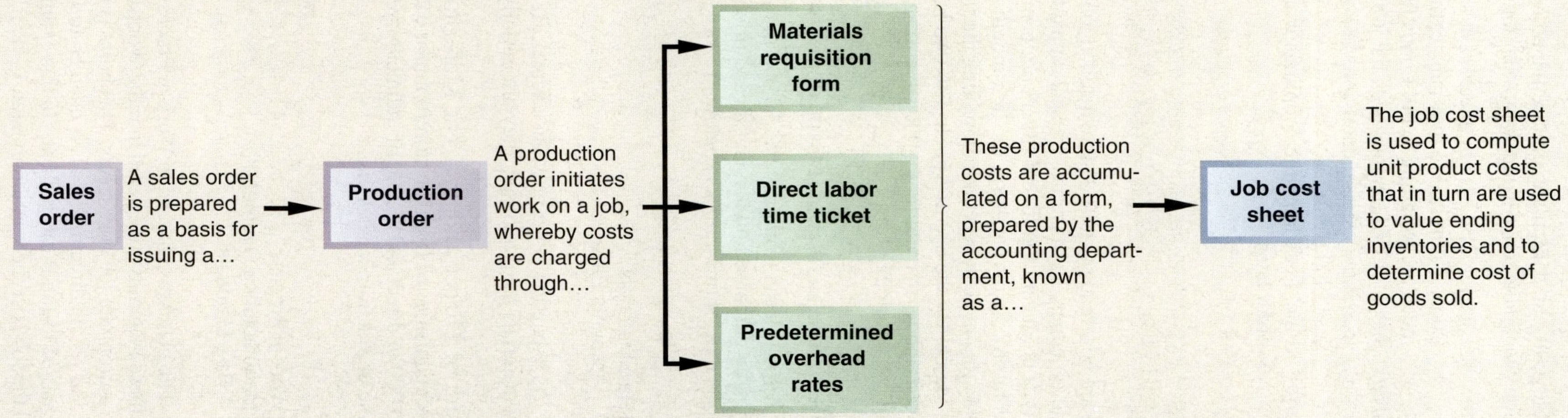

MANAGERIAL ACCOUNTING IN ACTION
The Wrap-up

YOST PRECISION MACHINING

In the 8:00 A.M. daily planning meeting on March 9, Jean Yost, the president of Yost Precision Machining, once again drew attention to job 2B47, the experimental couplings:

Jean: I see job 2B47 is completed. Let's get those couplings shipped immediately to Loops Unlimited so they can get their testing program under way. Marcus, how much are we going to bill Loops for those two units?

Marcus: Just a second, let me check the job cost sheet for that job. Here it is. We agreed to sell the experimental units at cost, so we will be charging Loops Unlimited just $900 a unit.

Jean: Fine. Let's hope the couplings work out and we make some money on the big order later.

Job-Order Costing—The Flow of Costs

LEARNING OBJECTIVE 4
Understand the flow of costs in a job-order costing system and prepare appropriate journal entries to record costs.

We are now ready to take a more detailed look at the flow of costs through the company's general ledger. To illustrate, we shall consider a single month's activity for Rand Company, a producer of gold and silver commemorative medallions. Rand Company has two jobs in process during April, the first month of its fiscal year. Job A, a special minting of 1,000 gold medallions commemorating the invention of motion pictures, was started during March. By the end of March, $30,000 in manufacturing costs had been recorded for the job. Job B, an order for 10,000 silver medallions commemorating the fall of the Berlin Wall, was started in April.

The Purchase and Issue of Materials

On April 1, Rand Company had $7,000 in raw materials on hand. During the month, the company purchased on account an additional $60,000 in raw materials. The purchase is recorded in journal entry (1) below:

(1)

Raw Materials	60,000	
Accounts Payable		60,000

As explained in the previous chapter, Raw Materials is an asset account. Thus, when raw materials are purchased, they are initially recorded as an asset—not as an expense.

Issue of Direct and Indirect Materials During April, $52,000 in raw materials were requisitioned from the storeroom for use in production. These raw materials include $50,000 of direct and $2,000 of indirect materials. Entry (2) records issuing the materials to the production departments.

(2)

Work in Process	50,000	
Manufacturing Overhead	2,000	
Raw Materials		52,000

The materials charged to Work in Process represent direct materials for specific jobs. As these materials are entered into the Work in Process account, they are also recorded on the appropriate job cost sheets. This point is illustrated in Exhibit 3–6, where $28,000 of the $50,000 in direct materials is charged to Job A's cost sheet and the remaining $22,000 is charged to Job B's cost sheet. (In this example, all data are presented in summary form and the job cost sheet is abbreviated.)

The $2,000 charged to Manufacturing Overhead in entry (2) represents indirect materials used in production during April. Observe that the Manufacturing Overhead account is separate from the Work in Process account. The purpose of the Manufacturing

EXHIBIT 3–6
Raw Materials Cost Flows

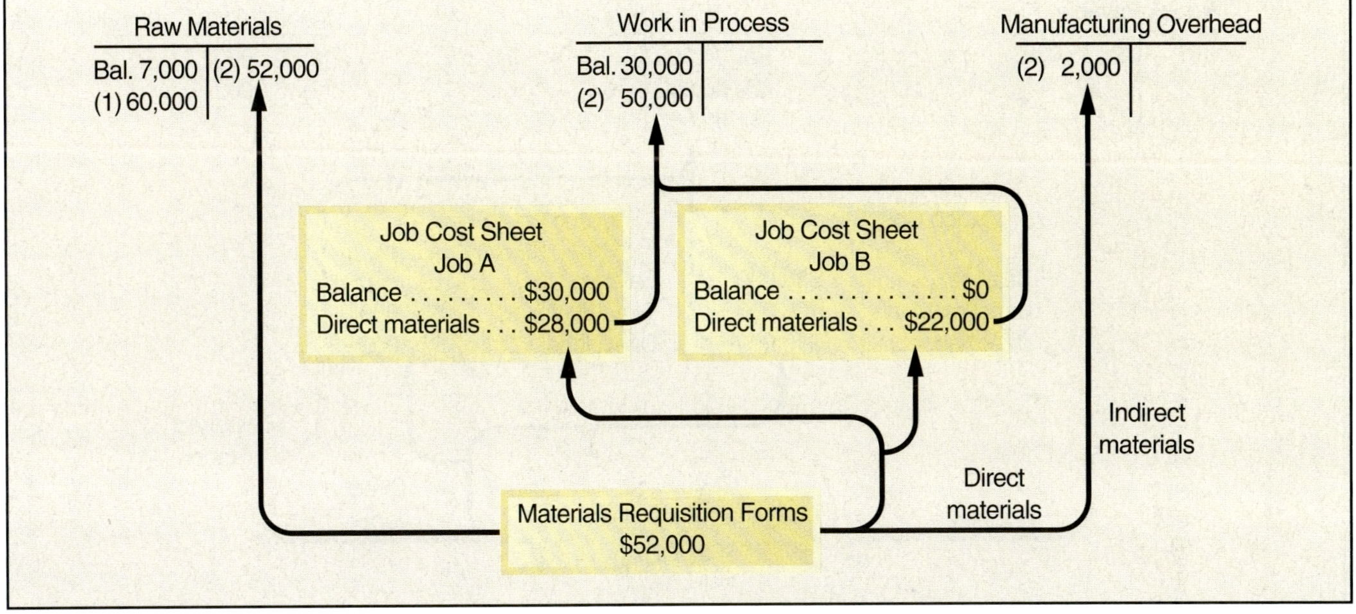

Overhead account is to accumulate all manufacturing overhead costs as they are incurred during a period.

Before leaving Exhibit 3–6 we need to point out one additional thing. Notice from the exhibit that the job cost sheet for Job A contains a beginning balance of $30,000. We stated earlier that this balance represents the cost of work done during March that has been carried forward to April. Also note that the Work in Process account contains the same $30,000 balance. *The reason the $30,000 appears in both places is that the Work in Process account is a control account and the job cost sheets form a subsidiary ledger. Thus, the Work in Process account contains a summarized total of all costs appearing on the individual job cost sheets for all jobs in process at any given point in time.* (Since Rand Company had only Job A in process at the beginning of April, Job A's $30,000 balance on that date is equal to the balance in the Work in Process account.)

Issue of Direct Materials Only Sometimes the materials drawn from the Raw Materials inventory account are all direct materials. In this case, the entry to record the issue of the materials into production would be as follows:

Work in Process	XXX	
Raw Materials		XXX

Labor Cost

As work is performed each day in various departments of Rand Company, employee time tickets are filled out by workers, collected, and forwarded to the Accounting Department. In the Accounting Department, wages are computed and the resulting costs are classified as either direct or indirect labor. In April, $60,000 was recorded for direct labor and $15,000 for indirect labor. This resulted in the following summary entry:

(3)

Work in Process	60,000	
Manufacturing Overhead	15,000	
Salaries and Wages Payable		75,000

EXHIBIT 3–7
Labor Cost Flows

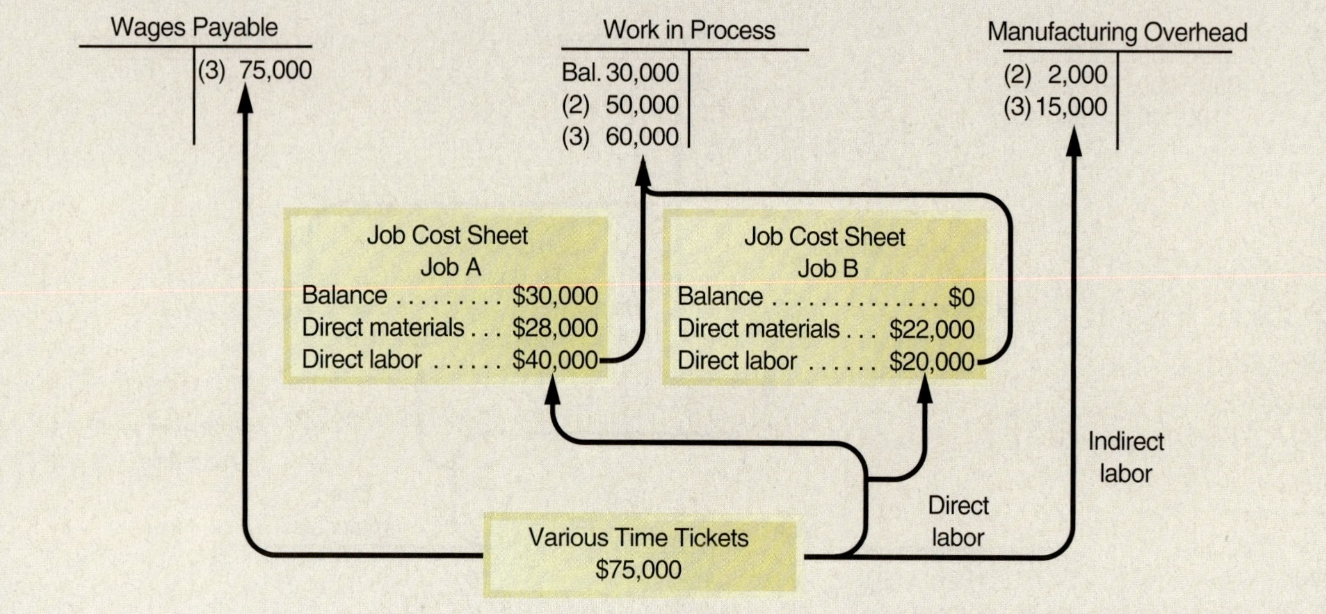

Only the direct labor of $60,000 is added to the Work in Process account. At the same time that direct labor costs are added to Work in Process, they are also added to the individual job cost sheets, as shown in Exhibit 3–7. During April, $40,000 of direct labor cost was charged to Job A and the remaining $20,000 was charged to Job B.

The labor costs charged to Manufacturing Overhead represent the indirect labor costs of the period, such as supervision, janitorial work, and maintenance.

Manufacturing Overhead Costs

Recall that all costs of operating the factory other than direct materials and direct labor are classified as manufacturing overhead costs. These costs are entered directly into the Manufacturing Overhead account as they are incurred. To illustrate, assume that Rand Company incurred the following general factory costs during April:

Utilities (heat, water, and power)	$21,000
Rent on factory equipment	16,000
Miscellaneous factory overhead costs	3,000
Total	$40,000

The following entry records the incurrence of these costs:

(4)

Manufacturing Overhead	40,000	
Accounts Payable		40,000

In addition, let us assume that during April, Rand Company recognized $13,000 in accrued property taxes and that $7,000 in prepaid insurance expired on factory buildings and equipment. The following entry records these items:

(5)

Manufacturing Overhead	20,000	
Property Taxes Payable		13,000
Prepaid Insurance		7,000

Finally, let us assume that the company recognized $18,000 in depreciation on factory equipment during April. The following entry records the accrual of this depreciation:

(6)

Manufacturing Overhead	18,000	
Accumulated Depreciation		18,000

In short, *all* manufacturing overhead costs are recorded directly into the Manufacturing Overhead account as they are incurred day by day throughout a period. It is important to understand that Manufacturing Overhead is a control account for many—perhaps thousands—of subsidiary accounts such as Indirect Materials, Indirect Labor, Factory Utilities, and so forth. As the Manufacturing Overhead account is debited for costs during a period, the various subsidiary accounts are also debited. In the example above and also in the assignment material for this chapter, we omit the entries to the subsidiary accounts for the sake of brevity.

The Application of Manufacturing Overhead

LEARNING OBJECTIVE 5
Apply overhead cost to Work in Process using a predetermined overhead rate.

Since actual manufacturing costs are charged to the Manufacturing Overhead control account rather than to Work in Process, how are manufacturing overhead costs assigned to Work in Process? The answer is, by means of the predetermined overhead rate. Recall from our discussion earlier in the chapter that a predetermined overhead rate is established at the beginning of each year. The rate is calculated by dividing the estimated total manufacturing overhead cost for the year by the estimated total units in the allocation base (measured in machine-hours, direct labor-hours, or some other base). The predetermined overhead rate is then used to apply overhead costs to jobs. For example, if direct labor-hours is the allocation base, overhead cost is applied to each job by multiplying the predetermined overhead rate by the number of direct labor-hours charged to the job.

To illustrate, assume that Rand Company has used machine-hours to compute its predetermined overhead rate and that this rate is $6 per machine-hour. Also assume that during April, 10,000 machine-hours were worked on Job A and 5,000 machine-hours were worked on Job B (a total of 15,000 machine-hours). Thus, $90,000 in overhead cost ($6 per machine-hour × 15,000 machine-hours = $90,000) would be applied to Work in Process. The following entry records the application of Manufacturing Overhead to Work in Process:

(7)

Work in Process	90,000	
Manufacturing Overhead		90,000

The flow of costs through the Manufacturing Overhead account is shown in Exhibit 3–8 (page 102).

The actual overhead costs in the Manufacturing Overhead account in Exhibit 3–8 are the costs that were added to the account in entries (2)–(6). Observe that the incurrence of these actual overhead costs [entries (2)–(6)] and the application of overhead to Work in Process [entry (7)] represent two separate and entirely distinct processes.

The Concept of a Clearing Account

The Manufacturing Overhead account operates as a clearing account. As we have noted, actual factory overhead costs are debited to the accounts as they are incurred day by day throughout the year. At certain intervals during the year, usually when a job is completed, overhead cost is applied to the job by means of the predetermined overhead rate, and Work in Process is debited and Manufacturing Overhead is credited. This sequence of events is illustrated below:

Manufacturing Overhead (a clearing account)

Actual overhead costs are charged to this account as they are incurred throughout the period.	Overhead is applied to Work in Process using the predetermined overhead rate.

EXHIBIT 3–8
The Flow of Costs in Overhead Application

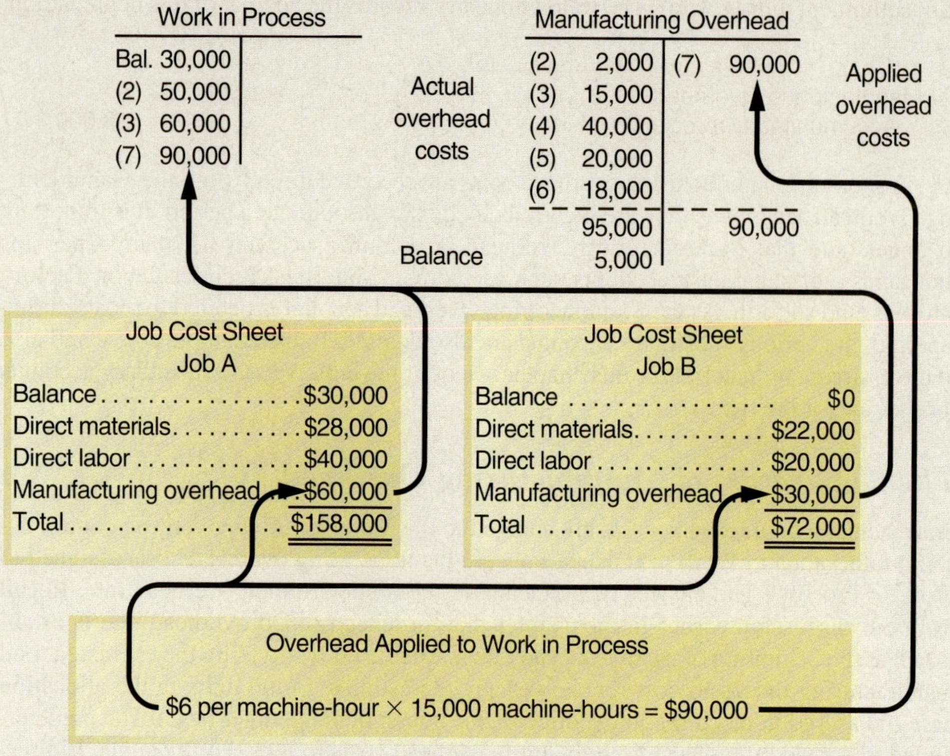

As we emphasized earlier, the predetermined overhead rate is based entirely on estimates of what overhead costs are *expected* to be, and it is established before the year begins. As a result, the overhead cost applied during a year will almost certainly turn out to be more or less than the overhead cost that is actually incurred. For example, notice from Exhibit 3–8 that Rand Company's actual overhead costs for the period are $5,000 greater than the overhead cost that has been applied to Work in Process, resulting in a $5,000 debit balance in the Manufacturing Overhead account. We will reserve discussion of what to do with this $5,000 balance until the next section, Problems of Overhead Application.

For the moment, we can conclude by noting from Exhibit 3–8 that the cost of a completed job consists of the actual direct materials cost of the job, the actual direct labor cost of the job, and the overhead cost *applied* to the job. Pay particular attention to the following subtle but important point: *Actual overhead costs are not charged to jobs; actual overhead costs do not appear on the job cost sheet nor do they appear in the Work in Process account. Only the applied overhead cost, based on the predetermined overhead rate, appears on the job cost sheet and in the Work in Process account.*

Nonmanufacturing Costs

In addition to manufacturing costs, companies also incur marketing and selling costs as well as administrative costs. As explained in the previous chapter, these costs should be treated as period expenses and charged directly to the income statement. *Nonmanufacturing costs should not go into the Manufacturing Overhead account.* To illustrate the correct treatment of nonmanufacturing costs, assume that Rand Company incurred $30,000 in selling and administrative salary costs during April. The following entry records these salaries:

(8)

Salaries Expense	30,000	
Salaries and Wages Payable		30,000

Assume that depreciation on office equipment during April was $7,000. The entry is as follows:

(9)

Depreciation Expense.	7,000	
Accumulated Depreciation		7,000

Pay particular attention to the difference between this entry and entry (6) where we recorded depreciation on factory equipment. In journal entry (6), depreciation on factory equipment was debited to Manufacturing Overhead and is therefore a product cost. In journal entry (9) above, depreciation on office equipment is debited to Depreciation Expense. Depreciation on office equipment is considered to be a period expense rather than a product cost.

Finally, assume that advertising was $42,000 and that other selling and administrative expenses in April totaled $8,000. The following entry records these items:

(10)

Advertising Expense.	42,000	
Other Selling and Administrative Expense	8,000	
Accounts Payable		50,000

Since the amounts in entries (8) through (10) all go directly into expense accounts, they will have no effect on product costs. The same will be true of any other selling and administrative expenses incurred during April, including sales commissions, depreciation on sales equipment, rent on office facilities, insurance on office facilities, and related costs.

Cost of Goods Manufactured

LEARNING OBJECTIVE 6
Prepare schedules of cost of goods manufactured and cost of goods sold.

When a job has been completed, the finished output is transferred from the production departments to the finished goods warehouse. By this time, the accounting department will have charged the job with direct materials and direct labor cost, and manufacturing overhead will have been applied using the predetermined rate. A transfer of costs is made within the costing system that *parallels* the physical transfer of the goods to the finished goods warehouse. The costs of the completed job are transferred out of the Work in Process account and into the Finished Goods account. The sum of all amounts transferred between these two accounts represents the cost of goods manufactured for the period.

In the case of Rand Company, let us assume that Job A was completed during April. The following entry transfers the cost of Job A from Work in Process to Finished Goods:

(11)

Finished Goods.	158,000	
Work in Process		158,000

The $158,000 represents the completed cost of Job A, as shown on the job cost sheet in Exhibit 3–8. Since Job A was the only job completed during April, the $158,000 also represents the cost of goods manufactured for the month. The $158,000 cost of goods manufactured for the month is added to the $10,000 in the beginning balance of Finished Goods from the previous month.

Job B was not completed by month-end, so its cost will remain in the Work in Process account and carry over to the next month. If a balance sheet is prepared at the end of April, the cost accumulated thus far on Job B will appear as "Work in process inventory" in the assets section.

Cost of Goods Sold

As finished goods are shipped to customers, their accumulated costs are transferred from the Finished Goods account to the Cost of Goods Sold account. If a complete job is shipped, as in the case where a job has been done to a customer's specifications, then the entire cost appearing on the job cost sheet is transferred into the Cost of Goods Sold account. In most cases, however, only a portion of the units involved in a particular job will be immediately sold. In these situations, the unit cost must be used to determine how much product cost should be removed from Finished Goods and charged to Cost of Goods Sold.

For Rand Company, we will assume 750 of the 1,000 gold medallions in Job A were shipped to customers by the end of the month for total sales revenue of $225,000. Since 1,000 units were produced and the total cost of the job from the job cost sheet was $158,000, the unit product cost was $158. The following journal entries would record the sale (all sales are on account):

(12)

Accounts Receivable	225,000	
Sales		225,000

(13)

Cost of Goods Sold.	118,500	
Finished Goods.		118,500
($158 per unit × 750 units = $118,500)		

With entry (13), the flow of costs through our job-order costing system is completed.

LEARNING OBJECTIVE 7
Use T-accounts to show the flow of costs in a job-order costing system.

Summary of Cost Flows

To pull the entire Rand Company example together, journal entries (1) through (13) are summarized in Exhibit 3–9. The flow of costs through the accounts is presented in T-account form in Exhibit 3–10 (page 106).

Exhibit 3–11 (page 107) presents a schedule of cost of goods manufactured and a schedule of cost of goods sold for Rand Company. Note particularly from Exhibit 3–11 that the manufacturing overhead cost on the schedule of cost of goods manufactured is the overhead applied to jobs during the month—not the actual manufacturing overhead costs incurred. The reason for this can be traced back to journal entry (7) and the T-account for Work in Process that appears in Exhibit 3–10. Under a normal costing system as illustrated in this chapter, applied—not actual—overhead costs are applied to jobs and thus to Work in Process inventory. Note also the cost of goods manufactured for the month ($158,000) agrees with the amount transferred from Work in Process to Finished Goods for the month as recorded earlier in entry (11). Also note that this $158,000 is used in computing the cost of goods sold for the month.

An income statement for April is presented in Exhibit 3–12 (page 107). Observe that the cost of goods sold on this statement ($123,500) is carried down from Exhibit 3–11.

Problems of Overhead Application

LEARNING OBJECTIVE 8
Compute under- or overapplied overhead cost and prepare the journal entry to close the balance in Manufacturing Overhead to the appropriate accounts.

We need to consider two complications relating to overhead application. These are (1) the computation of underapplied and overapplied overhead and (2) the disposition of any balance remaining in the Manufacturing Overhead account at the end of a period.

Underapplied and Overapplied Overhead

Since the predetermined overhead rate is established before a period begins and is based entirely on estimated data, the overhead cost applied to Work in Process will generally differ from the amount of overhead cost actually incurred during a period. In the case of Rand Company, for example, the predetermined overhead rate of $6 per hour resulted in $90,000 of overhead cost being applied to Work in Process, whereas actual overhead

EXHIBIT 3–9
Summary of Rand Company Journal Entries

		Debit	Credit
(1)	Raw Materials	60,000	
	Accounts Payable		60,000
(2)	Work in Process	50,000	
	Manufacturing Overhead	2,000	
	Raw Materials		52,000
(3)	Work in Process	60,000	
	Manufacturing Overhead	15,000	
	Salaries and Wages Payable		75,000
(4)	Manufacturing Overhead	40,000	
	Accounts Payable		40,000
(5)	Manufacturing Overhead	20,000	
	Property Taxes Payable		13,000
	Prepaid Insurance		7,000
(6)	Manufacturing Overhead	18,000	
	Accumulated Depreciation		18,000
(7)	Work in Process	90,000	
	Manufacturing Overhead		90,000
(8)	Salaries Expense	30,000	
	Salaries and Wages Payable		30,000
(9)	Depreciation Expense	7,000	
	Accumulated Depreciation		7,000
(10)	Advertising Expense	42,000	
	Other Selling and Administrative Expense	8,000	
	Accounts Payable		50,000
(11)	Finished Goods	158,000	
	Work in Process		158,000
(12)	Accounts Receivable	225,000	
	Sales		225,000
(13)	Cost of Goods Sold	118,500	
	Finished Goods		118,500

EXHIBIT 3–10

Summary of Cost Flows—Rand Company

Accounts Receivable

	XX*		
(12)	225,000		

Prepaid Insurance

	XX		
		(5)	7,000

Raw Materials

Bal.	7,000	(2)	52,000
(1)	60,000		
Bal.	15,000		

Work in Process

Bal.	30,000	(11)	158,000
(2)	50,000		
(3)	60,000		
(7)	90,000		
Bal.	72,000		

Finished Goods

Bal.	10,000	(13)	118,500
(11)	158,000		
Bal.	49,500		

Accumulated Depreciation

			XX
		(6)	18,000
		(9)	7,000

Manufacturing Overhead

(2)	2,000	(7)	90,000
(3)	15,000		
(4)	40,000		
(5)	20,000		
(6)	18,000		
Bal.	5,000		

Accounts Payable

			XX
		(1)	60,000
		(4)	40,000
		(10)	50,000

Salaries and Wages Payable

			XX
		(3)	75,000
		(8)	30,000

Property Taxes Payable

			XX
		(5)	13,000

Capital Stock

			XX

Retained Earnings

			XX

Sales

		(12)	225,000

Cost of Goods Sold

(13)	118,500		

Salaries Expense

(8)	30,000		

Depreciation Expense

(9)	7,000		

Advertising Expense

(10)	42,000		

Other Selling and Administrative Expense

(10)	8,000		

Explanation of entries:

(1) Raw materials purchased.
(2) Direct and indirect materials issued into production.
(3) Direct and indirect factory labor cost incurred.
(4) Utilities and other factory costs incurred.
(5) Property taxes and insurance incurred on the factory.
(6) Depreciation recorded on factory assets.
(7) Overhead cost applied to Work in Process.
(8) Administrative salaries expense incurred.
(9) Depreciation recorded on office equipment.
(10) Advertising and other expense incurred.
(11) Cost of goods manufactured transferred into finished goods.
(12) Sale of Job A recorded.
(13) Cost of goods sold recorded for Job A.

*XX = Normal balance in the account (for example, Accounts Receivable normally carries a debit balance).

EXHIBIT 3–11
Schedules of Cost of Goods Manufactured and Cost of Goods Sold

Cost of Goods Manufactured		
Direct materials:		
Raw materials inventory, beginning	$ 7,000	
Add: Purchases of raw materials	60,000	
Total raw materials available	67,000	
Deduct: Raw materials inventory, ending	15,000	
Raw materials used in production	52,000	
Less indirect materials included in manufacturing overhead	2,000	$ 50,000
Direct labor		60,000
Manufacturing overhead applied to work in process		90,000
Total manufacturing costs		200,000
Add: Beginning work in process inventory		30,000
		230,000
Deduct: Ending work in process inventory		72,000
Cost of goods manufactured		$158,000
Cost of Goods Sold		
Finished goods inventory, beginning		$ 10,000
Add: Cost of goods manufactured		158,000
Goods available for sale		168,000
Deduct: Finished goods inventory, ending		49,500
Unadjusted cost of goods sold		118,500
Add: Underapplied overhead		5,000
Adjusted cost of goods sold		$123,500

*Note that the underapplied overhead is added to cost of goods sold. If overhead were overapplied, it would be deducted from cost of goods sold.

EXHIBIT 3–12
Income Statement

RAND COMPANY
Income Statement
For the Month Ending April 30

Sales		$225,000
Less cost of goods sold ($118,500 + $5,000)		123,500
Gross margin		101,500
Less selling and administrative expenses:		
Salaries expense	$30,000	
Depreciation expense	7,000	
Advertising expense	42,000	
Other expense	8,000	87,000
Net operating income		$ 14,500

costs for April proved to be $95,000 (see Exhibit 3–8). The difference between the overhead cost applied to Work in Process and the actual overhead costs of a period is called either **underapplied** or **overapplied overhead.** For Rand Company, overhead was underapplied because the applied cost ($90,000) was $5,000 less than the actual cost ($95,000). If the situation had been reversed and the company had applied $95,000 in overhead cost to Work in Process while incurring actual overhead costs of only $90,000, then the overhead would have been overapplied.

What is the cause of underapplied or overapplied overhead? The causes can be complex, and a full explanation will have to wait for later chapters. Nevertheless, the basic problem is that the method of applying overhead to jobs using a predetermined overhead rate assumes that actual overhead costs will be proportional to the actual amount of the allocation base incurred during the period. If, for example, the predetermined overhead rate is $6 per machine-hour, then it is assumed that actual overhead costs incurred will be $6 for every machine-hour that is actually worked. There are at least two reasons why this may not be true. First, much of the overhead often consists of fixed costs that do not grow as the number of machine-hours incurred increases. Second, spending on overhead items may or may not be under control. If individuals who are responsible for overhead costs do a good job, those costs should be less than were expected at the beginning of the period. If they do a poor job, those costs will be more than expected. As we indicated above, however, a fuller explanation of the causes of underapplied and overapplied overhead will have to wait for later chapters.

To illustrate what can happen, suppose that two companies—Turbo Crafters and Black & Howell—have prepared the following estimated data for the coming year:

	Company	
	Turbo Crafters	Black & Howell
Predetermined overhead rate based on . . .	Machine-hours	Direct materials cost
Estimated manufacturing overhead	$300,000 (a)	$120,000 (a)
Estimated machine-hours	75,000 (b)	—
Estimated direct materials cost	—	$80,000 (b)
Predetermined overhead rate, (a) ÷ (b) . . .	$4 per machine-hour	150% of direct materials cost

Note that when the allocation base is dollars—such as direct materials cost in the case of Black & Howell—the predetermined overhead rate is a percentage. When dollars are divided by dollars, the result is a percentage.

Now assume that because of unexpected changes in overhead spending and changes in demand for the companies' products, the *actual* overhead cost and the *actual* activity recorded during the year in each company are as follows:

	Company	
	Turbo Crafters	Black & Howell
Actual manufacturing overhead costs	$290,000	$130,000
Actual machine-hours	68,000	—
Actual direct material costs	—	$ 90,000

For each company, note that the actual data for both cost and activity differ from the estimates used in computing the predetermined overhead rate. This results in underapplied and overapplied overhead as follows:

	Company	
	Turbo Crafters	Black & Howell
Actual manufacturing overhead costs	$290,000	$130,000
Manufacturing overhead cost applied to		
Work in Process during the year:		
68,000 *actual* machine-hours ×		
$4 per machine-hour	272,000	
$90,000 *actual* direct materials cost ×		
150% of direct materials cost		135,000
Underapplied (overapplied) overhead	$ 18,000	$ (5,000)

For Turbo Crafters, notice that the amount of overhead cost that has been applied to Work in Process ($272,000) is less than the actual overhead cost for the year ($290,000).

Therefore, overhead is underapplied. Also, notice that the original estimate of overhead for Turbo Crafters ($300,000) is not directly involved in this computation. Its impact is felt only through the $4 predetermined overhead rate.

For Black & Howell, the amount of overhead cost that has been applied to Work in Process ($135,000) is greater than the actual overhead cost for the year ($130,000), and so overhead is overapplied.

A summary of the concepts discussed above is presented in Exhibit 3–13.

Disposition of Under- or Overapplied Overhead Balances

The under- or overapplied balance remaining in the Manufacturing Overhead account at the end of a period is treated in one of two ways:

1. Closed out to Cost of Goods Sold.
2. Allocated between Work in Process, Finished Goods, and Cost of Goods Sold in proportion to the overhead applied during the current period that is in the ending balances of these accounts.

The second method, which allocates the under- or overapplied overhead among ending inventories and Cost of Goods Sold, is equivalent to using an "actual" overhead rate and is for that reason considered by many to be more accurate than the first method. Consequently, if the amount of underapplied or overapplied overhead is material, many accountants would insist that the second method be used. In problem assignments, we will always indicate which method you are to use for disposing of under- or overapplied overhead.

Closed Out to Cost of Goods Sold

As mentioned above, closing out the balance in Manufacturing Overhead to Cost of Goods Sold is simpler than the allocation method. Returning to the example of Rand Company, the entry to close the $5,000 of underapplied overhead to Cost of Goods Sold would be as follows:

(14)

Cost of Goods Sold.	5,000	
Manufacturing Overhead.		5,000

Note that since the Manufacturing Overhead account has a debit balance, Manufacturing Overhead must be credited to close out the account. This has the effect of increasing Cost of Goods Sold for April to $123,500:

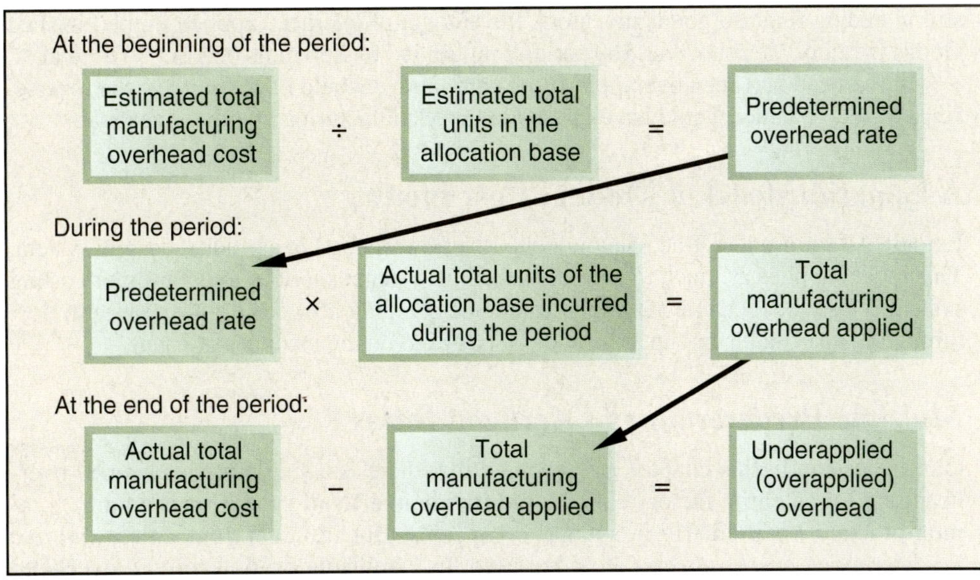

EXHIBIT 3–13
Summary of Overhead Concepts

Unadjusted cost of goods sold [from entry (13)]	$118,500
Add underapplied overhead [entry (14) above]	5,000
Adjusted cost of goods sold	$123,500

After this adjustment has been made, Rand Company's income statement for April will appear as shown earlier in Exhibit 3–12.

Allocated between Accounts Allocation of under- or overapplied overhead between Work in Process, Finished Goods, and Cost of Goods Sold is more accurate than closing the entire balance into Cost of Goods Sold. The reason is that allocation assigns overhead costs to where they would have gone in the first place had it not been for the errors in estimating the predetermined overhead rate.

Had Rand Company chosen to allocate the underapplied overhead among the inventory accounts and Cost of Goods Sold, it would first be necessary to determine the amount of overhead that had been applied during April to each of the accounts. The computations would have been as follows:

Overhead applied in work in process inventory, April 30	$30,000	33.33%
Overhead applied in finished goods inventory, April 30 ($60,000/1,000 units = $60 per unit) × 250 units	15,000	16.67%
Overhead applied in cost of goods sold, April ($60,000/1,000 units = $60 per unit) × 750 units	45,000	50.00%
Total overhead applied	$90,000	100.00%

Based on the above percentages, the underapplied overhead (i.e., the debit balance in Manufacturing Overhead) would be allocated as shown in the following journal entry:

Work in Process (33.33% × $5,000)	1,666.50	
Finished Goods (16.67% × $5,000)..............	833.50	
Cost of Goods Sold (50.00% × $5,000)...........	2,500.00	
Manufacturing Overhead.....................		5,000.00

Note that the first step in the allocation was to determine the amount of overhead applied in each of the accounts. For Finished Goods, for example, the total amount of overhead applied to Job A, $60,000, was divided by the total number of units in Job A, 1,000 units, to arrive at the average overhead applied of $60 per unit. Since 250 units from Job A were still in ending finished goods inventory, the amount of overhead applied in the Finished Goods Inventory account was $60 per unit multiplied by 250 units or $15,000 in total.

If overhead had been overapplied, the entry above would have been just the reverse, since a credit balance would have existed in the Manufacturing Overhead account.

A General Model of Product Cost Flows

Exhibit 3–14 presents a T-account model of the flow of costs in a product costing system. This model applies as much to a process costing system as it does to a job-order costing system. This model can be very helpful in understanding how costs enter a system, flow through it, and finally end up as Cost of Goods Sold on the income statement.

Multiple Predetermined Overhead Rates

Our discussion in this chapter has assumed that there is a single predetermined overhead rate for an entire factory called a **plantwide overhead rate.** This is a fairly common practice—particularly in smaller companies. But in larger companies, *multiple predetermined overhead rates* are often used. In a **multiple predetermined overhead**

EXHIBIT 3–14
A General Model of Cost Flows

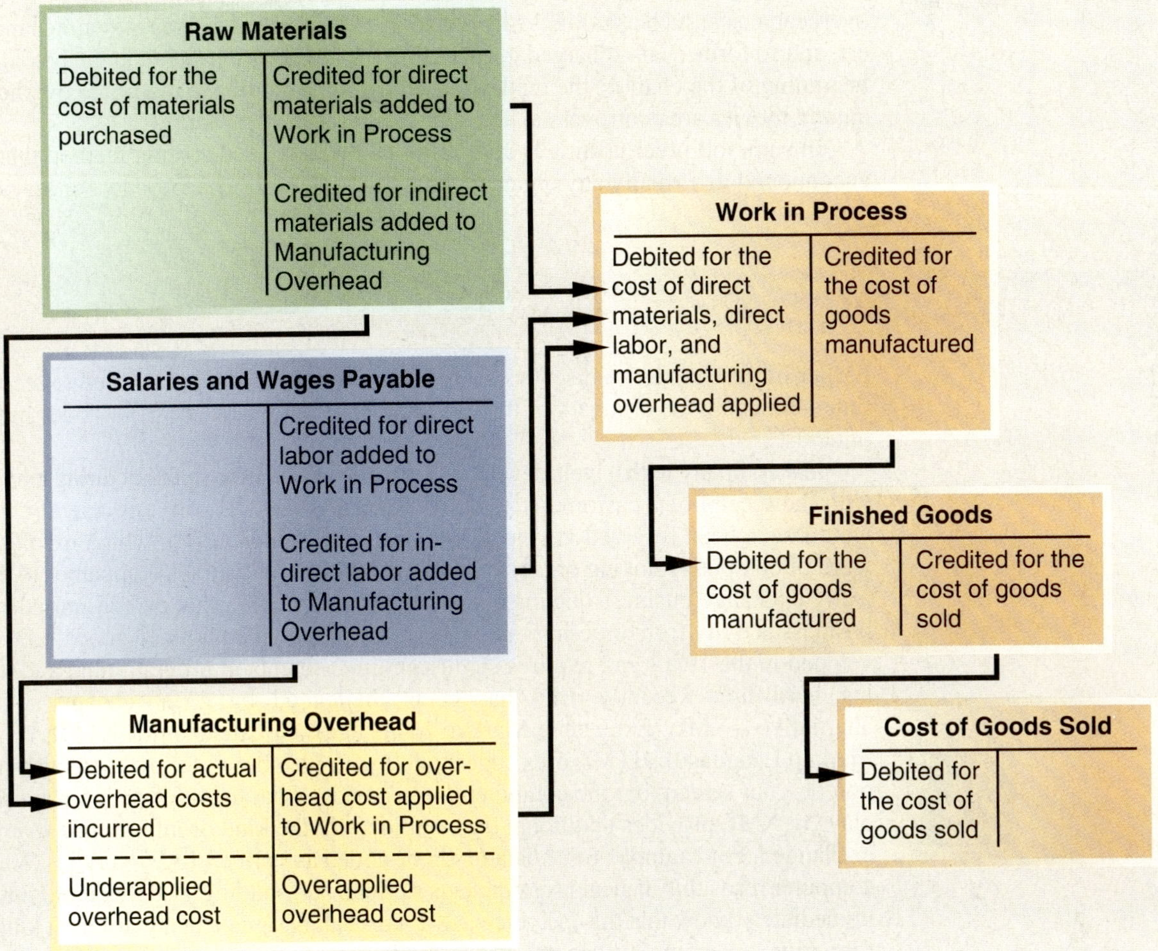

rate system each production department may have its own predetermined overhead rate. Such a system, while more complex, is considered to be more accurate, since it can reflect differences across departments in how overhead costs are incurred. For example, overhead might be allocated based on direct labor-hours in departments that are relatively labor intensive and based on machine-hours in departments that are relatively machine intensive. When multiple predetermined overhead rates are used, overhead is applied in each department according to its own overhead rate as a job proceeds through the department.

Job-Order Costing in Service Companies

Job-order costing is also used in service organizations such as law firms, movie studios, hospitals, and repair shops, as well as in manufacturing companies. In a law firm, for example, each client is considered to be a "job," and the costs of that job are accumulated day by day on a job cost sheet as the client's case is handled by the firm. Legal forms and similar inputs represent the direct materials for the job; the time expended by attorneys represents the direct labor; and the costs of secretaries, clerks, rent, depreciation, and so forth, represent the overhead.

In a movie studio such as Columbia Pictures, each film produced by the studio is a "job," and costs for direct materials (costumes, props, film, etc.) and direct labor (actors, directors, and extras) are charged to each film's job cost sheet. A share of the studio's overhead costs, such as utilities, depreciation of equipment, wages of maintenance workers, and so forth, is also charged to each film. However, as discussed in the box at the very beginning of the chapter, the methods used by some studios to distribute overhead costs among movies are controversial and sometimes result in lawsuits.

In sum, job-order costing is a versatile and widely used costing method that may be encountered in virtually any organization that provides diverse products or services.

Use of Information Technology

Earlier in the chapter we discussed how bar code technology can be used to record labor time—reducing the drudgery in that task and increasing accuracy. Bar codes have many other uses.

In a company with a well-developed bar code system, the manufacturing cycle begins with the receipt of a customer's order in electronic form. Until very recently, the order would have been received via electronic data interchange (EDI), which involves a network of computers linking organizations. An EDI network allows companies to electronically exchange business documents and other information that extend into all areas of business activity from ordering raw materials to shipping completed goods. EDI was developed in the 1980s and requires significant investments in programming and networking hardware. Recently, EDI has been challenged by a far cheaper web-based alternative—XML (Extensible Markup Language), an extension of HTML (Hypertext Markup Language). HTML uses codes to tell your web browser how to display information on your screen, but the computer doesn't know what the information is—it just displays it. XML provides additional tags that identify the kind of information that is being exchanged. For example, price data might be coded as <price> 14.95 <price>. When your computer reads this data and sees the tags <price> surrounding 14.95, your computer will immediately know that this is a price. XML tags can designate many different kinds of information—customer orders, medical records, bank statements, and so on—and the tags will indicate to your computer how to display, store, and retrieve the information. Office Depot is an early adopter of XML, which it is using to facilitate e-commerce with its big customers.

Once an order has been received via EDI or in the form of an XML file, the computer draws up a list of required raw materials and sends out electronic purchase orders to suppliers. When materials arrive at the company's plant from the suppliers, bar codes that have been applied by the suppliers are scanned to update inventory records and to trigger payment for the materials. The bar codes are scanned again when the materials are requisitioned for use in production. At that point, the computer credits the Raw Materials inventory account for the amount and type of goods requisitioned and charges the Work in Process inventory account.

A unique bar code is assigned to each job. This bar code is scanned to update Work in Process records for labor and other costs incurred in the manufacturing process. When goods are completed, another scan is performed that transfers both the cost and quantity of goods from the Work in Process inventory account to the Finished Goods inventory account, or charges Cost of Goods Sold for goods ready to be shipped.

Goods ready to be shipped are packed into containers that are bar coded with information that includes the customer number, the type and quantity of goods being shipped, and the order number. This bar code is then used for preparing billing information and for tracking the packed goods until placed on a carrier for shipment to the customer. Some customers require that the packed goods be bar coded with point-of-sale labels that can be scanned at retail check-out counters. These scans allow the retailer to update inventory records, verify price, and generate a customer receipt.

IN BUSINESS

USING XML TO ENHANCE WEB COMMERCE

W.W. Grainger Inc. is in the unglamorous, but important, business of selling maintenance and repair supplies to organizations. For an effective web-based catalog, the company needs up-to-date, detailed product descriptions from its own suppliers. Grainger is using software from OnDisplay Inc. to collect product descriptions from vendors' databases and to add XML tags. When Grainger's customers request product information on the web, this data can then be displayed in a standard format. This process cuts in half the amount of time required to post new product information to Grainger's web catalog.

If you would like to know more about XML, refer to the World Wide Web Consortium (W3C) web site www.w3c.org/xml.

Source: John J. Xenakis, *CFO*, October 1999, pp. 31–36.

In short, bar code technology is being integrated into many areas of business activity. When combined with EDI or XML, it eliminates a lot of clerical drudgery and allows companies to capture and exchange more data and to analyze and report information much more quickly and completely and with less error than with manual systems.

IN BUSINESS

MANAGING DIVERSITY WITH TECHNOLOGY

Andersen Windows, Inc. of Bayport, Minnesota, has a software program that enables it to produce just about any window configuration that a customer might order. The program—which works on most standard Microsoft® Windows platforms—allows customers to select from any of the company's large selection of standard window and door sizes and styles. Customers can add the features and options they want with an easy "point-and-click" until they've configured the desired units. Placing the order after final selections are made is just as easy—the window order can be sent electronically into Andersen's back office system where it is automatically fulfilled. The entire process is highly automated and very efficient, yet it enables the customer a high degree of flexibility.

Source: Andersen® Intelligent Quote, used by permission of Andersen Windows, Inc.

Summary

Job-order costing and process costing are widely used to track costs. Job-order costing is used in situations where the organization offers many different products or services, such as in furniture manufacturing, hospitals, and legal firms. Process costing is used where units of product are homogeneous, such as in flour milling or cement production.

Materials requisition forms and labor time tickets are used to assign direct materials and direct labor costs to jobs in a job-costing system. Manufacturing overhead costs are assigned to jobs using a predetermined overhead rate. The predetermined overhead rate is determined before the period begins by dividing the estimated total manufacturing cost for the period by the estimated total allocation base for the period. The most frequently used allocation bases are direct labor-hours and machine-hours. Overhead is applied to jobs by multiplying the predetermined overhead rate by the actual amount of the allocation base used by the job.

Since the predetermined overhead rate is based on estimates, the actual overhead cost incurred during a period may be more or less than the amount of overhead cost applied to production. Such a difference is referred to as under- or overapplied overhead. The under- or overapplied overhead for a period can be either (1) closed out to Cost of Goods Sold or (2) allocated between Work in Process, Finished Goods, and Cost of Goods Sold. When overhead is underapplied, manufacturing overhead costs have been understated and therefore inventories and/or expenses must be adjusted upwards. When overhead is overapplied, manufacturing overhead costs have been overstated and therefore inventories and/or expenses must be adjusted downwards.

Review Problem: Job-Order Costing

Hogle Company is a manufacturer that uses job-order costing. On January 1, the beginning of its fiscal year, the company's inventory balances were as follows:

Raw materials	$20,000
Work in process	$15,000
Finished goods	$30,000

The company applies overhead cost to jobs on the basis of machine-hours worked. For the current year, the company estimated that it would work 75,000 machine-hours and incur $450,000 in manufacturing overhead cost. The following transactions were recorded for the year:

a. Raw materials were purchased on account, $410,000.
b. Raw materials were requisitioned for use in production, $380,000 ($360,000 direct materials and $20,000 indirect materials).
c. The following costs were incurred for employee services: direct labor, $75,000; indirect labor, $110,000; sales commissions, $90,000; and administrative salaries, $200,000.
d. Sales travel costs were $17,000.
e. Utility costs in the factory were $43,000.
f. Advertising costs were $180,000.
g. Depreciation was recorded for the year, $350,000 (80% relates to factory operations, and 20% relates to selling and administrative activities).
h. Insurance expired during the year, $10,000 (70% relates to factory operations, and the remaining 30% relates to selling and administrative activities).
i. Manufacturing overhead was applied to production. Due to greater than expected demand for its products, the company worked 80,000 machine-hours during the year.
j. Goods costing $900,000 to manufacture according to their job cost sheets were completed during the year.
k. Goods were sold on account to customers during the year for a total of $1,500,000. The goods cost $870,000 to manufacture according to their job cost sheets.

Required:

1. Prepare journal entries to record the preceding transactions.
2. Post the entries in (1) above to T-accounts (don't forget to enter the beginning balances in the inventory accounts).
3. Is Manufacturing Overhead underapplied or overapplied for the year? Prepare a journal entry to close any balance in the Manufacturing Overhead account to Cost of Goods Sold. Do not allocate the balance between ending inventories and Cost of Goods Sold.
4. Prepare an income statement for the year.

Solution to Review Problem

1.	*a.*	Raw Materials	410,000	
		Accounts Payable		410,000
	b.	Work in Process	360,000	
		Manufacturing Overhead	20,000	
		Raw Materials		380,000
	c.	Work in Process	75,000	
		Manufacturing Overhead	110,000	
		Sales Commissions Expense	90,000	
		Administrative Salaries Expense	200,000	
		Salaries and Wages Payable		475,000
	d.	Sales Travel Expense	17,000	
		Accounts Payable		17,000
	e.	Manufacturing Overhead	43,000	
		Accounts Payable		43,000
	f.	Advertising Expense	180,000	
		Accounts Payable		180,000
	g.	Manufacturing Overhead	280,000	
		Depreciation Expense	70,000	
		Accumulated Depreciation		350,000

h.	Manufacturing Overhead	7,000	
	Insurance Expense	3,000	
	Prepaid Insurance		10,000

i. The predetermined overhead rate for the year would be computed as follows:

$$\text{Predetermined overhead rate} = \frac{\text{Estimated total manufacturing overhead cost}}{\text{Estimated total units in the allocation base}}$$

$$= \frac{\$450{,}000}{75{,}000 \text{ machine-hours}}$$

$$= \$6 \text{ per machine-hour}$$

Based on the 80,000 machine-hours actually worked during the year, the company would have applied $480,000 in overhead cost to production: $6 per machine-hour × 80,000 machine-hours = $480,000. The following entry records this application of overhead cost:

	Work in Process	480,000	
	Manufacturing Overhead		480,000
j.	Finished Goods	900,000	
	Work in Process		900,000
k.	Accounts Receivable	1,500,000	
	Sales		1,500,000
	Cost of Goods Sold	870,000	
	Finished Goods		870,000

2.

Accounts Receivable

(k)	1,500,000		

Finished Goods

Bal.	30,000	(k)	870,000
(j)	900,000		
Bal.	60,000		

Accounts Payable

		(a)	410,000
		(d)	17,000
		(e)	43,000
		(f)	180,000

Sales

		(k)	1,500,000

Sales Commissions Expense

(c)	90,000		

Advertising Expense

(f)	180,000		

Raw Materials

Bal.	20,000	(b)	380,000
(a)	410,000		
Bal.	50,000		

Prepaid Insurance

		(h)	10,000

Salaries and Wages Payable

		(c)	475,000

Cost of Goods Sold

(k)	870,000		

Administrative Salary Expense

(c)	200,000		

Depreciation Expense

(g)	70,000		

Work in Process

Bal.	15,000	(j)	900,000
(b)	360,000		
(c)	75,000		
(i)	480,000		
Bal.	30,000		

Accumulated Depreciation

		(g)	350,000

Manufacturing Overhead

(b)	20,000	(i)	480,000
(c)	110,000		
(e)	43,000		
(g)	280,000		
(h)	7,000		
	460,000		480,000
		Bal.	20,000

Insurance Expense

(h)	3,000		

Sales Travel Expense

(d)	17,000		

3. Manufacturing overhead is overapplied for the year. The entry to close it out to Cost of Goods Sold is as follows:

Manufacturing Overhead	20,000	
Cost of Goods Sold		20,000

4.

HOGLE COMPANY
Income Statement
For the Year Ended December 31

Sales		$1,500,000
Less cost of goods sold ($870,000 − $20,000)		850,000
Gross margin		650,000
Less selling and administrative expenses:		
Commissions expense	$ 90,000	
Administrative salaries expense	200,000	
Sales travel expense	17,000	
Advertising expense	180,000	
Depreciation expense	70,000	
Insurance expense	3,000	560,000
Net operating income		$ 90,000

Glossary

Absorption costing A costing method that includes all manufacturing costs—direct materials, direct labor, and both variable and fixed overhead—as part of the cost of a product. This term is synonymous with *full cost.* (p. 88)

Allocation base A measure of activity such as direct labor-hours or machine-hours that is used to assign costs to cost objects. (p. 93)

Bill of materials A document that shows the type and quantity of each major item of materials required to make a product. (p. 90)

Cost driver A factor, such as machine-hours, beds occupied, computer time, or flight-hours, that causes overhead costs. (p. 96)

Full cost See *Absorption costing.* (p. 88)

Job cost sheet A form prepared for each job that records the materials, labor, and overhead costs charged to the job. (p. 91)

Job-order costing system A costing system used in situations where many different products, jobs, or services are produced each period. (p. 89)

Materials requisition form A detailed source document that specifies the type and quantity of materials that are to be drawn from the storeroom and identifies the job to which the costs of materials are to be charged. (p. 90)

Multiple predetermined overhead rates A costing system in which there are multiple overhead cost pools with a different predetermined rate for each cost pool, rather than a single predetermined overhead rate for the entire company. Frequently, each production department is treated as a separate overhead cost pool. (p. 110)

Normal cost system A costing system in which overhead costs are applied to jobs by multiplying a predetermined overhead rate by the actual amount of the allocation base incurred by the job. (p. 94)

Overapplied overhead A credit balance in the Manufacturing Overhead account that occurs when the amount of overhead cost applied to Work in Process is greater than the amount of overhead cost actually incurred during a period. (p. 107)

Overhead application The process of charging manufacturing overhead cost to job cost sheets and to the Work in Process account. (p. 94)

Plantwide overhead rate A single predetermined overhead rate that is used throughout a plant. (p. 110)

Predetermined overhead rate A rate used to charge overhead cost to jobs; the rate is established in advance for each period using estimates of total manufacturing overhead cost and of the total allocation base for the period. (p. 94)

Process costing system A costing system used in situations where a single, homogeneous product (such as cement or flour) is produced for long periods of time. (p. 88)

Time ticket A detailed source document that is used to record the amount of time an employee spends on various activities. (p. 92)

Underapplied overhead A debit balance in the Manufacturing Overhead account that occurs when the amount of overhead cost actually incurred is greater than the amount of overhead cost applied to Work in Process during a period. (p. 107)

Appendix 3A: The Predetermined Overhead Rate and Capacity

LEARNING OBJECTIVE 9
Understand the implications of basing the predetermined overhead rate on activity at capacity rather than on estimated activity for the period.

Companies typically base their predetermined overhead rates on the estimated, or budgeted, amount of the allocation base for the upcoming period. This is the method that is used in the chapter, but it is a practice that has come under severe criticism.[1] An example will be very helpful in understanding why. Prahad Corporation manufactures music CDs for local recording studios. The company's CD duplicating machine is capable of producing a new CD every 10 seconds from a master CD. The company leases the CD duplicating machine for $180,000 per year, and this is the company's only manufacturing overhead cost. With allowances for setups and maintenance, the machine is theoretically capable of producing up to 900,000 CDs per year. However, due to weak retail sales of CDs, the company's commercial customers are unlikely to order more than 600,000 CDs next year. The company uses machine time as the allocation base for applying manufacturing overhead. These data are summarized below:

PRAHAD CORPORATION DATA	
Total manufacturing overhead cost	$180,000 per year
Allocation base: machine time per CD	10 seconds per CD
Capacity	900,000 CDs per year
Budgeted output for next year	600,000 CDs

If Prahad follows common practice and computes its predetermined overhead rate using estimated or budgeted figures, then its predetermined overhead rate for next year would be $0.03 per second of machine time computed as follows:

$$\text{Predetermined overhead rate} = \frac{\text{Estimated total manufacturing overhead cost}}{\text{Estimated total units in the allocation base}}$$

$$= \frac{\$180{,}000}{600{,}000 \text{ CDs} \times 10 \text{ seconds per CD}}$$

$$= \$0.03 \text{ per second}$$

Since each CD requires 10 seconds of machine time, each CD will be charged for $0.30 of overhead cost.

Critics charge that there are two problems with this procedure. First, if predetermined overhead rates are based on budgeted activity, then the unit product costs will fluctuate depending on the budgeted level of activity for the period. For example, if the budgeted output for the year was only 300,000 CDs, the predetermined overhead rate would be $0.06 per second of machine time or $0.60 per CD rather than $0.30 per CD. In general, if budgeted output falls, the overhead cost per unit will increase; it will appear that the CDs cost more to make. Managers may then be tempted to increase prices at the worst possible time—just as demand is falling.

---

[1] Institute of Management Accountants, *Measuring the Cost of Capacity: Statements on Management Accounting, Number 4Y,* March 31, 1996, Montvale, NJ; Thomas Klammer, ed., *Capacity Measurement and Improvement: A Manager's Guide to Evaluating and Optimizing Capacity Productivity* (Chicago: CAM-I, Irwin Professional Publishing, 1996); and C. J. McNair, "The Hidden Costs of Capacity," *The Journal of Cost Management* (Spring 1994), pp. 12–24.

Second, critics charge that under the traditional approach, products are charged for resources that they don't use. When the fixed costs of capacity are spread over estimated activity, the units that are produced must shoulder the costs of unused capacity. That is why the applied overhead cost per unit increases as the level of activity falls. The critics argue that products should be charged only for the capacity that they use; they should not be charged for the capacity they don't use. This can be accomplished by basing the predetermined overhead rate on capacity as follows:

$$\text{Predetermined overhead rate based on capacity} = \frac{\text{Estimated total manufacturing overhead cost at capacity}}{\text{Estimated total units in the allocation base at capacity}}$$

$$= \frac{\$180{,}000}{900{,}000 \text{ CDs} \times 10 \text{ seconds per CD}}$$

$$= \$0.02 \text{ per second}$$

Since the predetermined overhead rate is $0.02 per second, the overhead cost applied to each CD would be $0.20. This charge is constant and would not be affected by the level of activity during a period. If output falls, the charge would still be $0.20 per CD.

This method will almost certainly result in underapplied overhead. If actual output at Prahad Corporation is 600,000 CDs, then only $120,000 of overhead cost would be applied to products ($0.20 per CD × 600,000 CDs). Since the actual overhead cost is $180,000, there would be underapplied overhead of $60,000. In another departure from tradition, the critics suggest that the underapplied overhead that results from idle capacity should be separately disclosed on the income statement as the Cost of Unused Capacity—a period expense. Disclosing this cost as a lump sum on the income statement, rather than burying it in Cost of Goods Sold or ending inventories, makes it much more visible to managers.

Official pronouncements do not prohibit basing predetermined overhead rates on capacity for external reports.[2] Nevertheless, basing the predetermined overhead rate on estimated or budgeted activity is a long-established practice in industry, and some managers and accountants may object to the large amounts of underapplied overhead that would often result from using capacity to determine predetermined overhead rates. And some may insist that the underapplied overhead be allocated among Cost of Goods Sold and ending inventories—which would defeat the purpose of basing the predetermined overhead rate on capacity.

Questions

3–1 Why aren't actual overhead costs traced to jobs just as direct materials and direct labor costs are traced to jobs?

3–2 When would job-order costing be used in preference to process costing?

3–3 What is the purpose of the job cost sheet in a job-order costing system?

3–4 What is a predetermined overhead rate, and how is it computed?

3–5 Explain how a sales order, a production order, a materials requisition form, and a labor time ticket are involved in producing and costing products.

3–6 Explain why some production costs must be assigned to products through an allocation process. Give examples of such costs. Would such costs be classified as *direct* or *indirect* costs?

3–7 Why do companies use predetermined overhead rates rather than actual manufacturing overhead costs to apply overhead to jobs?

3–8 What factors should be considered in selecting a base to be used in computing the predetermined overhead rate?

---

[2] Institute of Management Accountants, *Measuring the Cost of Capacity,* pp. 46–47.

3–9 If a company fully allocates all of its overhead costs to jobs, does this guarantee that a profit will be earned for the period?

3–10 What account is credited when overhead cost is applied to Work in Process? Would you expect the amount applied for a period to equal the actual overhead costs of the period? Why or why not?

3–11 What is underapplied overhead? Overapplied overhead? What disposition is made of these amounts at the end of the period?

3–12 Provide two reasons why overhead might be underapplied in a given year.

3–13 What adjustment is made for underapplied overhead on the schedule of cost of goods sold? What adjustment is made for overapplied overhead?

3–14 Sigma Company applies overhead cost to jobs on the basis of direct labor cost. Job A, which was started and completed during the current period, shows charges of $5,000 for direct materials, $8,000 for direct labor, and $6,000 for overhead on its job cost sheet. Job B, which is still in process at year-end, shows charges of $2,500 for direct materials and $4,000 for direct labor. Should any overhead cost be added to Job B at year-end? Explain.

3–15 A company assigns overhead cost to completed jobs on the basis of 125% of direct labor cost. The job cost sheet for Job 313 shows that $10,000 in direct materials has been used on the job and that $12,000 in direct labor cost has been incurred. If 1,000 units were produced in Job 313, what is the unit product cost?

3–16 What is a plantwide overhead rate? Why are multiple overhead rates, rather than a plantwide rate, used in some companies?

3–17 What happens to overhead rates based on direct labor when automated equipment replaces direct labor?

3–18 (Appendix 3A) If the plant is operated at less than capacity and the predetermined overhead rate is based on the estimated total units in the allocation base at capacity, will overhead ordinarily be overapplied or underapplied?

3–19 (Appendix 3A) Rather than netting underapplied overhead against Cost of Goods Sold or Cost of Goods Sold and ending inventories, some critics suggest an alternative way to disclose underapplied overhead. What is this alternative method?

Exercises

EXERCISE 3–1 Process Costing and Job-Order Costing [LO1]

Which method of determining product costs, job-order costing or process costing, would be more appropriate in each of the following situations?

a. An Elmer's glue factory.
b. A textbook publisher such as McGraw-Hill.
c. An Exxon oil refinery.
d. A facility that makes Minute Maid frozen orange juice.
e. A Scott paper mill.
f. A custom home builder.
g. A shop that customizes vans.
h. A manufacturer of specialty chemicals.
i. An auto repair shop.
j. A Firestone tire manufacturing plant.
k. An advertising agency.
l. A law office.

EXERCISE 3–2 Job-Order Costing Documents [LO2]

Cycle Gear Corporation has incurred the following costs on job number W456, an order for 20 special sprockets to be delivered at the end of next month.

Direct materials:

On April 10, requisition number 15673 was issued for 20 titanium blanks to be used in the special order. The blanks cost $15.00 each.

On April 11, requisition number 15678 was issued for 480 hardened nibs also to be used in the special order. The nibs cost $1.25 each.

continued

Direct labor:

On April 12, Jamie Unser worked from 11:00 AM until 2:45 PM on Job W456. He is paid $9.60 per hour.

On April 18, Melissa Chan worked from 8:15 AM until 11:30 AM on Job W456. She is paid $12.20 per hour.

Required:
1. On what documents would these costs be recorded?
2. How much cost should have been recorded on each of the documents for Job W456?

EXERCISE 3–3 Compute the Predetermined Overhead Rate [LO3]

Harris Fabrics computes its predetermined overhead rate annually on the basis of direct labor hours. At the beginning of the year it estimated that its total manufacturing overhead would be $134,000 and the total direct labor would be 20,000 hours. Its actual total manufacturing overhead for the year was $123,900 and its actual total direct labor was 21,000 hours.

Required:

Compute the company's predetermined overhead rate for the year.

EXERCISE 3–4 Prepare Journal Entries [LO4]

Larned Corporation recorded the following transactions for the just completed month.

a. $80,000 in raw materials were purchased on account.
b. $71,000 in raw materials were requisitioned for use in production. Of this amount, $62,000 was for direct materials and the remainder was for indirect materials.
c. Total labor wages of $112,000 were incurred. Of this amount, $101,000 was for direct labor and the remainder was for indirect labor.
d. Additional manufacturing overhead costs of $175,000 were incurred.

Required:

Record the above transactions in journal entries.

EXERCISE 3–5 Apply Overhead [LO5]

Luthan Company uses a predetermined overhead rate of $23.40 per direct labor-hour. This predetermined rate was based on 11,000 estimated direct labor-hours and $257,400 of estimated total manufacturing overhead.

The company incurred actual total manufacturing overhead costs of $249,000 and 10,800 total direct labor-hours during the period.

Required:

Determine the amount of manufacturing overhead that would have been applied to units of product during the period.

EXERCISE 3–6 Applying Overhead; Cost of Goods Manufactured [LO5, LO6, LO8]

The following cost data relate to the manufacturing activities of Chang Company during the just completed year:

Manufacturing overhead costs incurred:	
Indirect materials	$15,000
Indirect labor	130,000
Property taxes, factory	8,000
Utilities, factory	70,000
Depreciation, factory	240,000
Insurance, factory	10,000
Total actual manufacturing overhead costs incurred	$473,000
Other costs incurred:	
Purchases of raw materials (both direct and indirect)	$400,000
Direct labor cost	$60,000
Inventories:	
Raw materials, beginning	$20,000
Raw materials, ending	$30,000
Work in process, beginning	$40,000
Work in process, ending	$70,000

The company uses a predetermined overhead rate to apply overhead cost to production. The rate for the year was $25 per machine-hour. A total of 19,400 machine-hours was recorded for the year.

Required:

1. Compute the amount of under- or overapplied overhead cost for the year.
2. Prepare a schedule of cost of goods manufactured for the year.

EXERCISE 3–7 Prepare T-Accounts [LO7, LO8]

Jurvin Enterprises recorded the following transactions for the just completed month. The company had no beginning inventories.

a. $94,000 in raw materials were purchased for cash.
b. $89,000 in raw materials were requisitioned for use in production. Of this amount, $78,000 was for direct materials and the remainder was for indirect materials.
c. Total labor wages of $132,000 were incurred and paid. Of this amount, $112,000 was for direct labor and the remainder was for indirect labor.
d. Additional manufacturing overhead costs of $143,000 were incurred and paid.
e. Manufacturing overhead costs of $152,000 were applied to jobs using the company's predetermined overhead rate.
f. All of the jobs in progress at the end of the month were completed and shipped to customers.
g. The underapplied or overapplied overhead for the period was closed out to Cost of Goods Sold.

Required:

1. Post the above transactions to T-accounts.
2. Determine the cost of goods sold for the period.

EXERCISE 3–8 Under- and Overapplied Overhead [LO8]

Osborn Manufacturing uses a predetermined overhead rate of $18.20 per direct labor-hour. This predetermined rate was based on 12,000 estimated direct labor-hours and $218,400 of estimated total manufacturing overhead.

The company incurred actual total manufacturing overhead costs of $215,000 and 11,500 total direct labor-hours during the period.

Required:

1. Determine the amount of underapplied or overapplied manufacturing overhead for the period.
2. Assuming that the entire amount of the underapplied or overapplied overhead is closed out to Cost of Goods Sold, what would be the effect of the underapplied or overapplied overhead on the company's gross margin for the period?

EXERCISE 3–9 Departmental Overhead Rates [LO2, LO3, LO5]

White Company has two departments, Cutting and Finishing. The company uses a job-order cost system and computes a predetermined overhead rate in each department. The Cutting Department bases its rate on machine-hours, and the Finishing Department bases its rate on direct labor cost. At the beginning of the year, the company made the following estimates:

	Department	
	Cutting	Finishing
Direct labor-hours	6,000	30,000
Machine-hours	48,000	5,000
Manufacturing overhead cost	$360,000	$486,000
Direct labor cost	$50,000	$270,000

Required:

1. Compute the predetermined overhead rate to be used in each department.
2. Assume that the overhead rates that you computed in (1) above are in effect. The job cost sheet for Job 203, which was started and completed during the year, showed the following:

	Department	
	Cutting	Finishing
Direct labor-hours	6	20
Machine-hours	80	4
Materials requisitioned	$500	$310
Direct labor cost	$70	$150

Compute the total overhead cost applied to Job 203.

3. Would you expect substantially different amounts of overhead cost to be assigned to some jobs if the company used a plantwide overhead rate based on direct labor cost, rather than using departmental rates? Explain. No computations are necessary.

EXERCISE 3–10 Journal Entries and T-accounts [LO4, LO5, LO7]

The Polaris Company uses a job-order costing system. The following data relate to October, the first month of the company's fiscal year.

a. Raw materials purchased on account, $210,000.
b. Raw materials issued to production, $190,000 ($178,000 direct materials and $12,000 indirect materials).
c. Direct labor cost incurred, $90,000; indirect labor cost incurred, $110,000.
d. Depreciation recorded on factory equipment, $40,000.
e. Other manufacturing overhead costs incurred during October, $70,000 (credit Accounts Payable).
f. The company applies manufacturing overhead cost to production on the basis of $8 per machine-hour. There were 30,000 machine-hours recorded for October.
g. Production orders costing $520,000 according to their job cost sheets were completed during October and transferred to Finished Goods.
h. Production orders that had cost $480,000 to complete according to their job cost sheets were shipped to customers during the month. These goods were sold on account at 25% above cost.

Required:

1. Prepare journal entries to record the information given above.
2. Prepare T-accounts for Manufacturing Overhead and Work in Process. Post the relevant information above to each account. Compute the ending balance in each account, assuming that Work in Process has a beginning balance of $42,000.

EXERCISE 3–11 Applying Overhead in a Service Company [LO2, LO3, LO5]

Leeds Architectural Consultants began operations on January 2. The following activity was recorded in the company's Work in Process account for the first month of operations:

Work in Process

Costs of subcontracted work	230,000	To completed projects	390,000
Direct staff costs	75,000		
Studio overhead	120,000		

Leeds Architectural Consultants is a service firm, so the names of the accounts it uses are different from the names used in manufacturing firms. Costs of Subcontracted Work is comparable to Direct Materials; Direct Staff Costs is the same as Direct Labor; Studio Overhead is the same as Manufacturing Overhead; and Completed Projects is the same as Finished Goods. Apart from the difference in terms, the accounting methods used by the company are identical to the methods used by manufacturing companies.

Leeds Architectural Consultants uses a job-order costing system and applies studio overhead to Work in Process on the basis of direct staff costs. At the end of January, only one job was still in process. This job (Lexington Gardens Project) had been charged with $6,500 in direct staff costs.

Required:

1. Compute the predetermined overhead rate that was in use during January.
2. Complete the following job cost sheet for the partially completed Lexington Gardens Project.

Job Cost Sheet—Lexington Gardens Project
As of January 31

Costs of subcontracted work	$?
Direct staff costs	?
Studio overhead	?
Total cost to January 31	$?

EXERCISE 3–12 Varying Predetermined Overhead Rates [LO3, LO5]

Kingsport Containers, Ltd, of the Bahamas experiences wide variation in demand for the 200-liter steel drums it fabricates. The leakproof, rustproof steel drums have a variety of uses from storing liquids and bulk materials to serving as makeshift musical instruments. The drums are made to order and are painted according to the customer's specifications—often in bright patterns and designs. The company is well known for the artwork that appears on its drums. Unit product costs are computed on a quarterly basis by dividing each quarter's manufacturing costs (materials, labor, and overhead) by the quarter's production in units. The company's estimated costs, by quarter, for the coming year follow:

	Quarter			
	First	Second	Third	Fourth
Direct materials	$240,000	$120,000	$60,000	$180,000
Direct labor	128,000	64,000	32,000	96,000
Manufacturing overhead	300,000	220,000	180,000	260,000
Total manufacturing costs	$668,000	$404,000	$272,000	$536,000
Number of units to be produced	80,000	40,000	20,000	60,000
Estimated unit product cost	$8.35	$10.10	$13.60	$8.93

Management finds the variation in unit costs to be confusing and difficult to work with. It has been suggested that the problem lies with manufacturing overhead, since it is the largest element of cost. Accordingly, you have been asked to find a more appropriate way of assigning manufacturing overhead cost to units of product. After some analysis, you have determined that the company's overhead costs are mostly fixed and therefore show little sensitivity to changes in the level of production.

Required:

1. The company uses a job-order costing system. How would you recommend that manufacturing overhead cost be assigned to production? Be specific, and show computations.
2. Recompute the company's unit product costs in accordance with your recommendations in (1) above.

EXERCISE 3–13 Applying Overhead; T-accounts; Journal Entries [LO3, LO4, LO5, LO7, LO8]

Harwood Company is a manufacturer that operates a job-order costing system. Overhead costs are applied to jobs on the basis of machine-hours. At the beginning of the year, management estimated that the company would incur $192,000 in manufacturing overhead costs and work 80,000 machine-hours.

Required:

1. Compute the company's predetermined overhead rate.
2. Assume that during the year the company works only 75,000 machine-hours and incurs the following costs in the Manufacturing Overhead and Work in Process accounts:

Manufacturing Overhead

(Maintenance)	21,000	?
(Indirect materials)	8,000	
(Indirect labor)	60,000	
(Utilities)	32,000	
(Insurance)	7,000	
(Depreciation)	56,000	

Work in Process

(Direct materials)	710,000	
(Direct labor)	90,000	
(Overhead)	?	

Copy the data in the T-accounts above onto your answer sheet. Compute the amount of overhead cost that would be applied to Work in Process for the year and make the entry in your T-accounts.

3. Compute the amount of under- or overapplied overhead for the year and show the balance in your Manufacturing Overhead T-account. Prepare a journal entry to close out the balance in this account to Cost of Goods Sold.
4. Explain why the manufacturing overhead was under- or overapplied for the year.

EXERCISE 3–14 Applying Overhead; Journal Entries; Disposition of Underapplied or Overapplied Overhead [LO4, LO7, LO8]

The following information is taken from the accounts of Latta Company. The entries in the T-accounts are summaries of the transactions that affected those accounts during the year.

Manufacturing Overhead

(a)	460,000	(b)	390,000
Bal.	70,000		

Work in Process

Bal.	15,000	(c)	710,000
	260,000		
	85,000		
(b)	390,000		
Bal.	40,000		

Finished Goods

Bal.	50,000	(d)	640,000
(c)	710,000		
Bal.	120,000		

Cost of Goods Sold

(d)	640,000		

The overhead that had been applied to production during the year is distributed among the ending balances in the accounts as follows:

Work in Process, ending	$ 19,500
Finished Goods, ending	58,500
Cost of Goods Sold	312,000
Overhead applied	$390,000

For example, of the $40,000 ending balance in Work in Process, $19,500 was overhead that had been applied during the year.

Required:

1. Identify reasons for entries (a) through (d).
2. Assume that the company closes any balance in the Manufacturing Overhead account directly to Cost of Goods Sold. Prepare the necessary journal entry.
3. Assume instead that the company allocates any balance in the Manufacturing Overhead account to the other accounts in proportion to the overhead applied in their ending balances. Prepare the necessary journal entry, with supporting computations.

EXERCISE 3–15 Applying Overhead; Journal Entries; T-accounts [LO3, LO4, LO5, LO7]

Dillon Products manufactures various machined parts to customer specifications. The company uses a job-order costing system and applies overhead cost to jobs on the basis of machine-hours. At the beginning of the year, it was estimated that the company would work 240,000 machine-hours and incur $4,800,000 in manufacturing overhead costs.

The company spent the entire month of January working on a large order for 16,000 custom-made machined parts. The company had no work in process at the beginning of January. Cost data relating to January follow:

a. Raw materials purchased on account, $325,000.
b. Raw materials requisitioned for production, $290,000 (80% direct materials and 20% indirect materials).
c. Labor cost incurred in the factory, $180,000 (one-third direct labor and two-thirds indirect labor).
d. Depreciation recorded on factory equipment, $75,000.
e. Other manufacturing overhead costs incurred, $62,000 (credit Accounts Payable).
f. Manufacturing overhead cost was applied to production on the basis of 15,000 machine-hours actually worked during the month.
g. The completed job was moved into the finished goods warehouse on January 31 to await delivery to the customer. (In computing the dollar amount for this entry, remember that the cost of a completed job consists of direct materials, direct labor, and *applied* overhead.)

Required:

1. Prepare journal entries to record items (a) through (f) above [ignore item (g) for the moment].

2. Prepare T-accounts for Manufacturing Overhead and Work in Process. Post the relevant items from your journal entries to these T-accounts.
3. Prepare a journal entry for item (g) above.
4. Compute the unit product cost that will appear on the job cost sheet.

EXERCISE 3–16 (Appendix 3A) Overhead Rates and Capacity Issues [LO3, LO5, LO8, LO9]

Security Pension Services helps clients to set up and administer pension plans that are in compliance with tax laws and regulatory requirements. The firm uses a job-order costing system in which overhead is applied to clients' accounts on the basis of professional staff hours charged to the accounts. Data concerning two recent years appear below:

	2005	2004
Estimated professional staff hours to be charged to clients' accounts	4,600	4,500
Estimated overhead cost	$310,500	$310,500
Professional staff hours available	6,000	6,000

"Professional staff hours available" is a measure of the capacity of the firm. Any hours available that are not charged to clients' accounts represent unused capacity.

Required:

1. Marta Brinksi is an established client whose pension plan was set up many years ago. In both 2004 and 2005, only 2.5 hours of professional staff time were charged to Ms. Brinksi's account. If the company bases its predetermined overhead rate on the estimated overhead cost and the estimated professional staff hours to be charged to clients, how much overhead cost would have been applied to Ms. Brinksi's account in 2004? In 2005?
2. Suppose that the company bases its predetermined overhead rate on the estimated overhead cost and the estimated professional staff hours to be charged to clients as in (1) above. Also suppose that the actual professional staff hours charged to clients' accounts and the actual overhead costs turn out to be exactly as estimated in both years. By how much would the overhead be under- or overapplied in 2004? In 2005?
3. Refer back to the data concerning Ms. Brinksi in (1) above. If the company bases its predetermined overhead rate on the estimated overhead cost and the *professional staff hours available,* how much overhead cost would have been applied to Ms. Brinksi's account in 2004? In 2005?
4. Suppose that the company bases its predetermined overhead rate on the estimated overhead cost and the professional staff hours available as in (3) above. Also suppose that the actual professional staff hours charged to clients' accounts and the actual overhead costs turn out to be exactly as estimated in both years. By how much would the overhead be under- or overapplied in 2004? In 2005?

EXERCISE 3–17 Applying Overhead in a Service Company; Journal Entries [LO4, LO5, LO8]

Vista Landscaping uses a job-order costing system to track the costs of its landscaping projects. The company provides garden design and installation services for its clients. The table below provides data concerning the three landscaping projects that were in progress during April. There was no work in process at the beginning of April.

	Project		
	Harris	Chan	James
Designer-hours	120	100	90
Direct materials cost	$4,500	$3,700	$1,400
Direct labor cost	$9,600	$8,000	$7,200

Actual overhead costs were $30,000 for April. Overhead costs are applied to projects on the basis of designer-hours since most of the overhead is related to the costs of the garden design studio. The predetermined overhead rate is $90 per designer-hour. The Harris and Chan projects were completed in April; the James project was not completed by the end of the month.

Required:

1. Compute the amount of overhead cost that would have been charged to each project during April.

2. Prepare a journal entry showing the completion of the Harris and Chan projects and the transfer of costs to the Completed Projects (i.e., Finished Goods) account.
3. What is the balance in the Work in Process account at the end of the month?
4. What is the balance in the Overhead account at the end of the month? What is this balance called?

Problems

PROBLEM 3–18 Comprehensive Problem [LO3, LO4, LO5, LO7, LO8]

Gold Nest Company of Guandong, China, is a family-owned enterprise that makes birdcages for the South China market. A popular pastime among older Chinese men is to take their pet birds on daily excursions to teahouses and public parks where they meet with other bird owners to talk and play mahjong. A great deal of attention is lavished on these birds, and the birdcages are often elaborately constructed from exotic woods and contain porcelain feeding bowls and silver roosts. Gold Nest Company makes a broad range of birdcages that it sells through an extensive network of street vendors who receive commissions on their sales. The Chinese currency is the renminbi, which is denoted by Rmb. All of the company's transactions with customers, employees, and suppliers are conducted in cash; there is no credit.

The company uses a job-order costing system in which overhead is applied to jobs on the basis of direct labor cost. At the beginning of the year, it was estimated that the total direct labor cost for the year would be Rmb200,000 and the total manufacturing overhead cost would be Rmb330,000. At the beginning of the year, the inventory balances were as follows:

Raw materials	Rmb25,000
Work in process	Rmb10,000
Finished goods	Rmb40,000

During the year, the following transactions were completed:

a. Raw materials purchased for cash, Rmb275,000.
b. Raw materials requisitioned for use in production, Rmb280,000 (materials costing Rmb220,000 were charged directly to jobs; the remaining materials were indirect).
c. Costs for employee services were incurred as follows:

Direct labor	Rmb180,000
Indirect labor	Rmb72,000
Sales commissions	Rmb63,000
Administrative salaries	Rmb90,000

d. Rent for the year was Rmb18,000 (Rmb13,000 of this amount related to factory operations, and the remainder related to selling and administrative activities).
e. Utility costs incurred in the factory, Rmb57,000.
f. Advertising costs incurred, Rmb140,000.
g. Depreciation recorded on equipment, Rmb100,000. (Rmb88,000 of this amount was on equipment used in factory operations; the remaining Rmb12,000 was on equipment used in selling and administrative activities.)
h. Manufacturing overhead cost was applied to jobs, Rmb __?__.
i. Goods that had cost Rmb675,000 to manufacture according to their job cost sheets were completed during the year.
j. Sales for the year totaled Rmb1,250,000. The total cost to manufacture these goods according to their job cost sheets was Rmb700,000.

Required:

1. Prepare journal entries to record the transactions for the year.
2. Prepare T-accounts for inventories, Manufacturing Overhead, and Cost of Goods Sold. Post relevant data from your journal entries to these T-accounts (don't forget to enter the beginning balances in your inventory accounts). Compute an ending balance in each account.
3. Is Manufacturing Overhead underapplied or overapplied for the year? Prepare a journal entry to close any balance in the Manufacturing Overhead account to Cost of Goods Sold.
4. Prepare an income statement for the year. (Do not prepare a schedule of cost of goods manufactured; all of the information needed for the income statement is available in the journal entries and T-accounts you have prepared.)

PROBLEM 3–19 Cost Flows; T-Accounts; Income Statement [LO3, LO5, LO6, LO7, LO8]
Supreme Videos, Inc., produces short musical videos for sale to retail outlets. The company's balance sheet accounts as of January 1, the beginning of its fiscal year, are given below.

SUPREME VIDEOS, INC.
Balance Sheet
January 1
Assets

Current assets:		
Cash		$ 63,000
Accounts receivable		102,000
Inventories:		
Raw materials (film, costumes)	$ 30,000	
Videos in process	45,000	
Finished videos awaiting sale	81,000	156,000
Prepaid insurance		9,000
Total current assets		330,000
Studio and equipment	730,000	
Less accumulated depreciation	210,000	520,000
Total assets		$850,000
Liabilities and Stockholders' Equity		
Accounts payable		$160,000
Capital stock	$420,000	
Retained earnings	270,000	690,000
Total liabilities and stockholders' equity		$850,000

Since the videos differ in length and in complexity of production, the company uses a job-order costing system to determine the cost of each video produced. Studio (manufacturing) overhead is charged to videos on the basis of camera-hours of activity. At the beginning of the year, the company estimated that it would work 7,000 camera-hours and incur $280,000 in studio overhead cost. The following transactions were recorded for the year:

a. Film, costumes, and similar raw materials purchased on account, $185,000.
b. Film, costumes, and other raw materials issued to production, $200,000 (85% of this material was considered direct to the videos in production, and the other 15% was considered indirect).
c. Utility costs incurred in the production studio, $72,000.
d. Depreciation recorded on the studio, cameras, and other equipment, $84,000. Three-fourths of this depreciation related to actual production of the videos, and the remainder related to equipment used in marketing and administration.
e. Advertising expense incurred, $130,000.
f. Costs for salaries and wages were incurred as follows:

Direct labor (actors and directors)	$82,000
Indirect labor (carpenters to build sets, costume designers, and so forth)	$110,000
Administrative salaries	$95,000

g. Prepaid insurance expired during the year, $7,000 (80% related to production of videos, and 20% related to marketing and administrative activities).
h. Miscellaneous marketing and administrative expenses incurred, $8,600.
i. Studio (manufacturing) overhead was applied to videos in production. The company recorded 7,250 camera-hours of activity during the year.
j. Videos that cost $550,000 to produce according to their job cost sheets were transferred to the finished videos warehouse to await sale and shipment.
k. Sales for the year totaled $925,000 and were all on account. The total cost to produce these videos according to their job cost sheets was $600,000.
l. Collections from customers during the year totaled $850,000.
m. Payments to suppliers on account during the year, $500,000; payments to employees for salaries and wages, $285,000.

Required:

1. Prepare a T-account for each account on the company's balance sheet and enter the beginning balances.
2. Record the transactions directly into the T-accounts. Prepare new T-accounts as needed. Key your entries to the letters (a) through (m) above. Find the ending balance in each account.
3. Is the Studio (manufacturing) Overhead account underapplied or overapplied for the year? Make an entry in the T-accounts to close any balance in the Studio Overhead account to Cost of Goods Sold.
4. Prepare an income statement for the year. (Do not prepare a schedule of cost of goods manufactured; all of the information needed for the income statement is available in the T-accounts.)

PROBLEM 3–20 Journal Entries; T-Accounts; Cost Flows [LO4, LO5, LO7]

Almeda Products, Inc., uses a job-order costing system. The company's inventory balances on April 1, the start of its fiscal year, were as follows:

Raw materials	$32,000
Work in process	$20,000
Finished goods	$48,000

During the year, the following transactions were completed:

a. Raw materials were purchased on account, $170,000.
b. Raw materials were issued from the storeroom for use in production, $180,000 (80% direct and 20% indirect).
c. Employee salaries and wages were accrued as follows: direct labor, $200,000; indirect labor, $82,000; and selling and administrative salaries, $90,000.
d. Utility costs were incurred in the factory, $65,000.
e. Advertising costs were incurred, $100,000.
f. Prepaid insurance expired during the year, $20,000 (90% related to factory operations, and 10% related to selling and administrative activities).
g. Depreciation was recorded, $180,000 (85% related to factory assets, and 15% related to selling and administrative assets).
h. Manufacturing overhead was applied to jobs at the rate of 175% of direct labor cost.
i. Goods that cost $700,000 to manufacture according to their job cost sheets were transferred to the finished goods warehouse.
j. Sales for the year totaled $1,000,000 and were all on account. The total cost to manufacture these goods according to their job cost sheets was $720,000.

Required:

1. Prepare journal entries to record the transactions for the year.
2. Prepare T-accounts for Raw Materials, Work in Process, Finished Goods, Manufacturing Overhead, and Cost of Goods Sold. Post the appropriate parts of your journal entries to these T-accounts. Compute the ending balance in each account. (Don't forget to enter the beginning balances in the inventory accounts.)
3. Is Manufacturing Overhead underapplied or overapplied for the year? Prepare a journal entry to close this balance to Cost of Goods Sold.
4. Prepare an income statement for the year. (Do not prepare a schedule of cost of goods manufactured; all of the information needed for the income statement is available in the journal entries and T-accounts you have prepared.)

PROBLEM 3–21 T-accounts; Applying Overhead [LO5, LO7, LO8]

Hudson Company's trial balance as of January 1, the beginning of its fiscal year, is given below:

Cash	$ 7,000	
Accounts Receivable	18,000	
Raw Materials	9,000	
Work in Process	20,000	
Finished Goods	32,000	
Prepaid Insurance	4,000	
Plant and Equipment	210,000	
Accumulated Depreciation		$ 53,000
Accounts Payable		38,000
Capital Stock		160,000
Retained Earnings		49,000
Total	$300,000	$300,000

Hudson Company is a manufacturer that uses a job-order costing system. During the year, the following transactions took place:

a. Raw materials purchased on account, $40,000.
b. Raw materials were requisitioned for use in production, $38,000 (85% direct and 15% indirect).
c. Factory utility costs incurred, $19,100.
d. Depreciation was recorded on plant and equipment, $36,000. Three-fourths of the depreciation related to factory equipment, and the remainder related to selling and administrative equipment.
e. Advertising expense incurred, $48,000.
f. Costs for salaries and wages were incurred as follows:

Direct labor	$45,000
Indirect labor	$10,000
Administrative salaries	$30,000

g. Prepaid insurance expired during the year, $3,000 (80% related to factory operations, and 20% related to selling and administrative activities).
h. Miscellaneous selling and administrative expenses incurred, $9,500.
i. Manufacturing overhead was applied to production. The company applies overhead on the basis of $8 per machine-hour; 7,500 machine-hours were recorded for the year.
j. Goods that cost $140,000 to manufacture according to their job cost sheets were transferred to the finished goods warehouse.
k. Sales for the year totaled $250,000 and were all on account. The total cost to manufacture these goods according to their job cost sheets was $130,000.
l. Collections from customers during the year totaled $245,000.
m. Payments to suppliers on account during the year, $150,000; payments to employees for salaries and wages, $84,000.

Required:

1. Prepare a T-account for each account in the company's trial balance and enter the opening balances shown above.
2. Record the transactions above directly into the T-accounts. Prepare new T-accounts as needed. Key your entries to the letters (a) through (m) above. Find the ending balance in each account.
3. Is manufacturing overhead underapplied or overapplied for the year? Make an entry in the T-accounts to close any balance in the Manufacturing Overhead account to Cost of Goods Sold.
4. Prepare an income statement for the year. (Do not prepare a schedule of cost of goods manufactured; all of the information needed for the income statement is available in the T-accounts.)

PROBLEM 3–22 T-accounts; Overhead Rates; Journal Entries [LO2, LO3, LO4, LO5, LO7]

AOZT Volzhskije Motory of St. Petersburg, Russia, makes marine motors for vessels ranging in size from harbor tugs to open-water icebreakers. (The Russian currency is the ruble, which is denoted by RUR. All currency amounts below are in thousands of RUR.)

The company uses a job-order costing system. Only three jobs—Job 208, Job 209, and Job 210—were worked on during May and June. Job 208 was completed on June 20; the other two jobs were uncompleted on June 30. Job cost sheets on the three jobs are given below:

	Job Cost Sheet		
	Job 208	Job 209	Job 210
May costs incurred:*			
Direct materials	RUR9,500	RUR5,100	RUR —
Direct labor	RUR8,000	RUR3,000	RUR —
Manufacturing overhead	RUR11,200	RUR4,200	RUR —
June costs incurred:			
Direct materials	RUR —	RUR6,000	RUR7,200
Direct labor	RUR4,000	RUR7,500	RUR8,500
Manufacturing overhead	RUR ?	RUR ?	RUR ?

*Jobs 208 and 209 were started during May.

The following additional information is available:

a. Manufacturing overhead is applied to jobs on the basis of direct labor cost.
b. Balances in the inventory accounts at May 31 were:

Raw Materials	RUR30,000
Work in Process	RUR?
Finished Goods	RUR50,000

Required:

1. Prepare T-accounts for Raw Materials, Work in Process, Finished Goods, and Manufacturing Overhead. Enter the May 31 balances given above; in the case of Work in Process, compute the May 31 balance and enter it into the Work in Process T-account.
2. Prepare journal entries for *June* as follows:
   a. Prepare an entry to record the issue of materials into production and post the entry to appropriate T-accounts. (In the case of direct materials, it is not necessary to make a separate entry for each job.) Indirect materials used during June totaled RUR3,600.
   b. Prepare an entry to record the incurrence of labor cost and post the entry to appropriate T-accounts. (In the case of direct labor cost, it is not necessary to make a separate entry for each job.) Indirect labor cost totaled RUR7,000 for June.
   c. Prepare an entry to record the incurrence of RUR19,400 in various actual manufacturing overhead costs for June. (Credit Accounts Payable.) Post this entry to the appropriate T-accounts.
3. What apparent predetermined overhead rate does the company use to assign overhead cost to jobs? Using this rate, prepare a journal entry to record the application of overhead cost to jobs for June (it is not necessary to make a separate entry for each job). Post this entry to appropriate T-accounts.
4. As stated earlier, Job 208 was completed during June. Prepare a journal entry to show the transfer of this job off of the production line and into the finished goods warehouse. Post the entry to appropriate T-accounts.
5. Determine the balance at June 30 in the Work in Process inventory account. How much of this balance consists of costs charged to Job 209? To Job 210?

PROBLEM 3–23 Multiple Departments; Applying Overhead [LO3, LO5, LO8]

High Desert Potteryworks makes a variety of pottery products that it sells to retailers such as Home Depot. The company uses a job-order costing system in which predetermined overhead rates are used to apply manufacturing overhead cost to jobs. The predetermined overhead rate in the Molding Department is based on machine-hours, and the rate in the Painting Department is based on direct labor cost. At the beginning of the year, the company's management made the following estimates:

	Department	
	Molding	Painting
Direct labor-hours	12,000	60,000
Machine-hours	70,000	8,000
Direct materials cost	$510,000	$650,000
Direct labor cost	$130,000	$420,000
Manufacturing overhead cost	$602,000	$735,000

Job 205 was started on August 1 and completed on August 10. The company's cost records show the following information concerning the job:

	Department	
	Molding	Painting
Direct labor-hours	30	85
Machine-hours	110	20
Materials placed into production	$470	$332
Direct labor cost	$290	$680

Required:

1. Compute the predetermined overhead rate used during the year in the Molding Department. Compute the rate used in the Painting Department.
2. Compute the total overhead cost applied to Job 205.
3. What would be the total cost recorded for Job 205? If the job contained 50 units, what would be the unit product cost?

4. At the end of the year, the records of High Desert Potteryworks revealed the following *actual* cost and operating data for all jobs worked on during the year:

	Department	
	Molding	Painting
Direct labor-hours	10,000	62,000
Machine-hours	65,000	9,000
Direct materials cost	$430,000	$680,000
Direct labor cost	$108,000	$436,000
Manufacturing overhead cost	$570,000	$750,000

What was the amount of under- or overapplied overhead in each department at the end of the year?

PROBLEM 3–24 T-Account Analysis of Cost Flows [LO3, LO6, LO8]
Selected ledger accounts of Moore Company are given below for the just completed year:

Raw Materials

Bal. 1/1	15,000	Credits	?
Debits	120,000		
Bal. 12/31	25,000		

Manufacturing Overhead

Debits	230,000	Credits	?

Work in Process

Bal. 1/1	20,000	Credits	470,000
Direct materials	90,000		
Direct labor	150,000		
Overhead	240,000		
Bal. 12/31	?		

Factory Wages Payable

Debits	185,000	Bal. 1/1	9,000
		Credits	180,000
		Bal. 12/31	4,000

Finished Goods

Bal. 1/1	40,000	Credits	?
Debits	?		
Bal. 12/31	60,000		

Cost of Goods Sold

Debits	?		

Required:
1. What was the cost of raw materials put into production during the year?
2. How much of the materials in (1) above consisted of indirect materials?
3. How much of the factory labor cost for the year consisted of indirect labor?
4. What was the cost of goods manufactured for the year?
5. What was the cost of goods sold for the year (before considering under- or overapplied overhead)?
6. If overhead is applied to production on the basis of direct labor cost, what rate was in effect during the year?
7. Was manufacturing overhead under- or overapplied? By how much?
8. Compute the ending balance in the Work in Process inventory account. Assume that this balance consists entirely of goods started during the year. If $8,000 of this balance is direct labor cost, how much of it is direct materials cost? Manufacturing overhead cost?

PROBLEM 3–25 Journal Entries; T-Accounts; Disposition of Underapplied or Overapplied Overhead [LO3, LO4, LO5, LO7, LO8]
Film Specialties, Inc., operates a small production studio in which advertising films are made for TV and other uses. The company uses a job-order costing system to accumulate costs for each

film produced. The company's trial balance as of May 1, the start of its fiscal year, is given as follows:

Cash	$ 60,000	
Accounts Receivable	210,000	
Materials and Supplies	130,000	
Films in Process	75,000	
Finished Films	860,000	
Prepaid Insurance	90,000	
Studio and Equipment	5,200,000	
Accumulated Depreciation		$1,990,000
Accounts Payable		700,000
Salaries and Wages Payable		35,000
Capital Stock		2,500,000
Retained Earnings		1,400,000
Total	$6,625,000	$6,625,000

Film Specialties, Inc., uses a Production Overhead account to record all transactions relating to overhead costs and applies overhead costs to jobs on the basis of camera-hours. For the current year, the company estimated that it would incur $1,350,000 in production overhead costs, and film 15,000 camera-hours. During the year, the following transactions were completed:

a. Materials and supplies purchased on account, $690,000.
b. Materials and supplies issued from the storeroom for use in production of various films, $700,000 (80% direct to the films and 20% indirect).
c. Utility costs incurred in the production studio, $90,000.
d. Costs for employee salaries and wages were incurred as follows:

Actors, directors, and camera crew	$1,300,000
Indirect labor costs of support workers	$230,000
Marketing and administrative salaries	$650,000

e. Advertising costs incurred, $800,000.
f. Prepaid insurance expired during the year, $70,000. Of this amount, $60,000 related to the operation of the production studio, and the remaining $10,000 related to the company's marketing and administrative activities.
g. Depreciation recorded for the year, $650,000 (80% represented depreciation of the production studio, cameras, and other production equipment; the remaining 20% represented depreciation of facilities and equipment used in marketing and administrative activities).
h. Rental costs incurred on various facilities and equipment used in production of films, $360,000; and rental costs incurred on equipment used in marketing and administrative activities, $40,000.
i. Production overhead was applied to jobs filmed during the year. The company recorded 16,500 camera-hours.
j. Films that cost $3,400,000 to produce according to their job cost sheets were completed during the year. The films were transferred to the finished films storeroom to await delivery to customers.
k. Sales of films for the year (all on account) totaled $6,000,000. The total cost to produce these films was $4,000,000 according to their job cost sheets.
l. Collections on account from customers during the year, $5,400,000.
m. Cash payments made during the year; to creditors on account, $2,500,000; and to employees for salaries and wages, $2,200,000.

Required:

1. Prepare journal entries to record the year's transactions.
2. Prepare a T-account for each account in the company's trial balance and enter the opening balances given above. Post your journal entries to the T-accounts. Prepare new T-accounts as needed. Compute the ending balance in each account.
3. Is production overhead underapplied or overapplied for the year? Prepare the necessary journal entry to close the balance in Production Overhead to Cost of Films Sold.
4. Prepare an income statement for the year. (Do not prepare a schedule of cost of goods manufactured; all of the information needed for the income statement is available in the T-accounts.)

PROBLEM 3–26 Predetermined Overhead Rate; Disposition of Under- or Overapplied Overhead [LO3, LO8]

Bieler & Cie of Altdorf, Switzerland, makes furniture using the latest automated technology. The company uses a job-order costing system and applies manufacturing overhead cost to products on the basis of machine-hours. The following estimates were used in preparing the predetermined overhead rate at the beginning of the year:

Machine-hours	75,000
Manufacturing overhead cost	Sfr900,000

The currency in Switzerland is the Swiss franc, which is denoted by Sfr.

During the year, a glut of furniture on the market resulted in cutting back production and a buildup of furniture in the company's warehouse. The company's cost records revealed the following actual cost and operating data for the year:

Machine-hours	60,000
Manufacturing overhead cost	Sfr850,000
Inventories at year-end:	
Raw materials	Sfr30,000
Work in process (includes overhead applied of 36,000)	Sfr100,000
Finished goods (includes overhead applied of 180,000)	Sfr500,000
Cost of goods sold (includes overhead applied of 504,000)	Sfr1,400,000

Required:

1. Compute the company's predetermined overhead rate.
2. Compute the under- or overapplied overhead.
3. Assume that the company closes any under- or overapplied overhead directly to Cost of Goods Sold. Prepare the appropriate journal entry.
4. Assume that the company allocates any under- or overapplied overhead to Work in Process, Finished Goods, and Cost of Goods Sold on the basis of the amount of overhead applied that remains in each account at the end of the year. Prepare the journal entry to show the allocation for the year.
5. How much higher or lower will net operating income be if the under- or overapplied overhead is allocated rather than closed directly to Cost of Goods Sold?

PROBLEM 3–27 Schedule of Cost of Goods Manufactured; Overhead Analysis [LO3, LO5, LO6, LO7]

Gitano Products operates a job-order costing system and applies overhead cost to jobs on the basis of direct materials *used in production* (*not* on the basis of raw materials purchased). In computing a predetermined overhead rate at the beginning of the year, the company's estimates were: manufacturing overhead cost, $800,000; and direct materials to be used in production, $500,000. The company has provided the following data in the form of an Excel worksheet:

	A	B	C
1		*Beginning*	*Ending*
2	Raw Materials	$20,000	$80,000
3	Work in Process	$150,000	$70,000
4	Finished Goods	$260,000	$400,000
5			
6	*The following actual costs were incurred during the year:*		
7	Purchase of raw materials (all direct)		$510,000
8	Direct labor cost		$90,000
9	Manufacturing overhead costs:		
10	Indirect labor		$170,000
11	Property taxes		$48,000
12	Depreciation of equipment		$260,000
13	Maintenance		$95,000
14	Insurance		$7,000
15	Rent, building		$180,000
16			

Required:

1. *a.* Compute the predetermined overhead rate for the year.
   b. Compute the amount of under- or overapplied overhead for the year.

2. Prepare a schedule of cost of goods manufactured for the year.
3. Compute the Cost of Goods Sold for the year. (Do not include any under- or overapplied overhead in your Cost of Goods Sold figure.) What options are available for disposing of under- or overapplied overhead?
4. Job 215 was started and completed during the year. What price would have been charged to the customer if the job required $8,500 in direct materials and $2,700 in direct labor cost and the company priced its jobs at 25% above the job's cost according to the accounting system?
5. Direct materials made up $24,000 of the $70,000 ending Work in Process inventory balance. Supply the information missing below:

Direct materials	$24,000
Direct labor	?
Manufacturing overhead	?
Work in process inventory	$70,000

PROBLEM 3–28 (Appendix 3A) Predetermined Overhead Rate and Capacity [LO3, LO5, LO8, LO9]

Platinum Tracks, Inc., is a small audio recording studio located in Los Angeles. The company handles work for advertising agencies—primarily for radio ads—and has a few singers and bands as clients. Platinum Tracks handles all aspects of recording from editing to making a digital master from which CDs can be copied. The competition in the audio recording industry in Los Angeles has always been tough, but it has been getting even tougher over the last several years. The studio has been losing customers to newer studios that are equipped with more up-to-date equipment and that are able to offer very attractive prices and excellent service. Summary data concerning the last two years of operations follow:

	2005	2004
Estimated hours of studio service	800	1,000
Estimated studio overhead cost	$160,000	$160,000
Actual hours of studio service provided	500	750
Actual studio overhead cost incurred	$160,000	$160,000
Hours of studio service at capacity	1,600	1,600

The company applies studio overhead to recording jobs on the basis of the hours of studio service provided. For example, 40 hours of studio time were required to record, edit, and master the *Verde Baja* music CD for a local Latino band. All of the studio overhead is fixed, and the actual overhead cost incurred was exactly as estimated at the beginning of the year in both 2004 and 2005.

Required:

1. Platinum Tracks computes its predetermined overhead rate at the beginning of each year based on the estimated studio overhead and the estimated hours of studio service for the year. How much overhead would have been applied to the *Verde Baja* job if it had been done in 2004? In 2005? By how much would overhead have been under- or overapplied in 2004? In 2005?
2. The president of Platinum Tracks has heard that some companies in the industry have changed to a system of computing the predetermined overhead rate at the beginning of each year based on the estimated studio overhead for the year and the hours of studio service that could be provided at capacity. He would like to know what effect this method would have on job costs. How much overhead would have been applied using this method to the *Verde Baja* job if it had been done in 2004? In 2005? By how much would overhead have been under- or overapplied in 2004 using this method? In 2005?
3. How would you interpret the under- or overapplied overhead that results from using studio hours at capacity to compute the predetermined overhead rate?
4. What fundamental business problem is Platinum Tracks facing? Which method of computing the predetermined overhead rate is likely to be more helpful in facing this problem? Explain.

PROBLEM 3–29 Multiple Departments; Overhead Rates; Under- or Overapplied Overhead [LO3, LO5, LO8]

eXcel

Hobart, Evans, and Nix is a small law firm that contains 10 partners and 12 support persons. The firm employs a job-order costing system to accumulate costs chargeable to each client, and it is organized into two departments—the Research and Documents Department and the Litigation Department. The firm uses predetermined overhead rates to charge the costs of these departments to its clients. At the beginning of the year, the firm's management made the following estimates for the year:

	Department	
	Research and Documents	Litigation
Research-hours	24,000	—
Direct attorney-hours	9,000	18,000
Legal forms and supplies	$16,000	$5,000
Direct attorney cost	$450,000	$900,000
Departmental overhead cost	$840,000	$360,000

The predetermined overhead rate in the Research and Documents Department is based on research-hours, and the rate in the Litigation Department is based on direct attorney cost.

The costs charged to each client are made up of three elements: legal forms and supplies used, direct attorney costs incurred, and an applied amount of overhead from each department in which work is performed on the case.

Case 418-3 was initiated on February 23 and completed on May 16. During this period, the following costs and time were recorded on the case:

	Department	
	Research and Documents	Litigation
Research-hours	26	—
Direct attorney-hours	7	114
Legal forms and supplies	$80	$40
Direct attorney cost	$350	$5,700

Required:

1. Compute the predetermined overhead rate used during the year in the Research and Documents Department. Compute the rate used in the Litigation Department.
2. Using the rates you computed in (1) above, compute the total overhead cost applied to Case 418-3.
3. What would be the total cost charged to Case 418-3? Show computations by department and in total for the case.
4. At the end of the year, the firm's records revealed the following actual cost and operating data for all cases handled during the year:

	Department	
	Research and Documents	Litigation
Research-hours	26,000	—
Direct attorney-hours	8,000	15,000
Legal forms and supplies	$19,000	$6,000
Direct attorney cost	$400,000	$750,000
Departmental overhead cost	$870,000	$315,000

Determine the amount of under- or overapplied overhead cost in each department for the year.

PROBLEM 3–30 Plantwide versus Departmental Overhead Rates; Under- or Overapplied Overhead [LO3, LO5, LO8]

"Blast it!" said David Wilson, president of Teledex Company. "We've just lost the bid on the Koopers job by $2,000. It seems we're either too high to get the job or too low to make any money on half the jobs we bid."

Teledex Company manufactures products to customers' specifications and operates a job-order costing system. Manufacturing overhead cost is applied to jobs on the basis of direct labor cost. The following estimates were made at the beginning of the year:

	Department			
	Fabricating	Machining	Assembly	Total Plant
Direct labor	$200,000	$100,000	$300,000	$600,000
Manufacturing overhead	$350,000	$400,000	$90,000	$840,000

Jobs require varying amounts of work in the three departments. The Koopers job, for example, would have required manufacturing costs in the three departments as follows:

	Department			
	Fabricating	Machining	Assembly	Total Plant
Direct materials	$3,000	$200	$1,400	$4,600
Direct labor	$2,800	$500	$6,200	$9,500
Manufacturing overhead	?	?	?	?

The company uses a plantwide overhead rate to apply manufacturing overhead cost to jobs.

Required:

1. Assuming use of a plantwide overhead rate:
   a. Compute the rate for the current year.
   b. Determine the amount of manufacturing overhead cost that would have been applied to the Koopers job.
2. Suppose that instead of using a plantwide overhead rate, the company had used a separate predetermined overhead rate in each department. Under these conditions:
   a. Compute the rate for each department for the current year.
   b. Determine the amount of manufacturing overhead cost that would have been applied to the Koopers job.
3. Explain the difference between the manufacturing overhead that would have been applied to the Koopers job using the plantwide rate in question 1 (b) above and using the departmental rates in question 2 (b).
4. Assume that it is customary in the industry to bid jobs at 150% of total manufacturing cost (direct materials, direct labor, and applied overhead). What was the company's bid price on the Koopers job? What would the bid price have been if departmental overhead rates had been used to apply overhead cost?
5. At the end of the year, the company assembled the following *actual* cost data relating to all jobs worked on during the year.

	Department			
	Fabricating	Machining	Assembly	Total Plant
Direct materials	$190,000	$16,000	$114,000	$320,000
Direct labor	$210,000	$108,000	$262,000	$580,000
Manufacturing overhead	$360,000	$420,000	$84,000	$864,000

Compute the under- or overapplied overhead for the year (a) assuming that a plantwide overhead rate is used, and (b) assuming that departmental overhead rates are used.

PROBLEM 3–31 Journal Entries; T-Accounts; Comprehensive Problem; Financial Statements; [LO3, LO4, LO5, LO6, LO7, LO8]

Froya Fabrikker A/S of Bergen, Norway, is a small company that manufactures specialty heavy equipment for use in North Sea oil fields. (The Norwegian currency is the krone, which is denoted by Nkr.) The company uses a job-order costing system and applies manufacturing overhead cost to jobs on the basis of direct labor-hours. At the beginning of the year, the following estimates were made for the purpose of computing the predetermined overhead rate: manufacturing overhead cost, Nkr360,000; and direct labor-hours, 900.

The following transactions took place during the year (all purchases and services were acquired on account):

a. Raw materials were purchased for use in production, Nkr200,000.
b. Raw materials were requisitioned for use in production (all direct materials), Nkr185,000.
c. Utility bills were incurred, Nkr70,000 (90% related to factory operations, and the remainder related to selling and administrative activities).
d. Salary and wage costs were incurred:

Direct labor (975 hours)	Nkr230,000
Indirect labor	Nkr90,000
Selling and administrative salaries	Nkr110,000

e. Maintenance costs were incurred in the factory, Nkr54,000.
f. Advertising costs were incurred, Nkr136,000.
g. Depreciation was recorded for the year, Nkr95,000 (80% related to factory equipment, and the remainder related to selling and administrative equipment).
h. Rental cost incurred on buildings, Nkr120,000 (85% related to factory operations, and the remainder related to selling and administrative facilities).
i. Manufacturing overhead cost was applied to jobs, Nkr __?__.
j. Cost of goods manufactured for the year, Nkr770,000.
k. Sales for the year (all on account) totaled Nkr1,200,000. These goods cost Nkr800,000 to manufacture according to their job cost sheets.

The balances in the inventory accounts at the beginning of the year were:

Raw Materials	Nkr30,000
Work in Process	Nkr21,000
Finished Goods	Nkr60,000

Required:

1. Prepare journal entries to record the preceding data.
2. Post your entries to T-accounts. (Don't forget to enter the beginning inventory balances above.) Determine the ending balances in the inventory accounts and in the Manufacturing Overhead account.
3. Prepare a schedule of cost of goods manufactured.
4. Prepare a journal entry to close any balance in the Manufacturing Overhead account to Cost of Goods Sold. Prepare a schedule of cost of goods sold.
5. Prepare an income statement for the year.
6. Job 412 was one of the many jobs started and completed during the year. The job required Nkr8,000 in direct materials and 39 hours of direct labor time at a total direct labor cost of Nkr9,200. The job contained only four units. If the company bills at a price 60% above the unit product cost on the job cost sheet, what price per unit would have been charged to the customer?

PROBLEM 3–32 Comprehensive Problem: T-Accounts, Job-Order Cost Flows; Financial Statements [LO3, LO5, LO6, LO8]

Chenko Products, Inc., manufactures goods to customers' orders and uses a job-order costing system. A beginning-of-the-year trial balance for the company is given below:

Cash	$ 35,000	
Accounts Receivable	127,000	
Raw Materials	10,000	
Work in Process	44,000	
Finished Goods	75,000	
Prepaid Insurance	9,000	
Plant and Equipment	400,000	
Accumulated Depreciation		$110,000
Accounts Payable		86,000
Salaries and Wages Payable		9,000
Capital Stock		375,000
Retained Earnings		120,000
Total	$700,000	$700,000

The company applies manufacturing overhead cost to jobs on the basis of direct materials cost. The following estimates were made at the beginning of the year for purposes of computing a predetermined overhead rate: manufacturing overhead cost, $510,000; and direct materials cost, $340,000. Summarized transactions of the company for the year are given below:

a. Raw materials purchased on account, $400,000.
b. Raw materials requisitioned for use in production, $370,000 ($320,000 direct materials and $50,000 indirect materials).
c. Salary and wage costs were incurred as follows:

Direct labor	$76,000
Indirect labor	$130,000
Selling and administrative salaries	$110,000

d. Maintenance costs incurred in the factory, $81,000.
e. Travel costs incurred by salespeople, $43,000.
f. Prepaid insurance on the factory expired during the year, $7,000.
g. Utility costs incurred, $70,000 (90% related to factory operations, and 10% related to selling and administrative activities).
h. Property taxes incurred on the factory building, $9,000.
i. Advertising costs incurred, $200,000.
j. Rental cost incurred on special factory equipment, $120,000.
k. Depreciation recorded for the year, $50,000 (80% related to factory assets, and 20% related to selling and administrative assets).
l. Manufacturing overhead cost applied to jobs, $? .
m. Cost of goods manufactured for the year, $890,000.
n. Sales for the year totaled $1,400,000 (all on account); the cost of goods sold totaled $930,000.
o. Cash collections from customers during the year totaled $1,350,000.
p. Cash payments during the year: to employees, $300,000; on accounts payable, $970,000.

Required:

1. Enter the company's transactions directly into T-accounts. (Don't forget to enter the beginning balances into the T-accounts.) Key your entries to the letters (a) through (p) above. Create new T-accounts as needed. Find the ending balance in each account.
2. Prepare a schedule of cost of goods manufactured.
3. Prepare a journal entry to close any balance in the Manufacturing Overhead account to Cost of Goods Sold. Prepare a schedule of cost of goods sold.
4. Prepare an income statement for the year.
5. Job 412 was one of the many jobs started and completed during the year. The job required $8,000 in direct materials and $1,600 in direct labor cost. If the job contained 400 units and the company billed the job at 175% of the unit product cost on the job cost sheet, what price per unit would have been charged to the customer?

Cases

CASE 3–33 Critical Thinking; Interpretation of Manufacturing Overhead Rates [LO3, LO5]

Kelvin Aerospace, Inc., manufactures parts such as rudder hinges for the aerospace industry. The company uses a job-order costing system with a plantwide predetermined overhead rate based on direct labor-hours. On December 16, 2005, the company's controller made a preliminary estimate of the predetermined overhead rate for the year 2006. The new rate was based on the estimated total manufacturing overhead cost of $3,402,000 and the estimated 63,000 total direct labor-hours for 2006:

$$\text{Predetermined overhead rate} = \frac{\$3{,}402{,}000}{63{,}000 \text{ hours}}$$

$$= \$54 \text{ per direct labor-hour}$$

This new predetermined overhead rate was communicated to top managers in a meeting on December 19. The rate did not cause any comment because it was within a few pennies of the overhead rate that had been used during 2005. One of the subjects discussed at the meeting was a proposal by the production manager to purchase an automated milling machine built by Sunghi Industries. The president of Kelvin Aerospace, Harry Arcany, agreed to meet with the sales representative from Sunghi Industries to discuss the proposal.

On the day following the meeting, Mr. Arcany met with Jasmine Chang, Sunghi Industries' sales representative. The following discussion took place:

Arcany: Wally, our production manager, asked me to meet with you since he is interested in installing an automated milling machine. Frankly, I'm skeptical. You're going to have to show me this isn't just another expensive toy for Wally's people to play with.

Chang: This is a great machine with direct bottom-line benefits. The automated milling machine has three major advantages. First, it is much faster than the manual methods you are using. It can process about twice as many parts per hour as your present milling machines. Second, it is much more flexible. There are some up-front programming costs, but once those have been incurred, almost no setup is required to run a standard operation. You just punch in the code for the standard operation, load the machine's hopper with raw material, and the machine does the rest.

Arcany: What about cost? Having twice the capacity in the milling machine area won't do us much good. That center is idle much of the time anyway.

Chang: I was getting there. The third advantage of the automated milling machine is lower cost. Wally and I looked over your present operations, and we estimated that the automated equipment would eliminate the need for about 6,000 direct labor-hours a year. What is your direct labor cost per hour?

Arcany: The wage rate in the milling area averages about $32 per hour. Fringe benefits raise that figure to about $41 per hour.

Chang: Don't forget your overhead.

Arcany: Next year the overhead rate will be $54 per hour.

Chang: So including fringe benefits and overhead, the cost per direct labor-hour is about $95.

Arcany: That's right.

Chang: Since you can save 6,000 direct labor-hours per year, the cost savings would amount to about $570,000 a year. And our 60-month lease plan would require payments of only $348,000 per year.

Arcany: That sounds like a no-brainer. When can you install the equipment?

Shortly after this meeting, Mr. Arcany informed the company's controller of the decision to lease the new equipment, which would be installed over the Christmas vacation period. The controller realized that this decision would require a recomputation of the predetermined overhead rate for the year 2006 since the decision would affect both the manufacturing overhead and the direct labor-hours for the year. After talking with both the production manager and the sales representative from Sunghi Industries, the controller discovered that in addition to the annual lease cost of $348,000, the new machine would also require a skilled technician/programmer who would have to be hired at a cost of $50,000 per year to maintain and program the equipment. Both of these costs would be included in factory overhead. There would be no other changes in total manufacturing overhead cost, which is almost entirely fixed. The controller assumed that the new machine would result in a reduction of 6,000 direct labor-hours for the year from the levels that had initially been planned.

When the revised predetermined overhead rate for the year 2006 was circulated among the company's top managers, there was considerable dismay.

Required:

1. Recompute the predetermined rate assuming that the new machine will be installed. Explain why the new predetermined overhead rate is higher (or lower) than the rate that was originally estimated for the year 2006.
2. What effect (if any) would this new rate have on the cost of jobs that do not use the new automated milling machine?
3. Why would managers be concerned about the new overhead rate?
4. After seeing the new predetermined overhead rate, the production manager admitted that he probably wouldn't be able to eliminate all of the 6,000 direct labor-hours. He had been hoping to accomplish the reduction by not replacing workers who retire or quit, but that had not been possible. As a result, the real labor savings would be only about 2,000 hours—one worker. Given this additional information, evaluate the original decision to acquire the automated milling machine from Sunghi Industries.

CASE 3–34 (Appendix 3A) Ethics; Predetermined Overhead Rate and Capacity [LO5, LO8, LO9]

Pat Miranda, the new controller of Vault Hard Drives, Inc., has just returned from a seminar on the choice of the activity level in the predetermined overhead rate. Even though the subject did not sound exciting at first, she found that there were some important ideas presented that should get a hearing at her company. After returning from the seminar, she arranged a meeting with the production manager, J. Stevens, and the assistant production manager, Marvin Washington.

Pat: I ran across an idea that I wanted to check out with both of you. It's about the way we compute predetermined overhead rates.

J.: We're all ears.

Pat: We compute the predetermined overhead rate by dividing the estimated total factory overhead for the coming year by the estimated total units produced for the coming year.

Marvin: We've been doing that as long as I've been with the company.

J.: And it has been done that way at every other company I've worked at, except at most places they divide by direct labor-hours.

Pat: We use units because it is simpler and we basically make one product with minor variations. But, there's another way to do it. Instead of dividing the estimated total factory overhead by the estimated total units produced for the coming year, we could divide by the total units produced at capacity.

Marvin: Oh, the Sales Department will love that. It will drop the costs on all of our products. They'll go wild over there cutting prices.

Pat: That is a worry, but I wanted to talk to both of you first before going over to Sales.

J.: Aren't you always going to have a lot of underapplied overhead?

Pat: That's correct, but let me show you how we would handle it. Here's an example based on our budget for next year.

Budgeted (estimated) production	160,000 units
Budgeted sales	160,000 units
Capacity	200,000 units
Selling price	$60 per unit
Variable manufacturing cost	$15 per unit
Total manufacturing overhead cost (all fixed)	$4,000,000
Administrative and selling expenses (all fixed)	$2,700,000
Beginning inventories	$0

Traditional Approach to Computation of the Predetermined Overhead Rate

$$\frac{\text{Estimated total manufacturing overhead cost, \$4,000,000}}{\text{Estimated total units produced, 160,000}} = \$25 \text{ per unit}$$

Budgeted Income Statement

Revenue (160,000 units × $60 per unit)		$9,600,000
Cost of goods sold:		
Variable manufacturing (160,000 units × $15 per unit)	$2,400,000	
Manufacturing overhead applied (160,000 units × $25 per unit)	4,000,000	6,400,000
Gross margin		3,200,000
Administrative and selling expenses		2,700,000
Net operating income		$ 500,000

New Approach to Computation of the Predetermined Overhead Rate Using Capacity in the Denominator

$$\frac{\text{Estimated total manufacturing overhead cost, \$4,000,000}}{\text{Total units at capacity, 200,000}} = \$20 \text{ per unit}$$

Budgeted Income Statement

Revenue (160,000 units × $60 per unit)		$9,600,000
Cost of goods sold:		
Variable manufacturing (160,000 units × $15 per unit)	$2,400,000	
Manufacturing overhead applied (160,000 units × $20 per unit)	3,200,000	5,600,000
Gross margin		4,000,000
Cost of unused capacity [(200,000 units − 160,000 units) × $20 per unit]		800,000
Administrative and selling expenses		2,700,000
Net operating income		$ 500,000

J.: Whoa!! I don't think I like the looks of that "Cost of unused capacity." If that thing shows up on the income statement, someone from headquarters is likely to come down here looking for some people to lay off.

Marvin: I'm worried about something else too. What happens when sales are not up to expectations? Can we pull the "hat trick"?

Pat: I'm sorry, I don't understand.

J.: Marvin's talking about something that happens fairly regularly. When sales are down and profits look like they are going to be lower than the president told the owners they were going to be, the president comes down here and asks us to deliver some more profits.

Marvin: And we pull them out of our hat.

J.: Yeah, we just increase production until we get the profits we want.

Pat: I still don't understand. You mean you increase sales?

J.: Nope, we increase production. We're the production managers, not the sales managers.

Pat: I get it. Since you have produced more, the sales force has more units it can sell.

J.: Nope, the marketing people don't do a thing. We just build inventories and that does the trick.

Required:

In all of the questions below, assume that the predetermined overhead rate under the traditional method is $25 per unit, and under the new method it is $20 per unit. Also assume that under the traditional method any under- or overapplied overhead is taken directly to the income statement as an adjustment to Cost of Goods Sold.

1. Suppose actual production is 160,000 units. Compute the net operating incomes that would be realized under the traditional and new methods if actual sales are 150,000 units and everything else turns out as expected.
2. How many units would have to be produced under each of the methods in order to realize the budgeted net operating income of $500,000 if actual sales are 150,000 units and everything else turns out as expected?
3. What effect does the new method based on capacity have on the volatility of net operating income?
4. Will the "hat trick" be easier or harder to perform if the new method based on capacity is used?
5. Do you think the "hat trick" is ethical?

CASE 3–35 Ethics and the Manager [LO3, LO5, LO8]

Terri Ronsin had recently been transferred to the Home Security Systems Division of National Home Products. Shortly after taking over her new position as divisional controller, she was asked to develop the division's predetermined overhead rate for the upcoming year. The accuracy of the rate is of some importance, since it is used throughout the year and any overapplied or underapplied overhead is closed out to Cost of Goods Sold at the end of the year. National Home Products uses direct labor-hours in all of its divisions as the allocation base for manufacturing overhead.

To compute the predetermined overhead rate, Terri divided her estimate of the total manufacturing overhead for the coming year by the production manager's estimate of the total direct labor-hours for the coming year. She took her computations to the division's general manager for approval but was quite surprised when he suggested a modification in the base. Her conversation with the general manager of the Home Security Systems Division, Harry Irving, went like this:

Ronsin: Here are my calculations for next year's predetermined overhead rate. If you approve, we can enter the rate into the computer on January 1 and be up and running in the job-order costing system right away this year.

Irving: Thanks for coming up with the calculations so quickly, and they look just fine. There is, however, one slight modification I would like to see. Your estimate of the total direct labor-hours for the year is 440,000 hours. How about cutting that to about 420,000 hours?

Ronsin: I don't know if I can do that. The production manager says she will need about 440,000 direct labor-hours to meet the sales projections for the year. Besides, there are going to be over 430,000 direct labor-hours during the current year and sales are projected to be higher next year.

Irving: Teri, I know all of that. I would still like to reduce the direct labor-hours in the base to something like 420,000 hours. You probably don't know that I had an agreement with your predecessor as divisional controller to shave 5% or so off the estimated direct labor-hours every year. That way, we kept a reserve that usually resulted in a big boost to net operating income at the end of the fiscal year in December. We called it our Christmas bonus. Corporate headquarters always seemed as pleased as punch that we could pull off such a miracle at the end of the year. This system has worked well for many years, and I don't want to change it now.

Required:

1. Explain how shaving 5% off the estimated direct labor-hours in the base for the predetermined overhead rate usually results in a big boost in net operating income at the end of the fiscal year.
2. Should Terri Ronsin go along with the general manager's request to reduce the direct labor-hours in the predetermined overhead rate computation to 420,000 direct labor-hours?

Group and Internet Exercises

GROUP EXERCISE 3–36 Talk with a Controller

Look in the yellow pages or contact your local chamber of commerce or local chapter of the Institute of Management Accountants to find the names of manufacturing companies in your area. Make an appointment to meet with the controller or chief financial officer of one of these companies.

Required:

Ask the following questions and write a brief report concerning what you found out.

1. Does the company use job-order costing, process costing, or some other method of determining product costs?
2. How is overhead assigned to products? What is the overhead rate? What is the basis of allocation? Is more than one overhead rate used?
3. Are product costs used in making any decisions? If so, what are those decisions and how are product costs used?
4. How are profits affected by changes in production volume? By changes in sales?
5. Has the company recently changed its cost system or is it considering changing its cost system? If so, why? What changes were made or what changes are being considered?

INTERNET EXERCISE 3–37

As you know, the World Wide Web is constantly evolving. Sites come and go, and change without notice. To enable periodic updating of site addresses, this problem has been posted to the textbook website (www.mhhe.com/garrison11e). After accessing the site, enter the Student Center and select this chapter. Select and complete the Internet Exercise.

Chapter

4 Systems Design: Process Costing

LEARNING OBJECTIVES

After studying Chapter 4, you should be able to:

LO1 Record the flow of materials, labor, and overhead through a process costing system.

LO2 Compute the equivalent units of production using the weighted-average method.

LO3 Prepare a quantity schedule using the weighted-average method.

LO4 Compute the costs per equivalent unit using the weighted-average method.

LO5 Prepare a cost reconciliation using the weighted-average method.

LO6 (Appendix 4A) Compute the equivalent units of production using the FIFO method.

LO7 (Appendix 4A) Prepare a quantity schedule using the FIFO method.

LO8 (Appendix 4A) Compute the costs per equivalent unit using the FIFO method.

LO9 (Appendix 4A) Prepare a cost reconciliation using the FIFO method.

Costing Cream Soda

BUSINESS FOCUS

Megan Harris started a company to produce cream soda from an old family recipe. At first the company struggled, but after favorable mention on a local newscast, the company expanded rapidly. Megan soon realized that to expand any further, it would be necessary to borrow money. The investment that would be required in additional equipment was too large for her to finance out of the company's current cash flows.

Megan was disappointed to find that few banks were willing to make a loan to such a small company, but she finally found a bank that would consider her loan application. However, Megan was informed that she would have to supply up-to-date financial statements with her loan application.

Megan had never bothered with financial statements before—she felt that as long as the balance in the company's checkbook kept increasing, the company was doing fine. She was puzzled how she was going to determine the value of the cream soda in the work in process and finished goods inventories. The valuation of the cream soda would affect both cost of goods sold and inventory balances. Megan thought of perhaps using job-order costing, which had been used at her previous employer, but her company produces only one product. Raw ingredients are continually being mixed to make more cream soda, and more bottled cream soda is always coming off the end of the bottling line. Megan didn't see how she could use a job-order costing system since the job never really ended. Perhaps there was another way to account for the costs of producing the cream soda. ■

As explained in Chapter 3, job-order costing and process costing are two common methods for determining unit product costs. A job-order costing system is used in situations where many different jobs or products are worked on each period. Examples of industries that would typically use job-order costing include furniture manufacturing, special-order printing, shipbuilding, and many types of service organizations.

By contrast, **process costing** is most commonly used in industries that produce essentially homogenous (i.e., uniform) products on a continuous basis, such as bricks, cornflakes, or paper. Process costing is particularly used in companies that convert basic raw materials into homogenous products, such as Reynolds Aluminum (aluminum ingots), Scott Paper (toilet paper), General Mills (flour), Exxon (gasoline and lubricating oils), Coppertone (sunscreens), and Kellogg (breakfast cereals). In addition, process costing is sometimes used in companies with assembly operations. A form of process costing may also be used in utilities that produce gas, water, and electricity.

Our purpose in this chapter is to explain how product costing works in a process costing system.

Comparison of Job-Order and Process Costing

In some ways process costing is very similar to job-order costing, and in some ways it is very different. In this section, we focus on these similarities and differences to provide a foundation for the detailed discussion of process costing that follows.

Similarities between Job-Order and Process Costing

Much of what was learned in Chapter 3 about costing and cost flows applies equally well to process costing in this chapter. We are not throwing out all that we have learned about costing and starting from "scratch" with a whole new system. The similarities between job-order and process costing can be summarized as follows:

1. Both systems have the same basic purposes—to assign material, labor, and overhead cost to products and to provide a mechanism for computing unit product costs.
2. Both systems use the same basic manufacturing accounts, including Manufacturing Overhead, Raw Materials, Work in Process, and Finished Goods.
3. The flow of costs through the manufacturing accounts is basically the same in both systems.

As can be seen from this comparison, much of the knowledge that we have already acquired about costing is applicable to a process costing system. Our task now is to refine and extend this knowledge to process costing.

Differences between Job-Order and Process Costing

The differences between job-order and process costing arise from two factors. The first is that the flow of units in a process costing system is more or less continuous, and the second is that completed units are indistinguishable from one another. Under process costing, it makes no sense to try to identify materials, labor, and overhead costs with a particular order from a customer (as we did with job-order costing), since each order is just one of many that are filled from a continuous flow of virtually identical units from the production line. Under process costing, we accumulate costs *by department,* rather than by order, and assign these costs uniformly to all units that pass through the department during a period.

EXHIBIT 4–1
Differences between Job-Order and Process Costing

Job-Order Costing	Process Costing
1. Many different jobs are worked on during each period, with each job having different production requirements.	1. A single product is produced either on a continuous basis or for long periods of time. All units of product are identical.
2. Costs are accumulated by individual job.	2. Costs are accumulated by department.
3. The *job cost sheet* is the key document controlling the accumulation of costs by a job.	3. The *department production report* is the key document showing the accumulation of costs in a department and how those costs were assigned to units of product.
4. Unit costs are computed *by job* on the job cost sheet.	4. Unit costs are computed *by department* on the department production report.

A further difference between the two costing systems is that the job cost sheet is not used in process costing, since the focal point of process costing is on departments. Instead of using job cost sheets, a **production report** is prepared for each department in which work is done on products. The production report serves several functions. It provides a summary of the number of units moving through a department during a period, and it also provides a computation of unit product costs. In addition, it shows what costs were charged to the department and what disposition was made of these costs. The department production report is the key document in a process costing system.

The major differences between job-order and process costing are summarized in Exhibit 4–1.

IN BUSINESS

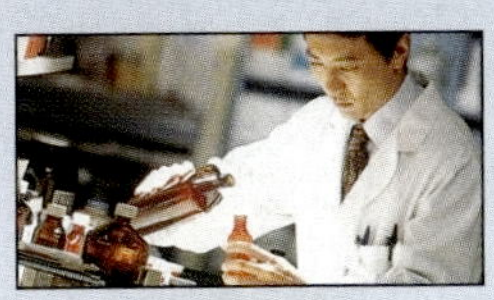

A HYBRID APPROACH

Managers of successful pharmacies understand product costs. Some pharmacies use a hybrid approach to costing drugs. For example, a hospital pharmacy may use process costing to develop the cost of formulating the base solution for parenterals (that is, drugs delivered by injection or through the blood stream) and then use job order costing to accumulate the additional costs incurred to create specific parenteral solutions. These additional costs include the ingredients added to the base solution and the time spent by the pharmacist to prepare the specific prescribed drug solution.

Source: "Pharmaceutical Care: Cost Estimation and Cost Management," *Drug Store News*, February 16, 1998, p. CP21, 5 p.

A Perspective of Process Cost Flows

Before going through a detailed example of process costing, it will be helpful to see how manufacturing costs flow through a process costing system.

Processing Departments

A **processing department** is part of an organization where work is performed on a product and where materials, labor, or overhead costs are added to the product. For example, a potato chip factory operated by Nalley's might have three processing departments—one for preparing potatoes, one for cooking, and one for inspecting and packaging. A brick factory might have two processing departments—one for mixing and molding clay into brick form and one for firing the molded brick. A company can have as many or as few processing departments as are needed to complete a product or service. Some products

EXHIBIT 4–2
Sequential Processing Departments

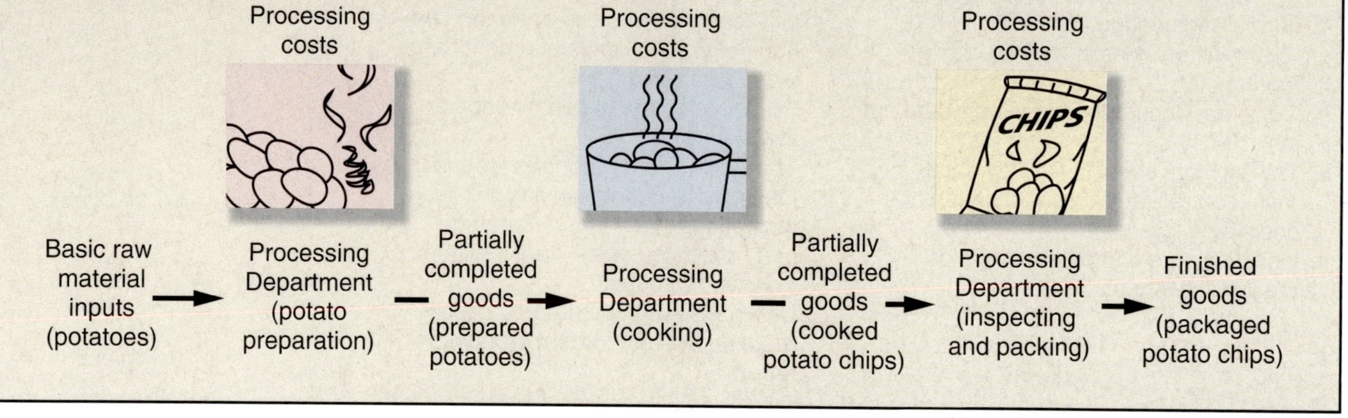

and services may go through several processing departments, while others may go through only one or two. Regardless of the number of departments involved, all processing departments in a process costing system have two essential features. First, the activity in the processing department must be performed uniformly on all of the units passing through it. Second, the output of the processing department must be homogeneous.

The processing departments involved in making a product such as bricks or potato chips would probably be organized in a *sequential* pattern in which units flow in sequence from one department to another. Exhibit 4–2 shows an example of processing departments arranged in a sequential pattern.

The Flow of Materials, Labor, and Overhead Costs

Cost accumulation is simpler in a process costing system than in a job-order costing system. In a process costing system, instead of having to trace costs to hundreds of different jobs, costs are traced to only a few processing departments.

A T-account model of materials, labor, and overhead cost flows in a process costing system is shown in Exhibit 4–3. Several key points should be noted from this exhibit. First, note that a separate Work in Process account is maintained for *each processing department.* In contrast, in a job-order costing system the entire company may have only one Work in Process account. Second, note that the completed production of the first processing department (Department A in the exhibit) is transferred to the Work in Process account of the second processing department (Department B), where it undergoes further work. After this further work, the completed units are then transferred to Finished Goods. (In Exhibit 4–3, we show only two processing departments, but a company can have many processing departments.)

Finally, note that materials, labor, and overhead costs can be added in *any* processing department—not just the first. Costs in Department B's Work in Process account would consist of the materials, labor, and overhead costs incurred in Department B plus the costs attached to partially completed units transferred in from Department A (called **transferred-in costs**).

Materials, Labor, and Overhead Cost Entries

LEARNING OBJECTIVE 1
Record the flow of materials, labor, and overhead through a process costing system.

To complete our discussion of cost flows in a process costing system, in this section we show journal entries relating to materials, labor, and overhead costs at Megan's Classic Cream Soda, the company mentioned at the very beginning of this chapter. Megan's Classic Cream Soda has two processing departments—Formulating and Bottling. In the Formulating Department, the various ingredients are checked for quality and then mixed and injected with carbon dioxide to create bulk cream soda. In the Bottling Department,

EXHIBIT 4–3
T-Account Model of Process Costing Flows

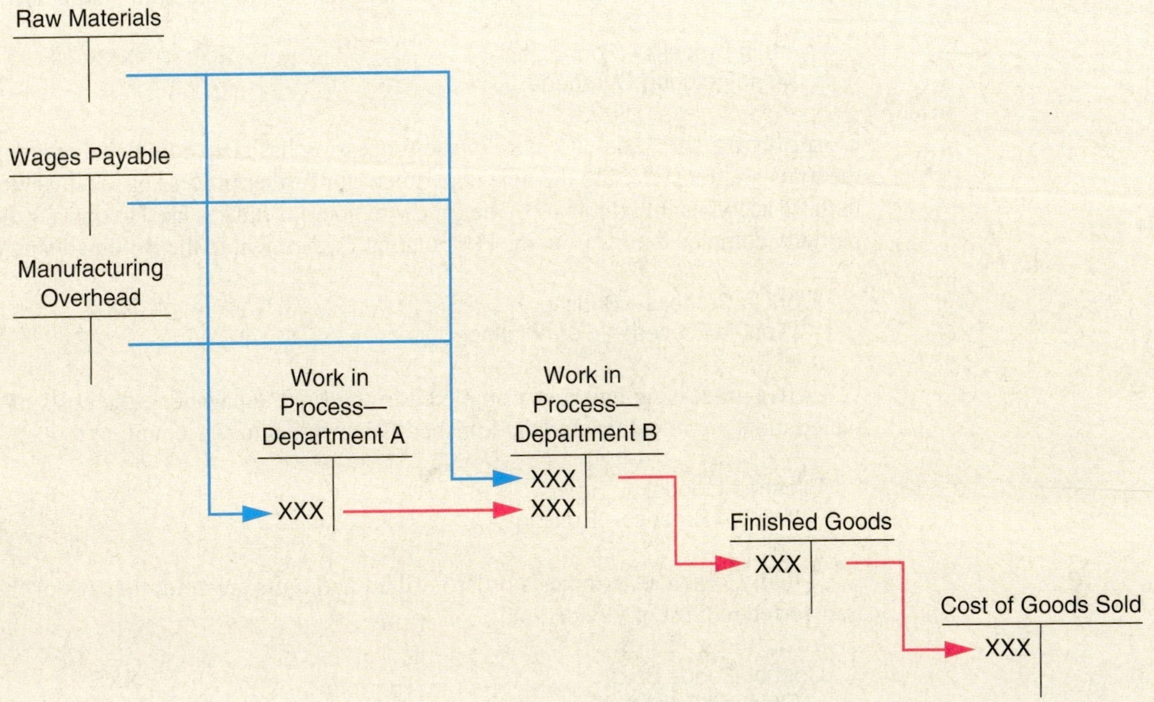

bottles are checked for defects, filled with cream soda, capped, visually inspected again for defects, and then packed for shipping.

Materials Costs As in job-order costing, materials are drawn from the storeroom using a materials requisition form. Materials can be added in any processing department, although it is not unusual for materials to be added only in the first processing department, with subsequent departments adding only labor and overhead costs as the partially completed units move along toward completion.

At Megan's Classic Cream Soda, some materials (i.e., water, flavors, sugar, and carbon dioxide) are added in the Formulating Department and some materials (i.e., bottles, caps, and packing materials) are added in the Bottling Department. The journal entry to record the materials used in the first processing department, the Formulating Department, is as follows:

Work in Process—Formulating	XXX	
Raw Materials		XXX

If other materials are subsequently added in another department, as at Megan's Classic Cream Soda, the entry is the following:

Work in Process—Bottling	XXX	
Raw Materials		XXX

Labor Costs In process costing, labor costs are traced to departments—not to individual jobs. The following journal entry records the labor costs in the Formulating Department at Megan's Classic Cream Soda:

Work in Process—Formulating	XXX	
Salaries and Wages Payable		XXX

Overhead Costs In process costing, as in job-order costing, predetermined overhead rates are usually used. Overhead cost is applied to units of product as they move through the department. The following journal entry records the cost for the Formulating Department:

Work in Process—Formulating	XXX	
Manufacturing Overhead		XXX

Completing the Cost Flows Once processing has been completed in a department, the units are transferred to the next department for further processing, as illustrated earlier in the T-accounts in Exhibit 4–3. The following journal entry is used to transfer the costs of partially completed units from the Formulating Department to the Bottling Department:

Work in Process—Bottling	XXX	
Work in Process—Formulating		XXX

After processing has been completed in the final department, the costs of the completed units are transferred to the Finished Goods inventory account:

Finished Goods	XXX	
Work in Process—Bottling		XXX

Finally, when a customer's order is filled and units are sold, the cost of the units is transferred to Cost of Goods Sold:

Cost of Goods Sold	XXX	
Finished Goods		XXX

To summarize, the cost flows between accounts are basically the same in a process costing system as they are in a job-order costing system. The only noticeable difference at this point is that in a process costing system each department has a separate Work in Process account.

MANAGERIAL ACCOUNTING IN ACTION
The Issue

DOUBLE DIAMOND skis

Samantha Trivers, president of Double Diamond Skis, was worried about the future of her company. After a rocky start, the company had come out with a completely redesigned ski called The Ultimate made of exotic materials and featuring flashy graphics. Exhibit 4–4 illustrates how this ski is manufactured. The ski was a runaway best seller—particularly among younger skiers—and had provided the company with much-needed cash for two years. However, last year a dismal snowfall in the Rocky Mountains had depressed sales, and Double Diamond was once again short of cash. Samantha was worried that another bad ski season would force Double Diamond into bankruptcy.

Just before starting production of next year's model of The Ultimate, Samantha called Jerry Madison, the company controller, into her office to discuss the reports she would need in the coming year.

Samantha: Jerry, I am going to need more frequent cost information this year. I really have to stay on top of things.

Jerry: What do you have in mind?

Samantha: I'd like reports at least once a month that detail our production costs for each department and for each pair of skis.

Jerry: That shouldn't be much of a problem. We already compile almost all of the necessary data for the annual report. The only complication is our work in process inventories. They haven't been a problem in our annual reports, since our fiscal year ends at a time when we have finished producing skis for the last model year and haven't yet started producing for the new model year. Consequently, there aren't any work in process inventories to value for the annual report. But that won't be true for monthly reports.

Samantha: I'm not sure why that is a problem, Jerry. But I'm confident you can figure out how to solve it.

EXHIBIT 4–4

The Production Process at Double Diamond Skis*

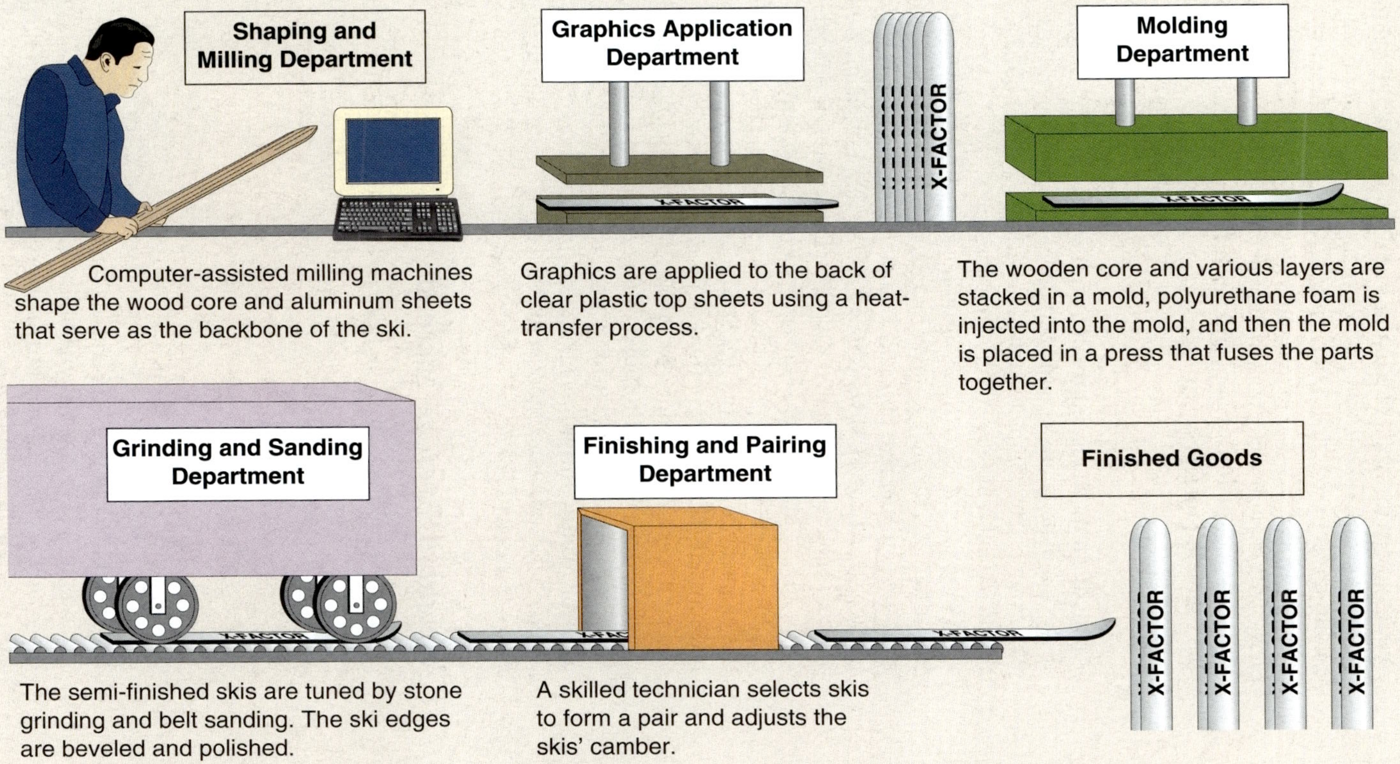

*Adapted from Bill Gout, Jesse James Doquilo, and Studio M D, "Capped Crusaders," *Skiing,* October 1993, pp. 138–144.

Equivalent Units of Production

Topic Tackler PLUS

4–1

Jerry Madison, the controller of Double Diamond Skis, was concerned with the following problem: After materials, labor, and overhead costs have been accumulated in a department, the department's output must be determined so that unit product costs can be computed. The difficulty is that a department usually has some partially completed units in its ending inventory. It does not seem reasonable to count these partially completed units as equivalent to fully completed units when counting the department's output. Therefore, Jerry will have to mathematically translate those partially completed units into an *equivalent* number of fully completed units. In process costing, this translation is done using the following formula:

Equivalent units = Number of partially completed units × Percentage completion

As the formula states, **equivalent units** is defined as the product of the number of partially completed units and the percentage completion of those units. The equivalent units is the number of complete units that could have been obtained from the materials and effort that went into the partially complete units.

For example, suppose the Molding Department at Double Diamond has 500 units in its ending work in process inventory that are 60% complete. These 500 partially complete units are equivalent to 300 fully complete units (500 × 60% = 300). Therefore, the ending work in process inventory contains 300 equivalent units. These equivalent units would be added to any units completed during the period to determine the period's output for the department—called the *equivalent units of production.*

Equivalent units of production for a period can be computed in two different ways. In this chapter, we discuss the *weighted-average method.* In Appendix 4A, the *FIFO method* is discussed. The **FIFO method** of process costing is a method in which equivalent units and unit costs relate only to work done during the current period. In contrast, the **weighted-average method** blends together units and costs from the current period with units and costs from the prior period. In the weighted-average method, the **equivalent units of production** for a department are the number of units transferred to the next department (or to finished goods) plus the equivalent units in the department's ending work in process inventory.

Weighted-Average Method

LEARNING OBJECTIVE 2
Compute the equivalent units of production using the weighted-average method.

Under the weighted-average method, a department's equivalent units are computed as follows:

Weighted-Average Method
(a separate calculation is made for each cost category in each processing department)

Equivalent units of production = Units transferred to the next department or to finished goods + Equivalent units in ending work in process inventory

We do not have to make an equivalent units calculation for units transferred to the next department. We can assume that they would not have been transferred unless they were 100% complete with respect to the work performed in the transferring department. However, an equivalent units calculation does need to be made for the partially completed units in ending inventory.

Consider the Shaping and Milling Department at Double Diamond. This department uses computerized milling machines to precisely shape the wooden core and metal sheets that will be used to form the backbone of the ski. (See Exhibit 4–4 for an overview of the production process at Double Diamond.) The following activity took place in the department in May, several months into the production of the new model of The Ultimate ski:

Shaping and Milling Department	Units	Percent Complete Materials	Conversion
Work in process, May 1	200	55%	30%
Units started into production during May	5,000		
Units completed during May and transferred to the next department	4,800	100%*	100%*
Work in process, May 31	400	40%	25%

*It is always assumed that units transferred out of a department are 100% complete with respect to the processing done in that department.

Note the use of the term *conversion* in the table above. **Conversion cost,** as defined in Chapter 2, is direct labor cost plus manufacturing overhead cost. In process costing, conversion cost is often—but not always—treated as a single element of product cost.

Also note that the May 1 beginning work in process was 55% complete with respect to materials costs and 30% complete with respect to conversion costs. This means that 55% of the materials costs required to complete the units in the department had already been incurred. Likewise, 30% of the conversion costs required to complete the units had already been incurred.

Since Double Diamond's work in process inventories are at different stages of completion in terms of the amounts of materials cost and conversion cost that have been added in the department, two equivalent unit figures must be computed. The equivalent units computations are shown in Exhibit 4–5.

Note from the computation in Exhibit 4–5 that units in the beginning work in process inventory are ignored. The weighted-average method is concerned only with the fact that there are 4,900 equivalent units for conversion cost in ending inventories and in units transferred to the next department—the method is not concerned with the additional fact that some of this work was accomplished in prior periods. This is a key point in the weighted-average method that is easy to overlook.

Computation of equivalent units of production is illustrated in Exhibit 4–6 (page 154). Study this exhibit carefully before going on.

EXHIBIT 4–5
Equivalent Units of Production: Weighted-Average Method

Shaping and Milling Department	Materials	Conversion
Units transferred to the next department	4,800	4,800
Work in process, May 31:		
400 units × 40% complete with respect to materials	160	
400 units × 25% complete with respect to conversion		100
Equivalent units of production	4,960	4,900

Production Report—Weighted-Average Method

The production report developed in this section contains the information requested by the president of Double Diamond Skis. The purpose of the production report is to summarize for management all of the activity that takes place in a department's Work in Process account for a period. This activity includes the units and costs that flow through the Work in Process account. As illustrated in Exhibit 4–7 (page 154), a separate production report is prepared for each department.

Earlier, when we outlined the differences between job-order costing and process costing, we stated that the production report takes the place of a job cost sheet in a process costing system. The production report is a key management document. It has three separate (though highly interrelated) parts:

EXHIBIT 4–6
Visual Perspective of Equivalent Units of Production

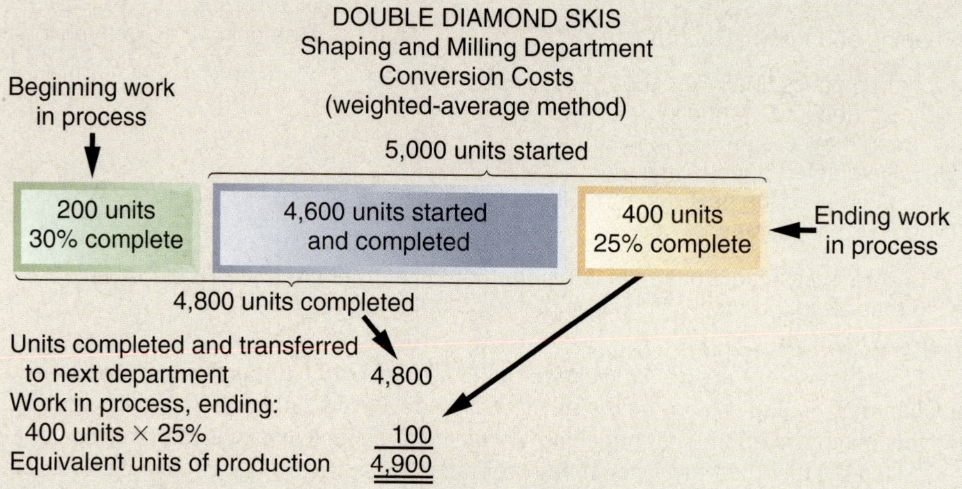

EXHIBIT 4–7
The Position of the Production Report in the Flow of Costs

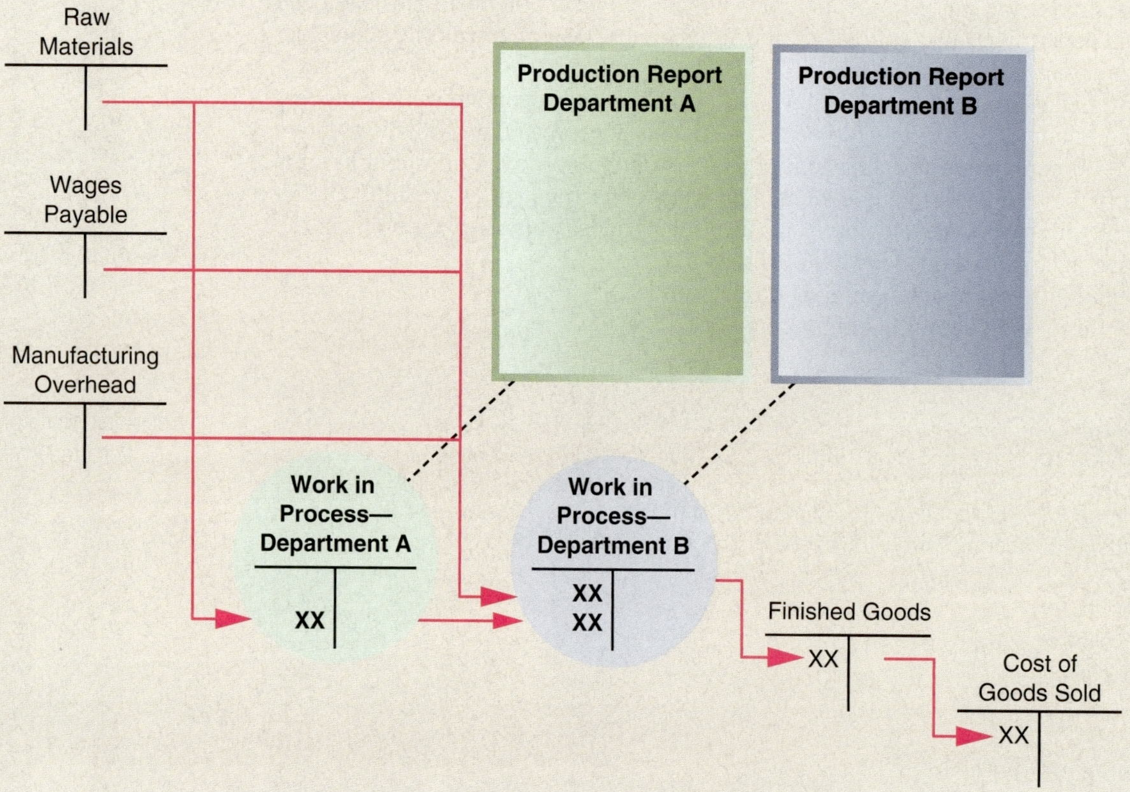

1. A quantity schedule, which shows the flow of units through the department and a computation of equivalent units.
2. A computation of costs per equivalent unit.
3. A reconciliation of all cost flows into and out of the department during the period.

We will use data for the May operations of the Shaping and Milling Department of Double Diamond Skis to illustrate the production report. Keep in mind that this report is only one of five reports that would be prepared for the company since the company has five processing departments.

Shaping and Milling Department Data for May Operations	
Work in process, beginning:	
Units in process	200
Stage of completion with respect to materials	55%
Stage of completion with respect to conversion	30%
Costs in the beginning inventory:	
Materials cost	$ 9,600
Conversion cost	5,575
Total cost in the beginning inventory	$ 15,175
Units started into production during May	5,000
Units completed and transferred out	4,800
Costs added to production during May:	
Materials cost	$368,600
Conversion cost	350,900
Total cost added in the department	$719,500
Work in process, ending:	
Units in process	400
Stage of completion with respect to materials	40%
Stage of completion with respect to conversion	25%

In this section, we show how a production report is prepared when the weighted-average method is used to compute equivalent units and unit costs. The preparation of a production report using the FIFO method is illustrated in Appendix 4A at the end of this chapter.

Step 1: Prepare a Quantity Schedule and Compute the Equivalent Units

LEARNING OBJECTIVE 3
Prepare a quantity schedule using the weighted-average method.

The first part of a production report consists of a **quantity schedule,** which shows the flow of units through a department and the computation of equivalent units. To illustrate, a quantity schedule combined with a computation of equivalent units is given below for the May operations of the Shaping and Milling Department of Double Diamond Skis.

Shaping and Milling Department
Quantity Schedule and Equivalent Units

	Quantity Schedule	Equivalent Units	
		Materials	Conversion
Units to be accounted for:			
Work in process, May 1 (materials 55% complete; conversion 30% complete)	200		
Started into production	5,000		
Total units to be accounted for	5,200		
Units accounted for as follows:			
Transferred to next department	4,800	4,800	4,800
Work in process, May 31 (materials 40% complete; conversion 25% complete)	400	160*	100†
Total units accounted for	5,200	4,960	4,900

*400 units × 40% = 160 equivalent units.
†400 units × 25% = 100 equivalent units.

The quantity schedule shows at a glance how many units moved through the department during the period as well as the stage of completion of any in-process units. In addition to providing this information, the quantity schedule serves as an essential guide in preparing and tying together the remaining parts of a production report.

Step 2: Compute Costs per Equivalent Unit

LEARNING OBJECTIVE 4
Compute the costs per equivalent unit using the weighted-average method.

As stated earlier, the weighted-average method blends together the work that was accomplished in the prior period with the work that was accomplished in the current period. That is why it is called the weighted-average method; it averages together units and costs from both the prior and current periods. These computations are shown below for the Shaping and Milling Department for May:

Shaping and Milling Department
Costs per Equivalent Unit

	Total Cost	Materials	Conversion	Whole Unit
Cost to be accounted for:				
Work in process, May 1	$ 15,175	$ 9,600	$ 5,575	
Cost added during the month in the Shaping and Milling Department	719,500	368,600	350,900	
Total cost to be accounted for (a) ...	$734,675	$378,200	$356,475	
Equivalent units (Step 1 above) (b) ..		4,960	4,900	
Cost per equivalent unit, (a) ÷ (b) ..		$76.25 +	$72.75	= $149.00

The cost per equivalent unit (EU) that we have computed for the Shaping and Milling Department will be used to apply costs to units that are transferred to the next department, Graphics Application, and will also be used to compute the cost in the ending work in process inventory. For example, each unit transferred out of the Shaping and Milling Department to the Graphics Application Department will carry with it a cost of $149. Since the costs are passed on from department to department, the unit cost of the last department, Finishing and Pairing, will represent the final cost of a completed unit of product.

Step 3: Prepare a Cost Reconciliation

LEARNING OBJECTIVE 5
Prepare a cost reconciliation using the weighted-average method.

The purpose of a **cost reconciliation** is to show how the costs that have been charged to a department during a period are accounted for. Typically, the costs charged to a department will consist of the following:

1. Cost in the beginning work in process inventory.
2. Materials, labor, and overhead costs added during the period.
3. Cost (if any) transferred in from the preceding department.

In a production report, these costs are titled "Cost to be accounted for." They are accounted for in the production report by computing the following amounts:

1. Cost transferred out to the next department (or to Finished Goods).
2. Cost remaining in the ending work in process inventory.

In short, when a cost reconciliation is prepared, the "Cost to be accounted for" from Step 2 is reconciled with the sum of the cost transferred out during the period plus the cost in the ending work in process inventory. This concept is illustrated in Exhibit 4–8. Study this exhibit carefully before going on to the cost reconciliation for the Shaping and Milling Department.

Topic Tackler PLUS
4–2

Example of a Cost Reconciliation To prepare a cost reconciliation, follow the quantity schedule line for line and show the cost associated with each group of units. This is done in Exhibit 4–9 (page 158), where we present a completed production report for the Shaping and Milling Department.

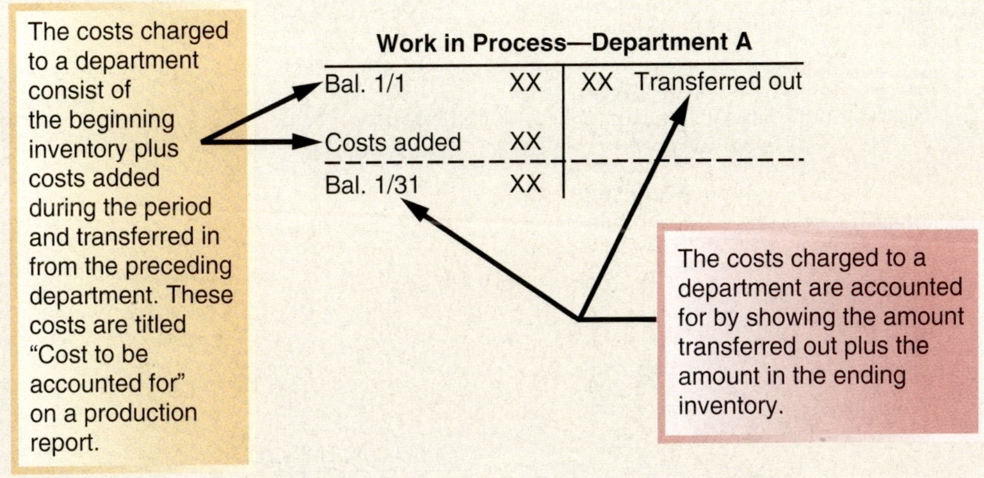

EXHIBIT 4–8
Graphic Illustration of the Cost Reconciliation Part of a Production Report

The quantity schedule in the exhibit shows that 200 units were in process on May 1 and that an additional 5,000 units were started into production during the month. Looking at the "Cost to be accounted for" in the middle part of the exhibit, notice that the units in process on May 1 had $15,175 in cost attached to them and that the Shaping and Milling Department added another $719,500 in cost to production during the month. Thus, the department has $734,675 ($15,175 + $719,500) in cost to be accounted for.

This cost is accounted for in two ways. As shown on the quantity schedule, 4,800 units were transferred to the Graphics Application Department, the next department in the production process. Another 400 units were still in process in the Shaping and Milling Department at the end of the month. Thus, part of the $734,675 "Cost to be accounted for" goes with the 4,800 units to the Graphics Application Department, and part of it remains with the 400 units in the ending work in process inventory in the Shaping and Milling Department.

Each of the 4,800 units transferred to the Graphics Application Department is assigned $149.00 in cost, for a total of $715,200. The 400 units still in process at the end of the month are assigned costs according to their stage of completion. To determine the stage of completion, we refer to the equivalent units computation and bring the equivalent units figures down to the cost reconciliation part of the report. We then assign costs to these units, using the cost per equivalent unit figures already computed.

After cost has been assigned to the ending work in process inventory, the total cost that we have accounted for ($734,675) agrees with the amount that we had to account for ($734,675). Thus, the cost reconciliation is complete.

MANAGERIAL ACCOUNTING IN ACTION
The Wrap-Up

Jerry: Here's an example of the kind of report I can put together for you every month. This particular report is for the Shaping and Milling Department. It follows a fairly standard format for industries like ours and is called a production report. I hope this is what you have in mind.

Samantha: The quantity schedule makes sense to me. I can see we had a total of 5,200 units to account for in the department, and 4,800 of those were transferred to the next department while 400 were still in process at the end of the month. What are these "equivalent units"?

Jerry: That's the problem I mentioned earlier. The 400 units that are still in process are far from complete. When we compute the unit costs, it wouldn't make sense to count them as whole units.

Samantha: I suppose not. I see what you are driving at. Since those 400 units are only 25% complete with respect to our conversion costs, they should only be counted as 100 units when we compute the unit costs for conversion.

Jerry: That's right. Is the rest of the report clear?

EXHIBIT 4–9
Production Report—Weighted-Average Method

DOUBLE DIAMOND SKIS
Shaping and Milling Department Production Report
(Weighted-Average Method)

Quantity Schedule and Equivalent Units	Quantity Schedule			
Units to be accounted for:				
Work in process, May 1 (materials 55% complete; conversion 30% complete)	200			
Started into production	5,000			
Total units to be accounted for	5,200			
		Equivalent Units (EU)		
		Materials	Conversion	
Units accounted for as follows:				
Transferred to next department	4,800	4,800	4,800	
Work in process, May 31 (materials 40% complete; conversion 25% complete)	400	160*	100†	
Total units accounted for	5,200	4,960	4,900	
Costs per Equivalent Unit	**Total Cost**	**Materials**	**Conversion**	**Whole Unit**
Cost to be accounted for:				
Work in process, May 1	$ 15,175	$ 9,600	$ 5,575	
Cost added in the department	719,500	368,600	350,900	
Total cost to be accounted for (a)	$734,675	$378,200	$356,475	
Equivalent units (b)		4,960	4,900	
Cost per EU, (a) ÷ (b)		$76.25	+ $72.75	= $149.00
		Equivalent Units (above)		
Cost Reconciliation	**Total Cost**	**Materials**	**Conversion**	
Cost accounted for as follows:				
Transferred to the next department:				
4,800 units × $149.00 per unit	$715,200	4,800	4,800	
Work in process, May 31:				
Materials, at $76.25 per EU	12,200	160		
Conversion, at $72.75 per EU	7,275		100	
Total work in process, May 31	19,475			
Total cost accounted for	$734,675			

*400 units × 40% = 160 equivalent units.
†400 units × 25% = 100 equivalent units.
EU = Equivalent unit.

Samantha: Yes, it does seem pretty clear, although I want to work the numbers through on my own to make sure I thoroughly understand the report.

Jerry: Does this report give you the information you wanted?

Samantha: Yes, it does. I can tell how many units are in process, how complete they are, what happened to them, and their costs. While I know the unit costs are averages and are heavily influenced by our volume, they still can give me some idea of how well we are doing on the cost side. Thanks, Jerry.

Operation Costing

The costing systems discussed in Chapters 3 and 4 represent the two ends of a continuum. On one end we have job-order costing, which is used by companies that produce many different items—generally to customers' specifications. On the other end we have process costing, which is used by companies that produce homogeneous products in large quantities. Between these two extremes there are many hybrid systems that include characteristics of both job-order and process costing. One of these hybrids is called *operation costing*.

Operation costing is used in situations where products have some common characteristics and also some individual characteristics. Shoes, for example, have common characteristics in that all styles involve cutting and sewing that can be done on a repetitive basis, using the same equipment and following the same basic procedures. Shoes also have individual characteristics—some are made of expensive leathers and others may be made using inexpensive synthetic materials. In a situation such as this, where products have some common characteristics but also must be handled individually, operation costing may be used to determine product costs.

As mentioned above, operation costing is a hybrid system that employs aspects of both job-order and process costing. Products are typically handled in batches when operation costing is in use, with each batch charged for its own specific materials. In this sense, operation costing is similar to job-order costing. However, labor and overhead costs are accumulated by operation or by department, and these costs are assigned to units as in process costing. If shoes are being produced, for example, each shoe is charged the same per unit conversion cost, regardless of the style involved, but it is charged with its specific materials cost. Thus, the company is able to distinguish between styles in terms of materials, but it is able to employ the simplicity of a process costing system for labor and overhead costs.

Examples of other products for which operation costing may be used include electronic equipment (such as semiconductors), textiles, clothing, and jewelry (such as rings, bracelets, and medallions). Products of this type are typically produced in batches, but they can vary considerably from model to model or from style to style in terms of the cost of raw material inputs. Therefore, an operation costing system is well suited for providing cost data.

Summary

Process costing is used in situations where homogeneous products or services are produced on a continuous basis. Costs flow through the manufacturing accounts in basically the same way in both job-order and process costing systems. A process costing system differs from a job-order system primarily in that costs are accumulated by department (rather than by job) and the department production report replaces the job cost sheet.

To compute unit costs in a department, the department's output in terms of equivalent units must be determined. In the weighted-average method, the equivalent units for a period are the sum of the units transferred out of the department during the period and the equivalent units in ending work in process inventory at the end of the period.

The activity in a department is summarized on a production report, which has three separate (though highly interrelated) parts. The first part is a quantity schedule, which includes a computation of equivalent units and shows the flow of units through a department during a period. The second part consists of a computation of costs per equivalent unit for materials, labor, and overhead as well as in total for the period. The third part consists of a cost reconciliation, which summarizes all cost flows through a department for a period.

Review Problem: Job-Order Costing

Luxguard Home Paint Company produces exterior latex paint, which it sells in one-gallon containers. The company has two processing departments—Base Fab and Finishing. White paint, which is used as a base for all the company's paints, is mixed from raw ingredients in the Base Fab Department. Pigments are then added to the basic white paint, the pigmented paint is squirted under pressure into one-gallon containers, and the containers are labeled and packed for shipping in the Finishing Department. Information relating to the company's operations for April follows:

a. Raw materials were issued for use in production: Base Fab Department, $851,000; and Finishing Department, $629,000.
b. Direct labor costs were incurred: Base Fab Department, $330,000; and Finishing Department, $270,000.
c. Manufacturing overhead cost was applied: Base Fab Department, $665,000; and Finishing Department, $405,000.
d. Basic white paint was transferred from the Base Fab Department to the Finishing Department, $1,850,000.
e. Paint that had been prepared for shipping was transferred from the Finishing Department to Finished Goods, $3,200,000.

Required:

1. Prepare journal entries to record items (a) through (e) above.
2. Post the journal entries from (1) above to T-accounts. The balance in the Base Fab Department's Work in Process account on April 1 was $150,000; the balance in the Finishing Department's Work in Process account was $70,000. After posting entries to the T-accounts, find the ending balance in each department's Work in Process account.
3. Prepare a production report for the Base Fab Department for April. The following additional information is available regarding production in the Base Fab Department during April:

Production data:	
Units (gallons) in process, April 1: materials 100% complete, labor and overhead 60% complete	30,000
Units (gallons) started into production during April	420,000
Units (gallons) completed and transferred to the Finishing Department	370,000
Units (gallons) in process, April 30: materials 50% complete, labor and overhead 25% complete	80,000
Cost data:	
Work in process inventory, April 1:	
Materials	$ 92,000
Labor	21,000
Overhead	37,000
Total cost of work in process	$ 150,000
Cost added during April:	
Materials	$ 851,000
Labor	330,000
Overhead	665,000
Total cost added during April	$1,846,000

Solution to Review Problem

1. a.	Work in Process—Base Fab Department	851,000	
	Work in Process—Finishing Department	629,000	
	Raw Materials		1,480,000
b.	Work in Process—Base Fab Department	330,000	
	Work in Process—Finishing Department	270,000	
	Salaries and Wages Payable		600,000
c.	Work in Process—Base Fab Department	665,000	
	Work in Process—Finishing Department	405,000	
	Manufacturing Overhead		1,070,000

d.	Work in Process—Finishing Department	1,850,000	
	Work in Process—Base Fab Department		1,850,000
e.	Finished Goods	3,200,000	
	Work in Process—Finishing Department		3,200,000

2.

Raw Materials

Bal.	XXX	1,480,000	(a)

Salaries and Wages Payable

		600,000	(b)

Work in Process—Base Fab Department

Bal.	150,000	1,850,000	(d)
(a)	851,000		
(b)	330,000		
(c)	665,000		
Bal.	146,000		

Manufacturing Overhead

(Various actual costs)		1,070,000	(c)

Work in Process—Finishing Department

Bal.	70,000	3,200,000	(e)
(a)	629,000		
(b)	270,000		
(c)	405,000		
(d)	1,850,000		
Bal.	24,000		

Finished Goods

Bal.	XXX		
(e)	3,200,000		

3.

LUXGUARD HOME PAINT COMPANY
Production Report—Base Fab Department
For the Month Ended April 30

Quantity Schedule and Equivalent Units	Quantity Schedule			
Units (gallons) to be accounted for:				
Work in process, April 1 (materials 100% complete, labor and overhead 60% complete)	30,000			
Started into production	420,000			
Total units to be accounted for	450,000			
		Equivalent Units (EU)		
		Materials	Labor	Overhead
Units (gallons) accounted for as follows:				
Transferred to Finishing Department	370,000	370,000	370,000	370,000
Work in process, April 30 (materials 50% complete, labor and overhead 25% complete)	80,000	40,000*	20,000*	20,000*
Total units accounted for	450,000	410,000	390,000	390,000

Costs per Equivalent Unit	Total Cost	Materials		Labor		Overhead		Whole Unit
Cost to be accounted for:								
Work in process, April 1	$ 150,000	$ 92,000		$ 21,000		$ 37,000		
Cost added by the Base Fab Department	1,846,000	851,000		330,000		665,000		
Total cost to be accounted for (a)	$1,996,000	$ 943,000		$351,000		$702,000		
Equivalent units of production (b)		410,000		390,000		390,000		
Cost per EU, (a) ÷ (b)		$2.30	+	$0.90	+	$1.80	=	$5.00

Cost Reconciliation	Total Cost	Equivalent Units (above) Materials	Labor	Overhead
Cost accounted for as follows:				
Transferred to Finishing Department:				
370,000 units × $5.00 per unit	$1,850,000	370,000	370,000	370,000
Work in process, April 30:				
Materials, at $2.30 per EU	92,000	40,000		
Labor, at $0.90 per EU	18,000		20,000	
Overhead, at $1.80 per EU	36,000			20,000
Total work in process	146,000			
Total cost accounted for	$1,996,000			

*Materials: 80,000 units × 50% = 40,000 EUs; labor and overhead: 80,000 units × 25% = 20,000 EUs.
EU = Equivalent unit.

Glossary

Conversion cost Direct labor cost plus manufacturing overhead cost. (p. 153)

Cost reconciliation The part of a department's production report that shows costs to be accounted for during a period and how those costs are accounted for. (p. 156)

Equivalent units The product of the number of partially completed units and their percentage of completion with respect to a particular cost. Equivalent units are the number of complete whole units one could obtain from the materials and effort contained in partially completed units. (p. 152)

Equivalent units of production (weighted-average method) The units transferred to the next department (or to finished goods) during the period plus the equivalent units in the department's ending work in process inventory. (p. 152)

FIFO method A method of accounting for cost flows in a process costing system in which equivalent units and unit costs relate only to work done during the current period. (p. 152)

Operation costing A hybrid costing system used when products are manufactured in batches and when the products have some common characteristics and some individual characteristics. This system handles materials the same as in job-order costing and labor and overhead the same as in process costing. (p. 159)

Process costing A costing method used in situations where essentially homogeneous products are produced on a continuous basis. (p. 146)

Processing department Any part of an organization where work is performed on a product and where materials, labor, or overhead costs are added to the product. (p. 147)

Production report A report that summarizes all activity in a department's Work in Process account during a period and that contains three parts: a quantity schedule and a computation of equivalent units, a computation of total and unit costs, and a cost reconciliation. (p. 147)

Quantity schedule The part of a production report that shows the flow of units through a department during a period and a computation of equivalent units. (p. 155)

Transferred-in cost The cost attached to products that have been received from a prior processing department. (p. 148)

Weighted-average method A method of process costing that blends together units and costs from both the current and prior periods. (p. 152)

Appendix 4A: FIFO Method

The FIFO method of process costing differs from the weighted-average method in two ways: (1) the computation of equivalent units, and (2) the way in which costs of beginning inventory are treated in the cost reconciliation report. The FIFO method is generally considered more accurate than the weighted-average method, but it is more complex. The complexity is not a problem for computers, but the FIFO method is a little more difficult to understand and to learn than the weighted-average method.

Equivalent Units—FIFO Method

LEARNING OBJECTIVE 6
Compute the equivalent units of production using the FIFO method.

The computation of equivalent units under the FIFO method differs from the computation under the weighted-average method in two ways.

First, the "units transferred out" is divided into two parts. One part consists of the units from the beginning inventory that were completed and transferred out, and the other part consists of the units that were both *started* and *completed* during the current period.

Second, full consideration is given to the amount of work expended during the current period on units in the *beginning* work in process inventory as well as on units in the ending inventory. Thus, under the FIFO method, both beginning and ending inventories are converted to an equivalent units basis. For the beginning inventory, the equivalent units represent the work done to *complete* the units; for the ending inventory, the equivalent units represent the work done to bring the units to a stage of partial completion at the end of the period (the same as with the weighted-average method):

The formula for computing the equivalent units of production under the FIFO method is more complex than under the weighted-average method:

FIFO Method
(a separate calculation is made for each cost category in each processing department)

Equivalent units of production = Equivalent units to complete beginning inventory*
+ Units started and completed during the period
+ Equivalent units in ending work in process inventory

$$\text{*Equivalent units to complete beginning inventory} = \text{Units in beginning inventory} \times \left(100\% - \text{Percentage completion of beginning inventory}\right)$$

Or, the equivalent units of production can also be determined as follows:

Equivalent units of production = Units transferred out
+ Equivalent units in ending work in process inventory
− Equivalent units in beginning inventory

To illustrate the FIFO method, refer again to the data for the Shaping and Milling Department at Double Diamond Skis. The department completed and transferred 4,800 units to the next department, the Graphics Application Department, during May. Since 200 of these units came from the beginning inventory, the Shaping and Milling Department must have started and completed 4,600 units during May. The 200 units in the beginning inventory were 55% complete with respect to materials and only 30% complete with respect to conversion costs when the month started. Thus, to complete these units the department must have added another 45% of materials costs (100% − 55% = 45%) and another 70% of conversion costs (100% − 30% = 70%). Following this line of reasoning, the equivalent units for the department for May would be computed as shown in Exhibit 4A–1 (page 164).

Comparison of Equivalent Units of Production under the Weighted-Average and FIFO Methods

Stop at this point and compare the data in Exhibit 4A–1 with the data in Exhibit 4–5 in the chapter, which shows the computation of equivalent units under the weighted-average method. Also refer to Exhibit 4A–2 (page 164), which compares the two methods.

EXHIBIT 4A–1
Equivalent Units of Production: FIFO Method

	Materials	Conversion
Work in process, May 1:		
200 units × (100% − 55%)*	90	
200 units × (100% − 30%)*		140
Units started and completed in May	4,600†	4,600†
Work in process, May 31:		
400 units × 40%	160	
400 units × 25%		100
Equivalent units of production	4,850	4,840

*This is the work needed to complete the units in beginning inventory.
†5,000 units started − 400 units in ending work in process = 4,600 units started and completed. The FIFO method assumes that the units in beginning inventory are finished first.

EXHIBIT 4A–2
Visual Perspective of Equivalent Units of Production

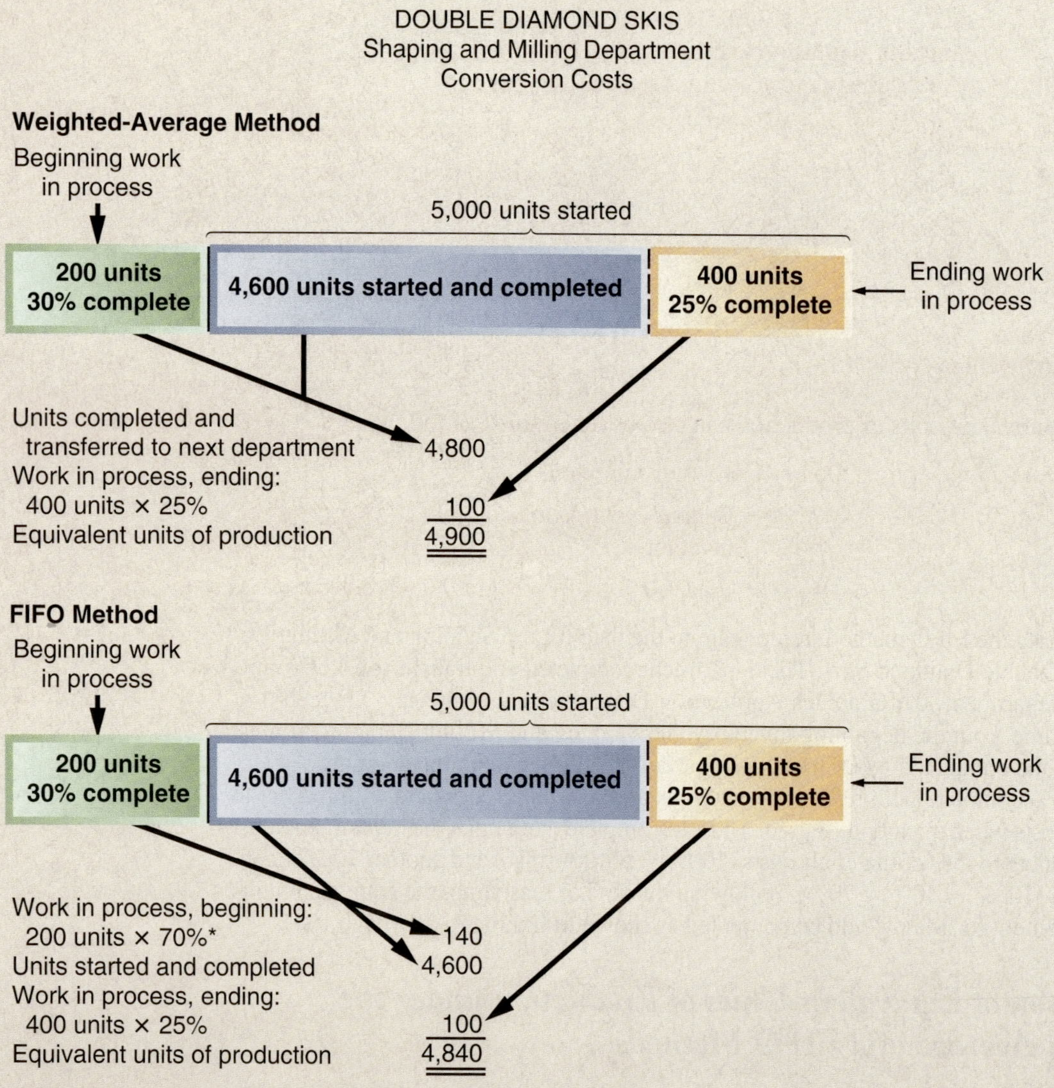

* 100% – 30% = 70%. This 70% represents the work needed to complete the units in the beginning inventory.

The essential difference between the two methods is that the weighted-average method blends work and costs from the prior period with work and costs in the current period, whereas the FIFO method separates the two periods. To see this more clearly, consider the following reconciliation of the two calculations of equivalent units:

Shaping and Milling Department	Materials	Conversion
Equivalent units—weighted-average method	4,960	4,900
Less equivalent units in beginning inventory:		
200 units × 55%	110	
200 units × 30%		60
Equivalent units of production—FIFO method	4,850	4,840

From the above, it is evident that the FIFO method removes the equivalent units that were already in beginning inventory from the equivalent units as defined using the weighted-average method. Thus, the FIFO method isolates the equivalent units due to work performed during the current period. The weighted-average method blends together the equivalent units already in beginning inventory with the equivalent units due to work performed in the current period.

Production Report—FIFO Method

LEARNING OBJECTIVE 7
Prepare a quantity schedule using the FIFO method.

The steps followed in preparing a production report under the FIFO method are the same as those discussed earlier for the weighted-average method. However, since the FIFO method makes a distinction between units in the beginning inventory and units started during the year, the cost reconciliation portion of the report is more complex under the FIFO method than it is under the weighted-average method. To illustrate the FIFO method, we will again use the data for Double Diamond Skis on page.

Step 1: Prepare a Quantity Schedule and Compute the Equivalent Units

There is only one difference between a quantity schedule prepared under the FIFO method and one prepared under the weighted-average method. This difference relates to units transferred out. As explained earlier in our discussion of equivalent units, the FIFO method divides units transferred out into two parts. One part consists of the units in the beginning inventory, and the other part consists of the units started and completed during the current period. A quantity schedule showing this format for units transferred out is presented in Exhibit 4A–3, along with a computation of equivalent units for the month.

LEARNING OBJECTIVE 8
Compute the costs per equivalent unit using the FIFO method.

We explained earlier that in computing equivalent units under the FIFO method, we must first show the amount of work required *to complete* the units in the beginning inventory. We then show the number of units started and completed during the period, and finally we show the amount of work *completed* on the units still in process at the end of the period. Carefully trace through these computations in Exhibit 4A–3.

Step 2: Compute the Costs per Equivalent Unit In computing unit costs under the FIFO method, we use only those costs that were incurred during the current period, and we ignore any costs in the beginning work in process inventory. Under the FIFO method, *unit costs relate only to work done during the current period.*

The costs per equivalent unit (EU) computed in Exhibit 4A–3 are used to cost units of product transferred to the next department; in addition, they are used to show the cost of partially completed units in the ending work in process inventory.

LEARNING OBJECTIVE 9
Prepare a cost reconciliation using the FIFO method.

Step 3: Prepare a Cost Reconciliation The purpose of cost reconciliation is to show how the costs charged to a department during a period are accounted for. With the FIFO method, two cost elements are associated with the units in the beginning work in process inventory. The first element is the cost carried over from the prior period. The second element is the cost needed *to complete* these units. For the Shaping and Milling

EXHIBIT 4A–3
Production Report—FIFO Method

DOUBLE DIAMOND SKIS
Shaping and Milling Department Production Report
(FIFO Method)

Quantity Schedule and Equivalent Units	Quantity Schedule			
Units to be accounted for:				
Work in process, May 1 (materials 55% complete; conversion 30% complete)	200			
Started into production	5,000			
Total units to be accounted for	5,200			
		Equivalent Units (EU)		
		Materials	Conversion	
Units accounted for as follows:				
Transferred to the next department:				
From the beginning inventory*	200	90	140	
Started and completed this month†	4,600	4,600	4,600	
Work in process, May 31 (materials 40% complete; conversion 25% complete)‡	400	160	100	
Total units accounted for	5,200	4,850	4,840	
Costs per Equivalent Unit	Total Cost	Materials	Conversion	Whole Unit
Cost to be accounted for:				
Work in process, May 1	$ 15,175			
Cost added in the department (a)	719,500	$368,600	$350,900	
Total cost to be accounted for	$734,675			
Equivalent units (b)		4,850	4,840	
Cost per EU, (a) ÷ (b)		$76.00	+ $72.50	= $148.50
		Equivalent Units (above)		
Cost Reconciliation	Total Cost	Materials	Conversion	
Cost accounted for as follows:				
Transferred to the next department:				
From the beginning inventory:				
Cost in the beginning inventory	$ 15,175			
Cost to complete these units:				
Materials, at $76.00 per EU	6,840	90*		
Conversion, at $72.50 per EU	10,150		140*	
Total cost from beginning inventory	32,165			
Units started and completed this month, at $148.50 per unit	683,100	4,600	4,600	
Total cost transferred to the next department	715,265			
Work in process, May 31:				
Materials, at $76.00 per EU	12,160	160‡		
Conversion, at $72.50 per EU	7,250		100‡	
Total work in process, May 31	19,410			
Total cost accounted for	$734,675			

*Materials: 200 units × (100% − 55%) = 90 EUs. Conversion: 200 units × (100% − 30%) = 140 EUs.
†5,000 units started − 400 units in ending work in process inventory = 4,600 units started and completed.
‡Materials: 400 units × 40% = 160 EUs. Conversion: 400 units × 25% = 100 EUs.
EU = Equivalent unit.

Department, $15,175 in cost was carried over from last month. In the cost reconciliation in Exhibit 4A–3, we add to this figure the $6,840 in materials cost and $10,150 in conversion cost needed to complete these units. Note from the exhibit that these materials and conversion cost figures are computed by multiplying the costs per equivalent unit for materials and conversion times the equivalent units of work needed *to complete* the items that were in the beginning inventory. (The equivalent units figures used in this computation are brought down from the "Equivalent units" portion of the production report.)

For units started and completed during the month, we simply multiply the number of units started and completed by the cost per whole unit to determine the amount transferred out. This would be $683,100 (4,600 units × $148.50 per unit = $683,100) for the department.

Finally, the amount of cost attached to the ending work in process inventory is computed by multiplying the cost per equivalent unit figures for the month times the equivalent units for materials and conversion costs in the ending inventory. Once again, the equivalent units needed for this computation are brought down from the "Equivalent units" portion of the production report.

Exhibit 4A–4 summarizes the major similarities and differences between production reports prepared under the weighted-average and FIFO methods.

A Comparison of Costing Methods

In most situations, the weighted-average and FIFO methods will produce very similar unit costs. If there never are any ending inventories, as in an ideal JIT environment, the two methods will produce identical results. The reason for this is that without any ending inventories, no costs can be carried forward into the next period and the weighted-average

EXHIBIT 4A–4
A Comparison of Production Report Content

Weighted-Average Method	FIFO Method
Quantity Schedule and Equivalent Units	
1. The quantity schedule includes all units transferred out in a single figure.	1. The quantity schedule separates the units transferred out into two parts. One part consists of units in the beginning inventory, and the other part consists of units started and completed during the current period.
2. In computing equivalent units, the units in the beginning inventory are treated as if they were started and completed during the current period.	2. Only work needed to *complete* units in the beginning inventory is included in the computation of equivalent units. Units started and completed during the current period are shown as a separate figure.
Total and Unit Costs	
1. The "Cost to be accounted for" part of the report is the same for both methods.	1. The "Cost to be accounted for" part of the report is the same for both methods.
2. Costs in the beginning inventory are added in with costs of the current period in computations of costs per equivalent unit.	2. Only costs of the current period are included in computations of costs per equivalent unit.
Cost Reconciliation	
1. All units transferred out are treated the same, regardless of whether they were part of the beginning inventory or started and completed during the period.	1. Units transferred out are divided into two groups: (a) units in the beginning inventory, and (b) units started and completed during the period.
2. Units in the ending inventory have cost applied to them in the same way under both methods.	2. Units in the ending inventory have cost applied to them in the same way under both methods.

method will base the unit costs on just the current period's costs—just as in the FIFO method. If there *are* ending inventories, either erratic input prices or erratic production levels would also be required to generate much of a difference in unit costs under the two methods. This is because the weighted-average method will blend the unit costs from the prior period with the unit costs of the current period. Unless these unit costs differ greatly, the blending will not make much difference.

Nevertheless, from the standpoint of cost control, the FIFO method is superior to the weighted-average method. Current performance should be measured in relation to costs of the current period only, and the weighted-average method mixes costs of the current period with costs of the prior period. Thus, under the weighted-average method, the manager's apparent performance in the current period is influenced by what happened in the prior period. This problem does not arise under the FIFO method, since it makes a clear distinction between costs of prior periods and costs incurred during the current period. For the same reason, the FIFO method also provides more up-to-date cost data for decision-making purposes.

On the other hand, the weighted-average method is simpler to apply than the FIFO method, but computers can handle the additional calculations with ease once they have been appropriately programmed.

Questions

4–1 Under what conditions would it be appropriate to use a process costing system?

4–2 In what ways are job-order and process costing similar?

4–3 Costs are accumulated by job in a job-order costing system; how are costs accumulated in a process costing system?

4–4 What two essential features characterize any processing department in a process costing system?

4–5 Why is cost accumulation easier in a process costing system than it is in a job-order costing system?

4–6 How many Work in Process accounts are maintained in a company using process costing?

4–7 Assume that a company has two processing departments—Mixing and Firing. Prepare a journal entry to show a transfer of partially completed units from the Mixing Department to the Firing Department.

4–8 Assume again that a company has two processing departments—Mixing followed by Firing. Explain what costs might be added to the Firing Department's Work in Process account during a period.

4–9 What is meant by the term *equivalent units of production* when the weighted-average method is used?

4–10 What is a quantity schedule, and what purpose does it serve?

4–11 Under process costing, it is often suggested that a product is like a rolling snowball as it moves from department to department. Why is this an apt comparison?

4–12 Watkins Trophies, Inc., produces thousands of medallions made of bronze, silver, and gold. The medallions are identical except for the materials used in their manufacture. What costing system would you advise the company to use?

4–13 Give examples of companies that might use operation costing.

4–14 (Appendix 4A) How does the computation of equivalent units under the FIFO method differ from the computation of equivalent units under the weighted-average method?

4–15 (Appendix 4A) On the cost reconciliation part of the production report, the weighted-average method treats all units transferred out in the same way. How does this differ from the FIFO method of handling units transferred out?

4–16 (Appendix 4A) From the standpoint of cost control, why is the FIFO method superior to the weighted-average method?

Exercises

EXERCISE 4–1 Process Costing Journal Entries [LO1]

Quality Brick Company produces bricks in two processing departments—Molding and Firing. Information relating to the company's operations in March follows:

a. Raw materials were issued for use in production: Molding Department, $23,000; and Firing Department, $8,000.
b. Direct labor costs were incurred: Molding Department, $12,000; and Firing Department, $7,000.
c. Manufacturing overhead was applied: Molding Department, $25,000; and Firing Department, $37,000.
d. Unfired, molded bricks were transferred from the Molding Department to the Firing Department. According to the company's process costing system, the cost of the unfired, molded bricks was $57,000.
e. Finished bricks were transferred from the Firing Department to the finished goods warehouse. According to the company's process costing system, the cost of the finished bricks was $103,000.
f. Finished bricks were sold to customers. According to the company's process costing system, the cost of the finished bricks sold was $101,000.

Required:

Prepare journal entries to record items (a) through (f) above.

EXERCISE 4–2 Computation of Equivalent Units—Weighted-Average Method [LO2]

Clonex Labs, Inc., uses a process costing system. The following data are available for one department for October:

		Percent Completed	
	Units	Materials	Conversion
Work in process, October 1 . . .	30,000	65%	30%
Work in process, October 31 . .	15,000	80%	40%

The department started 175,000 units into production during the month and transferred 190,000 completed units to the next department.

Required:

Compute the equivalent units of production for October assuming that the company uses the weighted-average method of accounting for units and costs.

EXERCISE 4–3 (Appendix 4A) Computation of Equivalent Units—FIFO Method [LO6]

Refer to the data for Clonex Labs, Inc., in Exercise 4–2.

Required:

Compute the equivalent units of production for October assuming that the company uses the FIFO method of accounting for units and costs.

EXERCISE 4–4 Preparation of Quantity Schedule—Weighted-Average Method [LO3]

Hielta Oy, a Finnish company, processes wood pulp for various manufacturers of paper products. Data relating to tons of pulp processed during June are provided below:

		Percent Completed	
	Tons of Pulp	Materials	Labor and Overhead
Work in process, June 1	20,000	90%	80%
Work in process, June 30	30,000	60%	40%
Started into production during June	190,000		

Required:

1. Compute the number of tons of pulp completed and transferred out during June.
2. Prepare a quantity schedule for June assuming that the company uses the weighted-average method.

EXERCISE 4–5 (Appendix 4A) Preparation of Quantity Schedule—FIFO Method [LO7]
Refer to the data for Hielta Oy in Exercise 4–4.

Required:
1. Compute the number of tons of pulp completed and transferred out during June.
2. Prepare a quantity schedule for June assuming that the company uses the FIFO method.

EXERCISE 4–6 Cost per Equivalent Unit—Weighted-Average Method [LO4]
Superior Micro Products uses the weighted-average method in its process costing system. Data for the Assembly Department for May appear below:

	Materials	Labor	Overhead
Work in process, May 1	$ 18,000	$ 5,500	$ 27,500
Cost added during May	$238,900	$80,300	$401,500
Equivalent units of production	35,000	33,000	33,000

Required:
1. Compute the cost per equivalent unit for materials, for labor, and for overhead.
2. Compute the total cost per equivalent whole unit.

EXERCISE 4–7 Cost Reconciliation—Weighted-Average Method [LO5]
Superior Micro Products uses the weighted-average method in its process costing system. During January, the Delta Assembly Department completed its processing of 25,000 units and transferred them to the next department. The cost of beginning inventory and the costs added during January amounted to $599,780 in total. The ending inventory in January consisted of 3,000 units, which were 80% complete with respect to materials and 60% complete with respect to labor and overhead. The costs per equivalent unit for the month were as follows:

	Materials	Labor	Overhead
Cost per equivalent unit	$12.50	$3.20	$6.40

Required:
1. Compute the total cost per equivalent unit for the month.
2. Compute the equivalent units of materials, labor, and overhead in the ending inventory for the month.
3. Prepare the cost reconciliation portion of the department's production report for January.

EXERCISE 4–8 (Appendix 4A) Cost per Equivalent Unit—FIFO Method [LO8]
Superior Micro Products uses the FIFO method in its process costing system. Data for the Assembly Department for May appear below:

	Materials	Labor	Overhead
Cost added during May	$193,320	$62,000	$310,000
Equivalent units of production	27,000	25,000	25,000

Required:
1. Compute the cost per equivalent unit for materials, labor, and overhead.
2. Compute the total cost per equivalent whole unit.

EXERCISE 4–9 (Appendix 4A) Cost Reconciliation—FIFO Method [LO9]
Jarvene Corporation uses the FIFO method in its process costing system. The following data are for the most recent month of operations in one of the company's processing departments:

Units in beginning inventory	400
Units started into production	3,000
Units in ending inventory	300
Units transferred to the next department	3,100

	Materials	Conversion
Percentage completion of beginning inventory	80%	40%
Percentage completion of ending inventory	70%	60%

The cost of beginning inventory according to the company's costing system was $11,040 and the costs added during the month amounted to $132,730. The costs per equivalent unit for the month were:

	Materials	Conversion
Cost per equivalent unit	$25.40	$18.20

Required:
1. Compute the total cost per equivalent unit for the month.
2. Compute the equivalent units of material and of conversion costs in the ending inventory.
3. Compute the equivalent units of material and of conversion costs that were required to complete the beginning inventory.
4. Determine the number of units started and completed during the month.
5. Prepare the cost reconciliation portion of the department's production report for the month.

EXERCISE 4–10 Process Costing Journal Entries [LO1]
Chocolaterie de Geneve, SA, is located in a French-speaking canton in Switzerland. The company makes chocolate truffles that are sold in popular embossed tins. The company has two processing departments—Cooking and Molding. In the Cooking Department, the raw ingredients for the truffles are mixed and then cooked in special candy-making vats. In the Molding Department, the melted chocolate and other ingredients from the Cooking Department are carefully poured into molds and decorative flourishes are applied by hand. After cooling, the truffles are packed for sale. The company uses a process costing system. The T-accounts below show the flow of costs through the two departments in April (all amounts are in Swiss francs):

Work in Process—Cooking

Balance 4/1	8,000	160,000	Transferred out
Direct materials	42,000		
Direct labor	50,000		
Overhead	75,000		

Work in Process—Molding

Balance 4/1	4,000	240,000	Transferred out
Transferred in	160,000		
Direct labor	36,000		
Overhead	45,000		

Required:
Prepare journal entries showing the flow of costs through the two processing departments during April.

EXERCISE 4–11 Quantity Schedule and Equivalent Units—Weighted-Average Method [LO2, LO3]
Alaskan Fisheries, Inc., processes salmon for various distributors. Two departments are involved—Cleaning and Packing. Data relating to pounds of salmon processed in the Cleaning Department during July are presented below:

	Pounds of Salmon	Percent Completed*
Work in process, July 1	20,000	30%
Started into production during July	380,000	—
Work in process, July 31	25,000	60%

*Labor and overhead only.

All materials are added at the beginning of processing in the Cleaning Department.

Required:

Prepare a quantity schedule and a computation of equivalent units for July for the Cleaning Department assuming that the company uses the weighted-average method of accounting for units.

EXERCISE 4–12 (Appendix 4A) Quantity Schedule and Equivalent Units—FIFO Method [LO6, LO7]
Refer to the data for Alaskan Fisheries, Inc., in Exercise 4–11.

Required:

Prepare a quantity schedule and a computation of equivalent units for July for the Cleaning Department assuming that the company uses the FIFO method of accounting for units.

EXERCISE 4–13 Equivalent Units and Cost per Equivalent Unit—Weighted-Average Method [LO2, LO4]
Helox, Inc., manufactures a product that passes through two production processes. A quantity schedule for the month of May for the first process follows:

	Quantity Schedule	Equivalent Units: Materials	Equivalent Units: Conversion
Units to be accounted for:			
Work in process, May 1 (materials 100% complete; conversion 40% complete)	5,000		
Started into production	180,000		
Total units to be accounted for	185,000		
Units accounted for as follows:			
Transferred to the next department	175,000	?	?
Work in process, May 31 (materials 100% complete; conversion 30% complete)	10,000	?	?
Total units accounted for	185,000	?	?

Costs in the beginning work in process inventory of the first processing department were: materials, $1,500; and conversion cost, $4,000. Costs added during the month were: materials, $54,000; and conversion cost, $352,000.

Required:

1. Assume that the company uses the weighted-average method of accounting for units and costs. Determine the equivalent units for the month for the first process.
2. Compute the costs per equivalent unit for the month for the first process.

EXERCISE 4–14 Cost Reconciliation—Weighted-Average Method [LO5]
(This exercise should be assigned only if Exercise 4–13 is also assigned.) Refer to the data for Helox, Inc., in Exercise 4–13 and to the equivalent units and costs per equivalent unit you have computed there.

Required:

Complete the following cost reconciliation for the first process:

Cost Reconciliation	Total Cost	Equivalent Units: Materials	Equivalent Units: Conversion
Cost accounted for as follows:			
Transferred to the next department: (? units × $? per unit)	$?		
Work in process, May 31:			
Materials, at _____ per EU	?	?	
Conversion, at _____ per EU	?		?
Total work in process, May 31	?		
Total cost accounted for	$?		

EXERCISE 4–15 (Appendix 4A) Quantity Schedule, Equivalent Units, Cost per Equivalent Unit—FIFO Method [LO6, LO7, LO8]

Refer to the data for Helox, Inc., in Exercise 4–13. Assume that the company uses the FIFO cost method.

Required:

1. Prepare a quantity schedule and a computation of equivalent units for the month for the first process.
2. Compute the costs per equivalent unit for the month for the first process.

EXERCISE 4–16 (Appendix 4A) Cost Reconciliation—FIFO Method [LO9]

(This exercise should be assigned only if Exercise 4–15 is also assigned.) Refer to the data for Helox, Inc., in Exercise 4–13 and to the equivalent units and costs per equivalent unit that you computed in Exercise 4–15.

Required:

Complete the following cost reconciliation for the first process:

	Total	Equivalent Units	
Cost Reconciliation	Cost	Materials	Conversion
Cost accounted for as follows:			
Transferred to the next department:			
From the beginning inventory:			
Cost in the beginning inventory	$?		
Cost to complete these units:			
Materials, at _____ per EU	?	?	
Conversion, at _____ per EU	?		?
Total cost from beginning inventory	?		
Units started and completed this month: _____ units × _____ per unit	?	?	?
Total cost transferred to the next department	?		
Work in process, May 31:			
Materials, at _____ per EU	?	?	
Conversion, at _____ per EU	?		?
Total work in process, May 31	?		
Total cost accounted for	$?		

EXERCISE 4–17 Quantity Schedule, Equivalent Units, and Cost per Equivalent Unit—Weighted-Average Method [LO2, LO3, LO4]

Pureform, Inc., manufactures a product that passes through two departments. Data for a recent month for the first department follow:

	Units	Materials	Labor	Overhead
Work in process, beginning	5,000	$4,320	$1,040	$1,790
Units started in process	45,000			
Units transferred out	42,000			
Work in process, ending	8,000			
Cost added during the month		$52,800	$21,500	$32,250

The beginning work in process inventory was 80% complete with respect to materials and 60% complete with respect to labor and overhead. The ending work in process inventory was 75% complete with respect to materials and 50% complete with respect to labor and overhead.

Required:

1. Assume that the company uses the weighted-average method of accounting for units and costs. Prepare a quantity schedule and a computation of equivalent units for the month for the first department.
2. Determine the costs per equivalent unit for the month.

EXERCISE 4–18 (Appendix 4A) Quantity Schedule, Equivalent Units, and Cost per Equivalent Unit—FIFO Method [LO6, LO7, LO8]
Refer to the data for Pureform, Inc., in Exercise 4–17.

Required:

1. Assume that the company uses the FIFO method of accounting for units and costs. Prepare a quantity schedule and a computation of equivalent units for the month for the first processing department.
2. Determine the costs per equivalent unit for the month.

Problems

PROBLEM 4–19 Step-by-Step Production Report—Weighted-Average Method [LO2, LO3, LO4, LO5]
Builder Products, Inc., manufactures a caulking compound that goes through three processing stages prior to completion. Information on work in the first department, Cooking, is given below for May:

Production data:	
Units in process, May 1; materials 100% complete; labor and overhead 80% complete	10,000
Units started into production during May	100,000
Units completed and transferred out	95,000
Units in process, May 31; materials 60% complete; labor and overhead 20% complete	?
Cost data:	
Work in process inventory, May 1:	
Materials cost	$1,500
Labor cost	$1,800
Overhead cost	$5,400
Cost added during May:	
Materials cost	$154,500
Labor cost	$22,700
Overhead cost	$68,100

Materials are added at several stages during the cooking process, whereas labor and overhead costs are incurred uniformly. The company uses the weighted-average method.

Required:

Prepare a production report for the Cooking Department for May. Use the following three steps in preparing your report:

1. Prepare a quantity schedule and a computation of equivalent units.
2. Compute the costs per equivalent unit for the month.
3. Using the data from (1) and (2) above, prepare a cost reconciliation.

PROBLEM 4–20 (Appendix 4A) Step-by-Step Production Report—FIFO Method [LO6, LO7, LO8, LO9]
Selzik Company makes super-premium cake mixes that go through two processing departments, Blending and Packaging. The following activity was recorded in the Blending Department during July:

eXcel

Production data:	
Units in process, July 1 (materials 100% complete; conversion 30% complete)	10,000
Units started into production	170,000
Units completed and transferred to Packaging	?
Units in process, July 31 (materials 100% complete; conversion 40% complete	20,000

continued

Cost data:		
Work in process inventory, July 1:		
Materials cost	$ 8,500	
Conversion cost	4,900	$ 13,400
Cost added during the month:		
Materials cost	139,400	
Conversion cost	244,200	383,600
Total cost		$397,000

All materials are added at the beginning of work in the Blending Department. The company uses the FIFO method.

Required:

Prepare a production report for the Blending Department for July. Use the following three steps as a guide in preparing your report:

1. Prepare a quantity schedule and compute the equivalent units.
2. Compute the costs per equivalent unit for the month.
3. Using the data from (1) and (2) above, prepare a cost reconciliation.

PROBLEM 4–21 Production Report—Weighted-Average Method [LO2, LO3, LO4, LO5]

Sunspot Beverages, Ltd., of Fiji makes blended tropical fruit drinks in two stages. Fruit juices are extracted from fresh fruits and then blended in the Blending Department. The blended juices are then bottled and packed for shipping in the Bottling Department. The following information pertains to the operations of the Blending Department for June. (The currency in Fiji is the Fijian dollar.)

Microsoft Excel - Problem 4-20 screen capture.xls

	A	B	C	D
1			*Percent Completed*	
2		*Units*	*Materials*	*Conversion*
3	Work in process, beginning	20,000	100%	75%
4	Started into production	180,000		
5	Completed and transferred out	160,000		
6	Work in process, ending	40,000	100%	25%
7				
8			*Materials*	*Conversion*
9	Work in process, beginning		$25,200	$24,800
10	Cost added during June		$334,800	$238,700
11				
12				

Required:

Prepare a production report for the Blending Department for June assuming that the company uses the weighted-average method.

PROBLEM 4–22 (Appendix 4A) Production Report—FIFO Method [LO6, LO7, LO8, LO9]

Refer to the data for the Blending Department of Sunspot Beverages, Ltd., in Problem 4–21. Assume that the company uses the FIFO method rather than the weighted-average method in its process costing.

Required:

Prepare a production report for the Blending Department for June.

PROBLEM 4–23 Analysis of Work in Process T-Account—Weighted-Average Method [LO2, LO3, LO4, LO5]

Weston Products manufactures an industrial cleaning compound that goes through three processing departments—Grinding, Mixing, and Cooking. All raw materials are introduced at the start of work in the Grinding Department. The Work in Process T-account for the Grinding Department for a recent month is given below:

Work in Process—Grinding Department

Inventory, May 1 (18,000 pounds, labor and overhead 1/3 complete)	21,800	?	Completed and transferred to mixing (? pounds)
May costs added:			
Raw materials (167,000 pounds)	133,400		
Labor and overhead	226,800		
Inventory, May 31 (15,000 pounds, labor and overhead 2/3 complete)	?		

The May 1 work in process inventory consists of $14,600 in materials cost and $7,200 in labor and overhead cost. The company uses the weighted-average method to account for units and costs.

Required:

1. Prepare a production report for the Grinding Department for the month.
2. What criticism can be made of the unit costs that you have computed on your production report if they are used to evaluate how well costs have been controlled?

PROBLEM 4–24 (Appendix 4A) Analysis of Work in Process T-Account—FIFO Method [LO6, LO7, LO8, LO9]

Superior Brands, Inc., manufactures paint. The paint goes through three processing departments—Cracking, Mixing, and Cooking. Activity in the Cracking Department during a recent month is summarized in the department's Work in Process account below:

Work in Process—Cracking Department

Inventory, April 1 (10,000 gallons, labor and overhead 80% complete)	39,000	?	Completed and transferred to mixing (? gallons)
April costs added:			
Materials (140,000 gallons)	259,000		
Labor and overhead	312,000		
Inventory, April 30 (30,000 gallons, labor and overhead 60% complete)	?		

The materials are added at the beginning of work in the Cracking Department. The company uses the FIFO method.

Required:

Prepare a production report for the Cracking Department for the month.

PROBLEM 4–25 Interpreting a Production Report—Weighted-Average Method [LO2, LO3, LO4]

Cooperative San José of southern Sonora state in Mexico makes a unique syrup using cane sugar and local herbs. The syrup is sold in small bottles and is prized as a flavoring for drinks and for use in desserts. The bottles are sold for $12 each. (The Mexican currency is the peso and is denoted by $.) The first stage in the production process is carried out in the Mixing Department, which removes foreign matter from the raw materials and mixes them in the proper proportions in large vats. The company uses the weighted-average method in its process costing system.

A hastily prepared report for the Mixing Department for April appears below:

Quantity Schedule	
Units to be accounted for:	
Work in process, April 1 (materials 90% complete; conversion 80% complete)	30,000
Started into production	200,000
Total units to be accounted for	230,000

continued

Units accounted for as follows:	
Transferred to next department	190,000
Work in process, April 30 (materials 75% complete; conversion 60% complete)	40,000
Total units accounted for	230,000
Total Cost	
Cost to be accounted for:	
Work in process, April 1	$ 98,000
Cost added during the month	827,000
Total cost to be accounted for	$925,000
Cost Reconciliation	
Cost accounted for as follows:	
Transferred to next department	$805,600
Work in process, April 30	119,400
Total cost accounted for	$925,000

Cooperative San José has just been acquired by another company, and the management of the acquiring company wants some additional information about Cooperative San José's operations.

Required:

1. What were the equivalent units for the month?
2. What were the costs per equivalent unit for the month? The beginning inventory consisted of the following costs: materials, $67,800; and conversion cost, $30,200. The costs added during the month consisted of: materials, $579,000; and conversion cost, $248,000.
3. How many of the units transferred to the next department were started and completed during the month?
4. The manager of the Mixing Department, anxious to make a good impression on the new owners, stated, "Materials prices jumped from about $2.50 per unit in March to $3 per unit in April, but due to good cost control I was able to hold our materials cost to less than $3 per unit for the month." Should this manager be rewarded for good cost control? Explain.

PROBLEM 4–26 Comprehensive Process Costing Problem—Weighted-Average Method [LO1, LO2, LO3, LO4, LO5]

Lubricants, Inc., produces a special kind of grease that is widely used by race car drivers. The grease is produced in two processing departments: Refining and Blending. Raw materials are introduced at various points in the Refining Department.

The following incomplete Work in Process account is available for the Refining Department for March:

Work in Process—Refining Department

March 1 inventory (20,000 gallons; materials 100% complete; labor and overhead 90% complete)	38,000	?	Completed and transferred to blending (? gallons)
March costs added:			
Raw oil materials (390,000 gallons)	495,000		
Direct labor	72,000		
Overhead	181,000		
March 31 inventory (40,000 gallons; materials 75% complete; labor and overhead 25% complete)	?		

The March 1 work in process inventory in the Refining Department consists of the following cost elements: raw materials, $25,000; direct labor, $4,000; and overhead, $9,000.

Costs incurred during March in the Blending Department were: materials used, $115,000; direct labor, $18,000; and overhead cost applied to production, $42,000. The company uses the weighted-average method in its process costing.

Required:

1. Prepare journal entries to record the costs incurred in both the Refining Department and Blending Department during March. Key your entries to the items (a) through (g) below.
   a. Raw materials were issued for use in production.
   b. Direct labor costs were incurred.
   c. Manufacturing overhead costs for the entire factory were incurred, $225,000. (Credit Accounts Payable.)
   d. Manufacturing overhead cost was applied to production using a predetermined overhead rate.
   e. Units that were complete with respect to processing in the Refining Department were transferred to the Blending Department, $740,000.
   f. Units that were complete with respect to processing in the Blending Department were transferred to Finished Goods, $950,000.
   g. Completed units were sold on account, $1,500,000. The Cost of Goods Sold was $900,000.
2. Post the journal entries from (1) above to T-accounts. The following account balances existed at the beginning of March. (The beginning balance in the Refining Department's Work in Process account is given above.)

Raw Materials	$618,000
Work in Process—Blending Department	$65,000
Finished Goods	$20,000

   After posting the entries to the T-accounts, find the ending balance in the inventory accounts and the manufacturing overhead account.
3. Prepare a production report for the Refining Department for March.

PROBLEM 4–27 Equivalent Units; Costing of Inventories; Journal Entries—Weighted-Average Method [LO1, LO2, LO4]

You are employed by Spirit Company, a manufacturer of digital watches. The company's chief financial officer is trying to verify the accuracy of the ending work in process and finished goods inventories prior to closing the books for the year. You have been asked to assist in this verification. The year-end balances shown on Spirit Company's books are as follows:

	Units	Costs
Work in process, December 31 (labor and overhead 50% complete)	300,000	$660,960
Finished goods, December 31	200,000	$1,009,800

Materials are added to production at the beginning of the manufacturing process, and overhead is applied to each product at the rate of 60% of direct labor cost. There was no finished goods inventory at the beginning of the year. A review of Spirit Company's inventory and cost records has disclosed the following data:

		Costs	
	Units	Materials	Labor
Work in process, January 1 (labor and overhead 80% complete)	200,000	$200,000	$315,000
Units started into production	1,000,000		
Cost added during the year:			
Materials cost		$1,300,000	
Labor cost			$1,995,000
Units completed during the year	900,000		

The company uses the weighted-average method.

Required:

1. Determine the equivalent units and costs per equivalent unit for materials, labor, and overhead for the year.

2. Determine the amount of cost that should be assigned to the ending work in process and finished goods inventories.
3. Prepare the necessary correcting journal entry to adjust the work in process and finished goods inventories to the correct balances as of December 31.
4. Determine the cost of goods sold for the year assuming there is no under- or overapplied overhead.

(CPA, adapted)

PROBLEM 4–28 Comprehensive Process Costing Problem—Weighted-Average Method [LO1, LO2, LO3, LO4, LO5]

Hilox, Inc., produces an antacid product that goes through two departments—Cooking and Bottling. The company has recently hired a new assistant accountant, who has prepared the following summary of production and costs for the Cooking Department for May using the weighted-average method.

Cooking Department costs:	
Work in process inventory, May 1: 70,000 quarts, materials 60% complete, labor and overhead 30% complete	$ 61,000*
Materials added during May	570,000
Labor added during May	100,000
Overhead applied during May	235,000
Total departmental costs	$966,000
Cooking Department costs assigned to:	
Quarts completed and transferred to the Bottling Department: 400,000 quarts at ? per quart	$?
Work in process inventory, May 31: 50,000 quarts, materials 70% complete, labor and overhead 40% complete	?
Total departmental costs assigned	$?

*Consists of materials, $39,000; labor, $5,000; and overhead, $17,000.

The new assistant accountant has determined the cost per quart transferred to be $2.415, as follows:

$$\frac{\text{Total departmental costs, \$966,000}}{\text{Quarts completed and transferred, 400,000}} = \$2.415$$

However, the assistant accountant is unsure how to use this unit cost figure in assigning cost to the ending work in process inventory. In addition, the company's general ledger shows only $900,000 in cost transferred from the Cooking Department to the Bottling Department, which does not agree with the $966,000 figure above.

The general ledger also shows the following costs incurred in the Bottling Department during May: materials used, $130,000; direct labor cost incurred, $80,000; and overhead cost applied to products, $158,000.

Required:

1. Prepare journal entries as follows to record activity in the company during May. Key your entries to the letters (a) through (g) below.
   a. Raw materials were issued to the two departments for use in production.
   b. Direct labor costs were incurred in the two departments.
   c. Manufacturing overhead costs were incurred, $400,000. (Credit Accounts Payable.) The company maintains a single Manufacturing Overhead account for the entire plant.
   d. Manufacturing overhead cost was applied to production in each department using predetermined overhead rates.
   e. Units completed as to processing in the Cooking Department were transferred to the Bottling Department, $900,000.
   f. Units completed as to processing in the Bottling Department were transferred to Finished Goods, $1,300,000.
   g. Units were sold on account, $2,000,000. The Cost of Good Sold was $1,250,000.

2. Post the journal entries from (1) above to T-accounts. Balances in selected accounts on May 1 are given below:

Raw Materials	$710,000
Work in Process—Bottling Department	$85,000
Finished Goods	$45,000

After posting the entries to the T-accounts, find the ending balance in the inventory accounts and the Manufacturing Overhead account.

3. Prepare a production report for the Cooking Department for May.

Cases

CASE 4–29 Ethics and the Manager, Understanding the Impact of Percentage Completion on Profit—Weighted-Average Method [LO2, LO4, LO5]

Gary Stevens and Mary James are production managers in the Consumer Electronics Division of General Electronics Company, which has several dozen plants scattered in locations throughout the world. Mary manages the plant located in Des Moines, Iowa, while Gary manages the plant in El Segundo, California. Production managers are paid a salary and get an additional bonus equal to 5% of their base salary if the entire division meets or exceeds its target profits for the year. The bonus is determined in March after the company's annual report has been prepared and issued to stockholders.

Shortly after the beginning of the new year, Mary received a phone call from Gary that went like this:

Gary: How's it going, Mary?

Mary: Fine, Gary. How's it going with you?

Gary: Great! I just got the preliminary profit figures for the division for last year and we are within $200,000 of making the year's target profits. All we have to do is pull a few strings, and we'll be over the top!

Mary: What do you mean?

Gary: Well, one thing that would be easy to change is your estimate of the percentage completion of your ending work in process inventories.

Mary: I don't know if I can do that, Gary. Those percentage completion figures are supplied by Tom Winthrop, my lead supervisor, who I have always trusted to provide us with good estimates. Besides, I have already sent the percentage completion figures to corporate headquarters.

Gary: You can always tell them there was a mistake. Think about it, Mary. All of us managers are doing as much as we can to pull this bonus out of the hat. You may not want the bonus check, but the rest of us sure could use it.

The final processing department in Mary's production facility began the year with no work in process inventories. During the year, 210,000 units were transferred in from the prior processing department and 200,000 units were completed and sold. Costs transferred in from the prior department totaled $39,375,000. No materials are added in the final processing department. A total of $20,807,500 of conversion cost was incurred in the final processing department during the year.

Required:

1. Tom Winthrop estimated that the units in ending inventory in the final processing department were 30% complete with respect to the conversion costs of the final processing department. If this estimate of the percentage completion is used, what would be the Cost of Goods Sold for the year?
2. Does Gary Stevens want the estimated percentage completion to be increased or decreased? Explain why.
3. What percentage completion would result in increasing reported net operating income by $200,000 over the net operating income that would be reported if the 30% figure were used?
4. Do you think Mary James should go along with the request to alter estimates of the percentage completion?

CASE 4–30 Production Report of Second Department—Weighted-Average Method [LO2, LO3, LO4, LO5]

eXcel

"I think we goofed when we hired that new assistant controller," said Ruth Scarpino, president of Provost Industries. "Just look at this production report that he prepared for last month for the Finishing Department. I can't make heads or tails out of it."

Finishing Department costs:	
Work in process inventory, April 1, 450 units; materials 100% complete; conversion 60% complete	$ 8,208*
Costs transferred in during the month from the preceding department, 1,950 units	17,940
Materials cost added during the month (materials are added when processing is 50% complete in the Finishing Department)	6,210
Conversion costs incurred during the month	13,920
Total departmental costs	$46,278
Finishing Department costs assigned to:	
Units completed and transferred to finished goods, 1,800 units at $25.71 per unit	$46,278
Work in process inventory, April 30, 600 units; materials 0% complete; conversion 35% complete	0
Total departmental costs assigned	$46,278

*Consists of cost transferred in, $4,068; materials cost, $1,980; and conversion cost, $2,160.

"He's struggling to learn our system," replied Frank Harrop, the operations manager. "The problem is that he's been away from process costing for a long time, and it's coming back slowly."

"It's not just the format of his report that I'm concerned about. Look at that $25.71 unit cost that he's come up with for April. Doesn't that seem high to you?" said Ms. Scarpino.

"Yes, it does seem high; but on the other hand, I know we had an increase in materials prices during April, and that may be the explanation," replied Mr. Harrop. "I'll get someone else to redo this report and then we may be able to see what's going on."

Provost Industries manufactures a ceramic product that goes through two processing departments—Molding and Finishing. The company uses the weighted-average method in its process costing.

Required:

1. Prepare a revised production report for the Finishing Department.
2. Explain to the president why the unit cost on the new assistant controller's report is so high.

CASE 4–31 (Appendix 4A) Production Report of Second Department—FIFO Method [LO6, LO7, LO8, LO9]

Refer to the data for Provost Industries in the preceding case. Assume that the company uses the FIFO method to account for units and costs.

Required:

1. Prepare a production report for the Finishing Department for April.
2. As stated in the case, the company experienced an increase in materials prices during April. Would the effects of this price increase tend to show up more under the weighted-average method or under the FIFO method? Why?

Group and Internet Exercises

GROUP EXERCISE 4–32 Operation Costing

Operation costing combines characteristics of both job-order costing and process costing. It is used in those situations where the products have some common characteristics and also some individual characteristics. Examples of industries where operation costing may be appropriate include shoes, clothing, jewelry, and semiconductors.

Required:

Select one of the above products and research how the product is made. Construct a flowchart of the production process. Indicate which steps in the production process would use job-order costing and which steps would use process costing.

INTERNET EXERCISE 4–33

As you know, the World Wide Web is a medium that is constantly evolving. Sites come and go, and change without notice. To enable the periodic updating of site addresses, this problem has been posted to the textbook website (www.mhhe.com/garrison11e). After accessing the site, enter the Student Center and select this chapter. Select and complete the Internet exercise.

Chapter 5

Cost Behavior: Analysis and Use

LEARNING OBJECTIVES

After studying Chapter 5, you should be able to:

LO1 Understand how fixed and variable costs behave and how to use them to predict costs.

LO2 Use a scattergraph plot to diagnose cost behavior.

LO3 Analyze a mixed cost using the high-low method.

LO4 Prepare an income statement using the contribution format.

LO5 (Appendix 5A) Analyze a mixed cost using the least-squares regression method.

BUSINESS FOCUS

A Costly Mistake

After spending countless hours tracking down the hardware and fixtures he needed to restore his Queen Anne-style Victorian house, Stephen Gordon recognized an opportunity. He opened Restoration Hardware, Inc., a specialty store carrying antique hardware and fixtures. The company's products are described by some as nostalgic, old-fashioned, and obscure. Customers can shop at one of the many Restoration Hardware stores, by catalog, or online at the company's website www.restorationhardware.com.

1998 was a year of phenomenal growth and change for Restoration Hardware. Twenty-four new stores were opened, increasing the total number in the chain to 65. The company's newly launched catalog business was an instant success. Net sales approached $200 million, an increase of almost 114% from the prior year. Gordon, chairman and CEO, took the company public.

The success enjoyed by the company in 1998 did not recur in 1999. Gordon believes his biggest mistake was a failure to consider cost behavior when making decisions to promote the company's products. The most popular furniture items in the store were discounted during the first quarter to encourage customer interest. The company spent $1 million to advertise this big sale, which was far more "successful" than Gordon had imagined. Sales for the first quarter increased by 84% to $60 million. However, much of the increase arose from sales of discounted goods. As a result, margins (that is, differences between sale prices and the cost of the goods that were sold) were lower than usual. Further, because the items placed on sale were larger and heavier than average, the costs to move them from the distribution centers to the stores were considerably higher. The company ended up reporting a loss of $2.7 million for the quarter. ■

Sources: Restoration Hardware website July 2000; Stephen Gordon, "My Biggest Mistake," *Inc.*, September 1999, p. 103; Heather Chaplin, "Past? Perfect," *American Demographics*, May 1999, pp. 68–69.

In Chapter 2, we stated that costs can be classified by behavior. Cost behavior refers to how a cost will change as the level of activity changes. Managers who understand how costs behave can predict how costs will change under various alternatives. Conversely, managers who attempt to make decisions without a thorough understanding of cost behavior patterns can create disastrous consequences. For example, cutting back production of a particular product line might result in far less cost savings than managers had assumed if they confused fixed costs with variable costs—leading to a decline in profits. To avoid such problems, managers must be able to accurately predict what costs will be at various activity levels.

This chapter briefly reviews the definitions of variable and fixed costs and then discusses the behavior of these costs in greater depth than was done in Chapter 2. The chapter also introduces the concept of a mixed cost, which is a cost that has variable and fixed cost elements. The chapter concludes by introducing a new income statement format—called the *contribution format*—in which costs are organized by behavior rather than by the traditional functions of production, sales, and administration.

Types of Cost Behavior Patterns

Topic Tackler PLUS 5–1

In Chapter 2 we mentioned only variable and fixed costs. In this chapter we will examine a third cost behavior pattern, known as a *mixed* or *semivariable* cost. All three cost behavior patterns—variable, fixed, and mixed—are found in most organizations. The relative proportion of each type of cost in an organization is known as its **cost structure.** For example, an organization might have many fixed costs but few variable or mixed costs. Alternatively, it might have many variable costs but few fixed or mixed costs. In this chapter, we will concentrate on gaining a fuller understanding of the behavior of each type of cost. In the next chapter, we will explore how cost structure impacts decisions.

IN BUSINESS

COST STRUCTURE: A MANAGEMENT CHOICE

Some managers are thriftier than others. Kenneth Iverson built Nucor Steel into the most successful U.S. steel company of recent years by developing a whole new approach to steel-making using cost-efficient minimills. Iverson ran his company with few layers of management and a commitment to employees that everyone would be treated alike. Workers were "dissuaded from joining a union by high wages and a series of No's—no management dining rooms, no company yachts, no company planes, no first-class travel for executives, and no support staff to pamper the upper echelons." Iverson ran the largest steel company in the U.S. with only 20 people in his headquarters. "By responding to market signals, focusing on a single major product line, and treating his employees with respect and compassion, Mr. Iverson contributed immensely to the industrial rebirth in this country."

Source: Donald F. Barnett and Robert W. Crandall, "Remembering a Man of Steel," *The Wall Street Journal*, April 23, 2002, p. B4.

Variable Costs

LEARNING OBJECTIVE 1
Understand how fixed and variable costs behave and how to use them to predict costs.

We explained in Chapter 2 that a variable cost is a cost whose total dollar amount varies in direct proportion to changes in the activity level. If the activity level doubles, the total variable cost also doubles. If the activity level increases by only 10%, then the total variable cost increases by 10% as well.

IN BUSINESS

SELLING ONLINE

By making investments in technology, cutting edge companies have created radically different cost structures from traditional companies. John Labbett, the CFO of Onsale, an Internet auctioneer of discontinued computers, was previously employed at House of Fabrics, a traditional retailer. The two companies have roughly the same total revenues of about $250 million. However, House of Fabrics, with 5,500 employees, has a revenue per employee of about $90,000. At Onsale, with only 200 employees, the figure is $1.18 million per employee. Additionally, Internet companies like Onsale are often able to grow at very little cost. If demand grows, an Internet company may not have to do much more than just add another computer server. If demand grows at a traditional retailer, the company may have to invest in a new building and additional inventory and may have to hire additional employees.

Source: George Donnelly, "New @ttitude," *CFO*, June 1999, pp. 42–54.

We also found in Chapter 2 that a variable cost remains constant if expressed on a *per unit* basis. To provide an example, consider Nooksack Expeditions, a small company that provides daylong whitewater rafting excursions on rivers in the North Cascade Mountains. The company provides all of the necessary equipment and experienced guides, and it serves gourmet meals to its guests. The meals are purchased from an exclusive caterer for $30 a person for a daylong excursion. If we look at the cost of the meals on a *per person* basis, it remains constant at $30. This $30 cost per person will not change, regardless of how many people participate in a daylong excursion. The behavior of this variable cost, on both a per unit and a total basis, is tabulated as follows:

Number of Guests	Cost of Meals per Guest	Total Cost of Meals
250	$30	$7,500
500	$30	$15,000
750	$30	$22,500
1,000	$30	$30,000

The idea that a variable cost is constant per unit but varies in total with the activity level is crucial to understanding cost behavior patterns. We shall rely on this concept repeatedly in this chapter and in chapters ahead.

Exhibit 5–1 illustrates variable cost behavior. Note that the graph of the total cost of the meals slants upward to the right. This is because the total cost of the meals is directly proportional to the number of guests. In contrast, the graph of the per unit cost of meals is flat because the cost of the meals per guest is constant at $30.

The Activity Base For a cost to be variable, it must be variable *with respect to something*. That "something" is its *activity base*. An **activity base** is a measure of whatever causes the incurrence of variable cost. In Chapter 3, we mentioned that an activity base is sometimes referred to as a *cost driver*. Some of the most common activity bases are direct labor-hours, machine-hours, units produced, and units sold. Other examples of activity bases (cost drivers) include the number of miles driven by salespersons, the number of pounds of laundry cleaned by a hotel, the number of calls handled by technical support staff at a software company, and the number of beds occupied in a hospital.

To plan and control variable costs, a manager must be well acquainted with the organization's various activity bases. People sometimes get the notion that if a cost doesn't vary with production or with sales, then it is not a variable cost. This is not correct. As suggested by the range of bases listed above, costs are caused by many different activities within an organization. Whether a cost is variable or fixed depends on whether it is caused by the activity under consideration. For example, if a manager is analyzing the cost of service calls under a product warranty, the relevant activity measure will be the number of

EXHIBIT 5–1
Variable Cost Behavior

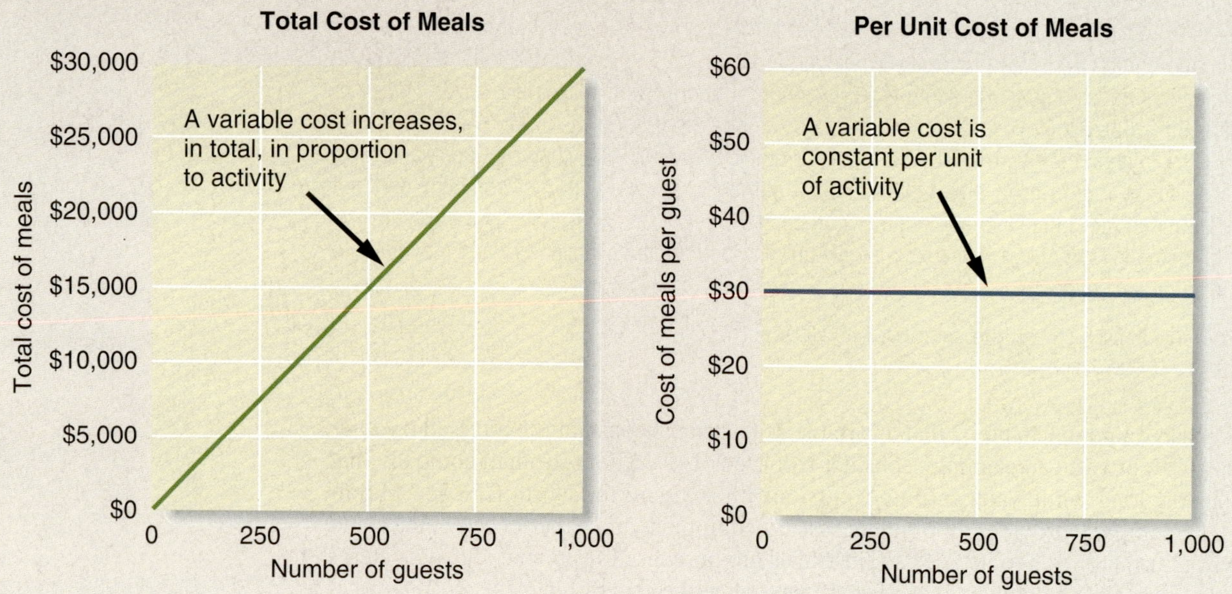

service calls made. Those costs that vary in total with the number of service calls made are the variable costs of making service calls.

Nevertheless, unless stated otherwise, you can assume that the activity base under consideration is the total volume of goods and services provided by the organization. So, for example, if we ask whether direct materials at Ford is a variable cost, the answer is yes, since the cost of direct materials is variable with respect to Ford's total volume of output. We will specify the activity base only when it is something other than total output.

IN BUSINESS

COPING WITH THE FALLOUT FROM SEPTEMBER 11

Costs can change for reasons that have nothing to do with changes in volume. Filterfresh is a company that services coffee machines located in commercial offices—providing milk, sugar, cups, and coffee. The company's operations were profoundly affected by the security measures many companies initiated after the terrorist attacks on the World Trade Center and the Pentagon on September 11, 2001. Heightened security at customer locations means that Filterfresh's 250 deliverymen can no longer casually walk through a customer's lobby with a load of supplies. Now a guard typically checks the deliveryman's identification and paperwork at the loading dock and may search the van before permitting the deliveryman access to the customer's building. These delays have added an average of about an hour per day to each route, which means that Filterfresh needs 24 more delivery people to do the same work it did prior to September 11. That's a 10% increase in cost without any increase in the amount of coffee sold.

Source: Anna Bernasek, "The Friction Economy," *Fortune*, February 18, 2002, pp. 104–112.

Extent of Variable Costs The number and type of variable costs in an organization will depend in large part on the organization's structure and purpose. A public utility like Florida Power and Light, with large investments in equipment, will tend to have few variable costs. Most of the costs are associated with its plant, and these costs tend to be insensitive to changes in levels of service provided. A manufacturing company like Black

EXHIBIT 5–2
Examples of Variable Costs

Type of Organization	Costs that Are Normally Variable with Respect to Volume of Output
Merchandising company	Cost of goods (merchandise) sold
Manufacturing company	Manufacturing costs: Direct materials Direct labor* Variable portion of manufacturing overhead: Indirect materials Lubricants Supplies Power
Both merchandising and manufacturing companies	Selling, general, and administrative costs: Commissions Clerical costs, such as invoicing Shipping costs
Service organizations	Supplies, travel, clerical

*Direct labor may or may not be variable in practice. See the discussion later in this chapter.

and Decker, by contrast, will often have many variable costs; these costs will be associated with both manufacturing and distributing its products to customers.

A merchandising company like Wal-Mart or J. K. Gill will usually have a high proportion of variable costs in its cost structure. In most merchandising companies, the cost of merchandise purchased for resale, a variable cost, constitutes a very large component of total cost. Service companies, by contrast, have diverse cost structures. Some service companies, such as the Skippers restaurant chain, have fairly large variable costs because of the costs of their raw materials. On the other hand, service companies involved in consulting, auditing, engineering, dental, medical, and architectural activities have very large fixed costs in the form of expensive facilities and highly trained salaried employees.

Some of the more frequently encountered variable costs are listed in Exhibit 5–2. This exhibit is not a complete listing of all costs that can be considered variable. Moreover, some of the costs listed in the exhibit may behave more like fixed than variable costs in some organizations and in some circumstances. We will see some examples of this later in the chapter. Nevertheless, Exhibit 5–2 provides a useful listing of many of the costs that normally would be considered variable with respect to the volume of output.

True Variable versus Step-Variable Costs

Not all variable costs have exactly the same behavior pattern. Some variable costs behave in a *true variable* or *proportionately variable* pattern. Other variable costs behave in a *step-variable* pattern.

True Variable Costs Direct materials is a true or proportionately variable cost because the amount used during a period will vary in direct proportion to the level of production activity. Moreover, any amounts purchased but not used can be stored and carried forward to the next period as inventory.

Step-Variable Costs The wages of maintenance workers are often considered to be a variable cost, but this labor cost doesn't behave in the same way as the cost of direct materials. Unlike direct materials, a maintenance worker's time can only be obtained in large chunks. Moreover, any maintenance time not utilized cannot be stored as inventory and carried forward to the next period. If the time is not used effectively, it is gone

EXHIBIT 5–3
True Variable versus Step-Variable Costs

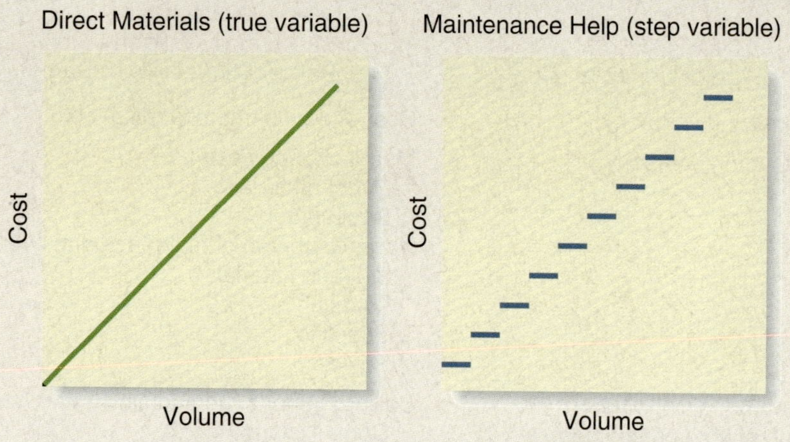

forever. Furthermore, a maintenance crew can work at a leisurely pace if pressures are light but intensify its efforts if pressures build up. For this reason, small changes in the level of production may have no effect on the number of maintenance people employed by the company.

A resource that is obtainable only in large chunks (such as maintenance workers) and whose costs increase or decrease only in response to fairly wide changes in activity is known as a **step-variable cost.** The behavior of a step-variable cost, contrasted with the behavior of a true variable cost, is illustrated in Exhibit 5–3.

Notice that the need for maintenance help changes only with fairly wide changes in volume and that when additional maintenance time is obtained, it comes in large, indivisible chunks. Great care must be taken in working with these kinds of costs to prevent "fat" from building up in an organization. There may be a tendency to employ additional help more quickly than needed, and there is a natural reluctance to lay people off when volume declines.

The Linearity Assumption and the Relevant Range

In dealing with variable costs, we have assumed a strictly linear relationship between cost and volume, except in the case of step-variable costs. Economists correctly point out that many costs that the accountant classifies as variable actually behave in a *curvilinear* fashion. The behavior of a **curvilinear cost** is shown in Exhibit 5–4.

Although many costs are not strictly linear when plotted as a function of volume, a curvilinear cost can be satisfactorily approximated with a straight line within a narrow band of activity known as the *relevant range.* The **relevant range** is that range of activity within which the assumptions made about cost behavior are valid. For example, note that the dashed line in Exhibit 5–4 can be used as an approximation to the curvilinear cost with very little loss of accuracy within the shaded relevant range. However, outside of the relevant range this particular straight line is a poor approximation to the curvilinear cost relationship. Managers should always keep in mind that a particular assumption made about cost behavior may be very inappropriate if activity falls outside of the relevant range.

Fixed Costs

In our discussion of cost behavior patterns in Chapter 2, we stated that total fixed costs remain constant within the relevant range of activity. To continue the Nooksack Expeditions example, assume the company decides to rent a building for $500 per month to store its equipment. Within the relevant range, the *total* amount of rent paid is the same regardless

IN BUSINESS

COSTING THE TREK

Jackson Hole Llamas is owned and operated by Jill Aanonsen/Hodges and David Hodges. The company provides guided tours to remote areas of Yellowstone National Park and the Jedediah Smith Wilderness, with the llamas carrying the baggage for the multiday treks.

Jill and David operate out of their ranch in Jackson Hole, Wyoming, leading about 10 trips each summer season. All food is provided as well as tents and sleeping pads. Based on the number of guests on a trip, Jill and David will decide how many llamas will go on the trip and how many will remain on the ranch. Llamas are transported to the trailhead in a special trailer.

The company has a number of costs, some of which are listed below:

Cost	Cost Behavior
Food and beverage costs	Variable with respect to the number of guests and the length of the trip in days.
Truck and trailer operating costs	Variable with respect to the number of miles to the trailhead.
Guide wages	Step variable; Jill and David serve as the guides on most trips and hire guides only for larger groups.
Costs of providing tents	Variable with respect to the number of guests and length of the trip in days. Jackson Hole Llamas owns its tents, but they wear out through use and must be repaired or eventually replaced.
Cost of feeding llamas	Variable with respect to the number of guests, and hence the number of llamas, on a trip. [Actually, the cost of feeding llamas may *decrease* with the number of guests on a trip. When a llama is on a trek, it lives off the land—eating grasses and other vegetation found in meadows and along the trail. When a llama is left on the ranch, it may have to be fed purchased feed.]
Property taxes	Fixed.

Source: Jill Aanonsen/Hodges and David Hodges, owners and operators of Jackson Hole Llamas, www.jhllamas.com.

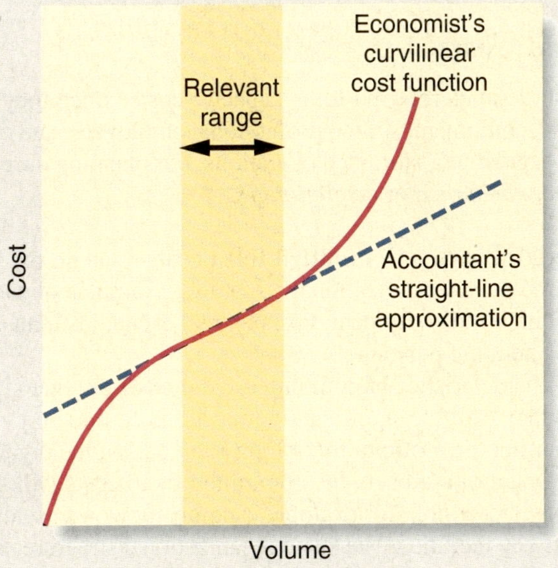

EXHIBIT 5–4
Curvilinear Costs and the Relevant Range

EXHIBIT 5–5
Fixed Cost Behavior

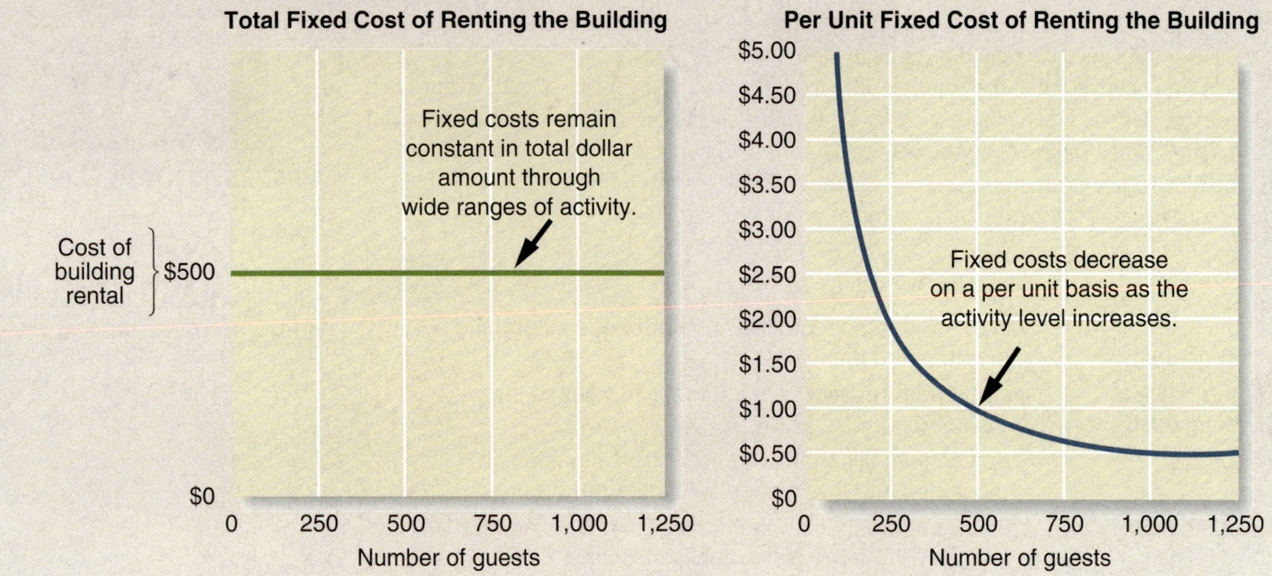

of the number of guests the company takes on its expeditions during any given month. This cost behavior pattern is shown graphically in Exhibit 5–5.

Since fixed costs remain constant in total, the amount of fixed cost computed on a *per unit* basis becomes progressively smaller as the level of activity increases. If Nooksack Expeditions has only 250 guests in a month, the $500 fixed rental cost would amount to $2 per guest. If there are 1,000 guests, the fixed rental cost would amount to only 50 cents per guest. This aspect of the behavior of fixed costs is also displayed in Exhibit 5–5. Note that as the number of guests increases, the average unit cost drops, but it drops at a decreasing rate. The first guests have the biggest impact on average unit costs.

This aspect of fixed costs can be confusing, although it is necessary in some contexts to express fixed costs on an average per unit basis. We found in Chapter 3, for example, that unit product costs for use in *external* financial statements contain both variable and fixed elements. However, to prevent confusion, fixed costs should be expressed in total rather than on a per-unit basis.

Types of Fixed Costs

Fixed costs are sometimes referred to as capacity costs, since they result from outlays made for buildings, equipment, skilled professional employees, and other items needed to provide the basic capacity for sustained operations. For planning purposes, fixed costs can be viewed as either *committed* or *discretionary.*

Committed Fixed Costs

Committed fixed costs relate to the investment in facilities, equipment, and basic organizational structure. Examples of such costs include depreciation of buildings and equipment, taxes on real estate, insurance, and salaries of top management and operating personnel.

The two key characteristics of committed fixed costs are that (1) they are long term in nature, and (2) they can't be significantly reduced even for short periods of time without seriously impairing the profitability or long-run goals of the organization. Even if operations are interrupted or cut back, the committed fixed costs will still continue largely unchanged. During a recession, for example, a company won't usually discharge key executives or sell off key facilities. The basic organizational structure and facilities ordinarily are kept intact. The costs of restoring them later are likely to be far greater than any short-run savings that might be realized.

Decisions to acquire major equipment or to take on other committed fixed costs involve a long planning horizon. Management should make such commitments only after careful analysis of the available alternatives. Once a decision is made to acquire committed fixed resources, the company may be locked into that decision for many years to come. Decisions relating to committed fixed costs will be examined in Chapter 14.

IN BUSINESS

SHARING OFFICE SPACE TO REDUCE COMMITTED FIXED COSTS

Even committed fixed costs may be more flexible than they would appear at first glance. Doctors in private practice have been under enormous pressure in recent years to cut costs. Dr. Edward Betz of Encino, California, reduced the committed fixed costs of maintaining his office by letting a urologist use the office on Wednesday afternoons and Friday mornings for $1,500 a month. Dr. Betz uses this time to work on paperwork at home and he makes up for the lost time in the office by treating some patients on Saturdays.

Source: Gloria Lau and Tim W. Ferguson, "Doc's Just an Employee Now," *Forbes,* May 18, 1998, pp. 162–172.

Since the amount of committed fixed costs cannot be changed in the short run, management is generally very concerned about utilizing these resources as effectively as possible.

Discretionary Fixed Costs

Discretionary fixed costs (often referred to as *managed fixed costs*) usually arise from *annual* decisions by management to spend in certain fixed cost areas. Examples of discretionary fixed costs include advertising, research, public relations, management development programs, and internships for students.

Two key differences exist between discretionary fixed costs and committed fixed costs. First, the planning horizon for a discretionary fixed cost is short term—usually a single year. By contrast, as we indicated earlier, committed fixed costs have a planning horizon that encompasses many years. Second, discretionary fixed costs can be cut for short periods of time with minimal damage to the long-run goals of the organization. For example, spending on management development programs can be reduced because of poor economic conditions. Although some unfavorable consequences may result from the cutback, it is doubtful that these consequences would be as great as those that would result if the company decided to economize during the year by laying off key personnel.

Whether a particular cost is regarded as committed or discretionary may depend on management's strategy. For example, during recessions when the level of home building is down, many construction companies lay off most of their workers and virtually disband operations. Other construction companies retain large numbers of employees on the payroll, even though the workers have little or no work to do. While these latter companies may be faced with short-term cash flow problems, it will be easier for them to respond quickly when economic conditions improve. And the higher morale and loyalty of their employees may give these companies a significant competitive advantage.

The most important characteristic of discretionary fixed costs is that management is not locked into its decisions regarding such costs. Discretionary costs can be adjusted from year to year or even perhaps during the course of a year if necessary.

IN BUSINESS

A TWIST ON FIXED AND VARIABLE COSTS

Mission Controls designs and installs automation systems for food and beverage manufacturers. At most companies, when sales drop and cost cutting is necessary, top managers lay off workers. The founders of Mission Controls decided to do something different when sales drop—they slash their own salaries before they even consider letting any of their employees go. This makes their own salaries somewhat variable, while the wages and salaries of workers act more like fixed costs. The payoff is a loyal and committed workforce.

Source: Christopher Caggiano, "Employment, Guaranteed for Life," *INC,* October 15, 2002, p. 74.

The Trend toward Fixed Costs The trend in many industries is toward greater fixed costs relative to variable costs. Chores that used to be performed by hand have been taken over by machines. For example, grocery clerks at stores like Safeway and Kroger used to key in prices by hand on cash registers. Now, most stores are equipped with bar-code readers that enter price and other product information automatically. In general, competition has created pressure to give customers more value for their money—a demand that often can only be satisfied by automating business processes. For example, an H & R Block employee used to fill out tax returns for customers by hand and the advice given to a customer largely depended on the knowledge of that particular employee. Now, sophisticated computer software is used to complete tax returns, and the software provides the customer with tax planning and other advice tailored to the customer's needs based on the accumulated knowledge of many experts.

As automation intensifies, the demand for "knowledge" workers—those who work primarily with their minds rather than their muscles—has grown tremendously. Since knowledge workers tend to be salaried, highly trained, and difficult to replace, the costs of compensating these workers are often relatively fixed and are committed rather than discretionary.

Is Labor a Variable or a Fixed Cost? As the preceding discussion suggests, wages and salaries may be fixed or variable. The behavior of wage and salary costs will differ from one country to another, depending on labor regulations, labor contracts, and custom. In some countries, such as France, Germany, and Japan, management has little flexibility in adjusting the labor force to changes in business activity. In countries such as the United States and the United Kingdom, management typically has much greater latitude. However, even in these less restrictive environments, managers may choose to treat employee compensation as a fixed cost for several reasons.

First, many managers are reluctant to decrease their workforce in response to short-term declines in sales. These managers realize that the success of their businesses hinges on retaining highly skilled and trained employees. If these valuable workers are laid off, it is unlikely that they would ever return or be easily replaced. Furthermore, laying off workers undermines the morale of those employees who remain.

Second, managers do not want to be caught with a bloated payroll in an economic downturn. Therefore, managers are reluctant to add employees in response to short-term increases in sales. Instead, more and more companies rely on temporary and part-time workers to take up the slack when their permanent, full-time employees are unable to handle all of the demand for their products and services. In such companies, labor costs are a curious mixture of fixed and variable costs.

IN BUSINESS

LABOR AT SOUTHWEST AIRLINES

Starting with a $10,000 investment in 1966, Herb Kelleher built Southwest Airlines into the most profitable airline in the United States. Prior to stepping down as president and CEO of the airline in 2001, Kelleher wrote: "The thing that would disturb me most to see after I'm no longer CEO is layoffs at Southwest. Nothing kills your company's culture like layoffs. Nobody has ever been furloughed here, and that is unprecedented in the airline industry. It's been a huge strength of ours . . . We could have furloughed at various times and been more profitable, but I always thought that was shortsighted. You want to show your people that you value them and you're not going to hurt them just to get a little money in the short run."

Because of this commitment by management to the company's employees, all wages and salaries are basically committed fixed costs at Southwest Airlines.

Source: Herb Kelleher, "The Chairman of the Board Looks Back," *Fortune*, May 28, 2001, pp. 63–76.

Many major companies have undergone waves of downsizing in recent years in which large numbers of employees—particularly middle managers—have lost their jobs.

This downsizing may seem to suggest that even management salaries should be regarded as variable costs, but this would not be a valid conclusion. Downsizing has largely been the result of attempts to reengineer business processes and cut costs rather than a response to a decline in sales activity. This underscores an important, but subtle, point. Fixed costs can change—they just don't change in response to small changes in activity.

In sum, there is no clear-cut answer to the question "Is labor a variable or fixed cost?" It depends on how much flexibility management has and management's strategy. Nevertheless, unless otherwise stated, we will assume in this text that direct labor is a variable cost. This assumption is more likely to be valid for companies in the United States than in countries where employment laws permit much less flexibility.

IN BUSINESS

THE REGULATORY BURDEN

Peter F. Drucker, a renowned observer of business and society, claims that "the driving force behind the steady growth of temps [and outsourcing of work] . . . is the growing burden of rules and regulations for employers." U.S. laws and regulations concerning employees require companies to file multiple reports—and any breach, even if unintentional, can result in punishment. According to the Small Business Administration, the owner of a small or midsize business spends up to a quarter of his or her time on employment-related paperwork and the cost of complying with government regulations (including tax report preparation) is over $5,000 per employee per year. "No wonder that employers . . . complain bitterly that they have no time to work on products and services. . . . They no longer chant the old mantra 'People are our greatest asset.' Instead, they claim 'People are our greatest liability.'" To the extent that the regulatory burden leads to a decline in permanent full-time employees and an increase in the use of temporary employees and outsourcing, labor costs are converted from fixed to variable costs. While this is not the intent of the regulations, it is a consequence.

Source: Peter F. Drucker, "They're Not Employees, They're People," *Harvard Business Review*, February 2002.

Fixed Costs and the Relevant Range

The concept of the relevant range, which was introduced in the discussion of variable costs, is also important in understanding fixed costs—particularly discretionary fixed costs. The levels of discretionary fixed costs are typically decided at the beginning of the year and depend on the needs of planned programs such as advertising and training. The scope of these programs will depend, in turn, on the overall anticipated level of activity for the year. At very high levels of activity, programs are often broadened or expanded. For example, if the company hopes to increase sales by 25%, it would probably plan for much larger advertising costs than if no sales increase were planned. So the *planned* level of activity might affect total discretionary fixed costs. However, once the total discretionary fixed costs have been budgeted, they are unaffected by the *actual* level of activity. For example, once the advertising budget has been established and spent, it will not be affected by how many units are actually sold. Therefore, the cost is fixed with respect to the *actual* number of units sold.

Discretionary fixed costs are easier to adjust than committed fixed costs. They also tend to be less "lumpy." Committed fixed costs consist of costs such as buildings, equipment, and the salaries of key personnel. It is difficult to buy half a piece of equipment or to hire a quarter of a product-line manager, so the step pattern depicted in Exhibit 5–6 is typical for such costs. The relevant range of activity for a fixed cost is the range of activity over which the graph of the cost is flat as in Exhibit 5–6. As a company expands its level of activity, it may outgrow its present facilities, or the key management team may need to be expanded. The result, of course, will be increased committed fixed costs as larger facilities are built and as new management positions are created.

One reaction to the step pattern depicted in Exhibit 5–6 is to say that discretionary and committed fixed costs are really just step-variable costs. To some extent this is true, since *almost* all costs can be adjusted in the long run. There are two major differences,

EXHIBIT 5–6
Fixed Costs and the Relevant Range

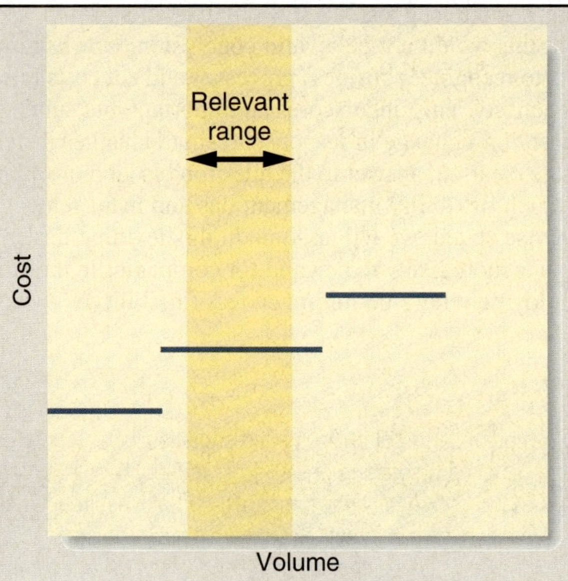

however, between the step-variable costs depicted earlier in Exhibit 5–3 and the fixed costs depicted in Exhibit 5–6.

The first difference is that the step-variable costs can often be adjusted quickly as conditions change, whereas once fixed costs have been set, they usually can't be changed easily. A step-variable cost such as maintenance labor, for example, can be adjusted upward or downward by hiring and laying off maintenance workers. By contrast, once a company has signed a lease for a building, it is locked into that level of lease cost for the life of the contract.

The second difference is that the *width of the steps* depicted for step-variable costs is much narrower than the width of the steps depicted for the fixed costs in Exhibit 5–6. The width of the steps relates to volume or level of activity. For step-variable costs, the width of a step might be 40 hours of activity or less if one is dealing, for example, with maintenance labor cost. For fixed costs, however, the width of a step might be *thousands* or even *tens of thousands* of hours of activity. In essence, the width of the steps for step-variable costs is generally so narrow that these costs can be treated essentially as variable costs for most purposes. The width of the steps for fixed costs, on the other hand, is so wide that these costs should be treated as entirely fixed within the relevant range.

Mixed Costs

A **mixed cost** contains both variable and fixed cost elements. Mixed costs are also known as semivariable costs. To continue the Nooksack Expeditions example, the company must pay a license fee of $25,000 per year plus $3 per rafting party to the state's Department of Natural Resources. If the company runs 1,000 rafting parties this year, then the total fees paid to the state would be $28,000, made up of $25,000 in fixed cost plus $3,000 in variable cost. The behavior of this mixed cost is shown graphically in Exhibit 5–7.

Even if Nooksack fails to attract any customers, the company will still have to pay the license fee of $25,000. This is why the cost line in Exhibit 5–7 intersects the vertical cost axis at the $25,000 point. For each rafting party the company organizes, the total cost of the state fees will increase by $3. Therefore, the total cost line slopes upward as the variable cost element is added to the fixed cost element.

Since the mixed cost in Exhibit 5–7 is represented by a straight line, the following equation for a straight line can be used to express the relationship between a mixed cost and the level of activity:

$$Y = a + bX$$

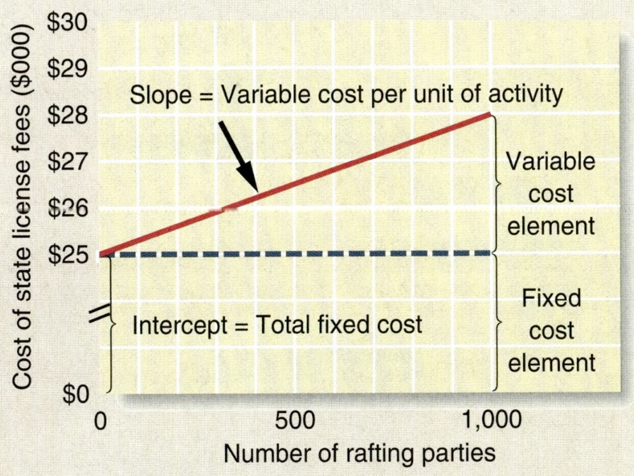

EXHIBIT 5–7
Mixed Cost Behavior

In this equation,

Y = The total mixed cost

a = The total fixed cost (the vertical intercept of the line)

b = The variable cost per unit of activity (the slope of the line)

X = The level of activity

Since the variable cost per unit equals the slope of the straight line, the steeper the slope, the higher the variable cost per unit.

In the case of the state fees paid by Nooksack Expeditions, the equation is written as follows:

$$Y = \$25{,}000 + \$3.00X$$

Y	\$25,000	\$3.00	X
Total mixed cost	Total fixed cost	Variable cost per unit of activity	Activity level

This equation makes it very easy to calculate what the total mixed cost would be for any level of activity within the relevant range. For example, suppose that the company expects to organize 800 rafting parties in the next year. The total state fees would be $27,400 calculated as follows:

$$Y = \$25{,}000 + (\$3.00 \text{ per rafting party} \times 800 \text{ rafting parties})$$
$$= \$27{,}400$$

IN BUSINESS

COST BEHAVIOR IN THE U.S. AND JAPAN

A total of 257 American and 40 Japanese manufacturing companies responded to a questionnaire concerning their management accounting practices. Among other things, the companies were asked whether they classified certain costs as variable, semivariable, or fixed. Some of the results are summarized in Exhibit 5–8. Note that companies do not all classify costs in the same way. For example, roughly 45% of the U.S. companies classify material-handling labor costs as variable, 35% as semivariable, and 20% as fixed. Also note that the Japanese companies are much more likely than U.S. companies to classify labor costs as fixed.

Source: NAA Tokyo Affiliate, "Management Accounting in the Advanced Management Surrounding—Comparative Study on Survey in Japan and U.S.A."

EXHIBIT 5–8
Percentages of Companies Classifying Specific Costs as Variable, Semivariable, or Fixed

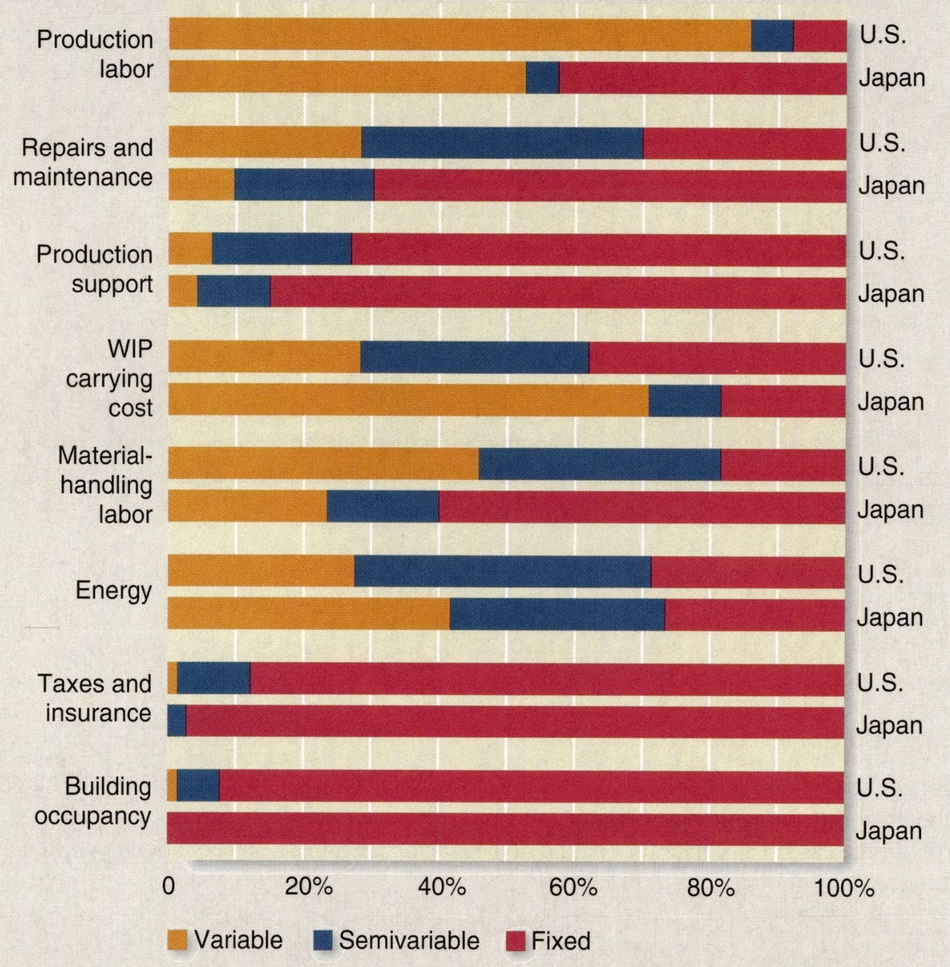

The Analysis of Mixed Costs

In practice, mixed costs are very common. For example, the cost of providing X-ray services to patients at the Harvard Medical School Hospital is a mixed cost. There are substantial fixed costs for equipment depreciation and for the salaries of radiologists and technicians, but there are also variable costs for X-ray film, power, and supplies. At Southwest Airlines, maintenance costs are a mixed cost. The company incurs fixed costs for renting maintenance facilities and for keeping skilled mechanics on the payroll, but the costs of replacement parts, lubricating oils, tires, and so forth, are variable with respect to how often and how far the company's aircraft are flown.

The fixed portion of a mixed cost represents the minimum cost of having a service *ready and available* for use. The variable portion represents the cost incurred for *actual consumption* of the service. The variable element varies in proportion to the amount of service that is consumed.

How does management go about actually estimating the fixed and variable components of a mixed cost? The most common methods used in practice and discussed later in this text are *account analysis* and the *engineering approach.*

In **account analysis,** each account under consideration is classified as either variable or fixed based on the analyst's prior knowledge of how the cost in the account behaves. For example, direct materials would be classified as variable and a building lease cost would be classified as fixed because of the nature of those costs. The total fixed cost of an organization is the sum of the costs for the accounts that have been classified as fixed. The variable cost per unit is estimated by dividing the sum of the costs for the accounts that have been classified as variable by the total activity.

The **engineering approach** to cost analysis involves a detailed analysis of what cost behavior should be, based on an industrial engineer's evaluation of the production methods to be used, the materials specifications, labor requirements, equipment usage, efficiency of production, power consumption, and so on. For example, Pizza Hut might use the engineering approach to estimate the cost of serving a particular take-out pizza. The cost of the pizza would be estimated by carefully costing the specific ingredients used to make the pizza, the power consumed to cook the pizza, and the cost of the container the pizza is delivered in. The engineering approach must be used in those situations where no past experience is available concerning activity and costs. In addition, it is sometimes used together with other methods to improve the accuracy of cost analysis.

Account analysis works best when analyzing costs at a fairly aggregated level, such as the cost of serving patients in the emergency room (ER) of Cook County General Hospital. The costs of drugs, supplies, forms, wages, equipment, and so on, can be roughly classified as variable or fixed and a mixed cost formula for the overall cost of the emergency room can be estimated fairly quickly. However, this method does not recognize that some of the accounts may have both fixed and variable cost elements. For example, the cost of electricity for the ER is a mixed cost. Most of the electricity is used for heating and lighting and is a fixed cost. However, the consumption of electricity increases with activity in the ER since diagnostic equipment, operating theater lights, defibrillators, and so on, all consume electricity. The most effective way to estimate the fixed and variable elements of such a mixed cost may be to analyze past records of cost and activity data. These records should reveal whether electrical costs vary significantly with the number of patients and if so, by how much. The remainder of this section will be concerned with how to conduct such an analysis of past cost and activity data.

IN BUSINESS

OPERATIONS DRIVE COSTS

White Grizzly Adventures is a snowcat skiing and snowboarding company in Meadow Creek, British Columbia, that is owned and operated by Brad and Carole Karafil. The company shuttles 12 guests to the top of the company's steep and tree-covered terrain in a single snowcat. Guests stay as a group at the company's lodge for a fixed number of days and are provided healthful gourmet meals.

Brad and Carole must decide each year when snowcat operations will begin in December and when they will end in early spring, and how many nonoperating days to schedule between groups of guests for maintenance and rest. This decision affects a variety of costs. Examples of costs that are fixed and variable with respect to the number of days of operation at White Grizzly include:

Cost	Cost Behavior—Fixed or Variable with Respect to Days of Operation
Property taxes	Fixed
Summer road maintenance and tree clearing	Fixed
Lodge depreciation	Fixed
Snowcat operator and guides	Variable
Cooks and lodge help	Variable
Snowcat depreciation	Variable
Snowcat fuel	Variable
Food*	Variable

*The costs of food served to guests theoretically depend on the number of guests in residence. However, the lodge is basically always filled to its capacity of 12 persons when the snowcat operation is running, so food costs can be considered to be driven by the days of operation.

Source: Brad & Carole Karafil, owners and operators of White Grizzly Adventures, www.whitegrizzly.com.

MANAGERIAL ACCOUNTING IN ACTION
The Issue

BRENTLINE HOSPITAL

Dr. Derek Chalmers, the chief executive officer of Brentline Hospital, motioned Kinh Nguyen, the chief financial officer of the hospital, into his office.

Derek: Kinh, come on in.

Kinh: What can I do for you?

Derek: Well for one, could you get the government to rescind the bookcase full of regulations against the wall over there?

Kinh: Sorry, that's a bit beyond my authority.

Derek: Just wishing, Kinh. Actually, I wanted to talk to you about our maintenance expenses. I don't usually pay attention to such things, but these expenses seem to be bouncing around a lot. Over the last half year or so they have been as low as $7,400 and as high as $9,800 per month.

Kinh: Actually, that's a pretty normal variation in those expenses.

Derek: Well, we budgeted a constant $8,400 a month. Can't we do a better job of predicting what these costs are going to be? And how do we know when we've spent too much in a month? Shouldn't there be some explanation for these variations?

Kinh: Now that you mention it, we are in the process of tightening up our budgeting process. Our first step is to break all of our costs down into fixed and variable components.

Derek: How will that help?

Kinh: Well, that will permit us to predict what the level of costs will be. Some costs are fixed and shouldn't change much. Other costs go up and down as our activity goes up and down. The trick is to figure out what is driving the variable component of the costs.

Derek: What about the maintenance costs?

Kinh: My guess is that the variations in maintenance costs are being driven by our overall level of activity. When we treat more patients, our equipment is used more intensively, which leads to more maintenance expense.

Derek: How would you measure the level of overall activity? Would you use patient-days?

Kinh: I think so. Each day a patient is in the hospital counts as one patient-day. The greater the number of patient-days in a month, the busier we are. Besides, our budgeting is all based on projected patient-days.

Derek: Okay, so suppose you are able to break the maintenance costs down into fixed and variable components. What will that do for us?

Kinh: Basically, I will be able to predict what maintenance costs should be as a function of the number of patient-days.

Derek: I can see where that would be useful. We could use it to predict costs for budgeting purposes.

Kinh: We could also use it as a benchmark. Based on the actual number of patient-days for a period, I can predict what the maintenance costs should have been. We can compare this to the actual spending on maintenance.

Derek: Sounds good to me. Let me know when you get the results.

Diagnosing Cost Behavior with a Scattergraph Plot

LEARNING OBJECTIVE 2
Use a scattergraph plot to diagnose cost behavior.

Kinh Nguyen began his analysis of maintenance costs by collecting cost and activity data for a number of recent months. Those data are displayed below:

Month	Activity Level: Patient-Days	Maintenance Cost Incurred
January	5,600	$7,900
February	7,100	$8,500
March	5,000	$7,400
April	6,500	$8,200
May	7,300	$9,100
June	8,000	$9,800
July	6,200	$7,800

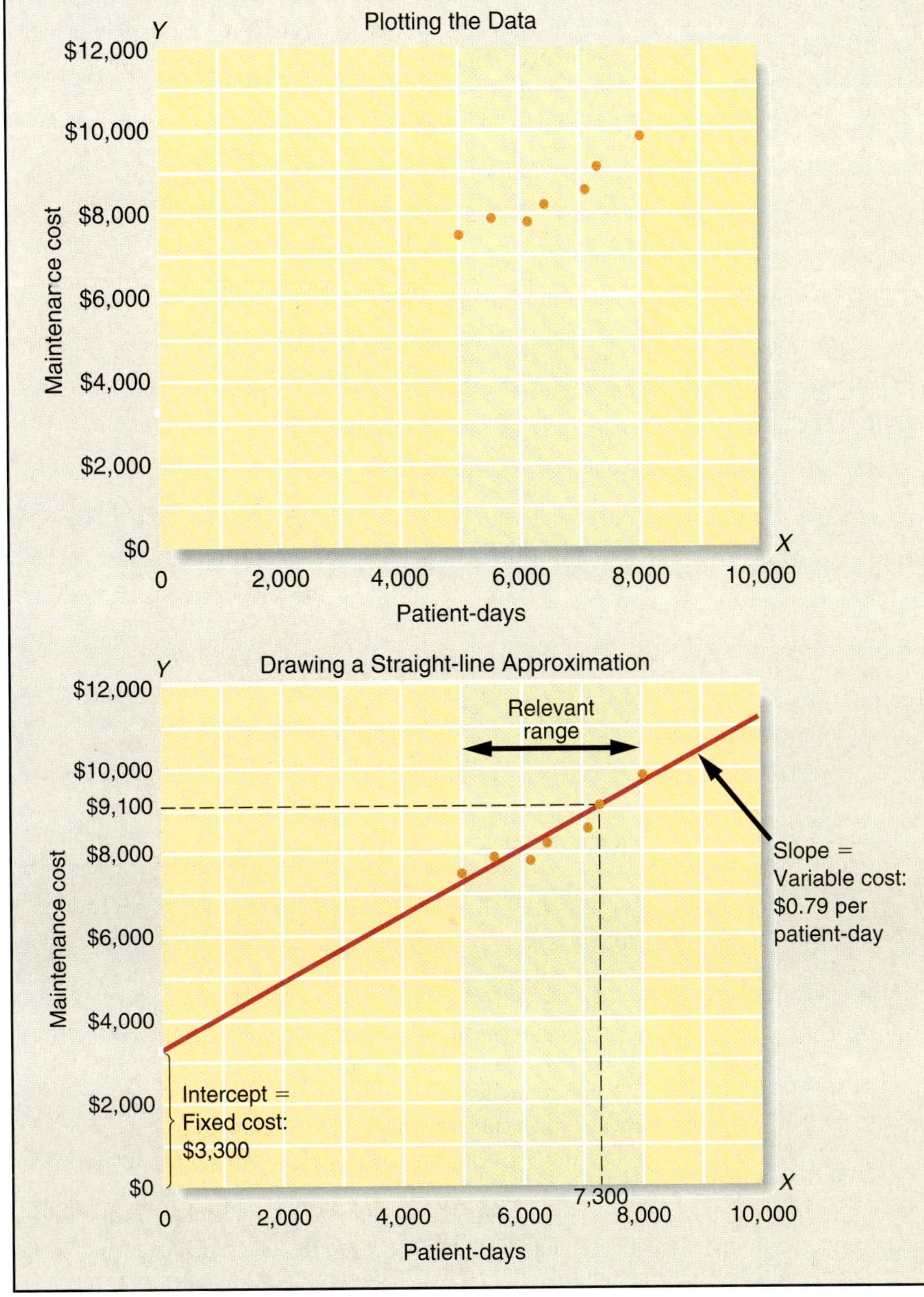

EXHIBIT 5–9
Scattergraph Method of Cost Analysis

The first step in analyzing the cost and activity data is to plot the data on a scattergraph. This plot will immediately reveal any nonlinearities or other problems with the data. The scattergraph of maintenance costs versus patient-days at Brentline Hospital is reproduced in the first panel of Exhibit 5–9. Two things should be noted about this scattergraph:

1. The total maintenance cost, *Y*, is plotted on the vertical axis. Cost is known as the **dependent variable,** since the amount of cost incurred during a period depends on the level of activity for the period. (That is, as the level of activity increases, total cost will also ordinarily increase.)
2. The activity, *X* (patient-days in this case), is plotted on the horizontal axis. Activity is known as the **independent variable,** since it causes variations in the cost.

From the scattergraph, it is evident that maintenance costs do increase with the number of patient-days. In addition, the scattergraph reveals that the relation between maintenance costs and patient-days is approximately *linear*. In other words, the points lie more or less along a straight line. Such a straight line has been drawn using a ruler in the second panel of Exhibit 5–9. Cost behavior is said to be **linear** whenever a straight line is a reasonable approximation for the relation between cost and activity. Note that the data points do not fall exactly on the straight line. This will almost always happen in practice; the relation is seldom perfectly linear.

Note that the straight line in Exhibit 5–9 has been drawn through the point representing 7,300 patient-days and a total maintenance cost of $9,100. Drawing the straight line through one of the data points allows the analyst to make a quick-and-dirty estimate of variable and fixed costs. The vertical intercept where the straight line crosses the *Y* axis—in this case, about $3,300—is the rough estimate of the fixed cost. The variable cost can be quickly estimated by subtracting the estimated fixed cost from the total cost at the point lying on the straight line.

Total maintenance cost for 7,300 patient-days (a point falling on the straight line)	$9,100
Less estimated fixed cost (the vertical intercept)	3,300
Estimated total variable cost for 7,300 patient-days	$5,800

The average variable cost per unit at 7,300 patient-days is computed as follows:

$$\text{Variable cost per unit} = \$5{,}800 \div 7{,}300 \text{ patient-days}$$
$$= \$0.79 \text{ per patient-day (rounded)}$$

Combining the estimate of the fixed cost and the estimate of the variable cost per patient-day, we can write the relation between cost and activity as follows:

$$Y = \$3{,}300 + \$0.79X$$

where *X* is the number of patient-days.

We hasten to add that this *is* a quick-and-dirty method of estimating the fixed and variable cost elements of a mixed cost; it is seldom used in practice when the financial implications of a decision based on the data are significant. However, setting aside the estimates of the fixed and variable cost elements, plotting the data on a scattergraph is an essential diagnostic step that is too often overlooked. Suppose, for example, we had been interested in the relation between total nursing wages and the number of patient-days at the hospital. The permanent, full-time nursing staff can handle up to 7,000 patient-days in a month. Beyond that level of activity, part-time nurses must be called in to help out. The cost and activity data for nurses are plotted on the scattergraph in Exhibit 5–10. Looking at that scattergraph, it is evident that two straight lines would do a much better job of fitting the data than a single straight line. Up to 7,000 patient-days, total nursing wages are essentially a fixed cost. Above 7,000 patient-days, total nursing wages are a mixed cost. This happens because, as stated above, the permanent, full-time nursing staff can handle up to 7,000 patient-days in a month. Above that level, part-time nurses are called in to help, which adds to the cost. Consequently, two straight lines (and two equations) would be used to represent total nursing wages—one for the relevant range of 5,600 to 7,000 patient-days and one for the relevant range of 7,000 to 8,000 patient-days.

As another example, suppose that Brentline Hospital management is interested in the relation between the hospital's telephone costs and patient-days. Patients are billed directly for their use of telephones, so those costs do not appear on the hospital's cost records. The telephone costs of concern to management are the charges for the staff's use of telephones. The data for this cost are plotted in Exhibit 5–11. It is evident from that plot that while the telephone costs do vary from month to month, they are not related to patient-days. Something other than patient-days is driving the telephone bills. Therefore,

EXHIBIT 5–10
More than One Relevant Range

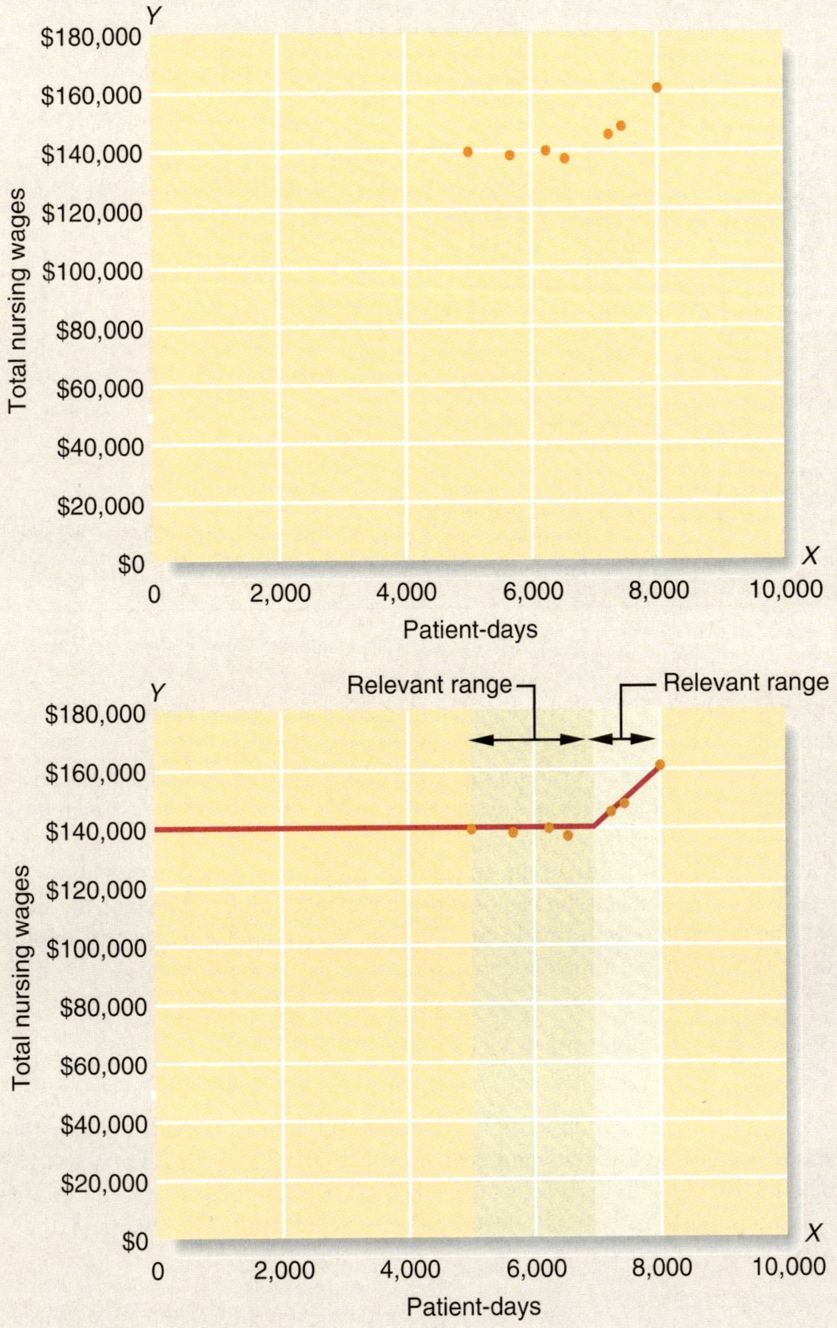

it would not make sense to analyze this cost any further by attempting to estimate a variable cost per patient-day for telephone costs. Plotting the data helps the cost analyst to diagnose such situations.

The High-Low Method

LEARNING OBJECTIVE 3
Analyze a mixed cost using the high-low method.

In addition to the quick-and-dirty method described in the preceding section, more precise methods are available for estimating fixed and variable costs. However, it must be emphasized that fixed and variable costs should be computed only if a scattergraph plot confirms that the relation is approximately linear. In the case of maintenance costs at Brentline Hospital, the relation does appear to be linear. In the case of telephone costs,

EXHIBIT 5–11
A Diagnostic Scattergraph Plot

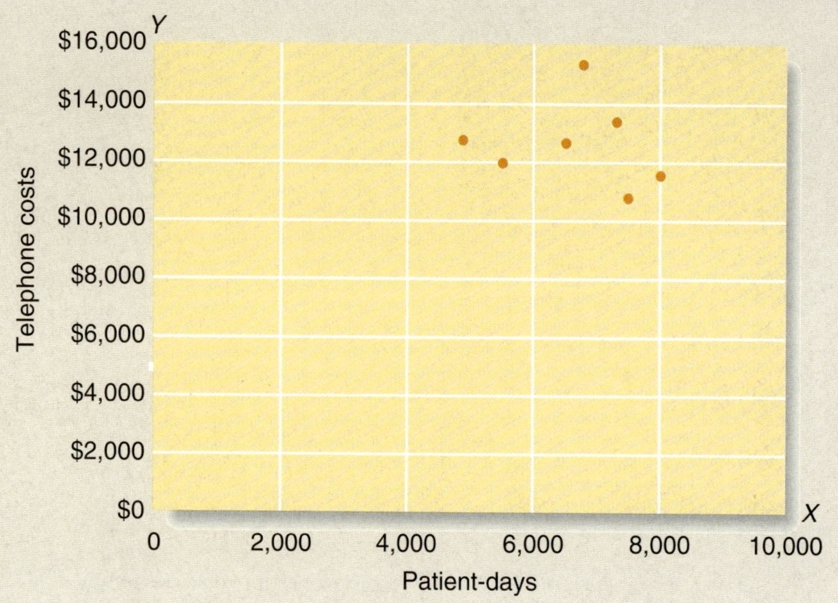

there isn't any clear relation between telephone costs and patient-days, so there is no point in estimating how much of the cost varies with patient-days.

Assuming that the scattergraph plot indicates a linear relation between cost and activity, the fixed and variable cost elements of a mixed cost can be estimated using the *high-low method* or the *least-squares regression method*. The high-low method is based on the rise-over-run formula for the slope of a straight line. As discussed above, if the relation between cost and activity can be represented by a straight line, then the slope of the straight line is equal to the variable cost per unit of activity. Consequently, the following formula can be used to estimate the variable cost.

$$\text{Variable cost} = \text{Slope of the line} = \frac{\text{Rise}}{\text{Run}} = \frac{Y_2 - Y_1}{X_2 - X_1}$$

To analyze mixed costs with the **high-low method,** you begin by identifying the period with the lowest level of activity and the period with the highest level of activity. The period with the lowest activity is selected as the first point in the above formula and the period with the highest activity is selected as the second point. Consequently, the formula becomes:

$$\text{Variable cost} = \frac{Y_2 - Y_1}{X_2 - X_1} = \frac{\text{Cost at the high activity level} - \text{Cost at the low activity level}}{\text{High activity level} - \text{Low activity level}}$$

or

$$\text{Variable cost} = \frac{\text{Change in cost}}{\text{Change in activity}}$$

Therefore, when the high-low method is used, the variable cost is estimated by dividing the difference in cost between the high and low levels of activity by the change in activity between those two points.

Using the high-low method, we first identify the periods with the highest and lowest *activity*—in this case, June and March. We then use the activity and cost data from these two periods to estimate the variable cost component as follows:

	Patient-Days	Maintenance Cost Incurred
High activity level (June)	8,000	$9,800
Low activity level (March)	5,000	7,400
Change	3,000	$2,400

$$\text{Variable cost} = \frac{\text{Change in cost}}{\text{Change in activity}} = \frac{\$2{,}400}{3{,}000 \text{ patient-days}} = \$0.80 \text{ per patient-day}$$

Having determined that the variable rate for maintenance cost is 80 cents per patient-day, we can now determine the amount of fixed cost. This is done by taking total cost at *either* the high or the low activity level and deducting the variable cost element. In the computation below, total cost at the high activity level is used in computing the fixed cost element:

$$\begin{aligned}\text{Fixed cost element} &= \text{Total cost} - \text{Variable cost element}\\ &= \$9{,}800 - (\$0.80 \text{ per patient-day} \times 8{,}000 \text{ patient-days})\\ &= \$3{,}400\end{aligned}$$

Both the variable and fixed cost elements have now been isolated. The cost of maintenance can be expressed as $3,400 per month plus 80 cents per patient-day.

The cost of maintenance can also be expressed in terms of the equation for a straight line as follows:

$$Y = \$3{,}400 + \$0.80X$$

↑ Y: Total maintenance cost

↑ X: Total patient-days

The data used in this illustration are shown graphically in Exhibit 5–12. Notice that a straight line has been drawn through the points corresponding to the low and high levels of activity. In essence, that is what the high-low method does—it draws a straight line through those two points.

Sometimes the high and low levels of activity don't coincide with the high and low amounts of cost. For example, the period that has the highest level of activity may not have the highest amount of cost. Nevertheless, the costs at the highest and lowest levels of *activity* are always used to analyze a mixed cost under the high-low method. The reason is that the analyst would like to use data that reflect the greatest possible variation in activity.

The high-low method is very simple to apply, but it suffers from a major (and sometimes critical) defect—it utilizes only two data points. Generally, two data points are not enough to produce accurate results. Additionally, periods in which the activity level is unusually low or unusually high will tend to produce inaccurate results. A cost formula that is estimated solely using data from these unusual periods may misrepresent the true cost relationship that holds during normal periods. Such a distortion is evident in Exhibit 5–12. The straight line should probably be shifted down somewhat so that it is closer to more of the data points. For these reasons, other methods of cost analysis that utilize a greater number of data points will generally be more accurate than the high-low method. A manager who chooses to use the high-low method should do so with a full awareness of the method's limitations.

Fortunately, modern computer software makes it very easy to use sophisticated statistical methods, such as *least-squares regression,* that use all of the data and that are capable of providing much more information than just the estimates of variable and fixed

EXHIBIT 5–12
High-Low Method of Cost Analysis

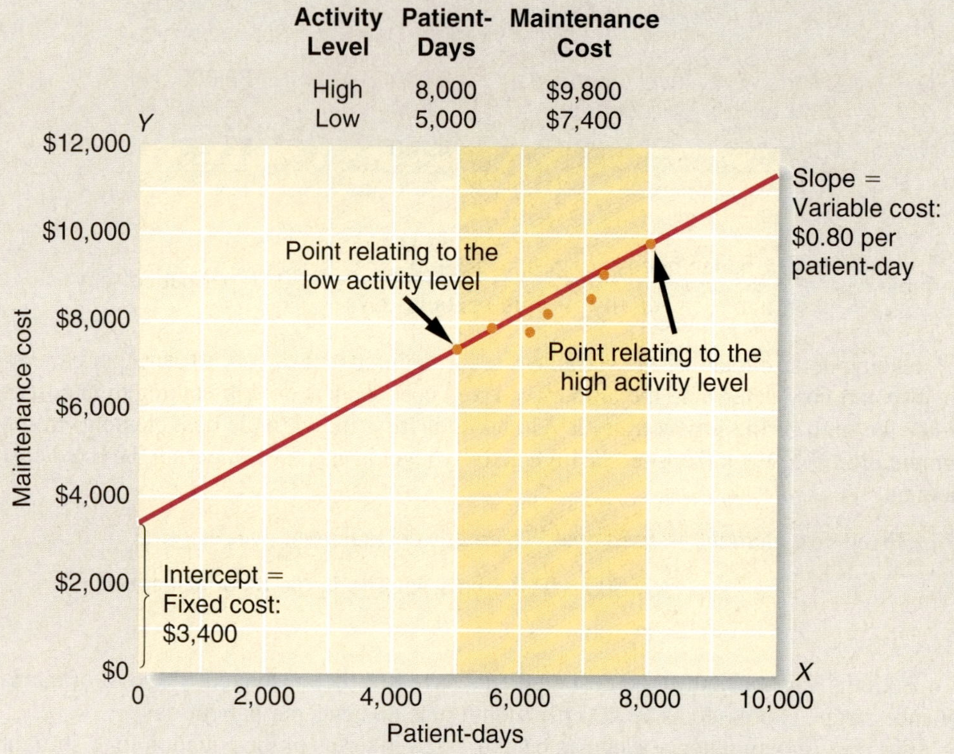

costs. The details of these statistical methods are beyond the scope of this text, but the basic approach is discussed below. Nevertheless, even if the least-squares regression approach is used, it is always a good idea to plot the data in a scattergraph. By simply looking at the scattergraph, you can quickly verify whether it makes sense to fit a straight line to the data using least-squares regression or some other method.

The Least-Squares Regression Method

The **least-squares regression method,** unlike the high-low method, uses all of the data to separate a mixed cost into its fixed and variable components. A *regression line* of the form $Y = a + bX$ is fitted to the data, where a represents the total fixed cost and b represents the variable cost per unit of activity. The basic idea underlying the least-squares regression method is illustrated in Exhibit 5–13 using hypothetical data points. Notice from the exhibit that the deviations from the plotted points to the regression line are measured vertically on the graph. These vertical deviations are called the regression errors. There is nothing mysterious about the least-squares regression method. It simply computes the regression line that minimizes the sum of these squared errors. The formulas that accomplish this are fairly complex and involve numerous calculations, but the principle is simple.

Fortunately, computers are adept at carrying out the computations required by the least-squares regression formulas. The data—the observed values of X and Y—are entered into the computer, and software does the rest. In the case of the Brentline Hospital maintenance cost data, a statistical software package on a personal computer can calculate the following least-squares regression estimates of the total fixed cost (a) and the variable cost per unit of activity (b):

$$a = \$3{,}431$$

$$b = \$0.759$$

Therefore, using the least-squares regression method, the fixed element of the maintenance cost is $3,431 per month and the variable portion is 75.9 cents per patient-day.

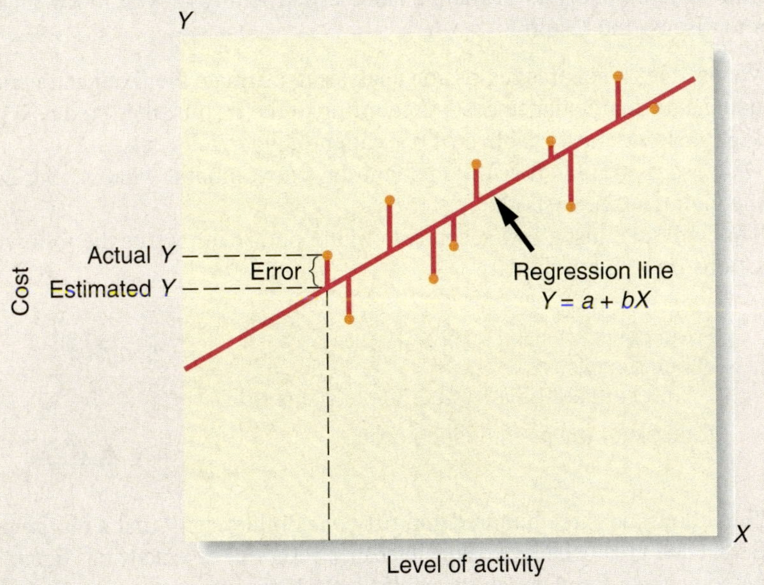

EXHIBIT 5–13
The Concept of Least-Squares Regression

In terms of the linear equation $Y = a + bX$, the cost formula can be written as

$$Y = \$3{,}431 + \$0.759X$$

where activity (X) is expressed in patient-days.

While a statistical software application was used in this example to calculate the values of a and b, the estimates can also be computed using a spreadsheet application such as Microsoft® Excel. In Appendix 5A to this chapter, we show how this can be done.

In addition to estimates of the intercept (fixed cost) and slope (variable cost per unit), least-squares regression software ordinarily provides a number of other very useful statistics. One of these statistics is the R^2, which is a measure of "goodness of fit." The $\boldsymbol{R^2}$ tells us the percentage of the variation in the dependent variable (cost) that is explained by variation in the independent variable (activity). The R^2 varies from 0% to 100%, and the higher the percentage, the better. In the case of the Brentline Hospital maintenance cost data, the R^2 is 0.90, which indicates that 90% of the variation in maintenance costs is explained by the variation in patient-days. This is reasonably high and is an indication of a good fit. On the other hand, a low R^2 would be an indication of a poor fit. You should always plot the data in a scattergraph, but it is particularly important to check the data visually when the R^2 is low. A quick look at the scattergraph can reveal that there is little real relation between the cost and the activity or that the relation is something other than a simple straight line. In such cases, additional analysis would be required.

IN BUSINESS

MANAGING POWER CONSUMPTION

The Tata Iron Steel Company Ltd. is one of the largest companies in India. Because of an unreliable electrical supply, the company is faced with frequent power shortages and must carefully manage its power consumption—allocating scarce power to the most profitable uses. Estimating the power requirements of each processing station in the steel mill was the first step in building a model to better manage power consumption. Management used simple least-squares regression to estimate the fixed and variable components of the power load. Total power consumption was the dependent variable and tons of steel processed was the independent variable. The fixed component estimated from the least-squares regression was the fixed power consumption (in KWHs) per month and the variable component was the power consumption (again in KWHs) per ton of steel processed.

Source: "How Tata Steel Optimized Its Results," *The Management Accountant* (India), May 1996, pp. 372–376.

MANAGERIAL ACCOUNTING IN ACTION
The Wrap-up

BRENTLINE HOSPITAL

After completing the analysis of maintenance costs, Kinh Nguyen met with Dr. Derek Chalmers to discuss the results.

Kinh: We used least-squares regression analysis to estimate the fixed and variable components of maintenance costs. According to the results, the fixed cost per month is $3,431 and the variable cost per patient-day is 75.9 cents.

Derek: Okay, so if we plan for 7,800 patient-days next month, what is your estimate of the maintenance costs?

Kinh: That will take just a few seconds to figure out. [Kinh wrote the following calculations on a pad of paper.]

Fixed costs	$3,431
Variable costs:	
7,800 patient-days × $0.759 per patient-day	5,920
Total expected maintenance costs	$9,351

Derek: Nine thousand three hundred and fifty *one* dollars; isn't that a bit *too* precise?

Kinh: Sure. I don't really believe the maintenance costs will be exactly this figure. However, based on the information we have, this is the best estimate we can come up with.

Derek: Don't let me give you a hard time. Even though it is an estimate, it will be a lot better than just guessing like we have done in the past. Thanks. I hope to see more of this kind of analysis.

Multiple Regression Analysis

In the discussion thus far, we have assumed that a single factor such as patient-days drives the variable cost component of a mixed cost. This assumption is acceptable for many mixed costs, but in some situations the variable cost element may be driven by a number of factors. For example, shipping costs may depend on both the number of units shipped *and* the weight of the units. In a situation such as this, *multiple regression* is necessary. **Multiple regression** is an analytical method that is used when the dependent variable (i.e., cost) is caused by more than one factor. Although adding more factors, or variables, makes the computations more complex, the principles involved are the same as in the simple least-squares regressions discussed above.

The Contribution Format Income Statement

LEARNING OBJECTIVE 4
Prepare an income statement using the contribution format.

Once costs have been separated into fixed and variable elements, what is done with the data? We have already answered this question somewhat by showing how a cost formula can be used to predict costs. To answer this question more fully will require most of the remainder of this text, since much of what the manager does requires an understanding of cost behavior. One immediate and very significant application of the ideas we have developed, however, is found in a new income statement format known as the **contribution approach.** The unique thing about the contribution approach is that it provides managers with an income statement geared directly to cost behavior.

Why a New Income Statement Format?

An income statement prepared using the *traditional approach,* as illustrated in Chapter 2, is not organized in terms of cost behavior. Rather, it is organized in a "functional" format—emphasizing the functions of production, administration, and sales. No attempt is made to distinguish between the behavior of costs included under each functional heading. Under the heading "Administrative expense," for example, both variable and fixed costs are lumped together.

Although an income statement prepared in the functional format may be useful for external reporting purposes, it has serious limitations when used for internal purposes. Internally, the manager needs cost data organized in a format that will facilitate planning, control, and decision-making. As we shall see in chapters ahead, these tasks are much easier when cost data are available in a fixed and variable format. The contribution approach to the income statement has been developed in response to these needs.

The Contribution Approach

Exhibit 5–14 uses a simple example to compare a contribution approach income statement to the traditional approach discussed in Chapter 2.

Notice that the contribution approach separates costs into fixed and variable categories, first deducting variable expenses from sales to obtain what is known as the *contribution margin.* The **contribution margin** is the amount remaining from sales revenues after variable expenses have been deducted. This amount *contributes* toward covering fixed expenses and then toward profits for the period.

The contribution approach to the income statement is used as an internal planning and decision-making tool. Its emphasis on costs by behavior facilitates cost-volume-profit analysis, such as we shall be doing in the next chapter. The approach is also very useful in appraising management performance, in segmented reporting of profit data, and in budgeting. Moreover, the contribution approach helps managers organize data pertinent to all kinds of special decisions such as product-line analysis, pricing, use of scarce resources, and make or buy analysis. All of these topics are covered in later chapters.

Topic Tackler PLUS 5–2

EXHIBIT 5–14

Comparison of the Contribution Income Statement with the Traditional Income Statement (the data are given)

Traditional Approach (costs organized by function)		
Sales		$12,000
Less cost of goods sold		6,000*
Gross margin		6,000
Less operating expenses:		
Selling	$3,100*	
Administrative	1,900*	5,000
Net operating income		$ 1,000

Contribution Approach (costs organized by behavior)		
Sales		$12,000
Less variable expenses:		
Variable production	$2,000	
Variable selling	600	
Variable administrative	400	3,000
Contribution margin		9,000
Less fixed expenses:		
Fixed production	4,000	
Fixed selling	2,500	
Fixed administrative	1,500	8,000
Net operating income		$ 1,000

*Contains both variable and fixed expenses. This is the income statement for a manufacturing company; thus, when the income statement is placed in the contribution format, the "cost of goods sold" figure is divided between variable production costs and fixed production costs. If this were the income statement for a *merchandising* company (which simply purchases completed goods from a supplier), then the cost of goods sold would be *all* variable.

Summary

As we shall see in later chapters, the ability to predict how costs will respond to changes in activity is critical for making decisions, controlling operations, and evaluating performance. Three major classifications of costs were discussed in this chapter—variable, fixed, and mixed. Mixed costs consist of variable and fixed elements and can be expressed in equation form as $Y = a + bX$, where X is the activity, Y is the cost, a is the fixed cost element, and b is the variable cost per unit of activity.

Several methods are available to estimate the fixed and variable cost components of a mixed cost using past records of cost and activity. If the relation between cost and activity appears to be linear based on a scattergraph plot, then the variable and fixed components of the mixed cost can be estimated using the quick-and-dirty method, the high-low method, or the least-squares regression method. The quick-and-dirty method is based on drawing a straight line and then using the slope and the intercept of the straight line to estimate the variable and fixed cost components of the mixed cost. The high-low method implicitly draws a straight line through the points of lowest activity and highest activity. In most situations, the least-squares regression method is preferred to both the quick-and-dirty and high-low methods. Computer software is widely available for using the least-squares method. These software applications provide a variety of useful statistics along with estimates of the intercept (fixed cost) and slope (variable cost per unit). Nevertheless, even when least-squares regression is used, the data should be plotted to confirm that the relationship is really a straight line.

Managers use costs organized by behavior as a basis for many decisions. To facilitate this use, the income statement can be prepared in a contribution format. The contribution format income statement classifies costs by cost behavior (i.e., variable versus fixed) rather than by the functions of production, administration, and sales.

Review Problem 1: Cost Behavior

Neptune Rentals offers a boat rental service. Consider the following costs of the company over the relevant range of 5,000 to 8,000 hours of operating time for its boats:

	Hours of Operating Time			
	5,000	6,000	7,000	8,000
Total costs:				
Variable costs	$ 20,000	$?	$?	$?
Fixed costs	168,000	?	?	?
Total costs	$188,000	$?	$?	$?
Cost per hour:				
Variable cost	$?	$?	$?	$?
Fixed cost	?	?	?	?
Total cost per hour	$?	$?	$?	$?

Required:

Compute the missing amounts, assuming that cost behavior patterns remain unchanged within the relevant range of 5,000 to 8,000 hours.

Solution to Review Problem 1

The variable cost per hour can be computed as follows:

$$\$20{,}000 \div 5{,}000 \text{ hours} = \$4 \text{ per hour}$$

Therefore, in accordance with the behavior of variable and fixed costs, the missing amounts are as follows:

	Hours of Operating Time			
	5,000	6,000	7,000	8,000
Total costs:				
Variable costs	$ 20,000	$ 24,000	$ 28,000	$ 32,000
Fixed costs	168,000	168,000	168,000	168,000
Total costs	$188,000	$192,000	$196,000	$200,000
Cost per hour:				
Variable cost	$ 4.00	$ 4.00	$ 4.00	$ 4.00
Fixed cost	33.60	28.00	24.00	21.00
Total cost per hour	$ 37.60	$ 32.00	$ 28.00	$ 25.00

Observe that the total variable costs increase in proportion to the number of hours of operating time, but that these costs remain constant at $4 if expressed on a per hour basis.

In contrast, the total fixed costs do not change with changes in the level of activity. They remain constant at $168,000 within the relevant range. With increases in activity, however, the fixed cost decreases per hour, dropping from $33.60 per hour when the boats are operated 5,000 hours a period to only $21.00 per hour when the boats are operated 8,000 hours a period. *Because of this troublesome aspect of fixed costs, they are most easily (and most safely) dealt with on a total basis, rather than on a unit basis, in cost analysis work.*

Review Problem 2: High-Low Method

The administrator of Azalea Hills Hospital would like a cost formula linking the costs involved in admitting patients to the number of patients admitted during a month. The admitting department's costs and the number of patients admitted during the immediately preceding eight months are given in the following table:

Month	Number of Patients Admitted	Admitting Department Costs
May	1,800	$14,700
June	1,900	$15,200
July	1,700	$13,700
August	1,600	$14,000
September	1,500	$14,300
October	1,300	$13,100
November	1,100	$12,800
December	1,500	$14,600

Required:

1. Use the high-low method to establish the fixed and variable components of admitting costs.
2. Express the fixed and variable components of admitting costs as a cost formula in the linear equation form $Y = a + bX$.

Solution to Review Problem 2

1. The first step in the high-low method is to identify the periods of the lowest and highest activity. Those periods are November (1,100 patients admitted) and June (1,900 patients admitted).

   The second step is to compute the variable cost per unit using those two data points:

Month	Number of Patients Admitted	Admitting Department Costs
High activity level (June)	1,900	$15,200
Low activity level (November)	1,100	12,800
Change	800	$ 2,400

$$\text{Variable cost} = \frac{\text{Change in cost}}{\text{Change in activity}} = \frac{\$2{,}400}{800 \text{ patients admitted}} = \$3 \text{ per patient admitted}$$

The third step is to compute the fixed cost element by deducting the variable cost element from the total cost at either the high or low activity. In the computation below, the high point of activity is used:

$$\begin{aligned}\text{Fixed cost element} &= \text{Total cost} - \text{Variable cost element}\\ &= \$15{,}200 - (\$3 \text{ per patient admitted} \times 1{,}900 \text{ patients admitted})\\ &= \$9{,}500\end{aligned}$$

2. The cost formula expressed in the linear equation form is $Y = \$9{,}500 + \$3X$.

Glossary

Account analysis A method for analyzing cost behavior in which each account under consideration is classified as either variable or fixed based on the analyst's prior knowledge of how the cost in the account behaves. (p. 196)

Activity base A measure of whatever causes the incurrence of a variable cost. For example, the total cost of X-ray film in a hospital will increase as the number of X-rays taken increases. Therefore, the number of X-rays is an activity base that explains the total cost of X-ray film. (p. 185)

Committed fixed costs Those fixed costs that are difficult to adjust and that relate to investment in facilities, equipment, and basic organizational structure. (p. 190)

Contribution approach An income statement format that is geared to cost behavior in that costs are separated into variable and fixed categories rather than being separated according to the functions of production, sales, and administration. (p. 206)

Contribution margin The amount remaining from sales revenues after all variable expenses have been deducted. (p. 207)

Cost structure The relative proportion of fixed, variable, and mixed costs found within an organization. (p. 184)

Curvilinear costs A relationship between cost and activity that is a curve rather than a straight line. (p. 188)

Dependent variable A variable that responds to some causal factor; total cost is the dependent variable, as represented by the letter *Y*, in the equation $Y = a + bX$. (p. 199)

Discretionary fixed costs Those fixed costs that arise from annual decisions by management to spend in certain fixed cost areas, such as advertising and research. (p. 191)

Engineering approach A detailed analysis of cost behavior based on an industrial engineer's evaluation of the inputs that are required to carry out a particular activity and of the prices of those inputs. (p. 197)

High-low method A method of separating a mixed cost into its fixed and variable elements by analyzing the change in cost between the high and low activity levels. (p. 202)

Independent variable A variable that acts as a causal factor; activity is the independent variable, as represented by the letter *X*, in the equation $Y = a + bX$. (p. 199)

Least-squares regression method A method of separating a mixed cost into its fixed and variable elements by fitting a regression line that minimizes the sum of the squared errors. (p. 204)

Linear cost behavior Cost behavior is said to be linear whenever a straight line is a reasonable approximation for the relation between cost and activity. (p. 200)

Mixed cost A cost that contains both variable and fixed cost elements. (p. 194)

Multiple regression An analytical method required in those situations where variations in a dependent variable are caused by more than one factor. (p. 206)

R^2 A measure of goodness of fit in least-squares regression analysis. It is the percentage of the variation in the dependent variable that is explained by variation in the independent variable. (p. 205)

Relevant range The range of activity within which assumptions about variable and fixed cost behavior are valid. (p. 188)

Step-variable cost The cost of a resource (such as a maintenance worker) that is obtainable only in large chunks and that increases and decreases only in response to fairly wide changes in the activity level. (p. 188)

Appendix 5A: Least-Squares Regression Using Microsoft® Excel

LEARNING OBJECTIVE 5
Analyze a mixed cost using the least-squares regression method.

The least-squares regression method for estimating a linear relationship is based on the equation for a straight line:

$$Y = a + bX$$

As explained in the chapter, least-squares regression selects the values for the intercept *a* and the slope *b* that minimize the sum of the squared errors. The following formulas, which are derived in statistics and calculus texts, accomplish that objective:

$$b = \frac{n(\Sigma XY) - (\Sigma X)(\Sigma Y)}{n(\Sigma X^2) - (\Sigma X)^2}$$

$$a = \frac{(\Sigma Y) - b(\Sigma X)}{n}$$

where:

X = The level of activity (independent variable)

Y = The total mixed cost (dependent variable)

a = The total fixed cost (the vertical intercept of the line)

b = The variable cost per unit of activity (the slope of the line)

n = Number of observations

Σ = Sum across all n observations

Manually completing the calculations required by the formulas is tedious at best. Fortunately, statistical software packages are widely available that perform the calculations automatically. Spreadsheet software, such as Microsoft® Excel, can also be used to do least-squares regression—although it requires a little more work than using a specialized statistical application.

To illustrate how Excel can be used to calculate the intercept *a*, the slope *b*, and the R^2, we will use the Brentline Hospital data for maintenance costs on page 198. The worksheet in Exhibit 5A–1 contains the data and the calculations.

As you can see, the *X* values (the independent variable) have been entered in cells B4 through B10. The *Y* values (the dependent variable) have been entered in cells C4 through C10. The slope, intercept, and R^2 are computed using the Excel functions INTERCEPT, SLOPE, and RSQ. You must specify the range of cells for the *Y* values and for the *X* values. In the worksheet below, cell B12 contains the formula =INTERCEPT(C4:C10,B4:B10); cell B13 contains the formula =SLOPE(C4:C10,B4:B10); and cell B14 contains the formula =RSQ(C4:C10,B4:B10).

According to the calculations carried out by Excel, the fixed maintenance cost (the intercept) is $3,431 per month and the variable cost (the slope) is $0.759 per patient-day.

EXHIBIT 5A–1
The Least-Squares Regression Worksheet for Brentline Hospital

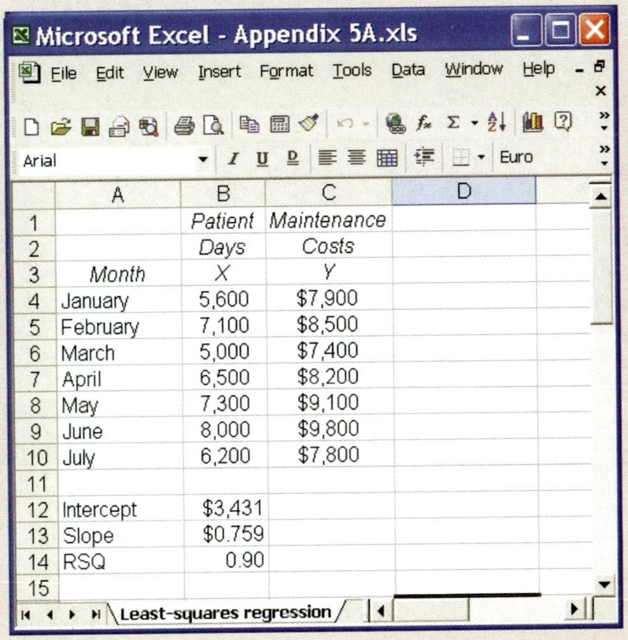

	A	B	C	D
1		Patient	Maintenance	
2		Days	Costs	
3	Month	X	Y	
4	January	5,600	$7,900	
5	February	7,100	$8,500	
6	March	5,000	$7,400	
7	April	6,500	$8,200	
8	May	7,300	$9,100	
9	June	8,000	$9,800	
10	July	6,200	$7,800	
11				
12	Intercept	$3,431		
13	Slope	$0.759		
14	RSQ	0.90		
15				

EXHIBIT 5A–2
A Scattergraph Plot of the Brentline Hospital Data

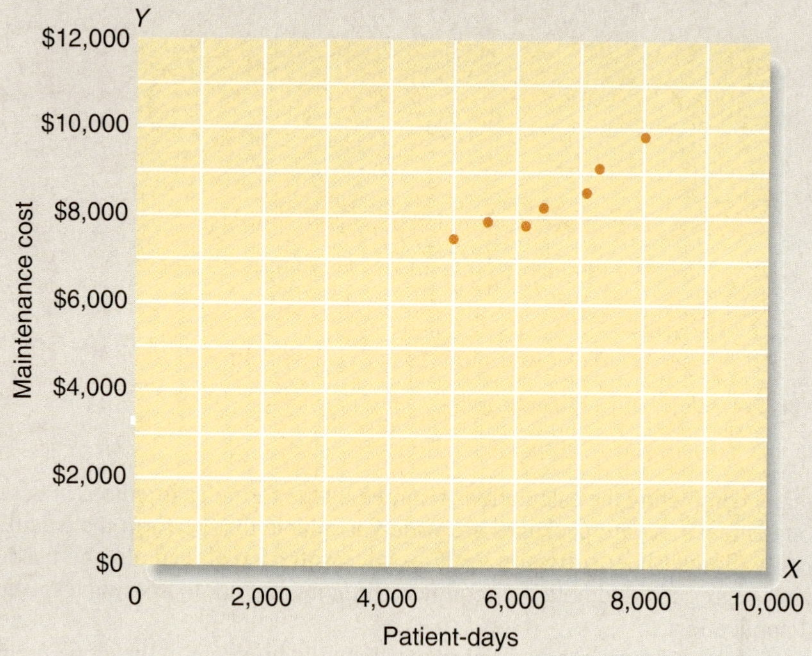

Therefore, the cost formula for maintenance cost is:

$$Y = a + bX$$

$$Y = \$3{,}431 + \$0.759X$$

Note that the R^2 (i.e., RSQ) is 0.90, which—as previously discussed—is quite good and indicates that 90% of the variation in maintenance costs is explained by the variation in patient-days.

Plotting the data is easy in Excel. Select the range of values that you would like to plot—in this case, cells B4:C10. Then select the Chart Wizard tool on the toolbar and make the appropriate choices in the various dialogue boxes that appear. When you are finished, you should have a scattergraph that looks like the plot in Exhibit 5A–2. Note that the relation between cost and activity is approximately linear, so it is reasonable to fit a straight line to the data as we have implicitly done with the least-squares regression.

Questions

5–1 Distinguish between (*a*) a variable cost, (*b*) a fixed cost, and (*c*) a mixed cost.

5–2 What effect does an increase in volume have on—
- *a.* Unit fixed costs?
- *b.* Unit variable costs?
- *c.* Total fixed costs?
- *d.* Total variable costs?

5–3 Define the following terms: (*a*) cost behavior and (*b*) relevant range.

5–4 What is meant by an *activity base* when dealing with variable costs? Give several examples of activity bases.

5–5 Distinguish between (*a*) a variable cost, (*b*) a mixed cost, and (*c*) a step-variable cost. Chart the three costs on a graph, with activity plotted horizontally and cost plotted vertically.

5–6 Managers often assume a strictly linear relationship between cost and volume. How can this practice be defended in light of the fact that many costs are curvilinear?

5–7 Distinguish between discretionary fixed costs and committed fixed costs.

5–8 Classify the following fixed costs as normally being either committed or discretionary:

a. Depreciation on buildings.
b. Advertising.
c. Research.
d. Long-term equipment leases.
e. Pension payments to the company's retirees.
f. Management development and training.

5–9 Does the concept of the relevant range apply to fixed costs? Explain.

5–10 What is the major disadvantage of the high-low method?

5–11 Give the general formula for a mixed cost. Which term represents the variable cost? The fixed cost?

5–12 What is meant by the term *least-squares regression?*

5–13 What is the difference between ordinary least-squares regression analysis and multiple regression analysis?

5–14 What is the difference between a contribution approach income statement and a traditional approach income statement?

5–15 What is the contribution margin?

Exercises

EXERCISE 5–1 Fixed and Variable Cost Behavior [LO1]

Espresso Express operates a number of espresso coffee stands in busy suburban malls. The fixed weekly expense of a coffee stand is $1,200 and the variable cost per cup of coffee served is $0.22.

Required:

1. Fill in the following table with your estimates of total costs and cost per cup of coffee at the indicated levels of activity for a coffee stand. Round off the cost of a cup of coffee to the nearest tenth of a cent.

	Cups of Coffee Served in a Week		
	2,000	2,100	2,200
Fixed cost	?	?	?
Variable cost	?	?	?
Total cost	?	?	?
Cost per cup of coffee served	?	?	?

2. Does the cost per cup of coffee served increase, decrease, or remain the same as the number of cups of coffee served in a week increases? Explain.

EXERCISE 5–2 High-Low Method; Scattergraph Analysis [LO2, LO3]

The following data relating to units shipped and total shipping expense have been assembled by Archer Company, a wholesaler of large, custom-built air-conditioning units for commercial buildings:

Month	Units Shipped	Total Shipping Expense
January	3	$1,800
February	6	$2,300
March	4	$1,700
April	5	$2,000
May	7	$2,300
June	8	$2,700
July	2	$1,200

Required:

1. Using the high-low method, estimate a cost formula for shipping expense.

2. The president of the company has no confidence in the high-low method and would like you to check out your results using a scattergraph.
   a. Prepare a scattergraph, using the data given above. Plot cost on the vertical axis and activity on the horizontal axis. Use a ruler to fit a straight line to your plotted points.
   b. Using your scattergraph, estimate the approximate variable cost per unit shipped and the approximate fixed cost per month with the quick-and-dirty method.
3. What factors, other than the number of units shipped, are likely to affect the company's total shipping expense? Explain.

EXERCISE 5–3 (Appendix 5A) Least-Square Regression [LO5]
Refer to the data for Archer Company in Exercise 5–2.

Required:
1. Using the least-squares regression method, estimate a cost formula for shipping expense.
2. If you also completed Exercise 5–2, prepare a simple table comparing the variable and fixed cost elements of shipping expense as computed under the quick-and-dirty scattergraph method, the high-low method, and the least-squares regression method.

EXERCISE 5–4 High-Low Method [LO3]
The Cheyenne Hotel in Big Sky, Montana, has accumulated records of the total electrical costs of the hotel and the number of occupancy-days over the last year. An occupancy-day represents a room rented out for one day. The hotel's business is highly seasonal, with peaks occurring during the ski season and in the summer.

Month	Occupancy-Days	Electrical Costs
January	1,736	$4,127
February	1,904	$4,207
March	2,356	$5,083
April	960	$2,857
May	360	$1,871
June	744	$2,696
July	2,108	$4,670
August	2,406	$5,148
September	840	$2,691
October	124	$1,588
November	720	$2,454
December	1,364	$3,529

Required:
1. Using the high-low method, estimate the fixed cost of electricity per month and the variable cost of electricity per occupancy-day. Round off the fixed cost to the nearest whole dollar and the variable cost to the nearest whole cent.
2. What other factors other than occupancy-days are likely to affect the variation in electrical costs from month to month?

EXERCISE 5–5 Contribution Format Income Statement [LO4]
The Alpine House, Inc., is a large retailer of winter sports equipment. An income statement for the company's Ski Department for a recent quarter is presented below:

THE ALPINE HOUSE, INC. Income Statement—Ski Department For the Quarter Ended March 31		
Sales		$150,000
Less cost of goods sold		90,000
Gross margin		60,000
Less operating expenses:		
Selling expenses	$30,000	
Administrative expenses	10,000	40,000
Net operating income		$ 20,000

Skis sell, on the average, for $750 per pair. Variable selling expenses are $50 per pair of skis sold. The remaining selling expenses are fixed. The administrative expenses are 20% variable and 80% fixed. The company does not manufacture its own skis; it purchases them from a supplier for $450 per pair.

Required:

1. Prepare an income statement for the quarter using the contribution approach.
2. For every pair of skis sold during the quarter, what was the contribution toward covering fixed expenses and toward earning profits?

EXERCISE 5–6 Cost Behavior; Contribution Format Income Statement [LO1, LO4]

Harris Company manufactures and sells a single product. A partially completed schedule of the company's total and per unit costs over the relevant range of 30,000 to 50,000 units produced and sold annually is given below:

	Units Produced and Sold		
	30,000	40,000	50,000
Total costs:			
Variable costs	$180,000	?	?
Fixed costs	300,000	?	?
Total costs	$480,000	?	?
Cost per unit:			
Variable cost	?	?	?
Fixed cost	?	?	?
Total cost per unit	?	?	?

Required:

1. Complete the schedule of the company's total and unit costs above.
2. Assume that the company produces and sells 45,000 units during the year at a selling price of $16 per unit. Prepare a contribution format income statement for the year.

EXERCISE 5–7 High-Low Method; Predicting Cost [LO1, LO3]

St. Mark's Hospital contains 450 beds. The average occupancy rate is 80% per month. In other words, on average, 80% of the hospital's beds are occupied by patients. At this level of occupancy, the hospital's operating costs are $32 per occupied bed per day, assuming a 30-day month. This $32 figure contains both variable and fixed cost elements.

During June, the hospital's occupancy rate was only 60%. A total of $326,700 in operating cost was incurred during the month.

Required:

1. Using the high-low method, estimate:
   a. The variable cost per occupied bed on a daily basis.
   b. The total fixed operating costs per month.
2. Assume an occupancy rate of 70% per month. What amount of total operating cost would you expect the hospital to incur?

EXERCISE 5–8 High-Low Method; Predicting Cost [LO1, LO3]

The Lakeshore Hotel's guest-days of occupancy and custodial supplies expense over the last seven months were:

Month	Guest-Days of Occupancy	Custodial Supplies Expense
March	4,000	$7,500
April	6,500	$8,250
May	8,000	$10,500
June	10,500	$12,000
July	12,000	$13,500
August	9,000	$10,750
September	7,500	$9,750

Guest-days is a measure of the overall activity at the hotel. For example, a guest who stays at the hotel for three days is counted as three guest-days.

Required:

1. Using the high-low method, estimate a cost formula for custodial supplies expense.
2. Using the cost formula you derived above, what amount of custodial supplies expense would you expect to be incurred at an occupancy level of 11,000 guest-days?

EXERCISE 5–9 Scattergraph Analysis; High-Low Method [LO2, LO3]
Refer to the data for Lakeshore Hotel in Exercise 5–8.

Required:

1. Prepare a scattergraph using the data from Exercise 5–8. Plot cost on the vertical axis and activity on the horizontal axis. Using a ruler, fit a line to your plotted points.
2. Using the quick-and-dirty method, what is the approximate monthly fixed cost? The approximate variable cost per guest-day?
3. Scrutinize the points on your graph and explain why the high-low method would or would not yield an accurate cost formula in this situation.

EXERCISE 5–10 Scattergraph Analysis [LO2]
Oki Products, Ltd., has observed the following processing costs at various levels of activity over the last 15 months:

Month	Units Produced	Processing Cost
1	4,500	$38,000
2	11,000	$52,000
3	12,000	$56,000
4	5,500	$40,000
5	9,000	$47,000
6	10,500	$52,000
7	7,500	$44,000
8	5,000	$41,000
9	11,500	$52,000
10	6,000	$43,000
11	8,500	$48,000
12	10,000	$50,000
13	6,500	$44,000
14	9,500	$48,000
15	8,000	$46,000

Required:

1. Prepare a scattergraph using the above data. Plot cost on the vertical axis and activity on the horizontal axis. Fit a line to your plotted points using a ruler.
2. Using the quick-and-dirty method, what is the approximate monthly fixed cost? The approximate variable cost per unit processed? Show your computations.

EXERCISE 5–11 Cost Behavior; High-Low Method [LO1, LO3]
Hoi Chong Transport, Ltd., operates a fleet of delivery trucks in Singapore. The company has determined that if a truck is driven 105,000 kilometers during a year, the average operating cost is 11.4 cents per kilometer. If a truck is driven only 70,000 kilometers during a year, the average operating cost increases to 13.4 cents per kilometer. (The Singapore dollar is the currency used in Singapore.)

Required:

1. Using the high-low method, estimate the variable and fixed cost elements of the annual cost of truck operation.
2. Express the variable and fixed costs in the form $Y = a + bX$.
3. If a truck were driven 80,000 kilometers during a year, what total cost would you expect to be incurred?

EXERCISE 5–12 (Appendix 5A) Least-Squares Regression [LO1, LO5]
George Caloz & Frères, located in Grenchen, Switzerland, makes prestige high-end custom watches in small lots. The company has been in operation since 1856. One of the company's

products, a platinum diving watch, goes through an etching process. The company has observed etching costs as follows over the last six weeks:

Week	Units	Total Etching Cost
1	4	SFr18
2	3	17
3	8	25
4	6	20
5	7	24
6	2	16
	30	SFr120

The Swiss currency is the Swiss Franc, which is denoted by SFr.

For planning purposes, management would like to know the amount of variable etching cost per unit and the total fixed etching cost per week.

Required:

1. Using the least-squares regression method, estimate the variable and fixed elements of etching cost.
2. Express the cost data in (1) above in the form $Y = a + bX$.
3. If the company processes five units next week, what would be the expected total etching cost?

Problems

PROBLEM 5–13 Cost Behavior; High-Low Method; Contribution Format Income Statement [LO1, LO3, LO4]

eXcel

Morrisey & Brown, Ltd., of Sydney is a merchandising company that is the sole distributor of a product that is increasing in popularity among Australian consumers. The company's income statements for the three most recent months follow:

MORRISEY & BROWN, LTD.
Income Statements
For the Three Months Ending September 30

	July	August	September
Sales in units	4,000	4,500	5,000
Sales revenue	A$400,000	A$450,000	A$500,000
Less cost of goods sold	240,000	270,000	300,000
Gross margin	160,000	180,000	200,000
Less operating expenses:			
Advertising expense	21,000	21,000	21,000
Shipping expense	34,000	36,000	38,000
Salaries and commissions	78,000	84,000	90,000
Insurance expense	6,000	6,000	6,000
Depreciation expense	15,000	15,000	15,000
Total operating expenses	154,000	162,000	170,000
Net operating income	A$ 6,000	A$ 18,000	A$ 30,000

(Note: Morrisey & Brown, Ltd.'s Australian-formatted income statement has been recast in the format common in the United States. The Australian dollar is denoted here by A$.)

Required:

1. Identify each of the company's expenses (including cost of goods sold) as either variable, fixed, or mixed.
2. Using the high-low method, separate each mixed expense into variable and fixed elements. State the cost formula for each mixed expense.
3. Redo the company's income statement at the 5,000-unit level of activity using the contribution format.

PROBLEM 5–14 Contribution Format versus Traditional Income Statement [LO4]

Marwick's Pianos, Inc., purchases pianos from a large manufacturer and sells them at the retail level. The pianos cost, on the average, $2,450 each from the manufacturer. Marwick's Pianos, Inc., sells the pianos to its customers at an average price of $3,125 each. The selling and administrative costs that the company incurs in a typical month are presented below:

Costs	Cost Formula
Selling:	
Advertising	$700 per month
Sales salaries and commissions	$950 per month, plus 8% of sales
Delivery of pianos to customers	$30 per piano sold
Utilities	$350 per month
Depreciation of sales facilities	$800 per month
Administrative:	
Executive salaries	$2,500 per month
Insurance	$400 per month
Clerical	$1,000 per month, plus $20 per piano sold
Depreciation of office equipment	$300 per month

During August, Marwick's Pianos, Inc., sold and delivered 40 pianos.

Required:

1. Prepare an income statement for Marwick's Pianos, Inc., for August. Use the traditional format, with costs organized by function.
2. Redo (1) above, this time using the contribution format, with costs organized by behavior. Show costs and revenues on both a total and a per unit basis down through contribution margin.
3. Refer to the income statement you prepared in (2) above. Why might it be misleading to show the fixed costs on a per unit basis?

PROBLEM 5–15 (Appendix 5A) Least-Squares Regression Method Scattergraph; Cost Behavior [LO1, LO2, LO5]

Professor John Morton has just been appointed chairperson of the Finance Department at Westland University. In reviewing the department's cost records, Professor Morton has found the following total cost associated with Finance 101 over the last several terms:

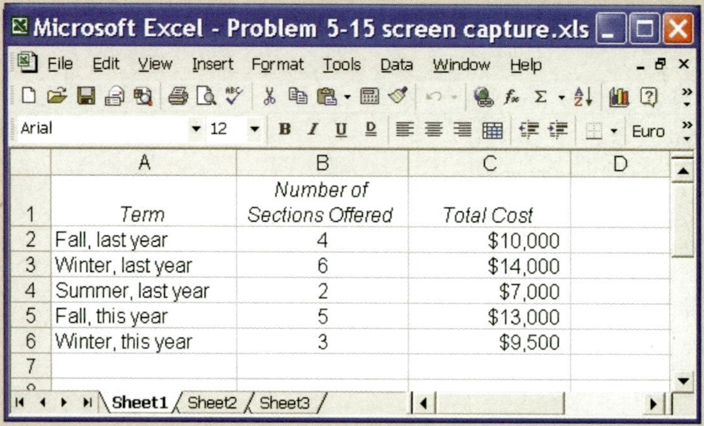

	A	B	C	D
1	Term	Number of Sections Offered	Total Cost	
2	Fall, last year	4	$10,000	
3	Winter, last year	6	$14,000	
4	Summer, last year	2	$7,000	
5	Fall, this year	5	$13,000	
6	Winter, this year	3	$9,500	
7				

Professor Morton knows that there are some variable costs, such as amounts paid to graduate assistants, associated with the course. He would like to have the variable and fixed costs separated for planning purposes.

Required:

1. Using the least-squares regression method, estimate the variable cost per section and the total fixed cost per term for Finance 101.
2. Express the cost data derived in (1) above in the linear equation form $Y = a + bX$.
3. Assume that because of the small number of sections offered during the Winter Term this year, Professor Morton will have to offer eight sections of Finance 101 during the Fall Term. Compute the expected total cost for Finance 101. Can you see any problem with using the cost formula from (2) above to derive this total cost figure? Explain.
4. Prepare a scattergraph and fit a line to the plotted points using the cost formula expressed in (2) above.

PROBLEM 5–16 Identifying Cost Behavior Patterns [LO1]

A number of graphs displaying cost behavior patterns are shown below. The vertical axis on each graph represents total cost, and the horizontal axis represents level of activity (volume).

Required:

1. For each of the following situations, identify the graph below that illustrates the cost behavior pattern involved. Any graph may be used more than once.
   a. Cost of raw materials used.
   b. Electricity bill—a flat fixed charge, plus a variable cost after a certain number of kilowatt-hours are used.
   c. City water bill, which is computed as follows:

First 1,000,000 gallons or less	$1,000 flat fee
Next 10,000 gallons	$0.003 per gallon used
Next 10,000 gallons	$0.006 per gallon used
Next 10,000 gallons	$0.009 per gallon used
Etc.	Etc.

   d. Depreciation of equipment, where the amount is computed by the straight-line method. When the depreciation rate was established, it was anticipated that the obsolescence factor would be greater than the wear and tear factor.
   e. Rent on a factory building donated by the city, where the agreement calls for a fixed fee payment unless 200,000 labor-hours or more are worked, in which case no rent need be paid.
   f. Salaries of maintenance workers, where one maintenance worker is needed for every 1,000 hours of machine-hours or less (that is, 0 to 1,000 hours requires one maintenance worker, 1,001 to 2,000 hours requires two maintenance workers, etc.)
   g. Cost of raw materials, where the cost starts at $7.50 per unit and then decreases by 5 cents per unit for each of the first 100 units purchased, after which it remains constant at $2.50 per unit.
   h. Rent on a factory building donated by the county, where the agreement calls for rent of $100,000 less $1 for each direct labor-hour worked in excess of 200,000 hours, but a minimum rental payment of $20,000 must be paid.
   i. Use of a machine under a lease, where a minimum charge of $1,000 is paid for up to 400 hours of machine time. After 400 hours of machine time, an additional charge of $2 per hour is paid up to a maximum charge of $2,000 per period.

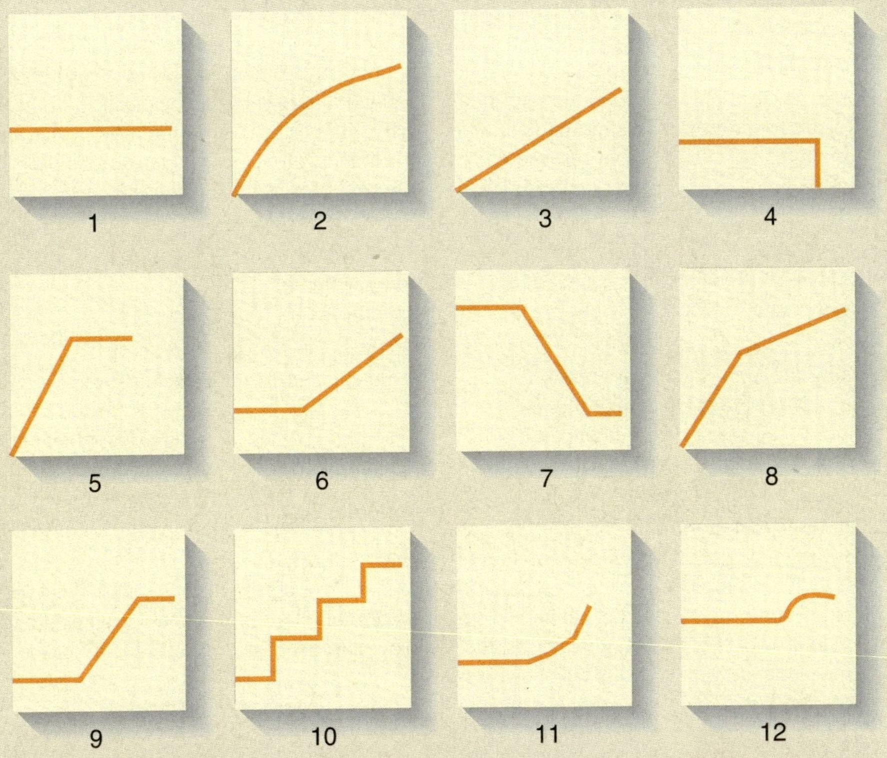

2. How would a knowledge of cost behavior patterns such as those above be of help to a manager in analyzing the cost structure of his or her company?

(CPA, adapted)

PROBLEM 5–17 High-Low and Scattergraph Analysis [LO2, LO3]

Pleasant View Hospital of British Columbia has just hired a new chief administrator who is anxious to employ sound management and planning techniques in the business affairs of the hospital. Accordingly, she has directed her assistant to summarize the cost structure of the various departments so that data will be available for planning purposes.

The assistant is unsure how to classify the utilities costs in the Radiology Department since these costs do not exhibit either strictly variable or fixed cost behavior. Utilities costs are very high in the department due to a CAT scanner that draws a large amount of power and is kept running at all times. The scanner can't be turned off due to the long warm-up period required for its use. When the scanner is used to scan a patient, it consumes an additional burst of power. The assistant has accumulated the following data on utilities costs and use of the scanner since the first of the year.

Month	Number of Scans	Utilities Cost
January	60	$2,200
February	70	$2,600
March	90	$2,900
April	120	$3,300
May	100	$3,000
June	130	$3,600
July	150	$4,000
August	140	$3,600
September	110	$3,100
October	80	$2,500

The chief administrator has informed her assistant that the utilities cost is probably a mixed cost that will have to be broken down into its variable and fixed cost elements by use of a scattergraph. The assistant feels, however, that if an analysis of this type is necessary, then the high-low method should be used, since it is easier and quicker. The controller has suggested that there may be a better approach.

Required:

1. Using the high-low method, estimate a cost formula for utilities. Express the formula in the form $Y = a + bX$. (The variable rate should be stated in terms of cost per scan.)
2. Prepare a scattergraph using the data above. (The number of scans should be placed on the horizontal axis, and utilities cost should be placed on the vertical axis.) Fit a straight line to the plotted points using a ruler and estimate a cost formula for utilities using the quick-and-dirty method.

PROBLEM 5–18 (Appendix 5A) Least-Squares Regression Method [LO5]

Refer to the data for Pleasant View Hospital in Problem 5–17.

Required:

1. Using the least-squares regression method, estimate a cost formula for utilities. (Round the variable cost to two decimal places.)
2. Refer to the graph prepared in part (2) of Problem 5–17. Explain why in this case the high-low method would be the least accurate of the three methods in deriving a cost formula.

PROBLEM 5–19 Scattergraph Analysis [LO2]

Molina Company is a value-added computer resaler that specializes in providing services to small companies. The company owns and maintains several autos for use by the sales staff. All expenses of operating these autos have been entered into an Automobile Expense account on the company's books. Along with this record of expenses, the company has also kept a careful record of the number of miles the autos have been driven each month.

The company's records of miles driven and total auto expenses over the past 10 months are given below:

Month	Total Mileage (000)	Total Cost
January	4	$3,000
February	8	$3,700
March	7	$3,300
April	12	$4,000
May	6	$3,300
June	11	$3,900
July	14	$4,200
August	10	$3,600
September	13	$4,100
October	15	$4,400

Molina Company's president wants to know the cost of operating the fleet of cars in terms of the fixed monthly cost and the variable cost per mile driven.

Required:

1. Prepare a scattergraph using the data given above. Place cost on the vertical axis and activity (miles driven) on the horizontal axis. Using a ruler, fit a straight line to the plotted points.
2. Estimate the fixed cost per month and the variable cost per mile driven using the quick-and-dirty method.

PROBLEM 5–20 (Appendix 5A) Least-Squares Regression Method [LO5]

Refer to the data for Molina Company in Problem 5–19.

Required:

1. Using the least-squares regression method, estimate the variable and fixed cost elements associated with the company's fleet of autos. (Since the Total Mileage is in thousands of miles, the variable cost you compute will also be in thousands of miles. The cost can be left in this form, or you can convert it to a per mile basis by dividing the cost you get by 1,000.)
2. From the data in (1) above, express the cost formula for auto use in the linear equation form $Y = a + bX$.

PROBLEM 5–21 (Appendix 5A) Least-Squares Regression Analysis; Contribution Format Income Statement [LO4, LO5]

Milden Company has an exclusive franchise to purchase a product from the manufacturer and distribute it on the retail level. As an aid in planning, the company has decided to start using the contribution format income statement internally. To have data to prepare such a statement, the company has analyzed its expenses and developed the following cost formulas:

Cost	Cost Formula
Cost of good sold	$35 per unit sold
Advertising expense	$210,000 per quarter
Sales commissions	6% of sales
Shipping expense	?
Administrative salaries	$145,000 per quarter
Insurance expense	$9,000 per quarter
Depreciation expense	$76,000 per quarter

Management has concluded that shipping expense is a mixed cost, containing both variable and fixed cost elements. Units sold and the related shipping expense over the last eight quarters follow:

Quarter	Units Sold (000)	Shipping Expense
Year 1:		
First	10	$119,000
Second	16	$175,000
Third	18	$190,000
Fourth	15	$164,000

continued

Quarter	Units Sold (000)	Shipping Expense
Year 2:		
First	11	$130,000
Second	17	$185,000
Third	20	$210,000
Fourth	13	$147,000

Milden Company's president would like a cost formula derived for shipping expense so that a budgeted income statement using the contribution approach can be prepared for the next quarter.

Required:

1. Using the least-squares regression method, estimate a cost formula for shipping expense. (Since the Units Sold above are in thousands of units, the variable cost you compute will also be in thousands of units. It can be left in this form, or you can convert your variable cost to a per unit basis by dividing it by 1,000.)
2. In the first quarter of Year 3, the company plans to sell 12,000 units at a selling price of $100 per unit. Prepare a contribution format income statement for the quarter.

PROBLEM 5–22 High-Low Method; Cost of Goods Manufactured [LO1, LO3]

Amfac Company manufactures a single product. The company keeps careful records of manufacturing activities from which the following information has been extracted:

	Level of Activity	
	March–Low	June–High
Number of units produced	6,000	9,000
Cost of goods manufactured	$168,000	$257,000
Work in process inventory, beginning	$9,000	$32,000
Work in process inventory, ending	$15,000	$21,000
Direct materials cost per unit	$6	$6
Direct labor cost per unit	$10	$10
Manufacturing overhead cost, total	? 78,000	? 102,000

The company's manufacturing overhead cost consists of both variable and fixed cost elements. To have data available for planning, management wants to determine how much of the overhead cost is variable with units produced and how much of it is fixed per month.

Required:

1. For both March and June, estimate the amount of manufacturing overhead cost added to production. The company had no under- or overapplied overhead in either month. (Hint: A useful way to proceed might be to construct a schedule of cost of goods manufactured.)
2. Using the high-low method, estimate a cost formula for manufacturing overhead. Express the variable portion of the formula in terms of a variable rate per unit of product.
3. If 7,000 units are produced during a month, what would be the cost of goods manufactured? (Assume that work in process inventories do not change and that there is no under- or overapplied overhead cost for the month.)

PROBLEM 5–23 High-Low Method; Predicting Cost [LO1, LO3]

Sawaya Co., Ltd., of Japan is a manufacturing company whose total factory overhead costs fluctuate considerably from year to year according to increases and decreases in the number of direct labor-hours worked in the factory. Total factory overhead costs (in Japanese yen, denoted ¥) at high and low levels of activity for recent years are given below:

	Level of Activity	
	Low	High
Direct labor-hours	50,000	75,000
Total factory overhead costs	¥14,250,000	¥17,625,000

The factory overhead costs above consist of indirect materials, rent, and maintenance. The company has analyzed these costs at the 50,000-hour level of activity as follows:

Indirect materials (variable)	¥5,000,000
Rent (fixed)	6,000,000
Maintenance (mixed)	3,250,000
Total factory overhead costs	¥14,250,000

To have data available for planning, the company wants to break down the maintenance cost into its variable and fixed cost elements.

Required:

1. Estimate how much of the ¥17,625,000 factory overhead cost at the high level of activity consists of maintenance cost. (Hint: To do this, it may be helpful to first determine how much of the ¥17,625,000 consists of indirect materials and rent. Think about the behavior of variable and fixed costs!)
2. Using the high-low method, estimate a cost formula for maintenance.
3. What total factory overhead costs would you expect the company to incur at an operating level of 70,000 direct labor-hours?

PROBLEM 5–24 High-Low Method; Predicting Cost [LO1, LO3]

Nova Company's total overhead costs at various levels of activity are presented below:

Month	Machine-Hours	Total Overhead Costs
April	70,000	$198,000
May	60,000	$174,000
June	80,000	$222,000
July	90,000	$246,000

Assume that the total overhead costs above consist of utilities, supervisory salaries, and maintenance. The breakdown of these costs at the 60,000 machine-hour level of activity is:

Utilities (variable)	$ 48,000
Supervisory salaries (fixed) . . .	21,000
Maintenance (mixed)	105,000
Total overhead costs	$174,000

Nova Company's management wants to break down the maintenance cost into its variable and fixed cost elements.

Required:

1. Estimate how much of the $246,000 of overhead cost in July was maintenance cost. (Hint: to do this, it may be helpful to first determine how much of the $246,000 consisted of utilities and supervisory salaries. Think about the behavior of variable and fixed costs!)
2. Using the high-low method, estimate a cost formula for maintenance.
3. Express the company's *total* overhead costs in the linear equation form $Y = a + bX$.
4. What *total* overhead costs would you expect to be incurred at an operating activity level of 75,000 machine-hours?

Cases

CASE 5–25 (Appendix 5A) Analysis of Mixed Costs, Job-Order Costing, and Activity-Based Costing [LO1, LO2, LO5]

Hokuriku-Seika Co., Ltd., of Yokohama, Japan, is a subcontractor to local manufacturing companies. The company specializes in precision metal cutting using focused high-pressure water jets and high-energy lasers. The company has a traditional job-order costing system in which direct labor and direct materials costs are assigned directly to jobs, but factory overhead is applied to jobs using a predetermined overhead rate with direct labor-hours as the activity base. Management uses this job cost data for valuing cost of goods sold and inventories for external reports. For internal decision making, management has largely ignored this cost data since direct labor costs are basically fixed and management believes overhead costs actually have little to do with direct labor-hours. Recently, management has become interested in activity-based costing (ABC) as a way of estimating job costs and other costs for decision-making purposes.

Management assembled a cross-functional team to design a prototype ABC system. Electrical costs were among the first factory overhead costs investigated by the team. Electricity is used to provide light, to power equipment, and to heat the building in the winter and cool it in the summer. The ABC team proposed allocating electrical costs to jobs based on machine-hours since running the machines consumes significant amounts of electricity. Data assembled by the team concerning actual direct labor-hours, machine-hours, and electrical costs over a recent eight-week period appear below. (The Japanese currency is the yen, which is denoted by ¥.)

	Direct Labor-Hours	Machine-Hours	Electrical Costs
Week 1	8,920	7,200	¥ 77,100
Week 2	8,810	8,200	84,400
Week 3	8,950	8,700	80,400
Week 4	8,990	7,200	75,500
Week 5	8,840	7,400	81,100
Week 6	8,890	8,800	83,300
Week 7	8,950	6,400	79,200
Week 8	8,990	7,700	85,500
Total	71,340	61,600	¥646,500

To help assess the effect of the proposed change to machine-hours as the allocation base, the eight-week totals were converted to annual figures by multiplying them by six.

	Direct Labor-Hours	Machine-Hours	Electrical Costs
Estimated annual total (eight-week total above × 6)	428,040	369,600	¥3,879,000

Required:

1. Assume that the estimated annual totals from the above table are used to compute the company's predetermined overhead rate. What would be the predetermined overhead rate for electrical costs if the allocation base is direct labor-hours? Machine-hours?
2. Hokuriku-Seika Co. intends to bid on a job for a shipyard that would require 350 direct labor-hours and 270 machine-hours. How much electrical cost would be charged to this job using the predetermined overhead rate computed in (1) above if the allocation base is direct labor-hours? Machine-hours?
3. Prepare a scattergraph in which you plot direct labor-hours on the horizontal axis and electrical costs on the vertical axis. Prepare another scattergraph in which you plot machine-hours on the horizontal axis and electrical costs on the vertical axis. Do you agree with the ABC team that machine-hours is a better allocation base for electrical costs than direct labor-hours? Why?
4. Using machine-hours as the measure of activity, estimate the fixed and variable components of electrical costs using least-squares regression.
5. How much electrical cost do you think would actually be caused by the shipyard job in (2) above? Explain.
6. What factors, apart from direct labor-hours and machine-hours, are likely to affect consumption of electrical power in the company?

CASE 5–26 Scattergraph Analysis; Selection of an Activity Base [LO2]

Angora Wraps of Pendleton, Oregon, makes fine sweaters out of pure angora wool. The business is seasonal, with the largest demand during the fall, the winter, and Christmas holidays. The company must ramp up production each summer to meet estimated demand.

The company has been analyzing its costs to determine which costs are fixed and variable for planning purposes. Below are data for the company's activity and direct labor costs over the last year.

Month	Thousands of Units Produced	Number of Paid Days	Direct Labor Cost
January	98	20	$14,162
February	76	20	$12,994
March	75	21	$15,184
April	80	22	$15,038
May	85	22	$15,768
June	102	21	$15,330
July	52	19	$13,724
August	136	21	$14,162
September	138	22	$15,476
October	132	23	$15,476
November	86	18	$12,972
December	56	21	$14,074

The number of workdays varies from month to month due to the number of weekdays, holidays, and days of vacation in the month. The paid days include paid vacations (in July) and paid holidays (in November and December). The number of units produced in a month varies depending on demand and the number of workdays in the month.

The company has eight workers who are classified as direct labor.

Required:

1. Plot the direct labor cost and units produced on a scattergraph. (Place cost on the vertical axis and units produced on the horizontal axis.)
2. Plot the direct labor cost and number of paid days on a scattergraph. (Place cost on the vertical axis and the number of paid days on the horizontal axis.)
3. Which measure of activity—number of units produced or paid days—should be used as the activity base for explaining direct labor cost? Explain

CASE 5–27 Analysis of Mixed Costs in a Pricing Decision [LO1 and LO2, LO3, or LO5]

Maria Chavez owns a catering company that serves food and beverages at parties and business functions. Chavez's business is seasonal, with a heavy schedule during the summer months and holidays and a lighter schedule at other times.

One of the major events Chavez's customers request is a cocktail party. She offers a standard cocktail party and has estimated the cost per guest as follows:

Food and beverages	$15.00
Labor (0.5 hrs. @ $10.00/hr.)	5.00
Overhead (0.5 hrs. @ $13.98/hr.)	6.99
Total cost per guest	$26.99

The standard cocktail party lasts three hours and Chavez hires one worker for every six guests, so that works out to one-half hour of labor per guest. These workers are hired only as needed and are paid only for the hours they actually work.

When bidding on cocktail parties, Chavez adds a 15% markup to yield a price of about $31 per guest. She is confident about her estimates of the costs of food and beverages and labor but is not as comfortable with the estimate of overhead cost. The $13.98 overhead cost per labor hour was determined by dividing total overhead expenses for the last 12 months by total labor hours for the same period. Monthly data concerning overhead costs and labor-hours follow:

Month	Labor-Hours	Overhead Expenses
January	2,500	$ 55,000
February	2,800	59,000
March	3,000	60,000
April	4,200	64,000
May	4,500	67,000
June	5,500	71,000
July	6,500	74,000
August	7,500	77,000
September	7,000	75,000
October	4,500	68,000
November	3,100	62,000
December	6,500	73,000
Total	57,600	$805,000

Chavez has received a request to bid on a 180-guest fund-raising cocktail party to be given next month by an important local charity. (The party would last the usual three hours.) She would like to win this contract because the guest list for this charity event includes many prominent individuals that she would like to land as future clients. Maria is confident that these potential customers would be favorably impressed by her company's services at the charity event.

Required:

1. Estimate the contribution to profit of a standard 180-guest cocktail party if Chavez charges her usual price of $31 per guest. (In other words, by how much would her overall profit increase?)
2. How low could Chavez bid for the charity event in terms of a price per guest and still not lose money on the event itself?
3. The individual who is organizing the charity's fund-raising event has indicated that he has already received a bid under $30 from another catering company. Do you think Chavez should bid below her normal $31 per guest price for the charity event? Why or why not?

(CMA, adapted)

CASE 5–28 (Appendix 5A) Mixed Cost Analysis Using Three Methods [LO2, LO3, LO5]

The Ramon Company manufactures a wide range of products at several locations. The Franklin plant, which manufactures electrical components, has been experiencing difficulties with fluctuating monthly overhead costs. These fluctuations have made it difficult to estimate the level of overhead that will be incurred for a month.

Management wants to be able to estimate overhead costs accurately to better plan its operational and financial needs. A trade publication indicates that for companies manufacturing electrical components, overhead tends to vary with direct labor-hours, but may contain both fixed and variable elements.

A member of the accounting staff has suggested that a good starting place for determining the cost behavior of overhead costs would be an analysis of historical data. The methods that have been proposed for determining the cost behavior pattern include high-low, scattergraph, and least-squares regression. Data on direct labor-hours and overhead costs have been collected for the past two years. The raw data are as follows:

	Last Year		This Year	
Month	Direct Labor-Hours	Overhead Costs	Direct Labor-Hours	Overhead Costs
January	20,000	$84,000	21,000	$86,000
February	25,000	$99,000	24,000	$93,000
March	22,000	$89,500	23,000	$93,000
April	23,000	$90,000	22,000	$87,000
May	20,000	$81,500	20,000	$80,000
June	19,000	$75,500	18,000	$76,500

continued

	Last Year		This Year	
Month	Direct Labor-Hours	Overhead Costs	Direct Labor-Hours	Overhead Costs
July	14,000	$70,500	12,000	$67,500
August	10,000	$64,500	13,000	$71,000
September	12,000	$69,000	15,000	$73,500
October	17,000	$75,000	17,000	$72,500
November	16,000	$71,500	15,000	$71,000
December	19,000	$78,000	18,000	$75,000

All equipment in the Franklin plant is leased under an arrangement calling for a flat fee up to 19,500 direct labor-hours, after which lease charges are assessed on an hourly basis. Lease expense is a major element of overhead cost.

Required:

1. Using the high-low method, estimate the cost formula for overhead in the Franklin plant.
2. Repeat (1) above, this time using the least-squares regression method.
3. Prepare a scattergraph using all of the data for the two-year period. Fit a straight line or lines to the plotted points using a ruler. In this part it is not necessary to compute the fixed and variable cost elements.
4. Assume that the Franklin plant works 22,500 direct labor-hours during a month. Estimate the expected overhead cost for the month using the cost formulas developed above with:
   a. The high-low method.
   b. The least-squares regression method.
   c. The scattergraph method [read the expected costs directly off the graph prepared in (3) above].
5. Of the three proposed methods, explain which one the Ramon Company should use to estimate monthly overhead costs in the Franklin plant. Explain why the other methods are less m desirable.

(CMA, adapted)

Group and Internet Exercises

GROUP EXERCISE 5–29 Variable and Fixed Costs in Practice

Form a team to investigate how an organization in your area handles variable and fixed costs. It may be in any industry and can be a business, a not-for-profit organization, or a part of the government. Research the organization on the Web and in periodicals to learn what the organization does and how it has performed financially. Make an appointment to meet with the controller, chief financial officer, or with another top manager who is familiar with the financial side of the organization. After meeting with that individual, write a memo in which you discuss the following issues.

Required:

1. Does the organization distinguish between variable and fixed costs in planning and controlling operations? If not, why not?
2. If the organization does distinguish between variable and fixed costs, how are variable and fixed costs estimated? What activity bases are used? How are these activity bases selected? What method does the company use for estimating the variable cost per unit of activity? How often are these estimates made? Does the company prepare scattergraphs of past cost and activity data?
3. If the organization does distinguish between variable and fixed costs, how does this help managers in planning and controlling operations?

INTERNET EXERCISE 5–30

As you know, the World Wide Web is a medium that is constantly evolving. Sites come and go, and change without notice. To enable the periodic updating of site addresses, this problem has been posted to the textbook website (www.mhhe.com/garrison11e). After accessing the site, enter the Student Center and select this chapter. Select and complete the Internet Exercise.

Chapter

6

Cost-Volume-Profit Relationships

LEARNING OBJECTIVES

After studying Chapter 6, you should be able to:

LO1 Explain how changes in activity affect contribution margin and net operating income.

LO2 Prepare and interpret a cost-volume-profit (CVP) graph.

LO3 Use the contribution margin ratio (CM ratio) to compute changes in contribution margin and net operating income resulting from changes in sales volume.

LO4 Show the effects on contribution margin of changes in variable costs, fixed costs, selling price, and volume.

LO5 Compute the break-even point in unit sales and sales dollars.

LO6 Determine the level of sales needed to achieve a desired target profit.

LO7 Compute the margin of safety and explain its significance.

LO8 Compute the degree of operating leverage at a particular level of sales and explain how the degree of operating leverage can be used to predict changes in net operating income.

LO9 Compute the break-even point for a multiple product company and explain the effects of shifts in the sales mix on contribution margin and the break-even point.

What Happened to the Profit?

BUSINESS FOCUS

Chip Conley is CEO of Joie de Vivre Hospitality, a company that owns and operates 28 hospitality businesses in northern California. Conley summed up the company's experience after the dot.com crash and 9/11 as follows: "In the history of American hotel markets, no hotel market has ever seen a drop in revenues as precipitous as the one in San Francisco and Silicon Valley in the last two years. On average, hotel revenues . . . dropped 40% to 45%. . . . We've been fortunate that our breakeven point is lower than our competition's. . . . But the problem is that the hotel business is a fixed-cost business. So in an environment where you have those precipitous drops and our costs are moderately fixed, our net incomes—well, they're not incomes anymore, they're losses." ■

Source: Karen Dillon, "Shop Talk," *Inc*, December 2002, pp. 111–114.

Cost-volume-profit (CVP) analysis is one of the most powerful tools that managers have at their command. It helps them understand the relationships among cost, volume, and profit by focusing on interactions among the following five elements:

1. Prices of products.
2. Volume or level of activity.
3. Per unit variable costs.
4. Total fixed costs.
5. Mix of products sold.

Because CVP analysis helps managers understand the interrelationships among cost, volume, and profit, it is a vital tool in many business decisions. These decisions include what products and services to offer, what pricing policy to follow, what marketing strategy to employ, and what basic cost structure to use. To help understand the role of CVP analysis in business decisions, consider the case of Acoustic Concepts, Inc., a company founded by Prem Narayan.

MANAGERIAL ACCOUNTING IN ACTION
The Issue

Accoustic Concepts, Inc.

Prem, who was a graduate student in engineering at the time, started Acoustic Concepts to market a radical new speaker he had designed for automobile sound systems. The speaker, called the Sonic Blaster, uses an advanced microprocessor and proprietary software to boost amplification to awesome levels. Prem contracted with a Taiwanese electronics manufacturer to produce the speaker. With seed money provided by his family, Prem placed an order with the manufacturer and ran advertisements in auto magazines.

The Sonic Blaster was an almost immediate success, and sales grew to the point that Prem moved the company's headquarters out of his apartment and into rented quarters in a nearby industrial park. He also hired a receptionist, an accountant, a sales manager, and a small sales staff to sell the speakers to retail stores. The accountant, Bob Luchinni, had worked for several small companies where he had acted as a business advisor as well as accountant and bookkeeper. The following discussion occurred soon after Bob was hired:

Prem: Bob, I've got a lot of questions about the company's finances that I hope you can help answer.

Bob: We're in great shape. The loan from your family will be paid off within a few months.

Prem: I know, but I am worried about the risks I've taken on by expanding operations. What would happen if a competitor entered the market and our sales slipped? How far could sales drop without putting us into the red? Another question I've been trying to resolve is how much our sales would have to increase to justify the big marketing campaign the sales staff is pushing for.

Bob: Marketing always wants more money for advertising.

Prem: And they are always pushing me to drop the selling price on the speaker. I agree with them that a lower price will boost our volume, but I'm not sure the increased volume will offset the loss in revenue from the lower price.

Bob: It sounds like these questions are all related in some way to the relationships among our selling prices, our costs, and our volume. We shouldn't have a problem coming up with some answers. I'll need a day or two, though, to gather some data.

Prem: Why don't we set up a meeting for three days from now? That would be Thursday.

Bob: That'll be fine. I'll have some preliminary answers for you as well as a model you can use for answering similar questions in the future.

Prem: Good. I'll be looking forward to seeing what you come up with.

The Basics of Cost-Volume-Profit (CVP) Analysis

Bob Luchinni's preparation for the Thursday meeting begins where our study of cost behavior in the preceding chapter left off—with the contribution income statement. The contribution income statement emphasizes the behavior of costs and therefore is extremely helpful to a manager in judging the impact on profits of changes in selling price, cost, or volume. Bob will base his analysis on the following contribution income statement he prepared last month:

ACOUSTIC CONCEPTS, INC.
Contribution Income Statement
For the Month of June

	Total	Per Unit
Sales (400 speakers)	$100,000	$250
Less variable expenses	60,000	150
Contribution margin	40,000	$100
Less fixed expenses	35,000	
Net operating income	$ 5,000	

Notice that sales, variable expenses, and contribution margin are expressed on a per unit basis as well as in total on this contribution income statement. The per unit figures will be very helpful in the work we will be doing in the following pages. Note that this contribution income statement has been prepared for management's use inside the company and would not ordinarily be made available to those outside the company.

Contribution Margin

LEARNING OBJECTIVE 1
Explain how changes in activity affect contribution margin and net operating income.

As explained in the previous chapter, contribution margin is the amount remaining from sales revenue after variable expenses have been deducted. Thus, it is the amount available to cover fixed expenses and then to provide profits for the period. Notice the sequence here—contribution margin is used *first* to cover the fixed expenses, and then whatever remains goes toward profits. If the contribution margin is not sufficient to cover the fixed expenses, then a loss occurs for the period. To illustrate with an extreme example, assume that Acoustic Concepts sells only one speaker during a particular month. The company's income statement would appear as follows:

	Total	Per Unit
Sales (1 speaker)	$ 250	$250
Less variable expenses	150	150
Contribution margin	100	$100
Less fixed expenses	35,000	
Net operating loss	$(34,900)	

For each additional speaker that the company is able to sell during the month, $100 more in contribution margin will become available to help cover the fixed expenses. If a second speaker is sold, for example, then the total contribution margin will increase by $100 (to a total of $200) and the company's loss will decrease by $100, to $34,800:

	Total	Per Unit
Sales (2 speakers)	$ 500	$250
Less variable expenses	300	150
Contribution margin	200	$100
Less fixed expenses	35,000	
Net operating loss	$(34,800)	

If enough speakers can be sold to generate $35,000 in contribution margin, then all of the fixed expenses will be covered and the company will *break even* for the month—that is, it will show neither profit nor loss but just cover all of its costs. To reach the break-even point, the company will have to sell 350 speakers in a month, since each speaker sold yields $100 in contribution margin:

	Total	Per Unit
Sales (350 speakers)	$87,500	$250
Less variable expenses	52,500	150
Contribution margin	35,000	$100
Less fixed expenses	35,000	
Net operating income	$ 0	

Computation of the break-even point is discussed in detail later in the chapter; for the moment, note that the **break-even point** is the level of sales at which profit is zero.

Once the break-even point has been reached, net operating income will increase by the amount of the unit contribution margin for each additional unit sold. For example, if 351 speakers are sold in a month, then we can expect that the net operating income for the month will be $100, since the company will have sold 1 speaker more than the number needed to break even:

	Total	Per Unit
Sales (351 speakers)	$87,750	$250
Less variable expenses	52,650	150
Contribution margin	35,100	$100
Less fixed expenses	35,000	
Net operating income	$ 100	

If 352 speakers are sold (2 speakers above the break-even point), then we can expect that the net operating income for the month will be $200, and so forth. It is not necessary to prepare a whole series of income statements to estimate profits at various activity levels. Rather, profits can be estimated by simply taking the number of units to be sold over the break-even point and multiplying that number by the unit contribution margin. The result represents the anticipated profits for the period. Or, to estimate the effect of a planned increase in sales on profits, simply multiply the increase in units sold by the unit contribution margin. The result will be the expected increase in profits. To illustrate, if Acoustic Concepts is currently selling 400 speakers per month and plans to increase sales to 425 speakers per month, the anticipated impact on profits can be computed as follows:

Increased number of speakers to be sold	25
Contribution margin per speaker	× $100
Increase in net operating income	$2,500

These calculations can be verified as follows:

	Sales Volume			
	400 Speakers	425 Speakers	Difference (25 Speakers)	Per Unit
Sales	$100,000	$106,250	$6,250	$250
Less variable expenses	60,000	63,750	3,750	150
Contribution margin	40,000	42,500	2,500	$100
Less fixed expenses	35,000	35,000	0	
Net operating income	$ 5,000	$ 7,500	$2,500	

To summarize these examples, if there were no sales, the company's loss would equal its fixed expenses. Each unit that is sold reduces the loss by the amount of the unit contribution margin. Once the break-even point has been reached, each additional unit sold increases the company's profit by the amount of the unit contribution margin.

CVP Relationships in Graphic Form

LEARNING OBJECTIVE 2
Prepare and interpret a cost-volume-profit (CVP) graph.

The relationships among revenue, cost, profit, and volume can be expressed graphically by preparing a **cost-volume-profit (CVP) graph.** A CVP graph highlights CVP relationships over wide ranges of activity and can give managers a perspective that can be obtained in no other way. To help explain his analysis to Prem Narayan, Bob Luchinni decided to prepare a CVP graph for Acoustic Concepts.

Preparing the CVP Graph In a CVP graph (sometimes called a *break-even chart*), unit volume is commonly represented on the horizontal (*X*) axis and dollars on the vertical (*Y*) axis. Preparing a CVP graph involves three steps. These steps are keyed to the graph in Exhibit 6–1:

1. Draw a line parallel to the volume axis to represent total fixed expenses. For Acoustic Concepts, total fixed expenses are $35,000.

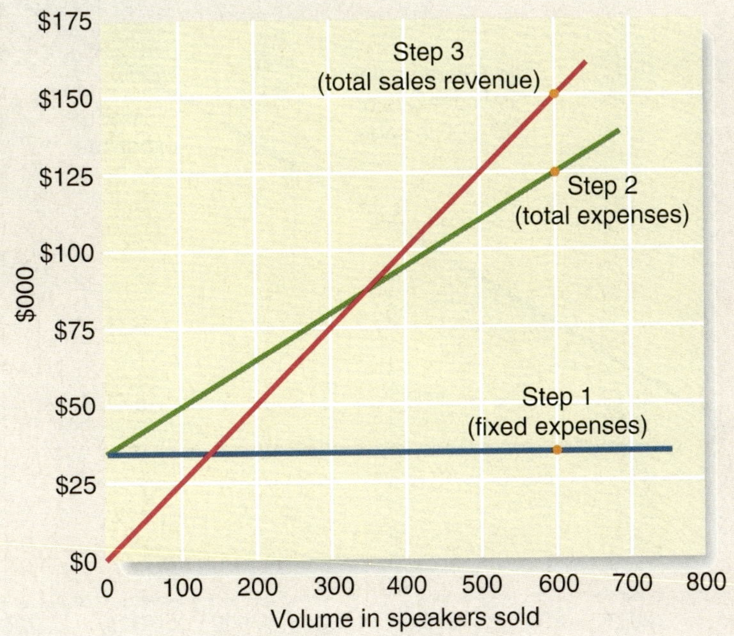

EXHIBIT 6–1
Preparing the CVP Graph

2. Choose some volume of unit sales and plot the point representing total expenses (fixed and variable) at the activity level you have selected. In Exhibit 6–1, Bob Luchinni chose a volume of 600 speakers. Total expenses at that activity level would be as follows:

Fixed expenses	$35,000
Variable expenses (600 speakers × $150 per speaker)	90,000
Total expenses	$125,000

After the point has been plotted, draw a line through it back to the point where the fixed expenses line intersects the dollars axis.

3. Again choose some volume of unit sales and plot the point representing total sales dollars at the activity level you have selected. In Exhibit 6–1, Bob Luchinni again chose a volume of 600 speakers. Sales at that activity level total $150,000 (600 speakers × $250 per speaker). Draw a line through this point back to the origin.

The interpretation of the completed CVP graph is given in Exhibit 6–2. The anticipated profit or loss at any given level of sales is measured by the vertical distance between the total revenue line (sales) and the total expenses line (variable expenses plus fixed expenses).

The break-even point is where the total revenue and total expenses lines cross. The break-even point of 350 speakers in Exhibit 6–2 agrees with the break-even point computed earlier.

As discussed earlier, when sales are below the break-even point—in this case, 350 units—the company suffers a loss. Note that the loss (represented by the vertical distance between the total expense and total revenue lines) worsens as sales decline. When sales are above the break-even point, the company earns a profit and the size of the profit (represented by the vertical distance between the total revenue and total expense lines) increases as sales increase.

EXHIBIT 6–2
The Completed CVP Graph

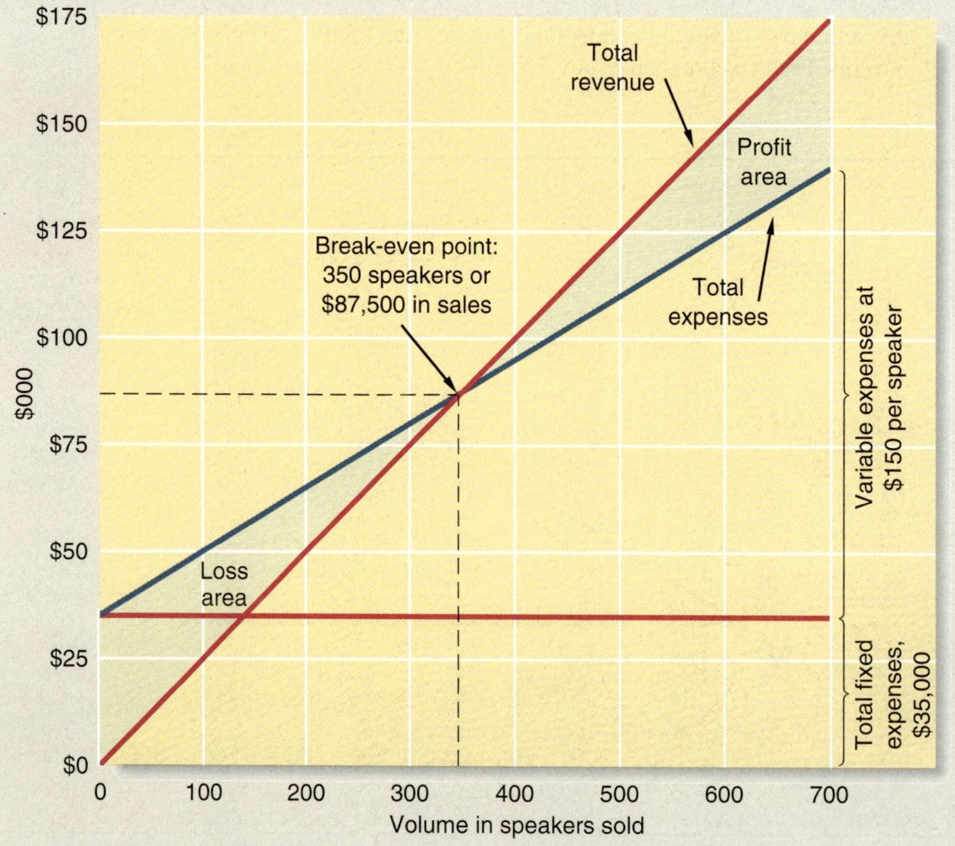

Contribution Margin Ratio (CM Ratio)

LEARNING OBJECTIVE 3
Use the contribution margin ratio (CM ratio) to compute changes in contribution margin and net operating income resulting from changes in sales volume.

In the previous section, we explored how cost-volume-profit relationships can be visualized. In this section, we show how the *contribution margin ratio* can be used in cost-volume-profit calculations. As the first step, we have added a column to Acoustic Concepts' contribution income statement in which sales revenues, variable expenses, and contribution margin are expressed as a percentage of sales:

	Total	Per Unit	Percent of Sales
Sales (400 speakers)	$100,000	$250	100%
Less variable expenses	60,000	150	60%
Contribution margin	40,000	$100	40%
Less fixed expenses	35,000		
Net operating income	$ 5,000		

The contribution margin as a percentage of total sales is referred to as the **contribution margin ratio (CM ratio).** This ratio is computed as follows:

$$\text{CM ratio} = \frac{\text{Contribution margin}}{\text{Sales}}$$

For Acoustic Concepts, the computations are:

$$\text{CM ratio} = \frac{\text{Total contribution margin}}{\text{Total sales}} = \frac{\$40{,}000}{\$100{,}000} = 40\%$$

In a company such as Acoustic Concepts that has only one product, the CM ratio can also be computed as follows:

$$\text{CM ratio} = \frac{\text{Unit contribution margin}}{\text{Unit selling price}} = \frac{\$100}{\$250} = 40\%$$

The CM ratio is extremely useful since it shows how the contribution margin will be affected by a change in total sales. To illustrate, notice that Acoustic Concepts has a CM ratio of 40%. This means that for each dollar increase in sales, total contribution margin will increase by 40 cents ($1 sales × CM ratio of 40%). Net operating income will also increase by 40 cents, assuming that fixed costs do not change.

As this illustration suggests, *the impact on net operating income of any given dollar change in total sales can be computed by simply applying the CM ratio to the dollar change.* For example, if Acoustic Concepts plans a $30,000 increase in sales during the coming month, the contribution margin should increase by $12,000 ($30,000 increase in sales × CM ratio of 40%). As we noted above, net operating income will also increase by $12,000 if fixed costs do not change. This is verified by the following table:

	Sales Volume			
	Present	Expected	Increase	Percent of Sales
Sales	$100,000	$130,000	$30,000	100%
Less variable expenses	60,000	78,000*	18,000	60%
Contribution margin	40,000	52,000	12,000	40%
Less fixed expenses	35,000	35,000	0	
Net operating income	$ 5,000	$ 17,000	$12,000	

*$130,000 expected sales ÷ $250 per unit = 520 units. 520 units × $150 per unit = $78,000.

The CM ratio is particularly valuable in situations where trade-offs must be made between more dollar sales of one product versus more dollar sales of another. Generally speaking, when trying to increase sales, products that yield the greatest amount of contribution margin per dollar of sales should be emphasized.

Some Applications of CVP Concepts

LEARNING OBJECTIVE 4
Show the effects on contribution margin of changes in variable costs, fixed costs, selling price, and volume.

Bob Luchinni, the accountant at Acoustic Concepts, wanted to demonstrate to the company's president Prem Narayan how the concepts developed on the preceding pages can be used in planning and decision making. Bob gathered the following basic data:

	Per Unit	Percent of Sales
Selling price	$250	100%
Less variable expenses	150	60%
Contribution margin	$100	40%

Recall that fixed expenses are $35,000 per month. Bob Luchinni will use these data to show the effects of changes in variable costs, fixed costs, sales price, and sales volume on the company's profitability in a variety of situations.

Change in Fixed Cost and Sales Volume

Acoustic Concepts is currently selling 400 speakers per month (monthly sales of $100,000). The sales manager feels that a $10,000 increase in the monthly advertising budget would increase monthly sales by $30,000 to a total of 520 units. Should the advertising budget be increased? The following table shows the effect of the proposed change in the monthly advertising budget:

	Current Sales	Sales with Additional Advertising Budget	Difference	Percent of Sales
Sales	$100,000	$130,000	$30,000	100%
Less variable expenses	60,000	78,000*	18,000	60%
Contribution margin	40,000	52,000	12,000	40%
Less fixed expenses	35,000	45,000†	10,000	
Net operating income	$ 5,000	$ 7,000	$ 2,000	

*520 units × $150 per unit = $78,000.
†$35,000 + additional $10,000 monthly advertising budget = $45,000.

Assuming no other factors need to be considered, the increase in the advertising budget should be approved since it would increase net operating income by $2,000. There are two shorter ways to present this solution. The first alternative solution follows:

Alternative Solution 1

Topic Tackler PLUS
6–1

Expected total contribution margin:	
$130,000 × 40% CM ratio	$52,000
Present total contribution margin:	
$100,000 × 40% CM ratio	40,000
Incremental contribution margin	12,000
Change in fixed expenses:	
Less incremental advertising expense	10,000
Increased net operating income	$ 2,000

Since in this case only the fixed costs and the sales volume change, the solution can be presented in an even shorter format, as follows:

Alternative Solution 2

Incremental contribution margin:	
$30,000 × 40% CM ratio	$12,000
Less incremental advertising expense	10,000
Increased net operating income	$2,000

Notice that this approach does not depend on knowledge of previous sales. Also note that it is unnecessary under either shorter approach to prepare an income statement. Both of the alternative solutions above involve an **incremental analysis**—they consider only those items of revenue, cost, and volume that will change if the new program is implemented. Although in each case a new income statement could have been prepared, the incremental approach is simpler and more direct and focuses attention on the specific changes involved in the decision.

Change in Variable Costs and Sales Volume Refer to the original data. Recall that Acoustic Concepts is currently selling 400 speakers per month. Management is considering the use of higher-quality components, which would increase variable costs (and thereby reduce the contribution margin) by $10 per speaker. However, the sales manager predicts that the higher overall quality would increase sales to 480 speakers per month. Should the higher-quality components be used?

The $10 increase in variable costs will decrease the unit contribution margin by $10—from $100 down to $90.

Solution

Expected total contribution margin with higher-quality components:	
480 speakers × $90 per speaker	$43,200
Present total contribution margin:	
400 speakers × $100 per speaker	40,000
Increase in total contribution margin	$ 3,200

According to this analysis, the higher-quality components should be used. Since fixed costs will not change, the $3,200 increase in contribution margin shown above should result in a $3,200 increase in net operating income.

Change in Fixed Cost, Sales Price, and Sales Volume Refer to the original data and recall again that the company is currently selling 400 speakers per month. To increase sales, the sales manager would like to cut the selling price by $20 per speaker and increase the advertising budget by $15,000 per month. The sales manager believes that if these two steps are taken, unit sales will increase by 50% to 600 speakers per month. Should the changes be made?

A decrease of $20 per speaker in the selling price will cause the unit contribution margin to decrease from $100 to $80.

Solution

Expected total contribution margin with lower selling price:	
600 speakers × $80 per speaker	$48,000
Present total contribution margin:	
400 speakers × $100 per speaker	40,000
Incremental contribution margin	8,000
Change in fixed expenses:	
Less incremental advertising expense	15,000
Reduction in net operating income	$(7,000)

According to this analysis, the changes should not be made. The same solution can be obtained by preparing comparative income statements as follows:

	Present 400 Speakers per Month		Expected 600 Speakers per Month		
	Total	Per Unit	Total	Per Unit	Difference
Sales	$100,000	$250	$138,000	$230	$38,000
Less variable expenses	60,000	150	90,000	150	30,000
Contribution margin	40,000	$100	48,000	$ 80	8,000
Less fixed expenses	35,000		50,000*		15,000
Net operating income (loss)	$ 5,000		$ (2,000)		$ (7,000)

*35,000 + Additional monthly advertising budget of $15,000 = $50,000.

Notice that the effect on net operating income is the same as that obtained by the incremental analysis above.

Change in Variable Cost, Fixed Cost, and Sales Volume

Refer to the original data. As before, the company is currently selling 400 speakers per month. The sales manager would like to pay a sales commission of $15 per speaker sold, rather than the flat salaries that now total $6,000 per month. The sales manager is confident that the change will increase monthly sales by 15% to 460 speakers per month. Should the change be made?

Solution Changing the sales staff from a salaried basis to a commission basis will affect both fixed and variable expenses. Fixed expenses will decrease by $6,000, from $35,000 to $29,000. Variable expenses will increase by $15, from $150 to $165, and the unit contribution margin will decrease from $100 to $85.

Expected total contribution margin with sales staff on commissions:	
460 speakers × $85 per speaker	$39,100
Present total contribution margin:	
400 speakers × $100 per speaker	40,000
Decrease in total contribution margin	(900)
Change in fixed expenses:	
Add salaries avoided if a commission is paid	6,000
Increase in net operating income	$ 5,100

According to this analysis, the changes should be made. Again, the same answer can be obtained by preparing comparative income statements:

	Present 400 Speakers per Month		Expected 460 Speakers per Month		
	Total	Per Unit	Total	Per Unit	Difference
Sales	$100,000	$250	$115,000	$250	$15,000
Less variable expenses	60,000	150	75,900	165	15,900
Contribution margin	40,000	$100	39,100	$85	900
Less fixed expenses	35,000		29,000		(6,000)*
Net operating income	$5,000		$10,100		$5,100

*Note: A *reduction* in fixed expenses has the effect of *increasing* net operating income.

Change in Regular Sales Price Refer to the original data where Acoustic Concepts is currently selling 400 speakers per month. The company has an opportunity to make a bulk sale of 150 speakers to a wholesaler if an acceptable price can be agreed on. This sale would not disturb the company's regular sales and would not affect the company's total fixed expenses. What price per speaker should be quoted to the wholesaler if Acoustic Concepts wants to increase its monthly profits by $3,000?

Solution

Variable cost per speaker	$150
Desired profit per speaker:	
$3,000 ÷ 150 speakers	20
Quoted price per speaker	$170

Notice that fixed expenses are not included in the computation. This is because fixed expenses are not affected by the bulk sale, so all of the additional revenue that is in excess of variable costs increases the company's profits.

Break-Even Analysis

Topic Tackler PLUS 6–2

CVP analysis is sometimes referred to simply as break-even analysis. This is unfortunate because break-even analysis is only one element of CVP analysis—although an important element. Break-even analysis is designed to answer questions such as, how far could sales drop before the company begins to lose money?

Break-Even Computations

LEARNING OBJECTIVE 5
Compute the break-even point in unit sales and sales dollars.

Earlier in the chapter we defined the break-even point as the level of sales at which the company's profit is zero. The break-even point can be computed using either the *equation method* or the *contribution margin method*—the two methods are equivalent.

The Equation Method The **equation method** centers on the contribution approach to the income statement illustrated earlier in the chapter. The format of this income statement can be expressed in equation form as follows:

$$\text{Profits} = (\text{Sales} - \text{Variable expenses}) - \text{Fixed expenses}$$

Rearranging this equation slightly yields the following equation, which is widely used in CVP analysis:

$$\text{Sales} = \text{Variable expenses} + \text{Fixed expenses} + \text{Profits}$$

At the break-even point, profits are zero. Therefore, the break-even point can be computed by finding that point where sales equal the total of the variable expenses plus the fixed expenses. For Acoustic Concepts, the break-even point in unit sales, Q, can be computed as follows:

$$\text{Sales} = \text{Variable expenses} + \text{Fixed expenses} + \text{Profits}$$

$$\$250Q = \$150Q + \$35{,}000 + \$0$$

$$\$100Q = \$35{,}000$$

$$Q = \$35{,}000 \div \$100 \text{ per speaker}$$

$$Q = 350 \text{ speakers}$$

where:

$$Q = \text{Quantity of speakers sold}$$
$$\$250 = \text{Unit selling price}$$
$$\$150 = \text{Unit variable expenses}$$
$$\$35{,}000 = \text{Total fixed expenses}$$

The break-even point in total sales dollars can be computed by multiplying the break-even level of unit sales by the selling price per unit:

$$350 \text{ speakers} \times \$250 \text{ per speaker} = \$87{,}500$$

The break-even point in total sales dollars, X, can also be computed as follows:

$$\text{Sales} = \text{Variable expenses} + \text{Fixed expenses} + \text{Profits}$$

$$X = 0.60X + \$35{,}000 + \$0$$
$$0.40X = \$35{,}000$$
$$X = \$35{,}000 \div 0.40$$
$$X = \$87{,}500$$

where:

$$X = \text{Total sales dollars}$$
$$0.60 = \text{Variable expense ratio (Variable expenses} \div \text{Sales)}$$
$$\$35{,}000 = \text{Total fixed expenses}$$

Organizations often have data available only in percentage or ratio form, and the approach we have just illustrated must then be used to find the break-even point. Notice that use of ratios in the equation yields a break-even point in sales dollars rather than in units sold. The break-even point in units sold is the following:

$$\$87{,}500 \div \$250 \text{ per speaker} = 350 \text{ speakers}$$

IN BUSINESS

BUYING ON THE GO—A DOT.COM TALE

*CD is a company set up by two young engineers, George Searle and Humphrey Chen, to allow customers to order music CDs on their cell phones. Suppose you hear a cut from a CD on your car radio that you would like to own. Pick up your cell phone, punch "*CD," enter the radio station's frequency, and the time you heard the song, and the CD will soon be on its way to you.

*CD charges about $17 for a CD, including shipping. The company pays its supplier about $13, leaving a contribution margin of $4 per CD. Because of the fixed costs of running the service, Searle expects the company to lose $1.5 million on sales of $1.5 million in its first year of operations. That assumes the company sells 88,000 CDs.

What is the company's break-even point? Working backwards, the company's fixed expenses would appear to be about $1,850,000 per year. Since the contribution margin per CD is $4, the company would have to sell over 460,000 CDs per year just to break even!

Source: Peter Kafka, "Play It Again," *Forbes*, July 26, 1999, p. 94.

The Contribution Margin Method The **contribution margin method** is just a shortcut version of the equation method already described. The approach centers on the idea discussed earlier that each unit sold provides a certain amount of contribution margin that goes toward covering fixed costs. To find how many units must be sold to break even, divide the total fixed expenses by the unit contribution margin:

$$\text{Break-even point in units sold} = \frac{\text{Fixed expenses}}{\text{Unit contribution margin}}$$

Each speaker generates a contribution margin of \$100 (\$250 selling price, less \$150 variable expenses). Since the total fixed expenses are \$35,000, the break-even point in units is computed as follows:

$$\frac{\text{Fixed expenses}}{\text{Unit contribution margin}} = \frac{\$35{,}000}{\$100 \text{ per speaker}} = 350 \text{ speakers}$$

A variation of this method uses the CM ratio instead of the unit contribution margin. The result is the break-even point in total sales dollars rather than in total units sold.

$$\text{Break-even point in total sales dollars} = \frac{\text{Fixed expenses}}{\text{CM ratio}}$$

In the Acoustic Concepts example, the calculation is as follows:

$$\frac{\text{Fixed expenses}}{\text{CM ratio}} = \frac{\$35{,}000}{0.40} = \$87{,}500$$

This approach, based on the CM ratio, is particularly useful when a company has multiple product lines and wishes to compute a single break-even point for the company as a whole. More is said on this point in a later section titled The Concept of Sales Mix.

Target Profit Analysis

LEARNING OBJECTIVE 6
Determine the level of sales needed to achieve a desired target profit.

CVP formulas can be used to determine the sales volume needed to achieve a target profit. Suppose that Prem Narayan of Acoustic Concepts would like to earn a target profit of \$40,000 per month. How many speakers would have to be sold?

The CVP Equation One approach is to use the equation method. Instead of solving for the unit sales where profits are zero, you instead solve for the unit sales where profits are \$40,000.

$$\begin{aligned}
\text{Sales} &= \text{Variable expenses} + \text{Fixed expenses} + \text{Profits} \\
\$250Q &= \$150Q + \$35{,}000 + \$40{,}000 \\
\$100Q &= \$75{,}000 \\
Q &= \$75{,}000 \div \$100 \text{ per speaker} \\
Q &= 750 \text{ speakers}
\end{aligned}$$

where:

$$\begin{aligned}
Q &= \text{Quantity of speakers sold} \\
\$250 &= \text{Unit selling price} \\
\$150 &= \text{Unit variable expenses} \\
\$35{,}000 &= \text{Total fixed expenses} \\
\$40{,}000 &= \text{Target profit}
\end{aligned}$$

Thus, the target profit can be achieved by selling 750 speakers per month, which represents \$187,500 in total sales (\$250 per speaker × 750 speakers).

IN BUSINESS

COSTS ON THE INTERNET

The company eToys, which sells toys over the Internet, lost $190 million in 1999 on sales of $151 million. One big cost was advertising. eToys spent about $37 on advertising for each $100 of sales. (Other e-tailers were spending even more—in some cases, up to $460 on advertising for each $100 in sales!)

eToys did have some advantages relative to bricks-and-mortar stores such as Toys "R" Us. eToys had much lower inventory costs since it only needed to keep on hand one or two of a slow-moving item, whereas a traditional store has to fully stock its shelves. And bricks-and-mortar retail spaces in malls and elsewhere do cost money—on average, about 7% of sales. However, e-tailers such as eToys have their own set of disadvantages. Customers "pick and pack" their own items at a bricks-and-mortar outlet, but e-tailers have to pay employees to carry out this task. This costs eToys about $33 for every $100 in sales. And the technology to sell over the net is not free. eToys spent about $29 on its website and related technology for every $100 in sales. However, many of these costs of selling over the net are fixed. Toby Lenk, the CEO of eToys, estimated that the company would pass its break-even point somewhere between $750 and $900 million in sales—representing less than 1% of the market for toys. eToys did not make this goal and laid off 70% of its employees in January 2001. Subsequently, eToys was acquired by KBKids.com.

Sources: Erin Kelly, "The Last e-Store on the Block," *Fortune*, September 18, 2000, pp. 214–220; Jennifer Couzin, *The Industry Standard*, January 4, 2001.

The Contribution Margin Approach A second approach involves expanding the contribution margin formula to include the target profit:

$$\text{Unit sales to attain the target profit} = \frac{\text{Fixed expenses} + \text{Target profit}}{\text{Unit contribution margin}}$$

$$= \frac{\$35{,}000 + \$40{,}000}{\$100 \text{ per speaker}}$$

$$= 750 \text{ speakers}$$

This approach gives the same answer as the equation method since it is simply a shortcut version of the equation method. Similarly, the dollar sales needed to attain the target profit can be computed as follows:

$$\text{Dollar sales to attain target profit} = \frac{\text{Fixed expenses} + \text{Target profit}}{\text{CM ratio}}$$

$$= \frac{\$35{,}000 + \$40{,}000}{0.40}$$

$$= \$187{,}500$$

The Margin of Safety

LEARNING OBJECTIVE 7
Compute the margin of safety and explain its significance.

The **margin of safety** is the excess of budgeted (or actual) sales dollars over the break-even volume of sales dollars. It states the amount by which sales can drop before losses are incurred. The higher the margin of safety, the lower the risk of not breaking even. The formula for its calculation is:

$$\text{Margin of safety} = \text{Total budgeted (or actual) sales} - \text{Break-even sales}$$

The margin of safety can also be expressed in percentage form by dividing the margin of safety in dollars by total sales:

$$\text{Margin of safety percentage} = \frac{\text{Margin of safety in dollars}}{\text{Total budgeted (or actual) sales}}$$

The calculation for the margin of safety for Acoustic Concepts is:

Sales (at the current volume of 400 speakers) (a)	$100,000
Break-even sales (at 350 speakers)	87,500
Margin of safety (in dollars) (b)	$ 12,500
Margin of safety as a percentage of sales, (b) ÷ (a) ...	12.5%

This margin of safety means that at the current level of sales and with the company's current prices and cost structure, a reduction in sales of $12,500, or 12.5%, would result in just breaking even.

In a single-product company like Acoustic Concepts, the margin of safety can also be expressed in terms of the number of units sold by dividing the margin of safety in dollars by the selling price per unit. In this case, the margin of safety is 50 speakers ($12,500 ÷ $250 per speaker = 50 speakers).

IN BUSINESS

SOUP NUTSY

Pak Melwani and Kumar Hathiramani, former silk merchants from Bombay, opened a soup store in Manhattan after watching a *Seinfeld* episode featuring the "soup Nazi." The episode parodied a real-life soup vendor, Ali Yeganeh, whose loyal customers put up with hour-long lines and "snarling customer service." Melwani and Hathiramani approached Yeganeh about turning his soup kitchen into a chain, but they were gruffly rebuffed. Instead of giving up, the two hired a French chef with a repertoire of 500 soups and opened a store called Soup Nutsy. For $6 per serving, Soup Nutsy offers 12 homemade soups each day, such as sherry crab bisque and Thai coconut shrimp. Melwani and Hathiramani report that in their first year of operation, they netted a profit of $210,000 on sales of $700,000. They report that it costs about $2 per serving to make the soup. So their variable expense ratio is one-third ($2 cost ÷ $6 selling price). If so, what are their fixed expenses? We can answer that question using the equation approach as follows:

$$\text{Sales} = \text{Variable expenses} + \text{Fixed expenses} + \text{Profits}$$

$$\$700{,}000 = \left(\frac{1}{3} \times \$700{,}000\right) + \text{Fixed expenses} + \$210{,}000$$

$$\text{Fixed expenses} = \$700{,}000 - \left(\frac{1}{3} \times \$700{,}000\right) - \$210{,}000$$

$$= \$256{,}667$$

With this information, you can determine that Soup Nutsy's break-even point is about $385,000 of sales. This gives the store a comfortable margin of safety of 45% of sales.

Source: Silva Sansoni, "The Starbucks of Soup?" *Forbes*, July 7, 1997, pp. 90–91.

MANAGERIAL ACCOUNTING IN ACTION
The Wrap Up

Accoustic Concepts, Inc.

It is Thursday morning, and Prem Narayan and Bob Luchinni are discussing the results of Bob's analysis.

Prem: Bob, everything you have shown me is pretty clear. I can see what impact some of the sales manager's suggestions would have on our profits. Some of those suggestions are quite good and some are not so good. I also understand that our break-even point is 350 speakers, so we have to make sure we don't slip below that level of sales. What really bothers me is that we are only selling 400 speakers a month now. What did you call the 50-speaker cushion?

Bob: That's the margin of safety.

Prem: Such a small cushion makes me very nervous. What can we do to increase the margin of safety?

Bob: We have to increase total sales or decrease the break-even point or both.
Prem: And to decrease the break-even point, we have to either decrease our fixed expenses or increase our unit contribution margin?
Bob: Exactly.
Prem: And to increase our unit contribution margin, we must either increase our selling price or decrease the variable cost per unit?
Bob: Correct.
Prem: So what do you suggest?
Bob: Well, the analysis doesn't tell us which of these to do, but it does indicate we have a potential problem here.
Prem: If you don't have any immediate suggestions, I would like to call a general meeting next week to discuss ways we can work on increasing the margin of safety. I think everyone will be concerned about how vulnerable we are to even small downturns in sales.
Bob: I agree. This is something everyone will want to work on.

CVP Considerations in Choosing a Cost Structure

Cost structure refers to the relative proportion of fixed and variable costs in an organization. An organization often has some latitude in trading off between these two types of costs. For example, fixed investments in automated equipment can reduce variable labor costs. In this section, we discuss the choice of a cost structure. We focus on the impact of cost structure on profit stability, in which *operating leverage* plays a key role.

Cost Structure and Profit Stability

When a manager has some latitude in trading off between fixed and variable costs, which cost structure is better—high variable costs and low fixed costs, or the opposite? No single answer to this question is possible; each approach has its advantages. To show what we mean, refer to the income statements given below for two blueberry farms. Bogside Farm depends on migrant workers to pick its berries by hand, whereas Sterling Farm has invested in expensive berry-picking machines. Consequently, Bogside Farm has higher variable costs, but Sterling Farm has higher fixed costs:

	Bogside Farm		Sterling Farm	
	Amount	Percent	Amount	Percent
Sales	$100,000	100%	$100,000	100%
Less variable expenses	60,000	60%	30,000	30%
Contribution margin	40,000	40%	70,000	70%
Less fixed expenses	30,000		60,000	
Net operating income	$ 10,000		$ 10,000	

Which farm has the better cost structure? The answer depends on many factors, including the long-run trend in sales, year-to-year fluctuations in the level of sales, and the attitude of the owners toward risk. If sales are expected to be above $100,000 in the future, then Sterling Farm probably has the better cost structure. The reason is that its CM ratio is higher, and its profits will therefore increase more rapidly as sales increase. To illustrate, assume that each farm experiences a 10% increase in sales without any increase in fixed costs. The new income statements would be as follows:

	Bogside Farm		Sterling Farm	
	Amount	Percent	Amount	Percent
Sales	$110,000	100%	$110,000	100%
Less variable expenses	66,000	60%	33,000	30%
Contribution margin	44,000	40%	77,000	70%
Less fixed expenses	30,000		60,000	
Net operating income	$ 14,000		$ 17,000	

Sterling Farm has experienced a greater increase in net operating income due to its higher CM ratio even though the increase in sales was the same for both farms.

What if sales drop below $100,000 from time to time? What are the break-even points of the two farms? What are their margins of safety? The computations needed to answer these questions are carried out below using the contribution margin method:

	Bogside Farm	Sterling Farm
Fixed expenses	$ 30,000	$ 60,000
Contribution margin ratio	÷ 0.40	÷ 0.70
Break-even in total sales dollars	$ 75,000	$ 85,714
Total current sales (a)	$100,000	$100,000
Break-even sales	75,000	85,714
Margin of safety in sales dollars (b)	$25,000	$14,286
Margin of safety as a percentage of sales, (b) ÷ (a)	25.0%	14.3%

This analysis makes it clear that Bogside Farm is less vulnerable to downturns than Sterling Farm. We can identify two reasons why it is less vulnerable. First, due to its lower fixed expenses, Bogside Farm has a lower break-even point and a higher margin of safety, as shown by the computations above. Therefore, it will not incur losses as quickly as Sterling Farm in periods of sharply declining sales. Second, due to its lower CM ratio, Bogside Farm will not lose contribution margin as rapidly as Sterling Farm when sales decline. Thus, Bogside Farm's income will be less volatile. We saw earlier that this is a drawback when sales increase, but it provides more protection when sales drop.

To summarize, without knowing the future, it is not obvious which cost structure is better. Both have advantages and disadvantages. Sterling Farm, with its higher fixed costs and lower variable costs, will experience wider swings in net operating income as sales fluctuate, with greater profits in good years and greater losses in bad years. Bogside Farm, with its lower fixed costs and higher variable costs, will enjoy greater stability in net operating income and will be more protected from losses during bad years, but at the cost of lower net operating income in good years.

IN BUSINESS

A LOSING COST STRUCTURE

Both JetBlue and United Airlines use an Airbus 235 to fly from Dulles International Airport near Washington, DC, to Oakland, California. Both planes have a pilot, copilot, and four flight attendants. That is where the similarity ends. Based on 2002 data, the pilot on the United flight earned $16,350 to $18,000 a month compared to $6,800 per month for the JetBlue pilot. United's senior flight attendants on the plane earned more than $41,000 per year; whereas the JetBlue attendants were paid $16,800 to $27,000 per year. Largely because of the higher labor costs at United, its costs of operating the flight were more than 60% higher than JetBlue's costs. Due to intense fare competition from JetBlue and other low-cost carriers, United was unable to cover its higher operating costs on this and many other flights. Consequently, United went into bankruptcy at the end of 2002.

Source: Susan Carey, "Costly Race in the Sky," *The Wall Street Journal*, September 9, 2002, pp. B1 and B3.

Operating Leverage

LEARNING OBJECTIVE 8
Compute the degree of operating leverage at a particular level of sales and explain how the degree of operating leverage can be used to predict changes in net operating income.

A lever is a tool for multiplying force. Using a lever, a massive object can be moved with only a modest amount of force. In business, *operating leverage* serves a similar purpose. **Operating leverage** is a measure of how sensitive net operating income is to percentage changes in sales. Operating leverage acts as a multiplier. If operating leverage is high, a small percentage increase in sales can produce a much larger percentage increase in net operating income.

Operating leverage can be illustrated by returning to the data given previously for the two blueberry farms. We previously showed that a 10% increase in sales (from $100,000 to $110,000 in each farm) results in a 70% increase in the net operating income of Sterling Farm (from $10,000 to $17,000) and only a 40% increase in the net operating income of Bogside Farm (from $10,000 to $14,000). Thus, for a 10% increase in sales, Sterling Farm experiences a much greater percentage increase in profits than does Bogside Farm. Therefore, Sterling Farm has greater operating leverage than Bogside Farm.

The **degree of operating leverage** at a given level of sales is computed by the following formula:

$$\text{Degree of operating leverage} = \frac{\text{Contribution margin}}{\text{Net operating income}}$$

The degree of operating leverage is a measure, at a given level of sales, *of how a percentage change in sales volume will affect profits.* To illustrate, the degree of operating leverage for the two farms at a $100,000 sales level would be computed as follows:

$$\text{Bogside Farm: } \frac{\$40,000}{\$10,000} = 4$$

$$\text{Sterling Farm: } \frac{\$70,000}{\$10,000} = 7$$

Since the degree of operating leverage for Bogside Farm is 4, the farm's net operating income grows four times as fast as its sales. Similarly, Sterling Farm's net operating income grows seven times as fast as its sales. Thus, if sales increase by 10%, then we can expect the net operating income of Bogside Farm to increase by four times this amount, or by 40%, and the net operating income of Sterling Farm to increase by seven times this amount, or by 70%.

	(1) Percent Increase in Sales	(2) Degree of Operating Leverage	(3) Percent Increase in Net Operating Income (1) × (2)
Bogside Farm	10%	4	40%
Sterling Farm	10%	7	70%

What is responsible for the higher operating leverage at Sterling Farm? The only difference between the two farms is their cost structure. If two companies have the same total revenue and same total expense but different cost structures, then the company with the higher proportion of fixed costs in its cost structure will have higher operating leverage. Referring back to the original example on page 244, when both farms have sales of $100,000 and total expenses of $90,000, one-third of Bogside Farm's costs are fixed but two-thirds of Sterling Farm's costs are fixed. As a consequence, Sterling's degree of operating leverage is higher than Bogside's.

The degree of operating leverage is not a constant; it is greatest at sales levels near the break-even point and decreases as sales and profits rise. This can be seen from the following tabulation, which shows the degree of operating leverage for Bogside Farm at various sales levels. (Data used earlier for Bogside Farm are shown in color.)

Sales	$75,000	$80,000	$100,000	$150,000	$225,000
Less variable expenses	45,000	48,000	60,000	90,000	135,000
Contribution margin (a)	30,000	32,000	40,000	60,000	90,000
Less fixed expenses	30,000	30,000	30,000	30,000	30,000
Net operating income (b)	$ 0	$ 2,000	$ 10,000	$ 30,000	$ 60,000
Degree of operating leverage, (a) ÷ (b)	∞	16	4	2	1.5

Thus, a 10% increase in sales would increase profits by only 15% (10% × 1.5) if the company were operating at a $225,000 sales level, as compared to the 40% increase we computed earlier at the $100,000 sales level. The degree of operating leverage will continue to decrease the farther the company moves from its break-even point. At the break-even point, the degree of operating leverage is infinitely large ($30,000 contribution margin ÷ $0 net operating income = ∞).

IN BUSINESS

FAN APPRECIATION

Operating leverage can be a good thing when business is booming but can turn the situation ugly when sales slacken. Jerry Colangelo, the managing partner of the Arizona Diamondbacks professional baseball team, spent over $100 million to sign six free agents—doubling the team's payroll cost—on top of the costs of operating and servicing the debt on the team's new stadium. With annual expenses of about $100 million, the team needs to average 40,000 fans per game to break even.

Faced with a financially risky situation, Colangelo decided to raise ticket prices by 12%. And he did it during Fan Appreciation Weekend! Attendance for the season dropped by 15%, turning what should have been a $20 million profit into a loss of over $10 million for the year. Note that a drop in attendance of 15% did not cut profit by just 15%—that's the magic of operating leverage at work.

Source: Mary Summers, "Bottom of the Ninth, Two Out," *Forbes*, November 1, 1999, pp. 69–70.

A manager can use the degree of operating leverage to quickly estimate what impact various percentage changes in sales will have on profits, without the necessity of preparing detailed income statements. As shown by our examples, the effects of operating leverage can be dramatic. If a company is near its break-even point, then even small percentage increases in sales can yield large percentage increases in profits. *This explains why management will often work very hard for only a small increase in sales volume.* If the degree of operating leverage is 5, then a 6% increase in sales would translate into a 30% increase in profits.

Structuring Sales Commissions

Companies generally compensate salespeople by paying them either a commission based on sales or a salary plus a sales commission. Commissions based on sales dollars can lead to lower profits. To illustrate, consider Pipeline Unlimited, a producer of surfing equipment. Salespeople for the company sell the company's product to retail sporting goods stores throughout North America and the Pacific Basin. Data for two of the company's surfboards, the XR7 and Turbo models, appear below:

	Model	
	XR7	Turbo
Selling price	$695	$749
Less variable expenses	344	410
Contribution margin	$351	$339

Which model will salespeople push hardest if they are paid a commission of 10% of sales revenue? The answer is the Turbo, since it has the higher selling price and hence the larger commission. On the other hand, from the standpoint of the company, profits will be greater if salespeople steer customers toward the XR7 model since it has the higher contribution margin.

To eliminate such conflicts, commissions can be based on contribution margin rather than on selling price alone. If this is done, the salespersons will want to sell the mix of products that will maximize contribution margin. Providing that fixed costs are not affected by the sales mix, maximizing the contribution margin will also maximize the company's profit. In effect, by maximizing their own compensation, salespersons will also maximize the company's profit.

The Concept of Sales Mix

LEARNING OBJECTIVE 9
Compute the break-even point for a multiple product company and explain the effects of shifts in the sales mix on contribution margin and the break-even point.

Before concluding our discussion of CVP concepts, we need to consider the impact of changes in *sales mix* on a company's profit.

The Definition of Sales Mix

The term **sales mix** refers to the relative proportions in which a company's products are sold. The idea is to achieve the combination, or mix, that will yield the greatest amount of profits. Most companies have many products, and often these products are not equally profitable. Hence, profits will depend to some extent on the company's sales mix. Profits will be greater if high-margin rather than low-margin items make up a relatively large proportion of total sales.

Changes in the sales mix can cause perplexing variations in a company's profits. A shift in the sales mix from high-margin items to low-margin items can cause total profits to decrease even though total sales may increase. Conversely, a shift in the sales mix from low-margin items to high-margin items can cause the reverse effect—total profits may increase even though total sales decrease. It is one thing to achieve a particular sales volume; it is quite another to sell the most profitable mix of products.

IN BUSINESS

KODAK: GOING DIGITAL

Kodak dominates the film industry in the U.S., selling two out of every three rolls of film. It also processes 40% of all film dropped off for developing. Unfortunately for Kodak, this revenue stream is threatened by digital cameras, which do not use film at all. To counter this threat, Kodak has moved into the digital market with its own line of digital cameras and various services, but sales of digital products undeniably cut into the company's film business. "Chief Financial Officer Robert Brust has 'stress-tested' profit models based on how quickly digital cameras may spread. If half of homes go digital, . . . Kodak's sales would rise 10% a year—but profits would go up only 8% a year. Cost cuts couldn't come fast enough to offset a slide in film sales and the margin pressure from selling cheap digital cameras." The sales mix is moving in the wrong direction, given the company's current cost structure and competitive prices.

Source: Bruce Upbin, "Kodak's Digital Moment," *Forbes*, August 21, 2000, pp. 106–112.

Sales Mix and Break-Even Analysis

If a company sells more than one product, break-even analysis is somewhat more complex than discussed earlier in this chapter. The reason is that different products will have different selling prices, different costs, and different contribution margins. Consequently, the break-even point will depend on the mix in which the various products are sold. To illustrate, consider Sound Unlimited, a small company that imports CDs from France for use in personal computers. At present, the company distributes the following CDs to retail computer stores: the Le Louvre CD, a multimedia free-form tour of the famous art museum in Paris; and the Le Vin CD, which features the wines and wine-growing regions of France. Both multimedia products have sound, photos, video clips, and sophisticated software. The company's September sales, expenses, and break-even point are shown in Exhibit 6–3.

As shown in the exhibit, the break-even point is $60,000 in sales. This is computed by dividing the fixed costs by the company's *overall* CM ratio of 45%. The sales mix is currently 20% for the Le Louvre CD and 80% for the Le Vin CD. If this sales mix does not change, then at the break-even total sales of $60,000, the sales of the Le Louvre CD would be $12,000 (20% of $60,000) and the sales of the Le Vin CD would be $48,000 (80% of $60,000). As shown in Exhibit 6–3, at these levels of sales, the company would indeed break even. But $60,000 in sales represents the break-even point for the company only if the sales mix does not change. *If the sales mix changes, then the break-even point will also change.* This is illustrated by the results for October in which the sales mix shifted away from the more profitable Le Vin CD (which has a 50% CM ratio) toward the less profitable Le Louvre CD (which has a 25% CM ratio). These results appear in Exhibit 6–4.

Although sales have remained unchanged at $100,000, the sales mix is exactly the reverse of what it was in Exhibit 6–3, with the bulk of the sales now coming from the less profitable Le Louvre CD. Notice that this shift in the sales mix has caused both the overall CM ratio and total profits to drop sharply from the prior month—the overall CM ratio

EXHIBIT 6–3
Multiple-Product Break-Even Analysis

SOUND UNLIMITED
Contribution Income Statement
For the Month of September

	Le Louvre CD		Le Vin CD		Total	
	Amount	Percent	Amount	Percent	Amount	Percent
Sales	$20,000	100%	$80,000	100%	$100,000	100%
Less variable expenses	15,000	75%	40,000	50%	55,000	55%
Contribution margin	$ 5,000	25%	$40,000	50%	45,000	45%
Less fixed expenses					27,000	
Net operating income					$ 18,000	

Computation of the break-even point:

$$\frac{\text{Fixed expenses}}{\text{Overall CM ratio}} = \frac{\$27,000}{0.45} = \$60,000$$

Verification of the break-even:

	Le Louvre CD	Le Vin CD	Total
Current dollar sales	$20,000	$80,000	$100,000
Percentage of total dollar sales	20%	80%	100%
Sales at break-even	$12,000	$48,000	$60,000

	Le Louvre CD		Le Vin CD		Total	
	Amount	Percent	Amount	Percent	Amount	Percent
Sales	$12,000	100%	$48,000	100%	$ 60,000	100%
Less variable expenses	9,000	75%	24,000	50%	33,000	55%
Contribution margin	$ 3,000	25%	$24,000	50%	27,000	45%
Less fixed expenses					27,000	
Net operating income					$ 0	

EXHIBIT 6–4
Multiple-Product Break-Even Analysis: A Shift in Sales Mix (see Exhibit 6–3)

SOUND UNLIMITED
Contribution Income Statement
For the Month of October

	Le Louvre CD		Le Vin CD		Total	
	Amount	Percent	Amount	Percent	Amount	Percent
Sales	$80,000	100%	$20,000	100%	$100,000	100%
Less variable expenses	60,000	75%	10,000	50%	70,000	70%
Contribution margin	$20,000	25%	$10,000	50%	30,000	30%
Less fixed expenses					27,000	
Net operating income					$ 3,000	

Computation of the break-even point:

$$\frac{\text{Fixed expenses}}{\text{Overall CM ratio}} = \frac{\$27,000}{0.30} = \$90,000$$

has dropped from 45% in September to only 30% in October, and net operating income has dropped from $18,000 to only $3,000. In addition, with the drop in the overall CM ratio, the company's break-even point is no longer $60,000 in sales. Since the company is now realizing less average contribution margin per dollar of sales, it takes more sales to cover the same amount of fixed costs. Thus, the break-even point has increased from $60,000 to $90,000 in sales per year.

In preparing a break-even analysis, some assumption must be made concerning the sales mix. Usually the assumption is that it will not change. However, if the sales mix is expected to change, then this must be explicitly considered in any CVP computations.

IN BUSINESS

PLAYING THE CVP GAME

In 2002, General Motors (GM) gave away almost $2,600 per vehicle in customer incentives such as price cuts and 0% financing. "The pricing sacrifices have been more than offset by volume gains, most of which have come from trucks and SUVs, like the Chevy Suburban and the GMC Envoy, which generate far more profit for the company than cars. Lehman Brothers analysts estimate that GM will sell an additional 395,000 trucks and SUVs and an extra 75,000 cars in 2002. The trucks, however, are the company's golden goose, hauling in an average [contribution margin] . . . of about $7,000, compared with just $4,000 for the cars. All told, the volume gains could bring in an additional $3 billion [in profits]."

Source: Janice Revell, "GM's Slow Leak," *Fortune,* October 28, 2002, pp. 105–110.

Assumptions of CVP Analysis

A number of assumptions underlie CVP analysis:

1. Selling price is constant. The price of a product or service will not change as volume changes.
2. Costs are linear and can be accurately divided into variable and fixed elements. The variable element is constant per unit, and the fixed element is constant in total over the entire relevant range.
3. In multiproduct companies, the sales mix is constant.
4. In manufacturing companies, inventories do not change. The number of units produced equals the number of units sold.

While some of these assumptions may be violated in practice, the violations are usually not serious enough to call into question the validity of CVP analysis. For example, in most multiproduct companies, the sales mix is constant enough so that the results of CVP analysis are reasonably valid.

Perhaps the greatest danger lies in relying on simple CVP analysis when a manager is contemplating a large change in volume that lies outside of the relevant range. For example, a manager might contemplate increasing the level of sales far beyond what the company has ever experienced before. However, even in these situations a manager can adjust the model as we have done in this chapter to take into account anticipated changes in selling prices, fixed costs, and the sales mix that would otherwise violate the assumptions. For example, in a decision that would affect fixed costs, the change in fixed costs can be explicitly taken into account as illustrated earlier in the chapter in the Acoustic Concepts example on pages 235–238.

Summary

CVP analysis as presented in this chapter is based on a simple model of how profits respond to prices, costs, and volume. This model can be used to answer a variety of critical questions such as what is the company's break-even volume, what is its margin of safety, and what is likely to happen if specified changes are made in prices, costs, and volume.

A CVP graph depicts the relationships between sales volume in units on the one hand and fixed expenses, variable expenses, total expenses, total sales, and profits on the other hand. The CVP graph is useful for developing intuition about how costs and profits respond to changes in sales volume.

The contribution margin ratio is the ratio of the total contribution margin to total sales. This ratio can be used to quickly estimate what impact a change in total sales would have on net operating income. The ratio is also useful in break-even analysis.

The break-even point is the level of sales (in units or in dollars) at which the company just breaks even. The break-even point can be computed using several different techniques that are all based on the simple CVP model. With slight modifications, the same techniques can be used to compute the level of sales required to attain a target profit.

The margin of safety is the amount by which the company's current sales exceeds the break-even point.

The degree of operating leverage allows quick estimation of what impact a given percentage change in sales would have on the company's net operating income. The higher the degree of operating leverage, the greater is the impact on the company's profits. The degree of operating leverage is not constant—it depends on the company's current level of sales.

The profits of a multiproduct company are affected by its sales mix. Changes in the sales mix can affect the break-even point, margin of safety, and other critical factors.

Review Problem: CVP Relationships

Voltar Company manufactures and sells a specialized cordless telephone for high electromagnetic radiation environments. The company's contribution format income statement for the most recent year is given below:

	Total	Per Unit	Percent of Sales
Sales (20,000 units)	$1,200,000	$60	100%
Less variable expenses	900,000	45	? %
Contribution margin	300,000	$15	? %
Less fixed expenses	240,000		
Net operating income	$ 60,000		

Management is anxious to improve the company's profit performance and has asked for an analysis of a number of items.

Required:

1. Compute the company's CM ratio and variable expense ratio.
2. Compute the company's break-even point in both units and sales dollars. Use the equation method.
3. Assume that sales increase by $400,000 next year. If cost behavior patterns remain unchanged, by how much will the company's net operating income increase? Use the CM ratio to determine your answer.
4. Refer to the original data. Assume that next year management wants the company to earn a minimum profit of $90,000. How many units will have to be sold to meet this target profit?
5. Refer to the original data. Compute the company's margin of safety in both dollar and percentage form.
6. *a.* Compute the company's degree of operating leverage at the present level of sales.
   b. Assume that through a more intense effort by the sales staff, the company's sales increase by 8% next year. By what percentage would you expect net operating income to increase? Use the degree of operating leverage to obtain your answer.
   c. Verify your answer to (*b*) by preparing a new contribution format income statement showing an 8% increase in sales.
7. In an effort to increase sales and profits, management is considering the use of a higher-quality speaker. The higher-quality speaker would increase variable costs by $3 per unit, but management could eliminate one quality inspector who is paid a salary of $30,000 per year. The sales manager estimates that the higher-quality speaker would increase annual sales by at least 20%.
   a. Assuming that changes are made as described above, prepare a projected contribution format income statement for next year. Show data on a total, per unit, and percentage basis.
   b. Compute the company's new break-even point in both units and dollars of sales. Use the contribution margin method.
   c. Would you recommend that the changes be made?

Solution to Review Problem

1.

$$\text{CM ratio} = \frac{\text{Contribution margin}}{\text{Selling price}} = \frac{\$15}{\$60} = 25\%$$

$$\text{Variable expense ratio} = \frac{\text{Variable expense}}{\text{Selling price}} = \frac{\$45}{\$60} = 75\%$$

2.

$$\text{Sales} = \text{Variable expenses} + \text{Fixed expenses} + \text{Profits}$$

$$\$60Q = \$45Q + \$240{,}000 + \$0$$

$$\$15Q = \$240{,}000$$

$$Q = \$240{,}000 \div \$15 \text{ per unit}$$

$$Q = 16{,}000 \text{ units; or at \$60 per unit, \$960,000}$$

Alternative solution:

$$X = 0.75X + \$240{,}000 + \$0$$

$$0.25X = \$240{,}000$$

$$X = \$240{,}000 \div 0.25$$

$$X = \$960{,}000\text{; or at \$60 per unit, 16,000 units}$$

3.

Increase in sales	$400,000
Multiply by the CM ratio	× 25%
Expected increase in contribution margin	$100,000

Since the fixed expenses are not expected to change, net operating income will increase by the entire $100,000 increase in contribution margin computed above.

4. Equation method:

$$\begin{aligned} \text{Sales} &= \text{Variable expenses} + \text{Fixed expenses} + \text{Profits} \\ \$60Q &= \$45Q + \$240{,}000 + \$90{,}000 \\ \$15Q &= \$330{,}000 \\ Q &= \$330{,}000 \div \$15 \text{ per unit} \\ Q &= 22{,}000 \text{ units} \end{aligned}$$

Contribution margin method:

$$\frac{\text{Fixed expenses} + \text{Target profit}}{\text{Contribution margin per unit}} = \frac{\$240{,}000 + \$90{,}000}{\$15 \text{ per unit}} = 22{,}000 \text{ units}$$

5.

$$\begin{aligned} \text{Margin of safety in dollars} &= \text{Total sales} - \text{Break-even sales} \\ &= \$1{,}200{,}000 - \$960{,}000 = \$240{,}000 \end{aligned}$$

$$\text{Margin of safety percentage} = \frac{\text{Margin of safety in dollars}}{\text{Total sales}} = \frac{\$240{,}000}{\$1{,}200{,}000} = 20\%$$

6. *a.*

$$\text{Degree of operating leverage} = \frac{\text{Contribution margin}}{\text{Net operating income}} = \frac{\$300{,}000}{\$60{,}000} = 5$$

b.

Expected increase in sales	8%
Degree of operating leverage	× 5
Expected increase in net operating income	40%

c. If sales increase by 8%, then 21,600 units (20,000 × 1.08 = 21,600) will be sold next year. The new contribution format income statement will be as follows:

	Total	Per Unit	Percent of Sales
Sales (21,600 units)	$1,296,000	$60	100%
Less variable expenses	972,000	45	75%
Contribution margin	324,000	$15	25%
Less fixed expenses	240,000		
Net operating income	$ 84,000		

Thus, the $84,000 expected net operating income for next year represents a 40% increase over the $60,000 net operating income earned during the current year:

$$\frac{\$84{,}000 - \$60{,}000}{\$60{,}000} = \frac{\$24{,}000}{\$60{,}000} = 40\% \text{ increase}$$

Note from the income statement above that the increase in sales from 20,000 to 21,600 units has resulted in increases in *both* total sales and total variable expenses. It is a common error to overlook the increase in variable expenses when preparing a projected contribution format income statement.

7. *a.* A 20% increase in sales would result in 24,000 units being sold next year: 20,000 units × 1.20 = 24,000 units.

	Total	Per Unit	Percent of Sales
Sales (24,000 units)	$1,440,000	$60	100%
Less variable expenses	1,152,000	48*	80%
Contribution margin	288,000	$12	20%
Less fixed expenses	210,000†		
Net operating income	$78,000		

*$45 + $3 = $48; $48 ÷ $60 = 80%.
†$240,000 − $30,000 = $210,000.

Note that the change in per unit variable expenses results in a change in both the per unit contribution margin and the CM ratio.

b.

$$\text{Break-even point in unit sales} = \frac{\text{Fixed expenses}}{\text{Contribution margin per unit}}$$

$$= \frac{\$210{,}000}{\$12 \text{ per unit}} = 17{,}500 \text{ units}$$

$$\text{Break-even point in dollar sales} = \frac{\text{Fixed expenses}}{\text{CM ratio}}$$

$$= \frac{\$210{,}000}{0.20} = \$1{,}050{,}000$$

c. Yes, based on these data the changes should be made. The changes will increase the company's net operating income from the present $60,000 to $78,000 per year. Although the changes will also result in a higher break-even point (17,500 units as compared to the present 16,000 units), the company's margin of safety will actually be wider than before:

$$\text{Margin of safety in dollars} = \text{Total sales} - \text{Break-even sales}$$

$$= \$1{,}440{,}000 - \$1{,}050{,}000 = \$390{,}000$$

As shown in (5) above, the company's present margin of safety is only $240,000. Thus, several benefits will result from the proposed changes.

Glossary

Break-even point The level of sales at which profit is zero. The break-even point can also be defined as the point where total sales equals total expenses or as the point where total contribution margin equals total fixed expenses. (p. 232)

Contribution margin method A method of computing the break-even point in which the fixed expenses are divided by the contribution margin per unit. (p. 240)

Contribution margin ratio (CM ratio) The contribution margin as a percentage of total sales. (p. 235)

Cost-volume-profit (CVP) graph The relationships between an organization's revenues, costs, and level of activity presented in graphic form. (p. 233)

Degree of operating leverage A measure, at a given level of sales, of how a percentage change in sales volume will affect profits. The degree of operating leverage is computed by dividing contribution margin by net operating income. (p. 246)

Equation method A method of computing the break-even point that relies on the equation Sales = Variable expenses + Fixed expenses + Profits. (p. 239)

Incremental analysis An analytical approach that focuses only on those items of revenue, cost, and volume that will change as a result of a decision. (p. 237)

Margin of safety The excess of budgeted (or actual) sales over the break-even volume of sales. (p. 242)

Operating leverage A measure of how sensitive net operating income is to a given percentage change in sales. It is computed by dividing the contribution margin by net operating income. (p. 246)

Sales mix The relative proportions in which a company's products are sold. Sales mix is computed by expressing the sales of each product as a percentage of total sales. (p. 248)

Questions

6–1 What is meant by a product's CM ratio? How is this ratio useful in planning business operations?

6–2 Often the most direct route to a business decision is an incremental analysis. What is meant by an *incremental analysis?*

6–3 Company A's cost structure includes costs that are mostly variable, whereas Company B's cost structure includes costs that are mostly fixed. In a time of increasing sales, which company will tend to realize the most rapid increase in profits? Explain.

6–4 What is meant by the term *operating leverage?*

6–5 A 10% decrease in the selling price of a product will have the same impact on net income as a 10% increase in the variable expenses. Do you agree? Why or why not?

6–6 What is meant by the term *break-even point*?

6–7 Name three approaches to break-even analysis. Briefly explain how each approach works.

6–8 In response to a request from your immediate supervisor, you have prepared a CVP graph portraying the cost and revenue characteristics of your company's product and operations. Explain how the lines on the graph and the break-even point would change if (*a*) the selling price per unit decreased, (*b*) fixed costs increased throughout the entire range of activity portrayed on the graph, and (*c*) variable costs per unit increased.

6–9 Al's Auto Wash charges $4 to wash a car. The variable costs of washing a car are $0.60 per car. Fixed expenses total $1,700 monthly. How many cars must be washed each month for Al to break even?

6–10 What is meant by the margin of safety?

6–11 Companies X and Y are in the same industry. Company X is highly automated, whereas Company Y relies primarily on labor to make its products. If sales and total expenses in the two companies are about the same, which would you expect to have the lower margin of safety? Why?

6–12 What is meant by the term *sales mix*? What assumption is usually made concerning sales mix in CVP analysis?

6–13 Explain how a shift in the sales mix could result in both a higher break-even point and a lower net income.

Exercises

EXERCISE 6–1 Preparing a Contribution Format Income Statement [LO1]

Whirly Corporation's most recent income statement is shown below:

	Total	Per Unit
Sales (10,000 units)	$350,000	$35.00
Less variable expenses	200,000	20.00
Contribution margin	150,000	$15.00
Less fixed expenses	135,000	
Net operating income	$ 15,000	

Required:

Prepare a new contribution format income statement under each of the following conditions (consider each case independently):

1. The sales volume increases by 100 units.
2. The sales volume decreases by 100 units.
3. The sales volume is 9,000 units.

EXERCISE 6–2 Prepare a Cost-Volume-Profit (CVP) Graph [LO2]

Karlik Enterprises has a single product whose selling price is $24 and whose variable cost is $18 per unit. The company's monthly fixed expense is $24,000.

Required:

1. Prepare a cost-volume-profit graph for the company up to a sales level of 8,000 units.
2. Estimate the company's break-even point in unit sales using your cost-volume-profit graph.

EXERCISE 6–3 Computing and Using the CM Ratio [LO3]

Last month when Holiday Creations, Inc., sold 50,000 units, total sales were $200,000, total variable expenses were $120,000, and total fixed expenses were $65,000.

Required:

1. What is the company's contribution margin (CM) ratio?
2. Estimate the change in the company's net income if it were to increase its total sales by $1,000.

EXERCISE 6–4 Changes in Variable Costs, Fixed Costs, Selling Price, and Volume [LO4]
Data for Hermann Corporation are shown below:

	Per Unit	Percent of Sales
Selling price	$90	100%
Less variable expenses	63	70
Contribution margin	$27	30%

Fixed expenses are $30,000 per month and the company is selling 2,000 units per month.

Required:

1. The marketing manager argues that a $5,000 increase in the monthly advertising budget would increase monthly sales by $9,000. Should the advertising budget be increased?
2. Refer to the original data. Management is considering using higher-quality components that would increase the variable cost by $2 per unit. The marketing manager believes the higher-quality product would increase sales by 10% per month. Should the higher-quality components be used?

EXERCISE 6–5 Compute the Break-Even Point [LO5]
Mauro Products has a single product, a woven basket whose selling price is $15 and whose variable cost is $12 per unit. The company's monthly fixed expenses are $4,200.

Required:

1. Solve for the company's break-even point in unit sales using the equation method.
2. Solve for the company's break-even point in sales dollars using the equation method and the CM ratio.
3. Solve for the company's break-even point in unit sales using the contribution margin method.
4. Solve for the company's break-even point in sales dollars using the contribution margin method and the CM ratio.

EXERCISE 6–6 Compute the Level of Sales Required to Attain a Target Profit [LO6]
Lin Corporation has a single product whose selling price is $120 and whose variable cost is $80 per unit. The company's monthly fixed expense is $50,000.

Required:

1. Using the equation method, solve for the unit sales that are required to earn a target profit of $10,000.
2. Using the contribution margin approach, solve for the dollar sales that are required to earn a target profit of $15,000.

EXERCISE 6–7 Compute the Margin of Safety [LO7]
Molander Corporation is a distributor of a sun umbrella used at resort hotels. Data concerning the next month's budget appear below:

Selling price	$30 per unit
Variable expense	$20 per unit
Fixed expense	$7,500 per month
Unit sales	1,000 units per month

Required:

1. Compute the company's margin of safety.
2. Compute the company's margin of safety as a percentage of its sales.

EXERCISE 6–8 Compute and Use the Degree of Operating Leverage [LO8]
Engberg Company installs lawn sod in home yards. The company's most recent monthly contribution format income statement follows:

	Amount	Percent of Sales
Sales	$80,000	100%
Less variable expenses	32,000	40%
Contribution margin	48,000	60%
Less fixed expenses	38,000	
Net operating income	$10,000	

Required:
1. Compute the company's degree of operating leverage.
2. Using the degree of operating leverage, estimate the impact on net income of a 5% increase in sales.
3. Verify your estimate from part (2) above by constructing a new contribution format income statement for the company assuming a 5% increase in sales.

EXERCISE 6–9 Compute the Break-Even Point for a Multiproduct Company [LO9]

Lucido Products markets two computer games: Claimjumper and Makeover. A contribution format income statement for a recent month for the two games appears below:

	Claimjumper	Makeover	Total
Sales	$30,000	$70,000	$100,000
Less variable expenses	20,000	50,000	70,000
Contribution margin	$10,000	$20,000	30,000
Less fixed expenses			24,000
Net operating income			$ 6,000

Required:
1. Compute the overall contribution margin (CM) ratio for the company.
2. Compute the overall break-even point for the company in sales dollars.
3. Verify the overall break-even point for the company by constructing a contribution format income statement showing the appropriate levels of sales for the two products.

EXERCISE 6–10 Using a Contribution Format Income Statement [LO1, LO4]

Miller Company's most recent contribution format income statement is shown below:

	Total	Per Unit
Sales (20,000 units)	$300,000	$15.00
Less variable expenses	180,000	9.00
Contribution margin	120,000	$6.00
Less fixed expenses	70,000	
Net operating income	$ 50,000	

Required:

Prepare a new contribution format income statement under each of the following conditions (consider each case independently):
1. The sales volume increases by 15%.
2. The selling price decreases by $1.50 per unit, and the sales volume increases by 25%.
3. The selling price increases by $1.50 per unit, fixed expenses increase by $20,000, and the sales volume decreases by 5%.
4. The selling price increases by 12%, variable expenses increase by 60 cents per unit, and the sales volume decreases by 10%.

EXERCISE 6–11 Break-Even Analysis and CVP Graphing [LO2, LO4, LO5]

The Hartford Symphony Guild is planning its annual dinner-dance. The dinner-dance committee has assembled the following expected costs for the event:

Dinner (per person)	$18
Favors and program (per person)	$2
Band	$2,800
Rental of ballroom	$900
Professional entertainment during intermission	$1,000
Tickets and advertising	$1,300

The committee members would like to charge $35 per person for the evening's activities.

Required:

1. Compute the break-even point for the dinner-dance (in terms of the number of persons who must attend).
2. Assume that last year only 300 persons attended the dinner-dance. If the same number attend this year, what price per ticket must be charged in order to break even?
3. Refer to the original data ($35 ticket price per person). Prepare a CVP graph for the dinner-dance from a zero level of activity up to 600 tickets sold. Number of persons should be placed on the horizontal *(X)* axis, and dollars should be placed on the vertical *(Y)* axis.

EXERCISE 6–12 Break-Even and Target Profit Analysis [LO3, LO4, LO5, LO6]

Lindon Company is the exclusive distributor for an automotive product that sells for $40 per unit and has a CM ratio of 30%. The company's fixed expenses are $180,000 per year.

Required:

1. What are the variable expenses per unit?
2. Using the equation method:
   a. What is the break-even point in units and sales dollars?
   b. What sales level in units and in sales dollars is required to earn an annual profit of $60,000?
   c. Assume that by using a more efficient shipper, the company is able to reduce its variable expenses by $4 per unit. What is the company's new break-even point in units and sales dollars?
3. Repeat (2) above using the contribution margin method.

EXERCISE 6–13 Break-Even and Target Profit Analysis [LO4, LO5, LO6]

Outback Outfitters sells recreational equipment. One of the company's products, a small camp stove, sells for $50 per unit. Variable expenses are $32 per stove, and fixed expenses associated with the stove total $108,000 per month.

Required:

1. Compute the break-even point in number of stoves and in total sales dollars.
2. If the variable expenses per stove increase as a percentage of the selling price, will it result in a higher or a lower break-even point? Why? (Assume that the fixed expenses remain unchanged.)
3. At present, the company is selling 8,000 stoves per month. The sales manager is convinced that a 10% reduction in the selling price would result in a 25% increase in monthly sales of stoves. Prepare two contribution income statements, one under present operating conditions, and one as operations would appear after the proposed changes. Show both total and per unit data on your statements.
4. Refer to the data in (3) above. How many stoves would have to be sold at the new selling price to yield a minimum net operating income of $35,000 per month?

EXERCISE 6–14 Missing Data; Basic CVP Concepts [LO1, LO9]

Fill in the missing amounts in each of the eight case situations below. Each case is independent of the others. (Hint: One way to find the missing amounts would be to prepare a contribution income statement for each case, enter the known data, and then compute the missing items.)

a. Assume that only one product is being sold in each of the four following case situations:

Case	Units Sold	Sales	Variable Expenses	Contribution Margin per Unit	Fixed Expenses	Net Operating Income (Loss)
1	15,000	$180,000	$120,000	?	$50,000	?
2	?	$100,000	?	$10	$32,000	$8,000
3	10,000	?	$70,000	$13	?	$12,000
4	6,000	$300,000	?	?	$100,000	$(10,000)

b. Assume that more than one product is being sold in each of the four following case situations:

Case	Sales	Variable Expenses	Average Contribution Margin (Percent)	Fixed Expenses	Net Operating Income (Loss)
1	$500,000	?	20%	?	$7,000
2	$400,000	$260,000	?	$100,000	?
3	?	?	60%	$130,000	$20,000
4	$600,000	$420,000	?	?	$(5,000)

EXERCISE 6–15 Break-Even Analysis; Target Profit; Margin of Safety; CM Ratio [LO1, LO3, LO5, LO6, LO7]

Menlo Company manufactures and sells a single product. The company's sales and expenses for last quarter follow:

	Total	Per Unit
Sales	$450,000	$30
Less variable expenses	180,000	12
Contribution margin	270,000	$18
Less fixed expenses	216,000	
Net operating income	$ 54,000	

Required:
1. What is the quarterly break-even point in units sold and in sales dollars?
2. Without resorting to computations, what is the total contribution margin at the break-even point?
3. How many units would have to be sold each quarter to earn a target profit of $90,000? Use the contribution margin method. Verify your answer by preparing a contribution format income statement at the target sales level.
4. Refer to the original data. Compute the company's margin of safety in both dollar and percentage terms.
5. What is the company's CM ratio? If sales increase by $50,000 per quarter and there is no change in fixed expenses, by how much would you expect quarterly net operating income to increase?

EXERCISE 6–16 Operating Leverage [LO4, LO8]

Magic Realm, Inc., has developed a new fantasy board game. The company sold 15,000 games last year at a selling price of $20 per game. Fixed costs associated with the game total $182,000 per year, and variable costs are $6 per game. Production of the game is entrusted to a printing contractor. Variable costs consist mostly of payments to this contractor.

Required:
1. Prepare a contribution format income statement for the game last year and compute the degree of operating leverage.
2. Management is confident that the company can sell 18,000 games next year (an increase of 3,000 games, or 20%, over last year). Compute:
   a. The expected percentage increase in net operating income for next year.
   b. The expected total dollar net operating income for next year. (Do not prepare an income statement; use the degree of operating leverage to compute your answer.)

EXERCISE 6–17 Multiproduct Break-Even Analysis [LO9]

Olongapo Sports Corporation is the distributor in the Philippines of two premium golf balls—the Flight Dynamic and the Sure Shot. Monthly sales and the contribution margin ratios for the two products follow:

	Product		
	Flight Dynamic	Sure Shot	Total
Sales	P150,000	P250,000	P400,000
CM ratio	80%	36%	?

Fixed expenses total P183,750 per month. (The currency in the Philippines is the peso, which is denoted by P.)

Required:

1. Prepare a contribution format income statement for the company as a whole. Carry computations to one decimal place.
2. Compute the break-even point for the company based on the current sales mix.
3. If sales increase by P100,000 a month, by how much would you expect net operating income to increase? What are your assumptions?

Problems

PROBLEM 6–18 Basic CVP Analysis; Graphing [LO1, LO2, LO4, LO5]

The Fashion Shoe Company operates a chain of women's shoe shops around the country. The shops carry many styles of shoes that are all sold at the same price. Sales personnel in the shops are paid a substantial commission on each pair of shoes sold (in addition to a small basic salary) in order to encourage them to be aggressive in their sales efforts.

The following worksheet contains cost and revenue data for Shop 48 and is typical of the company's many outlets:

Microsoft Excel - Problem 6-18 screen capture.xls

	A	B	C
1		*Per Pair of Shoes*	
2	Selling price	$ 30.00	
3			
4	Variable expenses:		
5	Invoice cost	$ 13.50	
6	Sales commission	4.50	
7	Total variable expenses	$ 18.00	
8			
9		*Annual*	
10	Fixed expenses:		
11	Advertising	$ 30,000	
12	Rent	20,000	
13	Salaries	100,000	
14	Total fixed expenses	$ 150,000	
15			

Sheet1 / Sheet2 / Sheet3

Required:

1. Calculate the annual break-even point in dollar sales and in unit sales for Shop 48.
2. Prepare a CVP graph showing cost and revenue data for Shop 48 from a zero level of activity up to 17,000 pairs of shoes sold each year. Clearly indicate the break-even point on the graph.
3. If 12,000 pairs of shoes are sold in a year, what would be Shop 48's net operating income or loss?
4. The company is considering paying the store manager of Shop 48 an incentive commission of 75 cents per pair of shoes (in addition to the salesperson's commission). If this change is made, what will be the new break-even point in dollar sales and in unit sales?
5. Refer to the original data. As an alternative to (4) above, the company is considering paying the store manager 50 cents commission on each pair of shoes sold in excess of the break-even point. If this change is made, what will be the shop's net operating income or loss if 15,000 pairs of shoes are sold?
6. Refer to the original data. The company is considering eliminating sales commissions entirely in its shops and increasing fixed salaries by $31,500 annually. If this change is made, what will be the new break-even point in dollar sales and in unit sales for Shop 48? Would you recommend that the change be made? Explain.

PROBLEM 6–19 Basics of CVP Analysis; Cost Structure [LO1, LO3, LO4, LO5, LO6]

Due to erratic sales of its sole product—a high-capacity battery for laptop computers—PEM, Inc., has been experiencing difficulty for some time. The company's contribution format income statement for the most recent month is given below:

Sales (19,500 units × $30 per unit)	$585,000
Less variable expenses	409,500
Contribution margin	175,500
Less fixed expenses	180,000
Net operating loss	$ (4,500)

Required:

1. Compute the company's CM ratio and its break-even point in both units and dollars.
2. The president believes that a $16,000 increase in the monthly advertising budget, combined with an intensified effort by the sales staff, will result in an $80,000 increase in monthly sales. If the president is right, what will be the effect on the company's monthly net operating income or loss? (Use the incremental approach in preparing your answer.)
3. Refer to the original data. The sales manager is convinced that a 10% reduction in the selling price, combined with an increase of $60,000 in the monthly advertising budget, will cause unit sales to double. What will the new contribution format income statement look like if these changes are adopted?
4. Refer to the original data. The Marketing Department thinks that a fancy new package for the laptop computer battery would help sales. The new package would increase packaging costs by 75 cents per unit. Assuming no other changes, how many units would have to be sold each month to earn a profit of $9,750?
5. Refer to the original data. By automating certain operations, the company could reduce variable costs by $3 per unit. However, fixed costs would increase by $72,000 each month.
   a. Compute the new CM ratio and the new break-even point in both units and dollars.
   b. Assume that the company expects to sell 26,000 units next month. Prepare two contribution format income statements, one assuming that operations are not automated and one assuming that they are. (Show data on a per unit and percentage basis, as well as in total, for each alternative.)
   c. Would you recommend that the company automate its operations? Explain.

PROBLEM 6–20 Basics of CVP Analysis [LO1, LO3, LO4, LO5, LO8]

Feather Friends, Inc., distributes a high-quality wooden birdhouse that sells for $20 per unit. Variable costs are $8 per unit, and fixed costs total $180,000 per year.

Required:

Answer the following independent questions:

1. What is the product's CM ratio?
2. Use the CM ratio to determine the break-even point in sales dollars.
3. Due to an increase in demand, the company estimates that sales will increase by $75,000 during the next year. By how much should net operating income increase (or net loss decrease) assuming that fixed costs do not change?
4. Assume that the operating results for last year were:

Sales	$400,000
Less variable expenses	160,000
Contribution margin	240,000
Less fixed expenses	180,000
Net operating income	$60,000

   a. Compute the degree of operating leverage at the current level of sales.
   b. The president expects sales to increase by 20% next year. By what percentage should net operating income increase?
5. Refer to the original data. Assume that the company sold 18,000 units last year. The sales manager is convinced that a 10% reduction in the selling price, combined with a $30,000 increase in advertising, would cause annual sales in units to increase by one-third. Prepare two contribution income statements, one showing the results of last year's operations and one showing

the results of operations if these changes are made. Would you recommend that the company do as the sales manager suggests?

6. Refer to the original data. Assume again that the company sold 18,000 units last year. The president does not want to change the selling price. Instead, he wants to increase the sales commission by $1 per unit. He thinks that this move, combined with some increase in advertising, would increase annual sales by 25%. By how much could advertising be increased with profits remaining unchanged? Do not prepare an income statement; use the incremental analysis approach.

PROBLEM 6–21 Sales Mix; Multiproduct Break-Even Analysis [LO9]
Gold Star Rice, Ltd., of Thailand exports Thai rice throughout Asia. The company grows three varieties of rice—Fragrant, White, and Loonzain. (The currency in Thailand is the baht, which is denoted by B.) Budgeted sales by product and in total for the coming month are shown below:

	Product							
	White		Fragrant		Loonzain		Total	
Percentage of total sales	20%		52%		28%		100%	
Sales	B150,000	100%	B390,000	100%	B210,000	100%	B750,000	100%
Less variable expenses	108,000	72%	78,000	20%	84,000	40%	270,000	36%
Contribution margin	B 42,000	28%	B312,000	80%	B126,000	60%	480,000	64%
Less fixed expenses							449,280	
Net operating income							B30,720	

$$\frac{\text{Break-even point}}{\text{in sales dollars}} = \frac{\text{Fixed expenses}}{\text{CM ratio}} = \frac{\text{B449,280}}{0.64} = \text{B702,000}$$

As shown by these data, net operating income is budgeted at B30,720 for the month and break-even sales at B702,000.

Assume that actual sales for the month total B750,000 as planned. Actual sales by product are: White, B300,000; Fragrant, B180,000; and Loonzain, B270,000.

Required:

1. Prepare a contribution format income statement for the month based on actual sales data. Present the income statement in the format shown above.
2. Compute the break-even point in sales dollars for the month based on your actual data.
3. Considering the fact that the company met its B750,000 sales budget for the month, the president is shocked at the results shown on your income statement in (1) above. Prepare a brief memo for the president explaining why both the operating results and the break-even point in sales dollars are different from what was budgeted.

PROBLEM 6–22 Break-Even Analysis; Pricing [LO1, LO4, LO5]
Minden Company introduced a new product last year for which it is trying to find an optimal selling price. Marketing studies suggest that the company can increase sales by 5,000 units for each $2 reduction in the selling price. The company's present selling price is $70 per unit, and variable expenses are $40 per unit. Fixed expenses are $540,000 per year. The present annual sales volume (at the $70 selling price) is 15,000 units.

Required:

1. What is the present yearly net operating income or loss?
2. What is the present break-even point in units and in dollar sales?
3. Assuming that the marketing studies are correct, what is the *maximum* profit that the company can earn yearly? At how many units and at what selling price per unit would the company generate this profit?
4. What would be the break-even point in units and in sales dollars using the selling price you determined in (3) above (e.g., the selling price at the level of maximum profits)? Why is this break-even point different from the break-even point you computed in (2) above?

PROBLEM 6–23 Interpretive Questions on the CVP Graph [LO2, LO5]

A CVP graph such as the one shown below is a useful technique for showing relationships between an organization's costs, volume, and profits.

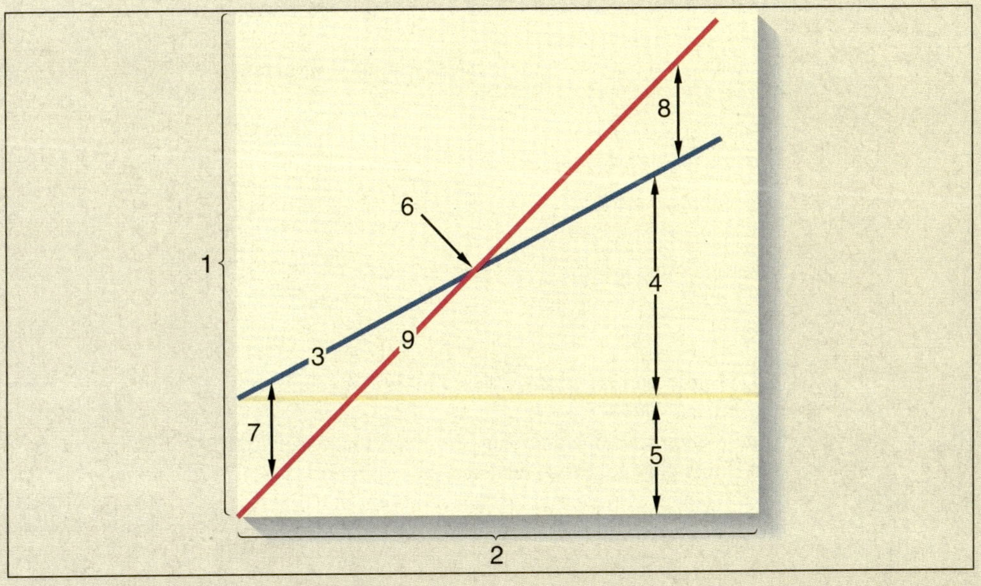

Required:

1. Identify the numbered components in the CVP graph.
2. State the effect of each of the following actions on line 3, line 9, and the break-even point. For line 3 and line 9, state whether the action will cause the line to:

   Remain unchanged.
   Shift upward.
   Shift downward.
   Have a steeper slope (i.e., rotate upward).
   Have a flatter slope (i.e., rotate downward).
   Shift upward *and* have a steeper slope.
   Shift upward *and* have a flatter slope.
   Shift downward *and* have a steeper slope.
   Shift downward *and* have a flatter slope.

   In the case of the break-even point, state whether the action will cause the break-even point to:

   Remain unchanged.
   Increase.
   Decrease.
   Probably change, but the direction is uncertain.

   Treat each case independently.

   x. *Example.* Fixed costs are reduced by $5,000 per period.
   Answer (see choices above): Line 3: Shift downward.
   Line 9: Remain unchanged.
   Break-even point: Decrease.

   a. The unit selling price is increased from $18 to $20.
   b. Unit variable costs are decreased from $12 to $10.
   c. Fixed costs are increased by $3,000 per period.
   d. Two thousand more units are sold during the period than were budgeted.
   e. Due to paying salespersons a commission rather than a flat salary, fixed costs are reduced by $8,000 per period and unit variable costs are increased by $3.
   f. Due to an increase in the cost of materials, both unit variable costs and the selling price are increased by $2.
   g. Advertising costs are increased by $10,000 per period, resulting in a 10% increase in the number of units sold.
   h. Due to automating an operation previously done by workers, fixed costs are increased by $12,000 per period and unit variable costs are reduced by $4.

PROBLEM 6–24 Various CVP Questions: Break-Even Point; Cost Structure; Target Sales [LO1, LO3, LO4, LO5, LO6, LO8]

Northwood Company manufactures basketballs. The company has a ball that sells for $25. At present, the ball is manufactured in a small plant that relies heavily on direct labor workers. Thus, variable costs are high, totaling $15 per ball.

Last year, the company sold 30,000 of these balls, with the following results:

Sales (30,000 balls)	$750,000
Less variable expenses	450,000
Contribution margin	300,000
Less fixed expenses	210,000
Net operating income	$ 90,000

Required:

1. Compute (a) the CM ratio and the break-even point in balls, and (b) the degree of operating leverage at last year's sales level.
2. Due to an increase in labor rates, the company estimates that variable costs will increase by $3 per ball next year. If this change takes place and the selling price per ball remains constant at $25, what will be the new CM ratio and break-even point in balls?
3. Refer to the data in (2) above. If the expected change in variable costs takes place, how many balls will have to be sold next year to earn the same net operating income ($90,000) as last year?
4. Refer again to the data in (2) above. The president feels that the company must raise the selling price of its basketballs. If Northwood Company wants to maintain *the same CM ratio as last year,* what selling price per ball must it charge next year to cover the increased labor costs?
5. Refer to the original data. The company is discussing the construction of a new, automated manufacturing plant. The new plant would slash variable costs per ball by 40%, but it would cause fixed costs per year to double. If the new plant is built, what would be the company's new CM ratio and new break-even point in balls?
6. Refer to the data in (5) above.
   a. If the new plant is built, how many balls will have to be sold next year to earn the same net operating income ($90,000) as last year?
   b. Assume the new plant is built and that next year the company manufactures and sells 30,000 balls (the same number as sold last year). Prepare a contribution income statement and compute the degree of operating leverage.
   c. If you were a member of top management, would you have been in favor of constructing the new plant? Explain.

PROBLEM 6–25 Graphing; Incremental Analysis; Operating Leverage [LO2, LO4, LO5, LO6, LO8]

Angie Silva has recently opened The Sandal Shop in Brisbane, Australia, a store that specializes in fashionable sandals. Angie has just received a degree in business and she is anxious to apply the principles she has learned to her business. In time, she hopes to open a chain of sandal shops. As a first step, she has prepared the following analysis for her new store:

Sales price per pair of sandals	$40
Variable expenses per pair of sandals	16
Contribution margin per pair of sandals	$24
Fixed expenses per year:	
Building rental	$15,000
Equipment depreciation	7,000
Selling	20,000
Administrative	18,000
Total fixed expenses	$60,000

Required:

1. How many pairs of sandals must be sold each year to break even? What does this represent in total sales dollars?

2. Prepare a CVP graph for the store from a zero level of activity up to 4,000 pairs of sandals sold each year. Indicate the break-even point on your graph.
3. Angie has decided that she must earn at least $18,000 the first year to justify her time and effort. How many pairs of sandals must be sold to reach this target profit?
4. Angie now has two salespersons working in the store—one full time and one part time. It will cost her an additional $8,000 per year to convert the part-time position to a full-time position. Angie believes that the change would bring in an additional $25,000 in sales each year. Should she convert the position? Use the incremental approach. (Do not prepare an income statement.)
5. Refer to the original data. During the first year, the store sold only 3,000 pairs of sandals and reported the following operating results:

Sales (3,000 pairs)	$120,000
Less variable expenses	48,000
Contribution margin	72,000
Less fixed expenses	60,000
Net operating income	$ 12,000

   a. What is the store's degree of operating leverage?
   b. Angie is confident that with a more intense sales effort and with a more creative advertising program she can increase sales by 50% next year. What would be the expected percentage increase in net operating income? Use the degree of operating leverage to compute your answer.

PROBLEM 6–26 Changes in Fixed and Variable Costs; Break-Even and Target Profit Analysis [LO4, LO5, LO6]

Neptune Company produces toys and other items for use in beach and resort areas. A small, inflatable toy has come onto the market that the company is anxious to produce and sell. The new toy will sell for $3 per unit. Enough capacity exists in the company's plant to produce 16,000 units of the toy each month. Variable costs to manufacture and sell one unit would be $1.25, and fixed costs associated with the toy would total $35,000 per month.

The company's Marketing Department predicts that demand for the new toy will exceed the 16,000 units that the company is able to produce. Additional manufacturing space can be rented from another company at a fixed cost of $1,000 per month. Variable costs in the rented facility would total $1.40 per unit, due to somewhat less efficient operations than in the main plant.

Required:

1. Compute the monthly break-even point for the new toy in units and in total sales dollars. Show all computations in good form.
2. How many units must be sold each month to make a monthly profit of $12,000?
3. If the sales manager receives a bonus of 10 cents for each unit sold in excess of the break-even point, how many units must be sold each month to earn a return of 25% on the monthly investment in fixed costs?

PROBLEM 6–27 Break-Even and Target Profit Analysis [LO5, LO6]

The Shirt Works sells a large variety of tee shirts and sweatshirts. Steve Hooper, the owner, is thinking of expanding his sales by hiring local high school students, on a commission basis, to sell sweatshirts bearing the name and mascot of the local high school.

These sweatshirts would have to be ordered from the manufacturer six weeks in advance, and they could not be returned because of the unique printing required. The sweatshirts would cost Mr. Hooper $8 each with a minimum order of 75 sweatshirts. Any additional sweatshirts would have to be ordered in increments of 75.

Since Mr. Hooper's plan would not require any additional facilities, the only costs associated with the project would be the costs of the sweatshirts and the costs of the sales commissions. The selling price of the sweatshirts would be $13.50 each. Mr. Hooper would pay the students a commission of $1.50 for each shirt sold.

Required:

1. To make the project worthwhile, Mr. Hooper would require a $1,200 profit for the first three months of the venture. What level of sales in units and in dollars would be required to reach this target net operating income? Show all computations.

2. Assume that the venture is undertaken and an order is placed for 75 sweatshirts. What would be Mr. Hooper's break-even point in units and in sales dollars? Show computations and explain the reasoning behind your answer.

PROBLEM 6–28 Changes in Cost Structure; Break-Even Analysis; Operating Leverage; Margin of Safety [LO4, LO5, LO7, LO8]

Morton Company's contribution format income statement for last month is given below:

Sales (15,000 units × $30 per unit)	$450,000
Less variable expenses	315,000
Contribution margin	135,000
Less fixed expenses	90,000
Net operating income	$ 45,000

The industry in which Morton Company operates is quite sensitive to cyclical movements in the economy. Thus, profits vary considerably from year to year according to general economic conditions. The company has a large amount of unused capacity and is studying ways of improving profits.

Required:

1. New equipment has come onto the market that would allow Morton Company to automate a portion of its operations. Variable costs would be reduced by $9 per unit. However, fixed costs would increase to a total of $225,000 each month. Prepare two contribution format income statements, one showing present operations and one showing how operations would appear if the new equipment is purchased. Show an Amount column, a Per Unit column, and a Percent column on each statement. Do not show percentages for the fixed costs.
2. Refer to the income statements in (1) above. For both present operations and the proposed new operations, compute (a) the degree of operating leverage, (b) the break-even point in dollars, and (c) the margin of safety in both dollar and percentage terms.
3. Refer again to the data in (1) above. As a manager, what factor would be paramount in your mind in deciding whether to purchase the new equipment? (Assume that ample funds are available to make the purchase.)
4. Refer to the original data. Rather than purchase new equipment, the marketing manager is thinking about changing the company's marketing strategy. Rather than pay sales commissions, which are currently included in variable expenses, the company would pay salespersons fixed salaries and would invest heavily in advertising. The marketing manager claims this new approach would increase unit sales by 30% without any change in selling price; the company's new monthly fixed expenses would be $180,000; and its net operating income would increase by 20%. Compute the break-even point in sales dollars for the company under the new marketing strategy. Do you agree with the marketing manager's proposal?

PROBLEM 6–29 Sales Mix; Break-Even Analysis; Margin of Safety [LO7, LO9]

Island Novelties, Inc., of Palau makes two products, Hawaiian Fantasy and Tahitian Joy. Present revenue, cost, and sales data for the two products follow:

	Hawaiian Fantasy	Tahitian Joy
Selling price per unit	$15	$100
Variable expenses per unit	$9	$20
Number of units sold annually	20,000	5,000

Fixed expenses total $475,800 per year. The Republic of Palau uses the U.S. dollar as its currency.

Required:

1. Assuming the sales mix given above, do the following:
   a. Prepare a contribution format income statement showing both dollar and percent columns for each product and for the company as a whole.
   b. Compute the break-even point in dollars for the company as a whole and the margin of safety in both dollars and percent.

2. The company has developed a new product to be called Samoan Delight. Assume that the company could sell 10,000 units at $45 each. The variable expenses would be $36 each. The company's fixed expenses would not change.
   a. Prepare another contribution format income statement, including sales of the Samoan Delight (sales of the other two products would not change).
   b. Compute the company's new break-even point in dollars and the new margin of safety in both dollars and percent.
3. The president of the company examines your figures and says, "There's something strange here. Our fixed costs haven't changed and you show greater total contribution margin if we add the new product, but you also show our break-even point going up. With greater contribution margin, the break-even point should go down, not up. You've made a mistake somewhere." Explain to the president what has happened.

PROBLEM 6–30 Sales Mix; Commission Structure; Multiproduct Break-Even Analysis [LO9]

Carbex, Inc., produces cutlery sets out of high-quality wood and steel. The company makes a standard cutlery set and a deluxe set and sells them to retail department stores throughout the country. The standard set sells for $60, and the deluxe set sells for $75. The variable expenses associated with each set are given below (in cost per set):

	Standard	Deluxe
Production costs	$15.00	$30.00
Sales commissions (15% of sales price)	$9.00	$11.25

The company's fixed expenses each month are:

Advertising	$105,000
Depreciation	$21,700
Administrative	$63,000

Salespersons are paid on a commission basis to encourage them to be aggressive in their sales efforts. Mary Parsons, the financial vice president, watches sales commissions carefully and has noted that they have risen steadily over the last year. For this reason, she was shocked to find that even though sales have increased, profits for the current month—May—are down substantially from April. Sales, in sets, for the last two months are given below:

	Standard	Deluxe	Total
April	4,000	2,000	6,000
May	1,000	5,000	6,000

Required:
1. Prepare contribution format income statements for April and May. Use the following headings:

	Standard		Deluxe		Total	
	Amount	Percent	Amount	Percent	Amount	Percent
Sales						
Etc						

   Place the fixed expenses only in the Total column. Do not show percentages for the fixed expenses.
2. Explain why there is a difference in net operating income between the two months, even though the same *total* number of sets was sold in each month.
3. What can be done to the sales commissions to optimize the sales mix?
4. *a.* Using April's figures, what was the break-even point for the month in sales dollars?
   b. Has May's break-even point gone up or down from that of April? Explain your answer without calculating the break-even point for May.

Cases

CASE 6–31 Detailed Income Statement; CVP Analysis [LO1, LO4, LO6]

The most recent income statement for Whitney Company appears below:

eXcel

WHITNEY COMPANY Income Statement For the Year Ended December 31			
Sales (45,000 units at $10 per unit)			$450,000
Less cost of goods sold:			
Direct materials		$90,000	
Direct labor		78,300	
Manufacturing overhead		98,500	266,800
Gross margin			183,200
Less operating expenses:			
Selling expenses:			
Variable:			
Sales commissions	$27,000		
Shipping	5,400	32,400	
Fixed (advertising, salaries)		120,000	
Administrative:			
Variable (billing and other)		1,800	
Fixed (salaries and other)		48,000	202,200
Net operating loss			$ (19,000)

All variable expenses in the company vary in terms of unit sold, except for sales commissions, which are based on sales dollars. Variable manufacturing overhead is 30 cents per unit. There were no beginning or ending inventories. Whitney Company's plant has a capacity of 75,000 units per year.

The company has been operating at a loss for several years. Management is studying several possible courses of action to determine what should be done to make next year profitable.

Required:

1. Redo Whitney Company's income statement in the contribution format. Show both a Total column and a Per Unit column on your statement. Leave enough space to the right of your numbers to enter the solution to both parts of (2) below.
2. The president is considering two proposals prepared by members of his staff:
   a. For next year, the vice president would like to reduce the unit selling price by 20%. She is certain that this would fill the plant to capacity.
   b. For next year, the sales manager would like to increase the unit selling price by 20%, increase the sales commission to 9% of sales, and increase advertising by $100,000. Based on marketing studies, he is confident this would increase unit sales by one-third.

   Prepare two contribution income statements, one showing what profits would be under the vice president's proposal and one showing what profits would be under the sales manager's proposal. On each statement, include both Total and Per Unit columns (do not show per unit data for the fixed costs).
3. Refer to the original data. The president believes it would be a mistake to change the unit selling price. Instead, he wants to use less costly raw materials, thereby reducing unit costs by 70 cents. How many units would have to be sold next year to earn a target profit of $30,200?
4. Refer to the original data. Whitney Company's board of directors believes that the company's problem lies in inadequate promotion. By how much can advertising be increased and still allow the company to earn a target profit of 4.5% on sales of 60,000 units?
5. Refer to the original data. The company has been approached by an overseas distributor who wants to purchase 9,500 units on a special price basis. There would be no sales commission on these units. However, shipping costs would be increased by 50% and variable administrative costs would be reduced by 25%. In addition, a $5,700 special insurance fee would have to be paid by Whitney Company to protect the goods in transit. What unit price would have to be quoted on the 9,500 units by Whitney Company to allow the company to earn a profit of $14,250 on total operations? Regular business would not be affected by this special order.

CASE 6–32 Missing Data; Break-Even Analysis; Target Profit; Margin of Safety; Operating Leverage [LO1, LO4, LO5, LO7, LO8]

You were employed just this morning by Pyrrhic Company, a prominent and rapidly growing organization. As your initial assignment, you were asked to complete an analysis of one of the company's products for the board of directors meeting later in the day. After completing the analysis, you left your office for a few moments only to discover on returning that a broken sprinkler in the ceiling has destroyed most of your work. Only the following bits remained:

PYRRHIC COMPANY
Actual Income Statement
For the Month Ended June 30

	Total	Per Unit	Percent
Sales (? units)	$?	$?	100%
Less variable expenses	?	?	?%
Contribution margin	?	$?	?%
Less fixed expenses	?		
Net operating income	$?		
Break-even point:			
In units	? units		
In dollars	$180,000		
Margin of safety:			
In dollars	$?		
In percentage	20%		
Degree of operating leverage	?		

The computations above are all based on actual results for June. The company's *projected* contribution format income statement for this product for July follows:

PYRRHIC COMPANY
Projected Income Statement
For the Month Ended July 31

	Total	Per Unit	Percent
Sales (33,000 units)	$?	$?	?%
Less variable expenses	?	?	?%
Contribution margin	?	$?	?%
Less fixed expenses	?		
Net operating income	$40,500		

To add to your woes, the company's mainframe computer is down so no data are available from that source. You do remember that sales for July are projected to increase by 10% over sales for June. You also remember that June's net operating income was $27,000—the same amount as your annual salary from the company. Finally, you remember that the degree of operating leverage is highly useful to the manager as a predictive tool.

Total fixed expenses, the unit selling price, and the unit variable expenses are planned to be the same in June and July.

The board of directors meets in just one hour.

Required:

1. For the June data, do the following:
   a. Complete the June contribution format income statement (all three columns).
   b. Compute the break-even point in units and verify the break-even point in sales dollars that is provided above. Use the contribution margin method.
   c. Compute the margin of safety in dollars and verify the margin of safety percentage that is provided above.
   d. Compute the degree of operating leverage as of June 30.
2. For the July data, do the following:
   a. Complete the July projected contribution format income statement (all three columns).

b. Compute the margin of safety in dollars and percent and compute the degree of operating leverage. Why has the margin of safety gone up and the degree of operating leverage gone down?

3. Brimming with confidence after having completed (1) and (2) above in less than one hour, you decide to give the board of directors some added data. You know that direct labor accounts for $1.80 of the company's per unit variable expenses. You have learned that direct labor costs may increase by one-third next year. Assuming that this cost increase takes place and that selling price and other cost factors remain unchanged, how many units will the company have to sell in a month to earn a net operating income equal to 20% of sales?

CASE 6–33 Cost Structure; Break-Even; Target Profits [LO4, LO5, LO6]

Pittman Company is a small but growing manufacturer of telecommunications equipment. The company has no sales force of its own; rather, it relies completely on independent sales agents to market its products. These agents are paid a commission of 15% of selling price for all items sold.

Barbara Cheney, Pittman's controller, has just prepared the company's budgeted income statement for next year. The statement follows:

PITTMAN COMPANY
Budgeted Income Statement
For the Year Ended December 31

Sales		$16,000,000
Manufacturing costs:		
Variable	$7,200,000	
Fixed overhead	2,340,000	9,540,000
Gross margin		6,460,000
Selling and administrative costs:		
Commissions to agents	2,400,000	
Fixed marketing costs	120,000*	
Fixed administrative costs	1,800,000	4,320,000
Net operating income		2,140,000
Less fixed interest cost		540,000
Income before income taxes		1,600,000
Less income taxes (30%)		480,000
Net income		$ 1,120,000

*Primarily depreciation on storage facilities.

As Barbara handed the statement to Karl Vecci, Pittman's president, she commented, "I went ahead and used the agents' 15% commission rate in completing these statements, but we've just learned that they refuse to handle our products next year unless we increase the commission rate to 20%."

"That's the last straw," Karl replied angrily. "Those agents have been demanding more and more, and this time they've gone too far. How can they possibly defend a 20% commission rate?"

"They claim that after paying for advertising, travel, and the other costs of promotion, there's nothing left over for profit," replied Barbara.

"I say it's just plain robbery," retorted Karl. "And I also say it's time we dumped those guys and got our own sales force. Can you get your people to work up some cost figures for us to look at?"

"We've already worked them up," said Barbara. "Several companies we know about pay a 7.5% commission to their own salespeople, along with a small salary. Of course, we would have to handle all promotion costs, too. We figure our fixed costs would increase by $2,400,000 per year, but that would be more than offset by the $3,200,000 (20% × $16,000,000) that we would avoid on agents' commissions."

The breakdown of the $2,400,000 cost follows:

Salaries:	
Sales manager	$ 100,000
Salespersons	600,000
Travel and entertainment	400,000
Advertising	1,300,000
Total	$2,400,000

"Super," replied Karl. "And I noticed that the $2,400,000 is just what we're paying the agents under the old 15% commission rate."

"It's even better than that," explained Barbara. "We can actually save $75,000 a year because that's what we're having to pay the auditing firm now to check out the agents' reports. So our overall administrative costs would be less."

"Pull all of these numbers together and we'll show them to the executive committee tomorrow," said Karl. "With the approval of the committee, we can move on the matter immediately."

Required:

1. Compute Pittman Company's break-even point in sales dollars for next year assuming:
   a. That the agents' commission rate remains unchanged at 15%.
   b. That the agents' commission rate is increased to 20%.
   c. That the company employs its own sales force.
2. Assume that Pittman Company decides to continue selling through agents and pays the 20% commission rate. Determine the volume of sales that would be required to generate the same net income as contained in the budgeted income statement for next year.
3. Determine the volume of sales at which net income would be equal regardless of whether Pittman Company sells through agents (at a 20% commission rate) or employs its own sales force.
4. Compute the degree of operating leverage that the company would expect to have on December 31 at the end of next year assuming:
   a. That the agents' commission rate remains unchanged at 15%.
   b. That the agents' commission rate is increased to 20%.
   c. That the company employs its own sales force.
   Use income *before* income taxes in your operating leverage computation.
5. Based on the data in (1) through (4) above, make a recommendation as to whether the company should continue to use sales agents (at a 20% commission rate) or employ its own sales force. Give reasons for your answer.

(CMA, adapted)

CASE 6–34 Break-Even Analysis with Step Fixed Costs [LO5, LO6]

The Pediatric Department at Wymont General Hospital has a capacity of 90 beds and operates 24 hours a day every day. The measure of activity in the department is patient-days, where one patient-day represents one patient occupying a bed for one day. The average revenue per patient-day is $130 and the average variable cost per patient-day is $50. The fixed cost of the department (not including personnel costs) is $454,000.

The only personnel directly employed by the Pediatric Department are aides, nurses, and supervising nurses. The hospital has minimum staffing requirements for the department based on total annual patient-days in Pediatrics. Hospital requirements, beginning at the minimum expected level of activity, follow:

Annual Patient-Days	Aides	Nurses	Supervising Nurses
10,000–14,000	21	11	4
14,001–17,000	22	12	4
17,001–23,725	22	13	4
23,726–25,550	25	14	5
25,551–27,375	26	14	5
27,376–29,200	29	16	6

These staffing levels represent full-time equivalents, and it should be assumed that the Pediatric Department always employs only the minimum number of required full-time equivalent personnel.

Average annual salaries for each class of employee are: aides, $18,000; nurses, $26,000; and supervising nurses, $36,000.

Required:

1. Compute the total fixed costs (including the salaries of aides, nurses, and supervising nurses) in the Pediatric Department for each level of activity shown above (i.e., total fixed costs at the 10,000–14,000 patient-day level of activity, total fixed costs at the 14,001–17,000 patient-day level of activity, etc.).
2. Compute the minimum number of patient-days required for the Pediatric Department to break even.

3. Determine the minimum number of patient-days required for the Pediatric Department to earn an annual "profit" of $200,000.

(CPA, adapted)

CASE 6–35 Break-Evens for Individual Products in a Multiproduct Company [LO5, LO9]

Cheryl Montoya picked up the phone and called her boss, Wes Chan, the vice president of marketing at Piedmont Fasteners Corporation: "Wes, I'm not sure how to go about answering the questions that came up at the meeting with the president yesterday."

"What's the problem?"

"The president wanted to know the break-even point for each of the company's products, but I am having trouble figuring them out."

"I'm sure you can handle it, Cheryl. And, by the way, I need your analysis on my desk tomorrow morning at 8:00 sharp in time for the follow-up meeting at 9:00."

Piedmont Fasteners Corporation makes three different clothing fasteners in its manufacturing facility in North Carolina. Data concerning these products appear below:

	Velcro	Metal	Nylon
Normal annual sales volume	100,000	200,000	400,000
Unit selling price	$1.65	$1.50	$0.85
Variable cost per unit	$1.25	$0.70	$0.25

Total fixed expenses are $400,000 per year.

All three products are sold in highly competitive markets, so the company is unable to raise its prices without losing unacceptable numbers of customers.

The company has an extremely effective just-in-time manufacturing system, so there are no beginning or ending work in process or finished goods inventories.

Required:

1. What is the company's over-all break-even in total sales dollars?
2. Of the total fixed costs of $400,000, $20,000 could be avoided if the Velcro product were dropped, $80,000 if the Metal product were dropped, and $60,000 if the Nylon product were dropped. The remaining fixed costs of $240,000 consist of common fixed costs such as administrative salaries and rent on the factory building that could be avoided only by going out of business entirely.
   a. What is the break-even point in units for each product?
   b. If the company sells exactly the break-even quantity of each product, what will be the overall profit of the company? Explain this result.

Group and Internet Exercises

GROUP EXERCISE 6–36 CVP and Collegiate Sports

Revenue from major intercollegiate sports is an important source of funds for many colleges. Most of the costs of putting on a football or basketball game are fixed and increase very little as the size of the crowd increases. Thus, the revenue from every extra ticket sold is almost pure profit.

Choose a sport played at your college or university, such as football or basketball, that generates significant revenue. Talk with the business manager of your college's sports programs before answering the following questions:

Required:

1. What is the maximum seating capacity of the stadium or arena in which the sport is played? During the past year, what was the average attendance at the games? On average, what percentage of the stadium or arena capacity was filled?
2. The number of seats sold often depends on the opponent. The attendance for a game with a traditional rival (e.g., Nebraska vs. Colorado, University of Washington vs. Washington State, or Texas vs. Texas A&M) is usually substantially above the average. Also, games against conference foes may draw larger crowds than other games. As a consequence, the number of tickets sold for a game is somewhat predictable. What implications does this have for the nature of the costs of putting on a game? Are most of the costs really fixed with respect to the number of tickets sold?
3. Estimate the variable cost per ticket sold.

4. Estimate the total additional revenue that would be generated in an average game if all of the tickets were sold at their normal prices. Estimate how much profit is lost because these tickets are not sold.
5. Estimate the ancillary revenue (parking and concessions) per ticket sold. Estimate how much profit is lost in an average game from these sources of revenue as a consequence of not having a sold-out game.
6. Estimate how much additional profit would be generated for your college if every game were sold out for the entire season.

GROUP EXERCISE 6–37 The Economics of Higher Education

The "baby bust" of the 1960s and early 1970s resulted in the number of college-age 18- and 19-year-olds contrasting sharply from 1980 to 1993. The number of graduating high school seniors peaked in 1979 and declined to a low of 6.9 million in 1992, a drop of nearly 40%. Throughout the eighties, tuition at private and public universities rose at an average of 9% per year, a figure far above the rise in household family incomes. Then, the demographics began to reverse themselves: the number of 18- and 19-year-olds began to increase in 1996 and will continue until they peak in 2010 at about 9.3 million for nearly a 33% increase in the college-eligible population. The four-year cost of attending a private college now often exceeds $100,000—including room and board.

Required:
1. If tuition and room and board costs increase at the rate of 9% per year, what will four years' tuition at a private college cost in 10 years? How affordable will a college education be at this level?
2. What is the cost of adding an extra student to a typical class? Explain this in terms of the cost structure of a university.
3. After two decades of almost uninterrupted expansion, the "baby bust" enrollment drop left many colleges with considerable underutilized capacity. What impact will increasing enrollment and economies of scale have on costs and tuition?
4. Which colleges do you expect will be helped the most by increasing enrollments—public or private?

GROUP EXERCISE 6–38 Airline Cost Structure

Airlines provide an excellent illustration of the concept of operating leverage, the sensitivity of a firm's operating profits to changes in demand, and the opportunities and risks presented by such a cost structure. The Uniform System of Accounts required by the Department of Transportation for airlines operating in the United States contains the following cost categories:

- Fuel and oil.
- Flying operations labor (flight crews—pilots, copilots, navigators, and flight engineers).
- Passenger service labor (flight attendants).
- Aircraft traffic and servicing labor (personnel servicing aircraft and handling passengers at gates, baggage, and cargo).
- Promotions and sales labor (reservations and sales agents, advertising and publicity).
- Maintenance labor (maintenance of flight equipment and ground property and equipment).
- Maintenance materials and overhead.
- Ground property and equipment (landing fees, rental expenses, and depreciation for ground property and equipment).
- Flight equipment (rental expenses and depreciation on aircraft frames and engines).
- General overhead (administrative personnel, utilities, insurance, communications, etc.).

Required:
1. Which of the above costs are likely to be affected if an airline adds an airport to its network?
2. Which of the above costs are likely to be affected if an airline schedules one more flight out of an airport that the airline already serves?
3. Which of the above costs are likely to be variable with respect to the number of passengers who actually fly on a particular scheduled flight?
4. Are airline profits likely to be affected very much by their load factors? Why? (The load factor refers to the percentage of scheduled seats filled by paying passengers.)

INTERNET EXERCISE 6–39

As you know, the World Wide Web is a medium that is constantly evolving. Sites come and go, and change without notice. To enable the periodic updating of site addresses, this problem has been posted to the textbook website (www.mhhe.com/garrison11e). After accessing the site, enter the Student Center and select this chapter. Select and complete the Internet exercise.

Chapter

7

Variable Costing: A Tool for Management

LEARNING OBJECTIVES

After studying Chapter 7, you should be able to:

LO1 Explain how variable costing differs from absorption costing and compute unit product costs under each method.

LO2 Prepare income statements using both variable and absorption costing.

LO3 Reconcile variable costing and absorption costing net operating incomes and explain why the two amounts differ.

LO4 Understand the advantages and disadvantages of both variable and absorption costing.

BUSINESS FOCUS

The House of Cards at Gillette

Alfred M. Zeien was the successful CEO of Gillette Co. for eight years, leading the company to earnings growth rates of 15% to 20% per year. However, as his successor discovered, some of this profit growth was an illusion based on building inventories. William H. Steele, an analyst with Bank of America Securities, alleges: "There is no question Gillette was making its numbers (in part) by aggressively selling to the trade, and building inventories." Within a three-year period, Gillette's inventories of finished goods had increased by over 40% (to $1.3 billion) even though Gillette's sales had barely increased.

How can building inventories increase profits without any increase in sales? As we will discover in this chapter, absorption costing—the most widely used method of determining product costs—can be used to manipulate profits in just this way. ■

Source: William C. Symonds, "The Big Trim at Gillette," *Business Week*, November 8, 1999, p. 42.

Two general approaches are used in manufacturing companies for costing products for the purposes of valuing inventories and cost of goods sold. One approach, called *absorption costing,* was discussed in Chapter 3. Absorption costing is generally used for external financial reports. The other approach, called *variable costing,* is preferred by some managers for internal decision making and must be used when an income statement is prepared in the contribution format. Ordinarily, absorption costing and variable costing produce different figures for net operating income, and the difference can be quite large. In addition to showing how these two methods differ, we will consider the arguments for and against each costing method and we will show how management decisions can be affected by the costing method chosen.

Overview of Absorption and Variable Costing

LEARNING OBJECTIVE 1
Explain how variable costing differs from absorption costing and compute unit product costs under each method.

In the last two chapters, we learned that the contribution format income statement and cost-volume-profit (CVP) analysis are valuable management tools. Both of these tools emphasize cost behavior and require that managers carefully distinguish between variable and fixed costs. Absorption costing, which was discussed in Chapters 2 and 3, assigns both variable and fixed manufacturing costs to products—mingling them in a way that makes it difficult for managers to distinguish between them. In contrast, variable costing focuses on *cost behavior*—clearly separating fixed from variable costs. One of the strengths of variable costing is that it harmonizes with both the contribution approach and the CVP concepts discussed in the preceding chapter.

Absorption Costing

In Chapter 3, we learned that **absorption costing** treats *all* manufacturing costs as product costs, regardless of whether they are variable or fixed. The cost of a unit of product under the absorption costing method consists of direct materials, direct labor, and *both* variable and fixed manufacturing overhead. Thus, absorption costing allocates a portion of fixed manufacturing overhead cost to each unit of product, along with the variable manufacturing costs. Because absorption costing includes all manufacturing costs in product costs, it is frequently referred to as the *full cost* method.

Variable Costing

Under **variable costing,** only those manufacturing costs that vary with output are treated as product costs. This would usually include direct materials, direct labor, and the variable portion of manufacturing overhead. Fixed manufacturing overhead is not treated as a product cost under this method. Rather, fixed manufacturing overhead is treated as a period cost and, like selling and administrative expenses, it is charged off in its entirety against revenue each period. Consequently, the cost of a unit of product in inventory or in cost of goods sold under the variable costing method does not contain any fixed manufacturing overhead cost. Variable costing is sometimes referred to as *direct costing* or *marginal costing.*

To complete this summary comparison of absorption and variable costing, we need to briefly consider the handling of selling and administrative expenses. These expenses are never treated as product costs, regardless of the costing method. Thus, under either absorption or variable costing, both variable and fixed selling and administrative expenses are always treated as period costs and deducted from revenues as incurred.

Exhibit 7–1 shows the classification of costs under both absorption and variable costing.

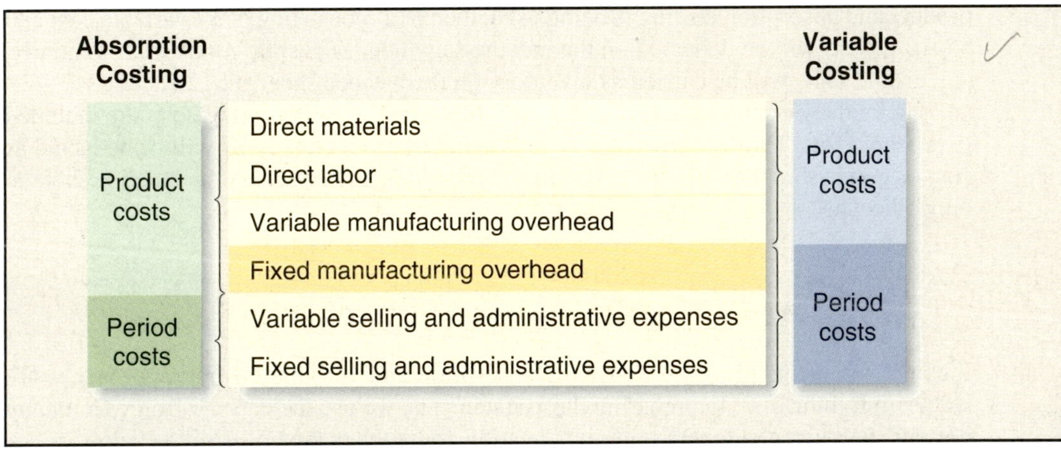

EXHIBIT 7–1
Cost Classifications—Absorption versus Variable Costing

Unit Cost Computations

To illustrate the computation of unit product costs under both absorption and variable costing, consider Boley Company, a small company that produces a single product and has the following cost structure:

Number of units produced each year	6,000
Variable costs per unit:	
Direct materials	$2
Direct labor	$4
Variable manufacturing overhead	$1
Variable selling and administrative expenses	$3
Fixed costs per year:	
Fixed manufacturing overhead	$30,000
Fixed selling and administrative expenses	$10,000

Topic Tackler PLUS 7–1

Required:
1. Compute the unit product cost under absorption costing.
2. Compute the unit product cost under variable costing.

Solution

Absorption Costing	
Direct materials	$ 2
Direct labor	4
Variable manufacturing overhead	1
Total variable manufacturing cost	7
Fixed manufacturing overhead ($30,000 ÷ 6,000 units of product)	5
Unit product cost	$12
Variable Costing	
Direct materials	$ 2
Direct labor	4
Variable manufacturing overhead	1
Unit product cost	$ 7

(Under variable costing, the $30,000 fixed manufacturing overhead will be charged off in total against income as a period expense along with selling and administrative expenses.)

Under the absorption costing method, *all* manfacturing costs, variable and fixed, are included when determining the unit product cost. Thus, if the company sells a unit of product and absorption costing is being used, then $12 (consisting of $7 variable cost and $5 fixed cost) will be deducted on the income statement as cost of goods sold. Similarly, any unsold units will be carried as inventory on the balance sheet at $12 each.

Under the variable costing method, only the variable manfacturing costs are included in product costs. Thus, if the company sells a unit of product, only $7 will be deducted as cost of goods sold, and unsold units will be carried as inventory on the balance sheet at only $7 each.

Income Comparison of Absorption and Variable Costing

LEARNING OBJECTIVE 2
Prepare income statements using both variable and absorption costing.

Income statements prepared under the absorption and variable costing approaches are shown in Exhibit 7–2. In preparing these statements, we use the data for Boley Company presented earlier, along with other information about the company as given below:

Units in beginning inventory	0
Units produced	6,000
Units sold	5,000
Units in ending inventory	1,000
Selling price per unit	$20
Selling and administrative expenses:	
Variable per unit	$3
Fixed per year	$10,000

	Absorption Costing	Variable Costing
Unit product cost:		
Direct materials	$ 2	$ 2
Direct labor	4	4
Variable manufacturing overhead	1	1
Fixed manufacturing overhead ($30,000 ÷ 6,000 units)	5	—
Unit product cost	$12	$ 7

Several facts can be learned by examining the financial statements in Exhibit 7–2:

1. Under the absorption costing method, if inventories increase then some of the fixed manufacturing costs of the current period will not appear on the income statement as part of cost of goods sold. Instead, these costs are deferred to a future period and are carried on the balance sheet as part of the inventory account. Such a deferral of costs is known as **fixed manufacturing overhead cost deferred in inventory.** The process can be explained by referring to the data for Boley Company. During the current period, Boley Company produced 6,000 units but sold only 5,000 units, thus leaving 1,000 unsold units in the ending inventory. Under the absorption costing method, each unit produced was assigned $5 of fixed overhead cost (see the unit cost computations above). Therefore, each of the 1,000 units going into inventory at the end of the period has $5 in fixed manufacturing overhead cost attached to it, or a total of $5,000 for the 1,000 units. *This fixed manufacturing overhead cost of the current period is deferred in inventory to the next period, when, hopefully, these units will be taken out of inventory and sold.* The deferral of $5,000 of fixed manufacturing overhead costs can be clearly seen by analyzing the ending inventory under the absorption costing method:

Variable manufacturing costs: 1,000 units × $7 per unit	$ 7,000
Fixed manufacturing overhead costs: 1,000 units × $5 per unit	5,000
Total value of ending inventory	$12,000

EXHIBIT 7–2
Comparison of Absorption and Variable Costing—Boley Company

Absorption Costing		
Sales (5,000 units × $20 per unit)		$100,000
Less cost of goods sold:		
Beginning inventory	$ 0	
Add cost of goods manufactured (6,000 units × $12 per unit)	72,000	
Goods available for sale	72,000	
Less ending inventory (1,000 units × $12 per unit)	12,000	
Cost of goods sold		60,000
Gross margin		40,000
Less selling and administrative expenses (5,000 units × $3 per unit variable + $10,000 fixed)		25,000
Net operating income		$ 15,000
Variable Costing		
Sales (5,000 units × $20 per unit)		$100,000
Less variable expenses:		
Variable cost of goods sold:		
Beginning inventory	$ 0	
Add variable manufacturing costs (6,000 units × $7 per unit)	42,000	
Goods available for sale	42,000	
Less ending inventory (1,000 units × $7 per unit)	7,000	
Variable cost of goods sold	35,000	
Variable selling and administrative expenses (5,000 units × $3 per unit)	15,000	50,000
Contribution margin		50,000
Less fixed expenses:		
Fixed manufacturing overhead	30,000	
Fixed selling and administrative expenses	10,000	40,000
Net operating income		$ 10,000

Note the difference in ending inventories. Fixed manufacturing overhead cost at $5 per unit is included under the absorption approach. This explains the difference in ending inventory and in net operating income (1,000 units × $5 per unit = $5,000).

In summary, under absorption costing, of the $30,000 in fixed manufacturing overhead costs incurred during the period, only $25,000 (5,000 units sold × $5 per unit) has been included in cost of goods sold. The remaining $5,000 (1,000 units *not* sold × $5 per unit) has been deferred in inventory to the next period.

2. Under the variable costing method, the entire $30,000 of fixed manufacturing overhead costs has been treated as an expense of the current period (see the bottom portion of the variable costing income statement).
3. The ending inventory figure under the variable costing method is $5,000 lower than it is under the absorption costing method. The reason is that under variable costing, only the variable manufacturing costs are assigned to units of product and therefore included in inventory:

Variable manufacturing costs: 1,000 units × $7 per unit	$7,000

Topic Tackler PLUS 7–2

The $5,000 difference in ending inventories explains the difference in net operating income reported between the two costing methods. Net operating income is $5,000 *higher* under absorption costing since, as explained above, $5,000 of fixed manufacturing overhead cost has been deferred in inventory to the next period.

4. The absorption costing income statement makes no distinction between fixed and variable costs; therefore, it is not well suited for CVP computations, which are important for good planning and control. To develop data for CVP analysis, it would be necessary to spend considerable time reworking and reclassifying costs on the absorption income statement.
5. The variable costing approach to costing units of product works very well with the contribution approach to the income statement, since both concepts are based on the idea of classifying costs by behavior. The variable costing data in Exhibit 7–2 could be used immediately in CVP computations.

Essentially, the difference between the absorption and variable costing methods centers on timing. Advocates of variable costing say that fixed manufacturing costs should be expensed immediately in total, whereas advocates of absorption costing say that fixed manufacturing costs should be charged against revenues gradually as units of product are sold. Any units of product not sold under absorption costing result in fixed manfacturing costs being inventoried and carried forward on the balance sheet *as assets* to the next period.

The following discussion of Emerald Isle Knitters expands on the discussion of the absorption and variable costing approaches to accounting for fixed manufacturing costs.

IN BUSINESS

DIRECT LABOR—A FIXED COST IN STATE-OWNED ENTERPRISES IN CHINA

The Shanghai Bund Steel Works (SBSW) of the Peoples' Republic of China is a large state-owned enterprise. In recent years, state-owned companies such as SBSW have been given a great deal of autonomy, providing that they meet their financial and nonfinancial targets. However, in state-owned enterprises, management has very little freedom to adjust the workforce—eliminating jobs would create political problems. Therefore, for internal management purposes, SBSW treats labor cost as a fixed cost that is part of fixed manufacturing overhead.

Source: Yau Shiu Wing Joseph, *Management Accounting* (UK), October 1996, pp. 52–54.

Extended Comparison of Income Data

MANAGERIAL ACCOUNTING IN ACTION
The Issue

Mary O'Meara is the owner and manager of Emerald Isle Knitters, Ltd., located in the Republic of Ireland. The company is very small, with only 10 employees. Mary started the company three years ago with cash loaned to her by a local bank. The company manufactures a traditional wool fisherman's sweater from a pattern Mary learned from her grandmother. Like most apparel manufacturers, Emerald Isle Knitters sells its product to department stores and clothing store chains rather than to retail customers.

The sweater was an immediate success, and the company sold all of the first year's production. However, in the second year of operations, one of the company's major customers canceled its order due to bankruptcy, and the company ended the year with large stocks of unsold sweaters. The third year of operations was a great year in contrast to the disastrous second year. Sales rebounded dramatically, and all of the unsold production carried over from the second year was sold by the end of the third year.

Shortly after the close of the third year, Mary met with her accountant Sean MacLafferty to discuss the results for the year. (Note: All of the company's business is transacted using the euro, denoted by €, as the currency. The euro is the common currency of many member countries of the European Union.)

Mary: Sean, the results for this year look a lot better than for last year, but I am frankly puzzled why this year's results aren't even better than the income statement shows.

Sean: I know what you mean. The net operating income for this year is just €90,000. Last year it was €30,000. That is a huge improvement, but it seems that profits this year should have been even higher and profits last year should have been much less. We were in big trouble last year. I was afraid we might not even break-even—yet we showed a healthy €30,000 profit. Somehow it doesn't seem quite right.

Mary: I wondered about that €30,000 profit last year, but I didn't question it since it was the only good news I had gotten for quite some time.

Sean: In case you're wondering, I didn't invent that profit last year just to make you feel better. Our auditor required that I follow certain accounting rules in preparing those reports for the bank. This may sound heretical, but we *could* use different rules for our own internal reports.

Mary: Wait a minute, rules are rules—especially in accounting.

Sean: Yes and no. For our internal reports, it might be better to use different rules than we use for the reports we send to the bank.

Mary: As I said, rules are rules. Still, I'm willing to listen if you want to show me what you have in mind.

Sean: It's a deal.

LEARNING OBJECTIVE 3
Reconcile variable costing and absorption costing net operating incomes and explain why the two amounts differ.

Immediately after the meeting with Mary, Sean put together the data and financial reports that appear in Exhibit 7–3. (All financial statements have been reformatted to U.S. standards.)

The basic data appear at the top of Exhibit 7–3, and the absorption costing income statements as reported to the bank for the last three years appear at the top of the exhibit

EXHIBIT 7–3
Absorption and Variable Costing Income Statements—Emerald Isle Knitters, Ltd.

Basic Data	
Selling price per unit sold	€20
Variable manufacturing cost per unit produced	€7
Fixed manufacturing overhead costs per year	€150,000
Variable selling and administrative expenses per unit sold	€1
Fixed selling and administrative expenses per year	€90,000

	Year 1	Year 2	Year 3	Three Years Together
Units in beginning inventory	0	0	5,000	0
Units produced	25,000	25,000	25,000	75,000
Units sold	25,000	20,000	30,000	75,000
Units in ending inventory	0	5,000	0	0

Unit Product Costs

	Year 1	Year 2	Year 3
Under variable costing (variable manufacturing costs only)	€7	€7	€7
Under absorption costing:			
Variable manufacturing costs	€7	€7	€7
Fixed manufacturing overhead costs (€150,000 spread over the number of units produced in each year)	6	6	6
Total absorption cost per unit	€13	€13	€13

continued

EXHIBIT 7–3
concluded

	Year 1		Year 2		Year 3		Three Years Together	
Absorption Costing								
Sales		€500,000		€400,000		€600,000		€1,500,000
Less cost of goods sold:								
Beginning inventory	€ 0		€ 0		€ 65,000		€ 0	
Add cost of goods manufactured (25,000 units × €13 per unit)	325,000		325,000		325,000		975,000	
Goods available for sale	325,000		325,000		390,000		975,000	
Less ending inventory (5,000 units × €13 per unit)	0		65,000		0		0	
Cost of goods sold		325,000		260,000		390,000		975,000
Gross margin		175,000		140,000		210,000		525,000
Less selling and administrative expenses		115,000*		110,000*		120,000*		345,000
Net operating income		€ 60,000		€ 30,000		€ 90,000		€ 180,000

*The selling and administrative expenses are computed as follows:
Year 1: 25,000 units × €1 per unit variable + €90,000 fixed = €115,000.
Year 2: 20,000 units × €1 per unit variable + €90,000 fixed = €110,000.
Year 3: 30,000 units × €1 per unit variable + €90,000 fixed = €120,000.

	Year 1		Year 2		Year 3		Three Years Together	
Variable Costing								
Sales		€500,000		€400,000		€600,000		€1,500,000
Less variable expenses:								
Variable cost of goods sold:								
Beginning inventory	€ 0		€ 0		€ 35,000		€ 0	
Add variable manufacturing costs (25,000 units × €7 per unit)	175,000		175,000		175,000		525,000	
Goods available for sale	175,000		175,000		210,000		525,000	
Less ending inventory (5,000 units × €7 per unit)	0		35,000		0		0	
Variable cost of goods sold	175,000*		140,000*		210,000*		525,000	
Variable selling and administrative expenses (€1 per unit *sold*)	25,000	200,000	20,000	160,000	30,000	240,000	75,000	600,000
Contribution margin		300,000		240,000		360,000		900,000
Less fixed expenses:								
Fixed manufacturing overhead	150,000		150,000		150,000		450,000	
Fixed selling and administrative expenses	90,000	240,000	90,000	240,000	90,000	240,000	270,000	720,000
Net operating income		€ 60,000		€ 0		€120,000		€ 180,000

*The variable cost of goods sold could have been computed more simply as follows:
Year 1: 25,000 units sold × €7 per unit = €175,000.
Year 2: 20,000 units sold × €7 per unit = €140,000.
Year 3: 30,000 units sold × €7 per unit = €210,000.

on page 281. Sean decided to try using the variable costing approach to see what effect it might have on net operating income. The variable costing income statements for the last three years appear in the last part of Exhibit 7–3.

Note that Emerald Isle Knitters maintained a steady rate of production of 25,000 sweaters per year. However, sales varied from year to year. In Year 1, production and sales were equal. In Year 2, production exceeded sales due to the canceled order. In Year 3, sales recovered and exceeded production. As a consequence, inventories did not change during Year 1, inventories increased during Year 2, and inventories decreased during Year 3. The change in inventories during the year is the key to understanding how absorption costing differs from variable costing. Note that when inventories increase in Year 2, absorption costing net operating income exceeds variable costing net operating income. When inventories decrease in Year 3, the opposite occurs—variable costing net operating income exceeds absorption costing net operating income. And when inventories do not change as in Year 1, there is no difference in net operating income between the two methods. Why is this? The reasons are discussed below and are briefly summarized in Exhibit 7–4.[1]

1. When production and sales are equal, as in Year 1 for Emerald Isle Knitters, net operating income will generally be the same regardless of whether absorption or variable costing is used. The reason is as follows: The *only* difference that can exist between absorption and variable costing net operating income is the amount of fixed manufacturing overhead recognized as expense on the income statement. When everything that is produced in the year is sold, all of the fixed manufacturing overhead assigned to units of product under absorption costing becomes part of the year's cost of goods sold. Under variable costing, the total fixed manufacturing overhead flows directly to the income statement as an expense. So under either method, when production equals sales (and hence inventories do not change), all the fixed manufacturing overhead incurred during the year flows through to the income

EXHIBIT 7–4
Comparative Income Effects—Absorption and Variable Costing

Relation between Production and Sales for the Period	Effect on Inventories	Relation between Absorption and Variable Costing Net Operating Incomes
Production = Sales	No change in inventories	Absorption costing net operating income = Variable costing net operating income
Production > Sales	Inventories increase	Absorption costing net operating income > Variable costing net operating income*
Production < Sales	Inventories decrease	Absorption costing net operating income < Variable costing net operating income†

*Net operating income is higher under absorption costing, since fixed manufacturing overhead cost is *deferred* in inventory under absorption costing as inventories increase.
†Net operating income is lower under absorption costing, since fixed manufacturing overhead cost is *released* from inventory under absorption costing as inventories decrease.

[1] The discussion in this section concerning differences between absorption and variable costing net operating incomes assumes that the LIFO inventory flow assumption is used.

EXHIBIT 7–5
Reconciliation of Variable Costing and Absorption Costing—Net Operating Income Data from Exhibit 7–3

	Year 1	Year 2	Year 3
Variable costing net operating income	€60,000	€ 0	€120,000
Add fixed manufacturing overhead costs deferred in inventory under absorption costing (5,000 units × €6 per unit)		30,000	
Deduct fixed manufacturing overhead costs released from inventory under absorption costing (5,000 units × €6 per unit)			(30,000)
Absorption costing net operating income	€60,000	€30,000	€ 90,000

statement as an expense. And therefore, the net operating income under the two methods is the same.

2. When production exceeds sales, the net operating income reported under absorption costing will generally be greater than the net operating income reported under variable costing (see Year 2 in Exhibit 7–3). This occurs because under absorption costing, part of the fixed manufacturing overhead costs of the current period is deferred in inventory. In Year 2, for example, €30,000 of fixed manufacturing overhead costs (5,000 units × €6 per unit) have been applied to units in ending inventory. These costs are excluded from cost of goods sold.

   Under variable costing, however, *all* of the fixed manufacturing overhead costs of Year 2 have been charged immediately against income as a period cost. As a result, the net operating income for Year 2 under variable costing is €30,000 *lower* than it is under absorption costing. Exhibit 7–5 contains a reconciliation of the variable costing and absorption costing net operating incomes.

3. When production is less than sales, the net operating income reported under the absorption costing approach will generally be less than the net operating income reported under the variable costing approach (see Year 3 in Exhibit 7–3). This happens because inventories are drawn down and fixed manufacturing overhead costs that were previously deferred in inventory under absorption costing are released and charged against income (known as **fixed manufacturing overhead cost released from inventory**). In Year 3, for example, the €30,000 in fixed manufacturing overhead costs deferred in inventory under the absorption approach from Year 2 to Year 3 is released from inventory because these units were sold. As a result, the cost of goods sold for Year 3 contains not only all of the fixed manufacturing overhead costs for Year 3 (since all that was produced in Year 3 was sold in Year 3) but €30,000 of fixed manufacturing overhead costs from Year 2 as well.

   By contrast, under variable costing only the fixed manufacturing overhead costs of Year 3 have been charged against Year 3. The result is that net operating income under variable costing is €30,000 *higher* than it is under absorption costing. Exhibit 7–5 contains a reconciliation of the variable costing and absorption costing net operating incomes for Year 3.

4. Over an *extended* period of time, the cumulative net operating incomes reported under absorption costing and variable costing will tend to be the same. The reason is that over the long run sales can't exceed production, nor can production much exceed sales. The shorter the time period, the more the net operating incomes will tend to differ.

Effect of Changes in Production on Net Operating Income

In the Emerald Isle Knitters example in the preceding section, production was constant and sales fluctuated over the three-year period. Since sales fluctuated, the data Sean

MacLafferty presented in Exhibit 7–3 allowed us to see the effect of changes in sales on net operating income under both variable and absorption costing.

To further investigate the differences between variable and absorption costing, Sean next put together the hypothetical example in Exhibit 7–6. In this hypothetical example, sales are constant and production fluctuates (the opposite of Exhibit 7–3). The purpose of Exhibit 7–6 is to illustrate for Mary O'Meara the effect of changes in *production* on net operating income under both variable and absorption costing.

Variable Costing

Net operating income is *not* affected by changes in production under variable costing. Notice from Exhibit 7–6 that net operating income is the same for all three years under variable costing, although production exceeds sales in one year and is less than sales in another year. In short, a change in production has no impact on net operating income when variable costing is used.

Absorption Costing

Net operating income *is* affected by changes in production under absorption costing. As shown in Exhibit 7–6, net operating income under absorption costing goes up in Year 2, in response to the increase in production for that year, and then goes down in Year 3, in response to the drop in production for that year. Note particularly that net operating income goes up and down between these two years *even though the same number of units is sold in each year.* The reason for this effect can be traced to fixed manufacturing overhead costs that shift between periods under absorption costing as a result of changes in inventory.

As shown in Exhibit 7–6, production exceeds sales in Year 2, resulting in an increase of 10,000 units in inventory. Each unit produced during Year 2 has €6 in fixed manufacturing

EXHIBIT 7–6
Sensitivity of Costing Methods to Changes in Production—Hypothetical Data

Basic Data			
Selling price per unit sold			€25
Variable manufacturing cost per unit produced			€10
Fixed manufacturing overhead costs per year			€300,000
Variable selling and administrative expenses per unit sold			€1
Fixed selling and administrative expenses per year			€200,000
	Year 1	Year 2	Year 3
Units in beginning inventory	0	0	10,000
Units produced	40,000	50,000	30,000
Units sold	40,000	40,000	40,000
Units in ending inventory	0	10,000	0
Unit Product Costs			
Under variable costing (variable manufacturing costs only)	€10.00	€10.00	€10.00
Under absorption costing			
Variable manufacturing costs	€10.00	€10.00	€10.00
Fixed manufacturing overhead costs (€300,000 total spread over the number of units produced in each year)	7.50	6.00	10.00
Total absorption cost per unit	€17.50	€16.00	€20.00

continued

EXHIBIT 7–6
concluded

	Year 1		Year 2		Year 3	
Absorption Costing						
Sales (40,000 units)		€1,000,000		€1,000,000		€1,000,000
Less cost of goods sold:						
Beginning inventory	€ 0		€ 0		€160,000	
Add cost of goods manufactured	700,000*		800,000*		600,000*	
Goods available for sale	700,000		800,000		760,000	
Less ending inventory	0		160,000†		0	
Cost of goods sold		700,000		640,000		760,000
Gross margin		300,000		360,000		240,000
Less selling and administrative expenses (40,000 units × €1 per unit variable + €200,000 fixed)		240,000		240,000		240,000
Net operating income		€ 60,000		€ 120,000		€ 0

*Cost of goods manufactured:
Year 1: 40,000 units × €17.50 per unit = €700,000.
Year 2: 50,000 units × €16.00 per unit = €800,000.
Year 3: 30,000 units × €20.00 per unit = €600,000.
†Ending inventory, Year 2: 10,000 units × €16 per unit = €160,000.

	Year 1		Year 2		Year 3	
Variable Costing						
Sales (40,000 units)		€1,000,000		€1,000,000		€1,000,000
Less variable expenses:						
Variable cost of goods sold:						
Beginning inventory	€ 0		€ 0		€100,000	
Add variable manufacturing costs at €10 per unit produced	400,000		500,000		300,000	
Goods available for sale	400,000		500,000		400,000	
Less ending inventory	0		100,000*		0	
Variable cost of goods sold	400,000		400,000		400,000	
Variable selling and administrative expenses	40,000	440,000	40,000	440,000	40,000	440,000
Contribution margin		560,000		560,000		560,000
Less fixed expenses:						
Fixed manufacturing overhead	300,000		300,000		300,000	
Fixed selling and administrative expenses	200,000	500,000	200,000	500,000	200,000	500,000
Net operating income		€ 60,000		€ 60,000		€ 60,000

*Ending inventory, Year 2: 10,000 units × €10 per unit = €100,000.

EXHIBIT 7–7
Reconciliation of Variable Costing and Absorption Costing—Net Operating Income Data from Exhibit 7–6

	Year 1	Year 2	Year 3
Variable costing net operating income	€60,000	€ 60,000	€60,000
Add fixed manufacturing overhead costs deferred in inventory under absorption costing (10,000 units × €6 per unit)		60,000	
Deduct fixed manufacturing overhead costs released from inventory under absorption costing (10,000 units × €6 per unit)			(60,000)
Absorption costing net operating income	€60,000	€120,000	€ 0

overhead costs attached to it (see the unit cost computations at the top of Exhibit 7–6). Therefore, €60,000 (10,000 units × €6 per unit) of the fixed manufacturing overhead costs of Year 2 are not charged against that year but rather are added to the inventory account (along with the variable manufacturing costs). The net operating income of Year 2 rises sharply, because of the deferral of these costs in inventories, even though the same number of units is sold in Year 2 as in the other years.

The reverse effect occurs in Year 3. Since sales exceed production in Year 3, that year is forced to cover all of its own fixed manufacturing overhead costs as well as the fixed manufacturing overhead costs carried forward in inventory from Year 2. A substantial drop in net operating income during Year 3 results from the release of fixed manufacturing overhead costs from inventories despite the fact that the same number of units is sold in that year as in the other years.

The variable costing and absorption costing net operating incomes are reconciled in Exhibit 7–7. This exhibit shows that the differences in net operating income can be traced to the effects of changes in inventories on absorption costing net operating income. Under absorption costing, fixed manufacturing overhead costs are deferred in inventory when inventories increase and are released from inventory when inventories decrease.

IN BUSINESS

CHAINSAW AL DUNLAP'S LEGACY AT SUNBEAM

Albert J. Dunlap, who relished his nickname "chainsaw Al," left Sunbeam Corp. under a cloud after three years as CEO. Dunlap was hired to turn around Sunbeam with his well-known cost-cutting and disregard for the sensibilities of existing employees. Three years later, Dunlap had been fired by the board of directors amid well-publicized concerns about his aggressive accounting practices. In addition to questionable accounting practices, Dunlap left a legacy of excess inventories. Dunlap's successors complain that eliminating those excess inventories has required the company to keep production levels well under capacity. Since Sunbeam, like almost all other companies, uses absorption costing to prepare its external financial reports, liquidating these excess inventories depresses the company's profits.

Source: Martha Brannigan, "Sunbeam Reports a $60.7 Million Loss Amid a Continued Excess Inventory," *The Wall Street Journal*, Tuesday, June 8, 1999, p. B10.

MANAGERIAL ACCOUNTING IN ACTION
The Wrap-Up

Emerald Isle KNITTERS

After checking all of his work, Sean discussed his results with Mary.

Sean: I have some calculations I would like to show you.

Mary: Will this take long? I only have a few minutes before I have to meet with the buyer from Neiman Marcus.

Sean: Well, we can at least get started. These exhibits should help explain why our net operating income didn't increase this year as much as you thought it should have.

Mary: This first exhibit (i.e., Exhibit 7–3) looks like it just summarizes our income statements for the last three years.

Sean: Not exactly. There are actually two sets of income statements on this exhibit. The absorption costing income statements are the ones I originally prepared and we submitted to the bank. Below the absorption costing income statements is another set of income statements.

Mary: Those are the ones labeled variable costing.

Sean: That's right. You can see that the net operating incomes are the same for the two sets of income statements in our first year of operations, but they differ for the other two years.

Mary: I'll say! The variable costing statements indicate that we just broke even in the second year instead of earning a €30,000 profit. And the increase in net operating income between the second and third years is €120,000 instead of just €60,000. I don't know how you came up with two different net operating income figures, but the variable costing net operating income seems to be much closer to the truth. The second year was almost a disaster. We barely sold enough sweaters to cover all of our fixed costs.

Sean: You and I both know that, but the accounting rules view the situation a little differently. If we produce more than we sell, the accounting rules require that we take some of the fixed manufacturing cost and assign it to the units that end up in inventories at year-end.

Mary: You mean that instead of appearing on the income statement as an expense, some of the fixed manufacturing costs wind up on the balance sheet as inventories?

Sean: Precisely.

Mary: I thought accountants were conservative. Since when was it conservative to call an expense an asset?

Sean: We accountants have been debating whether fixed manufacturing costs are an asset or an expense for over 50 years.

Mary: It must have been a *fascinating* debate.

Sean: I have to admit that it ranks right up there with watching grass grow in terms of excitement level.

Mary: I don't know what the arguments are, but I can tell you for sure that we don't make any money by just producing sweaters. If I understand what you have shown me, I can increase my net operating income under absorption costing by simply making more sweaters—we don't have to sell them.

Sean: Correct.

Mary: So all I have to do to enjoy the lifestyle of the rich and famous is to hire every unemployed knitter in Ireland to make sweaters I can't sell.

Sean: We would have a major cash flow problem, but our net operating income would certainly go up.

Mary: Well, if the banks want us to use absorption costing so be it. I don't know why they would want us to report that way, but if that's what they want, that's what they'll get. Is there any reason why we can't use the variable costing method inside the company? The statements are easier to understand, and the net operating income figures make more sense to me. Can't we do both?

Sean: I don't see why not. Making the adjustment from one method to the other is very simple.

Mary: Good. Let's talk about this some more after I get back from the meeting with Neiman Marcus.

Choosing a Costing Method

LEARNING OBJECTIVE 4
Understand the advantages and disadvantages of both variable and absorption costing.

The Impact on the Manager

Like Mary O'Meara, opponents of absorption costing argue that shifting fixed manufacturing overhead cost between periods can be confusing and can lead to misinterpretations and even to faulty decisions. Look again at the data in Exhibit 7–6; a manager might wonder why net operating income went up substantially in Year 2 under absorption costing when sales remained the same as in the prior year. Was it a result of lower selling costs, more efficient operations, or was some other factor involved? The manager is unable to tell, looking simply at the absorption costing income statement. Then in Year 3, net operating income drops sharply, even though the same number of units is sold as in the other two years. Why would income rise in one year and then drop in the next? The figures seem erratic and contradictory and can lead to confusion and a loss of confidence in the integrity of the financial data.

By contrast, the variable costing income statements in Exhibit 7–6 are clear and easy to understand. Sales remain constant over the three-year period covered in the exhibit, so both contribution margin and net operating income also remain constant. The statements are consistent with what the manager would expect to see under the circumstances, so they tend to generate confidence rather than confusion.

To avoid mistakes when absorption costing is used, readers of financial statements should be alert to changes in inventory levels. Under absorption costing, if inventories increase, fixed manufacturing overhead costs are deferred in inventories and net operating income is elevated. If inventories decrease, fixed manufacturing overhead costs are released from inventories and net operating income is depressed. Thus, fluctuations in net operating income can be due to changes in inventories rather than to changes in sales when absorption costing is used.

IN BUSINESS

THE PERVERSE EFFECTS OF ABSORPTION COSTING AT NISSAN

Jed Connelly, the top American executive at Nissan North America, admits: "We had a lot of excess production that we had to force on the market." Nissan liked to run its factories at capacity, regardless of how well the cars were selling, because under its bookkeeping rules (presumably absorption costing), the factories would then generate a profit. As a consequence, Nissan dealers had to slash prices and offer big rebates to sell their cars. According to *Fortune* magazine, "Years of discounting and distress sales seriously undercut the value of the Nissan brand. While Toyota stood for quality, customers came to Nissan to get a better deal."

Source: Alex Taylor III, "The Man Who Wants to Change Japan Inc.," *Fortune*, December 20, 1999, pp. 189–198.

CVP Analysis and Absorption Costing

Absorption costing is widely used for both internal and external reports. Many companies use the absorption approach exclusively because of its focus on *full* costing of units of product. A weakness of the method, however, is its inability to dovetail well with CVP analysis.

To illustrate, refer again to Exhibit 7–3. Let us compute the break-even point for Emerald Isle Knitters. To obtain the break-even point, we divide total fixed costs by the contribution margin per unit:

Selling price per unit	€ 20
Variable costs per unit (manufacturing and selling)	8
Contribution margin per unit	€ 12
Fixed manufacturing overhead costs	€150,000
Fixed selling and administrative costs	90,000
Total fixed costs	€240,000

$$\text{Break-even point in unit sales} = \frac{\text{Total fixed expenses}}{\text{Contribution margin per unit}} = \frac{€240{,}000}{€12\text{ per unit}} = 20{,}000\text{ units}$$

The break-even point is 20,000 units. Notice from Exhibit 7–3 that in Year 2 the company sold exactly 20,000 units, the break-even volume. Under the contribution approach, using variable costing, the company does break even in Year 2, showing zero net operating income. *Under absorption costing, however, the company shows a positive net operating income of €30,000 for Year 2.* How can this be? How can absorption costing produce a positive net operating income when the company sold exactly the break-even volume of units?

The answer lies in the fact that €30,000 in fixed manufacturing overhead costs were deferred in inventory during Year 2 under absorption costing and therefore did not appear as charges against income. By deferring these fixed manufacturing overhead costs in inventory, the income statement shows a profit even though the company sold exactly the break-even volume of units. Absorption costing runs into similar kinds of difficulty in other areas of CVP analysis, which assumes that variable costing is being used.

Decision Making

Under absorption costing, fixed manufacturing overhead costs appear to be variable with respect to the number of units sold, but they are not. For example, in Exhibit 7–3, the absorption unit product cost is €13, but the variable portion of this cost is only €7. Since the product costs are stated in terms of a per unit figure, managers may mistakenly believe that if another unit is produced, it will cost the company €13.

The misperception that absorption unit product costs are variable can lead to many managerial problems, including inappropriate pricing decisions and decisions to drop products that are in fact profitable. These problems with absorption costing product costs will be discussed more fully in later chapters.

External Reporting and Income Taxes

Practically speaking, absorption costing is required for external reports in the United States. A company that attempts to use variable costing on its external financial reports runs the risk that its auditors may not accept the financial statements as conforming to generally accepted accounting principles (GAAP).[2] Tax law on this issue is clear-cut. Under the Tax Reform Act of 1986, a form of absorption costing must be used when filling out income tax forms.

Even if a company must use absorption costing for its external reports, a manager can, as Mary O'Meara suggests, use variable costing income statements for internal reports. No particular accounting problems are created by using *both* costing methods—the variable costing method for internal reports and the absorption costing method for external reports. As we demonstrated earlier in Exhibits 7–5 and 7–7, the adjustment from variable costing net operating income to absorption costing net operating income is a simple one that can be easily made at the end of the accounting period.

Top executives are typically evaluated based on the earnings reported to shareholders on the company's external financial reports. This creates a problem for top executives who might otherwise favor using variable costing for internal reports. They may feel that since they are evaluated based on absorption costing reports, decisions should also be based on absorption costing data.

---

[2] The situation is actually slightly ambiguous concerning whether absorption costing is strictly required. Michael Schiff, "Variable Costing: A Closer Look," *Management Accounting,* February 1987, pp. 36–39, and Eric W. Noreen and Robert M. Bowen, "Tax Incentives and the Decision to Capitalize or Expense Manufacturing Overhead," *Accounting Horizons,* March 1989, pp. 29–42, argue that official pronouncements do not actually prohibit variable costing. And both articles provide examples of companies that expense significant elements of their fixed manufacturing costs on their external reports. Nevertheless, the reality is that most accountants believe that absorption costing is required for external reporting and a manager who argues otherwise is likely to be unsuccessful.

IN BUSINESS

ABSORPTION COSTING AROUND THE WORLD

Absorption costing is the norm for external financial reports around the world. After the fall of communism, accounting methods were changed in Russia to bring them into closer agreement with accounting methods used in the West. One result was the adoption of absorption costing.

Source: Adolf J. H. Enthoven, "Russia's Accounting Moves West," *Strategic Finance*, July 1999, pp. 32–37.

Advantages of Variable Costing and the Contribution Approach

As stated earlier, even if the absorption approach is used for external reporting purposes, variable costing, together with the contribution format income statement, is an appealing alternative for internal reports. The advantages of variable costing can be summarized as follows:

1. Data required for CVP analysis can be taken directly from a contribution format income statement. These data are not available on a conventional absorption costing income statement.
2. Under variable costing, the profit for a period is not affected by changes in inventories. Other things remaining the same (i.e., selling prices, costs, sales mix, etc.), profits move in the same direction as sales when variable costing is used.
3. Managers often assume that unit product costs are variable costs. This is a problem under absorption costing, since unit product costs are a combination of both fixed and variable costs. Under variable costing, unit product costs do not contain fixed costs.
4. The impact of fixed costs on profits is emphasized under the variable costing and contribution approach. The total amount of fixed costs appears explicitly on the income statement, highlighting that the whole amount of fixed costs must be covered for the company to be truly profitable. In contrast, under absorption costing the fixed costs are mingled together with the variable costs and are buried in cost of goods sold and ending inventories.
5. Variable costing data make it easier to estimate the profitability of products, customers, and other segments of the business. With absorption costing, profitability is obscured by arbitrary allocations of fixed costs. These issues will be discussed in later chapters.
6. Variable costing ties in with cost control methods such as standard costs and flexible budgets, which will be covered in later chapters.
7. Variable costing net operating income is closer to net cash flow than absorption costing net operating income. This is particularly important for companies with potential cash flow problems.

With all of these advantages, one might wonder why absorption costing continues to be used almost exclusively for external reporting and why it is the predominant choice for internal reports as well. This is partly due to tradition, but absorption costing is also attractive to many accountants and managers because they believe it better matches costs with revenues. Advocates of absorption costing argue that *all* manufacturing costs must be assigned to products in order to properly match the costs of producing units of product with their revenues when they are sold. The fixed costs of depreciation, taxes, insurance, supervisory salaries, and so on, are just as essential to manufacturing products as are the variable costs.

Advocates of variable costing argue that fixed manufacturing costs are not really the costs of any particular unit of product. These costs are incurred to have the *capacity* to make products during a particular period and will be incurred even if nothing is made during the period. Moreover, whether a unit is made or not, the fixed manufacturing costs will be exactly the same. Therefore, variable costing advocates argue that fixed manufacturing costs are not part of the costs of producing a particular unit of product and thus the matching principle dictates that fixed manufacturing costs should be charged to the current period.

At any rate, absorption costing is the generally accepted method for preparing mandatory external financial reports and income tax returns. Probably because of the cost and possible confusion of maintaining two separate costing systems—one for external reporting and one for internal reporting—most companies use absorption costing for both external and internal reports.

Variable Costing and the Theory of Constraints

The Theory of Constraints (TOC), which was introduced in Chapter 1, focuses on managing the constraints in a company as the key to improving profits. For reasons that will be discussed in Chapter 13, this requires careful identification of the variable costs of each product. Consequently, companies involved in TOC use a form of variable costing. One difference is that in the TOC approach, direct labor is generally considered to be a fixed cost. As discussed in earlier chapters, in many companies direct labor is not really a variable cost. Even though direct labor workers may be paid on an hourly basis, many companies have a commitment—sometimes enforced in labor contracts or by law—to guarantee workers a minimum number of paid hours. In TOC companies, there are two additional reasons to consider direct labor to be a fixed cost.

First, direct labor is not usually the constraint. In the simplest cases, the constraint is a machine. In more complex cases, the constraint is a policy (such as a poorly designed compensation scheme for salespersons) that prevents the company from using its resources more effectively. If direct labor is not the constraint, there is no reason to increase it. Hiring more direct labor would increase costs without increasing the output of salable products and services.

Second, TOC emphasizes continuous improvement to maintain competitiveness. Without committed and enthusiastic employees, sustained continuous improvement is virtually impossible. Since layoffs often have devastating effects on employee morale, managers involved in TOC are extremely reluctant to lay off employees.

For these reasons, most managers in TOC companies regard direct labor as a committed fixed cost rather than a variable cost. Hence, in the modified form of variable costing used in TOC companies, direct labor is not usually included as a part of product costs.

Impact of JIT Inventory Methods

As discussed in this chapter, variable and absorption costing will produce different net operating incomes whenever the number of units produced is different from the number of units sold—in other words, whenever there is a change in the number of units in inventory. We have also learned that absorption costing net operating income can be erratic, sometimes moving in a direction that is opposite from the movement in sales.

When companies use just-in-time (JIT) methods, these problems are reduced. The erratic movement of net operating income under absorption costing and the difference in net operating income between absorption and variable costing occur because of changes in the number of units in inventory. Under JIT, goods are produced to customers' orders and the goal is to eliminate finished goods inventories entirely and reduce work in process inventory to almost nothing. If there is very little inventory, then changes in inventories will be very small and both variable and absorption costing will show basically the same net operating income. With very little inventory, absorption costing net operating income usually moves in the same direction as movements in sales.

Of course, the cost of a unit of product will still be different between variable and absorption costing, as explained earlier in the chapter. But when JIT is used, the differences in net operating income will largely disappear.

Summary

Variable and absorption costing are alternative methods of determining unit product costs. Under variable costing, only those manufacturing costs that vary with output are treated as product costs. This includes direct materials, variable overhead, and ordinarily direct labor. Fixed manufacturing overhead is treated as a period cost and it is recorded on the income statement as incurred. By contrast, absorption costing treats fixed manufacturing overhead as a product cost, along with direct materials, direct labor, and variable overhead. Under both costing methods, selling and administrative expenses are treated as period costs and they are recorded on the income statement as incurred.

Since absorption costing treats fixed manufacturing overhead as a product cost, a portion of fixed manufacturing overhead is assigned to each unit as it is produced. If units of product are unsold at the end of a period, then the fixed manufacturing overhead cost attached to the units is carried with them into the inventory account and deferred to the next period. When these units are later sold, the fixed manufacturing overhead cost attached to them is released from the inventory account and charged against income as a part of cost of goods sold. Thus, under absorption costing, it is possible to defer a portion of the fixed manufacturing overhead cost from one period to the next period through the inventory account.

Unfortunately, this shifting of fixed manufacturing overhead cost between periods can cause erratic fluctuations in net operating income and can result in confusion and unwise decisions. To guard against mistakes when they interpret income statement data, managers should be alert to any changes that may have taken place in inventory levels or in unit product costs during the period.

Practically speaking, variable costing can't be used externally for either financial or tax reporting. However, it may be used internally by managers for planning and control purposes. The variable costing approach works well with CVP analysis.

Review Problem: Contrasting Variable and Absorption Costing

Dexter Company produces and sells a single product, a wooden hand loom for weaving small items such as scarves. Selected cost and operating data relating to the product for two years are given below:

Selling price per unit	$50
Manufacturing costs:	
Variable per unit produced:	
Direct materials	$11
Direct labor	$6
Variable overhead	$3
Fixed per year	$120,000
Selling and administrative costs:	
Variable per unit sold	$5
Fixed per year	$70,000

	Year 1	Year 2
Units in beginning inventory	0	2,000
Units produced during the year	10,000	6,000
Units sold during the year	8,000	8,000
Units in ending inventory	2,000	0

Required:

1. Assume that the company uses absorption costing.
   a. Compute the unit product cost in each year.
   b. Prepare an income statement for each year.
2. Assume that the company uses variable costing.
   a. Compute the unit product cost in each year.
   b. Prepare an income statement for each year.
3. Reconcile the variable costing and absorption costing net operating incomes.

Solution to Review Problem

1. *a.* Under absorption costing, all manufacturing costs, variable and fixed, are included in unit product costs:

	Year 1	Year 2
Direct materials	$11	$11
Direct labor	6	6
Variable manufacturing overhead	3	3
Fixed manufacturing overhead		
($120,000 ÷ 10,000 units)	12	
($120,000 ÷ 6,000 units)		20
Unit product cost	$32	$40

b. The absorption costing income statements follow:

	Year 1		Year 2	
Sales (8,000 units × $50 per unit)		$400,000		$400,000
Less cost of goods sold:				
Beginning inventory	$0		$ 64,000	
Add cost of goods manufactured (10,000 units × $32 per unit; 6,000 units × $40 per unit)	320,000		240,000	
Goods available for sale	320,000		304,000	
Less ending inventory (2,000 units × $32 per unit; 0 units × $40 per unit)	64,000	256,000	0	304,000
Gross margin		144,000		96,000
Less selling and administrative expenses (8,000 units × $5 per unit + $70,000)		110,000		110,000
Net operating income		$ 34,000		$ (14,000)

2. *a.* Under variable costing, only the variable manufacturing costs are included in unit product costs:

	Year 1	Year 2
Direct materials	$11	$11
Direct labor	6	6
Variable manufacturing overhead	3	3
Unit product cost	$20	$20

b. The variable costing income statements follow. Notice that the variable cost of goods sold is computed in a simpler, more direct manner than in the examples provided earlier. On a variable costing income statement, this simple approach or the more complex approach illustrated earlier to computing the cost of goods sold is acceptable.

	Year 1		Year 2	
Sales (8,000 units × $50 per unit)		$400,000		$400,000
Less variable expenses:				
Variable cost of goods sold (8,000 units × $20 per unit)	$160,000		$160,000	
Variable selling and administrative expenses (8,000 units × $5 per unit)	40,000		40,000	

continued

Contribution margin		200,000		200,000
Less fixed expenses:				
Fixed manufacturing overhead	120,000		120,000	
Fixed selling and administrative expenses	70,000	190,000	70,000	190,000
Net operating income		$ 10,000		$ 10,000

3. The reconciliation of the variable and absorption costing net operating incomes follows:

	Year 1	Year 2
Variable costing net operating income	$10,000	$ 10,000
Add fixed manufacturing overhead costs deferred in inventory under absorption costing (2,000 units × $12 per unit)	24,000	
Deduct fixed manufacturing overhead costs released from inventory under absorption costing (2,000 units × $12 per unit)		(24,000)
Absorption costing net operating income	$34,000	$(14,000)

Glossary

Absorption costing A costing method that includes all manufacturing costs—direct materials, direct labor, and both variable and fixed manufacturing overhead—in unit product costs. Absorption costing is also referred to as the *full cost* method. (p. 276)

Fixed manufacturing overhead cost deferred in inventory The portion of the fixed manufacturing overhead cost of a period that goes into inventory under the absorption costing method as a result of production exceeding sales. (p. 278)

Fixed manufacturing overhead cost released from inventory The portion of the fixed manufacturing overhead cost of a *prior* period that becomes an expense of the current period under the absorption costing method as a result of sales exceeding production. (p. 284)

Variable costing A costing method that includes only variable manufacturing costs—direct materials, direct labor, and variable manufacturing overhead—in unit product costs. (p. 276)

Questions

7–1 What is the basic difference between absorption costing and variable costing?

7–2 Are selling and administrative expenses treated as product costs or as period costs under variable costing?

7–3 Explain how fixed manufacturing overhead costs are shifted from one period to another under absorption costing.

7–4 What arguments can be advanced in favor of treating fixed manufacturing overhead costs as product costs?

7–5 What arguments can be advanced in favor of treating fixed manufacturing overhead costs as period costs?

7–6 If production and sales are equal, which method would you expect to show the higher net operating income, variable costing or absorption costing? Why?

7–7 If production exceeds sales, which method would you expect to show the higher net operating income, variable costing or absorption costing? Why?

7–8 If fixed manufacturing overhead costs are released from inventory under absorption costing, what does this tell you about the level of production in relation to the level of sales?

7–9 Parker Company had $5,000,000 in sales and reported a $300,000 loss in its annual report to stockholders. According to a CVP analysis prepared for management's use, $5,000,000 in sales is the break-even point for the company. Did the company's inventory level increase, decrease, or remain unchanged? Explain.

7–10 Under absorption costing, how is it possible to increase net operating income without increasing sales?

7–11 How is the use of variable costing limited?

7–12 How does the use of JIT reduce or eliminate the difference in reported net operating income between absorption and variable costing?

Exercises

EXERCISE 7–1 Variable and Absorption Costing Unit Product Costs [LO1]

Ida Sidha Karya Company is a family-owned company located in the village of Gianyar on the island of Bali in Indonesia. The company produces a handcrafted Balinese musical instrument called a gamelan that is similar to a xylophone. The sounding bars are cast from brass and hand-filed to attain just the right sound. The bars are then mounted on an intricately hand-carved wooden base. The gamelans are sold for 850 (thousand) rupiahs. (The currency in Indonesia is the rupiah, which is denoted by Rp.) Selected data for the company's operations last year follow (all currency values are in thousands of rupiahs):

Units in beginning inventory	0
Units produced	250
Units sold	225
Units in ending inventory	25
Variable costs per unit:	
Direct materials	Rp100
Direct labor	Rp320
Variable manufacturing overhead	Rp40
Variable selling and administrative	Rp20
Fixed costs:	
Fixed manufacturing overhead	Rp60,000
Fixed selling and administrative	Rp20,000

Required:

1. Assume that the company uses absorption costing. Compute the unit product cost for one gamelan.
2. Assume that the company uses variable costing. Compute the unit product cost for one gamelan.

EXERCISE 7–2 Variable Costing Income Statement; Explanation of Difference in Net Operating Income [LO2]

Refer to the data in Exercise 7–1 for Ida Sidha Karya Company. An absorption costing income statement prepared by the company's accountant appears below (all currency values are in thousands of rupiahs):

Sales (225 units × Rp850 per unit)		Rp191,250
Less cost of goods sold:		
Beginning inventory	Rp 0	
Add cost of goods manufactured (250 units × Rp _?_ per unit)	175,000	
Goods available for sale	175,000	
Less ending inventory (25 units × Rp _?_ per unit)	17,500	157,500
Gross margin		33,750
Less selling and administrative expenses:		
Variable selling and administrative	4,500	
Fixed selling and administrative	20,000	24,500
Net operating income		Rp 9,250

Required:

1. Determine how much of the ending inventory of Rp17,500 consists of fixed manufacturing overhead cost deferred in inventory to the next period.
2. Prepare an income statement for the year using the variable costing method. Explain the difference in net operating income between the two costing methods.

EXERCISE 7–3 Reconciliation of Absorption and Variable Costing Net Operating Incomes [LO3]

Jorgansen Lighting, Inc., manufactures heavy-duty street lighting systems for municipalities. The company uses variable costing for internal management reports and absorption costing for external reports to shareholders, creditors, and the government. The company has provided the following data:

	Year 1	Year 2	Year 3
Inventories:			
Beginning (units)	200	170	180
Ending (units)	170	180	220
Variable costing net operating income	$1,080,400	$1,032,400	$996,400

The company's fixed manufacturing overhead per unit was constant at $560 for all three years.

Required:

1. Determine each year's absorption costing net operating income. Present your answer in the form of a reconciliation report such as the one shown in Exhibit 7–5.
2. In Year 4, the company's variable costing net operating income was $984,400 and its absorption costing net operating income was $1,012,400. Did inventories increase or decrease during Year 4? How much fixed manufacturing overhead cost was deferred or released from inventory during Year 4?

EXERCISE 7–4 Evaluating Absorption and Variable Costing as Alternative Costing Methods [LO4]

The questions below pertain to two different scenarios involving a manufacturing company. In each scenario, the cost structure of the company is constant from year to year. Selling prices, unit variable costs, and total fixed costs are the same every year. However, unit sales and/or unit production levels may vary from year to year.

Required:

1. Consider the following data for scenario A:

	Year 1	Year 2	Year 3	Year 4
Variable costing net operating income	$510,600	$510,600	$510,600	$510,600
Absorption costing net operating income . . .	$577,290	$636,518	$471,082	$361,500

   a. Were unit sales constant from year to year? Explain.
   b. What was the relation between unit sales and unit production levels in each year? For each year, indicate whether inventories grew or shrank.

2. Consider the following data for scenario B:

	Year 1	Year 2	Year 3	Year 4
Variable costing net operating income	$770,600	$640,600	$380,600	$510,600
Absorption costing net operating income . . .	$603,745	$603,745	$603,745	$603,745

   a. Were unit sales constant from year to year? Explain.
   b. What was the relation between unit sales and unit production levels in each year? For each year, indicate whether inventories grew or shrank.

3. Given the patterns of net operating income in scenarios A and B above, which costing method, variable costing or absorption costing, do you believe provides a better reflection of economic reality? Explain.

EXERCISE 7–5 Variable and Absorption Costing Unit Product Costs and Income Statements [LO1, LO2]

Lynch Company manufactures and sells a single product. The following costs were incurred during the company's first year of operations:

Variable costs per unit:	
Manufacturing:	
Direct materials	$6
Direct labor	$9
Variable manufacturing overhead	$3
Variable selling and administrative	$4
Fixed costs per year:	
Fixed manufacturing overhead	$300,000
Fixed selling and administrative	$190,000

During the year, the company produced 25,000 units and sold 20,000 units. The selling price of the company's product is $50 per unit.

Required:

1. Assume that the company uses the absorption costing method:
   a. Compute the unit product cost.
   b. Prepare an income statement for the year.
2. Assume that the company uses the variable costing method:
   a. Compute the unit product cost.
   b. Prepare an income statement for the year.

EXERCISE 7–6 Variable Costing Income Statement; Reconciliation [LO2, LO3]

Whitman Company has just completed its first year of operations. The company's accountant has prepared an absorption costing income statement for the year:

WHITMAN COMPANY Income Statement		
Sales (35,000 units at $25 per unit)		$875,000
Less cost of goods sold:		
Beginning inventory	$ 0	
Add cost of goods manufactured (40,000 units at $16 per unit)	640,000	
Goods available for sale	640,000	
Less ending inventory (5,000 units at $16 per unit)	80,000	560,000
Gross margin		315,000
Less selling and administrative expenses		280,000
Net operating income		$ 35,000

The company's selling and administrative expenses consist of $210,000 per year in fixed expenses and $2 per unit sold in variable expenses. The $16 per unit product cost given above is computed as follows:

Direct materials	$ 5
Direct labor	6
Variable manufacturing overhead	1
Fixed manufacturing overhead ($160,000 ÷ 40,000 units)	4
Unit product cost	$16

Required:

1. Redo the company's income statement in the contribution format using variable costing.
2. Reconcile any difference between the net operating income on your variable costing income statement and the net operating income on the absorption costing income statement above.

EXERCISE 7–7 Inferring Costing Method; Unit Product Cost [LO1, LO4]
Sierra Company incurs the following costs to produce and sell a single product.

Variable costs per unit:	
Direct materials	$9
Direct labor	$10
Manufacturing overhead	$5
Selling and administrative expenses	$3
Fixed costs per year:	
Fixed manufacturing overhead	$150,000
Fixed selling and administrative expenses	$400,000

During the last year, 25,000 units were produced and 22,000 units were sold. The Finished Goods inventory account at the end of the year shows a balance of $72,000 for the 3,000 unsold units.

Required:
1. Is the company using absorption costing or variable costing to cost units in the Finished Goods inventory account? Show computations to support your answer.
2. Assume that the company wishes to prepare financial statements for the year to issue to its stockholders.
   a. Is the $72,000 figure for Finished Goods inventory the correct amount to use on these statements for external reporting purposes? Explain.
   b. At what dollar amount *should* the 3,000 units be carried in the inventory for external reporting purposes?

EXERCISE 7–8 Variable Costing Unit Product Cost and Income Statement; Break-Even [LO1, LO2]
Chuck Wagon Grills, Inc., makes a single product—a handmade specialty barbecue grill that it sells for $210. Data for last year's operations follow:

Units in beginning inventory	0
Units produced	20,000
Units sold	19,000
Units in ending inventory	1,000
Variable costs per unit:	
Direct materials	$ 50
Direct labor	80
Variable manufacturing overhead	20
Variable selling and administrative	10
Total variable cost per unit	$ 160
Fixed costs:	
Fixed manufacturing overhead	$700,000
Fixed selling and administrative	285,000
Total fixed costs	$985,000

Required:
1. Assume that the company uses variable costing. Compute the unit product cost for one barbecue grill.
2. Assume that the company uses variable costing. Prepare an income statement for the year using the contribution format.
3. What is the company's break-even point in terms of the number of barbecue grills sold?

EXERCISE 7–9 Absorption Costing Unit Product Cost and Income Statement [LO1, LO2]
Refer to the data in Exercise 7–8 for Chuck Wagon Grills. Assume in this exercise that the company uses absorption costing.

Required:
1. Compute the unit product cost for one barbecue grill.
2. Prepare an income statement for the year.

Problems

PROBLEM 7–10 Variable and Absorption Costing Unit Product Costs and Income Statements; Explanation of Difference in Net Operating Income [LO1, LO2, LO3]

High Country, Inc., produces and sells many recreational products. The company has just opened a new plant to produce a folding camp cot that will be marketed throughout the United States. The following cost and revenue data relate to May, the first month of the plant's operation:

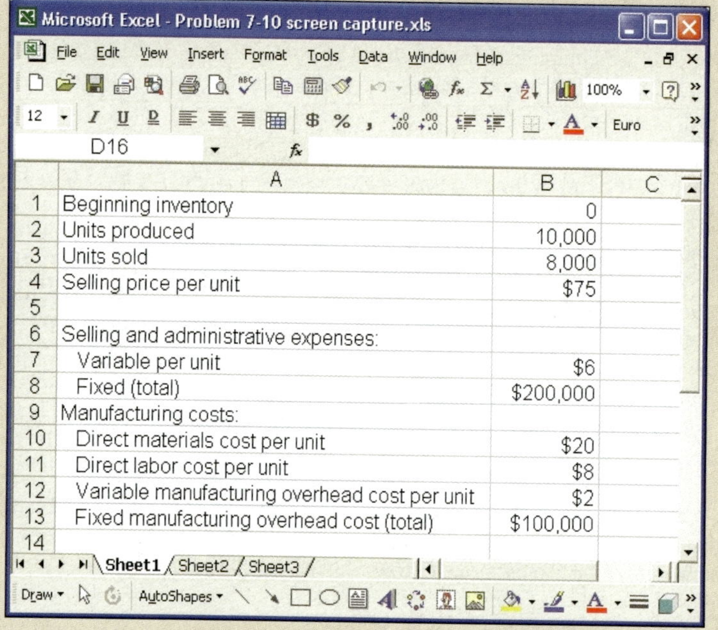

Microsoft Excel - Problem 7-10 screen capture.xls

	A	B	C
1	Beginning inventory	0	
2	Units produced	10,000	
3	Units sold	8,000	
4	Selling price per unit	$75	
5			
6	Selling and administrative expenses:		
7	Variable per unit	$6	
8	Fixed (total)	$200,000	
9	Manufacturing costs:		
10	Direct materials cost per unit	$20	
11	Direct labor cost per unit	$8	
12	Variable manufacturing overhead cost per unit	$2	
13	Fixed manufacturing overhead cost (total)	$100,000	
14			

Management is anxious to see how profitable the new camp cot will be and has asked that an income statement be prepared for May.

Required:

1. Assume that the company uses absorption costing.
   a. Determine the unit product cost.
   b. Prepare an income statement for May.
2. Assume that the company uses the contribution approach with variable costing.
   a. Determine the unit product cost.
   b. Prepare an income statement for May.
3. Explain the reason for any difference in the ending inventory balance under the two costing methods and the impact of this difference on reported net operating income.

PROBLEM 7–11 Variable Costing Income Statement; Reconciliation [LO2, LO3]

During Heaton Company's first two years of operations, the company reported absorption costing net operating income as follows:

	Year 1	Year 2
Sales (@ $25 per unit)	$1,000,000	$1,250,000
Less cost of goods sold:		
Beginning inventory	0	90,000
Add cost of goods manufactured (@ $18 per unit)	810,000	810,000
Goods available for sale	810,000	900,000
Less ending inventory (@ $18 per unit)	90,000	0
Cost of goods sold	720,000	900,000
Gross margin	280,000	350,000
Less selling and administrative expenses*	210,000	230,000
Net operating income	$ 70,000	$ 120,000

*$2 per unit variable; $130,000 fixed each year.

The company's $18 unit product cost is computed as follows:

Direct materials	$ 4
Direct labor	7
Variable manufacturing overhead	1
Fixed manufacturing overhead ($270,000 ÷ 45,000 units)	6
Unit product cost	$18

Production and cost data for the two years are:

	Year 1	Year 2
Units produced	45,000	45,000
Units sold	40,000	50,000

Required:
1. Prepare a variable costing income statement for each year.
2. Reconcile the absorption costing and the variable costing net operating income figures for each year.

PROBLEM 7–12 Absorption and Variable Costing; Production Constant, Sales Fluctuate [LO1, LO2, LO3, LO4]

Tami Tyler opened Tami's Creations, Inc., a small manufacturing company, at the beginning of the year. Getting the company through its first quarter of operations placed a considerable strain on Ms. Tyler's personal finances. The following income statement for the first quarter was prepared by a friend who has just completed a course in managerial accounting at State University.

TAMI'S CREATIONS, INC.
Income Statement
For the Quarter Ended March 31

Sales (28,000 units)		$1,120,000
Less variable expenses:		
Variable cost of goods sold*	$462,000	
Variable selling and administrative	168,000	630,000
Contribution margin		490,000
Less fixed expenses:		
Fixed manufacturing overhead	300,000	
Fixed selling and administrative	200,000	500,000
Net operating loss		$ (10,000)

*Consists of direct materials, direct labor, and variable manufacturing overhead.

Ms. Tyler is discouraged over the loss shown for the quarter, particularly since she had planned to use the statement as support for a bank loan. Another friend, a CPA, insists that the company should be using absorption costing rather than variable costing, and argues that if absorption costing had been used the company would probably have reported at least some profit for the quarter.

At this point, Ms. Tyler is manufacturing only one product, a swimsuit. Production and cost data relating to the swimsuit for the first quarter follow:

Units produced	30,000
Units sold	28,000
Variable costs per unit:	
Direct materials	$3.50
Direct labor	$12.00
Variable manufacturing overhead	$1.00
Variable selling and administrative	$6.00

Required:
1. Complete the following:
   a. Compute the unit product cost under absorption costing.

   b. Redo the company's income statement for the quarter using absorption costing.
   c. Reconcile the variable and absorption costing net operating income (loss) figures.
2. Was the CPA correct in suggesting that the company really earned a "profit" for the quarter? Explain.
3. During the second quarter of operations, the company again produced 30,000 units but sold 32,000 units. (Assume no change in total fixed costs.)
   a. Prepare an income statement for the quarter using variable costing.
   b. Prepare an income statement for the quarter using absorption costing.
   c. Reconcile the variable costing and absorption costing net operating income figures.

PROBLEM 7–13 Comprehensive Problem with Labor Fixed [LO1, LO2, LO3, LO4]
Far North Telecom, Ltd., of Ontario, has organized a new division to manufacture and sell specialty cellular telephones. The division's monthly costs are shown below:

Manufacturing costs:	
Variable costs per unit:	
Direct materials	$48
Variable manufacturing overhead	$2
Fixed manufacturing overhead costs (total)	$360,000
Selling and administrative costs:	
Variable	12% of sales
Fixed (total)	$470,000

Far North Telecom regards all of its workers as full-time employees and the company has a long-standing no layoff policy. Furthermore, production is highly automated. Accordingly, the company includes its labor costs in its fixed manufacturing overhead. The cellular phones sell for $150 each. During September, the first month of operations, the following activity was recorded:

Units produced	12,000
Units sold	10,000

Required:
1. Compute the unit product cost under:
   a. Absorption costing.
   b. Variable costing.
2. Prepare an income statement for September using absorption costing.
3. Prepare an income statement for September using variable costing.
4. Assume that the company must obtain additional financing in order to continue operations. As a member of top management, would you prefer to rely on the statement in (2) above or in (3) above when meeting with a group of prospective investors?
5. Reconcile the absorption costing and variable costing net operating income figures in (2) and (3) above.

PROBLEM 7–14 Prepare and Reconcile Variable Costing Statements [LO1, LO2, LO3, LO4]
Denton Company manufactures and sells a single product. Cost data for the product are given below:

Variable costs per unit:	
Direct materials	$ 7
Direct labor	10
Variable manufacturing overhead	5
Variable selling and administrative	3
Total variable cost per unit	$ 25
Fixed costs per month:	
Fixed manufacturing overhead	$315,000
Fixed selling and administrative	245,000
Total fixed cost per month	$560,000

The product sells for $60 per unit. Production and sales data for July and August, the first two months of operations, follow:

	Units Produced	Units Sold
July	17,500	15,000
August	17,500	20,000

The company's Accounting Department has prepared absorption costing income statements for July and August as presented below:

	July	August
Sales	$900,000	$1,200,000
Less cost of goods sold:		
Beginning inventory	0	100,000
Add cost of goods manufactured	700,000	700,000
Goods available for sale	700,000	800,000
Less ending inventory	100,000	0
Cost of goods sold	600,000	800,000
Gross margin	300,000	400,000
Less selling and administrative expenses	290,000	305,000
Net operating income	$ 10,000	$ 95,000

Required:

1. Determine the unit product cost under:
   a. Absorption costing.
   b. Variable costing.
2. Prepare variable costing income statements for July and August using the contribution approach.
3. Reconcile the variable costing and absorption costing net operating income figures.
4. The company's Accounting Department has determined the company's break-even point to be 16,000 units per month, computed as follows:

$$\frac{\text{Fixed cost per month, \$560,000}}{\text{Unit contribution margin, \$35 per unit}} = 16{,}000 \text{ units}$$

"I'm confused," said the president. "The accounting people say that our break-even point is 16,000 units per month, but we sold only 15,000 units in July, and the income statement they prepared shows a $10,000 profit for that month. Either the income statement is wrong or the break-even point is wrong." Prepare a brief memo for the president, explaining what happened on the July income statement.

PROBLEM 7–15 Variable Costing Income Statements; Sales Constant, Production Varies; JIT Impact [LO1, LO2, LO3, LO4]

"This makes no sense at all," said Bill Sharp, president of Essex Company. "We sold the same number of units this year as we did last year, yet our profits have more than doubled. Who made the goof—the computer or the people who operate it?" The statements to which Mr. Sharp was referring are shown below (absorption costing basis):

	Year 1	Year 2
Sales (20,000 units each year)	$700,000	$700,000
Less cost of goods sold	460,000	400,000
Gross margin	240,000	300,000
Less selling and administrative expenses	200,000	200,000
Net operating income	$ 40,000	$100,000

The statements above show the results of the first two years of operation. In the first year, the company produced and sold 20,000 units; in the second year, the company again sold 20,000 units, but it increased production as shown below:

	Year 1	Year 2
Production in units	20,000	25,000
Sales in units	20,000	20,000
Variable manufacturing cost per unit produced	$8	$8
Variable selling and administrative expense per unit sold	$1	$1
Fixed manufacturing overhead costs (total)	$300,000	$300,000

Essex Company applies fixed manufacturing overhead costs to its only product on the basis of *each year's production.* (Thus, a new fixed manufacturing overhead rate is computed each year, as in Exhibit 7–6.)

Required:

1. Compute the unit product cost for each year under:
   a. Absorption costing.
   b. Variable costing.
2. Prepare a variable costing income statement for each year, using the contribution approach.
3. Reconcile the variable costing and absorption costing net operating income figures for each year.
4. Explain to the president why, under absorption costing, the net operating income for Year 2 was higher than the net operating income for Year 1, although the same number of units was sold in each year.
5. *a.* Explain how operations would have differed in Year 2 if the company had been using JIT inventory methods.
   b. If JIT had been in use during Year 2, what would the company's net operating income have been under absorption costing? Explain the reason for any difference between this income figure and the figure reported by the company in the statements above.

PROBLEM 7–16 Incentives Created by Absorption Costing; Ethics and the Manager [LO2, LO4]
Carlos Cavalas, the manager of Echo Products' Brazilian Division, is trying to decide what production schedule to set for the last quarter of the year. The Brazilian Division had planned to sell 3,600 units during the year, but by September 30 only the following activity had been reported:

	Units
Inventory, January 1	0
Production	2,400
Sales	2,000
Inventory, September 30	400

The division can rent warehouse space to store up to 1,000 units. The minimum inventory level that the division should carry is 50 units. Mr. Cavalas is aware that production must be at least 200 units per quarter in order to retain a nucleus of key employees. Maximum production capacity is 1,500 units per quarter.

Demand has been soft, and the sales forecast for the last quarter is only 600 units. Due to the nature of the division's operations, fixed manufacturing overhead is a major element of product cost.

Required:

1. Assume that the division is using variable costing. How many units should be scheduled for production during the last quarter of the year? (The basic formula for computing the required production for a period in a company is: Expected sales + Desired ending inventory − Beginning inventory = Required production.) Show computations and explain your answer. Will the number of units scheduled for production affect the division's reported income or loss for the year? Explain.
2. Assume that the division is using absorption costing and that the divisional manager is given an annual bonus based on divisional operating income. If Mr. Cavalas wants to maximize his division's operating income for the year, how many units should be scheduled for production during the last quarter? [See the formula in (1) above.] Explain.

3. Identify the ethical issues involved in the decision Mr. Cavalas must make about the level of production for the last quarter of the year.

PROBLEM 7–17 Prepare and Interpret Income Statements; Changes in Both Sales and Production; JIT [LO1, LO2, LO3, LO4]

eXcel

Starfax, Inc., manufactures a small part that is widely used in various electronic products such as home computers. Operating results for the first three years of activity were as follows (absorption costing basis):

	Year 1	Year 2	Year 3
Sales	$800,000	$640,000	$800,000
Cost of goods sold:			
Beginning inventory	0	0	200,000
Add cost of goods manufactured	580,000	600,000	560,000
Goods available for sale	580,000	600,000	760,000
Less ending inventory	0	200,000	140,000
Cost of goods sold	580,000	400,000	620,000
Gross margin	220,000	240,000	180,000
Less selling and administrative expenses	190,000	180,000	190,000
Net operating income (loss)	$ 30,000	$ 60,000	$ (10,000)

In the latter part of Year 2, a competitor went out of business and in the process dumped a large number of units on the market. As a result, Starfax's sales dropped by 20% during Year 2 even though production increased during the year. Management had expected sales to remain constant at 50,000 units; the increased production was designed to provide the company with a buffer of protection against unexpected spurts in demand. By the start of Year 3, management could see that inventory was excessive and that spurts in demand were unlikely. To reduce the excessive inventories, Starfax cut back production during Year 3, as shown below:

	Year 1	Year 2	Year 3
Production in units	50,000	60,000	40,000
Sales in units	50,000	40,000	50,000

Additional information about the company follows:

a. The company's plant is highly automated. Variable manufacturing costs (direct materials, direct labor, and variable manufacturing overhead) total only $2 per unit, and fixed manufacturing overhead costs total $480,000 per year.
b. Fixed manufacturing overhead costs are applied to units of product on the basis of each year's production. (That is, a new fixed manufacturing overhead rate is computed each year, as in Exhibit 7–6.)
c. Variable selling and administrative expenses were $1 per unit sold in each year. Fixed selling and administrative expenses totaled $140,000 per year.
d. The company uses a FIFO inventory flow assumption.

Starfax's management can't understand why profits doubled during Year 2 when sales dropped by 20% and why a loss was incurred during Year 3 when sales recovered to previous levels.

Required:

1. Prepare variable costing income statements for each year using the contribution approach.
2. Refer to the absorption costing income statements above.
   a. Compute the unit product cost in each year under absorption costing. (Show how much of this cost is variable and how much is fixed.)
   b. Reconcile the variable costing and absorption costing net operating income figures for each year.
3. Refer again to the absorption costing income statements. Explain why net operating income was higher in Year 2 than it was in Year 1 under the absorption approach, in light of the fact that fewer units were sold in Year 2 than in Year 1.

4. Refer again to the absorption costing income statements. Explain why the company suffered a loss in Year 3 but reported a profit in Year 1 although the same number of units was sold in each year.
5. *a.* Explain how operations would have differed in Year 2 and Year 3 if the company had been using JIT inventory methods.
   b. If JIT had been used during Year 2 and Year 3, what would the company's net operating income (or loss) have been in each year under absorption costing? Explain the reason for any differences between these income figures and the figures reported by the company in the statements above.

Cases

CASE 7–18 Absorption and Variable Costing; Uneven Production; Break-Even Analysis; JIT Impact [LO2, LO3, LO4]

"Now this doesn't make any sense at all," said Flora Fisher, financial vice president for Warner Company. "Our sales have been steadily rising over the last several months, but profits have been going in the opposite direction. In September we finally hit $2,000,000 in sales, but the bottom line for that month drops off to a $100,000 loss. Why aren't profits more closely correlated with sales?"

The statements to which Ms. Fisher was referring are shown below (absorption costing basis):

WARNER COMPANY
Monthly Income Statements

	July	August	September
Sales (@ $25 per unit)	$1,750,000	$1,875,000	$2,000,000
Less cost of goods sold:			
Beginning inventory	80,000	320,000	400,000
Cost applied to production:			
Variable manufacturing costs (@ $9 per unit)	765,000	720,000	540,000
Fixed manufacturing overhead	595,000	560,000	420,000
Cost of goods manufactured	1,360,000	1,280,000	960,000
Goods available for sale	1,440,000	1,600,000	1,360,000
Less ending inventory	320,000	400,000	80,000
Cost of goods sold	1,120,000	1,200,000	1,280,000
Underapplied or (overapplied) fixed overhead cost	(35,000)	—	140,000
Adjusted cost of goods sold	1,085,000	1,200,000	1,420,000
Gross margin	665,000	675,000	580,000
Less selling and administrative expenses	620,000	650,000	680,000
Net operating income (loss)	$ 45,000	$ 25,000	$ (100,000)

Hal Taylor, a recent graduate from State University who has just been hired by Warner Company, has stated to Ms. Fisher that the contribution approach, with variable costing, is a much better way to report profit data to management. Sales and production data for the last quarter follow:

	July	August	September
Production in units	85,000	80,000	60,000
Sales in units	70,000	75,000	80,000

Additional information about the company's operations is given below:

a. Five thousand units were in inventory on July 1.

b. Fixed manufacturing overhead costs total $1,680,000 per quarter and are incurred evenly throughout the quarter. This fixed manufacturing overhead cost is applied to units of product on the basis of a budgeted production volume of 80,000 units per month.
c. Variable selling and administrative expenses are $6 per unit sold. The remainder of the selling and administrative expenses on the statements above are fixed.
d. The company uses a FIFO inventory flow assumption. Work in process inventories are insignificant and can be ignored.

"I know production is somewhat out of step with sales," said Carla Vorhees, the company's controller. "But we had to build inventory early in the quarter in anticipation of a strike in September. Since the union settled without a strike, we then had to cut back production in September in order to reduce the excess inventories. The income statements you have are completely accurate."

Required:

1. Prepare a variable costing income statement for each month using the contribution approach.
2. Compute the monthly break-even point under variable costing.
3. Explain to Ms. Fisher why profits have moved erratically over the three-month period shown in the absorption costing statements and why profits have not been more closely related to changes in sales volume.
4. Reconcile the variable costing and absorption costing net operating income (loss) figures for each month. Show all computations, and show how you derived each figure used in your reconciliation.
5. Assume that the company had decided to introduce JIT inventory methods at the beginning of September. (Sales and production during July and August were as shown above.)
   a. How many units would have been produced during September under JIT?
   b. Starting with the next quarter (October, November, and December), would you expect any difference between the income reported under absorption costing and under variable costing? Explain why there would or would not be any difference.
   c. Refer to your computations in (2) above. How would JIT help break-even analysis "make sense" under absorption costing?

CASE 7–19 Ethics and the Manager; Absorption Costing Income Statements [LO2, LO4]

Guochang Li was hired as chief executive officer (CEO) in late November by the board of directors of ContactGlobal, a company that produces an advanced global positioning system (GPS) device. The previous CEO had been fired by the board of directors due to a series of shady business practices including shipping defective GPS devices to dealers.

Guochang felt that his first priority was to restore employee morale—which had suffered during the previous CEO's reign. He was particularly anxious to build a sense of trust between himself and the company's employees. His second priority was to prepare the budget for the coming year, which the board of directors wanted to review in their December 15 meeting.

After hammering out the details in meetings with key managers, Guochang was able to put together a budget that he felt the company could realistically meet during the coming year. That budget appears below:

Basic budget data	
Units in beginning inventory	0
Units produced	400,000
Units sold	400,000
Units in ending inventory	0
Variable costs per unit:	
Direct materials	$ 57.20
Direct labor	15.00
Variable manufacturing overhead	5.00
Variable selling and administrative	10.00
Total variable cost per unit	$ 87.20
Fixed costs:	
Fixed manufacturing overhead	$ 6,888,000
Fixed selling and administrative	4,560,000
Total fixed costs	$11,448,000

CONTACTGLOBAL Budgeted Income Statement (absorption method)		
Sales (400,000 units × $120 per unit)		$48,000,000
Less cost of goods sold:		
Beginning inventory	$ 0	
Add cost of goods manufactured (400,000 units × $94.42 per unit)	37,768,000	
Goods available for sale	37,768,000	
Less ending inventory	0	37,768,000
Gross margin		10,232,000
Less selling and administrative expenses:		
Variable selling and administrative (400,000 units × $10 per unit)	4,000,000	
Fixed selling and administrative	4,560,000	8,560,000
Net operating income		$ 1,672,000

The board of directors made it clear that this budget was not as ambitious as they had hoped. The most influential member of the board stated that "managers should have to stretch to meet profit goals." After some discussion, the board decided to set a profit goal of $2,000,000 for the coming year. To provide strong incentives, the board agreed to pay out very substantial bonuses to top managers of $10,000 to $25,000 each if this profit goal was eventually met. The bonus would be all-or-nothing. If actual net operating income turned out to be $2,000,000 or more, the bonus would be paid. Otherwise, no bonus would be paid.

Required:

1. Assuming that the company does not build up its inventory (i.e., production equals sales) and its selling price and cost structure remain the same, how many units of the GPS device would have to be sold to meet the net operating income goal of $2,000,000?
2. Verify your answer to (1) above by constructing a revised budget and budgeted absorption costing income statement that yields a net operating income of $2,000,000.
3. Unfortunately, by October of the next year it had become clear that the company would not be able to make the $2,000,000 target profit. In fact, it looked like the company would wind up the year as originally planned, with sales of 400,000 units, no ending inventories, and a profit of $1,672,000.

   Several managers who were reluctant to lose their year-end bonuses approached Guochang and suggested that the company could still show a profit of $2,000,000. The managers pointed out that at the present rate of sales, there was enough capacity to produce tens of thousands of additional GPS devices for the warehouse and thereby shift fixed manufacturing overhead costs to another year. If sales are 400,000 units for the year and the selling price and cost structure remain the same, how many units would have to be produced in order to show a profit of at least $2,000,000 under absorption costing?
4. Verify your answer to (3) above by constructing an absorption costing income statement.
5. Do you think Guochang Li should approve the plan to build ending inventories in order to attain the target profit?
6. What advice would you give to the board of directors concerning how they determine bonuses in the future?

Case 7–20 The Case of the Plummeting Profits; JIT Impact [LO2, LO3, LO4]
"These statements can't be right," said Ben Yoder, president of Rayco, Inc. "Our sales in the second quarter were up by 25% over the first quarter, yet these income statements show a precipitous drop in net operating income for the second quarter. Those accounting people have fouled something up." Mr. Yoder was referring to the following statements (absorption costing basis):

RAYCO, INC. Income Statements For the First Two Quarters	First Quarter		Second Quarter	
Sales		$480,000		$600,000
Less cost of goods sold:				
Beginning inventory	$ 80,000		$140,000	
Add cost of goods manufactured	300,000		180,000	
Goods available for sale	380,000		320,000	
Less ending inventory	140,000		20,000	
Cost of goods sold	240,000		300,000	
Add underapplied overhead	—	240,000	72,000	372,000
Gross margin		240,000		228,000
Less selling and administrative expenses		200,000		215,000
Net operating income		$ 40,000		$ 13,000

After studying the statements briefly, Mr. Yoder called in the controller to see if the mistake in the second quarter could be located before the figures were released to the press. The controller stated, "I'm sorry to say that those figures are correct, Ben. I agree that sales went up during the second quarter, but the problem is in production. You see, we budgeted to produce 15,000 units each quarter, but a strike on the west coast among some of our suppliers forced us to cut production in the second quarter back to only 9,000 units. That's what caused the drop in net operating income."

Mr. Yoder was confused by the controller's explanation. He replied, "This doesn't make sense. I ask you to explain why net operating income dropped when sales went up and you talk about production! So what if we had to cut back production? We still were able to increase sales by 25%. If sales go up, then net operating income should go up. If your statements can't show a simple thing like that, then it's time for some changes in your department!"

Budgeted production and sales for the year, along with actual production and sales for the first two quarters, are given below:

	Quarter			
	First	Second	Third	Fourth
Budgeted sales (units)	12,000	15,000	15,000	18,000
Actual sales (units)	12,000	15,000	—	—
Budgeted production (units)	15,000	15,000	15,000	15,000
Actual production (units)	15,000	9,000	—	—

The company's plant is heavily automated, and fixed manufacturing overhead amounts to $180,000 each quarter. Variable manufacturing costs are $8 per unit. The fixed manufacturing overhead is applied to units of product at a rate of $12 per unit (based on the budgeted production shown above). Any under- or overapplied overhead is closed directly to cost of goods sold for the quarter. The company had 4,000 units in inventory to start the first quarter and uses the FIFO inventory flow assumption. Variable selling and administrative expenses are $5 per unit.

Required:

1. What characteristic of absorption costing caused the drop in net operating income for the second quarter and what could the controller have said to explain the problem?
2. Prepare a variable costing income statement for each quarter using the contribution approach.
3. Reconcile the absorption costing and the variable costing net operating income figures for each quarter.

4. Identify and discuss the advantages and disadvantages of using the variable costing method for internal reporting purposes.
5. Assume that the company had introduced JIT (just-in-time) at the beginning of the second quarter. (Sales and production during the first quarter remain the same.)
   a. How many units would have been produced during the second quarter under JIT?
   b. Starting with the third quarter, would you expect any difference between the net operating income reported under absorption costing and under variable costing? Explain why there would or would not be any difference.

Group and Internet Exercises

GROUP EXERCISE 7–21 Who Needs Customers? I Can Make Money without Them

Tough times always seem to bring out the worst in people. When companies are desperate to stay in business or to report more favorable earnings to Wall Street, some managers just can't seem to resist the temptation to manipulate reported profits. Unfortunately, inventory is sometimes a tempting source of such manipulations. It is important to know how such earnings distortions can occur, whether they result from intentional actions or innocent miscalculations.

Required:

1. What product costing method is used for external financial reporting purposes in the United States?
2. Excluding inflation and changes in the selling prices of products, how could a company with the same sales as last year report significantly higher profits without cutting any costs? Could a company with sales below the break-even point report profits? Explain.
3. Are all such "fictitious" profits an attempt to distort profits and mislead investors and creditors?
4. Could the reverse situation occur? That is, could lower accounting profits be reported even though the company is not economically worse off?

GROUP EXERCISE 7–22 Changing Cost Structures and Product Costing

As companies automate their operations with advanced manufacturing technology and information technology, cost structures are becoming more fixed with higher proportions of overhead.

Required:

1. What implications does this trend hold for arguments favoring absorption costing? What implications does this trend hold for arguments favoring variable costing?
2. If absorption costing continues to be used for external financial reporting, what impact will inventory buildups or inventory liquidations have on future reported earnings compared with the effects they have had on past reported earnings?
3. Most companies evaluate and compensate top management, in part, on the basis of net operating income. Would top management have a preference for basing its evaluations on variable costing or full absorption costing? Explain.

INTERNET EXERCISE 7–23

As you know, the World Wide Web is a medium that is constantly evolving. Sites come and go, and change without notice. To enable the periodic updating of site addresses, this problem has been posted to the textbook website (www.mhhe.com/garrison11e). After accessing the site, enter the Student Center and select this chapter. Select and complete the Internet Exercise.

Chapter

8

Activity-Based Costing: A Tool to Aid Decision Making

LEARNING OBJECTIVES

After studying Chapter 8, you should be able to:

LO1 Understand activity-based costing and how it differs from a traditional costing system.

LO2 Assign costs to cost pools using a first-stage allocation.

LO3 Compute activity rates for cost pools.

LO4 Assign costs to a cost object using a second-stage allocation.

LO5 Prepare a report showing activity-based costing margins from an activity view.

LO6 Compare product costs computed using traditional and activity-based costing methods.

LO7 (Appendix 8A) Prepare an action analysis report using activity-based costing data and interpret the report.

Bank of America Focuses on Profitability

BUSINESS FOCUS

Some companies track how much their customers spend on their products and how much it costs to serve these customers. Profitable customers are carefully nurtured. Unprofitable customers may be let go.

For example, "Bank of America calculates its profits every month on each of its more than 75 million accounts . . . By wading through all that data . . . BofA is able to zero in on the 10% of households that are most profitable. It assigns a financial adviser to track about 300 accounts at a time. Their job: to answer questions, coordinate the bank's efforts to sell more services, and—perhaps most important—watch for warning flags that these lucrative customers may be moving their business elsewhere . . . . The heavy intervention seems to be working . . . [C]ustomer defections are down, and account balances in the top 10% have grown . . . " ■

Source: Paul C. Judge, "What've You Done for Us Lately?" *Business Week*, September 14, 1998, pp. 140–146.

This chapter introduces the concept of *activity-based costing* which has been embraced by a wide variety of manufacturing, service, and nonprofit organizations including American Express, The Association of Neurological Surgeons, Cambridge Hospital Community Health Network, Carrier Corporation, Dana Corporation, Dialysis Clinic, GE Medical Systems, Hallmark, ITT Automotive North America, Maxwell Appliance Controls, Pillsbury, Tampa Electric Company, and the U.S. Postal Service. **Activity-based costing (ABC)** is a costing method that is designed to provide managers with cost information for strategic and other decisions that potentially affect capacity and therefore "fixed" as well as variable costs. Activity-based costing is ordinarily used as a supplement to, rather than as a replacement for, the company's usual costing system. Most organizations that use activity-based costing have two costing systems—the official costing system that is used for preparing external financial reports and the activity-based costing system that is used for internal decision making and for managing activities.

In practice, activity-based costing comes in many "flavors." Consultants emphasize different aspects of activity-based costing, and companies interpret activity-based costing differently. Since so much variation occurs in practice, we focus our attention in this chapter on what we consider to be "the best practice"—those techniques that provide managers with the most useful information for making strategic decisions. We will assume that the ABC system is used as a supplement to, rather than as a replacement for, the company's formal cost accounting system.

IN BUSINESS

ABC IN THE PUBLIC SECTOR

Robin Cooper and Robert S. Kaplan report that: "The U.S. Veterans Affairs Department has identified the cost of the 10 activities performed to process death benefits and uses this information to monitor and improve the underlying cost structure for performing this function. The U.S. Immigration and Naturalization Service (INS) uses its ABC cost information to set fees for all of its outputs, including administering citizenship exams and issuing permanent work permits (green cards)." The City of Indianapolis made ABC a cornerstone of its privatization efforts and its drive to provide more services at lower cost to citizens. The mayor of Indianapolis, Stephen Goldsmith, explains: "Introducing competition and privatization to government services requires real cost information. You can't compete if you are using fake money." When city workers became aware of the costs of carrying out activities such as filling potholes in streets and were faced with the possible transfer of such tasks to the private sector, they became highly motivated to reduce costs. Instead of going out to fill potholes with a five- or six-man repair crew, plus a supervisor, they started doing the same job with a three- or four-man crew without a supervisor. The number of politically appointed supervisors, which had stood at 36 for 75 employees, was slashed by half.

Source: Robert S. Kaplan and Robin Cooper, *Cost & Effect: Using Integrated Cost Systems to Drive Profitability and Performance*, Harvard Business School Press, Boston, 1998, pp. 245–250.

This chapter focuses primarily on ABC applications in manufacturing to provide a contrast with the material presented in earlier chapters. More specifically, Chapters 2, 3, and 4 focused on traditional absorption costing systems used by manufacturing companies to calculate unit product costs for the purpose of valuing inventories and determining cost of goods sold for external financial reports. In contrast, this chapter explains how manufacturing companies can use activity-based costing rather than traditional methods to calculate unit product costs for the purposes of managing overhead and making decisions. Chapter 7 had a similar purpose. That chapter focused on how to use variable costing to aid decisions that do not affect fixed costs. This chapter extends that idea to show how activity-based costing can be used to aid decisions that potentially affect fixed costs as well as variable costs. As a consequence of these differences in objectives, "best practice" activity-based costing differs in a number of ways from traditional cost accounting.

In activity-based costing:

1. Nonmanufacturing as well as manufacturing costs may be assigned to products.
2. Some manufacturing costs may be excluded from product costs.
3. A number of overhead cost pools are used, each of which is allocated to products and other cost objects using its own unique measure of activity.
4. The allocation bases often differ from those used in traditional costing systems.
5. The overhead rates, or *activity rates,* may be based on the level of activity at capacity rather than on the budgeted level of activity.

LEARNING OBJECTIVE 1
Understand activity-based costing and how it differs from a traditional costing system.

As we will see later in the chapter, these differences from traditional cost accounting systems can dramatically impact the apparent costs of products and the profitability of products and customers. But first, we will briefly discuss the reasons for these departures from traditional cost accounting practices.

IN BUSINESS

SHEDDING LIGHT ON PRODUCT PROFITABILITY

Reichhold, Inc., one of the world's leading suppliers of synthetic materials, adopted activity-based costing to help shed light on the profitability of its various products. Reichhold's prior cost system used one allocation base, reactor hours, to assign overhead costs to products. The ABC system uses four additional activity measures—preprocess preparation hours, thin-tank hours, filtration hours, and waste disposal costs per batch—to assign costs to products. Reichhold has rolled out ABC to all 19 of its North American plants because the management team believes that ABC helps improve the company's "capacity management, cycle times, value-added pricing decisions, and analysis of product profitability."

Source: Edward Blocher, Betty Wong, and Christopher McKittrick, "Making Bottom-Up ABC Work at Reichhold, Inc.," *Strategic Finance,* April 2002, pp. 51–55.

How Costs Are Treated under Activity-Based Costing

Nonmanufacturing Costs and Activity-Based Costing

In traditional cost accounting, only manufacturing costs are assigned to products. Selling and administrative expenses are treated as period expenses and are not assigned to products. However, many of these nonmanufacturing costs are also part of the costs of producing, selling, distributing, and servicing specific products. For example, commissions paid to salespersons, shipping costs, and warranty repair costs can be easily traced to individual products. In this chapter, we will use the term *overhead* to refer to nonmanufacturing costs as well as to indirect manufacturing costs. In activity-based costing, products are assigned all of the overhead costs—nonmanufacturing as well as manufacturing—that they can reasonably be supposed to have caused. In essence, we will be determining the entire cost of a product rather than just its manufacturing cost. The focus in Chapters 2, 3, and 4 was on determining just the manufacturing cost of a product.

Manufacturing Costs and Activity-Based Costing

In traditional cost accounting, *all* manufacturing costs are assigned to products—even manufacturing costs that are not caused by the products. For example, a portion of the factory security guard's wages would be allocated to each product even though the guard's wages are totally unaffected by which products are made or not made during a period. In activity-based costing, a cost is assigned to a product only if decisions concerning the product cause changes in the cost.

Plantwide Overhead Rate Our discussion in Chapter 3 assumed that a single overhead rate, called a *plantwide overhead rate,* was being used throughout an entire factory and that the allocation base was direct labor-hours or machine-hours. This simple approach to overhead assignment can result in distorted unit product costs when it is used for decision-making purposes.

When cost systems were developed in the 1800s, cost and activity data had to be collected by hand and all calculations were done with paper and pen. Consequently, the emphasis was on simplicity. Companies often established a single overhead cost pool for an entire facility or department as described in Chapter 3. Direct labor was the obvious choice as an allocation base for overhead costs. Direct labor-hours were already being recorded for purposes of determining wages and direct labor time spent on tasks was often closely monitored. In the labor-intensive production processes of that time, direct labor was a large component of product costs—larger than it is today. Moreover, managers believed direct labor and overhead costs were highly correlated. (Two variables, such as direct labor and overhead costs, are highly correlated if they tend to move together.) And finally, most companies produced a very limited variety of products that required similar resources to produce, so in fact there was probably little difference in the overhead costs attributable to different products. Under these conditions, it was not cost-effective to use a more elaborate costing system.

Conditions have changed. Many companies now sell a large variety of products and services that consume significantly different overhead resources. Consequently, a costing system that assigns essentially the same overhead cost to every product may no longer be adequate. Additionally, many managers now believe that overhead costs and direct labor are no longer highly correlated and that other factors drive overhead costs.

On an economywide basis, direct labor and overhead costs have been moving in opposite directions for a long time. As a percentage of total cost, direct labor has been declining, whereas overhead has been increasing.[1] Many tasks previously done by hand are now done with automated equipment—a component of overhead. Furthermore, product diversity has increased. Companies are creating new products and services at an ever-accelerating rate that differ in volume, batch size, and complexity. Managing and sustaining this product diversity requires many more overhead resources such as production schedulers and product design engineers, and many of these overhead resources have no obvious connection to direct labor. Finally, computers, bar code readers, and other technology have reduced the costs of collecting and manipulating data—making more complex (and accurate) costing systems such as activity-based costing less expensive to build and maintain.

Nevertheless, direct labor remains a viable base for applying overhead to products in some companies—particularly for external reports. Direct labor is an appropriate allocation base for overhead when overhead costs and direct labor are highly correlated. And indeed, most companies throughout the world continue to base overhead allocations on direct labor or machine-hours. However, if factorywide overhead costs do not move in tandem with factorywide direct labor or machine-hours, some other means of assigning overhead costs must be found or product costs will be distorted.

Departmental Overhead Rates Rather than use a plantwide overhead rate, many companies have a system in which each department has its own overhead rate. The nature of the work performed in a department will determine the department's allocation base. For example, overhead costs in a machining department may be allocated on the basis of the machine-hours incurred in that department. In contrast, the overhead costs in an assembly department may be allocated on the basis of direct labor-hours incurred in that department.

Unfortunately, even departmental overhead rates will not correctly assign overhead costs in situations where a company has a range of products that differ in volume, batch size, or complexity of production.[2] The reason is that the departmental approach usually

---

[1] Germain Böer provides some data concerning these trends in "Five Modern Management Accounting Myths," *Management Accounting,* January 1994, pp. 22–27. Data maintained by the U.S. Department of Commerce show that since 1849, on average, material cost has been fairly constant at 55% of sales. Labor cost has always been less important than direct materials and has declined steadily from 23% of sales in 1849 to about 10% in 1987. Overhead has grown from about 18% of sales in 1947 to about 33% of sales 50 years later.

[2] See Robin Cooper and Robert S. Kaplan, "How Cost Accounting Distorts Product Costs," *Management Accounting,* April 1988, pp. 20–27.

relies on volume as the base for allocating overhead cost to products. For example, if the machining department's overhead is applied to products on the basis of machine-hours, it is assumed that the department's overhead costs are caused by, and are directly proportional to, machine-hours. However, the department's overhead costs are probably more complex than this and are caused by a variety of factors, including the range of products processed in the department, the number of batch setups that are required, the complexity of the products, and so on. Activity-based costing is a technique that is designed to reflect these diverse factors more accurately when costing products. It attempts to accomplish this goal by identifying the major *activities* such as batch setups, purchase order processing, and so on, that consume overhead resources and thus cause costs. An **activity** is any event that causes the consumption of overhead resources. The costs of carrying out these activities are assigned to the products that cause the activities.

IN BUSINESS

ABC CHANGES THE FOCUS

Euclid Engineering makes parts and components for automobile manufacturers. As a result of its activity-based costing study, Euclid's managers "discovered that the company was spending more in launching new products than on direct labor expenses to produce existing products. Product development and launch expenses were 10% of expenses, whereas direct labor costs were only 9%. Of course, in the previous direct labor cost system, all attention had been focused on reducing direct labor costs. . . . Product development and launch costs were blended into the factory overhead rate applied to products based on direct labor cost. Now Euclid's managers realized that they had a major cost reduction opportunity by attacking the product launch cost directly."

Euclid shared the new information produced by the ABC study with customers. The detailed breakdown of the costs of design and engineering activities helped customers to make trade-offs, with the result that they would often ask that certain activities be skipped whose costs exceeded their benefits.

Source: Robert S. Kaplan and Robin Cooper, *Cost & Effect: Using Integrated Cost Systems to Drive Profitability and Performance* (Boston: Harvard Business School Press, 1998), pp. 219–222.

The Costs of Idle Capacity in Activity-Based Costing

In traditional cost accounting, predetermined overhead rates are computed by dividing budgeted overhead costs by a measure of budgeted activity such as budgeted direct labor-hours. This practice results in applying the costs of unused, or idle, capacity to products, and it results in unstable unit product costs as discussed in Appendix 3A. If budgeted activity falls, the overhead rate increases because the fixed components of overhead are spread over a smaller base, resulting in increased unit product costs.

In contrast to traditional cost accounting, activity-based costing charges products for the costs of capacity they use—not for the costs of capacity they don't use. In other words, the costs of idle capacity are not charged to products. This results in more stable unit costs and is consistent with the objective of assigning only those costs to products that are actually caused by the products. Instead of assigning the costs of idle capacity to products, in activity-based costing these costs are considered to be period costs that flow through to the income statement as an expense of the current period. This treatment highlights the cost of idle capacity rather than burying it in inventory and cost of goods sold.

Designing an Activity-Based Costing (ABC) System

Topic Tackler PLUS 8–1

Experts agree on several essential characteristics of any successful implementation of activity-based costing. First, the initiative to implement activity-based costing must be strongly supported by top management. Second, the design and implementation of an ABC system should be the responsibility of a cross-functional team rather than of the accounting department. The team should include representatives from each area that will use the data provided by the ABC system. Ordinarily, this would include representatives from marketing, production, engineering, and top management as well as technically trained accounting staff. An outside consultant who specializes in activity-based costing may serve as an advisor to the team. And third, the ABC data should be linked to how people are evaluated and rewarded. This ensures that the system will not be ignored.

The reason for insisting on strong top-management support and a multifunction team approach is rooted in the fact that it is difficult to implement changes in organizations unless those changes have the full support of those who are affected. This is particularly true if, as recommended above, the ABC system is used in evaluating and rewarding managers. Unless the managers who are directly affected by these changes have a say, resistance will be inevitable. In addition, designing a good ABC system requires intimate knowledge of many parts of the organization's overall operations. This knowledge can only come from the people who are familiar with those operations.

Top managers must support the initiative for two reasons. First, without leadership from top management, some managers may not see any reason to change. Second, if top managers do not support the ABC system and continue to evaluate and reward employees based on traditional (non-ABC) cost data, their subordinates will quickly get the message that ABC is not important and they will abandon the ABC initiative. Time after time, when accountants have attempted to implement an ABC system on their own without top-management support and active cooperation from other managers, the results have been ignored.

MANAGERIAL ACCOUNTING IN ACTION
The Issue

classic brass inc.

Classic Brass, Inc., makes finely machined brass fittings for a variety of applications including stanchions, cleats, and helms for luxury yachts. The president of the company, John Towers, recently attended a management conference at which activity-based costing was discussed. Following the conference, he called a meeting of the company's top managers to discuss what he had learned. Attending the meeting were the production manager Susan Ritcher, the marketing manager Tom Olafson, and the accounting manager Mary Goodman.

John: I'm glad we could all get together this morning. I just attended a conference that dealt with some issues that we have all been wondering about for some time.

Susan: Did anyone at the conference explain why my equipment always breaks down at the worst possible moment?

John: Sorry Susan, I guess it must be bad karma.

Tom: Did the conference tell you why we've been losing all those bids lately on our high-volume routine work?

John: Tom, you probably weren't expecting this answer, but, yes, there may be a simple reason why we've been losing those bids.

Tom: Let me guess. We've been losing the bids because we have more competition.

John: Yes, the competition has a lot to do with it. But Tom, we may have been shooting ourselves in the foot.

Tom: How so? I don't know about anyone else, but my salespeople have been hustling like crazy to get more business for the company.

Susan: Wait a minute Tom, my production people have been turning in tremendous improvements in defect rates, on-time delivery, and so on.

John: Whoa everybody. Calm down. I don't think anyone is to blame for losing the bids. Tom, when you talk with our customers, what reasons do they give for taking their business to our competitors? Is it a problem with the quality of our products or our on-time delivery?

Tom: No, they don't have any problem with our products or with our service—our customers readily admit we're among the best in the business.

Susan: Darn right!

John: Then what's the problem?

Tom: Price. The competition is undercutting our prices on the high-volume work.

John: Why are our prices too high?

Tom: Our prices aren't too high. Theirs are too low. Our competitors must be pricing below their cost.

John: Tom, why do you think that?

Tom: Well, if we charged the prices on high-volume work that our competitors are quoting, we'd be pricing below *our* cost, and I know we are just as efficient as any competitor.

Susan: Tom, why would our competitors price below their cost?

Tom: They are out to grab market share.

Susan: Does that make any sense? What good does more market share do if they are pricing below their cost?

John: I think Susan has a point, Tom. Mary, you're the expert with the numbers. Can you suggest another explanation?

Mary: I was afraid you would ask that. Those unit product cost figures our department reports to you are primarily intended to be used to value inventories and to determine cost of goods sold for our external financial statements. I am awfully uncomfortable about using them for bidding. In fact, I have mentioned this several times, but no one was interested.

John: Now I'm interested. Mary, are you telling us that the product cost figures we have been using for bidding are wrong? Perhaps the competition isn't pricing below our cost—we just don't know what our cost is?

Mary: Yes, that could be the problem. I just wish someone had listened earlier.

John: Does everyone agree with Mary that this is a problem we should work on?

Tom: Sure, if it means we can win more bids.

John: Okay, I want each of you to appoint one of your top people to a special team to investigate how we cost products.

Susan: Isn't this something Mary can handle with her staff?

John: Perhaps she could, but you know more about your operations than she does and besides, I want to make sure you agree with the results of the study and use them. Mary, do you agree?

Mary: Absolutely.

IN BUSINESS

PEDDLING TO OBLIVION

Claudia Post started a small bicycle-messenger service, Diamond Courier, in Philadelphia after having been unceremoniously fired by a local courier service. With her background in sales, a minimum of dollars to plunk down on starting her company, and an approach that demanded customer service every mile of the way, Claudia was looking at $1 million in sales within 17 months. Tracking delivery trends and anticipating customer needs, she added truck deliveries, airfreight services, a parts-distribution division, and a legal service that served subpoenas and prepared court filings for law firms in the Philadelphia region. Within three years, Diamond was booking $3.1 million in annual sales and had 40 bike messengers, an office staff of 25 employees, about 50 independent drivers, and one big problem. The company was losing money.

Post sold her jewelry to meet payroll and pay bills, and with input from an adviser, she took a close look at the profitability of each of the company's lines of business. Post had assumed that if she charged a competitive rate, kept clients happy, and increased sales, she would make money. However, an activity-based analysis indicated that the average cost of a bike delivery, including overhead, was $9.24, but she was charging only $4.60. Recalls Post: "The bicycle division, which I thought of as Diamond's core business, was generating just 10% of total revenues and barely covered its own direct-labor and insurance costs. Worse, the division created more logistical and customer-service nightmares than any other single aspect of Diamond, therefore generating a disproportionate share of overhead costs." She decided to drop the bicycle messenger service and concentrate on other more profitable lines of business. Further analysis later led to Post closing down the airfreight and parts distribution divisions, and the business was back on track with profits rolling in.

Today, barely 13 years after Diamond Courier made its first local messenger delivery, the company, now Diamond Transportation Group, Inc., is a leading national provider of transportation logistics management. States Post: "Today, as in 1990, Diamond delivers highly reliable and innovative solutions that meet our customers' objectives and enhance their profitability. And consistent with good business practices, we keep our eye on the numbers. Every day."

Sources: Susan Greco, "Are We Making Money Yet?" *INC.*, July 1996, pp. 52–61 and Cheryl A. Hodolitz, Diamond Transportation Group, private communication.

EXHIBIT 8–1
The Activity-Based Costing Model

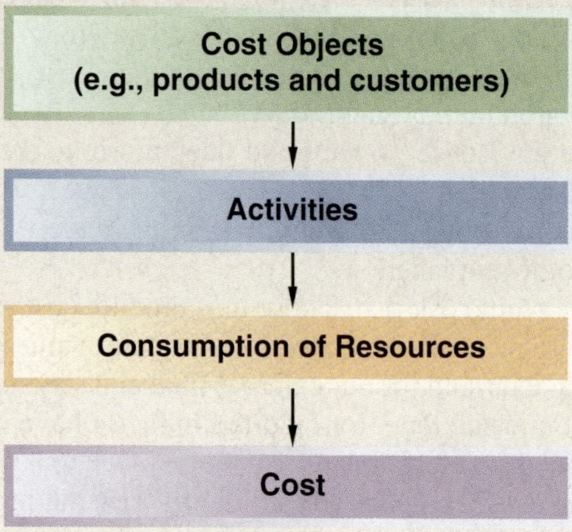

After studying the existing cost accounting system at Classic Brass and reviewing articles in professional and trade journals, the special team decided to implement an activity-based costing (ABC) system. Like most other ABC implementations, the new ABC system would supplement, rather than replace, the existing cost accounting system, which would continue to be used for external financial reports. The new ABC system would be used to prepare special reports for management decisions such as bidding on new business.

The accounting manager drew the chart appearing in Exhibit 8–1 to explain the general structure of the ABC model. Cost objects such as products generate activities. For example, a customer order for a brass cupholder requires the activity of preparing a production order. Such an activity consumes resources. A production order uses a sheet of paper and takes time to fill out. And consumption of resources causes costs. The greater the number of sheets used to fill out production orders and the greater the amount of time devoted to filling out such orders, the greater the cost. Activity-based costing attempts to trace through these relationships to identify how products and customers affect costs.

As in most other companies, the ABC team at Classic Brass felt that the company's traditional cost accounting system adequately measured the direct materials and direct labor costs of products since these costs are directly traced to products. Therefore, the ABC study would be concerned solely with the other costs of the company—manufacturing overhead and selling and administrative costs.

The team felt it was important to carefully plan how it would go about implementing the new ABC system at Classic Brass. Accordingly, the implementation process was broken down into six steps:

Steps for Implementing Activity-Based Costing:

1. Identify and define activities and activity cost pools.
2. Wherever possible, directly trace costs to activities and cost objects.
3. Assign costs to activity cost pools.
4. Calculate activity rates.
5. Assign costs to cost objects using the activity rates and activity measures.
6. Prepare management reports.

Step 1: Identify and Define Activities and Activity Cost Pools

The first major step in implementing an ABC system is to identify the activities that will form the foundation for the system. This can be difficult, time-consuming, and involves a great deal of judgment. A common procedure is for the individuals on the ABC implementation team to interview people who work in overhead departments and ask them to describe their major activities. Ordinarily, this results in a very long list of activities.

IN BUSINESS

IS E-TAILING REALLY EASIER?

The company art.com™ sells prints and framed prints over the web. An activity-based costing study identified the following 12 activities carried out in the company:

1. Service customers
2. Website optimization
3. Merchandise inventory selection and management
4. Purchasing and receiving
5. Customer acquisition and retention—paid-for marketing
6. Customer acquisition and retention—revenue share marketing (affiliate group)
7. Sustain information system
8. Sustain business—administration
9. Sustain business—production
10. Maintain facility—administrative
11. Maintain facility—production
12. Sustain business—executive

For example, the activity "merchandise inventory selection and management" involves scanning, describing, classifying, and linking each inventory item to search options on the company's website. "Staff must carefully manage each change to the database, which is similar to adding and removing inventory items from the shelf of a store. They annotate added inventory items and upload them into the system, as well as remove obsolete and discontinued items. . . . The number of inventory items for an e-tailer is typically much greater than for a brick-and-mortar [store], which is a competitive advantage, but experience shows managing a large inventory consumes substantial resources."

Source: Thomas L. Zeller, David R. Kublank, and Philip G. Makris, " How art.com™ Uses ABC to Succeed," *Strategic Finance*, March 2001, pp. 25–31. Reprinted with permission from the IMA, Montvale, NJ, USA, www.imanet.org.

The length of such lists of activities poses a problem. On the one hand, the greater the number of activities tracked in the ABC system, the more accurate the costs are likely to be. On the other hand, a complex system involving large numbers of activities is costly to design, implement, maintain, and use. Consequently, the original lengthy list of activities is usually reduced to a handful by combining similar activities. For example, several actions may be involved in handling and moving raw materials—from receiving raw materials on the loading dock to sorting them into the appropriate bins in the storeroom. All of these activities might be combined into a single activity called material handling.

A useful way to think about activities is to organize them into five general levels: *unit-level, batch-level, product-level, customer-level,* and *organization-sustaining* activities. These levels are described as follows:[3]

1. **Unit-level activities** are performed each time a unit is produced. The costs of unit-level activities should be proportional to the number of units produced. For example, providing power to run processing equipment would be a unit-level activity since power tends to be consumed in proportion to the number of units produced.
2. **Batch-level activities** are performed each time a batch is handled or processed, regardless of how many units are in the batch. For example, tasks such as placing purchase orders, setting up equipment, and arranging for shipments to customers are batch-level activities. They are incurred once for each batch (or customer order). Costs at the batch level depend on the number of batches processed rather than on the number of units produced, the number of units sold, or other measures of volume. For example, the cost of setting up a machine for batch processing is the same regardless of whether the batch contains one or thousands of items.
3. **Product-level activities** relate to specific products and typically must be carried out regardless of how many batches are run or units of product are produced or sold. For

[3] Robin Cooper, "Cost Classification in Unit-Based and Activity-Based Manufacturing Cost Systems," *Journal of Cost Management,* Fall 1990, pp. 4–14.

example, activities such as designing a product, advertising a product, and maintaining a product manager and staff are all product-level activities.

4. **Customer-level activities** relate to specific customers and include activities such as sales calls, catalog mailings, and general technical support that are not tied to any specific product.
5. **Organization-sustaining activities** are carried out regardless of which customers are served, which products are produced, how many batches are run, or how many units are made. This category includes activities such as heating the factory, cleaning executive offices, providing a computer network, arranging for loans, preparing annual reports to shareholders, and so on.

When combining activities in an ABC system, activities should be grouped together at the appropriate level. Batch-level activities should not be combined with unit-level activities or product-level activities with batch-level activities and so on. In general, it is best to combine only those activities that are highly correlated with each other within a level. For example, the number of customer orders received is likely to be highly correlated with the number of completed customer orders shipped, so these two batch-level activities (receiving and shipping orders) can usually be combined with little loss of accuracy.

At Classic Brass, the ABC team, in consultation with top managers, selected the following *activity cost pools* and *activity measures*:

Activity Cost Pools at Classic Brass	
Activity Cost Pool	Activity Measure
Customer orders	Number of customer orders
Product design	Number of product designs
Order size	Machine-hours
Customer relations	Number of active customers
Other	Not applicable

An **activity cost pool** is a "bucket" in which costs are accumulated that relate to a single activity measure in the ABC system. For example, the *Customer Orders* cost pool will be assigned all costs of resources that are consumed by taking and processing customer orders, including costs of processing paperwork and any costs involved in setting up machines for specific orders. The measure of activity for this cost pool is simply the number of customer orders received. This is a batch-level activity, since each order generates work that occurs regardless of whether the order is for one unit or 1,000 units. The number of customer orders received is an example of an *activity measure.* An **activity measure** is an allocation base in an activity-based costing system. The term *cost driver* is also used to refer to an activity measure. The activity measure should "drive" the cost being allocated.

Activity measures are often very rough measures of resource consumption. Probably the least accurate type of activity measure is known as a *transaction driver*. **Transaction drivers** are simple counts of the number of times an activity occurs such as the number of bills sent out to customers. This activity measure is satisfactory when all bills take about the same amount of time to prepare. However, if some bills are simple to prepare and others are very complex, a more accurate type of activity measure known as a *duration driver* may be used. **Duration drivers** measure the amount of time required to perform an activity such as the time spent preparing individual bills. In general, duration drivers are more accurate measures of the consumption of resources than transaction drivers, but they take more effort to record. For that reason, transaction drivers are often used in practice.

The *Product Design* cost pool will be assigned all costs of resources consumed by designing products. The activity measure for this cost pool is the number of products designed. This is a product-level activity, since the amount of design work on a new product does not depend on the number of units ultimately ordered or batches ultimately run.

The *Order Size* cost pool will be assigned all costs of resources consumed as a consequence of the number of units produced, including the costs of miscellaneous factory supplies, power to run machines, and some equipment depreciation. This is a unit-level activity since each unit requires some of these resources. The activity measure for this cost pool is machine-hours.

The *Customer Relations* cost pool will be assigned all costs associated with maintaining relations with customers, including the costs of sales calls and the costs of entertaining customers. The activity measure for this cost pool is the number of customers the company has on its active customer list. The Customer Relations cost pool represents a customer-level activity.

The *Other* cost pool will be assigned all overhead costs that are not associated with customer orders, product design, the size of the orders, or customer relations. These costs mainly consist of organization-sustaining costs and the costs of unused, idle capacity. These costs *will not* be assigned to products since they represent resources that are *not* consumed by products.

It is unlikely that any other company would use exactly the same activity cost pools and activity measures that were selected by Classic Brass. Because of the amount of judgment involved, the number and definitions of the activity cost pools and activity measures used by companies vary considerably.

The Mechanics of Activity-Based Costing

After the ABC system had been designed, the team was ready to begin the process of actually computing the costs of products, customers, and other objects of interest.

Step 2: Whenever Possible, Directly Trace Overhead Costs to Activities and Cost Objects

The second step in implementing an ABC system is to directly trace as many overhead costs as possible to the ultimate cost objects. At Classic Brass, the ultimate cost objects are products, customer orders, and customers. The company's annual manufacturing overhead and selling and administrative costs are listed in Exhibit 8–2. In the ABC system at

EXHIBIT 8–2
Annual Overhead Costs (both Manufacturing and Nonmanufacturing) at Classic Brass

Production Department:		
Indirect factory wages	$500,000	
Factory equipment depreciation	300,000	
Factory utilities	120,000	
Factory building lease	80,000	$1,000,000
Shipping costs*		40,000
General Administrative Department:		
Administrative wages and salaries	400,000	
Office equipment depreciation	50,000	
Administrative building lease	60,000	510,000
Marketing Department:		
Marketing wages and salaries	250,000	
Selling expenses	50,000	300,000
Total overhead costs		$1,850,000

*Shipping costs can be traced directly to customer orders.

Classic Brass all of these costs are considered to be "overhead" and will be assigned to cost objects where appropriate.

One of these overhead costs—shipping—can be traced directly to customer orders. Classic Brass is directly billed for each customer order it ships, so it is easy to trace these costs to the customer orders. Customers do not pay these actual shipping costs; instead they pay a standard shipping charge that can differ substantially from the actual bill that Classic Brass receives from the freight company.

No other overhead costs can be directly traced to products, customer orders, or customers. Consequently, the remainder of the overhead costs are assigned to cost objects using the ABC system.

IN BUSINESS

THE VIRTUAL BAKERY

Super Bakery, Inc., founded by former Pittsburgh Steelers running back Franco Harris, supplies donuts and other baked goods to schools, hospitals, and other institutions. The company is a virtual corporation—only the core, strategic functions of the business are performed inside the company. The remaining support activities are outsourced to a network of external companies. Super Bakery's products are sold by independent brokers, and the company contracts out baking, warehousing, and shipping. What does Super Bakery itself do? The company's master baker develops products, and the company formulates and produces its own dry mixes from ingredients it has purchased. The contracted bakeries simply add water to the mix and follow the baking instructions. Super Bakery maintains four regional sales managers, and a small office staff processes orders and handles bookkeeping and accounting.

As much as possible, actual costs are traced to individual customer accounts. The remaining costs of the company are assigned to customer accounts using the following activity cost pools and activity measures:

Activity Cost Pool	Activity Measure
Advertising, trade shows, and bonds	Projected number of cases sold
Order department	Number of orders
Sales management	Time spent in each sales territory
Research and development (R&D)	Hours of R&D for each product line

Since the independent sales brokers are paid a flat 5% commission on sales, they have little incentive to make sure that the sales are actually profitable to Super Bakery. To make sales, brokers tend to heavily discount prices. Consequently, Super Bakery's regional sales managers must approve all price discounts and they use the ABC data to evaluate the profitability of the deals proposed by the brokers.

Source: Tim R. V. Davis and Bruce L. Darling, "ABC in a Virtual Corporation," *Management Accounting*, October 1996, pp. 18–26.

Step 3: Assign Costs to Activity Cost Pools

LEARNING OBJECTIVE 2
Assign costs to cost pools using a first-stage allocation.

Most overhead costs are classified in a company's general ledger according to the departments in which they are incurred. For example, salaries, supplies, rent, and so forth incurred by the marketing department are charged to that department. In some cases, some or all of these costs can be directly traced to one of the activity cost pools in the ABC system—the third step in implementing activity-based costing. For example, if the ABC system has an activity called *purchase order processing*, then all of the costs of the purchasing department could probably be traced to that activity. To the extent possible, costs should be traced directly to activity cost pools. However, it is quite common for an overhead department to be involved in several of the activities that are tracked in the ABC system. In such situations, the costs of the department are divided among the activity cost pools via an allocation process called *first-stage allocation.* The **first-stage allocation** in an ABC system is the process by which overhead costs are assigned to activity cost pools.

In the case of Classic Brass, its shipping costs can be directly traced to customer orders (as noted in Exhibit 8–2). However, first-stage allocations will need to be performed for the remaining nine types of overhead costs shown in Exhibit 8–2. First-stage allocations are usually based on the results of interviews with employees who have first-hand knowledge of the activities. For example, Classic Brass needs to allocate $500,000 of indirect factory wages to its five activity cost pools. These allocations will be more accurate if the employees who are classified as indirect factory workers (e.g., supervisors, engineers, and quality inspectors) are asked to estimate what percentage of their time is spent dealing with customer orders, with product design, with processing units of product (i.e., order size), and with customer relations. These interviews are conducted with considerable care. Those who are interviewed must thoroughly understand what the activities encompass and what is expected of them in the interview. In addition, departmental managers are typically interviewed to determine how the nonpersonnel costs should be distributed across the activity cost pools. For example, the Classic Brass production manager would be interviewed to determine how the $300,000 of factory equipment depreciation (shown in Exhibit 8–2) should be allocated to the activity cost pools. The key question that the production manager would need to answer is "What percentage of the available machine capacity is consumed by each activity such as the number of customer orders or the number of units processed (i.e., size of orders)?"

The results of the interviews at Classic Brass are displayed in Exhibit 8–3. For example, factory equipment depreciation is distributed 20% to Customer Orders, 60% to Order Size, and 20% to the Other cost pool. The resource in this instance is machine time. According to the estimate made by the production manager, 60% of the total available time was used to actually process units to fill orders. Each customer order requires setting up, which also requires machine time. This activity consumes 20% of the total available machine time and is entered under the Customer Orders column. The remaining 20% of available machine time represents idle time and is entered under the Other column.

Exhibit 8–3 and many of the other exhibits in this chapter are presented in the form of Excel spreadsheets. All of the calculations required in activity-based costing can be done by hand. Nevertheless, setting up the activity-based costing system on a spreadsheet or using special ABC software can save a lot of work—particularly in situations involving many activity cost pools and in organizations that periodically update their ABC systems.

We will not go into the details of how all of the percentages in Exhibit 8–3 were determined. However, note that 100% of the factory building lease has been assigned to the Other cost pool. Classic Brass has a single production facility. It has no plans to expand or to sublease any excess space. The cost of this production facility is treated as an organization-sustaining cost since there is no way to avoid even a portion of this cost if a particular product or customer were to be dropped. (Remember that organization-sustaining costs are assigned to the Other cost pool and are not allocated to products.) In contrast, some companies have separate facilities for manufacturing specific products. The costs of these separate facilities could be directly traced to the specific products.

Topic Tackler PLUS

8–2

Once the percentage distributions in Exhibit 8–3 have been established, it is easy to allocate costs to the activity cost pools. The results of this first-stage allocation are displayed in Exhibit 8–4. Each cost is allocated across the activity cost pools by multiplying it by the percentages in Exhibit 8–3. For example, the indirect factory wages of $500,000 are multiplied by the 25% entry under Customer Orders in Exhibit 8–3 to arrive at the $125,000 entry under Customer Orders in Exhibit 8–4. Similarly, the indirect factory wages of $500,000 are multiplied by the 40% entry under Product Design in Exhibit 8–3 to arrive at the $200,000 entry under Product Design in Exhibit 8–4. All of the entries in Exhibit 8–4 are computed in this way.

LEARNING OBJECTIVE 3
Compute activity rates for cost pools.

EXHIBIT 8–3
Results of Interviews: Distribution of Resource Consumption across Activity Cost Pools

Microsoft Excel - ABC model-Classic Brass.XLS

	Activity Cost Pools					
	Customer Orders	Product Design	Order Size	Customer Relations	Other	Totals
Production Department:						
Indirect factory wages	25%	40%	20%	10%	5%	100%
Factory equipment depreciation	20%	0%	60%	0%	20%	100%
Factory utilities	0%	10%	50%	0%	40%	100%
Factory building lease	0%	0%	0%	0%	100%	100%
Shipping costs*	NA	NA	NA	NA	NA	NA
General Administrative Department:						
Administrative wages and salaries	15%	5%	10%	30%	40%	100%
Office equipment depreciation	30%	0%	0%	25%	45%	100%
Administrative building lease	0%	0%	0%	0%	100%	100%
Marketing Department:						
Marketing wages and salaries	20%	10%	0%	60%	10%	100%
Selling expenses	10%	0%	0%	70%	20%	100%

*Shipping costs are not included in this and subsequent tables because they are directly traced to customer orders rather than being allocated using the ABC system. NA = Not applicable.

EXHIBIT 8–4
First-Stage Allocations to Activity Cost Pools

Microsoft Excel - ABC model-Classic Brass.XLS

	Activity Cost Pools					
	Customer Orders	Product Design	Order Size	Customer Relations	Other	Totals
Production Department:						
Indirect factory wages	$ 125,000	$ 200,000	$ 100,000	$ 50,000	$ 25,000	$ 500,000
Factory equipment depreciation	60,000	0	180,000	0	60,000	300,000
Factory utilities	0	12,000	60,000	0	48,000	120,000
Factory building lease	0	0	0	0	80,000	80,000
General Administrative Department:						
Administrative wages and salaries	60,000	20,000	40,000	120,000	160,000	400,000
Office equipment depreciation	15,000	0	0	12,500	22,500	50,000
Administrative building lease	0	0	0	0	60,000	60,000
Marketing Department:						
Marketing wages and salaries	50,000	25,000	0	150,000	25,000	250,000
Selling expenses	5,000	0	0	35,000	10,000	50,000
Total	$ 315,000	$ 257,000	$ 380,000	$ 367,500	$ 490,500	$ 1,810,000

Exhibit 8–3 shows that Customer Orders consume 25% of the resources represented by the $500,000 of indirect factory wages.

25% × $500,000 = $125,000

Other entries in the table are computed in a similar fashion.

Now that the first-stage allocations to the activity cost pools have been completed, the fourth step is to compute the activity rates.

Step 4: Calculate Activity Rates

The activity rates that will be used for assigning overhead costs to products and customers are computed in Exhibit 8–5. The ABC team determined the total activity for each cost pool that would be required to produce the company's present product mix and to serve its present customers. These numbers are listed in Exhibit 8–5. For example, the ABC team found that 200 new product designs are required each year to serve the company's present customers. The activity rates are computed by dividing the *total* cost for each activity by its *total* activity. For example, the $315,000 total annual cost for the Customer Orders cost pool is divided by the total of 1,000 customer orders per year to arrive at the activity rate of $315 per customer order. Similarly, the $257,000 *total* cost for the Product Design cost pool is divided by the *total* number of designs (i.e., 200 product designs) to determine the activity rate of $1,285 per design. Note that activity rates are not computed for the *Other* category of costs. This is because the Other cost pool consists of organization-sustaining costs and costs of idle capacity that are not allocated to products and customers. Overall profits must be large enough to cover these unallocated costs. Also note that the activity rates represent *average* costs. For example, the average cost of a customer order is $315.

The entries in Exhibit 8–5 indicate that *on average* a customer order consumes resources that cost $315; a product design consumes resources that cost $1,285; a unit of product consumes resources that cost $19 per machine-hour; and maintaining relations with a customer consumes resources that cost $3,675. Note that these are *average* figures. Some members of the ABC design team at Classic Brass argued that it would be unfair to charge all new products the same $1,285 product design cost regardless of how much design time they actually require. After discussing the pros and cons, the team concluded that it would not be worth the effort at the present time to keep track of actual design time spent on each new product. They felt that the benefits of increased accuracy would not be great enough to justify the higher cost of implementing and maintaining the more detailed costing system. Similarly, some team members were uncomfortable assigning the same $3,675

EXHIBIT 8–5
Computation of Activity Rates

Microsoft Excel - ABC model-Classic Brass.XLS

Activity Cost Pools	(a) Total Cost*	(b) Total Activity		(a) ÷ (b) Activity Rate	
Customer orders	$315,000	1,000	orders	$315	per order
Product design	$257,000	200	designs	$1,285	per design
Order size	$380,000	20,000	MHs	$19	per MH
Customer relations	$367,500	100	customers	$3,675	per customer
Other	$490,500	Not applicable		Not applicable	

*From Exhibit 8-4.

EXHIBIT 8–6
The Activity-Based Costing Model at Classic Brass

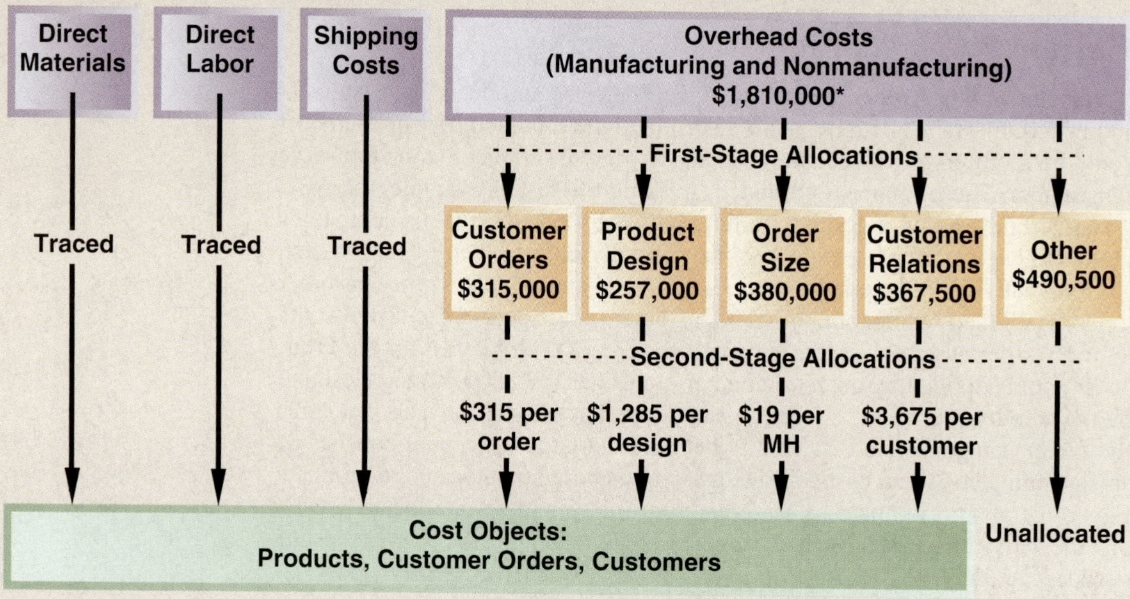

* Total overhead cost of $1,850,000 less $40,000 of shipping costs directly traced to customer orders.

cost to each customer. Some customers are undemanding—ordering standard products well in advance of their needs. Others are very demanding and consume large amounts of marketing and administrative staff time. These are generally customers who order customized products, who tend to order at the last minute, and who change their minds. While everyone agreed with this observation, the data that would be required to measure individual customers' demands on resources was not currently available. Rather than delay implementation of the ABC system, the team decided to defer such refinements to a later date.

LEARNING OBJECTIVE 4
Assign costs to a cost object using a second-stage allocation.

Before proceeding further, it would be helpful to get a better idea of the overall process of assigning costs to products and other cost objects in an ABC system. Exhibit 8–6 provides a visual perspective of the ABC system at Classic Brass. We recommend that you carefully go over this exhibit. In particular, note that the Other category, which contains organization-sustaining costs and costs of idle capacity, is not allocated to products or customers.

Step 5: Assign Costs to Cost Objects

The fifth step in the implementation of activity-based costing is called *second-stage allocation.* In the **second-stage allocation,** activity rates are used to apply costs to products and customers. At Classic Brass, the ABC system might be used to apply activity costs to all of the company's products, customer orders, and customers. For purposes of illustration, we will consider only one customer—Windward Yachts. This customer ordered two different products—stanchions and a compass housing. The stanchions are a standard product that does not require any design work. In contrast, the compass housing is a custom product that requires extensive designing. Data concerning these two products appear in Exhibit 8–7. Direct materials and direct labor costs are the same under the traditional cost accounting system and the ABC system. However, the two systems handle overhead very differently.

The overhead calculations for the stanchions and compass housings are carried out in Exhibit 8–8. Let's examine the ABC overhead calculations for the stanchions. For each activity cost pool, the amount of activity required by the product is multiplied by the activity rate to arrive at the amount of overhead cost applied to the product. For

EXHIBIT 8–7
Data Concerning the Products Ordered by Windward Yachts

Standard Stanchions

1. This is a standard design that does not require any new design resources.
2. Four hundred units were ordered during the year, comprising two separate orders.
3. Each stanchion required 0.5 machine-hours, for a total of 200 machine-hours.
4. The selling price per unit was $34, for a total of $13,600.
5. Direct materials for 400 units totaled $2,110.
6. Direct labor for 400 units totaled $1,850.
7. Shipping costs for the two orders totaled $180.

Custom Compass Housing

1. This is a custom product that requires new design resources.
2. There was only one order for a single unit during the year.
3. The compass housing required 4 machine-hours.
4. The selling price was $650.
5. Direct materials were $13.
6. Direct labor was $50.
7. Shipping costs were $25.

EXHIBIT 8–8
Computation of Overhead Costs

Overhead Cost for the Standard Stanchions

Activity Cost Pools	*(a) Activity Rate**		*(b) Activity***		*(a) × (b) ABC Cost*
Customer orders	$315	per order	2	orders	$630
Product design	$1,285	per design	0	designs	$0
Order size	$19	per MH	200	MHs	$3,800
Customer relations	$3,675	per customer	Not applicable		

Overhead Cost for the Custom Compass Housing

Activity Cost Pools	*(a) Activity Rate**		*(b) Activity***		*(a) × (b) ABC Cost*
Customer orders	$315	per order	1	order	$315
Product design	$1,285	per design	1	design	$1,285
Order size	$19	per MH	4	MHs	$76
Customer relations	$3,675	per customer	Not applicable		

*From Exhibit 8-5.
**From Exhibit 8-7.

example, since the stanchions involve 2 orders and the activity rate is $315 per order, the total Customer Order cost applied to the stanchions is $630 (2 × $315). Because the stanchion is a standard product that does not require a new design, no Product Design costs are assigned to this product. Also note that none of the Customer Relations costs have been allocated to the stanchions. A customer-level cost is assigned to customers directly; it is not assigned to products. Note how this procedure for assigning overhead costs differs from traditional costing. Instead of just a single overhead cost pool and a single predetermined overhead rate based on direct labor or machine-hours, now several cost pools and predetermined overhead rates are used to assign costs.

LEARNING OBJECTIVE 5
Prepare a report showing activity-based costing margins from an activity view.

The same procedure is followed in Exhibit 8–8 to determine the overhead cost for the custom compass housing.

Step 6: Prepare Management Reports

In Exhibit 8–9, the overhead costs computed in Exhibit 8–8 are combined with direct materials, direct labor, and shipping cost data. For each of the products, these combined costs are deducted from sales to arrive at product margins. Under the ABC system, the stanchions show a profit of $5,030, whereas the compass housing shows a loss of $1,114.

Note from Exhibit 8–9 that the new ABC system also includes a profitability analysis of Windward Yachts, the customer that ordered the stanchions and the custom compass housing. Such customer analyses can be easily accomplished by adding together the product margins for each of the products a customer has ordered and then subtracting the average charge of $3,675 for Customer Relations.

IN BUSINESS

FINDING THAT GOLDEN TOP 20%

According to Meridien Research of Newton, Massachusetts, 20% of a bank's customers generate about 150% of its revenue. At the other end of the spectrum, 30% of a bank's customers drain 50% of its profits. The question becomes how do banks identify which customers are in that golden top 20%? For many banks, the answer is revealed through customer relationship management software that provides activity-based costing capability.

"We had some customers that we thought, on the surface, would be very profitable, with an average of $300,000 in business accounts," said Jerry Williams, chairman and chief executive officer of First Bancorp. "What we didn't pull out was the fact that some write more than 275 checks a month. Once you apply the labor costs, it's not a profitable customer."

Meridien Research estimates that large commercial banks are increasing their spending on customer profitability systems by 14% a year with total annual expenditures exceeding $6 billion dollars.

Source: Joseph McKendrick, "Your Best Customers May Be Different Tomorrow," *Bank Technology News*, July 2001, pp. 1–4.

Comparison of Traditional and ABC Product Costs

Now that the product margins have been computed using activity-based costing, it would be interesting to compare them to the product margins computed using the company's traditional cost system.

Product Margins Computed Using the Traditional Cost System

LEARNING OBJECTIVE 6
Compare product costs computed using traditional and activity-based costing methods.

The costs of the two products ordered by Windward Yachts are computed under the company's traditional cost accounting system in Exhibit 8–10. The company's traditional system uses a plantwide predetermined overhead rate based on machine-hours. Since the total manufacturing overhead cost is $1,000,000 (see Exhibit 8–2) and the total machine time is 20,000 machine-hours (see Exhibit 8–5), the predetermined manufacturing overhead rate for the company is $50 per machine-hour ($1,000,000 ÷ 20,000 machine-hours = $50 per

EXHIBIT 8–9
Product and Customer Margins—Activity-Based Costing System (Activity View)

Product Profitability Analysis

		Standard Stanchions		Custom Compass Housing
Sales (from Exhibit 8-7)		$ 13,600		$ 650
Costs:				
Direct materials (from Exhibit 8-7)	$ 2,110		$ 13	
Direct labor (from Exhibit 8-7)	1,850		50	
Shipping costs (from Exhibit 8-7)	180		25	
Customer orders (from Exhibit 8-8)	630		315	
Product design (from Exhibit 8-8)	0		1,285	
Order size (from Exhibit 8-8)	3,800	8,570	76	1,764
Product margin		$ 5,030		$ (1,114)

Customer Profitability Analysis—Windward Yachts

Product margins of products ordered by Windward Yachts:	
Standard stanchion product margin (see above)	$ 5,030
Custom compass housing product margin (see above)	(1,114)
Total product margins	3,916
Less: Customer relations overhead (from Exhibit 8-5)	3,675
Customer margin	$ 241

machine-hour). From Exhibit 8–10, we see that when this predetermined manufacturing overhead rate is used to determine product costs, the stanchions show a loss of $360, whereas the compass housing shows a profit of $387.

The Differences between ABC and Traditional Product Costs

The costs of the products under the ABC system are dramatically different from the costs computed using the traditional costing system. The stanchions, which looked unprofitable under the traditional cost system, appear to be very profitable under the ABC system in

EXHIBIT 8–10
Product Margins—Traditional Cost Accounting System

		Standard Stanchions		Custom Compass Housing
Sales (from Exhibit 8–7)		$13,600		$650
Costs:				
Direct materials (from Exhibit 8–7)	$ 2,110		$ 13	
Direct labor (from Exhibit 8–7)	1,850		50	
Manufacturing overhead (see below)	10,000	13,960	200	263
Product margin*		$ (360)		$387

In the traditional costing system used at Classic Brass, manufacturing overhead is applied based on machine-hours. The predetermined rate is $50 per machine-hour, determined as follows:

$$\text{Predetermined manufacturing overhead rate} = \frac{\text{Total estimated manufacturing overhead}}{\text{Total estimated machine-hours}}$$

$$= \frac{\$1{,}000{,}000}{20{,}000 \text{ machine-hours}} = \$50 \text{ per machine-hour}$$

Referring back to Exhibit 8–7, the standard stanchions require 200 machine-hours in total and the custom compass housing requires 4 machine-hours. Therefore, $10,000 (200 machine-hours × $50 per machine-hour) of manufacturing overhead would be charged to the standard stanchions and $200 (4 machine-hours × $50 per machine-hour) to the custom compass housing.

*In a traditional costing system, the product margins do not include any nonmanufacturing costs such as shipping costs.

Exhibit 8–9. And the compass housing, which looked profitable under the traditional cost system, appears to be unprofitable under the ABC system.

There are two major reasons for these changes in apparent profitability. First, under the traditional cost system the costs of designing products were spread across all products without regard to whether they actually required design work. Under the ABC system, these costs are assigned only to products that actually require design work. Consequently, under the ABC system, design costs have been shifted from standard products like stanchions, which do not require any design work, to custom products like the compass housing.

Second, the Customer Orders costs, which are batch-level costs, were applied on the basis of machine-hours, a unit-level base, under the traditional cost system. This resulted in high-volume products absorbing the bulk of these batch-level costs even though they caused no more of these costs than low-volume products that were ordered as frequently. Under the ABC system, these batch-level costs are assigned as a lump-sum to each customer order. Consequently, the ABC system shifts these costs from high-volume orders like the stanchions to low-volume orders like the compass housing.

When batch-level or product-level costs are present, activity-based costing will ordinarily shift costs from high-volume products produced in large batches to low-volume products produced in small batches. This cost shifting will usually have a greater impact on the *per unit* costs of low-volume products than on the per unit costs of high-volume products. For example, suppose that a total of $100 in batch-level cost is shifted from a high-volume, 100-unit product to a low-volume, 1-unit product. This shifting of cost will decrease the cost of the high-volume product by $1 per unit, on average, but will increase the cost of the low-volume product by $100 for the single unit. In sum, implementing activity-based costing will typically shift costs from high-volume to low-volume products, but the effects will be much more dramatic on the per unit costs of the low-volume products. The per unit costs of the low-volume products will increase far more than the per unit costs of the high-volume products will decrease.

It is important to remember another major difference between the costs of products as computed under the ABC system at Classic Brass and product costs as computed under the traditional cost system. Under a traditional system, only manufacturing costs are assigned to products. Under the ABC system at Classic Brass, nonmanufacturing costs are assigned to products as well as the manufacturing costs. In addition, the organization-sustaining manufacturing costs and the costs of idle capacity are *not* assigned to products under the ABC system, whereas they *are* assigned to products under the traditional costing system. For these reasons, the term *product cost* in this chapter has a different meaning than it had in Chapters 2, 3, and 4. In the context of an ABC system like the one implemented at Classic Brass, product costs include the costs of *all* resources consumed by the product, whether they are manufacturing costs or not.

IN BUSINESS

COSTING CAN BE A GRIM BUSINESS

The Hospice of Central Kentucky (HCK) provides all medical needs to terminally ill patients so that patients can be at home with their families during their last days. HCK was being squeezed by increasing costs, without any compensating increases in reimbursements from insurance companies. As the first step in negotiating a better reimbursement plan, management decided to use ABC to get a better understanding of its costs. The following activity rates were computed:

Activity Cost Pool	Total Cost	Total Activity	Activity Rate
Prereferral	$ 24,611	74 referrals*	$332.58 per referral
Referral	10,873	74 referrals*	$146.93 per referral
Admission	1,960	46 admissions	$42.61 per admission
Post-admission	3,649	46 admissions	$79.33 per admission
Post-death	1,476	46 deaths	$32.09 per death
Bereavement	12,670	46 deaths	$275.43 per death
Medical services	5,588	2,080 service calls	$2.69 per service call
Reception	8,597	3,200 calls	$2.69 per call
Accounting/finance . . .	13,566	5,553 patient-days*	$2.44 per patient-day
Management	17,107	5,553 patient-days*	$3.08 per patient-day
Information systems . .	6,191	5,553 patient-days*	$1.11 per patient-day
Billing	2,899	192 billings	$15.10 per billing
Volunteer services . . .	3,378	75 volunteers	$45.04 per volunteer
Total	$112,565		

*Referrals and patient-days are weighted by the stage of the disease. For example, the actual number of patient-days is 3,593, but a day for a patient whose death is imminent is counted as equivalent to three patient-days for a patient in slow decline due to the more intensive care such patients receive.

The ABC system was then used to estimate the average cost per patient-day for patients in various stages of their diseases:

Stage of Disease	Cost per Patient-Day
Slow decline	$27.39
Rapid decline	$29.84
Imminent death	$62.88
Death	$381.57

This was a definite eye-opener for the hospice's management. The hospice's old cost system did not distinguish between costs at various stages of a disease and indeed would have given an answer of a flat $31.33 per patient-day ($112,565 ÷ 3,593 unweighted patient-days), regardless of the stage of the disease. This new information helped management to negotiate more favorable reimbursement rates from insurance companies.

Source: Sidney J. Baxendale and Victoria Dornbusch, "Activity-Based Costing for a Hospice," *Strategic Finance*, March 2000, pp. 65–70. Reprinted with permission from the IMA, Montvale, NJ, USA, www.imanet.org.

MANAGERIAL ACCOUNTING IN ACTION
The Wrap-Up

classic brass inc.

The ABC design team presented the results of its work in a meeting attended by all of the top managers of Classic Brass, including the president John Towers, the production manager Susan Richter, the marketing manager Tom Olafson, and the accounting manager Mary Goodman. The ABC team brought with them copies of the chart showing the ABC design (Exhibit 8–6), the tables showing the product margins for the stanchions and compass housing under the company's old cost accounting system (Exhibit 8–10), and the tables showing the ABC analysis of the same products (Exhibit 8–9). After the formal presentation by the ABC team, the following discussion took place:

John: I would like to personally thank the ABC team for all of the work they have done and for an extremely interesting presentation. I am now beginning to wonder about a lot of the decisions we have made in the past using our old cost accounting system.

Mary: I hope I don't have to remind anyone that I have been warning everyone for quite some time about this problem.

John: No, you don't have to remind us, Mary. I guess we just didn't understand the problem before.

John: Tom, why did we accept this order for standard stanchions in the first place if our old cost accounting system was telling us it was a big money loser?

Tom: Windward Yachts, the company that ordered the stanchions, has asked us to do a lot of custom work like the compass housing in the past. To get that work, we felt we had to accept their orders for money-losing standard products.

John: According to this ABC analysis, we had it all backwards. We are losing money on the custom products and making a fistful on the standard products.

Susan: I never did believe we were making a lot of money on the custom jobs. You ought to see all of the problems they create for us in production.

Tom: I hate to admit it, but the custom jobs always seem to give us headaches in marketing, too.

John: Why don't we just stop soliciting custom work? This seems like a no-brainer to me. If we are losing money on custom jobs like the compass housing, why not suggest to our customers that they go elsewhere for that kind of work?

Tom: Wait a minute, we would lose a lot of sales.

Susan: So what, we would save a lot more costs.

Mary: Maybe yes, maybe no. Some of the costs would not disappear if we were to drop all of those products.

Tom: Like what?

Mary: Well Tom, part of your salary is included in the costs of the ABC model.

Tom: Where? I don't see anything listed that looks like my salary.

Mary: Tom, when the ABC team interviewed you they asked you what percentage of your time was spent in handling customer orders and how much was spent dealing with new product design issues. Am I correct?

Tom: Sure, but what's the point?

Mary: I believe you said that about 10% of your time is spent dealing with new products. As a consequence, 10% of your salary was allocated to the Product Design cost pool. If we were to drop all of the products requiring design work, would you be willing to take a 10% pay cut?

Tom: I trust you're joking.

Mary: Do you see the problem? Just because 10% of your time is spent on custom products doesn't mean that the company would save 10% of your salary if the custom products were dropped. Before we take a drastic action like dropping the custom products, we should identify which costs are really relevant.

John: I think I see what you are driving at. We wouldn't want to drop a lot of products only to find that our costs really haven't changed much. It is true that dropping the products would free up resources like Tom's time, but we had better be sure we have some good use for those resources *before* we take such an action.

As this discussion among the managers of Classic Brass illustrates, caution should be exercised before taking an action based on an ABC analysis such as the one in Exhibit

8–9. The product and customer margins computed in that exhibit are a useful starting point for further analysis, but managers need to know what costs are really affected before taking any action such as dropping a product or customer or changing the prices of products or services. The appendix to this chapter shows how an *action analysis report* can be constructed to help managers make such decisions. An **action analysis report** provides more detail about costs and how they might adjust to changes in activity than the ABC analysis presented in Exhibit 8–9.

IN BUSINESS

CULLING THE CUSTOMER LIST

FedEx is now classifying its customers as the good, the bad, and the ugly based on their profitability. "At FedEx, customers who spend a lot with little service and marketing investment get different treatment than, say, those who spend just as much but cost more to keep. The 'good' can expect a phone call if their shipping volume falters, which can head off defections before they occur. As for the 'bad'—those who spend but are expensive to the company—FedEx is turning them into profitable customers, in many cases, by charging higher shipping prices. And the 'ugly'? . . . 'We just don't market to them anymore.'"

Source: Paul C. Judge, "What've You Done for Us Lately?" *Business Week*, September 14, 1998, pp. 137–146.

Targeting Process Improvements

Activity-based costing can be used to identify areas that would benefit from process improvements. Indeed, managers often cite this as the major benefit of activity-based costing.[4] **Activity-based management (ABM)** is used in conjunction with activity-based costing to improve processes and reduce costs. Activity-based management is used in organizations as diverse as manufacturing companies, hospitals, and the U.S. Marine Corps.[5] When "forty percent of the cost of running a hospital involves storing, collecting and moving information," there is obviously a great deal of room for eliminating waste and for improvement.[6]

The first step in any improvement program is to decide what to improve. The Theory of Constraints approach discussed in Chapter 1 is a powerful tool for targeting the area in an organization whose improvement will yield the greatest benefit. Activity-based management provides another approach. The activity rates computed in activity-based costing can provide valuable clues concerning where there is waste and the opportunity for improvement in an organization. For example, managers at Classic Brass were surprised at the high cost of customer orders. Some customer orders are for less than $100 worth of products, and yet it costs, on average, $315 to process an order according to the activity rates calculated in Exhibit 8–5. This seemed very expensive for an activity that adds no value to the product. As a consequence, the customer order processing activity was targeted for improvement using TQM and process reengineering as discussed in Chapter 1.

Benchmarking provides a systematic approach to identifying the activities with the greatest room for improvement. For example, the Marketing Resources Group of US WEST, a telephone company owned by Qwest, performed an ABC analysis of the

4 Dan Swenson, "The Benefits of Activity-Based Cost Management to the Manufacturing Industry," *Journal of Management Accounting Research* 7, pp. 168–180.

5 Julian Freeman, "Marines Embrace Continuous Improvement: Highlight of CAM-I's Meeting," *Management Accounting*, February 1997, p. 64.

6 Kambiz Foroohar, "Rx: Software," *Forbes*, April 7, 1997, p. 114.

activities carried out in the Accounting Department.[7] Managers computed the activity rates for the activities of the Accounting Department and then compared these rates to the costs of carrying out the same activities in other companies. Two benchmarks were used: (1) a sample of FORTUNE 100 companies, which are the largest 100 companies in the United States; and (2) a sample of "world-class" companies that had been identified by a consultant as having the best accounting practices in the world. These comparisons appear below:

Activity	Activity Measure	US WEST Cost	FORTUNE 100 Benchmark	World-Class Benchmark
Processing accounts receivable	Number of invoices processed	$3.80 per invoice	$15.00 per invoice	$4.60 per invoice
Processing accounts payable	Number of invoices processed	$8.90 per invoice	$7.00 per invoice	$1.80 per invoice
Processing payroll checks	Number of checks processed	$7.30 per check	$5.00 per check	$1.72 per check
Managing customer credit	Number of customer accounts	$12.00 per account	$16.00 per account	$5.60 per account

It is clear from this analysis that US WEST does a good job of processing accounts receivable. Its average cost per invoice is $3.80, whereas the cost in other companies that are considered world class is even higher—$4.60 per invoice. On the other hand, the cost of processing payroll checks is significantly higher at US WEST than at benchmark companies. The cost per payroll check at US WEST is $7.30 versus $5.00 at FORTUNE 100 companies and $1.72 at world-class companies. This suggests that it may be possible to wring some waste out of this activity using TQM, process reengineering, or some other method.

IN BUSINESS

COSTS IN HEALTH CARE

Owens & Minor, a $3 billion medical supplies distributor, offers an activity-based billing option to its customers. Instead of charging a fixed amount for items that are ordered by customers, the charges are based on activities required to fill the order as well as on the cost of the item ordered. For example, Owens & Minor charges extra for weekend deliveries. These charges encourage customers to reduce their weekend delivery requests. This results in decreased costs for Owens & Minor, which can then be passed on to customers in the form of lower charges for the specific items that are ordered. As many as 25% of Owens & Minor's 4,000 health care customers have used this billing option to identify and realize cost reduction opportunities. For example, Bill Wright of Sutter Health in Sacramento, California, said that Owens & Minor's activity-based billing has motivated his company to eliminate weekend deliveries, place more items per order, align purchase quantities with prepackaged specifications, and transmit orders electronically. The end result is that one Sutter affiliate decreased its purchasing costs from 4.25% of product costs to 3.75%. In all, Owens & Minor has identified about 250 activity-driven procurement costs that hospitals can manage more efficiently to reduce costs.

Source: Todd Shields, "Hospitals Turning to Activity-Based Costing to Save and Measure Distribution Costs," *Healthcare Purchasing News*, November 2001, pp. 14–15.

[7] Steve Coburn, Hugh Grove, and Cynthia Fukami, "Benchmarking with ABCM," *Management Accounting*, January 1995, pp. 56–60.

IN BUSINESS

DISCIPLINING THE SOFTWARE DEVELOPMENT PROCESS

Tata Consultancy Services (TCS) of India is the largest consulting organization in India, serving both Indian and international clients. The company used activity-based management to identify problem areas in its software development business. An early finding was that "quality assurance, testing, and error correction activities made up a significant chunk of the overall effort required to build a system, and this cost had to be kept under control to improve productivity and profitability." The company already had in place a Quality Management System that helped identify the types of errors that were occurring and the corrective action that would be required, but no costs were attached to these errors and actions. The activity-based management system provided this cost information, which allowed managers to set better priorities and to monitor the costs of error-detection and error-correction activities.

As another example of the usefulness of the system, 54 person-days in one software development project at TCS were charged to the activity "Waiting for client feedback"—a non-value-added activity. Investigation revealed that the client was taking a long time to review the Graphical User Interface (GUI) designed by TCS. The client was showing the GUI to various end users—often resulting in contradictory suggestions. The solution was to draw up guidelines for the GUI with the client, which were enforced. "As a result of this corrective action, subsequent client feedback was well within the time schedule. Most of our screens were accepted because they conformed to standards. . . ."

Source: Maha S. Mahalingam, Bala V. Balachandran, and Farooq C. Kohli, "Activity-Based Management for Systems Consulting Industry," *Journal of Cost Management*, May/June 1999, pp. 4–15.

Activity-Based Costing and External Reports

Since activity-based costing generally provides more accurate product costs than traditional costing methods, why isn't it used for external reports? Some companies *do* use activity-based costing in their external reports, but most do not. There are a number of reasons for this. First, external reports are less detailed than internal reports prepared for decision making. On the external reports, individual product costs are not reported. Cost of goods sold and inventory valuations are disclosed, but these accounts are not broken down by product. If some products are undercosted and some are overcosted, the errors tend to cancel each other when the product costs are added together.

Second, it is often very difficult to make changes in a company's accounting system. The official cost accounting systems in most large companies are usually embedded in complex computer programs that have been modified in-house over the course of many years. It is extremely difficult to make changes in such computer programs without causing numerous bugs.

Third, an ABC system such as the one described in this chapter does not conform to generally accepted accounting principles (GAAP). As discussed in Chapter 2, product costs computed for external reports must include all of the manufacturing costs and only manufacturing costs; but in an ABC system as described in this chapter, product costs exclude some manufacturing costs and include some nonmanufacturing costs. It is possible to adjust the ABC data at the end of the period to conform to GAAP, but that requires more work.

Fourth, auditors are likely to be uncomfortable with allocations that are based on interviews with the company's personnel. Such subjective data can be easily manipulated by management to make earnings and other key variables look more favorable.

For all of these reasons, most companies confine their ABC efforts to special studies for management, and they do not attempt to integrate activity-based costing into their formal cost accounting systems.

The Limitations of Activity-Based Costing

Implementing an activity-based costing system is a major project that requires substantial resources. And once implemented, an activity-based costing system is more costly to maintain than a traditional costing system—data concerning numerous activity measures must be periodically collected, checked, and entered into the system. The benefits of increased accuracy may not outweigh these costs.

Activity-based costing produces numbers, such as product margins, that are at odds with the numbers produced by traditional costing systems. But managers are accustomed to using traditional costing systems to run their operations and traditional costing systems are often used in performance evaluations. Essentially, activity-based costing changes the rules of the game. It is a fact of human nature that changes in organizations, particularly those that alter the rules of the game, inevitably face resistance. This underscores the importance of top management support and the full participation of line managers, as well as the accounting staff, in any activity-based costing initiative. If activity-based costing is viewed as an accounting initiative that does not have the full support of top management, it is doomed to failure.

In practice, most managers insist on fully allocating all costs to products, customers, and other costing objects in an activity-based costing system—including the costs of idle capacity and organization-sustaining costs. This results in overstated costs and understated margins and mistakes in pricing and other critical decisions.

Activity-based costing data can easily be misinterpreted and must be used with care when used in making decisions. Costs assigned to products, customers, and other cost objects are only *potentially* relevant. Before making any significant decisions using activity-based costing data, managers must identify which costs are really relevant for the decision at hand. See the appendix to this chapter for more details.

As discussed in the previous section, reports generated by the best activity-based costing systems do not conform to generally accepted accounting principles. Consequently, an organization involved in activity-based costing should have two cost systems—one for internal use and one for preparing external reports. This is costlier than maintaining just one system and may cause confusion about which system is to be believed and relied on.

IN BUSINESS

SOMETIMES ABC ISN'T THE BEST SOLUTION

Bertch Cabinet Mfg., Inc., makes high-quality wooden cabinets, marble tops, and mirrors for bathrooms and kitchens. The company experimented with activity-based costing (ABC) but found that it was too difficult to set up and maintain such a complex costing system. For example, 21 separate operations are required to make a single raised panel cabinet door. The costs of keeping track of each of these operations would far exceed any conceivable benefit. Instead of building a complex ABC system, Bertch Cabinet adopted a variation of variable costing that is used in the Theory of Constraints. This simpler system required far less effort to build and maintain, and it was much easier to understand. In the Bertch Cabinet Mfg. variable costing system, 70% of the direct labor cost was classified as variable and the rest as fixed.

Source: John B. MacArthur, "From Activity-Based Costing to Throughput Accounting," *Management Accounting*, April 1996, pp. 30–38.

IN BUSINESS

THE SURVEY SAYS . . .

Professors John Innes, Falconer Mitchell, and Donald Sinclair have conducted two surveys designed to study ABC adoption trends within the United Kingdom across a five-year time span. The professors' initial survey results are based on responses from 352 of the U.K.'s largest companies, while the follow-up survey results obtained five years later are based on responses from 177 of the U.K.'s largest companies.

The initial survey results indicated that 21% of respondents were currently using ABC, 29.6% were considering ABC adoption, 13.3% had rejected ABC after considering its implementation, and 36.1% were not considering ABC. Five years later the follow-up survey showed that 17.5% of respondents were currently using ABC, 20.3% were considering ABC adoption, 15.3% had rejected ABC after considering implementation, and 46.9% were not considering ABC. The professors summarized their findings by saying "These results are indicative of no growth in the popularity of ABC, and are consistent with both a leveling off in interest in it and the adoption of it over this five-year period."

Source: John Innes, Falconer Mitchell, and Donald Sinclair, "Activity-Based Costing in the U.K.'s Largest Companies: A Comparison of 1994 and 1999 Survey Results," *Management Accounting Research*, September 2000, pp. 349–362.

Summary

Traditional cost accounting methods suffer from several defects that can result in distorted costs for decision-making purposes. All manufacturing costs—even those that are not caused by any specific product—are allocated to products. And nonmanufacturing costs that are caused by products are not assigned to products. Traditional methods also allocate the costs of idle capacity to products. In effect, products are charged for resources that they don't use. And finally, traditional methods tend to place too much reliance on unit-level allocation bases such as direct labor and machine-hours. This results in overcosting high-volume products and undercosting low-volume products and can lead to mistakes when making decisions.

Activity-based costing estimates the costs of the resources consumed by cost objects such as products and customers. The activity-based costing approach assumes that cost objects generate activities that in turn consume costly resources. Activities form the link between costs and cost objects. Activity-based costing is concerned with overhead—both manufacturing overhead and selling and administrative overhead. The accounting for direct labor and direct materials is usually the same under traditional and ABC costing methods.

To build an ABC system, companies typically choose a small set of activities that summarize much of the work performed in overhead departments. Associated with each activity is an activity cost pool. To the extent possible, overhead costs are directly traced to these activity cost pools. The remaining overhead costs are allocated to the activity cost pools in the first-stage allocation. Interviews with managers often form the basis for these allocations.

An activity rate is computed for each cost pool by dividing the costs assigned to the cost pool by the measure of activity for the cost pool. Activity rates provide useful information to managers concerning the costs of performing overhead activities. A particularly high cost for an activity may trigger efforts to improve the way the activity is carried out in the organization.

In the second-stage allocation, the activity rates are used to apply costs to cost objects such as products and customers. The costs computed under activity-based costing are often quite different from the costs generated by a company's traditional cost accounting system. While the ABC system is almost certainly more accurate, managers should nevertheless exercise caution before making decisions based on the ABC data. Some of the costs may not be avoidable and hence would not be relevant.

Review Problem: Activity-Based Costing

Ferris Corporation makes a single product—a fire-resistant commercial filing cabinet—that it sells to office furniture distributors. The company has a simple ABC system that it uses for internal decision making. The company has two overhead departments whose costs are listed below:

Manufacturing overhead	$500,000
Selling and administrative overhead	300,000
Total overhead costs	$800,000

The company's ABC system has the following activity cost pools and activity measures:

Activity Cost Pool	Activity Measure
Assembling units	Number of units
Processing orders	Number of orders
Supporting customers	Number of customers
Other	Not applicable

Costs assigned to the "Other" activity cost pool have no activity measure; they consist of the costs of unused capacity and organization-sustaining costs—neither of which are assigned to products, orders, or customers.

Ferris Corporation distributes the costs of manufacturing overhead and of selling and administrative overhead to the activity cost pools based on employee interviews, the results of which are reported below:

Distribution of Resource Consumption Across Activity Cost Pools					
	Assembling Units	Processing Orders	Supporting Customers	Other	Total
Manufacturing overhead	50%	35%	5%	10%	100%
Selling and administrative overhead	10%	45%	25%	20%	100%
Total activity	1,000 units	250 orders	100 customers		

Required:

1. Perform the first-stage allocation of overhead costs to the activity cost pools as in Exhibit 8–4.
2. Compute activity rates for the activity cost pools as in Exhibit 8–5.
3. OfficeMart is one of Ferris Corporation's customers. Last year, OfficeMart ordered filing cabinets four different times. OfficeMart ordered a total of 80 filing cabinets during the year. Construct a table as in Exhibit 8–8 showing the overhead costs of these 80 units and four orders.
4. The selling price of a filing cabinet is $595. The cost of direct materials is $180 per filing cabinet, and direct labor is $50 per filing cabinet. What is the product margin on the 80 filing cabinets ordered by OfficeMart? How profitable is OfficeMart as a customer? See Exhibit 8–9 for an example of how to complete this report.

Solution to Review Problem

1. The first-stage allocation of costs to the activity cost pools appears below:

	Activity Cost Pools				
	Assembling Units	Processing Orders	Supporting Customers	Other	Total
Manufacturing overhead ...	$250,000	$175,000	$25,000	$50,000	$500,000
Selling and administrative overhead	30,000	135,000	75,000	60,000	300,000
Total cost	$280,000	$310,000	$100,000	$110,000	$800,000

2. The activity rates for the activity cost pools are:

Activity Cost Pools	(a) Total Cost	(b) Total Activity	(a) ÷ (b) Activity Rate
Assembling units	$280,000	1,000 units	$280 per unit
Processing orders	$310,000	250 orders	$1,240 per order
Supporting customers	$100,000	100 customers	$1,000 per customer

3. The overhead cost for the four orders of a total of 80 filing cabinets would be computed as follows:

Activity Cost Pools	(a) Activity Rate	(b) Activity	(a) × (b) ABC Cost
Assembling units	$280 per unit	80 units	$22,400
Processing orders	$1,240 per order	4 orders	$4,960
Supporting customers	$1,000 per customer	Not applicable	

4. The product and customer margins can be computed as follows:

Filing Cabinet Product Margin		
Sales ($595 per unit × 80 units)		$47,600
Cost:		
Direct materials ($180 per unit × 80 units)	$14,400	
Direct labor ($50 per unit × 80 units)	4,000	
Unit-related overhead (above)	22,400	
Order-related overhead (above)	4,960	45,760
Product margin		$ 1,840

Customer Profitability Analysis—OfficeMart	
Product margin (above)	$ 1,840
Less: Customer-related overhead (above)	1,000
Customer margin	$ 840

Glossary

Action analysis report A report showing what costs have been assigned to a cost object, such as a product or customer, and how difficult it would be to adjust the cost if there is a change in activity. (p. 335)

Activity An event that causes the consumption of overhead resources in an organization. (p. 317)

Activity-based costing (ABC) A costing method based on activities that is designed to provide managers with cost information for strategic and other decisions that potentially affect capacity and therefore fixed as well as variable costs. (p. 314)

Activity-based management (ABM) A management approach that focuses on managing activities as a way of eliminating waste and reducing delays and defects. (p. 335)

Activity cost pool A "bucket" in which costs are accumulated that relate to a single activity measure in an activity-based costing system. (p. 322)

Activity measure An allocation base in an activity-based costing system; ideally, a measure of the amount of activity that drives the costs in an activity cost pool. (p. 322)

Batch-level activities Activities that are performed each time a batch of goods is handled or processed, regardless of how many units are in the batch. The amount of resource consumed depends on the number of batches run rather than on the number of units in the batch. (p. 321)

Customer-level activities Activities that are carried out to support customers but that are not related to any specific product. (p. 322)

Duration driver A measure of the amount of time required to perform an activity. (p. 322)

First-stage allocation The process by which overhead costs are assigned to activity cost pools in an activity-based costing system. (p. 325)

Organization-sustaining activities Activities that are carried out regardless of which customers are served, which products are produced, how many batches are run, or how many units are made. (p. 322)

Product-level activities Activities that relate to specific products that must be carried out regardless of how many units are produced and sold or batches run. (p. 321)

Second-stage allocation The process by which activity rates are used to apply costs to products and customers in activity-based costing. (p. 328)

Transaction driver A simple count of the number of times an activity occurs. (p. 322)

Unit-level activities Activities that are performed each time a unit is produced. (p. 321)

Appendix 8A: ABC Action Analysis

LEARNING OBJECTIVE 7
Prepare an action analysis report using activity-based costing data and interpret the report.

A conventional ABC analysis, such as the one presented in Exhibit 8–9 in the chapter, has several important limitations. Referring back to that exhibit, recall that the custom compass housing shows a negative product margin of $1,114. Because of this apparent loss, managers were considering dropping this product. However, as the discussion among the managers revealed, it is unlikely that all of the $1,764 cost of the product would be avoided if the product were dropped. Some of these costs would continue even if the product were totally eliminated. *Before* taking action, it is vital to identify which costs would be avoided and which costs would continue. Only those costs that can be avoided are relevant in the decision. Moreover, many of the costs are managed costs that would require explicit management action to eliminate. If the custom compass housing product were eliminated, the direct materials cost would be avoided without any explicit management action—the materials simply wouldn't be ordered. On the other hand, if the custom compass housing product were dropped, explicit management action would be required to eliminate the salaries of overhead workers that have been assigned to the product.

Simply shifting these managed costs to other products would not solve anything. These costs would have to be eliminated or the resources *shifted to the constraint* to have any benefit to the company. While eliminating the cost is obviously beneficial, redeploying the resource is only beneficial if the resource is shifted to the constraint in the process. If the resource is redeployed to a work center that is not a constraint, it would have the effect of increasing the excess capacity in that work center—which has no direct benefit to the company.

In addition, if some overhead costs need to be eliminated as a result of dropping a product, specific managers must be held responsible for eliminating those costs or the reductions are unlikely to occur. If no one is specifically held responsible for eliminating the costs, they will almost certainly continue to be incurred. Without external pressure, managers usually avoid cutting costs in their areas of responsibility. The action analysis report developed in this appendix is intended to help top managers identify what costs are relevant in a decision and to place responsibility for the elimination of those costs on the appropriate managers.

Activity Rates—Action Analysis Report

Constructing an action analysis report begins with the results of the first-stage allocation, which is reproduced as Exhibit 8A–1. In contrast to the conventional ABC analysis covered in the chapter, the calculation of the activity rates for an action analysis report is a bit more involved. In addition to computing an overall activity rate for each activity cost pool, an activity rate is computed for each cell in Exhibit 8A–1. The computations of activity rates for the action analysis are carried out in Exhibit 8A–2. For example, the $125,000 cost of indirect factory wages for the Customer Orders cost pool is divided by the total activity for that cost pool—1,000 orders—to arrive at the activity rate of $125

EXHIBIT 8A–1
First-Stage Allocations to Activity Cost Pools

	Customer Orders	Product Design	Order Size	Customer Relations	Other	Total
	Activity Cost Pools					
Production Department:						
Indirect factory wages	$ 125,000	$ 200,000	$ 100,000	$ 50,000	$ 25,000	$ 500,000
Factory equipment depreciation	60,000	0	180,000	0	60,000	300,000
Factory utilities	0	12,000	60,000	0	48,000	120,000
Factory building lease	0	0	0	0	80,000	80,000
General Administrative Department:						
Administrative wages and salaries	60,000	20,000	40,000	120,000	160,000	400,000
Office equipment depreciation	15,000	0	0	12,500	22,500	50,000
Administrative building lease	0	0	0	0	60,000	60,000
Marketing Department:						
Marketing wages and salaries	50,000	25,000	0	150,000	25,000	250,000
Selling expenses	5,000	0	0	35,000	10,000	50,000
Total cost	$ 315,000	$ 257,000	$ 380,000	$ 367,500	$ 490,500	$ 1,810,000

EXHIBIT 8A–2
Computation of the Activity Rates for the Action Analysis Report

	Customer Orders	Product Design	Order Size	Customer Relations	Other
	Activity Cost Pools				
Total activity	1,000 orders	200 product designs	20,000 machine-hours	100 active customers	Not applicable*
Production Department:					
Indirect factory wages	$ 125	$ 1,000	$ 5	$ 500	
Factory equipment depreciation	60	0	9	0	
Factory utilities	0	60	3	0	
Factory building lease	0	0	0	0	
General Administrative Department:					
Administrative wages and salaries	60	100	2	1,200	
Office equipment depreciation	15	0	0	125	
Administrative building lease	0	0	0	0	
Marketing Department:					
Marketing wages and salaries	50	125	0	1,500	
Selling expenses	5	0	0	350	
Total (conventional ABC analysis)	$ 315	$ 1,285	$ 19	$ 3,675	

*Activity rates are not computed for the Other cost pool since these costs will not be allocated further.

$125,000 ÷ 1,000 orders = $125 per order.
Other entries in the table are computed similarly.

per customer order for indirect factory wages. Similarly, the $200,000 cost of indirect factory wages for the Product Design cost pool is divided by the total activity for that cost pool—200 designs—to arrive at the activity rate of $1,000 per design for indirect factory wages. Note that the totals at the bottom of Exhibit 8A–2 agree with the overall activity rates in Exhibit 8–5 in the chapter. Exhibit 8A–2, which shows the activity rates for the action analysis report, contains more detail than Exhibit 8–5, which contains the activity rates for the conventional ABC analysis.

Assignment of Overhead Costs to Products—Action Analysis Report

Similarly, computing the overhead costs to be assigned to products for an action analysis report involves more detail than for a conventional ABC analysis. The computations for Classic Brass are carried out in Exhibit 8A–3. For example, the activity rate of $125 per customer order for indirect factory wages is multiplied by 2 orders for the standard stanchions to arrive at the cost of $250 for indirect factory wages in Exhibit 8A–3. Instead of just a single cost number for each cost pool as in the conventional ABC analysis, we now have an entire cost matrix showing much more detail. Note that the column totals for the cost matrix in Exhibit 8A–3 agree with the ABC costs for stanchions in Exhibit 8–8. Indeed, the conventional ABC analysis of Exhibit 8–9 can be easily constructed using the column totals at the bottom of the cost matrices in Exhibit 8A–3. In contrast, the action analysis report will be based on the row totals at the right of the cost matrices in Exhibit 8A–3. In addition, the action analysis report will include a simple color-coding scheme that will help managers identify how easily the various costs can be adjusted.

Ease of Adjustment Codes

The ABC team constructed Exhibit 8A–4 to aid managers in the use of the ABC data. In this exhibit, each cost has been assigned an *ease of adjustment code*—Green, Yellow, or Red. The **ease of adjustment code** reflects how easily the cost could be adjusted to changes in activity.[8] "Green" costs are those costs that would adjust more or less automatically to changes in activity without any action by managers. For example, direct materials costs would adjust to changes in orders without any action being taken by managers. If a customer does not order stanchions, the direct materials for the stanchions would not be required and would not be ordered. "Yellow" costs are those costs that could be adjusted in response to changes in activity, but such adjustments require management action; the adjustment is not automatic. The ABC team believes, for example, that direct labor costs should be included in the Yellow category. Managers must make difficult decisions and take explicit action to increase or decrease, in aggregate, direct labor costs—particularly since the company has a no lay-off policy. "Red" costs are costs that could be adjusted to changes in activity only with a great deal of difficulty, and the adjustment would require management action. The building leases fall into this category, since it would be very difficult and expensive to break the leases.

The Action Analysis View of the ABC Data

Looking at Exhibit 8A–3, the totals on the right-hand side of the table indicate that the $1,676 of overhead cost for the custom compass housing consists of $1,145 of indirect factory wages, $96 of factory equipment depreciation, and so on. These data are displayed in Exhibit 8A–5, which shows an action analysis of the custom compass housing product. An action analysis report shows what costs have been assigned to the cost object, such as a product or customer, and how difficult it would be to adjust the cost if there is a change in activity. Note

[8] The idea of using colors to code how easily costs can be adjusted was suggested to us at a seminar put on by Boeing and by an article by Alfred King, "Green Dollars and Blue Dollars: The Paradox of Cost Reduction," *Journal of Cost Management,* Fall 1993, pp. 44–52.

EXHIBIT 8A–3
Action Analysis Cost Matrices

Action Analysis Cost Matrix for Standard Stanchions

	Activity Cost Pools				
	Customer Orders	*Product Design*	*Order Size*	*Customer Relations*	*Total*
Total activity for stanchions	2 orders	0 product designs	200 machine-hours	Not applicable	
Production Department:					
Indirect factory wages	$ 250	$ 0	$ 1,000		$ 1,250
Factory equipment depreciation	20	0	1,800		1,920
Factory utilities	0	0	600		600
Factory building lease	0	0	0		0
General Administrative Department:					
Administrative wages and salaries	120	0	400		520
Office equipment depreciation	30	0	0		30
Administrative building lease	0	0	0		0
Marketing Department:					
Marketing wages and salaries	100	0	0		100
Selling expenses	10	0	0		10
Total (conventional ABC analysis)	$ 630	$ 0	$ 3,800		$ 4,430

From Exhibit 8A–2, the activity rate for indirect factory wages for the Customer Orders cost pool is $125 per order.

$125 per order × 2 orders = $250

Other entries in the table are computed in a similar way.

Action Analysis Cost Matrix for the Custom Compass Housing

	Activity Cost Pools				
	Customer Orders	*Product Design*	*Order Size*	*Customer Relations*	*Total*
Total activity for custom compass housings	1 order	1 product design	4 machine-hours	Not applicable	
Production Department:					
Indirect factory wages	$ 125	$ 1,000	$ 20		$ 1,145
Factory equipment depreciation	60	0	36		96
Factory utilities	0	60	12		72
Factory building lease	0	0	0		0
General Administrative Department:					
Administrative wages and salaries	60	100	8		168
Office equipment depreciation	15	0	0		15
Administrative building lease	0	0	0		0
Marketing Department:					
Marketing wages and salaries	50	125	0		175
Selling expenses	5	0	0		5
Total (conventional ABC analysis)	$ 315	$ 1,285	$ 76		$ 1,676

From Exhibit 8A–2, the activity rate for indirect factory wages for the Customer Orders cost pool is $125 per order.

$125 per order × 1 order = $125

Other entries in the table are computed in a similar way.

EXHIBIT 8A–4
Ease of Adjustment Codes

***Green:** Costs that adjust automatically to changes in activity without management action.*

- Direct materials
- Shipping costs

***Yellow:** Costs that could, in principle, be adjusted to changes in activity, but management action would be required.*

- Direct labor
- Indirect factory wages
- Factory utilities
- Administrative wages and salaries
- Office equipment depreciation
- Marketing wages and salaries
- Selling expenses

***Red:** Costs that would be very difficult to adjust to changes in activity and management action would be required.*

- Factory equipment depreciation
- Factory building lease
- Administrative building lease

EXHIBIT 8A–5
Action Analysis of Custom Compass Housing: Activity-Based Costing System

Microsoft Excel - ABC model-Classic Brass.XLS

	A	B	C	D
1	**Custom Compass Housing**			
2	Sales (from Exhibit 8-7)		$ 650	
3				
4	Green costs:			
5	Direct materials (from Exhibit 8-7)	$ 13		
6	Shipping costs (from Exhibit 8-7)	25	38	
7	Green margin		612	
8				
9	Yellow costs:			
10	Direct labor (from Exhibit 8-7)	50		
11	Indirect factory wages (from Exhibit 8A-3)	1,145		
12	Factory utilities (from Exhibit 8A-3)	72		
13	Administrative wages and salaries (from Exhibit 8A-3)	168		
14	Office equipment depreciation (from Exhibit 8A-3)	15		
15	Marketing wages and salaries (from Exhibit 8A-3)	175		
16	Selling expenses (from Exhibit 8A-3)	5	1,630	
17	Yellow margin		(1,018)	
18				
19	Red costs:			
20	Factory equipment depreciation (from Exhibit 8A-3)	96		
21	Factory building lease (from Exhibit 8A-3)	0		
22	Administrative building lease (from Exhibit 8A-3)	0	96	
23	Red margin		$ (1,114)	
24				

Exhibit 8A-3B | Exhibit 8A-5 | Activity rates

that the Red margin at the bottom of Exhibit 8A–5, ($1,114), is exactly the same as the product margin for the custom compass housing in Exhibit 8–9 in the chapter.

The cost data in the action analysis in Exhibit 8A–5 are arranged by the color coded ease of adjustment. All of the Green costs—those that adjust more or less automatically to changes in activity—appear together at the top of the list of costs. These costs total $38 and are subtracted from the sales of $650 to yield a Green margin of $612. The same procedure is followed for the Yellow and Red costs. This action analysis indicates what costs would have to be cut and how difficult it would be to cut them if the custom compass housing product were dropped. Prior to making any decision about dropping products, the managers responsible for the costs must agree to either eliminate the resources represented by those costs or to transfer the resources to an area in the organization that really needs the resources—namely, a constraint. If managers do not make such a commitment, it is likely that the costs would continue to be incurred. As a result, the company would lose the sales from the products without really saving the costs.

MANAGERIAL ACCOUNTING IN ACTION
The Wrap-Up

After the action analysis was prepared by the ABC team, top management at Classic Brass met once again to review the results of the ABC analysis.

John: When we last met, we had discussed the advisability of discontinuing work like the custom compass housing for Windward Yachts. I understand that the ABC team has done some additional analysis to help us in making this decision.

Mary: That's right. The action analysis report we put together indicates how easy it would be to adjust each cost and where specific cost savings would have to come from if we were to drop jobs like the custom compass housing.

John: What's this red margin at the bottom of the action analysis? Isn't that a product margin?

Mary: Yes, it is. However, we call it a red margin because we should stop and think very, very carefully before taking any actions based on that margin.

John: Why is that?

Mary: As an example, we subtracted the costs of factory equipment depreciation to arrive at that red margin. We doubt that we could avoid any of that cost if we were to drop custom orders. We use the same machines on custom orders that we use on standard products. The factory equipment has no resale value, and it does not wear out through use.

John: What about this yellow margin?

Mary: Yellow means proceed with a great deal of caution. To get to the yellow margin we deducted from sales numerous costs that could be adjusted only if the managers involved are willing to eliminate resources or shift them to the constraint.

John: If I understand the yellow margin correctly, the apparent loss of $1,018 on the custom compass housing is the result of the indirect factory wages of $1,145.

Susan: Right, that's basically the wages of our design engineers.

John: I wouldn't want to lay off any of our designers. Could we turn them into salespersons?

Tom: I'd love to have Shueli Park join our marketing team.

Susan: No way, she's our best designer.

John: Okay, I get the picture. We are not going to be cutting anyone's wages, we aren't going to be laying off anyone, and it looks like we may have problems getting agreement about moving people around. Where does that leave us?

Mary: What about raising prices on our custom products?

Tom: We should be able to do that. We have been undercutting the competition to make sure that we won bids on custom work because we thought it was a very profitable thing to do.

John: Why don't we just charge directly for design work?

Tom: Some of our competitors already do that. However, I don't think we would be able to charge enough to cover our design costs.

John: Can we do anything to make our design work more efficient so it costs us less? I'm not going to lay anyone off, but if we make the design process more efficient, we could lower the charge for design work and spread those costs across more customers.

Susan: That may be possible. I'll form a TQM team to look at it.

John: Let's get some benchmark data on design costs. If we set our minds to it, I'm sure we can be world class in no time.

Susan: Okay. Mary, will you help with the benchmark data?

Mary: Sure.

Tom: There is another approach we can take too. Windward Yachts probably doesn't really need a custom compass housing. One of our standard compass housings would work just fine. If we start charging for the design work, I think they will see that it would be in their own best interest to use the lower-cost standard product.

John: Let's meet again in about a week to discuss our progress. Is there anything else on the agenda for today?

The points raised in the preceding discussion are extremely important. By measuring the resources consumed by products (and other cost objects), a "best practice" ABC system provides a much better basis for decision making than a traditional cost accounting system that spreads overhead costs around without much regard for what might be causing the overhead. A well-designed ABC system provides managers with estimates of potentially relevant costs that can be a very useful starting point for management analysis.

Summary

The action analysis report illustrated in this appendix is a valuable addition to the ABC toolkit. An action analysis report provides more information for decision making than a conventional ABC analysis. The action analysis report makes it clear where costs would have to be adjusted in the organization as a result of an action. In a conventional ABC analysis, a cost such as $315 for processing an order represents costs from many parts of the organization. If an order is dropped, there will be little pressure to actually eliminate the $315 cost unless it is clear where the costs are incurred and which managers would be responsible for reducing the cost. In contrast, an action analysis report traces the costs to where they are incurred in the organization and makes it much easier to assign responsibility to managers for reducing costs. In addition, an action analysis report provides information concerning how easily a cost can be adjusted. Costs that cannot be adjusted are not relevant in a decision.

Exhibit 8A–6 summarizes all of the steps required to create both an action analysis report as illustrated in this appendix and an activity analysis as shown in the chapter.

EXHIBIT 8A–6
Summary of the Steps to Produce an Action Analysis Report

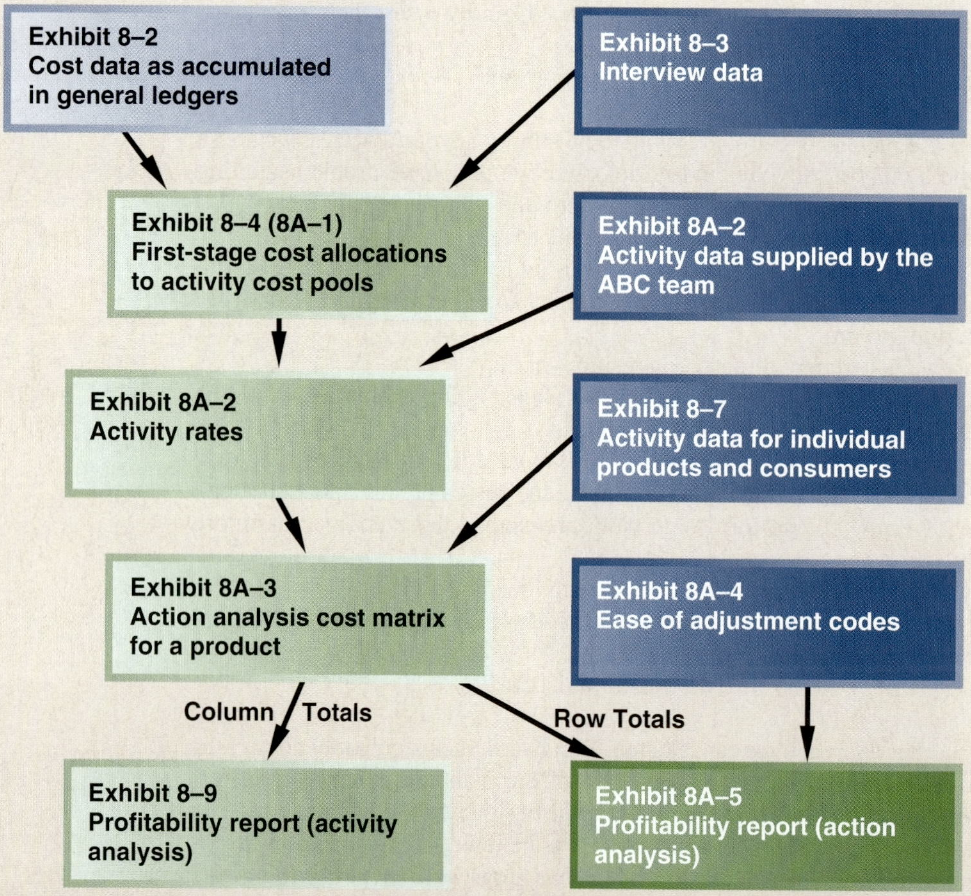

Review Problem: Activity Analysis Report

Refer to the data for Ferris Corporation in the Review Problem at the end of the chapter on pages 340–341.

Required:

1. Compute activity rates for Ferris Corporation as in Exhibit 8A–2.
2. Using Exhibit 8A–3 as a guide, construct a table showing the overhead costs for the OfficeMart orders described in requirement (3) of the Review Problem at the end of the chapter.
3. The management of Ferris Corporation has assigned ease of adjustment codes to costs as follows:

Cost	Ease of Adjustment Code
Direct materials	Green
Direct labor	Yellow
Manufacturing overhead	Yellow
Selling and administrative overhead	Red

Using Exhibit 8A–5 as a guide, prepare an action analysis of the OfficeMart orders.

Solution to Review Problem

1. The activity rates for the activity cost pools are:

	Assembling Units	Processing Orders	Supporting Customers
Total activity	1,000 units	250 orders	100 customers
Manufacturing overhead	$250	$ 700	$ 250
Selling and administrative overhead	30	540	750
Total	$280	$1,240	$1,000

2. The overhead cost for the four orders of a total of 80 filing cabinets would be computed as follows:

	Assembling Units	Processing Orders	Total
Activity	80 units	4 orders	
Manufacturing overhead	$20,000	$2,800	$22,800
Selling and administrative overhead	2,400	2,160	4,560
Total	$22,400	$4,960	$27,360

3. The action analysis of the four orders for 80 filing cabinets in total is:

Sales		$47,600
Green costs:		
Direct materials	$14,400	14,400
Green margin		33,200
Yellow costs:		
Direct labor	4,000	
Manufacturing overhead	22,800	26,800
Yellow margin		6,400
Red costs:		
Selling and administrative overhead	4,560	4,560
Red margin		$1,840

Note: An action analysis report can also be prepared for OfficeMart as a customer. The first step would be to calculate the overhead costs for OfficeMart as follows:

	Assembling Units	Processing Orders	Supporting Customers	Total
Activity	80 units	4 orders	1 customer	
Manufacturing overhead	$20,000	$2,800	$ 250	$23,050
Selling and administrative overhead	2,400	2,160	750	5,310
Total	$22,400	$4,960	$1,000	$28,360

The action analysis report can then be easily prepared as follows:

Sales		$47,600
Green costs:		
Direct materials	$14,400	14,400
Green margin		33,200
Yellow costs:		
Direct labor	4,000	
Manufacturing overhead	23,050	27,050
Yellow margin		6,150
Red costs:		
Selling and administrative overhead	5,310	5,310
Red margin		$ 840

Glossary

Ease of adjustment codes Costs are coded as Green, Yellow, or Red—depending on how easily the cost could be adjusted to changes in activity. "Green" costs adjust automatically to changes in activity. "Yellow" costs could be adjusted in response to changes in activity, but such adjustments require management action; the adjustment is not automatic. "Red" costs could be adjusted to changes in activity only with a great deal of difficulty and would require management action. (p. 344)

Questions

8–1 In what fundamental ways does activity-based costing differ from traditional costing methods such as those described in Chapters 2 and 3?

8–2 Why is direct labor a poor base for allocating overhead in many companies?

8–3 Why are overhead rates in activity-based costing based on the level of activity at capacity rather than on the budgeted level of activity?

8–4 Why is top management support crucial when attempting to implement an activity-based costing system?

8–5 What are unit-level, batch-level, product-level, customer-level, and organization-sustaining activities?

8–6 What types of costs should not be assigned to products in an activity-based costing system?

8–7 Why are there two stages of allocation in activity-based costing?

8–8 Why is the first stage of the allocation process in activity-based costing often based on interviews?

8–9 When activity-based costing is used, why do manufacturing overhead costs often shift from high-volume products to low-volume products?

8–10 How can the activity rates (i.e., cost per activity) for the various activities be used to target process improvements?

8–11 Why is the activity-based costing described in this chapter unacceptable for external financial reports?

8–12 (Appendix 8A) Why should an activity view of product margins such as in Exhibit 8–9 be supplemented with an action analysis such as in Exhibit 8A–5 when making decisions about products or customers?

Exercises

EXERCISE 8–1 ABC Cost Hierarchy [LO1]

The following activities occur at Greenwich Corporation, a company that manufactures a variety of products.

a. Receive raw materials from suppliers.
b. Manage parts inventories.
c. Do rough milling work on products.
d. Interview and process new employees in the personnel department.
e. Design new products.
f. Perform periodic preventive maintenance on general-use equipment.
g. Use the general factory building.
h. Issue purchase orders for a job.

Required:

Classify each of the activities above as either a unit-level, batch-level, product-level, or organization-sustaining activity.

EXERCISE 8–2 First Stage Allocation [LO2]

SecuriCorp operates a fleet of armored cars that make scheduled pickups and deliveries in the Los Angeles area. The company is implementing an activity-based costing system that has four activity cost pools: Travel, Pickup and Delivery, Customer Service, and Other. The activity measures are miles for the Travel cost pool, number of pickups and deliveries for the Pickup and Delivery cost pool, and number of customers for the Customer Service cost pool. The Other cost pool has no activity measure. The following costs will be assigned using the activity-based costing system:

Driver and guard wages	$ 720,000
Vehicle operating expense	280,000
Vehicle depreciation	120,000
Customer representative salaries and expenses	160,000
Office expenses	30,000
Administrative expenses	320,000
Total cost	$1,630,000

The distribution of resource consumption across the activity cost pools is as follows:

	Travel	Pickup and Delivery	Customer Service	Other	Totals
Driver and guard wages	50%	35%	10%	5%	100%
Vehicle operating expense	70%	5%	0%	25%	100%
Vehicle depreciation	60%	15%	0%	25%	100%
Customer representative salaries and expenses	0%	0%	90%	10%	100%
Office expenses	0%	20%	30%	50%	100%
Administrative expenses	0%	5%	60%	35%	100%

Required:

Carry out the first stage allocations of costs to activity cost pools as illustrated in Exhibit 8–4.

EXERCISE 8–3 Compute Activity Rates [LO3]

Green Thumb Gardening is a small gardening service that uses activity-based costing to estimate costs for pricing and other purposes. The proprietor of the company believes that costs are driven primarily by the size of customer lawns, the size of customer garden beds, the distance to travel to customers, and the number of customers. In addition, the costs of maintaining garden beds depends on whether the beds are low maintenance beds (mainly ordinary trees and shrubs) or high maintenance beds (mainly flowers and exotic plants). Accordingly, the company uses the five activity cost pools listed below:

Activity Cost Pool	Activity Measure
Caring for lawn	Square feet of lawn
Caring for garden beds–low maintenance	Square feet of low maintenance beds
Caring for garden beds–high maintenance	Square feet of high maintenance beds
Travel to jobs	Miles
Customer billing and service	Number of customers

The company has already carried out its first stage allocations of costs and has summarized its annual costs and activity as follows:

Activity Cost Pool	Estimated Overhead Cost	Expected Activity
Caring for lawn	$72,000	150,000 square feet of lawn
Caring for garden beds–low maintenance	$26,400	20,000 square feet of low maintenance beds
Caring for garden beds–high maintenance	$41,400	15,000 square feet of high maintenance beds
Travel to jobs	$3,250	12,500 miles
Customer billing and service	$8,750	25 customers

Required:

Compute the activity rate for each of the activity cost pools.

EXERCISE 8–4 Compute ABC Product Costs [LO4]

Klumper Corporation is a diversified manufacturer of industrial goods. The company's activity-based costing system contains the following six activity cost pools and activity rates:

Activity Cost Pool	Activity Rates
Labor related	$6.00 per direct labor-hour
Machine related	$4.00 per machine-hour
Machine setups	$50.00 per setup
Production orders	$90.00 per order
Shipments	$14.00 per shipment
Product sustaining	$840.00 per product

Activity data have been supplied for the following two products:

	Total Expected Activity	
	K425	M67
Number of units produced per year	200	2,000
Direct labor-hours	80	500
Machine-hours	100	1,500
Machine setups	1	4
Production orders	1	4
Shipments	1	10
Product sustaining	1	1

Required:
Compute the total and average per unit cost of each of the products listed.

EXERCISE 8–5 Product and Customer Profitability Analysis [LO4, LO5]
Thermal Rising, Inc., makes paragliders for sale through specialty sporting goods stores. The company has a standard paraglider model, but also makes custom-designed paragliders. Management has designed an activity-based costing system with the following activity cost pools and activity rates:

Activity Cost Pool	Activity Rate
Manufacturing volume	$26 per direct labor-hour
Order processing	$284 per order
Custom design processing	$186 per custom design
Customer service	$379 per customer

Management would like an analysis of the profitability of a particular customer, Big Sky Outfitters, which has ordered the following products over the last 12 months:

	Standard Model	Custom Design
Number of gliders	20	3
Number of orders	1	3
Number of custom designs	0	3
Direct labor-hours per glider	26.35	28.00
Selling price per glider	$1,850	$2,400
Direct materials cost per glider	$564	$634

The company's direct labor rate is $19.50 per hour.

Required:
Using the company's activity-based costing system, compute the profitability of each of the two products ordered by Big Sky Outfitters and the overall profitability of this customer.

EXERCISE 8–6 Contrasting Traditional and ABC Product Costs [LO6]

Superior Industrial Corporation makes two products—Model X100 and Model X200. Model X200 offers advanced features and is sold for a higher price than Model X100. Management expects to sell 50,000 units of Model X100 and 5,000 units of Model X200 next year. The company's total manufacturing overhead for the year is expected to be $1,920,000. A unit of Model X100 requires 0.2 direct labor-hours and a unit of Model X200 requires 0.4 direct labor-hours.

Required:
1. The company currently applies manufacturing overhead to products using direct labor-hours as the allocation base. If this method is followed, how much overhead cost would be applied to each product in total and per unit?
2. Management is considering an activity-based costing system and would like to know what impact this would have on product costs. Preliminary analysis suggests that under activity-based costing, a total of $1,340,000 in manufacturing overhead cost would be assigned to Model X100 and a total of $390,000 would be assigned to Model X200. In addition, a total of $160,000 in nonmanufacturing overhead would be applied to Model X100 and a total of $110,000 would be applied to Model X200. If this method is used, how much overhead cost would be applied to each product in total and per unit?
3. Explain the impact of switching from the traditional costing system based on direct labor-hours to the activity-based costing system on total and per unit overhead costs assigned to the two products.

EXERCISE 8–7 (Appendix 8A) Preparing an Action Analysis Report [LO7]
Hard Driver Corporation produces private label golf clubs for pro shops throughout North America. The company uses activity-based costing to evaluate the profitability of serving its customers. This analysis is based on categorizing the company's costs as follows, using the ease of adjustment color coding scheme described in Appendix 8A:

	Ease of Adjustment Code
Direct materials	Green
Direct labor	Yellow
Indirect labor	Yellow
Factory equipment depreciation	Red
Factory administration	Red
Selling and administrative wages and salaries	Red
Selling and administrative depreciation	Red
Marketing expenses	Yellow

Management would like to evaluate the profitability of a particular customer—the Grouse Mountain Golf Club of Avon, Colorado. Over the last 12 months, this customer submitted one order for 120 golf clubs that had to be produced in two batches due to differences in product labeling requested by the customer. Summary data concerning the order appear below:

Number of clubs	120
Number of orders	1
Number of batches	2
Direct labor-hour per club	0.4
Selling price per club	$49.00
Direct materials cost per club	$27.65
Direct labor rate per hour	$22.00

A cost analyst working in the controller's office at the company has already produced the action analysis cost matrix for the Grouse Mountain Golf Club that appears below:

Action Analysis Cost Matrix for Grouse Mountain Golf Club

	Activity Cost Pools				
	Volume	Batch Processing	Order Processing	Customer Service	Total
Activity	48 direct labor-hours	2 batches	1 order	1 customer	
Manufacturing overhead:					
Indirect labor	$57.60	$52.40	$3.40	$0.00	$113.40
Factory equipment depreciation	216.00	0.60	0.00	0.00	216.60
Factory administration	31.20	0.50	15.00	245.00	291.70
Selling and administrative overhead:					
Wages and salaries	21.60	0.00	42.00	324.00	387.60
Depreciation	0.00	0.00	7.00	21.00	28.00
Marketing expenses	268.80	0.00	65.00	376.00	709.80
Total	$595.20	$53.50	$132.40	$966.00	$1,747.10

Required:

Prepare an action analysis report showing the profitability of the Grouse Mountain Golf Club. Include direct materials and direct labor costs in the report. Use Exhibit 8A–5 as a guide for organizing the report.

EXERCISE 8–8 Cost Hierarchy [LO1]

CD Express, Inc., provides CD duplicating services to software companies. The customer provides a master CD from which CD Express makes copies. An order from a customer can be for a single copy or for thousands of copies. Most jobs are broken down into batches to allow smaller jobs, with higher priorities, to have access to the machines.

Following are listed a number of activities carried out at CD Express.

a. Sales representatives' periodic visits to customers to keep them informed about the services provided by CD Express.

b. Ordering labels from the printer for a particular CD.
c. Setting up the CD duplicating machine to make copies from a particular master CD.
d. Loading the automatic labeling machine with labels for a particular CD.
e. Visually inspecting CDs and placing them by hand into protective plastic cases prior to shipping.
f. Preparation of the shipping documents for the order.
g. Periodic maintenance of equipment.
h. Lighting and heating the company's production facility.
i. Preparation of quarterly financial reports.

Required:
Classify each of the activities above as either a unit-level, batch-level, product-level, customer-level, or organization-sustaining activity. (An order to duplicate a particular CD is a product-level activity.) Assume the order is large enough that it must be broken down into batches.

EXERCISE 8–9 First-Stage Allocations [LO2]

The operations vice president of Security Home Bank has been interested in investigating the efficiency of the bank's operations. She has been particularly concerned about the costs of handling routine transactions at the bank and would like to compare these costs at the bank's various branches. If the branches with the most efficient operations can be identified, their methods can be studied and then replicated elsewhere. While the bank maintains meticulous records of wages and other costs, there has been no attempt thus far to show how those costs are related to the various services provided by the bank. The operations vice president has asked your help in conducting an activity-based costing study of bank operations. In particular, she would like to know the cost of opening an account, the cost of processing deposits and withdrawals, and the cost of processing other customer transactions.

The Westfield branch of Security Home Bank has submitted the following cost data for last year:

Teller wages	$160,000
Assistant branch manager salary	75,000
Branch manager salary	80,000
Total	$315,000

Virtually all of the other costs of the branch—rent, depreciation, utilities, and so on—are organization-sustaining costs that cannot be meaningfully assigned to individual customer transactions such as depositing checks.

In addition to the cost data above, the employees of the Westfield branch have been interviewed concerning how their time was distributed last year across the activities included in the activity-based costing study. The results of those interviews appear below:

Distribution of Resource Consumption Across Activities

	Opening Accounts	Processing Deposits and Withdrawals	Processing Other Customer Transactions	Other Activities	Total
Teller wages	5%	65%	20%	10%	100%
Assistant branch manager salary	15%	5%	30%	50%	100%
Branch manager salary	5%	0%	10%	85%	100%

Required:
Prepare the first-stage allocation for the activity-based costing study. (See Exhibit 8–4 for an example of a first-stage allocation.)

EXERCISE 8–10 Computing and Interpreting Activity Rates [LO3]

(This exercise is a continuation of Exercise 8–9; it should be assigned *only* if Exercise 8–9 is also assigned.) The manager of the Westfield branch of Security Home Bank has provided the following data concerning the transactions of the branch during the past year:

Activity	Total Activity at the Westfield Branch
Opening accounts	500 new accounts opened
Processing deposits and withdrawals	100,000 deposits and withdrawals processed
Processing other customer transactions ...	5,000 other customer transactions processed

The lowest costs reported by other branches for these activities are displayed below:

Activity	Lowest Cost among All Security Home Bank Branches
Opening accounts	$26.75 per new account
Processing deposits and withdrawals	$1.24 per deposit or withdrawal
Processing other customer transactions	$11.86 per other customer transaction

Required:

1. Using the first-stage allocation from Exercise 8–9 and the above data, compute the activity rates for the activity-based costing system. (Use Exhibit 8–5 as a guide.) Round all computations to the nearest whole cent.
2. What do these results suggest to you concerning operations at the Westfield branch?

EXERCISE 8–11 Second-Stage Allocation to an Order [LO4]

Durban Metal Products, Ltd., of the Republic of South Africa makes specialty metal parts used in applications ranging from the cutting edges of bulldozer blades to replacement parts for Land Rovers. The company uses an activity-based costing system for internal decision-making purposes. The company has four activity cost pools as listed below:

Activity Cost Pool	Activity Measure	Activity Rate
Order size	Number of direct labor-hours	R16.85 per direct labor-hour
Customer orders	Number of customer orders	R320.00 per customer order
Product testing	Number of testing hours	R89.00 per testing hour
Selling	Number of sales calls	R1,090.00 per sales call

Note: The currency in South Africa is the Rand, denoted here by R.

The managing director of the company would like information concerning the cost of a recently completed order for heavy-duty trailer axles. The order required 200 direct labor-hours, 4 hours of product testing, and 2 sales calls.

Required:

Prepare a report showing the overhead cost of the order for heavy-duty trailer axles. (Use Exhibit 8–8 as a guide.) What is the total overhead cost assigned to the order?

EXERCISE 8–12 (Appendix 8A) Second-Stage Allocation to an Order Using the Action Analysis Approach [LO4, LO7]

This exercise should be assigned in conjunction with Exercise 8–11.

The results of the first-stage allocation of the activity-based costing system at Durban Metal Products, Ltd., in which the activity rates were computed, appear below:

	Order Size	Customer Orders	Product Testing	Selling
Manufacturing:				
Indirect labor	R 8.25	R180.00	R30.00	R 0.00
Factory depreciation	8.00	0.00	40.00	0.00
Factory utilities	0.10	0.00	1.00	0.00
Factory administration	0.00	48.00	18.00	30.00
Selling and administrative:				
Wages and salaries	0.50	80.00	0.00	800.00
Depreciation	0.00	12.00	0.00	40.00
Taxes and insurance	0.00	0.00	0.00	20.00
Selling expenses	0.00	0.00	0.00	200.00
Total overhead cost	R16.85	R320.00	R89.00	R1,090.00

Required:

1. Prepare a report showing the overhead cost of the order for heavy-duty trailer axles discussed in Exercise 8–11. (Use Exhibit 8A–3 as a guide.) What is the total overhead cost of the order according to the activity-based costing system?
2. Explain the two different perspectives this report gives to managers concerning the nature of the overhead costs involved in the order. (Hint: Look at the row and column totals of the report you have prepared.)

EXERCISE 8–13 Activity Measures [LO1]

Listed below are activities that you have observed at Ming Corporation, a manufacturing company. Each activity has been classified as a unit-level, batch-level, product-level, or customer-level activity.

Activity	Level of Activity	Examples of Activity Measures
a. Direct labor workers assemble a product	Unit	
b. Products are designed by engineers	Product	
c. Equipment is set up	Batch	
d. Machines are used to shape and cut materials	Unit	
e. Monthly bills are sent out to regular customers	Customer	
f. Materials are moved from the receiving dock to production lines	Batch	
g. All completed units are inspected for defects	Unit	

Required:

Complete the table by providing examples of activity measures for each activity.

EXERCISE 8–14 Computing ABC Product Costs [LO3, LO4]

Fogerty Company makes two products, titanium Hubs and Sprockets. Data regarding the two products follow:

	Direct Labor-Hours per Unit	Annual Production
Hubs	0.80	10,000 units
Sprockets	0.40	40,000 units

Additional information about the company follows:

a. Hubs require $32 in direct materials per unit, and Sprockets require $18.
b. The direct labor wage rate is $15 per hour.
c. Hubs are more complex to manufacture than Sprockets and they require special equipment.
d. The ABC system has the following activity cost pools:

Activity Cost Pool	Activity Measure	Estimated Overhead Cost	Activity		
			Total	Hubs	Sprockets
Machine setups	Number of setups	$72,000	400	100	300
Special processing	Machine-hours	$200,000	5,000	5,000	—
General factory	Direct labor-hours	$816,000	24,000	8,000	16,000

Required:

1. Compute the activity rate for each activity cost pool.
2. Determine the unit cost of each product according to the ABC system, including direct materials and direct labor.

EXERCISE 8–15 Cost Hierarchy and Activity Measures [LO1]

Vapo Ingman Oy, a Finnish manufacturing company, makes a variety of products at its plant outside Helsinki. Listed below are activities that you have observed at the plant.

a. Machine settings are changed between batches of different products.
b. Parts inventories are maintained in the storeroom. (Each product requires its own unique parts.)
c. Products are milled on a milling machine.
d. New employees are hired by the personnel office.

e. New products are designed.
f. Periodic maintenance is performed on general-purpose production equipment.
g. A bill is sent to a customer who is late in making payments.
h. Yearly taxes are paid on the company's facilities.
i. Purchase orders are issued for materials to be used in production.

Required:

1. Classify each of the activities above as either a unit-level, batch-level, product-level, customer-level, or organization-sustaining activity.
2. Where possible, for each activity name one or more activity measures that might be used to assign costs generated by the activity to products or customers.

EXERCISE 8–16 Calculating and Interpreting Activity-Based Costing Data [LO3, LO4]

Hiram's Lakeside is a popular restaurant located on Lake Washington in Seattle. The owner of the restaurant has been trying to better understand costs at the restaurant and has hired a student intern to conduct an activity-based costing study. The intern, in consultation with the owner, identified three major activities and then completed the first-stage allocations of costs to the activity cost pools. The results appear below.

Activity Cost Pool	Activity Measure	Total Cost	Total Activity
Serving a party of diners	Number of parties served	$33,000	6,000 parties
Serving a diner	Number of diners served	$138,000	15,000 diners
Serving drinks	Number of drinks ordered	$24,000	10,000 drinks

The above costs include all of the costs of the restaurant except for organization-sustaining costs such as rent, property taxes, and top-management salaries.

A group of diners who ask to sit at the same table are counted as a party. Some costs, such as the costs of cleaning linen, are the same whether one person is at a table or the table is full. Other costs, such as washing dishes, depend on the number of diners served.

Prior to the activity-based costing study, the owner knew very little about the costs of the restaurant. She knew that the total cost for the month (including organization-sustaining costs) was $240,000 and that 15,000 diners had been served. Therefore, the average cost per diner was $16.

Required:

1. According to the activity-based costing system, what is the total cost of serving each of the following parties of diners? (You can use the simplified approach described at the end of the chapter.)
   a. A party of four diners who order three drinks in total.
   b. A party of two diners who do not order any drinks.
   c. A lone diner who orders two drinks.
2. Convert the total costs you computed in (1) above to costs per diner. In other words, what is the average cost per diner for serving each of the following parties of diners?
   a. A party of four diners who order three drinks in total.
   b. A party of two diners who do not order any drinks.
   c. A lone diner who orders two drinks.
3. Why do the costs per diner for the three different parties differ from each other and from the overall average cost of $16 per diner?

EXERCISE 8–17 Activity-Based Costing as an Alternative to Traditional Product Costing [LO3, LO4, LO6]

This chapter emphasizes the use of activity-based costing in internal decisions. However, a modified form of activity-based costing can also be used to develop product costs for external financial reports. For this purpose, product costs include all manufacturing costs and exclude all nonmanufacturing costs. This problem illustrates such a costing system.

Harrison Company makes two products and uses a traditional costing system in which a single plantwide predetermined overhead rate is computed based on direct labor-hours. Data for the two products for the upcoming year follow:

	Rascon	Parcel
Direct materials cost per unit	$13.00	$22.00
Direct labor cost per unit	$6.00	$3.00
Direct labor-hours per unit	0.40	0.20
Number of units produced	20,000	80,000

These products are customized to some degree for specific customers.

Required:

1. The company's manufacturing overhead costs for the year are expected to be $576,000. Using the company's traditional costing system, compute the unit product costs for the two products.
2. Management is considering an activity-based costing system in which half of the overhead would continue to be allocated on the basis of direct labor-hours and half would be allocated on the basis of engineering design time. This time is expected to be distributed as follows during the upcoming year:

	Rascon	Parcel	Total
Engineering design time (in hours)	3,000	3,000	6,000

   Compute the unit product costs for the two products using the proposed ABC system.
3. Explain why the product costs differ between the two systems.

EXERCISE 8–18 Second-Stage Allocation and Margin Calculations [LO4, LO5]

Foam Products, Inc., makes foam seat cushions for the automotive and aerospace industries. The company's activity-based costing system has four activity cost pools, which are listed below along with their activity measures and activity rates:

Activity Cost Pool	Activity Measure	Activity Rate
Volume	Number of direct labor-hours	$5.55 per direct labor-hour
Batch processing	Number of batches	$107.00 per batch
Order processing	Number of orders	$275.00 per order
Customer service	Number of customers	$2,463.00 per customer

The company just completed a single order from Interstate Trucking for 1,000 custom seat cushions. The order was produced in two batches. Each seat cushion required 0.25 direct labor-hours. The selling price was $20 per unit, the direct materials cost was $8.50 per unit, and the direct labor cost was $6.00 per unit. This was Interstate Trucking's only order during the year.

Required:

1. Prepare a report showing the product margin for this order from an activity viewpoint. (Use the product profitability analysis in Exhibit 8–9 as a guide.) At this point, ignore the customer service costs.
2. Prepare a report showing the customer margin on sales to Interstate Trucking from an activity viewpoint. (Use the customer profitability analysis in Exhibit 8–9 as a guide.)

EXERCISE 8–19 (Appendix 8A) Second-Stage Allocations and Margin Calculations Using the Action Analysis Approach [LO4, LO7]

Refer to the data for Foam Products, Inc., in Exercise 8–18 and the following additional details concerning the activity rates in the activity-based costing system:

	Activity Rates			
	Volume	Batch Processing	Order Processing	Customer Service
Manufacturing overhead:				
Indirect labor	$0.60	$ 60.00	$ 20.00	$ 0.00
Factory equipment depreciation	4.00	17.00	0.00	0.00
Factory administration	0.10	7.00	25.00	150.00
Selling and administrative overhead:				
Wages and salaries	0.40	20.00	160.00	1,600.00
Depreciation	0.00	3.00	10.00	38.00
Marketing expenses	0.45	0.00	60.00	675.00
Total	$5.55	$107.00	$275.00	$2,463.00

Management has provided their ease of adjustment codes for the purpose of preparing action analyses.

	Ease of Adjustment Code
Direct materials	Green
Direct labor	Yellow
Manufacturing overhead:	
Indirect labor	Yellow
Factory equipment depreciation	Red
Factory administration	Red
Selling and administrative overhead:	
Wages and salaries	Red
Depreciation	Red
Marketing expenses	Yellow

Required:

1. Using Exhibit 8A–5 as a guide, prepare an action analysis report on the order from Interstate Trucking. Ignore customer service costs.
2. Management would like an action analysis report for the customer, Interstate Trucking, that is similar to those prepared for products, but is unsure of how this can be done. The customer service cost of $2,463 could be deducted directly from the product margin for the order, but this would obscure how much of the customer service cost consists of Green, Yellow, and Red costs. Prepare a report that clearly shows the adjustability of the various costs.

EXERCISE 8–20 Comprehensive Activity-Based Costing Exercise [LO2, LO3, LO4, LO5]
Advanced Products Corporation has supplied the following data from its activity-based costing system:

Overhead Costs	
Wages and salaries	$300,000
Other overhead costs	100,000
Total overhead costs	$400,000

Activity Cost Pool	Activity Measure	Total Activity for the Year
Volume related	Number of direct labor-hours	20,000 DLHs
Order related	Number of customer orders	400 orders
Customer support	Number of customers	200 customers
Other	These costs are not allocated to products or customers	Not applicable

Distribution of Resource Consumption Across Activities

	Volume Related	Order Related	Customer Support	Other	Total
Wages and salaries	40%	30%	20%	10%	100%
Other overhead costs	30%	10%	20%	40%	100%

During the year, Advanced Products completed one order for a new customer, Shenzhen Enterprises. This customer did not order any other products during the year. Data concerning that order follow:

Data concerning the Shenzhen Enterprises Order	
Units ordered	10 units
Direct labor-hours	2 DLHs per unit
Selling price	$300 per unit
Direct materials	$180 per unit
Direct labor	$50 per unit

Required:

1. Prepare a report showing the first-stage allocations of overhead costs to the activity cost pools. (Use Exhibit 8–4 as a guide.)
2. Compute the activity rates for the activity cost pools. (Use Exhibit 8–5 as a guide.)
3. Prepare a report showing the overhead costs for the order from Shenzhen Enterprises. (Use Exhibit 8–8 as a guide. Do not include the customer support costs at this point in the analysis.)
4. Prepare a report showing the product margin for the order and the customer margin for Shenzhen Enterprises. (Use Exhibit 8–9 as a guide.)

EXERCISE 8–21 (Appendix 8A) Comprehensive Activity-Based Costing Exercise [LO2, LO3, LO4, LO7]
Refer to the data for Advanced Products Corporation in Exercise 8–20.

Required:

1. Using Exhibit 8–4 as a guide, prepare a report showing the first-stage allocations of overhead costs to the activity cost pools.
2. Using Exhibit 8A–2 as a guide, compute the activity rates for the activity cost pools.
3. Using Exhibit 8A–3 as a guide, prepare a report showing the overhead costs for the order from Shenzhen Enterprises. Do not include customer support costs at this point in the analysis.
4. Using Exhibit 8–9 as a guide, prepare an activity analysis report showing the product margin for the order and the customer margin for Shenzhen Enterprises.
5. Using Exhibit 8A–5 as a guide, prepare an action analysis report showing the product margin for the order and the customer margin for Shenzhen Enterprises. Direct materials should be coded as a Green cost, direct labor and wages and salaries as Yellow costs, and other overhead costs as a Red cost.
6. Using Exhibit 8A–5 as a guide, prepare an action analysis report showing the customer margin for Shenzhen Enterprises. Direct materials should be coded as a Green cost, direct labor and wages and salaries as Yellow costs, and other overhead costs as a Red cost.
7. What action, if any, do you recommend as a result of the above analyses?

Problems

PROBLEM 8–22 Activity-Based Costing as an Alternative to Traditional Product Costing [LO3, LO4, LO5, LO6]
This chapter emphasizes the use of activity-based costing in internal decisions. However, a modified form of activity-based costing can also be used to develop product costs for external financial reports. For this purpose, product costs include all manufacturing overhead costs and exclude all nonmanufacturing costs. This problem illustrates such a costing system.

Siegel Company manufactures a product that is available in both a deluxe model and a regular model. The company has manufactured the regular model for years. The deluxe model was introduced several years ago to tap a new segment of the market. Since introduction of the deluxe model, the company's profits have steadily declined and management has become increasingly concerned about the accuracy of its costing system. Sales of the deluxe model have been increasing rapidly.

Manufacturing overhead is assigned to products on the basis of direct labor-hours. For the current year, the company has estimated that it will incur $900,000 in manufacturing overhead cost and produce 5,000 units of the deluxe model and 40,000 units of the regular model. The deluxe model requires two hours of direct labor time per unit, and the regular model requires one hour. Material and labor costs per unit are as follows:

	Model	
	Deluxe	Regular
Direct materials	$40	$25
Direct labor	$14	$7

Required:

1. Using direct labor-hours as the base for assigning overhead cost to products, compute the predetermined overhead rate. Using this rate and other data from the problem, determine the unit product cost of each model.
2. Management is considering using activity-based costing to apply manufacturing overhead cost to products for external financial reports. The activity-based costing system would have the following four activity cost pools:

Activity Cost Pool	Activity Measure	Estimated Overhead Cost
Purchasing	Purchase orders issued	$204,000
Processing	Machine-hours	182,000
Scrap/rework	Scrap/rework orders issued	379,000
Shipping	Number of shipments	135,000
		$900,000

	Expected Activity		
Activity Measure	Deluxe	Regular	Total
Purchase orders issued	200	400	600
Machine-hours	20,000	15,000	35,000
Scrap/rework orders issued	1,000	1,000	2,000
Number of shipments	250	650	900

Using Exhibit 8–5 as a guide, determine the predetermined overhead rate for each of the four activity cost pools.

3. Using the predetermined overhead rates you computed in part (2) above, do the following:
   a. Compute the total amount of manufacturing overhead cost that would be applied to each model using the activity-based costing system. After these totals have been computed, determine the amount of manufacturing overhead cost per unit of each model.
   b. Compute the unit product cost of each model (materials, labor, and manufacturing overhead).
4. From the data you have developed in parts (1) through (3) above, identify factors that may account for the company's declining profits.

PROBLEM 8–23 (Appendix 8A) Activity Rates and Activity-Based Management [LO2, LO3, LO7]
Aerotraiteur SA is a French company that provides passenger and crew meals to airlines operating out of the two international airports of Paris—Orly and Charles de Gaulle (CDG). The operations at Orly and CDG are managed separately, and top management believes that there may be benefits to greater sharing of information between the two operations.

To better compare the two operations, an activity-based costing system has been designed with the active participation of the managers at both Orly and CDG. The activity-based costing system is based on the following activity cost pools and activity measures:

Activity Cost Pool	Activity Measure
Meal preparation	Number of meals
Flight-related activities	Number of flights
Customer service	Number of customers
Other (costs of idle capacity and organization-sustaining costs)	Not applicable

The operation at CDG airport serves one million meals annually on 5,000 flights for 10 different airlines. (Each airline is considered one customer.) The annual cost of running the CDG airport operation, excluding only the costs of raw materials for meals, totals €2,940,000.

Note: The currency in France is the euro denoted by €.

Annual Cost of the CDG Operation	
Cooks and delivery personnel wages	€2,400,000
Kitchen supplies	30,000
Chef salaries	180,000
Equipment depreciation	60,000
Administrative wages and salaries	150,000
Building costs	120,000
Total cost	€2,940,000

To help determine the activity rates, employees were interviewed and asked how they divided their time among the four major activities. The results of employee interviews at CDG are displayed below:

Distribution of Resource Consumption Across Activities at the CDG Operation

	Meal Preparation	Flight Related	Customer Service	Other	Total
Cooks and delivery personnel wages . .	75%	20%	0%	5%	100%
Kitchen supplies	100%	0%	0%	0%	100%
Chef salaries	30%	20%	40%	10%	100%
Equipment depreciation	60%	0%	0%	40%	100%
Administrative wages and salaries	0%	20%	60%	20%	100%
Building costs	0%	0%	0%	100%	100%

Required:

1. Perform the first-stage allocation of costs to the activity cost pools. (Use Exhibit 8A–1 as a guide.)
2. Compute the activity rates for the activity cost pools. (Use Exhibit 8A–2 as a guide.) Do not round off.
3. The Orly operation has already concluded its activity-based costing study and has reported the following activity rates: €1.98 per meal for meal preparation; €115.60 per flight for flight-related activities; and €9,600 for customer service. Comparing the activity rates for the CDG operation you computed in part (2) above to the activity rates for Orly, do you have any suggestions for the top management of Aerotraiteur SA?

PROBLEM 8–24 Evaluating the Profitability of Services [LO2, LO3, LO4, LO5]

excel

Gallatin Carpet Cleaning is a small, family-owned business operating out of Bozeman, Montana. For its services, the company has always charged a flat fee per hundred square feet of carpet cleaned. The current fee is $28 per hundred square feet. However, there is some question about whether the company is actually making any money on jobs for some customers—particularly those located on remote ranches that require considerable travel time. The owner's daughter, home for the summer from college, has suggested investigating this question using activity-based costing. After some discussion, a simple system consisting of four activity cost pools seemed to be adequate. The activity cost pools and their activity measures appear below:

Activity Cost Pool	Activity Measure	Activity for the Year
Cleaning carpets	Square feet cleaned (00s)	20,000 hundred square feet
Travel to jobs	Miles driven	60,000 miles
Job support	Number of jobs	2,000 jobs
Other (costs of idle capacity and organization-sustaining costs)	None	Not applicable

The total cost of operating the company for the year is $430,000, which includes the following costs:

Wages	$150,000
Cleaning supplies	40,000
Cleaning equipment depreciation	20,000
Vehicle expenses	80,000
Office expenses	60,000
President's compensation	80,000
Total cost	$430,000

Resource consumption is distributed across the activities as follows:

Distribution of Resource Consumption Across Activities	Cleaning Carpets	Travel to Jobs	Job Support	Other	Total
Wages	70%	20%	0%	10%	100%
Cleaning supplies	100%	0%	0%	0%	100%
Cleaning equipment depreciation	80%	0%	0%	20%	100%
Vehicle expenses	0%	60%	0%	40%	100%
Office expenses	0%	0%	45%	55%	100%
President's compensation	0%	0%	40%	60%	100%

Job support consists of receiving calls from potential customers at the home office, scheduling jobs, billing, resolving issues, and so on.

Required:

1. Prepare the first-stage allocation of costs to the activity cost pools. (Use Exhibit 8–4 as a guide.)
2. Compute the activity rates for the activity cost pools. (Use Exhibit 8–5 as a guide.)
3. The company recently completed a 5 hundred square foot carpet-cleaning job at the Flying N ranch—a 75-mile round-trip journey from the company's offices in Bozeman. Compute the cost of this job using the activity-based costing system. (Use Exhibit 8–8 as a guide.)
4. The revenue from the Flying N ranch was $140 (5 hundred square feet @ $28 per hundred square feet). Prepare a report showing the margin from this job. (Use Exhibit 8–9 as a guide. Think of the job as a product.)
5. What do you conclude concerning the profitability of the Flying N ranch job? Explain.
6. What advice would you give the president concerning pricing jobs in the future?

PROBLEM 8–25 (Appendix 8A) Evaluating the Profitability of Services Using an Action Analysis [LO2, LO3, LO4, LO7]

Refer to the data for Gallatin Carpet Cleaning in Problem 8–24.

Required:

1. Using Exhibit 8A–1 as a guide, prepare the first-stage allocation of costs to the activity cost pools.
2. Using Exhibit 8A–2 as a guide, compute the activity rates for the activity cost pools.
3. The company recently completed a 5 hundred square foot carpet-cleaning job at the Flying N Ranch—a 75-mile round-trip journey from the company's offices in Bozeman. Using Exhibit 8A–3 as a guide, compute the cost of this job using the activity-based costing system.
4. The revenue from the Flying N Ranch was $140 (5 hundred square feet at $28 per hundred square feet). Using Exhibit 8A–5 as a guide, prepare an action analysis report of the Flying N Ranch job. The president of Gallatin Carpet Cleaning considers all of the company's costs to be Green costs except for office expenses, which are coded Yellow, and his own compensation, which is coded Red. The people who do the actual carpet cleaning are all trained part-time workers who are paid only for work actually done.
5. What do you conclude concerning the profitability of the Flying N Ranch job? Explain.
6. What advice would you give the president concerning pricing jobs in the future?

PROBLEM 8–26 Activity-Based Costing as an Alternative to Traditional Product Costing [LO3, LO4, LO6]

This chapter emphasizes the use of activity-based costing in internal decisions. However, a modified form of activity-based costing can also be used to develop product costs for external financial reports. For this purpose, product costs include all manufacturing overhead costs and exclude all nonmanufacturing costs. This problem illustrates such a costing system.

Ellix Company manufactures two models of ultra-high fidelity speakers, the X200 model and the X99 model. Data regarding the two products follow:

Product	Direct Labor-Hours	Annual Production	Total Direct Labor-Hours
X200	1.8 DLHs per unit	5,000 units	9,000 DLHs
X99	0.9 DLHs per unit	30,000 units	27,000 DLHs
			36,000 DLHs

Additional information about the company follows:

a. Model X200 requires $72 in direct materials per unit, and model X99 requires $50.
b. The direct labor rate is $10 per hour.
c. The company has always used direct labor-hours as the base for applying manufacturing overhead cost to products.
d. Model X200 is more complex to manufacture than model X99 and requires the use of special equipment.
e. Because of the special work required in (d) above, the company is considering the use of activity-based costing to apply manufacturing overhead cost to products. Three activity cost pools have been identified as follows:

Activity Cost Pool	Activity Measure	Total Cost
Machine setups	Number of setups	$ 360,000
Special processing	Machine-hours	180,000
General factory	Direct labor-hours	1,260,000
		$1,800,000

	Expected Activity		
Activity Measure	Model X200	Model X99	Total
Number of setups	50	100	150
Machine-hours	12,000	0	12,000
Direct labor-hours	9,000	27,000	36,000

Required:

1. Assume that the company continues to use direct labor-hours as the base for applying overhead cost to products.
   a. Compute the predetermined overhead rate.
   b. Compute the unit product cost of each model.
2. Assume that the company decides to use activity-based costing to apply overhead cost to products.
   a. Compute the activity rate for each activity cost pool and determine the amount of overhead cost that would be applied to each model using the activity-based costing system.
   b. Compute the unit product cost of each model.
3. Explain why overhead cost shifted from the high-volume model to the low-volume model under activity-based costing.

PROBLEM 8–27 Activity-Based Costing and Bidding on Jobs [LO2, LO3, LO4]

Mercer Asbestos Removal Company removes potentially toxic asbestos insulation and related products from buildings. There has been a long-simmering dispute between the company's estimator and the work supervisors. The on-site supervisors claim that the estimators do not adequately distinguish between routine work such as removal of asbestos insulation around heating pipes in older homes and nonroutine work such as removing asbestos-contaminated ceiling plaster in industrial buildings. The on-site supervisors believe that nonroutine work is far more expensive than routine work and should bear higher customer charges. The estimator sums up his position in this way: "My job is to measure the area to be cleared of asbestos. As directed by top management, I simply multiply the square footage by $2.50 to determine the bid price. Since our average cost is only $2.175 per square foot, that leaves enough cushion to take care of the additional costs of nonroutine work that shows up. Besides, it is difficult to know what is routine or not routine until you actually start tearing things apart."

To shed light on this controversy, the company initiated an activity-based costing study of all of its costs. Data from the activity-based costing system follow:

Activity Cost Pool	Activity Measure	Total Activity
Job size	Thousands of square feet	800 thousand square feet
Estimating and job setup	Number of jobs	500 jobs
Working on nonroutine jobs	Number of nonroutine jobs	100 nonroutine jobs
Other (costs of idle capacity and organization-sustaining costs) ...	Not applicable; these costs are not allocated to jobs	

Note: The 100 nonroutine jobs are included in the total of 500 jobs. Both nonroutine jobs and routine jobs require estimating and setup.

Costs for the Year	
Wages and salaries	$ 300,000
Disposal fees	700,000
Equipment depreciation	90,000
On-site supplies	50,000
Office expenses	200,000
Licensing and insurance	400,000
Total cost	$1,740,000

Distribution of Resource Consumption Across Activities

	Job Size	Estimating and Job Setup	Working on Nonroutine Jobs	Other	Total
Wages and salaries	50%	10%	30%	10%	100%
Disposal fees	60%	0%	40%	0%	100%
Equipment depreciation	40%	5%	20%	35%	100%
On-site supplies	60%	30%	10%	0%	100%
Office expenses	10%	35%	25%	30%	100%
Licensing and insurance	30%	0%	50%	20%	100%

Required:

1. Perform the first-stage allocation of costs to the activity cost pools. (Use Exhibit 8–4 as a guide.)
2. Compute the activity rates for the activity cost pools. (Use Exhibit 8–5 as a guide.)
3. Using the activity rates you have computed, determine the total cost and the average cost per thousand square feet of each of the following jobs according to the activity-based costing system.
   a. A routine 1,000-square-foot asbestos removal job.
   b. A routine 2,000-square-foot asbestos removal job.
   c. A nonroutine 2,000-square-foot asbestos removal job.
4. Given the results you obtained in (3) above, do you agree with the estimator that the company's present policy for bidding on jobs is adequate?

PROBLEM 8–28 Second Stage Allocations and Product Margins [LO4, LO5]

Pixel Studio, Inc., is a small company that creates computer-generated animations for films and television. Much of the company's work consists of short commercials for television, but the company also does realistic computer animations for special effects in movies.

The young founders of the company have become increasingly concerned with the economics of the business—particularly since many competitors have sprung up recently in the local area. To help understand the company's cost structure, an activity-based costing system has been designed. Three major activities are carried out in the company: animation concept, animation production, and contract administration. The animation concept activity is carried out at the contract proposal stage when the company bids on projects. This is an intensive activity that involves individuals from all parts of the company in creating story boards and prototype stills to be shown to the prospective client. Once a project is accepted by the client, the animation goes into production and contract administration begins. Almost all of the work involved in animation production is done by the technical staff, whereas the administrative staff is largely responsible for contract administration. The activity cost pools and their activity measures are listed below:

Activity Cost Pool	Activity Measure	Activity Rate
Animation concept	Number of proposals	$6,040 per proposal
Animation production	Minutes of completed animation	$7,725 per minute
Contract administration	Number of contracts	$6,800 per contract

These activity rates include all of the company' costs, except for the costs of idle capacity and organization-sustaining costs. There are no direct labor or direct materials costs.

Preliminary analysis using these activity rates has indicated that the local commercial segment of the market may be unprofitable. This segment is highly competitive. Producers of local commercials may ask three or four companies like Pixel Studio to bid, which results in an unusually low ratio of accepted contracts to bids. Furthermore, the animation sequences tend to be much shorter for local commercials than for other work. Since animation work is billed at fairly standard rates according to the running time of the completed animation, this means that the revenues from these short projects tend to be below average. Data concerning activity in the local commercial market appear below:

Activity Measure	Local Commercials
Number of proposals	25
Minutes of completed animation	5
Number of contracts	10

The total sales from the 10 contracts for local commercials was $180,000.

Required:

1. Using Exhibit 8–8 as a guide, determine the cost of the local commercial market. (Think of the local commercial market as a product.)
2. Using Exhibit 8–9 as a guide, prepare a report showing the margin of the local commercial market. (Remember, this company has no direct materials or direct labor costs.)
3. What would you recommend to management concerning the local commercial market?

PROBLEM 8–29 (Appendix 8A) Second Stage Allocations and Product Margins [LO4, LO7]

Refer to the data for Pixel Studio, Inc., in Problem 8–28. In addition, the company has provided the following details concerning its activity rates:

	Activity Rates		
	Animation Concept	Animation Production	Contract Administration
Technical staff salaries	$4,000	$6,000	$1,600
Animation equipment depreciation	360	1,125	0
Administrative wages and salaries	1,440	150	4,800
Supplies costs	120	300	160
Facility costs	120	150	240
Total	$6,040	$7,725	$6,800

Management has provided the following ease of adjustment codes for the various costs:

	Ease of Adjustment Code
Technical staff salaries	Red
Animation equipment depreciation	Red
Administrative wages and salaries	Yellow
Supplies costs	Green
Facility costs	Red

These codes created some controversy. In particular, some administrators objected to coding their own salaries Yellow, while the technical staff salaries were coded Red. However, the founders of the firm overruled these objections by pointing out that "our technical staff is our most valuable asset. Good animators are extremely difficult to find, and they would be the last to go if we had to cut back."

Required:

1. Using Exhibit 8A–3 as a guide, determine the cost of the local commercials market. (Think of the local commercial market as a product.)
2. Using Exhibit 8A–5 as a guide, prepare an action analysis report concerning the local commercial market. (This company has no direct materials or direct labor costs.)
3. What would you recommend to management concerning the local commercial market?

PROBLEM 8–30 Activity-Based Costing as an Alternative to Traditional Product Costing [LO3, LO4, LO6]

This chapter emphasizes the use of activity-based costing in internal decisions. However, a modified form of activity-based costing can also be used to develop product costs for external financial reports. For this purpose, product costs include all manufacturing overhead costs and exclude all nonmanufacturing costs. This problem illustrates such a costing system.

For many years, Zapro Company manufactured a single product called a mono-relay. Then three years ago, the company automated a portion of its plant and at the same time introduced a second product called a bi-relay which has become increasingly popular. The bi-relay is a more complex product, requiring one hour of direct labor time per unit to manufacture and extensive machining in the automated portion of the plant. The mono-relay requires only 0.75 hour of direct labor time per unit and only a small amount of machining. Manufacturing overhead costs are currently assigned to products on the basis of direct labor-hours.

Despite the growing popularity of the company's new bi-relay, profits have been declining steadily. Management is beginning to believe that there may be a problem with the company's costing system. Material and labor costs per unit are as follows:

	Mono-Relay	Bi-Relay
Direct materials	$35	$48
Direct labor (0.75 hour and 1.0 hour @ $12 per hour)	$9	$12

Management estimates that the company will incur $1,000,000 in manufacturing overhead costs during the current year and 40,000 units of the mono-relay and 10,000 units of the bi-relay will be produced and sold.

Required:

1. Compute the predetermined manufacturing overhead rate assuming that the company continues to apply manufacturing overhead cost on the basis of direct labor-hours. Using this rate and other data from the problem, determine the unit product cost of each product.
2. Management is considering using activity-based costing to apply manufacturing overhead cost to products for external financial reports. The activity-based costing system would have the following four activity cost pools:

Microsoft Excel - Problem 8-30 screen capture.xls

Activity Cost Pool (and Activity Measure)	Estimated Overhead Costs	Total	Mono-Relay	Bi-Relay
Maintaining parts inventory (number of part types)	$ 180,000	225	75	150
Processing purchase orders (number of orders)	90,000	1,000	800	200
Quality control (number of tests)	230,000	5,750	2,500	3,250
Machine-related (machine-hours)	500,000	10,000	4,000	6,000
Total overhead cost	$ 1,000,000			

Determine the predetermined overhead rate (i.e., activity rate) for each of the four activity cost pools.

3. Using the predetermined manufacturing overhead rates you computed in part (2) above, do the following:
   a. Determine the total amount of manufacturing overhead cost that would be applied to each product using the activity-based costing system. After these totals have been computed, determine the amount of manufacturing overhead cost per unit of each product.
   b. Compute the unit product cost of each product.
4. Look at the data you have computed in parts (1) through (3) above. In terms of manufacturing overhead costs, what factors make the bi-relay more costly to produce than the mono-relay? Is the bi-relay as profitable as management believes? Explain.

Cases

CASE 8–31 Activity-Based Costing and Pricing [LO3, LO4, LO5, LO6]

This chapter emphasizes the use of activity-based costing in internal decisions. However, a modified form of activity-based costing can also be used to develop product costs for external financial reports. For this purpose, product costs include all manufacturing overhead costs and exclude all nonmanufacturing costs. This problem illustrates such a costing system.

Java Source, Inc. (JSI), is a processor and distributor of a variety of blends of coffee. The company buys coffee beans from around the world and roasts, blends, and packages them for resale. JSI offers a large variety of different coffees that it sells to gourmet shops in one-pound bags. The major cost of the coffee is raw materials. However, the company's predominantly automated roasting, blending, and packing processes require a substantial amount of manufacturing overhead. The company uses relatively little direct labor.

Some of JSI's coffees are very popular and sell in large volumes, while a few of the newer blends sell in very low volumes. JSI prices its coffees at manufacturing cost plus a markup of 25%, with some adjustments made to keep the company's prices competitive.

For the coming year, JSI's budget includes estimated manufacturing overhead cost of $2,200,000. JSI assigns manufacturing overhead to products on the basis of direct labor-hours. The expected direct labor cost totals $600,000, which represents 50,000 hours of direct labor time. Based on the sales budget and expected raw materials costs, the company will purchase and use $5,000,000 of raw materials (mostly coffee beans) during the year.

The expected costs for direct materials and direct labor for one-pound bags of two of the company's coffee products appear below.

	Kenya Dark	Viet Select
Direct materials	$4.50	$2.90
Direct labor (0.02 hours per bag)	$0.24	$0.24

JSI's controller believes that the company's traditional costing system may be providing misleading cost information. To determine whether or not this is correct, the controller has prepared an analysis of the year's expected manufacturing overhead costs, as shown in the following table:

Activity Cost Pool	Activity Measure	Expected Activity for the Year	Expected Cost for the Year
Purchasing	Purchase orders	2,000 orders	$ 560,000
Material handling	Number of setups	1,000 setups	193,000
Quality control	Number of batches	500 batches	90,000
Roasting	Roasting hours	95,000 roasting hours	1,045,000
Blending	Blending hours	32,000 blending hours	192,000
Packaging	Packaging hours	24,000 packaging hours	120,000
Total manufacturing overhead cost			$2,200,000

Data regarding the expected production of Kenya Dark and Viet Select coffee are presented below.

	Kenya Dark	Viet Select
Expected sales	80,000 pounds	4,000 pounds
Batch size	5,000 pounds	500 pounds
Setups	2 per batch	2 per batch
Purchase order size	20,000 pounds	500 pounds
Roasting time per 100 pounds	1.5 roasting hours	1.5 roasting hours
Blending time per 100 pounds	0.5 blending hours	0.5 blending hours
Packaging time per 100 pounds	0.3 packaging hours	0.3 packaging hours

Required:

1. Using direct labor-hours as the base for assigning manufacturing overhead cost to products, do the following:
   a. Determine the predetermined overhead rate that will be used during the year.

b. Determine the unit product cost of one pound of the Kenya Dark coffee and one pound of the Viet Select coffee.

2. Using activity-based costing as the basis for assigning manufacturing overhead cost to products, do the following:
   a. Determine the total amount of manufacturing overhead cost assigned to the Kenya Dark coffee and to the Viet Select coffee for the year.
   b. Using the data developed in (2*a*) above, compute the amount of manufacturing overhead cost per pound of the Kenya Dark coffee and the Viet Select coffee. Round all computations to the nearest whole cent.
   c. Determine the unit product cost of one pound of the Kenya Dark coffee and one pound of the Viet Select coffee.
3. Write a brief memo to the president of JSI explaining what you have found in (1) and (2) above and discussing the implications to the company of using direct labor as the base for assigning manufacturing overhead cost to products.

(CMA, adapted)

CASE 8–32 Contrasting Activity-Based Costing and Traditional Costing [LO3, LO4, LO5]

This chapter emphasizes the use of activity-based costing in internal decisions. However, a modified form of activity-based costing can also be used to develop product costs for external financial reports. For this purpose, product costs include all manufacturing overhead costs and exclude all nonmanufacturing costs. This problem illustrates such a costing system.

"Wow! Is that X-20 model ever a loser! It's time to cut back its production and shift our resources toward the new Y-30 model," said Darrel Karter, executive vice president of Cutler Products, Inc. "Just look at this income statement I've received from accounting. The Y-30 is generating four times as much profit as the X-20, and it has only about one-sixth as much in sales. I'm convinced that our future depends on the Y-30." The year-end statement to which Darrel was referring follows:

		Model	
	Total	X-20	Y-30
Sales	$7,250,000	$6,000,000	$1,250,000
Cost of goods sold	4,600,000	3,660,000	940,000
Gross margin	2,650,000	2,340,000	310,000
Less selling and administrative expenses	2,450,000	2,300,000	150,000
Net operating income	$ 200,000	$ 40,000	$ 160,000
Number of units produced and sold		30,000	5,000

"The numbers sure look that way," replied Karen Carpenter, the company's sales manager. "But why isn't the competition more excited about the Y-30? I know we've only been producing the model for three years, but I'm surprised that more of our competitors haven't recognized what a cash cow it is."

"I think it's our new automated plant," replied Darrel. "Now it takes only two direct labor-hours to produce a unit of the X-20 and three direct labor-hours to produce a unit of the Y-30. That's considerably less than it used to take us."

"I agree that automation is wonderful," replied Karen. "I suppose that's how we're able to hold down the price of the Y-30. Branson Company in Germany tried to bring out a Y-30 but discovered they couldn't touch our price. But Branson is killing us on the X-20 by undercutting our price with some of our best customers. I suppose they'll pick up all of our X-20 business if we move out of that market. But who cares? We don't even have to advertise the Y-30; it just seems to sell itself."

"My only concern about automation is how our manufacturing overhead rate has shot up," said Darrel. "Our total manufacturing overhead cost is $1,800,000. That comes out to be a hefty amount per direct labor-hour, but Darlene down in accounting has been using direct labor-hours as the base for computing overhead rates for years and doesn't want to change. I don't suppose it matters so long as costs get assigned to products."

"I've never understood that debit and credit stuff," replied Karen. "But I think you've got a problem in production. I had lunch with Joanne yesterday and she complained about how complex the Y-30 is to produce. Apparently they have to do a lot of setups, special soldering, and other work on the Y-30 just to keep production moving. And they have to inspect every single unit."

"It'll have to wait," said Darrel. "I'm writing a proposal to the board of directors to phase out the X-20. We've got to increase our bottom line or we'll all be looking for jobs."

Required:

1. Compute the predetermined overhead rate based on direct labor-hours that the company used during the year. (There was no under- or overapplied overhead for the year.)
2. Direct materials and direct labor costs per unit for the two products are as follows:

	X-20	Y-30
Direct materials	$50	$80
Direct labor	$24	$36

   Using these data and the rate computed in part (1) above, determine the unit product cost of each product under the company's traditional costing system.
3. Assume that the company's $1,800,000 in manufacturing overhead cost can be assigned to six activity cost pools, as follows:

Activity Cost Pool (and Activity Measure)	Estimated Overhead Costs	Expected Activity Total	X-20	Y-30
Machine setups (number of setups)	$ 208,000	1,600	1,000	600
Quality control (number of inspections)	360,000	9,000	4,000	5,000
Purchase orders (number of orders)	90,000	1,200	840	360
Soldering (number of solder joints)	450,000	200,000	60,000	140,000
Shipments (number of shipments)	132,000	600	400	200
Machine related (machine-hours)	560,000	70,000	30,000	40,000
	$1,800,000			

   Given these data, would you support a recommendation to expand sales of the Y-30? Explain your position.
4. From the data you have prepared in part (3) above, why do you suppose the Y-30 "just seems to sell itself"?
5. If you were president of Cutler Products, Inc., what strategy would you follow from this point forward to improve the company's overall profits?

CASE 8–33 (Appendix 8A) Comprehensive Activity-Based Costing Case [LO2, LO3, LO4, LO6, LO7]

eXcel

Classic Windows is a small company that builds specialty wooden windows for local builders. For years the company has assigned overhead costs to products based on direct labor-hours (DLHs). However, the company's president became interested in activity-based costing after reading an article about activity-based costing in a trade journal. An activity-based costing design team was put together, and within a few months a simple system consisting of four activity cost pools had been created. The activity cost pools and their activity measures appear below:

Activity Cost Pool	Activity Measure	Activity for the Year
Making windows	Direct labor-hours	100,000 DLHs
Processing orders	Number of orders	2,000 orders
Customer relations	Number of customers	100 customers
Other (costs of idle capacity and organization-sustaining costs)	None	Not applicable

The Processing Orders activity cost pool includes order taking, job setup, job scheduling, and so on. Direct materials and direct labor are directly assigned to jobs in both the traditional and activity-based costing systems. The total overhead cost (both nonmanufacturing and manufacturing) for the year is $1,370,000 and includes the following costs:

Manufacturing overhead costs:		
Indirect factory wages	$400,000	
Production equipment depreciation	300,000	
Other factory costs	80,000	$ 780,000
Selling and administrative expenses:		
Administrative wages and salaries	300,000	
Office expenses	40,000	
Marketing expenses	250,000	590,000
Total overhead cost		$1,370,000

Based largely on interviews with employees, the distribution of resource consumption across the activities has been estimated as follows:

Distribution of Resource Consumption Across Activities

	Making Windows	Processing Orders	Customer Relations	Other	Total
Indirect factory wages	30%	40%	10%	20%	100%
Production equipment depreciation	90%	0%	0%	10%	100%
Other factory costs	30%	0%	0%	70%	100%
Administrative wages and salaries	0%	20%	30%	50%	100%
Office expenses	0%	30%	10%	60%	100%
Marketing expenses	0%	0%	60%	40%	100%

Management of the company is particularly interested in measuring the profitability of two customers. One of the customers, Kuszik Builders, is a low-volume purchaser. The other, Western Homes, is a relatively high-volume purchaser. Details of these two customers' orders for the year appear below:

	Kuszik Builders	Western Homes
Number of orders during the year	2 orders	3 orders
Total direct labor hours	300 DLHs	2,000 DLHs
Total sales	$12,500	$68,000
Total direct materials	$4,200	$18,500
Total direct labor cost	$5,400	$36,000

Required:

1. The company's traditional costing system applies manufacturing overhead to jobs using direct labor-hours. Using this traditional approach, carry out the following steps:
   a. Compute the predetermined manufacturing overhead rate.
   b. Compute the total margin for all of the windows ordered by Kuszik Builders according to the traditional costing system. Do the same for Western Homes.
2. Using activity-based costing, do the following:
   a. Perform the first-stage allocation of costs to the activity cost pools. (Use Exhibit 8–4 as a guide.)
   b. Compute the activity rates for the activity cost pools. (Use Exhibit 8–5 as a guide.)
   c. Compute the overhead costs of serving each of the two customers. (You will need to construct a table like Exhibit 8–8 for each of the customers. However, unlike Exhibit 8–8, you should fill in the column for Customer Relations as well as the other columns. Exhibit 8–8 was constructed for a product; in this case we are interested in a customer.)
   d. Prepare an action analysis report showing the margin on business with Kuszik Builders. (The ease of adjustment codes follow.) Repeat for Western Homes.

	Ease of Adjustment Code
Direct materials	Green
Direct labor	Yellow
Indirect factory wages	Yellow
Production equipment depreciation	Yellow
Other factory costs	Yellow
Administrative wages and salaries	Red
Office expenses	Yellow
Marketing expenses	Yellow

3. Does Classic Windows appear to be losing money on either customer? Do the traditional and activity-based costing systems agree concerning the profitability of the customers? If they do not agree, which costing system do you believe? Why?

CASE 8–34 Activity-Based Costing as an Alternative to Traditional Product Costing [LO3, LO4, LO5, LO6]*

This chapter emphasizes the use of activity-based costing in internal decisions. However, a modified form of activity-based costing can also be used to develop product costs for external financial reports. For this purpose, product costs include all manufacturing overhead costs and exclude all nonmanufacturing costs. This problem illustrates such a costing system.

"A dollar of gross margin per briefcase? That's ridiculous!" roared Art Dejans, president of CarryAll, Inc. "Why do we go on producing those standard briefcases when we're able to make over $15 per unit on our specialty items? Maybe it's time to get out of the standard line and focus the whole plant on specialty work."

Mr. Dejans is referring to a summary of unit costs and revenues that he had just received from the company's Accounting Department:

	Standard Briefcases	Specialty Briefcases
Selling price per unit	$36	$40
Unit product cost	35	25
Gross margin per unit	$ 1	$15

CarryAll produces briefcases from leather, fabric, and synthetic materials in a single plant. The basic product is a standard briefcase that is made from leather lined with fabric. The standard briefcase is a high-quality item and has sold well for many years.

Last year, the company decided to expand its product line and produce specialty briefcases for special orders. These briefcases differ from the standard in that they vary in size, they contain the finest leather and synthetic materials, and they are imprinted with the buyer's name. To reduce labor costs on the specialty briefcases, automated machines do most of the cutting and stitching. These machines are used to a much lesser degree in the production of standard briefcases.

"I agree that the specialty business is looking better and better," replied Sally Henrie, the company's marketing manager. "And there seems to be plenty of specialty work out there, particularly since the competition hasn't been able to touch our price. Did you know that Armor Company, our biggest competitor, charges over $50 a unit for its specialty items? Now that's what I call gouging the customer!"

---

* Adapted from a case written by Harold P. Roth and Imogene Posey, "Management Accounting Case Study: CarryAll Company," *Management Accounting Campus Report,* Institute of Management Accountants (Fall 1991), p. 9. Used by permission.

A breakdown of the manufacturing cost for each of CarryAll's product lines is given below:

	Standard Briefcases	Specialty Briefcases
Units produced each month	10,000	2,500
Direct materials:		
Leather	$15.00	$ 7.50
Fabric	5.00	5.00
Synthetic	0	5.00
Total direct materials	20.00	17.50
Direct labor 0.5 DLH and 0.25 DLH @ $12 per DLH	6.00	3.00
Manufacturing overhead 0.5 DLH and 0.25 DLH @ $18 per DLH	9.00	4.50
Total cost per unit	$35.00	$25.00

Manufacturing overhead is applied to products on the basis of direct labor-hours. The rate of $18 per direct labor-hour is determined by dividing the total manufacturing overhead cost for a month by the direct labor-hours:

$$\frac{\text{Predetermined}}{\text{overhead rate}} = \frac{\text{Manufacturing overhead}}{\text{Direct labor-hours}} = \frac{\$101{,}250}{5{,}625 \text{ DLHs}} = \$18 \text{ per DLH}$$

The following additional information is available about the company and its products:

a. Standard briefcases are produced in batches of 200 units, and specialty briefcases are produced in batches of 25 units. Thus, the company does 50 setups for the standard items each month and 100 setups for the specialty items. A setup for the standard items requires one hour of time, whereas a setup for the specialty items requires two hours of time.

b. All briefcases are inspected to ensure that quality standards are met. A total of 300 hours of inspection time is spent on the standard briefcases and 500 hours of inspection time is spent on the specialty briefcases each month.

c. A standard briefcase requires 0.5 hour of machine time, and a specialty briefcase requires 2 hours of machine time.

d. The company is considering the use of activity-based costing as an alternative to its traditional costing system for computing unit product costs. Since these unit product costs will be used for external financial reporting, all manufacturing overhead costs are to be allocated to products and nonmanufacturing costs are to be excluded from product costs. The activity-based costing system has already been designed and costs allocated to the activity cost pools. The activity cost pools and activity measures are detailed below:

Activity Cost Pool	Activity Measure	Estimated Overhead Cost
Purchasing	Number of orders	$12,000
Material handling	Number of receipts	15,000
Production orders and setup	Setup hours	20,250
Inspection	Inspection-hours	16,000
Frame assembly	Assembly-hours	8,000
Machine related	Machine-hours	30,000
		$101,250

Activity Measure	Expected Activity		
	Standard Briefcase	Specialty Briefcase	Total
Number of orders:			
Leather	34	6	40
Fabric	48	12	60
Synthetic material	0	100	100
Number of receipts:			
Leather	52	8	60
Fabric	64	16	80
Synthetic material	0	160	160
Setup hours	?	?	?
Inspection-hours	?	?	?
Assembly-hours	800	800	1,600
Machine-hours	?	?	?

Required:

1. Using activity-based costing, determine the amount of manufacturing overhead cost that would be applied to each standard briefcase and each specialty briefcase.
2. Using the data computed in (1) above and other data from the case as needed, determine the unit product cost of each product line from the perspective of the activity-based costing system.
3. Within the limitations of the data that have been provided, evaluate the president's concern about the profitability of the two product lines. Would you recommend that the company shift its resources entirely to production of specialty briefcases? Explain.
4. Sally Henrie stated that "the competition hasn't been able to touch our price" on specialty business. Why do you suppose the competition hasn't been able to touch CarryAll's price?

Group and Internet Exercises

GROUP EXERCISE 8–35 Dividing the Bill

Assume that you and your friends go to a restaurant as a group. At the end of the meal, you must decide how the bill for the group should be shared. One alternative is to figure out the cost of what each individual consumed and divide up the bill accordingly. Another alternative is to split the bill equally among the individuals.

Required:

Which system for dividing the bill is more equitable? Which system is easier to use? How does this issue relate to the material covered in this chapter?

GROUP EXERCISE 8–36 The Impact of Changing Cost Systems on Product Costs

A manufacturing company is thinking of changing its method of computing product costs for the purposes of making decisions. Under the company's traditional direct labor-based costing system, manufacturing overhead costs are applied to products on the basis of direct labor-hours. Under the proposed activity-based costing (ABC) system, manufacturing overhead costs would be applied to products using a variety of activity measures at the unit, batch, and product levels.

Required:

For each of the following products, indicate whether its unit product cost will increase or decrease when switching from a traditional direct labor-based costing system to an activity-based costing system.

1. A low-volume product that is produced in small batches.
2. A high-volume product that is produced in large batches with automated equipment and that requires very few direct labor-hours per unit.
3. A high-volume product that requires little machine work but a lot of direct labor.

INTERNET EXERCISE 8–37

As you know, the World Wide Web is a medium that is constantly evolving. Sites come and go, and change without notice. To enable the periodic updating of site addresses, this problem has been posted to the textbook website (www.mhhe.com/garrison11e). After accessing the site, enter the Student Center and select this chapter. Select and complete the Internet Exercise.

Chapter

9

Profit Planning

LEARNING OBJECTIVES

After studying Chapter 9, you should be able to:

LO1 Understand why organizations budget and the processes they use to create budgets.

LO2 Prepare a sales budget, including a schedule of expected cash collections.

LO3 Prepare a production budget.

LO4 Prepare a direct materials budget, including a schedule of expected cash disbursements for purchases of materials.

LO5 Prepare a direct labor budget.

LO6 Prepare a manufacturing overhead budget.

LO7 Prepare a selling and administrative expense budget.

LO8 Prepare a cash budget.

LO9 Prepare a budgeted income statement.

LO10 Prepare a budgeted balance sheet.

BUSINESS FOCUS

Lilo & Stitch on Budget

The full-length feature cartoon *Tarzan* grossed about $450 million worldwide for the Walt Disney Company. However, production costs got out of control. The company traditionally manages film production by focusing on meeting the planned release date—paying little attention to costs. In the case of *Tarzan,* production fell behind schedule due to the tendency of animation teams to add more eye-dazzling complexity to each production. At one point, it was estimated that 190,000 individual drawings would be needed to complete the film in contrast to the 130,000 drawings needed to complete *The Lion King*. To meet *Tarzan*'s release date, workers were pulled off other productions and were often paid at overtime rates. The size of the film crew eventually reached 573, which was nearly twice the size of the crew that had made *The Lion King*. With animators earning salaries in the hundreds of thousands of dollars, the cost implications were staggering.

Thomas S. Schumacher, Disney's feature-animation chief, was charged with dramatically reducing the cost of future films while making sure that the audience wouldn't notice any decline in quality. *Lilo & Stitch* was the first film to be produced with this goal in mind. The process began by prioritizing where the money was to be spent. The budget for music was kept generous; animation costs were cut by controlling the small details that add big costs with little effect on the quality of the film. For example, animators wanted to draw cute designs on the shirts worn by Nani, Lilo's big sister. However, adding this level of detail on every frame in which Nani appears in the film would have added about $250,000 in cost. By controlling such details, *Lilo & Stitch* was finished on time and at a cost of about $80 million. This contrasted with a cost of more than $150 million for *Tarzan*. ■

Source: Bruce Orwall, "Comics Stripped: At Disney, String of Weak Cartoons Leads to Cost Cuts," *The Wall Street Journal*, June 18, 2002, pp. A1 and A8.

In this chapter, we focus on the steps taken by businesses to achieve their planned levels of profits—a process called *profit planning*. We shall see that profit planning is accomplished through the preparation of a number of budgets, which, when brought together, form an integrated business plan known as the *master budget*. The master budget is an essential management tool that communicates management's plans throughout the organization, allocates resources, and coordinates activities.

The Basic Framework of Budgeting

LEARNING OBJECTIVE 1
Understand why organizations budget and the processes they use to create budgets.

A **budget** is a detailed plan for acquiring and using financial and other resources over a specified time period. It represents a plan for the future expressed in formal quantitative terms. The act of preparing a budget is called *budgeting*. The use of budgets to control an organization's activities is known as *budgetary control*.

The **master budget** is a summary of a company's plans that sets specific targets for sales, production, distribution, and financing activities. It generally culminates in a cash budget, a budgeted income statement, and a budgeted balance sheet. In short, it represents a comprehensive expression of management's plans for the future and how these plans are to be accomplished.

Personal Budgets

Nearly everyone budgets to some extent, even though many of the people who use budgets do not recognize what they are doing as budgeting. For example, most people make estimates of their income and plan expenditures for food, clothing, housing, and so on. As a result of this planning, people restrict their spending to some predetermined, allowable amount. While they may not be conscious of the fact, these people clearly go through a budgeting process. Income is estimated, expenditures are planned, and spending is restricted in accordance with the plan. Individuals also use budgets to forecast their future financial condition for purposes such as purchasing a home, financing college education, or setting aside funds for retirement. These budgets may exist only in the mind of the individual, but they are budgets nevertheless.

The budgets of a business or other organization serve much the same functions as the budgets prepared informally by individuals. Business budgets tend to be more detailed and to involve more work, but they are similar to the budgets prepared by individuals in most other respects. Like personal budgets, they assist in planning and controlling expenditures; they also assist in predicting operating results and financial condition in future periods.

Difference between Planning and Control

The terms *planning* and *control* are often confused, and occasionally are used as though they mean the same thing. Actually, planning and control are two quite distinct concepts. **Planning** involves developing objectives and preparing various budgets to achieve those objectives. **Control** involves the steps taken by management to increase the likelihood that the objectives set down at the planning stage are attained and that all parts of the organization are working together toward that goal. To be completely effective, a good budgeting system must provide for *both* planning and control. Good planning without effective control is time wasted.

Advantages of Budgeting

Companies realize many benefits from a budgeting program. Among these benefits are the following:

1. Budgets *communicate* management's plans throughout the organization.
2. Budgets force managers to *think about* and plan for the future. In the absence of the necessity to prepare a budget, many managers would spend all of their time dealing with daily emergencies.
3. The budgeting process provides a means of *allocating resources* to those parts of the organization where they can be used most effectively.
4. The budgeting process can uncover potential *bottlenecks* before they occur.
5. Budgets *coordinate* the activities of the entire organization by *integrating* the plans of its various parts. Budgeting helps to ensure that everyone in the organization is pulling in the same direction.
6. Budgets define goals and objectives that can serve as *benchmarks* for evaluating subsequent performance.

IN BUSINESS

BRINGING ORDER OUT OF CHAOS

Consider the following situation encountered by one of the authors at a mortgage banking company: For years, the company operated with virtually no system of budgets whatsoever. Management contended that budgeting wasn't well suited to the company's type of operation. Moreover, management pointed out that the company was already profitable. Indeed, outwardly the company gave every appearance of being a well-managed, smoothly operating organization. A careful look within, however, disclosed that day-to-day operations were far from smooth, and often approached chaos. The average day was nothing more than an exercise in putting out one brush fire after another. The Cash account was always at crisis levels. At the end of a day, no one ever knew whether enough cash would be available the next day to cover required loan closings. Departments were uncoordinated, and it was not uncommon to find that one department was pursuing a course of action that conflicted with the goals of another department. Employee morale was low, and turnover was high. Employees complained bitterly that when a job was well done, nobody ever knew about it.

The company was bought out by a new group of stockholders who required that an integrated budgeting system be established to control operations. Within one year's time, significant changes were evident. Brush fires were rare. Careful planning virtually eliminated the problems that had been experienced with cash, and departmental efforts were coordinated and directed toward predetermined overall company goals. Although the employees were initially wary of the new budgeting program, they became "converted" when they experienced its positive effects. The more efficient operations caused profits to jump dramatically. Communication increased throughout the organization. When a job was well done, everybody knew about it. As one employee stated, "For the first time, we know what the company expects of us."

Responsibility Accounting

Most of what we say in this chapter and in the next three chapters is concerned with *responsibility accounting.* The basic idea underlying **responsibility accounting** is that a manager should be held responsible for those items—and *only* those items—that the manager can actually control to a significant extent. Each line item (i.e., revenue or cost) in the budget is made the responsibility of a manager, and that manager is held responsible for subsequent deviations between budgeted goals and actual results. In effect, responsibility accounting *personalizes* accounting information by looking at revenues and costs from a *personal control* standpoint. This concept is central to any effective profit planning and control system. Someone must be held responsible for each cost or else no one will be responsible and the cost will inevitably grow out of control.

Being held responsible for financial performance does not mean that the manager is penalized if actual results do not measure up to the budgeted goals. However, the manager should take the initiative to correct any unfavorable discrepancies, should understand the source of significant favorable or unfavorable discrepancies, and should be prepared to explain the reasons for discrepancies to higher management. The point of an effective responsibility accounting system is to make sure that nothing "falls through the cracks," that the organization reacts quickly and appropriately to deviations from its plans, and that the organization learns from the feedback it gets by comparing budgeted goals to actual results. The point is *not* to penalize individuals for missing targets.

Choosing a Budget Period

Operating budgets ordinarily cover a one-year period corresponding to the company's fiscal year. Many companies divide their budget year into four quarters. The first quarter is then subdivided into months, and monthly budgets are developed. The last three quarters may be carried in the budget as quarterly totals only. As the year progresses, the figures for the second quarter are broken down into monthly amounts, then the third-quarter figures are broken down, and so forth. This approach has the advantage of requiring periodic review and reappraisal of budget data throughout the year.

IN BUSINESS

HEADING OFF A CRISIS

The Repertory Theatre of St. Louis is a not-for-profit professional theater that is supported by contributions from donors and by ticket sales. Financially, the theater appeared to be doing well. However, a five-year budget revealed that within a few years, expenses would exceed revenues and the theater would be facing a financial crisis. Realistically, additional contributions from donors would not fill the gap. Cutting costs would not work because of the theater's already lean operations; cutting costs even more would jeopardize the quality of the theater's productions. Raising ticket prices was ruled out due to competitive pressures and to the belief that this would be unpopular with many donors. The solution was to build a second mainstage performing space that would allow the theater to put on more performances to generate more revenue. By developing a long-range budget, the management of The Repertory Theatre of St. Louis was able to identify in advance a looming financial crisis and to develop a solution that would avert the crisis in time.

Source: Lawrence P. Carr, ed., "The Repertory Theatre of St. Louis (B): Strategic Budgeting," *Cases from Management Accounting Practice: Volumes 10 and 11*, Institute of Management Accountants, Montvale, NJ, 1997. See the theater's website at www.repstl.org for information concerning the current season.

Continuous or *perpetual budgets* are used by a significant number of organizations. A **continuous** or **perpetual budget** is a 12-month budget that rolls forward one month (or quarter) as the current month (or quarter) is completed. In other words, one month (or quarter) is added to the end of the budget as each month (or quarter) comes to a close. This approach keeps managers focused on the future at least one year ahead. Advocates of continuous budgets argue that with this approach there is less danger that managers will become too narrowly focused on short-term results.

In this chapter, we will look at one-year operating budgets. However, using basically the same techniques, operating budgets can be prepared for periods that extend over many years. It may be difficult to accurately forecast sales and required data much beyond a year, but even rough estimates can be invaluable in uncovering potential problems and opportunities that would otherwise be overlooked.

IN BUSINESS

KEEPING CURRENT

Jim Bell, Hunstman Corp.'s director of corporate finance, says that his company must frequently update its budgets and its forecasts to meet the demands of investors, creditors, and others. The company updates its annual budget each month, using the most recent data, to provide greater accuracy as the year unfolds. The budget is also used together with sophisticated modeling software to evaluate what effects decisions and various changes in input prices and other parameters might have on future results.

Source: Tim Reason, "Partial Clearing," *CFO*, December 2002, pp. 73–76.

The Self-Imposed Budget

The success of a budget program will be largely determined by the way in which the budget is developed. In the most successful budget programs, managers actively participate in preparing their own budgets. This is in contrast to the approach in which budgets are imposed from above. The participative approach to preparing budgets is particularly important if the budget is to be used to control and evaluate a manager's performance. If a budget is imposed on a manager from above, it will probably generate resentment rather than cooperation and commitment.

The budgeting approach in which managers prepare their own budget estimates—called a *self-imposed budget*—is generally considered to be the most effective method of budget preparation. A **self-imposed budget** or **participative budget,** as illustrated in Exhibit 9–1, is a budget that is prepared with the full cooperation and participation of managers at all levels.

A number of advantages are commonly cited for such self-imposed budgets:

1. Individuals at all levels of the organization are recognized as members of the team whose views and judgments are valued by top management.
2. Budget estimates prepared by front-line managers are often more accurate and reliable than estimates prepared by top managers who have less intimate knowledge of markets and day-to-day operations.
3. Motivation is generally higher when individuals participate in setting their own goals than when the goals are imposed from above. Self-imposed budgets create commitment.
4. A manager who is not able to meet a budget that has been imposed from above can always say that the budget was unrealistic and impossible to meet. With a self-imposed budget, this excuse is not available.

Once self-imposed budgets are prepared, are they subject to any kind of review? The answer is yes. Budget estimates prepared by lower-level managers should be scrutinized

EXHIBIT 9–1
The Initial Flow of Budget Data in a Participative Budgeting System

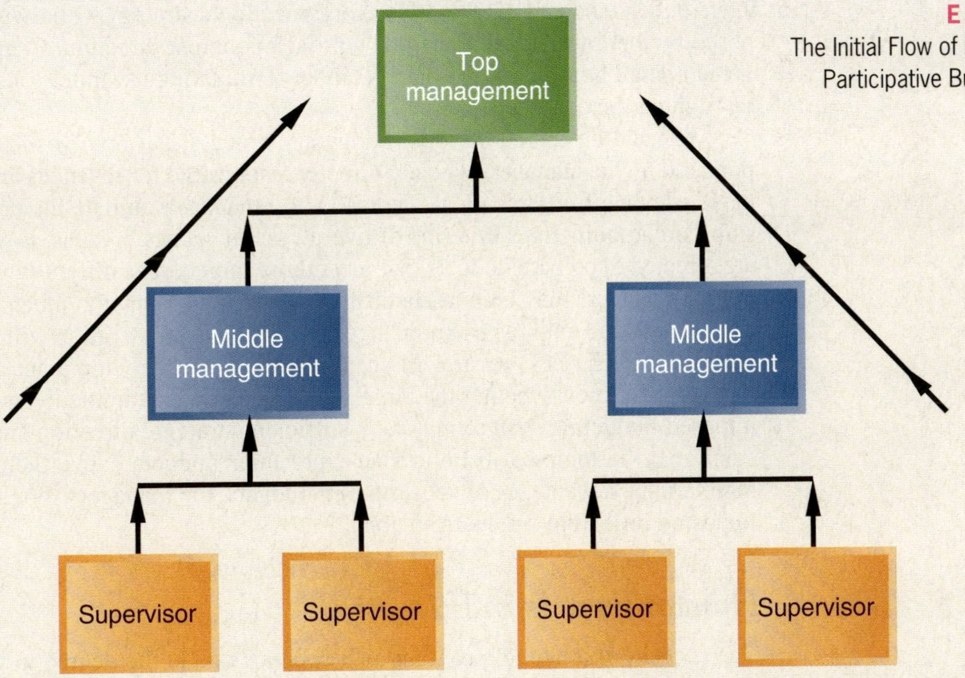

The initial flow of budget data in a participative system is from lower levels of responsibility to higher levels of responsibility. Each person with responsibility for cost control will prepare his or her own budget estimates and submit them to the next higher level of management. These estimates are reviewed and consolidated as they move upward in the organization.

by higher levels of management. Without such a review, self-imposed budgets may be too loose and allow too much "budgetary slack." The result will be inefficiency and waste. Therefore, before budgets are accepted, they must be carefully reviewed by immediate superiors. If changes from the original budget seem desirable, the items in question are discussed and modified as necessary.

IN BUSINESS

CUTTING SLACK IN IRELAND

A study of budgeting in four Irish businesses provides some interesting insights into controlling budgetary slack. It appears that one of the best ways to control budgetary slack is to train management accountants so that they fully understand the operational side of the business. As one operating manager put it, "Finance [i.e., management accountants] understand my budget completely. There is no slack or opportunity for slack." In contrast, budgetary slack was greatest in a subsidiary of a company headquartered in North America whose management accountants least understood the operating side of the business and yet always insisted that the budget be met. In fact, in this particular organization, corporate headquarters had previously ordered the Irish subsidiary midway through a year to deliver additional cost savings to make up for poor performance elsewhere in the corporation. Not surprisingly, the managers of the Irish subsidiary now routinely pad their budgets in case this happens again.

Source: Paul Pendergast, "Budget Padding: Is It a Job for the Finance Police?" *Management Accounting* (UK), November 1997, pp. 44–46.

In essence, all levels of an organization should work together to produce the budget. Since top management is generally unfamiliar with detailed, day-to-day operations, it should rely on subordinates to provide detailed budget data. On the other hand, top management has an overall strategic perspective that is also vital. Each level of responsibility in an organization should contribute its unique knowledge and perspective in a *cooperative* effort to develop an integrated budget.

To be successful, a self-imposed approach to setting budgets requires that all managers understand and agree with the organization's strategy. Otherwise, the budgets proposed by the lower-level managers will lack coherent direction. Chapter 10 discusses in greater detail how a company can go about formulating its strategy and communicating it throughout the organization.

We have described an ideal budgetary process that involves self-imposed budgets prepared by the managers who are directly responsible for revenues and costs. Most companies deviate from this ideal. Typically, top managers initiate the budget process by issuing broad guidelines in terms of overall target profits or sales. Lower-level managers are directed to prepare budgets that meet those targets. The difficulty is that the targets set by top managers may be unrealistically high or may allow too much slack. If the targets are too high and employees know they are unrealistic, motivation will suffer. If the targets allow too much slack, waste will occur. And unfortunately top managers are often not in a position to know whether the targets are appropriate. Admittedly, however, a pure self-imposed budgeting system may lack sufficient strategic direction and lower-level managers may be tempted to build slack into their budgets. Nevertheless, because of the motivational advantages of self-imposed budgets, top managers should be cautious about imposing inflexible targets from above.

Human Factors in Budgeting

The success of a budget program also depends on (1) the degree to which top management accepts the budget program as a vital part of the company's activities, and (2) the way in which top management uses budgeted data.

If a budget program is to be successful, it must have the complete acceptance and support of the persons who occupy key management positions. If lower or middle management personnel sense that top management is lukewarm about budgeting, or if they sense that top management simply tolerates budgeting as a necessary evil, then their own attitudes will reflect a similar lack of enthusiasm. Budgeting is hard work, and if top management is not enthusiastic about and committed to the budget program, then it is unlikely that anyone else in the organization will be either.

In administering the budget program, it is particularly important that top management not use the budget to pressure or blame employees. Using budgets in such negative ways will breed hostility, tension, and mistrust rather than greater cooperation and productivity. Unfortunately, the budget is too often used as a pressure device and excessive emphasis is placed on "meeting the budget" under all circumstances. Rather than being used as a weapon, the budget should be used as a positive instrument to assist in establishing goals, measuring operating results, and isolating areas that need attention.

Management must recognize that the human aspects of budgeting are extremely important. It is easy to become preoccupied with the technical aspects of the budget to the exclusion of the human aspects. Indeed, the use of budget data in a rigid and inflexible manner is often the greatest single complaint of persons whose performance is evaluated using budgets. Management should remember that the purposes of the budget are to motivate employees and to coordinate their efforts. Preoccupation with the dollars and cents in the budget, or being rigid and inflexible, is usually counterproductive.

IN BUSINESS

WHO CARES ABOUT BUDGETS?

Towers Perrin, a consulting firm, reports that the bonuses of more than two out of three corporate managers are based on meeting targets set in annual budgets. "Under this arrangement, managers at the beginning of a year all too often argue that their targets should be lowered because of tough business conditions, when in fact conditions are better than projected. If their arguments are successful, they can easily surpass the targets."

Source: Ronald Fink and Towers Perrin, "Riding the Bull: The 2000 Compensation Survey," *CFO*, June 2000, pp. 45–60.

In establishing a budget, how challenging should budget targets be? Some experts argue that budget targets should be very challenging and should require managers to stretch to meet goals. Even the most capable managers may have to scramble to meet such a "stretch budget" and they may not always succeed. In practice, most companies set their budget targets at a "highly achievable" level. A highly achievable budget may be challenging, but it can almost always be met by competent managers exerting reasonable effort.

Bonuses based on meeting and exceeding budgets are often a key element of management compensation. Typically, no bonus is paid unless the budget is met. The bonus often increases when the budget target is exceeded, but the bonus is usually capped out at some level. For obvious reasons, managers who have such a bonus plan or whose performance is evaluated based on meeting budget targets usually prefer to be evaluated based on highly achievable budgets than on stretch budgets. Moreover, highly achievable budgets may help build a manager's confidence and generate greater commitment to the budget. And finally, highly achievable budgets may result in less undesirable behavior at the end of budgetary periods by managers who are intent on earning their bonuses. Examples of such undesirable behaviors are presented in several of the In Business boxes in this chapter.

Zero-Based Budgeting

The traditional approach to budgeting starts with last year's budget and then adds to it (or subtracts from it) according to anticipated needs. This is an incremental approach to budgeting in which the previous year's budget is taken for granted as a baseline.

IN BUSINESS

BIASING FORECASTS

A manager's compensation is often tied to the budget. Typically, no bonus is paid unless a minimum performance hurdle such as 80% of the budget target is attained. Once that hurdle is passed, the manager's bonus increases until a cap is reached. That cap is often set at 120% of the budget target.

This common method of tying a manager's compensation to the budget has some serious negative side effects. For example, a marketing manager for a big beverage company intentionally grossly understated demand for the company's products for an upcoming major holiday so that the budget target for revenues would be low and easy to beat. Unfortunately, the company tied its production to this biased forecast and ran out of products to sell during the height of the holiday selling season.

As another example, near the end of the year another group of managers announced a price increase of 10% effective January 2 of the following year. Why would they do this? By announcing this price increase, managers hoped that customers would order before the end of the year, helping managers meet their sales targets for the current year. Sales in the following year would, of course, drop. What trick would managers pull to meet their sales targets next year in the face of this drop in demand?

Sources: Michael C. Jensen, "Corporate Budgeting Is Broken—Let's Fix It," *Harvard Business Review*, November, 2001 and Michael C. Jensen, "Why Pay People to Lie?" *The Wall Street Journal*, January 8, 2001, p. A32.

Zero-based budgeting is an alternative approach. Under a **zero-based budget,** managers are required to justify *all* budgeted expenditures, not just changes in the budget from the previous year. The baseline is zero rather than last year's budget.

A zero-based budget requires considerable documentation. In addition to all of the schedules in the usual master budget, the manager must prepare a series of "decision packages" in which all of the activities of the department are ranked according to their relative importance and their costs are identified. Higher-level managers can then review the decision packages and cut back in those areas that are less critical or whose costs do not appear to be justified.

Zero-based budgeting sounds like a good idea. However critics of zero-based budgeting charge that properly executed zero-based budgeting is too time-consuming and too costly to justify on an annual basis. In addition, it is argued that annual reviews soon become mechanical and that the whole purpose of zero-based budgeting is then lost.

Whether or not an organization should use an annual review is a matter of judgment. In some situations, annual zero-based reviews may be justified; in other situations, they may not be justified because of the time and cost involved. However, most managers would at least agree that on occasion zero-based reviews can be very helpful.

The Budget Committee

A standing **budget committee** is usually responsible for overall policy relating to the budget program and for coordinating the preparation of the budget itself. This committee may consist of the president; vice presidents in charge of various functions such as sales, production, and purchasing; and the controller. Difficulties and disputes relating to the budget are resolved by the budget committee. In addition, the budget committee approves the final budget and receives periodic reports on the progress of the organization in attaining budgeted goals.

Disputes can (and do) erupt over budget matters. Because budgets allocate resources, the budgeting process to a large extent determines which departments get more resources and which get less. Also, the budget sets the benchmarks by which managers and their departments will be at least partially evaluated. Therefore, it should not be surprising that managers take the budgeting process very seriously and invest considerable energy and emotion in ensuring that their interests, and those of their departments, are protected. Because of this, the budgeting process can easily degenerate into an interoffice brawl in which the ultimate goal of working together toward common goals is forgotten.

Running a successful budgeting program that avoids interoffice battles requires considerable interpersonal skills in addition to purely technical skills. But even the best interpersonal skills will fail if, as discussed earlier, top management uses the budget process to inappropriately pressure employees or to assign blame.

IN BUSINESS

THE POLITICS OF BUDGETING

Budgeting is often an intensely political process in which managers jockey for resources and relaxed goals for the upcoming year. One group of consultants describes the process in this way: Annual budgets "have a particular urgency in that they provide the standard and most public framework against which managers are assessed and judged. It is, therefore, not surprising that budget-setting is taken seriously . . . Often budgets are a means for managers getting what they want. A relaxed budget will secure a relatively easy twelve months, a tight one means that their names will constantly be coming up in the monthly management review meeting. Far better to shift the burden of cost control and financial discipline to someone else. Budgeting is an intensely political exercise conducted with all the sharper managerial skills not taught at business school, such as lobbying and flattering superiors, forced haste, regretted delay, hidden truth, half-truths, and lies."

Source: Michael Morrow, ed., *Activity-Based Management* (New York: Woodhead-Faulkner), p. 91.

IN BUSINESS

BETTER THAN BUDGETS?

Borealis is a company headquartered in Copenhagen, Denmark, that produces polymers for the plastics industry. Thomas Boesen, the company's financial controller, felt that the traditional budgeting process had outlived its usefulness—markets were changing so fast that the budget was out of date within weeks of its publication. Moreover, since budgets were used to control and evaluate the performance of managers, they were subject to considerable gaming behavior that reduced their accuracy and usefulness. So over a five-year period the company phased out its traditional budgets and replaced them with rolling forecasts and several other management tools. Instead of holding managers to a budget, targets based on competitors' performance were set for variable costs, fixed costs, and operating margins. Managers were given the freedom to spend money as needed to meet these competitive benchmarks. Since the rolling forecasts of financial results were not used to control spending or to evaluate managers' performance, managers had little incentive to "game the system," and hence the forecasts were more accurate than those obtained through the traditional budgeting process.

Source: Professor Bjorn Jorgensen, *Borealis*, Harvard Business School Case 9-102-048, Rev: May 9, 2002.

The Master Budget: An Overview

Topic Tackler PLUS 9–1

The master budget consists of a number of separate but interdependent budgets. Exhibit 9–2 provides an overview of the various parts of the master budget and how they are related.

The Sales Budget

A **sales budget** is a detailed schedule showing the expected sales for the budget period; typically, it is expressed in both dollars and units. An accurate sales budget is the key to the entire budgeting process. All of the other parts of the master budget are dependent on the sales budget, as illustrated in Exhibit 9–2. Thus, if the sales budget is sloppily done, then the rest of the budgeting process is largely a waste of time.

The sales budget helps determine how many units need to be produced. Thus, the production budget is prepared after the sales budget. The production budget in turn is used to determine the budgets for manufacturing costs including the direct materials budget, the direct labor budget, and the manufacturing overhead budget. These budgets are then combined with data from the sales budget and the selling and administrative expense budget to determine the cash budget. In essence, the sales budget triggers a chain reaction that leads to the development of the other budgets.

EXHIBIT 9–2
The Master Budget Interrelationships

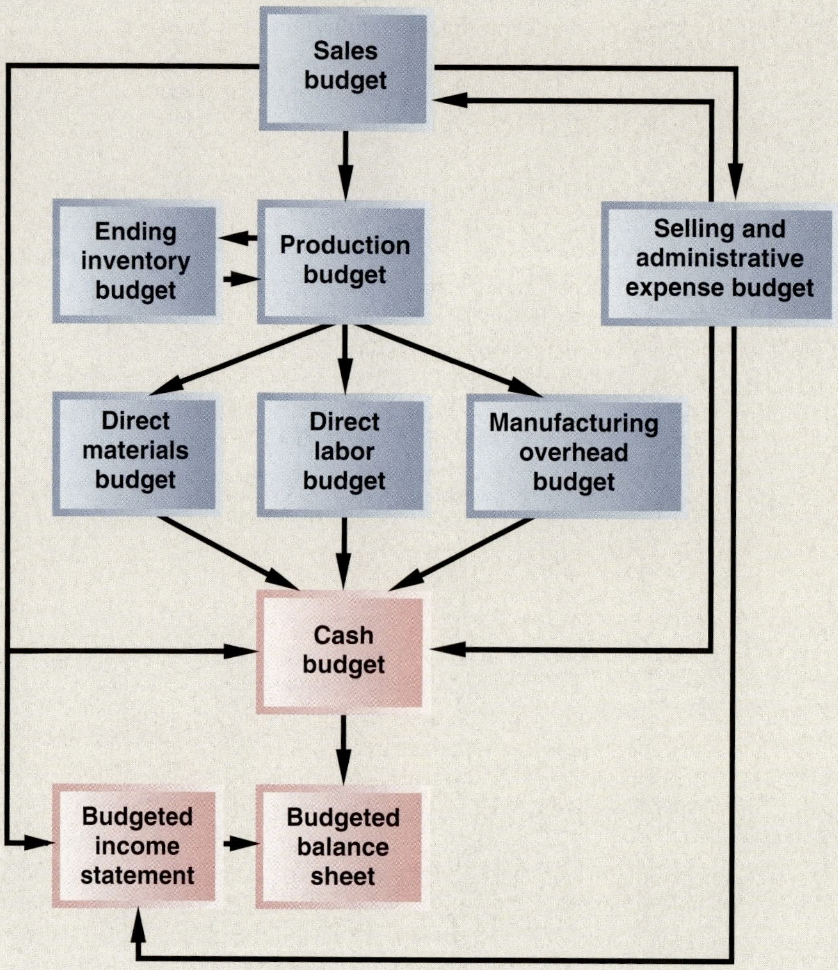

As shown in Exhibit 9–2, the selling and administrative expense budget is both dependent on and a determinant of the sales budget. This reciprocal relationship arises because sales will in part be determined by the funds committed to advertising and sales promotion.

The Cash Budget Once the operating budgets (sales, production, and so on) have been established, the cash budget and other financial budgets can be prepared. A **cash budget** is a detailed plan showing how cash resources will be acquired and used over some specified time period. Observe from Exhibit 9–2 that all of the operating budgets have an impact on the cash budget. In the case of the sales budget, the impact comes from the planned cash receipts to be received from sales. In the case of the other budgets, the impact comes from the planned cash expenditures within the budgets themselves.

Sales Forecasting—A Critical Step

The sales budget is usually based on the company's *sales forecast.* Sales from prior years are commonly used as a starting point in preparing the sales forecast. In addition, the analyst may examine the company's unfilled back orders, the company's pricing policy and marketing plans, trends in the industry, and general economic conditions. Sophisticated statistical tools may be used to analyze the data and to build models that are helpful in predicting key factors influencing the company's sales. Some companies use sophisticated computer simulations to enhance their marketing strategies and sales forecasts. We

IN BUSINESS

THE IMPORTANCE OF OWNERSHIP

Jack Stack, the president and CEO of Springfield Manufacturing, advises managers to accept the sales forecasts made by salespeople. He says that the forecasts should be substantiated, but that the forecasts should be accepted even when the manager disagrees with the forecasts. He admits that accepting a sales forecast that you disagree with can be very difficult, but he says that you have to do it. Why?

> Because if you don't, you let your salespeople off the hook. You take away their ownership of the forecast. It's not theirs anymore; it's yours—and so is the responsibility for hitting it. Oh, sure, your salespeople will go out and do their jobs, but something will be missing . . . . The pride, the desire to win that makes them dig deep down and pull off the big play when you need it. What you lose is passion—which is, ironically, the one thing you must have to achieve a reliable forecast.

Source: Jack Stack, "A Passion for Forecasting," *Inc.*, November 1997, pp. 37–38.

will not, however, go into the details of how sales forecasts are made. This is a subject that is more appropriately covered in marketing courses.

IN BUSINESS

BE REALISTIC

Gillette, the company that makes razors and other consumer products, got into trouble trying to meet increasingly unrealistic sales targets. The buyer at one of the company's big retail customers told Gillette's new CEO, Jim Kilts, that "he always waited until the last week of the quarter to order anything from Gillette 'because I know that you will always cut a deal.' To hit their numbers each quarter, [the Gillette salepersons] were willing to do anything—offer cut-rate deals, rearrange product packaging—whatever it took to make the sale." This resulted in artificially large sales at the end of the quarter—disrupting production schedules and loading the retail stores with excess inventory at discounted prices that would have to be sold off before more inventory would be ordered from Gillette.

Source: Katrina Brooker, "Jim Kilts Is an Old-School Curmudgeon," *Fortune*, December 30, 2002, pp. 95–102.

Preparing the Master Budget

MANAGERIAL ACCOUNTING IN ACTION
The Issue

Tom Wills is the majority stockholder and chief executive officer of Hampton Freeze, Inc., a company he started in 2004. The company makes premium popsicles using only natural ingredients and featuring exotic flavors such as tangy tangerine and minty mango. The company's business is highly seasonal, with most of the sales occurring in spring and summer.

In 2005, the company's second year of operations, a major cash crunch in the first and second quarters almost forced the company into bankruptcy. In spite of this cash crunch, 2005 turned out to be a very successful year in terms of both cash flow and net income. Partly as a result of that harrowing experience, Tom decided toward the end of 2005 to hire a professional financial manager. Tom interviewed several promising candidates for the job and settled on Larry Giano, who had considerable experience in the packaged foods industry. In the job interview, Tom questioned Larry about the steps he would take to prevent a recurrence of the 2005 cash crunch:

Hampton Freeze, Inc.

Tom: As I mentioned earlier, we are going to end 2005 with a very nice profit. What you may not know is that we had some very big financial problems this year.

Larry: Let me guess. You ran out of cash sometime in the first or second quarter.

Tom: How did you know?
Larry: Most of your sales are in the second and third quarter, right?
Tom: Sure, everyone wants to buy popsicles in the spring and summer, but nobody wants them when the weather turns cold.
Larry: So you don't have many sales in the first quarter?
Tom: Right.
Larry: And in the second quarter, which is the spring, you are producing like crazy to fill orders?
Tom: Sure.
Larry: Do your customers, the grocery stores, pay you the day you make your deliveries?
Tom: Are you kidding? Of course not.
Larry: So in the first quarter, you don't have many sales. In the second quarter, you are producing like crazy, which eats up cash, but you aren't paid by your customers until long after you have paid your employees and suppliers. No wonder you had a cash problem. I see this pattern all the time in food processing because of the seasonality of the business.
Tom: So what can we do about it?
Larry: The first step is to predict the magnitude of the problem before it occurs. If we can predict early in the year what the cash shortfall is going to be, we can go to the bank and arrange for credit before we really need it. Bankers tend to be leery of panicky people who show up begging for emergency loans. They are much more likely to make the loan if you look like you know what you are doing, you have done your homework, and you are in control of the situation.
Tom: How can we predict the cash shortfall?
Larry: You can put together a cash budget. While you're at it, you might as well do a master budget. You'll find it is well worth the effort.
Tom: I don't like budgets. They are too confining. My wife budgets everything at home, and I can't spend what I want.
Larry: Can I ask a personal question?
Tom: What?
Larry: Where did you get the money to start this business?
Tom: Mainly from our family's savings. I get your point. We wouldn't have had the money to start the business if my wife hadn't been forcing us to save every month.
Larry: Exactly. I suggest you use the same discipline in your business. It is even more important here because you can't expect your employees to spend your money as carefully as you would.

With the full backing of Tom Wills, Larry Giano set out to create a master budget for the company for the year 2006. In his planning for the budgeting process, Larry drew up the following list of documents that would be a part of the master budget:

1. A sales budget, including a schedule of expected cash collections.
2. A production budget (a merchandise purchases budget would be used in a merchandising company).
3. A direct materials budget, including a schedule of expected cash disbursements for raw materials.
4. A direct labor budget.
5. A manufacturing overhead budget.
6. An ending finished goods inventory budget.
7. A selling and administrative expense budget.
8. A cash budget.
9. A budgeted income statement.
10. A budgeted balance sheet.

Larry felt it was important to have everyone's cooperation in the budgeting process, so he asked Tom to call a companywide meeting in which the budgeting process would be explained. At the meeting there was initially some grumbling, but Tom was able to convince nearly everyone of the necessity for planning and getting better control over spending. It helped that the cash crisis earlier in the year was still fresh in everyone's minds. As much as some people disliked the idea of budgets, they liked their jobs more.

In the months that followed, Larry worked closely with all of the managers involved in the master budget, gathering data from them and making sure that they understood and fully supported the parts of the master budget that would affect them. In subsequent years, Larry hoped to turn the whole budgeting process over to the managers and to take a more advisory role.

The interdependent documents that Larry Giano prepared for Hampton Freeze are Schedules 1 through 10 of his company's master budget. In this section, we will study these schedules.

LEARNING OBJECTIVE 2
Prepare a sales budget, including a schedule of expected cash collections.

The Sales Budget

The sales budget is the starting point in preparing the master budget. As shown earlier in Exhibit 9–2, all other items in the master budget, including production, purchases, inventories, and expenses, depend on it.

The sales budget is constructed by multiplying the budgeted sales in units by the selling price. Schedule 1 below contains the quarterly sales budget for Hampton Freeze for the year 2006. Notice from the schedule that the company plans to sell 100,000 cases of popsicles during the year, with sales peaking in the third quarter.

A schedule of expected cash collections, such as the one that appears in Schedule 1 for Hampton Freeze, is prepared after the sales budget. This schedule will be needed later to prepare the cash budget. Cash collections consist of collections on credit sales made to customers in prior periods plus collections on sales made in the current budget period. At Hampton Freeze, experience has shown that 70% of sales are collected in the quarter in which the sale is made and the remaining 30% are collected in the following quarter. For example, 70% of the first quarter sales of $200,000 (or $140,000) is collected during the first quarter and 30% (or $60,000) is collected during the second quarter.

Schedule 1

Microsoft Excel - Hampton Freeze.xls

HAMPTON FREEZE, INC.
Sales Budget
For the Year Ended December 31, 2006

	Quarter 1	2	3	4	Year
Budgeted sales in cases	10,000	30,000	40,000	20,000	100,000
Selling price per case	$ 20.00	$ 20.00	$ 20.00	$ 20.00	$ 20.00
Total sales	$200,000	$600,000	$800,000	$400,000	$2,000,000
Percentage of sales collected in the period of the sale			70%		
Percentage of sales collected in the period after the sale			30%		

Schedule of Expected Cash Collections

	Quarter 1	2	3	4	Year
Accounts receivable, beginning balance[1]	$ 90,000				$ 90,000
First-quarter sales[2]	140,000	$ 60,000			200,000
Second-quarter sales[3]		420,000	$180,000		600,000
Third-quarter sales[4]			560,000	$240,000	800,000
Fourth-quarter sales[5]	-	-	-	280,000	280,000
Total cash collections[6]	$230,000	$480,000	$740,000	$520,000	$1,970,000

Schedule 1 / Schedule 2 / Schedule 3 / Schedule 4 / Schedule 5 / Sche

[1]Cash collections from last year's fourth-quarter sales. See the beginning-of-year balance sheet on page 400.
[2]$200,000 × 70%; $200,000 × 30%.
[3]$600,000 × 70%; $600,000 × 30%.
[4]$800,000 × 70%; $800,000 × 30%.
[5]$400,000 × 70%.
[6]Uncollected fourth-quarter sales appear as accounts receivable on the company's end-of-year balance sheet (see Schedule 10 on page 401).

IN BUSINESS

PREDICTING DEMAND

O'Reilly Auto Parts uses sophisticated demand software from Nonstop Solutions to forecast seasonal variations in sales. For example, monthly sales of windshield wiper blades vary from 25,000 in the summer to 50,000 in the winter. Demand software uses weather data, economic trends, and other information to make forecasts and can even learn from its past mistakes.

Source: Chana R. Schoenberger, "The Weakest Link," *Forbes*, October 1, 2001, pp. 114–115.

The Production Budget

LEARNING OBJECTIVE 3
Prepare a production budget.

The production budget is prepared after the sales budget. The **production budget** lists the number of units that must be produced during each budget period to meet sales needs and to provide for the desired ending inventory. Production needs can be determined as follows:

Budgeted unit sales	XXXX
Add desired ending inventory	XXXX
Total needs	XXXX
Less beginning inventory	XXXX
Required production	XXXX

Note that production requirements for a quarter are influenced by the desired level of the ending inventory. Inventories should be carefully planned. Excessive inventories tie up funds and create storage problems. Insufficient inventories can lead to lost sales or last-minute, high-cost crash production efforts. At Hampton Freeze, management believes that an ending inventory equal to 20% of the next quarter's sales strikes the appropriate balance.

Schedule 2 contains the production budget for Hampton Freeze. The first row in the production budget contains the budgeted sales, which have been taken directly from the sales budget (Schedule 1). The total needs for the first quarter are determined by adding together the budgeted sales of 10,000 cases for the quarter and the desired ending inventory of 6,000 cases. As discussed above, the ending inventory is intended to provide some cushion in case problems develop in production or sales increase unexpectedly. Since the budgeted sales for the second quarter are 30,000 cases and management would like the ending inventory in each quarter to be equal to 20% of the following quarter's sales, the desired ending inventory is 6,000 cases (20% of 30,000 cases). Consequently, the total needs for the first quarter are 16,000 cases. However, since the company already

Schedule 2

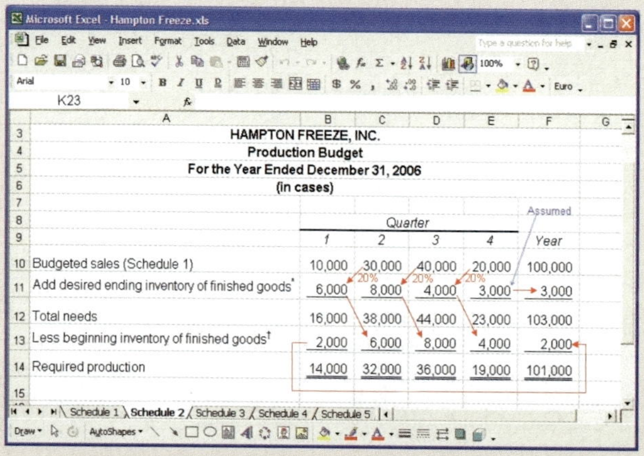

HAMPTON FREEZE, INC.
Production Budget
For the Year Ended December 31, 2006
(in cases)

	Quarter 1	Quarter 2	Quarter 3	Quarter 4	Year
Budgeted sales (Schedule 1)	10,000	30,000	40,000	20,000	100,000
Add desired ending inventory of finished goods*	6,000	8,000	4,000	3,000	3,000
Total needs	16,000	38,000	44,000	23,000	103,000
Less beginning inventory of finished goods†	2,000	6,000	8,000	4,000	2,000
Required production	14,000	32,000	36,000	19,000	101,000

*Twenty percent of the next quarter's sales. The ending inventory of 3,000 cases is assumed.
†The beginning inventory in each quarter is the same as the prior quarter's ending inventory.

has 2,000 cases in beginning inventory, only 14,000 cases need to be produced in the first quarter.

Pay particular attention to the Year column to the right of the production budget in Schedule 2. In some cases (e.g., budgeted sales, total needs, and required production), the amount listed for the year is the sum of the quarterly amounts for the item. In other cases (e.g., desired inventory of finished goods and beginning inventory of finished goods), the amount listed for the year is not simply the sum of the quarterly amounts. From the standpoint of the entire year, the beginning inventory of finished goods is the same as the beginning inventory of finished goods for the first quarter—it is *not* the sum of the beginning inventories of finished goods for all quarters. Similarly, from the standpoint of the entire year, the ending inventory of finished goods is the same as the ending inventory of finished goods for the fourth quarter—it is *not* the sum of the ending inventories of finished goods for all four quarters. It is important to pay attention to such distinctions in all of the schedules that follow.

Inventory Purchases—Merchandising Company

Hampton Freeze prepares a production budget, since it is a *manufacturing* company. If it were a *merchandising* company, it would instead prepare a **merchandise purchases budget** showing the amount of goods to be purchased from its suppliers during the period. The merchandise purchases budget has the same basic format as the production budget, as shown below:

Budgeted sales	XXXXX
Add desired ending merchandise inventory	XXXXX
Total needs	XXXXX
Less beginning merchandise inventory	XXXXX
Required purchases	XXXXX

Topic Tackler PLUS

9–2

A merchandising company would prepare a merchandise purchases budget such as the one above for each item carried in stock. The merchandise purchases budget can be expressed in terms of either units or the purchase cost of those units. So, for example, the Budgeted sales shown in the table above can be expressed in terms of either the number of units sold or the purchase cost of the units sold.

The Direct Materials Budget

LEARNING OBJECTIVE 4
Prepare a direct materials budget, including a schedule of expected cash disbursements for purchases of materials.

Returning to Hampton Freeze after the production requirements have been computed, a *direct materials budget* can be prepared. The **direct materials budget** details the raw materials that must be purchased to fulfill the production budget and to provide for adequate inventories. The required purchases of raw materials are computed as follows:

Raw materials needed to meet the production schedule	XXXXX
Add desired ending inventory of raw materials	XXXXX
Total raw materials needs	XXXXX
Less beginning inventory of raw materials	XXXXX
Raw materials to be purchased	XXXXX

Preparing a budget of this kind is one step in a company's overall **material requirements planning (MRP).** MRP is an operations management tool that uses a computer to help manage materials and inventories. The objective of MRP is to ensure that the right materials are on hand, in the right quantities, and at the right time to support the production budget. The detailed operation of MRP is covered in most operations management books.

Schedule 3 contains the direct materials budget for Hampton Freeze. The only raw material included in that budget is high fructose sugar, which is the major ingredient in

Schedule 3

HAMPTON FREEZE, INC.
Direct Materials Budget
For the Year Ended December 31, 2006

	Quarter 1	Quarter 2	Quarter 3	Quarter 4	Year
Required production in cases (Schedule 2)	14,000	32,000	36,000	19,000	101,000
Raw materials needed per case (pounds)	15	15	15	15	15
Production needs (pounds)	210,000	480,000	540,000	285,000	1,515,000
Add desired ending inventory of raw materials[1]	48,000	54,000	28,500	22,500	22,500
Total needs	258,000	534,000	568,500	307,500	1,537,500
Less beginning inventory of raw materials	21,000	48,000	54,000	28,500	21,000
Raw materials to be purchased	237,000	486,000	514,500	279,000	1,516,500
Cost of raw materials per pound	$ 0.20	$ 0.20	$ 0.20	$ 0.20	$ 0.20
Cost of raw materials to be purchased	$ 47,400	$ 97,200	$ 102,900	$ 55,800	$ 303,300

Percentage of purchases paid for in the period of the purchase	50%
Percentage of purchases paid for in the period after purchase	50%

Schedule of Expected Cash Disbursements for Materials

	Quarter 1	Quarter 2	Quarter 3	Quarter 4	Year
Accounts payable, beginning balance[2]	$ 25,800				$ 25,800
First-quarter purchases[3]	23,700	$ 23,700			47,400
Second-quarter purchases[4]		48,600	$ 48,600		97,200
Third-quarter purchases[5]			51,450	$ 51,450	102,900
Fourth-quarter purchases[6]	-	-	-	27,900	27,900
Total cash disbursements	$ 49,500	$ 72,300	$ 100,050	$ 79,350	$ 301,200

[1]Ten percent of the next quarter's production needs. For example, the second-quarter production needs are 480,000 pounds. Therefore, the desired ending inventory for the first quarter would be 10% × 480,000 pounds = 48,000 pounds. The ending inventory of 22,500 pounds for the fourth quarter is assumed.
[2]Cash payments for last year's fourth-quarter material purchases. See the beginning-of-year balance sheet on page 400.
[3]$47,400 × 50%; $47,400 × 50%.
[4]$97,200 × 50%; $97,200 × 50%.
[5]$102,900 × 50%; $102,900 × 50%.
[6]$55,800 × 50%. Unpaid fourth-quarter purchases appear as accounts payable on the company's end-of-year balance sheet.

popsicles other than water. The remaining raw materials are relatively insignificant and are included in variable manufacturing overhead. As with finished goods, management would like to maintain some minimum inventories of raw materials as a cushion. In this case, management would like to maintain ending inventories of sugar equal to 10% of the following quarter's production needs.

The first line in the direct materials budget contains the required production for each quarter, which is taken directly from the production budget (Schedule 2). Looking at the first quarter, since the production schedule calls for production of 14,000 cases of popsicles and each case requires 15 pounds of sugar, the total production needs are for 210,000 pounds of sugar (14,000 cases × 15 pounds per case). In addition, management wants to have ending inventories of 48,000 pounds of sugar, which is 10% of the following quarter's needs of 480,000 pounds. Consequently, the total needs are for 258,000 pounds (210,000 pounds for the current quarter's production plus 48,000 pounds for the desired ending inventory). However, since the company already has 21,000 pounds in beginning inventory, only 237,000 pounds of sugar (258,000 pounds − 21,000 pounds) will need to be purchased. Finally, the cost of the raw materials purchases is determined by multiplying the amount of raw material to be purchased by the cost per unit of the raw material. In this case, since 237,000 pounds of sugar will have to be purchased during the first quarter and sugar costs $0.20 per pound, the total cost will be $47,400 (237,000 pounds × $0.20 per pound).

As with the production budget, the amounts listed under the Year column are not always the sum of the quarterly amounts. The desired ending inventory of raw materials for the year is the same as the desired ending inventory of raw materials for the fourth quarter. Likewise, the beginning inventory of raw materials for the year is the same as the beginning inventory of raw materials for the first quarter.

The direct materials budget (and the merchandise purchases budget for a merchandising company) is usually accompanied by a schedule of expected cash disbursements for raw materials (or merchandise purchases). This schedule is needed to prepare the overall cash budget. Disbursements for raw materials (or merchandise purchases) consist of payments for purchases on account in prior periods plus any payments for purchases in the current budget period. Schedule 3 contains such a schedule of cash disbursements for Hampton Freeze.

Ordinarily, companies do not immediately pay their suppliers. At Hampton Freeze, the policy is to pay for 50% of purchases in the quarter in which the purchase is made and 50% in the following quarter, so while the company intends to purchase $47,400 worth of sugar in the first quarter, the company will only pay for half, $23,700, in the first quarter and the other half will be paid in the second quarter. The company will also pay $25,800 in the first quarter for sugar that was purchased on account in the previous quarter, but not yet paid for. This is the beginning balance in the accounts payable. Therefore, the total cash disbursements for sugar in the first quarter are $49,500—the $25,800 payment for sugar acquired in the previous quarter plus the $23,700 payment for sugar acquired during the first quarter.

The Direct Labor Budget

LEARNING OBJECTIVE 5
Prepare a direct labor budget.

The **direct labor budget** is also developed from the production budget. Direct labor requirements must be computed so that the company will know whether sufficient labor time is available to meet production needs. By knowing in advance how much labor time will be needed throughout the budget year, the company can develop plans to adjust the labor force as the situation requires. Companies that neglect to budget run the risk of facing labor shortages or having to hire and lay off workers at awkward times. Erratic labor policies lead to insecurity, low morale, and inefficiency.

The direct labor budget for Hampton Freeze is shown in Schedule 4. The first line in the direct labor budget consists of the required production for each quarter, which is taken directly from the production budget (Schedule 2). The direct labor requirement for each quarter is computed by multiplying the number of units to be produced in that quarter by the number of direct labor-hours required to make a unit. For example, 14,000 cases are to be produced in the first quarter and each case requires 0.40 direct labor-hour, so a total of 5,600 direct labor-hours (14,000 cases × 0.40 direct labor-hour per case) will be required in the first quarter. The direct labor requirements can then be translated into budgeted direct labor costs. How this is done will depend on the company's labor policy. In Schedule 4, the management of Hampton Freeze has assumed that the direct labor force will be adjusted as the work requirements change from quarter to quarter. In that case, the direct labor cost is computed by simply multiplying the direct labor-hour requirements by the direct labor rate per hour. For example, the direct labor cost in the first quarter is $84,000 (5,600 direct labor-hours × $15 per direct labor-hour).

Schedule 4

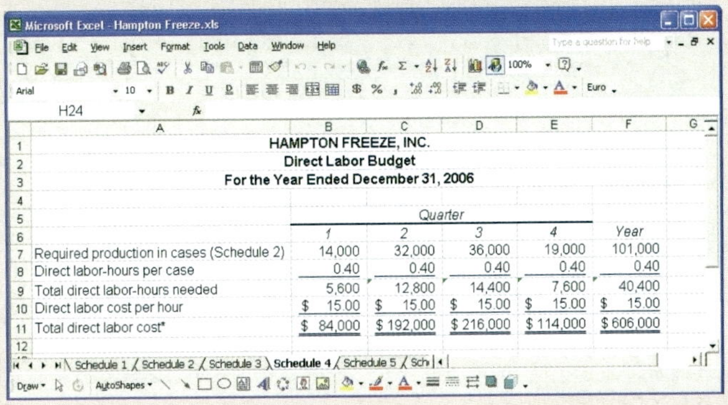

HAMPTON FREEZE, INC.
Direct Labor Budget
For the Year Ended December 31, 2006

	Quarter 1	2	3	4	Year
Required production in cases (Schedule 2)	14,000	32,000	36,000	19,000	101,000
Direct labor-hours per case	0.40	0.40	0.40	0.40	0.40
Total direct labor-hours needed	5,600	12,800	14,400	7,600	40,400
Direct labor cost per hour	$ 15.00	$ 15.00	$ 15.00	$ 15.00	$ 15.00
Total direct labor cost*	$ 84,000	$ 192,000	$ 216,000	$ 114,000	$ 606,000

*This schedule assumes that the direct labor work force will be fully adjusted to the total direct labor-hours needed each quarter.

However, many companies have employment policies or contracts that prevent them from laying off and rehiring workers as needed. Suppose, for example, that Hampton Freeze has 25 workers who are classified as direct labor and each of them is guaranteed at least 480 hours of pay each quarter at a rate of $15 per hour. In that case, the minimum direct labor cost for a quarter would be as follows:

$$25 \text{ workers} \times 480 \text{ hours per worker} \times \$15 \text{ per hour} = \$180{,}000$$

Note that in Schedule 4 the direct labor costs for the first and fourth quarters would have to be increased to $180,000 if Hampton Freeze's labor policy did not allow it to adjust the work force at will.

The Manufacturing Overhead Budget

LEARNING OBJECTIVE 6
Prepare a manufacturing overhead budget.

The **manufacturing overhead budget** provides a schedule of all costs of production other than direct materials and direct labor. Schedule 5 shows the manufacturing overhead budget for Hampton Freeze. At Hampton Freeze, manufacturing overhead is separated into variable and fixed components. The variable component is $4 per direct labor-hour and the fixed component is $60,600 per quarter. Because the variable component of the manufacturing overhead depends on direct labor, the first line in the manufacturing overhead budget consists of the budgeted direct labor-hours from the direct labor budget (Schedule 4). The budgeted direct labor-hours in each quarter are multiplied by the variable rate to determine the variable component of manufacturing overhead. For example, the variable manufacturing overhead for the first quarter is $22,400 (5,600 direct labor-hours × $4.00 per direct labor-hour). This is added to the fixed manufacturing overhead for the quarter to determine the total manufacturing overhead for the quarter. For example, the total manufacturing overhead for the first quarter is $83,000 ($22,400 + $60,600).

A few words about fixed costs and the budgeting process are in order. In most cases, fixed costs are the costs of supplying capacity to do things like make products, process purchase orders, handle customer calls, and so on. The amount of capacity that will be required depends on the expected level of activity for the period. If the expected level of activity is greater than the company's current capacity, then fixed costs may have to be increased. Or, if the expected level is appreciably below the company's current capacity, then it may be desirable to decrease fixed costs if that is possible. However, once the level of the fixed costs has been determined in the budget, the costs really are fixed. The time to adjust fixed costs is during the budgeting process. To determine the appropriate level of fixed costs at budget time, an activity-based costing system can be very helpful. It can help answer questions like, "How many clerks will we need to hire to process the anticipated number of purchase orders next year?" For simplicity, we assume in all of the budgeting examples in this book that the appropriate levels of fixed costs have already

Schedule 5

Microsoft Excel - Hampton Freeze.xls

HAMPTON FREEZE, INC.
Manufacturing Overhead Budget
For the Year Ended December 31, 2006

	Quarter				
	1	*2*	*3*	*4*	*Year*
Budgeted direct labor-hours (Schedule 4)	5,600	12,800	14,400	7,600	40,400
Variable overhead rate	$ 4.00	$ 4.00	$ 4.00	$ 4.00	$ 4.00
Variable manufacturing overhead	$ 22,400	$ 51,200	$ 57,600	$ 30,400	$ 161,600
Fixed manufacturing overhead	60,600	60,600	60,600	60,600	242,400
Total manufacturing overhead	83,000	111,800	118,200	91,000	404,000
Less depreciation	15,000	15,000	15,000	15,000	60,000
Cash disbursements for manufacturing overhead	$ 68,000	$ 96,800	$ 103,200	$ 76,000	$ 344,000
Total manufacturing overhead (a)					$ 404,000
Budgeted direct labor-hours (b)					40,400
Predetermined overhead rate for the year (a)÷(b)					$ 10.00

Schedule 1 / Schedule 2 / Schedule 3 / Schedule 4 / Schedule 5 / Schedule been determined for the budget with the aid of activity-based costing or some other method.

The last line of Schedule 5 for Hampton Freeze shows its budgeted cash disbursements for manufacturing overhead. Since some of the overhead costs are not cash outflows, the total budgeted manufacturing overhead costs must be adjusted to determine the cash disbursements for manufacturing overhead. At Hampton Freeze, the only significant noncash manufacturing overhead cost is depreciation, which is $15,000 per quarter. These noncash depreciation charges are deducted from the total budgeted manufacturing overhead to determine the expected cash disbursements. Hampton Freeze pays all overhead costs involving cash disbursements in the quarter incurred. Note that the company's predetermined overhead rate for the year will be $10 per direct labor-hour, which is determined by dividing the total budgeted manufacturing overhead for the year by the total budgeted direct labor-hours for the year.

The Ending Finished Goods Inventory Budget

After completing Schedules 1–5, Larry Giano had all of the data he needed to compute unit product costs. This computation was needed for two reasons: first, to determine cost of goods sold on the budgeted income statement; and second, to know what amount to put on the balance sheet inventory account for unsold units. The carrying cost of the unsold units is computed on the **ending finished goods inventory budget.**

Larry Giano considered using variable costing to prepare Hampton Freeze's budget statements, but he decided to use absorption costing instead since the bank would very likely require absorption costing. He also knew that it would be easy to convert the absorption costing financial statements to a variable costing basis later. At this point, the primary concern was to determine what financing, if any, would be required in the year 2006 and then to arrange for that financing from the bank.

The unit product cost computations are shown in Schedule 6. For Hampton Freeze, the absorption costing unit product cost is $13 per case of popsicles—consisting of $3 of direct materials, $6 of direct labor, and $4 of manufacturing overhead. The manufacturing overhead is applied to units of product on the basis of direct labor-hours at the rate of $10 per direct labor-hour. The budgeted carrying cost of the expected ending inventory is $39,000.

The Selling and Administrative Expense Budget

LEARNING OBJECTIVE 7
Prepare a selling and administrative expense budget.

The **selling and administrative expense budget** lists the budgeted expenses for areas other than manufacturing. In large organizations, this budget would be a compilation of many smaller, individual budgets submitted by department heads and other persons responsible for selling and administrative expenses. For example, the marketing manager in a large organization would submit a budget detailing the advertising expenses for each budget period.

Schedule 6

Microsoft Excel - Hampton Freeze.xls

HAMPTON FREEZE
Ending Finished Goods Inventory Budget
(absorption costing basis)
For the Year Ended December 31, 2006

Item	*Quantity*		*Cost*		*Total*
Production cost per case:					
Direct materials	15.00	pounds	$ 0.20	per pound	$ 3.00
Direct labor	0.40	hours	$ 15.00	per hour	6.00
Manufacturing overhead	0.40	hours	$ 10.00	per hour	4.00
Unit product cost					$ 13.00
Budgeted finished goods inventory:					
Ending finished goods inventory in cases (Schedule 2)					3,000
Unit product cost (see above)					$ 13.00
Ending finished goods inventory in dollars					$ 39,000

Schedule 1 / Schedule 2 / Schedule 3 / Schedule 4 / Schedule 5

Schedule 7

HAMPTON FREEZE
Selling and Administrative Expense Budget
For the Year Ended December 31, 2006

	Quarter 1	Quarter 2	Quarter 3	Quarter 4	Year
Budgeted sales in cases (Schedule 1)	10,000	30,000	40,000	20,000	100,000
Variable selling and administrative expense per case	$ 1.80	$ 1.80	$ 1.80	$ 1.80	$ 1.80
Budgeted variable expense	$ 18,000	$ 54,000	$ 72,000	$ 36,000	$180,000
Budgeted fixed selling and administrative expenses:					
Advertising	20,000	20,000	20,000	20,000	80,000
Executive salaries	55,000	55,000	55,000	55,000	220,000
Insurance		1,900	37,750		39,650
Property taxes				18,150	18,150
Depreciation	10,000	10,000	10,000	10,000	40,000
Total budgeted fixed selling and administrative expenses	85,000	86,900	122,750	103,150	397,800
Total budgeted selling and administrative expenses	103,000	140,900	194,750	139,150	577,800
Less depreciation	10,000	10,000	10,000	10,000	40,000
Cash disbursements for selling and administrative expenses	$ 93,000	$130,900	$184,750	$129,150	$537,800

Schedule 7 contains the selling and administrative expense budget for Hampton Freeze. Like the manufacturing overhead budget, the selling and administrative expense budget is divided into variable and fixed cost components. In the case of Hampton Freeze, the variable selling and administrative expense is $1.80 per case. Consequently, budgeted sales in cases for each quarter are entered at the top of the schedule. These data are taken from the sales budget (Schedule 1). The budgeted variable selling and administrative expenses are determined by multiplying the budgeted cases sold by the variable selling and administrative expense per case. For example, the budgeted variable selling and administrative expense for the first quarter is $18,000 (10,000 cases × $1.80 per case). The fixed selling and administrative expenses (all given data) are then added to the variable selling and administrative expenses to arrive at the total budgeted selling and administrative expenses. Finally, to determine the cash disbursements for selling and administrative items, the total budgeted selling and administrative expense is adjusted by subtracting any noncash selling and administrative expenses (in this case, just depreciation).

The Cash Budget

LEARNING OBJECTIVE 8
Prepare a cash budget.

As illustrated in Exhibit 9–2, the cash budget pulls together much of the data developed in the preceding steps. It is a good idea to review Exhibit 9–2 to get the big picture firmly in mind before moving on.

IN BUSINESS

CONCENTRATING ON THE CASH FLOW

Burlington Northern Santa Fe (BNSF) operates the second largest railroad in the United States. The company's senior vice president, CFO, and treasurer is Tom Hunt, who reports that "As a general theme, we've become very cash-flow-oriented." After the merger of the Burlington Northern and Santa Fe railroads, the company went through a number of years of heavy investments and negative cash flows. To keep on top of the company's cash position, Hunt has a cash forecast prepared every month. "Everything falls like dominoes from free cash flow," Hunt says. "It provides us with alternatives. Right now, the alternative of choice is buying back our own stock . . . [b]ut it could be increasing dividends or making acquisitions. All those things are not even on the radar screen if you don't have free cash flow."

Source: Randy Myers, "Cash Crop: The 2000 Working Capital Survey," *CFO*, August 2000, pp. 59–82.

The cash budget is composed of four major sections:

1. The receipts section.
2. The disbursements section
3. The cash excess or deficiency section.
4. The financing section.

The receipts section consists of a listing of all of the cash inflows, except for financing, expected during the budget period. Generally, the major source of receipts will be from sales.

The disbursements section consists of all cash payments that are planned for the budget period. These payments will include raw materials purchases, direct labor payments, manufacturing overhead costs, and so on, as contained in their respective budgets. In addition, other cash disbursements such as equipment purchases and dividends are listed.

The cash excess or deficiency section is computed as follows:

Cash balance, beginning	XXXX
Add receipts	XXXX
Total cash available	XXXX
Less disbursements	XXXX
Excess (deficiency) of cash available over disbursements	XXXX

If a cash deficiency exists during any budget period, the company will need to borrow funds. If there is a cash excess during any budget period, funds borrowed in previous periods can be repaid or the excess funds can be invested.

The financing section details the borrowings and repayments projected to take place during the budget period. It also lists interest payments that will be due on money borrowed.[1]

Generally speaking, the cash budget should be broken down into time periods that are as short as feasible. Considerable fluctuations in cash balances may be hidden by looking at a longer time period. While a monthly cash budget is most common, some organizations budget cash on a weekly or even daily basis. Larry Giano has prepared a quarterly cash budget for Hampton Freeze that can be further refined as necessary. This budget appears in Schedule 8. The cash budget builds on the earlier schedules and on additional data that are provided below:

- The beginning cash balance is $42,500.
- Management plans to spend $130,000 during the year on equipment purchases: $50,000 in the first quarter; $40,000 in the second quarter; $20,000 in the third quarter; and $20,000 in the fourth quarter.
- The board of directors has approved cash dividends of $8,000 per quarter.
- Management would like to have a cash balance of at least $40,000 at the beginning of each quarter for contingencies.
- Hampton Freeze has an open line of credit with a bank that enables the company to borrow at an interest rate of 10% per year. All borrowing and repayments are in round $1,000 amounts. All borrowing would occur at the beginning of quarters and all repayments would be made at the end of quarters. Interest would be due when repayments are made and only on the amount of principal that is repaid.

The cash budget is prepared one quarter at a time, starting with the first quarter. Larry began the cash budget by entering the beginning balance of cash for the first quarter of $42,500—a number that is given above. Receipts—in this case, just the $230,000 in cash collections from customers—are added to the beginning balance to arrive at the total cash available of $272,500. Since the total disbursements are $352,500 and the total cash

1 The format for the statement of cash flows, which is discussed in Chapter 16, may also be used for the cash budget.

Schedule 8

Microsoft Excel - Hampton Freeze.xls

HAMPTON FREEZE
Cash Budget
For the Year Ended December 31, 2006

	Schedule	Quarter 1	Quarter 2	Quarter 3	Quarter 4	Year
Cash balance, beginning		$42,500	$40,000	$ 40,000	$ 40,500	$ 42,500
Add receipts:						
Collections from customers	1	230,000	480,000	740,000	520,000	1,970,000
Total cash available		272,500	520,000	780,000	560,500	2,012,500
Less disbursements:						
Direct materials	3	49,500	72,300	100,050	79,350	301,200
Direct labor	4	84,000	192,000	216,000	114,000	606,000
Manufacturing overhead	5	68,000	96,800	103,200	76,000	344,000
Selling and administrative	7	93,000	130,900	184,750	129,150	537,800
Equipment purchases		50,000	40,000	20,000	20,000	130,000
Dividends		8,000	8,000	8,000	8,000	32,000
Total disbursements		352,500	540,000	632,000	426,500	1,951,000
Excess (deficiency) of cash available over disbursements		(80,000)	(20,000)	148,000	134,000	61,500
Financing:						
Borrowings (at beginning)*		120,000	60,000	-	-	180,000
Repayments (at ending)		-	-	(100,000)	(80,000)	(180,000)
Interest†		-	-	(7,500)	(6,500)	(14,000)
Total financing		120,000	60,000	(107,500)	(86,500)	(14,000)
Cash balance, ending		$40,000	$40,000	$ 40,500	$ 47,500	$ 47,500

Schedule 5 / Schedule 6 / Schedule 7 / Schedule 8 / Schedule 9 / Sheet10

*The company requires a minimum cash balance of $40,000. Therefore, borrowing must be sufficient to cover the cash deficiency of $80,000 in the first quarter and to provide for the minimum cash balance of $40,000. All borrowings and repayments of principal are in round $1,000 amounts.

†The interest payments relate only to the principal being repaid at the time it is repaid. For example, the interest in the third quarter relates only to the interest due on the $100,000 principal being repaid from the first quarter borrowing: $100,000 × 10% per year × ¾ year = $7,500. The interest paid in the fourth quarter is computed as follows:

$20,000 × 10% per year × 1 year	$2,000
$60,000 × 10% per year × ¾ year	4,500
Total interest paid	$6,500

available is only $272,500, there is a shortfall of $80,000. Since management would like to have a beginning cash balance of at least $40,000 for the second quarter, the company will need to borrow $120,000.

Required Borrowings at the End of the First Quarter	
Desired ending cash balance	$ 40,000
Plus deficiency of cash available over disbursements	80,000
Required borrowings	$120,000

The second quarter of the cash budget is handled similarly. Note that the ending cash balance for the first quarter is brought forward as the beginning cash balance for the second quarter. Also note that additional borrowing is required in the second quarter because of the continued cash shortfall.

Required Borrowings at the End of the Second Quarter	
Desired ending cash balance	$40,000
Plus deficiency of cash available over disbursements	20,000
Required borrowings	$60,000

In the third quarter, the cash flow situation improves dramatically and the excess of cash available over disbursements is $148,000. This makes it possible for the company to repay part of its loan from the bank, which now totals $180,000. How much can be repaid? The total amount of the principal *and* interest that can be repaid is determined as follows:

Total Maximum Feasible Loan Payments at the End of the Third Quarter	
Excess of cash available over disbursements	$148,000
Less desired ending cash balance	40,000
Maximum feasible principal and interest payment	$108,000

The next step—figuring out the exact amount of the loan payment—is tricky since interest must be paid on the principal amount that is repaid. In this case, the principal amount that is repaid must be less than $108,000, so we know that we would be paying off part of the loan that was taken out at the beginning of the first quarter. Since the repayment would be made at the end of the third quarter, interest would have accrued for three quarters. So the interest owed would be ¾ of 10%, or 7.5%. Either a trial-and-error or an algebraic approach will lead to the conclusion that the maximum principal repayment that can be made is $100,000.[2] The interest payment would be 7.5% of this amount, or $7,500—making the total payment $107,500.

In the fourth quarter, all of the loan and accumulated interest are paid off. If all loans are not repaid at the end of the year and budgeted financial statements are prepared, then interest must be accrued on the unpaid loans. This interest will not appear on the cash budget (since it has not yet been paid), but it will appear as interest expense on the budgeted income statement and as a liability on the budgeted balance sheet.

As with the production and raw materials budgets, the amounts under the Year column in the cash budget are not always the sum of the amounts for the four quarters. In particular, the beginning cash balance for the year is the same as the beginning cash balance for the first quarter and the ending cash balance for thc year is the same as the ending cash balance for the fourth quarter. Also note the beginning cash balance in any quarter is the same as the ending cash balance for the previous quarter.

The Budgeted Income Statement

LEARNING OBJECTIVE 9
Prepare a budgeted income statement.

A budgeted income statement can be prepared from the data developed in Schedules 1–8. *The budgeted income statement is one of the key schedules in the budget process.* It shows the company's planned profit for the upcoming budget period, and it stands as a benchmark against which subsequent company performance can be measured.

Schedule 9 contains the budgeted income statement for Hampton Freeze.

---

2 The algebraic approach to determining the amount that can be repaid on the loan follows:
Let X be the amount of the principal repayment. Then $10\% \times \frac{3}{4} \times X$ is the amount of interest owed on that principal amount. Since the company can afford to pay at most $108,000 to the bank, the sum of the principal repayment and the interest payment cannot exceed $108,000.

$$X + 10\% \times \tfrac{3}{4} \times X \leq \$108{,}000\text{, or}$$
$$X \leq \$100{,}465$$

Since all repayments must be in round $1,000 amounts, the appropriate principal repayment is $100,000.

Schedule 9

HAMPTON FREEZE		
Budgeted Income Statement		
For the Year Ended December 31, 2006		
	Schedules	
Sales	1	$ 2,000,000
Less cost of goods sold*	1,6	1,300,000
Gross margin		700,000
Less selling and administrative expenses	7	577,800
Net operating income		122,200
Less interest expense	8	14,000
Net income		$ 108,200

*100,000 cases sold × $13 per case = $1,300,000.

The Budgeted Balance Sheet

LEARNING OBJECTIVE 10
Prepare a budgeted balance sheet.

The budgeted balance sheet is developed by beginning with the balance sheet from the beginning of the budget period and adjusting it for the data contained in the various schedules. Hampton Freeze's budgeted balance sheet is presented in Schedule 10. Some of the data on the budgeted balance sheet have been taken from the company's previous end-of-year balance sheet for 2005 which appears below:

HAMPTON FREEZE, INC. Balance Sheet December 31, 2005		
Assets		
Current assets:		
Cash	$ 42,500	
Accounts receivable	90,000	
Raw materials inventory (21,000 pounds)	4,200	
Finished goods inventory (2,000 cases)	26,000	
Total current assets		$162,700
Plant and equipment:		
Land	80,000	
Buildings and equipment	700,000	
Accumulated depreciation	(292,000)	
Plant and equipment, net		488,000
Total assets		$650,700
Liabilities and Stockholders' Equity		
Current liabilities:		
Accounts payable (raw materials)		$ 25,800
Stockholders' equity:		
Common stock, no par	$175,000	
Retained earnings	449,900	
Total stockholders' equity		624,900
Total liabilities and stockholders' equity		$650,700

Schedule 10

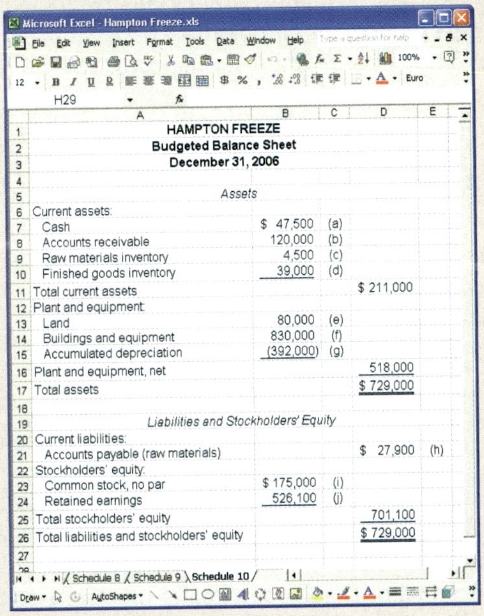

	A	B		C / D	
1	HAMPTON FREEZE				
2	Budgeted Balance Sheet				
3	December 31, 2006				
4					
5	*Assets*				
6	Current assets:				
7	Cash	$ 47,500	(a)		
8	Accounts receivable	120,000	(b)		
9	Raw materials inventory	4,500	(c)		
10	Finished goods inventory	39,000	(d)		
11	Total current assets			$ 211,000	
12	Plant and equipment:				
13	Land	80,000	(e)		
14	Buildings and equipment	830,000	(f)		
15	Accumulated depreciation	(392,000)	(g)		
16	Plant and equipment, net			518,000	
17	Total assets			$ 729,000	
18					
19	*Liabilities and Stockholders' Equity*				
20	Current liabilities:				
21	Accounts payable (raw materials)			$ 27,900	(h)
22	Stockholders' equity:				
23	Common stock, no par	$ 175,000	(i)		
24	Retained earnings	526,100	(j)		
25	Total stockholders' equity			701,100	
26	Total liabilities and stockholders' equity			$ 729,000	
27					

Explanation of December 31, 2006, balance sheet figures:

(a) The ending cash balance, as projected by the cash budget in Schedule 8.

(b) Thirty percent of fourth-quarter sales, from Schedule 1 ($400,000 × 30% = $120,000).

(c) From Schedule 3, the ending raw materials inventory will be 22,500 pounds. This material costs $0.20 per pound. Therefore, the ending inventory in dollars will be 22,500 pounds × $0.20 per pound = $4,500.

(d) From Schedule 6.

(e) From the December 31, 2005, balance sheet (no change).

(f) The December 31, 2005, balance sheet indicated a balance of $700,000. During 2006, $130,000 of additional equipment will be purchased (see Schedule 8), bringing the December 31, 2006, balance to $830,000.

(g) The December 31, 2005, balance sheet indicated a balance of $292,000. During 2006, $100,000 of depreciation will be taken ($60,000 on Schedule 5 and $40,000 on Schedule 7), bringing the December 31, 2006, balance to $392,000.

(h) One-half of the fourth-quarter raw materials purchases, from Schedule 3.

(i) From the December 31, 2005, balance sheet (no change).

(j)

December 31, 2005, balance	$449,900
Add net income, from Schedule 9	108,200
	558,100
Deduct dividends paid, from Schedule 8	32,000
December 31, 2006, balance	$526,100

MANAGERIAL ACCOUNTING IN ACTION
The Wrap-Up

After completing the master budget, Larry Giano took the documents to Tom Wills, chief executive officer of Hampton Freeze, for his review.

Larry: Here's the budget. Overall, the net income is excellent, and the net cash flow for the entire year is positive.

Tom: Yes, but I see on this cash budget that we have the same problem with negative cash flows in the first and second quarters that we had last year.

Larry: That's true. I don't see any way around that problem. However, there is no doubt in my mind that if you take this budget to the bank today, they'll approve an open line of credit that will allow you to borrow enough to make it through the first two quarters without any problem.

Tom: Are you sure? They didn't seem very happy to see me last year when I came in for an emergency loan.

Larry: Did you repay the loan on time?

Tom: Sure.

Larry: I don't see any problem. You won't be asking for an emergency loan this time. The bank will have plenty of warning. And with this budget, you have a solid plan that shows when and how you are going to pay off the loan. Trust me, they'll go for it.

Tom: Fantastic! It would sure make life a lot easier next year.

International Aspects of Budgeting

A multinational company faces special problems when preparing a budget. These problems arise because of fluctuations in foreign currency exchange rates, the high inflation rates found in some countries, and local economic conditions and governmental policies that affect everything from labor costs to marketing practices.

Fluctuations in foreign currency exchange rates create unique budgeting problems. Exporters may be able to predict with some accuracy their sales in the local foreign currency such as South African rands or Swiss francs. However, the amounts they eventually receive in their own currency will depend on the currency exchange rates that prevail at the time. If, for example, the currency exchange rates are less favorable than expected, the company will ultimately receive in its own currency less than it had anticipated.

Companies that are heavily involved in export operations often hedge their exposure to exchange rate fluctuations by buying and selling sophisticated financial contracts. These hedges ensure that if the company loses money in its exporting operations because of exchange rate fluctuations, it will make up that loss with gains on its financial contracts. The details of such hedging operations are covered in finance textbooks. When a multinational company uses hedging operations, the costs of those activities should be budgeted along with other expenses.

Some multinational companies have operations in countries with very high inflation rates—sometimes exceeding 100% a year. Such high inflation rates—called *hyperinflation*—can render a budget obsolete very quickly. A common budgeting tactic in such countries is to reduce the lead time for preparing the budget and to revise the budget frequently throughout the year in the light of the actual inflation experienced to date.

In addition to problems with exchange rates and inflation, multinational companies must be sensitive to government policies in the countries in which they operate that might affect labor costs, equipment purchases, cash management, or other budget items.

IN BUSINESS

AUTOMATING THE BUDGETING PROCESS

A number of companies, including Texaco, Fujitsu, Sprint, Nationwide Financial Services, Nortel Networks, Owens Corning, and Xilinx have been attempting to reengineer and automate the budgeting process. The goal is to eliminate the conventional iterative budgeting process that often finds preliminary budgets being passed up and down the management hierarchy many times before final agreement is reached—wasting much time and resulting in budgets that often don't reconcile. Apart from the tremendous technical challenges of integrating diverse budgets from many different operations, automation faces a high behavioral hurdle. As Greg Vesey of Texaco states, "Planning is the most political of all processes to fall under the finance function." Consequently, as many as half of all automation efforts fail. Companies such as National Semiconductor Corp. have given up entirely and have returned to their old budgeting methods.

Source: Russ Banham, "The Revolution in Planning," *CFO*, August 1999, pp. 46–56.

Summary

This chapter presents an overview of the budgeting process and shows how the various operating budgets relate to each other. The sales budget forms the foundation for profit planning. Once the sales budget has been set, the production budget and the selling and administrative expense budget can be prepared since they depend on how many units are to be sold. The production budget determines how many units are to be produced, so after it is prepared, the various manufacturing cost budgets can be prepared. All of these various budgets feed into the cash budget and the budgeted income statement and balance sheet. There are many connections between these various parts of the master budget. For example, the schedule of expected cash collections, which is completed in connection with the sales budget, provides data for both the cash budget and the budgeted balance sheet.

The material in this chapter is just an introduction to budgeting and profit planning. In later chapters, we will see how budgets are used to control day-to-day operations and how they are used in performance evaluation.

Review Problem: Budget Schedules

Mynor Company manufactures and sells a product that has seasonal variations in demand, with peak sales coming in the third quarter. The following information concerns operations for Year 2—the coming year—and for the first two quarters of Year 3:

a. The company's single product sells for $8 per unit. Budgeted sales in units for the next six quarters are as follows:

	Year 2 Quarter				Year 3 Quarter	
	1	2	3	4	1	2
Budgeted sales in units . . .	40,000	60,000	100,000	50,000	70,000	80,000

b. Sales are collected in the following pattern: 75% in the quarter the sales are made, and the remaining 25% in the following quarter. On January 1, Year 2, the company's balance sheet showed $65,000 in accounts receivable, all of which will be collected in the first quarter of the year. Bad debts are negligible and can be ignored.

c. The company desires an ending inventory of finished units on hand at the end of each quarter equal to 30% of the budgeted sales for the next quarter. On December 31, Year 1, the company had 12,000 units on hand.

d. Five pounds of raw materials are required to complete one unit of product. The company requires an ending inventory of raw materials on hand at the end of each quarter equal to 10% of the production needs of the following quarter. On December 31, Year 1, the company had 23,000 pounds of raw materials on hand.

e. The raw material costs $0.80 per pound. Purchases of raw material are paid for in the following pattern: 60% paid in the quarter the purchases are made, and the remaining 40% paid in the following quarter. On January 1, Year 2, the company's balance sheet showed $81,500 in accounts payable for raw material purchases, all of which will be paid for in the first quarter of the year.

Required:

Prepare the following budgets and schedules for the year, showing both quarterly and total figures:

1. A sales budget and a schedule of expected cash collections.
2. A production budget.
3. A direct materials purchases budget and a schedule of expected cash payments for material purchases.

Solution to Review Problem

1. The sales budget is prepared as follows:

	Year 2 Quarter 1	2	3	4	Year
Budgeted sales in units	40,000	60,000	100,000	50,000	250,000
Selling price per unit	× $8	× $8	× $8	× $8	× $8
Total sales	$320,000	$480,000	$800,000	$400,000	$2,000,000

Based on the budgeted sales above, the schedule of expected cash collections is prepared as follows:

	Year 2 Quarter 1	2	3	4	Year
Accounts receivable, beginning balance	$ 65,000				$ 65,000
First-quarter sales ($320,000 × 75%, 25%)	240,000	$ 80,000			320,000
Second-quarter sales ($480,000 × 75%, 25%)		360,000	$120,000		480,000
Third-quarter sales ($800,000 × 75%, 25%)			600,000	$200,000	800,000
Fourth-quarter sales ($400,000 × 75%)				300,000	300,000
Total cash collections	$305,000	$440,000	$720,000	$500,000	$1,965,000

2. Based on the sales budget in units, the production budget is prepared as follows:

	Year 2 Quarter 1	2	3	4	Year	Year 3 Quarter 1	2
Budgeted sales (units)	40,000	60,000	100,000	50,000	250,000	70,000	80,000
Add desired ending inventory of finished goods*	18,000	30,000	15,000	21,000†	21,000	24,000	
Total needs	58,000	90,000	115,000	71,000	271,000	94,000	
Less beginning inventory of finished goods	12,000	18,000	30,000	15,000	12,000	21,000	
Required production	46,000	72,000	85,000	56,000	259,000	73,000	

*30% of the following quarter's budgeted sales in units.
†30% of the budgeted Year 3 first-quarter sales.

3. Based on the production budget, raw materials will need to be purchased as follows during the year:

	Year 2 Quarter 1	2	3	4	Year 2	Year 3 Quarter 1
Required production (units)	46,000	72,000	85,000	56,000	259,000	73,000
Raw materials needed per unit (pounds)	× 5	× 5	× 5	× 5	× 5	× 5
Production needs (pounds)	230,000	360,000	425,000	280,000	1,295,000	365,000
Add desired ending inventory of raw materials (pounds)*	36,000	42,500	28,000	36,500†	36,500	
Total needs (pounds)	266,000	402,500	453,000	316,500	1,331,500	
Less beginning inventory of raw materials (pounds)	23,000	36,000	42,500	28,000	23,000	
Raw materials to be purchased (pounds)	243,000	366,500	410,500	288,500	1,308,500	

*Ten percent of the following quarter's production needs in pounds.
†Ten percent of the Year 3 first-quarter production needs in pounds.

Based on the raw material purchases above, expected cash payments are computed as follows:

	Year 2 Quarter				
	1	2	3	4	Year 2
Cost of raw materials to be purchased at $0.80 per pound	$194,400	$293,200	$328,400	$230,800	$1,046,800
Accounts payable, beginning balance	$ 81,500				$ 81,500
First-quarter purchases ($194,400 × 60%, 40%)	116,640	$ 77,760			194,400
Second-quarter purchases ($293,200 × 60%, 40%)		175,920	$117,280		293,200
Third-quarter purchases ($328,400 × 60%, 40%)			197,040	$131,360	328,400
Fourth-quarter purchases ($230,800 × 60%)				138,480	138,480
Total cash disbursements	$198,140	$253,680	$314,320	$269,840	$1,035,980

Glossary

Budget A detailed plan for the acquisition and use of financial and other resources over a specified time period. (p. 378)

Budget committee A group of key managers who are responsible for overall policy matters relating to the budget program and for coordinating the preparation of the budget. (p. 384)

Cash budget A detailed plan showing how cash resources will be acquired and used over some specific time period. (p. 386)

Continuous budget A 12-month budget that rolls forward one month as the current month is completed. (p. 380)

Control Those steps taken by management to increase the likelihood that the objectives set down at the planning stage are attained and that all parts of the organization are working together toward that goal. (p. 378)

Direct labor budget A detailed plan showing labor requirements over some specific time period. (p. 393)

Direct materials budget A detailed plan showing the amount of raw materials that must be purchased during a period to meet both production and inventory needs. (p. 391)

Ending finished goods inventory budget A budget showing the dollar amount of unsold finished goods inventory that will appear on the ending balance sheet. (p. 395)

Manufacturing overhead budget A detailed plan showing the production costs, other than direct materials and direct labor, that will be incurred over a specified time period. (p. 394)

Master budget A summary of a company's plans in which specific targets are set for sales, production, distribution, and financing activities and that generally culminates in a cash budget, budgeted income statement, and budgeted balance sheet. (p. 378)

Material requirements planning (MRP) An operations management tool that uses a computer to help manage materials and inventories. (p. 391)

Merchandise purchases budget A budget used by a merchandising company that shows the amount of goods that must be purchased from suppliers during the period. (p. 391)

Participative budget See *Self-imposed budget.* (p. 381)

Perpetual budget See *Continuous budget.* (p. 380)

Planning Developing objectives and preparing budgets to achieve those objectives. (p. 378)

Production budget A detailed plan showing the number of units that must be produced during a period in order to meet both sales and inventory needs. (p. 390)

Responsibility accounting A system of accountability in which managers are held responsible for those items of revenue and cost—and only those items—over which the manager can exert significant control. The managers are held responsible for differences between budgeted and actual results. (p. 379)

Sales budget A detailed schedule showing the expected sales for coming periods; these sales are typically expressed in both dollars and units. (p. 385)

Self-imposed budget A method of preparing budgets in which managers prepare their own budgets. These budgets are then reviewed by the manager's supervisor, and any issues are resolved by mutual agreement. (p. 381)

Selling and administrative expense budget A detailed schedule of planned expenses that will be incurred in areas other than manufacturing during a budget period. (p. 395)

Zero-based budget A method of budgeting in which managers are required to justify all costs as if the programs involved were being proposed for the first time. (p. 384)

Questions

9–1 What is a budget? What is budgetary control?

9–2 Discuss some of the major benefits to be gained from budgeting.

9–3 What is meant by the term *responsibility accounting?*

9–4 What is a master budget? Briefly describe its contents.

9–5 Why is the sales forecast the starting point in budgeting?

9–6 "As a practical matter, planning and control mean exactly the same thing." Do you agree? Explain.

9–7 Describe the flow of budget data in an organization. Who are the participants in the budgeting process, and how do they participate?

9–8 What is a self-imposed budget? What are the major advantages of self-imposed budgets? What caution must be exercised in their use?

9–9 How can budgeting assist a company in planning its work force staffing levels?

9–10 "The principal purpose of the cash budget is to see how much cash the company will have in the bank at the end of the year." Do you agree? Explain.

9–11 How does zero-based budgeting differ from traditional budgeting?

Exercises

EXERCISE 9–1 Schedule of Expected Cash Collections [LO2]

Silver Company makes a product that is very popular as a Mother's Day gift. Thus, peak sales occur in May of each year. These peak sales are shown in the company's sales budget for the second quarter given below (all sales are on account):

	April	May	June	Total
Budgeted sales	$300,000	$500,000	$200,000	$1,000,000

From past experience, the company has learned that 20% of a month's sales are collected in the month of sale, another 70% are collected in the month following sale, and the remaining 10% are collected in the second month following sale. Bad debts are negligible and can be ignored. February sales totaled $230,000, and March sales totaled $260,000.

Required:

1. Prepare a schedule of expected cash collections from sales, by month and in total, for the second quarter.
2. Assume that the company will prepare a budgeted balance sheet as of June 30. Compute the accounts receivable as of that date.

EXERCISE 9–2 Production Budget [LO3]

Down Under Products, Ltd., of Australia has budgeted sales of its popular boomerang for the next four months as follows:

	Sales in Units
April	50,000
May	75,000
June	90,000
July	80,000

The company is now in the process of preparing a production budget for the second quarter. Past experience has shown that end-of-month inventory levels must equal 10% of the following month's sales. The inventory at the end of March was 5,000 units.

Required:
Prepare a production budget for the second quarter; in your budget, show the number of units to be produced each month and for the quarter in total.

EXERCISE 9–3 Direct Materials Budget [LO4]
Three grams of musk oil are required for each bottle of Mink Caress, a very popular perfume made by a small company in western Siberia. The cost of the musk oil is 150 roubles per kilogram. (Siberia is located in Russia, whose currency is the rouble.) Budgeted production of Mink Caress is given below by quarters for Year 2 and for the first quarter of Year 3.

	Year 2 Quarter				Year 3 Quarter
	First	Second	Third	Fourth	First
Budgeted production, in bottles	60,000	90,000	150,000	100,000	70,000

Musk oil has become so popular as a perfume ingredient that it has become necessary to carry large inventories as a precaution against stock-outs. For this reason, the inventory of musk oil at the end of a quarter must be equal to 20% of the following quarter's production needs. Some 36,000 grams of musk oil will be on hand to start the first quarter of Year 2.

Required:
Prepare a direct materials budget for musk oil, by quarter and in total, for Year 2. At the bottom of your budget, show the amount of purchases in roubles for each quarter and for the year in total.

EXERCISE 9–4 Direct Labor Budget [LO5]
The production department of Rordan Corporation has submitted the following forecast of units to be produced by quarter for the upcoming fiscal year.

	1st Quarter	2nd Quarter	3rd Quarter	4th Quarter
Units to be produced	8,000	6,500	7,000	7,500

Each unit requires 0.35 direct labor-hours, and direct laborers are paid $12.00 per hour.

Required:
1. Construct the company's direct labor budget for the upcoming fiscal year, assuming that the direct labor work force is adjusted each quarter to match the number of hours required to produce the forecasted number of units produced.
2. Construct the company's direct labor budget for the upcoming fiscal year, assuming that the direct labor work force is not adjusted each quarter. Instead, assume that the company's direct labor work force consists of permanent employees who are guaranteed to be paid for at least 2,600 hours of work each quarter. If the number of required direct labor-hours is less than this number, the workers are paid for 2,600 hours anyway. Any hours worked in excess of 2,600 hours in a quarter are paid at the rate of 1.5 times the normal hourly rate for direct labor.

EXERCISE 9–5 Manufacturing Overhead Budget [LO6]
The direct labor budget of Yuvwell Corporation for the upcoming fiscal year contains the following details concerning budgeted direct labor-hours.

	1st Quarter	2nd Quarter	3rd Quarter	4th Quarter
Budgeted direct labor-hours	8,000	8,200	8,500	7,800

The company's variable manufacturing overhead rate is $3.25 per direct labor-hour and the company's fixed manufacturing overhead is $48,000 per quarter. The only noncash item included in the fixed manufacturing overhead is depreciation, which is $16,000 per quarter.

Required:
1. Construct the company's manufacturing overhead budget for the upcoming fiscal year.
2. Compute the company's manufacturing overhead rate (including both variable and fixed manufacturing overhead) for the upcoming fiscal year. Round off to the nearest whole cent.

EXERCISE 9–6 Selling and Administrative Expense Budget [LO7]
The budgeted unit sales of Weller Company for the upcoming fiscal year are provided below:

	1st Quarter	2nd Quarter	3rd Quarter	4th Quarter
Budgeted unit sales	15,000	16,000	14,000	13,000

The company's variable selling and administrative expense per unit is $2.50. Fixed selling and administrative expenses include advertising expenses of $8,000 per quarter, executive salaries of $35,000 per quarter, and depreciation of $20,000 per quarter. In addition, the company will make insurance payments of $5,000 in the first quarter and $5,000 in the third quarter. Finally, property taxes of $8,000 will be paid in the second quarter.

Required:
Prepare the company's selling and administrative expense budget for the upcoming fiscal year.

EXERCISE 9–7 Cash Budget Analysis [LO8]
A cash budget, by quarters, is given below for a retail company. (000 omitted). The company requires a minimum cash balance of at least $5,000 to start each quarter.

	Quarter				
	1	2	3	4	Year
Cash balance, beginning	$ 6	$?	$?	$?	$?
Add collections from customers	?	?	96	?	323
Total cash available	71	?	?	?	?
Less disbursements:					
Purchase of inventory	35	45	?	35	?
Operating expenses	?	30	30	?	113
Equipment purchases	8	8	10	?	36
Dividends	2	2	2	2	?
Total disbursements	?	85	?	?	?
Excess (deficiency) of cash available over disbursements	(2)	?	11	?	?
Financing:					
Borrowings	?	15	—	—	?
Repayments (including interest)*	—	—	(?)	(17)	(?)
Total financing	?	?	?	?	?
Cash balance, ending	$?	$?	$?	$?	$?

*Interest will total $1,000 for the year.

Required:
Fill in the missing amounts in the above table.

Problems

PROBLEM 9–8 Evaluating a Company's Budget Procedures [LO1]
Springfield Corporation operates on a calendar-year basis. It begins the annual budgeting process in late August, when the president establishes targets for total sales dollars and net operating income before taxes for the next year.

The sales target is given to the Marketing Department, where the marketing manager formulates a sales budget by product line in both units and dollars. From this budget, sales quotas by product line in units and dollars are established for each of the corporation's sales districts.

The marketing manager also estimates the cost of the marketing activities required to support the target sales volume and prepares a tentative marketing expense budget.

The executive vice president uses the sales and profit targets, the sales budget by product line, and the tentative marketing expense budget to determine the dollar amounts that can be devoted to manufacturing and corporate office expense. The executive vice president prepares the budget for corporate expenses, and then forwards to the Production Department the product-line sales budget in units and the total dollar amount that can be devoted to manufacturing.

The production manager meets with the factory managers to develop a manufacturing plan that will produce the required units when needed within the cost constraints set by the executive vice president. The budgeting process usually comes to a halt at this point because the Production Department does not consider the financial resources allocated to it to be adequate.

When this standstill occurs, the vice president of finance, the executive vice president, the marketing manager, and the production manager meet to determine the final budgets for each of the areas. This normally results in a modest increase in the total amount available for manufacturing costs, while the marketing expense and corporate office expense budgets are cut. The total sales and net operating income figures proposed by the president are seldom changed. Although the participants are seldom pleased with the compromise, these budgets are final. Each executive then develops a new detailed budget for the operations in his or her area.

None of the areas has achieved its budget in recent years. Sales often run below the target. When budgeted sales are not achieved, each area is expected to cut costs so that the president's profit target can still be met. However, the profit target is seldom met because costs are not cut enough. In fact, costs often run above the original budget in all functional areas. The president is disturbed that Springfield has not been able to meet the sales and profit targets. He hired a consultant with considerable relevant industry experience. The consultant reviewed the budgets for the past four years. He concluded that the product-line sales budgets were reasonable and that the cost and expense budgets were adequate for the budgeted sales and production levels.

Required:

1. Discuss how the budgeting process as employed by Springfield Corporation contributes to the failure to achieve the president's sales and profit targets.
2. Suggest how Springfield Corporation's budgeting process could be revised to correct the problem.
3. Should the functional areas be expected to cut their costs when sales volume falls below budget? Explain your answer.

(CMA, adapted)

PROBLEM 9–9 Schedule of Expected Cash Collections; Cash Budget [LO2, LO8]

Herbal Care Corp., a distributor of herb-based sunscreens, is ready to begin its third quarter, in which peak sales occur. The company has requested a $40,000, 90-day loan from its bank to help meet cash requirements during the quarter. Since Herbal Care has experienced difficulty in paying off its loans in the past, the loan officer at the bank has asked the company to prepare a cash budget for the quarter. In response to this request, the following data have been assembled:

a. On July 1, the beginning of the third quarter, the company will have a cash balance of $44,500.
b. Actual sales for the last two months and budgeted sales for the third quarter follow (all sales are on account):

May (actual)	$250,000
June (actual)	$300,000
July (budgeted)	$400,000
August (budgeted)	$600,000
September (budgeted)	$320,000

Past experience shows that 25% of a month's sales are collected in the month of sale, 70% in the month following sale, and 3% in the second month following sale. The remainder is uncollectible.

c. Budgeted merchandise purchases and budgeted expenses for the third quarter are given below:

	July	August	September
Merchandise purchases	$240,000	$350,000	$175,000
Salaries and wages	$45,000	$50,000	$40,000
Advertising	$130,000	$145,000	$80,000
Rent payments	$9,000	$9,000	$9,000
Depreciation	$10,000	$10,000	$10,000

Merchandise purchases are paid in full during the month following purchase. Accounts payable for merchandise purchases on June 30, which will be paid during July, total $180,000.

d. Equipment costing $10,000 will be purchased for cash during July.

e. In preparing the cash budget, assume that the $40,000 loan will be made in July and repaid in September. Interest on the loan will total $1,200.

Required:

1. Prepare a schedule of expected cash collections for July, August, and September and for the quarter in total.
2. Prepare a cash budget, by month and in total, for the third quarter.
3. If the company needs a minimum cash balance of $20,000 to start each month, can the loan be repaid as planned? Explain.

PROBLEM 9–10 Behavioral Aspects of Budgeting; Ethics and the Manager [LO1]

Norton Company, a manufacturer of infant furniture and carriages, is in the initial stages of preparing the annual budget for next year. Scott Ford has recently joined Norton's accounting staff and is interested to learn as much as possible about the company's budgeting process. During a recent lunch with Marge Atkins, sales manager, and Pete Granger, production manager, Ford initiated the following conversation.

Ford: Since I'm new around here and am going to be involved with the preparation of the annual budget, I'd be interested to learn how the two of you estimate sales and production numbers.

Atkins: We start out very methodically by looking at recent history, discussing what we know about current accounts, potential customers, and the general state of consumer spending. Then, we add that usual dose of intuition to come up with the best forecast we can.

Granger: I usually take the sales projections as the basis for my projections. Of course, we have to make an estimate of what this year's ending inventories will be, which is sometimes difficult.

Ford: Why does that present a problem? There must have been an estimate of ending inventories in the budget for the current year.

Granger: Those numbers aren't always reliable since Marge makes some adjustments to the sales numbers before passing them on to me.

Ford: What kind of adjustments?

Atkins: Well, we don't want to fall short of the sales projections so we generally give ourselves a little breathing room by lowering the initial sales projection anywhere from 5% to 10%.

Granger: So, you can see why this year's budget is not a very reliable starting point. We always have to adjust the projected production rates as the year progresses and, of course, this changes the ending inventory estimates. By the way, we make similar adjustments to expenses by adding at least 10% to the estimates; I think everyone around here does the same thing.

Required:

1. Marge Atkins and Pete Granger have described the use of what is sometimes called *budgetary slack.*
   a. Explain why Atkins and Granger behave in this manner and describe the benefits they expect to realize from the use of budgetary slack.
   b. Explain how the use of budgetary slack can adversely affect Atkins and Granger.
2. As a management accountant, Scott Ford believes that the behavior described by Marge Atkins and Pete Granger may be unethical. By referring to the Standards of Ethical Conduct for Practitioners of Management Accounting and Financial Management in Chapter 1, explain why the use of budgetary slack may be unethical.

(CMA, adapted)

PROBLEM 9–11 Production and Direct Materials Budgets [LO3, LO4]

Pearl Products Limited of Shenzhen, China, manufactures and distributes toys throughout South East Asia. Three cubic centimeters (cc) of solvent H300 are required to manufacture each unit of Supermix, one of the company's products. The company is now planning raw materials needs for the third quarter, the quarter in which peak sales of Supermix occur. To keep production and sales moving smoothly, the company has the following inventory requirements:

a. The finished goods inventory on hand at the end of each month must be equal to 3,000 units of Supermix plus 20% of the next month's sales. The finished goods inventory on June 30 is budgeted to be 10,000 units.

b. The raw materials inventory on hand at the end of each month must be equal to one-half of the following month's production needs for raw materials. The raw materials inventory on June 30 is budgeted to be 54,000 cc of solvent H300.
c. The company maintains no work in process inventories.

A sales budget for Supermix for the last six months of the year follows.

	Budgeted Sales in Units
July	35,000
August	40,000
September	50,000
October	30,000
November	20,000
December	10,000

Required:

1. Prepare a production budget for Supermix for the months July, August, September, and October.
2. Examine the production budget that you prepared in (1) above. Why will the company produce more units than it sells in July and August, and fewer units than it sells in September and October?
3. Prepare a direct materials budget showing the quantity of solvent H300 to be purchased for July, August, and September, and for the quarter in total.

PROBLEM 9–12 Direct Materials and Direct Labor Budgets [LO4, LO5]

The production department of Zan Corporation has submitted the following forecast of units to be produced by quarter for the upcoming fiscal year.

	1st Quarter	2nd Quarter	3rd Quarter	4th Quarter
Units to be produced	5,000	8,000	7,000	6,000

In addition, the beginning raw materials inventory for the 1st Quarter is budgeted to be 6,000 grams and the beginning accounts payable for the 1st Quarter is budgeted to be $2,880.

Each unit requires 8 grams of raw material that costs $1.20 per gram. Management desires to end each quarter with an inventory of raw materials equal to 25% of the following quarter's production needs. The desired ending inventory for the 4th Quarter is 8,000 grams. Management plans to pay for 60% of raw material purchases in the quarter acquired and 40% in the following quarter. Each unit requires 0.20 direct labor-hour and direct laborers are paid $11.50 per hour.

Required:

1. Prepare the company's direct materials budget and schedule of expected cash disbursements for materials for the upcoming fiscal year.
2. Prepare the company's direct labor budget for the upcoming fiscal year, assuming that the direct labor workforce is adjusted each quarter to match the number of hours required to produce the forecasted number of units produced.

PROBLEM 9–13 Direct Labor and Manufacturing Overhead Budgets [LO5, LO6]

The Production Department of Hruska Corporation has submitted the following forecast of units to be produced by quarter for the upcoming fiscal year.

	1st Quarter	2nd Quarter	3rd Quarter	4th Quarter
Units to be produced	12,000	10,000	13,000	14,000

Each unit requires 0.2 direct labor-hour and direct laborers are paid $12.00 per hour.

In addition, the variable manufacturing overhead rate is $1.75 per direct labor-hour. The fixed manufacturing overhead is $86,000 per quarter. The only noncash element of manufacturing overhead is depreciation, which is $23,000 per quarter.

Required:

1. Prepare the company's direct labor budget for the upcoming fiscal year, assuming that the direct labor work force is adjusted each quarter to match the number of hours required to produce the forecasted number of units produced.
2. Prepare the company's manufacturing overhead budget.

PROBLEM 9–14 Schedules of Expected Cash Collections and Disbursements [LO2, LO4, LO8]
You have been asked to prepare a December cash budget for Ashton Company, a distributor of exercise equipment. The following information is available about the company's operations:

a. The cash balance on December 1 is $40,000.

b. Actual sales for October and November and expected sales for December are as follows:

	October	November	December
Cash sales	$65,000	$70,000	$83,000
Sales on account	$400,000	$525,000	$600,000

Sales on account are collected over a three-month period as follows: 20% collected in the month of sale, 60% collected in the month following sale, and 18% collected in the second month following sale. The remaining 2% is uncollectible.

c. Purchases of inventory will total $280,000 for December. Thirty percent of a month's inventory purchases are paid during the month of purchase. The accounts payable remaining from November's inventory purchases total $161,000, all of which will be paid in December.

d. Selling and administrative expenses are budgeted at $430,000 for December. Of this amount, $50,000 is for depreciation.

e. A new web server for the Marketing Department costing $76,000 will be purchased for cash during December, and dividends totaling $9,000 will be paid during the month.

f. The company maintains a minimum cash balance of $20,000. An open line of credit is available from the company's bank to bolster the cash position as needed.

Required:

1. Prepare a schedule of expected cash collections for December.
2. Prepare a schedule of expected cash disbursements for merchandise purchases for December.
3. Prepare a cash budget for December. Indicate in the financing section any borrowing that will be needed during the month.

PROBLEM 9–15 Cash Budget; Income Statement; Balance Sheet [LO2, LO4, LO8, LO9, LO10]
Minden Company is a wholesale distributor of premium European chocolates. The company's balance sheet as of April 30 is given below:

MINDEN COMPANY
Balance Sheet
April 30

Assets	
Cash	$ 9,000
Accounts receivable	54,000
Inventory	30,000
Buildings and equipment, net of depreciation	207,000
Total assets	$300,000
Liabilities and Stockholders' Equity	
Accounts payable	$ 63,000
Note payable	14,500
Capital stock, no par	180,000
Retained earnings	42,500
Total liabilities and stockholders' equity	$300,000

The company is in the process of preparing budget data for May. A number of budget items have already been prepared, as stated below:

a. Sales are budgeted at $200,000 for May. Of these sales, $60,000 will be for cash; the remainder will be credit sales. One-half of a month's credit sales are collected in the month the sales are made, and the remainder is collected in the following month. All of the April 30 accounts receivable will be collected in May.

b. Purchases of inventory are expected to total $120,000 during May. These purchases will all be on account. Forty percent of all purchases are paid for in the month of purchase; the remainder are paid in the following month. All of the April 30 accounts payable to suppliers will be paid during May.

c. The May 31 inventory balance is budgeted at $40,000.

d. Operating expenses for May are budgeted at $72,000, exclusive of depreciation. These expenses will be paid in cash. Depreciation is budgeted at $2,000 for the month.
e. The note payable on the April 30 balance sheet will be paid during May, with $100 in interest. (All of the interest relates to May.)
f. New refrigerating equipment costing $6,500 will be purchased for cash during May.
g. During May, the company will borrow $20,000 from its bank by giving a new note payable to the bank for that amount. The new note will be due in one year.

Required:
1. Prepare a cash budget for May. Support your budget with a schedule of expected cash collections from sales and a schedule of expected cash disbursements for merchandise purchases.
2. Prepare a budgeted income statement for May. Use the absorption costing income statement format as shown in Schedule 9.
3. Prepare a budgeted balance sheet as of May 31.

PROBLEM 9–16 Cash Budget with Supporting Schedules [LO2, LO4, LO8]

Garden Sales, Inc., sells garden supplies. Management is planning its cash needs for the second quarter. The company usually has to borrow money during this quarter to support peak sales of lawn care equipment, which occur during May. The following information has been assembled to assist in preparing a cash budget for the quarter:

a. Budgeted monthly absorption costing income statements for April–July are:

	April	May	June	July
Sales	$600,000	$900,000	$500,000	$400,000
Cost of goods sold	420,000	630,000	350,000	280,000
Gross margin	180,000	270,000	150,000	120,000
Less operating expenses:				
Selling expense	79,000	120,000	62,000	51,000
Administrative expense*	45,000	52,000	41,000	38,000
Total operating expenses	124,000	172,000	103,000	89,000
Net operating income	$ 56,000	$ 98,000	$ 47,000	$ 31,000

*Includes $20,000 of depreciation each month.

b. Sales are 20% for cash and 80% on account.
c. Sales on account are collected over a three-month period with 10% collected in the month of sale; 70% collected in the first month following the month of sale; and the remaining 20% collected in the second month following the month of sale. February's sales totaled $200,000, and March's sales totaled $300,000.
d. Inventory purchases are paid for within 15 days. Therefore, 50% of a month's inventory purchases are paid for in the month of purchase. The remaining 50% is paid in the following month. Accounts payable at March 31 for inventory purchases during March total $126,000.
e. Each month's ending inventory must equal 20% of the cost of the merchandise to be sold in the following month. The merchandise inventory at March 31 is $84,000.
f. Dividends of $49,000 will be declared and paid in April.
g. Land costing $16,000 will be purchased for cash in May.
h. The cash balance at March 31 is $52,000; the company must maintain a cash balance of at least $40,000.
i. The company can borrow from its bank as needed to bolster the Cash account. Borrowings and repayments must be in multiples of $1,000. All borrowings take place at the beginning of a month, and all repayments are made at the end of a month. The annual interest rate is 12%. Compute interest on whole months ($\frac{1}{12}$, $\frac{2}{12}$, and so forth).

Required:
1. Prepare a schedule of expected cash collections for April, May, and June, and for the quarter in total.
2. Prepare the following for merchandise inventory:
   a. A merchandise purchases budget for April, May, and June.
   b. A schedule of expected cash disbursements for merchandise purchases for April, May, and June, and for the quarter in total.
3. Prepare a cash budget for April, May, and June as well as in total for the quarter. Show borrowings from the company's bank and repayments to the bank as needed to maintain the minimum cash balance.

PROBLEM 9–17 Integration of the Sales, Production, and Direct Materials Budgets [LO2, LO3, LO4]

Milo Company manufactures beach umbrellas. The company is preparing detailed budgets for the third quarter and has assembled the following information to assist in the budget preparation:

a. The Marketing Department has estimated sales as follows for the remainder of the year (in units):

July	30,000	October	20,000
August	70,000	November	10,000
September	50,000	December	10,000

The selling price of the beach umbrellas is $12 per unit.

b. All sales are on account. Based on past experience, sales are collected in the following pattern:

30% in the month of sale
65% in the month following sale
5% uncollectible

Sales for June totaled $300,000.

c. The company maintains finished goods inventories equal to 15% of the following month's sales. This requirement will be met at the end of June.

d. Each beach umbrella requires 4 feet of Gilden, a material that is sometimes hard to acquire. Therefore, the company requires that the ending inventory of Gilden be equal to 50% of the following month's production needs. The inventory of Gilden on hand at the beginning and end of the quarter will be:

June 30	72,000 feet
September 30	? feet

e. Gilden costs $0.80 per foot. One-half of a month's purchases of Gilden is paid for in the month of purchase; the remainder is paid for in the following month. The accounts payable on July 1 for purchases of Gilden during June will be $76,000.

Required:

1. Prepare a sales budget, by month and in total, for the third quarter. (Show your budget in both units and dollars.) Also prepare a schedule of expected cash collections, by month and in total, for the third quarter.
2. Prepare a production budget for each of the months July–October.
3. Prepare a direct materials budget for Gilden, by month and in total, for the third quarter. Also prepare a schedule of expected cash disbursements for Gilden, by month and in total, for the third quarter.

eXcel

PROBLEM 9–18 Cash Budget with Supporting Schedules [LO2, LO4, LO7, LO8]

Westex Products is a wholesale distributor of industrial cleaning products. When the treasurer of Westex Products approached the company's bank late in the current year seeking short-term financing, he was told that money was very tight and that any borrowing over the next year would have to be supported by a detailed statement of cash collections and disbursements. The treasurer also was told that it would be very helpful to the bank if borrowers would indicate the quarters in which they would be needing funds, as well as the amounts that would be needed, and the quarters in which repayments could be made.

Since the treasurer is unsure as to the particular quarters in which bank financing will be needed, he has assembled the following information to assist in preparing a detailed cash budget:

a. Budgeted sales and merchandise purchases for next year, as well as actual sales and purchases for the last quarter of the current year, are:

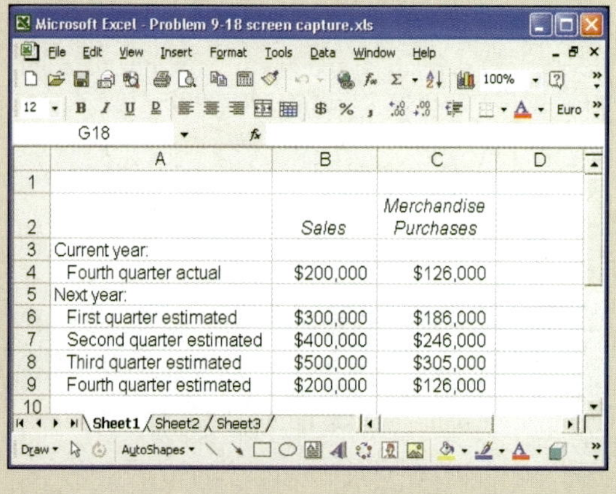

	Sales	Merchandise Purchases
Current year:		
Fourth quarter actual	$200,000	$126,000
Next year:		
First quarter estimated	$300,000	$186,000
Second quarter estimated	$400,000	$246,000
Third quarter estimated	$500,000	$305,000
Fourth quarter estimated	$200,000	$126,000

b. The company normally collects 65% of a quarter's sales before the quarter ends and another 33% in the following quarter. The remainder is uncollectible. This pattern of collections is now being experienced in the current year's fourth-quarter actual data.
c. Eighty percent of a quarter's merchandise purchases are paid for within the quarter. The remainder is paid for in the following quarter.
d. Operating expenses for next year are budgeted at $50,000 per quarter plus 15% of sales. Of the fixed amount, $20,000 each quarter is depreciation.
e. The company will pay $10,000 in dividends each quarter.
f. Equipment purchases of $75,000 will be made in the second quarter, and purchases of $48,000 will be made in the third quarter. These purchases will be for cash.
g. The Cash account contained $10,000 at the end of the current year. The treasurer feels that this represents a minimum balance that must be maintained.
h. Any borrowing will take place at the beginning of a quarter, and any repayments will be made at the end of a quarter at an annual interest rate of 10%. Interest is paid only when principal is repaid. All borrowings and all repayments of principal must be in round $1,000 amounts. Interest payments can be in any amount. (Compute interest on whole months, e.g., $\frac{1}{12}$, $\frac{2}{12}$.)
i. At present, the company has no loans outstanding.

Required:

1. Prepare the following by quarter and in total for next year:
   a. A schedule of expected cash collections.
   b. A schedule of expected cash disbursements for merchandise purchases.
2. Compute the expected cash disbursements for operating expenses, by quarter and in total, for next year.
3. Prepare a cash budget, by quarter and in total, for next year. Show clearly in your budget the quarter(s) in which borrowing will be necessary and the quarter(s) in which repayments can be made, as requested by the company's bank.

PROBLEM 9–19 Completing a Master Budget [LO2, LO4, LO7, LO8, LO9, LO10]

The following data relate to the operations of Shilow Company, a wholesale distributor of consumer goods:

Current assets as of March 31:	
Cash	$8,000
Accounts receivable	$20,000
Inventory	$36,000
Building and equipment, net	$120,000
Accounts payable	$21,750
Capital stock	$150,000
Retained earnings	$12,250

a. The gross margin is 25% of sales.
b. Actual and budgeted sales data:

March (actual)	$50,000
April	$60,000
May	$72,000
June	$90,000
July	$48,000

c. Sales are 60% for cash and 40% on credit. Credit sales are collected in the month following sale. The accounts receivable at March 31 are a result of March credit sales.
d. Each month's ending inventory should equal 80% of the following month's budgeted cost of goods sold.
e. One-half of a month's inventory purchases is paid for in the month of purchase; the other half is paid for in the following month. The accounts payable at March 31 are the result of March purchases of inventory.
f. Monthly expenses are as follows: commissions, 12% of sales; rent, $2,500 per month; other expenses (excluding depreciation), 6% of sales. Assume that these expenses are paid monthly. Depreciation is $900 per month (includes depreciation on new assets).
g. Equipment costing $1,500 will be purchased for cash in April.

h. The company must maintain a minimum cash balance of $4,000. An open line of credit is available at a local bank. All borrowing is done at the beginning of a month, and all repayments are made at the end of a month; borrowing must be in multiples of $1,000. The annual interest rate is 12%. Interest is paid only at the time of repayment of principal; figure interest on whole months (1/12, 2/12, and so forth).

Required:

Using the preceding data:

1. Complete the following schedule:

Schedule of Expected Cash Collections	April	May	June	Quarter
Cash sales	$36,000			
Credit sales	20,000			
Total collections	$56,000			

2. Complete the following:

Merchandise Purchases Budget	April	May	June	Quarter
Budgeted cost of goods sold	$45,000*	$54,000		
Add desired ending inventory	43,200†			
Total needs	88,200			
Less beginning inventory	36,000			
Required purchases	$52,200			

*For April sales: $60,000 sales × 75% cost ratio = $45,000.
†$54,000 × 80% = $43,200

Schedule of Expected Cash Disbursements—Merchandise Purchases	April	May	June	Quarter
March purchases	$21,750			$21,750
April purchases	26,100	$26,100		52,200
May purchases				
June purchases				
Total disbursements	$47,850			

3. Complete the following:

Schedule of Expected Cash Disbursements—Operating Expenses	April	May	June	Quarter
Commissions	$ 7,200			
Rent	2,500			
Other expenses	3,600			
Total disbursements	$13,300			

4. Complete the following cash budget:

Cash Budget	April	May	June	Quarter
Cash balance, beginning	$ 8,000			
Add cash collections	56,000			
Total cash available	64,000			

continued

	April	May	June	Quarter
Less cash disbursements:				
For inventory	47,850			
For expenses	13,300			
For equipment	1,500			
Total cash disbursements	62,650			
Excess (deficiency) of cash	1,350			
Financing:				
Etc.				

5. Prepare an absorption costing income statement, similar to the one shown in Schedule 9 in the text, for the quarter ended June 30.
6. Prepare a balance sheet as of June 30.

PROBLEM 9–20 Completing a Master Budget [LO2, LO4, LO7, LO8, LO9, LO10]

Hillyard Company, an office supplies specialty store, prepares its master budget on a quarterly basis. The following data have been assembled to assist in preparing the master budget for the first quarter:

a. As of December 31 (the end of the prior quarter), the company's general ledger showed the following account balances:

	Debits	Credits
Cash	$ 48,000	
Accounts Receivable	224,000	
Inventory	60,000	
Buildings and Equipment (net)	370,000	
Accounts Payable		$ 93,000
Capital Stock		500,000
Retained Earnings		109,000
	$702,000	$702,000

b. Actual sales for December and budgeted sales for the next four months are as follows:

December (actual)	$280,000
January	$400,000
February	$600,000
March	$300,000
April	$200,000

c. Sales are 20% for cash and 80% on credit. All payments on credit sales are collected in the month following sale. The accounts receivable at December 31 are a result of December credit sales.
d. The company's gross margin is 40% of sales. (In other words, cost of goods sold is 60% of sales.)
e. Monthly expenses are budgeted as follows: salaries and wages, $27,000 per month: advertising, $70,000 per month; shipping, 5% of sales; other expenses, 3% of sales. Depreciation, including depreciation on new assets acquired during the quarter, will be $42,000 for the quarter.
f. Each month's ending inventory should equal 25% of the following month's cost of goods sold.
g. One-half of a month's inventory purchases is paid for in the month of purchase; the other half is paid in the following month.
h. During February, the company will purchase a new copy machine for $1,700 cash. During March, other equipment will be purchased for cash at a cost of $84,500.
i. During January, the company will declare and pay $45,000 in cash dividends.
j. The company must maintain a minimum cash balance of $30,000. An open line of credit is available at a local bank for any borrowing that may be needed during the quarter. All borrowing is done at the beginning of a month, and all repayments are made at the end of a month. Borrowings and repayments of principal must be in multiples of $1,000. Interest is paid only at the time of payment of principal. The annual interest rate is 12%. (Figure interest on whole months, e.g., $\frac{1}{12}$, $\frac{2}{12}$.)

Required:

Using the data above, complete the following statements and schedules for the first quarter:

1. Schedule of expected cash collections:

	January	February	March	Quarter
Cash sales	$ 80,000			
Credit sales	224,000			
Total cash collections	$304,000			

2. *a.* Merchandise purchases budget:

	January	February	March	Quarter
Budgeted cost of goods sold	$240,000*	$360,000		
Add desired ending inventory	90,000†			
Total needs	330,000			
Less beginning inventory	60,000			
Required purchases	$270,000			

*$400,000 sales × 60% cost ratio = $240,000.

†$360,000 × 25% = $90,000.

b. Schedule of expected cash disbursements for merchandise purchases:

	January	February	March	Quarter
December purchases	$ 93,000			$ 93,000
January purchases	135,000	135,000		270,000
February purchases	—			
March purchases	—			
Total cash disbursements for purchases	$228,000			

3. Schedule of expected cash disbursements for operating expenses:

	January	February	March	Quarter
Salaries and wages	$ 27,000			
Advertising	70,000			
Shipping	20,000			
Other expenses	12,000			
Total cash disbursements for operating expenses	$129,000			

4. Cash budget:

	January	February	March	Quarter
Cash balance, beginning	$ 48,000			
Add cash collections	304,000			
Total cash available	352,000			
Less cash disbursements:				
Purchases of inventory	228,000			
Operating expenses	129,000			
Purchases of equipment	—			
Cash dividends	45,000			
Total cash disbursements	402,000			
Excess (deficiency) of cash	(50,000)			
Financing:				
Etc.				

5. Prepare an absorption costing income statement for the quarter ending March 31 as shown in Schedule 9 in the chapter.
6. Prepare a balance sheet as of March 31.

PROBLEM 9–21 Cash Budget for One Month [LO2, LO4, LO6, LO8]

Wallace Products, Ltd., is planning its cash needs for July. Since the company will be buying some new equipment during the month, the treasurer is sure that some borrowing will be needed, but he is uncertain how much. The following data have been assembled to assist the treasurer in preparing a cash budget for the month:

a. Equipment will be purchased during July for cash at a cost of $45,000.
b. Selling and administrative expenses will be:

Advertising	$110,000
Sales salaries	$50,000
Administrative salaries	$35,000
Shipping	$2,100

c. Sales are budgeted at $800,000 for July. Customers are allowed a 2½% cash discount on accounts paid within 10 days after the end of the month of sale. Only 50% of the payments made in the month following the sale fall within the discount period. (All of the company's sales are on account.)
d. On June 30, the company will have the following accounts receivable outstanding:

Month	Sales	Accounts Receivable at June 30	Percentage of Sales Uncollected at June 30	Percentage to Be Collected in July
March	$430,000	$6,450	1½%	?
April	$590,000	$35,400	6%	?
May	$640,000	$128,000	20%	?
June	$720,000	$720,000	100%	?

Bad debts are negligible. All March receivables shown above will have been collected by the end of July, and the collection pattern implicit in the schedule above will be the same in July as in previous months.

e. Production costs are budgeted as follows for July:

Prime costs:		
Raw materials to be used in production		$342,000
Direct labor		95,000
Overhead costs:		
Indirect labor	$36,000	
Utilities	1,900	
Payroll benefits	14,800	
Depreciation	28,000	
Property taxes	1,100	
Fire insurance	1,700	
Amortization of patents	3,500	
Scrapping of obsolete goods	2,600	89,600
Total production costs		$526,600

f. The raw materials inventory is budgeted to increase by $18,000 during July; other inventories will not change.
g. Half of the raw materials purchased each month is paid for in the month of purchase; the other half is paid for in the following month. Accounts payable at June 30 for raw materials purchases will be $172,000.
h. All July payroll amounts will be paid for within the month of July.
i. Utilities costs are paid for within the month.

j. The $14,800 monthly charge above for "Payroll benefits" includes the following items:

Company pension plan, including ⅟₁₂ of a $9,600 special adjustment that was paid in April	$7,000
Group insurance (payable semiannually, with the last payment having been made in January)	$900
Unemployment insurance (payable monthly)	$1,300
Vacation pay, which represents ⅟₁₂ of the annual cost (July's vacations will require $14,100)	$5,600

k. Property taxes are paid in June of each year.
l. Fire insurance premiums were prepaid in January.
m. The company has an open line of credit with the Royal Calgary Bank. All borrowing from the bank must be in round $1,000 amounts.
n. The cash balance on June 30 is $78,000; the company must maintain a cash balance of at least $75,000.

Required:

1. Prepare a schedule of expected cash collections for July.
2. Compute (a) budgeted cash disbursements for raw materials purchases, and (b) budgeted cash disbursements for overhead for July.
3. Prepare a cash budget for July.
4. A member of the board of directors of Wallace Products stated, "The monthly cash budget shows the company's cash surplus or deficiency and assures us that an unexpected cash shortage will not occur." Comment on this statement.

(SMA, adapted)

PROBLEM 9–22 Integrated Operating Budgets [LO3, LO4, LO5, LO6]

The West Division of Vader Corporation produces an intricate component part used in Vader's major product line. The divisional manager has recently been concerned about a lack of coordination between purchasing and production personnel and believes that a monthly budgeting system would be better than the present system.

The manager of the West Division has decided to develop budget information for the third quarter of the current year as a trial before the budget system is implemented for an entire fiscal year. In response to the manager's request for data that could be used to develop budget information, the controller of the West Division accumulated the following data:

Sales Sales through June 30, the first six months of the current year, were 24,000 units. Actual sales in units for May and June and estimated unit sales for the next five months are detailed as follows:

May (actual)	4,000
June (actual)	4,000
July (estimated)	5,000
August (estimated)	6,000
September (estimated)	7,000
October (estimated)	7,500
November (estimated)	8,000

The West Division expects to sell 65,000 units during the year ending December 31.

Direct Materials Data regarding the direct materials used in the component are shown in the following schedule. Each month's ending direct materials inventory should equal 50% of the next month's production needs.

Direct Material	Units of Direct Materials per Finished Component	Cost per Unit	Inventory Level June 30
No. 101	6 ounces	$2.40	35,000 ounces
No. 211	4 pounds	$5.00	30,000 pounds

Direct Labor Each component must pass through three processes to be completed. Data regarding the direct labor are as follows:

Process	Direct Labor-Hours per Finished Component	Cost per Direct Labor-Hour
Forming	0.40	$16.00
Assembly	1.00	$11.00
Finishing	0.10	$15.00

Manufacturing Overhead The West Division produced 27,000 components and incurred the variable overhead costs shown below during the six-month period ended June 30. The controller of the West Division believes that the variable overhead costs will be incurred at the same rate during the last six months of the year.

Supplies	$ 59,400
Electricity	27,000
Indirect labor	54,000
Other	8,100
Total variable overhead	$148,500

The fixed manufacturing overhead costs incurred during the first six months amounted to $93,500. Fixed manufacturing overhead costs are budgeted for the full year as follows:

Supervision	$ 60,000
Taxes	7,200
Depreciation	86,400
Other	32,400
Total fixed manufacturing overhead	$186,000

Finished Goods Inventory The desired monthly ending finished goods inventory in units is 80% of the next month's estimated sales. There are 4,000 finished units in inventory on June 30.

Required:

1. Prepare a production budget for the West Division for the third quarter ending September 30. Show computations by month and in total for the quarter.
2. Prepare a direct materials budget for each type of material for the third quarter ending September 30. Again show computations by month and in total for the quarter.
3. Prepare a direct labor budget for the third quarter ending September 30. This time it is *not* necessary to show monthly figures; show quarterly totals only. Assume that the workforce is adjusted as work requirements change.
4. Assume that the company plans to produce a total of 65,000 units for the year. Prepare a manufacturing overhead budget for the six-month period ending December 31. (Do not compute a predetermined overhead rate.) Again, it is *not* necessary to show monthly figures.

(CMA, adapted)

Cases

CASE 9–23 Evaluating a Company's Budget Procedures [LO1]

Tom Emory and Jim Morris strolled back to their plant from the administrative offices of Ferguson & Son Mfg. Company. Tom is manager of the machine shop in the company's factory; Jim is the manager of the equipment maintenance department.

The men had just attended the monthly performance evaluation meeting for plant department heads. These meetings had been held on the third Tuesday of each month since Robert Ferguson, Jr., the president's son, had become plant manager a year earlier.

As they were walking, Tom Emory spoke: "Boy, I hate those meetings! I never know whether my department's accounting reports will show good or bad performance. I'm beginning to expect the worst. If the accountants say I saved the company a dollar, I'm called 'Sir,' but if I spend even a little too much—boy, do I get in trouble. I don't know if I can hold on until I retire."

Tom had just been given the worst evaluation he had ever received in his long career with Ferguson & Son. He was the most respected of the experienced machinists in the company. He had been with Ferguson & Son for many years and was promoted to supervisor of the machine shop when the company expanded and moved to its present location. The president (Robert Ferguson, Sr.) had often stated that the company's success was due to the high quality of the work of machinists like Tom. As supervisor, Tom stressed the importance of craftsmanship and told his workers that he wanted no sloppy work coming from his department.

When Robert Ferguson, Jr., became the plant manager, he directed that monthly performance comparisons be made between actual and budgeted costs for each department. The departmental budgets were intended to encourage the supervisors to reduce inefficiencies and to seek cost reduction opportunities. The company controller was instructed to have his staff "tighten" the budget slightly whenever a department attained its budget in a given month; this was done to reinforce the plant manager's desire to reduce costs. The young plant manager often stressed the importance of continued progress toward attaining the budget; he also made it known that he kept a file of these performance reports for future reference when he succeeded his father.

Tom Emory's conversation with Jim Morris continued as follows:

Emory: I really don't understand. We've worked so hard to meet the budget, and the minute we do so they tighten it on us. We can't work any faster and still maintain quality. I think my men are ready to quit trying. Besides, those reports don't tell the whole story. We always seem to be interrupting the big jobs for all those small rush orders. All that setup and machine adjustment time is killing us. And quite frankly, Jim, you were no help. When our hydraulic press broke down last month, your people were nowhere to be found. We had to take it apart ourselves and got stuck with all that idle time.

Morris: I'm sorry about that, Tom, but you know my department has had trouble making budget, too. We were running well behind at the time of that problem, and if we'd spent a day on that old machine, we would never have made it up. Instead we made the scheduled inspections of the forklift trucks because we knew we could do those in less than the budgeted time.

Emory: Well, Jim, at least you have some options. I'm locked into what the scheduling department assigns to me and you know they're being harassed by sales for those special orders. Incidentally, why didn't your report show all the supplies you guys wasted last month when you were working in Bill's department?

Morris: We're not out of the woods on that deal yet. We charged the maximum we could to other work and haven't even reported some of it yet.

Emory: Well, I'm glad you have a way of getting out of the pressure. The accountants seem to know everything that's happening in my department, sometimes even before I do. I thought all that budget and accounting stuff was supposed to help, but it just gets me into trouble. It's all a big pain. I'm trying to put out quality work; they're trying to save pennies.

Required:

1. Identify the problems that appear to exist in Ferguson & Son Mfg. Company's budgetary control system and explain how the problems are likely to reduce the effectiveness of the system.
2. Explain how Ferguson & Son Mfg. Company's budgetary control system could be revised to improve its effectiveness.

(CMA, adapted)

CASE 9–24 Master Budget with Supporting Schedules [LO2, LO4, LO8, LO9, LO10]

You have just been hired as a new management trainee by Earrings Unlimited, a distributor of earrings to various retail outlets located in shopping malls across the country. In the past, the company has done very little in the way of budgeting and at certain times of the year has experienced a shortage of cash.

Since you are well trained in budgeting, you have decided to prepare comprehensive budgets for the upcoming second quarter in order to show management the benefits that can be gained from an integrated budgeting program. To this end, you have worked with accounting and other areas to gather the information assembled below.

The company sells many styles of earrings, but all are sold for the same price—$10 per pair. Actual sales of earrings for the last three months and budgeted sales for the next six months follow (in pairs of earrings):

January (actual)	20,000	June (budget)	50,000
February (actual)	26,000	July (budget)	30,000
March (actual)	40,000	August (budget)	28,000
April (budget)	65,000	September (budget)	25,000
May (budget)	100,000		

The concentration of sales before and during May is due to Mother's Day. Sufficient inventory should be on hand at the end of each month to supply 40% of the earrings sold in the following month.

Suppliers are paid \$4 for a pair of earrings. One-half of a month's purchases is paid for in the month of purchase; the other half is paid for in the following month. All sales are on credit, with no discount, and payable within 15 days. The company has found, however, that only 20% of a month's sales are collected in the month of sale. An additional 70% is collected in the following month, and the remaining 10% is collected in the second month following sale. Bad debts have been negligible.

Monthly operating expenses for the company are given below:

Variable:	
Sales commissions	4% of sales
Fixed:	
Advertising	\$200,000
Rent	\$18,000
Salaries	\$106,000
Utilities	\$7,000
Insurance	\$3,000
Depreciation	\$14,000

Insurance is paid on an annual basis, in November of each year.

The company plans to purchase \$16,000 in new equipment during May and \$40,000 in new equipment during June; both purchases will be for cash. The company declares dividends of \$15,000 each quarter, payable in the first month of the following quarter.

A listing of the company's ledger accounts as of March 31 is given below:

Assets	
Cash	\$ 74,000
Accounts receivable (\$26,000 February sales; \$320,000 March sales)	346,000
Inventory	104,000
Prepaid insurance	21,000
Property and equipment (net)	950,000
Total assets	\$1,495,000
Liabilities and Stockholders' Equity	
Accounts payable	\$ 100,000
Dividends payable	15,000
Capital stock	800,000
Retained earnings	580,000
Total liabilities and stockholders' equity	\$1,495,000

The company maintains a minimum cash balance of \$50,000. All borrowing is done at the beginning of a month; any repayments are made at the end of a month.

The annual interest rate is 12%. Interest is computed and paid at the end of each quarter on all loans outstanding during the quarter.

Required:

Prepare a master budget for the three-month period ending June 30. Include the following detailed budgets:

1. *a.* A sales budget, by month and in total.
   b. A schedule of expected cash collections from sales, by month and in total.
   c. A merchandise purchases budget in units and in dollars. Show the budget by month and in total.

d. A schedule of expected cash disbursements for merchandise purchases, by month and in total.

2. A cash budget. Show the budget by month and in total. Determine any borrowing that would be needed to maintain the minimum cash balance of $50,000.
3. A budgeted income statement for the three-month period ending June 30. Use the contribution approach.
4. A budgeted balance sheet as of June 30.

CASE 9–25 Cash Budget for a Growing Company [LO2, LO4, LO6, LO8]

CrossMan Corporation, a rapidly expanding crossbow distributor to retail outlets, is in the process of formulating plans for next year. Joan Caldwell, director of marketing, has completed her sales budget and is confident that sales estimates will be met or exceeded. The following budgeted sales figures show the growth expected and will provide the basis for planning within other corporate departments.

	Budgeted Sales		Budgeted Sales
January	$1,800,000	July	$3,000,000
February	$2,000,000	August	$3,000,000
March	$1,800,000	September	$3,200,000
April	$2,200,000	October	$3,200,000
May	$2,500,000	November	$3,000,000
June	$2,800,000	December	$3,400,000

George Brownell, assistant controller, has been given the responsibility for formulating the cash budget, a critical task during a period of rapid expansion. The following information provided by operating managers will be used in preparing the cash budget.

a. CrossMan collects 60% of credit sales in the month after the sale and 40% in the second month after the sale. Uncollectible accounts are negligible.
b. The purchase cost of the crossbows equals 50% of sales. Sixty percent of the crossbows are received one month prior to sale and 40% are received during the month of sale.
c. Prior experience shows that 80% of accounts payable are paid by CrossMan one month after receipt of the purchased crossbows, and the remaining 20% are paid the second month after receipt.
d. Hourly wages, including fringe benefits, depend on sales volume and are equal to 20% of the current month's sales. These wages are paid in the month incurred.
e. General and administrative expenses are budgeted to be $2,640,000 for the year. The composition of these expenses is given below. All of these expenses are incurred evenly throughout the year except the property taxes. Property taxes are paid in four equal installments in the last month of each quarter.

Salaries	$ 480,000
Promotion	660,000
Property taxes	240,000
Insurance	360,000
Utilities	300,000
Depreciation	600,000
Total	$2,640,000

f. Income tax payments are made by CrossMan in the first month of each quarter based on the income for the prior quarter. CrossMan's income tax rate is 40%. CrossMan's net operating income for the first quarter is projected to be $612,000.
g. Equipment and warehouse facilities are being acquired to support the company's rapidly growing sales. Purchases of equipment and facilities are budgeted at $28,000 for April and $324,000 for May.
h. CrossMan has a corporate policy of maintaining an end-of-month cash balance of $100,000. Cash is borrowed or invested monthly, as needed, to maintain this balance. Interest expense on borrowed funds is budgeted at $8,000 for the second quarter, all of which will be paid during June.

Required:

1. Prepare a cash budget for CrossMan Corporation by month and in total for the quarter ended June 30. Be sure that all receipts, disbursements, and borrowing/investing amounts are shown for each month. Ignore any interest income associated with amounts invested.
2. Discuss why cash budgeting is particularly important for a rapidly expanding company such as CrossMan Corporation.

(CMA, adapted)

Group and Internet Exercises

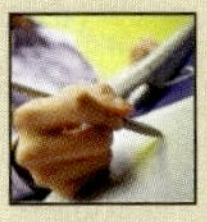

GROUP EXERCISE 9–26 Financial Pressures Hit Higher Education

In the late eighties and early nineties, public universities found that they were no longer immune to the financial stress faced by their private sister institutions and the rest of Corporate America. Budget cuts were in the air across the land. When the budget ax hit, the cuts often came without warning and their size was sometimes staggering. State support for some institutions dropped by 40% or more. Most university administrators had only experienced budget increases, never budget cuts. Also, the budget setbacks usually occurred at the most inopportune time—during the school year when contractual commitments with faculty and staff had been signed, programs had been planned, and students were enrolled and taking classes.

Required:

1. Should the university's administration be "fair" to all affected departments by declaring a round of across-the-board cuts whenever the state announces another subsidy reduction?
2. If not across-the-board cutbacks in programs, then would you recommend more focused reductions, and if so, what priorities would you establish for bringing spending in line with revenues?
3. Since these usually are not one-time-only cutbacks, how would you manage continuous, long-term reductions in budgets extending over a period of years?
4. Should the decision-making process be top-down (centralized with top administrators) or bottom-up (participative)? Why?
5. How should issues such as a protect-your-turf mentality, resistance to change, and consensus building be dealt with?

INTERNET EXERCISE 9–27

As you know, the World Wide Web is a medium that is constantly evolving. Sites come and go, and change without notice. To enable the periodic updating of site addresses, this problem has been posted to the textbook website (www.mhhe.com/garrison11e). After accessing the site, enter the Student Center and select this chapter. Select and complete the Internet Exercise.

Chapter

10

Standard Costs and the Balanced Scorecard

LEARNING OBJECTIVES

After studying Chapter 10, you should be able to:

LO1 Explain how direct materials standards and direct labor standards are set.

LO2 Compute the direct materials price and quantity variances and explain their significance.

LO3 Compute the direct labor rate and efficiency variances and explain their significance.

LO4 Compute the variable manufacturing overhead spending and efficiency variances.

LO5 Understand how a balanced scorecard fits together and how it supports a company's strategy.

LO6 Compute delivery cycle time, throughput time, and manufacturing cycle efficiency (MCE).

LO7 (Appendix 10A) Prepare journal entries to record standard costs and variances.

BUSINESS FOCUS

The Business End of Visual Effects

Special effects, such as the computer-generated action shots of dinosaurs in the movie *Jurassic Park,* are expensive to produce. A single visual effect, lasting three to seven seconds, can cost up to $50,000. And a high-profile film may contain hundreds of these shots.

With over 30 visual-effects companies in the United States, competition is fierce. Since visual effects are produced under fixed-price contracts, visual-effects companies must carefully estimate their costs. And once a bid has been accepted, costs must be zealously monitored to make sure they do not spin out of control. Buena Vista Visual Effects, a part of Walt Disney Studios, uses a standard cost system to estimate and control costs. A "storyboard" is created for each special-effects shot. The storyboard sketches the visual effect, details the length of the shot (measured in frames—24 frames equal one second of film), and describes the work that will need to be done to create the effect. A detailed budget is then prepared using standard costs. For example, a shot may require that a miniature model maker work full time for 12 weeks at a specified weekly wage. As the job progresses, this standard cost is compared to actual costs and significant cost overruns are investigated. Management attention is directed to significant variances. ■

Source: Ray Scalice, "Lights! Cameras! . . . Accountants?" *Management Accounting,* June 1996, pp. 42–46.

In this chapter we begin our study of management control and performance measures. Quite often, these terms carry with them negative connotations. Indeed, performance measurements can be used counterproductively to create fear, to cast blame, and to punish. However, if used properly, as explained in the following quotation, performance measurement serves a vital function in both daily life and in organizations:

> Imagine you want to improve your basketball shooting skill. You know that practice will help, so you [go] to the basketball court. There you start shooting toward the hoop, but as soon as the ball gets close to the rim your vision goes blurry for a second, so that you cannot observe where the ball ended up in relation to the target (left, right, in front, too far back, inside the hoop?). It would be pretty difficult to improve under those conditions. . . . (And by the way, how long would [shooting baskets] sustain your interest if you couldn't observe the outcome of your efforts?)
>
> Or imagine someone engaging in a weight loss program. A normal step in such programs is to purchase a scale to be able to track one's progress: Is this program working? Am I losing weight? A positive answer would be encouraging and would motivate me to keep up the effort, while a negative answer might lead me to reflect on the process: Am I working on the right diet and exercise program? Am I doing everything I am supposed to?, etc. Suppose you don't want to set up a sophisticated measurement system and decide to forgo the scale. You would still have some idea of how well you are doing from simple methods such as clothes feeling looser, a belt that fastens at a different hole, or simply via observation in a mirror! Now, imagine trying to sustain a weight loss program without *any* feedback on how well you are doing.
>
> In these . . . examples, availability of quantitative measures of performance can yield two types of benefits: First, performance feedback can help improve the "production process" through a better understanding of what works and what doesn't; e.g., shooting this way works better than shooting that way. Secondly, feedback on performance can sustain motivation and effort, because it is encouraging and/or because it suggests that more effort is required for the goal to be met.[1]

In the same way, performance measurement can be helpful in an organization. It can provide feedback concerning what works and what does not work, and it can help motivate people to sustain their efforts.

IN BUSINESS

FOCUSING ON THE NUMBERS

Joe Knight is the CEO of Setpoint, a company that designs and builds factory-automation equipment. Knight uses a large whiteboard, with about 20 rows and 10 columns, to focus worker attention on key factors involved in managing projects. A visitor to the plant, Steve Petersen, asked Knight to explain the board, but Knight instead motioned one of his workers to come over. The young man, with a baseball cap turned backward on his head, proceeded to walk the visitor through the board, explaining the calculation of gross margin and other key indicators on the board.

"'I was just amazed,' Petersen recalls. 'He knew that board inside and out. He knew every number on it. He knew exactly where the company was and where they had to focus their attention. There was no hesitation . . . . I was so impressed . . . that the people on the shop floor had it down like that. It was their scoreboard. It was the way they could tell if they were winning or losing. I talked to several of them, and I just couldn't get over the positive attitude they had and their understanding of the numbers.'"

Source: Bo Burlinghan, "What's Your Culture Worth?," *Inc.*, September 2001, pp. 124–133.

---

[1] Soumitra Dutta and Jean-François Manzoni, *Process Reengineering, Organizational Change and Performance Improvement* (New York: McGraw-Hill, 1999), Chapter IV.

In this chapter, our study of performance measurement begins with the lowest levels in the organization. We work our way up the organizational ladder in subsequent chapters. In this chapter we see how various measures are used to control operations and to evaluate performance. Even though we are starting with the lowest levels in the organization, keep in mind that performance measures should be derived from the organization's overall strategy. For example, a company like Sony that bases its strategy on rapid introduction of innovative consumer products should use different performance measures than a company like Federal Express where on-time delivery, customer convenience, and low cost are key competitive advantages. Sony may want to keep close track of the percentage of revenues from products introduced within the last year; whereas Federal Express may want to closely monitor the percentage of packages delivered on time. Later in this chapter when we discuss the *balanced scorecard,* we will have more to say concerning the role of strategy in the selection of performance measures. But first we will see how *standard costs* are used by managers to help control costs.

Companies in highly competitive industries like Federal Express, Southwest Airlines, Dell Computer, Shell Oil, and Toyota must be able to provide high-quality goods and services at low cost. If they do not, they will perish. Stated in the starkest terms, managers must obtain inputs such as raw materials and electricity at the lowest possible prices and must use them as effectively as possible—while maintaining or increasing the quality of what they sell. If inputs are purchased at prices that are too high or more input is used than is really necessary, higher costs will result.

How do managers control the prices that are paid for inputs and the quantities that are used? They could examine every transaction in detail, but this obviously would be an inefficient use of management time. For many companies, the answer to this control problem lies at least partially in *standard costs.*

Standard Costs—Management by Exception

A *standard* is a benchmark or "norm" for measuring performance. Standards are found everywhere. Your doctor evaluates your weight using standards that have been set for individuals of your age, height, and gender. The food we eat in restaurants must be prepared under specified standards of cleanliness. The buildings we live in must conform to standards set in building codes. Standards are also widely used in managerial accounting where they relate to the *quantity* and *cost* (or acquisition price) of inputs used in manufacturing goods or providing services.

Managers—often assisted by engineers and accountants—set quantity and cost standards for each major input such as raw materials and labor time. *Quantity standards* specify how much of an input should be used to make a product or provide a service. *Cost (price) standards* specify how much should be paid for each unit of the input. Actual quantities and actual costs of inputs are compared to these standards. If either the quantity or the cost of inputs departs significantly from the standards, managers investigate the discrepancy. The purpose is to find the cause of the problem and then eliminate it so that it does not recur. This process is called **management by exception.**

In our daily lives, we operate in a management by exception mode most of the time. Consider what happens when you sit down in the driver's seat of your car. You put the key in the ignition, you turn the key, and your car starts. Your expectation (standard) that the car will start is met; you do not have to open the car hood and check the battery, the connecting cables, the fuel lines, and so on. If you turn the key and the car does not start, then you have a discrepancy (variance). Your expectations are not met, and you need to investigate why. Note that even if the car starts after a second try, it would be wise to investigate. The fact that the expectation was not met should be viewed as an opportunity to uncover the cause of the problem rather than as simply an annoyance. If the underlying cause is not discovered and corrected, the problem may recur and become much worse.

EXHIBIT 10–1
The Variance Analysis Cycle

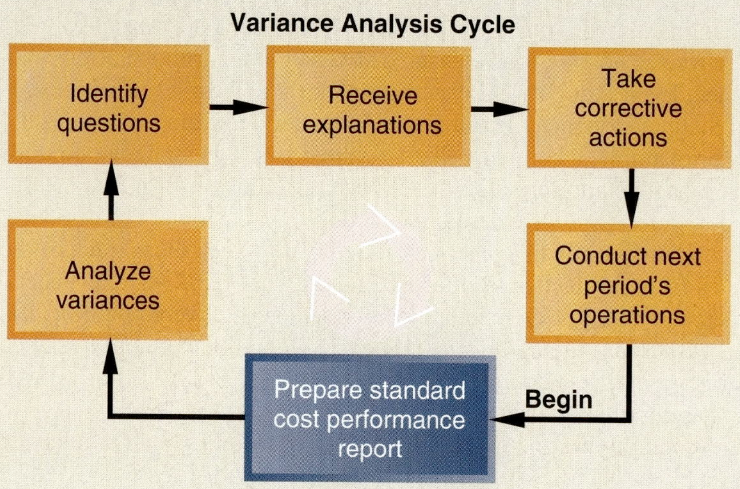

This basic approach to identifying and solving problems is the essence of the *variance analysis cycle*, which is illustrated in Exhibit 10–1. The cycle begins with the preparation of standard cost performance reports in the accounting department. These reports highlight the *variances*, which are the differences between actual results and what should have occurred according to the standards. The variances raise questions. Why did this variance occur? Why is this variance larger than it was last period? The significant variances are investigated to discover their root causes. Corrective actions are taken. And then next period's operations are carried out. The cycle then begins again with the preparation of a new standard cost performance report for the latest period. The emphasis should be on flagging problems for attention, finding their root causes, and then taking corrective action. The goal is to improve operations—not to assign blame.

Who Uses Standard Costs?

Manufacturing, service, food, and not-for-profit organizations all make use of standards to some extent. Auto service centers like Firestone and Sears, for example, often set specific labor time standards for the completion of certain work tasks, such as installing a carburetor or doing a valve job, and then measure actual performance against these standards. Fast-food outlets such as McDonald's have exacting standards for the quantity of meat going into a sandwich, as well as standards for the cost of the meat. Hospitals have standard costs for food, laundry, and other items, as well as standard time allowances for certain routine activities, such as laboratory tests. In short, you are likely to run into standard costs in virtually any line of business.

IN BUSINESS

STANDARD COSTING AT PARKER BRASS

The Brass Products Division at Parker Hannifin Corporation, known as Parker Brass, is a world-class manufacturer of tube and brass fittings, valves, hose and hose fittings. Management at the company uses variances from its standard costing system to target problem areas for improvement. If a production variance exceeds 5% of sales, the responsible manager is required to explain the variance and to propose a plan of action to correct the detected problems. In the past, variances were reported at the end of the month—often several weeks after a particular job had been completed. Now, a variance report is generated the day after a job is completed and summary variance reports are prepared weekly. These more frequent reports help managers take more timely corrective action.

Source: David Johnsen and Parvez Sopariwala, "Standard Costing Is Alive and Well at Parker Brass," *Management Accounting Quarterly*, Winter 2000, pp. 12–20.

Manufacturing companies often have highly developed standard costing systems in which standards relating to direct materials, direct labor, and overhead are established for each separate product. These standards are listed on a **standard cost card** that provides the manager with a great deal of information concerning the inputs that are required to produce a unit and their costs. In the following section, we provide a detailed example of setting standard costs and preparing a standard cost card.

Setting Standard Costs

Setting price and quantity standards requires the combined expertise of everyone who has responsibility for purchasing and using inputs. In a manufacturing setting, this might include accountants, purchasing managers, engineers, production supervisors, line managers, and production workers. Past records of purchase prices and input usage can be helpful in setting standards. However, the standards should be designed to encourage efficient *future* operations, not just a repetition of *past* inefficient operations.

Ideal versus Practical Standards

Should standards be attainable all of the time, should they be attainable only part of the time, or should they be so tight that they become, in effect, "the impossible dream"? Opinions vary, but standards tend to fall into one of two categories—either ideal or practical.

Ideal standards can be attained only under the best circumstances. They allow for no machine breakdowns or other work interruptions, and they call for a level of effort that can be attained only by the most skilled and efficient employees working at peak effort 100% of the time. Some managers feel that such standards have a motivational value. These managers argue that even though employees know they will rarely meet the standard, it is a constant reminder of the need for ever-increasing efficiency and effort. Few organizations use ideal standards. Most managers feel that ideal standards tend to discourage even the most diligent workers. Moreover, variances from ideal standards are difficult to interpret. Large variances from the ideal are normal and therefore it is difficult to "manage by exception."

Practical standards are defined as standards that are "tight but attainable." They allow for normal machine downtime and employee rest periods, and they can be attained through reasonable, though highly efficient, efforts by the average worker. Variances from such a standard represent deviations that fall outside of normal operating conditions, thereby signaling a need for management attention. Furthermore, practical standards can serve multiple purposes. In addition to signaling abnormal conditions, they can also be used in forecasting cash flows and in planning inventory. By contrast, ideal standards cannot be used in forecasting and planning; they do not allow for normal inefficiencies, and therefore they result in unrealistic planning and forecasting figures.

Throughout the remainder of this chapter, we will assume that practical rather than ideal standards are in use.

MANAGERIAL ACCOUNTING IN ACTION
The Issue

The Colonial Pewter Company was organized a year ago. The company's only product is a reproduction of an 18th century pewter bookend. The bookend is made largely by hand, using traditional metal-working tools. Consequently, the manufacturing process is labor intensive and requires a high level of skill.

Colonial Pewter has recently expanded its work force to take advantage of unexpected demand for the bookends as gifts. The company started with a small cadre of experienced pewter workers but has had to hire less experienced workers as a result of the expansion. The president of the company, J. D. Wriston, has called a meeting to discuss production problems. Attending the meeting are Tom Kuchel, the production manager; Janet Warner, the purchasing manager; and Terry Sherman, the corporate controller.

J. D.: I've got a feeling that we aren't getting the production we should out of our new people.

Tom: Give us a chance. Some of the new people have been with the company for less than a month.

Janet: Let me add that production seems to be wasting an awful lot of material—particularly pewter. That stuff is very expensive.

Tom: What about the shipment of defective pewter that you bought a couple of months ago—the one with the iron contamination? That caused us major problems.

Janet: That's ancient history. How was I to know it was off-grade? Besides, it was a great deal.

J. D.: Calm down everybody. Let's get the facts before we start sinking our fangs into each other.

Tom: I agree. The more facts the better.

J. D.: Okay, Terry, it's your turn. Facts are the controller's department.

Terry: I'm afraid I can't provide the answers off the top of my head, but it won't take me too long to set up a system that can routinely answer questions relating to worker productivity, material waste, and input prices.

J. D.: How long is "not too long"?

Terry: I will need all of your cooperation, but how about a week from today?

J. D.: That's okay with me. What about everyone else?

Tom: Sure.

Janet: Fine with me.

J. D.: Let's mark it on our calendars.

Setting Direct Materials Standards

LEARNING OBJECTIVE 1
Explain how direct materials standards and direct labor standards are set.

Terry Sherman's first task was to prepare price and quantity standards for the company's only significant raw material, pewter ingots. The **standard price per unit** for direct materials should reflect the final, delivered cost of the materials, net of any discounts taken. After consulting with purchasing manager Janet Warner, Terry prepared the following documentation for the standard price of a pound of pewter in ingot form:

Purchase price, top-grade pewter ingots, in 40-pound ingots . . .	$3.60
Freight, by truck, from the supplier's warehouse	0.44
Receiving and handling	0.05
Less purchase discount	(0.09)
Standard price per pound	$4.00

Notice that the standard price reflects a particular grade of material (top grade), purchased in particular lot sizes (40-pound ingots), and delivered by a particular type of carrier (truck). Allowances have also been made for handling and discounts. If everything proceeds according to these expectations, the net cost of a pound of pewter should therefore be $4.00.

The **standard quantity per unit** for direct materials should reflect the amount of material required for each unit of finished product, as well as an allowance for unavoidable waste, spoilage, and other normal inefficiencies. After consulting with the production manager, Tom Kuchel, Terry Sherman prepared the following documentation for the standard quantity of pewter in a pair of bookends:

Material requirements as specified in the bill of materials for a pair of bookends, in pounds	2.7
Allowance for waste and spoilage, in pounds	0.2
Allowance for rejects, in pounds	0.1
Standard quantity per pair of bookends, in pounds	3.0

A **bill of materials** is a list that shows the quantity of each type of material in a unit of finished product. It is a handy source for determining the basic material input per unit, but it should be adjusted for waste and other factors, as shown above, when determining the standard quantity per unit of product. "Waste and spoilage" in the table above refers to materials that are wasted as a normal part of the production process or that spoil before they are used. "Rejects" refers to the direct material contained in units that are defective and must be scrapped.

Although allowances for waste, spoilage, and rejects are often built into standards, this practice is now being questioned. Those involved in TQM (Total Quality Management) and similar improvement programs argue that no amount of waste or defects should be tolerated. If allowances for waste, spoilage, and rejects are built into the standard cost, the levels of those allowances should be periodically reviewed and reduced over time to reflect improved processes, better training, and better equipment.

Once the price and quantity standards have been set, the standard cost of material per unit of finished product can be computed as follows:

3.0 pounds per unit × \$4.00 per pound = \$12 per unit

This \$12 cost will appear as one item on the product's standard cost card.

IN BUSINESS

STANDARDS IN THE SPANISH ROYAL TOBACCO FACTORY

Standards have been used for centuries. For example, the Spanish Royal Tobacco Factory in Seville used standards to control costs in the 1700s. The Royal Tobacco Factory had a monopoly over snuff and cigar production in Spain and was housed in the largest industrial building in Europe. Employee theft of tobacco was a particular problem, due to its high value. Careful records were maintained of the amount of tobacco leaf issued to each worker, the number of cigars expected to be made based on standards, and the actual production. The worker was not paid if the actual production was less than expected. To minimize theft, tobacco was weighed after each production step to determine the amount of waste.

Source: Salvador Carmona, Mahmoud Ezzamel, and Fernando Gutiérrez, "Control and Cost Accounting Practices in the Spanish Royal Tobacco Factory," *Accounting, Organizations, and Society* 22, no. 5, 1997, pp. 411–446.

Setting Direct Labor Standards

Direct labor price and quantity standards are usually expressed in terms of a labor rate and labor-hours. The **standard rate per hour** for direct labor includes not only wages earned but also fringe benefits and other labor costs. Using last month's wage records and in consultation with the production manager, Terry Sherman determined the standard rate per direct labor hour at the Colonial Pewter Company as follows:

Basic wage rate per hour	\$10
Employment taxes at 10% of the basic rate	1
Fringe benefits at 30% of the basic rate	3
Standard rate per direct labor-hour	\$14

Many companies prepare a single standard rate for all employees in a department. This standard rate reflects the expected "mix" of workers, even though the actual wage rates may vary somewhat from individual to individual due to differing skills or seniority. According to the standard computed above, the direct labor rate for Colonial Pewter should average \$14 per hour.

The standard direct labor time required to complete a unit of product (called the **standard hours per unit**) is perhaps the single most difficult standard to determine. One approach is to break down each operation performed on the product into elemental body movements (such as reaching, pushing, and turning over). Standard times for such movements are available in reference works. These standard times can be applied to the movements and then added together to determine the total standard time allowed per operation. Another approach is for an industrial engineer to do a time and motion study, actually clocking the time required for certain tasks. As stated earlier, the standard time should include allowances for breaks, personal needs of employees, cleanup, and machine downtime.

After consulting with the production manager, Terry Sherman prepared the following documentation for the standard direct labor hours per unit:

Basic labor time per unit, in hours	1.9
Allowance for breaks and personal needs	0.1
Allowance for cleanup and machine downtime . . .	0.3
Allowance for rejects	0.2
Standard direct labor-hours per unit of product . . .	2.5

Once the rate and time standards have been set, the standard direct labor cost per unit of product can be computed as follows:

$$2.5 \text{ direct labor hours per unit} \times \$14 \text{ per hour} = \$35 \text{ per unit}$$

This $35 per unit standard direct labor cost appears along with direct materials on the standard cost card of the product.

IN BUSINESS

WATCHING THE PENNIES

Industrie Natuzzi SpA, founded and run by Pasquale Natuzzi, produces handmade leather furniture for the world market in Santaeramo Del Colle in southern Italy. Natuzzi is export-oriented and has, for example, about 25% of the U.S. leather furniture market. The company's furniture is handmade by craftsmen, each of whom has a networked computer terminal that provides precise instructions on how to accomplish a particular task and keeps track of how quickly the craftsman completes the task. If the craftsman beats the standard time for the task, the computer adds a bonus to the craftsman's pay.

The company's computers know exactly how much thread, screws, foam, leather, labor, and so on, is required for every model. "Should the price of Argentinean hides or German dyes rise one day, employees in Santaeramo enter the new prices into the computer, and the costs for all sofas with that leather and those colors are immediately recalculated. 'Everything has to be clear for me,' says Natuzzi. 'Why this penny? Where is it going?'"

Source: Richard C. Morais, "A Methodical Man," *Forbes*, August 11, 1997, pp. 70–72.

Setting Variable Manufacturing Overhead Standards

As with direct labor, the price and quantity standards for variable manufacturing overhead are usually expressed in terms of rate and hours. The rate represents *the variable portion of the predetermined overhead rate* discussed in Chapter 3; the hours relate to the activity base that is used to apply overhead to units of product (usually machine-hours or direct labor-hours, as we learned in Chapter 3). At Colonial Pewter, the variable portion of the predetermined overhead rate is $3 per direct labor-hour. Therefore, the standard variable manufacturing overhead cost per unit is computed as follows:

$$2.5 \text{ direct labor hours per unit} \times \$3 \text{ per hour} = \$7.50 \text{ per unit}$$

This $7.50 per unit cost for variable manufacturing overhead appears along with direct materials and direct labor on the standard cost card in Exhibit 10–2. Observe that the **standard cost per unit** is computed by multiplying the standard quantity of hours by the standard price or rate.

Inputs	(1) Standard Quantity or Hours	(2) Standard Price or Rate	(3) Standard Cost (1) × (2)
Direct materials	3.0 pounds	$4.00	$12.00
Direct labor	2.5 hours	$14.00	35.00
Variable manufacturing overhead	2.5 hours	$3.00	7.50
Total standard cost per unit			$54.50

EXHIBIT 10–2
Standard Cost Card—Variable Manufacturing Costs

Are Standards the Same as Budgets?

Standards and budgets are very similar. The major distinction between the two terms is that a standard is a *unit* amount, whereas a budget is a *total* amount. The standard cost for direct materials at Colonial Pewter is $12 per pair of bookends. If 1,000 pairs of bookends are to be made, then the budgeted cost of direct materials would be $12,000. In effect, *a standard can be viewed as the budgeted cost for one unit of product.*

A General Model for Variance Analysis

Two important reasons for separating standards into two categories—price and quantity—are that different managers are usually responsible for buying and for using inputs and that these two activities occur at different points in time. In the case of raw materials, for example, the purchasing manager is responsible for the price, and this responsibility is exercised at the time of purchase. In contrast, the production manager is responsible for the amount of the raw material used, and this responsibility is exercised when the materials are used in production, which may occur considerably after the purchase date. It is important, therefore, that we cleanly separate discrepancies due to deviations from price standards from those due to deviations from quantity standards. Differences between *standard* prices and *actual* prices and *standard* quantities and *actual* quantities are called **variances.** The act of computing and interpreting variances is called *variance analysis.*

Price and Quantity Variances

A general model for computing standard cost variances for variable costs is presented in Exhibit 10–3. This model isolates price variances from quantity variances and shows how each of these variances is computed.[2] We will be using this model throughout the chapter to compute variances for direct materials, direct labor, and variable manufacturing overhead.

Three things should be noted from Exhibit 10–3. First, a price variance and a quantity variance can be computed for all three variable cost elements—direct materials, direct labor, and variable manufacturing overhead—even though the variances have different names. For example, a price variance is called a *materials price variance* in the case of direct materials but a *labor rate variance* in the case of direct labor and an *overhead spending variance* in the case of variable manufacturing overhead.

Second, even though a price variance may be called by different names, it is computed in exactly the same way regardless of whether one is dealing with direct materials, direct labor, or variable manufacturing overhead. The same is true of the quantity variance.

Third, the input represents the actual quantity of direct materials, direct labor, and variable manufacturing overhead purchased or used; the output represents the good production of the period, expressed in terms of the *standard quantity* (or the *standard hours) allowed for the actual output* (see column 3 in Exhibit 10–3). The **standard quantity**

[2] Variance analysis of fixed costs will be discussed in the next chapter.

EXHIBIT 10–3
A General Model for Variance Analysis—Variable Manufacturing Costs

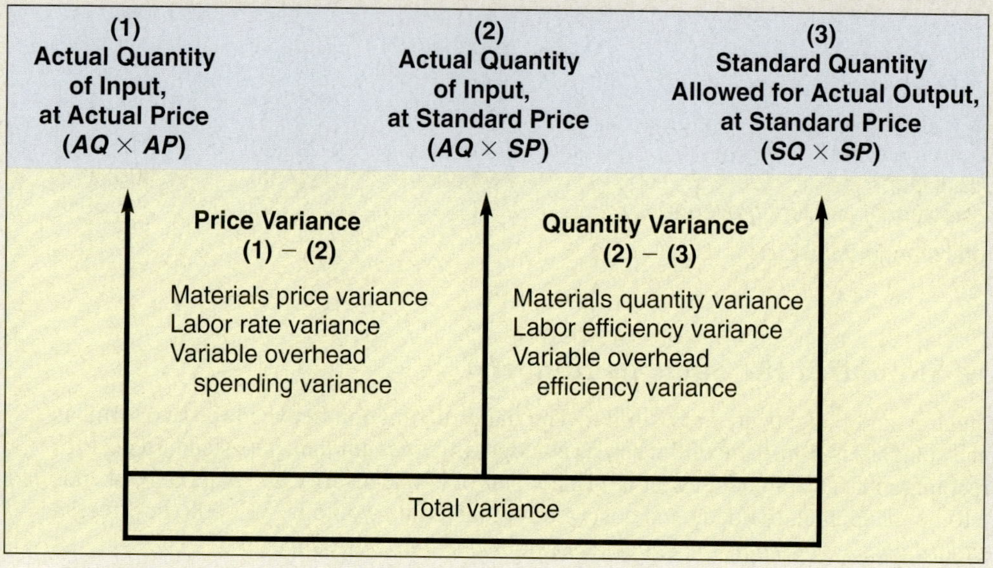

allowed or **standard hours allowed** means the amount of direct materials, direct labor, or variable manufacturing overhead *that should have been used* to produce the actual output of the period. This could be more or less than the actual materials, labor, or overhead, depending on the efficiency or inefficiency of operations. The standard quantity allowed is computed by multiplying the actual output in units by the standard input allowed per unit.

With this general model as the foundation, we will now examine the price and quantity variances in more detail.

Using Standard Costs—Direct Materials Variances

LEARNING OBJECTIVE 2
Compute the direct materials price and quantity variances and explain their significance.

Topic Tackler PLUS 10–1

After determining Colonial Pewter Company's standard costs for direct materials, direct labor, and variable manufacturing overhead, Terry Sherman's next step was to compute the company's variances for June, the most recent month. As discussed in the preceding section, variances are computed by comparing standard costs to actual costs. To facilitate this comparison, Terry referred to the standard cost data contained in Exhibit 10–2. This exhibit shows that the standard cost of direct materials per unit of product is as follows:

3.0 pounds per unit × $4.00 per pound = $12 per unit

Colonial Pewter's purchasing records for June showed that 6,500 pounds of pewter were purchased at a cost of $3.80 per pound. This cost included freight and handling and was net of the purchase discount. All of the material purchased was used during June to manufacture 2,000 pairs of pewter bookends. Using these data and the standard costs from Exhibit 10–2, Terry computed the price and quantity variances shown in Exhibit 10–4.

The three arrows in Exhibit 10–4 point to three different total cost figures. The first, $24,700, refers to the actual total cost of the pewter that was purchased during June. The second, $26,000, refers to what the pewter would have cost if it had been purchased at the standard price of $4.00 a pound rather than the actual price of $3.80 a pound. The difference between these two figures, $1,300 ($26,000 − $24,700), is the price variance. It exists because the actual purchase price was $0.20 per pound less than the standard purchase price. Since 6,500 pounds were purchased, the total amount of the variance is $1,300 ($0.20 per pound × 6,500 pounds). This variance is labeled favorable (denoted by F), since the actual purchase price was less than the standard purchase price. A price variance is labeled unfavorable (denoted by U) if the actual purchase price exceeds the standard purchase price.

EXHIBIT 10–4
Variance Analysis—Direct Materials

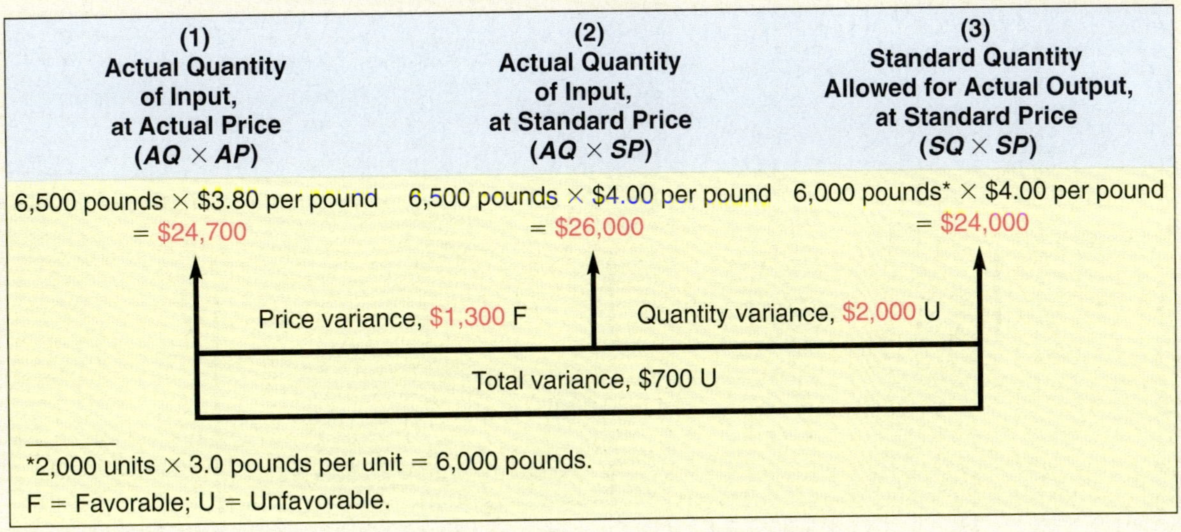

The third arrow in Exhibit 10–4 points to $24,000—the cost if the pewter had been purchased at the standard price *and* only the standard quantity allowed per unit had been used. The standards call for 3 pounds of pewter per unit. Since 2,000 units were produced, 6,000 pounds of pewter should have been used. This is referred to as the standard quantity allowed for the actual output. If this 6,000 pounds of pewter had been purchased at the standard price of $4.00 per pound, the company would have spent $24,000. The difference between this figure, $24,000, and the figure at the end of the middle arrow in Exhibit 10–4, $26,000, is the quantity variance of $2,000.

To understand this quantity variance, note that the actual amount of pewter used in production was 6,500 pounds. However, the standard amount of pewter allowed for the actual output is 6,000 pounds. Therefore, too much pewter was used to produce the actual output—by a total of 500 pounds. To express this in dollar terms, the 500 pounds is multiplied by the standard price of $4.00 per pound to yield the quantity variance of $2,000. Why is the standard price, rather than the actual price, of the pewter used in this calculation? The production manager is ordinarily responsible for the quantity variance. If the actual price were used in the calculation of the quantity variance, the production manager would be held responsible for the efficiency or inefficiency of the purchasing manager. Apart from being unfair, fruitless arguments between the production manager and purchasing manager would occur every time the actual price of an input was above its standard price. To avoid these arguments, the standard price is used when computing the quantity variance.

The quantity variance in Exhibit 10–4 is labeled unfavorable (denoted by U). This is because more pewter was used to produce the actual output than the standard allows. A quantity variance is labeled unfavorable (U) if the actual quantity exceeds the standard quantity and is labeled favorable (F) if the actual quantity is less than the standard quantity.

The computations in Exhibit 10–4 reflect the fact that all of the material purchased during June was also used during June. How are the variances computed if a different amount of material is purchased than is used? To illustrate, assume that during June the company purchased 6,500 pounds of materials, as before, but that it used only 5,000 pounds of material during the month and produced only 1,600 units. In this case, the price variance and quantity variance would be computed as shown in Exhibit 10–5.

Most companies compute the materials price variance when materials are *purchased* rather than when they are used in production. There are two reasons for this

EXHIBIT 10–5
Variance Analysis—Direct Materials, When the Amount Purchased Differs from the Amount Used

(1) Actual Quantity of Input, at Actual Price ($AQ \times AP$)	(2) Actual Quantity of Input, at Standard Price ($AQ \times SP$)	(3) Standard Quantity Allowed for Actual Output, at Standard Price ($SQ \times SP$)
6,500 pounds × \$3.80 per pound = \$24,700	6,500 pounds × \$4.00 per pound = \$26,000	4,800 pounds* × \$4.00 per pound = \$19,200

Price variance, \$1,300 F

5,000 pounds × 4.00 per pound = \$20,000

Quantity variance, \$800 U

A total variance, like the one shown in Exhibit 10–4, can't be computed in this situation since the amount of materials purchased (6,500 pounds) differs from the amount used in production (5,000 pounds).

*1,600 units × 3.0 pounds per unit = 4,800 pounds.

practice. First, delaying the computation of the price variance until the materials are used would result in less timely variance reports. Second, by computing the price variance when the materials are purchased, the materials can be carried in the inventory accounts at their standard cost. This greatly simplifies bookkeeping. (See Appendix 10A at the end of the chapter for an explanation of how the bookkeeping works in a standard costing system.)

Note from the exhibit that the price variance is computed on the entire amount of material purchased (6,500 pounds), as before, whereas the quantity variance is computed only on the portion of this material used in production during the month (5,000 pounds). What about the other 1,500 pounds of material that were purchased during the period, but that have not yet been used? When those materials are used in future periods, a quantity variance will be computed. However, a price variance will not be computed when the materials are finally used since the price variance was computed when the materials were purchased. The situation illustrated in Exhibit 10–5 is common for companies that purchase materials well in advance of when they are used in production.

Materials Price Variance—A Closer Look

A **materials price variance** measures the difference between what is paid for a given quantity of materials and what should have been paid according to the standard. From Exhibit 10–4, this difference can be expressed by the following formula:

$$\text{Materials price variance} = (AQ \times AP) - (AQ \times SP)$$

Actual quantity — Actual price — Standard price

The formula can be factored as follows:

$$\text{Materials price variance} = AQ(AP - SP)$$

Some managers prefer this simpler formula, since it permits variance computations to be made very quickly. Using the data from Exhibit 10–4 in this formula, we have the following:

6,500 pounds ($3.80 per pound − $4.00 per pound) = $1,300 F

Notice that the answer is the same as that shown in Exhibit 10–4. Also note that when using this formula approach, a negative variance is always labeled as favorable (F) and a positive variance is always labeled as unfavorable (U). This will be true of all variance formulas in this and later chapters.

Variance reports are often issued in a tabular format. An example of such a report follows, along with an explanation for the materials price variance that has been provided by the purchasing manager.

COLONIAL PEWTER COMPANY
Performance Report—Purchasing Department

Item Purchased	Quantity Purchased	(1) Actual Price	(2) Standard Price	(3) Difference in Price (2) − (3)	(4) Total Price Variance (1) × (4)	(5) Explanation
Pewter	6,500 pounds	$3.80	$4.00	$0.20	$1,300 F	Bargained for an especially good price.

F = Favorable; U = Unfavorable.

Isolation of Variances At what point should variances be isolated and brought to the attention of management? The answer is, the earlier the better. The sooner deviations from standard are brought to the attention of management, the sooner problems can be evaluated and corrected.

Once a performance report has been prepared, what does management do with the variance data? The most significant variances should be viewed as "red flags," calling attention to the fact that an exception has occurred that will require some explanation and perhaps follow-up effort. The performance report itself may contain some explanation of the reason for the variance, as shown above. In the case of Colonial Pewter Company, the purchasing manager, Janet Warner, said that the favorable price variance resulted from bargaining for an especially good price.

Responsibility for the Variance Who is responsible for the materials price variance? Generally speaking, the purchasing manager has control over the price paid for goods and is therefore responsible for any price variances. Many factors influence the prices paid for goods, including how many units are ordered in a lot, how the order is delivered, whether the order is a rush order, and the quality of materials purchased. A deviation in any of these factors from what was assumed when the standards were set can result in a price variance. For example, purchase of second-grade materials rather than top-grade materials may result in a favorable price variance, since the lower-grade materials would generally be less costly (but perhaps less suitable for production).

However, someone other than the purchasing manager could be responsible for a materials price variance. Production may be scheduled in such a way, for example, that the purchasing manager must request express delivery. In these cases, the production manager should be held responsible for the resulting price variances.

A word of caution is in order. Variance analysis should not be used as an excuse to conduct witch hunts or as a means of beating line managers and workers over the head. The emphasis must be on *supporting* the line managers and *assisting* them in meeting the goals that they have participated in setting for the company. In short, the emphasis should be positive rather than negative. Excessive dwelling on what has already happened, particularly in terms of trying to find someone to blame, can destroy morale and kill any cooperative spirit.

Materials Quantity Variance—A Closer Look

The **materials quantity variance** measures the difference between the quantity of materials used in production and the quantity that should have been used according to the standard. Although the variance is concerned with the physical usage of materials, it is generally stated in dollar terms to help gauge its importance, as shown in Exhibit 10–4. The formula for the materials quantity variance is as follows:

$$\text{Materials quantity variance} = (AQ \times SP) - (SQ \times SP)$$

Actual quantity Standard price Standard quantity allowed for actual output

Again, the formula can be factored as follows:

$$\text{Materials quantity variance} = SP(AQ - SQ)$$

Using the data from Exhibit 10–4 in the formula, we have the following:

$4.00 per pound (6,500 pounds − 6,000 pounds*) = $2,000 U

*2,000 units × 3.0 pounds per unit = 6,000 pounds.

The answer, of course, is the same as that yielded in Exhibit 10–4.

The data might appear as follows if a formal performance report were prepared:

COLONIAL PEWTER COMPANY
Performance Report—Production Department

Type of Materials	(1) Standard Price	(2) Actual Quantity	(3) Standard Quantity Allowed	(4) Difference in Quantity (2) − (3)	(5) Total Quantity Variance (1) × (4)	Explanation
Pewter	$4.00	6,500 pounds	6,000 pounds	500 pounds	$2,000 U	Low quality materials unsuitable for production.

F = Favorable; U = Unfavorable.

The materials quantity variance is best isolated when materials are used in production. Materials are drawn for the number of units to be produced, according to the standard bill of materials for each unit. Any additional materials are usually drawn with an excess materials requisition slip, which is different in color from the normal requisition slips. This procedure calls attention to the excessive usage of materials *while production is still in process* and provides an opportunity to correct any developing problem.

Excessive usage of materials can result from many factors, including faulty machines, inferior quality of materials, untrained workers, and poor supervision. Generally speaking, it is the responsibility of the production department to see that material usage is kept in line with standards. There may be times, however, when the *purchasing* department may be responsible for an unfavorable materials quantity variance. For example, if the purchasing department obtains inferior quality materials in an effort to economize on price, the materials may be unsuitable for use and may result in excessive waste. Thus, purchasing rather than production would be responsible for the quantity variance. At

Colonial Pewter, the production manager, Tom Kuchel, claimed that low quality materials were the cause of the unfavorable materials quantity variance for June.

IN BUSINESS

WHAT HAPPENED TO THE RAISINS?

Management at an unnamed breakfast cereal company became concerned about the apparent waste of raisins in one of its products. A box of the product was supposed to contain 10 ounces of cereal and 2 ounces of raisins. However, the production process had been using an average of 2.5 ounces of raisins per box. To correct the problem, a bonus was offered to employees if the consumption of raisins dropped to 2.1 ounces per box or less—which would allow for about 5% waste. Within a month, the target was hit and bonuses were distributed. However, another problem began to appear. Market studies indicated that customers had become dissatisfied with the amount of raisins in the product. Workers had hit the 2.1-ounce per box target by drastically reducing the amount of raisins in rush orders. Boxes of the completed product are ordinarily weighed and if the weight is less than 12 ounces, the box is rejected. However, rush orders aren't weighed since that would slow down the production process. Consequently, workers were reducing the raisins in rush orders so as to hit the overall target of 2.1 ounces of raisins per box. This resulted in substandard boxes of cereal in rush orders and customer complaints. Clearly, managers need to be very careful when they set targets and standards. They may not get what they bargained for. Subsequent investigation by an internal auditor revealed that, due to statistical fluctuations, an average of about 2.5 ounces of raisins must be used to ensure that every box contains at least 2 ounces of raisins.

Source: Harper A. Roehm and Joseph R. Castellano, "The Danger of Relying on Accounting Numbers Alone," *Management Accounting Quarterly*, Fall 1999, pp. 4–9.

Using Standard Costs—Direct Labor Variances

LEARNING OBJECTIVE 3
Compute the direct labor rate and efficiency variances and explain their significance.

Topic Tackler PLUS 10–2

Terry Sherman's next step in determining Colonial Pewter's variances for June was to compute the direct labor variances for the month. Recall from Exhibit 10–2 that the standard direct labor cost per unit of product is $35, computed as follows:

$$2.5 \text{ direct labor hours per unit} \times \$14.00 \text{ per hour} = \$35 \text{ per unit}$$

During June, the company paid its direct labor workers $74,250, including employment taxes and fringe benefits, for 5,400 hours of work. This was an average of $13.75 per hour. Using these data and the standard costs from Exhibit 10–2, Terry computed the direct labor rate and efficiency variances that appear in Exhibit 10–6.

Notice that the column headings in Exhibit 10–6 are the same as those used in the prior two exhibits, except that in Exhibit 10–6 the terms *hours* and *rate* are used in place of the terms *quantity* and *price.*

Labor Rate Variance—A Closer Look

As explained earlier, the price variance for direct labor is commonly termed a **labor rate variance.** This variance measures any deviation from standard in the average hourly rate paid to direct labor workers. The formula for the labor rate variance is expressed as follows:

$$\text{Labor rate variance} = (AH \times AR) - (AH \times SR)$$

Actual hours (AH) — Actual rate (AR) — Standard rate (SR)

The formula can be factored as follows:

$$\text{Labor rate variance} = AH(AR - SR)$$

EXHIBIT 10–6
Variance Analysis—Direct Labor

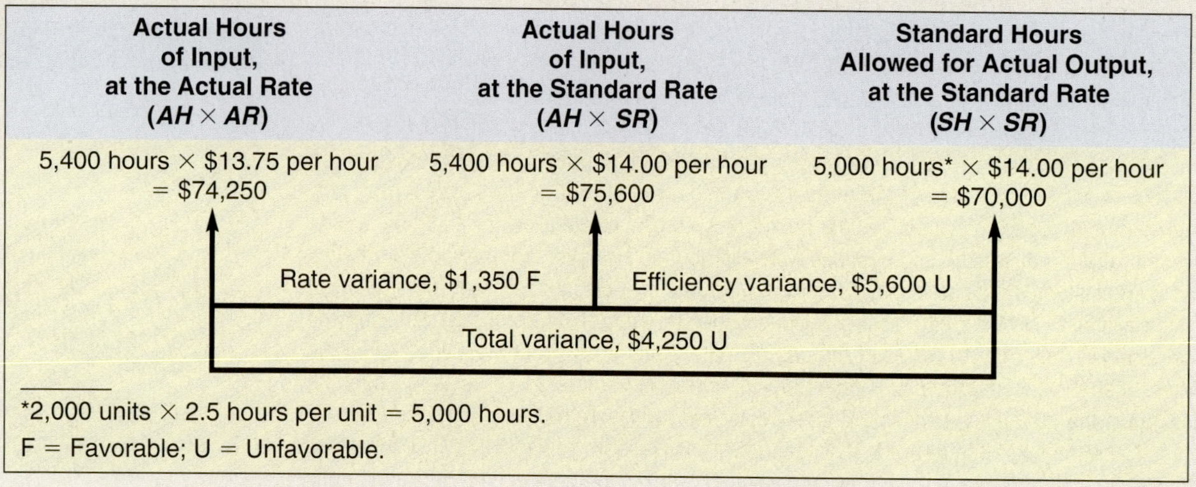

Using the data from Exhibit 10–6 in the formula, the labor rate variance can be computed as follows:

5,400 direct labor hours ($13.75 per hour − $14.00 per hour) = $1,350 F

In most companies, the wage rates paid to workers are quite predictable. Nevertheless, rate variances can arise because of the way labor is used. Skilled workers with high hourly rates of pay may be given duties that require little skill and call for lower hourly rates of pay. This will result in an unfavorable labor rate variance, since the actual hourly rate of pay will exceed the standard rate specified for the particular task. In contrast, a favorable rate variance would result when workers who are paid at a rate lower than specified in the standard are assigned to the task. However, the lower paid workers may not be as efficient. Finally, overtime work at premium rates will result in an unfavorable rate variance if the overtime premium is charged to the direct labor account.

Who is responsible for controlling the labor rate variance? Since labor rate variances generally arise as a result of how labor is used, production supervisors bear responsibility for seeing that labor rate variances are kept under control.

Labor Efficiency Variance—A Closer Look

The **labor efficiency variance** attempts to measure the productivity of direct labor. No variance is more closely watched by management, since it is widely believed that increasing direct labor productivity is vital to reducing costs. The formula for the labor efficiency variance is expressed as follows:

Labor efficiency variance = $(AH \times SR) - (SH \times SR)$

Actual hours — Standard rate — Standard hours allowed for actual output

The formula can be factored as follows:

Labor efficiency variance = $SR(AH - SH)$

Using the data from Exhibit 10–6 in the formula, we have the following:

$14.00 per hour (5,400 hours − 5,000 hours*) = $5,600 U

*2,000 units × 2.5 hours per unit = 5,000 hours.

Possible causes of an unfavorable labor efficiency variance include poorly trained or motivated workers; poor quality materials, requiring more labor time; faulty equipment, causing breakdowns and work interruptions; poor supervision of workers; and inaccurate standards. The managers in charge of production would usually be responsible for control of the labor efficiency variance. However, purchasing could be held responsible if acquisition of poor materials resulted in excessive labor processing time.

Another important cause of an unfavorable labor efficiency variance may be insufficient demand for the company's products. Managers in some companies argue that it is difficult, and perhaps unwise, to constantly adjust the work force in response to changes in the amount of work that needs to be done. In such companies, the direct labor work force is essentially fixed in the short run. If demand is insufficient to keep everyone busy, workers are not laid off. In this case, if demand falls below the level needed to keep everyone busy, an unfavorable labor efficiency variance will often be recorded.

If customer orders are insufficient to keep the workers busy, the work center manager has two options—either accept an unfavorable labor efficiency variance or build inventory.[3] A central lesson of just-in-time (JIT) is that building inventory with no immediate prospect of sale is a bad idea. Excessive inventory—particularly work in process inventory—leads to high defect rates, obsolete goods, and generally inefficient operations. As a consequence, when the work force is basically fixed in the short term, managers must be cautious about how labor efficiency variances are used. Some experts advocate eliminating labor efficiency variances in such situations—at least for the purposes of motivating and controlling workers on the shop floor.

Using Standard Costs—Variable Manufacturing Overhead Variances

LEARNING OBJECTIVE 4
Compute the variable manufacturing overhead spending and efficiency variances.

The final step in Terry Sherman's analysis of Colonial Pewter's variances for June was to compute the variable manufacturing overhead variances. The variable portion of manufacturing overhead can be analyzed using the same basic formulas that are used to analyze direct materials and direct labor. Recall from Exhibit 10–2 that the standard variable manufacturing overhead is $7.50 per unit of product, computed as follows:

$$2.5 \text{ direct labor hours per unit} \times \$3.00 \text{ per hour} = \$7.50 \text{ per unit}$$

Colonial Pewter's cost records showed that the total actual variable manufacturing overhead cost for June was $15,390. Recall from the earlier discussion of the direct labor variances that 5,400 hours of direct labor time were recorded during the month and that the company produced 2,000 pairs of bookends. Terry's analysis of this overhead data appears in Exhibit 10–7.

Notice the similarities between Exhibits 10–6 and 10–7. These similarities arise from the fact that direct labor-hours are being used as the base for allocating overhead cost to units of product; thus, the same hourly figures appear in Exhibit 10–7 for variable manufacturing overhead as in Exhibit 10–6 for direct labor. The main difference between the two exhibits is in the standard hourly rate being used, which in this company is much lower for variable manufacturing overhead than for direct labor.

Manufacturing Overhead Variances—A Closer Look

The formula for the **variable overhead spending variance** is expressed as follows:

$$\text{Variable overhead spending variance} = (AH \times AR) - (AH \times SR)$$

Actual hours (AH) Actual rate (AR) Standard rate (SR)

[3] For further discussion, see Eliyahu M. Goldratt and Jeff Cox, *The Goal,* 2nd rev. ed. (Croton-on-Hudson, NY: North River Press, 1992).

EXHIBIT 10–7
Variance Analysis—Variable Manufacturing Overhead

Actual Hours of Input, at the Actual Rate ($AH \times AR$)	Actual Hours of Input, at the Standard Rate ($AH \times SR$)	Standard Hours Allowed for Actual Output, at the Standard Rate ($SH \times SR$)
$15,390	5,400 hours × $3.00 per hour = $16,200	5,000 hours* × $3.00 per hour = $15,000
Spending variance, $810 F	Efficiency variance, $1,200 U	
Total variance, $390 U		

*2,000 units × 2.5 hours per unit = 5,000 hours.
F = Favorable; U = Unfavorable.

This formula can be factored as follows:

$$\text{Variable overhead spending variance} = AH(AR - SR)$$

Using the data from Exhibit 10–7 in the formula, the variable overhead spending variance can be computed as follows:

$$5{,}400 \text{ hours } (\$2.85 \text{ per hour}^* - \$3.00 \text{ per hour}) = \$810 \text{ F}$$

*$15,390 ÷ 5,400 hours = $2.85 per hour.

The formula for the **variable overhead efficiency variance** is expressed as follows:

$$\text{Variable overhead efficiency variance} = (AH \times SR) - (SH \times SR)$$

Actual hours (AH); Standard rate (SR); Standard hours allowed for actual output (SH)

This formula can be factored as follows:

$$\text{Variable overhead efficiency variance} = SR(AH - SH)$$

Again using the data from Exhibit 10–7, the variance could be computed as follows:

$$\$3.00 \text{ per hour } (5{,}400 \text{ hours} - 5{,}000 \text{ hours}^*) = \$1{,}200 \text{ U}$$

*2,000 units × 2.5 hours per unit = 5,000 hours.

We will reserve further discussion of the variable overhead spending and efficiency variances until the next chapter, where overhead analysis is discussed in depth.

Before proceeding further, we suggest that you pause at this point and go back and review the data contained in Exhibits 10–2 through 10–7. These exhibits and the accompanying text discussion provide a comprehensive, integrated illustration of standard setting and variance analysis.

MANAGERIAL ACCOUNTING IN ACTION
The Wrap-Up

In preparation for the scheduled meeting to discuss her analysis of Colonial Pewter's standard costs and variances, Terry distributed Exhibits 10–2 through 10–7 to the management group of Colonial Pewter. This included J. D. Wriston, the president of the company; Tom Kuchel, the production manager; and Janet Warner, the purchasing manager. J. D. Wriston opened the meeting with the following question:

J. D.: Terry, I think I understand the report you distributed, but just to make sure, would you mind summarizing the highlights of what you found?

Terry: As you can see, the biggest problems are the unfavorable materials quantity variance of $2,000 and the unfavorable labor efficiency variance of $5,600.

J. D.: Tom, you're the production boss. What do you think is causing the unfavorable labor efficiency variance?

Tom: It has to be the new production workers. Our experienced workers shouldn't have much problem meeting the standard of 2.5 hours per unit. We all knew that there would be some inefficiency for a while as we brought new people on board.

J. D.: No one is disputing that, Tom. However, $5,600 is a lot of money. Is this problem likely to go away very soon?

Tom: I hope so. If we were to contrast the last two weeks of June with the first two weeks, I'm sure we would see some improvement.

J. D.: I don't want to beat up on you, Tom, but this is a significant problem. Can you do something to accelerate the training process?

Tom: Sure. I could pair up each of the new guys with one of our old-timers and have them work together for a while. It would slow down our older guys a bit, but I'll bet the new workers would learn a lot.

J. D.: Let's try it. Now, what about that $2,000 unfavorable materials quantity variance?

Tom: Are you asking me?

J. D.: Well, I would like someone to explain it.

Tom: Don't look at me. It's that iron-contaminated pewter that Janet bought on her "special deal."

Janet: We got rid of that stuff months ago.

J. D.: Hold your horses. We're not trying to figure out who to blame here. I just want to understand what happened. If we can understand what happened, maybe we can fix it.

Terry: Tom, are the new workers generating a lot of scrap?

Tom: Yeah, I guess so.

J. D.: I think that could be part of the problem. Can you do anything about it?

Tom: I can watch the scrap closely for a few days to see where it's being generated. If it is the new workers, I can have the old-timers work with them on the problem when I team them up.

J. D.: Good. Let's reconvene in a few weeks to see what has happened. Hopefully, we can get those unfavorable variances under control.

Variance Analysis and Management by Exception

Variance analysis and performance reports are important elements of *management by exception.* Simply put, management by exception means that the manager's attention should be directed toward those parts of the organization where plans are not working for one reason or another. Time and effort should not be wasted focusing on those parts of the organization where things are going smoothly.

The budgets and standards discussed in this chapter and in the preceding chapter reflect management's plans. If all goes according to plan, there will be little difference between actual results and the results that would be expected according to the budgets and standards. If this happens, managers can concentrate on other issues. However, if actual results do not conform to the budget and to standards, the performance reporting system sends a signal to the manager that an "exception" has occurred. This signal is in the form of a variance from the budget or standards.

However, are all variances worth investigating? The answer is no. Differences between actual results and what was expected will almost always occur. If every variance were investigated, management would waste a great deal of time tracking down nickel-and-dime differences. Variances may occur for a variety of reasons—only some of which are significant and warrant management attention. For example, hotter-than-normal

EXHIBIT 10–8
A Statistical Control Chart

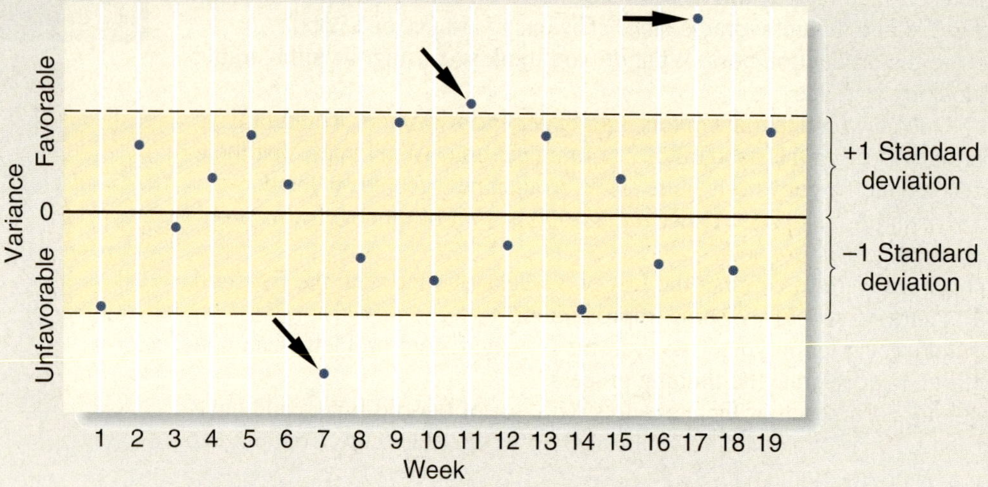

weather in the summer may result in higher-than-expected electrical bills for air conditioning. Or, workers may work slightly faster or slower on a particular day. Because of unpredictable random factors, one can expect that virtually every cost category will produce a variance of some kind.

How should managers decide which variances are worth investigating? One clue is the size of the variance. A variance of $5 is probably not big enough to warrant attention, whereas a variance of $5,000 might well be worth tracking down. Another clue is the size of the variance relative to the amount of spending. A variance that is only 0.1% of spending on an item is likely to be well within the bounds one would normally expect due to random factors. On the other hand, a variance of 10% of spending is much more likely to be a signal that something is wrong.

A more dependable approach is to plot variance data on a statistical control chart, such as illustrated in Exhibit 10–8. The basic idea underlying a statistical control chart is that some random fluctuations in variances from period to period are normal. A variance should only be investigated when it is unusual relative to that normal level of random fluctuation. Typically, the standard deviation of the variances is used as the measure of the normal level of fluctuations. A rule of thumb is adopted such as "investigate all variances that are more than *X* standard deviations from zero." In the control chart in Exhibit 10–8, *X* is 1.0. That is, the rule of thumb in this company is to investigate all variances that are more than one standard deviation in either direction (favorable or unfavorable) from zero. This means that the variances in weeks 7, 11, and 17 would have been investigated, but none of the others.

What value of *X* should be chosen? The bigger the value of *X*, the wider the band of acceptable variances that would not be investigated. Thus, the bigger the value of *X*, the less time will be spent tracking down variances, but the more likely it is that a real out-of-control situation will be overlooked. Ordinarily, if *X* is selected to be 1.0, roughly 30% of all variances will trigger an investigation even though there is no real problem. If *X* is set at 1.5, the figure drops to about 13%. If *X* is set at 2.0, the figure drops all the way to about 5%. Don't forget, however, that selecting a big value of *X* will result not only in fewer false alarms but also a higher probability that a real problem will be overlooked.

In addition to watching for unusually large variances, the pattern of the variances should be monitored. For example, a run of steadily mounting variances should trigger an investigation even though none of the variances is large enough by itself to warrant investigation.

EXHIBIT 10–9
Uses of Standard Costs in Four Countries

	United States	United Kingdom	Canada	Japan
Cost management	1*	2	2	1
Budgetary planning and control†	2	3	1	3
Pricing decisions	3	1	3	2
Financial statement preparation	4	4	4	4

*The numbers 1 through 4 denote importance of use, from greatest to least.
†Includes management planning.
Source: Compiled from data in a study by Shin'ichi Inoue, "Comparative Studies of Recent Development of Cost Management Problems in U.S.A., U.K., Canada, and Japan," Research Paper No. 29, Kagawa University, p. 20.

International Uses of Standard Costs

Standard costs are used by companies throughout the world. One study found that three-fourths of the companies surveyed in the United Kingdom, two-thirds of the companies surveyed in Canada, and 40% of the companies surveyed in Japan used standard cost systems.[4]

Standard costs were first introduced in Japan after World War II, with Nippon Electronics Company (NEC) being one of the first Japanese companies to adopt standard costs for all of its products. Many other Japanese companies followed NEC's lead and developed standard cost systems. The ways in which these standard costs are used in Japan—and also in the other countries cited above—are shown in Exhibit 10–9.

Over time, the pattern of use shown in Exhibit 10–9 may change, but at present managers can expect to encounter standard costs in most industrialized nations. Moreover, the most important uses are for cost management and budgetary planning purposes.

Evaluation of Controls Based on Standard Costs

Advantages of Standard Costs

Standard cost systems have a number of advantages.

1. Standard costs are a key element in a management by exception approach. If costs remain within the standards, managers can focus on other issues. When costs fall significantly outside the standards, managers are alerted that problems may exist that require attention. This approach helps managers focus on important issues.
2. Standards that are viewed as reasonable by employees can promote economy and efficiency. They provide benchmarks that individuals can use to judge their own performance.
3. Standard costs can greatly simplify bookkeeping. Instead of recording actual costs for each job, the standard costs for direct materials, direct labor, and overhead can be charged to jobs.
4. Standard costs fit naturally in an integrated system of "responsibility accounting." The standards establish what costs should be, who should be responsible for them, and whether actual costs are under control.

[4] Shin'ichi Inoue, "Comparative Studies of Recent Development of Cost Management Problems in U.S.A., U.K., Canada, and Japan," Research Paper No. 29, Kagawa University, p. 17. The study included 95 United States companies, 52 United Kingdom companies, 82 Canadian companies, and 646 Japanese companies.

Potential Problems with the Use of Standard Costs

The use of standard costs can present a number of potential problems. Most of these problems result from improper use of standard costs and the management by exception principle.

1. Standard cost variance reports are usually prepared on a monthly basis and often are released days or even weeks after the end of the month. As a consequence, the information in the reports may be so outdated that it is almost useless. Timely, frequent reports that are approximately correct are better than infrequent reports that are very precise but out of date by the time they are released. Some companies are now reporting variances and other key operating data daily or even more frequently.
2. If managers are insensitive and use variance reports as a club, morale may suffer. Employees should receive positive reinforcement for work well done. Management by exception, by its nature, tends to focus on the negative. If variances are used as a club, subordinates may be tempted to cover up unfavorable variances or take actions that are not in the best interests of the company to make sure the variances are favorable. For example, workers may put on a crash effort to increase output at the end of the month to avoid an unfavorable labor efficiency variance. In the rush to produce more output, quality may suffer.
3. Labor quantity standards and efficiency variances make two important assumptions. First, they assume that the production process is labor-paced; if labor works faster, output will go up. However, output in many companies is no longer determined by how fast labor works; rather, it is determined by the processing speed of machines. Second, the computations assume that labor is a variable cost. However, direct labor may be essentially fixed. If labor is fixed, then an undue emphasis on labor efficiency variances creates pressure to build excess inventories.
4. In some cases, a "favorable" variance can be as bad or worse than an "unfavorable" variance. For example, McDonald's has a standard for the amount of hamburger meat that should be in a Big Mac. A "favorable" variance would mean that less meat was used than the standard specifies. The result is a substandard Big Mac and possibly a dissatisfied customer.

5. Too much emphasis on meeting the standards may overshadow other important objectives such as maintaining and improving quality, on-time delivery, and customer satisfaction. This tendency can be reduced by using supplemental performance measures that focus on these other objectives.
6. Just meeting standards may not be sufficient; continual improvement may be necessary to survive in a competitive environment. For this reason, some companies focus on the trends in the standard cost variances—aiming for continual improvement rather than just meeting the standards. In other companies, engineered standards are being replaced either by a rolling average of actual costs, which is expected to decline, or by very challenging target costs.

In sum, managers should exercise considerable care in their use of a standard cost system. It is particularly important that managers go out of their way to focus on the positive, rather than just on the negative, and to be aware of possible unintended consequences.

Nevertheless, standard costs are still found in the vast majority of manufacturing companies and in many service companies, although their use is changing. For evaluating performance, standard cost variances may be supplanted in the future by a particularly interesting development known as the *balanced scorecard,* which is discussed in the next section. The balanced scorecard concept has been eagerly embraced by a wide variety of organizations including Analog Devices, KPMG, Tenneco, Allstate, AT&T, Elf Atochem, Conair-Franklin, CIGNA Corporation, London Life Insurance Co., Southern Gardens Citrus Processing, Duke Children's Hospital, JP Morgan Chase, 3COM, Rockwater, Apple Computer, Advanced Micro Devices (AMD), FMC, the Bank of Montreal, the Massachusetts Special Olympics, United Way of Southeastern New England, Boston Lyric Opera, Bridgeport Hospital and Healthcare Services, Housing Authority of Fiji, and Verizon Communications. It has been estimated that about half of all Fortune 1000 companies have implemented a balanced scorecard.

Balanced Scorecard

LEARNING OBJECTIVE 5
Understand how a balanced scorecard fits together and how it supports a company's strategy.

A **balanced scorecard** consists of an integrated set of performance measures that are derived from and support the company's strategy throughout the organization.[5,6] A strategy is essentially a theory about how to achieve the organization's goals. For example, Southwest Airlines' strategy is to offer passengers low prices and friendly service on short-haul jet service. The low prices result from the absence of costly frills such as meals, assigned seating, interline baggage checking, and a hub-and-spoke flight system. The friendly service is provided by flight attendants who go out of their way to entertain passengers with their antics. This is an interesting strategy. Southwest Airlines consciously hires people who have a sense of humor and who enjoy their work. Hiring and retaining such employees probably costs no more—and may cost less—than retaining grumpy flight attendants who view their jobs as a chore. Southwest Airlines' strategy is to build loyal customers through a combination of "fun"—which does not cost anything to provide—and low prices that are possible because of the lack of costly frills offered by competing airlines. The theory is that low prices and fun will lead to loyal customers, which, in combination with low costs, will lead to high profits. So far, this theory has worked.

Under the balanced scorecard approach, top management translates its strategy into performance measures that employees can understand and influence. For example, the amount of time passengers have to wait in line to have their baggage checked might be a performance measure for the supervisor in charge of the Southwest Airlines check-in counter at the Phoenix airport. This performance measure is easily understood by the supervisor, and can be improved by the supervisor's actions.

IN BUSINESS

THE BALANCED SCORECARD AT THE CITY OF CHARLOTTE

Governmental and nonprofit organizations as well as businesses can use the balanced scorecard approach to performance measurement. The City of Charlotte, North Carolina, developed a balanced scorecard with four major goals: (1) increase perception of safety; (2) strengthen neighborhoods; (3) promote economic opportunity; and (4) improve service quality. To strengthen neighborhoods, the city's managers set goals to: (a) promote safe, decent housing; (b) increase home ownership; and (c) increase job placements. The corresponding performance measures are: (a) the number of code compliances in housing; (b) the number of assisted purchases of homes; and (c) the number of adult job placements.

Pam Syfert, Charlotte's City Manager, states: "The Scorecard is a communication, information, and learning system. Building a scorecard helps managers link today's actions with the achievement of today's priorities. It encourages accountability. And, today, we define accountability by results."

Source: Robert S. Kaplan, *City of Charlotte (A)*, Harvard Business School case 9-199-036, December 15, 1998.

5 The balanced scorecard concept was developed by Robert Kaplan and David Norton. For further details, see their articles "The Balanced Scorecard—Measures that Drive Performance," *Harvard Business Review*, January/February 1992, pp. 71–79; "Using the Balanced Scorecard as a Strategic Management System," *Harvard Business Review*, January/February 1996, pp. 75–85; "Why Does a Business Need a Balanced Scorecard?" *Journal of Cost Management*, May/June 1997, pp. 5–10; and their books *Translating Strategy into Action: The Balanced Scorecard* (Boston, MA: Harvard Business School Press, 1996) and *The Strategy-Focussed Organization: How Balanced Scorecard Companies Thrive in the New Business Environment* (Boston, MA: Harvard Business School Press, 2001).

6 In the 1960s, the French developed a concept similar to the balanced scorecard called Tableau de Bord or "dashboard." For details, see Michel Lebas, "Managerial Accounting in France: Overview of Past Tradition and Current Practice," *The European Accounting Review*, 1994, 3, no. 3, pp. 471–487; and Marc Epstein and Jean-François Manzoni, "The Balanced Scorecard and the Tableau de Bord: Translating Strategy into Action," *Management Accounting*, August 1997, pp. 28–36.

EXHIBIT 10–10
From Strategy to Performance Measures: The Balanced Scorecard

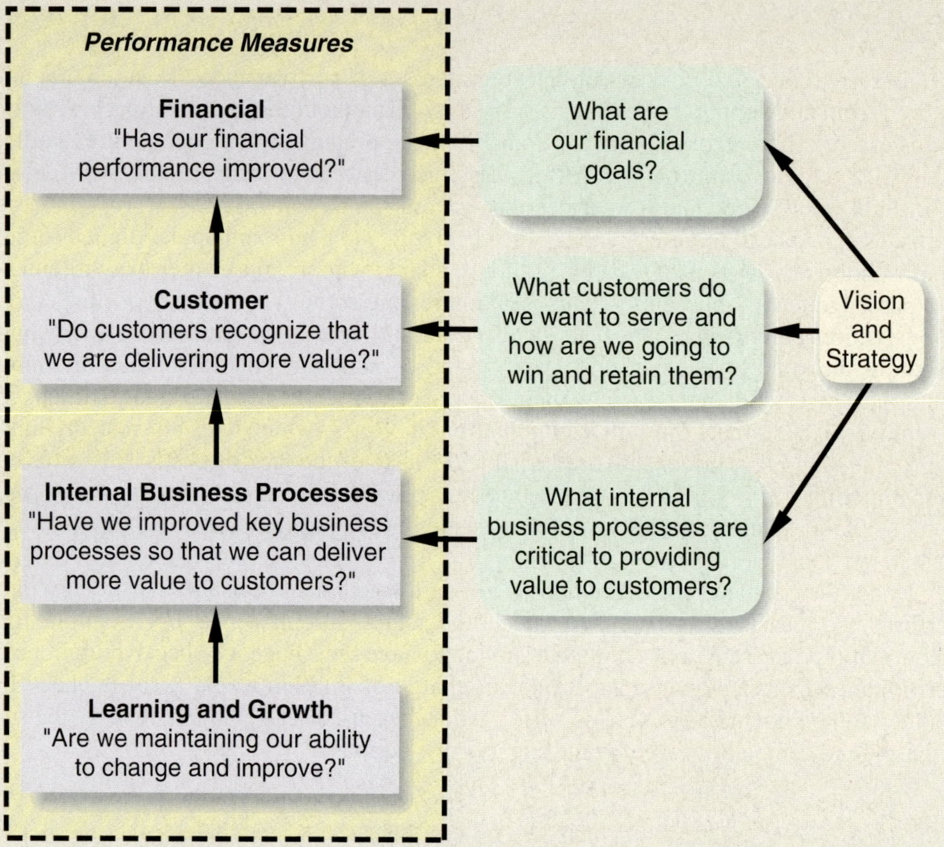

Common Characteristics of Balanced Scorecards

Performance measures used in the balanced scorecard approach tend to fall into the four groups illustrated in Exhibit 10–10: financial, customer, internal business processes, and learning and growth. Internal business processes are what the company does in an attempt to satisfy customers. For example, in a manufacturing company, assembling a product is an internal business process. In an airline, handling baggage is an internal business process. The idea underlying these groupings (as indicated by the vertical arrows in Exhibit 10–10) is that learning is necessary to improve internal business processes; improving business processes is necessary to improve customer satisfaction; and improving customer satisfaction is necessary to improve financial results.

Note that the emphasis in Exhibit 10–10 is on *improvement*—not on just attaining some specific objective such as profits of $10 million. In the balanced scorecard approach, continual improvement is encouraged. In many industries, this is a matter of survival. If an organization does not continually improve, it will eventually lose out to competitors that do.

Financial performance measures appear at the top of Exhibit 10–10. Ultimately, most companies exist to provide financial rewards to owners. There are exceptions. Some companies—for example, The Body Shop—may have loftier goals such as providing environmentally friendly products to consumers. However, even nonprofit organizations must generate enough financial resources to stay in operation.

However, for several reasons, financial performance measures are not sufficient in themselves—they should be integrated with nonfinancial measures in a well-designed balanced scorecard. First, financial measures are lag indicators that report on the results of past actions. In contrast, nonfinancial measures of key success drivers such as customer satisfaction are leading indicators of future financial performance. Second, top managers

EXHIBIT 10–11
Examples of Performance Measures for Balanced Scorecards

Customer Perspective	
Performance Measure	Desired Change
Customer satisfaction as measured by survey results	+
Number of customer complaints	–
Market share	+
Product returns as a percentage of sales	–
Percentage of customers retained from last period	+
Number of new customers	+

Internal Business Processes Perspective	
Performance Measure	Desired Change
Percentage of sales from new products	+
Time to introduce new products to market	–
Percentage of customer calls answered within 20 seconds	+
On-time deliveries as a percentage of all deliveries	+
Work in process inventory as a percentage of sales	–
Unfavorable standard cost variances	–
Defect-free units as a percentage of completed units	+
Delivery cycle time*	–
Throughput time*	–
Manufacturing cycle efficiency*	+
Quality costs†	–
Setup time	–
Time from call by customer to repair of product	–
Percent of customer complaints settled on first contact	+
Time to settle a customer claim	–

Learning and Growth Perspective	
Performance Measure	Desired Change
Suggestions per employee	+
Value-added employee‡	+
Employee turnover	–
Hours of in-house training per employee	+

*Explained later in this chapter.
†See Appendix 2B, Cost of Quality.
‡Value-added is revenue less externally purchased materials, supplies, and services.

are ordinarily responsible for the financial performance measures—not lower-level managers. The supervisor in charge of checking in passengers can be held responsible for how long passengers have to wait in line. However, this supervisor cannot reasonably be held responsible for the entire company's profit. That is the responsibility of the airline's top managers. We will have more to say about financial performance measures in later chapters.

Exhibit 10–11 lists some examples of performance measures that can be found on the balanced scorecards of companies. However, few companies, if any, would use all of these performance measures, and almost all companies would add other performance measures. Managers should carefully select the performance measures for their own company's balanced scorecard, keeping the following points in mind. First and foremost, the performance measures should be consistent with, and follow from, the company's strategy. If the performance measures are not consistent with the company's strategy, people will find themselves working at cross-purposes. Second, the performance measures should be understandable and controllable to a significant extent by those being evaluated. Third, the scorecard should not have too many performance measures. This can lead to a lack of focus and confusion.

While the entire organization will have an overall balanced scorecard, each responsible individual will have his or her own personal scorecard as well. This scorecard should consist of items the individual can personally influence that relate directly to the performance measures on the overall balanced scorecard. The performance measures on this personal scorecard should not be overly influenced by actions taken by others in the company or by events that are outside of the individual's control. And, using the performance measure should not lead employees to take actions that are counter to the organization's objectives.

With those broad principles in mind, we will now take a look at how a company's strategy affects its balanced scorecard.

IN BUSINESS

WHEN IMPROVEMENT ISN'T BETTER

Mark Graham Brown, a performance-measurement consultant, warns managers to focus on the right metrics when measuring performance. He relates the following story: "A fast-food chain gave lip service to many objectives, but what senior managers watched most rigorously was how much chicken its restaurants had to throw away . . . What happened? As one restaurant operator explained, it was easy to hit your . . . targets: just don't cook any chicken until somebody orders it. Customers might have to wait 20 minutes for their meal, and would probably never come back—but you'd sure make your numbers. Moral: a measurement may look good on paper, but you need to ask what behavior it will drive."

Source: "Using Measurement to Boost Your Unit's Performance," *Harvard Management Update*, October 1998.

IN BUSINESS

IN DENIAL

Larry Bossidy, the long-time CEO of Allied Signal, reports that "When I took over at Allied Signal . . . I got two different pictures from our people and our customers. While our people were saying that we were delivering an order-fill rate of 98%, our customers thought we were at 60%. The irony was, instead of trying to address the customers' complaints, we seemed to think we had to show that we were right and they were wrong." Note the two messages contained in this short quotation. First, make sure you measure the right thing. Apparently, the internal measure of order-fill rates that had been used at Allied Signal was deficient—it did not capture customer perceptions, which are of paramount importance. Second, if customers are unhappy, don't tell them they are wrong. Try to figure out why they are unhappy.

Source: Larry Bossidy and Ram Charan, "How Did Honeywell Chairman Larry Bossidy Turn the Company Around? By His Maniacal Focus on Just One Thing: Execution," *Fortune*, June 10, 2002, pp. 149–152.

A Company's Strategy and the Balanced Scorecard

Returning to the performance measures in Exhibit 10–10, each company must decide which customers to target and what internal business processes are crucial to attracting and retaining those customers. Different companies, having different strategies, will target different customers with different kinds of products and services. Take the automobile industry as an example. BMW stresses engineering and handling; Volvo, safety; Jaguar, luxury detailing; Corvette, racy styling; and Toyota, reliability. Because of these differences in emphases, a one-size-fits-all approach to performance measurement won't work

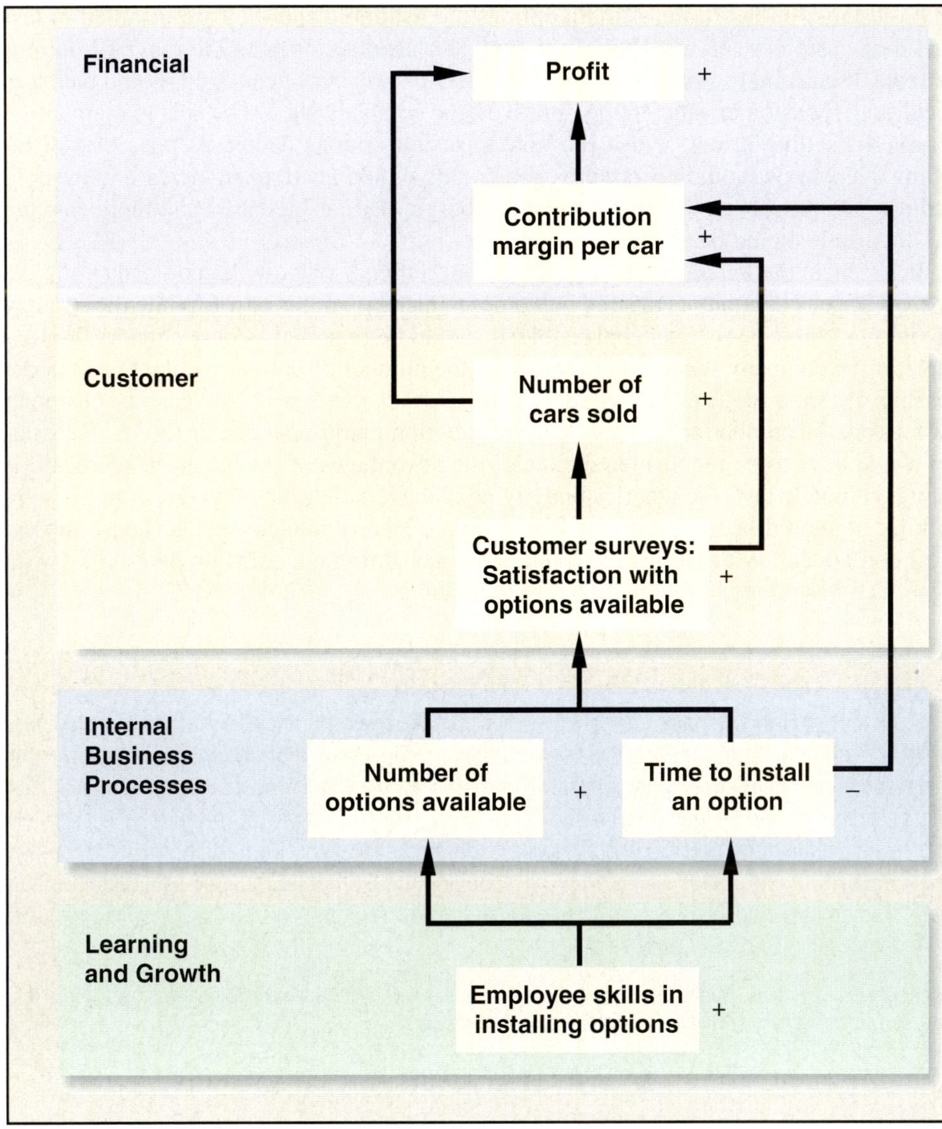

EXHIBIT 10–12
A Possible Strategy at Jaguar and the Balanced Scorecard

even within this one industry. Performance measures must be tailored to the specific strategy of each company.

Suppose, for example, that Jaguar's strategy is to offer distinctive, richly finished luxury automobiles to wealthy individuals who prize handcrafted, individualized products. Part of Jaguar's strategy might be to create such a large number of options for details, such as leather seats, interior and exterior color combinations, and wooden dashboards, that each car becomes virtually one of a kind. For example, instead of just offering tan or blue leather seats in standard cowhide, the company may offer customers the choice of an almost infinite palette of colors in any of a number of different exotic leathers. For such a system to work effectively, Jaguar would have to be able to deliver a completely customized car within a reasonable amount of time—and without incurring more cost for this customization than the customer is willing to pay. Exhibit 10–12 suggests how Jaguar might reflect this strategy in its balanced scorecard.

If the balanced scorecard is correctly constructed, the performance measures should be linked together on a cause-and-effect basis. Each link can then be read as a hypothesis in the form "If we improve this performance measure, then this other performance measure should also improve." Starting from the bottom of Exhibit 10–12, we can read the links between performance measures as follows. If employees acquire the skills to install new options more effectively, then the company can offer more options and the options can be installed in less time. If more options are available and they are installed in less time, then customer surveys should show greater satisfaction with the range of options available. If customer satisfaction improves, then the number of cars sold should increase. In addition, if customer satisfaction improves, the company should be able to maintain or increase its selling prices, and if the time to install options decreases, the costs of installing the options should decrease. Together, this should result in an increase in the contribution margin per car. If the contribution margin per car increases and more cars are sold, the result should be an increase in profits.

In essence, the balanced scorecard lays out a theory of how the company can take concrete actions to attain its desired outcomes (financial, in this case). While the strategy laid out in Exhibit 10–12 seems plausible, it should be regarded as only a theory. For example, if the company succeeds in increasing the number of options available and in decreasing the time required to install options and yet there is no increase in customer satisfaction, the number of cars sold, the contribution margin per car, or profits, the strategy would have to be reconsidered. One of the advantages of the balanced scorecard is that it continually tests the theories underlying management's strategy. If a strategy is not working, it should become evident when some of the predicted effects (i.e., more car sales) don't occur. Without this feedback, the organization may drift on indefinitely with an ineffective strategy based on faulty assumptions.

IN BUSINESS

BANNING BOREDOM—THE KEY TO PROFITS?

Store24 is one of New England's largest convenience-store chains. It adopted a strategy called "Ban Boredom"—attempting to differentiate itself from other convenience stores by providing an entertaining shopping experience. Unfortunately, this strategy bombed. Research indicated that customers overwhelmingly identified with Store24's traditional strengths—fast and efficient service—rather than the entertaining shopping experience that Store24 had attempted to create. The hypothesis "if we create an entertaining shopping experience, customer satisfaction will increase" turned out to be false. Store24 abandoned the new strategy and went back to its roots with the slogan "'Cause You Just Can't Wait."

Source: Dennis Campbell, "Putting Strategy Hypotheses to the Test with Cause-and-Effect Analysis," Harvard Business School Publishing, Balanced Scorecard Report, 2002.

Tying Compensation to the Balanced Scorecard

Incentive compensation for employees, such as bonuses, can, and probably should, be tied to balanced scorecard performance measures. However, this should be done only after the organization has been successfully managed with the scorecard for some time—perhaps a year or more. Managers must be confident that the performance measures are reliable, sensible, understood by those who are being evaluated, and not easily manipulated. As Robert Kaplan and David Norton, the originators of the balanced scorecard concept point out, "compensation is such a powerful lever that you have to be pretty confident that you have the right measures and have good data for the measures before making the link."[7]

Advantages of Timely and Graphic Feedback

Whatever performance measures are used, they should be reported on a frequent and timely basis. For example, data about defects should be reported to the responsible managers at least once a day so that action can be quickly taken if an unusual number of defects occurs. In the most advanced companies, any defect is reported *immediately,* and its cause is tracked down before any more defects occur. Another common characteristic of the performance measures under the balanced scorecard approach is that managers focus

[7] Lori Calabro, "On Balance: A CFO Interview," *CFO*, February 2001, pp. 73–78.

on *trends* in the performance measures over time. The emphasis is on progress and *improvement* rather than on meeting any specific standard.

For tracking trends and improvement over time, graphic displays are often far more informative than rows or columns of numbers. Consider, for example, the problem of passengers who reserve seats but do not show up to buy their tickets. Because of these "no-show" passengers, airlines routinely overbook popular flights. The airlines gamble that the number of overbooked passengers will be offset by the number of no-shows. Sometimes airlines lose this gamble. This results in the airline incurring substantial additional costs to either pay passengers to relinquish their reservations or to house and feed excess passengers until suitable replacement flights can be found. Because of these costs (and the ill will created among passengers), airlines carefully monitor the percentage of overbooked seats that actually turn out to be a problem and result in a passenger being bumped from a flight. Suppose, for example, that an airline has recorded the following data over the last 20 weeks:

Bumped passengers per hundred overbooked seats		Bumped passengers per hundred overbooked seats	
Week 1	7.1	Week 11	6.4
Week 2	6.5	Week 12	6.3
Week 3	6.7	Week 13	6.7
Week 4	7.2	Week 14	5.8
Week 5	7.0	Week 15	6.6
Week 6	7.3	Week 16	6.6
Week 7	6.7	Week 17	6.9
Week 8	6.5	Week 18	7.1
Week 9	6.2	Week 19	7.4
Week 10	5.8	Week 20	7.8

These data are plotted in Exhibit 10–13. Note how much easier it is to spot trends and unusual points when the data are plotted than when they are displayed in the form of a table. In particular, the worrisome increase in bumped passengers over the final seven weeks is very evident in the plotted data.

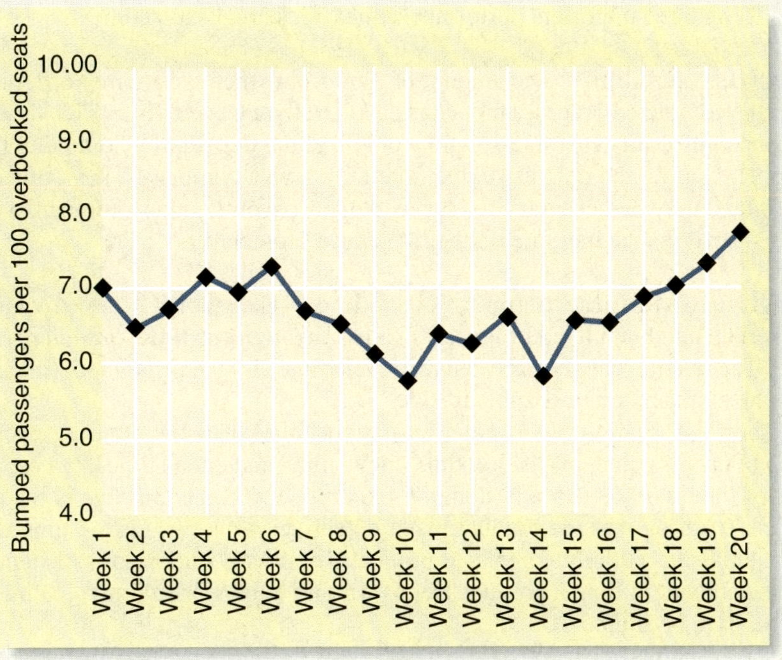

EXHIBIT 10–13
The Number of Passengers Bumped per Hundred Overbooked Seats

IN BUSINESS

A PICTURE IS WORTH A THOUSAND NUMBERS

Graphics are routinely integrated in Balanced Scorecard reports, with data often displayed on a "dashboard" with representations of gauges and digital readouts. At Beverage Can Americas Co. in Chicago, a division of London-based Rexam Plc., executive dashboards and scorecards are being rolled out to thousands of employees. "Each worker sees a handful of metrics that pertain to his or her job, which are represented as green, yellow, or red icons depending on whether they are satisfactory, borderline, or subpar."

Source: Scott Leibs, "Now You See It," *CFO*, July 2002, pp. 61–66.

IN BUSINESS

THE CUSTOMER PERSPECTIVE AT WELLS FARGO ONLINE FINANCIAL SERVICES

The Wells Fargo Online Financial Services group is responsible for developing online banking at Wells Fargo bank. Under the leadership of Mary D'Agostino, a vice president of the group, a balanced scorecard was developed that included adding and retaining high value customers as a major objective. The group uses two performance measures for this objective: (1) the number of incremental and total online customers and (2) the total bank profit per online customer. The first measure focuses on adding and retaining customers—the greater the number of incremental and total online customers, the more successful the group has been in adding and retaining online customers. The second measure focuses on the profitability (value) of the customers. In the first year of the operation of the balanced scorecard, the number of incremental and total online customers was well below the plan and hence was flagged for further action. On the other hand, the profit per customer was within 5% of the plan and was considered to be on target.

Sources: Nicole Tempest and Robert S. Kaplan, *Wells Fargo Online Financial Services (A)*, Harvard Business School cases 9-198-146, July 14, 1998. Nicole Tempest and Robert S. Kaplan, *Wells Fargo Online Financial Services (B)*, Harvard Business School cases 9-199-019, December 21, 1999.

Some Measures of Internal Business Process Performance

Most of the performance measures listed in Exhibit 10–11 are self-explanatory. However, three are not—*delivery cycle time, throughput time,* and *manufacturing cycle efficiency (MCE).* These three important performance measures are discussed next.

LEARNING OBJECTIVE 6
Compute delivery cycle time, throughput time, and manufacturing cycle efficiency (MCE).

Delivery Cycle Time

The amount of time from when a customer order is received to when the completed order is shipped is called **delivery cycle time.** This time is clearly a key concern to many customers, who would like the delivery cycle time to be as short as possible. Cutting the delivery cycle time may give a company a key competitive advantage—and may be necessary for survival. Consequently, many companies would include this performance measure on their balanced scorecard.

Throughput (Manufacturing Cycle) Time

The amount of time required to turn raw materials into completed products is called **throughput time,** or *manufacturing cycle time.* The relation between the delivery cycle time and the throughput (manufacturing cycle) time is illustrated in Exhibit 10–14.

As shown in Exhibit 10–14, the throughput time, or manufacturing cycle time, is made up of process time, inspection time, move time, and queue time. *Process time* is the amount of time work is actually done on the product. *Inspection time* is the amount of time spent ensuring that the product is not defective. *Move time* is the time required to move materials or partially completed products from workstation to workstation. *Queue time* is the amount of time a product spends waiting to be worked on, to be moved, to be inspected, or to be shipped.

As shown at the bottom of Exhibit 10–14, only one of these four activities adds value to the product—process time. The other three activities—inspecting, moving, and queuing—add no value and should be eliminated as much as possible.

EXHIBIT 10-14
Delivery Cycle Time and Throughput (Manufacturing Cycle) Time

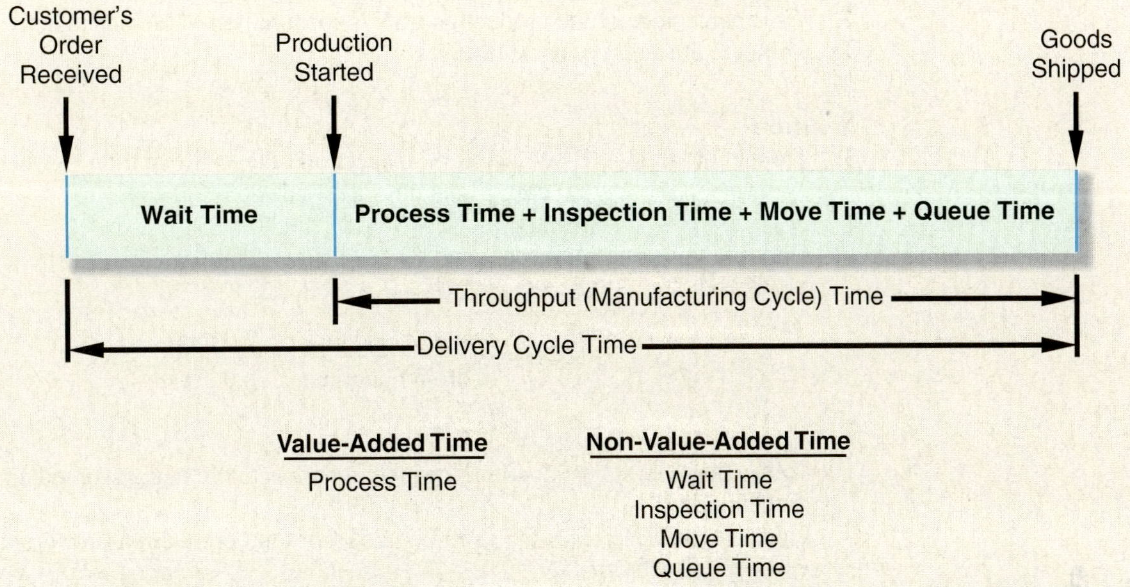

Manufacturing Cycle Efficiency (MCE) Through concerted efforts to eliminate the *non-value-added* activities of inspecting, moving, and queuing, some companies have reduced their throughput time to only a fraction of previous levels. In turn, this has helped to reduce the delivery cycle time from months to only weeks or hours. Throughput time, which is considered to be a key measure in delivery performance, can be put into better perspective by computing the **manufacturing cycle efficiency (MCE).** The MCE is computed by relating the value-added time to the throughout time. The formula is:

$$\text{MCE} = \frac{\text{Value-added time (Process time)}}{\text{Throughput (manufacturing cycle) time}}$$

An MCE of less than 1 indicates that non-value-added time is present in the production process. An MCE of 0.5, for example, would mean that half of the total production time consisted of inspection, moving, and similar non-value-added activities. In many manufacturing companies, the MCE is less than 0.1 (10%), which means that 90% of the time a unit is in process is spent on activities that do not add value to the product. Monitoring the MCE helps companies to reduce non-value-added activities and thus get products into the hands of customers more quickly and at a lower cost.

To provide an example of these measures, consider the following data for Novex Company:

Novex Company keeps careful track of the time to complete customer orders. During the most recent quarter, the following average times were recorded for each unit or order:

	Days
Wait time	17.0
Inspection time	0.4
Process time	2.0
Move time	0.6
Queue time	5.0

Goods are shipped as soon as production is completed.

Required:

1. Compute the throughput time.
2. Compute the manufacturing cycle efficiency (MCE).
3. What percentage of the production time is spent in non-value-added activities?
4. Compute the delivery cycle time.

Solution

1. Throughput time = Process time + Inspection time + Move time + Queue time
   = 2.0 days + 0.4 days + 0.6 days + 5.0 days
   = 8.0 days
2. Only process time represents value-added time; therefore, the computation of the MCE would be as follows:

$$\text{MCE} = \frac{\text{Value-added time}}{\text{Throughput time}} = \frac{2.0 \text{ days}}{8.0 \text{ days}}$$
$$= 0.25$$

   Thus, once put into production, a typical unit is actually being worked on only 25% of the time.
3. Since the MCE is 25%, 75% (100% − 25%) of total production time is spent in non-value-added activities.
4. Delivery cycle time = Wait time + Throughput time
   = 17.0 days + 8.0 days
   = 25.0 days

Some Final Observations Concerning the Balanced Scorecard We would like to emphasize a few points concerning the balanced scorecard. First, the balanced scorecard should be tailored to the company's strategy; each company's balanced scorecard should be unique. The examples given in this chapter are just that—examples. They should not be interpreted as general templates to be fitted to each company. Second, the balanced scorecard reflects a particular strategy, or theory, about how a company can further its objectives by taking specific actions. The theory should be viewed as tentative and subject to change if the actions do not in fact result in improvements in the company's financial and other goals. If the theory (i.e., strategy) changes, then the performance measures on the balanced scorecard should also change. The balanced scorecard should be viewed as a dynamic system that evolves as the company's strategy evolves.

IN BUSINESS

EXPEDITING LOAN APPLICATIONS

Banks ordinarily require three to four weeks to approve an application for a mortgage loan on a house. The application form includes the individual's employment history, income, and financial assets and liabilities. Personnel at the bank check credit references and review the entire application before granting the loan. A manager at one bank wondered why this process takes so long and asked employees to keep track of how much time they actually worked on processing an application. He discovered that processing an application took on average 26 days, but only about 15 minutes of this time was actual work. All of the remaining time the application was waiting in someone's in-basket. The manufacturing cycle efficiency (MCE) was therefore only 0.0004 (15 minutes/[26 days × 24 hours per day × 60 minutes per hour]). By redesigning and automating the process, the cycle time was cut down to 15 minutes and the MCE rose to 1.0. Loan applicants can now have a cup of coffee while waiting for approval.

Source: Kaplan and Norton, *Translating Strategy into Action: The Balanced Scorecard*, 1996, pp. 118–119.

Summary

A standard is a benchmark or "norm" for measuring performance. Standards are set for both the cost and the quantity of inputs needed to manufacture goods or to provide services. Quantity standards indicate how much of an input, such as labor time or raw materials, should be used to make a product or provide a service. Cost standards indicate what the cost of the input should be.

Standards are normally set so that they can be attained by reasonable, though highly efficient, efforts. Such "practical" standards are believed to positively motivate employees.

When standards are compared to actual performance, the difference is referred to as a *variance.* Variances are computed and reported to management on a regular basis for both the price and the quantity elements of direct materials, direct labor, and overhead. Price and rate variances for inputs are computed by taking the difference between the actual and standard prices of the inputs and multiplying the result by the amount of input purchased. Quantity and efficiency variances are computed by taking the difference between the actual amount of the input used and the amount of input that is allowed for the actual output, and then multiplying the result by the standard price of the input.

Not all variances require management time or attention. Only unusual or particularly significant variances should be investigated—otherwise a great deal of time would be spent investigating unimportant matters. Additionally, it should be emphasized that the point of the investigation should not be to find someone to blame. The point of the investigation is to pinpoint the problem so that it can be fixed and operations improved.

Traditional standard cost variance reports are often supplemented with other performance measures. Overemphasis on standard cost variances may lead to problems in other critical areas such as product quality, inventory levels, and on-time delivery.

The balanced scorecard is a promising approach to managing organizations. A balanced scorecard consists of an integrated system of performance measures that are derived from and support the company's strategy. Different companies will have different balanced scorecards because they have different strategies. A well-constructed balanced scorecard provides a means for guiding the company and also provides feedback concerning the effectiveness of the company's strategy.

Review Problem: Standard Costs

Xavier Company produces a single product. Variable manufacturing overhead is applied to products on the basis of direct labor-hours. The standard costs for one unit of product are as follows:

Direct material: 6 ounces at $0.50 per ounce	$3
Direct labor: 1.8 hours at $10 per hour	18
Variable manufacturing overhead: 1.8 hours at $5 per hour	9
Total standard variable cost per unit	$30

During June, 2,000 units were produced. The costs associated with June's operations were as follows:

Material purchased: 18,000 ounces at $0.60 per ounce	$10,800
Material used in production: 14,000 ounces	—
Direct labor: 4,000 hours at $9.75 per hour	$39,000
Variable manufacturing overhead costs incurred	$20,800

Required:

Compute the direct materials, direct labor, and variable manufacturing overhead variances.

Solution to the Review Problem

Direct Materials Variances

Actual Quantity of Input, at Actual Price ($AQ \times AP$)	**Actual Quantity of Input, at Standard Price ($AQ \times SP$)**	**Standard Quantity Allowed for Actual Output, at Standard Price ($SQ \times SP$)**
18,000 ounces × $0.60 per ounce	18,000 ounces × $0.50 per ounce	12,000 ounces* × $0.50 per ounce
= $10,800	= $9,000	= $6,000

Price variance, $1,800 U

14,000 ounces × $0.50 per ounce
= $7,000

Quantity variance, $1,000 U

*2,000 units × 6 ounces per unit = 12,000 ounces.

Using the formulas in the chapter, the same variances would be computed as follows:

Materials price variance = $AQ(AP - SP)$

18,000 ounces ($0.60 per ounce − $0.50 per ounce) = $1,800 U

Materials quantity variance = $SP(AQ - SQ)$

$0.50 per ounce (14,000 ounces − 12,000 ounces) = $1,000 U

Direct Labor Variances

Actual Hours of Input, at the Actual Rate ($AH \times AR$)	**Actual Hours of Input, at the Standard Rate ($AH \times SR$)**	**Standard Hours Allowed for Actual Output, at the Standard Rate ($SH \times SR$)**
4,000 hours × $9.75 per hour	4,000 hours × $10.00 per hour	3,600 hours* × $10.00 per hour
= $39,000	= $40,000	= $36,000

Rate variance, $1,000 F | Efficiency variance, $4,000 U

Total variance, $3,000 U

*2,000 units × 1.8 hours per unit = 3,600 hours.

Using the formulas in the chapter, the same variances would be computed as:

Labor rate variance = $AH(AR - SR)$

4,000 hours ($9.75 per hour − $10.00 per hour) = $1,000 F

Labor efficiency variance = $SR(AH - SH)$

$10.00 per hour (4,000 hours − 3,600 hours) = $4,000 U

Variable Manufacturing Overhead Variances

Actual Hours of Input, at the Actual Rate (*AH* × *AR*)	Actual Hours of Input, at the Standard Rate (*AH* × *SR*)	Standard Hours Allowed for Actual Output, at the Standard Rate (*SH* × *SR*)
	4,000 hours × $5.00 per hour	3,600 hours* × $5.00 per hour
$20,800	= $20,000	= $18,000

Spending variance, $800 U — Efficiency variance, $2,000 U

Total variance, $2,800 U

*2,000 units × 1.8 hours per unit = 3,600 hours.

Using the formulas in the chapter, the same variances would be computed as follows:

Variable overhead spending variance = *AH*(*AR* − *SR*)

4,000 hours ($5.20 per hour* − $5.00 per hour) = $800 U

*$20,800 ÷ 4,000 hours = $5.20 per hour.

Variable overhead efficiency variance = *SR*(*AH* − *SH*)

$5.00 per hour (4,000 hours − 3,600 hours) = $2,000 U

Glossary

Balanced scorecard An integrated set of performance measures that is derived from and supports the organization's strategy. (p. 449)

Bill of materials A listing of the amount of each type of material required to make a unit of product. (p. 433)

Delivery cycle time The elapsed time from receipt of a customer order to when the completed goods are shipped. (p. 456)

Ideal standards Standards that allow for no machine breakdowns or other work interruptions and that require peak efficiency at all times. (p. 431)

Labor efficiency variance A measure of the difference between the actual hours taken to complete a task and the standard hours allowed, multiplied by the standard hourly labor rate. (p. 442)

Labor rate variance A measure of the difference between the actual hourly labor rate and the standard rate, multiplied by the number of hours worked during the period. (p. 441)

Management by exception A system of management in which standards are set for various operating activities, with actual results compared to these standards. Any differences that are deemed significant are brought to the attention of management as "exceptions." (p. 429)

Manufacturing cycle efficiency (MCE) Process (value-added) time as a percentage of throughput time. (p. 457)

Materials price variance A measure of the difference between the actual unit price paid for an item and the standard price, multiplied by the quantity purchased. (p. 438)

Materials quantity variance A measure of the difference between the actual quantity of materials used in production and the standard quantity allowed, multiplied by the standard price per unit of materials. (p. 440)

Practical standards Standards that allow for normal machine downtime and other work interruptions and that can be attained through reasonable, though highly efficient, efforts by the average worker. (p. 431)

Standard cost card A detailed listing of the standard amounts of inputs that should go into a unit of product, multiplied by the standard price or rate that has been set for each input. (p. 431)

Standard cost per unit The standard cost of a unit of product as shown on the standard cost card; it is computed by multiplying the standard quantity or hours by the standard price or rate for each cost element. (p. 434)

Standard hours allowed The time that should have been taken to complete the period's output. It is computed by multiplying the actual number of units produced by the standard hours per unit. (p. 436)

Standard hours per unit The amount of labor time that should be required to complete a single unit of product, including allowances for breaks, machine downtime, cleanup, rejects, and other normal inefficiencies. (p. 433)

Standard price per unit The price that should be paid for a single unit of a material, including allowances for quality, quantity purchased, shipping, receiving, and other such costs, net of any discounts allowed. (p. 432)

Standard quantity allowed The amount of materials that should have been used to complete the period's actual output. It is computed by multiplying the actual number of units produced by the standard quantity per unit. (p. 435)

Standard quantity per unit The amount of materials that should be required to complete a single unit of product, including allowances for normal waste, spoilage, rejects, and similar inefficiencies. (p. 432)

Standard rate per hour The labor rate that should be incurred per hour of labor time, including employment taxes, fringe benefits, and other such labor costs. (p. 433)

Throughput time The amount of time required to turn raw materials into completed products. (p. 456)

Variable overhead efficiency variance The difference between the actual level of activity (direct labor-hours, machine-hours, or some other base) and the standard activity allowed, multiplied by the variable part of the predetermined overhead rate. (p. 444)

Variable overhead spending variance The difference between the actual variable overhead cost incurred during a period and the standard cost that should have been incurred based on the actual activity of the period. (p. 443)

Variance The difference between standard prices and quantities on the one hand and actual prices and quantities on the other hand. (p. 435)

Appendix 10A: General Ledger Entries to Record Variances

LEARNING OBJECTIVE 7
Prepare journal entries to record standard costs and variances.

Although standard costs and variances can be computed and used by management without being formally entered into the accounting records, many organizations prefer to make formal journal entries. Formal entry tends to give variances a greater emphasis than informal, off-the-record computations. This emphasis signals management's desire to keep costs within the limits that have been set. In addition, formal use of standard costs simplifies the bookkeeping process enormously. Inventories and cost of goods sold can be valued at their standard costs—eliminating the need to keep track of the actual cost of each unit.

Direct Materials Variances

To illustrate the general ledger entries needed to record standard cost variances, we will return to the data contained in the review problem at the end of the chapter. The entry to record the purchase of direct materials would be as follows:

Raw Materials (18,000 ounces at $0.50 per ounce)	9,000	
Materials Price Variance (18,000 ounces at $0.10 per ounce U)	1,800	
Accounts Payable (18,000 ounces at $0.60 per ounce) .		10,800

Notice that the price variance is recognized when purchases are made, rather than when materials are actually used in production and that the materials are carried in the inventory account at standard cost. As direct materials are later drawn from inventory and used in production, the quantity variance is isolated as follows:

Work in Process (12,000 ounces at $0.50 per ounce)	6,000	
Materials Quantity Variance (2,000 ounces U at $0.50 per ounce).	1,000	
Raw Materials (14,000 ounces at $0.50 per ounce)		7,000

Thus, direct materials are added to the Work in Process account at the standard cost of the materials that should have been used to produce the actual output.

Notice that both the price variance and the quantity variance above are unfavorable and are debit entries. If either of these variances had been favorable, it would have appeared as a credit entry.

Direct Labor Variances

Referring again to the cost data in the review problem at the end of the chapter, the general ledger entry to record the incurrence of direct labor cost would be:

Work in Process (3,600 hours at $10.00 per hour).	36,000	
Labor Efficiency Variance (400 hours U at $10.00 per hour) .	4,000	
Labor Rate Variance (4,000 hours at $0.25 per hour F) . . .		1,000
Wages Payable (4,000 hours at $9.75 per hour)		39,000

Thus, as with direct materials, direct labor costs enter into the Work in Process account at standard, both in terms of the rate and in terms of the hours allowed for the actual production of the period. Note that the unfavorable labor efficiency variance is a debit entry whereas the favorable labor rate variance is a credit entry.

Variable Manufacturing Overhead Variances

Variable manufacturing overhead variances usually are not recorded in the accounts separately but rather are determined as part of the general analysis of overhead, which is discussed in the next chapter.

Cost Flows in a Standard Cost System

The flows of costs through the company's accounts are illustrated in Exhibit 10A–1. Note that entries into the various inventory accounts are made at standard cost—not actual cost. The differences between actual and standard costs are entered into special accounts that accumulate the various standard cost variances. Ordinarily, these standard cost variance accounts are closed out to Cost of Goods Sold at the end of the period. Unfavorable variances increase Cost of Goods Sold, and favorable variances decrease Cost of Goods Sold.

EXHIBIT 10A–1
Cost Flows in a Standard Cost System*

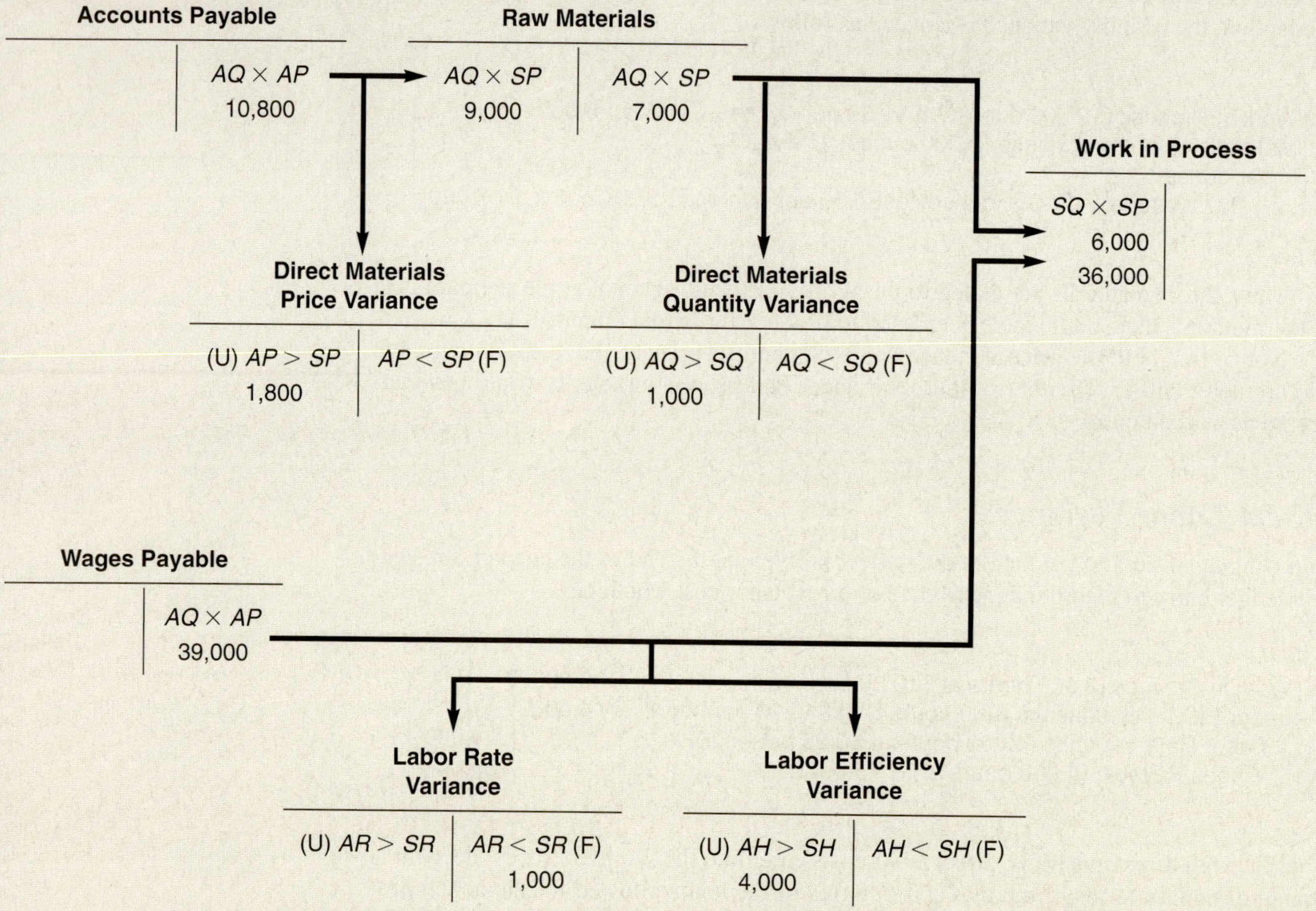

*The authors would like to thank Professor Rick French for suggesting this exhibit.

Questions

10–1 What is a quantity standard? What is a price standard?

10–2 Distinguish between ideal and practical standards.

10–3 If employees are chronically unable to meet a standard, what effect would you expect this to have on their productivity?

10–4 What is the difference between a standard and a budget?

10–5 What is meant by the term *variance?*

10–6 What is meant by the term *management by exception?*

10–7 Why are separate price and quantity variances computed?

10–8 Who is generally responsible for the materials price variance? The materials quantity variance? The labor efficiency variance?

10–9 The materials price variance can be computed at what two different points in time? Which point is better? Why?

10–10 An examination of the cost records of the Chittenden Furniture Company reveals that the materials price variance is favorable but that the materials quantity variance is unfavorable by a substantial amount. What might this indicate?

10–11 What dangers lie in using standards to identify who to blame for problems?

10–12 "Our workers are all under labor contracts; therefore, our labor rate variance is bound to be zero." Discuss.

10–13 What effect, if any, would you expect poor quality materials to have on direct labor variances?

10–14 If variable manufacturing overhead is applied to production on the basis of direct labor-hours and the direct labor efficiency variance is unfavorable, will the variable overhead efficiency variance be favorable or unfavorable, or could it be either? Explain.

10–15 What is a statistical control chart, and how is it used?

10–16 Why can undue emphasis on labor efficiency variances lead to excess work in process inventories?

10–17 Why do the measures used in a balanced scorecard differ from company to company?

10–18 Why does the balanced scorecard include financial performance measures as well as measures of how well internal business processes are doing?

10–19 What is the difference between delivery cycle time and throughput time? What four elements make up throughput time? Into what two classes can these four elements be placed?

10–20 If a company has a manufacturing cycle efficiency (MCE) of less than 1, what does it mean? How would you interpret an MCE of 0.40?

10–21 (Appendix 10A) What are the advantages of making formal journal entries in the accounting records for variances?

Exercises

EXERCISE 10–1 Setting Standards; Preparing a Standard Cost Card [LO1]

Martin Company manufactures a powerful cleaning solvent. The main ingredient in the solvent is a raw material called Echol. Information concerning the purchase and use of Echol follows:

Purchase of Echol Echol is purchased in 15-gallon containers at a cost of $115 per container. A discount of 2% is offered by the supplier for payment within 10 days, and Martin Company takes all discounts. Shipping costs, which Martin Company must pay, amount to $130 for an average shipment of 100 15-gallon containers of Echol.

Use of Echol The bill of materials calls for 7.6 quarts of Echol per bottle of cleaning solvent. (Each gallon contains four quarts.) About 5% of all Echol used is lost through spillage or evaporation (the 7.6 quarts above is the *actual* content per bottle). In addition, statistical analysis has shown that every 41st bottle is rejected at final inspection because of contamination.

Required:

1. Compute the standard purchase price for one quart of Echol.
2. Compute the standard quantity of Echol (in quarts) per salable bottle of cleaning solvent.
3. Using the data from (1) and (2) above, prepare a standard cost card showing the standard cost of Echol per bottle of cleaning solvent.

EXERCISE 10–2 Direct Materials Variances [LO2]

Bandar Industries Berhad of Malaysia manufactures sporting equipment. One of the company's products, a football helmet for the North American market, requires a special plastic. During the quarter ending June 30, the company manufactured 35,000 helmets, using 22,500 kilograms of plastic. The plastic cost the company RM 171,000. (The currency in Malaysia is the ringgit, which is denoted here by RM.)

According to the standard cost card, each helmet should require 0.6 kilograms of plastic, at a cost of RM 8 per kilogram.

Required:

1. What cost for plastic should have been incurred to make 35,000 helmets? How much greater or less is this than the cost that was incurred?
2. Break down the difference computed in (1) above into a materials price variance and a materials quantity variance.

EXERCISE 10–3 Direct Labor Variances [LO3]

SkyChefs, Inc., prepares in-flight meals for a number of major airlines. One of the company's products is grilled salmon in dill sauce with baby new potatoes and spring vegetables. During the most recent week, the company prepared 4,000 of these meals using 960 direct labor-hours. The company paid these direct labor workers a total of $9,600 for this work, or $10.00 per hour.

According to the standard cost card for this meal, it should require 0.25 direct labor-hours at a cost of $9.75 per hour.

Required:

1. What direct labor cost should have been incurred to prepare 4,000 meals? How much does this differ from the actual direct labor cost?
2. Break down the difference computed in (1) above into a labor rate variance and a labor efficiency variance.

EXERCISE 10–4 Variable Overhead Variances [LO4]

Logistics Solutions provides order fulfillment services for dot.com merchants. The company maintains warehouses that stock items carried by its dot.com clients. When a client receives an order from a customer, the order is forwarded to Logistics Solutions, which pulls the item from storage, packs it, and ships it to the customer. The company uses a predetermined variable overhead rate based on direct labor-hours.

In the most recent month, 120,000 items were shipped to customers using 2,300 direct labor-hours. The company incurred a total of $7,360 in variable overhead costs.

According to the company's standards, 0.02 direct labor-hours are required to fulfill an order for one item and the variable overhead rate is $3.25 per direct labor-hour.

Required:

1. What variable overhead cost should have been incurred to fill the orders for the 120,000 items? How much does this differ from the actual variable overhead cost?
2. Break down the difference computed in (1) above into a variable overhead spending variance and a variable overhead efficiency variance.

EXERCISE 10–5 Creating a Balanced Scorecard [LO5]

Historically, the Mason Paper Company (MPC) has manufactured commodity grade papers for use in computer printers and photocopiers. MPC has reported net operating losses for the last two years due to intense price pressure from much larger competitors. The MPC management team—including Kristen Townsend (CEO), Mike Martinez (vice president of Manufacturing), Tom Andrews (vice president of Marketing), and Wendy Chen (CFO)—is contemplating a change in strategy to save the company from impending bankruptcy. Excerpts from a recent management team meeting are shown below:

Townsend: As we all know, the commodity paper manufacturing business is all about economies of scale. The largest competitors with the lowest cost per unit win. The limited capacity of our older machines prohibits us from competing in the high-volume commodity paper grades. Furthermore, expanding our capacity by acquiring a new paper-making machine is out of the question given the extraordinarily high price tag. Therefore, I propose that we abandon cost reduction as a strategic goal and instead pursue manufacturing flexibility as the key to our future success.

Chen: Manufacturing flexibility? What does that mean?

Martinez: It means we have to abandon our "crank out as many tons of paper as possible" mentality. Instead, we need to pursue the low-volume business opportunities that exist in the nonstandard, specialized paper grades. To succeed in this regard, we'll need to improve our flexibility in three ways. First, we must improve our ability to switch between paper grades. Right now, we require an average of four hours to change over to another paper grade. Timely customer deliveries are a function of changeover performance. Second, we need to expand the range of paper grades that we can manufacture. Currently, we can only manufacture three paper grades. Our customers must perceive that we are a "one-stop shop" that can meet all of their paper grade needs. Third, we will need to improve our yields (e.g., tons of acceptable output relative to total tons processed) in the nonstandard paper grades. I am certain that our percentage of waste within these grades will be unacceptably high unless we do something to improve our processes. Our variable costs will go through the roof if we cannot increase our yields!

Chen: Wait just a minute! These changes are going to destroy our equipment utilization numbers!

Andrews: You're right Wendy; however, equipment utilization is not the name of the game when it comes to competing in terms of flexibility. Our customers don't care about our equipment utilization. Instead, as Mike just alluded to, they want just-in-time delivery of smaller quantities of a full range of paper grades. If we can shrink the elapsed time from order placement to order delivery and expand our product offerings, it will increase sales from current customers and bring in new customers. Furthermore, we will be able to charge a premium price because of the limited competition within this niche from our cost-focused larger competitors. Our contribution margin per ton should drastically improve!

Martinez: Of course, executing the change in strategy will not be easy. We'll need to make a substantial investment in training. It is imperative that we do not shortchange our commitment to training because ultimately it is our people who create our flexible manufacturing capabilities.

Chen: If we adopt this new strategy, it is definitely going to impact how we measure performance. We'll need to create measures that motivate our employees to make decisions that support our flexibility goals.

Townsend: Wendy, you hit the nail right on the head. For our next meeting, could you pull together some potential measures that support our new strategy?

Later that same day, Wendy shared the essence of the above conversation with the employees of her Finance Department. She indicated that she would welcome suggested performance measures from anyone within the department. As an employee in the Finance Department, you have decided to pursue this opportunity to enhance your career prospects within the organization.

Required:

1. Contrast MPC's previous manufacturing strategy with its new manufacturing strategy.
2. Generally speaking, why would a company that changes its strategic goals need to change its performance measurement system as well? What are some examples of measures that would have been appropriate for MPC prior to its change in strategy? Why would those measures fail to support MPC's new strategy?
3. Using Exhibit 10–12 as a guide, construct a balanced scorecard that would support MPC's new manufacturing strategy. Use arrows to show the causal links between the performance measures and show whether the performance measure should increase or decrease over time. Feel free to create measures that may not be specifically mentioned in the chapter, but nonetheless make sense given the strategic goals of the company.
4. What hypotheses are built into MPC's balanced scorecard? Which of these hypotheses do you believe are most questionable and why?

EXERCISE 10–6 Measures of Internal Business Process Performance [LO6]

Management of Mittel Rhein AG of Köln, Germany, would like to reduce the amount of time between when a customer places an order and when the order is shipped. For the first quarter of operations during the current year the following data were reported:

	Days
Inspection time	0.3
Wait time (from order to start of production)	14.0
Process time	2.7
Move time	1.0
Queue time	5.0

Required:

1. Compute the throughput time.
2. Compute the manufacturing cycle efficiency (MCE) for the quarter.
3. What percentage of the throughput time was spent in non-value-added activities?
4. Compute the delivery cycle time.
5. If by use of just-in-time (JIT) all queue time during production is eliminated, what will be the new MCE?

EXERCISE 10–7 (Appendix 10A) Recording Variances in the General Ledger [LO7]

Bliny Corporation makes a product with the following standard costs for direct material and direct labor:

Direct material: 2.00 meters at $3.25 per meter	$6.50
Direct labor: 0.40 hours at $12.00 per hour	$4.80

During the most recent month, 5,000 units were produced. The costs associated with the month's production of this product were as follows:

Material purchased: 12,000 meters at $3.15 per meter	$37,800
Material used in production: 10,500 meters	—
Direct labor: 1,975 hours at $12.20 per hour	$24,095

The standard cost variances for direct material and direct labor are:

Materials price variance: 12,000 meters at $0.10 per meter F	$1,200 F
Materials quantity variance: 500 meters at $3.25 per meter U	$1,625 U
Labor rate variance: 1,975 hours at $0.20 per hour U	$395 U
Labor efficiency variance: 25 hours at $12.00 per hour F	$300 F

Required:

1. Prepâre the general ledger entry to record the purchase of materials on account for the month.
2. Prepare the general ledger entry to record the use of materials for the month.
3. Prepare the general ledger entry to record the incurrence of direct labor cost for the month.

EXERCISE 10–8 Setting Standards [LO1]

Victoria Chocolates, Ltd., makes premium handcrafted chocolate confections in London. The owner of the company is setting up a standard cost system and has collected the following data for one of the company's products, the Empire Truffle. This product is made with the finest white chocolate and various fillings. The data below pertain only to the white chocolate used in the product (the currency is stated in pounds denoted here as £):

Material requirements, kilograms of white chocolate per dozen truffles .	0.70 kilograms
Allowance for waste, kilograms of white chocolate per dozen truffles ..	0.03 kilograms
Allowance for rejects, kilograms of white chocolate per dozen truffles ..	0.02 kilograms
Purchase price, finest grade white chocolate	£7.50 per kilogram
Purchase discount	8% of purchase price
Shipping cost from the supplier in Belgium	£0.30 per kilogram
Receiving and handling cost	£0.04 per kilogram

Required:

1. Determine the standard price of a kilogram of white chocolate.
2. Determine the standard quantity of white chocolate for a dozen truffles.
3. Determine the standard cost of the white chocolate in a dozen truffles.

EXERCISE 10–9 Direct Materials and Direct Labor Variances [LO2, LO3]

Dawson Toys, Ltd., produces a toy called the Maze. The company has recently established a standard cost system to help control costs and has established the following standards for the Maze toy:

Direct materials: 6 microns per toy at $0.50 per micron
Direct labor: 1.3 hours per toy at $8 per hour

During July, the company produced 3,000 Maze toys. Production data for the month on the toy follow:

Direct materials: 25,000 microns were purchased at a cost of $0.48 per micron. 5,000 of these microns were still in inventory at the end of the month.
Direct labor: 4,000 direct labor-hours were worked at a cost of $36,000.

Required:

1. Compute the following variances for July:
   a. Direct materials price and quantity variances.
   b. Direct labor rate and efficiency variances.
2. Prepare a brief explanation of the possible causes of each variance.

EXERCISE 10–10 Working Backwards from Labor Variances [LO3]

The auto repair shop of Quality Motor Company uses standards to control the labor time and labor cost in the shop. The standard labor cost for a motor tune-up is given below:

Job	Standard Hours	Standard Rate	Standard Cost
Motor tune-up	2.5	$9	$22.50

The record showing the time spent in the shop last week on motor tune-ups has been misplaced. However, the shop supervisor recalls that 50 tune-ups were completed during the week, and the controller recalls the following variance data relating to tune-ups:

Labor rate variance	$87 F
Total labor variance	$93 U

Required:
1. Determine the number of actual labor-hours spent on tune-ups during the week.
2. Determine the actual hourly rate of pay for tune-ups last week.

(Hint: A useful way to proceed would be to work from known to unknown data either by using the variance formulas or by using the columnar format shown in Exhibit 10–6.)

EXERCISE 10–11 Direct Labor and Variable Manufacturing Overhead Variances [LO3, LO4]
Erie Company manufactures a small CD player called the Jogging Mate. The company uses standards to control its costs. The labor standards that have been set for one Jogging Mate CD player are as follows:

Standard Hours	Standard Rate per Hour	Standard Cost
18 minutes	$12.00	$3.60

During August, 5,750 hours of direct labor time were needed to make 20,000 units of the Jogging Mate. The direct labor cost totaled $73,600 for the month.

Required:
1. What direct labor cost should have been incurred to make 20,000 units of the Jogging Mate? By how much does this differ from the cost that was incurred?
2. Break down the difference in cost from (1) above into a labor rate variance and a labor efficiency variance.
3. The budgeted variable manufacturing overhead rate is $4 per direct labor-hour. During August, the company incurred $21,850 in variable manufacturing overhead cost. Compute the variable overhead spending and efficiency variances for the month.

EXERCISE 10–12 Direct Materials and Direct Labor Variances [LO2, LO3]
Huron Company produces a commercial cleaning compound known as Zoom. The direct materials and direct labor standards for one unit of Zoom are given below:

	Standard Quantity or Hours	Standard Price or Rate	Standard Cost
Direct materials	4.6 pounds	$2.50 per pound	$11.50
Direct labor	0.2 hours	$12.00 per hour	$2.40

During the most recent month, the following activity was recorded:

a. Twenty thousand pounds of material were purchased at a cost of $2.35 per pound.
b. All of the material purchased was used to produce 4,000 units of Zoom.
c. 750 hours of direct labor time were recorded at a total labor cost of $10,425.

Required:
1. Compute the direct materials price and quantity variances for the month.
2. Compute the direct labor rate and efficiency variances for the month.

EXERCISE 10–13 Direct Materials Variances [LO2]
Refer to the data in Exercise 10–12. Assume that instead of producing 4,000 units during the month, the company produced only 3,000 units, using 14,750 pounds of material. (The rest of the material purchased remained in raw materials inventory.)

Required:
Compute the direct materials price and quantity variances for the month.

EXERCISE 10–14 Creating a Balanced Scorecard [LO5]

Ariel Tax Services prepares tax returns for individual and corporate clients. As the company has gradually expanded to 10 offices, the founder Max Jacobs has begun to feel as though he is losing control of operations. In response to this concern, he has decided to implement a performance measurement system that will help control current operations and facilitate his growth plans of expanding to 20 offices.

Jacobs describes the keys to the success of his business as follows:

"Our only real asset is our people. We must keep our employees highly motivated and we must continually replenish our human capital by hiring the 'cream of the crop.' Interestingly, employee morale and recruiting success are both driven by the same two factors—compensation and career advancement. In other words, providing superior compensation relative to the industry average coupled with fast-track career advancement opportunities keeps morale high and makes us a very attractive place to work. It drives a high rate of job offer acceptances relative to job offers tendered.

"Hiring highly qualified people and keeping them energized ensures operational success, which in our business is a function of productivity, efficiency, and effectiveness. Productivity boils down to employees being billable rather idle. Efficiency relates to the time required to complete a tax return. Finally, effectiveness is critical to our business in the sense that we cannot tolerate errors. Completing a tax return quickly is meaningless if the return contains errors.

"Our growth plans hinge upon acquiring new customers through word-of-mouth from satisfied repeat customers. We believe that our customers come back year after year because they value error-free, timely, and courteous tax return preparation. Common courtesy is an important aspect of our business! We call it service quality, and it all ties back to employee morale in the sense that happy employees treat their clients with care and concern.

"While sales growth is obviously important to our future plans, growth without a corresponding increase in profitability is useless. Therefore, we understand that increasing our profit margin is a function of cost-efficiency as well as sales growth. Given that payroll is our biggest expense, we must maintain an optimal balance between staffing levels and the revenue being generated. As I alluded to earlier, the key to maintaining this balance is employee productivity. If we can achieve cost-efficient sales growth, we should eventually have 20 profitable offices!"

Required:

1. Create a balanced scorecard for Ariel Tax Services. Link your scorecard measures using the framework from Exhibit 10–12. Indicate whether each measure is expected to increase or decrease. Feel free to create measures that may not be specifically mentioned in the chapter, but make sense given the strategic goals of the company.
2. What hypotheses are built into the balanced scorecard for Ariel Tax Services? Which of these hypotheses do you believe are most questionable and why?
3. Discuss the potential advantages and disadvantages of implementing an internal business process measure called *total dollar amount of tax refunds generated.* Would you recommend using this measure in Ariel's balanced scorecard?
4. Would it be beneficial to attempt to measure each office's individual performance with respect to the scorecard measures that you created? Why or why not?

EXERCISE 10–15 (Appendix 10A) Direct Materials and Direct Labor Variances; Journal Entries [LO2, LO3, LO7]

Genola Fashions began production of a new product on June 1. The company uses a standard cost system and has established the following standards for one unit of the new product:

	Standard Quantity or Hours	Standard Price or Rate	Standard Cost
Direct materials	2.5 yards	$14 per yard	$35.00
Direct labor	1.6 hours	$8 per hour	$12.80

During June, the following activity was recorded regarding the new product:

a. Purchasing acquired 10,000 yards of material at a cost of $13.80 per yard.
b. Production used 8,000 yards of the material to manufacture 3,000 units of the new product.
c. Production reported that 5,000 direct labor-hours were worked on the new product at a cost of $43,000.

Required:

1. For direct materials:
   a. Compute the direct materials price and quantity variances.
   b. Prepare journal entries to record the purchase of materials and the use of materials in production.
2. For direct labor:
   a. Compute the direct labor rate and efficiency variances.
   b. Prepare a journal entry to record the incurrence of direct labor cost for the month.
3. Post the entries you have prepared to the following T-accounts:

Raw Materials

?	?
Bal. ?	

Work in Process

Materials used ?	
Labor cost ?	

Accounts Payable

	138,000

Wages Payable

	43,000

Materials Price Variance

Materials Quantity Variance

Labor Rate Variance

Labor Efficiency Variance

Problems

PROBLEM 10–16 Variance Analysis in a Hospital [LO2, LO3, LO4]

John Fleming, chief administrator for Valley View Hospital, is concerned about the costs for tests in the hospital's lab. Charges for lab tests are consistently higher at Valley View than at other hospitals and have resulted in many complaints. Also, because of strict regulations on amounts reimbursed for lab tests, payments received from insurance companies and governmental units have not been high enough to cover lab costs.

Mr. Fleming has asked you to evaluate costs in the hospital's lab for the past month. The following information is available:

a. Two types of tests are performed in the lab—blood tests and smears. During the past month, 1,800 blood tests and 2,400 smears were performed in the lab.
b. Small glass plates are used in both types of tests. During the past month, the hospital purchased 12,000 plates at a cost of $28,200. This cost is net of a 6% quantity discount. 1,500 of these plates were unused at the end of the month; no plates were on hand at the beginning of the month.
c. During the past month, 1,150 hours of labor time were recorded in the lab at a cost of $13,800.
d. The lab's variable overhead cost last month totaled $7,820.

Valley View Hospital has never used standard costs. By searching industry literature, however, you have determined the following nationwide averages for hospital labs:

Plates: Two plates are required per lab test. These plates cost $2.50 each and are disposed of after the test is completed.

Labor: Each blood test should require 0.3 hours to complete, and each smear should require 0.15 hours to complete. The average cost of this lab time is $14 per hour.

Overhead: Overhead cost is based on direct labor-hours. The average rate for variable overhead is $6 per hour.

Required:

1. Compute a materials price variance for the plates purchased last month and a materials quantity variance for the plates used last month.
2. For labor cost in the lab:
   a. Compute a labor rate variance and a labor efficiency variance.
   b. In most hospitals, one-half of the workers in the lab are senior technicians and one-half are assistants. In an effort to reduce costs, Valley View Hospital employs only one-fourth senior technicians and three-fourths assistants. Would you recommend that this policy be continued? Explain.
3. Compute the variable overhead spending and efficiency variances. Is there any relation between the variable overhead efficiency variance and the labor efficiency variance? Explain.

PROBLEM 10–17 Basic Variance Analysis [LO2, LO3, LO4]
Becton Labs, Inc., produces various chemical compounds for industrial use. One compound, called Fludex, is prepared using an elaborate distilling process. The company has developed standard costs for one unit of Fludex, as follows:

Microsoft Excel - Problem 10-17 screen capture.xls

	A	B	C	D	E	F
1		*Standard Quantity*		*Standard Price or Rate*		*Standard Cost*
2	Direct materials	2.5	ounces	$20.00	per ounce	$ 50.00
3	Direct labor	1.4	hours	$12.50	per hour	17.50
4	Variable manufacturing overhead	1.4	hours	$3.50	per hour	4.90
5						$ 72.40
6						

During November, the following activity was recorded by the company relative to production of Fludex:

a. Materials purchased, 12,000 ounces at a cost of $225,000.
b. There was no beginning inventory of materials; however, at the end of the month, 2,500 ounces of material remained in ending inventory.
c. The company employs 35 lab technicians to work on the production of Fludex. During November, each worked an average of 160 hours at an average rate of $12 per hour.
d. Variable manufacturing overhead is assigned to Fludex on the basis of direct labor-hours. Variable manufacturing overhead costs during November totaled $18,200.
e. During November, 3,750 good units of Fludex were produced.

The company's management is anxious to determine the efficiency of the Fludex production activities.

Required:

1. For direct materials used in the production of Fludex:
   a. Compute the price and quantity variances.
   b. The materials were purchased from a new supplier who is anxious to enter into a long-term purchase contract. Would you recommend that the company sign the contract? Explain.
2. For direct labor employed in the production of Fludex:
   a. Compute the rate and efficiency variances.
   b. In the past, the 35 technicians employed in the production of Fludex consisted of 20 senior technicians and 15 assistants. During November, the company experimented with fewer senior technicians and more assistants in order to save costs. Would you recommend that the new labor mix be continued? Explain.
3. Compute the variable overhead spending and efficiency variances. What relation can you see between this efficiency variance and the labor efficiency variance?

PROBLEM 10–18 (Appendix 10A) Comprehensive Variance Analysis; Journal Entries [LO2, LO3, LO4, LO7]

Trueform Products, Inc., produces a broad line of sports equipment and uses a standard cost system for control purposes. Last year the company produced 8,000 varsity footballs. The standard costs associated with this football, along with the actual costs incurred last year, are given below (per football):

	Standard Cost	Actual Cost
Direct materials:		
Standard: 3.7 feet at $5.00 per foot	$18.50	
Actual: 4.0 feet at $4.80 per foot		$19.20
Direct labor:		
Standard: 0.9 hour at $7.50 per hour	6.75	
Actual: 0.8 hour at $8.00 per hour		6.40
Variable manufacturing overhead:		
Standard: 0.9 hour at $2.50 per hour	2.25	
Actual: 0.8 hour at $2.75 per hour		2.20
Total cost per football	$27.50	$27.80

The president was elated when he saw that actual costs exceeded standard costs by only $0.30 per football. He stated, "I was afraid that our unit cost might get out of hand when we gave out those raises last year in order to stimulate output. But it's obvious our costs are well under control."

There was no inventory of materials on hand to start the year. During the year, 32,000 feet of materials were purchased and used in production.

Required:

1. For direct materials:
   a. Compute the price and quantity variances for the year.
   b. Prepare journal entries to record all activity relating to direct materials for the year.
2. For direct labor:
   a. Compute the rate and efficiency variances.
   b. Prepare a journal entry to record the incurrence of direct labor cost for the year.
3. Compute the variable overhead spending and efficiency variances.
4. Was the president correct in his statement that "our costs are well under control"? Explain.
5. State possible causes of each variance that you have computed.

PROBLEM 10–19 Comprehensive Variance Analysis [LO2, LO3, LO4]

Miller Toy Company manufactures a plastic swimming pool at its Westwood Plant. The plant has been experiencing problems as shown by its June contribution format income statement below:

	Budgeted	Actual
Sales (15,000 pools)	$450,000	$450,000
Less variable expenses:		
Variable cost of goods sold*	180,000	196,290
Variable selling expenses	20,000	20,000
Total variable expenses	200,000	216,290
Contribution margin	250,000	233,710
Less fixed expenses:		
Manufacturing overhead	130,000	130,000
Selling and administrative	84,000	84,000
Total fixed expenses	214,000	214,000
Net operating income	$ 36,000	$ 19,710

*Contains direct materials, direct labor, and variable manufacturing overhead.

Janet Dunn, who has just been appointed general manager of the Westwood Plant, has been given instructions to "get things under control." Upon reviewing the plant's income statement, Ms. Dunn has concluded that the major problem lies in the variable cost of goods sold. She has been provided with the following standard cost per swimming pool:

	Standard Quantity or Hours	Standard Price or Rate	Standard Cost
Direct materials	3.0 pounds	$2.00 per pound	$ 6.00
Direct labor	0.8 hour	$6.00 per hour	4.80
Variable manufacturing overhead	0.4 hour*	$3.00 per hour	1.20
Total standard cost			$12.00

*Based on machine-hours.

Ms. Dunn has determined that during June the plant produced 15,000 pools and incurred the following costs:

a. Purchased 60,000 pounds of materials at a cost of $1.95 per pound.
b. Used 49,200 pounds of materials in production. (Finished goods and work in process inventories are insignificant and can be ignored.)
c. Worked 11,800 direct labor-hours at a cost of $7.00 per hour.
d. Incurred variable manufacturing overhead cost totaling $18,290 for the month. A total of 5,900 machine-hours was recorded.

It is the company's policy to close all variances to cost of goods sold on a monthly basis.

Required:

1. Compute the following variances for June:
   a. Direct materials price and quantity variances.
   b. Direct labor rate and efficiency variances.
   c. Variable overhead spending and efficiency variances.
2. Summarize the variances that you computed in (1) above by showing the net overall favorable or unfavorable variance for the month. What impact did this figure have on the company's income statement? Show computations.
3. Pick out the two most significant variances that you computed in (1) above. Explain to Ms. Dunn possible causes of these variances.

PROBLEM 10–20 Creating Balanced Scorecards that Support Different Strategies [LO5]

The Midwest Consulting Group (MCG) helps companies build balanced scorecards. As part of its marketing efforts, MCG conducts an annual balanced scorecard workshop for prospective clients. As MCG's newest employee, your boss has asked you to participate in this year's workshop by explaining to attendees how a company's strategy determines the measures that are appropriate for its balanced scorecard. Your boss has provided you with the excerpts below from the annual reports of two current MCG clients. She has asked you to use these excerpts as a basis for facilitating your portion of the workshop.

Excerpt from Applied Pharmaceuticals' annual report:

> The keys to our business are consistent and timely new product introductions and manufacturing process integrity. The new product introduction side of the equation is a function of research and development (R&D) yield (e.g., the number of marketable drug compounds created relative to the total number of potential compounds pursued). We seek to optimize our R&D yield and first-to-market capability by investing in state-of-the-art technology, hiring the highest possible percentage of the "best and the brightest" engineers that we pursue, and providing world-class training to those engineers. Manufacturing process integrity is all about establishing world-class quality specifications and then relentlessly engaging in prevention and appraisal activities to minimize defect rates. Our customers must have an awareness of and respect for our brand image of being "first to market and first in quality." If we deliver on this pledge to our customers, then our financial goal of increasing our return on stockholders' equity should take care of itself.

Excerpt from Destination Resorts International's annual report:

> Our business succeeds or fails based on the quality of the service that our front-line employees provide to customers. Therefore, it is imperative that we strive to maintain high employee

morale and minimize employee turnover. In addition, it is critical that we train our employees to use technology to create one seamless worldwide experience for our repeat customers. Once an employee enters a customer preference (e.g., provide two extra pillows in the room, deliver fresh brewed coffee to the room at 8:00 A.M., etc.) into our database, our worldwide workforce strives to ensure that a customer will never need to repeat it at any of our destination resorts. If we properly train and retain a motivated workforce, we should see continuous improvement in our percentage of error-free repeat customer check-ins, the time taken to resolve customer complaints, and our independently assessed room cleanliness. This in turn should drive improvement in our customer retention, which is the key to meeting our revenue growth goals.

Required:

1. Based on the excerpts above, compare and contrast the strategies of Applied Pharmaceuticals and Destination Resorts International.
2. Select balanced scorecard measures for each company and link the scorecard measures using the framework from Exhibit 10–12. Use arrows to show the causal links between the performance measures and show whether the performance measure should increase or decrease over time. Feel free to create measures that may not be specifically mentioned in the chapter, but nonetheless make sense given the strategic goals of each company.
3. What hypotheses are built into each balanced scorecard? Why do the hypotheses differ between the two companies?

PROBLEM 10–21 Measures of Internal Business Process Performance [LO6]

DataSpan, Inc., automated its plant at the start of the current year and installed a flexible manufacturing system. The company is also evaluating its suppliers and moving toward a just-in-time (JIT) inventory system. Many adjustment problems have been encountered, including problems relating to performance measurement. After much study, the company has decided to use the performance measures below as part of its balanced scorecard, and it has gathered data relating to these measures for the first four months of operations.

	Month			
	1	2	3	4
Throughput time (days)	?	?	?	?
Delivery cycle time (days)	?	?	?	?
Manufacturing cycle efficiency (MCE)	?	?	?	?
Percentage of on-time deliveries	91%	86%	83%	79%
Total sales (units)	3,210	3,072	2,915	2,806

Management has asked for your help in computing throughput time, delivery cycle time, and MCE. The following average times have been logged over the last four months:

	Average per Month (in days)			
	1	2	3	4
Move time per unit	0.4	0.3	0.4	0.4
Process time per unit	2.1	2.0	1.9	1.8
Wait time per order before start of production	16.0	17.5	19.0	20.5
Queue time per unit	4.3	5.0	5.8	6.7
Inspection time per unit	0.6	0.7	0.7	0.6

Required:

1. For each month, compute the following:
   a. The throughput time.
   b. The MCE.
   c. The delivery cycle time.
2. Evaluate the company's performance over the last four months.
3. Refer to the move time, process time, and so forth, given above for month 4.
   a. Assume that in month 5 the move time, process time, and so forth, are the same as in month 4, except that through the use of JIT inventory methods the company is able to

completely eliminate the queue time during production. Compute the new throughput time and MCE.

b. Assume in month 6 that the move time, process time, and so forth, are again the same as in month 4, except that the company is able to completely eliminate both the queue time during production and the inspection time. Compute the new throughput time and MCE.

PROBLEM 10–22 Setting Standards [LO1]

Danson Company is a chemical manufacturer that supplies various products to industrial users. The company plans to introduce a new chemical solution, called Nysap, for which it needs to develop a standard product cost. The following information is available on the production of Nysap:

a. Nysap is made by combining a chemical compound (nyclyn) and a solution (salex), and boiling the mixture. A 20% loss in volume occurs for both the salex and the nyclyn during boiling. After boiling, the mixture consists of 9.6 liters of salex and 12 kilograms of nyclyn per 10-liter batch of Nysap.

b. After the boiling process is complete, the solution is cooled slightly before 5 kilograms of protet are added per 10-liter batch of Nysap. The addition of the protet does not affect the total liquid volume. The resulting solution is then bottled in 10-liter containers.

c. The finished product is highly unstable, and one 10-liter batch out of five is rejected at final inspection. Rejected batches have no commercial value and are thrown out.

d. It takes a worker 35 minutes to process one 10-liter batch of Nysap. Employees work an eight-hour day, including one hour per day for rest breaks and cleanup.

Required:

1. Determine the standard quantity for each of the raw materials needed to produce an acceptable 10-liter batch of Nysap.
2. Determine the standard labor time allowed to produce an acceptable 10-liter batch of Nysap.
3. Assuming the following purchase prices and costs, prepare a standard cost card for direct materials and direct labor for one acceptable 10-liter batch of Nysap:

Salex	$1.50 per liter
Nyclyn	$2.80 per kilogram
Protet	$3.00 per kilogram
Direct labor cost	$9.00 per hour

(CMA, adapted)

PROBLEM 10–23 Variance Analysis with Multiple Lots [LO2, LO3]

Hillcrest Leisure Wear, Inc., manufactures men's clothing. The company has a single line of slacks that is produced in lots, with each lot representing an order from a customer. As a lot is completed, the customer's store label is attached to the slacks before shipment.

Hillcrest has a standard cost system and has established the following standards for a dozen slacks:

	Standard Quantity or Hours	Standard Price or Rate	Standard Cost
Direct materials	32 yards	$2.40 per yard	$76.80
Direct labor	6 hours	$7.50 per hour	$45.00

During October, Hillcrest worked on three orders for slacks. The company's job cost records for the month reveal the following:

Lot	Units in Lot (dozens)	Materials Used (yards)	Hours Worked
48	1,500	48,300	8,900
49	950	30,140	6,130
50	2,100	67,250	10,270

The following additional information is available:

a. Hillcrest purchased 180,000 yards of material during October at a cost of $424,800.

b. Direct labor cost incurred during the month for production of slacks amounted to $192,280.
c. There was no work in process inventory on October 1. During October, lots 48 and 49 were completed, and lot 50 was 100% complete with respect to materials and 80% complete with respect to labor.

Required:
1. Compute the materials price variance for the materials purchased during October.
2. Determine the materials quantity variance for October in both yards and dollars:
   a. For each lot worked on during the month.
   b. For the company as a whole.
3. Compute the labor rate variance for October.
4. Determine the labor efficiency variance for the month in both hours and dollars:
   a. For each lot worked on during the month.
   b. For the company as a whole.
5. In what situations might it be better to express variances in units (hours, yards, and so on) rather than in dollars? In dollars rather than in units?

(CPA, adapted)

PROBLEM 10–24 Direct Materials and Direct Labor Variances; Computations from Incomplete Data [LO1, LO2, LO3]

Sharp Company manufactures a product for which the following standards have been set:

	Standard Quantity or Hours	Standard Price or Rate	Standard Cost
Direct materials	3 feet	$5 per foot	$15
Direct labor	? hours	? per hour	?

During March, the company purchased direct materials at a cost of $55,650, all of which were used in the production of 3,200 units of product. In addition, 4,900 hours of direct labor time were worked on the product during the month. The cost of this labor time was $36,750. The following variances have been computed for the month:

Materials quantity variance	$4,500 U
Total labor variance	$1,650 F
Labor efficiency variance	$800 U

Required:
1. For direct materials:
   a. Compute the actual cost per foot for materials for March.
   b. Compute the materials price variance and a total variance for materials.
2. For direct labor:
   a. Compute the standard direct labor rate per hour.
   b. Compute the standard hours allowed for the month's production.
   c. Compute the standard hours allowed per unit of product.

(Hint: In completing the problem, it may be helpful to move from known to unknown data either by using the columnar format shown in Exhibits 10–4 and 10–6 or by using the variance formulas.)

PROBLEM 10–25 (Appendix 10A) Comprehensive Variance Analysis with Incomplete Data; Journal Entries [LO2, LO3, LO4, LO7]

eXcel

Maple Products, Ltd., manufactures a super-strong hockey stick. The standard cost of one hockey stick is:

	Standard Quantity or Hours	Standard Price or Rate	Standard Cost
Direct materials	? feet	$3.00 per foot	$?
Direct labor	2 hours	? per hour	?
Variable manufacturing overhead	? hours	$1.30 per hour	?
Total standard cost			$27.00

Last year, 8,000 hockey sticks were produced and sold. Selected cost data relating to last year's operations follow:

	Dr.	Cr.
Accounts payable—direct materials purchased (60,000 feet)		$174,000
Wages payable (? hours)		$79,200*
Work in process—direct materials	$115,200	
Direct labor rate variance		$3,300
Variable overhead efficiency variance	$650	

*Relates to the actual direct labor cost for the year.

The following additional information is available for last year's operations:

a. No materials were on hand at the start of last year. Some of the materials purchased during the year were still on hand in the warehouse at the end of the year.
b. The variable manufacturing overhead rate is based on direct labor-hours. Total actual variable manufacturing overhead cost for last year was $19,800.
c. Actual direct materials usage for last year exceeded the standard by 0.2 feet per stick.

Required:

1. For direct materials:
   a. Compute the price and quantity variances for last year.
   b. Prepare journal entries to record all activities relating to direct materials for last year.
2. For direct labor:
   a. Verify the rate variance given above and compute the efficiency variance for last year.
   b. Prepare a journal entry to record activity relating to direct labor for last year.
3. Compute the variable overhead spending variance for last year and verify the variable overhead efficiency variance given above.
4. State possible causes of each variance that you have computed.
5. Prepare a standard cost card for one hockey stick.

eXcel

PROBLEM 10–26 Comprehensive Variance Analysis [LO1, LO2, LO3, LO4]
Highland Company produces a lightweight backpack that is popular with college students. Standard variable costs relating to a single backpack are given below:

	Standard Quantity or Hours	Standard Price or Rate	Standard Cost
Direct materials	?	$6 per yard	$?
Direct labor	?	?	?
Variable manufacturing overhead	?	$3 per direct labor-hour	?
Total standard cost			$?

Overhead is applied to production on the basis of direct labor-hours. During March, 1,000 backpacks were manufactured and sold. Selected information relating to the month's production is given below:

	Materials Used	Direct Labor	Variable Manufacturing Overhead
Total standard cost allowed*	$16,800	$10,500	$4,200
Actual costs incurred	$15,000	?	$3,600
Materials price variance	?		
Materials quantity variance	$ 1,200 U		
Labor rate variance		?	
Labor efficiency variance		?	
Variable overhead spending variance			?
Variable overhead efficiency variance			?

*For the month's production.

The following additional information is available for March's production:

Actual direct labor-hours	1,500
Standard overhead rate per direct labor-hour	$3.00
Standard price of one yard of materials	$6.00
Difference between standard and actual cost per backpack produced during March	$0.15 F

Required:

1. What is the standard cost of a single backpack?
2. What was the actual cost per backpack produced during March?
3. How many yards of material are required at standard per backpack?
4. What was the materials price variance for March?
5. What is the standard direct labor rate per hour?
6. What was the labor rate variance for March? The labor efficiency variance?
7. What was the variable overhead spending variance for March? The variable overhead efficiency variance?
8. Prepare a standard cost card for one backpack.

PROBLEM 10–27 Variance Analysis and Internal Business Process Performance Measures [LO2, LO3, LO4, LO6]

"I've never seen such awful results," roared Ben Carrick, manufacturing vice president of Vorelli Industries. "I thought JIT and automation were supposed to make us more efficient, but just look at last month's efficiency report on Zets, our major product in this plant. The labor efficiency variance was $120,000 *unfavorable.* That's four times higher than it's ever been before. If you add on the $102,000 unfavorable materials price variance on Zets, that's over $220,000 down the drain in a single month on just one product. Have you people in purchasing and production lost control over everything?"

"Now take it easy, Ben," replied Sandi Shipp, the company's purchasing agent. "We knew when we adopted JIT that our material costs would go up somewhat. But we're locking onto the very best suppliers, and they're making deliveries three times a day for our Zets product. In a few months, we'll be able to offset most of our higher purchasing costs by completely vacating three rented warehouses."

"And I know our labor efficiency variance looks bad," responded Raul Duvall, the company's production superintendent, "but it doesn't tell the whole story. With JIT flow lines and our new equipment, we've never been more efficient in the plant."

"How can you say you're efficient when you took 90,000 direct labor-hours to produce just 30,000 Zets last month?" asked Ben Carrick. "That works out to be 3 hours per unit, but according to the standard cost card you should be able to produce a Zet in just 2.5 hours. Do you call that efficient?"

"The problem is that the president wants us to use JIT on the finished goods side of the plant as well as on the raw materials side," explained Raul. "So we're trying to gear production to demand, but at the moment we have to cut production back somewhat in order to work off our finished goods inventory of Zets. This will go on for several more months before we'll be able to get production completely in balance with current demand. And don't forget that our line people aren't just standing around when their machines are idle. Under the new system, they're doing their own inspections and they do maintenance on their own equipment."

"It had better *not* go on for several more months," roared Ben Carrick, "at least not if you people down in production want any bonuses this year. I've been looking at these reports for 30 years, and I know inefficiency when I see it. Let's get things back under control."

After leaving Ben Carrick's office, Raul Duvall has approached you for help in developing some performance measures that will show the actual efficiency of the company's production process. Working with Raul, you have gathered the following information:

a. The company manufactures several products in this plant. A standard cost card for Zets is given below:

	Standard Quantity or Hours	Standard Price or Rate	Standard Cost
Direct materials	18 feet	$3.00 per foot	$54.00
Direct labor	2.5 hours	$8.00 per hour	20.00
Variable manufacturing overhead	2.5 hours	$2.80 per hour	7.00
Total standard cost			$81.00

b. During June, the most recent month, the company purchased 510,000 feet of material for production of Zets at a cost of $3.20 per foot. All of this material was used in the production of 30,000 units during the month. A large part of the production process is now automated, and the company is experiencing less waste each month.
c. The company maintains a stable workforce to produce Zets. Persons who previously were inspectors and on the maintenance crew have been reassigned as direct labor workers. During June, 90,000 hours were logged by direct labor workers on the Zets flow lines. The average pay rate was $7.85 per hour.
d. Variable manufacturing overhead cost is assigned to products on the basis of direct labor-hours. During June, the company incurred $207,000 in variable manufacturing overhead costs associated with the manufacture of Zets.
e. Demand for Zets is increasing over time, and top management is discussing the possibility of constructing additional production facilities.
f. The following information has been gathered from computers located on the production line. This information is expressed in hours per unit of the Zets product.

   Processing: As workers have become more familiar with the new equipment and procedures, average processing time per unit has declined over the last three months, from 2.6 hours in April, to 2.5 hours in May, to 2.4 hours in June.

   Inspection: Workers are now directly responsible for quality control, which accounts for the following changes in inspection time per unit over the last three months: April, 1.3 hours; May, 0.9 hours; and June, 0.1 hours.

   Movement of goods: With the change to JIT flow lines, goods now move shorter distances between machines. Move time per unit over the past three months has been: April, 1.9 hours; May, 1.4 hours; and June, 0.6 hours.

   Queue time in cells: Better coordination of production with demand has resulted in less queue time as goods move along the production line. The data for the last three months are: April, 8.2 hours; May, 5.2 hours; and June, 1.9 hours.

Required:
1. Compute the materials price and quantity variances using traditional variance analysis. Is the decrease in waste apparent in this computation? Explain. If the company wants to compute the materials price variance, what should be done to make this computation more appropriate?
2. Compute the direct labor rate and efficiency variances using traditional variance analysis. Do you agree with Ben Carrick that the efficiency variance is still appropriate as a measure of performance for the company? Explain why you do or do not agree.
3. Compute the variable manufacturing overhead spending and efficiency variances using traditional variance analysis. Would you expect that a correlation still exists between direct labor and the incurrence of variable manufacturing overhead cost in the company? Explain, using data from your variance computations to support your position.
4. Compute the following for April, May, and June for Zets:
   a. The throughput time per unit.
   b. The manufacturing cycle efficiency (MCE).
5. Which performance measures do you think are more appropriate in this situation—the labor efficiency variance or throughput time per unit and manufacturing cycle efficiency?

PROBLEM 10–28 Building a Balanced Scorecard [LO5]

Lost Peak ski resort was for many years a small, family-owned resort serving day skiers from nearby towns. Lost Peak was recently acquired by Western Resorts, a major ski resort operator. The new owners have plans to upgrade the resort into a destination resort for vacationers. As part of this plan, the new owners would like to make major improvements in the Powder 8 Lodge, the resort's on-the-hill cafeteria. The menu at the lodge is very limited—hamburgers, hot dogs, chili, tuna fish sandwiches, pizzas, french fries, and packaged snacks. With little competition, the previous owners of the resort had felt no urgency to upgrade the food service at the lodge. If skiers want lunch on the mountain, the only alternatives are the Powder 8 Lodge or a brown bag lunch brought from home.

As part of the deal when acquiring Lost Peak, Western Resorts agreed to retain all of the current employees of the resort. The manager of the lodge, while hardworking and enthusiastic, has very little experience in the restaurant business. The manager is responsible for selecting the menu, finding and training employees, and overseeing daily operations. The kitchen staff prepare food and wash dishes. The dining room staff take orders, serve as cashiers, and clean the dining room area.

Shortly after taking over Lost Peak, management of Western Resorts held a day-long meeting with all of the employees of the Powder 8 Lodge to discuss the future of the ski resort and the new management's plans for the lodge. At the end of this meeting, management and lodge employees created a balanced scorecard for the lodge that would help guide operations for the coming ski season. Almost everyone who participated in the meeting seemed to be enthusiastic about the scorecard and management's plans for the lodge.

The following performance measures were included on the balanced scorecard for the Powder 8 Lodge:

a. Weekly Powder 8 Lodge sales
b. Weekly Powder 8 Lodge profit
c. Number of menu items
d. Dining area cleanliness as rated by a representative from Western Resorts management
e. Customer satisfaction with menu choices as measured by customer surveys
f. Customer satisfaction with service as measured by customer surveys
g. Average time to take an order
h. Average time to prepare an order
i. Percentage of kitchen staff completing basic cooking course at the local community college
j. Percentage of dining room staff completing basic hospitality course at the local community college

Western Resorts will pay for the costs of staff attending courses at the local community college.

Required:

1. Using the above performance measures, construct a balanced scorecard for the Powder 8 Lodge. Use Exhibit 10–12 as a guide. Use arrows to show causal links and indicate with a + or − whether the performance measure should increase or decrease.
2. What hypotheses are built into the balanced scorecard for the Powder 8 Lodge? Which of these hypotheses do you believe are most questionable? Why?
3. How will management know if one of the hypotheses underlying the balanced scorecard is false?

PROBLEM 10–29 Perverse Effects of Some Performance Measures [LO5]

There is often more than one way to improve a performance measure. Unfortunately, some of the actions taken by managers to make their performance look better may actually harm the organization. For example, suppose the marketing department is held responsible only for increasing the performance measure "total revenues." Increases in total revenues may be achieved by working harder and smarter, but they can also usually be achieved by simply cutting prices. The increase in volume from cutting prices almost always results in greater total revenues; however, it does not always lead to greater total profits. Those who design performance measurement systems need to keep in mind that managers who are under pressure to perform may take actions to improve performance measures that have negative consequences elsewhere.

Required:

For each of the following situations, describe actions that managers might take to show improvement in the performance measure but which do not actually lead to improvement in the organization's overall performance.

1. Concerned with the slow rate at which new products are brought to market, top management of a consumer electronics company introduces a new performance measure—speed-to-market. The research and development department is given responsibility for this performance measure, which measures the average amount of time a product is in development before it is released to the market for sale.
2. The CEO of a telephone company has been under public pressure from city officials to fix the large number of public pay phones that do not work. The company's repair people complain that the problem is vandalism and damage caused by theft of coins from coin boxes—particularly in high-crime areas in the city. The CEO says she wants the problem solved and has pledged to city officials that there will be substantial improvement by the end of the year. To ensure that this is done, she makes the managers in charge of installing and maintaining pay phones responsible for increasing the percentage of public pay phones that are fully functional.
3. A manufacturing company has been plagued by the chronic failure to ship orders to customers by the promised date. To solve this problem, the production manager has been given the responsibility of increasing the percentage of orders shipped on time. When a customer calls in an order, the production manager and the customer agree to a delivery date. If the order is not completed by that date, it is counted as a late shipment.

4. Concerned with the productivity of employees, the board of directors of a large multinational corporation has dictated that the manager of each subsidiary will be held responsible for increasing the revenue per employee of his or her subsidiary.

PROBLEM 10–30 Internal Business Process Performance Measures [LO6]

Tombro Industries is in the process of automating one of its plants and developing a flexible manufacturing system. The company is finding it necessary to make many changes in operating procedures. Progress has been slow, particularly in trying to develop new performance measures for the factory.

In an effort to evaluate performance and determine where improvements can be made, management has gathered the following data relating to activities over the last four months:

	Month			
	1	2	3	4
Quality control measures:				
Number of defects	185	163	124	91
Number of warranty claims	46	39	30	27
Number of customer complaints	102	96	79	58
Material control measures:				
Purchase order lead time	8 days	7 days	5 days	4 days
Scrap as a percent of total cost	1%	1%	2%	3%
Machine performance measures:				
Machine downtime as a percentage of availability	3%	4%	4%	6%
Use as a percentage of availability	95%	92%	89%	85%
Setup time (hours)	8	10	11	12
Delivery performance measures:				
Throughput time	?	?	?	?
Manufacturing cycle efficiency (MCE)	?	?	?	?
Delivery cycle time	?	?	?	?
Percentage of on-time deliveries	96%	95%	92%	89%

The president has read in industry journals that throughput time, MCE, and delivery cycle time are important measures of performance, but no one is sure how they are computed. You have been asked to assist the company, and you have gathered the following data relating to these measures:

	Average per Month (in days)			
	1	2	3	4
Wait time per order before start of production	9.0	11.5	12.0	14.0
Inspection time per unit	0.8	0.7	0.7	0.7
Process time per unit	2.1	2.0	1.9	1.8
Queue time per unit	2.8	4.4	6.0	7.0
Move time per unit	0.3	0.4	0.4	0.5

As part of its modernization process, the company is also moving toward a just-in-time (JIT) inventory system. Over the next year, the company hopes to have the bulk of its raw materials and parts on a JIT basis.

Required:

1. For each month, compute the following performance measures:
   a. Throughput time.
   b. MCE.
   c. Delivery cycle time.
2. Using the performance measures given in the main body of the problem and the performance measures computed in (1) above, do the following:
   a. Identify areas where the company seems to be improving.
   b. Identify areas where the company seems to be deteriorating.
3. Refer to the inspection time, process time, and so forth, given above for month 4.

a. Assume that in month 5 the inspection time, process time, and so forth, are the same as for month 4, except that the company is able to completely eliminate the queue time during production. Compute the new throughput time and MCE.

b. Assume that in month 6 the inspection time, process time, and so forth, are the same as in month 4, except that the company is able to eliminate both the queue time during production and the inspection time. Compute the new throughput time and MCE.

PROBLEM 10–31 Comprehensive Variance Analysis [LO2, LO3, LO4]

Marvel Parts, Inc., manufactures auto accessories. One of the company's products is a set of seat covers that can be adjusted to fit nearly any small car. The company has a standard cost system in use for all of its products. According to the standards that have been set for the seat covers, the factory should work 2,850 hours each month to produce 1,900 sets of covers. The standard costs associated with this level of production are:

	Total	Per Set of Covers
Direct materials	$42,560	$22.40
Direct labor	$17,100	9.00
Variable manufacturing overhead (based on direct labor-hours)	$6,840	3.60
		$35.00

During August, the factory worked only 2,800 direct labor-hours and produced 2,000 sets of covers. The following actual costs were recorded during the month:

	Total	Per Set of Covers
Direct materials (12,000 yards)	$45,600	$22.80
Direct labor	$18,200	9.10
Variable manufacturing overhead	$7,000	3.50
		$35.40

At standard, each set of covers should require 5.6 yards of material. All of the materials purchased during the month were used in production.

Required:

Compute the following variances for August:

1. The materials price and quantity variances.
2. The labor rate and efficiency variances.
3. The variable overhead spending and efficiency variances.

PROBLEM 10–32 Developing Standard Costs [LO1]

ColdKing Company is a small producer of fruit-flavored frozen desserts. For many years, ColdKing's products have had strong regional sales on the basis of brand recognition; however, other companies have begun marketing similar products in the area, and price competition has become increasingly intense. John Wakefield, the company's controller, is planning to implement a standard cost system for ColdKing and has gathered considerable information from his co-workers on production and material requirements for ColdKing's products. Wakefield believes that the use of standard costing will allow ColdKing to improve cost control and make better pricing decisions.

ColdKing's most popular product is raspberry sherbet. The sherbet is produced in 10-gallon batches, and each batch requires 6 quarts of good raspberries. The fresh raspberries are sorted by hand before they enter the production process. Because of imperfections in the raspberries and normal spoilage, 1 quart of berries is discarded for every 4 quarts of acceptable berries. Three minutes is the standard direct labor time for the sorting that is required to obtain 1 quart of acceptable raspberries. The acceptable raspberries are then blended with the other ingredients; blending requires 12 minutes of direct labor time per batch. After blending, the sherbet is packaged in quart containers. Wakefield has gathered the following pricing information:

a. ColdKing purchases raspberries at a cost of $0.80 per quart. All other ingredients cost a total of $0.45 per gallon of sherbet.
b. Direct labor is paid at the rate of $9.00 per hour.
c. The total cost of direct material and direct labor required to package the sherbet is $0.38 per quart.

Required:

1. Develop the standard cost for the direct cost components (materials, labor, and packaging) of a 10-gallon batch of raspberry sherbet. The standard cost should identify the standard quantity, standard rate, and standard cost per batch for each direct cost component of a batch of raspberry sherbet.
2. As part of the implementation of a standard cost system at ColdKing, John Wakefield plans to train those responsible for maintaining the standards on how to use variance analysis. Wakefield is particularly concerned with the causes of unfavorable variances.
   a. Discuss possible causes of unfavorable materials price variances and identify the individual(s) who should be held responsible for these variances.
   b. Discuss possible causes of unfavorable labor efficiency variances and identify the individual(s) who should be held responsible for these variances.

(CMA, adapted)

Cases

CASE 10–33 Balanced Scorecard [LO5]

Haglund Department Store is located in the downtown area of a small city. While the store had been profitable for many years, it is facing increasing competition from large national chains that have set up stores on the outskirts of the city. Recently the downtown area has been undergoing revitalization, and the owners of Haglund Department Store are somewhat optimistic that profitability can be restored.

In an attempt to accelerate the return to profitability, management of Haglund Department Store is in the process of designing a balanced scorecard for the company. Management believes the company should focus on two key problems. First, customers are taking longer and longer to pay the bills they incur using the department store's charge card, and the company has far more bad debts than are normal for the industry. If this problem were solved, the company would have more cash to make much needed renovations. Investigation has revealed that much of the problem with late payments and unpaid bills results from customers disputing incorrect charges on their bills. These incorrect charges usually occur because salesclerks incorrectly enter data on the charge account slip. Second, the company has been incurring large losses on unsold seasonal apparel. Such items are ordinarily resold at a loss to discount stores that specialize in such distress items.

The meeting in which the balanced scorecard approach was discussed was disorganized and ineffectively led—possibly because no one other than one of the vice presidents had read anything about how to build a balanced scorecard. Nevertheless, a number of potential performance measures were suggested by various managers. These potential performance measures are:

a. Percentage of charge account bills containing errors.
b. Percentage of salesclerks trained to correctly enter data on charge account slips.
c. Average age of accounts receivables.
d. Profit per employee.
e. Customer satisfaction with accuracy of charge account bills from monthly customer survey.
f. Total sales revenue.
g. Sales per employee.
h. Travel expenses for buyers for trips to fashion shows.
i. Unsold inventory at the end of the season as a percentage of total cost of sales.
j. Courtesy shown by junior staff members to senior staff members based on surveys of senior staff.
k. Percentage of suppliers making just-in-time deliveries.
l. Sales per square foot of floor space.
m. Written-off accounts receivable (bad debts) as a percentage of sales.
n. Quality of food in the staff cafeteria based on staff surveys.
o. Percentage of employees who have attended the city's cultural diversity workshop.
p. Total profit.

Required:

1. As someone with more knowledge of the balanced scorecard than almost anyone else in the company, you have been asked to build an integrated balanced scorecard. In your scorecard, use only performance measures listed previously. You do not have to use all of the performance measures suggested by the managers, but you should build a balanced scorecard that reveals a strategy for dealing with the problems with accounts receivable and with unsold merchandise. Construct the balanced scorecard following the format used in Exhibit 10–12. Do not be concerned with whether a specific performance measure falls within the learning and growth, internal business process, customer, or financial perspective. However, use arrows to show the causal links between performance measures within your balanced scorecard and explain whether the performance measures should show increases or decreases.
2. Assume that the company adopts your balanced scorecard. After operating for a year, some performance measures show improvements, but not others. What should management do next?
3. *a.* Suppose that customers express greater satisfaction with the accuracy of their charge account bills but the performance measures for the average age of accounts receivable and for bad debts do not improve. Explain why this might happen.
   b. Suppose that the performance measures for the average age of accounts receivable, bad debts, and unsold inventory improve, but total profits do not. Explain why this might happen. Assume in your answer that the explanation lies within the company.

CASE 10–34 Ethics and the Manager; Rigging Standards [LO1]

Stacy Cummins, the newly hired controller at Merced Home Products, Inc., was disturbed by what she had discovered about the standard costs at the Home Security Division. In looking over the past several years of quarterly earnings reports at the Home Security Division, she noticed that the first-quarter earnings were always poor, the second-quarter earnings were slightly better, the third-quarter earnings were again slightly better, and the fourth quarter always ended with a spectacular performance in which the Home Security Division managed to meet or exceed its target profit for the year. She also was concerned to find letters from the company's external auditors to top management warning about an unusual use of standard costs at the Home Security Division.

When Ms. Cummins ran across these letters, she asked the assistant controller, Gary Farber, if he knew what was going on at the Home Security Division. Gary said that it was common knowledge in the company that the vice president in charge of the Home Security Division, Preston Lansing, had rigged the standards at his division in order to produce the same quarterly earnings pattern every year. According to company policy, variances are taken directly to the income statement as an adjustment to cost of goods sold.

Favorable variances have the effect of increasing net operating income, and unfavorable variances have the effect of decreasing net operating income. Lansing had rigged the standards so that there were always large favorable variances. Company policy was a little vague about when these variances have to be reported on the divisional income statements. While the intent was clearly to recognize variances on the income statement in the period in which they arise, nothing in the company's accounting manuals actually explicitly required this. So for many years Lansing had followed a practice of saving up the favorable variances and using them to create a nice smooth pattern of earnings growth in the first three quarters, followed by a big "Christmas present" of an extremely good fourth quarter. (Financial reporting regulations forbid carrying variances forward from one year to the next on the annual audited financial statements, so all of the variances must appear on the divisional income statement by the end of the year.)

Ms. Cummins was concerned about these revelations and attempted to bring up the subject with the president of Merced Home Products but was told that "we all know what Lansing's doing, but as long as he continues to turn in such good reports, don't bother him." When Ms. Cummins asked if the board of directors was aware of the situation, the president somewhat testily replied, "Of course they are aware."

Required:

1. How did Preston Lansing probably "rig" the standard costs—are the standards set too high or too low? Explain.
2. Should Preston Lansing be permitted to continue his practice of managing reported earnings?
3. What should Stacy Cummins do in this situation?

CASE 10–35 (Appendix 10A) Variances and Journal Entries from Incomplete Data [LO2, LO3, LO7]

You are employed by Olster Company, which manufactures products for the senior citizen market. As a rising young executive in the company, you are scheduled to make a presentation in a few hours to your superior. This presentation relates to last week's production of Maxitol, a popular health tonic that is manufactured by Olster Company. Unfortunately, while studying ledger sheets and variance summaries by poolside in the company's fitness area, you were bumped and dropped the papers into the pool. In desperation, you fished the papers from the water, but you have discovered that only the following fragments are readable:

Maxitol—Standard Cost Card

	Standard Quantity or Hours	Standard Price or Rate	Standard Cost
Material A	6 gallons	$8 per gall	$
Material B		per pou	
Direct labor		per ho	
Standard cost per batc			$99.50

Maxitol—General Ledger Accounts

Raw Materials—Material A

Debit	Credit
Bal. 3/1 0	
Bal. 3/7 2,000	

Work in Process

Debit	Credit
Bal. 3/1 0	
Material A 5,760	
Bal. 3/7 0	

Material A—Price Variance

Debit	Credit
	300

Wages Payable

Debit	Credit
	4,100

Raw Materials—Material B

Debit	Credit
Bal. 3/1 700	2,500
Bal. 3/7 1,400	

Labor Rate Variance

Debit	Credit
500	

Material B—Quantity Variance

Debit	Credit
100	

Accounts Payable

Debit	Credit
	11,460

You remember that the accounts payable are for purchases of both Material A and Material B. You also remember that only 10 direct labor workers are involved in the production of Maxitol and that each worked 40 hours last week. The wages payable above are for wages earned by these workers.

You realize that to be ready for your presentation, you must reconstruct all data relating to Maxitol very quickly. As a start, you have called purchasing and found that 1,000 gallons of Material A and 800 pounds of Material B were purchased last week.

Required:

1. How many batches of Maxitol were produced last week? (This is a key figure; be sure it's right before going on.)
2. For Material A:
   a. What was the cost of Material A purchased last week?
   b. How many gallons were used in production last week?
   c. What was the quantity variance?
   d. Prepare journal entries to record all activity relating to Material A for last week.

3. For Material B:
   a. What is the standard cost per pound for Material B?
   b. How many pounds of Material B were used in production last week? How many pounds should have been used at standard?
   c. What is the standard quantity of Material B per batch?
   d. What was the price variance for Material B last week?
   e. Prepare journal entries to record all activity relating to Material B for last week.
4. For direct labor:
   a. What is the standard rate per direct labor-hour?
   b. What are the standard hours per batch?
   c. What were the standard hours allowed for last week's production?
   d. What was the labor efficiency variance for last week?
   e. Prepare a journal entry to record all activity relating to direct labor for last week.
5. Complete the standard cost card shown above for one batch of Maxitol.

CASE 10–36 Behavioral Impact of Standard Costs and Variances

Terry Travers is the manufacturing supervisor of Aurora Manufacturing Company, which produces a variety of plastic products. Some of these products are standard items that are listed in the company's catalog, while others are made to customer specifications. Each month, Travers receives a performance report showing the budget for the month, the actual activity, and the variance between budget and actual. Part of Travers' annual performance evaluation is based on his department's performance against budget. Aurora's purchasing manager, Sally Christensen, also receives monthly performance reports and she, too, is evaluated in part on the basis of these reports.

The monthly reports for June had just been distributed when Travers met Christensen in the hallway outside their offices. Scowling, Travers began the conversation, "I see we have another set of monthly performance reports hand-delivered by that not very nice junior employee in the budget office. He seemed pleased to tell me that I'm in trouble with my performance again."

Christensen: I got the same treatment. All I ever hear about are the things I've done wrong. Now I'll have to spend a lot of time reviewing the report and preparing explanations. The worst part is that it's now the 21st of July so the information is almost a month old, and we have to spend all this time on history.

Travers: My biggest gripe is that our production activity varies a lot from month to month, but we're given an annual budget that's written in stone. Last month we were shut down for three days when a strike delayed delivery of the basic ingredient used in our plastic formulation, and we had already exhausted our inventory. You know about that problem, though, because we asked you to call all over the country to find an alternate source of supply. When we got what we needed on a rush basis, we had to pay more than we normally do.

Christensen: I expect problems like that to pop up from time to time—that's part of my job—but now we'll both have to take a careful look at our reports to see where the charges are reflected for that rush order. Every month I spend more time making sure I should be charged for each item reported than I do making plans for my department's daily work. It's really frustrating to see charges for things I have no control over.

Travers: The way we get information doesn't help, either. I don't get copies of the reports you get, yet a lot of what I do is affected by your department, and by most of our other departments. Why do the budget and accounting people assume that I should only be told about my operations even though the president regularly gives us pep talks about how we all need to work together as a team?

Christensen: I seem to get more reports than I need, and I am never asked to comment on them until top management calls me on the carpet about my department's shortcomings. Do you ever hear comments when your department shines?

Travers: I guess they don't have time to review the good news. One of my problems is that all the reports are in dollars and cents. I work with people, machines, and materials. I need information to help me solve *this* month's problems—not another report of the dollars expended *last* month or the month before.

Required:

1. Based on the conversation between Terry Travers and Sally Christensen, describe the likely motivation and behavior of these two employees resulting from Aurora Manufacturing Company's standard cost and variance reporting system.
2. When properly implemented, both employees and companies should benefit from a system involving standard costs and variances.

a. Describe the benefits that can be realized from a standard cost system.

b. Based on the situation presented above, recommend ways for Aurora Manufacturing Company to improve its standard cost and variance reporting system so as to increase employee motivation.

(CMA, adapted)

Group and Internet Exercises

GROUP EXERCISE 10–37 Standards in an Auto Repair Shop

Make an appointment to meet with the manager of an auto repair shop that uses standards. In most cases, this would be an auto repair shop that is affiliated with a national chain such as Firestone or Sears or the service department of a new-car dealer.

Required:

At the scheduled meeting, seek answers to the following questions:

1. How are standards set?
2. Are standards practical or ideal?
3. How are the standards used?
4. Is the actual time taken to complete a task compared to the standard time?
5. What are the consequences of unfavorable variances? Of favorable variances?
6. Do the standards and variances create any potential problems?

GROUP EXERCISE 10–38 Standards in Practice

Identify a company in your local area that is likely to use standards such as a commercial bakery, commercial printer, chain restaurant, or manufacturer. After verifying that the company uses standards, make an appointment to meet with the manager, controller, or chief financial officer of the organization.

Required:

At the scheduled meeting, seek answers to the following questions:

1. How are standards set?
2. Are standards practical or ideal?
3. How are the standards used?
4. What are the consequences of unfavorable variances? Of favorable variances?
5. Do the standards and variances create any potential problems?

INTERNET EXERCISE 10–39

As you know, the World Wide Web is a medium that is constantly evolving. Sites come and go, and change without notice. To enable the periodic updating of site addresses, this problem has been posted to the textbook website (www.mhhe.com/garrison11e). After accessing the site, enter the Student Center and select this chapter. Select and complete the Internet Exercise.

Chapter

11

Flexible Budgets and Overhead Analysis

LEARNING OBJECTIVES

After studying Chapter 11, you should be able to:

LO1 Prepare a flexible budget and explain the advantages of the flexible budget approach over the static budget approach.

LO2 Prepare a performance report for both variable and fixed overhead costs using the flexible budget approach.

LO3 Use the flexible budget to prepare a variable overhead performance report containing only a spending variance.

LO4 Use the flexible budget to prepare a variable overhead performance report containing both a spending and an efficiency variance.

LO5 Compute the predetermined overhead rate and apply overhead to products in a standard cost system.

LO6 Compute and interpret the fixed overhead budget and volume variances.

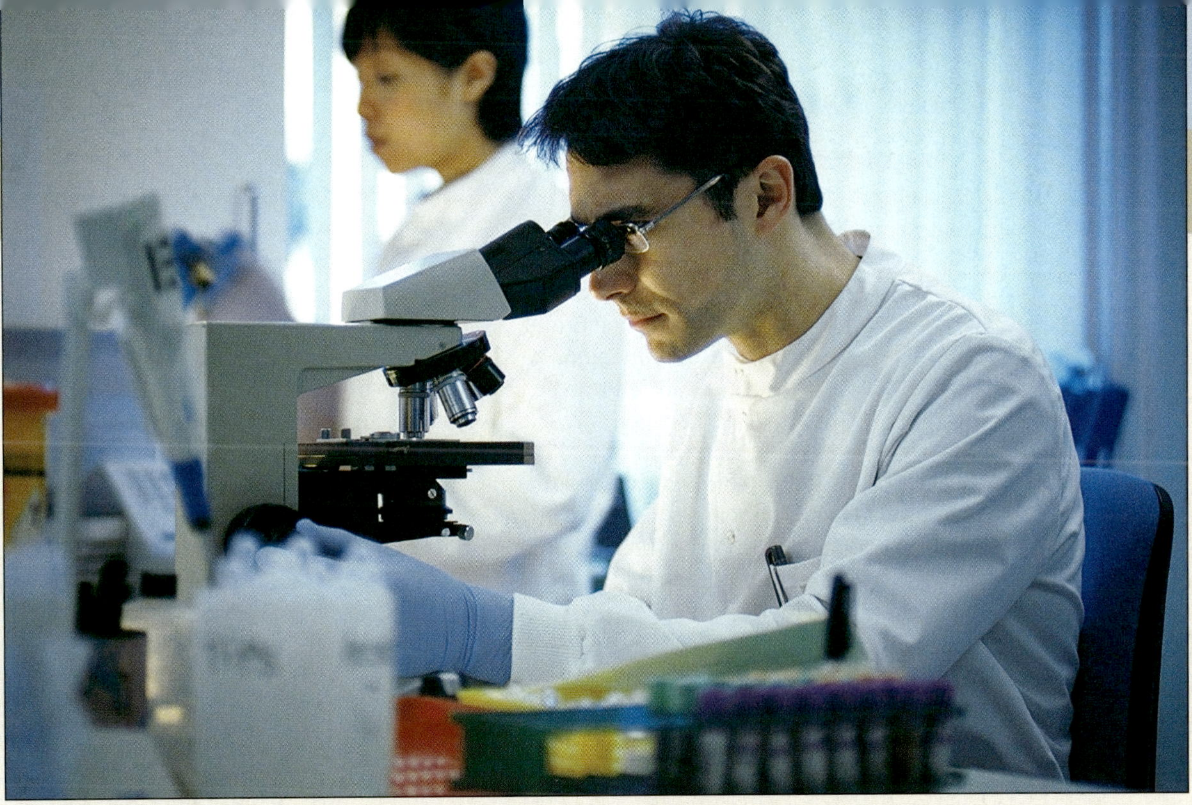

How Much Is Too Much?

BUSINESS FOCUS

Dr. Salinas had just been unexpectedly appointed director of Providence Medical Center. The previous director, who had instituted tight budgetary controls, was extremely unpopular with the hospital's staff, which led to his removal by the hospital's board of directors. Dr. Salinas suspected that he had been chosen for the job because of his popularity rather than any innate management ability. He thought of himself as a physician rather than as a manager.

Shortly after taking over as director, the hospital's lab supervisor came storming into Dr. Salinas' office, threw a computer-generated report on Dr. Salinas' desk, and angrily stated: "Here, look at this report. It says we spent too much money in the Lab Department. We spent 5% more than had been authorized in the annual budget. Well, of course we did! Practically every department in the hospital asked for more tests than they had predicted at budget time! What are we supposed to do, refuse to run tests as soon as we go over budget?" Dr. Salinas responded: "Of course not. You have to run the tests. However, we also have to keep some control over our spending. On the other hand, I agree it isn't fair to hold you to the original budget. I don't see the solution right now, but I will work on it." ■

Controlling overhead costs is a major preoccupation of managers in business, in government, and in not-for-profit organizations. Overhead is a major cost, if not *the* major cost, in many organizations. For example, it costs Microsoft very little to make copies of its software for sale to customers; almost all of Microsoft's costs are in research and development and marketing—elements of overhead. Or consider Disney World. The only direct cost of serving a particular guest is the cost of the food the guest consumes at the park; virtually all of the other costs of running the amusement park are overhead. Even Boeing, a manufacturer, has huge amounts of overhead in the form of engineering salaries, buildings, insurance, administrative salaries, and marketing costs.

IN BUSINESS

FOCUS ON OVERHEAD COSTS

Overhead costs now account for as much as 66% of the costs incurred by companies in service industries and up to 37% of the total costs of manufacturers. Consequently, overhead reduction is a recurring theme in many organizations. However, the extent of the reductions must be considered in light of competitive pressures to improve services and product quality. Managers must avoid cutting costs that add value to the organization.

Source: Nick Develin, "Unlocking Overhead Value," *Management Accounting*, December 1999, pp. 22–34.

Since overhead is usually made up of many separate costs, including everything from disposable coffee cups in the visitors' waiting area to the president's salary, it is more difficult to control than direct materials and direct labor. Overhead control is further complicated by the fact that overhead costs can be variable, fixed, or a mixture of variable and fixed. However, these complications can be largely overcome by using flexible budgets. In this chapter, we study flexible budgets in detail and learn how they can be used to control costs. We also expand the study of overhead variances that we started in Chapter 10.

Flexible Budgets

LEARNING OBJECTIVE 1
Prepare a flexible budget and explain the advantages of the flexible budget approach over the static budget approach.

Characteristics of a Flexible Budget

The budgets that we studied in Chapter 9 were *static budgets.* A **static budget** is prepared at the beginning of the budgeting period and is valid for only the planned level of activity. A static budget approach is suitable for planning, but it is inadequate for evaluating how well costs are controlled. If the actual level of activity during a period differs from what was planned, it would be misleading to simply compare actual costs to the static budget. If activity is higher than expected, variable costs should be higher than expected; and if activity is lower than expected, variable costs should be lower than expected.

Flexible budgets take into account changes in costs that should occur as a consequence of changes in activity. A **flexible budget** provides estimates of what costs should be for any level of activity within a specified range. When a flexible budget is used in performance evaluation, actual costs are compared to what the *costs should have been for the actual level of activity during the period* rather than to the budgeted costs from the original budget. This is a very important distinction—particularly for variable costs. If adjustments for the level of activity are not made, it is very difficult to interpret discrepancies between budgeted and actual costs.

EXHIBIT 11–1

RICK'S HAIRSTYLING Static Budget For the Month Ended March 31	
Budgeted number of client-visits	5,000
Budgeted variable overhead costs:	
Hairstyling supplies (@$1.20 per client-visit)	$ 6,000
Client gratuities (@$4.00 per client-visit)	20,000
Electricity (@$0.20 per client-visit)	1,000
Total variable overhead cost	27,000
Budgeted fixed overhead costs:	
Support staff wages and salaries	8,000
Rent	12,000
Insurance	1,000
Utilities other than electricity	500
Total fixed overhead cost	21,500
Total budgeted overhead cost	$48,500

Deficiencies of the Static Budget

To illustrate the difference between a static budget and a flexible budget, consider the case of Rick's Hairstyling, an upscale hairstyling salon located in Beverly Hills that is owned and managed by Rick Manzi. The salon has very loyal customers—many of whom are associated with the film industry. Despite the glamour associated with his salon, Rick is a very shrewd businessman. Recently he has been attempting to get better control of his overhead, and at the urging of his accounting and business adviser Victoria Kho, he has begun to prepare monthly budgets. Victoria Kho is an accountant in independent practice who specializes in small service-oriented businesses like Rick's Hairstyling.

At the end of February, Rick carefully prepared the March budget for overhead items that appears in Exhibit 11–1. Rick believes that the number of customers served in a month is the best way to measure the overall level of activity in his salon. Rick refers to these visits as client-visits. A customer who comes into the salon and has his or her hair styled is counted as one client-visit. After some discussion with Victoria Kho, Rick identified three major categories of variable overhead costs—hairstyling supplies, client gratuities, and electricity—and four major categories of fixed costs—support staff wages and salaries, rent, insurance, and utilities other than electricity. Client gratuities consist of flowers, candies, and glasses of champagne that Rick gives to his customers while they are in the salon. Rick considers electricity to be a variable cost, since almost all of the electricity in the salon is consumed by running blow-dryers, curling irons, and other hairstyling equipment.

To develop the budget for variable overhead, Rick estimated that the average cost per client-visit should be $1.20 for hairstyling supplies, $4.00 for client gratuities, and $0.20 for electricity. Based on his estimate of 5,000 client-visits in March, Rick budgeted for $6,000 ($1.20 per client-visit × 5,000 client-visits) in hairstyling supplies, $20,000 ($4.00 per client-visit × 5,000 client-visits) in client gratuities, and $1,000 ($0.20 per client-visit × 5,000 client-visits) in electricity.

The budget for fixed overhead items was based on Rick's records of how much he had spent on these items in the past. The budget included $8,000 for support staff wages and salaries, $12,000 for rent, $1,000 for insurance, and $500 for utilities other than electricity.

At the end of March, Rick prepared a report comparing actual to budgeted costs. That report appears in Exhibit 11–2. The problem with that report, as Rick immediately

EXHIBIT 11–2

RICK'S HAIRSTYLING
Static Budget Performance Report
For the Month Ended March 31

	Actual	Budgeted	Variance
Client-visits	5,200	5,000	200 F
Variable overhead costs:			
Hairstyling supplies	$ 6,400	$ 6,000	$ 400 U*
Client gratuities	22,300	20,000	2,300 U*
Electricity	1,020	1,000	20 U*
Total variable overhead cost	29,720	27,000	2,720 U*
Fixed overhead costs:			
Support staff wages and salaries	8,100	8,000	100 U
Rent	12,000	12,000	0
Insurance	1,000	1,000	0
Utilities other than electricity	470	500	30 F
Total fixed overhead cost	21,570	21,500	70 U
Total overhead cost	$51,290	$48,500	$2,790 U*

*The cost variances for variable costs and for total overhead are useless for evaluating how well costs were controlled since they have been derived by comparing actual costs at one level of activity to budgeted costs at a different level of activity.

realized, is that it compares costs at one level of activity (5,200 client-visits) to costs at a different level of activity (5,000 client-visits). Since Rick had 200 more client-visits than expected, his variable costs *should* be higher than budgeted. The static budget performance report confuses control over activity and control over costs. From Rick's standpoint, the increase in activity was good and should be counted as a favorable variance, but the increase in activity has an apparently negative impact on the costs in the report. Rick knew that something would have to be done to make the report more meaningful, but he was unsure of what to do. So he made an appointment to meet with Victoria Kho to discuss the next step.

MANAGERIAL ACCOUNTING IN ACTION
The Issue

RICK'S hairstyling salon

Victoria: How is the budgeting going?

Rick: Pretty well. I didn't have any trouble putting together the overhead budget for March. I also made out a report comparing the actual costs for March to the budgeted costs, but that report isn't giving me what I really want to know.

Victoria: Because your actual level of activity didn't match your budgeted activity?

Rick: Right. I know the level of activity shouldn't affect my fixed costs, but we had a lot more client-visits than I had expected and that had to affect my variable costs.

Victoria: So you want to know whether the actual costs are justified by the actual level of activity you had in March?

Rick: Precisely.

Victoria: If you leave your reports and data with me, I can work on it later today, and by tomorrow I'll have a report to show to you. Actually, I have a styling appointment for later this week. Why don't I move my appointment up to tomorrow, and I will bring along the analysis so we can discuss it.

Rick: That's great.

How a Flexible Budget Works

A flexible budget approach recognizes that a budget does not have to be static. Depending on the actual level of activity, a budget can be adjusted to show what costs *should be* for that specific level of activity. To illustrate how flexible budgets work, Victoria

EXHIBIT 11–3
Illustration of the Flexible Budgeting Concept

RICK'S HAIRSTYLING
Flexible Budget
For the Month Ended March 31

Budgeted number of client-visits	5,000				
	Cost Formula (per client-visit)	Activity (in client-visits)			
Overhead Costs		4,900	5,000	5,100	5,200
Variable overhead costs:					
Hairstyling supplies	$1.20	$ 5,880	$ 6,000	$ 6,120	$ 6,240
Client gratuities	4.00	19,600	20,000	20,400	20,800
Electricity (variable)	0.20	980	1,000	1,020	1,040
Total variable overhead cost	$5.40	26,460	27,000	27,540	28,080
Fixed overhead costs:					
Support staff wages and salaries		8,000	8,000	8,000	8,000
Rent		12,000	12,000	12,000	12,000
Insurance		1,000	1,000	1,000	1,000
Utilities other than electricity		500	500	500	500
Total fixed overhead cost		21,500	21,500	21,500	21,500
Total overhead cost		$47,960	$48,500	$49,040	$49,580

prepared the report in Exhibit 11–3. It shows how overhead costs can be expected to change, depending on the monthly level of activity. Within the activity range of 4,900 to 5,200 client-visits, the fixed costs are expected to remain the same. For the variable overhead costs, Victoria multiplied Rick's per-client costs ($1.20 for hairstyling supplies, $4.00 for client gratuities, and $0.20 for electricity) by the appropriate number of client-visits in each column. For example, the $1.20 cost of hairstyling supplies was multiplied by 4,900 client-visits to give the total cost of $5,880 for hairstyling supplies at that level of activity.

Topic Tackler PLUS
11–1

Using the Flexible Budgeting Concept in Performance Evaluation

LEARNING OBJECTIVE 2
Prepare a performance report for both variable and fixed overhead costs using the flexible budget approach.

To get a better idea of how well Rick controlled his variable overhead costs in March, Victoria applied the flexible budgeting concept to create a budget based on the *actual* number of client-visits for the month (Exhibit 11–4). The budget is prepared by multiplying the actual level of activity by the cost formula for each of the variable cost categories. For example, using the $1.20 per client-visit for hairstyling supplies, the total cost for this item *should be* $6,240 for 5,200 client-visits ($1.20 per client-visit × 5,200 client-visits). Since the actual cost for hairstyling supplies was $6,400, the unfavorable variance was $160.

Contrast the flexible budget performance report in Exhibit 11–4 with the static budget approach in Exhibit 11–2. The variance for hairstyling supplies was $400 unfavorable using the static budget approach. However, actual costs at one level of activity were being compared to budgeted costs at a different level of activity. This is like comparing apples to oranges. Because actual activity was higher by 200 client-visits than budgeted activity, the total cost of hairstyling supplies *should* have been $240 ($1.20 per client-visit × 200 client-visits) higher than budgeted. As a result, $240 of the $400 "unfavorable" variance in the static budget performance report in Exhibit 11–2 was spurious.

EXHIBIT 11–4

RICK'S HAIRSTYLING
Flexible Budget Performance Report
For the Month Ended March 31

Budgeted number of client-visits	5,000			
Actual number of client-visits	5,200			
Overhead Costs	Cost Formula (per client-visit)	Actual Costs Incurred for 5,200 Client-Visits	Budget Based on 5,200 Client-Visits	Variance
Variable overhead costs:				
Hairstyling supplies	$1.20	$ 6,400	$ 6,240	$ 160 U
Client gratuities	4.00	22,300	20,800	1,500 U
Electricity (variable)	0.20	1,020	1,040	20 F
Total variable overhead cost	$5.40	29,720	28,080	1,640 U
Fixed overhead costs:				
Support staff wages and salaries		8,100	8,000	100 U
Rent		12,000	12,000	0
Insurance		1,000	1,000	0
Utilities other than electricity		470	500	30 F
Total fixed overhead cost		21,570	21,500	70 U
Total overhead cost		$51,290	$49,580	$1,710 U

In contrast, the flexible budget performance report in Exhibit 11–4 provides a more valid assessment of performance. Apples are compared to apples. Actual costs are compared to what costs should have been at the actual level of activity. When this is done, we see that the variance is $160 unfavorable rather than $400 unfavorable as it was in the original static budget performance report. In some cases, as with electricity in Rick's report, an unfavorable variance may be transformed into a favorable variance when an increase in activity is properly taken into account.

MANAGERIAL ACCOUNTING IN ACTION
The Wrap-Up

RICK'S
hairstyling salon

The following discussion took place the next day at Rick's salon.

Victoria: Let me show you what I've got. [Victoria shows the report contained in Exhibit 11–4.] All I did was multiply the costs per client-visit by the number of client-visits you actually had in March for the variable costs. That allowed me to come up with a better benchmark for what the variable costs should have been.

Rick: That's what you labeled the "budget based on 5,200 client-visits"?

Victoria: That's right. Your original budget was based on 5,000 client-visits, so it understated what the variable overhead costs should be when you actually serve 5,200 customers.

Rick: That's clear enough. These variances aren't quite as shocking as the variances on my first report.

Victoria: Yes, but you still have an unfavorable variance of $1,500 for client gratuities.

Rick: I know how that happened. In March there was a big Democratic Party fund-raising dinner that I forgot about when I prepared the March budget. Everyone in the film industry was there.

Victoria: Even Arnold Schwarzenegger?

Rick: Well, all the Democrats were there. At any rate, to fit all of our regular clients in, we had to push them through here pretty fast. Everyone still got top-rate service, but I felt pretty bad about not being able to spend as much time with each customer. I wanted to give my customers a little extra something to compensate them for the less personal service, so I ordered a lot of flowers which I gave away by the bunch.

Victoria: With the prices you charge, Rick, I am sure the gesture was appreciated.

Rick: One thing bothers me about the report. Why are some of my actual fixed costs different from what I budgeted? Doesn't fixed mean that they are not supposed to change?

Victoria: We call these costs *fixed* because they shouldn't be affected by *changes in the level of activity.* However, that doesn't mean that they can't change for other reasons. For example, your utilities bill, which includes natural gas for heating, varies with the weather.

Rick: I can see that. March was warmer than normal, so my utilities bill was lower than I had expected.

Victoria: The use of the term *fixed* also suggests to people that the cost can't be controlled, but that isn't true. It is often easier to control fixed costs than variable costs. For example, it would be fairly easy for you to change your insurance bill by adjusting the amount of insurance you carry. It would be much more difficult for you to have much of an impact on the variable electricity bill, which is a necessary part of serving customers.

Rick: I think I understand, but it *is* confusing.

Victoria: Just remember that a cost is called variable if it is proportional to activity; it is called fixed if it does not depend on the level of activity. However, fixed costs can change for reasons having nothing to do with changes in the level of activity. And controllability has little to do with whether a cost is variable or fixed. Fixed costs are often more controllable than variable costs.

IN BUSINESS

FOCUS ON OPPORTUNITIES

Legendary management guru Peter F. Drucker cautions managers that "almost without exception, the first page of the [monthly] report presents the areas in which results fall below expectations or in which expenditures exceed the budget. It focuses on problems. Problems cannot be ignored. But . . . enterprises have to focus on opportunities. That requires a small but fundamental procedural change: a new first page to the monthly report, one that precedes the page that shows the problems. The new page should focus on where results are better than expected. As much time should be spent on that new first page as traditionally was spent on the problem page."

Source: Peter F. Drucker, "Change Leaders," *Inc.*, June 1999, pp. 65–72.

Using the flexible budget approach, Rick Manzi now has a much better way of assessing whether overhead costs are under control. The analysis is not so simple, however, in companies that provide a variety of products and services. The number of units produced or customers served may not be an adequate measure of overall activity. For example, does it make sense to count a Sony floppy diskette, worth less than a dollar, as equivalent to a large-screen Sony TV? If the number of units produced is used as a measure of overall activity, then the floppy diskette and the large-screen TV would be counted as equivalent. Clearly, the number of units produced (or customers served) may not be appropriate as an overall measure of activity when the organization has a variety of products or services; a common denominator may be needed.

The Measure of Activity—A Critical Choice

What should be used as the measure of activity when the company produces a variety of products and services? At least three factors are important in selecting an activity base for an overhead flexible budget:

1. The activity base and variable overhead costs should be causally related. Changes in the activity base should cause, or at least be highly correlated with, changes in the variable overhead costs in the flexible budget. Ideally, the variable overhead costs in the flexible budget should vary in direct proportion to changes in the activity base. For example, in a carpentry shop specializing in handmade wood furniture, the costs of miscellaneous supplies such as glue, wooden dowels, and sandpaper can be expected to vary with the number of direct labor-hours. Direct labor-hours would therefore be a good measure of activity to use in a flexible budget for the costs of such supplies.
2. The activity base should not be expressed in dollars or other currency. For example, direct labor cost is usually a poor choice for an activity base in flexible budgets. Changes in wage rates affect the activity base but do not usually result in a proportionate change in overhead. For example, we would not ordinarily expect to see a 5% increase in the consumption of glue in a carpentry shop if the workers receive a 5% increase in pay. Therefore, it is normally best to use physical rather than financial measures of activity in flexible budgets.
3. The activity base should be simple and easily understood. A base that is not easily understood will probably result in confusion and misunderstanding. It is difficult to control costs if people don't understand the reports or do not accept them as valid.

Variable Overhead Variances—A Closer Look

Topic Tackler PLUS 11–2

When the flexible budget is based on *hours* of activity (such as direct labor-hours) rather than on units of product or number of customers served, the flexible budget on the performance report can be based on either the actual hours used *or* the standard hours allowed for the actual output. Which should be used?

Actual versus Standard Hours

The nature of the problem can best be seen through a specific example. MicroDrive Corporation makes precision computer disk-drive motors for military applications. Data concerning the company's variable manufacturing overhead costs are shown in Exhibit 11–5.

MicroDrive Corporation uses machine-hours as the activity base in its flexible budget because its managers believe most of the overhead costs are driven by machine-hours. Based on the budgeted production of 25,000 motors and the standard of 2 machine-hours per motor, the budgeted level of activity was 50,000 machine-hours. However, actual production for the year was only 20,000 motors, and 42,000 hours of machine time were used to produce these motors. According to the standard, only 40,000 hours of machine time should have been used (40,000 machine-hours = 2 machine-hours per motor × 20,000 motors).

In preparing an overhead performance report for the year, MicroDrive could use the 42,000 machine-hours actually worked during the year *or* the 40,000 machine-hours that should have been worked according to the standard. If the actual hours are used, only a spending variance will be computed. If the standard hours are used, both a spending *and* an efficiency variance will be computed. Both of these approaches are illustrated in the following sections.

EXHIBIT 11–5
MicroDrive Corporation Data

Budgeted production	25,000 motors
Actual production	20,000 motors
Standard machine-hours per motor	2 machine-hours per motor
Budgeted machine-hours (2 × 25,000)	50,000 machine-hours
Standard machine-hours allowed for the actual output (2 × 20,000)	40,000 machine-hours
Actual machine-hours	42,000 machine-hours
Variable overhead costs per machine-hour:	
Indirect labor	$0.80 per machine-hour
Lubricants	$0.30 per machine-hour
Power	$0.40 per machine-hour
Actual total variable overhead costs:	
Indirect labor	$36,000
Lubricants	11,000
Power	24,000
Total actual variable overhead cost	$71,000

EXHIBIT 11–6

MICRODRIVE CORPORATION
Variable Overhead Performance Report
For the Year Ended December 31

Budget allowances are based on 42,000 machine-hours actually worked.

Comparing the budget to actual overhead cost yields only a spending variance.

Budgeted machine-hours	50,000
Actual machine-hours	42,000
Standard machine-hours allowed	40,000

Overhead Costs	Cost Formula (per machine-hour)	Actual Costs Incurred 42,000 Machine-Hours (AH × AR)	Budget Based on 42,000 Machine-Hours (AH × SR)	Spending Variance
Variable overhead costs:				
Indirect labor	$0.80	$36,000	$33,600*	$2,400 U
Lubricants	0.30	11,000	12,600	1,600 F
Power	0.40	24,000	16,800	7,200 U
Total variable overhead cost	$1.50	$71,000	$63,000	$8,000 U

*42,000 machine-hours × $0.80 per machine-hour = $33,600. Other budget allowances are computed in the same way.

Spending Variance Alone

LEARNING OBJECTIVE 3
Use the flexible budget to prepare a variable overhead performance report containing only a spending variance.

If MicroDrive Corporation bases its overhead performance report on the 42,000 machine-hours actually worked during the year, then the performance report will show only a spending variance for variable overhead. A performance report prepared in this way is shown in Exhibit 11–6.

The formula for the spending variance was introduced in the preceding chapter. That formula is:

$$\text{Variable overhead spending variance} = (AH \times AR) - (AH \times SR)$$

Actual hours — Actual rate — Standard rate

Or, in factored form:

$$\text{Variable overhead spending variance} = AH(AR - SR)$$

The report in Exhibit 11–6 is structured around the first, or unfactored, format.

Interpreting the Spending Variance The variable overhead spending variance is useful only to the extent that the cost driver for variable overhead really is the actual hours worked. Then the flexible budget based on the actual hours worked is a valid benchmark that tells us how much *should* have been spent in total on variable overhead items during the period. The actual overhead costs would be larger than this benchmark, resulting in an unfavorable variance, if either (1) the variable overhead items cost more to purchase than the standards allow or (2) more variable overhead items were used than the standards allow. So the spending variance includes both price and quantity variances.

Both Spending and Efficiency Variances

LEARNING OBJECTIVE 4
Use the flexible budget to prepare a variable overhead performance report containing both a spending and an efficiency variance.

If management of MicroDrive Corporation wants both a spending and an efficiency variance for variable overhead, then it should compute budget allowances for *both* the 40,000 machine-hour and the 42,000 machine-hour levels of activity. A performance report prepared in this way is shown in Exhibit 11–7.

Note from Exhibit 11–7 that the spending variance is the same as the spending variance shown in Exhibit 11–6. The performance report in Exhibit 11–7 has simply been expanded to also include an efficiency variance. Together, the spending and efficiency variances make up the total variance.

Interpreting the Efficiency Variance Like the variable overhead spending variance, the variable overhead efficiency variance is useful only to the extent that the cost driver for variable overhead really is the actual hours worked. Then any increase in hours actually worked should result in additional variable overhead costs. Consequently, if too many hours are used to create the actual output, this is presumed to result in an increase in variable overhead. The variable overhead efficiency variance is an estimate of the effect on variable overhead costs of inefficiency in the use of the base (i.e., hours). In a sense, the term *variable overhead efficiency variance* is a misnomer. It seems to suggest that it measures the efficiency with which variable overhead resources are used. It does not. It is an estimate of the indirect effect on variable overhead costs of inefficiency in the use of the activity base.

Recall from the preceding chapter that the variable overhead efficiency variance is a function of the difference between the actual hours incurred and the hours that should have been used to produce the period's output:

$$\text{Variable overhead efficiency variance} = (AH \times SR) - (SH \times SR)$$

Actual hours — Standard rate — Standard hours allowed for actual output

EXHIBIT 11–7

MICRODRIVE CORPORATION
Variable Overhead Performance Report
For the Year Ended December 31

Budget allowances are based on 40,000 machine-hours—the time it *should have taken* to produce the year's actual output of 20,000 motors—as well as on the 42,000 *actual* machine-hours worked.

This approach yields both a spending and an efficiency variance.

Budgeted machine-hours	50,000
Actual machine-hours	42,000
Standard machine-hours allowed	40,000

Overhead Costs	Cost Formula (per machine-hour)	(1) Actual Costs Incurred 42,000 Machine-Hours (*AH* × *AR*)	(2) Budget Based on 42,000 Machine-Hours (*AH* × *SR*)	(3) Budget Based on 40,000 Machine-Hours (*SH* × *SR*)	Total Variance (1) − (3)	Breakdown of the Total Variance: Spending Variance (1) − (2)	Breakdown of the Total Variance: Efficiency Variance (2) − (3)
Variable overhead costs:							
Indirect labor	$0.80	$36,000	$33,600*	$32,000	$ 4,000 U	$2,400 U	$1,600 U
Lubricants	0.30	11,000	12,600	12,000	1,000 F	1,600 F	600 U
Power	0.40	24,000	16,800	16,000	8,000 U	7,200 U	800 U
Total variable overhead cost	$1.50	$71,000	$63,000	$60,000	$11,000 U	$8,000 U	$3,000 U

*42,000 machine-hours × $0.80 per machine-hour = $33,600. Other budget allowances are computed in the same way.

Or, in factored form:

$$\text{Variable overhead efficiency variance} = SR(AH - SH)$$

If more hours are worked than are allowed at standard, then the overhead efficiency variance will be unfavorable. However, as discussed above, the inefficiency is not in the use of overhead *but rather in the use of the base itself.*

This point can be illustrated by looking again at Exhibit 11–7. Two thousand more machine-hours were used during the period than should have been used to produce the period's output. Each of these hours presumably required the incurrence of $1.50 of variable overhead cost, resulting in an unfavorable variance of $3,000 (2,000 machine-hours × $1.50 per machine-hour = $3,000). Although this $3,000 variance is called an overhead efficiency variance, it could better be called a machine-hours efficiency variance, since it results from using too many machine-hours rather than from inefficient use of overhead resources. However, the term *overhead efficiency variance* is so firmly ingrained that a change is unlikely. Even so, be careful to interpret the variance with a clear understanding of what it really measures.

Control of the Efficiency Variance Who is responsible for control of the overhead efficiency variance? Since the variance really reflects efficiency in the utilization of the base underlying the flexible budget, whoever is responsible for control of this base is responsible for control of the variance. If the base is direct labor-hours, then the supervisor responsible for the use of labor time will be responsible for any overhead efficiency variance.

Activity-Based Costing and the Flexible Budget

It is unlikely that all of the variable overhead in a complex organization is driven by a single factor such as the number of units produced or the number of labor-hours or machine-hours. Activity-based costing provides a way of recognizing a variety of overhead cost drivers and thereby increasing the accuracy of the costing system. In activity-based costing, each overhead cost pool has its own measure of activity. The actual spending in each overhead cost pool can be independently evaluated using the techniques discussed in this chapter. The only difference is that the cost formulas for variable overhead costs will be stated in terms of different kinds of activities instead of all being stated in terms of units or a common measure of activity such as direct labor-hours or machine-hours. If done properly, activity-based costing can greatly enhance the usefulness of overhead performance reports by recognizing multiple causes of overhead costs. In general, the usefulness of overhead performance reports depends on how carefully the reports are designed and prepared. In particular, managers must take care to separate the variable from the fixed costs in the flexible budgets.

IN BUSINESS

POOLS WITHIN POOLS

Caterpillar, Inc. a manufacturer of heavy equipment and a pioneer in the development and use of activity-based costing, separates its overhead costs into three large pools—the logistics cost pool, the manufacturing cost pool, and the general cost pool. In turn, these three cost pools are subdivided into scores of activity centers, with each center having its own flexible budget from which variable and fixed overhead rates are developed. "The many manufacturing cost center rates are the unique elements that set Caterpillar's system apart from simple cost systems."

Source: Lou F. Jones, "Product Costing at Caterpillar," *Management Accounting* 72, no. 8, p. 39.

Overhead Rates and Fixed Overhead Analysis

Fixed overhead variances are different from variable overhead variances because of the difference in the nature of the costs. To provide a background for our discussion, we will first briefly review the need for, and computation of, predetermined overhead rates. This review will be helpful, since the predetermined overhead rate plays a major role in fixed overhead analysis. We will then show how fixed overhead variances are computed and make some observations about their usefulness to managers.

LEARNING OBJECTIVE 5
Compute the predetermined overhead rate and apply overhead to products in a standard cost system.

Flexible Budgets and Overhead Rates

Fixed costs come in large, indivisible pieces that by definition do not vary with changes in the level of activity within the relevant range. This creates a problem in product costing, since the average fixed cost per unit will vary with the level of activity. Consider the data in the following table:

Month	(1) Total Fixed Overhead Cost	(2) Number of Units Produced	(3) Average Fixed Cost per Unit (1) ÷ (2)
January	$6,000	1,000	$6.00
February	$6,000	1,500	$4.00
March	$6,000	800	$7.50

Notice that the large number of units produced in February results in a low unit cost ($4.00), whereas the small number of units produced in March results in a high unit cost ($7.50). This phenomenon arises only in connection with the fixed portion of overhead, since by definition the variable portion of overhead remains constant on a per unit basis, rising and falling in total proportionately with changes in the activity level. Most managers feel that the fixed portion of unit cost should be stabilized so that a single unit cost can be used throughout the year. As we learned in Chapter 3, this stability can be accomplished through use of the predetermined overhead rate.

Throughout the remainder of this chapter, we will be analyzing the fixed overhead costs of MicroDrive Corporation. To assist us in that task, the flexible budget of the company—including fixed costs—is displayed in Exhibit 11–8. Note that the total fixed overhead costs amount to $300,000 within the range of activity in the flexible budget.

Denominator Activity The formula that we used in Chapter 3 to compute the predetermined overhead rate was:

$$\text{Predetermined overhead rate} = \frac{\text{Estimated total manufacturing overhead cost}}{\text{Estimated total units in the base (MH, DLH, etc.)}}$$

The estimated total units in the base in the formula for the predetermined overhead rate is called the **denominator activity.** Recall from our discussion in Chapter 3 that once an estimated activity level (denominator activity) has been chosen, it remains unchanged throughout the year, even if the actual level of activity turns out to be different from what

EXHIBIT 11–8

MICRODRIVE CORPORATION
Flexible Budgets at Various Levels of Activity

Overhead Costs	Cost Formula (per machine-hour)	Activity (in machine-hours) 40,000	45,000	50,000	55,000
Variable overhead costs:					
Indirect labor	$0.80	$ 32,000	$ 36,000	$ 40,000	$ 44,000
Lubricants	0.30	12,000	13,500	15,000	16,500
Power	0.40	16,000	18,000	20,000	22,000
Total variable overhead cost . .	$1.50	60,000	67,500	75,000	82,500
Fixed overhead costs:					
Depreciation		100,000	100,000	100,000	100,000
Supervisory salaries		160,000	160,000	160,000	160,000
Insurance		40,000	40,000	40,000	40,000
Total fixed overhead cost		300,000	300,000	300,000	300,000
Total overhead cost		$360,000	$367,500	$375,000	$382,500

was estimated. The reason for not changing the denominator is to keep the amount of overhead applied to each unit of product the same regardless of when it is produced during the year.

IN BUSINESS

KNOW YOUR COSTS

Understanding the difference between fixed and variable costs can be critical. Kennard T. Wing, of OMG Center for Collaborative Learning, reports that a large health care system made the mistake of classifying all of its costs as variable. As a consequence, when volume dropped, managers felt that costs should be cut proportionately and more than 1,000 people were laid off—even though "the workload of most of them had no direct relation to patient volume. The result was that morale of the survivors plummeted and within a year the system was scrambling to replace not only those it had let go, but many others who had quit. The point is, the accounting systems we design and implement really do affect management decisions in significant ways. A system built on a bad model of the business will either not be used or, if used, will lead to bad decisions."

Source: Kennard T. Wing, "Using Enhanced Cost Models in Variance Analysis for Better Control and Decision Making," *Management Accounting Quarterly*, Winter 2000, pp. 27–35.

Computing the Overhead Rate When we discussed predetermined overhead rates in Chapter 3, we didn't explain how the estimated total manufacturing cost was determined. This figure can be derived from the flexible budget. Once the denominator level of activity has been chosen, the flexible budget can be used to determine the total amount of overhead cost that should be incurred at that level of activity. The predetermined overhead rate can then be computed using the following variation on the basic formula for the predetermined overhead rate:

$$\text{Predetermined overhead rate} = \frac{\text{Overhead from the flexible budget at the denominator level of activity}}{\text{Denominator level of activity}}$$

To illustrate, refer to MicroDrive Corporation's flexible budget for manufacturing overhead in Exhibit 11–8. Suppose that the budgeted activity level for the year is 50,000 machine-hours and that this will be used as the denominator activity in the formula for the predetermined overhead rate. The numerator in the formula is the estimated total overhead cost of $375,000 when the activity level is 50,000 machine-hours. This amount is taken from the flexible budget in Exhibit 11–8. Thus, the predetermined overhead rate for MicroDrive Corporation will be computed as follows:

$$\frac{\$375{,}000}{50{,}000 \text{ MHs}} = \$7.50 \text{ per machine-hour (MH)}$$

Or the company can break its predetermined overhead rate down into variable and fixed elements rather than using a single combined figure:

$$\text{Variable element: } \frac{\$75{,}000}{50{,}000 \text{ MHs}} = \$1.50 \text{ per MH}$$

$$\text{Fixed element: } \frac{\$300{,}000}{50{,}000 \text{ MHs}} = \$6 \text{ per MH}$$

For every standard machine-hour of operation, work in process will be charged with $7.50 of overhead, of which $1.50 will be variable overhead and $6.00 will be fixed overhead. Since a disk-drive motor should take two machine-hours to complete, its cost will include $3 of variable overhead and $12 of fixed overhead, as shown on the following standard cost card:

Standard Cost Card—Per Motor	
Direct materials (assumed)	$14
Direct labor (assumed)	6
Variable overhead (2 MHs at $1.50 per MH)	3
Fixed overhead (2 MHs at $6 per MH)	12
Total standard cost per motor	$35

In sum, the flexible budget provides the estimated overhead cost needed to compute the predetermined overhead rate. Thus, the flexible budget plays a key role in determining the amount of fixed and variable overhead cost that will be charged to units of product.

Overhead Application in a Standard Cost System

To understand fixed overhead variances, it is necessary first to understand how overhead is applied to work in process in a standard cost system. Recall that in Chapter 3 we applied overhead to work in process on the basis of actual hours of activity (multiplied by the predetermined overhead rate). This procedure was correct, since at the time we were dealing with a normal cost system.[1] However, we are now dealing with a standard cost system. In such a system, overhead is applied to work in process on the basis of the *standard hours allowed for the output of the period* rather than on the basis of the actual number of hours worked. This point is illustrated in Exhibit 11–9. In a standard cost system, every unit of product is charged with the same amount of overhead cost, regardless of how much time the unit actually requires for processing.

The Fixed Overhead Variances

LEARNING OBJECTIVE 6
Compute and interpret the fixed overhead budget and volume variances.

To illustrate the computation of fixed overhead variances, we will refer again to the data for MicroDrive Corporation.

Denominator activity in machine-hours	50,000
Budgeted fixed overhead costs	$300,000
Fixed portion of the predetermined overhead rate (computed earlier)	$6 per machine-hour

EXHIBIT 11–9
Applied Overhead Costs: Normal Cost System versus Standard Cost System

Normal Cost System
Manufacturing Overhead

Actual overhead costs incurred.	Applied overhead costs: Actual hours × Predetermined overhead rate.

Under- or overapplied overhead

Standard Cost System
Manufacturing Overhead

Actual overhead costs incurred.	Applied overhead costs: Standard hours allowed for actual output × Predetermined overhead rate.

Under- or overapplied overhead

1 Normal cost systems are discussed on page 94 in Chapter 3.

Let us assume that the following actual operating results were recorded for the year:

Actual machine-hours	42,000
Standard machine-hours allowed*	40,000
Actual fixed overhead costs:	
Depreciation	$100,000
Supervisory salaries	172,000
Insurance	36,000
Total actual fixed overhead cost	$308,000

*For the actual production of the year.

From these data, two variances can be computed for fixed overhead—a *budget variance* and a *volume variance.* The variances are shown in Exhibit 11–10.

Notice from the exhibit that overhead has been applied to work in process on the basis of 40,000 standard hours allowed for the actual output of the year rather than on the basis of 42,000 actual hours worked. As stated earlier, this keeps unit costs from being affected by variations in efficiency.

The Budget Variance—A Closer Look

The **budget variance** is the difference between the actual fixed overhead costs incurred during the period and the original budgeted fixed overhead costs for the period. It can be computed as shown in Exhibit 11–10 or by using the following formula:

$$\text{Budget variance} = \text{Actual fixed overhead cost} - \text{Budgeted fixed overhead cost}$$

Applying this formula to MicroDrive Corporation, the budget variance would be computed as follows:

$$\$308,000 - \$300,000 = \$8,000\ \text{U}$$

The variances computed for the fixed costs at Rick's Hairstyling in Exhibit 11–4 are all budget variances, since they represent the difference between the actual fixed overhead cost and the budgeted fixed overhead cost.

An expanded overhead performance report for MicroDrive Corporation appears in Exhibit 11–11. This report now includes the budget variances for fixed overhead as well as the spending variances for variable overhead that were in Exhibit 11–6.

EXHIBIT 11–10
Computation of the Fixed Overhead Variances

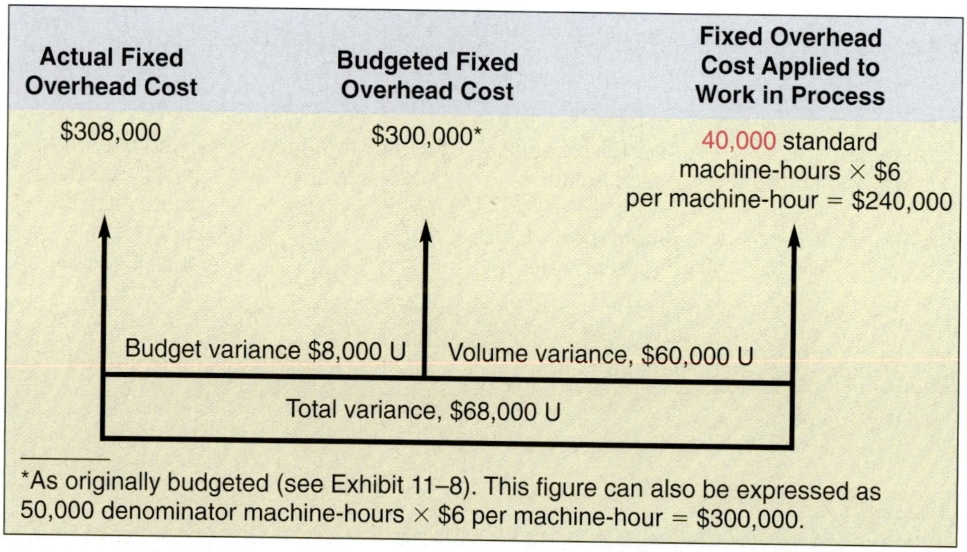

*As originally budgeted (see Exhibit 11–8). This figure can also be expressed as 50,000 denominator machine-hours × $6 per machine-hour = $300,000.

The budget variances for fixed overhead can be very useful, since they represent the difference between how much *should* have been spent (according to the original budget) and how much was actually spent. For example, supervisory salaries has a $12,000 unfavorable variance. There should be some explanation for this large variance. Was it due to an increase in salaries? Was it due to overtime? Was another supervisor hired? If so, why was another supervisor hired?

The Volume Variance—A Closer Look

The **volume variance** is a measure of utilization of facilities. The variance arises whenever the standard hours allowed for the output of a period are different from the denominator activity level that was planned when the period began. It can be computed as shown in Exhibit 11–10 or by using the following formula:

$$\text{Volume variance} = \text{Fixed portion of the predetermined overhead rate} \times \left(\text{Denominator hours} - \text{Standard hours allowed}\right)$$

Applying this formula to MicroDrive Corporation, the volume variance would be computed as follows:

$$\$6 \text{ per MH } (50{,}000 \text{ MHs} - 40{,}000 \text{ MHs}) = \$60{,}000 \text{ U}$$

Note that this computation agrees with the volume variance as shown in Exhibit 11–10. As stated earlier, the volume variance is a measure of utilization of facilities. An unfavorable variance, as above, means that the company operated at an activity level *below* that planned for the period. A favorable variance would mean that the company operated at an activity level *greater* than that planned for the period.

It is important to note that the volume variance does not measure over- or underspending. A company normally would incur the same dollar amount of fixed overhead cost regardless of whether the period's activity was above or below the planned

EXHIBIT 11–11
Fixed Overhead Costs on the Overhead Performance Report

MICRODRIVE CORPORATION
Overhead Performance Report
For the Year Ended December 31

Budgeted machine-hours	50,000
Actual machine-hours	42,000
Standard machine-hours allowed	40,000

Overhead Costs	Cost Formula (per machine-hour)	Actual Costs 42,000 Machine-Hours	Budget Based on 42,000 Machine-Hours	Spending or Budget Variance
Variable overhead costs:				
Indirect labor	$0.80	$ 36,000	$ 33,600	$ 2,400 U
Lubricants	0.30	11,000	12,600	1,600 F
Power	0.40	24,000	16,800	7,200 U
Total variable overhead cost	$1.50	71,000	63,000	8,000 U
Fixed overhead costs:				
Depreciation		100,000	100,000	0
Supervisory salaries		172,000	160,000	12,000 U
Insurance		36,000	40,000	4,000 F
Total fixed overhead cost		308,000	300,000	8,000 U
Total overhead cost		$379,000	$363,000	$16,000 U

(denominator) level. In short, the volume variance is an activity-related variance. It is explainable only by activity and is controllable only through activity.

To summarize:

1. If the denominator activity and the standard hours allowed for the output of the period are the same, the volume variance is zero.
2. If the denominator activity is greater than the standard hours allowed for the output of the period, then the volume variance is unfavorable. This indicates that facilities were utilized less than was planned.
3. If the denominator activity is less than the standard hours allowed for the output of the period, then the volume variance is favorable. This indicates that facilities were utilized more than was planned.

Graphic Analysis of Fixed Overhead Variances

Graphic analysis can provide insights into the budget and volume variances. A graph containing these variances is presented in Exhibit 11–12.

As shown in the graph, fixed overhead cost is applied to work in process at the predetermined rate of $6 for each standard hour of activity. (The applied-cost line is the upward-sloping line on the graph.) Since a denominator level of 50,000 machine-hours was used in computing the $6 rate, the applied-cost line crosses the budget-cost line at exactly 50,000 machine-hours. If the denominator hours and the standard hours allowed for the output are the same, there can be no volume variance. It is only when the standard hours differ from the denominator hours that a volume variance can arise.

In the case at hand, the standard hours allowed for the actual output (40,000 hours) are less than the denominator hours (50,000 hours). The result is an unfavorable volume variance, since less cost was applied to production than was originally budgeted. If the situation had been reversed and the standard hours allowed for the actual output had exceeded the denominator hours, then the volume variance on the graph would have been favorable.

EXHIBIT 11–12
Graphic Analysis of Fixed Overhead Variances

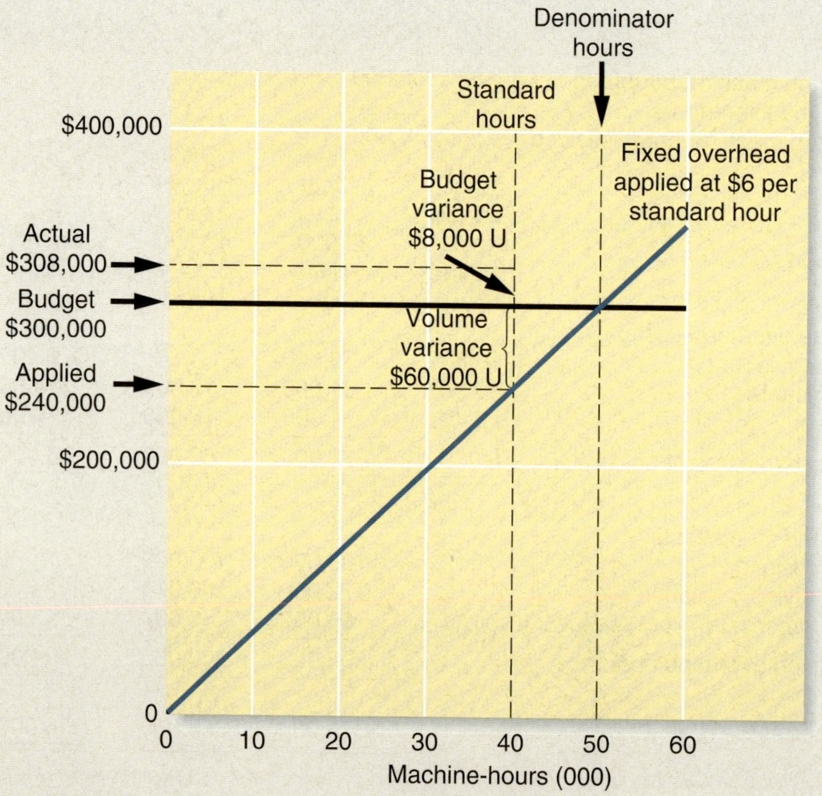

Cautions in Fixed Overhead Analysis

A volume variance for fixed overhead arises because when applying the costs to work in process, we act *as if* the fixed costs were variable and depended on activity. This point can be seen from the graph in Exhibit 11–12. Notice from the graph that the fixed overhead costs are applied to work in process at a rate of $6 per hour *as if* they were variable. Treating these costs as if they were variable is necessary for product costing purposes, but some real dangers lurk here. Managers can easily be misled into thinking that fixed costs are *in fact* variable.

Keep clearly in mind that fixed overhead costs come in large, indivisible pieces. Expressing fixed costs on a unit or per hour basis, though necessary for product costing for external reports, is artificial. Increases or decreases in activity in fact have no effect on total fixed costs within the relevant range of activity. Even though fixed costs are expressed on a unit or per hour basis, they are *not* proportional to activity. In a sense, the volume variance is the error that occurs as a result of treating fixed costs as variable costs in the costing system.

Overhead Variances and Under- or Overapplied Overhead Cost

Four variances relating to overhead cost have been computed for MicroDrive Corporation in this chapter. These four variances are as follows:

Variable overhead spending variance (p. 499)	$ 8,000 U
Variable overhead efficiency variance (p. 501)	3,000 U
Fixed overhead budget variance (p. 506)	8,000 U
Fixed overhead volume variance (p. 506)	60,000 U
Total overhead variance	$79,000 U

Recall from Chapter 3 that under- or overapplied overhead is the difference between the amount of overhead applied to products and the actual overhead costs incurred during a period. Basically, the overhead variances we have computed in this chapter break the under- or overapplied overhead down into variances that can be used by managers for control purposes. *The sum of the overhead variances equals the under- or overapplied overhead cost for a period.*

Furthermore, in a standard cost system, unfavorable variances are equivalent to underapplied overhead and favorable variances are equivalent to overapplied overhead. Unfavorable variances occur because more was spent on overhead than the standards allow. Underapplied overhead occurs when more was spent on overhead than was applied to products during the period. But in a standard costing system, the standard amount of overhead allowed is exactly the same amount of overhead applied to products. Therefore, in a standard costing system, unfavorable variances and underapplied overhead are the same thing, as are favorable variances and overapplied overhead.

For MicroDrive Corporation, the total overhead variance was $79,000 unfavorable. Therefore, its overhead cost was underapplied by $79,000 for the year. To solidify this point in your mind, *carefully study the review problem at the end of the chapter!* This review problem provides a comprehensive summary of overhead analysis, including the computation of under- or overapplied overhead cost in a standard cost system.

Summary

When analyzing overhead costs, it is vital to distinguish between variable overhead and fixed overhead. Variable overhead costs vary in total in proportion to changes in activity whereas total fixed costs do not change within the relevant range. This distinction is important when constructing flexible budgets and when computing overhead variances.

A flexible budget shows what costs should be for various levels of activity. The flexible budget amount for a specific level of activity is determined differently depending on whether a cost is variable or fixed. If a cost is variable, the flexible budget amount is computed by multiplying the cost per unit of activity by the level of activity specified for the flexible budget. If a cost is fixed, the original total budgeted fixed cost is used as the flexible budget amount.

The two variances for variable overhead discussed in the chapter are the variable overhead spending and variable overhead efficiency variances. These variances were also covered in the previous chapter.

Two variances for fixed overhead are covered in the chapter. One—the budget variance—is quite simple; the other is considerably more complex. The budget variance is the difference between the actual total fixed overhead cost incurred and the total amount of fixed overhead cost that was originally budgeted. The volume variance is the difference between the amount of fixed overhead cost applied to inventory and the total amount of fixed overhead cost that was originally budgeted. The budget variance is a straightforward measure of the degree to which fixed overhead spending was under control. The volume variance is a consequence of treating a fixed cost as if it were variable and is more difficult to interpret meaningfully.

The sum of all four overhead variances equals the overhead over- or underapplied for the period. Unfavorable variances are equivalent to underapplied overhead and favorable variances are equivalent to overapplied overhead.

Review Problem: Overhead Analysis

(This problem provides a comprehensive review of Chapter 11, including the computation of under- or overapplied overhead and its breakdown into the four overhead variances.)

Data for the manufacturing overhead of Aspen Company are given below:

Overhead Costs	Cost Formula (per machine-hour)	Machine-Hours 5,000	6,000	7,000
Variable overhead costs:				
Supplies	$0.20	$ 1,000	$ 1,200	$ 1,400
Indirect labor	0.30	1,500	1,800	2,100
Total variable overhead cost	$0.50	2,500	3,000	3,500
Fixed overhead costs:				
Depreciation		4,000	4,000	4,000
Supervision		5,000	5,000	5,000
Total fixed overhead cost		9,000	9,000	9,000
Total overhead cost		$11,500	$12,000	$12,500

Five hours of machine time are required per unit of product. The company has set its denominator activity for the coming period at 6,000 machine-hours (or 1,200 units). The predetermined overhead rate is computed as follows:

$$\text{Total: } \frac{\$12{,}000}{6{,}000 \text{ MHs}} = \$2.00 \text{ per machine-hour}$$

$$\text{Variable element: } \frac{\$3{,}000}{6{,}000 \text{ MHs}} = \$0.50 \text{ per machine-hour}$$

$$\text{Fixed element: } \frac{\$9{,}000}{6{,}000 \text{ MHs}} = \$1.50 \text{ per machine-hour}$$

Assume the following *actual* results for the period:

Number of units produced	1,300 units
Actual machine-hours	6,800 machine-hours
Standard machine-hours allowed*	6,500 machine-hours
Actual variable overhead cost	$4,200
Actual fixed overhead cost	$9,400

*1,300 units × 5 machine-hours per unit.

Therefore, the company's Manufacturing Overhead account would appear as follows at the end of the period:

	Manufacturing Overhead		
Actual overhead costs	13,600*	13,000†	Applied overhead costs
Underapplied overhead	600		

*$4,200 variable + $9,400 fixed = $13,600.
†6,500 standard machine-hours × $2 per machine-hour = $13,000. In a standard cost system, overhead is applied on the basis of standard hours, not actual hours.

Required:

Analyze the $600 underapplied overhead in terms of:

1. A variable overhead spending variance.
2. A variable overhead efficiency variance.
3. A fixed overhead budget variance.
4. A fixed overhead volume variance.

Solution to Review Problem

Variable Overhead Variances

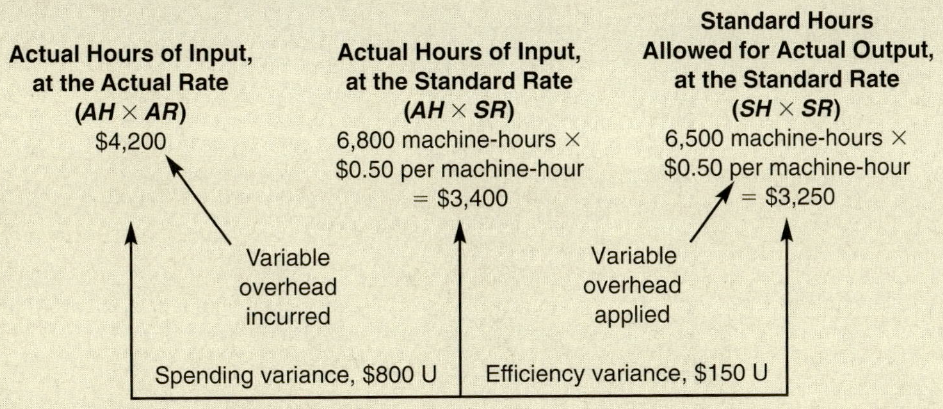

These same variances in the alternative format would be computed as follows:

Variable overhead spending variance:

$$\text{Spending variance} = (AH \times AR) - (AH \times SR)$$

$$(\$4{,}200^*) - (6{,}800 \text{ machine-hours} \times \$0.50 \text{ per machine-hour}) = \$800\text{ U}$$

*$AH \times AR$ equals the total actual cost for the period.

Variable overhead efficiency variance:

$$\text{Efficiency variance} = SR(AH - SH)$$

$$\$0.50 \text{ per machine-hour } (6{,}800 \text{ machine-hours} - 6{,}500 \text{ machine-hours}) = \$150\text{ U}$$

Fixed Overhead Variances

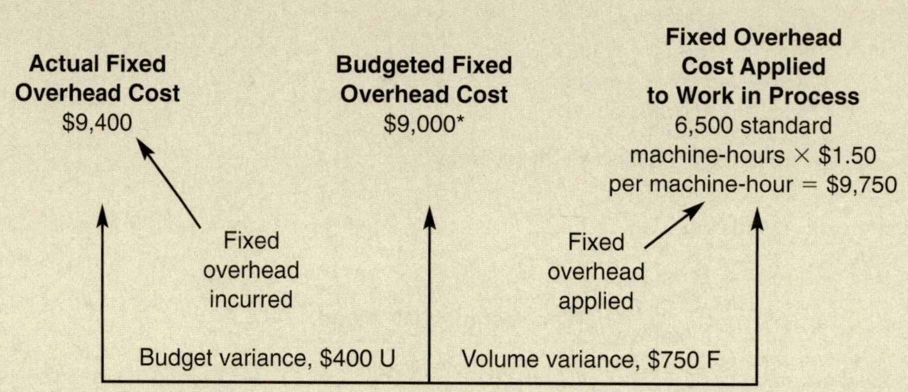

*Can be expressed as: 6,000 denominator machine-hours × $1.50 per machine-hour = $9,000.

These same variances in the alternative format would be computed as follows:

Fixed overhead budget variance:

$$\text{Budget variance} = \text{Actual fixed overhead cost} - \text{Budgeted fixed overhead cost}$$

$$= \$9{,}400 - \$9{,}000 = \$400\text{ U}$$

Fixed overhead volume variance:

$$\text{Volume variance} = \text{Fixed portion of the predetermined overhead rate} \times (\text{Denominator hours} - \text{Standard hours})$$

$$\$1.50 \text{ per machine-hour } (6{,}000 \text{ machine-hours} - 6{,}500 \text{ machine-hours}) = \$750\text{ F}$$

Summary of Variances The four overhead variances are summarized below:

Variable overhead:	
Spending variance	$800 U
Efficiency variance	150 U
Fixed overhead:	
Budget variance	400 U
Volume variance	750 F
Underapplied overhead	$600

Notice that the $600 summary variance figure agrees with the underapplied balance in the company's Manufacturing Overhead account. This agreement verifies the accuracy of our variance analysis.

Glossary

Budget variance A measure of the difference between the actual fixed overhead costs incurred during the period and budgeted fixed overhead costs as contained in the flexible budget. (p. 506)

Denominator activity The activity figure used to compute the predetermined overhead rate. (p. 503)

Flexible budget A budget that is designed to cover a range of activity and that can be used to develop budgeted costs at any point within that range to compare to actual costs incurred. (p. 492)

Static budget A budget created at the beginning of the budgeting period that is valid only for the planned level of activity. (p. 492)

Volume variance The variance that arises whenever the standard hours allowed for the output of a period are different from the denominator activity level that was used to compute the predetermined overhead rate. (p. 507)

Questions

11–1 What is a static budget?
11–2 What is a flexible budget and how does it differ from a static budget?
11–3 Name three criteria that should be considered in choosing an activity base on which to construct a flexible budget.
11–4 In a performance report for variable overhead, what variance(s) will be produced if the flexible budget is based on actual hours worked? On both actual hours worked and standard hours allowed?
11–5 What is meant by the term *standard hours allowed?*
11–6 How does the variable manufacturing overhead spending variance differ from the materials price variance?
11–7 Why is the term *overhead efficiency variance* a misnomer?
11–8 In what way is a flexible budget involved in product costing?
11–9 What is meant by the term *denominator level of activity?*
11–10 Why do we apply overhead to work in process on the basis of standard hours allowed in Chapter 11 when we applied it on the basis of actual hours in Chapter 3? What is the difference in costing systems between the two chapters?
11–11 In a standard cost system, what two variances are computed for fixed manufacturing overhead?
11–12 What does the fixed overhead budget variance measure?
11–13 Under what circumstances would you expect the volume variance to be favorable? Unfavorable? Does the variance measure deviations in spending for fixed overhead items? Explain.
11–14 What is the danger in expressing fixed costs on a per unit basis?
11–15 Under- or overapplied overhead can be broken down into what four variances?
11–16 If factory overhead is overapplied for August, would you expect the total of the overhead variances to be favorable or unfavorable?

Exercises

EXERCISE 11–1 Prepare a Flexible Budget [LO1]
The cost formulas for Emory Company's manufacturing overhead costs are given below. These cost formulas cover a relevant range of 15,000 to 25,000 machine-hours each year.

Overhead Costs	Cost Formula
Utilities	$0.30 per machine-hour
Indirect labor	$52,000 plus $1.40 per machine-hour
Supplies	$0.20 per machine-hour
Maintenance	$18,000 plus $0.10 per machine-hour
Depreciation	$90,000

Required:
Prepare a flexible budget in increments of 5,000 machine-hours. Include all costs in your budget.

EXERCISE 11–2 Preparing a Flexible Budget Performance Report [LO2]
Orcas Boat Charter Service rents live-aboard boats for cruising in the San Juan Islands of Washington State. The company bases its overhead cost budgets on the following data:

Variable overhead costs:	
Cleaning	$60.50 per charter
Maintenance	$35.25 per charter
Port fees	$15.75 per charter
Fixed overhead costs:	
Salaries and wages	$9,150 per month
Depreciation	$12,100 per month
Utilities	$860 per month
Moorage	$4,980 per month

Each time a boat is chartered, whether it is for one day or a week, certain costs must be incurred. Those costs are listed above under the variable overhead costs. For example, each time a boat returns from a charter, it must be thoroughly cleaned, which costs on average $60.50.

In July, the following actual costs were incurred for 160 charters:

Cleaning	$9,440
Maintenance	$5,980
Port fees	$2,670
Salaries and wages	$9,200
Depreciation	$12,800
Utilities	$835
Moorage	$5,360

Due to an unanticipated surge in demand for charters, the company purchased a new boat in July to add to its charter fleet.

Required:

1. Construct a Flexible Budget Performance Report for Orcas Boat Charter Service for July, following the format in Exhibit 11–4.
2. What is apparently the major cause of the overall variance for the month? Explain.

EXERCISE 11–3 Variable Overhead Performance Report with Just a Spending Variance [LO3]

Yung Corporation bases its variable overhead performance report on the actual direct labor-hours of the period. Data concerning the most recent year that ended on December 31 appear below:

Budgeted direct labor-hours	38,000
Actual direct labor-hours	34,000
Standard direct labor-hours allowed	35,000

Cost formula (per direct labor-hour):

Indirect labor	$0.60
Supplies	$0.10
Electricity	$0.05

Actual costs incurred:

Indirect labor	$21,200
Supplies	$3,200
Electricity	$1,600

Required:

Prepare a variable overhead performance report using the format in Exhibit 11–6. Compute just the variable overhead spending variances (do not compute the variable overhead efficiency variances).

EXERCISE 11–4 Variable Overhead Performance Report with Both Spending and Efficiency Variances [LO4]

Refer to the data for Yung Corporation in Exercise 11–3. Management would like to compute both spending and efficiency variances for variable overheads in the company's variable overhead performance report.

Required:
Prepare a variable overhead performance report using the format in Exhibit 11–7. Compute both the variable overhead spending variances and the overhead efficiency variances.

EXERCISE 11–5 Applying Overhead in a Standard Costing System [LO5]
Privack Corporation has a standard cost system in which it applies overhead to products based on the standard direct labor-hours allowed for the actual output of the period. Data concerning the most recent year appear below:

Variable overhead cost per direct labor-hour	$2.00
Total fixed overhead cost per year	$250,000
Budgeted standard direct labor-hours (denominator level of activity)	40,000
Actual direct labor-hours	39,000
Standard direct labor-hours allowed for the actual output	38,000

Required:
1. Compute the predetermined overhead rate for the year.
2. Determine the amount of overhead that would be applied to the output of the period.

EXERCISE 11–6 Fixed Overhead Variances [LO6]
Primara Corporation has a standard cost system in which it applies overhead to products based on the standard direct labor-hours allowed for the actual output of the period. Data concerning the most recent year appear below:

Total budgeted fixed overhead cost for the year	$250,000
Actual fixed overhead cost for the year	$254,000
Budgeted standard direct labor-hours (denominator level of activity)	25,000
Actual direct labor-hours	27,000
Standard direct labor-hours allowed for the actual output	26,000

Required:
1. Compute the fixed portion of the predetermined overhead rate for the year.
2. Compute the fixed overhead budget variance and volume variance.

EXERCISE 11–7 Preparing a Flexible Budget [LO1]

An incomplete flexible budget is given below for Lavage Rapide, a Swiss company that owns and operates a large automatic carwash facility near Geneva. The Swiss currency is the Swiss franc, which is denoted by SFr.

LAVAGE RAPIDE
Flexible Budget
For the Month Ended August 31

Overhead Costs	Cost Formula (per car)	Activity (cars) 8,000	9,000	10,000
Variable overhead costs:				
Cleaning supplies	?	?	7,200 SFr	?
Electricity	?	?	2,700	?
Maintenance	?	?	1,800	?
Total variable overhead cost	?	?	?	?
Fixed overhead costs:				
Operator wages		?	9,000	?
Depreciation		?	6,000	?
Rent		?	8,000	?
Total fixed overhead cost		?	?	?
Total overhead cost		?	? SFr	?

Required:
Fill in the missing data.

EXERCISE 11–8 Using a Flexible Budget [LO2]

Refer to the data in Exercise 11–7. Lavage Rapide's owner-manager would like to prepare a budget for August assuming an activity level of 8,800 cars.

Required:

Prepare a static budget for August. Use Exhibit 11–1 in the chapter as your guide.

EXERCISE 11–9 Flexible Budget Performance Report [LO2]

Refer to the data in Exercise 11–7. Lavage Rapide's actual level of activity during August was 8,900 cars, although the owner had constructed his static budget for the month assuming the level of activity would be 8,800 cars. The actual overhead costs incurred during August are given below:

	Actual Costs Incurred for 8,900 Cars
Variable overhead costs:	
Cleaning supplies	7,080 SFr
Electricity	2,460 SFr
Maintenance	1,550 SFr
Fixed overhead costs:	
Operator wages	9,100 SFr
Depreciation	7,000 SFr
Rent	8,000 SFr

Required:

Prepare a flexible budget performance report for both the variable and fixed overhead costs for August. Use Exhibit 11–4 in the chapter as your guide.

EXERCISE 11–10 Variable Overhead Performance Report [LO3]

The variable portion of Murray Company's flexible budget for manufacturing overhead is given below:

	Cost Formula (per machine-hour	Machine-Hours		
Variable Overhead Costs		10,000	12,000	14,000
Supplies	$0.20	$ 2,000	$ 2,400	$ 2,800
Maintenance	0.80	8,000	9,600	11,200
Utilities	0.10	1,000	1,200	1,400
Rework	0.40	4,000	4,800	5,600
Total variable overhead cost	$1.50	$15,000	$18,000	$21,000

During a recent period, the company recorded 11,500 machine-hours of activity. The variable overhead costs incurred were:

Supplies	$2,400
Maintenance	$8,000
Utilities	$1,100
Rework time	$5,300

The budgeted activity for the period had been 12,000 machine-hours.

Required:

1. Prepare a variable overhead performance report for the period. Indicate whether variances are favorable (F) or unfavorable (U). Show only a spending variance on your report.
2. Discuss the significance of the variances. Might some variances be the result of others? Explain.

EXERCISE 11–11 Variable Overhead Performance Report with Both Spending and Efficiency Variances [LO4]

The check-clearing office of Columbia National Bank is responsible for processing all checks that come to the bank for payment. Managers at the bank believe that variable overhead costs are essentially proportional to the number of labor-hours worked in the office, so labor-hours are used as the activity base when preparing variable overhead budgets and performance reports. Data for September, the most recent month, appear below:

Budgeted labor-hours	3,080	
Actual labor-hours	3,100	
Standard labor-hours allowed for the actual number of checks processed	3,200	
	Cost Formula (per labor-hour)	**Actual Costs Incurred in September**
Variable overhead costs:		
Office supplies	$0.10	$ 365
Staff coffee lounge	0.20	520
Indirect labor	0.90	2,710
Total variable overhead cost	$1.20	$3,595

Required:

Prepare a variable overhead performance report for September for the check-clearing office that includes both spending and efficiency variances. Use Exhibit 11–7 as a guide.

EXERCISE 11–12 Predetermined Overhead Rate [LO5]

Operating at a normal level of 30,000 direct labor-hours, Lasser Company produces 10,000 units of product each period. The direct labor wage rate is $12 per hour. Two and one-half yards of direct materials go into each unit of product; the material costs $8.60 per yard. The flexible budget used to plan and control manufacturing overhead costs is given below (in condensed form):

	Cost Formula (per direct labor-hour)	Direct Labor-Hours		
Overhead Costs		20,000	30,000	40,000
Variable costs	$1.90	$ 38,000	$ 57,000	$ 76,000
Fixed costs		168,000	168,000	168,000
Total overhead cost		$206,000	$225,000	$244,000

Required:

1. Using 30,000 direct labor-hours as the denominator activity, compute the predetermined overhead rate and break it down into variable and fixed elements.
2. Complete the standard cost card below for one unit of product:

Direct materials, 2.5 yards at $8.60 per yard	$21.50
Direct labor, ?	?
Variable overhead, ?	?
Fixed overhead, ?	?
Total standard cost per unit	$?

EXERCISE 11–13 Using Fixed Overhead Variances [LO6]
The standard cost card for the single product manufactured by Cutter, Inc., is given below:

Standard Cost Card—per Unit	
Direct materials, 3 yards at $6 per yard	$ 18
Direct labor, 4 hours at $15.50 per hour	62
Variable overhead, 4 hours at $1.50 per hour	6
Fixed overhead, 4 hours at $5 per hour	20
Total standard cost per unit	$106

Manufacturing overhead is applied to production on the basis of standard direct labor-hours. During the year, the company worked 37,000 hours and manufactured 9,500 units of product. Selected data relating to the company's fixed manufacturing overhead cost for the year are shown below:

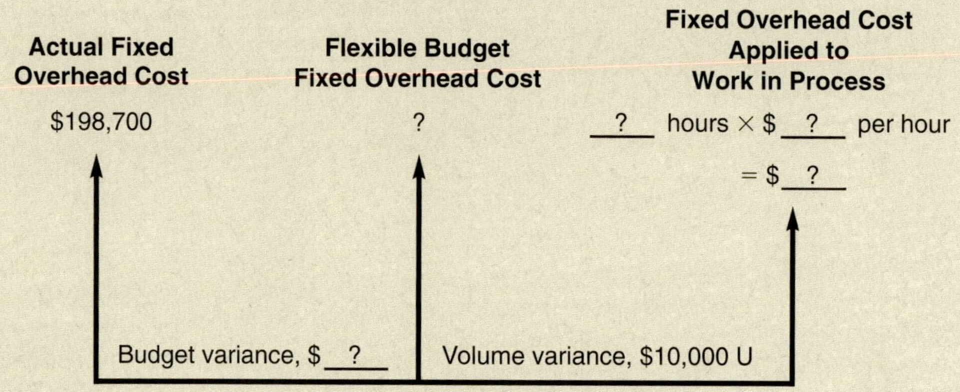

Required:
1. What were the standard hours allowed for the year's production?
2. What was the amount of fixed overhead cost contained in the flexible budget for the year?
3. What was the fixed overhead budget variance for the year?
4. What denominator activity level did the company use in setting the predetermined overhead rate for the year?

EXERCISE 11–14 Predetermined Overhead Rate; Overhead Variances [LO4, LO5, LO6]
Norwall Company's flexible budget for manufacturing overhead (in condensed form) is given below:

Overhead Costs	Cost Formula (per machine-hour)	Machine-Hours 50,000	60,000	70,000
Variable costs	$3	$150,000	$180,000	$210,000
Fixed costs		300,000	300,000	300,000
Total overhead cost		$450,000	$480,000	$510,000

The following information is available for a recent period:

a. The denominator activity of 60,000 machine-hours is used to compute the predetermined overhead rate.
b. At the 60,000 standard machine-hours level of activity, the company should produce 40,000 units of product.
c. The company's actual operating results were:

Number of units produced	42,000
Actual machine-hours	64,000
Actual variable overhead costs	$185,600
Actual fixed overhead costs	$302,400

Required:

1. Compute the predetermined overhead rate and break it down into variable and fixed cost elements.
2. Compute the standard hours allowed for the actual production.
3. Compute the variable overhead spending and efficiency variances and the fixed overhead budget and volume variances.

EXERCISE 11–15 Relations Among Fixed Overhead Variances [LO5, LO6]

Selected information relating to Yost Company's operations for the most recent year is given below:

Activity:	
Denominator activity (machine-hours)	45,000
Standard hours allowed per unit	3
Number of units produced	14,000
Costs:	
Actual fixed overhead costs incurred	$267,000
Fixed overhead budget variance	$3,000 F

The company applies overhead cost to products on the basis of standard machine-hours.

Required:

1. What were the standard machine-hours allowed for the actual production?
2. What was the fixed portion of the predetermined overhead rate?
3. What was the volume variance?

EXERCISE 11–16 Fixed Overhead Variances [LO6]

Selected operating information on three different companies for a recent year is given below:

	Company		
	A	B	C
Full-capacity machine-hours	10,000	18,000	20,000
Budgeted machine-hours*	9,000	17,000	20,000
Actual machine-hours	9,000	17,800	19,000
Standard machine-hours allowed for actual production	9,500	16,000	20,000

*Denominator activity for computing the predetermined overhead rate.

Required:

For each company, state whether the company would have a favorable or unfavorable volume variance and why.

Problems

PROBLEM 11–17 Applying the Flexible Budget Approach [LO2]

The St. Lucia Blood Bank, a private charity partly supported by government grants, is located on the Caribbean island of St. Lucia. The Blood Bank has just finished its operations for September, which was a particularly busy month due to a powerful hurricane that hit neighboring islands causing many injuries. The hurricane largely bypassed St. Lucia, but residents of St. Lucia willingly donated their blood to help people on other islands. As a consequence, the blood bank collected and processed over 20% more blood than had been originally planned for the month.

A report prepared by a government official comparing actual costs to budgeted costs for the Blood Bank appears below. (The currency on St. Lucia is the East Caribbean dollar.) Continued support from the government depends on the Blood Bank's ability to demonstrate control over its costs.

ST. LUCIA BLOOD BANK Cost Control Report For the Month Ended September 30	Actual	Budget	Variance
Liters of blood collected	620	500	120
Variable costs:			
Medical supplies	$ 9,350	$ 7,500	$1,850 U
Lab tests	6,180	6,000	180 U
Refreshments for donors	1,340	1,000	340 U
Administrative supplies	400	250	150 U
Total variable cost	17,270	14,750	2,520 U
Fixed costs:			
Staff salaries	10,000	10,000	0
Equipment depreciation	2,800	2,500	300 U
Rent	1,000	1,000	0
Utilities	570	500	70 U
Total fixed cost	14,370	14,000	370 U
Total cost	$31,640	$28,750	$2,890 U

The managing director of the Blood Bank was very unhappy with this report, claiming that his costs were higher than expected due to the emergency on the neighboring islands. He also pointed out that the additional costs had been fully covered by payments from grateful recipients on the other islands. The government official who prepared the report countered that all of the figures had been submitted by the Blood Bank to the government; he was just pointing out that actual costs were a lot higher than promised in the budget.

Required:

1. Prepare a new performance report for September using the flexible budget approach. (Note: Even though some of these costs might be classified as direct costs rather than as overhead, the flexible budget approach can still be used to prepare a flexible budget performance report.)
2. Do you think any of the variances in the report you prepared should be investigated? Why?

PROBLEM 11–18 Comprehensive Standard Cost Variances [LO4, LO6]

"Wonderful! Not only did our salespeople do a good job in meeting the sales budget this year, but our production people did a good job in controlling costs as well," said Kim Clark, president of Martell Company. "Our $18,300 overall manufacturing cost variance is only 1.2% of the $1,536,000 standard cost of products made during the year. That's well within the 3% parameter set by management for acceptable variances. It looks like everyone will be in line for a bonus this year."

The company produces and sells a single product. The standard cost card for the product follows:

Standard Cost Card—per Unit of Product	
Direct materials, 2 feet at $8.45 per foot	$16.90
Direct labor, 1.4 direct labor hours at $16 per direct labor-hour	22.40
Variable overhead, 1.4 direct labor-hours at $2.50 per direct labor-hour	3.50
Fixed overhead, 1.4 direct labor-hours at $6 per direct labor-hour	8.40
Standard cost per unit	$51.20

The following additional information is available for the year just completed:

a. The company manufactured 30,000 units of product during the year.
b. A total of 64,000 feet of material was purchased during the year at a cost of $8.55 per foot. All of this material was used to manufacture the 30,000 units. There were no beginning or ending inventories for the year.

c. The company worked 43,500 direct labor-hours during the year at a direct labor cost of $15.80 per hour.
d. Overhead is applied to products on the basis of standard direct labor-hours. Data relating to manufacturing overhead costs follow:

Denominator activity level (direct labor-hours)	35,000
Budgeted fixed overhead costs (from the overhead flexible budget)	$210,000
Actual variable overhead costs incurred	$108,000
Actual fixed overhead costs incurred	$211,800

Required:
1. Compute the direct materials price and quantity variances for the year.
2. Compute the direct labor rate and efficiency variances for the year.
3. For manufacturing overhead compute:
   a. The variable overhead spending and efficiency variances for the year.
   b. The fixed overhead budget and volume variances for the year.
4. Total the variances you have computed, and compare the net amount with the $18,300 mentioned by the president. Do you agree that bonuses should be given to everyone for good cost control during the year? Explain.

PROBLEM 11–19 Comprehensive Standard Cost Variances [LO4, LO5, LO6]
Flandro Company uses a standard cost system and sets predetermined overhead rates on the basis of direct labor-hours. The following data are taken from the company's budget for the current year:

Denominator activity (direct labor-hours)	5,000
Variable manufacturing overhead cost	$25,000
Fixed manufacturing overhead cost	$59,000

The standard cost card for the company's only product is given below:

Direct materials, 3 yards at $4.40 per yard	$13.20
Direct labor, 1 hour at $12 per hour	12.00
Manufacturing overhead, 140% of direct labor cost	16.80
Standard cost per unit	$42.00

During the year, the company produced 6,000 units of product and incurred the following costs:

Materials purchased, 24,000 yards at $4.80 per yard	$115,200
Materials used in production (in yards)	18,500
Direct labor cost incurred, 5,800 hours at $13 per hour	$75,400
Variable manufacturing overhead cost incurred	$29,580
Fixed manufacturing overhead cost incurred	$60,400

Required:
1. Redo the standard cost card in a clearer, more usable format by detailing the variable and fixed overhead cost elements.
2. Prepare an analysis of the variances for materials and labor for the year.
3. Prepare an analysis of the variances for variable and fixed overhead for the year.
4. What effect, if any, does the choice of a denominator activity level have on unit standard costs? Is the volume variance a controllable variance from a spending point of view? Explain.

PROBLEM 11–20 Preparing an Overhead Performance Report [LO2]
Several years ago, Westmont Company developed a comprehensive budgeting system for profit planning and control purposes. The line supervisors have been very happy with the system and with the reports being prepared on their performance, but both middle and upper management have expressed considerable dissatisfaction with the information being generated by the system. A typical manufacturing overhead performance report for a recent period follows:

WESTMONT COMPANY
Overhead Performance Report—Assembly Department
For the Quarter Ended March 31

	Actual	Budget	Variance
Machine-hours	35,000	40,000	
Variable overhead costs:			
Indirect materials	$ 29,700	$ 32,000	$2,300 F
Rework	7,900	8,000	100 F
Utilities	51,800	56,000	4,200 F
Machine setup	11,600	12,000	400 F
Total variable overhead cost	101,000	108,000	7,000 F
Fixed overhead costs:			
Maintenance	79,200	80,000	800 F
Inspection	60,000	60,000	0
Total fixed overhead cost	139,200	140,000	800 F
Total overhead cost	$240,200	$248,000	$7,800 F

After receiving a copy of this overhead performance report, the supervisor of the Assembly Department stated, "These reports are super. It makes me feel really good to see how well things are going in my department. I can't understand why those people upstairs complain so much."

The budget data above are for the original planned level of activity for the quarter.

Required:

1. The company's vice president is uneasy about the performance reports being prepared and would like you to evaluate their usefulness to the company.
2. What changes, if any, should be made in the overhead performance report to give better insight into how well the supervisor is controlling costs?
3. Prepare a new overhead performance report for the quarter, incorporating any changes you suggested in (2) above. (Include both the variable and the fixed costs in your report.)

PROBLEM 11–21 Applying Overhead; Overhead Variances [LO4, LO5, LO6]
Chilczuk, S.A., of Gdansk, Poland, is a major producer of classic Polish sausage. The company uses a standard cost system to help control costs. Manufacturing overhead is applied to production on the basis of standard direct labor-hours. According to the company's flexible budget, the following manufacturing overhead costs should be incurred at an activity level of 35,000 labor-hours (the denominator activity level):

Variable manufacturing overhead costs	PZ 87,500
Fixed manufacturing overhead costs	210,000
Total manufacturing overhead cost	PZ297,500

The currency in Poland is the zloty, which is denoted here by PZ.

During the most recent year, the following operating results were recorded:

Activity:	
Actual labor-hours worked	30,000
Standard labor-hours allowed for output	32,000
Cost:	
Actual variable manufacturing overhead cost incurred	PZ78,000
Actual fixed manufacturing overhead cost incurred	PZ209,400

At the end of the year, the company's Manufacturing Overhead account contained the following data:

Manufacturing Overhead

Actual	287,400	Applied	272,000
	15,400		

Management would like to determine the cause of the PZ15,400 underapplied overhead.

Required:

1. Compute the predetermined overhead rate. Break the rate down into variable and fixed cost elements.
2. Show how the PZ272,000 Applied figure in the Manufacturing Overhead account was computed.
3. Analyze the PZ15,400 underapplied overhead figure in terms of the variable overhead spending and efficiency variances and the fixed overhead budget and volume variances.
4. Explain the meaning of each variance that you computed in (3) above.

PROBLEM 11–22 Flexible Budget and Overhead Analysis [LO1, LO4, LO5, LO6]

eXcel

Harper Company assembles all of its products in the Assembly Department. Budgeted costs for the operation of this department for the year have been set as follows:

Variable costs:	
Direct materials	$ 900,000
Direct labor	675,000
Utilities	45,000
Indirect labor	67,500
Supplies	22,500
Total variable cost	1,710,000
Fixed costs:	
Insurance	8,000
Supervisory salaries	90,000
Depreciation	160,000
Equipment rental	42,000
Total fixed cost	300,000
Total budgeted cost	$2,010,000
Budgeted direct labor-hours	75,000

Since the assembly work is done mostly by hand, operating activity in this department is best measured by direct labor-hours. The cost formulas used to develop the budgeted costs above are valid over a relevant range of 60,000 to 90,000 direct labor-hours per year.

Required:

1. Prepare a manufacturing overhead flexible budget for the Assembly Department using increments of 15,000 direct labor-hours. (The company does not include direct materials and direct labor costs in the flexible budget.)
2. Assume that the company computes predetermined overhead rates by department. Compute the rates that will be used to apply Assembly Department overhead costs to production. Break this rate down into variable and fixed cost elements.
3. Suppose that during the year the following actual activity and costs are recorded by the Assembly Department:

Actual direct labor-hours worked	73,000
Standard direct labor-hours allowed for the output of the year	70,000
Actual variable manufacturing overhead cost incurred	$124,100
Actual fixed manufacturing overhead cost incurred	$301,600

Complete the following:

a. A T-account for manufacturing overhead costs in the Assembly Department for the year is given below. Determine the amount of applied overhead cost for the year, and compute the under- or overapplied overhead.

Manufacturing Overhead

Actual cost	425,700	

b. Analyze the under- or overapplied overhead in terms of the variable overhead spending and efficiency variances and the fixed overhead budget and volume variances.

PROBLEM 11–23 Evaluating an Overhead Performance Report [LO2, LO4]

Frank Western, supervisor of the Machining Department for Freemont Company, was visibly upset after being reprimanded for his department's poor performance over the prior month. The department's performance report is given below:

FREEMONT COMPANY
Performance Report—Machining Department

	Cost Formula (per machine-hour)	Actual	Budget	Variance
Machine-hours		38,000	35,000	
Variable overhead costs:				
Utilities	$0.40	$ 15,700	$ 14,000	$ 1,700 U
Indirect labor	2.30	86,500	80,500	6,000 U
Supplies	0.60	26,000	21,000	5,000 U
Maintenance	1.20	44,900	42,000	2,900 U
Total variable overhead cost	$4.50	173,100	157,500	15,600 U
Fixed overhead costs:				
Supervision		38,000	38,000	0
Maintenance		92,400	92,000	400 U
Depreciation		80,000	80,000	0
Total fixed overhead cost		210,400	210,000	400 U
Total overhead cost		$383,500	$367,500	$16,000 U

"I just can't understand all the red ink," said Western to Sarah Mason, supervisor of another department. "When the boss called me in, I thought he was going to give me a pat on the back because I know for a fact that my department worked more efficiently last month than it has ever worked before. Instead, he tore me apart. I thought for a minute that it might be over the supplies that were stolen out of our warehouse last month. But they only amounted to a couple of thousand dollars, and just look at this report. *Everything* is unfavorable."

The budget for the Machining Department had called for production of 14,000 units last month, which is equal to a budgeted activity level of 35,000 machine-hours (at a standard time of 2.5 machine-hours per unit). Actual production in the Machining Department for the month was 16,000 units.

Required:

1. Evaluate the overhead performance report given above and explain why the variances are all unfavorable.
2. Prepare a new overhead performance report that will help Mr. Western's superiors assess efficiency and cost control in the Machining Department. (Hint: Exhibit 11–7 may be helpful in structuring your report; however, the report you prepare should include both variable and fixed costs.)

3. Would the supplies stolen out of the warehouse be included as part of the variable overhead spending variance or as part of the variable overhead efficiency variance for the month? Explain.

PROBLEM 11–24 Variable Overhead Performance Report [LO4]
The cost formulas for variable overhead costs in a machine shop are given below:

Variable Overhead Cost	Cost Formula (per machine-hour)
Power	$0.30
Setup time	0.20
Polishing wheels	0.16
Maintenance	0.18
Total variable overhead cost	$0.84

During August, the machine shop was scheduled to work 11,250 machine-hours and to produce 4,500 units of product. The standard machine time per unit of product is 2.5 hours. A strike near the end of the month forced a cutback in production. Actual results for the month were:

Actual machine-hours worked	9,250
Actual number of units produced	3,600

Actual costs for the month were:

Variable Overhead Cost	Total Actual Costs	Per Machine-Hour
Power	$2,405	$0.26
Setup time	2,035	0.22
Polishing wheels	1,110	0.12
Maintenance	925	0.10
Total variable overhead cost	$6,475	$0.70

Required:
Prepare an overhead performance report for the machine shop for August. Use column headings in your report as shown below:

Overhead Item	Cost Formula (per machine-hour)	Actual Costs Incurred 9,250 Machine-Hours	Budget Based on ? Machine-Hours	Budget Based on ? Machine-Hours	Total Variance	Breakdown of the Total Variance: Spending Variance	Breakdown of the Total Variance: Efficiency Variance

PROBLEM 11–25 Standard Cost Card; Fixed Overhead Analysis; Graphing [LO5, LO6]
When planning operations for the year, Southbrook Company chose a denominator activity of 40,000 direct labor-hours. According to the company's flexible budget, the following manufacturing overhead costs should be incurred at this activity level:

Variable manufacturing overhead costs	$72,000
Fixed manufacturing overhead costs	$360,000

The company produces a single product that requires 2.5 hours to complete. The direct labor rate is $12 per hour. Eight yards of material are needed to complete one unit of product; the material has a standard cost of $4.50 per yard. Overhead is applied to production on the basis of standard direct labor-hours.

Required:

1. Compute the predetermined overhead rate. Break the rate down into variable and fixed cost elements.
2. Prepare a standard cost card for one unit of product using the following format:

Direct materials, 8 yards at $4.50 per yard	$36
Direct labor, ?	?
Variable manufacturing overhead, ?	?
Fixed manufacturing overhead, ?	?
Standard cost per unit	$?

3. Prepare a graph with cost on the vertical (*Y*) axis and direct labor-hours on the horizontal (*X*) axis. Plot a line on your graph from a zero level of activity to 60,000 direct labor-hours for each of the following costs:
   a. Budgeted fixed overhead (in total).
   b. Applied fixed overhead [applied at the hourly rate computed in (1) above].
4. Assume that during the year actual activity is as follows:

Number of units produced	14,000
Actual direct labor-hours worked	33,000
Actual fixed manufacturing overhead cost incurred	$361,800

   a. Compute the fixed overhead budget and volume variances for the year.
   b. Show the volume variance on the graph you prepared in (3) above.
5. Disregard the data in (4) above. Assume instead that actual activity during the year is as follows:

Number of units produced	20,000
Actual direct labor-hours worked	52,000
Actual fixed manufacturing overhead costs incurred	$361,800

   a. Compute the fixed overhead budget and volume variances for the year.
   b. Show the volume variance on the graph you prepared in (3) above.

PROBLEM 11–26 Comprehensive Problem; Flexible Budget; Overhead Performance Report [LO1, LO2, LO3, LO4]

Gant Products, Inc., has recently introduced budgeting as an integral part of its corporate planning process. The company's first effort at constructing a flexible budget for manufacturing overhead is shown below:

Percentage of capacity	80%	100%
Machine-hours	4,800	6,000
Maintenance	$1,480	$ 1,600
Supplies	1,920	2,400
Utilities	1,940	2,300
Supervision	3,000	3,000
Machine setup	960	1,200
Total manufacturing overhead cost	$9,300	$10,500

The budgets above are relevant over a range of 80% to 100% of capacity. The managers who will be working under these budgets have control over both fixed and variable costs. The company applies manufacturing overhead to products on the basis of standard machine-hours.

Required:

1. Redo the company's flexible budget, presenting it in better format. Show the budget at 80%, 90%, and 100% levels of capacity. (Use the high-low method to separate fixed and variable costs.)

2. Express the flexible budget prepared in (1) above using a single cost formula for all overhead costs.
3. The company operated at 95% of machine-hour capacity during April. Five thousand six hundred standard machine-hours were allowed for the output of the month. Actual overhead costs incurred were:

Maintenance	$ 2,083
Supplies	3,420
Utilities	2,666
Supervision	3,000
Machine setup	855
Total overhead cost	$12,024

The fixed costs had no budget variances. Prepare an overhead performance report for April. Structure your report so that it shows only a spending variance for overhead. You may assume that the master budget for April called for an activity level during the month of 6,000 machine-hours.

4. Upon receiving the performance report you have prepared, the production manager commented, "I have two observations to make. First, I think there's an error on your report. You show an unfavorable spending variance for supplies, yet I know that we paid exactly the budgeted price for all the supplies we used last month. Pat Stevens, the purchasing agent, made a comment to me that our supplies prices haven't changed in over a year. Second, I wish you would modify your report to include an efficiency variance for overhead. The reason is that waste has been a problem in the factory for years and the efficiency variance would help us get overhead waste under control."
   a. Explain the probable cause of the unfavorable spending variance for supplies.
   b. Compute an efficiency variance for *total* variable overhead and explain to the production manager why it would or would not contain elements of overhead waste.

PROBLEM 11–27 Applying Overhead; Overhead Variances [LO4, LO5, LO6]

Lane Company manufactures a single product that requires a great deal of hand labor. Overhead cost is applied on the basis of standard direct labor-hours. The company's condensed flexible budget for manufacturing overhead is given below:

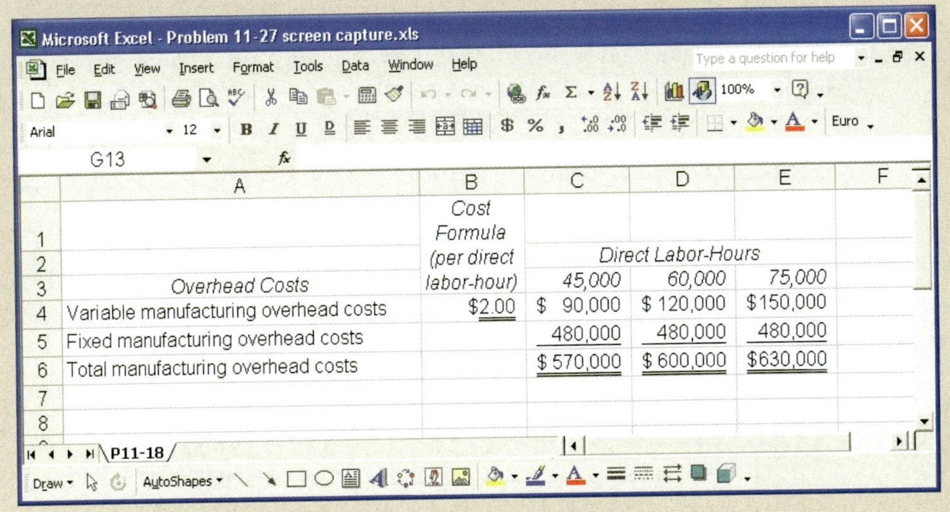

	A	B	C	D	E
1		Cost Formula			
2		(per direct		Direct Labor-Hours	
3	Overhead Costs	labor-hour)	45,000	60,000	75,000
4	Variable manufacturing overhead costs	$2.00	$ 90,000	$ 120,000	$150,000
5	Fixed manufacturing overhead costs		480,000	480,000	480,000
6	Total manufacturing overhead costs		$ 570,000	$ 600,000	$630,000

The company's product requires 3 pounds of material that has a standard cost of $7 per pound and 1.5 hours of direct labor time that has a standard rate of $12 per hour.

The company planned to operate at a denominator activity level of 60,000 direct labor-hours and to produce 40,000 units of product during the most recent year. Actual activity and costs for the year were as follows:

Number of units produced	42,000
Actual direct labor-hours worked	65,000
Actual variable manufacturing overhead cost incurred	$123,500
Actual fixed manufacturing overhead cost incurred	$483,000

Required:

1. Compute the predetermined overhead rate for the year. Break the rate down into variable and fixed elements.
2. Prepare a standard cost card for the company's product; show the details for all manufacturing costs on your standard cost card.
3. Do the following:
   a. Compute the standard direct labor-hours allowed for the year's production.
   b. Complete the following Manufacturing Overhead T-account for the year:

Manufacturing Overhead

?	?
?	?

4. Determine the reason for any under- or overapplied overhead for the year by computing the variable overhead spending and efficiency variances and the fixed overhead budget and volume variances.
5. Suppose the company had chosen 65,000 direct labor-hours as the denominator activity rather than 60,000 hours. State which, if any, of the variances computed in (4) above would have changed, and explain how the variance(s) would have changed. No computations are necessary.

PROBLEM 11–28 Flexible Budget and Overhead Performance Report [LO1, LO2, LO4]
You have just been hired by FAB Company, the manufacturer of a revolutionary new garage door opening device. John Foster, the president, has asked that you review the company's costing system and "do what you can to help us get better control of our manufacturing overhead costs." You find that the company has never used a flexible budget, and you suggest that preparing such a budget would be an excellent first step in overhead planning and control.

After much effort and analysis, you are able to determine the following cost formulas for the company's normal operating range of 20,000 to 30,000 machine-hours each month:

Overhead Costs	Cost Formula
Utilities	$0.90 per machine-hour
Maintenance	$1.60 per machine-hour plus $40,000 per month
Machine setup	$0.30 per machine-hour
Indirect labor	$0.70 per machine-hour plus $130,000 per month
Depreciation	$70,000 per month

To show the president how the flexible budget concept works, you have gathered the following actual manufacturing overhead cost data for the most recent month, March, in which the company worked 26,000 machine-hours and produced 15,000 units:

Utilities	$ 24,200
Maintenance	78,100
Machine setup	8,400
Indirect labor	149,600
Depreciation	71,500
Total manufacturing overhead cost	$331,800

The only variance in the fixed costs for the month was with depreciation, which increased as a result of purchasing new equipment.

The company had originally planned to work 30,000 machine-hours during March.

Required:

1. Prepare a flexible budget for the company in increments of 5,000 hours.
2. Prepare an overhead performance report for the company for March. (Use the format illustrated in Exhibit 11–11.)
3. What additional information would you need to compute an overhead efficiency variance for the company?

PROBLEM 11–29 Selection of a Denominator; Overhead Analysis; Standard Cost Card [LO4, LO5, LO6]

Morton Company's condensed flexible budget for manufacturing overhead is given below:

Overhead Costs	Cost Formula (per direct labor-hour)	Direct Labor-Hours 20,000	30,000	40,000
Variable manufacturing overhead costs	$4.50	$ 90,000	$135,000	$180,000
Fixed manufacturing overhead costs		270,000	270,000	270,000
Total manufacturing overhead cost		$360,000	$405,000	$450,000

The company manufactures a single product that requires two direct labor-hours to complete. The direct labor wage rate is $15 per hour. Four feet of raw material are required for each unit of product; the standard cost of the material is $8.75 per foot.

Although normal activity is 30,000 direct labor-hours each year, the company expects to operate at a 40,000-hour level of activity this year.

Required:

1. Assume that the company chooses 30,000 direct labor-hours as the denominator level of activity. Compute the predetermined overhead rate, breaking it down into variable and fixed cost elements.
2. Assume that the company chooses 40,000 direct labor-hours as the denominator level of activity. Repeat the computations in (1) above.
3. Complete two standard cost cards as outlined below.

Denominator Activity: 30,000 Direct Labor-Hours	
Direct materials, 4 feet at $8.75 per foot	$35.00
Direct labor, ?	?
Variable overhead, ?	?
Fixed overhead, ?	?
Standard cost per unit	$?

Denominator Activity: 40,000 Direct Labor-Hours	
Direct materials, $4 feet at $8.75 per foot	$35.00
Direct labor, ?	?
Variable overhead, ?	?
Fixed overhead, ?	?
Standard cost per unit	$?

4. Assume that the company actually produces 18,000 units and works 38,000 direct labor-hours during the year. Actual manufacturing overhead costs for the year are:

Variable manufacturing overhead costs	$174,800
Fixed manufacturing overhead costs	271,600
Total manufacturing overhead cost	$446,400

Do the following:

a. Compute the standard direct labor-hours allowed for this year's production.

b. Complete the Manufacturing Overhead account below. Assume that the company uses 30,000 direct labor-hours (normal activity) as the denominator activity figure in computing predetermined overhead rates, as you have done in (1) above.

Manufacturing Overhead

Actual costs 446,400	?
?	?

c. Determine the cause of the under- or overapplied overhead for the year by computing the variable overhead spending and efficiency variances and the fixed overhead budget and volume variances.

5. Looking at the variances you have computed, what appears to be the major disadvantage of using normal activity rather than expected actual activity as a denominator in computing the predetermined overhead rate? What advantages can you see to offset this disadvantage?

PROBLEM 11–30 Activity-Based Costing and the Flexible Budget Approach [LO2]
The Little Theatre is a nonprofit organization devoted to staging plays for children in Manchester, England. The theater has a very small full-time professional administrative staff. Through a special arrangement with the actors' union, actors and directors rehearse without pay and are paid only for actual performances.

The costs of 2004's operations appear below. (The currency in England is the pound, denoted £.) During 2004, The Little Theatre had six different productions—each of which was performed 18 times. For example, one of the productions was Peter the Rabbit, which had the usual six-week run with three performances on each weekend.

THE LITTLE THEATRE
Cost Report
For the Year Ended 31 December 2004

Number of productions	6
Number of performances of each production	18
Total number of performances	108
Actual costs incurred:	
Actors' and directors' wages	£216,000
Stagehands' wages	32,400
Ticket booth personnel and ushers' wages	16,200
Scenery, costumes, and props	108,000
Theater hall rent	54,000
Printed programs	27,000
Publicity	12,000
Administrative expenses	43,200
Total actual cost incurred	£508,800

Some of the costs vary with the number of productions, some with the number of performances, and some are relatively fixed and depend on neither the number of productions nor the number of performances. The costs of scenery, costumes, props, and publicity vary with the number of productions. It doesn't make any difference how many times Peter the Rabbit is performed, the cost of the scenery is the same. Likewise, the cost of publicizing a play with posters and radio commercials is the same whether there are 10, 20, or 30 performances of the play. On the other hand, the wages of the actors, directors, stagehands, ticket booth personnel, and ushers vary with the number of performances. The greater the number of performances, the higher the wage costs will be. Similarly, the costs of renting the hall and printing the programs will vary with the number of performances. Administrative expenses are more difficult to pin down, but the best estimate is that approximately 75% of these costs are fixed, 15% depend on the number of productions staged, and the remaining 10% depend on the number of performances.

At the end of 2004, the board of directors of the theater authorized expanding the theater's program in 2005 to seven productions, with 24 performances each. Not surprisingly, actual costs for 2005 were considerably higher than the costs for 2004. (Grants from donors and ticket sales were also correspondingly higher.) Data concerning 2005's operations appear below:

THE LITTLE THEATRE Cost Report For the Year Ended 31 December 2005	
Number of productions	7
Number of performances of each production	24
Total number of performances	168
Actual costs incurred:	
Actors' and directors' wages	£341,800
Stagehands' wages	49,700
Ticket booth personnel and ushers' wages	25,900
Scenery, costumes, and props	130,600
Theater hall rent	78,000
Printed programs	38,300
Publicity	15,100
Administrative expenses	47,500
Total actual cost incurred	£726,900

Even though many of the costs above may be considered direct costs rather than overhead, the flexible budget approach covered in the chapter can still be used to evaluate how well these costs are controlled. The principles are the same whether a cost is a direct cost or is overhead.

Required:

1. Use the actual results from 2004 to estimate the cost formulas for the flexible budget for The Little Theatre. Keep in mind that the theater has two measures of activity—the number of productions and the number of performances.
2. Prepare a performance report for 2005 using the flexible budget approach and both measures of activity. Assume there was no inflation. (Note: To evaluate administrative expenses, first determine the flexible budget amounts for the three elements of administrative expenses. Then compare the total of the three elements to the actual administrative expense of £47,500.)
3. If you were on the board of directors of the theater, would you be pleased with how well costs were controlled during 2005? Why or why not?
4. The cost formulas provide figures for the average cost per production and average cost per performance. How accurate do you think these figures would be for predicting the cost of a new production or of an additional performance of a particular production?

Cases

CASE 11–31 Ethics and the Manager [LO2]

Tom Kemper is the controller of the Wichita manufacturing facility of Prudhom Enterprises, Incorporated. Among the many reports that must be filed with corporate headquarters is the annual overhead performance report. The report covers the year ended December 31, and is due at corporate headquarters shortly after the beginning of the New Year. Kemper does not like putting work off to the last minute, so just before Christmas he put together a preliminary draft of the overhead performance report. Some adjustments would later be required for transactions that occur between Christmas and New Year's Day, but there are generally very few of these. A copy of the preliminary draft report, which Kemper completed on December 21, follows:

WICHITA MANUFACTURING FACILITY
Overhead Performance Report
December 21 Preliminary Draft

Budgeted machine-hours 200,000
Actual machine-hours 180,000

Overhead Costs	Cost Formula (per machine-hour)	Actual Costs 180,000 Machine-Hours	Budget Based on 180,000 Machine-Hours	Spending or Budget Variance
Variable overhead costs:				
Power	$0.10	$ 19,750	$ 18,000	$ 1,750 U
Supplies	0.25	47,000	45,000	2,000 U
Abrasives	0.30	58,000	54,000	4,000 U
Total variable overhead cost	$0.65	124,750	117,000	7,750 U
Fixed overhead costs:				
Depreciation		345,000	332,000	13,000 U
Supervisory salaries		273,000	275,000	2,000 F
Insurance		37,000	37,000	0
Industrial engineering		189,000	210,000	21,000 F
Factory building lease		60,000	60,000	0
Total fixed overhead cost		904,000	914,000	10,000 F
Total overhead cost		$1,028,750	$1,031,000	$ 2,250 F

Melissa Ilianovitch, the general manager at the Wichita facility, asked to see a copy of the preliminary draft report at 4:45 P.M. on December 23. Kemper carried a copy of the report to her office where the following discussion took place:

Ilianovitch: Ouch! Almost all of the variances on the report are unfavorable. The only thing that looks good at all are the favorable variances for supervisory salaries and for industrial engineering. How did we have an unfavorable variance for depreciation?

Kemper: Do you remember that milling machine that broke down because the wrong lubricant was used by the machine operator?

Ilianovitch: Only vaguely.

Kemper: It turned out we couldn't fix it. We had to scrap the machine and buy a new one.

Ilianovitch: This report doesn't look good. I was raked over the coals last year when we had just a few unfavorable variances.

Kemper: I'm afraid the final report is going to look even worse.

Ilianovitch: Oh?

Kemper: The line item for industrial engineering on the report is for work we hired Ferguson Engineering to do for us on a contract basis. The original contract was for $210,000, but we asked them to do some additional work that was not in the contract. Under the terms of the contract, we have to reimburse Ferguson Engineering for the costs of the additional work. The $189,000 in actual costs that appear on the preliminary draft report reflects only their billings up through December 21. The last bill they had sent us was on November 28, and they completed the project just last week. Yesterday I got a call from Laura Sunder over at Ferguson and she said they would be sending us a final bill for the project before the end of the year. The total bill, including the reimbursements for the additional work, is going to be . . .

Ilianovitch: I am not sure I want to hear this.

Kemper: $225,000

Ilianovitch: Ouch! Ouch! Ouch!

Kemper: The additional work we asked them to do added $15,000 to the cost of the project.

Ilianovitch: No way can I turn in a performance report with an overall unfavorable variance. They'll kill me at corporate headquarters. Call up Laura at Ferguson and ask her not to send the bill until after the first of the year. We have to have that $21,000 favorable variance for industrial engineering on the performance report.

Required:

What should Tom Kemper do? Explain.

CASE 11–32 Preparing a Performance Report Using Activity-Based Costing [LO2]

Boyne University offers an extensive continuing education program in many cities throughout the state. For the convenience of its faculty and administrative staff and to save costs, the university employs a supervisor to operate a motor pool. The motor pool operated with 20 vehicles until February, when an additional automobile was acquired. The motor pool furnishes gasoline, oil, and other supplies for its automobiles. A mechanic does routine maintenance and minor repairs. Major repairs are done at a nearby commercial garage.

Each year, the supervisor prepares an operating budget that informs the university administration of the funds needed for operating the motor pool. Depreciation (straight line) on the automobiles is recorded in the budget in order to determine the cost per mile of operating the vehicles.

The following schedule presents the operating budget for the current year, which has been approved by the university. The schedule also shows actual operating costs for March of the current year compared to one-twelfth of the annual operating budget.

UNIVERSITY MOTOR POOL
Budget Report for March

	Annual Operating Budget	Monthly Budget*	March Actual	(Over) Under Budget
Gasoline	$ 42,000	$ 3,500	$ 4,300	$(800)
Oil, minor repairs, parts	3,600	300	380	(80)
Outside repairs	2,700	225	50	175
Insurance	6,000	500	525	(25)
Salaries and benefits	30,000	2,500	2,500	0
Depreciation of vehicles	26,400	2,200	2,310	(110)
Total cost	$110,700	$ 9,225	$10,065	$(840)
Total miles	600,000	50,000	63,000	
Cost per mile	$ 0.1845	$0.1845	$0.1598	
Number of automobiles in use	20	20	21	

*Annual operating budget ÷ 12 months.

The annual operating budget was constructed on the following assumptions:

a. Twenty automobiles in the motor pool.
b. Thirty thousand miles driven per year per automobile.
c. Twenty-five miles per gallon per automobile.
d. $1.75 per gallon of gasoline.
e. $0.006 cost per mile for oil, minor repairs, and parts.
f. $135 cost per automobile per year for outside repairs.
g. $300 cost per automobile per year for insurance.

The supervisor of the motor pool is unhappy with the monthly report comparing budget and actual costs for March, claiming it presents an unfair picture of performance. A previous employer used flexible budgeting to compare actual costs to budgeted amounts.

Required:

1. Prepare a new performance report for March showing budgeted costs, actual costs, and variances. In preparing your report, use flexible budgeting techniques to compute the monthly budget figures.
2. What are the deficiencies in the performance report presented above? How does the report that you prepared in (1) above overcome these deficiencies?

(CMA, adapted)

CASE 11–33 Working Backwards from Variance Data [LO4, LO5, LO6]

You have recently graduated from State University and have accepted a position with Vitex, Inc., the manufacturer of a popular consumer product. During your first week on the job, the vice president has been favorably impressed with your work. She has been so impressed, in fact, that yesterday she called you into her office and asked you to attend the executive committee meeting this morning for the purpose of leading a discussion on the variances reported for last period. Anxious to favorably impress the executive committee, you took the variances and supporting data home last night to study.

On your way to work this morning, the papers were laying on the seat of your new, red convertible. As you were crossing a bridge on the highway, a sudden gust of wind caught the papers and blew them over the edge of the bridge and into the stream below. You managed to retrieve only one page, which contains the following information:

STANDARD COST CARD

Direct materials, 6 pounds at $3 per pound	$18.00
Direct labor, 0.8 direct labor-hours at $15 per direct labor-hour	12.00
Variable manufacturing overhead, 0.8 direct labor-hours at $3 per direct labor-hour	2.40
Fixed manufacturing overhead, 0.8 direct labor-hours at $7 per direct labor-hour	5.60
Standard cost per unit	$38.00

	Total Standard Cost*	Variances Reported			
		Price or Rate	Spending or Budget	Quantity or Efficiency	Volume
Direct materials	$405,000	$6,900 F		$9,000 U	
Direct labor	$270,000	$14,550 U		$21,000 U	
Variable manufacturing overhead	$54,000		$1,300 F	$?† U	
Fixed manufacturing overhead	$126,000		$500 F		$14,000 U

*Applied to Work in Process during the period.
†Entry obliterated.

You recall that manufacturing overhead cost is applied to production on the basis of direct labor-hours and that all of the materials purchased during the period were used in production. Since the company uses JIT to control work flows, work in process inventories are insignificant and can be ignored.

It is now 8:30 A.M. The executive committee meeting starts in just one hour; you realize that to avoid looking like a bungling fool you must somehow generate the necessary "backup" data for the variances before the meeting begins. Without backup data it will be impossible to lead the discussion or answer any questions.

Required:

1. How many units were produced last period? (Think hard about this one!)
2. How many pounds of direct material were purchased and used in production?
3. What was the actual cost per pound of material?
4. How many actual direct labor-hours were worked during the period?
5. What was the actual rate paid per direct labor-hour?
6. How much actual variable manufacturing overhead cost was incurred during the period?
7. What is the total fixed manufacturing overhead cost in the company's flexible budget?
8. What were the denominator direct labor-hours for last period?

CASE 11–34 Comprehensive Variance Analysis; Incomplete Data [LO4, LO5, LO6]

Each of the cases below is independent. Each company uses a standard cost system and each company's flexible budget for manufacturing overhead is based on standard machine-hours.

Item	Company A	Company B
1. Denominator activity in machine-hours	?	40,000
2. Standard machine-hours allowed for units produced	32,000	?
3. Actual machine-hours worked	30,000	?
4. Flexible budget variable overhead per machine-hour	$?	$2.80
5. Flexible budget fixed overhead (total)	$?	$?
6. Actual variable overhead cost incurred	$54,000	$117,000
7. Actual fixed overhead cost incurred	$209,400	$302,100
8. Variable overhead cost applied to production*	$?	$117,600
9. Fixed overhead cost applied to production*	$192,000	$?
10. Variable overhead spending variance	$?	$?
11. Variable overhead efficiency variance	$3,500 F	$8,400 U
12. Fixed overhead budget variance	$?	$2,100 U
13. Fixed overhead volume variance	$18,000 U	$?
14. Variable portion of the predetermined overhead rate	$?	$?
15. Fixed portion of the predetermined overhead rate	$?	$?
16. Underapplied (or overapplied) overhead	$?	$?

*Based on standard hours allowed for units produced

Required:

Compute the unknown amounts. (Hint: One way to proceed would be to use the format for variance analysis found in Exhibit 10–7 for variable overhead and in Exhibit 11–10 for fixed overhead.)

Group and Internet Exercises

GROUP EXERCISE 11–35 Choice of Denominator Activity Level

American Widget, Inc., makes a number of high-volume standard products that are sold in highly competitive markets. As a result, its cost system stresses cost control. American uses a standard cost system and updates standards on a regular and timely basis. Until recently, expected annual capacity was the basis for determining predetermined factory overhead rates. This rate was used for internal planning and reporting and performance evaluation purposes, as well as for inventory valuation.

John Phillips, controller, has proposed changing the basis for internal planning and reporting from expected annual capacity to practical capacity. Since practical capacity remains relatively constant unless there is a plant expansion or purchase of new manufacturing machinery, Phillips believes this change would facilitate planning and budgeting.

Phillips has held one meeting with department managers and presented them with their new annual budgets prepared on the basis of the proposed practical capacity standard. There was little discussion. Later, a member of the cost accounting staff pointed out that the new standard for fixed manufacturing costs would be tighter than the old standard.

Required:

1. If the new annual budgets for American Widget reflect the implementation of tighter standards based on practical capacity:
   a. What negative behavioral implications for employees and department managers could occur as a result of this change?
   b. What could American Widget management do to reduce the negative behavioral effects?
2. Explain how tight cost standards within an organization could have positive behavioral effects.

3. Identify the individuals who should participate in setting standards and describe the benefits to an organization of their participation in the standard-setting process.

(CMA, adapted)

GROUP EXERCISE 11–36 Analyzing Your College's Budget

Obtain a copy of your college or university's budget and actual results for the most recently completed year.

Required:

1. Determine the major assumptions used in the last budget (e.g., number of students; tuition per student; number of employees; increases in wages, salaries, benefits; changes in occupancy costs; etc.).
2. Compare the budgeted revenue amounts with the actual results. Try to determine the reasons for any differences.
3. Compare budgeted expenses with the actual results using the basic approach shown in Exhibit 11–4. Try to determine the reasons for any differences.

INTERNET EXERCISE 11–37

As you know, the World Wide Web is a medium that is constantly evolving. Sites come and go, and change without notice. To enable the periodic updating of site addresses, this problem has been posted to the textbook website (www.mhhe.com/garrison11e). After accessing the site, enter the Student Center and select this chapter. Select and complete the Internet Exercise.

Chapter 12

Segment Reporting and Decentralization

LEARNING OBJECTIVES

After studying Chapter 12, you should be able to:

LO1 Prepare a segmented income statement using the contribution format, and explain the difference between traceable fixed costs and common fixed costs.

LO2 Compute return on investment (ROI) and show how changes in sales, expenses, and assets affect ROI.

LO3 Compute residual income and understand the strengths and weaknesses of this method of measuring performance.

LO4 (Appendix 12A) Determine the range, if any, within which a negotiated transfer price should fall.

Tracing Changes the Picture

BUSINESS FOCUS

E & A Company (the name has been changed to conceal the company's true identity) provides a wide range of engineering and architectural consulting services to both government and industry. For many years, the company pooled all operating costs and allocated them to its three branch offices on the basis of labor cost. When it abandoned this practice and started tracing costs such as rent directly to the offices, while at the same time assigning other costs on a more appropriate basis, the reported profits of one branch office doubled, the reported profits of another branch office changed from a loss to a profit, and the reported profits of the third branch office changed from a profit to a loss. ■

Source: Beth M. Chaffman and John Talbott, "Activity-Based Costing in a Service Organization," *CMA* 64, no. 10, p. 18.

Once an organization grows beyond a few people, it becomes impossible for the top manager to make decisions about everything. For example, the CEO of the Hyatt Hotel chain cannot be expected to decide whether a particular hotel guest at the Hyatt Hotel on Maui should be allowed to check out later than the normal checkout time. It makes sense for the CEO to authorize employees at Maui to make this decision. As in this example, managers in large organizations have to delegate some decisions to those who are at lower levels in the organization.

Decentralization in Organizations

In a **decentralized organization,** decision-making authority is not confined to a few top executives; rather, decision-making authority is spread throughout the organization. All large organizations are decentralized to some extent out of necessity. At one extreme, a strongly decentralized organization is one in which even the lowest-level managers and employees are empowered to make decisions. At the other extreme, in a strongly centralized organization, lower-level managers have little freedom to make a decision. Although most organizations fall somewhere between these two extremes, the trend is towards decentralization.

Advantages and Disadvantages of Decentralization

Decentralization has five major advantages:

1. Top management is relieved of day-to-day problem solving and is able to concentrate on strategy, higher-level decision making, and coordinating activities.
2. Lower-level managers generally have more detailed and up-to-date information about local conditions than top managers. Therefore, lower-level managers are often capable of making better operational decisions.
3. Delegating decision-making authority to lower-level managers enables them to quickly respond to customers.
4. Decentralization provides lower-level managers with the decision-making experience they will need when promoted to higher-level positions.
5. Delegating decision-making authority to lower-level managers often increases their motivation, resulting in increased job satisfaction and retention, as well as improved performance.

Decentralization has four major disadvantages:

1. Lower-level managers may make decisions without fully understanding the big picture. While top-level managers typically have less detailed information about local operations than the lower-level managers, they usually have more information about the company as a whole and should have a better understanding of the company's strategy.
2. In a truly decentralized organization, there may be a lack of coordination among autonomous managers. This problem can be reduced by clearly defining the company's strategy and communicating it effectively throughout the organization through the use of a well-designed Balanced Scorecard (see Chapter 10).
3. Lower-level managers may have objectives that are different from the objectives of the entire organization. For example, some managers may be more interested in

increasing the sizes of their departments than in increasing the profits of the company.[1] To some degree, this problem can be overcome by designing performance evaluation systems that motivate managers to make decisions that are in the best interests of the company.

4. It may be difficult to effectively spread innovative ideas in a strongly decentralized organization. Someone in one part of the organization may have a terrific idea that would benefit other parts of the organization, but without strong central direction the idea may not be shared with, and adopted by, other parts of the organization. This problem can be reduced through the effective use of intranet systems, which allow globally dispersed employees to electronically share their ideas and knowledge.

Responsibility Accounting

Since decentralized organizations delegate decision-making responsibility to lower-level managers, they need *responsibility accounting systems* that link lower-level managers' decision-making authority with accountability for the outcomes of those decisions. The term **responsibility center** is used for any part of an organization whose manager has control over and is accountable for cost, profit, or investments. The three primary types of responsibility centers are *cost centers*, *profit centers*, and *investment centers*.[2]

Cost, Profit, and Investment Centers

Cost Center The manager of a **cost center** has control over costs, but not over revenue or investment funds. Service departments such as accounting, finance, general administration, legal, and personnel are usually classified as cost centers. In addition, manufacturing facilities are often considered to be cost centers. The managers of cost centers are expected to minimize costs while providing the level of products and services demanded by other parts of the organization. For example, the manager of a manufacturing facility would be evaluated at least in part by comparing actual costs to how much costs should have been for the actual level of output during the period. Standard cost variances and flexible budget variances, such as those discussed in Chapters 10 and 11, are often used to evaluate cost center performance.

Profit Center The manager of a **profit center** has control over both costs and revenue. Like a cost center manager, a profit center manager does not have control over investment funds. For example, the manager in charge of a Six Flags amusement park would be responsible for both the revenues and costs, and hence the profits, of the amusement park,

---

[1] Similar problems exist with top-level managers as well. The shareholders of the company delegate their decision-making authority to the top managers. Unfortunately, top managers may abuse that trust by rewarding themselves and their friends too generously, spending too much company money on palatial offices, and so on. The issue of how to ensure that top managers act in the best interests of the company's owners continues to puzzle experts. To a large extent, the owners rely on performance evaluation using return on investment and residual income measures as discussed later in the chapter and on bonuses and stock options. The stock market is also an important disciplining mechanism. If top managers squander the company's resources, the price of the company's stock will almost surely fall—resulting in a loss of prestige, bonuses, and possibly a job. And, of course, particularly outrageous self-dealing may land a CEO in court, as recent events have demonstrated.

[2] Some companies classify business segments that are responsible mainly for generating revenue, such as an insurance sales office, as *revenue centers*. Other companies would consider this to be just another type of profit center, since costs of some kind (salaries, rent, utilities) are usually deducted from the revenues in the segment's income statement.

but may not have control over major investments in the park. Profit center managers are often evaluated by comparing actual profit to targeted or budgeted profit.

Investment Center The manager of an **investment center** has control over cost, revenue, and investments in operating assets. For example, the vice president of the Truck Division at General Motors would have a great deal of discretion over investments in the division. This vice president would be responsible for initiating investment proposals, such as funding research into more fuel-efficient engines for sport-utility vehicles. Once the proposal has been approved by General Motor's top-level managers and board of directors, the vice president of the Truck Division would then be responsible for making sure that the investment pays off. Investment center managers are usually evaluated using return on investment (ROI) or residual income measures, as discussed later in the chapter.

IN BUSINESS

EXTREME INCENTIVES

In 2003, Tyco International, Ltd., was rocked by a series of scandals including disclosure of $2 billion of accounting-related problems, investigations by the Securities and Exchange Commission, and a criminal trial of its ex-CEO, Dennis Kozlowski, on charges of more than $600 million in unauthorized compensation and fraudulent stock sales. Was any of this foreseeable? Well, in a word, yes.

BusinessWeek reported in 1999 that the CEO of Tyco International, Ltd., was putting unrelenting pressure on his managers to deliver growth. "Each year, [the CEO] sets targets for how much each manager must increase his or her unit's earnings in the coming year. The targets are coupled with a powerful incentive system. If they meet or exceed these targets, managers are promised a bonus that can be many times their salary. But if they fall even a bit short, the bonus plummets." This sounds good, but "to many accounting experts, the sort of all-or-nothing bonus structure set up at Tyco is a warning light. If top executives set profit targets too high or turn a blind eye to how managers achieve them, the incentive for managers to cut corners is enormous. Indeed, a blue-ribbon panel of accounting experts who were trying to improve corporate auditing standards several years ago . . . identified just such extreme incentives as a red flag. 'If you're right under the target, there's a tremendous economic interest to accelerate earnings," says David F. Larcker, a professor of accounting at the Wharton School. 'If you're right over it, there is an incentive to push earnings into the next period.'"

Sources: *Reuters*, "Tyco Says to Restate Several Years of Results," June 16, 2003; Jeanne King, *Reuters*, "New York Trial of ex-Tyco CEO Koslowski Can Proceed," June 23, 2003; and, William C. Symonds, Diane Brady, Geoffrey Smith, and Lorraine Woellert, "Tyco: Aggressive or Out of Line?" *BusinessWeek*, November 1, 1999, pp. 160–165.

An Organizational View of Responsibility Centers

Superior Foods Corporation provides an example of the various kinds of responsibility centers that exist in an organization. Superior Foods generates $500 million in annual sales by manufacturing and distributing snack foods and beverages. Exhibit 12–1 shows a partial organization chart for Superior Foods that displays cost, profit, and investment centers. Note that the departments and work centers that do not generate significant revenues by themselves are classified as cost centers. These are staff departments, such as finance, legal, and personnel, and operating units, such as the bottling plant, warehouse, and beverage distribution center. The profit centers generate revenues, and they include the salty snacks, beverages, and confections product families. The vice president of operations oversees the allocation of investment funds across the product families and is responsible for the profits of those product families. And finally, corporate headquarters is an investment center, since it is responsible for all revenues, costs, and investments.

EXHIBIT 12–1
Business Segments Classified as Cost, Profit, and Investment Centers

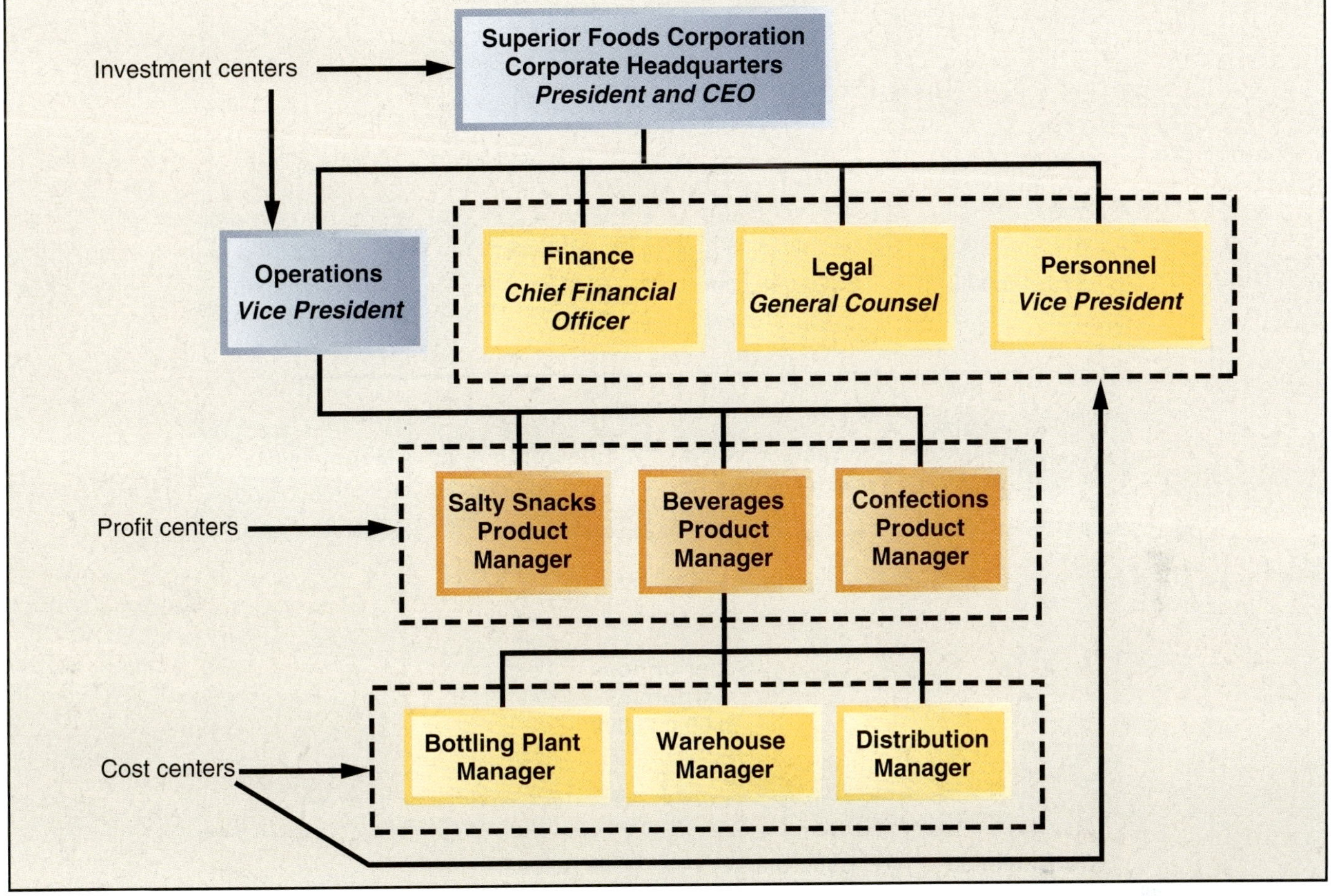

Decentralization and Segment Reporting

LEARNING OBJECTIVE 1
Prepare a segmented income statement using the contribution format, and explain the difference between traceable fixed costs and common fixed costs.

Effective decentralization requires *segmented reporting.* In addition to the companywide income statement, reports are needed for individual segments of the organization. A **segment** is a part or activity of an organization about which managers would like cost, revenue, or profit data. Examples of segments include divisions of a company, sales territories, individual stores, service centers, manufacturing plants, marketing departments, individual customers, and product lines. A company's operations can be segmented in many ways. For example, Exhibit 12–2 shows several ways in which Superior Foods could segment its business. The top half of the exhibit shows Superior segmenting its $500 million in revenue by geographical region, and the bottom half shows Superior segmenting its total revenue by customer channel. With the appropriate database and software, managers could easily drill even further down into the organization. For example, the sales in California could be segmented by product family, then by product line. This drilldown capability helps managers to identify the sources of strong or weak overall financial performance. In this chapter, we learn how to construct income statements for business segments. These segmented income statements are useful in analyzing the profitability of segments and in measuring the performance of segment managers.

Building a Segmented Income Statement

Several important principles are involved in constructing a segmented income statement that would be useful to managers. These principles are illustrated in the following example.

EXHIBIT 12–2
Superior Foods Corporation: Revenue Segmented by Geographic Region and Customer Channel

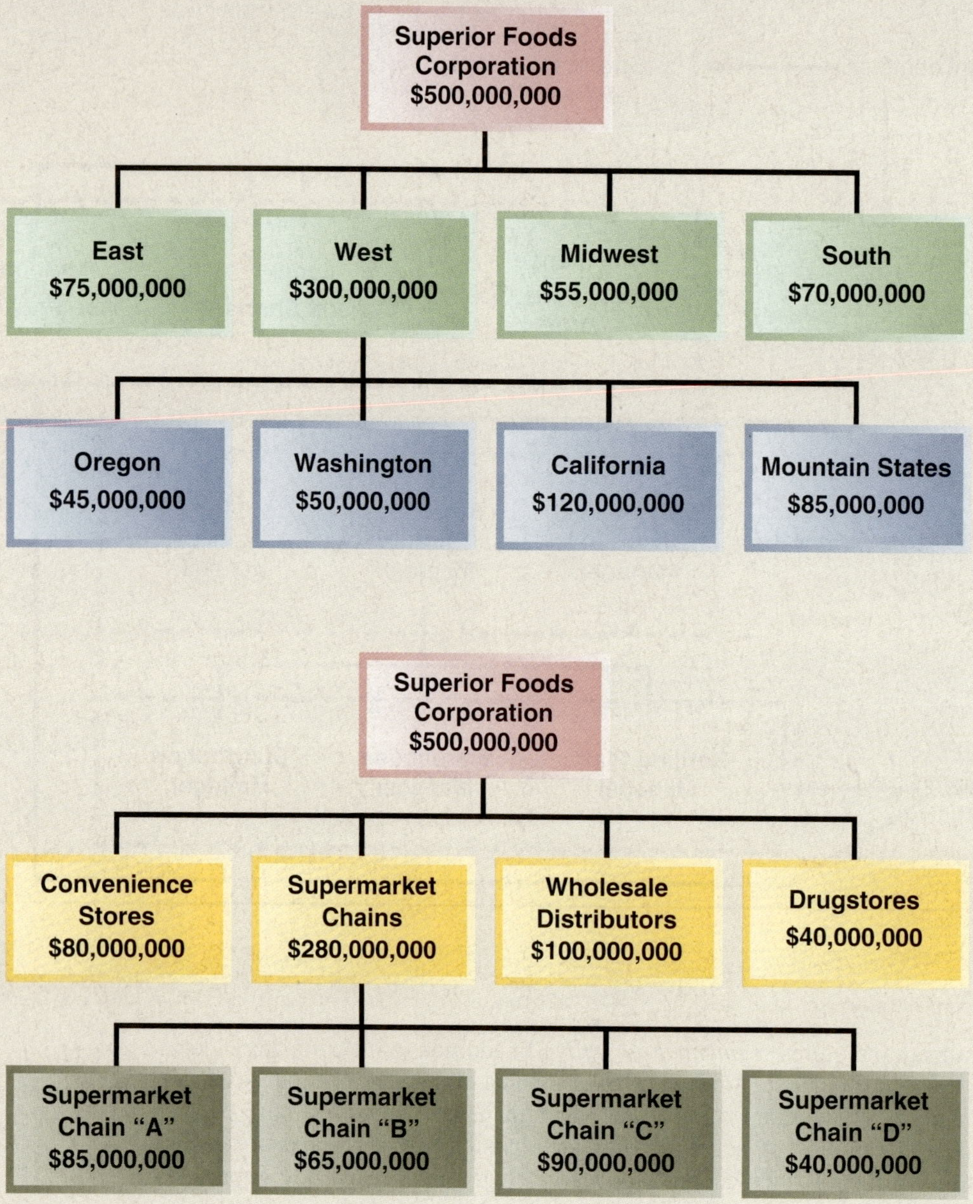

MANAGERIAL ACCOUNTING IN ACTION
The Issue

Soft Solutions Inc.

SoftSolutions, Inc., is a rapidly growing computer software company founded by Lori Saffer, who had previously worked in a large software company, and Marjorie Matsuo, who had previously worked in the hotel industry as a general manager. They formed the company to develop and market user-friendly accounting and operations software designed specifically for hotels. They quit their jobs, pooled their savings, hired several programmers, and got down to work.

The first sale was by far the most difficult. No hotel wanted to be the first to use an untested product from an unknown company. After overcoming this obstacle with persistence, good luck, dedication to customer service, and a very low introductory price, the company's sales burgeoned.

The company quickly developed similar business software for other specialized markets and then branched out into clip art and computer games. Within four years of its founding, the organization had grown to the point where Saffer and Matsuo were no longer able to personally direct all of the company's activities. Decentralization had become a necessity.

Accordingly, the company was split into two divisions—Business Products and Consumer Products. By mutual consent, Matsuo took the title president and Saffer took the title vice president of the Business Products Division. Chris Worden, a programmer who had spearheaded the drive into the clip art and computer games markets, was designated vice president of the Consumer Products Division.

Almost immediately, the issue arose of how best to evaluate the performance of the divisions. Matsuo called a meeting to consider this issue and asked Saffer, Worden, and the controller, Bill Carson, to attend. The following discussion took place at that meeting:

Marjorie Matsuo: We need to find a better way to measure the performance of the divisions.

Chris Worden: I agree. Consumer Products has been setting the pace in this company for the last two years, and we should be getting more recognition.

Lori Saffer: Chris, we are delighted with the success of the Consumer Products Division.

Chris Worden: I know. But it is hard to figure out just how successful we are with the present accounting reports. All we have are sales and cost of goods sold figures for the division.

Bill Carson: What's the matter with those figures? They are prepared using generally accepted accounting principles.

Chris Worden: The sales figures are fine. However, cost of goods sold includes some costs that really aren't the costs of our division, and it excludes some costs that are. Let's take a simple example. Everything we sell in the Consumer Products Division has to pass through the automatic bar-coding machine, which applies a unique bar code to the product.

Lori Saffer: We know. Every item we ship must have a unique identifying bar code. That's true for items from the Business Products Division as well as for items from the Consumer Products Division.

Chris Worden: That's precisely the point. Whether an item comes from the Business Products Division or the Consumer Products Division, it must pass through the automatic bar-coding machine after the software has been packaged. How much of the cost of the automatic bar coder would be saved if we didn't have any consumer products?

Marjorie Matsuo: Since we have only one automatic bar coder and we would need it anyway to code the business products, I guess none of the cost would be saved.

Chris Worden: That's right. And since none of the cost could be saved even if the entire Consumer Products Division were eliminated, how can we logically say that some of the cost of the automatic bar coder is a cost of the Consumer Products Division?

Lori Saffer: Just a minute, Chris, are you saying that my Business Products Division should be charged with the entire cost of the automatic bar coder?

Chris Worden: No, that's not what I am saying.

Marjorie Matsuo: But Chris, I don't see how we can have sensible performance reports without making someone responsible for costs like the cost of the automatic bar coder. Bill, as our accounting expert, what do you think?

Bill Carson: I have some ideas for handling issues like the automatic bar coder. The best approach would probably be for me to put together a draft performance report. We can discuss it at the next meeting when everyone has something concrete to look at.

Marjorie Matsuo: Okay, let's see what you come up with.

Bill Carson, the controller of SoftSolutions, realized that segmented income statements would be required to more appropriately evaluate the performance of the two divisions. To construct the segmented reports, he would have to carefully segregate costs that are attributable to the segments from costs that are not. Since most of the disputes over costs would be about fixed costs such as the automatic bar-coding machine, he knew he would also have to separate fixed from variable costs. Under the conventional absorption costing income statement prepared for the entire company, variable and fixed manufacturing costs were commingled in the cost of goods sold.

Largely for these reasons, Bill Carson decided to use the contribution format income statement based on variable costing that was discussed in earlier chapters. Recall that when the contribution format is used: (1) the cost of goods sold consists only of the variable manufacturing costs; (2) variable and fixed costs are listed in separate sections; and (3) a contribution margin is computed. When such a statement is segmented as in this chapter, fixed costs are broken down further into what are called traceable and common costs as discussed later. This breakdown allows a *segment margin* to be computed for each segment of the company. The segment margin is a valuable tool for assessing the long-run profitability of a segment and is also a much better tool for evaluating performance than the usual absorption costing reports.

Levels of Segmented Statements

A portion of the segmented report Bill Carson prepared is shown in Exhibit 12–3. The contribution format income statement for the entire company appears at the very top of the exhibit under the column labeled Total Company. Immediately to the right of this column are two columns—one for each of the two divisions. We can see that the divisional segment margin is $60,000 for the Business Products Division and $40,000 for the Consumer Products Division. This is the portion of the report that was specifically requested by the company's divisional managers. They wanted to know how much each of their divisions was contributing to the company's profits.

However, segmented income statements can be prepared for activities at many levels in a company. To provide more information to the company's divisional managers, Bill Carson has further segmented the divisions according to their major product lines. In the case of the Consumer Products Division, the product lines are clip art and computer games. Going even further, Bill Carson has segmented each of the product lines according to how they are sold—in retail computer stores or by catalog sales. In Exhibit 12–3, this further segmentation is illustrated for the computer games product line. Notice that as we go from one segmented statement to another, we look at smaller and smaller pieces of the company. While not shown in Exhibit 12–3, Bill Carson also prepared segmented income statements for the major product lines in the Business Products Division.

Substantial benefits are received from a series of statements such as those contained in Exhibit 12–3. By carefully examining trends and results in each segment, a manager is able to gain considerable insight into the company's operations viewed from many different angles.

IN BUSINESS

PUTTING SEGMENTS ON TRIAL

Segment margins should be regularly examined. Management guru Peter F. Drucker urges managers to "put every product, every service, every process, every market, every distribution channel, every customer, and every end use on trial for its life. And the change leader does so on a regular schedule. The question . . . is 'If we did not do this already, would we, knowing what we now know, go into it?'"

Source: Peter F. Drucker, "Change Leaders," *Inc.*, June 1999, p. 66.

Sales and Contribution Margin

To prepare an income statement for a particular segment, variable expenses are deducted from sales to yield the contribution margin for the segment. It is important to keep in mind that the contribution margin tells us what happens to profits as volume changes—holding a segment's capacity and fixed costs constant. The contribution margin is especially useful in decisions involving temporary uses of capacity such as special orders. Decisions concerning the most effective uses of existing capacity often involve only variable costs and revenues, which of course are the very elements involved in contribution margin. Such decisions will be discussed in detail in Chapter 13.

EXHIBIT 12–3
SoftSolutions, Inc.—Segmented Income Statements in the Contribution Format

Segments Defined as Divisions

	Total Company	Divisions: Business Products Division	Divisions: Consumer Products Division
Sales	$500,000	$300,000	$200,000
Less variable expenses:			
Variable cost of goods sold	180,000	120,000	60,000
Other variable expenses	50,000	30,000	20,000
Total variable expenses	230,000	150,000	80,000
Contribution margin	270,000	150,000	120,000
Less traceable fixed expenses	170,000	90,000	80,000*
Divisional segment margin	100,000	$ 60,000	$ 40,000
Less common fixed expenses not traceable to the individual divisions	85,000		
Net operating income	$ 15,000		

Segments Defined as Product Lines of the Consumer Products Division

	Consumer Products Division	Product Line: Clip Art	Product Line: Computer Games
Sales	$200,000	$ 75,000	$125,000
Less variable expenses:			
Variable cost of goods sold	60,000	20,000	40,000
Other variable expenses	20,000	5,000	15,000
Total variable expenses	80,000	25,000	55,000
Contribution margin	120,000	50,000	70,000
Less traceable fixed expenses	70,000	30,000	40,000
Product-line segment margin	50,000	$ 20,000	$ 30,000
Less common fixed expenses not traceable to the individual product lines	10,000		
Divisional segment margin	$ 40,000		

Segments Defined as Sales Channels for One Product Line, Computer Games, of the Consumer Products Division

	Computer Games	Sales Channels: Retail Stores	Sales Channels: Catalog Sales
Sales	$125,000	$100,000	$ 25,000
Less variable expenses:			
Variable cost of goods sold	40,000	32,000	8,000
Other variable expenses	15,000	5,000	10,000
Total variable expenses	55,000	37,000	18,000
Contribution margin	70,000	63,000	7,000
Less traceable fixed expenses	25,000	15,000	10,000
Sales-channel segment margin	45,000	$ 48,000	$ (3,000)
Less common fixed expenses not traceable to the individual sales channels	15,000		
Product-line segment margin	$ 30,000		

*Notice that this $80,000 in traceable fixed expenses is divided into two parts when the Consumer Products Division is broken down into product lines—$70,000 traceable and $10,000 common. The reasons for this are discussed later in the section "Traceable Costs Can Become Common Costs."

Traceable and Common Fixed Costs

The most puzzling aspect of Exhibit 12–3 is probably the treatment of fixed costs. The report has two kinds of fixed costs—traceable and common. Only the *traceable fixed costs* are charged to the segments in the segmented income statements in the report. If a cost is not traceable to a segment, then it is not assigned to the segment.

A **traceable fixed cost** of a segment is a fixed cost that is incurred because of the existence of the segment—if the segment had never existed, the fixed cost would not have been incurred; and if the segment were eliminated, the fixed cost would disappear. Examples of traceable fixed costs include the following:

- The salary of the Fritos product manager at PepsiCo is a *traceable* fixed cost of the Fritos business segment of PepsiCo.
- The maintenance cost for the building in which Boeing 747s are assembled is a *traceable* fixed cost of the 747 business segment of Boeing.
- The liability insurance at Disney World is a *traceable* fixed cost of the Disney World business segment of the Disney Corporation.

A **common fixed cost** is a fixed cost that supports the operations of more than one segment, but is not traceable in whole or in part to any one segment. Even if a segment were entirely eliminated, there would be no change in a true common fixed cost. For example:

- The salary of the CEO of General Motors is a *common* fixed cost of the various divisions of General Motors.
- The cost of heating a Safeway or Kroger grocery store is a *common* fixed cost of the various departments—groceries, produce, bakery, meat, etc.—in the store.
- The cost of the automatic bar-coding machine at SoftSolutions is a *common* fixed cost of the Consumer Products Division and of the Business Products Division.
- The cost of the receptionist's salary at an office shared by a number of doctors is a *common* fixed cost of the doctors. The cost is traceable to the office, but not to individual doctors.

Identifying Traceable Fixed Costs

The distinction between traceable and common fixed costs is crucial in segment reporting, since traceable fixed costs are charged to the segments and common fixed costs are not. In an actual situation, it is sometimes hard to determine whether a cost should be classified as traceable or common.

The general guideline is to treat as traceable costs *only those costs that would disappear over time if the segment itself disappeared.* For example, if the Consumer Products Division were sold or discontinued, it would no longer be necessary to pay the division manager's salary. Therefore the division manager's salary should be classified as a traceable fixed cost of the division. On the other hand, the president of the company undoubtedly would continue to be paid even if the Consumer Products Division were dropped. In fact, he or she might even be paid more if dropping the division was a good idea. Therefore, the president's salary is common to both divisions and should not be charged to either division.

In assigning costs to segments, the key point is to resist the temptation to allocate costs (such as depreciation of corporate facilities) that are clearly common and that will continue regardless of whether the segment exists or not. *Any allocation of common costs to segments will reduce the value of the segment margin as a guide to long-run segment profitability and segment performance.*

Activity-Based Costing

Some costs are easy to identify as traceable costs. For example, the cost of advertising Crest toothpaste on television is clearly traceable to Crest. A more difficult situation arises when a building, machine, or other resource is shared by two or more segments. For example, assume that a multiproduct company leases warehouse space that is used for storing the full range of its products. Would the lease cost of the warehouse be a traceable or a common cost of the products? Managers familiar with activity-based costing might argue that the lease cost is traceable and should be assigned to the products according to how much space the products use in the warehouse. In like manner, these managers would argue that order processing costs, sales support costs, and other selling, general, and administrative (SG&A) expenses should also be charged to segments according to the segments' consumption of SG&A resources.

To illustrate, consider Holt Corporation, a company that manufactures concrete pipe for industrial uses. The company has three products—9-inch pipe, 12-inch pipe, and 18-inch pipe. Space is rented in a large warehouse on a yearly basis as needed. The rental cost of this space is $4 per square foot per year. The 9-inch pipe occupies 1,000 square feet of space, the 12-inch pipe occupies 4,000 square feet, and the 18-inch pipe occupies 5,000 square feet. The company also has an order processing department that incurred $150,000 in order processing costs last year. Management believes that order processing costs are driven by the number of orders placed by customers. Last year 2,500 orders were placed, of which 1,200 were for 9-inch pipe, 800 were for 12-inch pipe, and 500 were for 18-inch pipe. Given these data, the following costs would be assigned to each product using the activity-based costing approach:

Warehouse space cost:	
9-inch pipe: $4 per square foot × 1,000 square feet	$ 4,000
12-inch pipe: $4 per square foot × 4,000 square feet	16,000
18-inch pipe: $4 per square foot × 5,000 square feet	20,000
Total cost assigned	$ 40,000
Order processing costs:	
$150,000 ÷ 2,500 orders = $60 per order	
9-inch pipe: $60 per order × 1,200 orders	$ 72,000
12-inch pipe: $60 per order × 800 orders	48,000
18-inch pipe: $60 per order × 500 orders	30,000
Total cost assigned	$150,000

This method of assigning costs combines the strength of activity-based costing with the power of the contribution approach and greatly enhances the manager's ability to measure the profitability and performance of segments. However, managers must still ask themselves if the costs would in fact disappear over time if the segment itself disappeared. In the case of Holt Corporation, it is clear that the $20,000 in warehousing costs for the 18-inch pipe would be eliminated if 18-inch pipes were no longer being produced. The company would simply rent less warehouse space the following year. However, suppose the company owns the warehouse. Then it is not so clear that $20,000 of warehousing cost would really disappear if the 18-inch pipes were discontinued. The company might be able to sublease the space, or use it for other products, but then again the space might simply be empty while the costs of the warehouse continue to be incurred.

IN BUSINESS

USING ABC TO ASSIGN DATA CENTER COSTS

Harris Corporation consolidated its division-level data centers into a centralized data center called the Computing and Communication Services (CCS) Department. CCS is a cost center that recovers its operating costs by charging other divisions within Harris for the use of its resources. To facilitate the "chargeback" process, CCS developed an activity-based costing system. Activities such as "test systems," "monitor network," "schedule jobs," "install software," "administer servers," and "print reports" were used to ensure that internal customers were only charged for the dollar value of the resources that they consumed.

Source: Peter Brewer, "Developing a Data Center Chargeback System Using ABC," *Journal of Cost Management*, May/June 1998, pp. 41–47.

Traceable Costs Can Become Common Costs

Fixed costs that are traceable to one segment may be a common cost of another segment. For example, an airline might want a segmented income statement that shows the segment margin for a particular flight from Los Angeles to Paris further broken down into first-class, business-class, and economy-class segment margins. The airline must pay a substantial landing fee at Charles DeGaulle airport in Paris. This fixed landing fee is a traceable cost of the flight, but it is a common cost of the first-class, business-class, and economy-class segments. Even if the first-class cabin is empty, the entire landing fee must be paid. So the landing fee is not a traceable cost of the first-class cabin. But on the other hand, paying the fee is necessary in order to have any first-class, business-class, or economy-class passengers. So the landing fee is a common cost of these three classes.

The dual nature of some fixed costs can be seen in Exhibit 12–4. Notice from the diagram that when segments are defined as divisions, the Consumer Products Division has $80,000 in traceable fixed expenses. However, when we drill down to the product lines, only $70,000 of the $80,000 cost that was traceable to the Consumer Products Division is traceable to the product lines. Notice that the other $10,000 becomes a common cost of the two product lines of the Consumer Products Division.

Why would $10,000 of traceable fixed cost become a common cost when the division is divided into product lines? The $10,000 is the monthly salary of the manager of the Consumer Products Division. This salary is a traceable cost of the division as a whole, but it is a common cost of the division's product lines. The manager's salary is a necessary cost of having the two product lines, but even if one of the product lines were discontinued entirely, the manager's salary would probably not be cut. Therefore, none of the manager's salary can really be traced to the individual products.

The $70,000 traceable fixed cost of the product lines consists of the costs of product-specific advertising. A total of $30,000 was spent on advertising clip art and $40,000 was spent on advertising computer games. These costs can clearly be traced to the individual product lines.

Segment Margin

Observe from Exhibit 12–3 that the **segment margin** is obtained by deducting the traceable fixed costs of a segment from the segment's contribution margin. It represents the margin available after a segment has covered all of its own costs. *The segment margin is the best gauge of the long-run profitability of a segment,* since it includes only those costs that are caused by the segment. If a segment can't cover its own costs, then that segment

EXHIBIT 12–4
Reclassification of Traceable Fixed Expenses from Exhibit 12–3

		Segment	
	Total Company	Business Products Division	Consumer Products Division
Contribution margin	$270,000	$150,000	$120,000
Less traceable fixed expenses	170,000	90,000	80,000

		Segment	
	Consumer Products Division	Clip Art	Computer Games
Contribution margin	$120,000	$50,000	$70,000
Less traceable fixed expenses	70,000	30,000	40,000
Product-line segment margin	50,000	$20,000	$30,000
Less common fixed expenses	10,000		
Divisional segment margin	$ 40,000		

probably should not be retained (unless it has important side effects on other segments). Notice from Exhibit 12–3, for example, that Catalog Sales has a negative segment margin. This means that the segment is not generating enough revenue to cover its own costs. Retention or elimination of product lines and other segments is covered in more depth in Chapter 13.

From a decision-making point of view, the segment margin is most useful in major decisions that affect capacity such as dropping a segment. By contrast, as we noted earlier, the contribution margin is most useful in decisions relating to short-run changes in volume, such as pricing special orders that involve temporary use of existing capacity.

IN BUSINESS

SEGMENT INFORMATION MAKES PROFITS RISE

Great Harvest bakeries use freshly milled Montana whole wheat to make soft-crust specialty breads. The company was founded by Pete and Laura Wakeman and is headquartered in Dillon, Montana. Great Harvest encourages each of its over 100 franchised bakeries to experiment with new approaches to business management, customer service, and marketing and uses several methods to spread the best innovations throughout the system. Staffers at the headquarters in Dillon "provide franchisees with a **top 10 list** of the 10 best-performing bakeries in 14 statistical and financial categories. . . . Got a problem controlling labor expenses at your store? Call up the bakery owners who've got that figured out and get their advice." In addition, bakery owners who join the Numbers Club agree to open their books to the other owners in the club. "Franchisees can spot other owners whose situations might be similar to theirs (same size bakery and market, say, or the same level of owner's labor)—and who appear to have found better solutions to problems. They can identify the perfectly useful peer—and call him or her up."

Source: Michael Hopkins, "Zen and the Art of the Self-Managing Company," *Inc.*, November 2000, pp. 54–63.

IN BUSINESS

DAILY SEGMENT FEEDBACK FUELS INNOVATION

Steve Briley, the department manager of Cracking Plant 3B at Texas Eastman Company's chemical plant in Longview, Texas, created an innovative daily performance report to help guide his department. Instead of relying on rules and orders to run operations, Briley turned his department into a minicompany called the "Threebee Company" and made his employees the "owners"—complete with official-looking stock certificates. An income statement for the company was issued at the beginning of each day to the owners. The daily income statement assigned revenues to the output of the previous day and costs to the inputs used in the department that day. Briley promised that he would reward the department with a new kitchen if the daily profit hit an ambitious goal after 90 days. This approach was very successful—for a variety of reasons. First, the daily income statement provided rapid, easily understood feedback to the workers in the department. If they did something that increased—or decreased—profit such as changing operating temperatures, they would know the next day. Second, this approach empowered employees to make decisions quickly in response to changes in the operating environment. For example, if a critical machine broke down, workers now knew the lost output would have a tremendous impact on profits and would take immediate steps to get the machine working. Third, the daily income statement helped employees make trade-offs and set priorities. After some experience with the income statement, they realized what problems were important in terms of their impact on profits.

Source: Robert S. Kaplan and Robin Cooper, *Cost & Effect: Using Integrated Cost Systems to Drive Profitability and Performance*, Harvard Business School Press, 1998, pp. 64–71.

MANAGERIAL ACCOUNTING IN ACTION
The Wrap-Up

Shortly after Bill Carson, the SoftSolutions, Inc., controller, completed the draft segmented income statement, he sent copies to the other managers and scheduled a meeting in which the report could be explained. The meeting was held on the Monday following the first meeting; and Marjorie Matsuo, Lori Saffer, and Chris Worden were all in attendance.

Soft Solutions Inc.

Lori Saffer: I think these segmented income statements are fairly self-explanatory. However, there is one thing I wonder about.

Bill Carson: What's that?

Lori Saffer: What is this common fixed expense of $85,000 listed under the total company? And who is going to be responsible for it if neither Chris nor I have responsibility?

Bill Carson: The $85,000 of common fixed expenses represents expenses like administrative salaries and the costs of common production equipment such as the automatic bar-coding machine. Marjorie, do you want to respond to the question about responsibility for these expenses?

Marjorie Matsuo: Sure. Since I'm the president of the company, I'm responsible for those costs. Some things can be delegated, others cannot be. It wouldn't make any sense for either you or Chris to make strategic decisions about the bar coder, since it affects both of you. That's an important part of my job—making decisions about resources that affect all parts of the organization. This report makes it much clearer who is responsible for what. I like it.

Chris Worden: So do I—my division's segment margin is higher than the net operating income for the entire company.

Marjorie Matsuo: Don't get carried away, Chris. Let's not misinterpret what this report means. The segment margins *have* to be big to cover the common costs of the company. We can't let the big segment margins lull us into a sense of complacency. If we use these reports, we all have to agree that our objective is to increase all of the segment margins over time.

Lori Saffer: I'm willing to give it a try.

Chris Worden: The reports make sense to me.

Marjorie Matsuo: So be it. Then the first item of business would appear to be a review of catalog sales of computer games, where we appear to be losing money. Chris, could you brief us on this at our next meeting?

Chris Worden: I'd be happy to. I have been suspecting for some time that our catalog sales strategy could be improved.

Marjorie Matsuo: We look forward to hearing your analysis.

IN BUSINESS

WHAT'S IN A SEGMENT?

Continental Airlines could figure out the profitability of a specific route on a monthly basis—for example, Houston to Los Angeles—but management did not know the profitability of a particular flight on that route. The company's new chief financial officer (CFO), Larry Kellner, placed top priority on developing a flight profitability system that would break out the profit (or loss) for each individual flight. Once completed, the flight profitability system revealed such money-losing flights as two December flights that left Houston for London within a four-hour period with only about 30 passengers each. "If those flights are blurred in with the whole month of December, they just don't jump off the page," says Kellner. With the data on the profitability of individual flights, Continental was able to design more appropriate schedules.

Source: Tim Reason, "Making Continental Airlines' Turnaround Permanent Meant Installing Some High-Flying IT Systems," *CFO*, October 2000, pp. 61–64.

Segmented Financial Information on External Reports

The Financial Accounting Standards Board (FASB) now requires that companies in the United States include segmented financial and other data in their annual reports and that the segmented reports prepared for external users *must use the same methods and definitions that the companies use in internal segmented reports that are prepared to aid in making operating decisions.* This is a very unusual requirement. Companies are not ordinarily required to report the same data to external users that are reported internally for decision-making purposes. This may seem like a reasonable requirement for the FASB to make, but it has some serious drawbacks. First, segmented data are often highly sensitive and companies are reluctant to release such data to the public for the simple reason that their competitors will then have access to the data. Second, segmented statements prepared in accordance with GAAP do not distinguish between fixed and variable costs and between traceable and common costs. Indeed, the segmented income statements illustrated earlier in this chapter do not conform to GAAP for that reason. To avoid the complications of reconciling non-GAAP segment earnings with GAAP consolidated earnings, it is likely that at least some managers will choose to construct their segmented financial statements in a manner that conforms with GAAP. This will result in more occurrences of the problems discussed in the following section.

Hindrances to Proper Cost Assignment

For segment reporting to accomplish its intended purposes, costs must be properly assigned to segments. If the purpose is to determine the profits being generated by a particular division, then all of the costs attributable to that division—and only those costs—should be assigned to it. Unfortunately, companies often make mistakes when assigning costs to responsibility centers. They omit some costs, inappropriately assign traceable fixed costs, and arbitrarily allocate common fixed costs.

Omission of Costs

The costs assigned to a segment should include all costs attributable to that segment from the company's entire *value chain.* The **value chain,** which is illustrated in Exhibit 12–5, consists of the major business functions that add value to a company's products and services. All of these functions, from research and development, through product design, manufacturing, marketing, distribution, and customer service, are required to bring a product or service to the customer and generate revenues.

However, as discussed in Chapters 2, 3, and 7, only manufacturing costs are included in product costs under absorption costing, which is widely regarded as required for external financial reporting. To avoid having to maintain two costing systems and to provide consistency between internal and external reports, many companies also use absorption costing for their internal reports such as segmented income statements. As a result, such companies omit from their profitability analysis part or all of the "upstream" costs in the value chain, which consist of research and development and product design, and the "downstream" costs, which consist of marketing, distribution, and customer service. Yet these nonmanufacturing costs are just as essential in determining product profitability as are the manufacturing costs. These upstream and downstream costs, which are usually titled *Selling, General, and Administrative (SG&A)* on the income statement, can represent half or more of the total costs of an organization. If either the upstream or downstream costs are omitted in profitability analysis, then the product is undercosted and management may unwittingly develop and maintain products that in the long run result in losses rather than profits for the company.

EXHIBIT 12–5
Business Functions Making Up the Value Chain

Inappropriate Methods for Assigning Traceable Costs among Segments

Companies inappropriately assign traceable fixed costs to responsibility centers in two ways. First, they may fail to trace costs to responsibility centers when feasible to do so. Second, they may rely on inappropriate allocation bases to assign traceable fixed costs.

Failure to Trace Costs Directly Costs that can be traced directly to a specific segment of a company should not be allocated to other segments. Rather, such costs should be charged directly to the responsible segment. For example, the rent for a branch office of an insurance company should be charged directly against the branch office rather than included in a companywide overhead pool and then spread throughout the company.

Inappropriate Allocation Base Some companies allocate costs to segments using arbitrary bases. For example, some companies allocate SG&A expenses on the basis of sales revenues. Thus, if a segment generates 20% of total company sales, it would be allocated 20% of the company's SG&A expenses as its "fair share." This same basic procedure is followed if cost of goods sold or some other measure is used as the allocation base.

Costs should be allocated to segments for internal decision-making purposes only when the allocation base actually drives the cost being allocated (or is very highly correlated with the real cost driver). For example, sales should be used to allocate SG&A expenses only if a 10% increase in sales will result in a 10% increase in SG&A expenses. To the extent that SG&A expenses are not driven by sales volume, these expenses will be improperly allocated to responsibility centers. In all likelihood, a disproportionately high percentage of the SG&A expenses will be assigned to the responsibility centers with the highest amount of sales. Conversely, the responsibility centers with the least amount of sales will receive a "free ride," in the sense that some of their traceable SG&A expenses will be borne by responsibility centers with higher sales.

IN BUSINESS

STOPPING THE BICKERING

AT&T Power Systems, a subsidiary of AT&T, makes electronic power supplies and components for the data processing and telecommunications industries. Independent business units (i.e., segments) at AT&T Power Systems are evaluated as profit centers, however, "more time was being spent debating the appropriate overhead-allocation scheme than was being spent on strategies to increase contribution margins." If, in fact, no cause-and-effect relation exists between an overhead expense and the activity in any particular segment, then any allocation of this overhead expense to the segments is completely arbitrary and can be endlessly debated by segment managers. Consequently, a change was made to evaluate the segments on the basis of just contribution margin and controllable expenses—eliminating arbitrary allocations of overhead from the performance measure.

Source: Richard L. Jenson, James W. Brackner, and Clifford R. Skousen, *Managerial Accounting in Support of Manufacturing Excellence,* The IMA Foundation for Applied Research, Inc., Montvale, NJ, pp. 97–101.

Arbitrarily Dividing Common Costs among Segments

The third business practice that leads to distorted segment costs is the practice of assigning nontraceable costs to segments. For example, some companies allocate the common costs of the corporate headquarters building to products on segment reports. However, in a multiproduct company, no single product is likely to be really responsible for any significant amount of this cost. Even if a product were eliminated entirely, there would usually be no significant effect on any of the costs of the corporate headquarters building. In short, there is no cause-and-effect relation between the cost of the corporate headquarters building and the existence of any one product. As a consequence, any allocation of the cost of the corporate headquarters building to the products must be arbitrary.

Common costs like the costs of the corporate headquarters building are necessary, of course, to have a functioning organization. The practice of arbitrarily allocating common costs to segments is often justified on the grounds that "someone" has to "cover the common costs." While it is undeniably true that the common costs must be covered, arbitrarily allocating common costs to segments does not ensure that this will happen. In fact, adding a share of common costs to the real costs of a segment may make an otherwise profitable segment appear to be unprofitable. If a manager eliminates the apparently unprofitable segment, the real traceable costs of the segment will be saved, but its revenues will be lost. And what happens to the common fixed costs that were allocated to the segment? They don't disappear; they are reallocated to the remaining segments of the company. That makes all of the remaining segments appear to be less profitable—possibly resulting in dropping other segments. The net effect will be to reduce the overall profits of the company and make it even more difficult to "cover the common costs."

Additionally, common fixed costs are not manageable by the manager to whom they are arbitrarily allocated; they are the responsibility of higher-level managers. Allocating common fixed costs to responsibility centers is counterproductive in a responsibility accounting system. When common fixed costs are allocated to managers, they are held responsible for those costs even though they cannot control them.

In sum, the way many companies handle segment reporting results in cost distortion. This distortion results from three practices—the failure to trace costs directly to a specific segment when it is feasible to do so, the use of inappropriate bases for allocating costs, and the allocation of common costs to segments. These practices are widespread. One study found that 60% of the companies surveyed made no attempt to assign SG&A costs to segments on a cause-and-effect basis.[3]

IN BUSINESS

THE BIG GOUGE?

The Big Dig in Boston is a $14 billion-plus project to bury major roads underground in downtown Boston. Two companies—Bechtel and Parsons Brinckerhoff (PB)—manage the 20-year project, which is $1.6 billion over budget. The two companies will likely collect in excess of $120 million in fixed fees for their work on the project—not including reimbursements for overhead costs. Bechtel and PB have many projects underway at any one time and many common fixed costs. These common fixed costs are not actually caused by the Big Dig project and yet portions of these costs have been claimed as reimbursable expenses. "Bechtel and PB say they don't collect a penny more for overhead than they are entitled to." A Bechtel spokesman says, "Our allocation of overhead [on the Big Dig] is rigorously audited . . . " This is undoubtedly true; in practice, fixed common costs are routinely (and arbitrarily) allocated to segments for cost reimbursement and other purposes. Managers at Bechtel, PB, and other companies argue that someone must pay for these costs. While this too is true, who actually pays for these costs will depend on how the common fixed costs are arbitrarily allocated among segments. Massachusetts has lodged a number of complaints concerning Bechtel's cost recovery claims. Such complaints are almost inevitable when common fixed costs are allocated to segments. It might be better to simply set an all-inclusive fixed fee up front with no cost recovery and hence no issues concerning what costs are really attributable to the project.

Source: Nathan Vardi, *Forbes*, "Desert Storm," June 23, 2003, pp. 63–66.

Evaluating Investment Center Performance—Return on Investment

LEARNING OBJECTIVE 2
Compute return on investment (ROI) and show how changes in sales, expenses, and assets affect ROI.

Thus far, the chapter has focused on how to properly assign costs to responsibility centers and how to construct segmented income statements. These are vital steps when evaluating cost and profit centers. However, evaluating an investment center's performance

3 James R. Emore and Joseph A. Ness, "The Slow Pace of Meaningful Change in Cost Systems," *Journal of Cost Management* 4, no. 4, p. 39.

requires more than accurate cost and segment margin reporting. In addition, an investment center is responsible for earning an adequate return on investment. This section and the next section of the chapter present two methods for evaluating this aspect of an investment center's performance. The first method, covered in this section, is called *return on investment (ROI).* The second method, covered in the next section, is called *residual income.*

Topic Tackler PLUS 12–1

The Return on Investment (ROI) Formula

The **return on investment (ROI)** is defined as net operating income divided by average operating assets:

$$\text{ROI} = \frac{\text{Net operating income}}{\text{Average operating assets}}$$

The higher the return on investment (ROI) of a business segment, the greater the profit earned per dollar invested in the segment's operating assets.

Net Operating Income and Operating Assets Defined

Note that *net operating income,* rather than net income, is used in the ROI formula. **Net operating income** is income before interest and taxes and is sometimes referred to as EBIT (earnings before interest and taxes). Net operating income is used in the formula because the base (i.e., denominator) consists of *operating assets.* Thus, to be consistent we use net operating income in the numerator.

Operating assets include cash, accounts receivable, inventory, plant and equipment, and all other assets held for operating purposes. Examples of assets that would not be included in the operating assets category (i.e., examples of nonoperating assets) would include land held for future use, an investment in another company, or a building rented to someone else. These assets are not held for operating purposes and therefore are excluded from operating assets. The operating assets base used in the formula is typically computed as the average of the operating assets between the beginning and the end of the year.

Most companies use the net book value (i.e., acquisition cost less accumulated depreciation) of depreciable assets to calculate average operating assets. This approach has drawbacks. An asset's net book value decreases over time as the accumulated depreciation increases. This decreases the denominator in the ROI calculation, thus increasing ROI. Consequently, ROI mechanically increases over time. Moreover, replacing old depreciated equipment with new equipment increases the book value of depreciable assets and decreases ROI. Hence, it is argued that using net book value in the calculation of average operating assets results in a predictable pattern of increasing ROI over time as accumulated depreciation grows and discourages replacing old equipment with new, updated equipment. An alternative to the net book value is the gross cost of the asset, which ignores accumulated depreciation. Gross cost stays constant over time because depreciation is ignored; therefore, ROI does not grow automatically over time, and replacing a fully depreciated asset with a comparably priced new asset will not adversely affect ROI.

Nevertheless, most companies use the net book value approach to computing average operating assets because it is consistent with their financial reporting practices of recording the net book value of assets on the balance sheet and including depreciation as an operating expense on the income statement. In this text, we will use the net book value approach unless a specific exercise or problem directs otherwise.

Understanding ROI—The DuPont Perspective

The equation for ROI, net operating income divided by average operating assets, does not provide much help to managers interested in taking actions to improve their ROI. It only offers two levers for improving performance—net operating income and average operating assets. Fortunately, ROI can also be expressed as follows:

$$\text{ROI} = \text{Margin} \times \text{Turnover}$$

where

$$\text{Margin} = \frac{\text{Net operating income}}{\text{Sales}}$$

and

$$\text{Turnover} = \frac{\text{Sales}}{\text{Average operating assets}}$$

Note that the sales terms in the margin and turnover formulas cancel out when they are multiplied together, yielding the original formula for ROI stated in terms of net operating income and average operating assets. So either formula for ROI will always give the same answer. However, the margin and turnover formulation provides some additional insights.

From a manager's perspective, margin and turnover are very important concepts. Margin is improved by increasing sales or reducing operating expenses, including cost of goods sold and selling and administrative expenses. The lower the operating expenses per dollar of sales, the higher the margin earned. Some managers tend to focus too much on margin and ignore turnover. However, turnover incorporates a crucial area of a manager's responsibility—the investment in operating assets. Excessive funds tied up in operating assets (e.g., cash, accounts receivable, inventories, plant and equipment, and other assets) depress turnover and lower ROI. In fact, inefficient use of operating assets can be just as much of a drag on profitability as excessive operating expenses, which depress margin.

The E.I. du Pont de Nemours and Company (better know as DuPont) pioneered the use of ROI and recognized the importance of looking at both margin and turnover in assessing the performance of a manager. ROI is now widely used as the key measure of investment center performance. ROI reflects in a single figure many aspects of the manager's responsibilities. It can be compared to the returns of other investment centers in the organization, the returns of other companies in the industry, and to the past returns of the investment center itself.

DuPont also developed the diagram that appears in Exhibit 12–6. This exhibit helps managers understand how they can work to improve ROI. Any increase in ROI must involve at least one of the following:

1. Increased sales
2. Reduced operating expenses
3. Reduced operating assets

Many actions involve combinations of changes in sales, expenses, and operating assets. For example, a manager may make an investment in (i.e., increase) operating assets to reduce operating expenses or increase sales. Whether the net effect is favorable or not is judged in terms of its overall impact on ROI.

To illustrate how ROI is impacted by various actions, we will use the Monthaven outlet of the Burger Grill chain as an example. Burger Grill is a small chain of upscale casual restaurants that has been rapidly adding outlets via franchising. The Monthaven franchise is owned by a group of local surgeons who have little time to devote to management and little expertise in business matters. Therefore, they delegate operating decisions—including decisions concerning investment in operating assets such as inventories—to a professional manager they have hired. The manager is evaluated largely based on the ROI the franchise generates.

The following data represent the results of operations for the most recent month:

Sales	$100,000
Operating expenses	$90,000
Net operating income	$10,000
Average operating assets	$50,000

EXHIBIT 12–6
Elements of Return on Investment (ROI)

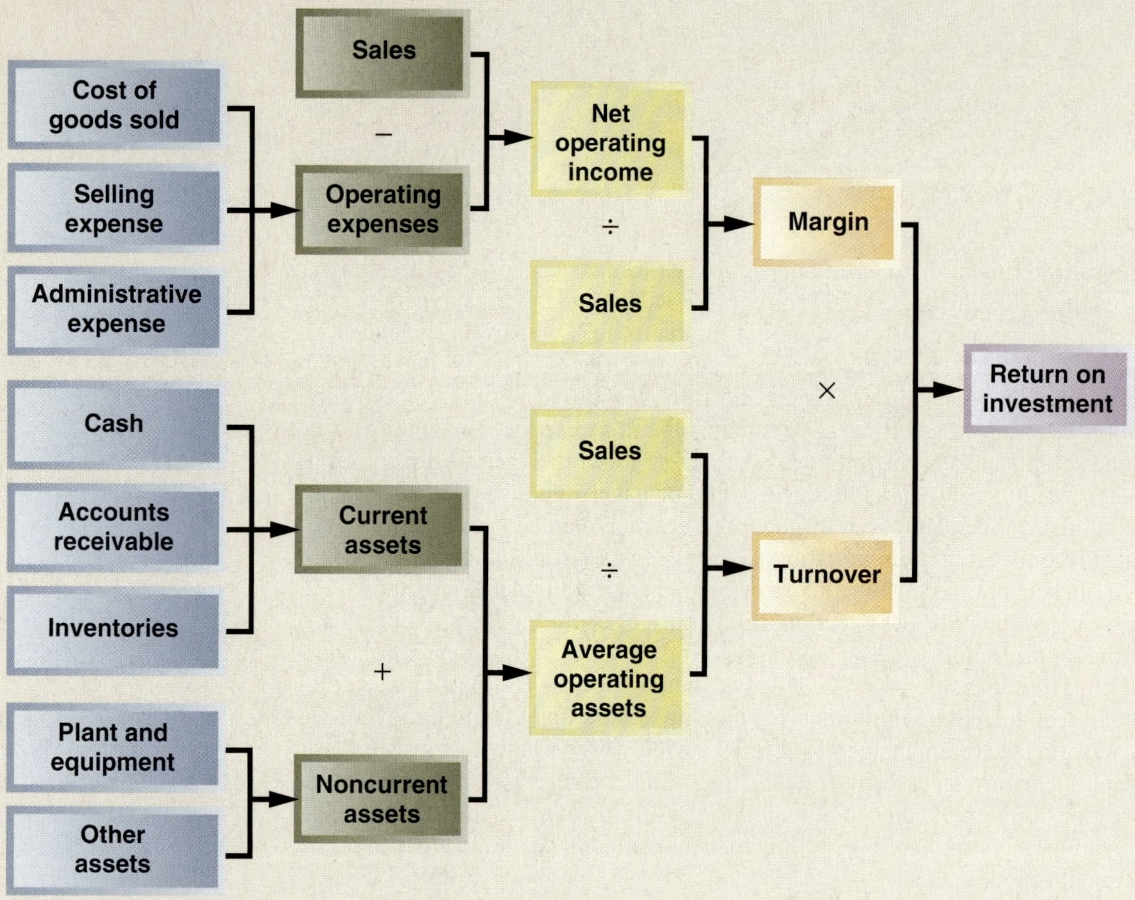

The return on investment (ROI) for the month is computed as follows:

$$\begin{aligned}
\text{ROI} &= \frac{\text{Net operating income}}{\text{Sales}} \times \frac{\text{Sales}}{\text{Average operating assets}} \\
&= \frac{\$10{,}000}{\$100{,}000} \times \frac{\$100{,}000}{\$50{,}000} \\
&= 10\% \times 2 = 20\%
\end{aligned}$$

Example 1: Increased Sales without Any Increase in Operating Assets

Assume that the manager of the Monthaven Burger Grill is able to increase sales by 10% without any increase in operating assets. The increase in sales will require additional operating expenses, but as long as fixed costs are not affected by the increase in sales and the manager exercises effective control over costs, operating expenses will increase by less than 10% and therefore the increase in net operating income will be greater than 10%. (Recall the concept of operating leverage from Chapter 6.) Assume that the increase in operating expenses will be 7.8% rather than 10%. The new net operating income would therefore be $12,980, an increase of 29.8%, determined as follows:

Sales (1.10 × $100,000)	$110,000
Operating expenses (1.078 × $90,000)	97,020
Net operating income	$ 12,980

In this case, the new ROI will be:

$$\text{ROI} = \frac{\text{Net operating income}}{\text{Sales}} \times \frac{\text{Sales}}{\text{Average operating assets}}$$
$$= \frac{\$12{,}980}{\$110{,}000} \times \frac{\$110{,}000}{\$50{,}000}$$
$$= 11.8\% \times 2.2 = 25.96\% \text{ (as compared to 20\% originally)}$$

Note that the key to improved ROI in the case of an increase in sales is that the percentage increase in operating expenses must be less than the percentage increase in sales.

Example 2: Decreased Operating Expenses with No Change in Sales or Operating Assets Assume that by improving business processes, the manager of the Monthaven Burger Grill is able to reduce operating expenses by $1,000 without any effect on sales or operating assets. This reduction in operating expenses will result in increasing net operating income by $1,000, from $10,000 to $11,000. The new ROI will be:

$$\text{ROI} = \frac{\text{Net operating income}}{\text{Sales}} \times \frac{\text{Sales}}{\text{Average operating assets}}$$
$$= \frac{\$11{,}000}{\$100{,}000} \times \frac{\$100{,}000}{\$50{,}000}$$
$$= 11\% \times 2 = 22\% \text{ (as compared to 20\% originally)}$$

When margins are being squeezed, cutting expenses is often the first line of attack adopted by a manager. Discretionary fixed costs (i.e., fixed costs that arise from annual decisions by management) usually come under scrutiny first, and various programs are either curtailed or eliminated in an effort to cut costs. Managers must be careful, however, not to cut too much or in the wrong place. That may have the effect of decreasing sales or indirectly causing increased costs elsewhere. Also, managers must remember that indiscriminate cost-cutting can destroy morale.

Example 3: Decreased Operating Assets with No Change in Sales or Operating Expenses Assume that the manager of the Monthaven Burger Grill is able to reduce inventories by $10,000 using just-in-time techniques. This might actually have a positive effect on sales (through fresher ingredients) and on operating expenses (through reduced inventory spoilage), but for the sake of illustration, suppose the reduction in inventories has no effect on sales or operating expenses. The reduction in inventories will reduce average operating assets by $10,000, from $50,000 down to $40,000. The new ROI will be:

$$\text{ROI} = \frac{\text{Net operating income}}{\text{Sales}} \times \frac{\text{Sales}}{\text{Average operating assets}}$$
$$= \frac{\$10{,}000}{\$100{,}000} \times \frac{\$100{,}000}{\$40{,}000}$$
$$= 10\% \times 2.5 = 25\% \text{ (as compared to 20\% originally)}$$

In this example, JIT was used to reduce operating assets. Another common tactic for reducing operating assets is to speed up the collection of accounts receivable. For example, many companies now encourage customers to pay electronically rather than to use the much slower method of sending checks by mail.

IN BUSINESS

JIT AND ROI IMPROVEMENT

A study of companies that adopted just-in-time (JIT) in comparison to a control group that did not adopt JIT, found that the JIT adopters improved their ROIs more. The JIT adopters' success resulted from improvements in both profit margins and asset turnover. The elimination of inventories in JIT reduces total assets, but more important, it leads to process improvements as production problems are exposed. When production problems and non-value-added activities are eliminated, costs go down.

Source: Michael R. Kinney and William F. Wempe, "Further Evidence on the Extent and Origins of JIT's Profitability Effects," *The Accounting Review*, January 2002, pp. 203–225.

Example 4: Invest in Operating Assets to Increase Sales Assume that the manager of the Monthaven Burger Grill invests $2,000 in a state-of-the-art soft-serve ice cream machine that is capable of dispensing a number of different flavors. This new machine will result in additional sales of $4,000 and additional operating expenses of $1,000. Thus, net operating income will increase by $3,000, to $13,000. The new ROI will be:

$$\text{ROI} = \frac{\text{Net operating income}}{\text{Sales}} \times \frac{\text{Sales}}{\text{Average operating assets}}$$

$$= \frac{\$13{,}000}{\$104{,}000} \times \frac{\$104{,}000}{\$52{,}000}$$

$$= 12.5\% \times 2 = 25\% \text{ (as compared to 20\% originally)}$$

In this particular example, the investment had no effect on turnover, which remained at 2, so there had to be an increase in margin in order to improve the ROI.

IN BUSINESS

MCDONALD CHIC

McDonald's France has been spending lavishly to remodel its restaurants to blend with local architecture and to make their interiors less uniform and sterile. For example, some outlets in the Alps have wood-and-stone interiors similar to those of alpine chalets. The idea is to defuse the negative feelings many of the French people have toward McDonald's as a symbol of American culture and, perhaps more importantly, to try to entice customers to linger over their meals and spend more. This investment in operating assets has apparently been successful—even though a Big Mac costs about the same in Paris as in New York, the average French customer spends about $9 per visit versus only about $4 in the U.S.

Source: Carol Matlack and Pallavi Gogoi, "What's This? The French Love McDonald's?" *BusinessWeek*, January 13, 2003, p. 50.

ROI and the Balanced Scorecard

Simply exhorting managers to increase ROI is not sufficient. Managers who are told to increase ROI will naturally wonder how this is to be accomplished. The Du Pont scheme, which is illustrated in Exhibit 12–6, provides managers with *some* guidance. Generally speaking, ROI can be increased by increasing sales, decreasing costs, and/or decreasing investments in operating assets. However, it may not be obvious to managers *how* they are supposed to increase sales, decrease costs, and decrease investments in a way that is consistent with the company's strategy. For example, a manager who is given inadequate guidance may cut back on investments that are critical to implementing the company's strategy.

For that reason, as discussed in Chapter 10, when managers are evaluated based on ROI, a balanced scorecard approach is advised. And indeed, ROI, or residual income (discussed below), is typically included as one of the financial performance measures on a company's balanced scorecard. As briefly discussed in Chapter 10, the balanced scorecard provides a way of communicating a company's strategy to managers throughout the organization. The scorecard indicates *how* the company intends to improve its financial performance. A well-constructed balanced scorecard should answer questions like: "What internal business processes should be improved?" and "Which customer should be targeted and how will they be attracted and retained at a profit?" In short, a well-constructed balanced scorecard can provide managers with a road map that indicates how the company intends to increase its ROI. In the absence of such a road map of the company's strategy, managers may have difficulty understanding what they are supposed to do to increase ROI and they may work at cross-purposes rather than in harmony with the overall strategy of the company.

Criticisms of ROI

Although ROI is widely used in evaluating performance, it is not a perfect tool. The method is subject to the following criticisms:

1. Just telling managers to increase ROI may not be enough. Managers may not know how to increase ROI; they may increase ROI in a way that is inconsistent with the company's strategy; or they may take actions that increase ROI in the short run but harm the company in the long run (such as cutting back on research and development). This is why ROI is best used as part of a balanced scorecard as discussed above. A balanced scorecard can provide concrete guidance to managers, making it more likely that actions taken are consistent with the company's strategy and reducing the likelihood that short-run performance will be enhanced at the expense of long-term performance.
2. A manager who takes over a business segment typically inherits many committed costs over which the manager has no control. These committed costs may be relevant in assessing the performance of the business segment as an investment but make it difficult to fairly assess the performance of the manager relative to other managers.
3. As discussed in the next section, a manager who is evaluated based on ROI may reject investment opportunities that are profitable for the whole company but that would have a negative impact on the manager's performance evaluation.

IN BUSINESS

LET THE BUYER BEWARE

Those who sell products and services to businesses are well aware that many potential customers look very carefully at the impact the purchase would have on ROI before making a purchase. Unfortunately, some salespersons make extravagant ROI claims. For example, businesspeople complain that software salespersons routinely exaggerate the impact that new software will have on ROI. Some of the tricks used by salespersons include: inflating the salaries of workers who are made redundant by productivity gains; omitting costs such as training costs and implementation costs; inflating expected sales increases; and using former clients as examples of ROI gains when the clients were given the software for free or for nominal cost. The message? Be skeptical of salespersons' claims with respect to ROI gains from purchasing their products and services.

Source: Scott Leibs, "All Hail the ROI," *CFO*, April 2002, pp. 27–28.

Residual Income

LEARNING OBJECTIVE 3
Compute residual income and understand the strengths and weaknesses of this method of measuring performance.

Another approach to measuring an investment center's performance focuses on a concept known as *residual income.* **Residual income** is the net operating income that an investment center earns above the minimum required return on its operating assets. In equation form, residual income is calculated as follows:

$$\text{Residual income} = \text{Net operating income} - \left(\text{Average operating assets} \times \text{Minimum required rate of return}\right)$$

Economic Value Added (EVA®) is an adaptation of residual income that has recently been adopted by many companies.[4] Under EVA, companies often modify their accounting principles in various ways. For example, funds used for research and development are often treated as investments rather than as expenses under EVA.[5] These complications are best dealt with in a more advanced course; in this text we will focus on the basics and will not draw any distinction between residual income and EVA.

When residual income or EVA is used to measure performance, the objective is to maximize the total amount of residual income or EVA, not to maximize ROI. This is an important distinction. If the objective were to maximize ROI, then every company should divest all of its products except the single product with the highest ROI. A wide variety of organizations have embraced some version of residual income or EVA, including Bausch & Lomb, Best Buy, Boise Cascade, Coca-Cola, Dun and Bradstreet, Eli Lilly, Federated Mogul, Georgia-Pacific, Guidant Corporation, Hershey Foods, Husky Injection Molding, J.C. Penney, Kansas City Power & Light, Olin, Quaker Oats, Silicon Valley Bank, Sprint, Toys R Us, Tupperware, and the United States Postal Service. In addition, financial institutions such as Credit Suisse First Boston now use EVA—and its allied concept, market value added—to evaluate potential investments in other companies.

For purposes of illustration, consider the following data for an investment center—the Ketchican Division of Alaskan Marine Services Corporation.

ALASKAN MARINE SERVICES CORPORATION Ketchican Division Basic Data for Performance Evaluation	
Average operating assets	$100,000
Net operating income	$20,000
Minimum required rate of return	15%

Alaskan Marine Services Corporation has long had a policy of evaluating investment center managers based on ROI, but it is considering a switch to residual income. The controller of the company, who is in favor of the change to residual income, has provided the following table that shows how the performance of the division would be evaluated under each of the two methods:

ALASKAN MARINE SERVICES CORPORATION Ketchican Division	Alternative Performance Measures	
	ROI	Residual Income
Average operating assets (a)	$100,000	$100,000
Net operating income (b)	$ 20,000	$ 20,000
ROI, (b) ÷ (a)	20%	
Minimum required return (15% × $100,000)		15,000
Residual income		$ 5,000

[4] The basic idea underlying residual income and economic value added has been around for over 100 years. In recent years, economic value added has been popularized and trademarked by the consulting firm Stern, Stewart & Co.

[5] Over 100 different adjustments could be made for deferred taxes, LIFO reserves, provisions for future liabilities, mergers and acquisitions, gains or losses due to changes in accounting rules, operating leases, and other accounts, but most companies make only a few. For further details, see John O'Hanlon and Ken Peasnell, "Wall Street's Contribution to Management Accounting: the Stern Stewart EVA® Financial Management System," *Management Accounting Research* 9, 1998, pp. 421–444.

The reasoning underlying the residual income calculation is straightforward. The company is able to earn a rate of return of at least 15% on its investments. Since the company has invested $100,000 in the Ketchican Division in the form of operating assets, the company should be able to earn at least $15,000 (15% × $100,000) on this investment. Since the Ketchican Division's net operating income is $20,000, the residual income above and beyond the minimum required return is $5,000. If residual income is adopted as the performance measure to replace ROI, the manager of the Ketchican Division would be evaluated based on the growth in residual income from year to year.

Motivation and Residual Income

Topic Tackler PLUS 12–2

One of the primary reasons why the controller of Alaskan Marine Services Corporation would like to switch from ROI to residual income has to do with how managers view new investments under the two performance measurement schemes. The residual income approach encourages managers to make investments that are profitable for the entire company but that would be rejected by managers who are evaluated by the ROI formula.

To illustrate this problem with ROI, suppose that the manager of the Ketchican Division is considering purchasing a computerized diagnostic machine to aid in servicing marine diesel engines. The machine would cost $25,000 and is expected to generate additional operating income of $4,500 a year. From the standpoint of the company, this would be a good investment since it promises a rate of return of 18% ($4,500 ÷ $25,000), which is in excess of the company's minimum required rate of return of 15%.

If the manager of the Ketchican Division is evaluated based on residual income, she would be in favor of the investment in the diagnostic machine as shown below:

ALASKAN MARINE SERVICES CORPORATION
Ketchican Division
Performance Evaluated Using Residual Income

	Present	New Project	Overall
Average operating assets	$100,000	$25,000	$125,000
Net operating income	$ 20,000	$ 4,500	$ 24,500
Minimum required return	15,000	3,750*	18,750
Residual income	$ 5,000	$ 750	$ 5,750

*$25,000 × 15% = $3,750.

Since the project would increase the residual income of the Ketchican Division, the manager would want to invest in the new diagnostic machine.

Now suppose that the manager of the Ketchican Division is evaluated based on ROI. The effect of the diagnostic machine on the division's ROI is computed below:

ALASKAN MARINE SERVICES CORPORATION
Ketchican Division
Performance Evaluated Using ROI

	Present	New Project	Overall
Average operating assets (a)	$100,000	$25,000	$125,000
Net operating income (b)	$20,000	$4,500	$24,500
ROI, (b) ÷ (a)	20%	18%	19.6%

The new project reduces the division's ROI from 20% to 19.6%. This happens because the 18% rate of return on the new diagnostic machine, while above the company's 15% minimum required rate of return, is below the division's present ROI of 20%. Therefore, the new diagnostic machine would drag the division's ROI down even though it would be a good investment from the standpoint of the company as a whole. If the manager of the division is evaluated based on ROI, she will be reluctant to even propose such an investment.

Generally, a manager who is evaluated based on ROI will reject any project whose rate of return is below the division's current ROI even if the rate of return on the project is above the minimum required rate of return for the entire company. In contrast, any project whose rate of return is above the minimum required rate of return for the company will result in an increase in residual income. Since it is in the best interests of the company as a whole to accept any project whose rate of return is above the minimum required rate of return, managers who are evaluated based on residual income will tend to make better decisions concerning investment projects than managers who are evaluated based on ROI.

Divisional Comparison and Residual Income

The residual income approach has one major disadvantage. It can't be used to compare the performance of divisions of different sizes. You would expect larger divisions to have more residual income than smaller divisions, not necessarily because they are better managed but simply because they are bigger.

As an example, consider the following residual income computations for the Wholesale Division and the Retail Division of Sisal Marketing Corporation:

	Wholesale Division	Retail Division
Average operating assets (a)	$1,000,000	$250,000
Net operating income	$ 120,000	$ 40,000
Minimum required return: 10% × (a)	100,000	25,000
Residual income	$ 20,000	$ 15,000

Observe that the Wholesale Division has slightly more residual income than the Retail Division, but that the Wholesale Division has $1,000,000 in operating assets as compared to only $250,000 in operating assets for the Retail Division. Thus, the Wholesale Division's greater residual income is probably more a result of its size than the quality of its management. In fact, it appears that the smaller division may be better managed, since it has been able to generate nearly as much residual income with only one-fourth as much in operating assets to work with. This problem can be reduced by focusing on the percentage change in residual income from year to year rather than on the absolute amount of the residual income.

IN BUSINESS

REACTING TO THE USE OF EVA

One study found that, relative to companies that did not adopt EVA, a sample of companies adopting Economic Value Added as a performance measure "(1) increased their dispositions of assets and decreased their new investment, (2) increased their payouts to shareholders through share repurchases, and (3) used their assets more intensively. These actions are consistent with the strong rate of return discipline associated with the capital charge in residual income-based measures."

Source: James S. Wallace, "Adopting Residual Income-Based Compensation Plans: Do You Get What You Pay For?" *Journal of Accounting and Economics* 24, 1997, pp. 275–300.

IN BUSINESS

HEADS I WIN, TAILS YOU LOSE

A number of companies, including AT&T, Armstrong Holdings, and Baldwin Technology, have stopped using residual income measures of performance after trying them. Why? Reasons differ, but "bonus evaporation is often seen as the Achilles' heel of value-based metrics [like residual income and EVA]—and a major cause of plans being dropped." Managers tend to love residual income and EVA when their bonuses are big, but clamor for changes in performance measures when bonuses shrink.

Source: Bill Richard and Alix Nyberg, "Do EVA and Other Value Metrics Still Offer a Good Mirror of Company Performance?" *CFO,* March 2001, pp. 56–64.

Summary

For purposes of evaluating performance, business units are classified as cost centers, profit centers, and investment centers. Cost centers are commonly evaluated using standard cost and flexible budget variances as discussed in prior chapters. Profit centers and investment centers are evaluated using the techniques discussed in this chapter.

Segmented income statements provide information for evaluating the profitability and performance of divisions, product lines, sales territories, and other segments of a company. Under the contribution approach covered in this chapter, variable costs and fixed costs are clearly distinguished from each other and only those costs that are traceable to a segment are assigned to the segment. A cost is considered traceable to a segment only if the cost is caused by the segment and could be avoided by eliminating the segment. Fixed common costs are not allocated to segments. The segment margin consists of revenues, less variable expenses, less traceable fixed expenses of the segment.

Return on investment (ROI) and residual income and its cousin EVA are widely used to evaluate the performance of investment centers. ROI suffers from the underinvestment problem—managers are reluctant to invest in projects that would drag down their ROI but whose returns exceed the company's required rate of return. The residual income and EVA approaches solve this problem by giving managers full credit for any returns in excess of the company's required rate of return.

Review Problem 1: Segmented Statements

The business staff of the legal firm Frampton, Davis & Smythe has constructed the following report which breaks down the firm's overall results for last month in terms of its two main business segments—family law and commercial law:

	Total	Family Law	Commercial Law
Revenues from clients	$1,000,000	$400,000	$600,000
Less variable expenses	220,000	100,000	120,000
Contribution margin	780,000	300,000	480,000
Less traceable fixed expenses	670,000	280,000	390,000
Segment margin	110,000	20,000	90,000
Less common fixed expenses	60,000	24,000	36,000
Net operating income	$ 50,000	$ (4,000)	$ 54,000

However, this report is not quite correct. The common fixed expenses such as the managing partner's salary, general administrative expenses, and general firm advertising have been allocated to the two segments based on revenues from clients.

Required:

1. Redo the segment report, eliminating the allocation of common fixed expenses. Show both Amount and Percent columns for the firm as a whole and for each of the segments. Would the firm be better off financially if the family law segment were dropped? (Note: Many of the firm's commercial law clients also use the firm for their family law requirements such as drawing up wills.)
2. The firm's advertising agency has proposed an ad campaign targeted at boosting the revenues of the family law segment. The ad campaign would cost $20,000, and the advertising agency claims that it would increase family law revenues by $100,000. The managing partner of Frampton, Davis & Smythe believes this increase in business could be accommodated without any increase in fixed expenses. What effect would this ad campaign have on the family law segment margin and on overall net operating income of the firm?

Solution to Review Problem 1

1. The corrected segmented income statement appears below:

	Total		Family Law		Commercial Law	
	Amount	Percent	Amount	Percent	Amount	Percent
Revenues from clients	$1,000,000	100%	$400,000	100%	$600,000	100%
Less variable expenses	220,000	22%	100,000	25%	120,000	20%
Contribution margin	780,000	78%	300,000	75%	480,000	80%
Less traceable fixed expenses	670,000	67%	280,000	70%	390,000	65%
Segment margin	110,000	11%	$ 20,000	5%	$ 90,000	15%
Less common fixed expenses	60,000	6%				
Net operating income	$ 50,000	5%				

No, the firm would not be financially better off if the family law practice were dropped. The family law segment is covering all of its own costs and is contributing $20,000 per month to covering the common fixed expenses of the firm. While the segment margin as a percent of sales is much lower for family law than for commercial law, it is still profitable. Moreover, family law may be a service that the firm must provide to its commercial clients in order to remain competitive.

2. The ad campaign would be expected to add $55,000 to the family law segment as follows:

Increased revenues from clients	$100,000
Family law contribution margin ratio	× 75%
Incremental contribution margin	$ 75,000
Less cost of the ad campaign	20,000
Increased segment margin	$ 55,000

Since there would be no increase in fixed expenses (including common fixed expenses), the increase in overall net operating income should also be $55,000.

Review Problem 2: Return on Investment (ROI) and Residual Income

The Magnetic Imaging Division of Medical Diagnostics, Inc., has reported the following results for last year's operations:

Sales	$25 million
Net operating income	$3 million
Average operating assets	$10 million

Required:

1. Compute the margin, turnover, and ROI for the Magnetic Imaging Division.
2. Top management of Medical Diagnostics, Inc., has set a minimum required rate of return on average operating assets of 25%. What is the Magnetic Imaging Division's residual income for the year?

Solution to Review Problem 2

1. The required calculations follow:

$$\text{Margin} = \frac{\text{Net operating income}}{\text{Sales}}$$

$$= \frac{\$3{,}000{,}000}{\$25{,}000{,}000}$$

$$= 12\%$$

$$\text{Turnover} = \frac{\text{Sales}}{\text{Average operating assets}}$$

$$= \frac{\$25{,}000{,}000}{\$10{,}000{,}000}$$

$$= 2.5$$

$$\text{ROI} = \text{Margin} \times \text{Turnover}$$

$$= 12\% \times 2.5$$

$$= 30\%$$

2. The residual income for the Magnetic Imaging Division is computed as follows:

Average operating assets	$10,000,000
Net operating income	$ 3,000,000
Minimum required return (25% × $10,000,000)	2,500,000
Residual income	$ 500,000

Glossary

Common fixed cost A fixed cost that supports more than one business segment, but is not traceable in whole or in part to any one of the business segments. (p. 548)

Cost center A business segment whose manager has control over cost but has no control over revenue or the use of investment funds. (p. 541)

Decentralized organization An organization in which decision making authority is not confined to a few top executives but rather is spread throughout the organization. (p. 540)

Economic Value Added (EVA) A concept similar to residual income in which a variety of adjustments may be made to GAAP financial statements for performance evaluation purposes. (p. 562)

Investment center A business segment whose manager has control over cost, revenue, and the use of investment funds. (p. 542)

Margin Net operating income divided by sales. (p. 557)

Net operating income Income before interest and income taxes have been deducted. (p. 556)

Operating assets Cash, accounts receivable, inventory, plant and equipment, and all other assets held for productive use in an organization. (p. 556)

Profit center A business segment whose manager has control over cost and revenue but has no control over the use of investment funds. (p. 541)

Residual income The net operating income that an investment center earns above the required return on its operating assets. (p. 561)

Responsibility center Any business segment whose manager has control over cost, revenue, or the use of investment funds. (p. 541)

Return on investment (ROI) Net operating income divided by average operating assets. It also equals margin multiplied by turnover. (p. 556)

Segment Any part or activity of an organization about which the manager seeks cost, revenue, or profit data. (p. 543)

Segment margin A segment's contribution margin less its traceable fixed costs. It represents the margin available after a segment has covered all of its own traceable costs. (p. 550)

Traceable fixed cost A fixed cost that is incurred because of the existence of a particular business segment and would be eliminated if the segment were eliminated. (p. 548)

Turnover Sales divided by average operating assets. (p. 557)

Value chain The major business functions that add value to a company's products and services such as research and development, product design, manufacturing, marketing, distribution, and customer service. (p. 553)

Appendix 12A: Transfer Pricing

Divisions in a company often supply goods and services to other divisions within the same company. For example, the truck division of Toyota supplies trucks to other Toyota divisions to use in their operations. When the divisions are evaluated based on their profit, return on investment, or residual income, a price must be established for such a transfer—otherwise, the division that produces the good or service will receive no credit. The price in such a situation is called a *transfer price.* A **transfer price** is the price charged when one segment of a company provides goods or services to another segment of the same company. For example, most companies in the oil industry, such as Shell, have petroleum refining and retail sales divisions that are evaluated on the basis of ROI or residual income. The petroleum refining division processes crude oil into gasoline, kerosene, lubricants, and other end products. The retail sales division takes gasoline and other products from the refining division and sells them through the company's chain of service stations. Each product has a price for transfers within the company. Suppose the transfer price for gasoline is $0.80 a gallon. Then the refining division gets credit for $0.80 a gallon of revenue on its segment report and the retailing division must deduct $0.80 a gallon as an expense on its segment report. Clearly, the refining division would like the transfer price to be as high as possible, whereas the retailing division would like the transfer price to be as low as possible. However, the transaction has no direct effect on the entire company's reported profit. It is like taking money out of one pocket and putting it into the other.

Managers are intensely interested in how transfer prices are set, since transfer prices can have a dramatic effect on the reported profitability of a division. Three common approaches are used to set transfer prices:

1. Allow the managers involved in the transfer to negotiate their own transfer price.
2. Set transfer prices at cost using either variable cost or full (absorption) cost.
3. Set transfer prices at the market price.

We will consider each of these transfer pricing methods in turn, beginning with negotiated transfer prices. Throughout the discussion we should keep in mind that *the fundamental objective in setting transfer prices is to motivate the managers to act in the best interests of the overall company.* In contrast, **suboptimization** occurs when managers do not act in the best interests of the overall company or even in the best interests of their own division.

Negotiated Transfer Prices

LEARNING OBJECTIVE 4
Determine the range, if any, within which a negotiated transfer price should fall.

A **negotiated transfer price** results from discussions between the selling and buying divisions. Negotiated transfer prices have several important advantages. First, this approach preserves the autonomy of the divisions and is consistent with the spirit of decentralization. Second, the managers of the divisions are likely to have much better information about the potential costs and benefits of the transfer than others in the company.

When negotiated transfer prices are used, the managers who are involved in a proposed transfer within the company meet to discuss the terms and conditions of the transfer. They may decide not to go through with the transfer, but if they do, they must agree to a transfer price. Generally speaking, we cannot predict the exact transfer price they will agree to. However, we can confidently predict two things: (1) the selling division will agree to the transfer only if the profits of the selling division increase as a result of the transfer, and (2) the buying division will agree to the transfer only if the profits of the buying division also increase as a result of the transfer. This may seem obvious, but it is an important point.

Clearly, if the transfer price is below the selling division's cost, a loss will occur on the transaction and the selling division will refuse to agree to the transfer. Likewise, if the transfer price is set too high, it will be impossible for the buying division to make any profit on the transferred item. For any given proposed transfer, the transfer price has both a lower limit (determined by the selling division) and an upper limit (determined by the buying division). The actual transfer price agreed to by the two division managers can fall anywhere between those two limits. These limits determine the **range of acceptable**

transfer prices—the range of transfer prices within which the profits of both divisions participating in a transfer would increase.

An example will help us to understand negotiated transfer prices. Harris & Louder, Ltd., owns fast-food restaurants and snack food and beverage manufacturers in the United Kingdom. One of the restaurants, Pizza Maven, serves a variety of beverages along with pizzas. One of the beverages is ginger beer, which is served on tap. Harris & Louder has just purchased a new division, Imperial Beverages, that produces ginger beer. The managing director of Imperial Beverages has approached the managing director of Pizza Maven about purchasing Imperial Beverages ginger beer for sale at Pizza Maven restaurants rather than its usual brand of ginger beer. Managers at Pizza Maven agree that the quality of Imperial Beverages' ginger beer is comparable to the quality of their regular brand. It is just a question of price. The basic facts are as follows (the currency in this example is pounds denoted here as £):

Imperial Beverages:	
Ginger beer production capacity per month	10,000 barrels
Variable cost per barrel of ginger beer	£8 per barrel
Fixed costs per month	£70,000
Selling price of Imperial Beverages ginger beer on the outside market	£20 per barrel
Pizza Maven:	
Purchase price of regular brand of ginger beer	£18 per barrel
Monthly consumption of ginger beer	2,000 barrels

The Selling Division's Lowest Acceptable Transfer Price The selling division, Imperial Beverages, will be interested in a proposed transfer only if its profit increases. Clearly, the transfer price must not fall below the variable cost per barrel of £8. In addition, if Imperial Beverages has insufficient capacity to fill the Pizza Maven order, then it would have to sacrifice some of its regular sales. Imperial Beverages would expect to be compensated for the contribution margin on these lost sales. In sum, if the transfer has no effect on fixed costs, then from the selling division's standpoint, the transfer price must cover both the variable costs of producing the transferred units and any opportunity costs from lost sales.

Seller's perspective:

$$\text{Transfer price} \geq \begin{array}{c}\text{Variable cost}\\ \text{per unit}\end{array} + \frac{\text{Total contribution margin on lost sales}}{\text{Number of units transferred}}$$

The Buying Division's Highest Acceptable Transfer Price The buying division, Pizza Maven, will be interested in a transfer only if its profit increases. In cases like this where a buying division has an outside supplier, the buying division's decision is simple. Buy from the inside supplier if the price is less than the price offered by the outside supplier.

Purchaser's perspective:

$$\text{Transfer price} \leq \text{Cost of buying from outside supplier}$$

Or, if an outside supplier does not exist:

$$\text{Transfer price} \leq \text{Profit to be earned per unit sold (not including the transfer price)}$$

We will consider several different hypothetical situations and see what the range of acceptable transfer prices would be in each situation.

Selling Division with Idle Capacity Suppose that Imperial Beverages has sufficient idle capacity to satisfy the demand for ginger beer from Pizza Maven without sacrificing sales of ginger beer to its regular customers. To be specific, let's suppose that Imperial Beverages is selling only 7,000 barrels of ginger beer a month on the outside market. That leaves unused capacity of 3,000 barrels a month—more than enough to satisfy Pizza Maven's requirement of 2,000 barrels a month. What range of transfer prices, if any, would make both divisions better off with the transfer of 2,000 barrels a month?

1. The selling division, Imperial Beverages, will be interested in the transfer only if:

$$\text{Transfer price} \geq \begin{matrix}\text{Variable cost}\\ \text{per unit}\end{matrix} + \frac{\text{Total contribution margin on lost sales}}{\text{Number of units transferred}}$$

   Since Imperial Beverages has ample idle capacity, there are no lost outside sales. And since the variable cost per unit is £8, the lowest acceptable transfer price as far as the selling division is concerned is also £8.

$$\text{Transfer price} \geq £8 + \frac{£0}{2{,}000} = £8$$

2. The buying division, Pizza Maven, can buy similar ginger beer from an outside vendor for £18. Therefore, Pizza Maven would be unwilling to pay more than £18 per barrel for Imperial Beverages' ginger beer.

$$\text{Transfer price} \leq \text{Cost of buying from outside supplier} = £18$$

3. Combining the requirements of both the selling division and the buying division, the acceptable range of transfer prices in this situation is:

$$£8 \leq \text{Transfer price} \leq £18$$

   Assuming that the managers understand their own businesses and that they are cooperative, they should be able to agree on a transfer price within this range.

Selling Division with No Idle Capacity Suppose that Imperial Beverages has *no* idle capacity; it is selling 10,000 barrels of ginger beer a month on the outside market at £20 per barrel. To fill the order from Pizza Maven, Imperial Beverages would have to divert 2,000 barrels from its regular customers. What range of transfer prices, if any, would make both divisions better off transferring the 2,000 barrels within the company?

1. The selling division, Imperial Beverages, will be interested in the transfer only if:

$$\text{Transfer price} \geq \begin{matrix}\text{Variable cost}\\ \text{per unit}\end{matrix} + \frac{\text{Total contribution margin on lost sales}}{\text{Number of units transferred}}$$

   Since Imperial Beverages has no idle capacity, there *are* lost outside sales. The contribution margin per barrel on these outside sales is £12 (£20 − £8).

$$\text{Transfer price} \geq £8 + \frac{(£20 - £8) \times 2{,}000}{2{,}000} = £8 + (£20 - £8) = £20$$

   Thus, as far as the selling division is concerned, the transfer price must at least cover the revenue on the lost sales, which is £20 per barrel. This makes sense since the cost of producing the 2,000 barrels is the same whether they are sold on the inside market or on the outside. The only difference is that the selling division loses the revenue of £20 per barrel if it transfers the barrels to Pizza Maven.
2. As before, the buying division, Pizza Maven, would be unwilling to pay more than the £18 per barrel it is already paying for similar ginger beer from its regular supplier.

$$\text{Transfer price} \leq \text{Cost of buying from outside supplier} = £18$$

3. Therefore, the selling division would insist on a transfer price of at least £20. But the buying division would refuse any transfer price above £18. It is impossible to satisfy both division managers simultaneously; there can be no agreement on a transfer price and no transfer will take place. Is this good? The answer is yes. From the standpoint of the entire company, the transfer doesn't make sense. Why give up sales of £20 to save costs of £18?

Basically, the transfer price is a mechanism for dividing between the two divisions any profit the entire company earns as a result of the transfer. If the company as a whole loses money on the transfer, there will be no profit to divide up, and it will be impossible for the two divisions to come to an agreement. On the other hand, if the company as a whole makes money on the transfer, there will be a profit to share, and it will always be possible for the two divisions to find a mutually agreeable transfer price that increases the profits of both divisions. If the pie is bigger, it is always possible to divide it up in such a way that everyone has a bigger piece.

Selling Division Has Some Idle Capacity Suppose now that Imperial Beverages is selling 9,000 barrels of ginger beer a month on the outside market. Pizza Maven can only sell one kind of ginger beer on tap. It cannot buy 1,000 barrels from Imperial Beverages and 1,000 barrels from its regular supplier; it must buy all of its ginger beer from one source.

To fill the entire 2,000-barrel a month order from Pizza Maven, Imperial Beverages would have to divert 1,000 barrels from its regular customers who are paying £20 per barrel. The other 1,000 barrels can be made using idle capacity. What range of transfer prices, if any, would make both divisions better off transferring the 2,000 barrels within the company?

1. As before, the selling division, Imperial Beverages, will insist on a transfer price that at least covers its variable cost and opportunity cost:

$$\text{Transfer price} \geq \begin{matrix}\text{Variable cost}\\ \text{per unit}\end{matrix} + \frac{\text{Total contribution margin on lost sales}}{\text{Number of units transferred}}$$

   Since Imperial Beverages does not have enough idle capacity to fill the entire order for 2,000 barrels, there *are* lost outside sales. The contribution margin per barrel on the 1,000 barrels of lost outside sales is £12 (£20 − £8).

$$\text{Transfer price} \geq £8 + \frac{(£20 - £8) \times 1{,}000}{2{,}000} = £8 + £6 = £14$$

   Thus, as far as the selling division is concerned, the transfer price must cover the variable cost of £8 plus the average opportunity cost of lost sales of £6.

2. As before, the buying division, Pizza Maven, would be unwilling to pay more than the £18 per barrel it pays its regular supplier.

$$\text{Transfer price} \leq \text{Cost of buying from outside suppliers} = £18$$

3. Combining the requirements for both the selling and buying divisions, the range of acceptable transfer prices is:

$$£14 \leq \text{Transfer price} \leq £18$$

   Again, assuming that the managers understand their own businesses and that they are cooperative, they should be able to agree on a transfer price within this range.

No Outside Supplier If Pizza Maven has no outside supplier for the ginger beer, the highest price the buying division would be willing to pay depends on how much the buying division expects to make on the transferred units—excluding the transfer price. If, for example, Pizza Maven expects to earn £30 per barrel of ginger beer after paying its own expenses, then it should be willing to pay up to £30 per barrel to Imperial Beverages. Remember, however, that this assumes Pizza Maven cannot buy ginger beer from other sources.

Evaluation of Negotiated Transfer Prices As discussed earlier, if a transfer within the company would result in higher overall profits for the company, there is always a range of transfer prices within which both the selling and buying division would also have higher profits if they agree to the transfer. Therefore, if the managers understand their own businesses and are cooperative, then they should always be able to agree on a transfer price if it is in the best interests of the company that they do so.

Unfortunately, not all managers understand their own businesses and not all managers are cooperative. As a result, negotiations often break down even when it would be in the managers' own best interests to come to an agreement. Sometimes that is the fault of the way managers are evaluated. If managers are pitted against each other rather than against their own past performance or reasonable benchmarks, a noncooperative atmosphere is almost guaranteed. Nevertheless, it must be admitted that even with the best performance evaluation system, some people by nature are not cooperative.

Given the disputes that often accompany the negotiation process, most companies rely on some other means of setting transfer prices. Unfortunately, as we will see below, all of the alternatives to negotiated transfer prices have their own serious drawbacks.

Transfers at the Cost to the Selling Division

Many companies set transfer prices at either the variable cost or full (absorption) cost incurred by the selling division. Although the cost approach to setting transfer prices is relatively simple to apply, it has some major defects.

First, the use of cost—particularly full cost—as a transfer price can lead to bad decisions and thus suboptimization. Return to the example involving the ginger beer. The full cost of ginger beer can never be less than £15 per barrel (£8 per barrel variable cost + £7 per barrel fixed cost at capacity). What if the cost of buying the ginger beer from an outside supplier is less than £15—for example, £14 per barrel? If the transfer price were set at full cost, then Pizza Maven would never want to buy ginger beer from Imperial Beverages, since it could buy its ginger beer from an outside supplier at less cost. However, from the standpoint of the company as a whole, ginger beer should be transferred from Imperial Beverages to Pizza Maven whenever Imperial Beverages has idle capacity. Why? Because when Imperial Beverages has idle capacity, it only costs the company £8 in variable cost to produce a barrel of ginger beer, but it costs £14 per barrel to buy from outside suppliers.

Second, if cost is used as the transfer price, the selling division will never show a profit on any internal transfer. The only division that shows a profit is the division that makes the final sale to an outside party.

Third, cost-based prices do not provide incentives to control costs. If the actual costs of one division are simply passed on to the next, there is little incentive for anyone to work to reduce costs. This problem can be overcome by using standard costs rather than actual costs for transfer prices.

Despite these shortcomings, cost-based transfer prices are commonly used in practice. Advocates argue that they are easily understood and convenient to use.

IN BUSINESS

ABC-BASED TRANSFER PRICES

Teva Pharmaceutical Industries Ltd. of Israel rejected the negotiated transfer price approach because senior executives believed that this approach would lead to endless, nonproductive arguments. Instead, the company uses activity-based costing to set its transfer prices. Marketing divisions are charged for unit-level costs based on the actual quantities of each product they acquire. In addition, they are charged batch-level costs based on the actual number of batches their orders require. Product-level and organization-sustaining costs are charged to the marketing divisions annually in lump sums—the details will be covered in Chapter 16. Essentially, Teva Pharmaceutical Industries sets its transfer prices at carefully computed variable costs. As long as Teva Pharmaceutical Industries has unused capacity, this system sends the marketing managers the correct signals about how much it really costs the company to produce each product. With this information, the marketing managers are much better equipped to make pricing and other decisions regarding the products.

Source: Robert S. Kaplan, Dan Weiss, and Eyal Desheh, "Transfer Pricing with ABC," *Management Accounting*, May 1997, pp. 20–28.

Transfers at Market Price

Some form of competitive **market price** (i.e., the price charged for an item on the open market) is often regarded as the best approach to the transfer pricing problem—particularly if transfer price negotiations routinely become bogged down.

The market price approach is designed for situations in which there is an *outside market* for the transferred product or service; the product or service is sold in its present form to outside customers. If the selling division has no idle capacity, the market price is the perfect choice for the transfer price. This is because, from the company's perspective, the real cost of the transfer is the opportunity cost of the lost revenue on the outside sale. Whether the item is transferred internally or sold on the outside market, the production costs are exactly the same. If the market price is used as the transfer price, the selling division manager will not lose anything by making the transfer, and the buying division manager will get the correct signal about how much it really costs the company for the transfer to take place.

While the market price works beautifully when the selling division has no idle capacity, difficulties occur when the selling division has idle capacity. Recalling once again the ginger beer example, the outside market price for the ginger beer produced by Imperial Beverages is £20 per barrel. However, Pizza Maven can purchase all of the ginger beer it wants from outside suppliers for £18 per barrel. Why would Pizza Maven ever buy from Imperial Beverages if Pizza Maven is forced to pay Imperial Beverages' market price? In some market price-based transfer pricing schemes, the transfer price would be lowered to £18, the outside vendor's market price, and Pizza Maven would be directed to buy from Imperial Beverages as long as Imperial Beverages is willing to sell. This scheme can work reasonably well, but a drawback is that managers at Pizza Maven will regard the cost of ginger beer as £18 rather than the £8, which is the real cost to the company when the selling division has idle capacity. Consequently, the managers of Pizza Maven will make pricing and other decisions based on an incorrect cost.

Unfortunately, none of the possible solutions to the transfer pricing problem are perfect—not even market-based transfer prices.

Divisional Autonomy and Suboptimization

The principles of decentralization suggest that companies should grant managers autonomy to set transfer prices and to decide whether to sell internally or externally. It may be very difficult for top managers to accept this principle when their subordinate managers are about to make a suboptimal decision. However, if top management intervenes, the purposes of decentralization are defeated. Furthermore, to impose the correct transfer price, top managers would have to know details about the buying and selling divisions' outside market, variable costs, and capacity utilization. The whole premise of decentralization is that local managers have access to better information for operational decisions than top managers at corporate headquarters.

Of course, if a division manager consistently makes suboptimal decisions, the performance of the division will suffer. The offending manager's compensation will be adversely affected and promotion will become less likely. Thus, a performance evaluation system based on divisional profits, ROI, or residual income provides some built-in checks and balances. Nevertheless, if top managers wish to create a culture of autonomy and independent profit responsibility, they must allow their subordinate managers to control their own destiny—even to the extent of granting their managers the right to make mistakes.

International Aspects of Transfer Pricing

The objectives of transfer pricing change when a multinational corporation is involved and the goods and services being transferred cross international borders. The objectives

EXHIBIT 12A–1
Domestic and International Transfer Pricing Objectives

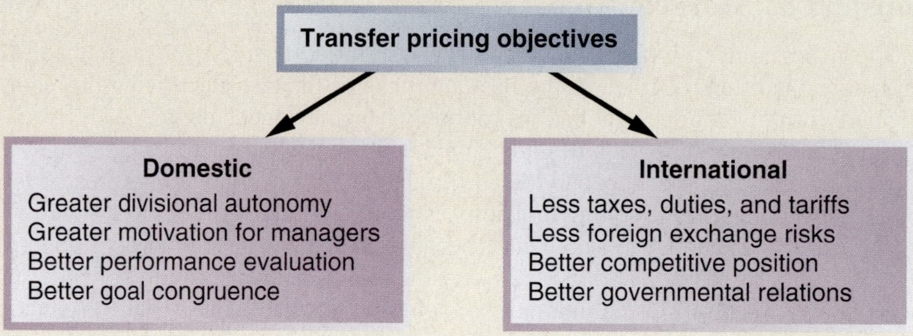

of international transfer pricing, as compared to domestic transfer pricing, are summarized in Exhibit 12A–1.[6]

As shown in the exhibit, the objectives of international transfer pricing focus on minimizing taxes, duties, and foreign exchange risks, along with enhancing a company's competitive position and improving its relations with foreign governments. Although domestic objectives such as managerial motivation and divisional autonomy are always important, they often become secondary when international transfers are involved. Companies will focus instead on charging a transfer price that will slash its total tax bill or that will strengthen a foreign subsidiary.

For example, charging a low transfer price for parts shipped to a foreign subsidiary may reduce customs duty payments as the parts cross international borders, or it may help the subsidiary to compete in foreign markets by keeping the subsidiary's costs low. On the other hand, charging a high transfer price may help a multinational corporation draw profits out of a country that has stringent controls on foreign remittances, or it may allow a multinational corporation to shift income from a country that has high income tax rates to a country that has low rates.

Review Problem 3: Transfer Pricing

Situation A

Collyer Products, Inc., has a Valve Division that manufactures and sells a standard valve:

Capacity in units	100,000
Selling price to outside customers	$30
Variable costs per unit	$16
Fixed costs per unit (based on capacity)	$9

The company has a Pump Division that could use this valve in one of its pumps. The Pump Division is currently purchasing 10,000 valves per year from an overseas supplier at a cost of $29 per valve.

Required:

1. Assume that the Valve Division has ample idle capacity to handle all of the Pump Division's needs. What is the acceptable range, if any, for the transfer price between the two divisions?
2. Assume that the Valve Division is selling all of the valves that it can produce to outside customers. What is the acceptable range, if any, for the transfer price between the two divisions?
3. Assume again that the Valve Division is selling all of the valves that it can produce to outside customers. Also assume that $3 in variable expenses can be avoided on transfers within the

[6] The exhibit is adapted from Wagdy M. Abdallah, "Guidelines for CEOs in Transfer Pricing Policies," *Management Accounting* 70, no. 3, p. 61.

company, due to reduced selling costs. What is the acceptable range, if any, for the transfer price between the two divisions?

Solution to Situation A

1. Since the Valve Division has idle capacity, it does not have to give up any outside sales to take on the Pump Division's business. Applying the formula for the lowest acceptable transfer price from the viewpoint of the selling division, we get:

$$\text{Transfer price} \geq \begin{matrix}\text{Variable cost}\\ \text{per unit}\end{matrix} + \frac{\text{Total contribution margin on lost sales}}{\text{Number of units transferred}}$$

$$\text{Transfer price} \geq \$16 + \frac{\$0}{10{,}000} = \$16$$

The Pump Division would be unwilling to pay more than $29, the price it is currently paying an outside supplier for its valves. Therefore, the transfer price must fall within the range:

$$\$16 \leq \text{Transfer price} \leq \$29$$

2. Since the Valve Division is selling all of the valves that it can produce on the outside market, it would have to give up some of these outside sales to take on the Pump Division's business. Thus, the Valve Division has an opportunity cost, which is the total contribution margin on lost sales:

$$\text{Transfer price} \geq \begin{matrix}\text{Variable cost}\\ \text{per unit}\end{matrix} + \frac{\text{Total contribution margin on lost sales}}{\text{Number of units transferred}}$$

$$\text{Transfer price} \geq \$16 + \frac{(\$30 - \$16) \times 10{,}000}{10{,}000} = \$16 + \$14 = \$30$$

Since the Pump Division can purchase valves from an outside supplier at only $29 per unit, no transfers will be made between the two divisions.

3. Applying the formula for the lowest acceptable transfer price from the viewpoint of the selling division, we get:

$$\text{Transfer price} \geq \begin{matrix}\text{Variable cost}\\ \text{per unit}\end{matrix} + \frac{\text{Total contribution margin on lost sales}}{\text{Number of units transferred}}$$

$$\text{Transfer price} \geq (\$16 - \$3) + \frac{(\$30 - \$16) \times 10{,}000}{10{,}000} = \$13 + \$14 = \$27$$

In this case, the transfer price must fall within the range:

$$\$27 \leq \text{Transfer price} \leq \$29$$

Situation B

Refer to the original data in situation A above. Assume that the Pump Division needs 20,000 special high-pressure valves per year. The Valve Division's variable costs to manufacture and ship the special valve would be $20 per unit. To produce these special valves, the Valve Division would have to reduce its production and sales of regular valves from 100,000 units per year to 70,000 units per year.

Required:
As far as the Valve Division is concerned, what is the lowest acceptable transfer price?

Solution to Situation B

To produce the 20,000 special valves, the Valve Division will have to give up sales of 30,000 regular valves to outside customers. Applying the formula for the lowest acceptable transfer price from the viewpoint of the selling division, we get:

$$\text{Transfer price} \geq \begin{matrix}\text{Variable cost}\\ \text{per unit}\end{matrix} + \frac{\text{Total contribution margin on lost sales}}{\text{Number of units transferred}}$$

$$\text{Transfer price} \geq \$20 + \frac{(\$30 - \$16) \times 30{,}000}{20{,}000} = \$20 + \$21 = \$41$$

Glossary (Appendix 12A)

Market price The price being charged for an item on the open market. (p. 573)

Negotiated transfer price A transfer price agreed on between buying and selling divisions. (p. 568)

Range of acceptable transfer prices The range of transfer prices within which the profits of both the selling division and the buying division would increase as a result of a transfer. (p. 568)

Suboptimization An overall level of profits that is less than a segment or a company is capable of earning. (p. 568)

Transfer price The price charged when one division or segment provides goods or services to another division or segment of an organization. (p. 568)

Questions

12–1 What is meant by the term *decentralization?*

12–2 What benefits result from decentralization?

12–3 Distinguish between a cost center, a profit center, and an investment center.

12–4 Define a segment of an organization. Give several examples of segments.

12–5 How does the contribution approach assign costs to segments of an organization?

12–6 Distinguish between a traceable cost and a common cost. Give several examples of each.

12–7 Explain how the segment margin differs from the contribution margin.

12–8 Why aren't common costs allocated to segments under the contribution approach?

12–9 How is it possible for a cost that is traceable to a segment to become a common cost if the segment is divided into further segments?

12–10 What is meant by the terms *margin* and *turnover* in ROI calculations?

12–11 What is meant by residual income?

12–12 In what way can the use of ROI as a performance measure for investment centers lead to bad decisions? How does the residual income approach overcome this problem?

12–13 (Appendix 12A) What is meant by the term *transfer price,* and why are transfer prices needed?

12–14 (Appendix 12A) From the standpoint of a selling division that has idle capacity, what is the lowest acceptable transfer price for an item?

12–15 (Appendix 12A) From the standpoint of a selling division that has *no* idle capacity, what is the lowest acceptable transfer price for an item?

12–16 (Appendix 12A) What are the advantages and disadvantages of cost-based transfer prices?

12–17 (Appendix 12A) If a market price for a product can be determined, why isn't it always the best transfer price?

Exercises

EXERCISE 12–1 Basic Segmented Income Statement [LO1]

Royal Lawncare Company produces and sells two packaged products, Weedban and Greengrow. Revenue and cost information relating to the products follow:

	Product	
	Weedban	Greengrow
Selling price per unit	$6.00	$7.50
Variable expenses per unit	$2.40	$5.25
Traceable fixed expenses per year	$45,000	$21,000

Common fixed expenses in the company total $33,000 annually. Last year the company produced and sold 15,000 units of Weedban and 28,000 units of Greengrow.

Required:

Prepare a contribution format income statement segmented by product lines. Show both Amount and Percent columns for the company as a whole and for each of the products.

EXERCISE 12–2 Compute the Return on Investment (ROI) [LO2]

Alyeska Services Company, a division of a major oil company, provides various services to the operators of the North Slope oil field in Alaska. Data concerning the most recent year appear below:

Sales	$7,500,000
Net operating income	$600,000
Average operating assets	$5,000,000

Required:

1. Compute the margin for Alyeska Services Company.
2. Compute the turnover for Alyeska Services Company.
3. Compute the return on investment (ROI) for Alyeska Services Company.

EXERCISE 12–3 Residual Income [LO3]

Juniper Design Ltd. of Manchester, England, is a company specializing in providing design services to residential developers. Last year the company had net operating income of £600,000 on sales of £3,000,000. The company's average operating assets for the year were £2,800,000 and its minimum required rate of return was 18%. (The currency used in England is the pound sterling, denoted by £.)

Required:

Compute the company's residual income for the year.

EXERCISE 12–4 (Appendix 12A) Transfer Pricing Basics [LO4]

Sako Company's Audio Division produces a speaker that is used by manufacturers of various audio products. Sales and cost data on the speaker follow:

Selling price per unit on the intermediate market	$60
Variable costs per unit	$42
Fixed costs per unit (based on capacity)	$8
Capacity in units	25,000

Sako Company has a Hi-Fi Division that could use this speaker in one of its products. The Hi-Fi Division will need 5,000 speakers per year. It has received a quote of $57 per speaker from another manufacturer. Sako Company evaluates division managers on the basis of divisional profits.

Required:

1. Assume that the Audio Division is now selling only 20,000 speakers per year to outside customers.
   a. From the standpoint of the Audio Division, what is the lowest acceptable transfer price for speakers sold to the Hi-Fi Division?
   b. From the standpoint of the Hi-Fi Division, what is the highest acceptable transfer price for speakers acquired from the Audio Division?
   c. If left free to negotiate without interference, would you expect the division managers to voluntarily agree to the transfer of 5,000 speakers from the Audio Division to the Hi-Fi Division? Why or why not?
   d. From the standpoint of the entire company, should the transfer take place? Why or why not?
2. Assume that the Audio Division is selling all of the speakers it can produce to outside customers.
   a. From the standpoint of the Audio Division, what is the lowest acceptable transfer price for speakers sold to the Hi-Fi Division?
   b. From the standpoint of the Hi-Fi Division, what is the highest acceptable transfer price for speakers acquired from the Audio Division?
   c. If left free to negotiate without interference, would you expect the division managers to voluntarily agree to the transfer of 5,000 speakers from the Audio Division to the Hi-Fi Division? Why or why not?
   d. From the standpoint of the entire company, should the transfer take place? Why or why not?

EXERCISE 12–5 Segmented Income Statement [LO1]

Wingate Company, a wholesale distributor of videotapes, has been experiencing losses for some time, as shown by its most recent monthly contribution format income statement, which follows:

Sales	$1,000,000
Less variable expenses	390,000
Contribution margin	610,000
Less fixed expenses	625,000
Net operating income (loss)	$ (15,000)

In an effort to isolate the problem, the president has asked for an income statement segmented by division. Accordingly, the Accounting Department has developed the following information:

	Division		
	East	Central	West
Sales	$250,000	$400,000	$350,000
Variable expenses as a percentage of sales	52%	30%	40%
Traceable fixed expenses	$160,000	$200,000	$175,000

Required:

1. Prepare a contribution format income statement segmented by divisions, as desired by the president. Show both Amount and Percent columns for the company as a whole and for each division.
2. As a result of a marketing study, the president believes that sales in the West Division could be increased by 20% if monthly advertising in that division were increased by $15,000. Would you recommend the increased advertising? Show computations.

EXERCISE 12–6 Effects of Changes in Sales, Expenses, and Assets on ROI [LO2]

CommercialServices.com Corporation provides business-to-business services on the Internet. Data concerning the most recent year appear below:

Sales	$3,000,000
Net operating income	$150,000
Average operating assets	$750,000

Required:

Consider each question below independently. Carry out all computations to two decimal places.

1. Compute the company's return on investment (ROI).
2. The entrepreneur who founded the company is convinced that sales will increase next year by 50% and that net operating income will increase by 200%, with no increase in average operating assets. What would be the company's ROI?
3. The chief financial officer of the company believes a more realistic scenario would be a $1,000,000 increase in sales, requiring a $250,000 increase in average operating assets, with a resulting $200,000 increase in net operating income. What would be the company's ROI in this scenario?

EXERCISE 12–7 Working with a Segmented Income Statement [LO1]

Raner, Harris, & Chan is a consulting firm that specializes in information systems for medical and dental clinics. The firm has two offices—one in Chicago and one in Minneapolis. The firm classifies the direct costs of consulting jobs as variable costs. A contribution format segmented income statement for the company's most recent year is given below:

	Total Company		Office			
			Chicago		Minneapolis	
Sales	$450,000	100%	$150,000	100%	$300,000	100%
Less variable expenses	225,000	50%	45,000	30%	180,000	60%
Contribution margin	225,000	50%	105,000	70%	120,000	40%
Less traceable fixed expenses	126,000	28%	78,000	52%	48,000	16%
Office segment margin	99,000	22%	$ 27,000	18%	$ 72,000	24%
Less common fixed expenses not traceable to offices	63,000	14%				
Net operating income	$ 36,000	8%				

Required:

1. By how much would the company's net operating income increase if Minneapolis increased its sales by $75,000 per year? Assume no change in cost behavior patterns.
2. Refer to the original data. Assume that sales in Chicago increase by $50,000 next year and that sales in Minneapolis remain unchanged. Assume no change in fixed costs.
   a. Prepare a new segmented income statement for the company using the format shown previously. Show both amounts and percentages.
   b. Observe from the income statement you have prepared that the contribution margin ratio for Chicago has remained unchanged at 70% (the same as in the previous data) but that the segment margin ratio has changed. How do you explain the change in the segment margin ratio?

EXERCISE 12–8 Working with a Segmented Income Statement [LO1]

Refer to the data in Exercise 12–7. Assume that Minneapolis' sales by major market are:

			Market			
	Minneapolis		Medical		Dental	
Sales	$300,000	100%	$200,000	100%	$100,000	100%
Less variable expenses	180,000	60%	128,000	64%	52,000	52%
Contribution margin	120,000	40%	72,000	36%	48,000	48%
Less traceable fixed expenses	33,000	11%	12,000	6%	21,000	21%
Market segment margin	87,000	29%	$ 60,000	30%	$ 27,000	27%
Less common fixed expenses not traceable to markets	15,000	5%				
Office segment margin	$ 72,000	24%				

The company would like to initiate an intensive advertising campaign in one of the two market segments during the next month. The campaign would cost $5,000. Marketing studies indicate that such a campaign would increase sales in the Medical market by $40,000 or increase sales in the Dental market by $35,000.

Required:

1. In which of the markets would you recommend that the company focus its advertising campaign? Show computations to support your answer.
2. In Exercise 12–7, Minneapolis shows $48,000 in traceable fixed expenses. What happened to the $48,000 in this exercise?

EXERCISE 12–9 Effects of Changes in Profits and Assets on Return on Investment (ROI) [LO2]

Pecs Alley is a regional chain of health clubs. The managers of the clubs, who have authority to make investments as needed, are evaluated based largely on return on investment (ROI). The Springfield Club reported the following results for the past year:

Sales	$1,400,000
Net operating income	$70,000
Average operating assets	$350,000

Required:

The following questions are to be considered independently. Carry out all computations to two decimal places.

1. Compute the club's return on investment (ROI).
2. Assume that the manager of the club is able to increase sales by $70,000 and that, as a result, net operating income increases by $18,200. Further assume that this is possible without any increase in operating assets. What would be the club's return on investment (ROI)?
3. Assume that the manager of the club is able to reduce expenses by $14,000 without any change in sales or operating assets. What would be the club's return on investment (ROI)?
4. Assume that the manager of the club is able to reduce operating assets by $70,000 without any change in sales or net operating income. What would be the club's return on investment (ROI)?

Exercise 12–10 Cost-Volume Profit Analysis and Return on Investment (ROI) [LO2]

Posters.com is a small Internet retailer of high-quality posters. The company has $1,000,000 in operating assets and fixed expenses of $150,000 per year. With this level of operating assets and fixed expenses, the company can support sales of up to $3,000,000 per year. The company's contribution margin ratio is 25%, which means that an additional dollar of sales results in additional contribution margin, and net operating income, of 25 cents.

Required:

1. Complete the following table showing the relation between sales and return on investment (ROI).

Sales	Net Operating Income	Average Operating Assets	ROI
$2,500,000	$475,000	$1,000,000	?
$2,600,000	$?	$1,000,000	?
$2,700,000	$?	$1,000,000	?
$2,800,000	$?	$1,000,000	?
$2,900,000	$?	$1,000,000	?
$3,000,000	$?	$1,000,000	?

2. What happens to the company's return on investment (ROI) as sales increase? Explain.

EXERCISE 12–11 Return on Investment (ROI) [LO2]

Provide the missing data in the following table for a distributor of martial arts products:

	Division		
	Alpha	Bravo	Charlie
Sales	$?	$11,500,000	$?
Net operating income	$?	$ 920,000	$210,000
Average operating assets	$800,000	$?	$?
Margin	4%	?	7%
Turnover	5	?	?
Return on investment (ROI)	?	20%	14%

EXERCISE 12–12 Evaluating New Investments Using Return on Investment (ROI) and Residual Income [LO2, LO3]

Selected sales and operating data for three divisions of different structural engineering firms are given below:

	Division A	Division B	Division C
Sales	$12,000,000	$14,000,000	$25,000,000
Average operating assets	$3,000,000	$7,000,000	$5,000,000
Net operating income	$600,000	$560,000	$800,000
Minimum required rate of return	14%	10%	16%

Required:

1. Compute the return on investment (ROI) for each division using the formula stated in terms of margin and turnover.
2. Compute the residual income for each division.
3. Assume that each division is presented with an investment opportunity that would yield a 15% rate of return.
   a. If performance is being measured by ROI, which division or divisions will probably accept the opportunity? Reject? Why?
   b. If performance is being measured by residual income, which division or divisions will probably accept the opportunity? Reject? Why?

EXERCISE 12–13 Computing and Interpreting Return on Investment (ROI) [LO2]

Selected operating data for two divisions of Outback Brewing, Ltd., of Australia are given below:

	Division	
	Queensland	New South Wales
Sales	$4,000,000	$7,000,000
Average operating assets	$2,000,000	$2,000,000
Net operating income	$360,000	$420,000
Property, plant, and equipment (net)	$950,000	$800,000

Required:

1. Compute the rate of return for each division using the return on investment (ROI) formula stated in terms of margin and turnover.
2. Which divisional manager seems to be doing the better job? Why?

EXERCISE 12–14 Contrasting Return on Investment (ROI) and Residual Income [LO2, LO3]

Meiji Isetan Corp. of Japan has two regional divisions with headquarters in Osaka and Yokohama. Selected data on the two divisions follow (in millions of yen, denoted by ¥):

	Division	
	Osaka	Yokohama
Sales	¥3,000,000	¥9,000,000
Net operating income	¥210,000	¥720,000
Average operating assets	¥1,000,000	¥4,000,000

Required:

1. For each division, compute the return on investment (ROI) in terms of margin and turnover. Where necessary, carry computations to two decimal places.
2. Assume that the company evaluates performance using residual income and that the minimum required rate of return for any division is 15%. Compute the residual income for each division.
3. Is Yokohama's greater amount of residual income an indication that it is better managed? Explain.

EXERCISE 12–15 (Appendix 12A) Transfer Pricing from the Viewpoint of the Entire Company [LO4]

Division A manufactures electronic circuit boards. The boards can be sold either to Division B of the same company or to outside customers. Last year, the following activity occurred in Division A:

Selling price per circuit board	$125
Production cost per circuit board	$90
Number of circuit boards:	
Produced during the year	20,000
Sold to outside customers	16,000
Sold to Division B	4,000

Sales to Division B were at the same price as sales to outside customers. The circuit boards purchased by Division B were used in an electronic instrument manufactured by that division (one board per instrument). Division B incurred $100 in additional cost per instrument and then sold the instruments for $300 each.

Required:

1. Prepare income statements for Division A, Division B, and the company as a whole.
2. Assume that Division A's manufacturing capacity is 20,000 circuit boards. Next year, Division B wants to purchase 5,000 circuit boards from Division A rather than 4,000. (Circuit boards of this type are not available from outside sources.) From the standpoint of the company as a whole, should Division A sell the 1,000 additional circuit boards to Division B or continue to sell them to outside customers? Explain.

EXERCISE 12–16 Return on Investment (ROI) and Residual Income Relations [LO2, LO3]

A family friend has asked your help in analyzing the operations of three anonymous companies operating in the same service sector industry. Supply the missing data in the table below:

	Company		
	A	B	C
Sales	$9,000,000	$7,000,000	$4,500,000
Net operating income	$?	$ 280,000	$?
Average operating assets	$3,000,000	$?	$1,800,000
Return on investment (ROI)	18%	14%	?
Minimum required rate of return:			
Percentage	16%	?	15%
Dollar amount	$?	$ 320,000	$?
Residual income	$?	$?	$ 90,000

EXERCISE 12–17 (Appendix 12A) Transfer Pricing Situations [LO4]

In each of the cases below, assume that Division X has a product that can be sold either to outside customers or to Division Y of the same company for use in its production process. The managers of the divisions are evaluated based on their divisional profits.

	Case	
	A	B
Division X:		
Capacity in units	200,000	200,000
Number of units being sold to outside customers	200,000	160,000
Selling price per unit to outside customers	$90	$75
Variable costs per unit	$70	$60
Fixed costs per unit (based on capacity)	$13	$8
Division Y:		
Number of units needed for production	40,000	40,000
Purchase price per unit now being paid to an outside supplier	$86	$74

Required:

1. Refer to the data in case A above. Assume in this case that $3 per unit in variable selling costs can be avoided on intracompany sales. If the managers are free to negotiate and make decisions on their own, will a transfer take place? If so, within what range will the transfer price fall? Explain.
2. Refer to the data in case B above. In this case there will be no savings in variable selling costs on intracompany sales. If the managers are free to negotiate and make decisions on their own, will a transfer take place? If so, within what range will the transfer price fall? Explain.

Problems

eXcel  

PROBLEM 12–18 Segment Reporting and Decision-Making [LO1]

Vulcan Company's contribution format income statement for June is given below:

VULCAN COMPANY
Income Statement
For the Month Ended June 30

Sales	$750,000
Less variable expenses	336,000
Contribution margin	414,000
Less fixed expenses	378,000
Net operating income	$ 36,000

Management is disappointed with the company's performance and is wondering what can be done to improve profits. By examining sales and cost records, you have determined the following:

a. The company is divided into two sales territories—Northern and Southern. The Northern territory recorded $300,000 in sales and $156,000 in variable expenses during June; the remaining sales and variable expenses were recorded in the Southern territory. Fixed expenses of $120,000 and $108,000 are traceable to the Northern and Southern territories, respectively. The rest of the fixed expenses are common to the two territories.
b. The company is the exclusive distributor for two products—Paks and Tibs. Sales of Paks and Tibs totaled $50,000 and $250,000, respectively, in the Northern territory during June. Variable expenses are 22% of the selling price for Paks and 58% for Tibs. Cost records show that $30,000 of the Northern territory's fixed expenses are traceable to Paks and $40,000 to Tibs, with the remainder common to the two products.

Required:

1. Prepare contribution format segmented income statements first showing the total company broken down between sales territories and then showing the Northern territory broken down by product line. Show both Amount and Percent columns for the company in total and for each segment.
2. Look at the statement you have prepared showing the total company segmented by sales territory. What insights revealed by this statement should be brought to the attention of management?
3. Look at the statement you have prepared showing the Northern territory segmented by product lines. What insights revealed by this statement should be brought to the attention of management?

PROBLEM 12–19 Comparison of Performance Using Return on Investment (ROI) [LO2]

Comparative data on three companies in the same service industry are given below:

	Company		
	A	B	C
Sales	$600,000	$500,000	$?
Net operating income	$ 84,000	$ 70,000	$?
Average operating assets	$300,000	$?	$1,000,000
Margin	?	?	3.5%
Turnover	?	?	2
ROI	?	7%	?

Required:

1. What advantages are there to breaking down the ROI computation into two separate elements, margin and turnover?
2. Fill in the missing information above, and comment on the relative performance of the three companies in as much detail as the data permit. Make *specific recommendations* about how to improve the return on investment.

(Adapted from National Association of Accountants, *Research Report No. 35,* p. 34)

PROBLEM 12–20 Return on Investment (ROI) and Residual Income [LO2, LO3]

"I know headquarters wants us to add that new product line," said Dell Havasi, manager of Billings Company's Office Products Division. "But I want to see the numbers before I make any move. Our division's return on investment (ROI) has led the company for three years, and I don't want any letdown."

Billings Company is a decentralized wholesaler with five autonomous divisions. The divisions are evaluated on the basis of ROI, with year-end bonuses given to the divisional managers who have the highest ROIs. Operating results for the company's Office Products Division for the most recent year are given below:

Sales	$10,000,000
Less variable expenses	6,000,000
Contribution margin	4,000,000
Less fixed expenses	3,200,000
Net operating income	$ 800,000
Divisional operating assets	$ 4,000,000

The company had an overall return on investment (ROI) of 15% last year (considering all divisions). The Office Products Division has an opportunity to add a new product line that would require an additional investment in operating assets of $1,000,000. The cost and revenue characteristics of the new product line per year would be:

Sales	$2,000,000
Variable expenses	60% of sales
Fixed expenses	$640,000

Required:

1. Compute the Office Products Division's ROI for the most recent year; also compute the ROI as it would appear if the new product line is added.
2. If you were in Dell Havasi's position, would you accept or reject the new product line? Explain.
3. Why do you suppose headquarters is anxious for the Office Products Division to add the new product line?
4. Suppose that the company's minimum required rate of return on operating assets is 12% and that performance is evaluated using residual income.
   a. Compute the Office Products Division's residual income for the most recent year; also compute the residual income as it would appear if the new product line is added.
   b. Under these circumstances, if you were in Dell Havasi's position, would you accept or reject the new product line? Explain.

PROBLEM 12–21 (Appendix 12A) Transfer Price with an Outside Market [LO4]
Hrubec Products, Inc., operates a Pulp Division that manufactures wood pulp for use in the production of various paper goods. Revenue and costs associated with a ton of pulp follow:

Selling price		$70
Less expenses:		
Variable	$42	
Fixed (based on a capacity of 50,000 tons per year)	18	60
Net operating income		$10

Hrubec Products has just acquired a small company that manufactures paper cartons. This company will be treated as a division of Hrubec with full profit responsibility. The newly formed Carton Division is currently purchasing 5,000 tons of pulp per year from a supplier at a cost of $70 per ton, less a 10% quantity discount. Hrubec's president is anxious for the Carton Division to begin purchasing its pulp from the Pulp Division if an acceptable transfer price can be worked out.

Required:

For (1) and (2) below, assume that the Pulp Division can sell all of its pulp to outside customers for $70 per ton.

1. Are the managers of the Carton and Pulp Divisions likely to voluntarily agree to a transfer price for 5,000 tons of pulp next year? Why or why not?
2. If the Pulp Division meets the price that the Carton Division is currently paying to its supplier and sells 5,000 tons of pulp to the Carton Division each year, what will be the effect on the profits of the Pulp Division, the Carton Division, and the company as a whole?

For (3)–(6) below, assume that the Pulp Division is currently selling only 30,000 tons of pulp each year to outside customers at the stated $70 price.

3. Are the managers of the Carton and Pulp Divisions likely to voluntarily agree to a transfer price for 5,000 tons of pulp next year? Why or why not?
4. Suppose that the Carton Division's outside supplier drops its price (net of the quantity discount) to only $59 per ton. Should the Pulp Division meet this price? Explain. If the Pulp Division does *not* meet the $59 price, what will be the effect on the profits of the company as a whole?
5. Refer to (4) above. If the Pulp Division refuses to meet the $59 price, should the Carton Division be required to purchase from the Pulp Division at a higher price for the good of the company as a whole?
6. Refer to (4) above. Assume that due to inflexible management policies, the Carton Division is required to purchase 5,000 tons of pulp each year from the Pulp Division at $70 per ton. What will be the effect on the profits of the company as a whole?

PROBLEM 12–22 Basic Segment Reporting; Activity-Based Cost Assignment [LO1]
Diversified Products, Inc., has recently acquired a small publishing company that Diversified Products intends to operate as one of its investment centers. The newly acquired company has three books that it offers for sale—a cookbook, a travel guide, and a handy speller. Each book sells for $10. The publishing company's most recent monthly income statement is given below:

	Total Company		Product Line		
			Cookbook	Travel Guide	Handy Speller
Sales	$300,000	100%	$90,000	$150,000	$60,000
Less expenses:					
Printing costs	102,000	34%	27,000	63,000	12,000
Advertising	36,000	12%	13,500	19,500	3,000
General sales	18,000	6%	5,400	9,000	3,600
Salaries	33,000	11%	18,000	9,000	6,000
Equipment depreciation	9,000	3%	3,000	3,000	3,000
Sales commissions	30,000	10%	9,000	15,000	6,000
General administration	42,000	14%	14,000	14,000	14,000
Warehouse rent	12,000	4%	3,600	6,000	2,400
Depreciation—office facilities	3,000	1%	1,000	1,000	1,000
Total expenses	285,000	95%	94,500	139,500	51,000
Net operating income (loss)	$ 15,000	5%	$ (4,500)	$ 10,500	$ 9,000

The following additional information is available about the company:

a. Only printing costs and sales commissions are variable; all other costs are fixed. The printing costs (which include materials, labor, and variable overhead) are traceable to the three product lines as shown in the statement above. Sales commissions are 10% of sales for any product.

b. The same equipment is used to produce all three books, so the equipment depreciation cost has been allocated equally among the three product lines. An analysis of the company's activities indicates that the equipment is used 30% of the time to produce cookbooks, 50% of the time to produce travel guides, and 20% of the time to produce handy spellers.

c. The warehouse is used to store finished units of product, so the rental cost has been allocated to the product lines on the basis of sales dollars. The warehouse rental cost is $3 per square foot per year. The warehouse contains 48,000 square feet of space, of which 7,200 square feet is used by the cookbook line, 24,000 square feet by the travel guide line, and 16,800 square feet by the handy speller line.

d. The general sales cost above includes the salary of the sales manager and other sales costs not traceable to any specific product line. This cost has been allocated to the product lines on the basis of sales dollars.

e. The general administration cost and depreciation of office facilities both relate to overall administration of the company as a whole. These costs have been allocated equally to the three product lines.

f. All other costs are traceable to the three product lines in the amounts shown on the statement above.

The management of Diversified Products, Inc., is anxious to improve the new investment center's 5% return on sales.

Required:

1. Prepare a new contribution format segmented income statement for the month. Show both an Amount column and a Percent column for the company as a whole and for each product line. Adjust allocations of equipment depreciation and of warehouse rent as indicated by the additional information provided.
2. After seeing the income statement in the main body of the problem, management has decided to eliminate the cookbook, since it is not returning a profit, and to focus all available resources on promoting the travel guide.
   a. Based on the statement you have prepared, do you agree with the decision to eliminate the cookbook? Explain.
   b. Based on the statement you have prepared, do you agree with the decision to focus all available resources on promoting the travel guide? Explain. (You may assume that an ample market is available for all three product lines.)
3. What additional points would you bring to the attention of management that might help to improve profits?

PROBLEM 12–23 Return on Investment (ROI) and Residual Income [LO2, LO3]
Financial data for Joel de Paris, Inc., for last year follow:

JOEL DE PARIS, INC. Balance Sheet	Ending Balance	Beginning Balance
Assets		
Cash	$ 120,000	$ 140,000
Accounts receivable	530,000	450,000
Inventory	380,000	320,000
Plant and equipment, net	620,000	680,000
Investment in Buisson, S.A.	280,000	250,000
Land (undeveloped)	170,000	180,000
Total assets	$2,100,000	$2,020,000
Liabilities and Stockholders' Equity		
Accounts payable	$ 310,000	$ 360,000
Long-term debt	1,500,000	1,500,000
Stockholders' equity	290,000	160,000
Total liabilities and stockholders' equity	$2,100,000	$2,020,000

JOEL DE PARIS, INC. Income Statement		
Sales		$4,050,000
Less operating expenses		3,645,000
Net operating income		405,000
Less interest and taxes:		
Interest expense	$150,000	
Tax expense	110,000	260,000
Net operating income		$ 145,000

The company paid dividends of $15,000 last year. The "Investment in Buisson, S.A.," on the balance sheet represents an investment in the stock of another company.

Required:

1. Compute the company's margin, turnover, and return on investment (ROI) for last year.
2. The board of directors of Joel de Paris, Inc., has set a minimum required rate of return of 15%. What was the company's residual income last year?

PROBLEM 12–24 (Appendix 12A) Basic Transfer Pricing [LO4]
Alpha and Beta are divisions within the same company. The managers of both divisions are evaluated based on their own division's return on investment (ROI). Assume the following information relative to the two divisions:

	Case 1	Case 2	Case 3	Case 4
Alpha Division:				
Capacity in units	80,000	400,000	150,000	300,000
Number of units now being sold to outside customers	80,000	400,000	100,000	300,000
Selling price per unit to outside customers	$30	$90	$75	$50
Variable costs per unit	$18	$65	$40	$26
Fixed costs per unit (based on capacity)	$6	$15	$20	$9
Beta Division:				
Number of units needed annually	5,000	30,000	20,000	120,000
Purchase price now being paid to an outside supplier	$27	$89	$75*	—

*Before any quantity discount.

Managers are free to decide if they will participate in any internal transfers. All transfer prices are negotiated.

Required:

1. Refer to case 1 shown previously. Alpha Division can avoid $2 per unit in commissions on any sales to Beta Division. Will the managers agree to a transfer and if so, within what range will the transfer price be? Explain.
2. Refer to case 2 shown previously. A study indicates that Alpha Division can avoid $5 per unit in shipping costs on any sales to Beta Division.
   a. Would you expect any disagreement between the two divisional managers over what the transfer price should be? Explain.
   b. Assume that Alpha Division offers to sell 30,000 units to Beta Division for $88 per unit and that Beta Division refuses this price. What will be the loss in potential profits for the company as a whole?
3. Refer to case 3 shown previously. Assume that Beta Division is now receiving an 8% quantity discount from the outside supplier.
   a. Will the managers agree to a transfer? If so, what is the range within which the transfer price would be?
   b. Assume that Beta Division offers to purchase 20,000 units from Alpha Division at $60 per unit. If Alpha Division accepts this price, would you expect its ROI to increase, decrease, or remain unchanged? Why?
4. Refer to case 4 shown previously. Assume that Beta Division wants Alpha Division to provide it with 120,000 units of a *different* product from the one that Alpha Division is now producing. The new product would require $21 per unit in variable costs and would require that Alpha Division cut back production of its present product by 45,000 units annually. What is the lowest acceptable transfer price from Alpha Division's perspective?

PROBLEM 12–25 Restructuring a Segmented Income Statement [LO1]

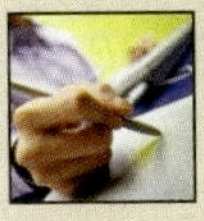

Losses have been incurred at Millard Corporation for some time. In an effort to isolate the problem and improve the company's performance, management has requested that the monthly income statement be segmented by sales region. The company's first effort at preparing a segmented statement is given below. This statement is for May, the most recent month of activity.

	Sales Region		
	West	Central	East
Sales	$450,000	$800,000	$750,000
Less regional expenses (traceable):			
Cost of goods sold	162,900	280,000	376,500
Advertising	108,000	200,000	210,000
Salaries	90,000	88,000	135,000
Utilities	13,500	12,000	15,000
Depreciation	27,000	28,000	30,000
Shipping expense	17,100	32,000	28,500
Total regional expenses	418,500	640,000	795,000
Regional income (loss) before corporate expenses	31,500	160,000	(45,000)
Less corporate expenses:			
Advertising (general)	18,000	32,000	30,000
General administrative expense	50,000	50,000	50,000
Total corporate expenses	68,000	82,000	80,000
Net operating income (loss)	$ (36,500)	$ 78,000	$(125,000)

Cost of goods sold and shipping expense are both variable; other costs are all fixed.

Millard Corporation is a wholesale distributor of office products. It purchases office products from manufacturers and distributes them in the three regions given above. The three regions are about the same size, and each has its own manager and sales staff. The products that the company distributes vary widely in profitability.

Required:

1. List any disadvantages or weaknesses that you see to the statement format illustrated previously.
2. Explain the basis that is apparently being used to allocate the corporate expenses to the regions. Do you agree with these allocations? Explain.
3. Prepare a new contribution format segmented income statement for May. Show a Total column as well as data for each region. Include percentages on your statement for all columns.
4. Analyze the statement that you prepared in part (3) shown previously. What points that might help to improve the company's performance would you bring to management's attention?

PROBLEM 12–26 Segment Reporting; Activity-Based Cost Assignment [LO1]

"That commercial market has been dragging us down for years," complained Shanna Reynolds, president of Morley Products. "Just look at that anemic income figure for the commercial market. That market had three million dollars more in sales than the home market, but only a few thousand dollars more in profits. What a loser it is!"

The income statement to which Ms. Reynolds was referring follows:

	Total Company		Commercial Market	Home Market	School Market
Sales	$20,000,000	100.0%	$8,000,000	$5,000,000	$7,000,000
Less expenses:					
Cost of goods sold	9,500,000	47.5%	3,900,000	2,400,000	3,200,000
Sales support	3,600,000	18.0%	1,440,000	900,000	1,260,000
Order processing	1,720,000	8.6%	688,000	430,000	602,000
Warehousing	940,000	4.7%	376,000	235,000	329,000
Packing and shipping . .	520,000	2.6%	208,000	130,000	182,000
Advertising	1,690,000	8.5%	676,000	422,500	591,500
General management . .	1,310,000	6.6%	524,000	327,500	458,500
Total expenses	19,280,000	96.4%	7,812,000	4,845,000	6,623,000
Net operating income	$ 720,000	3.6%	$ 188,000	$ 155,000	$ 377,000

"I agree," said Walt Divot, the company's vice president. "We need to focus more of our attention on the school market, since it's our best segment. Maybe that will bolster profits and get the stockholders off our backs."

The following additional information is available about the company:

a. Morley Products is a wholesale distributor of various goods; the cost of goods sold figures above are traceable to the markets in the amounts shown.

b. Sales support, order processing, and packing and shipping are variable costs. Warehousing, general management, and advertising are fixed costs. These costs have all been allocated to the markets on the basis of sales dollars—a practice that the company has followed for years.

c. You have compiled the following data.

		Amount of Activity			
Cost Pool and Allocation Base	Total Cost	Total	Commercial Market	Home Market	School Market
Sales support (number of calls)	$3,600,000	24,000	8,000	5,000	11,000
Order processing (number of orders)	$1,720,000	8,600	1,750	5,200	1,650
Warehousing (square feet of space)	$940,000	117,500	35,000	65,000	17,500
Packing and shipping (pounds shipped)	$520,000	104,000	24,000	16,000	64,000

d. You have determined the following breakdown of the company's advertising expense and general management expense:

		Market		
	Total	Commercial	Home	School
Advertising:				
Traceable	$1,460,000	$700,000	$180,000	$580,000
Common	$230,000			
General management:				
Traceable—salaries	$410,000	$150,000	$120,000	$140,000
Common	$900,000			

The company is searching for ways to improve profit, and you have suggested that a contribution format segmented income statement in which costs are assigned on the basis of activities might provide some useful insights for management.

Required:

1. Refer to the data in part (c) shown previously. Determine a rate for each cost pool. Then, using this rate, compute the amount of cost assignable to each market.
2. Using the data from (1) above and other data from the problem, prepare a revised contribution format segmented income statement for the company. Show an Amount column and a Percent column for the company as a whole and for each market segment. Carry percentage figures to one decimal place. (Remember to include warehousing among the fixed expenses.)
3. What, if anything, in your segmented income statement should be brought to management's attention? Explain.

PROBLEM 12–27 Return on Investment (ROI) Analysis [LO2]

The contribution format income statement for Huerra Company for last year is given below:

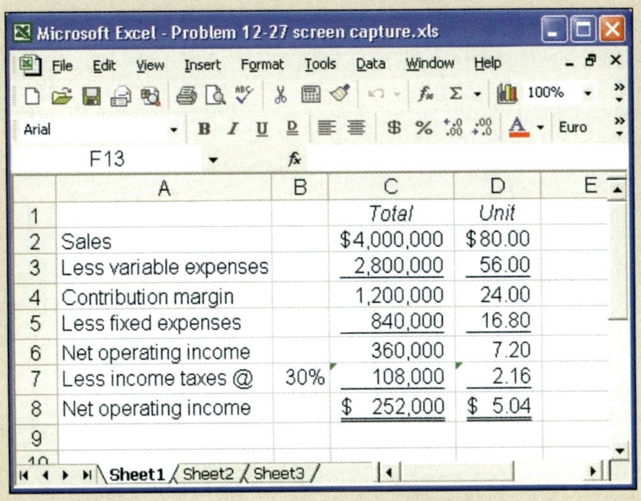

	A	B	C	D
1			*Total*	*Unit*
2	Sales		$4,000,000	$80.00
3	Less variable expenses		2,800,000	56.00
4	Contribution margin		1,200,000	24.00
5	Less fixed expenses		840,000	16.80
6	Net operating income		360,000	7.20
7	Less income taxes @	30%	108,000	2.16
8	Net operating income		$ 252,000	$ 5.04
9				

The company had average operating assets of $2,000,000 during the year.

Required:

1. Compute the company's return on investment (ROI) for the period using the ROI formula stated in terms of margin and turnover.

   For each of the following questions, indicate whether the margin and turnover will increase, decrease, or remain unchanged as a result of the events described, and then compute the new ROI figure. Consider each question separately, starting in each case from the data used to compute the original ROI in (1) above.
2. Using just-in-time (JIT), the company is able to reduce the average level of inventory by $400,000. (The released funds are used to pay off short-term creditors.)
3. The company achieves a cost savings of $32,000 per year by using less costly materials.
4. The company issues bonds and uses the proceeds to purchase $500,000 in machinery and equipment at the beginning of the period. Interest on the bonds is $60,000 per year. Sales remain unchanged. The new, more efficient equipment reduces production costs by $20,000 per year.
5. As a result of a more intense effort by salespeople, sales are increased by 20%; operating assets remain unchanged.

6. Obsolete inventory carried on the books at a cost of $40,000 is scrapped and written off as a loss.
7. The company uses $200,000 of cash (received on accounts receivable) to repurchase and retire some of its common stock.

PROBLEM 12–28 Return on Investment (ROI) and Residual Income; Decentralization [LO2, LO3]
Raddington Industries produces tool and die machinery for manufacturers. The company expanded vertically several years ago by acquiring Reigis Steel Company, one of its suppliers of alloy steel plates. Raddington decided to maintain Reigis' separate identity and therefore established the Reigis Steel Division as one of its investment centers.

Raddington evaluates its divisions on the basis of ROI. Management bonuses are also based on ROI. All investments in operating assets are expected to earn a minimum required rate of return of 11%.

Reigis' ROI has ranged from 14% to 17% since it was acquired by Raddington. During the past year, Reigis had an investment opportunity that would yield an estimated rate of return of 13%. Reigis' management decided against the investment because it believed the investment would decrease the division's overall ROI.

Last year's absorption costing income statement for Reigis Steel Division is given below. The division's operating assets employed were $12,960,000 at the end of the year, which represents an 8% increase over the previous year-end balance.

REIGIS STEEL DIVISION
Divisional Income Statement
For the Year Ended December 31

Sales		$31,200,000
Cost of goods sold		16,500,000
Gross margin		14,700,000
Less operating expenses:		
Selling expenses	$5,620,000	
Administrative expenses	7,208,000	12,828,000
Net operating income		$ 1,872,000

Required:

1. Compute the following performance measures for the Reigis Steel Division:
   a. ROI. (Remember, ROI is based on the *average* operating assets, computed from the beginning-of-year and end-of-year balances.) State ROI in terms of margin and turnover.
   b. Residual income.
2. Would the management of Reigis Steel Division have been more likely to accept the investment opportunity it had last year if residual income were used as a performance measure instead of ROI? Explain.
3. The Reigis Steel Division is a separate investment center within Raddington Industries. Identify the items Reigis must be free to control if it is to be evaluated fairly by either the ROI or residual income performance measures.

(CMA, adapted)

PROBLEM 12–29 (Appendix 12A) Market-Based Transfer Price [LO4]
Stavos Company's Cabinet Division manufactures a standard cabinet for television sets. The cost per cabinet is:

Variable cost per cabinet	$ 70
Fixed cost per cabinet	30*
Total cost per cabinet	$100

*Based on a capacity of 10,000 cabinets per year.

Part of the Cabinet Division's output is sold to outside manufacturers of television sets and part is sold to Stavos Company's Quark Division, which produces a TV set under its own name. The Cabinet Division charges $140 per cabinet for all sales.

The costs, revenue, and net operating income associated with the Quark Division's TV set is given below:

Selling price per TV set		$480
Less variable cost per TV set:		
Cost of the cabinet	$140	
Variable cost of electronic parts	210	
Total variable cost		350
Contribution margin		130
Less fixed costs per TV set		80*
Net operating income per TV set		$ 50

*Based on a capacity of 3,000 sets per year.

The Quark Division has an order from an overseas source for 1,000 TV sets. The overseas source wants to pay only $340 per set.

Required:

1. Assume that the Quark Division has enough idle capacity to fill the 1,000-set order. Is the division likely to accept the $340 price or to reject it? Explain.
2. Assume that both the Cabinet Division and the Quark Division have idle capacity. Under these conditions, would it be advantageous for the company as a whole if the Quark Division rejects the $340 price? Show computations to support your answer.
3. Assume that the Quark Division has idle capacity but that the Cabinet Division is operating at capacity and could sell all of its cabinets to outside manufacturers. Compute the profit impact to the Quark Division of accepting the 1,000-set order at the $340 unit price.
4. What conclusions do you draw concerning the use of market price as a transfer price in intracompany transactions?

PROBLEM 12–30 Multiple Segmented Income Statements [LO1]

eXcel

Companhia Bradesco, S.A., of Brazil, an industrial supply store chain, has two divisions. The company's contribution format income statement segmented by divisions for last year is given below (the currency in Brazil is the real, denoted here by R):

	Total Company	Division	
		Plastics	Glass
Sales	R1,500,000	R900,000	R600,000
Less variable expenses	700,000	400,000	300,000
Contribution margin	800,000	500,000	300,000
Less traceable fixed expenses:			
Advertising	300,000	180,000	120,000
Depreciation	140,000	92,000	48,000
Administration	220,000	118,000	102,000
Total	660,000	390,000	270,000
Divisional segment margin	140,000	R110,000	R 30,000
Less common fixed expenses	100,000		
Net operating income	R 40,000		

Top management doesn't understand why the Glass Division has such a low segment margin when its sales are only one-third less than sales in the Plastics Division. Accordingly, management has directed that the Glass Division be further segmented into product lines. The following information is available on the product lines in the Glass Division:

	Glass Division Product Lines		
	Flat Glass	Auto Glass	Specialty Glass
Sales	R200,000	R300,000	R100,000
Traceable fixed expenses:			
Advertising	R30,000	R42,000	R48,000
Depreciation	R10,000	R24,000	R14,000
Administration	R14,000	R21,000	R7,000
Variable expenses as a percentage of sales	65%	40%	50%

Analysis shows that R60,000 of the Glass Division's administration expenses are common to the product lines.

Required:

1. Prepare a contribution format segmented income statement for the Glass Division with segments defined as product lines. Show both an Amount column and a Percent column for the division in total and for each product line.
2. Management is surprised by Specialty Glass's poor showing and would like to have the product line segmented by market. The following information is available about the two markets in which Specialty Glass is sold:

	Specialty Glass Markets	
	Domestic	Foreign
Sales	R60,000	R40,000
Traceable fixed expenses:		
Advertising	R18,000	R30,000
Variable expenses as a percentage of sales	50%	50%

All of Specialty Glass's depreciation and administration expenses are common to the markets in which the product is sold. Prepare a contribution format segmented income statement for Specialty Glass with segments defined as markets. Show both Amount and Percent columns.
3. Refer to the statement prepared in (1) above. The sales manager wants to run a special promotional campaign on one of the products over the next month. A market study indicates that such a campaign would increase sales of Flat Glass by R40,000 or sales of Auto Glass by R30,000. The campaign would cost R8,000. Show computations to determine which product line should be chosen.

PROBLEM 12–31 (Appendix 12A) Cost-Volume-Profit Analysis; Return on Investment (ROI); Transfer Pricing [LO2, LO4]

The Valve Division of Bendix, Inc., produces a small valve that is used by various companies as a component part in their products. Bendix, Inc., operates its divisions as autonomous units, giving its divisional managers great discretion in pricing and other decisions. Each division is expected to generate a minimum required rate of return of at least 14% on its operating assets. The Valve Division has average operating assets of $700,000. The valves are sold for $5 each. Variable costs are $3 per valve, and fixed costs total $462,000 per year. The division has a capacity of 300,000 valves each year.

Required:

1. How many valves must the Valve Division sell each year to generate the desired rate of return on its assets?
   a. What is the margin earned at this level of sales?
   b. What is the turnover at this level of sales?
2. Assume that the Valve Division's current ROI equals the minimum required rate of 14%. In order to increase the division's ROI, the divisional manager wants to increase the selling price per valve by 4%. Market studies indicate that an increase in the selling price would cause sales to drop by 20,000 units each year. However, operating assets could be reduced by $50,000 due to decreased needs for accounts receivable and inventory. Compute the margin, turnover, and ROI if these changes are made.

3. Refer to the original data. Assume again that the Valve Division's current ROI equals the minimum required rate of 14%. Rather than increase the selling price, the sales manager wants to reduce the selling price per valve by 4%. Market studies indicate that this would fill the plant to capacity. In order to carry the greater level of sales, however, operating assets would increase by $50,000. Compute the margin, turnover, and ROI if these changes are made.
4. Refer to the original data. Assume that the normal volume of sales is 280,000 valves each year at a price of $5 per valve. Another division of the company is currently purchasing 20,000 valves each year from an overseas supplier, at a price of $4.25 per valve. The manager of the Valve Division has refused to meet this price, pointing out that it would result in a loss for his division:

Selling price per valve		$4.25
Cost per valve:		
Variable	$3.00	
Fixed ($462,000 ÷ 300,000 valves)	1.54	4.54
Net loss per valve		$(0.29)

The manager of the Valve Division also points out that the normal $5 selling price barely allows his division to earn the required 14% rate of return. "If we take on some business at only $4.25 per unit, then our ROI is obviously going to suffer," he reasons, "and maintaining that ROI figure is the key to my future. Besides, taking on these extra units would require us to increase our operating assets by at least $50,000 due to the larger inventories and accounts receivable we would be carrying." Would you recommend that the Valve Division sell to the other division at $4.25? Show ROI computations to support your answer.

PROBLEM 12–32 (Appendix 12A) Negotiated Transfer Price [LO4]

Ditka Industries has several independent divisions. The company's Tube Division manufactures a picture tube used in television sets. The Tube Division's absorption costing income statement for last year, in which 8,000 tubes were sold, is given below:

	Total	Unit
Sales	$1,360,000	$170.00
Less cost of goods sold	840,000	105.00
Gross margin	520,000	65.00
Less selling and administrative expenses	390,000	48.75
Divisional net operating income	$ 130,000	$ 16.25

As shown above, it costs the Tube Division $105 to produce a single tube. This figure consists of the following costs:

Direct materials	$ 38
Direct labor	27
Manufacturing overhead (75% fixed)	40
Total cost per tube	$105

The Tube Division has fixed selling and administrative expenses of $350,000 per year.

Ditka Industries has just formed a new division, called the TV Division, that will produce a television set that requires a high-resolution picture tube. The Tube Division has been asked to manufacture 2,500 of these tubes each year and sell them to the TV Division. As one step in determining the price that should be charged to the TV Division, the Tube Division has estimated the following cost for each of the new high-resolution tubes:

Direct materials	$ 60
Direct labor	49
Manufacturing overhead (2/3 fixed)	54
Total cost per tube	$163

To manufacture the new tubes, the Tube Division would have to reduce production of its regular tubes by 3,000 units per year. There would be no variable selling and administrative expenses on the intracompany business, and total fixed overhead costs would not change. Assume direct labor is a variable cost.

Required:

1. Determine the lowest acceptable transfer price from the perspective of the Tube Division for each of the new high-resolution tubes.
2. Assume that the TV Division has found an outside supplier that will provide the new tubes for $200 each. If the Tube Division meets this price, what will be the effect on the profits of the company as a whole?

Cases

CASE 12–33 Segmented Statements; Product-Line Analysis [LO1]

"At last, I can see some light at the end of the tunnel," said Steve Adams, president of Jelco Products. "Our losses have shrunk from over $75,000 a month at the beginning of the year to only $26,000 for August. If we can just isolate the remaining problems with products A and C, we'll be in the black by the first of next year."

The company's absorption costing income statement for the latest month (August) is presented below:

JELCO PRODUCTS
Income Statement
For August

	Total Company	Product A	Product B	Product C
Sales	$1,500,000	$600,000	$400,000	$500,000
Less cost of goods sold	922,000	372,000	220,000	330,000
Gross margin	578,000	228,000	180,000	170,000
Less operating expenses:				
Selling	424,000	162,000	112,000	150,000
Administrative	180,000	72,000	48,000	60,000
Total operating expenses	604,000	234,000	160,000	210,000
Net operating income (loss)	$ (26,000)	$ (6,000)	$ 20,000	$(40,000)

"What recommendations did that business consultant make?" asked Mr. Adams. "We paid the guy $100 an hour; surely he found something wrong." "He says our problems are concealed by the way we make up our income statements," replied Sally Warren, the executive vice president. "He left us some data on what he calls 'traceable' and 'common' costs that he says we should be isolating in our reports." The data to which Ms. Warren was referring are shown below:

	Total Company	Product A	Product B	Product C
Variable costs:*				
Manufacturing (materials, labor, and variable overhead)		18%	32%	20%
Selling		10%	8%	10%
Traceable fixed costs:				
Manufacturing	$376,000	$180,000	$36,000	$160,000
Selling	$282,000	$102,000	$80,000	$100,000
Common fixed costs:				
Manufacturing	$210,000	—	—	—
Administrative	$180,000	—	—	—

*As a percentage of sales.

"I don't see anything wrong with our income statements," said Mr. Adams. "Bill, our chief accountant, says that he has been using this format for over 30 years. He's also very careful to allocate all of our costs to the products."

"I'll admit that Bill always seems to be on top of things," replied Ms. Warren. "By the way, purchasing says that the X7 chips we use in products A and B are on back order and won't be available for several weeks. From the looks of August's income statement, we had better concentrate our remaining inventory of X7 chips on product B." (Two X7 chips are used in both product A and product B.)

The following additional information is available on the company:

a. Work in process and finished goods inventories are negligible and can be ignored.
b. Products A and B each sell for $250 per unit, and product C sells for $125 per unit. Strong market demand exists for all three products.

Required:

1. Prepare a new contribution format income statement for August, segmented by product. Show Amount and Percent columns for the company in total and for each product.
2. Assume that Mr. Adams is considering the elimination of product C due to the losses it is incurring. Based on the statement you prepared in (1) above, what points would you make for or against elimination of product C?
3. Do you agree with the company's decision to concentrate the remaining inventory of X7 chips on product B? Why or why not?
4. Product C is sold in both a vending and a home market with sales and cost data as follows:

	Market	
	Vending	Home
Sales	$50,000	$450,000
Variable costs:*		
Manufacturing	20%	20%
Selling	28%	8%
Traceable fixed costs:		
Selling	$45,000	$30,000

*As a percentage of sales.

The remainder of product C's fixed selling costs and all of product C's fixed manufacturing costs are common to the markets in which product C is sold.

a. Prepare a contribution format income statement showing product C segmented by market. Show both Amount and Percent columns for the product in total and for each market.
b. What insights revealed by this statement would you bring to management's attention?

CASE 12–34 (Appendix 12A) Transfer Pricing; Divisional Performance [LO4]

Weller Industries is a decentralized organization with six divisions. The company's Electrical Division produces a variety of electrical items, including an X52 electrical fitting. The Electrical Division (which is operating at capacity) sells this fitting to its regular customers for $7.50 each; the fitting has a variable manufacturing cost of $4.25.

The company's Brake Division has asked the Electrical Division to supply it with a large quantity of X52 fittings for only $5 each. The Brake Division, which is operating at 50% of capacity, will put the fitting into a brake unit that it will produce and sell to a large commercial airline manufacturer. The cost of the brake unit being built by the Brake Division follows:

Purchased parts (from outside vendors)	$22.50
Electrical fitting X52	5.00
Other variable costs	14.00
Fixed overhead and administration	8.00
Total cost per brake unit	$49.50

Although the $5 price for the X52 fitting represents a substantial discount from the regular $7.50 price, the manager of the Brake Division believes that the price concession is necessary if his division is to get the contract for the airplane brake units. He has heard "through the grapevine" that the airplane manufacturer plans to reject his bid if it is more than $50 per brake unit. Thus, if the Brake Division is forced to pay the regular $7.50 price for the X52 fitting, it will either not get the contract or it will suffer a substantial loss at a time when it is already operating at only 50% of capacity. The manager of the Brake Division argues that the price concession is imperative to the well-being of both his division and the company as a whole.

Weller Industries uses return on investment (ROI) to measure divisional performance.

Required:

1. Assume that you are the manager of the Electrical Division. Would you recommend that your division supply the X52 fitting to the Brake Division for $5 each as requested? Why or why not? Show all computations.
2. Would it be profitable for the company as a whole for the Electrical Division to supply the fittings to the Brake Division if the airplane brakes can be sold for $50? Show all computations, and explain your answer.
3. In principle, should it be possible for the two managers to agree to a transfer price in this particular situation? If so, within what range would that transfer price lie?
4. Discuss the organizational and manager behavior problems, if any, inherent in this situation. What would you advise the company's president to do in this situation?

(CMA, adapted)

eXcel  

CASE 12–35 Service Organization; Segment Reporting [LO1]

Music Teachers, Inc., is an educational association for music teachers that has 20,000 members. The association operates from a central headquarters but has local membership chapters throughout the United States. Monthly meetings are held by the local chapters to discuss recent developments on topics of interest to music teachers. The association's journal, *Teachers' Forum,* is issued monthly with features about recent developments in the field. The association publishes books and reports and also sponsors professional courses that qualify for continuing professional education credit. The association's statement of revenues and expenses for the current year is presented below.

MUSIC TEACHERS, INC.
Statement of Revenues and Expenses
For the Year Ended November 30

Revenues	$3,275,000
Less expenses:	
Salaries	920,000
Personnel costs	230,000
Occupancy costs	280,000
Reimbursement of member costs to local chapters	600,000
Other membership services	500,000
Printing and paper	320,000
Postage and shipping	176,000
Instructors' fees	80,000
General and administrative	38,000
Total expenses	3,144,000
Excess of revenues over expenses	$ 131,000

The board of directors of Music Teachers, Inc., has requested that a segmented income statement be prepared showing the contribution of each profit center to the association. The association has four profit centers: Membership Division, Magazine Subscriptions Division, Books and Reports Division, and Continuing Education Division. Mike Doyle has been assigned responsibility for preparing the segmented income statement, and he has gathered the following data prior to its preparation.

a. Membership dues are $100 per year, of which $20 is considered to cover a one-year subscription to the association's journal. Other benefits include membership in the association and chapter affiliation. The portion of the dues covering the magazine subscription ($20) should be assigned to the Magazine Subscription Division.
b. One-year subscriptions to *Teachers' Forum* were sold to nonmembers and libraries at $30 per subscription. A total of 2,500 of these subscriptions were sold last year. In addition to subscriptions, the magazine generated $100,000 in advertising revenues. The costs per magazine subscription were $7 for printing and paper and $4 for postage and shipping.
c. A total of 28,000 technical reports and professional texts were sold by the Books and Reports Division at an average unit selling price of $25. Average costs per publication were $4 for printing and paper and $2 for postage and shipping.

d. The association offers a variety of continuing education courses to both members and nonmembers. The one-day courses had a tuition cost of $75 each and were attended by 2,400 students. A total of 1,760 students took two-day courses at a tuition cost of $125 for each student. Outside instructors were paid to teach some courses.

e. Salary costs and space occupied by division follow:

	Salaries	Space Occupied (square feet)
Membership	$210,000	2,000
Magazine Subscriptions	150,000	2,000
Books and Reports	300,000	3,000
Continuing Education	180,000	2,000
Corporate staff	80,000	1,000
Total	$920,000	10,000

Personnel costs are 25% of salaries in the separate divisions as well as for the corporate staff. The $280,000 in occupancy costs includes $50,000 in rental cost for a warehouse used by the Books and Reports Division for storage purposes.

f. Printing and paper costs other than for magazine subscriptions and for books and reports relate to the Continuing Education Division.

g. General and administrative expenses include costs relating to overall administration of the association as a whole. The company's corporate staff does some mailing of materials for general administrative purposes.

The expenses that can be traced or assigned to the corporate staff, as well as any other expenses that are not traceable to the profit centers, will be treated as common costs. It is not necessary to distinguish between variable and fixed costs.

Required:

1. Prepare a segmented income statement for Music Teachers, Inc. This statement should show the segment margin for each division as well as results for the association as a whole.
2. Give arguments for and against allocating *all* costs of the association to the four divisions.

(CMA, adapted)

Group and Internet Exercises

GROUP EXERCISE 12–36 College Segment Reports

Obtain a copy of your college or university's most recent financial report prepared for internal use.

Required:

1. Does the financial report break down the results into major segments such as schools, academic departments, intercollegiate sports, and so on? Can you determine the financial contribution (i.e., revenues less expenses) of each segment from the report?
2. If the report attempts to show the financial contribution of each major segment, does the report follow the principles for segment reporting in this chapter? If not, what principles are violated and what harm, if any, can occur as a result from violating those principles?

GROUP EXERCISE 12–37 (Appendix 12A) Transfer Pricing Role Playing

Divide your team into two groups—one will play the part of the managers of the Consumer Products Division of Highstreet Enterprises, Inc., and the other will play the part of the managers of the Industrial Products Division of the same company.

The Consumer Products Division would like to acquire an advanced electric motor from the Industrial Products Division that would be used to make a state-of-the-art sorbet maker. At the expected selling price of $89, the Consumer Products Division would sell 50,000 sorbet makers per year. Each sorbet maker would require one advanced electric motor. The only possible source for the advanced electric motor is the Industrial Products Division, which holds a critical patent. The variable cost of the sorbet maker (not including the cost of the electric motor) would be $54. The sorbet maker project would require additional fixed costs of $180,000 per year and additional operating assets of $3,000,000.

The Industrial Products Division has plenty of spare capacity to make the electric motors requested by the Consumer Products Division. The variable cost of producing the motors would be $13 per unit. The additional fixed costs that would have to be incurred to fill the order from the Consumer Products Division would amount to $30,000 per year and the additional operating assets would be $400,000.

The division managers of Highstreet Enterprises are evaluated based on residual income, with a minimum required rate of return of 20%.

Required:

The two groups—those representing the managers of the Consumer Products Division and those representing the managers of the Industrial Products Division—should negotiate the transfer price for the 50,000 advanced electric motors per year. (The groups may or may not be able to come to an agreement.) Whatever the outcome of the negotiations, each group should write a memo to the instructor justifying the outcome in terms of what would be in the best interests of their division.

INTERNET EXERCISE 12–38

As you know, the World Wide Web is a medium that is constantly evolving. Sites come and go, and change without notice. To enable the periodic updating of site addresses, this problem has been posted to the textbook website (www.mhhe.com/garrison11e). After accessing the site, enter the Student Center and select this chapter. Select and complete the Internet Exercise.

Chapter

13

Relevant Costs for Decision Making

LEARNING OBJECTIVES

After studying Chapter 13, you should be able to:

LO1 Identify relevant and irrelevant costs and benefits in a decision situation.

LO2 Prepare an analysis showing whether a product line or other organizational segment should be dropped or retained.

LO3 Prepare a make or buy analysis.

LO4 Prepare an analysis showing whether a special order should be accepted.

LO5 Determine the most profitable use of a constrained resource and the value of obtaining more of the constrained resource.

LO6 Prepare an analysis showing whether joint products should be sold at the split-off point or processed further.

BUSINESS FOCUS

Traveling on a Sunk Cost

A failure to recognize the existence of sunk costs can lead to bad business decisions. As evidence, consider the following incident described by a business consultant after encountering a frustrated and angry fellow traveler ("Mr. Smith") whose flight home faced a lengthy delay:

Mr. Smith had recently flown into St. Louis on a commercial airline for a two-day business trip. While there, he learned that his company's private airplane had flown in the day before and would leave on the same day that he was scheduled to leave. Mr. Smith immediately cashed in his $200 commercial airline ticket and made arrangements to fly back on the company plane. He flew home feeling pretty good about saving his company the $200 fare and being able to depart on schedule.

About two weeks later, however, Mr. Smith's boss asked him why the department had been cross-charged $400 for his return trip when the commercial airfare was only $200. Mr. Smith explained that "the company plane was flying back regardless, and there were a number of empty seats."

How could Mr. Smith's attempt to save his company $200 end up "costing" his department $400? The problem is that Mr. Smith recognized something that his company's cost allocation system did not: namely, that the vast majority of the costs associated with flying the plane home were already sunk and, thus, unavoidable at the time he made the decision to fly home. By failing to distinguish between sunk (i.e., unavoidable) and avoidable costs, the cost allocation system was causing the company and its managers to make uneconomic business decisions.

It is now clear why Mr. Smith was so frustrated the day I ran into him in St. Louis. His company's plane was sitting on the runway with a number of empty seats and ready to take off for the very same destination. Yet there was no way Mr. Smith was going to fly on that plane even though doing so was the "best business decision." ■

Source: Dennis L. Weisman, "How Cost Allocation Systems Can Lead Managers Astray," *Journal of Cost Management* 5, no. 1, p. 4. Used by permission.

Making decisions is one of the basic functions of a manager. Managers are constantly faced with problems of deciding what products to sell, whether to make or buy component parts, what prices to charge, what channels of distribution to use, whether to accept special orders at special prices, and so forth. Decision making is often a difficult task that is complicated by numerous alternatives and massive amounts of data, only some of which may be relevant.

Every decision involves choosing from among at least two alternatives. In making a decision, the costs and benefits of one alternative must be compared to the costs and benefits of other alternatives. Costs that differ between alternatives are called **relevant costs.** Distinguishing between relevant and irrelevant costs and benefits is critical for two reasons. First, irrelevant data can be ignored—saving decision makers tremendous amounts of time and effort. Second, bad decisions can easily result from erroneously including irrelevant costs and benefits when analyzing alternatives. To be successful in decision making, managers must be able to tell the difference between relevant and irrelevant data and must be able to correctly use the relevant data in analyzing alternatives. The purpose of this chapter is to develop these skills by illustrating their use in a wide range of decision-making situations. We hasten to add that these decision-making skills are as important in your personal life as they are to managers in business. After completing your study of this chapter, you should be able to think more clearly about decisions in many facets of your life.

Cost Concepts for Decision Making

LEARNING OBJECTIVE 1
Identify relevant and irrelevant costs and benefits in a decision situation.

Four cost terms discussed in Chapter 2 are particularly applicable to this chapter. These terms are *differential costs, incremental costs, opportunity costs,* and *sunk costs.* You may find it helpful to turn back to Chapter 2 and refresh your memory concerning these terms before reading on.

Identifying Relevant Costs and Benefits

Only those costs and benefits that differ in total between alternatives are relevant in a decision. If a cost will be the same regardless of the alternative selected, then the decision has no effect on the cost and it can be ignored. For example, if you are trying to decide whether to go to a movie or to rent a videotape for the evening, the rent on your apartment is irrelevant. Whether you go to a movie or rent a videotape, the rent on your apartment will be exactly the same and is therefore irrelevant to the decision. On the other hand, the cost of the movie ticket and the cost of renting the videotape would be relevant in the decision since they are *avoidable costs.*

An **avoidable cost** is a cost that can be eliminated in whole or in part by choosing one alternative over another. By choosing the alternative of going to the movie, the cost of renting the videotape can be avoided. By choosing the alternative of renting the videotape, the cost of the movie ticket can be avoided. Therefore, the cost of the movie ticket and the cost of renting the videotape are both avoidable costs. On the other hand, the rent on the apartment is not an avoidable cost of either alternative. You would continue to rent your apartment under either alternative. Avoidable costs are relevant costs. Unavoidable costs are irrelevant costs.

Two broad categories of costs are never relevant in decisions. These irrelevant costs are:

1. Sunk costs.
2. Future costs that do not differ between the alternatives.

As we learned in Chapter 2, a **sunk cost** is a cost that has already been incurred and cannot be avoided regardless of what a manager decides to do. Sunk costs are always the same, no matter what alternatives are being considered, and they are therefore always irrelevant and should be ignored. On the other hand, future costs that do differ between alternatives *are* relevant. For example, when deciding whether to go to a movie or rent a videotape, the cost of buying a movie ticket and the cost of renting a videotape have not yet been incurred. These are future costs that differ between the alternatives and therefore they are relevant.

Along with sunk cost, the term **differential cost** was introduced in Chapter 2. In managerial accounting, the terms *avoidable cost, differential cost, incremental cost,* and *relevant cost* are often used interchangeably. To identify the costs that are avoidable in a particular decision situation and are therefore relevant, these steps should be followed:

1. Eliminate costs and benefits that do not differ between alternatives. These irrelevant costs consist of (a) sunk costs and (b) future costs that do not differ between alternatives.
2. Use the remaining costs and benefits that do differ between alternatives in making the decision. The costs that remain are the differential, or avoidable, costs.

IN BUSINESS

IT ISN'T EASY TO BE SMART ABOUT MONEY

Most of us commonly suffer from psychological quirks that make it very difficult for us to actually ignore irrelevant costs when making decisions. As Dan Seligman puts it: "Higher primates do not like to admit, even to themselves, that they have screwed up." Humans have "the deep-seated, egoistic human need—evidenced in numerous psychological experiments—to justify the sunk costs in one's life. . . . Many people do not feel liberated by the news that sunk costs are irrelevant. Quite the contrary—they wish to resist the news."

What's the evidence? A lot of human behavior. As Paula Zakaria reports: "If you put your house on the market but refuse offers below the price you paid, you are guilty of *anchoring*. The amount you paid is irrelevant; a house, like a stock, is worth what the market will bear at the time of sale. Do you hold onto stocks that fall in the hope that they will recover? It's called *loss aversion,* and stop doing it. . . . [W]e are only selectively rational. . . . At times, it seems, we favor habit, emotional comfort or near-term pleasure over precise reasoning, consistent preference, or long-term financial security."

Sources: Dan Seligman, "Of Mice and Economics," *Forbes,* August 24, 1998, p. 62; Brian O'Reilley, "Why Johnny Can't Invest," *FORTUNE,* November 9, 1998, pp. 173–178; John S. Hammond, Ralph L. Keeney, and Howard Raiffa, "The Hidden Traps in Decision Making," *Harvard Business Review,* September–October 1998, pp. 47–58; and Paula Throckmorton Zakaria, "Strange Calculations," *The Wall Street Journal,* Tuesday, March 2, 1999, p. A17.

Different Costs for Different Purposes

We need to recognize from the outset of our discussion that costs that are relevant in one decision situation are not necessarily relevant in another. Simply put, this means that *the manager needs different costs for different purposes.* For one purpose, a particular group of costs may be relevant; for another purpose, an entirely different group of costs may be relevant. Thus, in *each* decision situation the data must be carefully examined to isolate the relevant costs. Otherwise, there is the risk of being misled by irrelevant data.

The concept of "different costs for different purposes" is basic to managerial accounting; we shall see its application frequently in the pages that follow.

An Example of Identifying Relevant Costs and Benefits

Cynthia is currently a student in an MBA program in Boston and would like to visit a friend in New York City over the weekend. She is trying to decide whether to drive or take the train. Because she is on a tight budget, she wants to carefully consider the costs of the two alternatives. If one alternative is far less expensive than the other, that may be decisive in her choice. By car, the distance between her apartment in Boston and her friend's apartment in New York City is 230 miles. Cynthia has compiled the following list of items to consider:

Automobile Costs		
Item	Annual Cost of Fixed Items	Cost per Mile (based on 10,000 miles per year)
(a) Annual straight-line depreciation on car [($18,000 original cost − $4,000 estimated resale value in 5 years)/5 years]	$2,800	$0.280
(b) Cost of gasoline ($1.60 per gallon ÷ 32 miles per gallon)		0.050
(c) Annual cost of auto insurance and license	$1,380	0.138
(d) Maintenance and repairs		0.065
(e) Parking fees at school ($45 per month × 8 months)	$360	0.036
(f) Total average cost per mile		$0.569

Additional Data	
Item	
(g) Reduction in the resale value of car due solely to wear and tear	$0.026 per mile
(h) Cost of round-trip Amtrak ticket from Boston to New York City	$104
(i) Benefit of relaxing and being able to study during the train ride rather than having to drive	?
(j) Cost of putting the dog in a kennel while gone	$40
(k) Benefit of having a car available in New York City	?
(l) Hassle of parking the car in New York City	?
(m) Cost of parking the car in New York City	$25 per day

Which costs and benefits are relevant in this decision? Remember, only those costs and benefits that differ between alternatives are relevant. Everything else is irrelevant and can be ignored.

Start at the top of the list with item (a): the original cost of the car is a sunk cost. This cost has already been incurred and therefore can never differ between alternatives. Consequently, it is irrelevant and can be ignored. The same is true of the accounting depreciation of $2,800 per year, which simply spreads the sunk cost across a number of years.

Move down the list to item (b): the cost of gasoline consumed by driving to New York City. This would clearly be a relevant cost in this decision. If Cynthia takes the train, this cost would not be incurred. Hence, the cost differs between alternatives and is therefore relevant.

Item (c), the annual cost of auto insurance and license, is not relevant. Whether Cynthia takes the train or drives on this particular trip, her annual auto insurance premium and her auto license fee will remain the same.[1]

Item (d), the cost of maintenance and repairs, is relevant. While maintenance and repair costs have a large random component, over the long run they should be more or less

[1] If Cynthia has an accident while driving to New York City or back, this might affect her insurance premium when the policy is renewed. The increase in the insurance premium would be a relevant cost of this particular trip, but the normal amount of the insurance premium is not relevant in any case.

proportional to the amount of miles the car is driven. Thus, the average cost of $0.065 per mile is a reasonable estimate to use.

Item (e), the monthly fee that Cynthia pays to park at her school during the academic year, would not be relevant in the decision of how to get to New York City. Regardless of which alternative she selects—driving or taking the train—she will still need to pay for parking at school.

Item (f) is the total average cost of $0.569 per mile. As discussed above, some elements of this total are relevant, but some are not relevant. Since it contains some irrelevant costs, it would be incorrect to estimate the cost of driving to New York City and back by simply multiplying the $0.569 by 460 miles (230 miles each way × 2). This erroneous approach would yield a cost of driving of $261.74. Unfortunately, such mistakes are often made in both personal life and in business. Since the total cost is stated on a per-mile basis, people are easily misled. Often people think that if the cost is stated as $0.569 per mile, the cost of driving 100 miles is $56.90. But it is not. Many of the costs included in the $0.569 cost per mile are sunk and/or fixed and will not increase if the car is driven another 100 miles. The $0.569 is an average cost, not an incremental cost. Beware of such unitized costs (i.e., costs stated in terms of a dollar amount per unit, per mile, per direct labor-hour, per machine-hour, and so on)—they are often misleading.

Item (g), the decline in the resale value of the car that occurs as a consequence of driving more miles, is relevant in the decision. Because she uses the car, its resale value declines. Eventually, she will be able to get less for the car when she sells it or trades it in on another car. This reduction in resale value is a real cost of using the car that should be taken into account. Cynthia estimates this cost by accessing the *Kelly Blue Book* website at www.kbb.com. The reduction in resale value of an asset through use or over time is often called *real* or *economic depreciation.* This is different from accounting depreciation, which attempts to match the sunk cost of the asset with the periods that benefit from that cost.

Item (h), the $104 cost of a round-trip ticket on Amtrak, is clearly relevant in this decision. If she drives, she would not have to buy the ticket.

Item (i) is relevant to the decision, even if it is difficult to put a dollar value on relaxing and being able to study while on the train. It is relevant because it is a benefit that is available under one alternative but not under the other.

Item (j), the cost of putting Cynthia's dog in the kennel while she is gone, is clearly irrelevant in this decision. Whether she takes the train or drives to New York City, she will still need to put her dog in a kennel.

Like item (i), items (k) and (l) are relevant to the decision even if it is difficult to measure their dollar impacts.

Item (m), the cost of parking in New York City, is relevant to the decision.

Bringing together all of the relevant data, Cynthia would estimate the relative costs of driving and taking the train as follows:

Relevant financial cost of driving to New York City:	
Gasoline (460 miles at $0.050 per mile)	$ 23.00
Maintenance and repairs (460 miles @ $0.065 per mile)	29.90
Reduction in the resale value of car due solely to wear and tear (460 miles @ $0.026 per mile)	11.96
Cost of parking the car in New York City (2 days @ $25 per day)	50.00
Total	$114.86
Relevant financial cost of taking the train to New York City:	
Cost of round-trip Amtrak ticket from Boston to New York City	$104.00

What should Cynthia do? From a purely financial standpoint, it would be cheaper by $10.86 ($114.86 − $104.00) to take the train than to drive. Cynthia has to decide if the convenience of having a car in New York City outweighs the additional cost and the disadvantages of being unable to relax and study on the train and the hassle of finding parking in the city.

In this example, we focused on identifying the relevant costs and benefits—everything else was ignored. In the next example, we will begin the analysis by including all of the costs and benefits—relevant or not. We will see that if we are very careful, we will still get the correct answer because the irrelevant costs and benefits will cancel out when we compare the alternatives.

IN BUSINESS

CRUISING ON THE CHEAP

Cruise ship operators such as Princess Cruises sometimes offer deep discounts on popular cruises. Recently, a 10-day Mediterranean cruise on the Norwegian Dream was being offered at up to 75% off the list price. A seven-day cruise to Alaska could be booked for a $499–$700 discount. The cause? "An ambitious fleet expansion left the cruise industry grappling with a tidal wave of capacity. . . . Most cruise costs are fixed whether all the ship's berths are filled or not, so it is better to sell cheap than not at all. . . . In the current glut, discounting has made it possible for the cruise lines to keep berths nearly full."

Source: Martin Brannigan, *The Wall Street Journal,* July 17, 2000, pp. B1 & B4.

Reconciling the Total and Differential Approaches

Oak Harbor Woodworks is considering a new labor-saving machine that rents for $3,000 per year. The machine will be used on the company's butcher block production line. Data concerning the company's annual sales and costs of butcher blocks with and without the new machine are shown below:

	Current Situation	Situation with the New Machine
Units produced and sold	5,000	5,000
Selling price per unit	$40	$40
Direct materials cost per unit	$14	$14
Direct labor cost per unit	$8	$5
Variable overhead cost per unit	$2	$2
Fixed costs, other	$62,000	$62,000
Fixed costs, rental of new machine	—	$3,000

Given the annual sales and the price and cost data above, the net operating income for the product under the two alternatives can be computed as shown in Exhibit 13–1.

Note that the net operating income is $12,000 higher with the new machine, so that is the better alternative. Note also that the $12,000 advantage for the new machine can be obtained in two different ways. It is the difference between the $30,000 net operating income with the new machine and the $18,000 net operating income for the current situation. It is also the sum of the differential costs and benefits as shown in the last column of Exhibit 13–1. A positive number in the Differential Costs and Benefits column indicates that the difference between the alternatives favors the new machine; a negative number indicates that the difference favors the current situation. A zero in that column simply means that the total amount for the item is exactly the same for both alternatives. Thus, since the difference in the net operating incomes equals the sum of the differences for the individual items, any cost or benefit that is the same for both alternatives will have no impact on which alternative is preferred. This is the reason that costs and benefits that do not differ between alternatives are irrelevant and can be ignored. If we properly account for them, they will cancel out when we compare the alternatives.

We could have arrived at the same solution much more quickly by ignoring altogether the irrelevant costs and benefits.

EXHIBIT 13–1
Total and Differential Costs

	Current Situation	Situation with New Machine	Differential Costs and Benefits
Sales (5,000 units @ $40 per unit)	$200,000	$200,000	$ 0
Less variable expenses:			
Direct materials (5,000 units @ $14 per unit)	70,000	70,000	0
Direct labor (5,000 units @ $8 and $5 per unit)	40,000	25,000	15,000
Variable overhead (5,000 units @ $2 por unit)	10,000	10,000	0
Total variable expenses	120,000	105,000	
Contribution margin	80,000	95,000	
Less fixed expenses:			
Other	62,000	62,000	0
Rent of new machine	0	3,000	(3,000)
Total fixed expenses	62,000	65,000	
Net operating income	$ 18,000	$ 30,000	$12,000

- The selling price per unit and the number of units sold do not differ between the alternatives. Therefore, the total sales revenues are exactly the same for the two alternatives as shown in Exhibit 13–1. Since the sales revenues are exactly the same, they have no effect on the difference in net operating income between the two alternatives. That is shown in the last column in Exhibit 13–1, which shows a $0 differential benefit.
- The direct materials cost per unit, the variable overhead cost per unit, and the number of units produced and sold do not differ between the alternatives. Consequently, the direct materials cost and the variable overhead cost will be the same for the two alternatives and can be ignored.
- The "other" fixed expenses do not differ between the alternatives, so they can be ignored as well.

Indeed, the only costs that do differ between the alternatives are direct labor costs and the fixed rental cost of the new machine. Hence, the two alternatives can be compared based only on these relevant costs:

Net advantage to renting the new machine:	
Decrease in direct labor costs (5,000 units at a cost savings of $3 per unit)	$15,000
Increase in fixed expenses	(3,000)
Net annual cost savings from renting the new machine	$12,000

If we focus on just the relevant costs and benefits, we get exactly the same answer as when we listed all of the costs and benefits—including those that do not differ between the alternatives and hence are irrelevant. We get the same answer because the only costs and benefits that matter in the final comparison of the net operating incomes are those that differ between the two alternatives and hence are not zero in the last column of Exhibit 13–1. Those two relevant costs are both listed in the above analysis showing the net advantage to renting the new machine.

Why Isolate Relevant Costs?

In the preceding example, we used two different approaches to analyze the alternatives. First, we considered all costs, both those that were relevant and those that were not; and second, we considered only the relevant costs. We obtained the same answer under both approaches. It would be natural to ask, "Why bother to isolate relevant costs when total costs will do the job just as well?" Isolating relevant costs is desirable for at least two reasons.

First, only rarely will enough information be available to prepare a detailed income statement for both alternatives such as we have done in the preceding examples. Assume, for example, that you are called on to make a decision relating to a portion of a single operation of a multidepartmental, multiproduct company. Under these circumstances, it would be virtually impossible to prepare an income statement of any type. You would have to rely on your ability to recognize which costs are relevant and which are not in order to assemble the data necessary to make a decision.

Second, mingling irrelevant costs with relevant costs may cause confusion and distract attention from the information that is really critical. Furthermore, the danger always exists that an irrelevant piece of data may be used improperly, resulting in an incorrect decision. The best approach is to ignore irrelevant data and base the decision entirely on relevant data.

Relevant cost analysis, combined with the contribution approach to the income statement, provides a powerful tool for making decisions. We will investigate various uses of this tool in the remaining sections of this chapter.

IN BUSINESS

ENVIRONMENTAL COSTS ADD UP

A decision analysis can be flawed by incorrectly including irrelevant costs such as sunk costs and future costs that do not differ between alternatives. It can also be flawed by omitting future costs that *do* differ between alternatives. This is a problem particularly with environmental costs that have dramatically increased in recent years and about which many managers have little knowledge.

Consider the environmental complications posed by a decision of whether to install a solvent-based or powder-based system for spray-painting parts. In a solvent painting system, parts are sprayed as they move along a conveyor. The paint that misses the part is swept away by a wall of water, called a water curtain. The excess paint accumulates in a pit as sludge that must be removed each month. Environmental regulations classify this sludge as hazardous waste. As a result, a permit must be obtained to produce the waste and meticulous records must be maintained of how the waste is transported, stored, and disposed of. The annual costs of complying with these regulations can easily exceed $140,000 in total for a painting facility that initially costs only $400,000 to build. The costs of complying with environmental regulations include the following:

- The waste sludge must be hauled to a special disposal site. The typical disposal fee is about $300 per barrel, or $55,000 per year for a modest solvent-based painting system.
- Workers must be specially trained to handle the paint sludge.
- The company must carry special insurance.
- The company must pay substantial fees to the state for releasing pollutants (i.e., the solvent) into the air.
- The water in the water curtain must be specially treated to remove contaminants. This can cost tens of thousands of dollars per year.

In contrast, a powder-based painting system avoids almost all of these environmental costs. Excess powder used in the painting process can be recovered and reused without creating a hazardous waste. Additionally, the powder-based system does not release contaminants into the atmosphere. Therefore, even though the cost of building a powder-based system may be higher than the cost of building a solvent-based system, over the long run the costs of the powder-based system may be far lower due to the high environmental costs of a solvent-based system. Managers need to be aware of such environmental costs and take them fully into account when making decisions.

Source: Germain Böer, Margaret Curtin, and Louis Hoyt, "Environmental Cost Management," *Management Accounting,* September 1998, pp. 28–38.

30 questions

Adding and Dropping Product Lines and Other Segments

LEARNING OBJECTIVE 2
Prepare an analysis showing whether a product line or other organizational segment should be dropped or retained.

Decisions relating to whether old product lines or other segments of a company should be dropped and new ones added are among the most difficult that a manager has to make. In such decisions, many qualitative and quantitative factors must be considered. Ultimately, however, any final decision to drop an old segment or to add a new one is going to hinge primarily on the impact the decision will have on net operating income. To assess this impact, costs must be carefully analyzed.

An Illustration of Cost Analysis

Consider the three major product lines of the Discount Drug Company—drugs, cosmetics, and housewares. Sales and cost information for the preceding month for each separate product line and for the store in total are given in Exhibit 13–2.

What can be done to improve the company's overall performance? One product line—housewares—shows a net operating loss for the month. Perhaps dropping this line would increase the company's profits. However, the report in Exhibit 13–2 may be misleading. No attempt has been made in Exhibit 13–2 to distinguish between fixed expenses that may be avoided if a product line is dropped and common fixed expenses that cannot be avoided by dropping any particular product line. The two alternatives are keeping the housewares product line and dropping the housewares product line. Only those costs that differ between these two alternatives (i.e., that can be avoided by dropping the housewares product line) are relevant. In deciding whether to drop a product line, it is crucial for managers to clearly identify which costs can be avoided, and hence are relevant to the decision, and which costs cannot be avoided, and hence are irrelevant. The decision should be approached as follows:

Topic Tackler PLUS 13–1

If the housewares line is dropped, then the company will lose $20,000 per month in contribution margin, but by dropping the line it may be possible to avoid some fixed costs. It may be possible, for example, to discharge certain employees, or it may be possible to reduce advertising costs. If by dropping the housewares line the company is able to avoid more in fixed costs than it loses in contribution margin, then it will be better off if the product line is eliminated, since overall net operating income should improve. On the other hand, if the company is not able to avoid as much in fixed costs as it loses in contribution margin, then the housewares line should be kept. In short, the manager should ask, "What costs can I avoid if I drop this product line?"

EXHIBIT 13–2
Discount Drug Company Product Lines

		Product Line		
	Total	Drugs	Cosmetics	Housewares
Sales	$250,000	$125,000	$75,000	$50,000
Less variable expenses	105,000	50,000	25,000	30,000
Contribution margin	145,000	75,000	50,000	20,000
Less fixed expenses:				
Salaries	50,000	29,500	12,500	8,000
Advertising	15,000	1,000	7,500	6,500
Utilities	2,000	500	500	1,000
Depreciation—fixtures	5,000	1,000	2,000	2,000
Rent	20,000	10,000	6,000	4,000
Insurance	3,000	2,000	500	500
General administrative	30,000	15,000	9,000	6,000
Total fixed expenses	125,000	59,000	38,000	28,000
Net operating income (loss)	$ 20,000	$ 16,000	$12,000	$ (8,000)

As we have seen from our earlier discussion, not all costs are avoidable. For example, some of the costs associated with a product line may be sunk costs. Other costs may be allocated fixed costs that will not differ in total regardless of whether the product line is dropped or retained.

To show how to proceed in a product-line analysis, suppose that Discount Drug Company has analyzed the fixed costs being charged to the three product lines and has determined the following:

1. The salaries expense represents salaries paid to employees working directly on the product. All of the employees working in housewares would be discharged if the product line is dropped.
2. The advertising expense represents product advertising specific to each product line and is avoidable if the line is dropped.
3. The utilities expense represents utilities costs for the entire company. The amount charged to each product line is an allocation based on space occupied and is not avoidable if the product line is dropped.
4. The depreciation expense represents depreciation on fixtures used for display of the various product lines. Although the fixtures are nearly new, they are custom-built and will have no resale value if the housewares line is dropped.
5. The rent expense represents rent on the entire building housing the company; it is allocated to the product lines on the basis of sales dollars. The monthly rent of $20,000 is fixed under a long-term lease agreement.
6. The insurance expense represents insurance carried on inventories within each of the three product-lines.
7. The general administrative expense represents the costs of accounting, purchasing, and general management, which are allocated to the product lines on the basis of sales dollars. These costs will not change if the housewares line is dropped.

With this information, management can identify fixed costs that can and cannot be avoided if the product line is dropped:

Fixed Expenses	Total Cost Assigned to Housewares	Not Avoidable*	Avoidable
Salaries	$ 8,000		$ 8,000
Advertising	6,500		6,500
Utilities	1,000	$ 1,000	
Depreciation—fixtures	2,000	2,000	
Rent	4,000	4,000	
Insurance	500		500
General administrative	6,000	6,000	
Total	$28,000	$13,000	$15,000

*These fixed costs represent either (1) sunk costs or (2) future costs that will not change whether the housewares line is retained or discontinued.

To determine how dropping the line will affect the overall profits of the company, we can compare the contribution margin that will be lost to the costs that can be avoided if the line is dropped:

Contribution margin lost if the housewares line is discontinued (see Exhibit 13–2)	$(20,000)
Less fixed costs that can be avoided if the housewares line is discontinued (see above)	15,000
Decrease in overall company net operating income	$ (5,000)

In this case, the fixed costs that can be avoided by dropping the product line are less than the contribution margin that will be lost. Therefore, based on the data given, the housewares line should not be discontinued unless a more profitable use can be found for the floor and counter space that it is occupying.

A Comparative Format

Some managers prefer to approach decisions of this type by preparing comparative income statements showing the effects on the company as a whole of either keeping or dropping the product line in question as we did in Exhibit 13–1. A comparative analysis of this type for the Discount Drug Company is shown in Exhibit 13–3.

As shown in the last column of the exhibit, overall company net operating income will decrease by $5,000 each period if the housewares line is dropped. This is the same answer, of course, as we obtained when we focused just on the lost contribution margin and avoidable fixed costs.

Beware of Allocated Fixed Costs

Our conclusion that the housewares line should not be dropped seems to conflict with the data shown earlier in Exhibit 13–2, which indicates that the housewares line is showing a loss. Why keep a line that is showing a loss? The explanation for this apparent inconsistency lies in part with the common fixed costs that are being allocated to the product lines. As we observed in Chapter 12, one of the great dangers in allocating common fixed costs is that such allocations can make a product line (or other segment of a business) *look* less profitable than it really is. In this instance, a consequence of allocating the common fixed costs among all product lines is to make the housewares line *look* unprofitable, whereas, in fact, dropping the product line would result in a decrease in overall company net operating income. This point can be seen clearly if we recast the data in Exhibit 13–2 and eliminate the allocation of the common fixed costs. This recasting of data—using the segmented approach from Chapter 12—is shown in Exhibit 13–4 (page 612).

Exhibit 13–4 gives us a much different perspective of the housewares line than does Exhibit 13–2. As shown in Exhibit 13–4, the housewares line is covering all of its own traceable fixed costs and is generating a $3,000 segment margin toward covering the common fixed costs of the company. Unless another product line can be found that will

EXHIBIT 13–3
A Comparative Format for Product-Line Analysis

	Keep Housewares	Drop Housewares	Difference: Net Operating Income Increase (or Decrease)
Sales	$50,000	$ 0	$(50,000)
Less variable expenses	30,000	0	30,000
Contribution margin	20,000	0	(20,000)
Less fixed expenses:			
Salaries	8,000	0	8,000
Advertising	6,500	0	6,500
Utilities	1,000	1,000	0
Depreciation—fixtures	2,000	2,000	0
Rent	4,000	4,000	0
Insurance	500	0	500
General administrative	6,000	6,000	0
Total fixed expenses	28,000	13,000	15,000
Net operating income (loss)	$ (8,000)	$(13,000)	$ (5,000)

EXHIBIT 13–4
Discount Drug Company Product Lines—Recast in Contribution Format (from Exhibit 13–2)

		Product Line		
	Total	Drugs	Cosmetics	Housewares
Sales	$250,000	$125,000	$75,000	$50,000
Less variable expenses	105,000	50,000	25,000	30,000
Contribution margin	145,000	75,000	50,000	20,000
Less traceable fixed expenses:				
Salaries	50,000	29,500	12,500	8,000
Advertising	15,000	1,000	7,500	6,500
Depreciation—fixtures	5,000	1,000	2,000	2,000
Insurance	3,000	2,000	500	500
Total traceable fixed expenses	73,000	33,500	22,500	17,000
Product-line segment margin	72,000	$41,500	$27,500	$ 3,000*
Less common fixed expenses:				
Utilities	2,000			
Rent	20,000			
General administrative	30,000			
Total common fixed expenses	52,000			
Net operating income	$ 20,000			

*If the housewares line is dropped, this $3,000 in segment margin will be lost to the company. In addition, we have seen that the $2,000 depreciation on the fixtures is a sunk cost that cannot be avoided. The sum of these two figures ($3,000 + $2,000 = $5,000) would be the decrease in the company's overall profits if the housewares line were discontinued.

generate a segment margin greater than $3,000, the company would be better off keeping the housewares line. By keeping the line, the company's overall net operating income will be higher than if the product line were dropped.

IN BUSINESS

FAKING OUT TAXPAYERS

Owners of sports teams often tap the general taxpayer to help build fancy new stadiums that include luxurious skyboxes for wealthy fans. How do they do this? Partly by paying consultants to produce studies that purport to show the big favorable economic impact on the area of the new stadium. The trouble is that these studies are bogus. Voters in the state of Washington turned down public funding for the new Safeco baseball field in Seattle, but the state legislature went into special session to pass a tax bill to fund construction anyway. And shortly thereafter, taxpayers were asked to pay $325 million to tear down the old Kingdome football stadium to build a new stadium for the Seattle Seahawks. When asked why public funds should finance private facilities for professional sports, the response was: "Even if you aren't a football fan, the high level of economic activity generated by the Seahawks does affect you. . . . The Seahawks' total annual economic impact in Washington State is $129 million." Sounds impressive, but the argument contains a fallacy. Most of this money would have been spent in Washington State anyway even if the Seahawks had left Seattle for another city. If a local fan did not have a Seahawks game to attend, what would he/she have done with the money? Burn it? Hardly. Almost all of this money would have been spent locally anyway. An independent estimate of the *additional* spending that would come to Washington State as a result of keeping the Seahawks in Seattle put the total economic impact at less than half the amount that was erroneously claimed by proponents of the stadium. To put this in perspective, Seattle's Fred Hutchinson Cancer Research Center alone has over twice the economic impact of professional sports teams in Seattle.

Source: Tom Griffin, "Only a Game," *Columns—The University of Washington Alumni Magazine*, June 1997, pp. 15–17. An online version of this article is available at www.washington.edu/alumni/columns/june97/game1.html.

Additionally, we should note that managers may choose to retain an unprofitable product line if the line helps sell other products or if it serves as a "magnet" to attract customers. Bread, for example, may not be an especially profitable line in some food stores, but customers expect it to be available, and many of them would undoubtedly shift their buying elsewhere if a particular store decided to stop carrying it.

The Make or Buy Decision

LEARNING OBJECTIVE 3
Prepare a make or buy analysis.

Providing a product or service to a customer involves many steps. For example, consider all of the steps that are necessary to develop and sell a product such as tax preparation software in retail stores. First the software must be developed, which involves highly skilled software engineers and a great deal of project management effort. Then the product must be put into a form that can be delivered to customers. This involves burning the application onto a blank CD or DVD, applying a label, and packaging the result in an attractive box. Then the product must be distributed to retail stores. Then the product must be sold. And finally, help lines and other forms of after-sale service may have to be provided. And we should not forget that the blank CD or DVD, the label, and the box must of course be made by someone before any of this can happen. All of these activities, from development, to production, to after-sales service are called a *value chain.*

Separate companies may carry out each of the activities in the value chain or a single company may carry out several. When a company is involved in more than one activity in the entire value chain, it is **vertically integrated.** Vertical integration is very common. Some companies control all of the activities in the value chain from producing basic raw materials right up to the final distribution of finished goods and provision of after-sales service. Other companies are content to integrate on a smaller scale by purchasing many of the parts and materials that go into their finished products. A decision to carry out one of the activities in the value chain internally, rather than to buy externally from a supplier, is called a **make or buy decision.** Quite often these decisions involve whether to buy a particular part or to make it internally. Make or buy decisions also involve decisions concerning whether to outsource development tasks, after-sales service, or other activities.

Topic Tackler PLUS
13–2

IN BUSINESS

EMPLOYEE HEALTH BENEFITS—MAKE OR BUY?

With health care insurance premiums rising by over 10% per year, companies have been searching for ways to reduce the costs of providing health care to their employees. Some companies have adopted the unconventional approach of providing health care services in-house. Quad/Graphics, a printing company with 14,000 employees, hired its own doctors and nurses to provide primary health care on-site. By "making" its own health care for employees rather than "buying" it through the purchase of insurance, the company claims that its health care costs have risen just 6% annually and that their spending on health care is now 17% less than the industry average.

Source: Kimberly Weisul, "There's a Doctor in the House," *BusinessWeek,* December 16, 2002, p. 8

Strategic Aspects of the Make or Buy Decision

Vertical integration provides certain advantages. An integrated company is less dependent on its suppliers and may be able to ensure a smoother flow of parts and materials for production than a nonintegrated company. For example, a strike against a major parts supplier can interrupt the operations of a nonintegrated company for many months, whereas an integrated company that is producing its own parts might be able to continue operations. Also, some companies feel that they can control quality better by producing their own parts and materials, rather than by relying on the quality control standards of outside suppliers. In addition, the integrated company realizes profits from the parts and materials that it is "making" rather than "buying," as well as profits from its regular operations.

The advantages of vertical integration are counterbalanced by the advantages of using external suppliers. By pooling demand from a number of companies, a supplier may be able to enjoy economies of scale. These economies of scale can result in higher quality and lower costs than would be possible if the company were to attempt to make the parts or provide the service on its own. A company must be careful, however, to retain control over activities that are essential to maintaining its competitive position. For example, Hewlett-Packard controls the software for laser printers that it makes in cooperation with Canon Inc. of Japan. The present trend appears to be toward less vertical integration, with companies like Sun Microsystems and Hewlett-Packard concentrating on hardware and software design and relying on outside suppliers for almost everything else in the value chain. These factors suggest that the make or buy decision should be weighed very carefully.

An Example of Make or Buy

To provide an illustration of a make or buy decision, consider Mountain Goat Cycles. The company is now producing the heavy-duty gear shifters used in its most popular line of mountain bikes. The company's Accounting Department reports the following costs of producing 8,000 units of the shifter internally each year:

	Per Unit	8,000 Units
Direct materials	$ 6	$ 48,000
Direct labor	4	32,000
Variable overhead	1	8,000
Supervisor's salary	3	24,000
Depreciation of special equipment	2	16,000
Allocated general overhead	5	40,000
Total cost	$21	$168,000

An outside supplier has offered to sell 8,000 shifters a year to Mountain Goat Cycles at a price of only $19 each. Should the company stop producing the shifters internally and start purchasing them from the outside supplier? As always, the focus should be on the relevant costs. As we have seen, the relevant (i.e., differential or avoidable) costs can be obtained by eliminating those costs that are not avoidable—that is, by eliminating (1) the sunk costs and (2) the future costs that will continue regardless of whether the shifters are produced internally or purchased outside. The costs that remain are avoidable by purchasing outside. If these avoidable costs are less than the outside purchase price, then the company should continue to manufacture its own shifters and reject the outside supplier's offer. That is, the company should purchase outside only if the outside purchase price is less than the costs that can be avoided by halting its own production of the shifters.

Looking at the cost data, note that depreciation of special equipment is listed as one of the costs of producing the shifters internally. Since the equipment has already been purchased, this depreciation is a sunk cost and is therefore irrelevant. If the equipment could be sold, its salvage value would be relevant. Or if the machine could be used to make other products, this could be relevant as well. However, we will assume that the equipment has no salvage value and that it has no other use except making the heavy-duty gear shifters.

Also note that the company is allocating a portion of its general overhead costs to the shifters. Any portion of this general overhead cost that would actually be eliminated if the gear shifters were purchased rather than made would be relevant in the analysis. However, it is likely that the general overhead costs allocated to the gear shifters are in fact common to all items produced in the factory and would continue unchanged even if the shifters were purchased from the outside. Such allocated common costs are not relevant costs (since they do not differ between the make or buy alternatives) and should be eliminated from the analysis along with the sunk costs.

EXHIBIT 13–5
Mountain Goat Cycles Make or Buy Analysis

	Total Relevant Costs—8,000 units	
	Make	Buy
Direct materials (8,000 units @ $6 per unit)	$ 48,000	
Direct labor (8,000 units @ $4 per unit)	32,000	
Variable overhead (8,000 units @ $1 per unit)	8,000	
Supervisor's salary	24,000	
Depreciation of special equipment (not relevant)		
Allocated general overhead (not relevant)		
Outside purchase price		$152,000
Total cost	$112,000	$152,000
Difference in favor of continuing to make	$40,000	

The variable costs of producing the shifters (direct materials, direct labor, and variable overhead) are relevant costs, since they can be avoided by buying the shifters from the outside supplier. If the supervisor can be discharged and his or her salary avoided by buying the shifters, then it too is relevant to the decision. Assuming that both the variable costs and the supervisor's salary can be avoided by buying from the outside supplier, then the analysis takes the form shown in Exhibit 13–5.

Since it costs $40,000 less to continue to make the shifters internally than to buy them from the outside supplier, Mountain Goat Cycles should reject the outside supplier's offer. However, the company may wish to consider one additional factor before coming to a final decision. This factor is the opportunity cost of the space now being used to produce the shifters.

Opportunity Cost

If the space now being used to produce the shifters *would otherwise be idle,* then Mountain Goat Cycles should continue to produce its own shifters and the supplier's offer should be rejected, as stated above. Idle space that has no alternative use has an opportunity cost of zero.

But what if the space now being used to produce shifters could be used for some other purpose? In that case, the space would have an opportunity cost equal to the segment margin that could be derived from the best alternative use of the space.

IN BUSINESS

THE OTHER SIDE OF THE COIN

This section of the chapter focuses on a company's decision of whether to make or buy a part. We can also look at this situation from the standpoint of the potential supplier for the part. It isn't always easy to be a supplier. Steven Keller, founder and CEO of Keller Design, a small maker of pet accessories, found this out the hard way after landing a contract with Target, the big retailing chain. Eventually, sales to Target grew to be 80% of Keller Design's business. "Then reality bit. Target suddenly decided to drop . . . four kinds of can lids and food scoops. . . . Later, an unexpected $100,000 charge for airfreighting devoured Keller's profits on a $300,000 shipment. Target also changed its mind about 6,000 specially made ceramic dog bowls, which will probably have to be dumped on a close-out firm for a fraction of Keller's investment. . . . " "The odds are pretty well stacked against you. Contracts with large customers tend to be boilerplate, shifting most of the risk to the supplier." Protect yourself by having your own lawyer go over all contracts, contest unreasonable charges, and don't rely too much on one big customer.

Source: Leigh Gallagher, "Holding the Bag," *Forbes,* June 14, 1999, pp. 164 and 168.

To illustrate, assume that the space now being used to produce shifters could be used to produce a new cross-country bike that would generate a segment margin of $60,000 per year. Under these conditions, Mountain Goat Cycles would be better off to accept the supplier's offer and to use the available space to produce the new product line:

	Make	Buy
Total annual cost (see Exhibit 13–5)	$112,000	$152,000
Opportunity cost—segment margin forgone on a potential new product line	60,000	
Total cost	$172,000	$152,000
Difference in favor of purchasing from the outside supplier	$20,000	

Opportunity costs are not recorded in the organization's general ledger since they do not represent actual dollar outlays. Rather, they represent economic benefits that are *forgone* as a result of pursuing some course of action. The opportunity costs of Mountain Goat Cycles are sufficiently large in this case to change the decision.

IN BUSINESS

TOUGH CHOICES

Brad and Carole Karafil own and operate White Grizzly Adventures, a snowcat skiing and snowboarding company in Meadow Creek, British Columbia. While rare, it does sometimes happen that the company is unable to operate due to bad weather. Guests are housed and fed, but no one can ski. The contract signed by each guest stipulates that no refund is given in the case of an unavoidable cancellation that is beyond the control of the operators. So technically, Brad and Carole are not obligated to provide any refund if they must cancel operations due to bad weather. However, 70% of their guests are repeat customers and a guest who has paid roughly $300 a day to ski is likely to be unhappy if skiing is cancelled even though it is no fault of White Grizzly.

What costs, if any, are saved if skiing is cancelled and the snowcat does not operate? Not much. Guests are still housed and fed and the guides, who are independent contractors, are still paid. Some snowcat operating costs are avoided, but little else. Therefore, there would be little cost savings to pass on to guests.

Brad and Carole could issue a credit to be used for one day of skiing at another time. If a customer with such a credit occupied a seat on a snowcat that would otherwise be empty, the only significant cost to Brad and Carole would be the cost of feeding the customer. However, an empty seat basically doesn't exist—the demand for seats far exceeds the supply and the schedule is generally fully booked far in advance of the ski season. Consequently, the real cost of issuing a credit for one day of skiing is high. Brad and Carole would be giving up $300 from a paying customer for every guest they issue a credit voucher to. Issuing a credit voucher involves an opportunity cost of $300 in forgone sales revenues.

What would you do if you had to cancel skiing due to bad weather? Would you issue a refund or a credit voucher, losing money in the process, or would you risk losing customers? It's a tough choice.

Source: Brad and Carole Karafil, owners and operators of White Grizzly Adventures, www.whitegrizzly.com.

Special Orders

Managers must often evaluate whether a *special order* should be accepted, and if the order is accepted, the price that should be charged. A **special order** is a one-time order that is not considered part of the company's normal ongoing business. To illustrate, Mountain Goat Cycles has just received a request from the Seattle Police Department to produce 100 specially modified mountain bikes at a price of $179 each. The bikes would be used to patrol some of the more densely populated residential sections of the city. Mountain Goat Cycles can easily modify its City Cruiser model to fit the specifications of the Seattle Police. The normal selling price of the City Cruiser bike is $249, and its unit product cost is $182 as shown below:

LEARNING OBJECTIVE 4
Prepare an analysis showing whether a special order should be accepted.

Direct materials	$ 86
Direct labor	45
Manufacturing overhead	51
Unit product cost	$182

The variable portion of the above manufacturing overhead is $6 per unit. The order would have no effect on the company's total fixed manufacturing overhead costs.

The modifications requested by the Seattle Police Department consist of welded brackets to hold radios, nightsticks, and other gear. These modifications would require $17 in incremental variable costs. In addition, the company would have to pay a graphics design studio $1,200 to design and cut stencils that would be used for spray painting the Seattle Police Department's logo and other identifying marks on the bikes.

This order should have no effect on the company's other sales. The production manager says that she can handle the special order without disrupting any of the company's regular scheduled production.

What effect would accepting this order have on the company's net operating income?

Only the incremental costs and benefits are relevant. Since the existing fixed manufacturing overhead costs would not be affected by the order, they are not relevant. The incremental net operating income can be computed as follows:

	Per Unit	Total 100 Bikes
Incremental revenue	$179	$17,900
Less incremental costs:		
Variable costs:		
Direct materials	86	8,600
Direct labor	45	4,500
Variable manufacturing overhead	6	600
Special modifications	17	1,700
Total variable cost	$154	15,400
Fixed cost:		
Purchase of stencils		1,200
Total incremental cost		16,600
Incremental net operating income		$ 1,300

Therefore, even though the $179 price on the special order is below the normal $182 unit product cost and the order would require additional costs, the order would result in an increase in net operating income. In general, a special order is profitable as long as the incremental revenue from the special order exceeds the incremental costs of the order. We must note, however, that it is important to make sure that there is indeed idle capacity and that the special order does not cut into normal sales or undercut prices on normal sales. For example, if the company was operating at capacity, opportunity costs would have to be taken into account as well as the incremental costs that have already been detailed above.

IN BUSINESS

FLY THE FRIENDLY AISLES

Shoppers at Safeway can now earn United Airlines frequent flier miles when they buy their groceries. Airlines charge marketing partners such as Safeway about 2¢ per mile. Since airlines typically require 25,000 frequent flier miles for a domestic round-trip ticket, United is earning about $500 per frequent-flier ticket issued to Safeway customers. This income to United is higher than many discounted fares. Moreover, United carefully manages its frequent flier program so that few frequent flier passengers displace regular fare-paying customers. The only costs of adding a frequent flier passenger to a flight may be food, a little extra fuel, and some administrative costs. All of the other costs of the flight would be incurred anyway. Thus, the miles that United sells to Safeway are almost pure profit.

Source: Wendy Zellner, *Business Week,* March 6, 2000, pp. 152–154.

Utilization of a Constrained Resource

LEARNING OBJECTIVE 5
Determine the most profitable use of a constrained resource and the value of obtaining more of the constrained resource.

Managers are routinely faced with the problem of deciding how constrained resources are going to be utilized. A department store, for example, has a limited amount of floor space and therefore cannot stock every product that may be available. A manufacturer has a limited number of machine-hours and a limited number of direct labor-hours at its disposal. When a limited resource of some type restricts the company's ability to satisfy demand, the company is said to have a **constraint.** Since the company cannot fully satisfy demand, the manager must decide how the constrained resource should be used. Fixed costs are usually unaffected by such choices, so the course of action that will maximize the company's *total* contribution margin should ordinarily be selected.

Contribution in Relation to a Constrained Resource

To maximize total contribution margin, a company should not necessarily promote those products that have the highest *unit* contribution margins. Rather, total contribution margin will be maximized by promoting those products or accepting those orders that provide the highest contribution margin *per unit of the constrained resource.* To illustrate, Mountain Goat Cycles makes a line of panniers—saddlebags for bicycles. There are two models of panniers—a touring model and a mountain model. Cost and revenue data for the two models of panniers follow:

	Model	
	Mountain Pannier	Touring Pannier
Selling price per unit	$25	$30
Variable cost per unit	10	18
Contribution margin per unit	$15	$12
Contribution margin (CM) ratio	60%	40%

The mountain pannier appears to be much more profitable than the touring pannier. It has a $15 per unit contribution margin as compared to only $12 per unit for the touring model, and it has a 60% CM ratio as compared to only 40% for the touring model.

But now let us add one more piece of information—the plant that makes the panniers is operating at capacity. This does not mean that every machine and every person in the plant is working at the maximum possible rate. Because machines have different capacities, some machines will be operating at less than 100% of capacity. However, if the plant as a whole cannot produce any more units, some machine or process must be operating at capacity. The machine or process that is limiting overall output is called the **bottleneck**—it is the constraint.

At Mountain Goat Cycles, the bottleneck is a stitching machine. The mountain pannier requires 2 minutes of stitching time, and the touring pannier requires 1 minute of stitching time. Since the stitching machine already has more work than it can handle, something will have to be cut back. In this situation, which product is more profitable? To answer this question, focus on the *contribution margin per unit of the constrained resource*. This figure is computed by dividing the contribution margin by the amount of the constrained resource a unit of product requires. These calculations are carried out below for the mountain and touring panniers.

	Model	
	Mountain Pannier	Touring Pannier
Contribution margin per unit (above) (a)	$15.00	$12.00
Stitching machine time required to produce one unit (b)	2 minutes	1 minute
Contribution margin per unit of the constrained resource, (a) ÷ (b)	$7.50 per minute	$12.00 per minute

It is now easy to decide which product is less profitable and should be deemphasized. Each minute on the stitching machine that is devoted to the touring pannier results in an increase of $12 in contribution margin and profits. The comparable figure for the mountain pannier is only $7.50 per minute. Therefore, the touring model should be emphasized. Even though the mountain model has the larger contribution margin per unit and the larger CM ratio, the touring model provides the larger contribution margin in relation to the constrained resource.

To verify that the touring model is indeed the more profitable product, suppose an hour of additional stitching time is available and that unfilled orders exist for both products. The additional hour on the stitching machine could be used to make either 30 mountain panniers (60 minutes ÷ 2 minutes per mountain pannier) or 60 touring panniers (60 minutes ÷ 1 minute per touring pannier), with the following consequences:

	Model	
	Mountain Pannier	Touring Pannier
Contribution margin per unit (above)	$ 15	$ 12
Additional units that can be processed in one hour	× 30	× 60
Additional contribution margin	$450	$720

Since the additional contribution margin would be $720 for the touring panniers and only $450 for the mountain panniers, the touring panniers make the most profitable use of the company's constraining resource—the stitching machine.

This example clearly shows that looking at unit contribution margins alone is not enough; the contribution margin must be viewed in relation to the amount of the constrained resource each product requires.

IN BUSINESS

THEORY OF CONSTRAINTS SOFTWARE

Indalex Aluminum Solutions Group is the largest producer of soft alloy extrusions in North America. The company has installed a new generation of business intelligence software created by pVelocity, Inc., of Toronto, Canada. The software "provides decision makers across our entire manufacturing enterprise with time-based financial metrics using TOC concepts to identify bottlenecks." And, it "shifts the focus of a manufacturing company from traditional cost accounting measurements to measuring the generation of dollars per unit of time." For example, instead of emphasizing products with the largest gross margins or contribution margins, the software helps managers to identify and emphasize the products that maximize the contribution margin per unit of the constrained resource.

Source: Mike Alger, "Managing a Business as a Portfolio of Customers," *Strategic Finance*, June 2003, pp. 54–57.

Managing Constraints

Profits can be increased by effectively managing the organization's constraints. One aspect of managing a constraint is to decide how to best utilize it. As discussed above, if the constraint is a bottleneck in the production process, the manager should select the product mix that maximizes the total contribution margin. In addition, the manager should take an active role in managing the constraint itself. Management should focus efforts on increasing the efficiency of the bottleneck operation and on increasing its capacity. Such efforts directly increase the output of finished goods and will often pay off in an almost immediate increase in profits.

It is often possible for a manager to increase the capacity of the bottleneck, which is called **relaxing (or elevating) the constraint.** For example, the stitching machine operator could be asked to work overtime. This would result in more available stitching time and hence more finished goods that can be sold. The benefits from relaxing the constraint are often enormous and can be easily quantified. The manager should first ask, "What would I do with additional capacity at the bottleneck if it were available?" In the example, if unfilled orders exist for both the touring and mountain panniers, the additional capacity would be used to process more touring panniers, since they earn a contribution margin of $12 per minute, or $720 per hour. Given that the overtime pay for the operator is likely to be much less than $720 per hour, running the stitching machine on overtime would be an excellent way to increase the profits of the company while at the same time satisfying more customers.

To reinforce this concept, suppose that there are only unfilled orders for the mountain pannier. How much would it be worth to the company to run the stitching machine overtime in this situation? Since the additional capacity would be used to make the mountain pannier, the value of that additional capacity would drop to $7.50 per minute or $450 per hour. Nevertheless, the value of relaxing the constraint would still be quite high.

These calculations indicate that managers should pay great attention to the bottleneck operation. If a bottleneck machine breaks down or is ineffectively utilized, the losses to the company can be quite large. In our example, for every minute the stitching machine is down due to breakdowns or setups, the company loses between $7.50 and $12.00. The losses on an hourly basis are between $450 and $720! In contrast, there is no such loss of contribution margin if time is lost on a machine that is not a bottleneck—such machines have excess capacity anyway.

The implications are clear. Managers should focus much of their attention on managing the bottleneck. As we have discussed, managers should emphasize products that most profitably utilize the constrained resource. They should also make sure that products are processed smoothly through the bottleneck, with minimal lost time due to breakdowns and setups. And they should try to find ways to increase the capacity at the bottleneck.

The capacity of a bottleneck can be effectively increased in a number of ways, including:

- Working overtime on the bottleneck.
- Subcontracting some of the processing that would be done at the bottleneck.
- Investing in additional machines at the bottleneck.
- Shifting workers from processes that are not bottlenecks to the process that is the bottleneck.
- Focusing business process improvement efforts such as TQM and Business Process Reengineering on the bottleneck.
- Reducing defective units. Each defective unit that is processed through the bottleneck and subsequently scrapped takes the place of a good unit that could be sold.

The last three methods of increasing the capacity of the bottleneck are particularly attractive, since they are essentially free and may even yield additional cost savings.

The methods and ideas discussed in this section are all part of the Theory of Constraints, which was introduced in Chapter 1. A number of organizations have successfully used the Theory of Constraints to improve their performance, including Avery Dennison, Bethlehem Steel, Binney & Smith, Boeing, Champion International, Ford Motor Company, General Motors, ITT, Monster Cable, National Semiconductor, Pratt and Whitney Canada, Pretoria Academic Hospital, Procter and Gamble, Texas Instruments, United Airlines, United Electrical Controls, the United States Air Force Logistics Command, and the United States Navy Transportation Corps.

IN BUSINESS

COPING WITH POWER SHORTAGES

Tata Iron and Steel Company Ltd. is one of the largest companies in India, employing about 75,000 people. The company has had to cope with electrical power shortages severe enough to force it to shut down some of its mills. But which ones? In these situations, electrical power is the company's constraint and it became imperative to manage this constraint effectively. The first step was to estimate the electrical loads of running each of the company's mills using least-squares regression. These data were then used to compute the contribution margin per KWH (kilowatt-hour) for each mill. The model indicated which mills should be shut down, and in what order, and which products should be cut back. The model also indicated that it would be profitable for the company to install its own diesel generating units—the contribution margin from the additional output more than paid for the costs of buying and running the diesel generators.

Source: "How Tata Steel Optimized Its Results," *The Management Accountant (India)*, July 1997, pp. 372–375.

The Problem of Multiple Constraints

What does a company do if it has more than one potential constraint? For example, a company may have limited raw materials, limited direct labor-hours available, limited floor space, and limited advertising dollars to spend on product promotion. How would it determine the right combination of products to produce? The proper combination or "mix" of products can be found by use of a quantitative method known as *linear programming,* which is covered in quantitative methods and operations management courses.

IN BUSINESS

LOOK BEFORE YOU LEAP

The constraint can often be elevated at very low cost. Western Textile Products makes pockets, waistbands, and other clothing components. The constraint at the company's plant in Greenville, South Carolina, was the slitting machines. These large machines slit huge rolls of textiles into appropriate widths for use on other machines. Management was contemplating adding a second shift to elevate the constraint. However, investigation revealed that the slitting machines were actually being run only about one hour in a nine-hour shift. "The other eight hours were required to get materials, load and unload the machine, and do setups. Instead of adding a second shift, a second person was assigned to each machine to fetch materials and do as much of the setting up as possible offline while the machine was running." This approach resulted in increasing the run time to four hours. If another shift had been added without any improvement in how the machines were being used, the cost would have been much higher and run time would have increased by only one hour.

Source: Eric Noreen, Debra Smith, and James T. Mackey, *The Theory of Constraints and Its Implications for Management Accounting* (Croton-on-Hudson, NY: The North River Press), pp. 84–85.

Joint Product Costs and the Contribution Approach

LEARNING OBJECTIVE 6
Prepare an analysis showing whether joint products should be sold at the split-off point or processed further.

In some industries, a number of end products are produced from a single raw material input. For example, in the petroleum refining industry a large number of products are extracted from crude oil, including gasoline, jet fuel, home heating oil, lubricants, asphalt, and various organic chemicals. Another example is provided by the Santa Maria Wool Cooperative of New Mexico. The company buys raw wool from local sheepherders, separates the wool into three grades—coarse, fine, and superfine—and then dyes the wool using traditional methods that rely on pigments from local materials. The production process, together with cost and revenue data, is diagrammed in Exhibit 13–6.

At Santa Maria Wool Cooperative, coarse wool, fine wool, and superfine wool are produced from one input—raw wool. Two or more products that are produced from a common input are known as **joint products.** The **split-off point** is the point in the manufacturing process at which the joint products can be recognized as separate products. This does not occur at Santa Maria Cooperative until the raw wool has been processed through the separating process. The term **joint cost** is used to describe the costs incurred up to the split-off point. At Santa Maria Wool Cooperative, the joint costs are the $200,000 cost of the raw wool and the $40,000 cost of separating the wool. The undyed wool is called an *intermediate product* because it is not finished at this point. Nevertheless, a market does exist for undyed wool—albeit at a significantly lower price than finished, dyed wool.

The Pitfalls of Allocation

Joint costs are common costs that are incurred to simultaneously produce a variety of end products. These joint costs are traditionally allocated among the different products at the split-off point. A typical approach is to allocate the joint costs according to the relative sales value of the end products.

Although allocation of joint product costs is needed for some purposes, such as balance sheet inventory valuation, allocations of this kind are extremely misleading for decision making. The In Business box on page 623 illustrates an incorrect decision that resulted from using such an allocated joint cost.

Sell or Process Further Decisions

Joint costs are irrelevant in decisions regarding what to do with a product from the split-off point forward. Regardless of what is done with the product after the split-off point, the

IN BUSINESS

GETTING IT ALL WRONG

A company located on the Gulf of Mexico produces soap products. Its six main soap product lines are produced from common inputs. Joint product costs up to the split-off point constitute the bulk of the production costs for all six product lines. These joint product costs are allocated to the six product lines on the basis of the relative sales value of each line at the split-off point.

A waste product results from the production of the six main product lines. The company loaded the waste onto barges and dumped it into the Gulf of Mexico, since the waste was thought to have no commercial value. The dumping was stopped, however, when the company's research division discovered that with some further processing the waste could be sold as a fertilizer ingredient. The further processing costs $175,000 per year. The waste was then sold to fertilizer manufacturers for $300,000.

The accountants responsible for allocating manufacturing costs included the sales value of the waste product along with the sales value of the six main product lines in their allocation of the joint product costs at the split-off point. This allocation resulted in the waste product being allocated $150,000 in joint product cost. This $150,000 allocation, when added to the further processing costs of $175,000 for the waste, made it appear that the waste product was unprofitable—as shown in the table below. When presented with this analysis, the company's management decided that further processing of the waste should be stopped. The company went back to dumping the waste in the Gulf.

Sales value of the waste product after further processing . . .	$300,000
Less costs assignable to the waste product	325,000
Net loss	$(25,000)

joint costs must be incurred to get the product to the split-off point. Moreover, even if the product were disposed of in a landfill without any further processing, all of the joint costs must be incurred to obtain the other products that come out of the joint process. Therefore, none of the joint costs are economically attributable to any one of the intermediate or end products that emerge from the system. The joint costs are a common cost of all of the intermediate and end products and should not be allocated to them for purposes of making decisions about the products. In the case of the soap company (see the accompanying In Business box "Getting It All Wrong"), the $150,000 in allocated joint costs should not have been permitted to influence what was done with the waste product from the split-off point forward. The analysis should have been as follows:

	Dump in Gulf	Process Further
Sales value of fertilizer ingredient	0	$300,000
Additional processing costs	0	175,000
Contribution margin	0	$125,000
Advantage of processing further	$125,000	

Decisions of this type are known as **sell or process further decisions.** It is profitable to continue processing a joint product after the split-off point *so long as the incremental revenue from such processing exceeds the incremental processing cost incurred after the split-off point.* Joint costs that have already been incurred up to the split-off point are always irrelevant in decisions concerning what to do from the split-off point forward.

To provide a detailed example of the sell or process further decision, return to the data for Santa Maria Wool Cooperative in Exhibit 13–6. We can answer several important questions using this data. First, is the company making money if it runs the entire process

EXHIBIT 13–6
Santa Maria Wool Cooperative

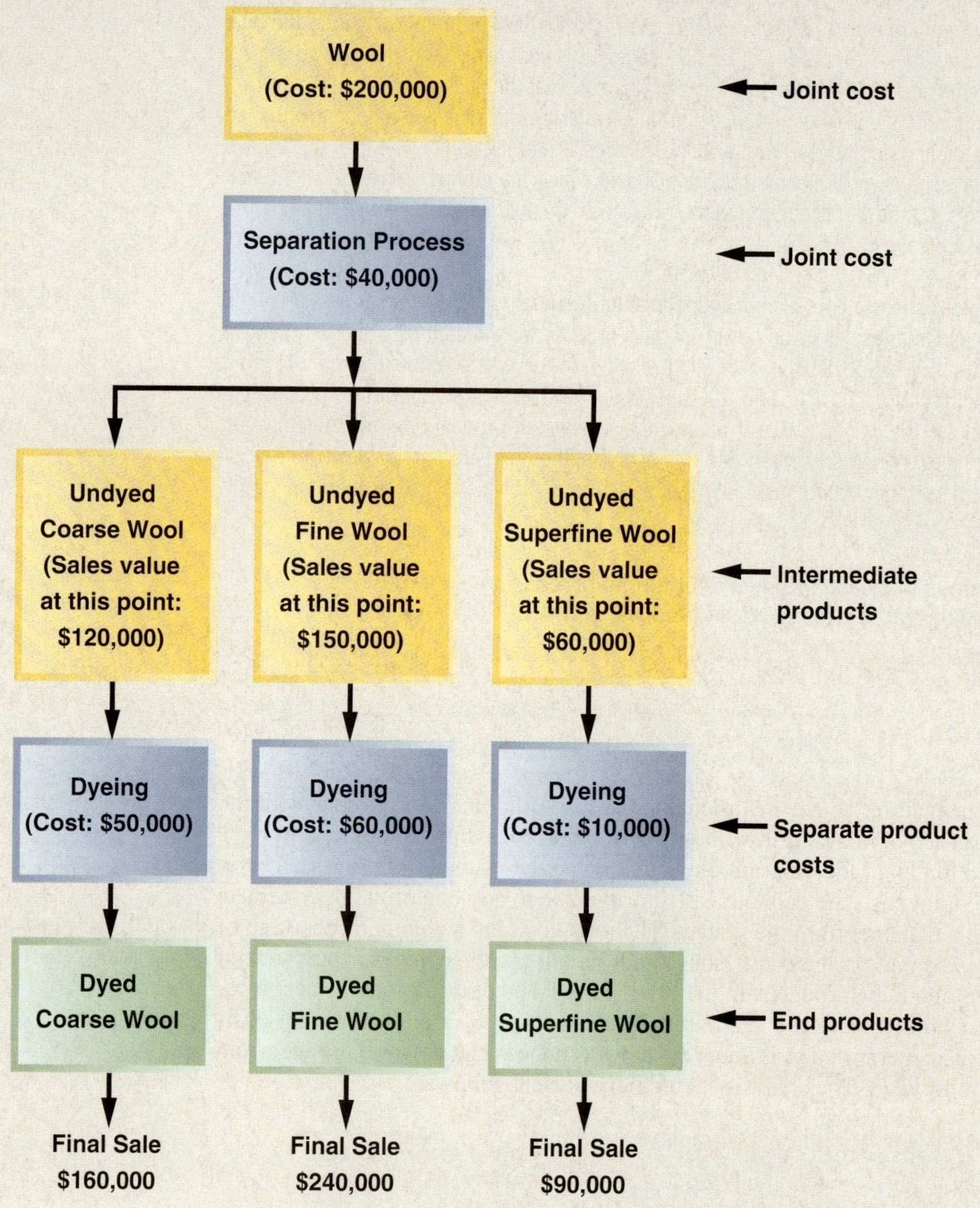

from beginning to end? Assuming there are no costs other than those displayed in Exhibit 13–6, the company is indeed making money as follows:

Analysis of the profitability of the overall operation:		
Combined final sales value		
($160,000 + $240,000 + $90,000)		$490,000
Less costs of producing the end products:		
Cost of wool	$200,000	
Cost of separating wool	40,000	
Combined costs of dyeing		
($50,000 + $60,000 + $10,000)	120,000	360,000
Profit		$130,000

However, even though the company is making money overall, it may be losing money on one or more of the products. If the company buys wool and runs the separation process, it will get all three intermediate products. Nothing can be done about that. However, each of these products can be sold *as is* without further processing. It may be that the company would be better off selling one or more of the products prior to dyeing to avoid the dyeing costs. The appropriate way to make this choice is to compare the incremental revenues to the incremental costs from further processing as follows:

Analysis of sell or process further:

	Coarse Wool	Fine Wool	Superfine Wool
Final sales value after further processing	$160,000	$240,000	$90,000
Less sales value at the split-off point	120,000	150,000	60,000
Incremental revenue from further processing .	40,000	90,000	30,000
Less cost of further processing (dyeing)	50,000	60,000	10,000
Profit (loss) from further processing	$(10,000)	$ 30,000	$20,000

As this analysis shows, the company would be better off selling the undyed coarse wool as is rather than processing it further. The other two products should be processed further and dyed before selling them.

Note that the joint costs of the wool ($200,000) and of the wool separation process ($40,000) play no role in the decision of whether to sell or further process the intermediate products. These joint costs are relevant in a decision of whether to buy wool and to run the wool separation process, but they are not relevant in decisions about what to do with the intermediate products once they have been separated.

Activity-Based Costing and Relevant Costs

As discussed in Chapter 8, activity-based costing can be used to help identify potentially relevant costs for decision-making purposes. Activity-based costing improves the traceability of costs by focusing on the activities caused by a product or other segment. However, managers should exercise caution against reading more into this "traceability" than really exists. People have a tendency to assume that if a cost is traceable to a segment, then the cost is automatically an avoidable cost. That is not true. As emphasized in Chapter 8, the costs provided by a well-designed activity-based costing system are only *potentially* relevant. Before making a decision, managers must still decide which of the potentially relevant costs are actually avoidable. Only those costs that are avoidable are relevant and the others should be ignored.

To illustrate, refer again to the data relating to the housewares line in Exhibit 13–4. The $2,000 fixtures depreciation is a traceable cost of the housewares lines because it directly relates to activities in that department. We found, however, that the $2,000 is not avoidable if the housewares line is dropped. The key lesson here is that the method used to assign a cost to a product or other segment does not change the basic nature of the cost. A sunk cost such as depreciation of old equipment is still a sunk cost regardless of whether it is traced directly to a particular segment on an activity basis, allocated to all segments on the basis of labor-hours, or treated in some other way in the costing process. Regardless of the method used to assign costs to products or other segments, the principles discussed in this chapter must be applied to determine the costs that are avoidable in each situation.

Summary

Everything in this chapter consists of applications of one simple but powerful idea. Only those costs and benefits that differ between alternatives are relevant in a decision. All other costs and benefits are irrelevant and should be ignored. In particular, sunk costs are irrelevant as are future costs that do not differ between alternatives.

This simple idea was applied in a variety of situations including decisions that involve making or buying a component, adding or dropping a product line, processing a joint product further, and using a constrained resource. This list includes only a small sample of the possible applications of the relevant cost concept. Indeed, any decision involving costs hinges on the proper identification and analysis of the costs that are relevant. We will continue to focus on the concept of relevant costs in the following chapter where long-run investment decisions are considered.

Review Problem: Relevant Costs

Charter Sports Equipment manufactures round, rectangular, and octagonal trampolines. Data on sales and expenses for the past month follow:

		Trampoline		
	Total	Round	Rectangular	Octagonal
Sales	$1,000,000	$140,000	$500,000	$360,000
Less variable expenses	410,000	60,000	200,000	150,000
Contribution margin	590,000	80,000	300,000	210,000
Less fixed expenses:				
Advertising—traceable	216,000	41,000	110,000	65,000
Depreciation of special equipment	95,000	20,000	40,000	35,000
Line supervisors' salaries	19,000	6,000	7,000	6,000
General factory overhead*	200,000	28,000	100,000	72,000
Total fixed expenses	530,000	95,000	257,000	178,000
Net operating income (loss)	$ 60,000	$ (15,000)	$ 43,000	$ 32,000

*A common fixed cost that is allocated on the basis of sales dollars.

Management is concerned about the continued losses shown by the round trampolines and wants a recommendation as to whether or not the line should be discontinued. The special equipment used to produce the trampolines has no resale value. If the round trampoline model is dropped, the two line supervisors assigned to the model would be discharged.

Required:

1. Should production and sale of the round trampolines be discontinued? The company has no other use for the capacity now being used to produce the round trampolines. Show computations to support your answer.
2. Recast the above data in a format that would be more useful to management in assessing the long-run profitability of the various product lines.

Solution to Review Problem

1. No, production and sale of the round trampolines should not be discontinued. Computations to support this answer follow:

Contribution margin lost if the round trampolines are discontinued		$(80,000)
Less fixed costs that can be avoided:		
Advertising—traceable	$41,000	
Line supervisors' salaries	6,000	47,000
Decrease in net operating income for the company as a whole		$(33,000)

The depreciation of the special equipment represents a sunk cost, and therefore it is not relevant to the decision. The general factory overhead is allocated and will presumably continue regardless of whether or not the round trampolines are discontinued; thus, it is not relevant.

2. If management wants a clear picture of the profitability of the segments, the general factory overhead should not be allocated. It is a common cost and therefore should be deducted from the total product-line segment margin, as shown in Chapter 12. A more useful income statement format would be as follows:

		Trampoline		
	Total	Round	Rectangular	Octagonal
Sales	$1,000,000	$140,000	$500,000	$360,000
Less variable expenses	410,000	60,000	200,000	150,000
Contribution margin	590,000	80,000	300,000	210,000
Less traceable fixed expenses:				
Advertising—traceable	216,000	41,000	110,000	65,000
Depreciation of special equipment	95,000	20,000	40,000	35,000
Line supervisors' salaries	19,000	6,000	7,000	6,000
Total traceable fixed expenses	330,000	67,000	157,000	106,000
Product-line segment margin	260,000	$13,000	$143,000	$104,000
Less common fixed expenses	200,000			
Net operating income (loss)	$ 60,000			

Glossary

Avoidable cost A cost that can be eliminated (in whole or in part) by choosing one alternative over another in a decision. This term is synonymous with *relevant cost* and *differential cost.* (p. 602)

Bottleneck A machine or some other part of a process that limits the total output of the entire system. (p. 619)

Constraint A limitation under which a company must operate, such as limited available machine time or raw materials, that restricts the company's ability to satisfy demand. (p. 618)

Differential cost Any cost that differs between alternatives in a decision-making situation. This term is synonymous with *avoidable cost* and *relevant cost.* (p. 603)

Joint costs Costs that are incurred up to the split-off point in a process that produces joint products. (p. 622)

Joint products Two or more items that are produced from a common input. (p. 622)

Make or buy decision A decision concerning whether an item should be produced internally or purchased from an outside supplier. (p. 613)

Relaxing (or elevating) the constraint An action that increases the amount of a constrained resource. (p. 620)

Relevant cost A cost that differs between alternatives in a particular decision. This term is synonymous with *avoidable cost* and *differential cost.* (p. 602)

Sell or process further decision A decision as to whether a joint product should be sold at the split-off point or sold after further processing. (p. 623)

Special order A one-time order that is not considered part of the company's normal ongoing business. (p. 616)

Split-off point That point in the manufacturing process where some or all of the joint products can be recognized as individual products. (p. 622)

Sunk cost Any cost that has already been incurred and that cannot be changed by any decision made now or in the future. (p. 603)

Vertical integration The involvement by a company in more than one of the activities in the entire value chain from development through production, distribution, sales, and after-sales service. (p. 613)

Questions

13–1 What is a *relevant cost?*

13–2 Define the following terms: *incremental cost, opportunity cost,* and *sunk cost.*

13–3 Are variable costs always relevant costs? Explain.

13–4 "Sunk costs are easy to spot—they're simply the fixed costs associated with a decision." Do you agree? Explain.

13–5 "Variable costs and differential costs mean the same thing." Do you agree? Explain.

13–6 "All future costs are relevant in decision making." Do you agree? Why?

13–7 Prentice Company is considering dropping one of its product lines. What costs of the product line would be relevant to this decision? Irrelevant?

13–8 "If a product line is generating a loss, then it should be discontinued." Do you agree? Explain.

13–9 What is the danger in allocating common fixed costs among product lines or other segments of an organization?

13–10 How does opportunity cost enter into the make or buy decision?

13–11 Give at least four examples of possible constraints.

13–12 How will relating product contribution margins to the amount of the constrained resource they consume help a company maximize its profits?

13–13 Define the following terms: *joint products, joint costs,* and *split-off point.*

13–14 From a decision-making point of view, should joint costs be allocated among joint products?

13–15 What guideline should be used in determining whether a joint product should be sold at the split-off point or processed further?

13–16 Airlines sometimes offer reduced rates during certain times of the week to members of a businessperson's family if they accompany him or her on trips. How does the concept of relevant costs enter into the decision by the airline to offer reduced rates of this type?

Exercises

EXERCISE 13–1 Identifying Relevant Costs [LO1]

A number of costs are listed below that may be relevant in decisions faced by the management of Svahn, AB, a Swedish manufacturer of sailing yachts:

	Case 1		Case 2	
Item	Relevant	Not Relevant	Relevant	Not Relevant
a. Sales revenue				
b. Direct materials				
c. Direct labor				
d. Variable manufacturing overhead				
e. Depreciation—Model B100 machine				
f. Book value—Model B100 machine				
g. Disposal value—Model B100 machine				
h. Market value—Model B300 machine (cost)				
i. Fixed manufacturing overhead (general)				
j. Variable selling expense				
k. Fixed selling expense				
l. General administrative overhead				

Required:

Copy the information above onto your answer sheet and place an X in the appropriate column to indicate whether each item is relevant or not relevant in the following situations. Requirement 1 relates to Case 1 above, and requirement 2 relates to Case 2.

1. The company chronically has no idle capacity and the old Model B100 machine is the company's constraint. Management is considering purchasing a Model B300 machine to use in addition to the company's present Model B100 machine. The old Model B100 machine will continue to be used to capacity as before, with the new Model B300 machine being used to expand production. This will increase the company's production and sales. The increase in

volume will be large enough to require increases in fixed selling expenses and in general administrative overhead, but not in the fixed manufacturing overhead.

2. The old Model B100 machine is not the company's constraint, but management is considering replacing it with a new Model B300 machine because of the potential savings in direct materials with the new machine. The Model B100 machine would be sold. This change will have no effect on production or sales, other than some savings in direct materials costs due to less waste.

EXERCISE 13–2 Dropping or Retaining a Segment [LO2]

The Regal Cycle Company manufactures three types of bicycles—a dirt bike, a mountain bike, and a racing bike. Data on sales and expenses for the past quarter follow:

	Total	Dirt Bikes	Mountain Bikes	Racing Bikes
Sales	$300,000	$90,000	$150,000	$60,000
Less variable manufacturing and selling expenses	120,000	27,000	60,000	33,000
Contribution margin	180,000	63,000	90,000	27,000
Less fixed expenses:				
Advertising, traceable	30,000	10,000	14,000	6,000
Depreciation of special equipment	23,000	6,000	9,000	8,000
Salaries of product-line managers	35,000	12,000	13,000	10,000
Allocated common fixed expenses*	60,000	18,000	30,000	12,000
Total fixed expenses	148,000	46,000	66,000	36,000
Net operating income (loss)	$ 32,000	$17,000	$ 24,000	$ (9,000)

*Allocated on the basis of sales dollars.

Management is concerned about the continued losses shown by the racing bikes and wants a recommendation as to whether or not the line should be discontinued. The special equipment used to produce racing bikes has no resale value and does not wear out.

Required:

1. Should production and sale of the racing bikes be discontinued? Explain. Show computations to support your answer.
2. Recast the above data in a format that would be more usable to management in assessing the long-run profitability of the various product lines.

EXERCISE 13–3 Make or Buy a Component [LO3]

Troy Engines, Ltd., manufactures a variety of engines for use in heavy equipment. The company has always produced all of the necessary parts for its engines, including all of the carburetors. An outside supplier has offered to sell one type of carburetor to Troy Engines, Ltd., for a cost of $35 per unit. To evaluate this offer, Troy Engines, Ltd., has gathered the following information relating to its own cost of producing the carburetor internally:

	Per Unit	15,000 Units per Year
Direct materials	$14	$210,000
Direct labor	10	150,000
Variable manufacturing overhead	3	45,000
Fixed manufacturing overhead, traceable	6*	90,000
Fixed manufacturing overhead, allocated	9	135,000
Total cost	$42	$630,000

*One-third supervisory salaries; two-thirds depreciation of special equipment (no resale value).

Required:

1. Assuming that the company has no alternative use for the facilities that are now being used to produce the carburetors, should the outside supplier's offer be accepted? Show all computations.
2. Suppose that if the carburetors were purchased, Troy Engines, Ltd., could use the freed capacity to launch a new product. The segment margin of the new product would be $150,000 per year. Should Troy Engines, Ltd., accept the offer to buy the carburetors for $35 per unit? Show all computations.

EXERCISE 13–4 Evaluating a Special Order [LO4]

Imperial Jewelers is considering a special order for 20 handcrafted gold bracelets to be given as gifts to members of a wedding party. The normal selling price of a gold bracelet is $189.95 and its unit product cost is $149.00 as shown below:

Direct materials	$ 84.00
Direct labor	45.00
Manufacturing overhead	20.00
Unit product cost	$149.00

Most of the manufacturing overhead is fixed and unaffected by variations in how much jewelry is produced in any given period. However, $4.00 of the overhead is variable with respect to the number of bracelets produced. The customer who is interested in the special bracelet order would like special filigree applied to the bracelets. This filigree would require additional materials costing $2.00 per bracelet and would also require acquisition of a special tool costing $250 that would have no other use once the special order is completed. This order would have no effect on the company's regular sales and the order could be fulfilled using the company's existing capacity without affecting any other order.

Required:

What effect would accepting this order have on the company's net operating income if a special price of $169.95 per bracelet is offered for this order? Should the special order be accepted at this price?

EXERCISE 13–5 Utilization of a Constrained Resource [LO5]

Barlow Company manufactures three products: A, B, and C. The selling price, variable costs, and contribution margin for one unit of each product follow:

	Product		
	A	B	C
Selling price	$180	$270	$240
Less variable expenses:			
Direct materials	24	72	32
Other variable expenses	102	90	148
Total variable expenses	126	162	180
Contribution margin	$ 54	$108	$ 60
Contribution margin ratio	30%	40%	25%

The same raw material is used in all three products. Barlow Company has only 5,000 pounds of raw material on hand and will not be able to obtain any more of it for several weeks due to a strike in its supplier's plant. Management is trying to decide which product(s) to concentrate on next week in filling its backlog of orders. The material costs $8 per pound.

Required:

1. Compute the amount of contribution margin that will be obtained per pound of material used in each product.
2. Which orders would you recommend that the company work on next week—the orders for product A, product B, or product C? Show computations.
3. A foreign supplier could furnish Barlow with additional stocks of the raw material at a substantial premium over the usual price. If there is unfilled demand for all three products, what is the highest price that Barlow Company should be willing to pay for an additional pound of materials? Explain.

EXERCISE 13–6 Sell or Process Further [LO6]
Dorsey Company manufactures three products from a common input in a joint processing operation. Joint processing costs up to the split-off point total $350,000 per quarter. The company allocates these costs to the joint products on the basis of their relative sales value at the split-off point. Unit selling prices and total output at the split-off point are as follows:

Product	Selling Price	Quarterly Output
A	$16 per pound	15,000 pounds
B	$8 per pound	20,000 pounds
C	$25 per gallon	4,000 gallons

Each product can be processed further after the split-off point. Additional processing requires no special facilities. The additional processing costs (per quarter) and unit selling prices after further processing are given below:

Product	Additional Processing Costs	Selling Price
A	$63,000	$20 per pound
B	$80,000	$13 per pound
C	$36,000	$32 per gallon

Required:
Which product or products should be sold at the split-off point and which product or products should be processed further? Show computations.

EXERCISE 13–7 Identification of Relevant Costs [LO1]

Hollings Company sells and delivers office furniture in the Rocky Mountain area.

The costs associated with the acquisition and annual operation of a delivery truck are given below:

Insurance	$1,600
Licenses	$250
Taxes (vehicle)	$150
Garage rent for parking (per truck)	$1,200
Depreciation ($9,000 ÷ 5 years)	$1,800*
Gasoline, oil, tires, and repairs	$0.07 per mile

*Based on obsolescence rather than on wear and tear.

Required:
1. Assume that Hollings Company has purchased one truck that has been driven 50,000 miles during the first year. Compute the average cost per mile of owning and operating the truck.
2. At the beginning of the second year, Hollings Company is unsure whether to use the truck or leave it parked in the garage and have all hauling done commercially. (The state requires the payment of vehicle taxes even if the vehicle isn't used.) What costs from the previous list are relevant to this decision? Explain.
3. Assume that the company decides to use the truck during the second year. Near year-end an order is received from a customer over 1,000 miles away. What costs from the previous list are relevant in a decision between using the truck to make the delivery and having the delivery done commercially? Explain.
4. Occasionally, the company could use two trucks at the same time. For this reason, some thought is being given to purchasing a second truck. The total miles driven would be the same as if only one truck were owned. What costs from the previous list are relevant to a decision over whether to purchase the second truck? Explain.

EXERCISE 13–8 Dropping or Retaining a Segment [LO2]
Thalassines Kataskeves, S.A., of Greece makes marine equipment. The company has been experiencing losses on its bilge pump product line for several years. The most recent quarterly contribution format income statement for the bilge pump product line follows:

THALASSINES KATASKEVES, S.A. Income Statement—Bilge Pump For the Quarter Ended March 31		
Sales		€850,000
Less variable expenses:		
Variable manufacturing expenses	€330,000	
Sales commissions	42,000	
Shipping	18,000	
Total variable expenses		390,000
Contribution margin		460,000
Less fixed expenses:		
Advertising	270,000	
Depreciation of equipment (no resale value)	80,000	
General factory overhead	105,000*	
Salary of product-line manager	32,000	
Insurance on inventories	8,000	
Purchasing department expenses	45,000†	
Total fixed expenses		540,000
Net operating loss		€ (80,000)

*Common costs allocated on the basis of machine-hours.
†Common costs allocated on the basis of sales dollars.

The currency in Greece is the euro, denoted here by €. Discontinuing the bilge pump product line would not affect sales of other product lines and would have no effect on the company's total general factory overhead or total Purchasing Department expenses.

Required:

Would you recommend that the bilge pump product line be discontinued? Support your answer with appropriate computations.

EXERCISE 13–9 Make or Buy a Component [LO3]

Han Products manufactures 30,000 units of part S-6 each year for use on its production line. At this level of activity, the cost per unit for part S-6 is as follows:

Direct materials	$ 3.60
Direct labor	10.00
Variable manufacturing overhead	2.40
Fixed manufacturing overhead	9.00
Total cost per part	$25.00

An outside supplier has offered to sell 30,000 units of part S-6 each year to Han Products for $21 per part. If Han Products accepts this offer, the facilities now being used to manufacture part S-6 could be rented to another company at an annual rental of $80,000. However, Han Products has determined that two-thirds of the fixed manufacturing overhead being applied to part S-6 would continue even if part S-6 were purchased from the outside supplier.

Required:

Prepare computations showing how much profits will increase or decrease if the outside supplier's offer is accepted.

EXERCISE 13–10 Special Order [LO4]

Delta Company produces a single product. The cost of producing and selling a single unit of this product at the company's normal activity level of 60,000 units per year is:

Direct materials	$5.10
Direct labor	$3.80
Variable manufacturing overhead	$1.00
Fixed manufacturing overhead	$4.20
Variable selling and administrative expense	$1.50
Fixed selling and administrative expense	$2.40

The normal selling price is $21 per unit. The company's capacity is 75,000 units per year. An order has been received from a mail-order house for 15,000 units at a special price of $14 per unit. This order would not affect regular sales.

Required:

1. If the order is accepted, by how much will annual profits be increased or decreased? (The order will not change the company's total fixed costs.)
2. Assume the company has 1,000 units of this product left over from last year that are vastly inferior to the current model. The units must be sold through regular channels at reduced prices. What unit cost figure is relevant for establishing a minimum selling price for these units? Explain.

EXERCISE 13–11 Utilization of a Constrained Resource [LO5]

Benoit Company produces three products, A, B, and C. Data concerning the three products follow (per unit):

	Product		
	A	B	C
Selling price	$80	$56	$70
Less variable expenses:			
Direct materials	24	15	9
Other variable expenses	24	27	40
Total variable expenses	48	42	49
Contribution margin	$32	$14	$21
Contribution margin ratio	40%	25%	30%

Demand for the company's products is very strong, with far more orders each month than the company has raw materials available to produce. The same material is used in each product. The material costs $3 per pound with a maximum of 5,000 pounds available each month.

Required:

Which orders would you advise the company to accept first, those for A, for B, or for C? Which orders second? Third?

EXERCISE 13–12 Sell or Process Further [LO6]

Wexpro, Inc., produces several products from processing 1 ton of clypton, a rare mineral. Material and processing costs total $60,000 per ton, one-fourth of which is allocated to product X. Seven thousand units of product X are produced from each ton of clypton. The units can either be sold at the split-off point for $9 each, or processed further at a total cost of $9,500 and then sold for $12 each.

Required:

Should product X be processed further or sold at the split-off point?

EXERCISE 13–13 Identification of Relevant Costs [LO1]

Bill has just returned from a duck hunting trip. He has brought home eight ducks. Bill's friend, John, disapproves of duck hunting, and to discourage Bill from further hunting, John has presented him with the following cost estimate per duck:

Camper and equipment:	
Cost, $12,000; usable for eight seasons; 10 hunting trips per season	$150
Travel expense (pickup truck):	
100 miles at $0.31 per mile (gas, oil, and tires—$0.21 per mile; depreciation and insurance—$0.10 per mile)	31
Shotgun shells (two boxes)	20
Boat:	
Cost, $2,320, usable for eight seasons; 10 hunting trips per season	29
Hunting license:	
Cost, $30 for the season; 10 hunting trips per season	3
Money lost playing poker:	
Loss, $24 (Bill plays poker every weekend)	24
Bottle of whiskey:	
Cost, $15 (used to ward off the cold)	15
Total cost	$272
Cost per duck ($272 ÷ 8 ducks)	$ 34

Required:

1. Assuming that the duck hunting trip Bill has just completed is typical, what costs are relevant to a decision as to whether Bill should go duck hunting again this season?
2. Suppose that Bill gets lucky on his next hunting trip and shoots 10 ducks in the amount of time it took him to shoot 8 ducks on his last trip. How much would it have cost him to shoot the last two ducks? Explain.
3. Which costs are relevant in a decision of whether Bill should give up hunting? Explain.

EXERCISE 13–14 Dropping or Retaining a Segment [LO2]

Bed & Bath, a retailing company, has two departments, Hardware and Linens. A recent monthly contribution format income statement for the company follows:

		Department	
	Total	Hardware	Linens
Sales	$4,000,000	$3,000,000	$1,000,000
Less variable expenses	1,300,000	900,000	400,000
Contribution margin	2,700,000	2,100,000	600,000
Less fixed expenses	2,200,000	1,400,000	800,000
Net operating income (loss)	$ 500,000	$ 700,000	$ (200,000)

A study indicates that $340,000 of the fixed expenses being charged to Linens are sunk costs or allocated costs that will continue even if the Linens Department is dropped. In addition, the elimination of the Linens Department will result in a 10% decrease in the sales of the Hardware Department.

Required:

If the Linens Department is dropped, what will be the effect on the net operating income of the company as a whole?

EXERCISE 13–15 Make or Buy a Component [LO3]

For many years Futura Company has purchased the starters that it installs in its standard line of farm tractors. Due to a reduction in output, the company has idle capacity that could be used to produce the starters. The chief engineer has recommended against this move, however, pointing out that the cost to produce the starters would be greater than the current $8.40 per unit purchase price:

	Per Unit	Total
Direct materials	$3.10	
Direct labor	2.70	
Supervision	1.50	$60,000
Depreciation	1.00	40,000
Variable manufacturing overhead	0.60	
Rent	0.30	12,000
Total production cost	$9.20	

A supervisor would have to be hired to oversee production of the starters. However, the company has sufficient idle tools and machinery that no new equipment would have to be purchased. The rent charge above is based on space utilized in the plant. The total rent on the plant is $80,000 per period. Depreciation is due to obsolescence rather than wear and tear.

Required:

Prepare computations showing how much profits will increase or decrease as a result of making the starters.

Problems

PROBLEM 13–16 Dropping or Retaining a Flight [LO2]

Profits have been decreasing for several years at Pegasus Airlines. In an effort to improve the company's performance, consideration is being given to dropping several flights that appear to be unprofitable.

A typical income statement for one such flight (flight 482) is given below (per flight):

Ticket revenue (175 seats × 40% occupancy × $200 ticket price)	$14,000	100.0%
Less variable expenses ($15 per person)	1,050	7.5
Contribution margin	12,950	92.5%
Less flight expenses:		
Salaries, flight crew	1,800	
Flight promotion	750	
Depreciation of aircraft	1,550	
Fuel for aircraft	5,800	
Liability insurance	4,200	
Salaries, flight assistants	1,500	
Baggage loading and flight preparation	1,700	
Overnight costs for flight crew and assistants at destination	300	
Total flight expenses	17,600	
Net operating loss	$ (4,650)	

The following additional information is available about flight 482:

a. Members of the flight crew are paid fixed annual salaries, whereas the flight assistants are paid by the flight.

b. One-third of the liability insurance is a special charge assessed against flight 482 because in the opinion of the insurance company, the destination of the flight is in a "high-risk" area. The remaining two-thirds would be unaffected by a decision to drop flight 482.

c. The baggage loading and flight preparation expense is an allocation of ground crews' salaries and depreciation of ground equipment. Dropping flight 482 would have no effect on the company's total baggage loading and flight preparation expenses.

d. If flight 482 is dropped, Pegasus Airlines has no authorization at present to replace it with another flight.

e. Aircraft depreciation is due entirely to obsolescence. Depreciation due to wear and tear is negligible.

f. Dropping flight 482 would not allow Pegasus Airlines to reduce the number of aircraft in its fleet or the number of flight crew on its payroll.

Required:

1. Prepare an analysis showing what impact dropping flight 482 would have on the airline's profits.
2. The airline's scheduling officer has been criticized because only about 50% of the seats on Pegasus' flights are being filled compared to an industry average of 60%. The scheduling officer has explained that Pegasus' average seat occupancy could be improved considerably by eliminating about 10% of its flights, but that doing so would reduce profits. Explain how this could happen.

PROBLEM 13–17 Sell or Process Further [LO6]

(Prepared from a situation suggested by Professor John W. Hardy.) Lone Star Meat Packers is a major processor of beef and other meat products. The company has a large amount of T-bone steak on hand, and it is trying to decide whether to sell the T-bone steaks as they are initially cut or to process them further into filet mignon and the New York cut.

If the T-bone steaks are sold as initially cut, the company figures that a 1-pound T-bone steak would yield the following profit:

Selling price ($2.25 per pound)	$2.25
Less joint costs incurred up to the split-off point where T-bone steak can be identified as a separate product	1.80
Profit per pound	$0.45

As mentioned above, instead of being sold as initially cut, the T-bone steaks could be further processed into filet mignon and New York cut steaks. Cutting one side of a T-bone steak provides the filet mignon, and cutting the other side provides the New York cut. One 16-ounce T-bone steak cut in this way will yield one 6-ounce filet mignon and one 8-ounce New York cut; the remaining ounces are waste. The cost of processing the T-bone steaks into these cuts is $0.25 per pound. The filet mignon can be sold for $4.00 per pound, and the New York cut can be sold for $2.80 per pound.

Required:

1. Determine the profit per pound from processing the T-bone steaks into filet mignon and New York cut steaks.
2. Would you recommend that the T-bone steaks be sold as initially cut or processed further? Why?

PROBLEM 13–18 Close or Retain a Store [LO2]

Superior Markets, Inc., operates three stores in a large metropolitan area. A segmented absorption costing income statement for the company for the last quarter is given below:

SUPERIOR MARKETS, INC.
Income Statement
For the Quarter Ended September 30

	Total	North Store	South Store	East Store
Sales	$3,000,000	$720,000	$1,200,000	$1,080,000
Cost of goods sold	1,657,200	403,200	660,000	594,000
Gross margin	1,342,800	316,800	540,000	486,000
Operating expenses:				
Selling expenses	817,000	231,400	315,000	270,600
Administrative expenses	383,000	106,000	150,900	126,100
Total expenses	1,200,000	337,400	465,900	396,700
Net operating income (loss)	$ 142,800	$(20,600)	$ 74,100	$ 89,300

The North Store has consistently shown losses over the past two years. For this reason, management is giving consideration to closing the store. The company has retained you to make a recommendation as to whether the store should be closed or kept open. The following additional information is available for your use:

a. The breakdown of the selling and administrative expenses is as follows:

	Total	North Store	South Store	East Store
Selling expenses:				
Sales salaries	$239,000	$ 70,000	$ 89,000	$ 80,000
Direct advertising	187,000	51,000	72,000	64,000
General advertising*	45,000	10,800	18,000	16,200
Store rent	300,000	85,000	120,000	95,000
Depreciation of store fixtures	16,000	4,600	6,000	5,400
Delivery salaries	21,000	7,000	7,000	7,000
Depreciation of delivery equipment	9,000	3,000	3,000	3,000
Total selling expenses	$817,000	$231,400	$315,000	$270,600

*Allocated on the basis of sales dollars.

	Total	North Store	South Store	East Store
Administrative expenses:				
Store management salaries	$ 70,000	$ 21,000	$ 30,000	$ 19,000
General office salaries*	50,000	12,000	20,000	18,000
Insurance on fixtures and inventory	25,000	7,500	9,000	8,500
Utilities	106,000	31,000	40,000	35,000
Employment taxes	57,000	16,500	21,900	18,600
General office—other*	75,000	18,000	30,000	27,000
Total administrative expenses	$383,000	$106,000	$150,900	$126,100

*Allocated on the basis of sales dollars.

b. The lease on the building housing the North Store can be broken with no penalty.
c. The fixtures being used in the North Store would be transferred to the other two stores if the North Store were closed.
d. The general manager of the North Store would be retained and transferred to another position in the company if the North Store were closed. She would be filling a position that would otherwise be filled by hiring a new employee at a salary of $11,000 per quarter. The general manager of the North Store would be retained at her normal salary of $12,000 per quarter. All other employees in the store would be discharged.
e. The company has one delivery crew that serves all three stores. One delivery person could be discharged if the North Store were closed. This person's salary is $4,000 per quarter. The delivery equipment would be distributed to the other stores. The equipment does not wear out through use, but does eventually become obsolete.
f. The company's employment taxes are 15% of salaries.
g. One-third of the insurance in the North Store is on the store's fixtures.
h. The "General office salaries" and "General office—other" relate to the overall management of Superior Markets, Inc. If the North Store were closed, one person in the general office could be discharged because of the decrease in overall workload. This person's compensation is $6,000 per quarter.

Required:

1. Prepare a schedule showing the change in revenues and expenses and the impact on the company's overall net operating income that would result if the North Store were closed.
2. Assuming that the store space can't be subleased, what recommendation would you make to the management of Superior Markets, Inc.?
3. Disregard requirement 2. Assume that if the North Store were closed, at least one-fourth of its sales would transfer to the East Store, due to strong customer loyalty to Superior Markets. The East Store has ample capacity to handle the increased sales. You may assume that the increased sales in the East Store would yield the same gross margin percentage as present sales in that store. What effect would these factors have on your recommendation concerning the North Store? Show all computations to support your answer.

PROBLEM 13–19 Make or Buy Analysis [LO3]

"In my opinion, we ought to stop making our own drums and accept that outside supplier's offer," said Wim Niewindt, managing director of Antilles Refining, N.V., of Aruba. "At a price of 18 florins per drum, we would be paying 5 florins less than it costs us to manufacture the drums in our own plant. (The currency in Aruba is the florin, denoted below by fl.) Since we use 60,000 drums a year, that would be an annual cost savings of 300,000 florins." Antilles Refining's present cost to manufacture one drum is given below (based on 60,000 drums per year):

Direct materials	fl10.35
Direct labor	6.00
Variable overhead	1.50
Fixed overhead (fl2.80 general company overhead, fl1.60 depreciation and, fl0.75 supervision)	5.15
Total cost per drum	fl23.00

A decision about whether to make or buy the drums is especially important at this time since the equipment being used to make the drums is completely worn out and must be replaced. The choices facing the company are:

Alternative 1: Rent new equipment and continue to make the drums. The equipment would be rented for fl135,000 per year.

Alternative 2: Purchase the drums from an outside supplier at fl18 per drum.

The new equipment would be more efficient than the equipment that Antilles Refining has been using and, according to the manufacturer, would reduce direct labor and variable overhead costs by 30%. The old equipment has no resale value. Supervision cost (fl45,000 per year) and direct materials cost per drum would not be affected by the new equipment. The new equipment's capacity would be 90,000 drums per year.

The company's total general company overhead would be unaffected by this decision.

Required:

1. To assist the managing director in making a decision, prepare an analysis showing the total cost and the cost per drum for each of the two alternatives given above. Assume that 60,000 drums are needed each year. Which course of action would you recommend to the managing director?
2. Would your recommendation in (1) above be the same if the company's needs were: (a) 75,000 drums per year or (b) 90,000 drums per year? Show computations to support your answer, with costs presented on both a total and a per unit basis.
3. What other factors would you recommend that the company consider before making a decision?

PROBLEM 13–20 Relevant Cost Analysis in a Variety of Situations [LO2, LO3, LO4]

Andretti Company has a single product called a Dak. The company normally produces and sells 60,000 Daks each year at a selling price of $32 per unit. The company's unit costs at this level of activity are given below:

Direct materials	$10.00	
Direct labor	4.50	
Variable manufacturing overhead	2.30	
Fixed manufacturing overhead	5.00	($300,000 total)
Variable selling expenses	1.20	
Fixed selling expenses	3.50	($210,000 total)
Total cost per unit	$26.50	

A number of questions relating to the production and sale of Daks follow. Each question is independent.

Required:

1. Assume that Andretti Company has sufficient capacity to produce 90,000 Daks each year without any increase in fixed manufacturing overhead costs. The company could increase its sales by 25% above the present 60,000 units each year if it were willing to increase the fixed selling expenses by $80,000. Would the increased fixed selling expenses be justified?
2. Assume again that Andretti Company has sufficient capacity to produce 90,000 Daks each year. A customer in a foreign market wants to purchase 20,000 Daks. Import duties on the Daks would be $1.70 per unit, and costs for permits and licenses would be $9,000. The only selling costs that would be associated with the order would be $3.20 per unit shipping cost. Compute the per unit break-even price on this order.
3. The company has 1,000 Daks on hand that have some irregularities and are therefore considered to be "seconds." Due to the irregularities, it will be impossible to sell these units at the normal price through regular distribution channels. What unit cost figure is relevant for setting a minimum selling price? Explain.
4. Due to a strike in its supplier's plant, Andretti Company is unable to purchase more material for the production of Daks. The strike is expected to last for two months. Andretti Company has enough material on hand to operate at 30% of normal levels for the two-month period. As an alternative, Andretti could close its plant down entirely for the two months. If the plant were closed, fixed manufacturing overhead costs would continue at 60% of their normal level during the two-month period and the fixed selling expenses would be reduced by 20%. What would be the impact on profits of closing the plant for the two-month period?
5. An outside manufacturer has offered to produce Daks and ship them directly to Andretti's customers. If Andretti Company accepts this offer, the facilities that it uses to produce Daks would be idle; however, fixed manufacturing overhead costs would be reduced by 75%. Since the outside manufacturer would pay for all shipping costs, the variable selling expenses would be only two-thirds of their present amount. Compute the unit cost that is relevant for comparison to the price quoted by the outside manufacturer.

PROBLEM 13–21 Shutting Down or Continuing to Operate a Plant [LO2]

(Note: This type of decision is similar to dropping a product line.)

Birch Company normally produces and sells 30,000 units of RG-6 each month. RG-6 is a small electrical relay used as a component part in the automotive industry. The selling price is $22 per unit, variable costs are $14 per unit, fixed manufacturing overhead costs total $150,000 per month, and fixed selling costs total $30,000 per month.

Employment-contract strikes in the companies that purchase the bulk of the RG-6 units have caused Birch Company's sales to temporarily drop to only 8,000 units per month. Birch Company estimates that the strikes will last for two months, after which time sales of RG-6 should return to normal. Due to the current low level of sales, Birch Company is thinking about closing down its own plant during the strike, which would reduce its fixed manufacturing overhead costs by $45,000 per month and its fixed selling costs by 10%. Start-up costs at the end of the shutdown period would total $8,000. Since Birch Company uses just-in-time (JIT) production methods, no inventories are on hand.

Required:

1. Assuming that the strikes continue for two months, would you recommend that Birch Company close its own plant? Explain. Show computations in good form.
2. At what level of sales (in units) for the two-month period should Birch Company be indifferent between closing the plant or keeping it open? Show computations. (Hint: This is a type of break-even analysis, except that the fixed cost portion of your break-even computation should include only those fixed costs that are relevant [i.e., avoidable] over the two-month period.)

PROBLEM 13–22 Make or Buy Decision [LO3]

Silven Industries, which manufactures and sells a highly successful line of summer lotions and insect repellents, has decided to diversify in order to stabilize sales throughout the year. A natural area for the company to consider is the production of winter lotions and creams to prevent dry and chapped skin.

After considerable research, a winter products line has been developed. However, Silven's president has decided to introduce only one of the new products for this coming winter. If the product is a success, further expansion in future years will be initiated.

The product selected (called Chap-Off) is a lip balm that will be sold in a lipstick-type tube. The product will be sold to wholesalers in boxes of 24 tubes for $8 per box. Because of excess capacity, no additional fixed manufacturing overhead costs will be incurred to produce the product. However, a $90,000 charge for fixed manufacturing overhead will be absorbed by the product under the company's absorption costing system.

Using the estimated sales and production of 100,000 boxes of Chap-Off, the Accounting Department has developed the following cost per box:

Direct material	$3.60
Direct labor	2.00
Manufacturing overhead	1.40
Total cost	$7.00

The costs above include costs for producing both the lip balm and the tube that contains it. As an alternative to making the tubes, Silven has approached a supplier to discuss the possibility of purchasing the tubes for Chap-Off. The purchase price of the empty tubes from the supplier would be $1.35 per box of 24 tubes. If Silven Industries accepts the purchase proposal, direct labor and variable manufacturing overhead costs per box of Chap-Off would be reduced by 10% and direct materials costs would be reduced by 25%.

Required:

1. Should Silven Industries make or buy the tubes? Show calculations to support your answer.
2. What would be the maximum purchase price acceptable to Silven Industries? Explain.
3. Instead of sales of 100,000 boxes, revised estimates show a sales volume of 120,000 boxes. At this new volume, additional equipment must be acquired to manufacture the tubes at an annual rental of $40,000. Assuming that the outside supplier will not accept an order for less than 100,000 boxes, should Silven Industries make or buy the tubes? Show computations to support your answer.
4. Refer to the data in (3) above. Assume that the outside supplier will accept an order of any size for the tubes at $1.35 per box. How, if at all, would this change your answer? Show computations.
5. What qualitative factors should Silven Industries consider in determining whether they should make or buy the tubes?

(CMA, adapted)

PROBLEM 13–23 Accept or Reject a Special Order [LO4]

Polaski Company manufactures and sells a single product called a Ret. Operating at capacity, the company can produce and sell 30,000 Rets per year. Costs associated with this level of production and sales are given below:

	Unit	Total
Direct materials	$15	$ 450,000
Direct labor	8	240,000
Variable manufacturing overhead	3	90,000
Fixed manufacturing overhead	9	270,000
Variable selling expense	4	120,000
Fixed selling expense	6	180,000
Total cost	$45	$1,350,000

The Rets normally sell for $50 each. Fixed manufacturing overhead is constant at $270,000 per year within the range of 25,000 through 30,000 Rets per year.

Required:

1. Assume that due to a recession, Polaski Company expects to sell only 25,000 Rets through regular channels next year. A large retail chain has offered to purchase 5,000 Rets if Polaski is willing to accept a 16% discount off the regular price. There would be no sales commissions on this order; thus, variable selling expenses would be slashed by 75%. However, Polaski Company would have to purchase a special machine to engrave the retail chain's name on the 5,000 units. This machine would cost $10,000. Polaski Company has no assurance that the retail chain will purchase additional units in the future. Determine the impact on profits next year if this special order is accepted.
2. Refer to the original data. Assume again that Polaski Company expects to sell only 25,000 Rets through regular channels next year. The U.S. Army would like to make a one-time-only purchase of 5,000 Rets. The Army would pay a fixed fee of $1.80 per Ret, and it would reimburse Polaski Company for all costs of production (variable and fixed) associated with the units. Since the army would pick up the Rets with its own trucks, there would be no variable selling expenses associated with this order. If Polaski Company accepts the order, by how much will profits increase or decrease for the year?
3. Assume the same situation as that described in (2) above, except that the company expects to sell 30,000 Rets through regular channels next year. Thus, accepting the U.S. Army's order would require giving up regular sales of 5,000 Rets. If the Army's order is accepted, by how much will profits increase or decrease from what they would be if the 5,000 Rets were sold through regular channels?

PROBLEM 13–24 Utilization of a Constrained Resource [LO5]

The Walton Toy Company manufactures a line of dolls and a doll dress sewing kit. Demand for the dolls is increasing, and management requests assistance from you in determining an economical sales and production mix for the coming year. The company has provided the following data:

Microsoft Excel - Problem 13-24 screen capture.xls

	A	B	C	D	E	F
1	*Product*	*Demand Next Year (units)*	*Selling Price per Unit*	*Direct Materials*	*Direct Labor*	
2	Debbie	50,000	$13.50	$4.30	$3.20	
3	Trish	42,000	$5.50	$1.10	$2.00	
4	Sarah	35,000	$21.00	$6.44	$5.60	
5	Mike	40,000	$10.00	$2.00	$4.00	
6	Sewing kit	325,000	$8.00	$3.20	$1.60	
7						

The following additional information is available:

a. The company's plant has a capacity of 130,000 direct labor-hours per year on a single-shift basis. The company's present employees and equipment can produce all five products.
b. The direct labor rate of $8 per hour is expected to remain unchanged during the coming year.
c. Fixed costs total $520,000 per year. Variable overhead costs are $2 per direct labor-hour.
d. All of the company's nonmanufacturing costs are fixed.
e. The company's finished goods inventory is negligible and can be ignored.

Required:

1. Determine the contribution margin per direct labor-hour expended on each product.
2. Prepare a schedule showing the total direct labor-hours that will be required to produce the units estimated to be sold during the coming year.
3. Examine the data you have computed in (1) and (2) above. How would you allocate the 130,000 direct labor hours of capacity to Walton Toy Company's various products?
4. What is the highest price, in terms of a rate per hour, that Walton Toy Company would be willing to pay for additional capacity (that is, for added direct labor time)?
5. Assume again that the company does not want to reduce sales of any product. Identify ways in which the company could obtain the additional output.

(CPA, adapted)

PROBLEM 13–25 Sell or Process Further [LO6]

Come-Clean Corporation produces a variety of cleaning compounds and solutions for both industrial and household use. While most of its products are processed independently, a few are related, such as the company's Grit 337 and its Sparkle silver polish.

Grit 337 is a coarse cleaning powder with many industrial uses. It costs $1.60 a pound to make, and it has a selling price of $2.00 a pound. A small portion of the annual production of Grit 337 is retained in the factory for further processing. It is combined with several other ingredients to form a paste that is marketed as Sparkle silver polish. The silver polish sells for $4.00 per jar.

This further processing requires one-fourth pound of Grit 337 per jar of silver polish. The additional direct costs involved in the processing of a jar of silver polish are:

Other ingredients	$0.65
Direct labor	1.48
Total direct cost	$2.13

Overhead costs associated with the processing of the silver polish are:

Variable manufacturing overhead cost	25% of direct labor cost
Fixed manufacturing overhead cost (per month):	
Production supervisor	$3,000
Depreciation of mixing equipment	$1,400

The production supervisor has no duties other than to oversee production of the silver polish. The mixing equipment is special-purpose equipment acquired specifically to produce the silver polish. Its resale value is negligible and it does not wear out through use.

Direct labor is a variable cost at Come-Clean Corporation.

Advertising costs for the silver polish total $4,000 per month. Variable selling costs associated with the silver polish are 7.5% of sales.

Due to a recent decline in the demand for silver polish, the company is wondering whether its continued production is advisable. The sales manager feels that it would be more profitable to sell all of the Grit 337 as a cleaning powder.

Required:

1. What is the incremental contribution margin per jar from further processing of Grit 337 into silver polish?
2. What is the minimum number of jars of silver polish that must be sold each month to justify the continued processing of Grit 337 into silver polish? Explain. Show all computations in good form.

(CMA, adapted)

PROBLEM 13–26 Dropping or Retaining a Product [LO2]

Tracey Douglas is the owner and managing director of Heritage Garden Furniture, Ltd., a South African company that makes museum-quality reproductions of antique outdoor furniture. Ms. Douglas would like advice concerning the advisability of eliminating the model C3 lawnchair. These lawnchairs have been among the company's best-selling products, but they seem to be unprofitable.

A condensed absorption costing income statement for the company and for the model C3 lawnchair for the quarter ended June 30 follows:

	All Products	Model C3 Lawnchair
Sales	R2,900,000	R300,000
Cost of goods sold:		
Direct materials	759,000	122,000
Direct labor	680,000	72,000
Fringe benefits (20% of direct labor)	136,000	14,400
Variable manufacturing overhead	28,000	3,600
Building rent and maintenance	30,000	4,000
Depreciation	75,000	19,100
Total cost of goods sold	1,708,000	235,100
Gross margin	1,192,000	64,900
Selling and administrative expenses:		
Product managers' salaries	75,000	10,000
Sales commissions (5% of sales)	145,000	15,000
Fringe benefits (20% of salaries and commissions)	44,000	5,000
Shipping	120,000	10,000
General administrative expenses	464,000	48,000
Total selling and administrative expenses	848,000	88,000
Net operating income (loss)	R 344,000	R (23,100)

The currency in South Africa is the rand, denoted here by R.

The following additional data have been supplied by the company:

a. Direct labor is a variable cost.
b. All of the company's products are manufactured in the same facility and use the same equipment. Building rent and maintenance and depreciation are allocated to products using various bases. The equipment does not wear out through use; it eventually becomes obsolete.
c. There is ample capacity to fill all orders.
d. Dropping the model C3 lawnchair would have no effect on sales of other product lines.
e. Work in process and finished goods inventories are insignificant.
f. Shipping costs are traced directly to products.
g. General administrative expenses are allocated to products on the basis of sales dollars. There would be no effect on the total general administrative expenses if the model C3 lawnchair were dropped.
h. If the model C3 lawnchair were dropped, the product manager would be laid off.

Required:

1. Given the current level of sales, would you recommend that the model C3 lawnchair be dropped? Prepare appropriate computations to support your answer.
2. What would sales of the model C3 lawnchair have to be, at minimum, in order to justify retaining the product? Explain. (Hint: Set this up as a break-even problem but include only the relevant costs.)

Cases

CASE 13–27 Ethics and the Manager; Shut Down or Continue Operations [LO2]

Haley Romeros had just been appointed vice president of the Rocky Mountain Region of the Bank Services Corporation (BSC). The company provides check processing services for small banks. The banks send checks presented for deposit or payment to BSC, which records the data on each check in a computerized database. BSC then sends the data electronically to the nearest Federal Reserve Bank check-clearing center where the appropriate transfers of funds are made between banks. The Rocky Mountain Region has three check processing centers, which are located in Billings, Montana; Great Falls, Montana; and Clayton, Idaho. Prior to her promotion to vice president, Ms. Romeros had been the manager of a check processing center in New Jersey.

Immediately upon assuming her new position, Ms. Romeros requested a complete financial report for the just-ended fiscal year from the region's controller, John Littlebear. Ms. Romeros specified that the financial report should follow the standardized format required by corporate headquarters for all regional performance reports. That report follows:

BANK SERVICES CORPORATION (BSC)
Rocky Mountain Region
Financial Performance

		Check Processing Centers		
	Total	Billings	Great Falls	Clayton
Sales	$50,000,000	$20,000,000	$18,000,000	$12,000,000
Operating expenses:				
Direct labor	32,000,000	12,500,000	11,000,000	8,500,000
Variable overhead	850,000	350,000	310,000	190,000
Equipment depreciation	3,900,000	1,300,000	1,400,000	1,200,000
Facility expense	2,800,000	900,000	800,000	1,100,000
Local administrative expense*	450,000	140,000	160,000	150,000
Regional administrative expense†	1,500,000	600,000	540,000	360,000
Corporate administrative expense‡	4,750,000	1,900,000	1,710,000	1,140,000
Total operating expense	46,250,000	17,690,000	15,920,000	12,640,000
Net operating income	$ 3,750,000	$ 2,310,000	$ 2,080,000	$ (640,000)

*Local administrative expenses are the administrative expenses incurred at the check processing centers.
†Regional administrative expenses are allocated to the check processing centers based on sales.
‡Corporate administrative expenses are charged to segments of the company such as the Rocky Mountain Region and the check processing centers at the rate of 9.5% of their sales.

Upon seeing this report, Ms. Romeros summoned John Littlebear for an explanation.

Romeros: What's the story on Clayton? It didn't have a loss the previous year did it?

Littlebear: No, the Clayton facility has had a nice profit every year since it was opened six years ago, but Clayton lost a big contract this year.

Romeros: Why?

Littlebear: One of our national competitors entered the local market and bid very aggressively on the contract. We couldn't afford to meet the bid. Clayton's costs—particularly their facility expenses—are just too high. When Clayton lost the contract, we had to lay off a lot of employees, but we could not reduce the fixed costs of the Clayton facility.

Romeros: Why is Clayton's facility expense so high? It's a smaller facility than either Billings or Great Falls and yet its facility expense is higher.

Littlebear: The problem is that we are able to rent suitable facilities very cheaply at Billings and Great Falls. No such facilities were available at Clayton; we had them built. Unfortunately, there were big cost overruns. The contractor we hired was inexperienced at this kind of work and in fact went bankrupt before the project was completed. After hiring another contractor to finish the work, we were way over budget. The large depreciation charges on the facility didn't matter at first because we didn't have much competition at the time and could charge premium prices.

Romeros: Well we can't do that anymore. The Clayton facility will obviously have to be shut down. Its business can be shifted to the other two check processing centers in the region.

Littlebear: I would advise against that. The $1,200,000 in depreciation at the Clayton facility is misleading. That facility should last indefinitely with proper maintenance. And it has no resale value; there is no other commercial activity around Clayton.

Romeros: What about the other costs at Clayton?

Littlebear: If we shifted Clayton's business over to the other two processing centers in the region, we wouldn't save anything on direct labor or variable overhead costs. We might save $90,000 or so in local administrative expense, but we would not save any regional administrative expense and corporate headquarters would still charge us 9.5% of our sales as corporate administrative expense.

In addition, we would have to rent more space in Billings and Great Falls in order to handle the work transferred from Clayton; that would probably cost us at least $600,000 a year. And don't forget that it will cost us something to move the equipment from Clayton to Billings and Great Falls. And the move will disrupt service to customers.

Romeros: I understand all of that, but a money-losing processing center on my performance report is completely unacceptable.

Littlebear: And if you shut down Clayton, you are going to throw some loyal employees out of work.

Romeros: That's unfortunate, but we have to face hard business realities.

Littlebear: And you would have to write off the investment in the facilities at Clayton.

Romeros: I can explain a write-off to corporate headquarters; hiring an inexperienced contractor to build the Clayton facility was my predecessor's mistake. But they'll have my head at headquarters if I show operating losses every year at one of my processing centers. Clayton has to go. At the next corporate board meeting, I am going to recommend that the Clayton facility be closed.

Required:

1. From the standpoint of the company as a whole, should the Clayton processing center be shut down and its work redistributed to other processing centers in the region? Explain.
2. Do you think Haley Romeros's decision to shut down the Clayton facility is ethical? Explain.
3. What influence should the depreciation on the facilities at Clayton have on prices charged by Clayton for its services?

CASE 13–28 Plant Closing Decision [LO1, LO2]

QualSupport Corporation manufactures seats for automobiles, vans, trucks, and various recreational vehicles. The company has a number of plants around the world, including the Denver Cover Plant, which makes seat covers.

Ted Vosilo is the plant manager of the Denver Cover Plant, but also serves as the regional production manager for the company. His budget as the regional manager is charged to the Denver Cover Plant.

Vosilo has just heard that QualSupport has received a bid from an outside vendor to supply the equivalent of the entire annual output of the Denver Cover Plant for $35 million. Vosilo was astonished at the low outside bid because the budget for the Denver Cover Plant's operating costs for the upcoming year was set at $52 million. If this bid is accepted, the Denver Cover Plant will be closed down.

The budget for Denver Cover's operating costs for the coming year is presented below. Additional facts regarding the plant's operations are as follows:

a. Due to Denver Cover's commitment to use high-quality fabrics in all of its products, the Purchasing Department was instructed to place blanket purchase orders with major suppliers to ensure the receipt of sufficient materials for the coming year. If these orders are canceled as a consequence of the plant closing, termination charges would amount to 20% of the cost of direct materials.
b. Approximately 400 plant employees will lose their jobs if the plant is closed. This includes all of the direct laborers and supervisors as well as the plumbers, electricians, and other skilled workers classified as indirect plant workers. Some would be able to find new jobs while many others would have difficulty. All employees would have difficulty matching Denver Cover's base pay of $18.80 per hour, which is the highest in the area. A clause in Denver Cover's contract with the union may help some employees; the company must provide employment assistance to its former employees for 12 months after a plant closing. The estimated cost to administer this service would be $1.5 million for the year.
c. Some employees would probably choose early retirement because QualSupport has an excellent pension plan. In fact, $3 million of the annual pension expense would continue whether Denver Cover is open or not.
d. Vosilo and his staff would not be affected by the closing of Denver Cover. They would still be responsible for administering three other area plants.
e. If the Denver Cover Plant were closed, the company would realize about $3.2 million salvage value for the equipment and building. If the plant remains open, there are no plans to make any significant investments in new equipment or buildings. The old equipment is adequate and should last indefinitely.

DENVER COVER PLANT Annual Budget for Operating Costs		
Materials		$14,000,000
Labor:		
Direct	$13,100,000	
Supervision	900,000	
Indirect plant	4,000,000	18,000,000
Overhead:		
Depreciation—equipment	3,200,000	
Depreciation—building	7,000,000	
Pension expense	5,000,000	
Plant manager and staff	800,000	
Corporate allocation	4,000,000	20,000,000
Total budgeted costs		$52,000,000

Required:

1. Without regard to costs, identify the advantages to QualSupport Corporation of continuing to obtain covers from its own Denver Cover Plant.
2. QualSupport Corporation plans to prepare a financial analysis that will be used in deciding whether or not to close the Denver Cover Plant. Management has asked you to identify:
   a. The annual budgeted costs that are relevant to the decision regarding closing the plant (show the dollar amounts).
   b. The annual budgeted costs that are *not* relevant to the decision regarding closing the plant and explain why they are not relevant (again show the dollar amounts).
   c. Any nonrecurring costs that would arise due to the closing of the plant, and explain how they would affect the decision (again show any dollar amounts).
3. Looking at the data you have prepared in (2) above, should the plant be closed? Show computations and explain your answer.
4. Identify any revenues or costs not specifically mentioned in the problem that QualSupport should consider before making a decision.

(CMA, adapted)

CASE 13–29 Decentralization and Relevant Costs [LO4]

Uberin Corporation consists of three decentralized divisions—Grathin Division, Able Division, and Facet Division. The president of Uberin has given the managers of the three divisions the authority to decide whether they will sell to outside customers on the intermediate market or sell to other divisions within the company. The divisions are autonomous in that each divisional manager has power to set selling prices to outside customers and to set transfer prices to other divisions. (A transfer price is a price one division charges another division of the same company for a product or service it supplies to that division.) Divisional managers are evaluated and compensated on the basis of their divisions' profits.

The manager of the Able Division is considering two alternative orders. Data on the orders are provided below:

a. The Facet Division needs 2,000 motors that can be supplied by the Able Division at a transfer price of $1,600 per motor. To manufacture these motors, Able would purchase component parts from the Grathin Division at a transfer price of $400 per part. (Each motor would require one part.) Grathin would incur variable costs for these parts of $200 each. In addition, each part would require 2.5 hours of machine time at the Grathin Division's general fixed overhead rate of $38 per hour. Able Division would then further process these parts, incurring variable costs of $450 per motor. The motors would require 5 hours of machine time each in Able's plant at its general fixed overhead rate of $23 per hour.

   If the Facet Division can't obtain the motors from the Able Division, it will purchase the motors from Waverly Corporation, which has offered to supply the same motors to Facet Division at a price of $1,500 per motor. To manufacture these motors, Waverly Corporation would also have to purchase a component part from Grathin Division. This would be a different component part than that needed by the Able Division. It would cost Grathin $175 in variable cost to produce, and Grathin would sell it to Waverly Corporation for $350 per part on an order of 2,000 parts. Because of its intricate design, this part would also require 2.5 hours of machine time.

b. HighTech Corporation wants to place an order with the Able Division for 2,500 units of a motor that is similar to the motor needed by the Facet Division. HighTech has offered to pay $1,200 per motor. To manufacture these motors, Able Division would again have to purchase a component part from the Grathin Division. This part would cost Grathin Division $100 per part in variable cost to produce, and Grathin would sell it to Able Division at a transfer price of $200 per part. This part would require 2 hours of machine time in Grathin's plant. Able Division would further process these parts, incurring variable costs of $500 per motor. This work would require 4 hours of machine time in Able Division.

The Able Division's plant capacity is limited, and the division can accept only the order from the Facet Division or the order from HighTech, but not both. The president of Uberin and the manager of the Able Division both agree that it would not be beneficial to increase capacity at this time. The company's total general fixed overhead would not be affected by this decision.

Required:

1. If the manager of the Able Division wants to maximize the division's profits, which order should be accepted—the order from the Facet Division or the order from HighTech Corporation? Support your answer with appropriate computations.
2. For the sake of discussion, assume that the Able Division decides to accept the order from HighTech Corporation. Determine if this decision is in the best interests of Uberin *as a whole.* Explain your answer. Support your answer with appropriate computations.

(CMA, adapted)

CASE 13–30 Sell or Process Further Decision [LO6]

The Scottie Sweater Company produces sweaters under the "Scottie" label. The company buys raw wool and processes it into wool yarn from which the sweaters are woven. One spindle of wool yarn is required to produce one sweater. The costs and revenues associated with the sweaters are given below:

		Per Sweater
Selling price		$30.00
Cost to manufacture:		
Raw materials:		
Buttons, thread, lining	$ 2.00	
Wool yarn	16.00	
Total raw materials	18.00	
Direct labor	5.80	
Manufacturing overhead	8.70	32.50
Manufacturing profit (loss)		$ (2.50)

Originally, all of the wool yarn was used to produce sweaters, but in recent years a market has developed for the wool yarn itself. The yarn is purchased by other companies for use in production of wool blankets and other wool products. Since the development of the market for the wool yarn, a continuing dispute has existed in the Scottie Sweater Company as to whether the yarn should be sold simply as yarn or processed into sweaters. Current cost and revenue data on the yarn are given below:

		Per Spindle of Yarn
Selling price		$20.00
Cost to manufacture:		
Raw materials (raw wool)	$7.00	
Direct labor	3.60	
Manufacturing overhead	5.40	16.00
Manufacturing profit		$ 4.00

The market for sweaters is temporarily depressed, due to unusually warm weather in the western states where the sweaters are sold. This has made it necessary for the company to discount the selling price of the sweaters to $30 from the normal $40 price. Since the market for wool yarn has remained strong, the dispute has again surfaced over whether the yarn should be sold outright rather than processed into sweaters. The sales manager thinks that the production of sweaters should be discontinued; she is upset about having to sell sweaters at a $2.50 loss when the yarn could be sold for a $4.00 profit. However, the production superintendent does not want to close down a large portion of the factory. He argues that the company is in the sweater business, not the yarn business, and that the company should focus on its core strength.

All of the manufacturing overhead costs are fixed and would not be affected even if sweaters were discontinued. Manufacturing overhead is assigned to products on the basis of 150% of direct labor cost. Materials and direct labor costs are variable.

Required:

1. Would you recommend that the wool yarn be sold outright or processed into sweaters? Support your answer with appropriate computations and explain your reasoning.
2. What is the lowest price that the company should accept for a sweater? Support your answer with appropriate computations and explain your reasoning.

CASE 13–31 Integrative Case: Relevant Costs; Pricing [LO1, LO4]

Wesco Incorporated's only product is a combination fertilizer-weed killer called GrowNWeed. GrowNWeed is sold nationwide to retail nurseries and garden stores.

Zwinger Nursery plans to sell a similar fertilizer weed killer compound through its regional nursery chain under its own private label. Zwinger does not have manufacturing facilities of its own, so it has asked Wesco (and several other companies) to submit a bid for manufacturing and delivering a 20,000-pound order of the private brand compound to Zwinger. While the chemical composition of the Zwinger compound differs from that of GrowNWeed, the manufacturing processes are very similar.

The Zwinger compound would be produced in 1,000-pound lots. Each lot would require 25 direct labor-hours and the following chemicals:

Chemicals	Quantity in Pounds
AG-5	300
KL-2	200
CW-7	150
DF-6	175

The first three chemicals (AG-5, KL-2, and CW-7) are all used in the production of GrowNWeed. DF-6 was used in another compound that Wesco discontinued several months ago. The supply of DF-6 that Wesco had on hand when the other compound was discontinued was not discarded. Wesco could sell its supply of DF-6 at the prevailing market price less $0.10 per pound selling and handling expenses.

Wesco also has on hand a chemical called BH-3, which was manufactured for use in another product that is no longer produced. BH-3, which cannot be used in GrowNWeed, can be substituted for AG-5 on a one-for-one basis without affecting the quality of the Zwinger compound. The BH-3 in inventory has a salvage value of $600.

Inventory and cost data for the chemicals that can be used to produce the Zwinger compound are shown below:

Raw Material	Pounds in Inventory	Actual Price per Pound When Purchased	Current Market Price per Pound
AG-5	18,000	$1.15	$1.20
KL-2	6,000	$1.10	$1.05
CW-7	7,000	$1.35	$1.35
DF-6	3,000	$0.80	$0.70
BH-3	3,500	$0.90	(Salvage)

The current direct labor wage rate is $14 per hour. The predetermined overhead rate is based on direct labor-hours (DLH). The predetermined overhead rate for the current year, based on a two-shift capacity with no overtime, is as follows:

Variable manufacturing overhead	$ 3.00 per DLH
Fixed manufacturing overhead	10.50 per DLH
Combined predetermined overhead rate	$13.50 per DLH

Wesco's production manager reports that the present equipment and facilities are adequate to manufacture the Zwinger compound. Therefore, the order would have no effect on total fixed manufacturing overhead costs. However, Wesco is within 400 hours of its two-shift capacity this month. Any additional hours beyond the 400 hours must be done in overtime. If need be, the Zwinger compound could be produced on regular time by shifting a portion of GrowNWeed production to overtime. Wesco's direct labor wage rate for overtime is $21 per hour. There is no allowance for any overtime premium in the predetermined overhead rate.

Required:

1. Wesco has decided to submit a bid for the 20,000-pound order of Zwinger's new compound. The order must be delivered by the end of the current month. Zwinger has indicated that this is a one-time order that will not be repeated. Calculate the lowest price that Wesco could bid for the order without reducing its net operating income.
2. Refer to the original data. Assume that Zwinger Nursery plans to place regular orders for 20,000-pound lots of the new compound. Wesco expects the demand for GrowNWeed to remain strong. Therefore, the recurring orders from Zwinger would put Wesco over its two-shift capacity. However, production could be scheduled so that 90% of each Zwinger order could be completed during regular hours. As another option, some GrowNWeed production could be shifted temporarily to overtime so that the Zwinger orders could be produced on regular time. Current market prices are the best available estimates of future market prices.

   Wesco's standard markup policy for new products is 40% of the full manufacturing cost, including fixed manufacturing overhead. Calculate the price that Wesco, Inc., would quote Zwinger Nursery for each 20,000-pound lot of the new compound, assuming that it is to be treated as a new product and this pricing policy is followed.

(CMA, adapted)

CASE 13–32 Make or Buy; Utilization of a Constrained Resource [LO1, LO3, LO5]

TufStuff, Inc., sells a wide range of drums, bins, boxes, and other containers that are used in the chemical industry. One of the company's products is a heavy-duty corrosion-resistant metal drum, called the WVD drum, used to store toxic wastes. Production is constrained by the capacity of an automated welding machine that is used to make precision welds. A total of 2,000 hours of welding time is available annually on the machine. Since each drum requires 0.4 hour of welding time, annual production is limited to 5,000 drums. At present, the welding machine is used exclusively to make the WVD drums. The accounting department has provided the following financial data concerning the WVD drums:

WVD Drums		
Selling price per drum		$149.00
Cost per drum:		
Direct materials	$52.10	
Direct labor ($18 per hour)	3.60	
Manufacturing overhead	4.50	
Selling and administrative expense	29.80	90.00
Margin per drum		$ 59.00

Management believes 6,000 WVD drums could be sold each year if the company had sufficient manufacturing capacity. As an alternative to adding another welding machine, management has considered buying additional drums from an outside supplier. Harcor Industries, Inc., a supplier of quality products, would be able to provide up to 4,000 WVD-type drums per year at a price of $138 per drum, which TufStuff would resell to its customers at its normal selling price after appropriate relabeling.

Megan Flores, TufStuff's production manager, has suggested that the company could make better use of the welding machine by manufacturing bike frames, which would require only 0.5

hour of welding time per frame and yet sell for far more than the drums. Megan believes that TufStuff could sell up to 1,600 bike frames per year to bike manufacturers at a price of $239 each. The accounting department has provided the following data concerning the proposed new product:

Bike Frames		
Selling price per frame		$239.00
Cost per frame:		
Direct materials	$99.40	
Direct labor ($18 per hour)	28.80	
Manufacturing overhead	36.00	
Selling and administrative expense . . .	47.80	212.00
Margin per frame		$ 27.00

The bike frames could be produced with existing equipment and personnel. Manufacturing overhead is allocated to products on the basis of direct labor-hours. Most of the manufacturing overhead consists of fixed common costs such as rent on the factory building, but some of it is variable. The variable manufacturing overhead has been estimated at $1.35 per WVD drum and $1.90 per bike frame. The variable manufacturing overhead cost would not be incurred on drums acquired from the outside supplier.

Selling and administrative expenses are allocated to products on the basis of revenues. Almost all of the selling and administrative expenses are fixed common costs, but it has been estimated that variable selling and administrative expenses amount to $0.75 per WVD drum whether made or purchased and would be $1.30 per bike frame.

All of the company's employees—direct and indirect—are paid for full 40-hour workweeks and the company has a policy of laying off workers only in major recessions.

Required:

1. Given the margins of the two products as indicated in the reports submitted by the accounting department, does it make sense to consider producing the bike frames? Explain.
2. Compute the contribution margin per unit for:
   a. Purchased WVD drums.
   b. Manufactured WVD drums.
   c. Manufactured bike frames.
3. Determine the number of WVD drums (if any) that should be purchased and the number of WVD drums and/or bike frames (if any) that should be manufactured. What is the increase in net operating income that would result from this plan over current operations?

   As soon as your analysis was shown to the top management team at TufStuff, several managers got into an argument concerning how direct labor costs should be treated when making this decision. One manager argued that direct labor is always treated as a variable cost in textbooks and in practice and has always been considered a variable cost at TufStuff. After all, "direct" means you can directly trace the cost to products. "If direct labor is not a variable cost, what is?" Another manager argued just as strenuously that direct labor should be considered a fixed cost at TufStuff. No one had been laid off in over a decade, and for all practical purposes, everyone at the plant is on a monthly salary. Everyone classified as direct labor works a regular 40-hour workweek and overtime has not been necessary since the company adopted just-in-time techniques. Whether the welding machine is used to make drums or frames, the total payroll would be exactly the same. There is enough slack, in the form of idle time, to accommodate any increase in total direct labor time that the bike frames would require.
4. Redo requirements (2) and (3) above, making the opposite assumption about direct labor from the one you originally made. In other words, if you treated direct labor as a variable cost, redo the analysis treating it as a fixed cost. If you treated direct labor as a fixed cost, redo the analysis treating it as a variable cost.
5. What do you think is the correct way to treat direct labor cost in this situation—as variable or as fixed?

Group and Internet Exercises

GROUP EXERCISE 13–33 Outsourcing May Be Hazardous to Your Health

Outsourcing, when a company contracts with third parties to produce some of its parts or products, has become commonplace among U.S. manufacturers. Thirty years ago, when factories were less complex, predetermined manufacturing overhead rates of 50% or less of direct labor cost were deemed reasonable. But today, predetermined manufacturing overhead rates of 200% of direct labor cost are common and rates of 500% or more are not unusual. As a result, outsourcing has gained widespread acceptance over the past several decades. Products with high direct labor content are especially susceptible to being outsourced to parts of the world where labor rates are much lower than they are in the United States.

Required:

1. What is the meaning of manufacturing overhead rates of 500% or more of direct labor?
2. What implications do such high manufacturing overhead rates hold for products high in direct labor content?
3. What happens to the costs of the remaining products when a product is outsourced?
4. Can you think of any drawbacks to outsourcing in a less-developed foreign land or any limitations to a strategy dependent on labor cost savings?
5. Continuing with the line of thinking developed in (1)–(3) above, what happens next?

INTERNET EXERCISE 13–34

As you know, the World Wide Web is a medium that is constantly evolving. Sites come and go, and change without notice. To enable periodic updating of site addresses, this problem has been posted to the textbook website (www.mhhe.com/garrison11e). After accessing the site, enter the Student Center and select this chapter. Select and complete the Internet Exercise.

Chapter

14

Capital Budgeting Decisions

LEARNING OBJECTIVES

After studying Chapter 14, you should be able to:

LO1 Evaluate the acceptability of an investment project using the net present value method.

LO2 Evaluate the acceptability of an investment project using the internal rate of return method.

LO3 Evaluate an investment project that has uncertain cash flows.

LO4 Rank investment projects in order of preference.

LO5 Determine the payback period for an investment.

LO6 Compute the simple rate of return for an investment.

LO7 (Appendix 14A) Understand present value concepts and the use of present value tables.

LO8 (Appendix 14D) Include income taxes in a capital budgeting analysis.

Invest Less, Make More

BUSINESS FOCUS

When Steven Burd became the CEO of Safeway, he slashed annual capital spending from \$550 million to \$290 million. Burd gave the following reason: "We had projects that were not returning the cost of money. So we cut spending back, which made the very best projects come to the surface."

Safeway set a minimum 22.5% pretax return on investment in all new store and remodeling projects. With that discipline in place, Safeway again increased capital spending. Recently it spent about \$1 billion in a single year, adding 40 to 45 new stores and remodeling more than 200. Burd says he has emphasized expanding existing stores because the older stores generally have excellent real estate locations and the added size brings strong increases in sales. ■

Source: Robert Berner, "Safeway's Resurgence Is Built on Attention to Detail," *The Wall Street Journal,* October 2, 1998, p. B4.

The term capital budgeting is used to describe how managers plan significant outlays on projects that have long-term implications such as the purchase of new equipment and the introduction of new products. Most companies have many more potential projects than can actually be funded. Hence, managers must carefully select those projects that promise the greatest future return. How well managers make these capital budgeting decisions is a critical factor in the long-run profitability of the company.

Capital budgeting involves *investment*—a company must commit funds now in order to receive a return in the future. Investments are not limited to stocks and bonds. Purchase of inventory or equipment is also an investment. For example, Tri-Con Global Restaurants, Inc. makes an investment when it opens a new Pizza Hut restaurant. L. L. Bean makes an investment when it installs a new computer to handle customer billing. DaimlerChrysler makes an investment when it redesigns a product such as the Jeep Eagle and must retool its production lines. Merck & Co. invests in medical research. Amazon.com makes an investment when it redesigns its website. All of these investments are characterized by a commitment of funds today in the expectation of receiving a return in the future in the form of additional cash inflows or reduced cash outflows.

Capital Budgeting—Planning Investments

Typical Capital Budgeting Decisions

What types of business decisions require capital budgeting analysis? Virtually any decision that involves an outlay now in order to obtain some return (increase in revenue or reduction in costs) in the future. Typical capital budgeting decisions include:

1. Cost reduction decisions. Should new equipment be purchased to reduce costs?
2. Expansion decisions. Should a new plant, warehouse, or other facility be acquired to increase capacity and sales?
3. Equipment selection decisions. Which of several available machines should be purchased?
4. Lease or buy decisions. Should new equipment be leased or purchased?
5. Equipment replacement decisions. Should old equipment be replaced now or later?

Capital budgeting decisions tend to fall into two broad categories—*screening decisions* and *preference decisions*. **Screening decisions** relate to whether a proposed project passes a preset hurdle. For example, a company may have a policy of accepting projects only if they promise a return of 20% on the investment. The required rate of return is the minimum rate of return a project must yield to be acceptable.

Preference decisions, by contrast, relate to selecting from among several *competing* courses of action. To illustrate, a company may be considering several different machines to replace an existing machine on the assembly line. The choice of which machine to purchase is a *preference* decision.

In this chapter, we initially discuss ways of making screening decisions. Preference decisions are discussed toward the end of the chapter.

The Time Value of Money

As stated earlier, investments commonly involve returns that extend over fairly long periods of time. Therefore, in approaching capital budgeting decisions, it is necessary to use techniques that best recognize *the time value of money.* A dollar today is worth more than a dollar a year from now. The same concept applies in choosing between investment projects. Projects that promise earlier returns are preferable to those that promise later returns.

The capital budgeting techniques that recognize the above two characteristics of business investments are those that involve *discounted cash flows.* We will spend most of this chapter showing how to use discounted cash flow methods in making capital budgeting decisions. If you are not already familiar with discounting and the use of present value tables, you should read Appendix 14A, The Concept of Present Value, at the end of this chapter before proceeding any further.

IN BUSINESS

CHOOSING A CAT

Sometimes a long-term decision does not have to involve present value calculations or any other sophisticated analytical technique. White Grizzly Adventures of Meadow Creek, British Columbia, needs two snowcats for its powder skiing operations—one for shuttling guests to the top of the mountain and one to be held in reserve in case of mechanical problems with the first. Bombardier of Canada sells new snowcats for $250,000 and used, reconditioned snowcats for $150,000. In either case, the snowcats are good for about 5,000 hours of operation before they need to be reconditioned. From White Grizzly's perspective, the choice is clear. Since both new and reconditioned snowcats last about 5,000 hours, but the reconditioned snowcats cost $100,000 less, the reconditioned snowcats are the obvious choice. They may not have all of the latest bells and whistles, but they get the job done at a price a small operation can afford.

Bombardier snowcats do not have passenger cabs as standard equipment. To save money, White Grizzly builds its own custom-designed passenger cab for about $15,000, using recycled Ford Escort seats and industrial-strength aluminum for the frame and siding. If purchased retail, a passenger cab would cost about twice as much and would not be as well-suited for snowcat skiing.

Source: Brad & Carole Karafil, owners and operators of White Grizzly Adventures, www.whitegrizzly.com.

Discounted Cash Flows—The Net Present Value Method

LEARNING OBJECTIVE 1
Evaluate the acceptability of an investment project using the net present value method.

Two approaches to making capital budgeting decisions use discounted cash flows. One is the *net present value method,* and the other is the *internal rate of return method* (sometimes called the *time-adjusted rate of return method*). The net present value method is discussed in this section; the internal rate of return method is discussed in the following section.

The Net Present Value Method Illustrated

Under the net present value method, the present value of a project's cash inflows is compared to the present value of the project's cash outflows. The difference between the present value of these cash flows, called the **net present value,** determines whether or not the project is an acceptable investment. To illustrate, consider the following data:

Example A: Harper Company is contemplating the purchase of a machine capable of performing certain operations that are now performed manually. The machine will cost $50,000, and it will last for five years. At the end of the five-year period, the machine will have a zero scrap value. Use of the machine will reduce labor costs by $18,000 per year. Harper Company requires a minimum pretax return of 20% on all investment projects.[1]

1 For simplicity, we ignore inflation and taxes. The impact of inflation on discounted cash flow analysis is discussed in Appendix 14B. The impact of income taxes on capital budgeting decisions is discussed in Appendix 14D.

EXHIBIT 14–1
Net Present Value Analysis of a Proposed Project

Topic Tackler PLUS 14–1

Initial cost	$50,000
Life of the project	5 years
Annual cost savings	$18,000
Salvage value	$0
Required rate of return	20%

Item	Year(s)	Amount of Cash Flow	20% Factor	Present Value of Cash Flows
Annual cost savings	1–5	$ 18,000	2.991*	$53,838
Initial investment	Now	$(50,000)	1.000	(50,000)
Net present value				$ 3,838

*From Table 14C–4 in Appendix 14C at the end of this chapter.

Should the machine be purchased? Harper Company must determine whether a cash investment now of $50,000 can be justified if it will result in an $18,000 reduction in cost each year over the next five years. It may appear that the answer is obvious since the total cost savings is $90,000 ($18,000 per year × 5 years). However, the company can earn a 20% return by investing its money elsewhere. It is not enough that the cost reductions cover just the original cost of the machine; they must also yield a return of at least 20% or the company would be better off investing the money elsewhere.

To determine whether the investment is desirable, the stream of annual $18,000 cost savings should be discounted to its present value and then compared to the cost of the new machine. Since Harper Company requires a minimum return of 20% on all investment projects, this rate is used in the discounting process and is called the *discount rate.* Exhibit 14–1 shows how this analysis is done.

According to the analysis, Harper Company should purchase the new machine. The present value of the cost savings is $53,838, whereas the present value of the required investment (cost of the machine) is only $50,000. Deducting the present value of the required investment from the present value of the cost savings gives the *net present value* of $3,838. Whenever the net present value is zero or greater, as in our example, an investment project is acceptable. Whenever the net present value is negative (the present value of the cash outflows exceeds the present value of the cash inflows), an investment project is not acceptable. In sum:

If the Net Present Value Is . . .	Then the Project Is . . .
Positive	Acceptable, since it promises a return greater than the required rate of return.
Zero	Acceptable, since it promises a return equal to the required rate of return.
Negative	Not acceptable, since it promises a return less than the required rate of return.

There is another way to interpret the net present value. The new machine promises more than the required 20% rate of return. This is evident from the positive net present value of $3,838. Harper Company could spend up to $53,838 for the new machine and still obtain the minimum required 20% rate of return. The net present value of $3,838, therefore, shows the amount of "cushion" or "margin of error." One way to look at this is that the company could underestimate the cost of the new machine by up to $3,838, or overestimate the net present value of the future cash savings by up to $3,838, and the project would still be financially attractive.

Emphasis on Cash Flows

In capital budgeting decisions, the focus is on cash flows and not on accounting net income. The reason is that accounting net income is based on accruals that ignore the timing of cash flows into and out of an organization. From a capital budgeting standpoint, the timing of cash flows is important, since a dollar received today is more valuable than a dollar received in the future. Therefore, even though accounting net income is useful for many things, it is not ordinarily used in discounted cash flow analysis.[2] Instead of focusing on accounting net income, the analyst should concentrate on identifying the specific cash flows of the investment project.

What kinds of cash flows should the analyst look for? Although the specific cash flows will vary from project to project, certain types of cash flows tend to recur as explained in the following paragraphs.

Typical Cash Outflows Most projects will have an immediate cash outflow in the form of an initial investment in equipment or other assets. Any salvage value realized from the sale of old equipment can be recognized as a cash inflow or as a reduction in the required investment. In addition, some projects require that a company expand its working capital. **Working capital** is current assets (cash, accounts receivable, and inventory) less current liabilities. When a company takes on a new project, the balances in the current asset accounts will often increase. For example, opening a new Nordstrom's department store would require additional cash in sales registers and more inventory. These additional working capital needs should be treated as part of the initial investment in a project. Also, many projects require periodic outlays for repairs and maintenance and for additional operating costs. These should all be treated as cash outflows for capital budgeting purposes.

Typical Cash Inflows On the cash inflow side, a project will normally either increase revenues or reduce costs. Either way, the amount involved should be treated as a cash inflow for capital budgeting purposes. Notice that from a cash flow standpoint, a reduction in costs is equivalent to an increase in revenues. Cash inflows are also frequently realized from selling equipment for its salvage value when a project ends, although the company may actually have to pay to dispose of some low-value or hazardous items. In addition, any working capital that was tied up in the project can be released for use elsewhere at the end of the project and should be treated as a cash inflow at that time. Working capital is released, for example, when a company sells off its inventory or collects its accounts receivable.

IN BUSINESS

HAZARDOUS PCS

Disposing of old equipment can be difficult and costly—particularly when disposal is governed by environmental regulations. For example, computer equipment often contains lead and other substances that could contaminate the air, soil, or groundwater. Cindy Brethauer, the network administrator for 1st Choice Bank, in Greeley, Colorado, was faced with the mounting problem of storing old monitors, printers, and personal computers that could not be simply thrown away. These bulky items were constantly being shuttled back and forth from one storage space to another. For help, she turned to Technology Recycling LLC, which hauls away old computers and peripherals for $35 per component. Technology LLC strips the machines, recycling some of the materials and taking environmentally sensitive materials to disposal facilities approved by the Environmental Protection Agency. Technology LLC handles the complicated paperwork for its customers.

Source: Jill Hecht Maxwell, *Inc. Tech*, 2000, 1, p. 25.

[2] Under certain conditions, capital budgeting decisions can be correctly made by discounting appropriately defined accounting net income. However, this approach requires advanced techniques that are beyond the scope of this book.

In summary, the following types of cash flows are common in business investment projects:

Cash outflows:
- Initial investment (including installation costs).
- Increased working capital needs.
- Repairs and maintenance.
- Incremental operating costs.

Cash inflows:
- Incremental revenues.
- Reduction in costs.
- Salvage value.
- Release of working capital.

Recovery of the Original Investment

When computing the net present value of a project, depreciation is not deducted for two reasons.

First, depreciation is not a current cash outflow.[3] As discussed above, discounted cash flow methods focus on *cash flows.* Although depreciation is used to compute net income for financial statements, it is not relevant in an analytical framework that focuses on cash flows.

A second reason for not deducting depreciation is that discounted cash flow methods *automatically* provide for return of the original investment, thereby making a deduction for depreciation unnecessary. To demonstrate this point, consider the following data:

Example B: Carver Hospital is considering the purchase of an attachment for its X-ray machine that will cost $3,170. The attachment will be usable for four years, after which time it will have no salvage value. It will increase net cash inflows by $1,000 per year in the X-ray department. The hospital's board of directors requires a rate of return of at least 10% on investments.

A net present value analysis of the desirability of purchasing the X-ray attachment is presented in Exhibit 14–2. Notice that the attachment promises exactly a 10% return on the original investment, since the net present value is zero at a 10% discount rate.

Each annual $1,000 cash inflow arising from use of the attachment is made up of two parts. One part represents a recovery of a portion *of* the original $3,170 paid for the attachment, and the other part represents a return *on* this investment. The breakdown of each year's $1,000 cash inflow between recovery *of* investment and return *on* investment is shown in Exhibit 14–3.

The first year's $1,000 cash inflow consists of interest in the amount of $317 that represents a 10% return *on* the $3,170 original investment, plus a $683 return *of* that investment. Since the amount of the unrecovered investment decreases over the four years, the dollar amount of the interest return also decreases. By the end of the fourth year, all $3,170 of the original investment has been recovered.

Simplifying Assumptions

Two simplifying assumptions are usually made in net present value analysis.

The first assumption is that all cash flows other than the initial investment occur at the end of periods. This is somewhat unrealistic in that cash flows typically occur *throughout* a period rather than just at its end. The purpose of this assumption is to simplify computations.

The second assumption is that all cash flows generated by an investment project are immediately reinvested at a rate of return equal to the discount rate. Unless these conditions are met, the net present value computed for the project will not be accurate. We used

3 Although depreciation itself is not a cash outflow, it does have an effect on income taxes. This is discussed in Appendix 14D.

EXHIBIT 14–2
Carver Hospital—Net Present Value Analysis of X-Ray Attachment

Initial cost	$3,170
Life of the project	4 years
Annual net cash inflow	$1,000
Salvage value	$0
Required rate of return	10%

Item	Year(s)	Amount of Cash Flow	10% Factor	Present Value of Cash Flows
Annual net cash inflow	1–4	$ 1,000	3.170*	$3,170
Initial investment	Now	$(3,170)	1.000	(3,170)
Net present value				$ 0

*From Table 14C–4 in Appendix 14C.

EXHIBIT 14–3
Carver Hospital—Breakdown of Annual Cash Inflows

Year	(1) Investment Outstanding during the Year	(2) Cash Inflow	(3) Return on Investment (1) × 10%	(4) Recovery of Investment during the Year (2) − (3)	(5) Unrecovered Investment at the End of the Year (1) − (4)
1	$3,170	$1,000	$317	$ 683	$2,487
2	$2,487	$1,000	$249	751	$1,736
3	$1,736	$1,000	$173	827	$909
4	$909	$1,000	$91	909	$0
Total investment recovered				$3,170	

a discount rate of 10% for Carver Hospital in Exhibit 14–2. Unless the cash flows in each period are immediately reinvested at a 10% return, the net present value computed for the X-ray attachment will be misstated.

Choosing a Discount Rate

A positive net present value indicates that the project's return exceeds the discount rate. A negative net present value indicates that the project's return is less than the discount rate. Therefore, if the company's minimum required rate of return is used as the discount rate, a project with a positive net present value is acceptable and a project with a negative net present value is unacceptable.

What is a company's minimum required rate of return? The company's *cost of capital* is usually regarded as the minimum required rate of return. The **cost of capital** is the average rate of return the company must pay to its long-term creditors and to shareholders for the use of their funds. The cost of capital is the minimum required rate of return because if a project's rate of return is less than the cost of capital, the company does not earn enough to compensate its creditors and shareholders. Therefore, any project with a rate of return less than the cost of capital should not be accepted.

The cost of capital serves as a *screening device* in net present value analysis. When the cost of capital is used as the discount rate, any project with a negative net present value does not cover the company's cost of capital and should be discarded as unacceptable.

An Extended Example of the Net Present Value Method

To conclude our discussion of the net present value method, we present below an extended example of how it is used to analyze an investment proposal. This example will also help to tie together (and to reinforce) many of the ideas developed thus far.

Example C: Under a special licensing arrangement, Swinyard Company has an opportunity to market a new product in the western United States for a five-year period. The product would be purchased from the manufacturer, with Swinyard Company responsible for promotion and distribution costs. The licensing arrangement could be renewed at the end of the five-year period. After careful study, Swinyard Company has estimated the following costs and revenues for the new product:

Cost of equipment needed	$60,000
Working capital needed	$100,000
Overhaul of the equipment in four years	$5,000
Salvage value of the equipment in five years	$10,000
Annual revenues and costs:	
Sales revenues	$200,000
Cost of goods sold	$125,000
Out-of-pocket operating costs (for salaries, advertising, and other direct costs)	$35,000

At the end of the five-year period, the working capital would be released for investment elsewhere if Swinyard decides not to renew the licensing arrangement. Swinyard Company uses a 14% discount rate. Would you recommend that the new product be introduced?

This example involves a variety of cash inflows and cash outflows. The solution is given in Exhibit 14–4.

Notice particularly how the working capital is handled in this exhibit. It is counted as a cash outflow at the beginning of the project and as a cash inflow when it is released at the end of the project. Also notice how the sales revenues, cost of goods sold, and out-of-pocket costs are handled. **Out-of-pocket costs** are actual cash outlays for salaries, advertising, and other operating expenses. Depreciation would not be an out-of-pocket cost, since it involves no current cash outlay.

Since the net present value is positive, the new product should be added assuming the company has no better use for the investment funds.

EXHIBIT 14–4

The Net Present Value Method—An Extended Example

Sales revenues	$200,000
Less cost of goods sold	125,000
Less out-of-pocket costs for salaries, advertising, etc.	35,000
Annual net cash inflows	$ 40,000

Item	Year(s)	Amount of Cash Flow	14% Factor	Present Value of Cash Flows
Purchase of equipment	Now	$(60,000)	1.000	$ (60,000)
Working capital needed	Now	$(100,000)	1.000	(100,000)
Overhaul of equipment	4	$(5,000)	0.592*	(2,960)
Annual net cash inflows from sales of the product line	1–5	$40,000	3.433†	137,320
Salvage value of the equipment	5	$10,000	0.519*	5,190
Working capital released	5	$100,000	0.519*	51,900
Net present value				$ 31,450

*From Table 14C–3 in Appendix 14C.
†From Table 14C–4 in Appendix 14C.

Discounted Cash Flows—The Internal Rate of Return Method

LEARNING OBJECTIVE 2
Evaluate the acceptability of an investment project using the internal rate of return method.

The **internal rate of return** is the rate of return promised by an investment project over its useful life. It is sometimes referred to simply as the *yield* on a project. The internal rate of return is computed by finding the discount rate that equates the present value of a project's cash outflows with the present value of its cash inflows. In other words, the internal rate of return is the discount rate that will result in a net present value of zero.

The Internal Rate of Return Method Illustrated

To illustrate the internal rate of return method, consider the following data:

Example D: Glendale School District is considering the purchase of a large tractor-pulled lawn mower. At present, the lawn is mowed using a small hand-pushed gas mower. The large, tractor-pulled mower will cost $16,950 and will have a useful life of 10 years. It will have a negligible scrap value, which can be ignored. The tractor-pulled mower would do the job much more quickly than the old mower, resulting in labor savings of $3,000 per year.

To compute the internal rate of return promised by the new mower, we must find the discount rate that will cause the net present value of the project to be zero. How do we do this? The simplest and most direct approach *when the net cash inflow is the same every year* is to divide the investment in the project by the expected net annual cash inflow. This computation will yield a factor from which the internal rate of return can be determined. The formula is as follows:

$$\text{Factor of the internal rate of return} = \frac{\text{Investment required}}{\text{Net annual cash inflow}} \qquad (1)$$

The factor derived from formula (1) is then located in the present value tables to see what rate of return it represents. Using formula (1) and the data for Glendale School District's proposed project, we get:

$$\frac{\text{Investment required}}{\text{Net annual cash inflow}} = \frac{\$16{,}950}{\$3{,}000} = 5.650$$

Thus, the discount factor that will equate a series of $3,000 cash inflows with a present investment of $16,950 is 5.650. Now we need to find this factor in Table 14C–4 in Appendix 14C to see what rate of return it represents. We should use the 10-period line in Table 14C–4 since the cash flows for the project continue for 10 years. If we scan along the 10-period line, we find that a factor of 5.650 represents a 12% rate of return. Therefore, the internal rate of return promised by the mower project is 12%. We can verify this by computing the project's net present value using a 12% discount rate. This computation is shown in Exhibit 14–5 (page 662).

Notice from Exhibit 14–5 that using a 12% discount rate equates the present value of the annual cash inflows with the present value of the investment required in the project, leaving a zero net present value. The 12% rate therefore represents the internal rate of return promised by the project.

Salvage Value and Other Cash Flows

The technique just demonstrated works very well if a project's cash flows are identical every year. But what if they are not? For example, what if a project will have some salvage value at the end of its life in addition to the annual cash inflows? Under these circumstances, a trial-and-error process may be used to find the rate of return that will equate the cash inflows with the cash outflows. The trial-and-error process can be carried out by hand; however, computer software programs such as spreadsheets can perform the necessary computations in seconds. In short, erratic or uneven cash flows should not prevent an analyst from determining a project's internal rate of return.

EXHIBIT 14–5
Evaluation of the Mower Purchase Using a 12% Discount Rate

Initial cost	$16,950
Life of the project	10 years
Annual cost savings	$3,000
Salvage value	$0

Item	Year(s)	Amount of Cash Flow	12% Factor	Present Value of Cash Flows
Annual cost savings	1–10	$3,000	5.650*	$16,950
Initial investment	Now	$(16,950)	1.000	(16,950)
Net present value				$ 0

*From Table 14C–4 in Appendix 14C.

Using the Internal Rate of Return

Once the internal rate of return has been computed, what do managers do with the information? The internal rate of return is compared to the company's *required rate of return.* The **required rate of return** is the minimum rate of return that an investment project must yield to be acceptable. If the internal rate of return is *equal* to or *greater* than the required rate of return, then the project is considered acceptable. If it is less than the required rate of return, then the project is rejected. Quite often, the company's cost of capital is used as the required rate of return. The reasoning is that if a project can't provide a rate of return at least as great as the cost of the funds invested in it, then it is not profitable.

In the case of the Glendale School District example used earlier, let us assume that the district has set a minimum required rate of return of 15% on all projects. Since the large mower promises a rate of return of only 12%, it does not clear this hurdle and would therefore be rejected as a project.

The Cost of Capital as a Screening Tool

As we have seen in preceding examples, the cost of capital often operates as a *screening* device, helping the manager screen out undesirable investment projects. This screening is accomplished in different ways, depending on whether the company is using the internal rate of return method or the net present value method in its capital budgeting analysis.

When the internal rate of return method is used, the cost of capital is used as the *hurdle rate* that a project must clear for acceptance. If the internal rate of return of a project is not great enough to clear the cost of capital hurdle, then the project is ordinarily rejected. We saw the application of this idea in the Glendale School District example, where the hurdle rate was set at 15%.

When the net present value method is used, the cost of capital is the *discount rate* used to compute the net present value of a proposed project. Any project yielding a negative net present value is rejected unless other factors are significant enough to warrant its acceptance.

The use of the cost of capital as a screening tool is summarized in Exhibit 14–6.

Comparison of the Net Present Value and the Internal Rate of Return Methods

The net present value method has several important advantages over the internal rate of return method.

EXHIBIT 14–6
Capital Budgeting Screening Decisions

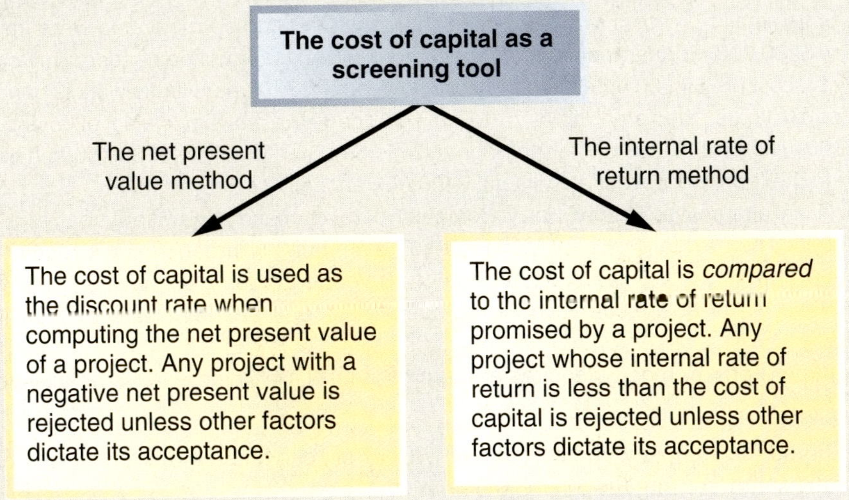

First, the net present value method is often simpler to use. As mentioned earlier, the internal rate of return method may require hunting for the discount rate that results in a net present value of zero. This can be a very laborious trial-and-error process, although it can be automated using a computer.

Second, the internal rate of return method makes a questionable assumption. Both methods assume that cash flows generated by a project during its useful life are immediately reinvested elsewhere. However, the two methods make different assumptions concerning the rate of return that is earned on those cash flows. The net present value method assumes the rate of return is the discount rate, whereas the internal rate of return method assumes the rate of return is the internal rate of return on the project. Specifically, if the internal rate of return of the project is high, this assumption may not be realistic. It is generally more realistic to assume that cash inflows can be reinvested at a rate of return equal to the discount rate—particularly if the discount rate is the company's cost of capital or an opportunity rate of return. For example, if the discount rate is the company's cost of capital, this rate of return can be actually realized by paying off the company's creditors and buying back the company's stock with cash flows from the project. In short, when the net present value method and the internal rate of return method do not agree concerning the attractiveness of a project, it is best to go with the net present value method. Of the two methods, it makes the more realistic assumption about the rate of return that can be earned on cash flows from the project.

Expanding the Net Present Value Method

So far all of our examples have involved only a single investment alternative. We will now expand the net present value method to include two alternatives. In addition, we will integrate the concept of relevant costs into the discounted cash flow analysis.

The net present value method can be used to compare competing investment projects in two ways. One is the *total-cost approach,* and the other is the *incremental-cost approach.* Each approach is illustrated below.

The Total-Cost Approach

The total-cost approach is the most flexible method for comparing competing projects. To illustrate the mechanics of the approach, consider the following data:

Example E: Harper Ferry Company provides a ferry service across the Mississippi River. One of its small ferryboats is in poor condition. This ferry can be renovated at an immediate cost of $200,000. Further repairs and an overhaul of the motor will be needed five years from now at a cost of $80,000. In all, the ferry will be usable for 10 years if this work is done. At the end of 10 years, the ferry will have to be scrapped at a salvage value of approximately $60,000. The scrap value of the ferry right now is $70,000. It will cost $300,000 each year to operate the ferry, and revenues will total $400,000 annually.

As an alternative, Harper Ferry Company can purchase a new ferryboat at a cost of $360,000. The new ferry will have a life of 10 years, but it will require some repairs costing $30,000 at the end of 5 years. At the end of 10 years, the ferry will have a scrap value of $60,000. It will cost $210,000 each year to operate the ferry, and revenues will total $400,000 annually.

Harper Ferry Company requires a return of at least 14% before taxes on all investment projects.

Should the company purchase the new ferry or renovate the old ferry? Exhibit 14–7 gives the solution using the total-cost approach.

Two points should be noted from the exhibit. First, *all* cash inflows and *all* cash outflows are included in the solution under each alternative. No effort has been made to isolate those cash flows that are relevant to the decision and those that are not relevant. The inclusion of all cash flows associated with each alternative gives the approach its name—the *total-cost* approach.

Second, notice that a net present value is computed for each of the two alternatives. This is a distinct advantage of the total-cost approach in that an unlimited number of alternatives can be compared side by side to determine the best option. For example, another alternative for Harper Ferry Company would be to get out of the ferry business entirely. If management desired, the net present value of this alternative could be com-

EXHIBIT 14–7
The Total-Cost Approach to Project Selection

	New Ferry	Old Ferry
Annual revenues	$400,000	$400,000
Annual cash operating costs	210,000	300,000
Net annual cash inflows	$190,000	$100,000

Item	Year(s)	Amount of Cash Flows	14% Factor*	Present Value of Cash Flows
Buy the new ferry:				
Initial investment	Now	$(360,000)	1.000	$(360,000)
Salvage value of the old ferry	Now	$70,000	1.000	70,000
Repairs in five years	5	$(30,000)	0.519	(15,570)
Net annual cash inflows	1–10	$190,000	5.216	991,040
Salvage value of the new ferry	10	$60,000	0.270	16,200
Net present value				701,670
Keep the old ferry:				
Renovation	Now	$(200,000)	1.000	(200,000)
Repairs in five years	5	$(80,000)	0.519	(41,520)
Net annual cash inflows	1–10	$100,000	5.216	521,600
Salvage value of the old ferry	10	$60,000	0.270	16,200
Net present value				296,280
Net present value in favor of buying the new ferry				$ 405,390

*All present value factors are from Tables 14C–3 and 14C–4 in Appendix 14C.

puted to compare with the alternatives shown in Exhibit 14–7. Still other alternatives might be open to the company. Once management has determined the net present value of each alternative that it wishes to consider, it can select the course of action that promises to be the most profitable. In the case at hand, given only two alternatives, the data indicate that the most profitable choice is to purchase the new ferry.[4]

IN BUSINESS

DOES IT REALLY NEED TO BE NEW?

Tom Copeland, the director of Corporate Finance Practice at the consulting firm Monitor Group, observes: "If they could afford it, most people would like to drive a new car. Managers are no different . . . [I]n my experience, . . . [managers] routinely spend millions of dollars on new machines years earlier than they need to. In most cases, the overall cost (including the cost of breakdowns) is 30% to 40% lower if a company continues servicing an existing machine for five more years instead of buying a new one. In order to fight impulsive acquisitions of new machinery, companies should require unit managers to run the numbers on all alternative investment options open to them—including maintaining the existing assets or buying used ones."

Source: Tom Copeland, "Cutting Costs Without Drawing Blood," *Harvard Business Review*, September-October 2000, pp. 3–7.

The Incremental-Cost Approach

When only two alternatives are being considered, the incremental-cost approach offers a simpler and more direct route to a decision. Unlike the total-cost approach, it includes in the discounted cash flow analysis only those costs and revenues that *differ* between the two alternatives being considered. To illustrate, refer again to the data in Example E relating to Harper Ferry Company. The solution using only differential costs is presented in Exhibit 14–8.[5]

Two things should be noted from the data in this exhibit. First, notice that the net present value in favor of buying the new ferry of $405,390 shown in Exhibit 14–8 agrees with the net present value shown under the total-cost approach in Exhibit 14–7. This agreement should be expected, since the two approaches are just different roads to the same destination.

EXHIBIT 14–8
The Incremental-Cost Approach to Project Selection

Item	Year(s)	Amount of Cash Flows	14% Factor*	Present Value of Cash Flows
Incremental investment to buy the new ferry	Now	$(160,000)	1.000	$(160,000)
Salvage value of the old ferry now	Now	$70,000	1.000	70,000
Difference in repairs in five years	5	$50,000	0.519	25,950
Increase in net annual cash inflows	1–10	$90,000	5.216	469,440
Difference in salvage value in 10 years	10	$0	0.270	0
Net present value in favor of buying the new ferry				$ 405,390

*All present value factors are from Tables 14C–3 and 14C–4 in Appendix 14C.

[4] The alternative with the highest net present value is not always the best choice, although it is the best choice in this case. For further discussion, see the section Preference Decisions—The Ranking of Investment Projects.

[5] Technically, the incremental-cost approach is misnamed, since it focuses on differential costs (that is, on both cost increases and decreases) rather than just on incremental costs. As used here, the term *incremental costs* should be interpreted broadly to include both cost increases and cost decreases.

Second, notice that the costs used in Exhibit 14–8 are just the differences between the costs shown for the two alternatives in the prior exhibit. For example, the $160,000 incremental investment required to purchase the new ferry in Exhibit 14–8 is the difference between the $360,000 cost of the new ferry and the $200,000 cost required to renovate the old ferry from Exhibit 14–7. The other figures in Exhibit 14–8 have been computed in the same way.

Least-Cost Decisions

Revenues are not directly involved in some decisions. For example, a company that does not charge for delivery service may need to replace an old delivery truck, or a company may be trying to decide whether to lease or to buy its fleet of executive cars. In situations such as these, where no revenues are involved, the most desirable alternative will be the one that promises the *least total cost* from the present value perspective. Hence, these are known as least-cost decisions. To illustrate a least-cost decision, consider the following data:

Example F: Val-Tek Company is considering replacing an old threading machine with a new threading machine that would substantially reduce annual operating costs. Selected data relating to the old and the new machines are presented below:

	Old Machine	New Machine
Purchase cost when new	$200,000	$250,000
Salvage value now	$30,000	—
Annual cash operating costs	$150,000	$90,000
Overhaul needed immediately	$40,000	—
Salvage value in six years	$0	$50,000
Remaining life	6 years	6 years

Val-Tek Company uses a 10% discount rate.

Exhibit 14–9 analyzes the alternatives using the total-cost approach.

EXHIBIT 14–9
The Total-Cost Approach (Least-Cost Decision)

Item	Year(s)	Amount of Cash Flows	10% Factor*	Present Value of Cash Flows
Buy the new machine:				
Initial investment	Now	$(250,000)	1.000	$(250,000)†
Salvage value of the old machine	Now	$30,000	1.000	30,000†
Annual cash operating costs	1–6	$(90,000)	4.355	(391,950)
Salvage value of the new machine	6	$50,000	0.564	28,200
Present value of net cash outflows				(583,750)
Keep the old machine:				
Overhaul needed now	Now	$(40,000)	1.000	$ (40,000)
Annual cash operating costs	1–6	$(150,000)	4.355	(653,250)
Present value of net cash outflows				(693,250)
Net present value in favor of buying the new machine				$ 109,500

*All factors are from Tables 14C–3 and 14C–4 in Appendix 14C.
†These two items could be netted into a single $220,000 incremental-cost figure ($250,000 − $30,000 = $220,000).

As shown in the exhibit, the new machine has the lowest total cost when the present value of the net cash outflows is considered. An analysis of the two alternatives using the incremental-cost approach is presented in Exhibit 14–10. As before, the data in this exhibit represent the differences between the alternatives as shown under the total-cost approach.

IN BUSINESS

TRADING IN THAT OLD CAR?

Consumer Reports magazine provides the following data concerning the alternatives of keeping a four-year-old Ford Taurus for three years or buying a similar new car to replace it. The illustration assumes the car would be purchased and used in suburban Chicago.

	Keep the Old Taurus	Buy a New Taurus
Annual maintenance	$1,180	$650
Annual insurance	$370	$830
Annual license	$15	$100
Trade-in value in three years	$605	$7,763
Purchase price, including sales tax		$17,150

Consumer Reports is ordinarily extremely careful in its analysis, but in this instance it has omitted one financial item that differs substantially between the alternatives. What is it? To check your answer, go to the textbook website at www.mhhe.com/garrison11e. After accessing the site, click on the link to the Internet Exercises and then the link to this chapter.

Source: "When to Give Up on Your Clunker," *Consumer Reports*, August 2000, pp. 12–16.

Uncertain Cash Flows

LEARNING OBJECTIVE 3
Evaluate an investment project that has uncertain cash flows.

Thus far, the chapter has assumed that all future cash flows are known with certainty. However, future cash flows are often uncertain or difficult to estimate. A number of techniques are available for handling this complication. Some of these techniques are quite technical—involving computer simulations or advanced mathematical skills—and are beyond the scope of this book. However, we can provide some very useful information to managers without getting too technical.

EXHIBIT 14–10
The Incremental-Cost Approach (Least-Cost Decision)

Item	Year(s)	Amount of Cash Flows	10% Factor*	Present Value of Cash Flows
Incremental investment required to purchase the new machine	Now	$(210,000)	1.000	$(210,000)†
Salvage value of the old machine	Now	$30,000	1.000	30,000†
Savings in annual cash operating costs	1–6	$60,000	4.355	261,300
Difference in salvage value in six years	6	$50,000	0.564	28,200
Net present value in favor of buying the new machine				$ 109,500

*All factors are from Tables 14C–3 and 14C–4 in Appendix 14C.
†These two items could be netted into a single $180,000 incremental-cost figure ($210,000 − $30,000 = $180,000).

An Example

As an example of difficult-to-estimate future cash flows, consider the case of investments in automated equipment. The up-front costs of automated equipment and the tangible benefits, such as reductions in operating costs and waste, tend to be relatively easy to estimate. However, the intangible benefits, such as greater reliability, greater speed, and higher quality, are more difficult to quantify in terms of future cash flows. These intangible benefits certainly impact future cash flows—particularly in terms of increased sales and perhaps higher selling prices—but the cash flow effects are difficult to estimate. What can be done?

A fairly simple procedure can be followed when the intangible benefits are likely to be significant. Suppose, for example, that a company with a 12% discount rate is considering purchasing automated equipment that would have a 10-year useful life. Also suppose that a discounted cash flow analysis of just the tangible costs and benefits shows a negative net present value of $226,000. Clearly, if the intangible benefits are large enough, they could turn this negative net present value into a positive net present value. In this case, the amount of additional cash flow per year from the intangible benefits that would be needed to make the project financially attractive can be computed as follows:

Net present value excluding the intangible benefits (negative)	$(226,000)
Present value factor for an annuity at 12% for 10 periods (from Table 14C–4 in Appendix 14C)	5.650

$$\frac{\text{Negative net present value to be offset, \$226,000}}{\text{Present value factor, 5.650}} = \$40,000$$

Thus, if the intangible benefits of the automated equipment are worth at least $40,000 a year to the company, then the automated equipment should be purchased. If, in the judgment of management, these intangible benefits are not worth $40,000 a year, then the automated equipment should not be purchased.

This technique can be used in other situations in which future cash flows are difficult to estimate. For example, this technique can be used when the salvage value is difficult to estimate. To illustrate, suppose that all of the cash flows from an investment in a supertanker have been estimated—other than its salvage value in 20 years. Using a discount rate of 12%, management has determined that the net present value of all of these cash flows is a negative $1.04 million. This negative net present value would be offset by the salvage value of the supertanker. How large would the salvage value have to be to make this investment attractive?

Net present value excluding salvage value (negative)	$(1,040,000)
Present value factor at 12% for 20 periods (from Table 14C–3 in Appendix 14C)	0.104

$$\frac{\text{Negative net present value to be offset, \$1,040,000}}{\text{Present value factor, 0.104}} = \$10,000,000$$

Thus, if the salvage value of the tanker is at least $10 million, its net present value would be positive and the investment would be made. However, if management believes the salvage value is unlikely to be as large as $10 million, the investment should not be made.

Real Options

The analysis in this chapter has assumed that an investment cannot be postponed and that, once started, nothing can be done to alter the course of the project. In reality, investments can often be postponed. Postponement is a particularly attractive option when the net present value of a project is modest using current estimates of future cash flows and the future cash flows involve a great deal of uncertainty that may be resolved over time. Similarly, once an investment is made, management can often exploit changes in the business environment and take actions that enhance future cash flows. For example, buying a supertanker provides management with a number of options, some of which may become more attractive as time unfolds. Instead of operating the supertanker itself, the company may decide to lease it to another operator if the rental rates become high enough. Or, if a supertanker shortage develops, management may decide to sell the supertanker and take a gain. In the case of an investment in automated equipment, management may initially buy only the basic model without costly add-ons, but keep the option open to add more capacity and capability later. The ability to delay the start of a project, to expand it if conditions are favorable, to cut losses if they are unfavorable, and to otherwise modify plans as business conditions change adds value to many investments. These advantages can be quantified using what is called *real options* analysis, but the techniques are beyond the scope of this book.

IN BUSINESS

THINKING AHEAD

With an eye on environmental concerns, the board of directors of Royal Dutch/Shell, the Anglo-Dutch energy company, has decided that all big projects must explicitly take into account the likely future costs of abating carbon emissions. Calculations must assume a cost of $5 per ton of carbon dioxide emission in 2005 through 2009, rising to $20 per ton from 2010 onward. A Shell manager explains: "We know that $5 and $20 are surely the wrong price, but everyone else who assumes a carbon price of zero in the future will be more wrong. This is not altruism. We see it as giving us a competitive edge."

Source: "Big Business Bows to Global Warming," *The Economist*, December 2, 2000, p. 81.

Preference Decisions—The Ranking of Investment Projects

LEARNING OBJECTIVE 4
Rank investment projects in order of preference.

Recall that when considering investment opportunities, managers must make two types of decisions—screening decisions and preference decisions. Screening decisions, which come first, pertain to whether or not some proposed investment is acceptable. Preference decisions come *after* screening decisions and attempt to answer the following question: "How do the remaining investment proposals, all of which have been screened and provide an acceptable rate of return, rank in terms of preference? That is, which one(s) would be *best* for the company to accept?"

Preference decisions are more difficult to make than screening decisions because investment funds are usually limited. This often requires that some (perhaps many) otherwise very profitable investment opportunities must be passed up.

Sometimes preference decisions are called rationing decisions, or ranking decisions. Limited investment funds must be rationed among many competing alternatives. Hence, the alternatives must be ranked. Either the internal rate of return method or the net present value method can be used in making preference decisions. However, as discussed earlier, if the two methods are in conflict, it is best to use the net present value method, which is more reliable.

Internal Rate of Return Method

When using the internal rate of return method to rank competing investment projects, the preference rule is: *The higher the internal rate of return, the more desirable the project.* An investment project with an internal rate of return of 18% is usually considered preferable to another project that promises a return of only 15%. Internal rate of return is widely used to rank projects.

Net Present Value Method

Unfortunately, the net present value of one project cannot be directly compared to the net present value of another project unless the investments are equal. For example, assume that a company is considering two competing investments, as shown below:

	Investment	
	A	B
Investment required	$(10,000)	$(5,000)
Present value of cash inflows	11,000	6,000
Net present value	$ 1,000	$ 1,000

Although each project has a net present value of $1,000, the projects are not equally desirable if the funds available for investment are limited. The project requiring an investment of only $5,000 is much more desirable than the project requiring an investment of $10,000. This fact can be highlighted by dividing the net present value of the project by the investment required. The result, shown below in equation form, is called the **project profitability index.**

$$\text{Project profitability index} = \frac{\text{Net present value of the project}}{\text{Investment required}} \qquad (2)$$

The project profitability indexes for the two investments above would be computed as follows:

	Investment	
	A	B
Net present value (a)	$1,000	$1,000
Investment required (b)	$10,000	$5,000
Project profitability index, (a) ÷ (b)	0.10	0.20

When using the project profitability index to rank competing investments projects, the preference rule is: *The higher the project profitability index, the more desirable the project.*[6] Applying this rule to the two investments above, investment B should be chosen over investment A.

The project profitability index is an application of the techniques for utilizing constrained resources discussed in Chapter 13. In this case, the constrained resource is the limited funds available for investment, and the project profitability index is similar to the contribution margin per unit of the constrained resource.

A few details should be clarified with respect to the computation of the project profitability index. The "Investment required" refers to any cash outflows that occur at the beginning of the project, reduced by any salvage value recovered from the sale of old equipment. The "Investment required" also includes any investment in working capital that the project may need.

Other Approaches to Capital Budgeting Decisions

The net present value and internal rate of return methods are widely used as decision-making tools. Other methods of making capital budgeting decisions are also used, however, and

[6] Because of the "lumpiness" of projects, the project profitability index ranking may not be perfect. Nevertheless, it is a good starting point. For further details, see the Profitability Analysis Appendix at the end of the book.

are preferred by some managers. In this section, we discuss two such methods known as *payback* and *simple rate of return.* Both methods have been used for many years, but have been declining in popularity.

The Payback Method

LEARNING OBJECTIVE 5
Determine the payback period for an investment.

The payback method focuses on the *payback period.* The **payback period** is the length of time that it takes for a project to recoup its initial cost out of the cash receipts that it generates. This period is sometimes referred to as "the time that it takes for an investment to pay for itself." The basic premise of the payback method is that the more quickly the cost of an investment can be recovered, the more desirable is the investment.

The payback period is expressed in years. *When the net annual cash inflow is the same every year,* the following formula can be used to compute the payback period:

$$\text{Payback period} = \frac{\text{Investment required}}{\text{Net annual cash inflow*}} \qquad (3)$$

*If new equipment is replacing old equipment, this becomes incremental net annual cash inflow.

Topic Tackler PLUS
14–2

To illustrate the payback method, consider the following data:

Example G: York Company needs a new milling machine. The company is considering two machines: machine A and machine B. Machine A costs $15,000 and will reduce operating costs by $5,000 per year. Machine B costs only $12,000 but will also reduce operating costs by $5,000 per year.

Required:
Which machine should be purchased according to the payback method?

$$\text{Machine A payback period} = \frac{\$15{,}000}{\$5{,}000} = 3.0 \text{ years}$$

$$\text{Machine B payback period} = \frac{\$12{,}000}{\$5{,}000} = 2.4 \text{ years}$$

According to the payback calculations, York Company should purchase machine B, since it has a shorter payback period than machine A.

IN BUSINESS

INVESTING IN AN MBA

The financial benefit of earning an MBA degree is enhanced earning power; the costs include both tuition and the opportunity cost of lost salary for two years. *Forbes* magazine computed both the net present value and the payback period for 80 full-time MBA programs. *Forbes* looked at the first five years of enhanced earnings after the degree is granted and the costs of getting the degree. The net present value of an MBA varies a great deal—ranging from over $100,000 at Harvard to $1,000 or less at some institutions. The payback periods show less variation. The quickest paybacks are at Harvard and Ohio State—3.3 years. The slowest payback is about five years. Earnings that extend beyond the five-year horizon are ignored in the *Forbes* analysis. If these earnings had been included, the net present values of degrees would have increased substantially.

Source: Kurt Brandenhausen, "The Bottom Line on B-Schools," *Forbes*, February 7, 2000, pp. 100–104.

Evaluation of the Payback Method

The payback method is not a true measure of the profitability of an investment. Rather, it simply tells a manager how many years will be required to recover the original investment. Unfortunately, a shorter payback period does not always mean that one investment is more desirable than another.

To illustrate, consider again the two machines used in the example above. Since machine B has a shorter payback period than machine A, it *appears* that machine B is more desirable than machine A. But if we add one more piece of information, this illusion quickly disappears. Machine A has a projected 10-year life, and machine B has a projected 5-year life. It would take two purchases of machine B to provide the same length of service as would be provided by a single purchase of machine A. Under these circumstances, machine A would be a much better investment than machine B, even though machine B has a shorter payback period. Unfortunately, the payback method has no inherent mechanism for highlighting differences in useful life between investments. Such differences can be very important, and relying on payback alone may result in incorrect decisions.

A further criticism of the payback method is that it does not consider the time value of money. A cash inflow to be received several years in the future is weighed equally with a cash inflow to be received right now. To illustrate, assume that for an investment of $8,000 you can purchase either of the two following streams of cash inflows:

Year	0	1	2	3	4	5	6	7	8
Stream 1 . .					$8,000	$2,000	$2,000	$2,000	$2,000
Stream 2 . .		$2,000	$2,000	$2,000	$2,000	$8,000			

Which stream of cash inflows would you prefer to receive in return for your $8,000 investment? Each stream has a payback period of 4.0 years. Therefore, if payback alone were relied on in making the decision, the streams would be viewed as equally desirable. However, from the point of view of the time value of money, stream 2 is much more desirable than stream 1.

On the other hand, under certain conditions the payback method can be very useful. For one thing, it can help identify which investment proposals are in the "ballpark." That is, it can be used as a screening tool to help answer the question, "Should I consider this proposal further?" If a proposal doesn't provide a payback within some specified period, then there may be no need to consider it further. In addition, the payback period is often of great importance to new companies that are "cash poor." When a company is cash poor, a project with a short payback period but a low rate of return might be preferred over another project with a high rate of return but a long payback period. The reason is that the company may simply need a faster return of its cash investment. And finally, the payback method is sometimes used in industries where products become obsolete very rapidly—such as consumer electronics. Since products may last only a year or two, the payback period on investments must be very short.

IN BUSINESS

CONSERVATION IS NOT SELF-DENIAL

Amory Lovins, the director of the Rocky Mountain Institute in Snowmass, Colorado, is a passionate advocate of energy efficiency as a means of conserving natural resources and reducing pollution. Rather than cutting energy consumption by adopting more austere lifestyles, Lovins believes that energy consumption can be radically cut by using energy more efficiently. This approach has the virtues of combining energy conservation with cash savings and better living standards. He claims that America's annual electric bill of $220 billion could be cut in half by making investments with a payback period of one year or less. To illustrate his point, Lovins designed the institute's headquarters to require no furnace or air conditioning. During the cold winters, daytime solar heat enters the building through a built-in greenhouse, is soaked up by massive stone walls and foundations, and is then released at night. The institute is hardly a chilling, austere structure. Its passive heating system supports a small stand of tropical fruit trees, a mini fish farm, an indoor waterfall, and a hot tub. Lovins claims that the building's efficient design added only $6,000 to its construction costs and the payback period on this investment was only 10 months.

Source: David Stipp, "Can This Man Solve America's Energy Crisis?" *Fortune*, May 13, 2002, pp. 100–110.

An Extended Example of Payback

As shown by formula (3) given earlier, the payback period is computed by dividing the investment in a project by the net annual cash inflows that the project will generate. If new equipment is replacing old equipment, then any salvage value to be received on disposal of the old equipment should be deducted from the cost of the new equipment, and only the *incremental* investment should be used in the payback computation. In addition, any depreciation deducted in arriving at the project's net operating income must be added back to obtain the project's expected net annual cash inflow. To illustrate, consider the following data:

Example H: Goodtime Fun Centers, Inc., operates amusement parks. Some of the vending machines in one of its parks provide very little revenue, so the company is considering removing the machines and installing equipment to dispense soft ice cream. The equipment would cost $80,000 and have an eight-year useful life. Incremental annual revenues and costs associated with the sale of ice cream would be as follows:

Sales	$150,000
Less cost of ingredients	90,000
Contribution margin	60,000
Less fixed expenses:	
Salaries	27,000
Maintenance	3,000
Depreciation	10,000
Total fixed expenses	40,000
Net operating income	$ 20,000

The vending machines can be sold for a $5,000 scrap value. The company will not purchase equipment unless it has a payback period of three years or less. Does the equipment to dispense ice cream pass this hurdle?

An analysis of the payback period for the proposed equipment is given in Exhibit 14–11. Several things should be noted. First, depreciation is added back to net operating income to obtain the net annual cash inflow from the new equipment. Depreciation is not

EXHIBIT 14–11
Computation of the Payback Period

Step 1: *Compute the net annual cash inflow.* Since the net annual cash inflow is not given, it must be computed before the payback period can be determined:

Net operating income (given above)	$20,000
Add: Noncash deduction for depreciation	10,000
Net annual cash inflow	$30,000

Step 2: *Compute the payback period.* Using the net annual cash inflow figure from above, the payback period can be determined as follows:

Cost of the new equipment	$80,000
Less salvage value of old equipment	5,000
Investment required	$75,000

$$\text{Payback period} = \frac{\text{Investment required}}{\text{Net annual cash inflow}}$$

$$= \frac{\$75,000}{\$30,000} = 2.5 \text{ years}$$

a cash outlay; thus, it must be added back to adjust net operating income to a cash basis. Second, the payback computation deducts the salvage value of the old machines from the cost of the new equipment so that only the incremental investment is used in computing the payback period.

Since the proposed equipment has a payback period of less than three years, the company's payback requirement has been met.

IN BUSINESS

COUNTING THE ENVIRONMENTAL COSTS

Companies often grossly underestimate how much they are spending on environmental costs. Many of these costs are buried in broad cost categories such as manufacturing overhead. Kestrel Management Services, LLC, a management consulting firm specializing in environmental matters, found that one chemical facility was spending five times as much on environmental expenses as its cost system reported. At another site, a small manufacturer with $840,000 in pretax profits thought that its annual safety and environmental compliance expenses were about $50,000 but, after digging into the accounts, found that the total was closer to $300,000. Alerted to this high cost, management of the company invested about $125,000 in environmental improvements, anticipating a three- to six-month payback period. By taking steps such as more efficient dust collection, the company improved its product quality, reduced scrap rates, decreased its consumption of city water for cooling, and reduced the expense of discharging wastewater into the city's sewer system. Further analysis revealed that spending $50,000 to improve energy efficiency would reduce annual energy costs by about $45,000. Few of these costs were visible in the company's traditional cost accounting system.

Source: Thomas P. Kunes, "A Green and *Lean* Workplace?" *Strategic Finance*, February 2001, pp. 71–73, 83.

Payback and Uneven Cash Flows

When the cash flows associated with an investment project change from year to year, the simple payback formula that we outlined earlier cannot be used. Consider the following data:

Year	Investment	Cash Inflow
1	$4,000	$1,000
2		$0
3		$2,000
4	$2,000	$1,000
5		$500
6		$3,000
7		$2,000

What is the payback period on this investment? The answer is 5.5 years, but to obtain this figure it is necessary to track the unrecovered investment year by year. The steps involved in this process are shown in Exhibit 14–12. By the middle of the sixth year, sufficient cash inflows will have been realized to recover the entire investment of $6,000 ($4,000 + $2,000).

The Simple Rate of Return Method

LEARNING OBJECTIVE 6
Compute the simple rate of return for an investment.

The **simple rate of return** method is another capital budgeting technique that does not involve discounting cash flows. The simple rate of return is also known as the accounting rate of return or the unadjusted rate of return.

Unlike the other capital budgeting methods that we have discussed, the simple rate of return method does not focus on cash flows. Rather, it focuses on accounting net operating income. The approach is to estimate the revenues that will be generated by a proposed investment and then to deduct from these revenues all of the projected operating expenses associated with the project. The net operating income is then related to the initial investment in the project, as shown in the following formula:

EXHIBIT 14–12
Payback and Uneven Cash Flows

Year	Investment	Cash Inflow	Unrecovered Investment
1	$4,000	$1,000	$3,000
2		$0	$3,000
3		$2,000	$1,000
4	$2,000	$1,000	$2,000
5		$500	$1,500
6		$3,000	$0
7		$2,000	$0

$$\text{Simple rate of return} = \frac{\begin{array}{c}\text{Annual incremental}\\\text{revenues}\end{array} - \begin{array}{c}\text{Annual incremental expenses,}\\\text{including depreciation}\end{array} = \begin{array}{c}\text{Annual incremental net}\\\text{operating income}\end{array}}{\text{Initial investment*}} \qquad (4)$$

*The initial investment should be reduced by any salvage value from the sale of old equipment.

Or, if a cost reduction project is involved, formula (4) becomes:

$$\text{Simple rate of return} = \frac{\begin{array}{c}\text{Annual}\\\text{cost savings}\end{array} - \begin{array}{c}\text{Annual depreciation on}\\\text{new equipment}\end{array}}{\text{Initial investment*}} \qquad (5)$$

*The initial investment should be reduced by any salvage value from the sale of old equipment.

Example I: Brigham Tea, Inc., is a processor of low-acid tea. The company is contemplating purchasing equipment for an additional processing line. The additional processing line would increase revenues by $90,000 per year. Incremental cash operating expenses would be $40,000 per year. The equipment would cost $180,000 and have a nine-year life. No salvage value is projected.

$$\text{Simple rate of return} = \frac{\left[\begin{array}{c}\$90{,}000\text{ Annual}\\\text{incremental revenues}\end{array}\right] - \left[\begin{array}{c}\$40{,}000\text{ Annual cash operating expenses}\\+\ \$20{,}000\text{ Annual depreciation}\end{array}\right]}{\$180{,}000\text{ Initial investment}}$$

$$= \frac{\$30{,}000}{\$180{,}000}$$

$$= 16.7\%$$

Example J: Midwest Farms, Inc., hires people on a part-time basis to sort eggs. The cost of this hand-sorting process is $30,000 per year. The company is investigating an egg-sorting machine that would cost $90,000 and have a 15-year useful life. The machine would have negligible salvage value, and it would cost $10,000 per year to operate and maintain. The egg-sorting equipment currently being used could be sold now for a scrap value of $2,500.

A cost reduction project is involved in this situation. By applying equation (5), we can compute the simple rate of return as follows:

$$\text{Simple rate of return} = \frac{\begin{array}{c}\$20{,}000^{*}\text{ Annual}\\\text{cost savings}\end{array} - \begin{array}{c}\$6{,}000^{\dagger}\text{ Annual depreciation}\\\text{on new equipment}\end{array}}{\$90{,}000 - \$2{,}500}$$

$$= 16.0\%$$

*$30,000 − $10,000 = $20,000 cost savings.
†$90,000 ÷ 15 years = $6,000 depreciation.

IN BUSINESS

AN AMAZING RETURN

Ipswitch, Inc., a software developer and seller, has moved much of its business to the Web. Potential customers can download free trial copies of the company's software at www.ipswitch.com. After the trial period, a customer must return to the Web site to purchase and download a permanent copy of the software. The initial investment in setting up a Web site was modest—roughly \$190,000. The cost of keeping the Web site up and running and updated with the latest product information is about \$1.3 million a year—mainly in the form of salaries and benefits for eight employees. The company estimates that additional revenues brought in by the Web amount to about \$13 million per year and that the company saves about \$585,000 per year in direct mail advertising costs by using the Web for much of its advertising instead. Assuming that the cost of sales is almost zero for downloaded software, the accounting rate of return on the initial investment in the Web site is 6,466% ([\$13,000,000 − \$1,300,000 + \$585,000] ÷ \$190,000)!

Source: Karen N. Kroll, "Many Happy Returns," *INC*, November 30, 2001, pp. 150–152.

Criticisms of the Simple Rate of Return

The most damaging criticism of the simple rate of return method is that it does not consider the time value of money. The simple rate of return method considers a dollar received 10 years from now to be as valuable as a dollar received today. Thus, the simple rate of return method can be misleading if the alternatives being considered have different cash flow patterns. Additionally, many projects do not have constant incremental revenues and expenses over their useful lives. As a result, the simple rate of return will fluctuate from year to year, with the possibility that a project may appear to be desirable in some years and undesirable in others. In contrast, the net present value method provides a single number that summarizes all of the cash flows over the entire useful life of the project.

IN BUSINESS

WATCHING THE REALLY LONG TERM

Forest product companies have some of the longest time horizons of any industry since trees they plant today may not reach their peak for decades. Of the 29 forest product companies that responded to a questionnaire, 9% use the simple rate of return as the primary criterion to evaluate timber investments, 15% use the payback period, 38% use the internal rate of return, and 38% use the net present value. None of the largest forest products companies use either the simple rate of return or the payback method to evaluate timber projects. For other investment decisions—that typically have shorter time horizons—the method used shifted away from net present value and toward the payback period.

Source: Jack Bailes, James Nielsen, and Stephen Lawton, "How Forest Product Companies Analyze Capital Budgets," *Management Accounting*, October 1998, pp. 24–30.

Postaudit of Investment Projects

After an investment project has been approved and implemented, a *postaudit* should be conducted. A **postaudit** involves checking whether or not expected results are actually realized. This is a key part of the capital budgeting process. It helps to keep managers honest in their investment proposals. Any tendency to inflate the benefits or downplay the costs in a proposal should become evident after a few postaudits have been conducted. The postaudit also provides an opportunity to reinforce and possibly expand successful projects and to cut losses on floundering projects.

The same technique should be used in the postaudit as was used in the original approval process. That is, if a project was approved on the basis of a net present value analysis, then the same procedure should be used in performing the postaudit. However, the data used in the postaudit analysis should be *actual observed data* rather than estimated data. This gives management an opportunity to make a side-by-side comparison to see how well the project has succeeded. It also helps assure that estimated data received on future proposals will be carefully prepared, since the persons submitting the data will know that their estimates will be given careful scrutiny in the postaudit process. Actual results that are far out of line with original estimates should be carefully reviewed.

IN BUSINESS

CAPITAL BUDGETING IN PRACTICE

A survey of Fortune 1000 companies—the largest companies in the United States—asked CFOs how often various capital budgeting methods are used in their companies. Some of the results of that survey are displayed below:

	Frequency of Use				
Capital Budgeting Tool	Always	Often	Sometimes	Rarely	Never
Net present value	50%	35%	11%	3%	1%
Internal rate of return	45%	32%	15%	6%	2%
Payback	19%	33%	22%	17%	9%
Accounting rate of return	5%	9%	19%	16%	50%

Many companies use more than one method—for example, they may use both the net present value and the internal rate of return methods to evaluate capital budgeting projects. Note that the two discounted cash flow methods—net present value and internal rate of return—are by far the most commonly used in practice.

A similar survey of companies in the United Kingdom yielded the following results:

	Frequency of Use			
Capital Budgeting Tool	Always	Mostly	Often	Rarely
Net present value	43%	20%	14%	7%
Internal rate of return	48%	20%	10%	5%
Payback	30%	16%	17%	14%
Accounting rate of return	26%	15%	18%	7%

Note that while the results were quite similar for the U.S. and U.K. companies, the U.K. companies were more likely to use the payback and accounting rate of return methods than the U.S. companies.

Sources: Patricia A. Ryan and Glenn P. Ryan, "Capital Budgeting Practices of the Fortune 1000: How Have Things Changed?" *Journal of Business and Management,* Fall 2002, pp. 355–364. Glen C. Arnold and Panos D. Hatzopoulus, "The Theory-Practice Gap in Capital Budgeting: Evidence from the United Kingdom," *Journal of Business Finance & Accounting* 27(5) & 27(6), June/July 2000, pp. 603–626.

Summary

Investment decisions should take into account the time value of money since a dollar today is more valuable than a dollar received in the future. The net present value and internal rate of return methods both reflect this fact. In the net present value method, future cash flows are discounted to their present value so that they can be compared with current cash outlays. The difference between the present value of the cash inflows and the present value of the cash outflows is called the project's net present value. If the net present value of the project is negative, the project is rejected. The discount rate in the net present value method is usually based on a minimum required rate of return such as the company's cost of capital.

The internal rate of return is the rate of return that equates the present value of the cash inflows and the present value of the cash outflows, resulting in a zero net present value. If the internal rate of return is less than the company's minimum required rate of return, the project is rejected.

After rejecting projects whose net present values are negative or whose internal rates of return are less than the minimum required rate of return, the company may still have more projects than can be supported with available funds. The remaining projects can be ranked using either the project profitability index or internal rate of return. The project profitability index is computed by dividing the present value of the project's future net cash inflows by the required initial investment.

Some companies prefer to use either payback or the simple rate of return to evaluate investment proposals. The payback period is the number of periods that are required to fully recover the initial investment in the project. The simple rate of return is determined by dividing a project's accounting net operating income by the initial investment in the project.

Review Problem 1: Basic Present Value Computations

Each of the following situations is independent. Work out your own solution to each situation, and then check it against the solution provided.

1. In 12 years, John plans to retire. Upon retiring, he would like to take an extended vacation, which he expects will cost at least $40,000. What lump-sum amount must he invest now to have the needed $40,000 at the end of 12 years if the rate of return is:
   a. Eight percent?
   b. Twelve percent?
2. The Morgans would like to send their daughter to a music camp at the end of each of the next five years. The camp costs $1,000 a year. What lump-sum amount would have to be invested now to have the $1,000 at the end of each year if the rate of return is:
   a. Eight percent?
   b. Twelve percent?
3. You have just received an inheritance from a relative. You can invest the money and either receive a $200,000 lump-sum amount at the end of 10 years or receive $14,000 at the end of each year for the next 10 years. If your minimum desired rate of return is 12%, which alternative would you prefer?

Solution to Review Problem 1

1. *a.* The amount that must be invested now would be the present value of the $40,000, using a discount rate of 8%. From Table 14C–3 in Appendix 14C, the factor for a discount rate of 8% for 12 periods is 0.397. Multiplying this discount factor by the $40,000 needed in 12 years will give the amount of the present investment required: $40,000 × 0.397 = $15,880.
   b. We will proceed as we did in (*a*) above, but this time we will use a discount rate of 12%. From Table 14C–3 in Appendix 14C, the factor for a discount rate of 12% for 12 periods is 0.257. Multiplying this discount factor by the $40,000 needed in 12 years will give the amount of the present investment required: $40,000 × 0.257 = $10,280.
   Notice that as the discount rate (desired rate of return) increases, the present value decreases.
2. This part differs from (1) above in that we are now dealing with an annuity rather than with a single future sum. The amount that must be invested now will be the present value of the $1,000 needed at the end of each year for five years. Since we are dealing with an annuity, or a series of annual cash flows, we must refer to Table 14C–4 in Appendix 14C for the appropriate discount factor.
   a. From Table 14C–4 in Appendix 14C, the discount factor for 8% for five periods is 3.993. Therefore, the amount that must be invested now to have $1,000 available at the end of each year for five years is $1,000 × 3.993 = $3,993.
   b. From Table 14C–4 in Appendix 14C, the discount factor for 12% for five periods is 3.605. Therefore, the amount that must be invested now to have $1,000 available at the end of each year for five years is $1,000 × 3.605 = $3,605.
   Again, notice that as the discount rate (desired rate of return) increases, the present value decreases. At a higher rate of return we can invest less than would have been needed if a lower rate of return were being earned.

3. For this part we will need to refer to both Tables 14C–3 and 14C–4 in Appendix 14C. From Table 14C–3, we will need to find the discount factor for 12% for 10 periods, then apply it to the $200,000 lump sum to be received in 10 years. From Table 14C–4, we will need to find the discount factor for 12% for 10 periods, then apply it to the series of $14,000 payments to be received over the 10-year period. Whichever alternative has the higher present value is the one that should be selected.

$$\$200{,}000 \times 0.322 = \$64{,}400$$

$$\$14{,}000 \times 5.650 = \$79{,}100$$

Thus, you should prefer to receive the $14,000 per year for 10 years rather than the $200,000 lump sum.

Review Problem 2: Comparison of Capital Budgeting Methods

Lamar Company is studying a project that would have an eight-year life and require a $2,400,000 investment in equipment. At the end of eight years, the project would terminate and the equipment would have no salvage value. The project would provide net operating income each year as follows:

Sales		$3,000,000
Less variable expenses		1,800,000
Contribution margin		1,200,000
Less fixed expenses:		
Advertising, salaries, and other fixed out-of-pocket costs	$700,000	
Depreciation	300,000	
Total fixed expenses		1,000,000
Net operating income		$ 200,000

The company's discount rate is 12%.

Required:

1. Compute the net annual cash inflow from the project.
2. Compute the project's net present value. Is the project acceptable?
3. Find the project's internal rate of return to the nearest whole percent.
4. Compute the project's payback period.
5. Compute the project's simple rate of return.

Solution to Review Problem 2

1. The net annual cash inflow can be computed by deducting the cash expenses from sales:

Sales	$3,000,000
Less variable expenses	1,800,000
Contribution margin	1,200,000
Less advertising, salaries, and other fixed out-of-pocket costs	700,000
Net annual cash inflow	$ 500,000

Or it can be computed by adding depreciation back to net operating income:

Net operating income	$200,000
Add: Noncash deduction for depreciation	300,000
Net annual cash inflow	$500,000

2. The net present value can be computed as follows:

Item	Year(s)	Amount of Cash Flows	12% Factor	Present Value of Cash Flows
Cost of new equipment	Now	$(2,400,000)	1.000	$(2,400,000)
Net annual cash inflow	1–8	$500,000	4.968	2,484,000
Net present value				$ 84,000

Yes, the project is acceptable since it has a positive net present value.

3. The formula for computing the factor of the internal rate of return is:

$$\text{Factor of the internal rate of return} = \frac{\text{Investment required}}{\text{Net annual cash inflow}}$$

$$= \frac{\$2{,}400{,}000}{\$500{,}000} = 4.800$$

Looking in Table 14C–4 in Appendix 14C at the end of the chapter and scanning along the 8-period line, we find that a factor of 4.800 represents a rate of return of about 13%.

4. The formula for the payback period is:

$$\text{Payback period} = \frac{\text{Investment required}}{\text{Net annual cash inflow}}$$

$$= \frac{\$2{,}400{,}000}{\$500{,}000}$$

$$= 4.8 \text{ years}$$

5. The formula for the simple rate of return is:

$$\text{Simple rate of return} = \frac{\begin{array}{c}\text{Annual} \\ \text{incremental} \\ \text{revenues}\end{array} - \begin{array}{c}\text{Annual incremental} \\ \text{expenses, including} \\ \text{depreciation}\end{array} = \begin{array}{c}\text{Annual} \\ \text{incremental net} \\ \text{operating income}\end{array}}{\text{Initial investment}}$$

$$= \frac{\$200{,}000}{\$2{,}400{,}000}$$

$$= 8.3\%$$

Glossary

Capital budgeting The process of planning significant outlays on projects that have long-term implications such as the purchase of new equipment or the introduction of a new product. (p. 654)

Cost of capital The average rate of return a company must pay to its long-term creditors and shareholders for the use of their funds. (p. 659)

Internal rate of return The discount rate at which the net present value of an investment project is zero; the rate of return promised by a project over its useful life. (p. 661)

Net present value The difference between the present value of the cash inflows and the present value of the cash outflows of an investment project. (p. 655)

Out-of-pocket costs Actual cash outlays for salaries, advertising, repairs, and similar costs. (p. 660)

Payback period The length of time that it takes for a project to fully recover its initial cost out of the cash receipts that it generates. (p. 671)

Postaudit The follow-up after a project has been approved and implemented to determine whether expected results were actually realized. (p. 676)

Preference decision A decision as to which of several competing acceptable investment proposals is best. (p. 654)

Project profitability index The ratio of the net present value of a project's cash flows to the investment required. (p. 670)
Required rate of return The minimum rate of return that an investment project must yield to be acceptable. (p. 662)
Screening decision A decision as to whether a proposed investment passes a preset hurdle. (p. 654)
Simple rate of return The rate of return computed by dividing a project's annual accounting net operating income by the initial investment required. (p. 674)
Working capital The excess of current assets over current liabilities. (p. 657)

Appendix 14A: The Concept of Present Value

LEARNING OBJECTIVE 7
Understand present value concepts and the use of present value tables.

A dollar received today is more valuable than a dollar received a year from now for the simple reason that if you have a dollar today, you can put it in the bank and have more than a dollar a year from now. Since dollars today are worth more than dollars in the future, we must weight cash flows that are received at different times so that they can be compared.

The Mathematics of Interest

If a bank pays 5% interest, then a deposit of \$100 today will be worth \$105 one year from now. This can be expressed as follows:

$$F_1 = P(1 + r) \qquad (1)$$

where F_1 = the balance at the end of one period, P = the amount invested now, and r = the rate of interest per period.

If the investment made now is \$100 deposited in a savings account that earns 5% interest, then P = \$100 and r = 0.05. Under these conditions, F_1 = \$105, the amount to be received in one year.

The \$100 present outlay is called the **present value** of the \$105 amount to be received in one year. It is also known as the *discounted value* of the future \$105 receipt. The \$100 represents the value in present terms of \$105 to be received a year from now when the interest rate is 5%.

Compound Interest

What if the \$105 is left in the bank for a second year? In that case, by the end of the second year the original \$100 deposit will have grown to \$110.25:

Original deposit	\$100.00
Interest for the first year:	
\$100 × 0.05	5.00
Balance at the end of the first year	105.00
Interest for the second year:	
\$105 × 0.05	5.25
Balance at the end of the second year	\$110.25

Notice that the interest for the second year is \$5.25, as compared to only \$5.00 for the first year. The reason for the greater interest earned during the second year is that during the second year, interest is being paid *on interest.* That is, the \$5.00 interest earned during the first year has been left in the account and has been added to the original \$100 deposit when computing interest for the second year. This is known as **compound interest.** In this case, the compounding is annual. Interest can be compounded on a semiannual, quarterly, monthly, or even more frequent basis. The more frequently compounding is done, the more rapidly the balance will grow.

EXHIBIT 14A–1
The Relationship between Present Value and Future Value

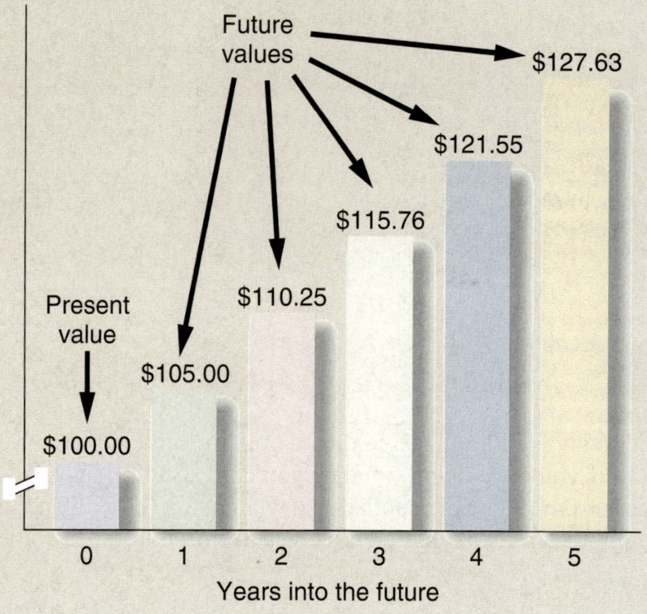

We can determine the balance in an account after n periods of compounding using the following equation:

$$F_n = P(1 + r)^n \tag{2}$$

where n = the number of periods of compounding.

If $n = 2$ years and the interest rate is 5% per year, then the balance in two years will be computed as follows:

$$F_2 = \$100(1 + 0.05)^2$$
$$F_2 = \$110.25$$

Present Value and Future Value Exhibit 14A–1 shows the relationship between present value and future value. As shown in the exhibit, if $100 is deposited in a bank at 5% interest, it will grow to $127.63 by the end of five years if interest is compounded annually.

Computation of Present Value

An investment can be viewed in two ways. It can be viewed either in terms of its future value or in terms of its present value. We have seen from our computations above that if we know the present value of a sum (such as our $100 deposit), the future value in n years can be computed by using equation (2). But what if the tables are reversed and we know the *future* value of some amount but we do not know its present value?

For example, assume that you are to receive $200 two years from now. You know that the future value of this sum is $200, since this is the amount that you will be receiving in two years. But what is the sum's present value—what is it worth *right now?* The present value of any sum to be received in the future can be computed by turning equation (2) around and solving for P:

$$P = \frac{F_n}{(1 + r)^n} \tag{3}$$

In our example, F_n = \$200 (the amount to be received in the future), $r = 0.05$ (the annual rate of interest), and $n = 2$ (the number of years in the future that the amount is to be received).

$$P = \frac{\$200}{(1 + 0.05)^2}$$

$$P = \frac{\$200}{1.1025}$$

$$P = \$181.40$$

As shown by the computation above, the present value of a \$200 amount to be received two years from now is \$181.40 if the interest rate is 5%. In effect, \$181.40 received *right now* is equivalent to \$200 received two years from now if the rate of return is 5%. The \$181.40 and the \$200 are just two ways of looking at the same thing.

The process of finding the present value of a future cash flow, which we have just completed, is called **discounting.** We have *discounted* the \$200 to its present value of \$181.40. The 5% interest that we have used to find this present value is called the **discount rate.** Discounting future sums to their present value is a common practice in business, particularly in capital budgeting decisions.

If you have a power key (y^x) on your calculator, the above calculations are fairly easy. However, some of the present value formulas we will be using are more complex and difficult to use. Fortunately, tables are available in which many of the calculations have already been done for you. For example, Table 14C–3 in Appendix 14C shows the discounted present value of \$1 to be received at various periods in the future at various interest rates. The table indicates that the present value of \$1 to be received two periods from now at 5% is 0.907. Since in our example we want to know the present value of \$200 rather than just \$1, we need to multiply the factor in the table by \$200:

$$\$200 \times 0.907 = \$181.40$$

This answer is the same as we obtained earlier using the formula in equation (3).

Present Value of a Series of Cash Flows

Although some investments involve a single sum to be received (or paid) at a single point in the future, other investments involve a *series* of cash flows. A series (or stream) of identical cash flows is known as an **annuity.** To provide an example, assume that a company has just purchased some government bonds in order to temporarily invest funds that are being held for future plant expansion. The bonds will yield interest of \$15,000 each year and will be held for five years. What is the present value of the stream of interest receipts from the bonds? As shown in Exhibit 14A–2, if the discount rate is 12%, the present value of this stream is \$54,075. The discount factors used in this exhibit were taken from Table 14C–3 in Appendix 14C.

Two points are important in connection with Exhibit 14A–2. First, the present value of the \$15,000 interest declines the further it is into the future. The present value of

EXHIBIT 14A–2
Present Value of a Series of Cash Receipts

Year	Factor at 12% (Table 14C–3)	Interest Received	Present Value
1	0.893	\$15,000	\$13,395
2	0.797	\$15,000	11,955
3	0.712	\$15,000	10,680
4	0.636	\$15,000	9,540
5	0.567	\$15,000	8,505
			\$54,075

$15,000 received a year from now is $13,395, as compared to only $8,505 if received five years from now. This point simply underscores the fact that money has a time value.

The second point is that the computations used in Exhibit 14A–2 involved unnecessary work. The same present value of $54,075 could have been obtained more easily by referring to Table 14C–4 in Appendix 14C. Table 14C–4 contains the present value of $1 to be received each year over a *series* of years at various interest rates. Table 14C–4 has been derived by simply adding together the factors from Table 14C–3, as follows:

Year	Table 14C–3 Factors at 12%
1	0.893
2	0.797
3	0.712
4	0.636
5	0.567
	3.605

The sum of the five factors above is 3.605. Notice from Table 14C–4 that the factor for $1 to be received each year for five years at 12% is also 3.605. If we use this factor and multiply it by the $15,000 annual cash inflow, then we get the same $54,075 present value that we obtained earlier in Exhibit 14A–2.

$$\$15{,}000 \times 3.605 = \$54{,}075$$

Therefore, when computing the present value of a series (or stream) of equal cash flows that begins at the end of period 1, Table 14C–4 should be used.

To summarize, the present value tables in Appendix 14C should be used as follows:

Table 14C–3: This table should be used to find the present value of a single cash flow (such as a single payment or receipt) occurring in the future.

Table 14C–4: This table should be used to find the present value of a series (or stream) of identical cash flows beginning at the end of the current period and continuing into the future.

The use of both of these tables is illustrated in various exhibits in the main body of the chapter. *When a present value factor appears in an exhibit, you should take the time to trace it back into either Table 14C–3 or Table 14C–4 to get acquainted with the tables and how they work.* (Review Problem 1 at the end of the chapter is designed for those who would like some practice in present value analysis before attempting the homework exercises and problems.)

Glossary (Appendix 14A)

Annuity A series, or stream, of identical cash flows. (p. 683)
Compound interest The process of paying interest on interest in an investment. (p. 681)
Discount rate The rate of return that is used to find the present value of a future cash flow. (p. 683)
Discounting The process of finding the present value of a future cash flow. (p. 683)
Present value The value now of an amount that will be received in some future period. (p. 681)

Appendix 14B: Inflation and Capital Budgeting

Does inflation impact capital budgeting analysis? The answer is a qualified yes in that inflation does have an impact on the *numbers* that are used in a capital budgeting analysis,

EXHIBIT 14B–1
Capital Budgeting and Inflation

Reconciliation of the Market-Based and Real Costs of Capital

The real cost of capital	12.0%
The inflation factor	10.0
The combined effect (12% × 10% = 1.2%)	1.2
The market-based cost of capital	23.2%

Solution A: Inflation Not Considered

Item	Year(s)	Amount of Cash Flows	12% Factor	Present Value of Cash Flows
Initial investment	Now	$(36,000)	1.000	$(36,000)
Annual cost savings	1–3	$ 20,000	2.402	48,040
Net present value				$ 12,040‡

Solution B: Inflation Considered

Item	Year(s)	Amount of Cash Flows	Price Index Number*	Price-Adjusted Cash Flows	23.2% Factor†	Present Value of Cash Flows
Initial investment	Now	$(36,000)	1.000	$(36,000)	1.000	$(36,000)
Annual cost savings	1	$ 20,000	1.100	$ 22,000	0.812	17,864
	2	$ 20,000	1.210	$ 24,200	0.659	15,948
	3	$ 20,000	1.331	$ 26,620	0.535	14,242
Net present value						$ 12,054‡

*Computation of the price-index numbers, assuming a 10% inflation rate each year: Year 1, $(1.10)^1 = 1.10$; Year 2, $(1.10)^2 = 1.21$; and Year 3, $(1.10)^3 = 1.331$.
†Discount formulas are computed using the formula $1/(1 + r)^n$, where r is the discount factor and n is the number of years. The computations are $1/1.232 = 0.812$ for Year 1; $1/(1.232)^2 = 0.659$ for Year 2; and $1/(1.232)^3 = 0.535$ for Year 3.
‡These amounts are different only because of rounding error.

but it does not have an impact on the *results* of the analysis if certain conditions are satisfied. To show what we mean by this statement, we will use the following data:

Example K: Martin Company wants to purchase a new machine that costs $36,000. The machine would provide annual cost savings of $20,000, and it would have a three-year life with no salvage value. For each of the next three years, the company expects a 10% inflation rate in the cash flows associated with the new machine. If the company's cost of capital is 23.2%, should the new machine be purchased?

To answer this question, it is important to know how the cost of capital was derived. Ordinarily, it is based on the market rates of return on the company's various sources of financing—both debt and equity. This market rate of return includes expected inflation; the higher the expected rate of inflation, the higher the market rate of return on debt and equity. When the inflationary effect is removed from the market rate of return, the result is called a real rate of return. For example, if the inflation rate of 10% is removed from Martin's cost of capital of 23.2%, the "real cost of capital" is only 12%, as shown in Exhibit 14B–1. (You can't simply subtract the inflation rate from the market cost of capital to obtain the real cost of capital. The computations are a bit more complex than that.)

When performing a net present value analysis, one must be consistent. The market-based cost of capital reflects inflation. Therefore, if a market-based cost of capital is used to discount cash flows, then the cash flows should be adjusted upwards to reflect the effects of inflation in forthcoming periods. Computations for Martin Company under this approach are given in solution B in Exhibit 14B–1.

On the other hand, there is no need to adjust the cash flows upward if the "real cost of capital" is used in the analysis (since the inflationary effects have been taken out of the discount rate). Computations for Martin Company under this approach are given in solution A in Exhibit 14B–1. Note that under solutions A and B that the answer will be the same (within rounding error) regardless of which approach is used, so long as one is consistent and all of the cash flows associated with the project are affected in the same way by inflation.

Several points should be noted about solution B, where the effects of inflation are explicitly taken into account. First, note that the annual cost savings are adjusted for the effects of inflation by multiplying each year's cash savings by a price-index number that reflects a 10% inflation rate. (Observe from the footnotes to the exhibit how the index number is computed for each year.) Second, note that the net present value obtained in solution B, where inflation is explicitly taken into account, is the same, within rounding error, to that obtained in solution A, where the inflation effects are ignored. This result may seem surprising, but it is logical. The reason is that we have adjusted both the cash flows and the discount rate so that they are consistent, and these adjustments cancel each other out across the two solutions.

Throughout the chapter we assume for simplicity that there is no inflation. In that case, the market-based and real costs of capital are the same, and there is no reason to adjust the cash flows for inflation since there is none. When there is inflation, the unadjusted cash flows can be used in the analysis if all of the cash flows are affected identically by inflation and the real cost of capital is used to discount the cash flows. Otherwise, the cash flows should be adjusted for inflation and the market-based cost of capital should be used in the analysis.

EXHIBIT 14C–1

Future Value of \$1; $(1 + r)^n$

Periods	4%	5%	6%	7%	8%	9%	10%	11%	12%	13%	14%	15%	16%	17%	18%	19%	20%
1	1.040	1.050	1.060	1.070	1.080	1.090	1.100	1.110	1.120	1.130	1.140	1.150	1.160	1.170	1.180	1.190	1.200
2	1.082	1.103	1.124	1.145	1.166	1.188	1.210	1.232	1.254	1.277	1.300	1.323	1.346	1.369	1.392	1.416	1.440
3	1.125	1.158	1.191	1.225	1.260	1.295	1.331	1.368	1.405	1.443	1.482	1.521	1.561	1.602	1.643	1.685	1.728
4	1.170	1.216	1.262	1.311	1.360	1.412	1.464	1.518	1.574	1.630	1.689	1.749	1.811	1.874	1.939	2.005	2.074
5	1.217	1.276	1.338	1.403	1.469	1.539	1.611	1.685	1.762	1.842	1.925	2.011	2.100	2.192	2.288	2.386	2.488
6	1.265	1.340	1.419	1.501	1.587	1.677	1.772	1.870	1.974	2.082	2.195	2.313	2.436	2.565	2.700	2.840	2.986
7	1.316	1.407	1.504	1.606	1.714	1.828	1.949	2.076	2.211	2.353	2.502	2.660	2.826	3.001	3.185	3.379	3.583
8	1.369	1.477	1.594	1.718	1.851	1.993	2.144	2.305	2.476	2.658	2.853	3.059	3.278	3.511	3.759	4.021	4.300
9	1.423	1.551	1.689	1.838	1.999	2.172	2.358	2.558	2.773	3.004	3.252	3.518	3.803	4.108	4.435	4.785	5.160
10	1.480	1.629	1.791	1.967	2.159	2.367	2.594	2.839	3.106	3.395	3.707	4.046	4.411	4.807	5.234	5.695	6.192
11	1.539	1.710	1.898	2.105	2.332	2.580	2.853	3.152	3.479	3.836	4.226	4.652	5.117	5.624	6.176	6.777	7.430
12	1.601	1.796	2.012	2.252	2.518	2.813	3.138	3.498	3.896	4.335	4.818	5.350	5.936	6.580	7.288	8.064	8.916
13	1.665	1.886	2.133	2.410	2.720	3.066	3.452	3.883	4.363	4.898	5.492	6.153	6.886	7.699	8.599	9.596	10.699
14	1.732	1.980	2.261	2.579	2.937	3.342	3.797	4.310	4.887	5.535	6.261	7.076	7.988	9.007	10.147	11.420	12.839
15	1.801	2.079	2.397	2.759	3.172	3.642	4.177	4.785	5.474	6.254	7.138	8.137	9.266	10.539	11.974	13.590	15.407
16	1.873	2.183	2.540	2.952	3.426	3.970	4.595	5.311	6.130	7.067	8.137	9.358	10.748	12.330	14.129	16.172	18.488
17	1.948	2.292	2.693	3.159	3.700	4.328	5.054	5.895	6.866	7.986	9.276	10.761	12.468	14.426	16.672	19.244	22.186
18	2.026	2.407	2.854	3.380	3.996	4.717	5.560	6.544	7.690	9.024	10.575	12.375	14.463	16.879	19.673	22.901	26.623
19	2.107	2.527	3.026	3.617	4.316	5.142	6.116	7.263	8.613	10.197	12.056	14.232	16.777	19.748	23.214	27.252	31.948
20	2.191	2.653	3.207	3.870	4.661	5.604	6.727	8.062	9.646	11.523	13.743	16.367	19.461	23.106	27.393	32.429	38.338
30	3.243	4.322	5.743	7.612	10.063	13.268	17.449	22.892	29.960	39.116	50.950	66.212	85.850	111.065	143.371	184.675	237.376

EXHIBIT 14C–2

Future Value of an Annuity of $1 in Arrears; $\frac{(1+r)^n - 1}{r}$

Periods	4%	5%	6%	7%	8%	9%	10%	11%	12%	13%	14%	15%	16%	17%	18%	19%	20%
1	1.000	1.000	1.000	1.000	1.000	1.000	1.000	1.000	1.000	1.000	1.000	1.000	1.000	1.000	1.000	1.000	1.000
2	2.040	2.050	2.060	2.070	2.080	2.090	2.100	2.110	2.120	2.130	2.140	2.150	2.160	2.170	2.180	2.190	2.200
3	3.122	3.153	3.184	3.215	3.246	3.278	3.310	3.342	3.374	3.407	3.440	3.473	3.506	3.539	3.572	3.606	3.640
4	4.246	4.310	4.375	4.440	4.506	4.573	4.641	4.710	4.779	4.850	4.921	4.993	5.066	5.141	5.215	5.291	5.368
5	5.416	5.526	5.637	5.751	5.867	5.985	6.105	6.228	6.353	6.480	6.610	6.742	6.877	7.014	7.154	7.297	7.442
6	6.633	6.802	6.975	7.153	7.336	7.523	7.716	7.913	8.115	8.323	8.536	8.754	8.977	9.207	9.442	9.683	9.930
7	7.898	8.142	8.394	8.654	8.923	9.200	9.487	9.783	10.089	10.405	10.730	11.067	11.414	11.772	12.142	12.523	12.916
8	9.214	9.549	9.897	10.260	10.637	11.028	11.436	11.859	12.300	12.757	13.233	13.727	14.240	14.773	15.327	15.902	16.499
9	10.583	11.027	11.491	11.978	12.488	13.021	13.579	14.164	14.776	15.416	16.085	16.786	17.519	18.285	19.086	19.923	20.799
10	12.006	12.578	13.181	13.816	14.487	15.193	15.937	16.722	17.549	18.420	19.337	20.304	21.321	22.393	23.521	24.709	25.959
11	13.486	14.207	14.972	15.784	16.645	17.560	18.531	19.561	20.655	21.814	23.045	24.349	25.733	27.200	28.755	30.404	32.150
12	15.026	15.917	16.870	17.888	18.977	20.141	21.384	22.713	24.133	25.650	27.271	29.002	30.850	32.824	34.931	37.180	39.581
13	16.627	17.713	18.882	20.141	21.495	22.953	24.523	26.212	28.029	29.985	32.089	34.352	36.786	39.404	42.219	45.244	48.497
14	18.292	19.599	21.015	22.550	24.215	26.019	27.975	30.095	32.393	34.883	37.581	40.505	43.672	47.103	50.818	54.841	59.196
15	20.024	21.579	23.276	25.129	27.152	29.361	31.772	34.405	37.280	40.417	43.842	47.580	51.660	56.110	60.965	66.261	72.035
16	21.825	23.657	25.673	27.888	30.324	33.003	35.950	39.190	42.753	46.672	50.980	55.717	60.925	66.649	72.939	79.850	87.442
17	23.698	25.840	28.213	30.840	33.750	36.974	40.545	44.501	48.884	53.739	59.118	65.075	71.673	78.979	87.068	96.022	105.931
18	25.645	28.132	30.906	33.999	37.450	41.301	45.599	50.396	55.750	61.725	68.394	75.836	84.141	93.406	103.740	115.266	128.117
19	27.671	30.539	33.760	37.379	41.446	46.018	51.159	56.939	63.440	70.749	78.969	88.212	98.603	110.285	123.414	138.166	154.740
20	29.778	33.066	36.786	40.995	45.762	51.160	57.275	64.203	72.052	80.947	91.025	102.444	115.380	130.033	146.628	165.418	186.688
30	56.085	66.439	79.058	94.461	113.283	136.308	164.494	199.021	241.333	293.199	356.787	434.745	530.312	647.439	790.948	966.712	1181.882

if its a lump sum - cash flow in or out.

EXHIBIT 14C-3

Present Value of $1; $\frac{1}{(1 + r)^n}$

Periods	4%	5%	6%	7%	8%	9%	10%	11%	12%	13%	14%	15%	16%	17%	18%	19%	20%	21%	22%	23%	24%	25%
1	0.962	0.952	0.943	0.935	0.926	0.917	0.909	0.901	0.893	0.885	0.877	0.870	0.862	0.855	0.847	0.840	0.833	0.826	0.820	0.813	0.806	0.800
2	0.925	0.907	0.890	0.873	0.857	0.842	0.826	0.812	0.797	0.783	0.769	0.756	0.743	0.731	0.718	0.706	0.694	0.683	0.672	0.661	0.650	0.640
3	0.889	0.864	0.840	0.816	0.794	0.772	0.751	0.731	0.712	0.693	0.675	0.658	0.641	0.624	0.609	0.593	0.579	0.564	0.551	0.537	0.524	0.512
4	0.855	0.823	0.792	0.763	0.735	0.708	0.683	0.659	0.636	0.613	0.592	0.572	0.552	0.534	0.516	0.499	0.482	0.467	0.451	0.437	0.423	0.410
5	0.822	0.784	0.747	0.713	0.681	0.650	0.621	0.593	0.567	0.543	0.519	0.497	0.476	0.456	0.437	0.419	0.402	0.386	0.370	0.355	0.341	0.328
6	0.790	0.746	0.705	0.666	0.630	0.596	0.564	0.535	0.507	0.480	0.456	0.432	0.410	0.390	0.370	0.352	0.335	0.319	0.303	0.289	0.275	0.262
7	0.760	0.711	0.665	0.623	0.583	0.547	0.513	0.482	0.452	0.425	0.400	0.376	0.354	0.333	0.314	0.296	0.279	0.263	0.249	0.235	0.222	0.210
8	0.731	0.677	0.627	0.582	0.540	0.502	0.467	0.434	0.404	0.376	0.351	0.327	0.305	0.285	0.266	0.249	0.233	0.218	0.204	0.191	0.179	0.168
9	0.703	0.645	0.592	0.544	0.500	0.460	0.424	0.391	0.361	0.333	0.308	0.284	0.263	0.243	0.225	0.209	0.194	0.180	0.167	0.155	0.144	0.134
10	0.676	0.614	0.558	0.508	0.463	0.422	0.386	0.352	0.322	0.295	0.270	0.247	0.227	0.208	0.191	0.176	0.162	0.149	0.137	0.126	0.116	0.107
11	0.650	0.585	0.527	0.475	0.429	0.388	0.350	0.317	0.287	0.261	0.237	0.215	0.195	0.178	0.162	0.148	0.135	0.123	0.112	0.103	0.094	0.086
12	0.625	0.557	0.497	0.444	0.397	0.356	0.319	0.286	0.257	0.231	0.208	0.187	0.168	0.152	0.137	0.124	0.112	0.102	0.092	0.083	0.076	0.069
13	0.601	0.530	0.469	0.415	0.368	0.326	0.290	0.258	0.229	0.204	0.182	0.163	0.145	0.130	0.116	0.104	0.093	0.084	0.075	0.068	0.061	0.055
14	0.577	0.505	0.442	0.388	0.340	0.299	0.263	0.232	0.205	0.181	0.160	0.141	0.125	0.111	0.099	0.088	0.078	0.069	0.062	0.055	0.049	0.044
15	0.555	0.481	0.417	0.362	0.315	0.275	0.239	0.209	0.183	0.160	0.140	0.123	0.108	0.095	0.084	0.074	0.065	0.057	0.051	0.045	0.040	0.035
16	0.534	0.458	0.394	0.339	0.292	0.252	0.218	0.188	0.163	0.141	0.123	0.107	0.093	0.081	0.071	0.062	0.054	0.047	0.042	0.036	0.032	0.028
17	0.513	0.436	0.371	0.317	0.270	0.231	0.198	0.170	0.146	0.125	0.108	0.093	0.080	0.069	0.060	0.052	0.045	0.039	0.034	0.030	0.026	0.023
18	0.494	0.416	0.350	0.296	0.250	0.212	0.180	0.153	0.130	0.111	0.095	0.081	0.069	0.059	0.051	0.044	0.038	0.032	0.028	0.024	0.021	0.018
19	0.475	0.396	0.331	0.277	0.232	0.194	0.164	0.138	0.116	0.098	0.083	0.070	0.060	0.051	0.043	0.037	0.031	0.027	0.023	0.020	0.017	0.014
20	0.456	0.377	0.312	0.258	0.215	0.178	0.149	0.124	0.104	0.087	0.073	0.061	0.051	0.043	0.037	0.031	0.026	0.022	0.019	0.016	0.014	0.012
21	0.439	0.359	0.294	0.242	0.199	0.164	0.135	0.112	0.093	0.077	0.064	0.053	0.044	0.037	0.031	0.026	0.022	0.018	0.015	0.013	0.011	0.009
22	0.422	0.342	0.278	0.226	0.184	0.150	0.123	0.101	0.083	0.068	0.056	0.046	0.038	0.032	0.026	0.022	0.018	0.015	0.013	0.011	0.009	0.007
23	0.406	0.326	0.262	0.211	0.170	0.138	0.112	0.091	0.074	0.060	0.049	0.040	0.033	0.027	0.022	0.018	0.015	0.012	0.010	0.009	0.007	0.006
24	0.390	0.310	0.247	0.197	0.158	0.126	0.102	0.082	0.066	0.053	0.043	0.035	0.028	0.023	0.019	0.015	0.013	0.010	0.008	0.007	0.006	0.005
25	0.375	0.295	0.233	0.184	0.146	0.116	0.092	0.074	0.059	0.047	0.038	0.030	0.024	0.020	0.016	0.013	0.010	0.009	0.007	0.006	0.005	0.004
26	0.361	0.281	0.220	0.172	0.135	0.106	0.084	0.066	0.053	0.042	0.033	0.026	0.021	0.017	0.014	0.011	0.009	0.007	0.006	0.005	0.004	0.003
27	0.347	0.268	0.207	0.161	0.125	0.098	0.076	0.060	0.047	0.037	0.029	0.023	0.018	0.014	0.011	0.009	0.007	0.006	0.005	0.004	0.003	0.002
28	0.333	0.255	0.196	0.150	0.116	0.090	0.069	0.054	0.042	0.033	0.026	0.020	0.016	0.012	0.010	0.008	0.006	0.005	0.004	0.003	0.002	0.002
29	0.321	0.243	0.185	0.141	0.107	0.082	0.063	0.048	0.037	0.029	0.022	0.017	0.014	0.011	0.008	0.006	0.005	0.004	0.003	0.002	0.002	0.002
30	0.308	0.231	0.174	0.131	0.099	0.075	0.057	0.044	0.033	0.026	0.020	0.015	0.012	0.009	0.007	0.005	0.004	0.003	0.003	0.002	0.002	0.001
40	0.208	0.142	0.097	0.067	0.046	0.032	0.022	0.015	0.011	0.008	0.005	0.004	0.003	0.002	0.001	0.001	0.001	0.000	0.000	0.000	0.000	0.000

0.552

If its in series go to year and look for value.

EXHIBIT 14C–4

Present Value of an Annuity of $1 in Arrears; $\frac{1}{r}\left[1 - \frac{1}{(1 + r)^n}\right]$

Periods	4%	5%	6%	7%	8%	9%	10%	11%	12%	13%	14%	15%	16%	17%	18%	19%	20%	21%	22%	23%	24%	25%
1	0.962	0.952	0.943	0.935	0.926	0.917	0.909	0.901	0.893	0.885	0.877	0.870	0.862	0.855	0.847	0.840	0.833	0.826	0.820	0.813	0.806	0.800
2	1.886	1.859	1.833	1.808	1.783	1.759	1.736	1.713	1.690	1.668	1.647	1.626	1.605	1.585	1.566	1.547	1.528	1.509	1.492	1.474	1.457	1.440
3	2.775	2.723	2.673	2.624	2.577	2.531	2.487	2.444	2.402	2.361	2.322	2.283	2.246	2.210	2.174	2.140	2.106	2.074	2.042	2.011	1.981	1.952
4	3.630	3.546	3.465	3.387	3.312	3.240	3.170	3.102	3.037	2.974	2.914	2.855	2.798	2.743	2.690	2.639	2.589	2.540	2.494	2.448	2.404	2.362
5	4.452	4.329	4.212	4.100	3.993	3.890	3.791	3.696	3.605	3.517	3.433	3.352	3.274	3.199	3.127	3.058	2.991	2.926	2.864	2.803	2.745	2.689
6	5.242	5.076	4.917	4.767	4.623	4.486	4.355	4.231	4.111	3.998	3.889	3.784	3.685	3.589	3.498	3.410	3.326	3.245	3.167	3.092	3.020	2.951
7	6.002	5.786	5.582	5.389	5.206	5.033	4.868	4.712	4.564	4.423	4.288	4.160	4.039	3.922	3.812	3.706	3.605	3.508	3.416	3.327	3.242	3.161
8	6.733	6.463	6.210	5.971	5.747	5.535	5.335	5.146	4.968	4.799	4.639	4.487	4.344	4.207	4.078	3.954	3.837	3.726	3.619	3.518	3.421	3.329
9	7.435	7.108	6.802	6.515	6.247	5.995	5.759	5.537	5.328	5.132	4.946	4.772	4.607	4.451	4.303	4.163	4.031	3.905	3.786	3.673	3.566	3.463
10	8.111	7.722	7.360	7.024	6.710	6.418	6.145	5.889	5.650	5.426	5.216	5.019	4.833	4.659	4.494	4.339	4.192	4.054	3.923	3.799	3.682	3.571
11	8.760	8.306	7.887	7.499	7.139	6.805	6.495	6.207	5.938	5.687	5.453	5.234	5.029	4.836	4.656	4.486	4.327	4.177	4.035	3.902	3.776	3.656
12	9.385	8.863	8.384	7.943	7.536	7.161	6.814	6.492	6.194	5.918	5.660	5.421	5.197	4.988	4.793	4.611	4.439	4.278	4.127	3.985	3.851	3.725
13	9.986	9.394	8.853	8.358	7.904	7.487	7.103	6.750	6.424	6.122	5.842	5.583	5.342	5.118	4.910	4.715	4.533	4.362	4.203	4.053	3.912	3.780
14	10.563	9.899	9.295	8.745	8.244	7.786	7.367	6.982	6.628	6.302	6.002	5.724	5.468	5.229	5.008	4.802	4.611	4.432	4.265	4.108	3.962	3.824
15	11.118	10.380	9.712	9.108	8.559	8.061	7.606	7.191	6.811	6.462	6.142	5.847	5.575	5.324	5.092	4.876	4.675	4.489	4.315	4.153	4.001	3.859
16	11.652	10.838	10.106	9.447	8.851	8.313	7.824	7.379	6.974	6.604	6.265	5.954	5.668	5.405	5.162	4.938	4.730	4.536	4.357	4.189	4.033	3.887
17	12.166	11.274	10.477	9.763	9.122	8.544	8.022	7.549	7.120	6.729	6.373	6.047	5.749	5.475	5.222	4.990	4.775	4.576	4.391	4.219	4.059	3.910
18	12.659	11.690	10.828	10.059	9.372	8.756	8.201	7.702	7.250	6.840	6.467	6.128	5.818	5.534	5.273	5.033	4.812	4.608	4.419	4.243	4.080	3.928
19	13.134	12.085	11.158	10.336	9.604	8.950	8.365	7.839	7.366	6.938	6.550	6.198	5.877	5.584	5.316	5.070	4.843	4.635	4.442	4.263	4.097	3.942
20	13.590	12.462	11.470	10.594	9.818	9.129	8.514	7.963	7.469	7.025	6.623	6.259	5.929	5.628	5.353	5.101	4.870	4.657	4.460	4.279	4.110	3.954
21	14.029	12.821	11.764	10.836	10.017	9.292	8.649	8.075	7.562	7.102	6.687	6.312	5.973	5.665	5.384	5.127	4.891	4.675	4.476	4.292	4.121	3.963
22	14.451	13.163	12.042	11.061	10.201	9.442	8.772	8.176	7.645	7.170	6.743	6.359	6.011	5.696	5.410	5.149	4.909	4.690	4.488	4.302	4.130	3.970
23	14.857	13.489	12.303	11.272	10.371	9.580	8.883	8.266	7.718	7.230	6.792	6.399	6.044	5.723	5.432	5.167	4.925	4.703	4.499	4.311	4.137	3.976
24	15.247	13.799	12.550	11.469	10.529	9.707	8.985	8.348	7.784	7.283	6.835	6.434	6.073	5.746	5.451	5.182	4.937	4.713	4.507	4.318	4.143	3.981
25	15.622	14.094	12.783	11.654	10.675	9.823	9.077	8.422	7.843	7.330	6.873	6.464	6.097	5.766	5.467	5.195	4.948	4.721	4.514	4.323	4.147	3.985
26	15.983	14.375	13.003	11.826	10.810	9.929	9.161	8.488	7.896	7.372	6.906	6.491	6.118	5.783	5.480	5.206	4.956	4.728	4.520	4.328	4.151	3.988
27	16.330	14.643	13.211	11.987	10.935	10.027	9.237	8.548	7.943	7.409	6.935	6.514	6.136	5.798	5.492	5.215	4.964	4.734	4.524	4.332	4.154	3.990
28	16.663	14.898	13.406	12.137	11.051	10.116	9.307	8.602	7.984	7.441	6.961	6.534	6.152	5.810	5.502	5.223	4.970	4.739	4.528	4.335	4.157	3.992
29	16.984	15.141	13.591	12.278	11.158	10.198	9.370	8.650	8.022	7.470	6.983	6.551	6.166	5.820	5.510	5.229	4.975	4.743	4.531	4.337	4.159	3.994
30	17.292	15.372	13.765	12.409	11.258	10.274	9.427	8.694	8.055	7.496	7.003	6.566	6.177	5.829	5.517	5.235	4.979	4.746	4.534	4.339	4.160	3.995
40	19.793	17.159	15.046	13.332	11.925	10.757	9.779	8.951	8.244	7.634	7.105	6.642	6.233	5.871	5.548	5.258	4.997	4.760	4.544	4.347	4.166	3.999

Appendix 14D: Income Taxes in Capital Budgeting Decisions

LEARNING OBJECTIVE 8
Include income taxes in a capital budgeting analysis.

We ignored income taxes in this chapter for two reasons. First, many organizations do not pay income taxes. Not-for-profit organizations, such as hospitals and charitable foundations, and governmental agencies are exempt from income taxes. Second, capital budgeting is complex and is best absorbed in small doses. Now that we have a solid foundation in the concepts of present value and discounting, we can explore the effects of income taxes on capital budgeting decisions.

The U.S. income tax code is enormously complex. We only scratch the surface here. To keep the subject within reasonable bounds, we have made many simplifying assumptions about the tax code. Among the most important of these assumptions are: (1) taxable income equals net income as computed for financial reports; and (2) the tax rate is a flat percentage of taxable income. The actual tax code is far more complex than this; indeed, experts acknowledge that no one person knows or can know it all. However, the simplifications that we make throughout this appendix allow us to cover the most important implications of income taxes for capital budgeting without getting bogged down in details.

The Concept of After-Tax Cost

Businesses, like individuals, must pay income taxes. In the case of businesses, the amount of income tax that must be paid is determined by the company's net taxable income. Tax deductible expenses (tax deductions) decrease the company's net taxable income and hence reduce the taxes the company must pay. For this reason, expenses are often stated on an *after-tax* basis. For example, if a company pays rent of $10 million a year but this expense results in a reduction in income taxes of $3 million, the after-tax cost of the rent is $7 million. An expenditure net of its tax effect is known as **after-tax cost.**

To illustrate, assume that a company with a tax rate of 30% is contemplating a training program that costs $60,000. What impact will this have on the company's taxes? To keep matters simple, let's suppose the training program has no immediate effect on sales. How much does the company actually pay for the training program after taking into account the impact of this expense on taxes? The answer is $42,000 as shown in Exhibit 14D–1. While the training program costs $60,000 before taxes, it would reduce the company's taxes by $18,000, so its *after-tax* cost would be only $42,000.

EXHIBIT 14D–1
The Computation of After-Tax Cost

	Without Training Program		With Training Program
Sales	$850,000		$850,000
Less tax deductible expenses:			
Salaries, insurance, and other	700,000		700,000
New training program			60,000
Total expenses	700,000		760,000
Taxable income	$150,000		$ 90,000
Income taxes (30%)	$ 45,000		$ 27,000
Cost of new training program		$60,000	
Less: Reduction in income taxes ($45,000 − $27,000)		18,000	
After-tax cost of the new training program		$42,000	

The after-tax cost of any tax-deductible cash expense can be determined using the following formula:[1]

$$\text{After-tax cost (net cash outflow)} = (1 - \text{Tax rate}) \times \text{Tax-deductible cash expense} \quad (1)$$

We can verify the accuracy of this formula by applying it to the $60,000 training program expenditure:

$$(1 - 0.30) \times \$60{,}000 = \$42{,}000 \text{ after-tax cost of the training program}$$

This formula is very useful since it provides the actual amount of cash a company must pay after considering tax effects. It is this actual, after-tax, cash outflow that should be used in capital budgeting decisions.

Similar reasoning applies to revenues and other *taxable* cash inflows. Since these cash receipts are taxable, the company must pay out a portion of them in taxes. The **after-tax benefit,** or net cash inflow, realized from a particular cash receipt can be obtained by applying a simple variation of the cash expenditure formula used above:

$$\text{After-tax benefit (net cash inflow)} = (1 - \text{Tax rate}) \times \text{Taxable cash receipt} \quad (2)$$

We emphasize the term *taxable cash receipts* because not all cash inflows are taxable. For example, the release of working capital at the end of an investment project would not be a taxable cash inflow. It is not counted as income for either financial accounting or income tax reporting purposes since it is simply a recovery of the initial investment.

Depreciation Tax Shield

Depreciation is not a cash flow. For this reason, depreciation was ignored in Chapter 14 in all discounted cash flow computations. However, depreciation does affect the taxes that must be paid and therefore has an indirect effect on the company's cash flows.

To illustrate the effect of depreciation deductions on tax payments, consider a company with annual cash sales of $500,000 and cash operating expenses of $310,000. In addition, the company has a depreciable asset on which the depreciation deduction is $90,000 per year. The tax rate is 30%. As shown in Exhibit 14D–2, the depreciation deduction reduces the company's taxes by $27,000. In effect, the depreciation deduction of $90,000 *shields* $90,000 in revenues from taxation and thereby *reduces* the amount of taxes that the company must pay. Because depreciation deductions shield revenues from taxation, they are generally referred to as a **depreciation tax shield.**[2] The reduction in tax payments made possible by the depreciation tax shield is equal to the amount of the depreciation deduction, multiplied by the tax rate as follows:

$$\text{Tax savings from the depreciation tax shield} = \text{Tax rate} \times \text{Depreciation deduction} \quad (3)$$

We can verify this formula by applying it to the $90,000 depreciation deduction in our example:

$$0.30 \times \$90{,}000 = \$27{,}000 \text{ reduction in tax payments}$$

In this appendix, when we estimate after-tax cash flows for capital budgeting decisions, we will include the tax savings provided by the depreciation tax shield.

---

[1] This formula assumes that a company is operating at a profit; if it is operating at a loss, the tax situation can be very complex. For simplicity, we assume in all examples, exercises, and problems that the company is operating at a profit.

[2] The term *depreciation tax shield* may convey the impression that there is something underhanded about depreciation deductions—that companies are getting some sort of a special tax break. However, to use the depreciation deduction, a company must have already acquired a depreciable asset—which typically requires a cash outflow. Essentially, the tax code requires companies to delay recognizing the cash outflow as an expense until depreciation charges are recorded.

EXHIBIT 14D–2
The Impact of Depreciation Deductions on Tax Payments

	Without Depreciation Deduction	With Depreciation Deduction
Sales	$500,000	$500,000
Cash operating expenses	310,000	310,000
Cash flow from operations	190,000	190,000
Depreciation expense	—	90,000
Taxable income	$190,000	$100,000
Income taxes (30%)	$ 57,000	$ 30,000

$27,000 lower taxes with the depreciation deduction

	Without Depreciation Deduction	With Depreciation Deduction
Cash flow comparison:		
Cash flow from operations (above)	$190,000	$190,000
Income taxes (above)	57,000	30,000
Net cash flow	$133,000	$160,000

$27,000 greater cash flow with the depreciation deduction

EXHIBIT 14D–3
Tax Adjustments Required in a Capital Budgeting Analysis

Item	Treatment
Tax-deductible cash expense*	Multiply by (1 − Tax rate) to get after-tax cost.
Taxable cash receipt*	Multiply by (1 − Tax rate) to get after-tax cash inflow.
Depreciation deduction	Multiply by the tax rate to get the tax savings from the depreciation tax shield.

*Cash expenses can be deducted from the cash receipts and the difference multiplied by (1 − Tax rate). See the example at the top of Exhibit 14D–4.

To keep matters simple, we will assume in all of our examples and problem materials that depreciation reported for tax purposes is straight-line depreciation, with no deduction for salvage value. In other words, we will assume that the entire original cost of the asset is written off evenly over its useful life. Since the net book value of the asset at the end of its useful life will be zero under this depreciation method, we will assume that any proceeds received on disposal of the asset at the end of its useful life will be taxed as ordinary income.

In actuality, the rules for depreciation are more complex than this and most companies take advantage of accelerated depreciation methods allowed under the tax code. These accelerated methods usually result in a reduction in current taxes and an offsetting increase in future taxes. This shifting of part of the tax burden from the current year to future years is advantageous from a present value point of view, since a dollar today is worth more than a dollar in the future. A summary of the concepts we have introduced so far is given in Exhibit 14D–3.

Example of Income Taxes and Capital Budgeting

Armed with an understanding of after-tax cost, after-tax revenue, and the depreciation tax shield, we are now prepared to examine a comprehensive example of income taxes and capital budgeting.

Holland Company owns the mineral rights to land that has a deposit of ore. The company is uncertain as to whether it should purchase equipment and open a mine on the property. After careful study, the following data have been assembled by the company:

Cost of equipment needed ...	$300,000
Working capital needed ...	$75,000
Estimated annual cash receipts from sales of ore ...	$250,000
Estimated annual cash expenses for salaries, insurance, utilities, and other cash expenses of mining the ore ...	$170,000
Cost of road repairs needed in 6 years ...	$40,000
Salvage value of the equipment in 10 years ...	$100,000

The ore in the mine would be exhausted after 10 years of mining activity, at which time the mine would be closed. The equipment would then be sold for its salvage value. Holland Company uses the straight-line method, assuming no salvage value, to compute depreciation deductions for tax purposes. The company's after-tax cost of capital is 12% and its tax rate is 30%.

Should Holland Company purchase the equipment and open a mine on the property? The solution to the problem is given in Exhibit 14D–4. We suggest that you go through this solution item by item and note the following points:

Cost of new equipment. The initial investment of $300,000 in the new equipment is included in full with no reductions for taxes. This represents an *investment,* not an expense, so no tax adjustment is made. (Only revenues and expenses are adjusted for the effects of taxes.) However, this investment does affect taxes through the depreciation deductions that are considered below.

Working capital. Observe that the working capital needed for the project is included in full with no reductions for taxes. Like the cost of new equipment, working capital is an investment and not an expense so no tax adjustment is made. Also observe that no tax adjustment is made when the working capital is released at the end of the project's life. The release of working capital is not a taxable cash flow, since it is a return of investment funds back to the company.

EXHIBIT 14D–4
Example of Income Taxes and Capital Budgeting

	Per Year
Cash receipts from sales of ore ...	$250,000
Less payments for salaries, insurance, utilities, and other cash expenses ...	170,000
Net cash receipts ...	$ 80,000

Items and Computations	Year(s)	(1) Amount	(2) Tax Effect*	After-Tax Cash Flows (1) × (2)	12% Factor	Present Value of Cash Flows
Cost of new equipment ...	Now	$(300,000)	—	$(300,000)	1.000	$(300,000)
Working capital needed ...	Now	$(75,000)	—	$(75,000)	1.000	(75,000)
Net annual cash receipts (above) ...	1–10	$80,000	1 − 0.30	$56,000	5.650	316,400
Road repairs ...	6	$(40,000)	1 − 0.30	$(28,000)	0.507	(14,196)
Annual depreciation deductions ...	1–10	$30,000	0.30	$9,000	5.650	50,850
Salvage value of equipment ...	10	$100,000	1 − 0.30	$70,000	0.322	22,540
Release of working capital ...	10	$75,000	—	$75,000	0.322	24,150
Net present value ...						$ 24,744

*Taxable cash receipts and tax-deductible cash expenses are multiplied by (1 − Tax rate) to determine the after-tax cash flow. Depreciation deductions are multiplied by the tax rate itself to determine the after-tax cash flow (i.e., tax savings from the depreciation tax shield).

Net annual cash receipts. The net annual cash receipts from sales of ore are adjusted for the effects of income taxes, as discussed earlier in the chapter. Note at the top of Exhibit 14D–4 that the annual cash expenses are deducted from the annual cash receipts to obtain the net cash receipts. This simplifies computations.

Road repairs. Since the road repairs occur just once (in the sixth year), they are treated separately from other expenses. Road repairs would be a tax-deductible cash expense, and therefore they are adjusted for the effects of income taxes, as discussed earlier in the chapter.

Depreciation deductions. The tax savings provided by depreciation deductions is essentially an annuity that is included in the present value computations in the same way as other cash flows.

Salvage value of equipment. Since the company does not consider salvage value when computing depreciation deductions, book value will be zero at the end of the life of an asset. Thus, any salvage value received is taxable as income to the company. The after-tax benefit is determined by multiplying the salvage value by (1 − Tax rate).

Since the net present value of the proposed mining project is positive, the equipment should be purchased and the mine opened. Study Exhibit 14D–4 thoroughly. *Exhibit 14D–4 is the key exhibit!*

Summary (Appendix 14D)

Unless a company is a tax-exempt organization, such as a not-for-profit school or a governmental unit, income taxes should be considered in making capital budgeting decisions. Tax-deductible cash expenditures and taxable cash receipts are placed on an after-tax basis by multiplying them by (1 − Tax rate). Only the after-tax amount should be used in determining the desirability of an investment proposal.

Although depreciation is not a cash outflow, it is a valid deduction for tax purposes and as such affects income tax payments. The depreciation tax shield—computed by multiplying the depreciation deduction by the tax rate itself—also results in savings in income taxes.

Glossary (Appendix 14D)

After-tax benefit The amount of net cash inflow realized from a taxable cash receipt after income tax effects have been considered. The amount is determined by multiplying the taxable cash receipt by (1 − Tax rate). (p. 692)

After-tax cost The amount of net cash outflow resulting from a tax-deductible cash expense after income tax effects have been considered. The amount is determined by multiplying the tax-deductible cash expense by (1 − Tax rate). (p. 691)

Depreciation tax shield A reduction in tax that results from depreciation deductions. The reduction in tax is computed by multiplying the depreciation deduction by the tax rate. (p. 692)

Questions

14–1 What is the difference between capital budgeting screening decisions and capital budgeting preference decisions?

14–2 What is meant by the term *time value of money?*

14–3 What is meant by the term *discounting?*

14–4 Why isn't accounting net income used in the net present value and internal rate of return methods of making capital budgeting decisions?

14–5 Why are discounted cash flow methods of making capital budgeting decisions superior to other methods?

14–6 What is net present value? Can it ever be negative? Explain.

14–7 Identify two simplifying assumptions associated with discounted cash flow methods of making capital budgeting decisions.

14–8 If a company has to pay interest of 14% on long-term debt, then its cost of capital is 14%. Do you agree? Explain.

14–9 What is meant by an investment project's internal rate of return? How is the internal rate of return computed?

14–10 Explain how the cost of capital serves as a screening tool when dealing with (*a*) the net present value method and (*b*) the internal rate of return method.

14–11 As the discount rate increases, the present value of a given future cash flow also increases. Do you agree? Explain.

14–12 Refer to Exhibit 14–4. Is the return on this investment proposal exactly 14%, more than 14%, or less than 14%? Explain.

14–13 How is the project profitability index computed, and what does it measure?

14–14 Can an investment with a negative project profitability index be an acceptable investment? Explain.

14–15 What is meant by the term *payback period?* How is the payback period determined? How can the payback method be useful?

14–16 What is the major criticism of the payback and simple rate of return methods of making capital budgeting decisions?

14–17 (Appendix 14D) What is meant by after-tax cost and how is the concept used in capital budgeting decisions?

14–18 (Appendix 14D) What is a depreciation tax shield and how does it affect capital budgeting decisions?

14–19 (Appendix 14D) Ludlow Company is considering the introduction of a new product line. Would an increase in the income tax rate tend to make the new investment more or less attractive? Explain.

14–20 (Appendix 14D) Assume that an old piece of equipment is sold at a loss. From a capital budgeting point of view, what two cash inflows will be associated with the sale?

14–21 (Appendix 14D) Assume that a new piece of equipment costs $40,000 and that the tax rate is 30%. Should the new piece of equipment be included in the capital budgeting analysis as a cash outflow of $40,000, or as a cash outflow of $28,000 [$40,000 × (1 − 0.30)]? Explain.

Exercises

EXERCISE 14–1 Net Present Value Method [LO1]

The management of Kunkel Company is considering the purchase of a $40,000 machine that would reduce operating costs by $7,000 per year. At the end of the machine's eight-year useful life, it will have zero scrap value. The company's required rate of return is 12% on all investment projects.

Required:

(Ignore income taxes.)

1. Determine the net present value of the investment in the machine.
2. What is the difference between the total, undiscounted cash inflows and cash outflows over the entire life of the machine?

EXERCISE 14–2 Internal Rate of Return [LO2]

Wendell's Donut Shoppe is investigating the purchase of a new $18,600 donut-making machine. The new machine would permit the company to reduce the amount of part-time help needed, at a cost savings of $3,800 per year. In addition, the new machine would allow the company to produce one new style of donut, resulting in the sale of at least 1,000 dozen more donuts each year. The company realizes a contribution margin of $1.20 per dozen donuts sold. The new machine would have a six-year useful life.

Required:

(Ignore income taxes.)

1. What would be the total annual cash inflows associated with the new machine for capital budgeting purposes?
2. Find the internal rate of return promised by the new machine to the nearest whole percent.

3. In addition to the data given previously, assume that the machine will have a $9,125 salvage value at the end of six years. Under these conditions, compute the internal rate of return to the nearest whole percent. (Hint: You may find it helpful to use the net present value approach; find the discount rate that will cause the net present value to be closest to zero. Use the format shown in Exhibit 14–4.)

EXERCISE 14–3 Present Value Potpourri [LO1, LO3]

Solve each of the following present value exercises independently:

Required:

(Ignore income taxes.)

1. The Cambro Foundation, a nonprofit organization, is planning to invest $104,950 in a project that will last for three years. The project will provide cash inflows as follows:

Year 1	$30,000
Year 2	$40,000
Year 3	?

   Assuming that the project will yield exactly a 12% rate of return, what is the expected cash inflow for Year 3?

2. Lukow Products is investigating the purchase of a piece of automated equipment that will save $400,000 each year in direct labor and inventory carrying costs. This equipment costs $2,500,000 and is expected to have a 15-year useful life with no salvage value. The company's required rate of return is 20% on all equipment purchases. Management anticipates that this equipment will provide intangible benefits such as greater flexibility and higher quality output. What dollar value per year would these intangible benefits have to have to make the equipment an acceptable investment?
3. The Matchless Dating Service has made an investment in video and recording equipment that costs $106,700. The equipment is expected to generate cash inflows of $20,000 per year. How many years will the equipment have to be used to provide the company with a 10% rate of return on its investment?

EXERCISE 14–4 Preference Ranking [LO4]

Information on four investment proposals is given below:

	Investment Proposal			
	A	B	C	D
Investment required	$(90,000)	$(100,000)	$(70,000)	$(120,000)
Present value of cash inflows	126,000	90,000	105,000	160,000
Net present value	$ 36,000	$ (10,000)	$ 35,000	$ 40,000
Life of the project	5 years	7 years	6 years	6 years

Required:

1. Compute the project profitability index for each investment proposal.
2. Rank the proposals in terms of preference.

EXERCISE 14–5 Payback Method [LO5]

The management of Unter Corporation is considering an investment with the following cash flows:

Year	Investment	Cash Inflow
1	$15,000	$1,000
2	$8,000	$2,000
3		$2,500
4		$4,000
5		$5,000
6		$6,000
7		$5,000
8		$4,000
9		$3,000
10		$2,000

Required:

1. Determine the payback period of the investment.
2. Would the payback period be affected if the cash inflow in the last year were several times as large?

EXERCISE 14–6 Simple Rate of Return Method [LO6]

The management of Ballard MicroBrew is considering the purchase of an automated bottling machine for $120,000. The machine would replace an old piece of equipment that costs $30,000 per year to operate. The new machine would cost $12,000 per year to operate. The old machine currently in use could be sold now for a scrap value of $40,000. The new machine would have a useful life of 10 years with no salvage value.

Required:

Compute the simple rate of return on the new automated bottling machine.

EXERCISE 14–7 (Appendix 14A) Basic Present Value Concepts [LO7]

Solve each of the following parts independently. (Ignore income taxes.)

1. The Atlantic Medical Clinic can purchase a new computer system that will save $7,000 annually in billing costs. The computer system will last for eight years and have no salvage value. Up to how much should the Atlantic Medical Clinic be willing to pay for the new computer system if the clinic's required rate of return is:
   a. Sixteen percent?
   b. Twenty percent?
2. The Caldwell *Herald* newspaper reported the following story:
   Frank Ormsby of Caldwell is the state's newest millionaire. By choosing the six winning numbers on last week's state lottery, Mr. Ormsby has won the week's grand prize totaling $1.6 million. The State Lottery Commission has indicated that Mr. Ormsby will receive his prize in 20 annual installments of $80,000 each.
   a. If Mr. Ormsby can invest money at a 12% rate of return, what is the present value of his winnings?
   b. Is it correct to say that Mr. Ormsby is the "state's newest millionaire"? Explain your answer.
3. Fraser Company will need a new warehouse in five years. The warehouse will cost $500,000 to build. What lump-sum amount should the company invest now to have the $500,000 available at the end of the five-year period? Assume that the company can invest money at:
   a. Ten percent.
   b. Fourteen percent.

EXERCISE 14–8 (Appendix 14D) After-Tax Costs [LO8]

Solve each of the following parts independently:

a. Neal Company would like to initiate a management development program for its executives. The program would cost $100,000 per year to operate. What would be the after-tax cost of the program if the company's income tax rate is 30%?

b. Smerk's Department Store has rearranged the merchandise display cases on the first floor of its building, placing fast turnover items near the front door. This rearrangement has caused the company's contribution margin (and taxable income) to increase by $40,000 per month. If the company's income tax rate is 30%, what is the after-tax benefit from this rearrangement of facilities?

c. Perfect Press, Inc., has just purchased a new binding machine at a cost of $210,000. For tax purposes, the entire original cost of the machine will be depreciated over seven years using the straight-line method. Determine the yearly tax savings from the depreciation tax shield. Assume that the income tax rate is 30%.

EXERCISE 14–9 Basic Net Present Value Analysis [LO1]

Kathy Myers frequently purchases stocks and bonds, but she is uncertain how to determine the rate of return that she is earning. For example, three years ago she paid $13,000 for 200 shares of Malti Company's common stock. She received a $420 cash dividend on the stock at the end of each year for three years. At the end of three years, she sold the stock for $16,000. Kathy would like to earn a return of at least 14% on all of her investments. She is not sure whether the Malti Company stock provided a 14% return and would like some help with the necessary computations.

Required:
(Ignore income taxes.) Using the net present value method, determine whether or not the Malti Company stock provided a 14% return. Use the general format illustrated in Exhibit 14–4 and round all computations to the nearest whole dollar.

EXERCISE 14–10 Basic Payback Period and Simple Rate of Return Computations [LO5, LO6]
A piece of laborsaving equipment has just come onto the market that Mitsui Electronics, Ltd., could use to reduce costs in one of its plants in Japan. Relevant data relating to the equipment follow (currency is in thousands of yen, denoted by ¥):

Purchase cost of the equipment	¥432,000
Annual cost savings that will be provided by the equipment	¥90,000
Life of the equipment	12 years

Required:
(Ignore income taxes.)
1. Compute the payback period for the equipment. If the company requires a payback period of four years or less, would the equipment be purchased?
2. Compute the simple rate of return on the equipment. Use straight-line depreciation based on the equipment's useful life. Would the equipment be purchased if the company's required rate of return is 14%?

EXERCISE 14–11 Net Present Value Analysis of Two Alternatives [LO1]
Perit Industries has $100,000 to invest. The company is trying to decide between two alternative uses of the funds. The alternatives are:

	Project A	Project B
Cost of equipment required	$100,000	
Working capital investment required	—	$100,000
Annual cash inflows	$21,000	$16,000
Salvage value of equipment in six years	$8,000	
Life of the project	6 years	6 years

The working capital needed for project B will be released at the end of six years for investment elsewhere. Perit Industries' discount rate is 14%.

Required:
(Ignore income taxes.) Which investment alternative (if either) would you recommend that the company accept? Show all computations using the net present value format. Prepare separate computations for each project.

EXERCISE 14–12 Basic Net Present Value and Internal Rate of Return Analysis [LO1, LO2, LO3]

Consider each part below independently. Ignore income taxes.
1. Preston Company's required rate of return is 14% on all investments. The company can purchase a new machine at a cost of $84,900. The new machine would generate cash inflows of $15,000 per year and have a 12-year useful life with no salvage value. Compute the machine's net present value. (Use the format shown in Exhibit 14–1.) Is the machine an acceptable investment? Explain.
2. The Walton *Daily News* is investigating the purchase of a new auxiliary press that has a projected life of 18 years. It is estimated that the new press will save $30,000 per year in cash operating costs. If the new press costs $217,500, what is its internal rate of return? Is the press an acceptable investment if the company's required rate of return is 16%? Explain.
3. Refer to the data above for the Walton *Daily News*. How much would the annual cash inflows (cost savings) have to be for the new press to provide the required 16% rate of return? Round your answer to the nearest whole dollar.

EXERCISE 14–13 Payback Period and Simple Rate of Return [LO5, LO6]
Nick's Novelties, Inc., is considering the purchase of electronic pinball machines to place in amusement houses. The machines would cost a total of $300,000, have an eight-year useful life,

and have a total salvage value of $20,000. The company estimates that annual revenues and expenses associated with the machines would be as follows:

Revenues		$200,000
Less operating expenses:		
Commissions to amusement houses ...	$100,000	
Insurance	7,000	
Depreciation	35,000	
Maintenance	18,000	160,000
Net operating income		$ 40,000

Required:
(Ignore income taxes.)

1. Assume that Nick's Novelties, Inc., will not purchase new equipment unless it provides a payback period of five years or less. Would the company purchase the pinball machines?
2. Compute the simple rate of return promised by the pinball machines. If the company requires a simple rate of return of at least 12%, will the pinball machines be purchased?

EXERCISE 14–14 (Appendix 14A) Basic Present Value Concepts [LO7]
Consider each of the following situations independently. (Ignore income taxes.)

1. In three years, when he is discharged from the Air Force, Steve wants to buy an $8,000 power boat. What lump-sum amount must he invest now to have the $8,000 at the end of three years if he can invest money at:
   a. Ten percent?
   b. Fourteen percent?
2. Annual cash inflows that will arise from two competing investment projects are given below:

	Investment	
Year	A	B
1	$ 3,000	$12,000
2	6,000	9,000
3	9,000	6,000
4	12,000	3,000
	$30,000	$30,000

   Each investment project will require the same investment outlay. The discount rate is 18%. Compute the present value of the cash inflows for each investment.
3. Julie has just retired. Her company's retirement program has two options as to how retirement benefits can be received. Under the first option, Julie would receive a lump sum of $150,000 immediately as her full retirement benefit. Under the second option, she would receive $14,000 each year for 20 years plus a lump-sum payment of $60,000 at the end of the 20-year period. If she can invest money at 12%, which option would you recommend that she accept? Use present value analysis.

EXERCISE 14–15 Comparison of Projects Using Net Present Value [LO1]
Labeau Products, Ltd., of Perth, Australia, has $35,000 to invest. The company is trying to decide between two alternative uses for the funds as follows:

	Invest in Project X	Invest in Project Y
Investment required	$35,000	$35,000
Annual cash inflows	$9,000	
Single cash inflow at the end of 10 years ...		$150,000
Life of the project	10 years	10 years

The company's discount rate is 18%.

Required:

(Ignore income taxes.) Which alternative would you recommend that the company accept? Show all computations using the net present value approach. Prepare separate computations for each project.

EXERCISE 14–16 Internal Rate of Return and Net Present Value [LO1, LO2]

Henrie's Drapery Service is investigating the purchase of a new machine for cleaning and blocking drapes. The machine would cost $130,400, including freight and installation. Henrie's has estimated that the new machine would increase the company's cash inflows, net of expenses, by $25,000 per year. The machine would have a 10-year useful life and no salvage value.

Required:

(Ignore income taxes.)

1. Compute the machine's internal rate of return to the nearest whole percent.
2. Compute the machine's net present value. Use a discount rate of 14% and the format shown in Exhibit 14–5. Why do you have a zero net present value?
3. Suppose that the new machine would increase the company's annual cash inflows, net of expenses, by only $22,500 per year. Under these conditions, compute the internal rate of return to the nearest whole percent.

EXERCISE 14–17 (Appendix 14D) After-Tax Cash Flows in Net Present Value Analysis [LO8]

Dwyer Company is considering two investment projects. Relevant cost and cash flow information on the two projects is given below:

	Project A	Project B
Investment in heavy trucks	$130,000	
Investment in working capital		$130,000
Net annual cash inflows	$25,000	$25,000
Life of the project	9 years*	9 years

*Useful life of the trucks

The trucks will have a $15,000 salvage value in nine years. For tax purposes, the company computes depreciation deductions assuming zero salvage value and uses straight-line depreciation. The trucks will be depreciated over five years. At the end of nine years, the working capital will be released for use elsewhere. The company requires an after-tax return of 12% on all investments. The tax rate is 30%.

Required:

Compute the net present value of each investment project. Round all dollar amounts to the nearest whole dollar.

EXERCISE 14–18 (Appendix 14D) Net Present Value Analysis Including Income Taxes [LO8]

The Midtown Cafeteria employs five people to operate antiquated dishwashing equipment. The cost of wages for these people and for maintenance of the equipment is $85,000 per year. Management is considering the purchase of a single, highly automated dishwashing machine that would cost $140,000 and have a useful life of 12 years. This machine would require the services of only three people to operate at a cost of $48,000 per year. A maintenance contract on the machine would cost an additional $2,000 per year. New water jets would be needed on the machine in six years at a total cost of $15,000.

The old equipment is fully depreciated and has no resale value. The new machine will have a salvage value of $9,000 at the end of its 12-year useful life. For tax purposes, the company computes depreciation deductions assuming zero salvage value and uses straight-line depreciation. The new dishwashing machine would be depreciated over seven years. Management requires a 14% after-tax return on all equipment purchases. The company's tax rate is 30%.

Required:

1. Determine the before-tax net annual cost savings that the new dishwashing machine will provide.
2. Using the data from (1) above and other data from the exercise, compute the new dishwashing machine's net present value. Round all dollar amounts to the nearest whole dollar. Would you recommend that it be purchased?

Problems

PROBLEM 14–19 Basic Net Present Value Analysis [LO1]

Windhoek Mines, Ltd., of Namibia, is contemplating the purchase of equipment to exploit a mineral deposit on land to which the company has mineral rights. An engineering and cost analysis has been made, and it is expected that the following cash flows would be associated with opening and operating a mine in the area:

Cost of new equipment and timbers	R275,000
Working capital required	R100,000
Net annual cash receipts	R120,000*
Cost to construct new roads in three years	R40,000
Salvage value of equipment in four years	R65,000

*Receipts from sales of ore, less out-of-pocket costs for salaries, utilities, insurance, and so forth.

The currency in Namibia is the rand, denoted here by R.

It is estimated that the mineral deposit would be exhausted after four years of mining. At that point, the working capital would be released for reinvestment elsewhere. The company's required rate of return is 20%.

Required:

(Ignore income taxes.) Determine the net present value of the proposed mining project. Should the project be accepted? Explain.

PROBLEM 14–20 Net Present Value Analysis; Uncertain Cash Flows [LO1, LO3]

"I'm not sure we should lay out $500,000 for that automated welding machine," said Jim Alder, president of the Superior Equipment Company. "That's a lot of money, and it would cost us $80,000 for software and installation, and another $3,000 every month just to maintain the thing. In addition, the manufacturer admits that it would cost $45,000 more at the end of seven years to replace worn-out parts."

"I admit it's a lot of money," said Franci Rogers, the controller. "But you know the turnover problem we've had with the welding crew. This machine would replace six welders at a cost savings of $108,000 per year. And we would save another $6,500 per year in reduced material waste. When you figure that the automated welder would last for 12 years, I'm sure the return would be greater than our 16% required rate of return."

"I'm still not convinced," countered Mr. Alder. "We can only get $12,000 scrap value out of our old welding equipment if we sell it now, and in 12 years the new machine will only be worth $20,000 for parts. But have your people work up the figures and we'll talk about them at the executive committee meeting tomorrow."

Required:

(Ignore income taxes.)

1. Compute the net annual cost savings promised by the automated welding machine.
2. Using the data from (1) above and other data from the problem, compute the automated welding machine's net present value. (Use the incremental-cost approach.) Would you recommend purchasing the automated welding machine? Explain.
3. Assume that management can identify several intangible benefits associated with the automated welding machine, including greater flexibility in shifting from one type of product to another, improved quality of output, and faster delivery as a result of reduced throughput time. What dollar value per year would management have to attach to these intangible benefits in order to make the new welding machine an acceptable investment?

PROBLEM 14–21 Preference Ranking of Investment Projects [LO4]

The management of Revco Products is exploring five different investment opportunities. Information on the five projects under study follows:

	Project Number				
	1	2	3	4	5
Investment required . . .	$(270,000)	$(450,000)	$(400,000)	$(360,000)	$(480,000)
Present value of cash inflows at a 10% discount rate	336,140	522,970	379,760	433,400	567,270
Net present value	$ 66,140	$ 72,970	$ (20,240)	$ 73,400	$ 87,270
Life of the project	6 years	3 years	5 years	12 years	6 years
Internal rate of return . . .	18%	19%	8%	14%	16%

The company's required rate of return is 10%; thus, a 10% discount rate has been used in the present value computations above. Limited funds are available for investment, so the company can't accept all of the available projects.

Required:

1. Compute the project profitability index for each investment project.
2. Rank the five projects according to preference, in terms of:
   a. Net present value
   b. Project profitability index
   c. Internal rate of return
3. Which ranking do you prefer? Why?

PROBLEM 14–22 Simple Rate of Return; Payback [LO5, LO6]

Paul Swanson has an opportunity to acquire a franchise from The Yogurt Place, Inc., to dispense frozen yogurt products under The Yogurt Place name. Mr. Swanson has assembled the following information relating to the franchise:

a. A suitable location in a large shopping mall can be rented for $3,500 per month.
b. Remodeling and necessary equipment would cost $270,000. The equipment would have a 15-year life and an $18,000 salvage value. Straight-line depreciation would be used, and the salvage value would be considered in computing depreciation.
c. Based on similar outlets elsewhere, Mr. Swanson estimates that sales would total $300,000 per year. Ingredients would cost 20% of sales.
d. Operating costs would include $70,000 per year for salaries, $3,500 per year for insurance, and $27,000 per year for utilities. In addition, Mr. Swanson would have to pay a commission to The Yogurt Place, Inc., of 12.5% of sales.

Required:

(Ignore income taxes.)

1. Prepare a contribution format income statement that shows the expected net operating income each year from the franchise outlet.
2. Compute the simple rate of return promised by the outlet. If Mr. Swanson requires a simple rate of return of at least 12%, should he acquire the franchise?
3. Compute the payback period on the outlet. If Mr. Swanson wants a payback of four years or less, will he acquire the franchise?

PROBLEM 14–23 (Appendix 14D) Basic Net Present Value Analysis Including Income Taxes [LO8]

The Diamond Freight Company has been offered a seven-year contract to haul munitions for the government. Since this contract would represent new business, the company would have to purchase several new heavy-duty trucks at a cost of $350,000 if the contract were accepted. Other data relating to the contract follow:

Net annual cash receipts (before taxes) from the contract	$105,000
Cost of replacing the motors in the trucks in four years	$45,000
Salvage value of the trucks at termination of the contract	$18,000

With the motors being replaced after four years, the trucks will have a useful life of seven years. To raise money to assist in the purchase of the new trucks, the company will sell several old, fully depreciated trucks for a total selling price of $16,000. The company requires a 16% after-tax return on all equipment purchases. The tax rate is 30%. For tax purposes, the company computes depreciation deductions assuming zero salvage value and using straight-line depreciation. The new trucks would be depreciated over five years.

Required:

Compute the net present value of this investment opportunity. Round all dollar amounts to the nearest whole dollar. Would you recommend that the contract be accepted?

PROBLEM 14–24 Basic Net Present Value Analysis [LO1]

The Sweetwater Candy Company would like to buy a new machine that would automatically "dip" chocolates. The dipping operation is currently done largely by hand. The machine the company is considering costs $120,000. The manufacturer estimates that the machine would be usable for 12 years but would require the replacement of several key parts at the end of the sixth year. These parts would cost $9,000, including installation. After 12 years, the machine could be sold for $7,500.

The company estimates that the cost to operate the machine will be $7,000 per year. The present method of dipping chocolates costs $30,000 per year. In addition to reducing costs, the new machine will increase production by 6,000 boxes of chocolates per year. The company realizes a contribution margin of $1.50 per box. A 20% rate of return is required on all investments.

Required:

(Ignore income taxes.)

1. What are the net annual cash inflows that will be provided by the new dipping machine?
2. Compute the new machine's net present value. Use the incremental cost approach and round all dollar amounts to the nearest whole dollar.

PROBLEM 14–25 Net Present Value Analysis of a Lease or Buy Decision [LO1]

The Riteway Ad Agency provides cars for its sales staff. In the past, the company has always purchased its cars from a dealer and then sold the cars after three years of use. The company's present fleet of cars is three years old and will be sold very shortly. To provide a replacement fleet, the company is considering two alternatives:

Alternative 1: The company can purchase the cars, as in the past, and sell the cars after three years of use. Ten cars will be needed, which can be purchased at a discounted price of $17,000 each. If this alternative is accepted, the following costs will be incurred on the fleet as a whole:

Annual cost of servicing, taxes, and licensing	$3,000
Repairs, first year	$1,500
Repairs, second year	$4,000
Repairs, third year	$6,000

At the end of three years, the fleet could be sold for one-half of the original purchase price.

Alternative 2: The company can lease the cars under a three-year lease contract. The lease cost would be $55,000 per year (the first payment due at the end of Year 1). As part of this lease cost, the owner would provide all servicing and repairs, license the cars, and pay all the taxes. Riteway would be required to make a $10,000 security deposit at the beginning of the lease period, which would be refunded when the cars were returned to the owner at the end of the lease contract.

Required:

(Ignore income taxes.)

1. Riteway Ad Agency has an 18% required rate of return. Use the total-cost approach to determine the present value of the cash flows associated with each alternative. Round all dollar amounts to the nearest whole dollar. Which alternative should the company accept?
2. Using the data in (1) above and other data as needed, explain why it is often less costly for a company to lease equipment and facilities rather than to buy them.

PROBLEM 14–26 Internal Rate of Return; Sensitivity Analysis [LO2]

"In my opinion, a tanning salon would be a natural addition to our spa and very popular with our customers," said Stacey Winder, manager of the Lifeline Spa. "Our figures show that we could remodel the building next door to our spa and install all of the necessary equipment for $330,000. I have contacted tanning salons in other areas, and I am told that the tanning beds will be usable for about nine years. I am also told that a four-bed salon such as we are planning would generate a cash inflow of about $80,000 per year after all expenses."

"It does sound very appealing," replied Kevin Leblanc, the spa's accountant. "Let me push the numbers around a bit and see what kind of a return the salon would generate."

Required:

(Ignore income taxes.)

1. Compute the internal rate of return promised by the tanning salon to the nearest whole percent.
2. Assume that Ms. Winder will not open the salon unless it promises a return of at least 14%. Compute the amount of annual cash inflow that would provide this return on the $330,000 investment.
3. Although nine years is the average life of tanning salon equipment, Ms. Winder has found that this life can vary substantially. Compute the internal rate of return to the nearest whole percent if the life were (a) 6 years and (b) 12 years rather than 9 years. Is there any information provided by these computations that you would be particularly anxious to show Ms. Winder?
4. Ms. Winder has also found that although $80,000 is an average cash inflow from a four-bed salon, some salons vary as much as 20% from this figure. Compute the internal rate of return to the nearest whole percent if the annual cash inflows were (a) 20% less and (b) 20% greater than $80,000.
5. Assume that the $330,000 investment is made and that the salon is opened as planned. Because of concerns about the effects of excessive tanning, however, the salon is not able to attract as many customers as planned. Cash inflows are only $50,000 per year, and after eight years the salon equipment is sold to a competitor for $135,440. Compute the internal rate of return to the nearest whole percent earned on the investment over the eight-year period. (Hint: A useful way to proceed is to find the discount rate that will cause the net present value to be equal to, or near, zero.)

PROBLEM 14–27 Net Present Value; Uncertain Future Cash Flows; Postaudit [LO1, LO3]

Saxon Products, Inc., is investigating the purchase of a robot for use on the company's assembly line. Selected data relating to the robot are provided below:

Cost of the robot	$1,800,000
Installation and software	$900,000
Annual savings in labor costs	?
Annual savings in inventory carrying costs	$210,000
Monthly increase in power and maintenance costs	$2,500
Salvage value in 10 years	$70,000
Useful life	10 years

Engineering studies suggest that use of the robot will result in a savings of 25,000 direct labor-hours each year. The labor rate is $16 per hour. Also, the smoother work flow made possible by the use of automation will allow the company to reduce the amount of inventory on hand by $400,000. This inventory reduction will take place at the end of the first year of operation; the released funds will be available for use elsewhere in the company. Saxon Products has a 20% required rate of return on all purchases of equipment.

Shelly Martins, the controller, has noted that all of Saxon's competitors are automating their plants. She is pessimistic, however, about whether Saxon's management will allow it to automate. In preparing the proposal for the robot, she stated to a colleague, "Let's just hope that reduced labor and inventory costs can justify the purchase of this automated equipment. Otherwise, we'll never get it. You know how the president feels about equipment paying for itself out of reduced costs."

Required:

(Ignore income taxes.)

1. Determine the net *annual* cost savings if the robot is purchased. (Do not include the $400,000 inventory reduction or the salvage value in this computation.)
2. Compute the net present value of the proposed investment in the robot. Based on these data, would you recommend that the robot be purchased? Explain.

3. Assume that the robot is purchased. At the end of the first year, Shelly Martins has found that some items didn't work out as planned. Due to unforeseen problems, software and installation costs were $75,000 more than estimated and direct labor has been reduced by only 22,500 hours per year, rather than by 25,000 hours. Assuming that all other cost data were accurate, does it appear that the company made a wise investment? Show computations using the net present value format as in (2) above. (Hint: It might be helpful to place yourself back at the beginning of the first year with the new data.)
4. Upon seeing your analysis in (3) above, Saxon's president stated, "That robot is the worst investment we've ever made. And now we'll be stuck with it for years."
   a. Explain to the president what benefits other than cost savings might accrue from using the new automated equipment.
   b. Compute for the president the dollar amount of cash inflow that would be needed each year from the benefits in (a) above for the automated equipment to yield a 20% rate of return.

PROBLEM 14–28 Preference Ranking of Investment Projects [LO4]

Oxford Company has limited funds available for investment and must ration the funds among five competing projects. Selected information on the five projects follows:

Project	Investment Required	Net Present Value	Life of the Project (years)	Internal Rate of Return (percent)
A	$160,000	$44,323	7	18%
B	$135,000	$42,000	12	16%
C	$100,000	$35,035	7	20%
D	$175,000	$38,136	3	22%
E	$150,000	$(8,696)	6	8%

The net present values above have been computed using a 10% discount rate. The company wants your assistance in determining which project to accept first, second, and so forth.

Required:

1. Compute the project profitability index for each project.
2. In order of preference, rank the five projects in terms of:
   a. Net present value.
   b. Project profitability index.
   c. Internal rate of return.
3. Which ranking do you prefer? Why?

PROBLEM 14–29 Simple Rate of Return; Payback [LO5, LO6]

Sharkey's Fun Center contains a number of electronic games as well as a miniature golf course and various rides located outside the building. Paul Sharkey, the owner, would like to construct a water slide on one portion of his property. Mr. Sharkey has gathered the following information about the slide:

a. Water slide equipment could be purchased and installed at a cost of $330,000. According to the manufacturer, the slide would be usable for 12 years after which it would have no salvage value.
b. Mr. Sharkey would use straight-line depreciation on the slide equipment.
c. To make room for the water slide, several rides would be dismantled and sold. These rides are fully depreciated, but they could be sold for $60,000 to an amusement park in a nearby city.
d. Mr. Sharkey has concluded that about 50,000 more people would use the water slide each year than have been using the rides. The admission price would be $3.60 per person (the same price that the Fun Center has been charging for the old rides).
e. Based on experience at other water slides, Mr. Sharkey estimates that annual incremental operating expenses for the slide would be: salaries, $85,000; insurance, $4,200; utilities, $13,000; and maintenance, $9,800.

Required:

(Ignore income taxes.)

1. Prepare an income statement showing the expected net operating income each year from the water slide.

2. Compute the simple rate of return expected from the water slide. Based on this computation, would the water slide be constructed if Mr. Sharkey requires a simple rate of return of at least 14% on all investments?
3. Compute the payback period for the water slide. If Mr. Sharkey accepts any project with a payback period of five years or less, would the water slide be constructed?

PROBLEM 14–30 Net Present Value Analysis [LO1]

In eight years, Kent Duncan will retire. He is exploring the possibility of opening a self-service car wash. The car wash could be managed in the free time he has available from his regular occupation, and it could be closed easily when he retires. After careful study, Mr. Duncan has determined the following:

a. A building in which a car wash could be installed is available under an eight-year lease at a cost of $1,700 per month.
b. Purchase and installation costs of equipment would total $200,000. In eight years the equipment could be sold for about 10% of its original cost.
c. An investment of an additional $2,000 would be required to cover working capital needs for cleaning supplies, change funds, and so forth. After eight years, this working capital would be released for investment elsewhere.
d. Both a wash and a vacuum service would be offered with a wash costing $2.00 and the vacuum costing $1.00 per use.
e. The only variable costs associated with the operation would be 20 cents per wash for water and 10 cents per use of the vacuum for electricity.
f. In addition to rent, monthly costs of operation would be: cleaning, $450; insurance, $75; and maintenance, $500.
g. Gross receipts from the wash would be about $1,350 per week. According to the experience of other car washes, 60% of the customers using the wash would also use the vacuum.

Mr. Duncan will not open the car wash unless it provides at least a 10% return.

Required:

(Ignore income taxes.)

1. Assuming that the car wash will be open 52 weeks a year, compute the expected net annual cash receipts (gross cash receipts less cash disbursements) from its operation. (Do not include the cost of the equipment, the working capital, or the salvage value in these computations.)
2. Would you advise Mr. Duncan to open the car wash? Show computations using the net present value method of investment analysis. Round all dollar figures to the nearest whole dollar.

PROBLEM 14–31 Simple Rate of Return; Payback; Internal Rate of Return [LO2, LO5, LO6]

The Elberta Fruit Farm of Ontario has always hired transient workers to pick its annual cherry crop. Francie Wright, the farm manager, has just received information on a cherry picking machine that is being purchased by many fruit farms. The machine is a motorized device that shakes the cherry tree, causing the cherries to fall onto plastic tarps that funnel the cherries into bins. Ms. Wright has gathered the following information to decide whether a cherry picker would be a profitable investment for the Elberta Fruit Farm:

a. Currently, the farm is paying an average of $40,000 per year to transient workers to pick the cherries.
b. The cherry picker would cost $94,500, and it would have an estimated 12-year useful life. The farm uses straight-line depreciation on all assets and considers salvage value in computing depreciation deductions. The estimated salvage value of the cherry picker is $4,500.
c. Annual out-of-pocket costs associated with the cherry picker would be: cost of an operator and an assistant, $14,000; insurance, $200; fuel, $1,800; and a maintenance contract, $3,000.

Required:

(Ignore income taxes.)

1. Determine the annual savings in cash operating costs that would be realized if the cherry picker were purchased.
2. Compute the simple rate of return expected from the cherry picker. (Hint: Note that this is a cost reduction project.) Would the cherry picker be purchased if Elberta Fruit Farm's required rate of return is 16%?
3. Compute the payback period on the cherry picker. The Elberta Fruit Farm will not purchase equipment unless it has a payback period of five years or less. Would the cherry picker be purchased?
4. Compute (to the nearest whole percent) the internal rate of return promised by the cherry picker. Based on this computation, does it appear that the simple rate of return is an accurate guide in investment decisions?

PROBLEM 14–32 Net Present Value; Total and Incremental Approaches [LO1]

Bilboa Freightlines, S.A., of Panama, has a small truck that it uses for intracity deliveries. The truck is worn out and must be either overhauled or replaced with a new truck. The company has assembled the following information. (Panama uses the U.S. dollar as its currency):

Microsoft Excel - Problem 14-32 screen capture.xls

	A	B	C
1		*Present Truck*	*New Truck*
2	Purchase cost new	$21,000	$30,000
3	Remaining book value	$11,500	
4	Overhaul needed now	$7,000	
5	Annual cash operating costs	$10,000	$6,500
6	Salvage value-now	$9,000	
7	Salvage value-eight years from now	$1,000	$4,000

If the company keeps and overhauls its present delivery truck, then the truck will be usable for eight more years. If a new truck is purchased, it will be used for eight years, after which it will be traded in on another truck. The new truck would be diesel-operated, resulting in a substantial reduction in annual operating costs, as shown above.

The company computes depreciation on a straight-line basis. All investment projects are evaluated using a 16% discount rate.

Required:

(Ignore income taxes.)

1. Should Bilboa Freightlines keep the old truck or purchase the new one? Use the total-cost approach to net present value in making your decision. Round to the nearest whole dollar.
2. Redo (1) above, this time using the incremental-cost approach.

PROBLEM 14–33 (Appendix 14D) A Comparison of Investment Alternatives Including Income Taxes [LO8]

Julia Vanfleet is professor of mathematics. She has received a $225,000 inheritance from her father's estate, and she is anxious to invest it between now and the time she retires in 12 years. Professor Vanfleet is considering two alternatives for investing her inheritance.

Alternative 1. Corporate bonds can be purchased that mature in 12 years and that bear interest at 10%. This interest would be taxable and paid annually.

Alternative 2. A small retail business is available for sale that can be purchased for $225,000. The following information relates to this alternative:

a. Of the purchase price, $80,000 would be for fixtures and other depreciable items. The remainder would be for the company's working capital (inventory, accounts receivable, and cash). The fixtures and other depreciable items would have a remaining useful life of at least 12 years but would be depreciated for tax reporting purposes over eight years using the following allowances published by the Internal Revenue Service:

Year	Percentage of Original Cost Depreciated
1	14.3%
2	24.5%
3	17.5%
4	12.5%
5	8.9%
6	8.9%
7	8.9%
8	4.5%
	100.0%

Salvage value is not taken into account when computing depreciation for tax purposes. At any rate, at the end of 12 years these depreciable items would have a negligible salvage value; however, the working capital would be recovered (either through sale or liquidation of the business) for reinvestment elsewhere.

b. The store building would be leased. At the end of 12 years, if Professor Vanfleet could not find someone to buy the business, it would be necessary to pay $2,000 to the owner of the building to break the lease.

c. Store records indicate that sales have averaged $850,000 per year and out-of-pocket costs (including wages and rent on the building) have averaged $780,000 per year (*not* including income taxes). Management of the store would be entrusted to employees.

d. Professor Vanfleet's tax rate is 40%.

Required:

Advise Professor Vanfleet as to which alternative should be selected. Use the total-cost approach to net present value in your analysis, and a discount rate of 8%. Round all dollar amounts to the nearest whole dollar.

PROBLEM 14–34 Net Present Value Analysis of a New Product [LO1]

eXcel

Matheson Electronics has just developed a new electronic device which, when mounted on an automobile, will tell the driver how many miles the automobile is traveling per gallon of gasoline.

The company is anxious to begin production of the new device. To this end, marketing and cost studies have been made to determine probable costs and market potential. These studies have provided the following information:

a. New equipment would have to be acquired to produce the device. The equipment would cost $315,000 and have a 12-year useful life. After 12 years, it would have a salvage value of about $15,000.

b. Sales in units over the next 12 years are projected to be as follows:

Year	Sales in Units
1	6,000
2	12,000
3	15,000
4–12	18,000

c. Production and sales of the device would require working capital of $60,000 to finance accounts receivable, inventories, and day-to-day cash needs. This working capital would be released at the end of the project's life.

d. The devices would sell for $35 each; variable costs for production, administration, and sales would be $15 per unit.

e. Fixed costs for salaries, maintenance, property taxes, insurance, and straight-line depreciation on the equipment would total $135,000 per year. (Depreciation is based on cost less salvage value.)

f. To gain rapid entry into the market, the company would have to advertise heavily. The advertising program would be:

Year	Amount of Yearly Advertising
1–2	$180,000
3	$150,000
4–12	$120,000

g. Matheson Electronics' board of directors has specified a required rate of return of 14% on all new products.

Required:

(Ignore income taxes.)

1. Compute the net cash inflow (cash receipts less yearly cash operating expenses) anticipated from sale of the device for each year over the next 12 years.
2. Using the data computed in (1) above and other data provided in the problem, determine the net present value of the proposed investment. Would you recommend that Matheson accept the device as a new product?

PROBLEM 14–35 (Appendix 14D) Comparison of Total-Cost and Incremental-Cost Approaches Including Income Taxes [LO8]

Reliable Waste Systems provides a solid waste collection service in a large metropolitan area. The company is considering the purchase of several new trucks to replace an equal number of old trucks now in use. The new trucks would cost $650,000, but they would require only one operator per truck (compared to two operators for the trucks now being used), as well as provide other cost savings. A comparison of total annual cash operating costs between the old trucks that would be replaced and the new trucks is provided below:

	Old Trucks	New Trucks
Salaries—operators	$170,000	$ 85,000
Fuel	14,000	9,000
Insurance	6,000	11,000
Maintenance	10,000	5,000
Total annual cash operating costs	$200,000	$110,000

If the new trucks are purchased, the old trucks will be sold to a company in a nearby city for $85,000. These trucks cost $300,000 when they were new and have a current book value of $120,000. If the new trucks are not purchased, the company will take depreciation deductions for tax purposes on the old trucks of $60,000 a year over the next two years.

If the new trucks are not purchased, the old trucks will be used for seven more years and then sold for an estimated $15,000 scrap value. However, to keep the old trucks operating, extensive repairs will be needed in one year that will cost $170,000. These repairs will be expensed for tax purposes in the year incurred.

The new trucks would have a useful life of seven years and would have an estimated $60,000 salvage value at the end of their useful life. The company's tax rate is 30%, and its after-tax cost of capital is 12%. For tax purposes, the company would depreciate the equipment over five years using straight-line depreciation and assuming zero salvage value.

Required:

1. Use the total-cost approach to net present value analysis to determine whether the new trucks should be purchased. Round all dollar amounts to the nearest whole dollar.
2. Repeat the computations in (1) above, this time using the incremental-cost approach to net present value analysis.

Cases

CASE 14–36 Ethics and the Manager

The Fore Corporation is an integrated food processing company that has operations in over two dozen countries. Fore's corporate headquarters is in Chicago, and the company's executives frequently travel to visit Fore's foreign and domestic facilities.

Fore has a fleet of aircraft that consists of two business jets with international range and six smaller turboprop aircraft that are used on shorter flights. Company policy is to assign aircraft to trips on the basis of minimizing cost, but the practice is to assign the aircraft based on the organizational rank of the traveler. Fore offers its aircraft for short-term lease or for charter by other organizations whenever Fore itself does not plan to use the aircraft. Fore surveys the market often in order to keep its lease and charter rates competitive.

William Earle, Fore's vice president of finance, has claimed that a third business jet can be justified financially. However, some people in the controller's office have surmised that the real reason for a third business jet was to upgrade the aircraft used by Earle. Presently, the people outranking Earle keep the two business jets busy with the result that Earle usually flies in smaller turboprop aircraft.

The third business jet would cost $11 million. A capital expenditure of this magnitude requires a formal proposal with projected cash flows and net present value computations using Fore's minimum required rate of return. If Fore's president and the finance committee of the board of directors approve the proposal, it will be submitted to the full board of directors. The board has final approval on capital expenditures exceeding $5 million and has established a firm policy of rejecting any discretionary proposal that has a negative net present value.

Earle asked Rachel Arnett, assistant corporate controller, to prepare a proposal on a third business jet. Arnett gathered the following data:

- Acquisition cost of the aircraft, including instrumentation and interior furnishing.
- Operating cost of the aircraft for company use.
- Projected avoidable commercial airfare and other avoidable costs from company use of the plane.
- Projected value of executive time saved by using the third business jet.
- Projected contribution margin from incremental lease and charter activity.
- Estimated resale value of the aircraft.

When Earle reviewed Arnett's completed proposal and saw the large negative net present value figure, he returned the proposal to Arnett. With a glare, Earle commented, "You must have made an error. The proposal should look better than that."

Feeling some pressure, Arnett went back and checked her computations; she found no errors. However, Earle's message was clear. Arnett discarded her projections that she believed were reasonable and replaced them with figures that had a remote chance of actually occurring but were more favorable to the proposal. For example, she used first-class airfares to refigure the avoidable commercial airfare costs, even though company policy was to fly coach. She found revising the proposal to be distressing.

The revised proposal still had a negative net present value. Earle's anger was evident as he told Arnett to revise the proposal again, and to start with a $100,000 positive net present value and work backwards to compute supporting projections.

Required:

1. Explain whether Rachel Arnett's revision of the proposal was in violation of the Standards of Ethical Conduct for Practitioners of Management Accounting and Financial Management.
2. Was William Earle in violation of the Standards of Ethical Conduct for Practitioners of Management Accounting and Financial Management by telling Arnett specifically how to revise the proposal? Explain your answer.
3. Identify specific internal controls that Fore Corporation could implement to prevent unethical behavior on the part of the vice president of finance.

(CMA, adapted)

CASE 14–37 Comparison of Alternatives Using Net Present Value Analysis [LO1]

Kingsley Products, Ltd., is using a model 400 shaping machine to make one of its products. The company is expecting to have a large increase in demand for the product and is anxious to expand its productive capacity. Two possibilities are under consideration:

Alternative 1. Purchase another model 400 shaping machine to operate along with the currently owned model 400 machine.

Alternative 2. Purchase a model 800 shaping machine and use the currently owned model 400 machine as standby equipment. The model 800 machine is a high-speed unit with double the capacity of the model 400 machine.

The following additional information is available on the two alternatives:

a. Both the model 400 machine and the model 800 machine have a 10-year life from the time they are first used in production. The scrap value of both machines is negligible and can be ignored. Straight-line depreciation is used.
b. The cost of a new model 800 machine is $300,000.
c. The model 400 machine now in use cost $160,000 three years ago. Its present book value is $112,000, and its present market value is $90,000.
d. A new model 400 machine costs $170,000 now. If the company decides not to buy the model 800 machine, then the old model 400 machine will have to be replaced in seven years at a cost of $200,000. The replacement machine will be sold at the end of the tenth year for $140,000.
e. Production over the next 10 years is expected to be:

Year	Production in Units
1	40,000
2	60,000
3	80,000
4–10	90,000

f. The two models of machines are not equally efficient. Comparative variable costs per unit are:

	Model	
	400	800
Direct materials per unit	$0.25	$0.40
Direct labor per unit	0.49	0.16
Supplies and lubricants per unit	0.06	0.04
Total variable cost per unit	$0.80	$0.60

g. The model 400 machine is less costly to maintain than the model 800 machine. Annual repairs and maintenance costs on a model 400 machine are $2,500.
h. Repairs and maintenance costs on a model 800 machine, with a model 400 machine used as standby, would total $3,800 per year.
i. No other costs will change as a result of the decision between the two machines.
j. Kingsley Products has a 20% required rate of return on all investments.

Required:
(Ignore income taxes.)

1. Which alternative should the company choose? Use the net present value approach.
2. Suppose that the cost of labor increases by 10%. Would this make the model 800 machine more or less desirable? Explain. No computations are needed.
3. Suppose that the cost of direct materials doubles. Would this make the model 800 machine more or less desirable? Explain. No computations are needed.

CASE 14–38 (Appendix 14D) Make or Buy Decision Including Income Taxes [LO8]
Jonfran Company manufactures three different models of paper shredders, including the waste container which serves as the base. While the shredder heads are different for all three models, the waste container is the same. The number of waste containers that Jonfran will need during the next five years is estimated as follows:

Year 1	50,000	Year 4	55,000
Year 2	50,000	Year 5	55,000
Year 3	52,000		

The equipment used to manufacture the waste containers must be replaced because it has broken and can't be repaired. The new equipment has a list price of $945,000 but will be purchased at a 2% discount. The freight on the equipment would be $11,000, and installation costs would total $22,900. The equipment would be purchased and placed into service in January of Year 1. The equipment would have a salvage value of $15,000 at the end of its useful life.

For tax reporting purposes, the cost of the new equipment net of discounts, but including freight and installation costs, would be depreciated over four years using the straight-line method and assuming no salvage value.

The new equipment would be more efficient than the old equipment and it would slash both direct labor and variable overhead costs in half. However, the new equipment would require the use of a slightly heavier gauge of metal, which would increase direct material costs by 30%. The company uses JIT inventory methods, but the heavier gauge metal is sometimes hard to get so the company would have to keep a small quantity on hand, which would increase working capital needs by $20,000.

The old equipment is fully depreciated and is not included in the fixed overhead. The old equipment can be sold now for $1,500; Jonfran has no alternative use for the manufacturing space at this time, so if the new equipment is not purchased, the old equipment will be left in place.

Rather than replace the old equipment, one of Jonfran's production managers has suggested that the waste containers be purchased. One supplier has quoted a price of $28 per container. This price is $7 less than Jonfran's current manufacturing cost, which follows:

Direct materials		$10
Direct labor		8
Variable overhead		6
Fixed overhead:		
Supervision	$2	
Facilities	5	
General	4	11
Total cost per unit		$35

Jonfran uses a plantwide predetermined fixed overhead rate. If the waste containers are purchased outside, the salary and benefits of one supervisor, included in the fixed overhead at $45,000, would be eliminated. No other changes would be made in the other cash and noncash items included in fixed overhead except depreciation on the new equipment.

Jonfran is subject to a 30% tax rate and requires a 14% after-tax return on all equipment purchases.

Required:

Using net present value analysis, determine whether the company should purchase the new equipment and make the waste containers or purchase the containers from the outside supplier. Use the total-cost approach and round all dollar amounts to the nearest whole dollar.

(CMA, adapted)

CASE 14–39 Net Present Value Analysis of a Lease or Buy Decision [LO1]

Top-Quality Stores, Inc., owns a nationwide chain of supermarkets. The company is going to open another store soon, and a suitable building site has been located in an attractive and rapidly growing area. In discussing how the company can acquire the desired building and other facilities needed to open the new store, Sam Watkins, the company's vice president in charge of sales, stated, "I know most of our competitors are starting to lease facilities rather than buy, but I just can't see the economics of it. Our development people tell me that we can buy the building site, put a building on it, and get all the store fixtures we need for just $850,000. They also say that property taxes, insurance, and repairs would run $20,000 a year. When you figure that we plan to keep a site for 18 years, that's a total cost of $1,210,000. But then when you realize that the property will be worth at least a half million in 18 years, that's a net cost to us of only $710,000. What would it cost to lease the property?"

"I understand that Beneficial Insurance Company is willing to purchase the building site, construct a building and install fixtures to our specifications, and then lease the facility to us for 18 years at an annual lease payment of $120,000," replied Lisa Coleman, the company's executive vice president.

"That's just my point," said Sam. "At $120,000 a year, it would cost us a cool $2,160,000 over the 18 years. That's three times what it would cost to buy, and what would we have left at the end? Nothing! The building would belong to the insurance company!"

"You're overlooking a few things," replied Lisa. "For one thing, the treasurer's office says that we could only afford to put $350,000 down if we buy the property, and then we would have to pay the other $500,000 off over four years at $175,000 a year. So there would be some interest involved on the purchase side that you haven't figured in."

"But that little bit of interest is nothing compared to over 2 million bucks for leasing," said Sam. "Also, if we lease I understand we would have to put up an $8,000 security deposit that we wouldn't get back until the end. And besides that, we would still have to pay all the yearly repairs and maintenance costs just like we owned the property. No wonder those insurance companies are so rich if they can swing deals like this."

"Well, I'll admit that I don't have all the figures sorted out yet," replied Lisa. "But I do have the operating cost breakdown for the building, which includes $7,500 annually for property taxes, $8,000 for insurance, and $4,500 for repairs and maintenance. If we lease, Beneficial will handle its own insurance costs and of course the owner will have to pay the property taxes. I'll put all this together and see if leasing makes any sense with our required rate of return of 16%. The president wants a presentation and recommendation in the executive committee meeting tomorrow. Let's see, development said the first lease payment would be due now and the remaining ones due in years 1–17. Development also said that this store should generate a net cash inflow that's well above the average for our stores."

Required:

(Ignore income taxes.)

1. Using the net present value approach, determine whether Top-Quality Stores, Inc., should lease or buy the new facility. Assume that you will be making your presentation before the company's executive committee.
2. How will you reply in the meeting if Sam Watkins brings up the issue of the building's future sales value?

Group and Internet Exercises

GROUP EXERCISE 14–40 Capital Budgets in Colleges

In recent years, your college or university has probably undertaken a capital budgeting project such as building or renovating a facility. Investigate one of these capital budgeting projects. You will probably need the help of your university's or college's accounting or finance office.

Required:

1. Determine the total cost of the project and the source of the funds for the project. Did the money come from state funds, gifts, grants, endowments, or the school's general fund?
2. Did the costs of the project stay within budget?
3. What financial criteria were used to evaluate the project?
4. If the net present value method or internal rate of return method was used, review the calculations. Do you agree with the calculations and methods used?
5. If the net present value method was not used to evaluate the project, estimate the project's net present value. If all of the required data are not available, make reasonable estimates for the missing data. What discount rate did you use? Why?
6. Evaluate the capital budgeting procedures that were actually used by your college or university.

INTERNET EXERCISE 14–41

As you know, the World Wide Web is a medium that is constantly evolving. Sites come and go, and change without notice. To enable periodic updating of site addresses, this problem has been posted to the textbook website (www.mhhe.com/garrison11e). After accessing the site, enter the Student Center and select this chapter. Select and complete the Internet Exercise.

Chapter

15

Service Department Costing: An Activity Approach

LEARNING OBJECTIVES

After studying Chapter 15, you should be able to:

LO1 Allocate service department costs to other departments, using the direct method.

LO2 Allocate service department costs to other departments, using the step method.

LO3 Allocate variable and fixed service department costs separately at the beginning of a period and at the end of the period.

What Difference Does It Make?

BUSINESS FOCUS

Prior to 1995, Boeing billed internal organizational units for their phone usage using 29 different rates that reflected how much of each type of service was used, such as international long distance, domestic long distance, and voice mailboxes. In 1995, this system was replaced by a much simpler system in which all of the costs of voice services were allocated to units based on the number of salaried employees. The rate in 1995 was $76.84 per salaried employee per month; by 1998, the rate had increased to $91.84. A department with 10 salaried employees would therefore be charged $918.40 per month for voice services regardless of how many phone lines were in use, how many long distance phone calls were made, or how many voice mailboxes were in use. The simplified billing was thought to save Boeing several million dollars a year in administrative costs. However, managers complained about the new system for several reasons. First, the new billing system removed any incentives to economize on the use of voice services. Purchases of cell phones more than doubled and long distance usage outpaced the growth in employees. Second, some managers complained that the new system overcharged them for voice services and did not provide any way for them to reduce phone costs other than to reduce the number of salaried employees. A manager who tried to control the use of long distance calling in his or her department would find that those efforts had absolutely no effect on how much the department was charged for voice services.

Boeing abandoned its simplified billing system in 1999, returning to a system that charged for voice services actually used. ■

Source: William R. Ortega, "Alternative Chargeback Systems for Shared Services at the Boeing Company: The Case of Voice Telecommunication Services," Management Accounting Section 2001 Research and Case Conference, Institute of Management Accountants, January 18–20, 2000.

Most large organizations have both *operating departments* and *service departments.* The central purposes of the organization are carried out in the **operating departments.** In contrast, **service departments** do not directly engage in operating activities. Instead, they provide services or assistance to the operating departments. Examples of operating departments include the Surgery Department at Mt. Sinai Hospital, the Geography Department at the University of Washington, the Marketing Department at Allstate Insurance Company, and production departments at manufacturers such as Mitsubishi, Hewlett-Packard, and Michelin. Examples of service departments include Cafeteria, Internal Auditing, Human Resources, Cost Accounting, and Purchasing.

Service department costs are allocated to operating departments for a variety of reasons including:

- To encourage operating departments to make wise use of service department resources. If the services were provided for free, operating managers would be inclined to waste these resources.
- To provide operating departments with more complete cost data for making decisions. Actions taken by operating departments have impacts on service department costs. For example, hiring another employee will increase costs in the human resources department. Such service department costs should be charged to the operating departments, otherwise the operating departments will not take them into account when making decisions.
- To help measure the profitability of operating departments. Allocating service department costs to operating departments provides a more complete accounting of the costs incurred as a consequence of activities in the operating departments.
- To create an incentive for service departments to operate efficiently. Allocating service department costs to operating departments provides a system of checks and balances in the sense that cost-conscious operating departments will take an active interest in keeping service department costs low.
- To value inventory for external financial reporting purposes. Generally Accepted Accounting Principles (GAAP) require that all manufacturing overhead costs be assigned to products. Allocating service department costs to operating departments ensures that these manufacturing overhead costs are included in the operating departments' overhead rates, which are used to apply costs to products.
- When cost-plus pricing is used, service department costs are commonly allocated to the operating departments so as to include these costs in the cost base.

Several different allocation methods will be considered in this chapter. The method that is selected can have a significant impact on the computed costs of goods and services and can affect an operating department's performance evaluation.

Allocations Using the Direct and Step Methods

All allocations require the use of an allocation base. We have discussed the principles involved in selecting an allocation base in earlier chapters, but those principles are worth repeating.

Selecting Allocation Bases

An allocation base should "drive" the cost that is being allocated. For example, when allocating the costs of the employee cafeteria, the number of meals served would be a good choice for the allocation base. Many of the costs of the cafeteria, such as the costs of ingredients used, are driven by how many meals are served. Ideally, *all* of the costs that are being allocated should be driven by the allocation base in the sense that the costs being

EXHIBIT 15–1
Examples of Bases Commonly Used to Allocate Service Department Costs

Service Department	Allocation Bases
Laundry	Pounds of laundry
Airport Ground Services	Number of flights
Cafeteria	Number of meals
Medical Facilities	Cases handled; number of employees; hours worked
Materials Handling	Hours of service; volume handled
Information Technology	Number of personal computers; applications installed
Custodial Services	Square footage occupied
Cost Accounting	Labor-hours; customers served
Power	KWH used; capacity of machines
Human Resources	Number of employees; training hours
Receiving, Shipping, and Stores	Units handled; number of requisitions; space occupied
Factory Administration	Total labor-hours
Maintenance	Machine-hours

allocated are directly proportional to the allocation base. For example, if the number of meals served increases (or decreases) by 10%, then the total cost of the employee cafeteria should also increase (or decrease) by 10%. Managers also often argue that an allocation base should reflect as accurately as possible the benefits received from the service department.

For example, most managers would argue that the appropriate allocation base for janitorial services is the square feet of building space occupied by each department because both the costs and benefits of janitorial services tend to be proportional to the amount of space occupied by a department. Examples of allocation bases for some service departments are listed in Exhibit 15–1. Note that a given service department's costs may be allocated using more than one base. For example, the costs of a human resources department might be divided into two parts, with one part allocated on the basis of the number of employees in each department and the other part allocated on the basis of hours spent in training programs run by the human resources department.

IN BUSINESS

INCREASING ACCURACY AT HUGHES AIRCRAFT

For many years, Hughes Aircraft allocated service department costs to operating departments using headcount as the allocation base. This method, while simple, was inaccurate because most service department costs are not driven by the number of employees (i.e., headcount) in the operating departments. To overcome this problem, the company adopted an activity-based approach in which each service department's costs are allocated based on the activities that are believed to drive the service department's costs. For example, the costs of the Human Resources Department are now allocated on the basis of headcount, new hires, union employees, and training hours in each operating department. Operating managers can control the amount of Human Resources cost allocated to their departments by controlling headcount, number of new hires, number of union employees, and number of training hours in their departments.

Source: Jack Haedicke and David Feil, "Hughes Aircraft Sets the Standard for ABC," *Management Accounting* 72, no. 8, pp. 31–32.

Interdepartmental Services

LEARNING OBJECTIVE 1
Allocate service department costs to other departments, using the direct method.

Many service departments provide services to each other, as well as to operating departments. The Cafeteria Department, for example, provides food for all employees, including those assigned to other service departments. In turn, the Cafeteria Department may receive services from other service departments, such as from Custodial Services or from Personnel. Services provided between service departments are known as **interdepartmental** or **reciprocal services.**

Three approaches are used to allocate the costs of service departments to other departments. These are known as the *direct method,* the *step method,* and the *reciprocal method.* These three methods are discussed in the following sections.

Direct Method The **direct method** is the simplest of the three cost allocation methods. It ignores the services provided by a service department to other service departments and allocates all of its costs directly to operating departments. Even if a service department (such as Personnel) provides a large amount of service to another service department (such as the cafeteria), no allocations are made between the two departments. Rather, all costs are allocated *directly* to the operating departments, bypassing the other service departments. Hence the term *direct method.*

IN BUSINESS

A LOSING FOOTBALL PROGRAM

At Georgia Tech, service department costs are allocated to intercollegiate sports programs using the direct method. For example, the costs of the Sports Medicine Department are allocated on the basis of the number of student athletes in each intercollegiate sport. Some costs, such as a sport's operating budget, recruiting costs, scholarships, and salaries, can be traced directly to the sport and are called direct costs. Service department costs, which are allocated, include Sports Medicine, Facilities, Sports Information, Academic Center, Student-Athlete Program, Office Supplies, Legal and Audit, Accounting Office, Marketing, and Administrative. Allocations of these service department costs to the sports programs can make a big difference in their apparent profitability. For example, the football program shows a margin of over $1 million based on just its direct costs, but a loss of over $800,000 when service department costs are allocated to the program.

Source: C. David Strupeck, Ken Milani, and James E. Murphy III, "Financial Management at Georgia Tech," *Management Accounting* 74, no. 8, pp. 58–63.

For an example of the direct method, consider Mountain View Hospital, which has two service departments and two operating departments as shown below:

	Service Departments		Operating Departments		
	Hospital Administration	Custodial Services	Laboratory	Patient Care	Total
Departmental costs before allocation	$360,000	$90,000	$261,000	$689,000	$1,400,000
Employee hours. .	12,000	6,000	18,000	30,000	66,000
Space occupied—square feet . . .	10,000	200	5,000	45,000	60,200

Hospital Administration costs will be allocated on the basis of employee-hours and Custodial Services costs will be allocated on the basis of square feet occupied.

The direct method of allocating the hospital's service department costs to the operating departments is shown in Exhibit 15–2. Several things should be carefully noted in this exhibit. First, the employee-hours of the Hospital Administration Department and the Custodial Services Department are ignored when allocating the costs of Hospital Administration using the direct method. *Under the direct method, any of the allocation base attributable to the service departments themselves is ignored; only the amount of the allocation base attributable to the operating departments is used in the allocation.* Note that the same rule is used when allocating the costs of the Custodial Services Department.

Topic Tackler PLUS
15–1

EXHIBIT 15–2
Direct Method of Allocation

	Service Departments		Operating Departments		
	Hospital Administration	Custodial Services	Laboratory	Patient Care	Total
Departmental costs before allocation	$360,000	$90,000	$261,000	$689,000	$1,400,000
Allocation:					
Hospital Administration costs (18/48, 30/48)*	(360,000)		135,000	225,000	
Custodial Services costs (5/50, 45/50)†		(90,000)	9,000	81,000	
Total costs after allocation	$ 0	$ 0	$405,000	$995,000	$1,400,000

*Based on the employee-hours in the two operating departments, which are 18,000 hours + 30,000 hours = 48,000 hours.
†Based on the square feet occupied by the two operating departments, which is 5,000 square feet + 45,000 square feet = 50,000 square feet.

Even though the Hospital Administration and Custodial Services departments occupy some space, this is ignored when the Custodial Services costs are allocated. Finally, note that after all allocations have been completed, all of the service department costs are contained in the two operating departments.

Although the direct method is simple, it is less accurate than the other methods since it ignores interdepartmental services.

LEARNING OBJECTIVE 2
Allocate service department costs to other departments, using the step method.

Step Method Unlike the direct method, the **step method** provides for allocation of a service department's costs to other service departments, as well as to operating departments. The step method is sequential. The sequence typically begins with the department that provides the greatest amount of service to other service departments. After its costs have been allocated, the process continues, step by step, ending with the department that provides the least amount of services to other service departments. This step procedure is illustrated in graphic form in Exhibit 15–3 (page 722).

Exhibit 15–4 (page 722) shows the details of the step method. Note the following three key points about these allocations. First, under the Allocation heading in Exhibit 15–4, you see two allocations, or steps. In the first step, the costs of Hospital Administration are allocated to another service department (Custodial Services) as well as to the operating departments. In contrast to the direct method, the allocation base for Hospital Administration costs now includes the employee-hours for Custodial Services as well as for the operating departments. However, the allocation base still excludes the employee-hours for Hospital Administration itself. *In both the direct and step methods, any amount of the allocation base attributable to the service department whose cost is being allocated is always ignored.* Second, looking again at Exhibit 15–4, note that in the second step under the Allocation heading, the cost of Custodial Services is allocated to the two operating departments, and none of the cost is allocated to Hospital Administration even though Hospital Administration occupies space in the building. *In the step method, any amount of the allocation base that is attributable to a service department whose cost has already been allocated is ignored.* After a service department's costs have been allocated, costs of other service departments are not reallocated back to it. Third, note that the cost of Custodial Services allocated to other departments in the second step ($130,000) in Exhibit 15–4 includes the costs of Hospital Administration that were allocated to Custodial Services in the first step in Exhibit 15–4.

Topic Tackler PLUS
15–2

EXHIBIT 15–3
Graphic Illustration—Step Method

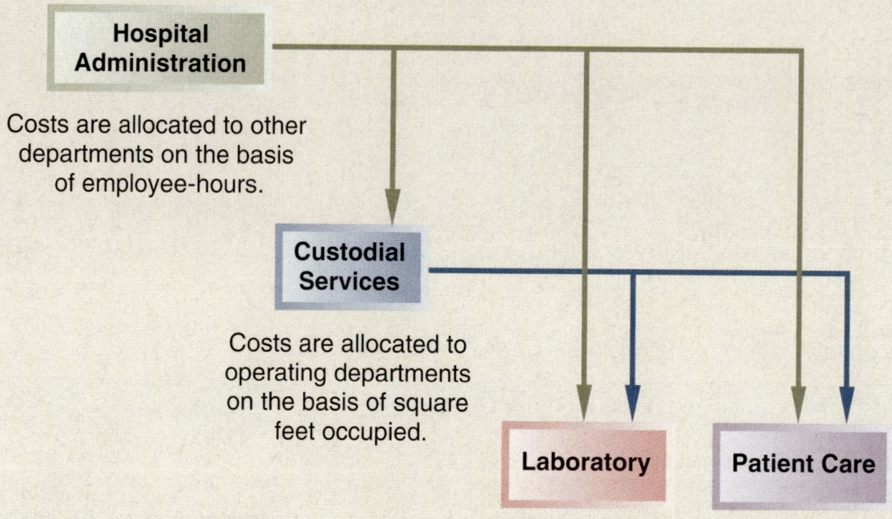

EXHIBIT 15–4
Step Method of Allocation

	Service Departments		Operating Departments		
	Hospital Administration	Custodial Services	Laboratory	Patient Care	Total
Departmental costs before allocation	$360,000	$ 90,000	$261,000	$ 689,000	$1,400,000
Allocation:					
Hospital Administration costs (6/54, 18/54, 30/54)* .	(360,000)	40,000	120,000	200,000	
Custodial Services costs (5/50, 45/50)†		(130,000)	13,000	117,000	
Total costs after allocation	$ 0	$ 0	$394,000	$1,006,000	$1,400,000

*Based on the employee-hours in Custodial Services and the two operating departments, which are 6,000 hours + 18,000 hours + 30,000 hours = 54,000 hours.
†As in Exhibit 15–2, this allocation is based on the square feet occupied by the two operating departments.

IN BUSINESS

STEPPING DOWN AT GROUP HEALTH

Group Health Cooperative of Puget Sound is a large health maintenance organization with 500 service departments that account for 30% of Group Health's total costs. The step method is used to allocate these costs to patient care departments and then to patients. These allocations are done so that costs can be summarized in a variety of ways including "by consumers, by diagnostic groupings, by employer groups, and by specific populations, such as Medicare, Medicaid, AIDS, Heart Care, and so on."

Source: John Y. Lee and Pauline Nefcy, "The Anatomy of an Effective HMO Cost Management System," *Management Accounting*, January 1997, p. 52.

Reciprocal Method The **reciprocal method** gives full recognition to interdepartmental services. Under the step method discussed above only partial recognition of interdepartmental services is possible. The step method always allocates costs forward—never backward. The reciprocal method, by contrast, allocates service department costs in *both* directions. Thus, since Custodial Services in the prior example provides services for Hospital Administration, part of Custodial Services' costs will be allocated *back* to Hospital Administration if the reciprocal method is used. At the same time, part of Hospital Administration's costs will be allocated *forward* to Custodial Services. Reciprocal allocation requires the use of simultaneous linear equations and is beyond the scope of this book. Examples of the reciprocal method can be found in more advanced cost accounting texts.

The reciprocal method is rarely used in practice for two reasons. First, the computations are relatively complex. Although the complexity issue can be overcome by use of computers, there is no evidence that computers have made the reciprocal method more popular. Second, the step method usually provides results that are close to the results that the reciprocal method would provide. Thus, companies have little motivation to use the more complex reciprocal method.

Revenue Producing Departments To conclude our discussion of allocation methods, it is important to note that even though most service departments are cost centers and therefore generate no revenues, a few service departments such as the cafeteria may charge for the services they perform. If a service department generates revenues, those revenues should be offset against the department's costs, and only the net amount of cost remaining after this offset should be allocated to other departments. Otherwise, the other departments would be charged for costs that have already been reimbursed.

Allocating Costs by Behavior

Whenever possible, variable and fixed service department costs should be allocated separately to provide more useful data for planning and control of departmental operations.

Variable Costs

Variable costs vary in total in proportion to changes in the level of service provided. For example, the cost of food in a cafeteria is a variable cost that varies in proportion to the number of persons using the cafeteria or the number of meals served.

As a general rule, a variable cost should be charged to consuming departments according to whatever activity causes the incurrence of the cost. For example, variable costs of a maintenance department that are caused by the number of machine-hours worked in the operating departments should be allocated to the operating departments using machine-hours as the allocation base. This will ensure that these costs are properly traced to departments, products, and customers.

Fixed Costs

The fixed costs of service departments represent the costs of making capacity available for use. These costs should be allocated to consuming departments in *predetermined lump-sum amounts.* By predetermined lump-sum amounts we mean that the total amount charged to each consuming department is determined in advance and, once determined, does not change. The lump-sum amount charged to a department can be based either on the department's peak-period or long-run average servicing needs. The logic behind lump-sum allocations of this type is as follows:

When a service department is first established, its capacity will be determined by the needs of the departments that it will serve. This capacity may reflect the peak-period needs of the other departments, or it may reflect their long-run average or "normal" servicing needs. Depending on how much servicing capacity is provided for, it will be necessary to make a commitment of resources, which will be reflected in the service department's fixed costs. These fixed costs should be borne by the consuming departments in proportion to the amount of capacity each consuming department requires. That is, if available capacity in the service department has been provided to meet the peak-period needs of consuming departments, then the fixed costs of the service department should be allocated in predetermined lump-sum amounts to consuming departments on that basis. If available capacity has been provided only to meet "normal" or long-run average needs, then the fixed costs should be allocated on that basis.

Once set, allocations should not vary from period to period, since they represent the cost of having a certain level of service capacity available and on line for each consuming department. The fact that a consuming department does not need the peak level or even the "normal" level of service every period is immaterial; the capacity to deliver this level of service must be available. The consuming departments should bear the cost of that availability.

To illustrate this idea, assume that Novak Company has just organized a Maintenance Department to service all machines in the Cutting, Assembly, and Finishing Departments. In determining the capacity of the newly organized Maintenance Department, the various operating departments estimated that they would have the following peak-period needs for maintenance:

Department	Peak-Period Maintenance Needs in Terms of Number of Hours of Maintenance Work Required	Percent of Total Hours
Cutting	900	30%
Assembly	1,800	60
Finishing	300	10
	3,000	100%

Therefore, in allocating the Maintenance Department fixed costs to the operating departments, 30% (i.e., 900/3,000 = 30%) should be allocated to the Cutting Department, 60% to the Assembly Department, and 10% to the Finishing Department. These lump-sum allocations *will not change* from period to period unless peak-period servicing needs change.

Should Actual or Budgeted Costs Be Allocated?

Should the *actual* or *budgeted* costs of a service department be allocated to operating departments? The answer is that budgeted costs should be allocated because allocating actual costs would burden the operating departments with any inefficiencies in the service department. In other words, if actual costs are allocated, any lack of cost control on the part of the service department is simply buried in a routine allocation to other departments.

Any variance over budgeted costs is the responsibility of the service department. The variance should be retained in the service department and closed out at year-end against the company's revenues or against cost of goods sold, along with other variances. Operating department managers justifiably complain bitterly if they are forced to absorb service department inefficiencies.

Technically, preset charges based on budgeted costs are not allocations. Instead of dividing actual costs among the operating departments, they are charged a fixed amount per unit of service provided. In effect, management says, "You will be charged X dollars for every unit of service that you consume or capacity that you require. You can consume as much or as little as you desire; the total charge you bear will vary proportionately." The purpose of making such charges is to ensure that the managers of the operating departments are fully aware of all of the costs of their actions—including costs that are incurred in service departments. This helps operating department managers make appropriate trade-offs when deciding, for example, whether to purchase a service from an external provider or to obtain it from a service department inside the company.

A Summary of Cost Allocation Guidelines

The following guidelines summarize the preceding discussion concerning allocations of service department costs.

1. Variable and fixed service department costs should be allocated separately when feasible.
2. Variable costs should be allocated at the budgeted rate, according to whatever activity (e.g., miles driven, direct labor-hours, number of employees) causes the incurrence of the cost.
   a. If the allocations are being made at the beginning of the year, they should be based on the budgeted activity level planned for the consuming departments. The allocation formula is:

   $$\text{Variable cost allocated at the beginning of the period} = \text{Budgeted rate} \times \text{Budgeted activity}$$

   b. If the allocations are being made at the end of the year, they should be based on the actual activity level that has occurred during the year. The allocation formula is:

   $$\text{Variable cost allocated at the end of the period} = \text{Budgeted rate} \times \text{Actual activity}$$

   Allocations made at the beginning of the year provide data for pricing and other decisions. Allocations made at the end of the year provide data for comparing actual performance to planned performance.
3. Fixed costs represent the costs of having service capacity available. Where feasible, these costs should be allocated in predetermined lump-sum amounts. The lump-sum amount allocated to each department should be in proportion to the servicing needs that gave rise to the fixed costs. (This might be either peak-period needs or long-run average needs.) Budgeted fixed costs, rather than actual fixed costs, should always be allocated.

Implementing the Allocation Guidelines

LEARNING OBJECTIVE 3
Allocate variable and fixed service department costs separately at the beginning of a period and at the end of the period.

Specific examples will show how to implement the three guidelines given above. First, we focus on the allocation of costs for a single department, and then we provide a more extended example involving multiple departments.

Basic Allocation Techniques

Seaboard Airlines has two operating divisions: a Freight Division and a Passenger Division. The company has a Maintenance Department that provides servicing to both divisions. Variable servicing costs are budgeted at $10 per flight-hour. The department's fixed costs are budgeted at $750,000 for the year. The fixed costs of the Maintenance Department are budgeted based on the peak-period demand, which occurs during the Thanksgiving to New Year's holiday period. The airline wants to make sure that none of its aircraft are grounded during this key period due to unavailability of maintenance facilities. Approximately 40% of the maintenance during this period is performed on the Freight Division's equipment, and 60% is performed on the Passenger Division's equipment. These figures and the budgeted flight-hours for the coming year are as follows:

	Percent of Peak Period Capacity Required	Budgeted Flight-Hours
Freight Division	40%	9,000
Passenger Division	60	15,000
Total	100%	24,000

Given these data, the amount of cost that would be allocated to each division from the Maintenance Department at the beginning of the coming year would be as follows:

		Budgeted activity	Division Freight	Division Passenger
Budgeted variable rate	Variable cost allocation:			
	$10 per flight-hour ×	9,000 flight-hours . .	$ 90,000	
	$10 per flight-hour ×	15,000 flight-hours . .		$150,000
	Fixed cost allocation:			
Peak-period capacity required	40% × $750,000		300,000	
	60% × $750,000			450,000
	Total cost allocated		$390,000	$600,000
	Budgeted fixed cost			

These allocated Maintenance Department costs would be included in the flexible budgets of the respective divisions and included in the computation of divisional overhead rates.

At the end of the year, Seaboard Airlines' management may want to make a second allocation, this time based on actual activity, in order to compare actual performance for the year against planned performance. To illustrate, year-end records show that actual variable and fixed costs in the aircraft Maintenance Department for the year were $260,000 and $780,000, respectively. One division logged more flight-hours during the year than planned, and the other division logged fewer flight-hours than planned, as shown below:

	Flight-Hours Budgeted (see above)	Flight-Hours Actual
Freight Division	9,000	8,000
Passenger Division	15,000	17,000
Total flight-hours	24,000	25,000

The amount of actual Maintenance Department cost charged to each division for the year would be as follows:

		Actual activity	Division Freight	Division Passenger
Budgeted variable rate	Variable cost allocation:			
	$10 per flight-hour ×	8,000 flight-hours . .	$ 80,000	
	$10 per flight-hour ×	17,000 flight-hours . .		$170,000
	Fixed cost allocation:			
Peak-period capacity required	40% × $750,000		300,000	
	60% × $750,000			450,000
	Total cost allocated		$380,000	$620,000
	Budgeted fixed cost			

Notice that variable servicing costs are charged to the operating divisions based on the budgeted rate ($10 per hour) and the *actual activity* for the year. In contrast, the charges for fixed costs are exactly the same as they were at the beginning of the year. Also note that the two operating divisions are *not* charged for the actual costs of the service department, which may be influenced by inefficiency in the service department and may be beyond the control of the managers of the operating divisions. Instead, the service department is held responsible for the unallocated actual costs as shown below:

	Variable	Fixed
Total actual costs incurred	$260,000	$780,000
Costs allocated (above)	250,000*	750,000
Spending variance—not allocated	$ 10,000	$ 30,000

*$10 per flight-hour × 25,000 actual flight-hours = $250,000.

These variances will be closed out against the company's revenues or cost of goods sold for the year, along with any other variances that may occur.

Effect of Allocations on Operating Departments

Once allocations have been completed, what do the operating departments do with the allocated service department costs? The allocations are typically included in performance evaluations of the operating departments and also included in determining their profitability.

In addition, if the operating departments are responsible for developing overhead rates for costing products or services, then the allocated costs are combined with the other costs of the operating departments, and the total is used as the basis for rate computations. This rate development process is illustrated in Exhibit 15–5.

The budget serves as the means for combining allocated service department costs with operating department costs and for computing overhead rates. An example is presented in Exhibit 15–6 (page 728). Note from the exhibit that both variable and fixed service department costs have been allocated to Superior Company's Milling Department and are included on the latter's budget. Since allocated service department costs are an integral part of the budget, they are automatically included in overhead rate computations, as shown at the bottom of the exhibit.

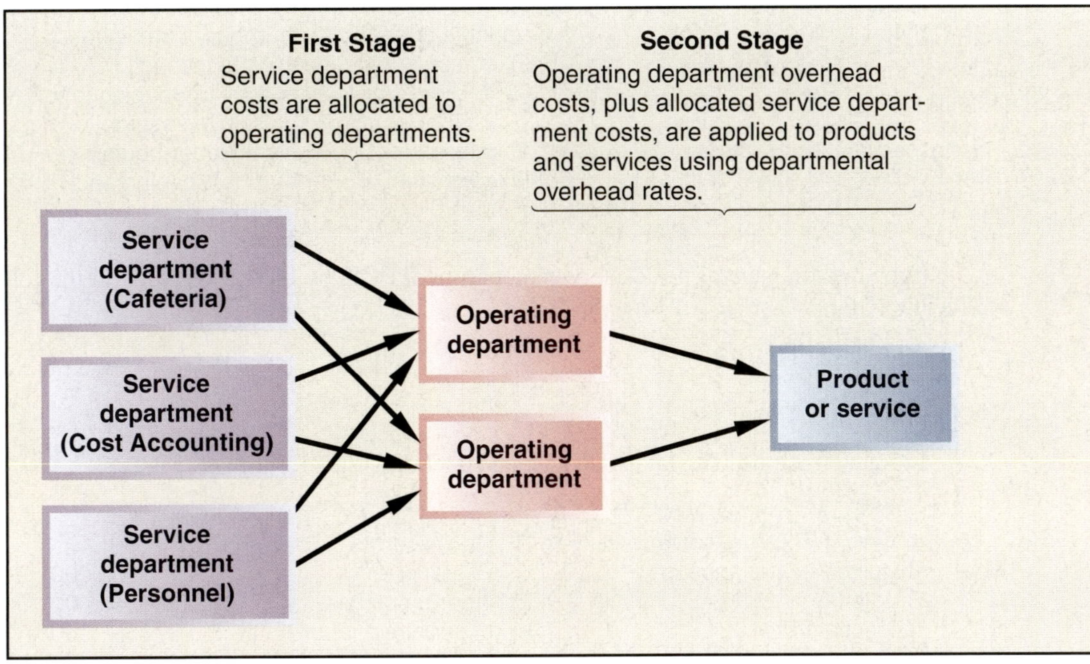

EXHIBIT 15–5
Effect of Allocations on Products and Services

EXHIBIT 15–6
Budget Containing Allocated Service Department Costs

SUPERIOR COMPANY
Budget—Milling Department

	Cost Formula (per direct labor-hour)	Overhead
Budgeted direct labor-hours	50,000	
Variable overhead costs:		
Indirect labor	$1.45	$ 72,500
Indirect material	0.90	45,000
Utilities	0.10	5,000
Allocation—Cafeteria	0.15	7,500
Total variable overhead cost	$2.60	130,000
Fixed overhead costs:		
Depreciation		85,000
Supervisory salaries		110,000
Property taxes		9,000
Allocation—Cafeteria		21,000
Allocation—Human Resources		45,000
Total fixed overhead cost		270,000
Total overhead cost		$400,000

$$\text{Predetermined overhead rate} = \frac{\$400,000}{50,000 \text{ DLHs}} = \$8 \text{ per direct labor-hour}$$

An Extended Example

Proctor Company has three service departments—Building Maintenance, Cafeteria, and Inspection. The company also has two operating departments—Shaping and Assembly. The service departments provide services to each other, as well as to the operating departments. Types of costs in the service departments and allocation bases are given below:

Department	Type of Cost	Allocation Bases
Building Maintenance	Fixed costs	Square feet occupied
Cafeteria	Variable costs	Number of employees
	Fixed costs	10% to Inspection, 40% to Shaping, and 50% to Assembly
Inspection	Variable costs	Direct labor-hours
	Fixed costs	70% to Shaping and 30% to Assembly

Proctor Company allocates service department costs by the step method in the following order:

1. Building Maintenance.
2. Cafeteria.
3. Inspection.

Assume the following budgeted cost and operating data for the year:

Department	Variable Cost	Fixed Cost
Building Maintenance	—	$130,000
Cafeteria	$200 per employee	$250,000
Inspection	$0.06 per direct labor-hour	$548,000

Department	Number of Employees	Direct Labor-Hours	Square Feet Occupied
Building Maintenance	6	—	3,000
Cafeteria	9	—	4,000
Inspection	30	—	1,000
Shaping	190	300,000	8,000
Assembly	250	500,000	13,000
Total	485	800,000	29,000

In addition to the service department costs listed above, the company's Shaping Department has budgeted $1,340,000 in overhead costs, and its Assembly Department has budgeted $1,846,000 in overhead costs.

Cost allocations from the service departments to the operating departments are shown in Exhibit 15–7. In the first panel of Exhibit 15–7 (page 730), the variable costs of the service departments are allocated using the step method and budgeted rates and budgeted activity. For example, the variable cost of the Cafeteria Department is $200 per employee, so the Inspection Department, with 30 employees, is allocated $6,000 of this variable cost. In the second panel of Exhibit 15–7, the fixed costs of the service departments are allocated. Building Maintenance is allocated first using the square feet occupied by each of the other departments as the allocation base. Then the fixed costs of the Cafeteria and Inspection departments are allocated based on the given percentages. After both the variable and fixed service department costs have been allocated, the predetermined overhead rates for the two operating departments are computed toward the bottom of the exhibit.

Some Cautions in Allocating Service Department Costs

Pitfalls in Allocating Fixed Costs

Rather than charge fixed costs to using departments in predetermined lump-sum amounts, some companies allocate them using a *variable* allocation base that fluctuates from period to period. This practice can distort decisions and create serious inequities between departments. The inequities will arise from the fact that the fixed costs allocated to one department will be heavily influenced by what happens in *other* departments.

To illustrate, assume that Kolby Products has an auto service center that provides maintenance work on the fleet of autos used in the company's two sales territories. The auto service center costs are all fixed. Contrary to good practice, the company allocates these fixed costs to the sales territories on the basis of actual miles driven (a variable allocation base). Selected cost data for the last two years follow:

	Year 1	Year 2
Auto service center costs (all fixed) (a)	$120,000	$120,000
Western sales territory—miles driven	1,500,000	1,500,000
Eastern sales territory—miles driven	1,500,000	900,000
Total miles driven (b)	3,000,000	2,400,000
Allocation rate per mile, (a) ÷ (b)	$0.04	$0.05

Notice that the Western sales territory maintained an activity level of 1,500,000 miles driven in both years. On the other hand, activity in the Eastern sales territory dropped from 1,500,000 miles in Year 1 to only 900,000 miles in Year 2. The auto service center

EXHIBIT 15–7

THE PROCTOR COMPANY
Beginning-of-Year Cost Allocations for Purposes of Preparing Predetermined Overhead Rates

	Building Maintenance	Cafeteria	Inspection	Shaping	Assembly
Variable costs to be allocated	$ 0	$ 94,000	$ 42,000		
Cafeteria allocation:					
$200 per employee × 30 employees		(6,000)	6,000		
$200 per employee × 190 employees		(38,000)		$ 38,000	
$200 per employee × 250 employees		(50,000)			$ 50,000
Inspection allocation:					
$0.06 per DLH × 300,000 DLH			(18,000)	18,000	
$0.06 per DLH × 500,000 DLH			(30,000)		30,000
Total	0	0	0	56,000	80,000
Fixed costs to be allocated	130,000	250,000	548,000		
Building Maintenance allocation:*					
$5 per square foot × 4,000 square feet	(20,000)	20,000			
$5 per square foot × 1,000 square feet	(5,000)		5,000		
$5 per square foot × 8,000 square feet	(40,000)			40,000	
$5 per square foot × 13,000 square feet	(65,000)				65,000
Cafeteria allocation:†					
10% × $270,000		(27,000)	27,000		
40% × $270,000		(108,000)		108,000	
50% × $270,000		(135,000)			135,000
Inspection allocation:‡					
70% × $580,000			(406,000)	406,000	
30% × $580,000			(174,000)		174,000
Total	0	0	0	554,000	374,000
Total allocated costs	$ 0	$ 0	$ 0	610,000	454,000
Other budgeted costs				1,340,000	1,846,000
Total budgeted overhead costs (a)				$1,950,000	$2,300,000
Budgeted direct labor-hours (b)				300,000	500,000
Predetermined overhead rate, (a) ÷ (b)				$6.50	$4.60

* Square footage of space	29,000 square feet
Less Building Maintenance space	3,000 square feet
Net space for allocation	26,000 square feet

$$\frac{\text{Building Maintenance fixed costs, \$130,000}}{\text{Net space for allocation, 26,000 square feet}} = \text{\$5 per square foot}$$

† Cafeteria fixed costs	$250,000
Allocated from Building Maintenance	20,000
Total cost to be allocated	$270,000

Allocation percentages are given.

‡ Inspection fixed costs	$548,000
Allocated from Building Maintenance	5,000
Allocated from Cafeteria	27,000
Total cost to be allocated	$580,000

Allocation percentages are given.

costs that would have been allocated to the two sales territories over the two-year span using actual miles driven as the allocation base are as follows:

Year 1:	
Western sales territory: 1,500,000 miles at $0.04 per mile	$ 60,000
Eastern sales territory: 1,500,000 miles at $0.04 per mile	60,000
Total cost allocated	$120,000

Year 2:	
Western sales territory: 1,500,000 miles at $0.05 per mile	$ 75,000
Eastern sales territory: 900,000 miles at $0.05 per mile	45,000
Total cost allocated	$120,000

In Year 1, the two sales territories share the service department costs equally. In Year 2, however, the bulk of the service department costs are allocated to the Western sales territory. This is not because of any increase in activity in the Western sales territory; rather, it is because of the *decrease* in activity in the Eastern sales territory. Even though the Western sales territory maintained the same level of activity in both years, it is penalized with a heavier cost allocation in Year 2 because of what has happened in *another* part of the company.

This kind of inequity is almost inevitable when a variable allocation base is used to allocate fixed costs. The manager of the Western sales territory undoubtedly will be upset about the inequity forced on his territory, but he will feel powerless to do anything about it. The result will be a loss of confidence in the system and considerable ill will.

IN BUSINESS

FRUSTRATION IN THE PATHOLOGY LAB

Hospitals in New Zealand, as elsewhere, are under considerable pressure to reduce costs. Consequently, managers are being held responsible for the costs of their departments and performance evaluations are often heavily influenced by cost control efforts. How these costs are computed can have a dramatic impact on evaluations. According to the accounting department of Waikato Hospital, the average cost per test in the hospital's pathology lab had increased from NZ$5.90 to NZ$7.29 over a three-year period. On the other hand, according to the management of the pathology lab, the cost per test had decreased from NZ$1.44 to NZ$1.42 over the same period. (NZ$ denotes a New Zealand dollar.) What accounts for this huge discrepancy in both the cost per test and the trend over time? The accounting department included allocations of the hospital's general overhead costs in the costs of the pathology lab; the managers of the pathology lab did not. The hospital's accounting staff conceded that the pathology laboratory was indeed more efficient in terms of its direct costs, but "Unfortunately, they're getting more indirect costs [allocated to them]." The manager of the pathology lab, who had taken aggressive steps to improve efficiency and control costs, was outraged.

Source: Necia France, Graham Francis, Stewart Lawrence, and Sydney Sacks, "Cost Counting and Comparability: Aspects of Performance Measurement in a Pathology Laboratory," *Pacific Accounting Review* 14, no. 2, December 2002, pp. 1–31.

Beware of Sales Dollars as an Allocation Base

Sales dollars is a popular allocation base for service department costs. One reason is that a sales dollars base is simple, straightforward, and easy to work with. Another reason is that people tend to view sales dollars as a measure of ability to pay, and, hence, as a measure of how readily costs can be absorbed from other parts of the organization.

Unfortunately, sales dollars are often a very poor allocation base, for the reason that sales dollars vary from period to period, whereas the costs being allocated are often largely *fixed.* As discussed earlier, if a variable allocation base is used to allocate fixed costs, the costs allocated to one department will depend in large part on what happens in *other* departments. A letup in sales effort in one department will shift allocated costs from that department to other, more successful departments. In effect, the departments putting forth the best sales efforts are penalized in the form of higher allocations. The result is often bitterness and resentment on the part of the managers of the better departments.

Consider the following situation encountered by one of the authors:

A large men's clothing store has one service department and three sales departments—Suits, Shoes, and Accessories. The service department's costs total $60,000 per

period and are allocated to the three sales departments according to sales dollars. A recent period showed the following allocation:

	Departments			
	Suits	Shoes	Accessories	Total
Sales by department	$260,000	$40,000	$100,000	$400,000
Percentage of total sales	65%	10%	25%	100%
Allocation of service department costs, based on percentage of total sales	$39,000	$6,000	$15,000	$60,000

In the following period, the manager of the Suits Department launched a very successful program to expand sales by $100,000 in his department. Sales in the other two departments remained unchanged. Total service department costs also remained unchanged, but the allocation of these costs changed substantially, as shown below:

	Departments			
	Suits	Shoes	Accessories	Total
Sales by department	$360,000	$40,000	$100,000	$500,000
Percentage of total sales	72%	8%	20%	100%
Allocation of service department costs, based on percentage of total sales	$43,200	$4,800	$12,000	$60,000
Increase (or decrease) from prior allocation	$4,200	$(1,200)	$(3,000)	$0

The manager of the Suits Department complained that as a result of his successful effort to expand sales in his department, he was being forced to carry a larger share of the service department costs. On the other hand, the managers of the departments that showed no improvement in sales were relieved of a portion of the costs that they had been carrying. Yet there had been no change in the amount of services provided for any department.

The manager of the Suits Department viewed the increased service department cost allocation to his department as a penalty for his outstanding performance, and he wondered whether his efforts had really been worthwhile in the eyes of top management.

Sales dollars should be used as an allocation base only in those cases where service department costs are driven by sales. In those situations where service department costs are fixed, they should be allocated according to the three guidelines discussed earlier in the chapter.

Summary

Service departments are organized to provide some needed service in a single, centralized place, rather than having all units within the organization provide the service for themselves. Service department costs are charged to operating departments by an allocation process. In turn, the operating departments include the allocated costs in their budgets, from which overhead rates are computed for purposes of costing products or services.

Variable and fixed service department costs should be allocated separately. The variable costs should be allocated according to whatever activity causes their incurrence. The fixed costs should be allocated in predetermined lump-sum amounts according to either the peak-period or the long-run average servicing needs of the consuming departments. Budgeted costs, rather than actual costs, should always be allocated. If actual costs were allocated, the operating departments would be implicitly held responsible for any inefficiency in the service departments. Any variances between budgeted and actual service department costs should be kept within the service departments and should be the responsibility of the service department managers.

Review Problem: Direct and Step Methods

Kovac Printing Company has three service departments and two operating departments. Selected data for the five departments relating to the most recent period follow:

	Service Departments			Operating Departments		
	Training	Janitorial	Maintenance	Offset Printing	Lithography	Total
Overhead costs	$360,000	$210,000	$96,000	$400,000	$534,000	$1,600,000
Number of employees	120	70	280	630	420	1,520
Square feet of space occupied	10,000	20,000	40,000	80,000	200,000	350,000
Hours of press time	—	—	—	30,000	60,000	90,000

The company allocates service department costs in the following order and using the bases indicated: Training (number of employees), Janitorial (space occupied), and Maintenance (hours of press time). Contrary to best practice, the company makes no distinction between variable and fixed service department costs in its allocations.

Required:

1. Use the direct method to allocate service department costs to the operating departments.
2. Use the step method to allocate service department costs to the operating departments.

Solution to Review Problem

1. Under the direct method, service department costs are allocated directly to the operating departments. Supporting computations for these allocations follow:

	Allocation Bases					
	Training		Janitorial		Maintenance	
Offset Printing data	630 employees	3/5	80,000 square feet	2/7	30,000 hours	1/3
Lithography data	420 employees	2/5	200,000 square feet	5/7	60,000 hours	2/3
Total	1,050 employees	5/5	280,000 square feet	7/7	90,000 hours	3/3

Given these allocation rates, the allocations to the operating departments would be as follows:

	Service Departments			Operating Departments		
	Training	Janitorial	Maintenance	Offset Printing	Lithography	Total
Overhead costs	$360,000	$210,000	$ 96,000	$400,000	$534,000	$1,600,000
Allocation:						
Training (3/5; 2/5)	(360,000)			216,000	144,000	
Janitorial (2/7; 5/7)		(210,000)		60,000	150,000	
Maintenance (1/3; 2/3)			(96,000)	32,000	64,000	
Total overhead cost after allocations	$ 0	$ 0	$ 0	$708,000	$892,000	$1,600,000

2. Under the step method, services rendered between service departments are recognized when costs are allocated to other departments. Starting with the Training service department, supporting computations for these allocations follow:

	Allocation Bases					
	Training		Janitorial		Maintenance	
Janitorial data	70 employees	5%	—		—	
Maintenance data ..	280 employees	20%	40,000 square feet	1/8	—	
Offset Printing data .	630 employees	45%	80,000 square feet	2/8	30,000 hours	1/3
Lithography data ...	420 employees	30%	200,000 square feet	5/8	60,000 hours	2/3
Total	1,400 employees	100%	320,000 square feet	8/8	90,000 hours	3/3

Given these ratios, the allocations to the various departments would be as follows:

	Service Departments			Operating Departments		
	Training	Janitorial	Maintenance	Offset Printing	Lithography	Total
Overhead costs	$360,000	$210,000	$ 96,000	$400,000	$534,000	$1,600,000
Allocation:						
Training (5%; 20%; 45%; 30%)* ..	(360,000)	18,000	72,000	162,000	108,000	
Janitorial (1/8; 2/8; 5/8)		(228,000)	28,500	57,000	142,500	
Maintenance (1/3; 2/3)			(196,500)	65,500	131,000	
Total overhead cost after allocations .	$ 0	$ 0	$ 0	$684,500	$915,500	$1,600,000

*Allocation rates can be shown either in percentages, in fractions, or as a dollar rate per unit of activity. Both percentages and fractions are shown in this problem for sake of illustration. *It is better to use fractions if the use of percentages would result in rounding errors.*

Glossary

Direct method The allocation of a service department's costs directly to operating departments without recognizing services provided to other service departments. (p. 720)

Interdepartmental services Services provided between service departments. Also see *Reciprocal services.* (p. 719)

Operating department A department or similar unit in an organization within which the central purposes of the organization are carried out. (p. 718)

Reciprocal method A method of allocating service department costs that gives full recognition to interdepartmental services. (p. 722)

Reciprocal services Services provided between service departments. Also see *Interdepartmental services.* (p. 719)

Service department A department that provides support or assistance to operating departments and that does not engage directly in production or in other operating activities of an organization. (p. 718)

Step method The allocation of service department costs to other service departments, as well as to operating departments, in a sequential manner. (p. 721)

Questions

15–1 What is the difference between a service department and an operating department? Give several examples of service departments.

15–2 How are service department costs assigned to products and services?

15–3 What are interdepartmental service costs? How are such costs allocated to other departments under the step method?

15–4 How are service department costs allocated to other departments under the direct method?

15–5 If a service department generates revenues, how do these revenues enter into the allocation of the department's costs to other departments?

15–6 What guidelines should govern the allocation of fixed service department costs to other departments? The allocation of variable service department costs?

15–7 "A variable allocation base should never be used in allocating fixed service department costs to operating departments." Explain.

Exercises

EXERCISE 15–1 Direct Method [LO1]

Seattle Western University has provided the following data to be used in its service department cost allocations:

	Service Departments		Operating Departments	
	Administration	Facility Services	Undergraduate Programs	Graduate Programs
Departmental costs before allocations	$2,400,000	$1,600,000	$26,800,000	$5,700,000
Student credit-hours			20,000	5,000
Space occupied—square feet .	25,000	10,000	70,000	30,000

Required:

Using the direct method, allocate the costs of the service departments to the two operating departments. Allocate administrative costs on the basis of student credit-hours and facility services costs on the basis of space occupied.

EXERCISE 15–2 Step Method [LO2]

Madison Park Co-op, a whole foods grocery and gift shop, has provided the following data to be used in its service department cost allocations:

	Service Departments		Operating Departments	
	Administration	Janitorial	Groceries	Gifts
Departmental costs before allocations . . .	$150,000	$40,000	$2,320,000	$950,000
Employee-hours	320	160	3,100	740
Space occupied—square feet	250	100	4,000	1,000

Required:

Using the step method, allocate the costs of the service departments to the two operating departments. Allocate administrative costs first on the basis of employee-hours and then janitorial costs on the basis of space occupied.

EXERCISE 15–3 Allocations by Cost Behavior at the Beginning of the Period [LO3]

Hannibal Steel Company has a Transport Services Department that provides trucks to haul ore from the company's mine to its two steel mills—the Northern Plant and the Southern Plant. Budgeted costs for the Transport Services Department total $350,000 per year, consisting of $0.25 per ton variable cost and $300,000 fixed cost. The level of fixed cost is determined by peak-period requirements. During the peak period, the Northern Plant requires 70% of the Transport Services Department's capacity and the Southern Plant requires 30%.

During the coming year, 120,000 tons of ore are budgeted to be hauled for the Northern Plant and 60,000 tons of ore for the Southern Plant.

Required:

Compute the amount of Transport Services Department cost that should be allocated to each plant at the beginning of the year for purposes of computing predetermined overhead rates. (The company allocates variable and fixed costs separately.)

EXERCISE 15–4 Allocations by Cost Behavior at the End of the Period [LO3]

Refer to the data in Exercise 15-3. Assume that it is now the end of the year. During the year, the Transport Services Department actually hauled the following amounts of ore for the two plants: Northern Plant, 130,000 tons; Southern Plant, 50,000 tons. The Transport Services Department

incurred $364,000 in cost during the year, of which $54,000 was variable cost and $310,000 was fixed cost.

Management wants end-of-year service department cost allocations in order to compare actual performance to planned performance.

Required:

1. Determine how much of the $54,000 in variable cost should be allocated to each plant.
2. Determine how much of the $310,000 in fixed cost should be allocated to each plant.
3. Should any of the $364,000 in the Transport Services Department cost not be allocated to the plants? Explain.

EXERCISE 15–5 Step Method [LO2]

The Ferre Publishing Company has three service departments and two operating departments. Selected data from a recent period on the five departments follow:

	Service Departments			Operating Departments		
	Administration	Janitorial	Maintenance	Binding	Printing	Total
Overhead costs	$140,000	$105,000	$48,000	$275,000	$430,000	$998,000
Number of employees	60	35	140	315	210	760
Square feet of space occupied	15,000	10,000	20,000	40,000	100,000	185,000
Hours of press time				30,000	60,000	90,000

The company allocates service department costs by the step method in the following order: Administration (number of employees), Janitorial (space occupied), and Maintenance (hours of press time). The company makes no distinction between variable and fixed service department costs.

Required:

Using the step method, allocate the service department costs to the operating departments.

EXERCISE 15–6 Direct Method [LO1]

Refer to the data for the Ferre Publishing Company in Exercise 15–5.

Required:

Assuming that the company uses the direct method rather than the step method to allocate service department costs, how much overhead cost would be assigned to each operating department?

EXERCISE 15–7 Sales Dollars as an Allocation Base for Fixed Costs [LO3]

Konig Enterprises, Ltd., owns and operates three restaurants in Vancouver, B.C. The company allocates its fixed administrative expenses to the three restaurants on the basis of sales dollars. During 2004, the fixed administrative expenses totaled $2,000,000. These expenses were allocated as follows:

	Restaurants			
	Rick's Harborside	Imperial Garden	Ginger Wok	Total
Total sales—2004	$16,000,000	$15,000,000	$9,000,000	$40,000,000
Percentage of total sales .	40%	37.5%	22.5%	100%
Allocation (based on the above percentages) ...	$800,000	$750,000	$450,000	$2,000,000

During 2005, the following year, the Imperial Garden restaurant increased its sales by $10 million. The sales levels in the other two restaurants remained unchanged. The company's 2005 sales data were as follows:

	Restaurants			
	Rick's Harborside	Imperial Garden	Ginger Wok	Total
Total sales—2005	$16,000,000	$25,000,000	$9,000,000	$50,000,000
Percentage of total sales .	32%	50%	18%	100%

Fixed administrative expenses remained unchanged at $2,000,000 during 2005.

Required:
1. Using sales dollars as an allocation base, show the allocation of the fixed administrative expenses among the three restaurants for 2005.
2. Compare your allocation from (1) above to the allocation for 2004. As the manager of the Imperial Garden, how would you feel about the allocation that has been charged to you for 2005?
3. Comment on the usefulness of sales dollars as an allocation base.

EXERCISE 15–8 Allocating Variable Costs at the End of the Year [LO3]

Westlake Hospital has a Radiology Department that provides X-ray services to the hospital's three operating departments. The variable costs of the Radiology Department are allocated to the operating departments on the basis of the number of X-rays provided for each department. Budgeted and actual data relating to the cost of X-rays taken last year are given below:

	Variable Costs	
	Budgeted	Actual
Radiology Department	$18 per X-ray	$20 per X-ray

The budgeted and actual number of X-rays provided for each operating department last year follow:

	Pediatrics	OB Care	General Hospital
Budgeted number of X-rays	7,000	4,500	12,000
Actual number of X-rays taken . .	6,000	3,000	15,000

Required:

Determine the amount of Radiology Department variable cost that should have been allocated to each of the three operating departments at the end of last year for purposes of comparing actual performance to planned performance.

EXERCISE 15–9 Allocations of Fixed Costs [LO3]

Refer to Westlake Hospital in Exercise 15–8. In addition to the Radiology Department, the hospital also has a Janitorial Services Department that provides services to all other departments in the hospital. The fixed costs of the two service departments are allocated using the following bases:

Department	Basis for Allocation	
Janitorial Services	Square feet of space occupied:	
	Radiology Department	6,000 square feet
	Pediatrics	30,000 square feet
	OB Care	24,000 square feet
	General Hospital	90,000 square feet
Radiology	Long-run average X-ray needs per year:	
	Pediatrics	9,000 X-rays
	OB Care	6,000 X-rays
	General Hospital	15,000 X-rays

Budgeted and actual fixed costs in the two service departments for the year follow:

	Janitorial Services	Radiology
Budgeted fixed costs	$375,000	$590,000
Actual fixed costs	$381,000	$600,000

Required:
1. Show the allocation of the fixed costs of the two service departments at the beginning of the year. The hospital uses the step method of allocation.
2. Show the allocation of the fixed costs of the two service departments at the end of the year for purposes of comparing actual performance to planned performance.

Problems

PROBLEM 15–10 Step Method versus Direct Method; Predetermined Overhead Rates [LO1, LO2]
The Sendai Co., Ltd., of Japan has budgeted costs in its various departments as follows for the coming year:

Factory Administration	¥270,000,000
Custodial Services	68,760,000
Personnel	28,840,000
Maintenance	45,200,000
Machining—overhead	376,300,000
Assembly—overhead	175,900,000
Total cost	¥965,000,000

The Japanese currency is the yen, denoted by ¥. The company allocates service department costs to other departments in the order listed below.

Department	Number of Employees	Total Labor-Hours	Square Feet of Space Occupied	Direct Labor-Hours	Machine-hours
Factory Administration	12	—	5,000	—	—
Custodial Services	4	3,000	2,000	—	—
Personnel	5	5,000	3,000	—	—
Maintenance	25	22,000	10,000	—	—
Machining	40	30,000	70,000	20,000	70,000
Assembly	60	90,000	20,000	80,000	10,000
	146	150,000	110,000	100,000	80,000

Machining and Assembly are operating departments; the other departments are service departments. The company does not make a distinction between fixed and variable service department costs. Factory Administration is allocated on the basis of labor-hours; Custodial Services on the basis of square feet occupied; Personnel on the basis of number of employees; and Maintenance on the basis of machine-hours.

Required:

1. Allocate service department costs to consuming departments by the step method. Then compute predetermined overhead rates in the operating departments using a machine-hours basis in Machining and a direct labor-hours basis in Assembly.
2. Repeat (1) above, this time using the direct method. Again compute predetermined overhead rates in Machining and Assembly.
3. Assume that the company doesn't bother with allocating service department costs but simply computes a single plantwide overhead rate based on total overhead costs (both service department and operating department costs) divided by total direct labor-hours. Compute the plantwide overhead rate.
4. Suppose a job requires machine and labor time as follows:

	Machine-hours	Direct Labor-Hours
Machining Department	190	25
Assembly Department	10	75
Total hours	200	100

Using the overhead rates computed in (1), (2), and (3) above, compute the amount of overhead cost that would be assigned to the job if the overhead rates were developed using the step method, the direct method, and the plantwide method.

PROBLEM 15–11 Allocating by Cost Behavior [LO3]

Sharp Motor Company has two operating divisions—an Auto Division and a Truck Division. The company has a cafeteria that serves the employees of both divisions. The costs of operating the cafeteria are budgeted at $40,000 per month plus $3 per meal served. The company pays all the cost of the meals.

The fixed costs of the cafeteria are determined by peak-period requirements. The Auto Division is responsible for 65% of the peak-period requirements, and the Truck Division is responsible for the other 35%.

For June, the Auto Division has estimated that it will need 35,000 meals served, and the Truck Division has estimated that it will need 20,000 meals served.

Required:

1. At the beginning of June, how much cafeteria cost should be allocated to each division for planning purposes?
2. Assume that it is now the end of June. Cost records in the cafeteria show that actual fixed costs for the month totaled $42,000 and that actual meal costs totaled $128,000. Due to unexpected layoffs of employees during the month, only 20,000 meals were served to the Auto Division. Another 20,000 meals were served to the Truck Division, as planned. How much of the actual cafeteria costs for the month should be allocated to each division? (Management uses these end-of-month allocations to compare actual performance with planned performance.)
3. Refer to the data in (2) above. Assume that the company follows the practice of allocating *all* cafeteria costs to the divisions in proportion to the number of meals served to each division during the month. On this basis, how much cost would be allocated to each division for June?
4. What criticisms can you make of the allocation method used in (3) above?
5. If managers of operating departments know that fixed service costs are going to be allocated on the basis of peak-period requirements, what will be their probable strategy as they report their estimate of peak-period requirements to the company's budget committee? As a member of top management, what would you do to neutralize such strategies?

PROBLEM 15–12 Allocating Costs Equitably Among Divisions [LO3]

"These allocations don't make any sense at all," said Bob Cosic, manager of National Airlines' Freight Division. "We used the maintenance hangar less during the second quarter than we did during the first quarter, yet we were allocated more cost. Is that fair? In fact, we picked up the lion's share of the hangar's cost during the second quarter, even though we're a lot smaller than the Domestic Passenger Division."

National Airlines established the maintenance hangar to service its three operating divisions. The company allocates the cost of the hangar to the divisions on the basis of the number of hours of use each quarter. Allocations for the first two quarters to which Mr. Cosic was referring are given below:

Microsoft Excel - Problem 15-12 screen capture.xls

	A	B	C	D	E
1		*Freight*	*Domestic Passenger*	*Overseas Passenger*	*Total*
2	First quarter actual results:				
3	Hours of hangar use	900	1,800	300	3,000
4	Percent of total	30%	60%	10%	100%
5	Hangar cost allocated	$51,600	$103,200	$17,200	$172,000
6					
7	Second quarter actual results:				
8	Hours of hangar use	800	700	500	2,000
9	Percent of total	40%	35%	25%	100%
10	Hangar cost allocated	$67,200	$58,800	$42,000	$168,000
11					

National Airlines

"Now don't get upset, Bob," replied Colleen Rogers, the controller. "Those allocations are fair. As you can see, your division used the hangar more than any other division during the second quarter and therefore it has been allocated the largest share of cost. Although use of the hangar was off somewhat during the second quarter, keep in mind that most of the hangar's costs are fixed and therefore continue regardless of how much the hangar is used. Also, remember that we built enough capacity into the hangar to handle the divisions' peak-period needs, and that cost has to be absorbed by someone. The fairest way to handle it is to charge according to usage from quarter to quarter. When you use the hangar more, you get charged more; it's as simple as that."

"That's just the point," replied Cosic. "I didn't use the hangar more, I used it less. So why am I charged more?"

The Freight Division requires 30% of the hangar's capacity during peak periods; the Domestic Passenger Division, 50%; and the Overseas Passenger Division, 20%. The peak period occurs in the fourth quarter of the year.

Required:

1. Is there any merit to Mr. Cosic's complaint? Explain.
2. Using the high-low method, determine the cost formula for the hangar in terms of a variable rate per hour and total fixed cost each quarter.
3. Reallocate the hangar costs for the first and second quarters in accordance with the cost allocation principles discussed in the chapter. Allocate the variable and fixed costs separately.

eXcel

PROBLEM 15–13 Step Method [LO2, LO3]
Woodbury Hospital has three service departments and three operating departments. Estimated cost and operating data for all departments in the hospital for the forthcoming quarter are presented in the table below:

	Service Departments			Operating Departments			
	Housekeeping Services	Food Services	Admin. Services	Laboratory	Radiology	General Hospital	Total
Variable costs	$ 0	$193,860	$158,840	$243,600	$304,800	$ 74,500	$ 975,600
Fixed costs	87,000	107,200	90,180	162,300	215,700	401,300	1,063,680
Total cost	$87,000	$301,060	$249,020	$405,900	$520,500	$475,800	$2,039,280
Meals served			800	2,000	1,000	68,000	71,800
Percentage of peak-period needs—Food Services			0.8%	2.4%	1.6%	95.2%	100%
Square feet of space	5,000	13,000	6,500	10,000	7,500	108,000	150,000
Files processed				14,000	7,000	25,000	46,000
Percentage of peak-period needs—Admin. Services				30%	20%	50%	100%

The costs of the service departments are allocated by the step method using the allocation bases and in the order shown in the following table:

Service Department	Costs Incurred	Allocation Bases
Housekeeping Services	Fixed	Square feet of space
Food Services	Variable	Meals served
	Fixed	Peak-period needs—Food Services
Administrative Services	Variable	Files processed
	Fixed	Peak-period needs—Admin. Services

All billing in the hospital is done through Laboratory, Radiology, or General Hospital. The hospital's administrator wants the costs of the three service departments allocated to these three billing centers.

Required:

Prepare the cost allocation desired by the hospital administrator. (Use the step method.) Include under each billing center the direct costs of the center, as well as the costs allocated from the service departments.

PROBLEM 15–14 Beginning- and End-of-Year Allocations [LO3]
Tasman Products, Ltd., of Australia has a Maintenance Department that services the equipment in the company's Forming Department and Assembly Department. The cost of this servicing is allocated to the operating departments on the basis of machine-hours. Cost and other data relating to

the Maintenance Department and to the other two departments for the most recent year are presented below. (The currency in Australia is the Australian dollar.)

Data for the Maintenance Department follow:

	Budget	Actual
Variable costs for lubricants	$96,000*	$110,000
Fixed costs for salaries and other	$150,000	$153,000

*Budgeted at $0.40 per machine-hour.

Data for the Forming and Assembly departments follow:

	Percentage of Peak-Period Capacity Required	Machine-Hours	
		Budget	Actual
Forming Department	70%	160,000	190,000
Assembly Department	30%	80,000	70,000
Total	100%	240,000	260,000

The company allocates variable and fixed costs separately. The level of fixed costs in the Maintenance Department is determined by peak-period requirements.

Required:

1. Assume that it is the beginning of the year. How much of the budgeted Maintenance Department cost would be allocated to each department?
2. Assume that it is now the end of the year. Management would like data to assist in comparing actual performance to planned performance in the Maintenance Department and in the other departments.
   a. How much of the actual Maintenance Department costs should be allocated to the Forming Department and to the Assembly Department? Show all computations.
   b. Should any portion of the actual Maintenance Department costs not be allocated to the other departments? If all costs should be allocated, explain why; if a portion should not be allocated, compute the amount and explain why it should not be allocated.

PROBLEM 15–15 Step Method; Predetermined Overhead Rates [LO2, LO3]

Bombay Castings, Ltd., has two operating departments, Fabrication and Finishing, and three service departments. The service departments and the bases on which their costs are allocated to consuming departments are listed below:

Department	Cost	Allocation Bases
Building and Grounds	Fixed	Square feet occupied
Administration	Variable	Number of employees
	Fixed	Employees at full capacity
Equipment Maintenance	Variable	Machine-hours
	Fixed	40% to Fabrication 60% to Finishing

Indian currency is denominated in rupees, denoted here by R.

Service department costs are allocated to consuming departments by the step method in the order shown. The company has developed the cost and operating data given in the following table for purposes of preparing overhead rates in the two operating departments:

	Building and Grounds	Adminis-tration	Equipment Maintenance	Fabrication	Finishing	Total
Variable costs	R 0	R22,200	R16,900	R146,000	R320,000	R 505,100
Fixed costs	88,200	60,000	24,000	420,000	490,000	1,082,200
Total cost	R88,200	R82,200	R40,900	R566,000	R810,000	R1,587,300
Budgeted employees	6	4	30	450	630	1,120
Employees at full capacity	8	4	45	570	885	1,512
Square feet occupied	600	500	1,400	12,000	15,500	30,000
Budgeted machine-hours				70,000	105,000	175,000

Required:

1. Show the allocation of service department costs to operating departments for purposes of preparing overhead rates in Fabrication and Finishing.
2. Assuming that overhead rates are calculated using machine-hours as the allocation base, compute the overhead rate for each operating department.
3. Assume the following *actual* data for the year for the Administration Department:

Actual variable costs	R23,800
Actual employees for the year:	
Building and Grounds	6
Administration	4
Equipment Maintenance	32
Fabrication	460
Finishing	625
	1,127

Compute the amount of end-of-year Administration Department variable cost that should be allocated to each department. (Management uses these end-of-year allocations to compare actual performance to planned performance.)

PROBLEM 15–16 Step Method [LO2, LO3]
The Bayview Resort has three operating units—the Convention Center, Food Services, and Guest Lodging. These three operating units are supported by three service units—General Administration, Cost Accounting, and Laundry. The costs of the service units are allocated by the step method using the allocation bases and in the order shown below:

General Administration:
- Fixed costs—allocated 10% to Cost Accounting, 4% to the Laundry, 30% to the Convention Center, 16% to Food Services, and 40% to Guest Lodging.

Cost Accounting:
- Variable costs—allocated on the basis of the number of items processed each period.
- Fixed costs—allocated on the basis of peak-period requirements.

Laundry:
- Variable costs—allocated on the basis of the number of pounds of laundry processed each period.
- Fixed costs—allocated on the basis of peak-period requirements.

Cost and operating data for all units in the resort for a recent quarter are given in the following table:

	Service Units			Operating Units			
	General Administration	Cost Accounting	Laundry	Convention Center	Food Services	Guest Lodging	Total
Variable costs	$ 0	$ 70,000	$143,000	$ 0	$ 52,000	$ 24,000	$ 289,000
Fixed costs	200,000	110,000	65,900	95,000	375,000	486,000	1,331,900
Total overhead cost	$200,000	$180,000	$208,900	$95,000	$427,000	$510,000	$1,620,900
Pounds of laundry processed				20,000	15,000	210,000	245,000
Percentage of peak-period requirements—Laundry				10%	6%	84%	100%
Number of items processed	1,000		800	1,200	3,000	9,000	15,000
Percentage of peak-period requirements—Cost Accounting	*		7%	13%	20%	60%	100%

*General administration is excluded from the computation of peak-period requirements due to the order in which the service unit costs are allocated.

Since all billing is done through the Convention Center, Food Services, and Guest Lodging, the resort's general manager wants the costs of the three service units allocated to these three billing centers.

Required:

Prepare the cost allocation desired by the resort's general manager. Include under each billing center the direct costs of the center, as well as the costs allocated from the service units.

Cases

CASE 15–17 Direct Method; Plantwide versus Departmental Overhead Rates [LO1, LO3]

Hobart Products manufactures a complete line of fiberglass attaché cases and suitcases. Hobart has three manufacturing (or operating) departments—Molding, Component, and Assembly—and two service departments—Power and Maintenance.

The sides of the cases are manufactured in the Molding Department. The frames, hinges, locks, and so forth, are manufactured in the Component Department. The cases are completed in the Assembly Department. Varying amounts of materials, time, and effort are required for each of the various cases. The Power Department and Maintenance Department provide services to the manufacturing departments.

Hobart has always used a plantwide overhead rate. Direct labor-hours are used to assign the overhead to products. The overhead rate is computed by dividing the company's total estimated overhead cost by the total estimated direct labor-hours to be worked in the three manufacturing departments.

Whit Portlock, manager of Cost Accounting, has recommended that the company use departmental overhead rates rather than a single, plantwide rate. Planned operating costs and expected levels of activity for the coming year have been developed by Mr. Portlock and are presented below:

	Service Departments	
	Power	Maintenance
Departmental activity measures:		
Estimated usage in the coming year	80,000 KWh	12,500 hours*
Departmental costs:		
Materials and supplies	$ 500,000	$ 25,000
Variable labor	140,000	0
Fixed overhead	1,200,000	375,000
Total service department cost	$1,840,000	$400,000

*Hours of maintenance time.

	Manufacturing Departments		
	Molding	Component	Assembly
Departmental activity measures:			
Direct labor-hours	50,000	200,000	150,000
Machine-hours	87,500	12,500	0
Departmental costs:			
Raw materials	$1,630,000	$3,000,000	$ 25,000
Direct labor	350,000	2,000,000	1,300,000
Variable overhead	210,500	1,000,000	1,650,000
Fixed overhead	1,750,000	620,000	749,500
Total departmental cost	$3,940,500	$6,620,000	$3,724,500

	Manufacturing Departments		
	Molding	Component	Assembly
Use of service departments:			
Maintenance:			
Estimated usage in hours of maintenance time for the coming year	9,000	2,500	1,000
Percentage of peak-period Maintenance Department capacity required	70%	20%	10%
Power:			
Estimated usage in kilowatt-hours for the coming year	36,000	32,000	12,000
Percentage of peak-period Power Department capacity required	50%	35%	15%

Required:

1. If the company uses a single, plantwide overhead rate for the coming year, what plantwide overhead rate would be used?
2. Assume that Whit Portlock has been asked to develop departmental overhead rates for the three manufacturing departments for comparison with the plantwide rate. In order to develop these rates, do the following:
   a. Using the direct method, allocate the service department costs to the manufacturing departments. In each case, allocate the variable and fixed costs separately.
   b. Compute overhead rates for the three manufacturing departments for the coming year. In computing the rates, use machine-hours as the allocation base in the Molding Department and direct labor-hours as the allocation base in the other two departments.
3. Assume that Hobart Products has one small attaché case that has the following annual requirements for machine time and direct labor time in the various departments:

	Machine-hours	Direct Labor-Hours
Molding Department	3,000	1,000
Component Department	800	2,500
Assembly Department	0	4,000
Total hours	3,800	7,500

   a. Compute the amount of overhead cost that would be allocated to this attaché case if a plantwide overhead rate is used. Repeat the computation, assuming that departmental overhead rates are used.

b. Hobart Products bases its selling prices on its computed costs—adding a percentage markup. Management is concerned because this attaché case is priced well below competing products of competitors. On the other hand, Hobart has other products that are priced well above its competitors, resulting in lost sales and declining profits. Looking at the computations in (a), what effect is a plantwide rate having on the costing of products and therefore on selling prices?

4. What additional steps could Hobart Products take to improve its overhead costing?

(CMA, adapted)

CASE 15–18 Step Method versus Direct Method [LO1, LO2]

eXcel

"This is really an odd situation," said Jim Carter, general manager of Highland Publishing Company. "We get most of the jobs we bid on that require a lot of press time in the Printing Department, yet profits on those jobs are never as high as they ought to be. On the other hand, we lose most of the jobs we bid on that require a lot of time in the Binding Department. I would be inclined to think that the problem is with our overhead rates, but we're already computing separate overhead rates for each department. So what else could be wrong?"

Highland Publishing Company is a large organization that offers a variety of printing and binding work. The Printing and Binding departments are supported by three service departments. The costs of these service departments are allocated to other departments in the order listed below. (For each service department, use the allocation base that provides the best measure of service provided, as discussed in the chapter.)

Department	Total Labor-Hours	Square Feet of Space Occupied	Number of Employees	Machine-Hours	Direct Labor-Hours
Personnel	20,000	4,000	10		
Custodial Services	30,000	6,000	15		
Maintenance	50,000	20,000	25		
Printing	90,000	80,000	40	150,000	60,000
Binding	260,000	40,000	120	30,000	175,000
	450,000	150,000	210	180,000	235,000

Budgeted overhead costs in each department for the current year are shown below (no distinction is made between variable and fixed costs):

Personnel	$ 360,000
Custodial Services	141,000
Maintenance	201,000
Printing	525,000
Binding	373,500
Total budgeted cost	$1,600,500

Because of its simplicity, the company has always used the direct method to allocate service department costs to the two operating departments.

Required:

1. Using the step method, allocate the service department costs to the consuming departments. Then compute predetermined overhead rates for the current year using machine-hours as the allocation base in the Printing Department and direct labor-hours as the allocation base in the Binding Department.
2. Repeat (1) above, this time using the direct method. Again compute predetermined overhead rates in the Printing and Binding departments.
3. Assume that during the current year the company bids on a job that requires machine and labor time as follows:

	Machine-hours	Direct Labor-Hours
Printing Department	15,400	900
Binding Department	800	2,000
Total hours	16,200	2,900

a. Determine the amount of overhead cost that would be assigned to the job if the company used the overhead rates developed in (1) above. Then determine the amount of overhead cost that would be assigned to the job if the company used the overhead rates developed in (2) above.

b. Explain to Mr. Carter, the general manager, why the step method provides a better basis for computing predetermined overhead rates than the direct method.

Group and Internet Exercises

GROUP EXERCISE 15–19 Understanding the Cost of Complexity

Service departments (or production support departments in the case of a manufacturer) make up a large and growing part of the cost structure of most businesses. This is as true in hospitals, financial institutions, universities, and other service industries as it is in manufacturing where production support department costs can average 40% or more of total manufacturing costs.

In an effort to reduce costs, many companies seek to reduce head count, which is a demoralizing experience not only for those who lose their jobs, but also for those who remain employed. One sure sign of problems with this head-count-reduction approach is that more than half of companies refill these positions within a year after eliminating them.

Required:

1. Choose an industry with which you are somewhat familiar (or with which someone you know is familiar) and list seven or eight major production support or service departments in the factory or other facility in this industry. What is the output of each of these support or service departments?
2. Assume a relatively uncomplicated factory (facility) where just a single, standard product (or service) is mass produced. Describe the activity or work being done in each of the service areas of this focused company.
3. Now assume a more complicated operation for another factory located close by where a wide range of products are made or services are offered—some are standard products/services while others are made to order, some are high-volume products/services while others are low volume, and some are fairly complex products/services while others are relatively simple. Describe the activity or work being done in the various service functions for this full-service company.
4. Which factory or facility has higher production support costs? Why?
5. Explain the relationship between the range of products produced and the size of the support departments. When does the output of each of these support departments increase? When does the cost of each of these support departments increase?
6. Most companies are under increasing pressure to reduce costs. How would you go about bringing the overall level of service department costs down?

INTERNET EXERCISE 15–20

As you know, the World Wide Web is a medium that is constantly evolving. Sites come and go, and change without notice. To enable periodic updating of site addresses, this problem has been posted to the textbook website (www.mhhe.com/garrison11e). After accessing the site, enter the Student Center and select this chapter. Select and complete the Internet Exercise.

Chapter

16

"How Well Am I Doing?" Statement of Cash Flows

LEARNING OBJECTIVES

After studying Chapter 16, you should be able to:

LO1 Classify changes in noncash balance sheet accounts as sources or uses of cash.

LO2 Classify transactions as operating, investing, or financing activities.

LO3 Prepare a statement of cash flows using the indirect method to determine the net cash provided by operating activities.

LO4 (Appendix 16A) Use the direct method to determine the net cash provided by operating activities.

Focus on Cash

BUSINESS FOCUS

George Pilla is a finance consultant who works with new businesses like AP Engines, a company that provides billing software for Internet Protocol phone and cable service. He has found that the burn rate (the rate at which cash is consumed by a company) is critical. "Running out of cash is the worst thing," says Pilla, "and we are usually working three to six months ahead, trying to figure out when we're going to run out of cash and how we're going to fund [the company]." ■

Source: George Donnelly, "Start Me Up," *CFO,* July 2000, pp. 77–84.

Three major financial statements are ordinarily required for external reports—an income statement, a balance sheet, and a statement of cash flows. The **statement of cash flows** highlights the major activities that directly and indirectly impact cash flows and hence affect the overall cash balance. Managers focus on cash for a very good reason—without sufficient cash at the right times, a company may miss golden opportunities or may even go bankrupt.

The statement of cash flows answers questions that cannot be easily answered by the income statement and balance sheet alone. For example, the statement of cash flows can be used to answer questions like the following: Where did Delta Airlines get the cash to pay a dividend of nearly $140 million in a year in which, according to its income statement, it lost more than $1 billion? How was The Walt Disney Company able to invest nearly $800 million in expansion of its theme parks, including a major renovation of Epcot Center, despite a loss of more than $500 million on its investment in EuroDisney? Where did Wendy's International, Inc., get $125 million to expand its chain of fast-food restaurants in a year in which its net income was only $79 million and it did not raise any new debt? To answer such questions, familiarity with the statement of cash flows is required.

The statement of cash flows is a valuable analytical tool for managers as well as for investors and creditors, although managers tend to be more concerned with forecasted statements of cash flows that are prepared as part of the budgeting process. The statement of cash flows can be used to answer crucial questions such as:

1. Is the company generating sufficient positive cash flows from its ongoing operations to remain viable?
2. Will the company be able to repay its debts?
3. Will the company be able to pay its usual dividend?
4. Why do net income and net cash flow differ?
5. To what extent will the company have to borrow money in order to make needed investments?

This chapter focuses on how to prepare the statement of cash flows and on how to use it to assess a company's finances.

The Basic Approach to a Statement of Cash Flows

LEARNING OBJECTIVE 1
Classify changes in noncash balance sheet accounts as sources or uses of cash.

For the statement of cash flows to be useful to managers and others, it is important that companies employ a common definition of cash. It is also important that the statement be constructed using consistent guidelines for identifying activities that are *sources* of cash and *uses* of cash. The proper definition of cash and the guidelines to use in identifying sources and uses of cash are discussed in this section.

Definition of Cash

In a statement of cash flows, *cash* is broadly defined to include both cash and cash equivalents. **Cash equivalents** consist of short-term, highly liquid investments such as Treasury bills, commercial paper, and money market funds that are made solely for the purpose of generating a return on temporarily idle funds. Instead of simply holding cash, most companies invest their excess cash reserves in these types of interest-bearing assets that can be easily converted into cash. These short-term, liquid assets are usually included in *marketable securities* on the balance sheet. Since such assets are equivalent to cash, they are included with cash in a statement of cash flows.

Constructing the Statement of Cash Flows Using Changes in Noncash Balance Sheet Accounts

A type of statement of cash flows could be constructed by simply summarizing all of the debits and credits to the Cash and Cash Equivalents accounts during a period. However, this approach would overlook all of the transactions that involved an implicit exchange of cash. For example, when a company purchases inventory on credit, cash is implicitly exchanged. In essence, the supplier loans the company cash, which the company then uses to acquire inventory from the supplier. Rather than just looking at the transactions that explicitly involve cash, financial statement users are interested in all of the transactions that implicitly or explicitly involve cash. When inventory is purchased on credit, the Inventory account increases, which is an implicit *use* of cash. At the same time, Accounts Payable increases, which is an implicit *source* of cash. In general, increases in the Inventory account are classified as uses of cash and increases in the Accounts Payable account are classified as sources of cash. This suggests that analyzing changes in balance sheet accounts, such as Inventory and Accounts Payable, will uncover both the explicit and implicit sources and uses of cash. And this is indeed the basic approach taken in the statement of cash flows. The logic underlying this approach is demonstrated in Exhibit 16–1.

Exhibit 16–1 shows how net cash flow can be explained in terms of net income, dividends, and changes in balance sheet accounts. The first line in the exhibit consists of the balance sheet equation: Assets = Liabilities + Stockholders' Equity. The first step is to recognize that assets consist of cash and noncash assets. This is shown in the second line of the exhibit. The third line in the exhibit recognizes that if the account balances are always equal, then the changes in the account balances must be equal too. The next step is simply to note that the change in cash for a period is by definition the company's net cash flow, which yields line 4 in the exhibit. The only difference between line 4 and line 5 is that the changes in noncash assets is moved from the left-hand side of the equation to the right-hand side. This is done because we are attempting to explain net cash flow, so it should be isolated on the left-hand side of the equation. To get from line 5 to line 6, we need to remember that stockholders' equity is affected by net income, dividends, and changes in capital stock. Net income increases stockholders' equity, while dividends reduce stockholders' equity. To get from line 6 of the exhibit to line 7, a few terms on the right-hand side of the equation are rearranged.

EXHIBIT 16–1

Explaining Net Cash Flow by Analysis of the Noncash Balance Sheet Accounts

1.	Assets			=	Liabilities	+	Stockholders' Equity					
2.	Cash	+	Noncash Assets	=	Liabilities	+	Stockholders' Equity					
3.	Change in Cash	+	Changes in Noncash Assets	=	Changes in Liabilities	+	Changes in Stockholders' Equity					
4.	Net Cash Flow	+	Changes in Noncash Assets	=	Changes in Liabilities	+	Changes in Stockholders' Equity					
5.	Net Cash Flow	=	Changes in Liabilities	−	Changes in Noncash Assets	+	Changes in Stockholders' Equity					
6.	Net Cash Flow	=	Changes in Liabilities	−	Changes in Noncash Assets	+	Net Income	−	Dividends	+	Changes in Capital Stock	
7.	Net Cash Flow	=	Net Income	−	Changes in Noncash Assets	+	Changes in Liabilities	−	Dividends	+	Changes in Capital Stock	

IN BUSINESS

WHAT'S UP AT AMAZON?

Amazon.com, the online retailer of books and other merchandise, may have the best chance of eventually succeeding of any Internet retailer. Even so, "[I]t's no news that Amazon has had troubles, but the numbers are worse than many on Wall Street have admitted." Robert Tracy, a CPA and an analyst on the staff of grantsinvestor.com, took a close look at Amazon's financial statements and found that the company was holding its bills longer than it used to, especially at year-end. The cash flow from this increase in accounts payable exceeded the cash flow from all other operating sources combined. "Bulls [i.e., those who are positive about Amazon.com stock] will commend the company on imaginative cash management. Bears [i.e., those who are skeptical about the stock] will accuse it of financial engineering. What is not debatable is that, by stretching out payments into the new year, Amazon has presented a more liquid face to the world than it could otherwise have done."

Source: James Grant, "Diving into Amazon," *Forbes*, January 22, 2001, p. 153.

According to equation 7 in Exhibit 16–1, the net cash flow for a period can be determined by starting with net income, then deducting changes in noncash assets, adding changes in liabilities, deducting dividends paid to stockholders, and finally adding changes in capital stock. It is important to realize that changes in accounts can be either increases (positive) or decreases (negative), and this affects how we should interpret equation 7 in Exhibit 16–1. For example, increases in liabilities are added back to net income, whereas decreases in liabilities are deducted from net income to arrive at the net cash flow. On the other hand, increases in noncash assets are deducted from net income while decreases in noncash assets are added back to net income. Exhibit 16–2 summarizes the appropriate classifications—in terms of sources and uses—of net income, dividends, and changes in the noncash balance sheet accounts.

The classifications in Exhibit 16–2 seem to make sense. Positive net income generates cash, whereas a net loss consumes cash. Decreases in noncash assets, such as sale of inventories or property, are a source of cash. Increases in noncash assets, such as purchase of inventories or property, are a use of cash. Increases in liabilities, such as taking out a loan, are a source of cash. Decreases in liabilities, such as paying off a loan, are a use of cash. Increases in capital stock accounts, such as sale of common stock, are a source of cash. And payments of dividends to stockholders use cash.

EXHIBIT 16–2
Classifications of Sources and Uses of Cash

	Sources		Uses		
Net income	Always				
Net loss			Always		
Changes in noncash assets	Decreases		Increases		
Changes in liabilities*	Increases		Decreases		
Changes in capital stock accounts	Increases		Decreases		
Dividends paid to stockholders			Always		
	Total sources	−	Total uses	=	Net cash flow

*Contra asset accounts, such as the Accumulated Depreciation and Amortization account, follow the rules for liabilities.

Constructing a simple statement of cash flows is a straightforward process. Begin with net income (or net loss) and then add to it everything listed as sources in Exhibit 16–2 and subtract from it everything listed as uses. This will be illustrated with an example in the next section.

An Example of a Simplified Statement of Cash Flows

To illustrate the ideas introduced in the preceding section, we will now construct a *simplified* statement of cash flows for Nordstrom, Inc., one of the leading fashion retailers in the United States. This simplified statement does not follow the format required by the Financial Accounting Standards Board for external financial reports, but it shows where the numbers come from in a statement of cash flows and how they fit together. In later sections, we will show how the same basic data can be used to construct a full-fledged statement of cash flows that would be acceptable for external reports.

Constructing a Simplified Statement of Cash Flows

According to Exhibit 16–2, to construct a statement of cash flows we need the company's net income or loss, the changes in each of its balance sheet accounts, and the dividends paid to stockholders for the year. We can obtain this information from the Nordstrom financial statements that appear in Exhibits 16–3, 16–4, and 16–5. In a few instances, the actual statements have been simplified for ease of computation and discussion.

EXHIBIT 16–3

NORDSTROM, INC.*
Income Statement
(dollars in millions)

Net sales	$3,638
Less cost of goods sold	2,469
Gross margin	1,169
Less operating expenses	941
Net operating income	228
Nonoperating items:	
Gain on sale of store	3
Income before taxes	231
Less income taxes	91
Net income	$ 140

*This statement is loosely based on an actual income statement published by Nordstrom. Among other differences, there was no "Gain on sale of store" in the original statement. This "gain" has been included here to illustrate how to handle gains and losses on a statement of cash flows.

EXHIBIT 16–4

NORDSTROM, INC.*
Comparative Balance Sheet
(dollars in millions)

	Ending Balance	Beginning Balance	Change	Source or Use?
Assets				
Current assets:				
Cash and cash equivalents	$ 91	$ 29	+62	
Accounts receivable	637	654	−17	Source
Merchandise inventory	586	537	+49	Use
Total current assets	1,314	1,220		
Property, buildings, and equipment	1,517	1,394	+123	Use
Less accumulated depreciation and amortization	654	561	+93	Source
Net property, buildings, and equipment	863	833		
Total assets	$2,177	$2,053		
Liabilities and Stockholders' Equity				
Current liabilities:				
Accounts payable	$ 264	$ 220	+44	Source
Accrued wages and salaries payable	193	190	+3	Source
Accrued income taxes payable	28	22	+6	Source
Notes payable	40	38	+2	Source
Total current liabilities	525	470		
Long-term debt	439	482	−43	Use
Deferred income taxes	47	49	−2	Use
Total liabilities	1,011	1,001		
Stockholders' equity:				
Common stock	157	155	+2	Source
Retained earnings	1,009	897	+112	†
Total stockholders' equity	1,166	1,052		
Total liabilities and stockholders' equity	$2,177	$2,053		

*This statement differs from the actual statement published by Nordstrom.
†The change in retained earnings of $112 million equals the net income of $140 million less the cash dividends paid to stockholders of $28 million. Net income is classified as a source and dividends as a use.

EXHIBIT 16–5

NORDSTROM, INC.*
Statement of Retained Earnings
(dollars in millions)

Retained earnings, beginning balance	$ 897
Add: Net income	140
	1,037
Deduct: Dividends paid	28
Retained earnings, ending balance	$1,009

*This statement differs in a few details from the actual statement published by Nordstrom.

EXHIBIT 16–6

NORDSTROM, INC.
Simplified Statement of Cash Flows
(dollars in millions)

Note: This simplified statement is for illustration purposes only. It should *not* be used to complete end-of-chapter homework assignments or for preparing an actual statement of cash flows. See Exhibit 16–12 for the proper format for a statement of cash flows.

Sources		
Net income	$140	
Decreases in noncash assets:		
Decrease in accounts receivable	17	
Increases in liabilities (and contra asset accounts):		
Increase in accumulated depreciation and amortization	93	
Increase in accounts payable	44	
Increase in accrued wages and salaries	3	
Increase in accrued income taxes	6	
Increase in notes payable	2	
Increases in capital stock accounts:		
Increase in common stock	2	
Total sources		$307
Uses		
Increases in noncash assets:		
Increase in merchandise inventory	49	
Increase in property, buildings, and equipment	123	
Decreases in liabilities:		
Decrease in long-term debt	43	
Decrease in deferred income taxes	2	
Dividends	28	
Total uses		245
Net cash flow		$ 62

Note that changes between the beginning and ending balances have been computed for each of the balance sheet accounts in Exhibit 16–4, and each change has been classified as a source or use of cash. For example, the $17 million decrease in accounts receivable has been classified as a source of cash. This is because, as shown in Exhibit 16–2, decreases in noncash accounts, such as accounts receivable, are classified as sources of cash.

A *simplified* statement of cash flows appears in Exhibit 16–6. This statement was constructed by gathering together all of the entries listed as sources in Exhibit 16–4 and all of the entries listed as uses. The sources exceeded the uses by $62 million. This is the net cash flow for the year and is also, by definition, the change in cash and cash equivalents for the year. (Trace this $62 million back to Exhibit 16–4.)

The Need for a More Detailed Statement

While the simplified statement of cash flows in Exhibit 16–6 is not difficult to construct, it is not acceptable for external financial reports and is not as useful as it could be for internal reports. The FASB requires that the statement of cash flows follow a different format and that a few of the entries be modified. Nevertheless, almost all of the entries on a full-fledged statement of cash flows are the same as the entries on the simplified statement of cash flows—they are just in a different order.

In the following sections, we will discuss the modifications to the simplified statement of cash flows that are necessary to conform to external reporting requirements.

IN BUSINESS

PLUGGING THE CASH FLOW LEAK

Modern synthetic fabrics such as polyester fleece and Gore-Tex have almost completely replaced wool in ski clothing. John Fernsell started Ibex Outdoor Clothing in Woodstock, Vermont, to buck this trend. Fernsell's five-person company designs and sells jackets made of high-grade wool from Europe.

Fernsell quickly discovered an unfortunate fact of life about the wool clothing business—he faces a potentially ruinous cash crunch every year. Ibex orders wool from Europe in February but does not pay the mills until June when they ship fabric to the garment makers in California. The garment factories send finished goods to Ibex in July and August, and Ibex pays for them on receipt. Ibex ships to retailers in September and October, but doesn't get paid until November, December, or even January. That means from June to December the company spends like crazy—and takes in virtually nothing. Fernsell tried to get by with a line of credit, but it was insufficient. To survive, he had to ask his suppliers to let him pay late, which was not a long-term solution. To reduce this cash flow problem, Fernsell is introducing a line of wool *summer* clothing so that some cash will be flowing in from May through July, when he must pay his suppliers for the winter clothing.

Source: Daniel Lyons, "Wool Gatherer," *Forbes*, April 16, 2001, p. 310.

Organization of the Full-Fledged Statement of Cash Flows

LEARNING OBJECTIVE 2
Classify transactions as operating, investing, or financing activities.

To make it easier to compare statements of cash flows from different companies, the Financial Accounting Standards Board (FASB) requires that companies follow prescribed rules for preparing the statement of cash flows.

One of the FASB requirements is that the statement of cash flows be divided into three sections: *operating activities, investing activities,* and *financing activities.* The guidelines for applying these classifications are summarized in Exhibit 16–7 and discussed below.

Operating Activities

Generally, **operating activities** are those activities that enter into the determination of net income. Technically, however, the FASB defines operating activities as all the transactions that are not classified as investing or financing activities. Generally speaking, this

EXHIBIT 16–7
Guidelines for Classifying Transactions as Operating, Investing, and Financing Activities

Operating activities:
- Net income
- Changes in current assets
- Changes in noncurrent assets that affect net income (e.g., depreciation)
- Changes in current liabilities (except for debts to lenders and dividends payable)
- Changes in noncurrent liabilities that affect net income

Investing activities:
- Changes in noncurrent assets that are not included in net income

Financing activities:
- Changes in the current liabilities that are debts to lenders rather than obligations to suppliers, employees, or the government
- Changes in noncurrent liabilities that are not included in net income
- Changes in capital stock accounts
- Dividends

includes all transactions affecting current assets. It also includes all transactions affecting current liabilities except for issuing and repaying a note payable. Operating activities also include changes in noncurrent balance sheet accounts that directly affect net income such as the Accumulated Depreciation and Amortization account.

Topic Tackler PLUS

16–1

IN BUSINESS

KEEP AN EYE ON THE CASH FLOW

BusinessWeek advises taking a very close look at the statement of cash flows:

> If you really want to put the quality of a company's earnings to the test, you need to examine the cash flow statement. . . .
>
> To get a feeling for whether a company is playing games with its earnings, compare net income on the income statement with "cash flow from operating activities" . . . . "Generally, the closer a ratio of these two numbers is to one, the higher quality the earnings," says David Zion, a Bear Sterns accounting analyst.
>
> Next, compare the rates at which net income and operating cash are growing. If the two normally move in lockstep but cash flow lags, "it's a terrific early warning sign," says Howard Schilit, who heads the Center for Financial Research & Analysis. . . .
>
> [N]egative cash flow from operations isn't always bad. Because of the high costs of building a business, it is perfectly normal—even desirable—for fast-growing companies to consume more cash than they generate. Typically, such companies tide themselves over with bank loans or equity sales. In other words, they run a surplus in "financing" cash flows. Still, if operating cash doesn't pick up, bail out. Eventually, lenders lose patience with companies whose operations hemorrhage cash.

Source: Anne Tergeson, "The Ins and Outs of Cash Flow," *Business Week,* January 22, 2001, p. 102.

Investing Activities

Generally speaking, transactions that involve acquiring or disposing of noncurrent assets are classified as **investing activities.** These transactions include acquiring or selling property, plant, and equipment; acquiring or selling securities held for long-term investment, such as bonds and stocks of other companies; and lending money to another entity (such as a subsidiary) and the subsequent collection of the loan. However, as previously discussed, changes in noncurrent assets that directly affect net income, such as depreciation and amortization charges, are classified as operating activities.

Financing Activities

As a general rule, borrowing from creditors or repaying creditors as well as transactions with the company's owners are classified as **financing activities.** For example, when a company borrows money by issuing a bond, the transaction is classified as a financing activity. However, transactions with creditors that affect net income are classified as operating activities. For example, interest on the company's debt is included in operating activities rather than financing activities because interest is deducted as an expense in computing net income. In contrast, dividend payments to owners do not affect net income and therefore are classified as a financing rather than an operating activity.

Most changes in current liabilities are considered to be operating activities unless the transaction involves borrowing money directly from a lender, as with a note payable, or repaying such a debt. Transactions involving accounts payable, wages payable, and taxes payable are included in operating activities rather than financing activities, since these transactions occur on a routine basis and involve the company's suppliers, employees, and the government rather than lenders.

Other Issues in Preparing the Statement of Cash Flows

We must consider several other issues before illustrating the preparation of a statement of cash flows that would be acceptable for external financial reports. These issues are (1) whether amounts on the statement should be presented gross or net, (2) whether operating activities should be presented using the direct or indirect method, and (3) whether direct exchanges should be reported on the statement.

Cash Flows: Gross or Net?

For both financing and investing activities, items on the statement of cash flows should be presented in gross amounts rather than in net amounts. To illustrate, suppose that Macy's Department Stores purchases $50 million in property during the year and sells other property for $30 million. Instead of showing the net change of $20 million, the company must show the gross amounts of both the purchases and the sales. The purchases would be recorded as a use of cash, and the sales would be recorded as a source of cash. In like manner, if Alcoa receives $80 million from the issue of long-term bonds and then pays out $30 million to retire other bonds, the two transactions must be reported separately on the statement of cash flows rather than being netted against each other.

The gross method of reporting does *not* extend to operating activities, where debits and credits to an account are ordinarily netted against each other on the statement of cash flows. For example, if Sears adds $600 million to its accounts receivable as a result of sales during the year and $520 million of accounts receivable are collected, only the net increase of $80 million would be reported on the statement of cash flows.

Operating Activities: Direct or Indirect Method?

The net amount of the cash inflows and outflows arising from operating activities, which is known formally as the **net cash provided by operating activities,** can be computed by either the *direct* or the *indirect* method.

Under the **direct method,** the income statement is reconstructed on a cash basis from top to bottom. For example, in the direct method, cash collected from customers is used instead of revenue, and payments to suppliers is used instead of cost of goods sold. In essence, cash receipts are counted as revenues and cash disbursements are counted as expenses. The difference between the cash receipts and cash disbursements is the net cash provided by operating activities for the period.

Under the **indirect method,** the operating activities section of the statement of cash flows is constructed by starting with net income and adjusting it to a cash basis. That is, rather than directly computing cash sales, cash expenses, and so forth, these amounts are arrived at *indirectly* by removing from net income any items that do not affect cash flows. The indirect method has an advantage over the direct method because it shows the reasons for any differences between net income and the net cash provided by operating activities. The indirect method is also known as the **reconciliation method.**

Topic Tackler PLUS 16–2

Which method should be used for constructing the operating activities section of the statement of cash flows—the direct method or the indirect method? Both methods will result in exactly the same amount of net cash provided by operating activities. However, for external reporting purposes, the FASB *recommends* and *encourages* the use of the direct method. But there is a catch. If the direct method is used, there must be a supplementary reconciliation of net income with operating cash flows. In essence, if a company chooses to use the direct method, it must also go to the trouble of constructing a statement in which a form of the indirect method is used. However, if a company chooses to use the indirect method for determining the net cash flows from operating activities, there is no requirement that it also report the results of using the direct method.

Not surprisingly only about 1% of companies use the direct method to construct the statement of cash flows for external reports.[1] The remaining 99% probably use the indirect method because it is simply less work. While there are some good reasons for using the direct method, we use the indirect method in this chapter. The direct method is discussed and illustrated in Appendix 16A at the end of the chapter.

Direct Exchange Transactions

Companies sometimes enter into **direct exchange transactions** in which noncurrent balance sheet items are swapped. For example, a company might issue common stock in exchange for property. Or creditors might swap their long-term debt for common stock of the company. Or a company might acquire equipment under a long-term lease contract offered by the seller.

Direct exchange transactions are not reported on the statement of cash flows. However, such direct exchanges are disclosed in a separate schedule that accompanies the statement.

An Example of a Full-Fledged Statement of Cash Flows

LEARNING OBJECTIVE 3
Prepare a statement of cash flows using the indirect method to determine the net cash provided by operating activities.

In this section, we apply the FASB rules to construct a statement of cash flows for Nordstrom that would be acceptable for external reporting. The approach we take is based on an analysis of changes in balance sheet accounts, as in our earlier discussion of the simplified statement of cash flows. Indeed, as you will see, the full-fledged statement of cash flows is for the most part just a reorganized form of the simplified statement that appears in Exhibit 16–6.

The format for the operating activities part of the statement of cash flows is shown in Exhibit 16–8. For example, consider the effect of an increase in the Accounts Receivable account on the net cash provided by operating activities. Since the Accounts Receivable account is a noncash asset, we know from Exhibit 16–2 that increases in this account are treated as *uses* of cash. In other words, increases in Accounts Receivable are deducted when determining net cash flows. Intuitive explanations for this and other adjustments are sometimes slippery; nonetheless, some commonly given explanations are listed in Exhibit 16–9. For example, Exhibit 16–9 suggests that an increase in Accounts Receivable is deducted from net income because sales have been recorded for which no cash has been collected. Therefore, to adjust net income to a cash basis, the increase in the Accounts Receivable account must be deducted from net income to show that cash-basis sales are less than reported sales. However, we can more simply state that an increase in Accounts Receivable is deducted when computing net cash flows because, according to the logic of Exhibits 16–1 and 16–2, increases in all noncash assets must be deducted.

Eight Basic Steps to Preparing the Statement of Cash Flows

Preparing a statement of cash flows can be confusing and it is easy to overlook important details. For that reason, we recommend that you use a worksheet such as the one in Exhibit 16–10 to help prepare the statement of cash flows. To use this worksheet, follow these eight steps:

1. Copy onto the worksheet the title of each account appearing on the comparative balance sheet except for cash and cash equivalents and retained earnings. Contra asset accounts such as the Accumulated Depreciation and Amortization account should be

[1] American Institute of Certified Public Accountants, *Accounting Trends and Techniques: 2000* (Jersey City, NJ, 2000), p. 523.

EXHIBIT 16–8
General Model: Indirect Method of Determining the "Net Cash Provided by Operating Activities"

	Add (+) or Deduct (−) to Adjust Net Income
Net income	$XXX
Adjustments needed to convert net income to a cash basis:	
Depreciation, depletion, and amortization charges	+
Add (deduct) changes in current asset accounts affecting revenue or expense:*	
Increase in the account	−
Decrease in the account	+
Add (deduct) changes in current liability accounts affecting revenue or expense:†	
Increase in the account	+
Decrease in the account	−
Add (deduct) gains or losses on sales of assets:	
Gain on sales of assets	−
Loss on sales of assets	+
Add (deduct) changes in the Deferred Income Taxes account:	
Increase if a liability; decrease if an asset	+
Decrease if a liability; increase if an asset	−
Net cash provided by operating activities	$XXX

*Examples include accounts receivable, accrued receivables, inventory, and prepaid expenses.
†Examples include accounts payable, accrued liabilities, and taxes payable.

listed with the liabilities because they are treated the same way as liabilities on the statement of cash flows.

2. Compute the change from the beginning balance to the ending balance in each balance sheet account. Break down the change in retained earnings into net income and dividends paid to stockholders.
3. Using Exhibit 16–2 as a guide, code each entry on the worksheet as a source or a use of cash.
4. Under the Cash Flow Effect column, write sources as positive numbers and uses as negative numbers.
5. Make any necessary adjustments to reflect gross, rather than net, amounts involved in transactions—including adjustments for gains and losses. Some of these adjustments may require adding new entries to the bottom of the worksheet. The net effect of all such adjusting entries must be zero.
6. Classify each entry on the worksheet as an operating, investing, or financing activity according to the FASB's criteria, as given in Exhibit 16–7.
7. Copy the data from the worksheet to the statement of cash flows section by section, starting with the operating activities section.
8. At the bottom of the statement of cash flows prepare a reconciliation of the beginning and ending balances of cash and cash equivalents. The net change in cash and cash equivalents shown at the bottom of this statement should equal the change in the Cash and Cash Equivalents accounts during the year.

On the following pages we will apply these eight steps to the data contained in the comparative balance sheet for Nordstrom, Inc., found in Exhibit 16–4. *As we discuss each step, refer to Exhibit 16–4 and trace the data from this exhibit into the worksheet in Exhibit 16–10.*

EXHIBIT 16–9
Explanation of Adjustments for Changes in Current Asset and Current Liability Accounts (see Exhibit 16–8)

	Change in the Account	This Change Means That . . .	Therefore, to Adjust to a Cash Basis under the Indirect Method, We Must . . .
Accounts Receivable and Accrued Receivables	Increase	Sales (revenues) have been reported for which no cash has been collected.	Deduct the amount from net income to show that cash-basis sales are less than reported sales (revenues).
	Decrease	Cash has been collected for which no sales (revenues) have been reported for the current period.	Add the amount to net income to show that cash-basis sales are greater than reported sales (revenues).
Inventory	Increase	Goods have been purchased that are not included in cost of goods sold (COGS).	Deduct the amount from net income to show that cash-basis COGS is greater than reported COGS.
	Decrease	Goods have been included in COGS that were purchased in a prior period.	Add the amount to net income to show that cash-basis COGS is less than reported COGS.
Prepaid Expenses	Increase	More cash has been paid out for services than has been reported as expense.	Deduct the amount from net income to show that cash-basis expenses are greater than reported expenses.
	Decrease	More has been reported as expense for services than has been paid out in cash.	Add the amount to net income to show that cash-basis expenses are less than reported expenses.
Accounts Payable and Accrued Liabilities	Increase	More has been reported as expense for goods and services than has been paid out in cash.	Add the amount to net income to show that cash-basis expenses for goods and services are less than reported expenses.
	Decrease	More cash has been paid out for goods and services than has been reported as expense.	Deduct the amount from net income to show that cash-basis expenses for goods and services are greater than reported expenses.
Taxes Payable	Increase	More income tax expense has been reported than has been paid out in cash.	Add the amount to net income to show that cash-basis expenses are less than reported expenses.
	Decrease	More cash has been paid to the tax authorities than has been reported as income tax expense.	Deduct the amount from net income to show that cash-basis expenses are greater than reported expenses.

Setting Up the Worksheet (Steps 1–4)

As indicated above, step 1 in preparing the worksheet is to simply list all of the relevant account titles from the company's balance sheet. Note that we have done this for Nordstrom, Inc., on the worksheet in Exhibit 16–10. (The titles of Nordstrom's accounts have been taken from the company's comparative balance sheet, which is found in Exhibit 16–4 on page 754.) The only significant differences between Nordstrom's balance sheet accounts and the worksheet listing are that (1) the Accumulated Depreciation and Amortization account has been moved down with the liabilities on the worksheet, (2) the Cash and Cash Equivalents accounts have been omitted, and (3) the change in retained earnings has been broken down into net income and dividends.

As stated in step 2, the change in each account's balance during the year is listed in the first column of the worksheet. We have entered these changes for Nordstrom's accounts onto the worksheet in Exhibit 16–10. (Refer to Nordstrom's comparative balance sheet in Exhibit 16–4 to see how these changes were computed.)

Then, as indicated in step 3, each change on the worksheet is classified as either a source or a use of cash. Whether a change is a source or a use can be determined by

EXHIBIT 16–10

NORDSTROM, INC.
Statement of Cash Flows Worksheet
(dollars in millions)

	(1) Change	(2) Source or Use?	(3) Cash Flow Effect	(4) Adjust-ments	(5) Adjusted Effect (3) + (4)	(6) Classi-fication*
Assets (except cash and cash equivalents)						
Current assets:						
Accounts receivable	−17	Source	$ +17		$ +17	Operating
Merchandise inventory	+49	Use	−49		−49	Operating
Noncurrent assets:						
Property, buildings, and equipment	+123	Use	−123	$−15	−138	Investing
Contra Assets, Liabilities, and Stockholders' Equity						
Contra assets:						
Accumulated depreciation and amortization	+93	Source	+93	+10	+103	Operating
Current liabilities:						
Accounts payable	+44	Source	+44		+44	Operating
Accrued wages and salaries payable	+3	Source	+3		+3	Operating
Accrued income taxes payable	+6	Source	+6		+6	Operating
Notes payable	+2	Source	+2		+2	Financing
Noncurrent liabilities:						
Long-term debt	−43	Use	−43		−43	Financing
Deferred income taxes	−2	Use	−2		−2	Operating
Stockholders' equity:						
Common stock	+2	Source	+2		+2	Financing
Retained earnings:						
Net income	+140	Source	+140		+140	Operating
Dividends	−28	Use	−28		−28	Financing
Additional Entries						
Proceeds from sale of store				+8	+8	Investing
Gain on sale of store				−3	−3	Operating
Total (net cash flow)			$ +62	$ 0	$ +62	

*See Exhibit 16–11 for the reasons for these classifications.

referring back to Exhibit 16–2 on page 752, where we first discussed these classifications. For example, Nordstrom's Merchandise Inventory account increased by $49 million during the year. According to Exhibit 16–2, increases in noncash asset accounts are classified as uses of cash, so an entry has been made to that effect in the second column of the worksheet for the Merchandise Inventory account.

So far, nothing is new. All of this was done in Exhibit 16–4 when we constructed the simplified statement of cash flows. Step 4 is mechanical, but it helps prevent careless errors. Sources are coded as positive changes and uses as negative changes in the Cash Flow Effect column on the worksheet.

Adjustments to Reflect Gross, Rather than Net, Amounts (Step 5)

As discussed earlier, the FASB requires that gross, rather than net, amounts be disclosed in the investing and financing sections. This rule requires special treatment of gains and losses. To illustrate, suppose that Nordstrom decided to sell an old store and move its retail operations to a new location. Assume that the original cost of the old store was $15 million, its accumulated depreciation was $10 million, and that it was sold for $8 million in cash. The journal entry to record this transaction appears below:

Cash Proceeds	8,000,000	
Accumulated Depreciation and Amortization	10,000,000	
Property, Buildings, and Equipment		15,000,000
Gain on Sale		3,000,000

The $3 million gain is reflected in the income statement in Exhibit 16–3 on page 753.

We can reconstruct the gross additions to the Property, Buildings, and Equipment account and the gross charges to the Accumulated Depreciation and Amortization account with the help of T-accounts:

Property, Buildings, and Equipment

Balance	1,394		
Additions (plug*)	138	15	Disposal of store
Balance	1,517		

Accumulated Depreciation and Amortization

		561	Balance
Disposal of store	10	103	Depreciation charges (plug*)
		654	Balance

*By *plug* we mean the balancing figure in the account.

According to the FASB rules, the gross additions of $138 million to the Property, Buildings, and Equipment account should be disclosed on the statement of cash flows rather than the net change in the account of $123 million ($1,517 million − $1,394 million = $123 million). Likewise, the gross depreciation charges of $103 million should be disclosed rather than the net change in the Accumulated Depreciation and Amortization account of $93 million ($654 million − $561 million = $93 million). And the cash proceeds of $8 million from sale of the building should also be disclosed on the statement of cash flows. All of this is accomplished, while preserving the correct overall net cash flows on the statement, by using the above journal entry to make adjusting entries on the worksheet. The debits are recorded as positive adjustments, and the credits are recorded as negative adjustments. These adjusting entries are recorded under the Adjustments column in Exhibit 16–10.

It may not be clear why the gain on the sale is *deducted* in the operating activities section of the statement of cash flows. The company's $140 million net income, which is part of the operating activities section, includes the $3 million gain on the sale of the store. But this $3 million gain must be reported in the *investing* activities section of the statement of cash flows as part of the $8 million proceeds from the sale transaction. Therefore, to avoid double counting, the $3 million gain is deducted from net income in the operating activities section of the statement. The adjustments we have made on the worksheet accomplish this. The $3 million gain will be deducted in the operating activities section, and all $8 million of the sale proceeds will be shown as an investing item. As a result, all of the gain will be included in the investing section of the statement of cash flows and none of it will be in the operating activities section. There will be no double-counting of the gain.

In the case of a loss on the sale of an asset, we do the opposite. The loss is added back to the net income figure in the operating activities section of the statement of cash flows. Whatever cash proceeds are received from the sale of the asset are reported in the investing activities section.

Before turning to step 6 in the process of building the statement of cash flows, one small step is required. Add the Adjustments in column (4) to the Cash Flow Effect in column (3) to arrive at the Adjusted Effect in column (5).

Classifying Entries as Operating, Investing, or Financing Activities (Step 6)

In step 6, each entry on the worksheet is classified as an operating, investing, or financing activity using the guidelines in Exhibit 16–7. These classifications are entered directly on the worksheet in Exhibit 16–10 and are explained in Exhibit 16–11. Most of these classifications are straightforward, but the classification of the change in the Deferred Income Taxes account may require some additional explanation. Because of the way income tax expense is determined for financial reporting purposes, the expense that appears on the income statement often differs from the taxes that are actually owed to the government. Usually, the income tax expense overstates the company's actual income tax liability for the year. When this happens, the journal entry to record income taxes includes a credit to Deferred Income Taxes:

Income Tax Expense	XXX	
Income Taxes Payable		XXX
Deferred Income Taxes (plug)		XXX

EXHIBIT 16–11
Classifications of Entries on Nordstrom's Statement of Cash Flows

Entry	Classification	Reason
• Changes in Accounts Receivable and Merchandise Inventory	Operating activity	Changes in current assets are included in operating activities.
• Change in Property, Buildings, and Equipment	Investing activity	Changes in noncurrent assets that do not directly affect net income are included in investing activities.
• Change in Accumulated Depreciation and Amortization	Operating activity	Depreciation and amortization directly affect net income and are therefore included in operating activities.
• Changes in Accounts Payable, Accrued Wages and Salaries Payable, and Accrued Income Taxes Payable	Operating activity	Changes in current liabilities (except for notes payable) are included in operating activities.
• Change in Notes Payable	Financing activity	Issuing or repaying notes payable is classified as a financing activity.
• Change in Long-Term Debt	Financing activity	Changes in noncurrent liabilities that do not directly affect net income are included in financing activities.
• Change in Deferred Income Taxes	Operating activity	Deferred income taxes result from income tax expense that directly affects net income. Therefore, this entry is included in operating activities.
• Change in Common Stock	Financing activity	Changes in capital stock accounts are always included in financing activities.
• Net income	Operating activity	Net income is always included in operating activities.
• Dividends	Financing activity	Dividends paid to stockholders are always included in financing activities.
• Proceeds from sale of store	Investing activity	The gross amounts received on disposal of noncurrent assets are included in investing activities.
• Gains from sale of store	Operating activity	Gains and losses directly affect net income and are therefore included in operating activities.

Since deferred income taxes arise directly from the computation of an expense, the change in the Deferred Income Taxes account is included in the operating activities section of the statement of cash flows.

In the case of Nordstrom, the Deferred Income Taxes account decreased during the year. Deferred Income Taxes is a liability account for Nordstrom. Since this liability account decreased during the year, the change is counted as a use of cash and is deducted in determining net cash flow for the year.

IN BUSINESS

EVAPORATING CASH FLOW

Investors often assume that it is harder for management to manipulate operating cash flows than reported net earnings. That is often true, but some skepticism is in order. After an investigation by the Securities and Exchange Commission, Dynergy Inc. moved $300 million tied to a complex natural-gas trading arrangement from the operating cash flow section of its already-published statement of cash flows to the financing section. This reduced the company's reported operating cash flow for the year by 37%. And Enron's cash flow from operations was overstated by almost 50% prior to revelations concerning its fraudulent accounting practices.

Sources: Henny Sender, "Cash Flow? It Isn't Always What It Seems," *The Wall Street Journal,* May 8, 2002, pp. C1 & C3 and Tim Reason, "See-Through Finance," *CFO,* October 2002, pp. 45–52.

The Completed Statement of Cash Flows (Steps 7 and 8)

Once the worksheet is completed, the actual statement of cash flows is easy to complete. Nordstrom's statement of cash flows appears in Exhibit 16–12 (page 766). Trace each item from the worksheet into this statement.

The operating activities section of the statement follows the format laid out in Exhibit 16–8, beginning with net income. The other entries in the operating activities section are adjustments required to convert net income to a cash basis. The sum of all of the entries under the operating activities section is called the "Net cash provided by operating activities."

The investing activities section comes next on the statement of cash flows. The worksheet entries that have been classified as investing activities are recorded in this section in any order. The sum of all the entries in this section is called the "Net cash used in investing activities."

The financing activities section of the statement follows the investing activities section. The worksheet entries that have been classified as financing activities are recorded in this section in any order. The sum of all of the entries in this section is called the "Net cash used in financing activities."

Finally, for step 8, the bottom of the statement of cash flows contains a reconciliation of the beginning and ending balances of cash and cash equivalents.

Interpretation of the Statement of Cash Flows

The completed statement of cash flows in Exhibit 16–12 provides a very favorable picture of Nordstrom's cash flows. The net cash flow from operations is a healthy $259 million. This positive cash flow permitted the company to make substantial additions to its property, buildings, and equipment and to pay off a substantial portion of its long-term debt. If similar conditions prevail in the future, the company can continue to finance substantial growth from its own cash flows without the necessity of raising debt or selling stock.

When interpreting a statement of cash flows, it is particularly important to examine the net cash provided by operating activities. This figure indicates how successful the company is in generating cash on a continuing basis. A negative cash flow from

EXHIBIT 16–12

NORDSTROM, INC.*
Statement of Cash Flows—Indirect Method
(dollars in millions)

Operating Activities		
Net income		$140
Adjustments to convert net income to a cash basis:		
Depreciation and amortization charges	103	
Decrease in accounts receivable	17	
Increase in merchandise inventory	(49)	
Increase in accounts payable	44	
Increase in accrued wages and salaries payable	3	
Increase in accrued income taxes payable	6	
Decrease in deferred income taxes	(2)	
Gain on sale of store	(3)	119
Net cash provided by operating activities		259
Investing Activities		
Additions to property, buildings, and equipment	(138)	
Proceeds from sale of store	8	
Net cash used in investing activities		(130)
Financing Activities		
Increase in notes payable	2	
Decrease in long-term debt	(43)	
Increase in common stock	2	
Cash dividends paid	(28)	
Net cash used in financing activities		(67)
Net increase in cash and cash equivalents		62
Cash and cash equivalents at beginning of year		29
Cash and cash equivalents at end of year		$ 91

Reconciliation of the beginning and ending cash balances

*This statement differs from the actual statement published by Nordstrom.

operations may be a sign of fundamental difficulties. A positive cash flow from operations is necessary to avoid liquidating assets or borrowing money just to sustain day-to-day operations.

Depreciation, Depletion, and Amortization

A few pitfalls can trap the unwary when reading a statement of cash flows. Perhaps the most common pitfall is to misinterpret the nature of the depreciation charges on the statement of cash flows. Since depreciation is added back to net income, you might think that all you have to do to increase net cash flow is to increase depreciation charges. This is false. In a merchandising company like Nordstrom, increasing the depreciation charge by X dollars would decrease net income by X dollars because of the added expense. Adding back the depreciation charge to net income on the statement of cash flows simply cancels out the reduction in net income caused by the depreciation charge. Referring back to Exhibit 16–2, depreciation, depletion, and amortization charges are added back to net income on the statement of cash flows because they are a decrease in an asset (or an increase in a contra asset)—not because they generate cash.

IN BUSINESS

WHAT'S WRONG WITH THIS PICTURE?

Getty Images is the world's biggest stock photo company—owning the rights to over 70 million images and 30,000 hours of film. The company gets its revenues from licensing the use of these images. The stock market is impressed with the potential in this market—despite losses of $63 million in the first six months of the year, the company's stock was worth $1.8 billion. "What is there for a growth company to talk about if earnings are so rotten? Anything but earnings. . . . Getty Images declared victory in its cash from operations, which it said had swelled to a robust $17.1 million in the second quarter, up from a deficit of $2.6 million in the first. Does that mean Getty collected its bills and whittled down its inventory? Nope. Both receivables and inventory are rising. The cash flow from operations, rather, comes from not paying bills."

Source: Elizabeth MacDonald, "Image Problem," *Forbes*, October 16, 2000, pp. 104–106.

Summary

The statement of cash flows is one of the three major financial statements prepared by organizations. It explains how cash was generated and how it was used during a period. The statement of cash flows is widely used as a tool for assessing the financial health of organizations.

In general, sources of cash include net income, decreases in assets, increases in liabilities, and increases in stockholders' capital accounts. Uses of cash include increases in assets, decreases in liabilities, decreases in stockholders' capital accounts, and dividends. A simplified form of the statement of cash flows can be easily constructed using just these definitions and a comparative balance sheet.

For external reporting purposes, the statement of cash flows must be organized in terms of operating, investing, and financing activities. While some exceptions exist, changes in noncurrent assets are generally included in investing activities and changes in noncurrent liabilities are generally included in financing activities. And, with a few exceptions, operating activities include net income and changes in current assets and current liabilities.

An analyst should pay particularly close attention to the net cash provided by operating activities, since this provides a measure of how successful the company is in generating cash on a continuing basis.

Review Problem

Rockford Company's comparative balance sheet for 2005 and the company's income statement for the year follow:

ROCKFORD COMPANY
Comparative Balance Sheet
December 31, 2005, and 2004
(dollars in millions)

	2005	2004
Assets		
Cash	$ 26	$ 10
Accounts receivable	180	270
Inventory	205	160
Prepaid expenses	17	20
Plant and equipment	430	309
Less accumulated depreciation	(218)	(194)
Long-term investments	60	75
Total assets	$ 700	$ 650
Liabilities and Stockholders' Equity		
Accounts payable	$ 230	$ 310
Accrued liabilities	70	60
Bonds payable	135	40
Deferred income taxes	15	8
Common stock	140	140
Retained earnings	110	92
Total liabilities and stockholders' equity	$ 700	$ 650

ROCKFORD COMPANY
Income Statement
For the Year Ended December 31, 2005
(dollars in millions)

Sales	$1,000
Less cost of goods sold	530
Gross margin	470
Less operating expenses	352
Net operating income	118
Nonoperating items:	
Loss on sale of equipment	(4)
Income before taxes	114
Less income taxes	48
Net income	$66

Notes: Dividends of $48 million were paid in 2005. The loss on sale of equipment of $4 million reflects a transaction in which equipment with an original cost of $12 million and accumulated depreciation of $5 million was sold for $3 million in cash.

Required:

Using the indirect method, determine the net cash provided by operating activities for 2005 and construct a statement of cash flows for the year.

Solution to Review Problem

A worksheet for Rockford Company appears below. Using the worksheet, it is a simple matter to construct the statement of cash flows, including the net cash provided by operating activities.

ROCKFORD COMPANY
Statement of Cash Flows Worksheet
For the Year Ended December 31, 2005
(dollars in millions)

	(1) Change	(2) Source or Use?	(3) Cash Flow Effect	(4) Adjustments	(5) Adjusted Effect (3) + (4)	(6) Classification
Assets (except cash and cash equivalents)						
Current assets:						
Accounts receivable	−90	Source	$ +90		$ +90	Operating
Inventory	+45	Use	−45		−45	Operating
Prepaid expenses	−3	Source	+3		+3	Operating
Noncurrent assets:						
Property, buildings, and equipment	+121	Use	−121	$−12	−133	Investing
Long-term investments	−15	Source	+15		+15	Investing
Contra Assets, Liabilities, and Stockholders' Equity						
Contra assets:						
Accumulated depreciation	+24	Source	+24	+5	+29	Operating
Current liabilities:						
Accounts payable	−80	Use	−80		−80	Operating
Accrued liabilities	+10	Source	+10		+10	Operating
Noncurrent liabilities:						
Bonds payable	+95	Source	+95		+95	Financing
Deferred income taxes	+7	Source	+7		+7	Operating
Stockholders' equity:						
Common stock	+0	—	+0		+0	Financing
Retained earnings:						
Net income	+66	Source	+66		+66	Operating
Dividends	−48	Use	−48		−48	Financing
Additional Entries						
Proceeds from sale of equipment				+3	+3	Investing
Loss on sale of equipment				+4	+4	Operating
Total (net cash flow)			$ +16	$ 0	$ +16	

ROCKFORD COMPANY
Statement of Cash Flows—Indirect Method
For the Year Ended December 31, 2005
(dollars in millions)

Operating Activities:		
Net income		$ 66
Adjustments to convert net income to a cash basis:		
Depreciation and amortization charges	$ 29	
Decrease in accounts receivable	90	
Increase in inventory	(45)	
Decrease in prepaid expenses	3	
Decrease in accounts payable	(80)	
Increase in accrued liabilities	10	
Increase in deferred income taxes	7	
Loss on sale of equipment	4	18
Net cash provided by operating activities		84
Investing Activities:		
Additions to property, buildings, and equipment	(133)	
Decrease in long-term investments	15	
Proceeds from sale of equipment	3	
Net cash used in investing activities		(115)
Financing Activities:		
Increase in bonds payable	95	
Cash dividends paid	(48)	
Net cash provided by financing activities		47
Net increase in cash and cash equivalents		16
Cash and cash equivalents at beginning of year		10
Cash and cash equivalents at end of year		$ 26

Note that the $16 million increase in cash and cash equivalents agrees with the $16 million increase in the company's Cash account shown in the balance sheet on page 768, and it agrees with the total in column (5) of the worksheet shown on page 769.

Glossary

Cash equivalents Short-term, highly liquid investments such as Treasury bills, commercial paper, and money market funds that are made solely for the purpose of generating a return on temporarily idle funds. (p. 750)

Direct exchange transactions Transactions involving only noncurrent balance sheet accounts. For example, a company might issue common stock that is directly exchanged for property. (p. 759)

Direct method A method of computing the cash provided by operating activities in which the income statement is reconstructed on a cash basis from top to bottom. (p. 758)

Financing activities All transactions (other than payment of interest) involving borrowing from creditors or repaying creditors as well as transactions with the company's owners (except stock dividends and stock splits). (p. 757)

Indirect method A method of computing the cash provided by operating activities that starts with net income and adjusts it to a cash basis. It is also known as the *reconciliation method.* (p. 758)

Investing activities Transactions that involve acquiring or disposing of noncurrent assets. (p. 757)

Net cash provided by operating activities The net result of the cash inflows and outflows arising from day-to-day operations. (p. 758)

Operating activities Transactions that enter into the determination of net income. (p. 756)

Reconciliation method See *Indirect method.* (p. 758)

Statement of cash flows A financial statement that highlights the major activities that directly and indirectly impact cash flows and hence affect the overall cash balance. (p. 750)

Appendix 16A: The Direct Method of Determining the Net Cash Provided by Operating Activities

LEARNING OBJECTIVE 4
Use the direct method to determine the net cash provided by operating activities.

To compute the net cash provided by operating activities under the direct method, we must reconstruct the income statement on a cash basis from top to bottom. Exhibit 16A–1 shows the adjustments that must be made to adjust sales, expenses, and so forth, to a cash basis. To illustrate, we have included in the exhibit the Nordstrom data from the chapter.

Note that the net cash provided by operating activities of $259 million agrees with the amount computed in the chapter by the indirect method. The two amounts agree, since the direct and indirect methods are just different roads to the same destination. The investing and financing activities sections of the statement will be exactly the same as shown for the indirect method in Exhibit 16–12. The only difference between the indirect and direct methods is in the operating activities section.

Similarities and Differences in the Handling of Data

Although we arrive at the same destination under either the direct or the indirect method, not all data are handled in the same way in the adjustment process. Stop for a moment,

EXHIBIT 16A–1
General Model: Direct Method of Determining the Net Cash Provided by Operating Activities

Revenue or Expense Item	Add (+) or Deduct (−) to Adjust to a Cash Basis	Illustration—Nordstrom (in millions)	
Sales revenue (as reported)		$3,638	
Adjustments to a cash basis:			
1. Increase in accounts receivable	−		
2. Decrease in accounts receivable	+	+17	
Total			$3,655
Cost of goods sold (as reported)		2,469	
Adjustments to a cash basis:			
3. Increase in merchandise inventory	+	+49	
4. Decrease in merchandise inventory	−		
5. Increase in accounts payable	−	−44	
6. Decrease in accounts payable	+		
Total			2,474
Operating expenses (as reported)		941	
Adjustments to a cash basis:			
7. Increase in prepaid expenses	+		
8. Decrease in prepaid expenses	−		
9. Increase in accrued liabilities	−	−3	
10. Decrease in accrued liabilities	+		
11. Period's depreciation, depletion, and amortization charges	−	−103	
Total			835
Income tax expense (as reported)		91	
Adjustments to a cash basis:			
12. Increase in accrued taxes payable	−	−6	
13. Decrease in accrued taxes payable	+		
14. Increase in deferred income taxes	−		
15. Decrease in deferred income taxes	+	+2	
Total			87
Net cash provided by operating activities			$ 259

flip back to the general model for the indirect method in Exhibit 16–8 on page 760 and compare the adjustments made in that exhibit to the adjustments made for the direct method in Exhibit 16A–1. The adjustments for accounts that affect revenue are the same in the two methods. In either case, increases in the accounts are deducted and decreases in the accounts are added. The adjustments for accounts that affect expenses, however, are handled in *opposite* ways in the indirect and direct methods. This is because under the indirect method the adjustments are made to *net income,* whereas under the direct method the adjustments are made to the *expense accounts* themselves.

To illustrate this difference, note the handling of prepaid expenses and depreciation in the indirect and direct methods. Under the indirect method (Exhibit 16–8 on page 760), an increase in the Prepaid Expenses account is *deducted* from net income in computing the amount of net cash provided by operating activities. Under the direct method (Exhibit 16A–1), an increase in Prepaid Expenses is *added* to operating expenses. The reason for the difference can be explained as follows: An increase in Prepaid Expenses means that more cash has been paid out for items such as insurance than has been included as expense for the period. Therefore, to adjust net income to a cash basis, we must either deduct this increase from net income (indirect method) or we must add this increase to operating expenses (direct method). Either way, we will end up with the same figure for net cash provided by operating activities. Similarly, depreciation is added to net income under the indirect method to cancel out its effect (Exhibit 16–8), whereas it is deducted from operating expenses under the direct method to cancel out its effect (Exhibit 16A–1). These differences in the handling of data are true for all other expense items in the two methods.

In the matter of gains and losses on sales of assets, no adjustments are needed at all under the direct method. These gains and losses are simply ignored, since they are not part of sales, cost of goods sold, operating expenses, or income taxes. Observe that in Exhibit 16A–1, Nordstrom's $3 million gain on the sale of the store is not listed as an adjustment in the operating activities section.

Special Rules—Direct and Indirect Methods

As stated earlier, when the direct method is used, the FASB requires a reconciliation between net income and the net cash provided by operating activities, as determined by the indirect method. Thus, *when a company elects to use the direct method, it must also present the indirect method* in a separate schedule accompanying the statement of cash flows.

On the other hand, if a company elects to use the indirect method to compute the net cash provided by operating activities, then it must also provide a special breakdown of data. The company must provide a separate disclosure of the amount of interest and the amount of income taxes paid during the year. The FASB requires this separate disclosure so that users can take the data provided by the indirect method and make estimates of what the amounts for sales, income taxes, and so forth, would have been if the direct method had been used instead.

Questions

16–1 What is the purpose of a statement of cash flows?

16–2 What are *cash equivalents,* and why are they included with cash on a statement of cash flows?

16–3 What are the three major sections on a statement of cash flows, and what are the general rules that determine the transactions that should be included in each section?

16–4 Why is interest paid on amounts borrowed from banks and other lenders considered to be an operating activity when the amounts borrowed are financing activities?

16–5 If an asset is sold at a gain, why is the gain deducted from net income when computing the net cash provided by operating activities under the indirect method?

16–6 Why aren't transactions involving accounts payable considered to be financing activities?

16–7 Give an example of a direct exchange and explain how such exchanges are handled when preparing a statement of cash flows.

16–8 Assume that a company repays a $300,000 loan from its bank and then later in the same year borrows $500,000. What amount(s) would appear on the statement of cash flows?

16–9 How do the direct and the indirect methods differ in their approach to computing the net cash provided by operating activities?

16–10 A business executive once stated, "Depreciation is one of our biggest sources of cash." Do you agree that depreciation is a source of cash? Explain.

16–11 If the balance in Accounts Receivable increases during a period, how will this increase be recognized using the indirect method of computing the net cash provided by operating activities?

16–12 (Appendix 16A) If the balance in Accounts Payable decreases during a period, how will this decrease be recognized using the direct method of computing the net cash provided by operating activities?

16–13 During the current year, a company declared and paid a $60,000 cash dividend and a 10% stock dividend. How will these two items be treated on the current year's statement of cash flows?

16–14 Would a sale of equipment for cash be considered a financing activity or an investing activity? Why?

16–15 (Appendix 16A) A merchandising company showed $250,000 in cost of goods sold on its income statement. The company's beginning inventory was $75,000, and its ending inventory was $60,000. The accounts payable balance was $50,000 at the beginning of the year and $40,000 at the end of the year. Using the direct method, adjust the company's cost of goods sold to a cash basis.

Exercises

EXERCISE 16–1 Classifying Transactions [LO1, LO2]

Below are transactions that took place in Placid Company during the past year:

a. Equipment was purchased.
b. A cash dividend was declared and paid.
c. Accounts receivable decreased.
d. Short-term investments were purchased.
e. Equipment was sold.
f. Preferred stock was sold to investors.
g. A stock dividend was declared and issued.
h. Interest was paid to long-term creditors.
i. Salaries and wages payable decreased.
j. Stock of another company was purchased.
k. Bonds were issued that will be due in 10 years.
l. Rent was received from subleasing office space, reducing rents receivable.
m. Common stock was repurchased and retired.

Required:

Prepare an answer sheet with the following headings:

	Activity					
Transaction	Operating	Investing	Financing	Not Reported	Source	Use
a.						
b.						
etc.						

Enter the transactions above on your answer sheet and indicate how the effects of each transaction would be classified on a statement of cash flows. Place an *X* in the Operating, Investing, or Financing column and an *X* in the Source or Use column as appropriate.

EXERCISE 16–2 Net Cash Provided by Operating Activities (Indirect Method) [LO3]
For the just completed year, Hanna Company had a net income of $35,000. Balances in the company's current asset and current liability accounts at the beginning and end of the year were:

	End of Year	Beginning of Year
Current assets:		
Cash	$30,000	$40,000
Accounts receivable	$125,000	$106,000
Inventory	$213,000	$180,000
Prepaid expenses	$6,000	$7,000
Current liabilities:		
Accounts payable	$210,000	$195,000
Accrued liabilities	$4,000	$6,000

The Deferred Income Taxes liability account on the balance sheet increased by $4,000 during the year, and depreciation charges were $20,000.

Required:
Using the indirect method, determine the net cash provided by operating activities for the year.

EXERCISE 16–3 (Appendix 16A) Net Cash Provided by Operating Activities (Direct Method) [LO4]
Refer to the data for Hanna Company in Exercise 16–2. The company's income statement for the year appears below:

Sales	$350,000
Less cost of goods sold	140,000
Gross margin	210,000
Less operating expenses	160,000
Income before taxes	50,000
Less income taxes	15,000
Net income	$ 35,000

Required:
Using the direct method (and the data from Exercise 16–2), convert the company's income statement to a cash basis.

EXERCISE 16–4 Net Cash Provided by Operating Activities (Indirect Method) [LO3]
Changes in various accounts and gains and losses on the sale of assets during the year for Argon Company are given below:

Item	Amount
Accounts Receivable	$90,000 decrease
Accrued Interest Receivable	$4,000 increase
Inventory	$120,000 increase
Prepaid Expenses	$3,000 decrease
Accounts Payable	$65,000 decrease
Accrued Liabilities	$8,000 increase
Deferred Income Taxes Payable	$12,000 increase
Sale of equipment	$7,000 gain
Sale of long-term investments	$10,000 loss

Required:
Prepare an answer sheet using the following column headings:

Item	Amount	Add	Deduct

For each item, place an X in the Add or Deduct column to indicate whether the dollar amount should be added to or deducted from net income under the indirect method when computing the net cash provided by operating activities for the year.

EXERCISE 16–5 Prepare a Statement of Cash Flows (Indirect Method) [LO2, LO3]
The following changes took place during the year in Pavolik Company's balance sheet accounts:

Cash	$5 D	Accounts Payable	$35 I
Accounts Receivable	$110 I	Accrued Liabilities	$4 D
Inventory	$70 D	Bonds Payable	$150 I
Prepaid Expenses	$9 I	Deferred Income Taxes	$8 I
Long-Term Investments	$6 D	Common Stock	$80 D
Plant and Equipment	$200 I	Retained Earnings	$54 I
Accumulated Depreciation	$(60) I		
Land	$15 D		

D = Decrease; I = Increase.

Long-term investments that had cost the company $6 were sold during the year for $16, and land that had cost $15 was sold for $9. In addition, the company declared and paid $30 in cash dividends during the year. No sales or retirements of plant and equipment took place during the year.

The company's income statement for the year follows:

Sales		$700
Less cost of goods sold		400
Gross margin		300
Less operating expenses		184
Net operating income		116
Nonoperating items:		
Gain on sale of investments	$10	
Loss on sale of land	6	4
Income before taxes		120
Less income taxes		36
Net income		$ 84

The company's beginning cash balance was $90, and its ending balance was $85.

Required:

1. Use the indirect method to determine the net cash provided by operating activities for the year.
2. Prepare a statement of cash flows for the year.

EXERCISE 16–6 (Appendix 16A) Adjust Net Income to a Cash Basis (Direct Method) [LO4]
Refer to the data for Pavolik Company in Exercise 16–5.

Required:

Use the direct method to convert the company's income statement to a cash basis.

EXERCISE 16–7 Prepare a Statement of Cash Flows (Indirect Method) [LO2, LO3]
Comparative financial statement data for Carmono Company follow:

	2005	2004
Cash	$ 3	$ 6
Accounts receivable	22	24
Inventory	50	40
Plant and Equipment	240	200
Less accumulated depreciation	(65)	(50)
Total assets	$250	$220
Accounts payable	$ 40	$ 36
Common stock	150	145
Retained earnings	60	39
Total liabilities and stockholders' equity	$250	$220

For 2005, the company reported net income as follows:

Sales	$275
Cost of goods sold	150
Gross margin	125
Operating expenses	90
Net income	$ 35

Dividends of $14 were declared and paid during 2005.

Required:
Using the indirect method, prepare a statement of cash flows for 2005.

EXERCISE 16–8 (Appendix 16A) Net Cash Provided by Operating Activities (Direct Method) [LO4]
Refer to the data for Carmono Company in Exercise 16–7.

Required:
Using the direct method, convert the company's income statement to a cash basis.

Problems

PROBLEM 16–9 Classifying Transactions on a Statement of Cash Flows [LO1, LO2]
Below are a number of transactions that took place in Seneca Company during the past year:

a. Common stock was sold for cash.
b. Interest was paid on a note, decreasing Interest Payable.
c. Bonds were retired.
d. A long-term loan was made to a subsidiary.
e. Interest was received on the loan in (d) above, reducing Interest Receivable.
f. A stock dividend was declared and issued on common stock.
g. A building was acquired by issuing shares of common stock.
h. Equipment was sold for cash.
i. Short-term investments were sold.
j. Cash dividends were declared and paid.
k. Preferred stock was converted into common stock.
l. Deferred Income Taxes, a long-term liability, was reduced.
m. Dividends were received on stock of another company held as an investment.
n. Equipment was purchased by giving a long-term note to the seller.

Required:
Prepare an answer sheet with the following column headings:

Transaction	Source, Use, or Neither	Activity: Operating	Activity: Investing	Activity: Financing	Reported in a Separate Schedule	Not on the Statement

Enter the letter of the transaction in the left column and indicate whether the transaction would be a source, use, or neither. Then place an X in the appropriate column to show the proper classification of the transaction on the statement of cash flows, or to show if it would not appear on the statement at all.

PROBLEM 16–10 Prepare a Statement of Cash Flows (Indirect Method) [LO2, LO3]

Balance sheet accounts for Joyner Company contained the following amounts at the end of Years 1 and 2:

Microsoft Excel - Problem 16-10 screen capture.xls

	A	B	C
1		*Year 2*	*Year 1*
2	*Debit Balance Accounts*		
3	Cash	$ 4,000	$ 21,000
4	Accounts Receivable	250,000	170,000
5	Inventory	310,000	260,000
6	Prepaid Expenses	7,000	14,000
7	Loan to Hymas Company	40,000	-
8	Plant and Equipment	510,000	400,000
9	Total debits	$1,121,000	$ 865,000
10			
11	*Credit Balance Accounts*		
12	Accumulated Depreciation	$ 132,000	$ 120,000
13	Accounts Payable	310,000	250,000
14	Accrued Liabilities	20,000	30,000
15	Bonds Payable	190,000	70,000
16	Deferred Income Taxes	45,000	42,000
17	Common Stock	300,000	270,000
18	Retained Earnings	124,000	83,000
19	Total credits	$1,121,000	$ 865,000
20			

The company's income statement for Year 2 follows:

Sales	$900,000
Less cost of goods sold	500,000
Gross margin	400,000
Less operating expenses	328,000
Net operating income	72,000
Gain on sale of equipment	8,000
Income before taxes	80,000
Less income taxes	24,000
Net income	$ 56,000

Equipment that had cost $40,000 and on which there was accumulated depreciation of $30,000 was sold during Year 2 for $18,000. Cash dividends totaling $15,000 were declared and paid during Year 2.

Required:

1. Using the indirect method, compute the net cash provided by operating activities for Year 2.
2. Prepare a statement of cash flows for Year 2.
3. Briefly explain why cash declined so sharply during the year.

PROBLEM 16–11 (Appendix 16A) Prepare and Interpret a Statement of Cash Flows (Direct Method) [LO2, LO4]

Refer to the financial statement data for Joyner Company in Problem 16–10. Sam Conway, president of the company, considers $15,000 to be the minimum cash balance for operating purposes. As can be seen from the balance sheet data, only $4,000 in cash was available at the end of the current year. The sharp decline is puzzling to Mr. Conway, particularly since sales and profits are at a record high.

Required:

1. Using the direct method, adjust the company's income statement to a cash basis for Year 2.
2. Using the data from (1) above and other data from the problem as needed, prepare a statement of cash flows for Year 2.
3. Explain why cash declined so sharply during the year.

PROBLEM 16–12 Prepare a Statement of Cash Flows (Indirect Method) [LO2, LO3]
Comparative financial statements for Weaver Company follow:

WEAVER COMPANY
Comparative Balance Sheet
December 31, 2005 and 2004

	2005	2004
Assets		
Cash	$ 9	$ 15
Accounts receivable	340	240
Inventory	125	175
Prepaid expenses	10	6
Plant and equipment	610	470
Less accumulated depreciation	(93)	(85)
Long-term investments	16	19
Total assets	$1,017	$840
Liabilities and Stockholders' Equity		
Accounts payable	$ 310	$230
Accrued liabilities	60	72
Bonds payable	290	180
Deferred income taxes	40	34
Common stock	210	250
Retained earnings	107	74
Total liabilities and stockholders' equity	$1,017	$840

WEAVER COMPANY
Income Statement
For the Year Ended December 31, 2005

Sales		$800
Less cost of goods sold		500
Gross margin		300
Less operating expenses		213
Net operating income		87
Nonoperating items:		
Gain on sale of investments	$7	
Loss on sale of equipment	4	3
Income before taxes		90
Less income taxes		27
Net income		$ 63

During 2005, the company sold some equipment for $20 that had cost $40 and on which there was accumulated depreciation of $16. In addition, the company sold long-term investments for $10 that had cost $3 when purchased several years ago. Cash dividends totaling $30 were paid during 2005.

Required:

1. Using the indirect method, determine the net cash provided by operating activities for 2005.
2. Using the information in (1) above, along with an analysis of the remaining balance sheet accounts, prepare a statement of cash flows for 2005.

PROBLEM 16–13 (Appendix 16A) Prepare a Statement of Cash Flows (Direct Method) [LO2, LO4]
Refer to the financial statement data for Weaver Company in Problem 16–12.

Required:
1. Using the direct method, adjust the company's income statement for 2005 to a cash basis.
2. Using the information obtained in (1) above, along with an analysis of the remaining balance sheet accounts, prepare a statement of cash flows for 2005.

PROBLEM 16–14 Prepare and Interpret a Statement of Cash Flows (Indirect Method) [LO2, LO3]

Mary Walker, president of Rusco Products, considers $14,000 to be the minimum cash balance for operating purposes. As can be seen from the statements below, only $8,000 in cash was available at the end of 2005. Since the company reported a large net income for the year, and also issued both bonds and common stock, the sharp decline in cash is puzzling to Ms. Walker.

RUSCO PRODUCTS
Comparative Balance Sheet
July 31, 2005 and 2004

	2005	2004
Assets		
Current assets:		
Cash	$ 8,000	$ 21,000
Accounts receivable	120,000	80,000
Inventory	140,000	90,000
Prepaid expenses	5,000	9,000
Total current assets	273,000	200,000
Long-term investments	50,000	70,000
Plant and equipment	430,000	300,000
Less accumulated depreciation	60,000	50,000
Net plant and equipment	370,000	250,000
Total assets	$693,000	$520,000
Liabilities and Stockholders' Equity		
Current liabilities:		
Accounts payable	$123,000	$ 60,000
Accrued liabilities	8,000	17,000
Total current liabilities	131,000	77,000
Bonds payable	70,000	
Deferred income taxes	20,000	12,000
Stockholders' equity:		
Preferred stock	80,000	96,000
Common stock	286,000	250,000
Retained earnings	106,000	85,000
Total stockholders' equity	472,000	431,000
Total liabilities and stockholders' equity	$693,000	$520,000

RUSCO PRODUCTS Income Statement For the Year Ended July 31, 2005		
Sales		$500,000
Less cost of goods sold		300,000
Gross margin		200,000
Less operating expenses		158,000
Net operating income		42,000
Nonoperating items:		
Gain on sale of investments	$ 10,000	
Loss on sale of equipment	2,000	8,000
Income before taxes		50,000
Less income taxes		20,000
Net income		$ 30,000

The following additional information is available for the year 2005.

a. Dividends totaling $9,000 were declared and paid in cash.
b. Equipment was sold during the year for $8,000. The equipment had originally cost $20,000 and had accumulated depreciation of $10,000.
c. The decrease in the Preferred Stock account is the result of a conversion of preferred stock into an equal dollar amount of common stock.
d. Long-term investments that had cost $20,000 were sold during the year for $30,000.

Required:

1. Using the indirect method, compute the net cash provided by operating activities for 2005.
2. Using the data from (1) above, and other data from the problem as needed, prepare a statement of cash flows for 2005.
3. Explain the major reasons for the decline in the company's cash position.

PROBLEM 16–15 (Appendix 16A) Prepare and Interpret a Statement of Cash Flows (Direct Method) [LO2, LO4]

Refer to the financial statements for Rusco Products in Problem 16–14. Since the Cash account decreased so dramatically during 2005, the company's executive committee is anxious to see how the income statement would appear on a cash basis.

Required:

1. Using the direct method, adjust the company's income statement for 2005 to a cash basis.
2. Using the data from (1) above, and other data from the problem as needed, prepare a statement of cash flows for 2005.
3. Briefly explain the major reasons for the sharp decline in cash during the year.

eXcel

PROBLEM 16–16 Missing Data; Statement of Cash Flows (Indirect Method) [LO2, LO3]

Oxident Products manufactures a vitamin supplement. The following *changes* have taken place in the company's balance sheet accounts as a result of the past year's activities:

Debit Balance Accounts	Net Increase (Decrease)
Cash	$ (10,000)
Accounts Receivable	(81,000)
Inventory	230,000
Prepaid Expenses	(6,000)
Long-Term Loans to Subsidiaries	100,000
Long-Term Investments	(120,000)
Plant and Equipment	500,000
Net increase	$ 613,000

Credit Balance Accounts	Net Increase (Decrease)
Accumulated Depreciation	$ 90,000
Accounts Payable	(70,000)
Accrued Liabilities	35,000
Bonds Payable	400,000
Deferred Income Taxes	8,000
Preferred Stock	(180,000)
Common Stock	270,000
Retained Earnings	60,000
Net increase	$ 613,000

The following additional information is available about last year's activities:

a. The company sold equipment during the year for $40,000. The equipment originally cost $100,000 and it had $70,000 in accumulated depreciation at the time of sale.
b. Net income for the year was $____?____.
c. The balance in the Cash account at the beginning of the year was $52,000; the balance at the end of the year was $____?____.
d. The company declared and paid $30,000 in cash dividends during the year.
e. Long-term investments that had cost $120,000 were sold during the year for $80,000.
f. The balances in the Plant and Equipment and Accumulated Depreciation accounts for the past year are given below:

	Ending	Beginning
Plant and Equipment	$3,200,000	$2,700,000
Accumulated Depreciation	$1,500,000	$1,410,000

g. If data are not given explaining the change in an account, make the most reasonable assumption as to the cause of the change.

Required:
Using the indirect method, prepare a statement of cash flows for the past year. Show all computations for items that appear on your statement.

PROBLEM 16–17 Worksheet; Prepare and Interpret a Statement of Cash Flows (Indirect Method) [LO2, LO3]

"See, I told you things would work out," said Barry Kresmier, president of Lomax Company. "We expanded sales from $1.6 million to $2.0 million in 2005, nearly doubled our warehouse space, and ended the year with more cash in the bank than we started with. A few more years of expansion like this and we'll be the industry leaders."

"Yes, I'll admit our statements look pretty good," replied Sheri Colson, the company's vice president. "But we're doing business with a lot of companies we don't know much about and that worries me. I'll admit, though, that we're certainly moving a lot of merchandise; our inventory is actually down from last year."

A comparative balance sheet for Lomax Company containing data for the last two years follows:

LOMAX COMPANY
Comparative Balance Sheet
December 31, 2005 and 2004

	2005	2004
Assets		
Current assets:		
Cash	$ 42,000	$ 27,000
Marketable securities	19,000	13,000
Accounts receivable	710,000	530,000
Inventory	848,000	860,000
Prepaid expenses	10,000	5,000
Total current assets	1,629,000	1,435,000
Long-term investments	60,000	110,000
Loans to subsidiaries	130,000	80,000
Plant and equipment	3,170,000	2,600,000
Less accumulated depreciation	810,000	755,000
Net plant and equipment	2,360,000	1,845,000
Goodwill	84,000	90,000
Total assets	$4,263,000	$3,560,000
Liabilities and Stockholders' Equity		
Current liabilities:		
Accounts payable	$ 970,000	$ 670,000
Accrued liabilities	65,000	82,000
Total current liabilities	1,035,000	752,000
Long-term notes	820,000	600,000
Deferred income taxes	95,000	80,000
Total liabilities	1,950,000	1,432,000
Stockholders' equity:		
Common stock	1,740,000	1,650,000
Retained earnings	573,000	478,000
Total stockholders' equity	2,313,000	2,128,000
Total liabilities and stockholders' equity	$4,263,000	$3,560,000

The following additional information is available about the company's activities during 2005:

a. Cash dividends declared and paid to the common stockholders totaled $75,000.
b. Long-term notes with a value of $380,000 were repaid during the year.
c. Equipment was sold during the year for $70,000. The equipment had cost $130,000 and had $40,000 in accumulated depreciation on the date of sale.
d. Long-term investments were sold during the year for $110,000. These investments had cost $50,000 when purchased several years ago.
e. The company's income statement for 2005 follows:

Sales		$2,000,000
Less cost of goods sold		1,300,000
Gross margin		700,000
Less operating expenses		490,000
Net operating income		210,000
Nonoperating items:		
Gain on sale of investments	$60,000	
Loss on sale of equipment	20,000	40,000
Income before taxes		250,000
Less income taxes		80,000
Net income		$170,000

Required:

1. Prepare a worksheet like Exhibit 16–10 for Lomax Company.
2. Using the indirect method, prepare a statement of cash flows for the year 2005.
3. What problems relating to the company's activities are revealed by the statement of cash flows that you have prepared?

PROBLEM 16–18 (Appendix 16A) Adjusting Net Income to a Cash Basis (Direct Method) [LO4]
Refer to the data for the Lomax Company in Problem 16–17. All of the long-term notes issued during 2005 are being held by Lomax's bank. The bank's management wants the income statement adjusted to a cash basis so that it can compare the cash basis statement to the accrual basis statement.

Required:
Use the direct method to convert Lomax Company's 2005 income statement to a cash basis.

PROBLEM 16–19 Missing Data; Statement of Cash Flows (Indirect Method) [LO2, LO3]
Below are listed the *changes* in Yoric Company's balance sheet accounts for the past year:

	Debits	Credits
Cash	$ 17,000	
Accounts Receivable	110,000	
Inventory		$ 65,000
Prepaid Expenses		8,000
Long-Term Loans to Subsidiaries		30,000
Long-Term Investments	80,000	
Plant and Equipment	220,000	
Accumulated Depreciation		5,000
Accounts Payable		32,000
Accrued Liabilities	9,000	
Bonds Payable		400,000
Deferred Income Taxes		16,000
Common Stock	170,000	
Retained Earnings		50,000
	$606,000	$606,000

The following additional information is available about last year's activities:

a. Net income for the year was $____?____.
b. The company sold equipment during the year for $15,000. The equipment originally cost $50,000 and it had $37,000 in accumulated depreciation at the time of sale.
c. Cash dividends of $20,000 were declared and paid during the year.
d. Depreciation charges for the year were $____?____.
e. The balances in the Plant and Equipment and Accumulated Depreciation accounts are given below:

	Ending	Beginning
Plant and Equipment	$1,800,000	$1,580,000
Accumulated Depreciation	$680,000	$675,000

f. The balance in the Cash account at the beginning of the year was $23,000; the balance at the end of the year was $____?____.
g. If data are not given explaining the change in an account, make the most reasonable assumption as to the cause of the change.

Required:
Using the indirect method, prepare a statement of cash flows for the year.

Group and Internet Exercises

GROUP EXERCISE 16–20 Reconciling the Statement of Cash Flows with the Balance Sheet
As shown in the chapter, it should be possible to reconcile the statement of cash flows with the changes in noncash balance sheet accounts. In practice, this is often difficult because the net change

in a balance sheet account may have been decomposed into increases and decreases in the account or it may be netted against some other change in a balance sheet account when shown on the statement of cash flows. Find the most recent annual report of a company that interests you.

Required:

As far as you can, trace the changes in the company's noncash balance sheet accounts to the statement of cash flows.

INTERNET EXERCISE 16–21

As you know, the World Wide Web is a medium that is constantly evolving. Sites come and go, and change without notice. To enable periodic updating of site addresses, this problem has been posted to the textbook website (www.mhhe.com/garrison11e). After accessing the site, enter the Student Center and select this chapter. Select and complete the Internet Exercise.

Chapter

17

"How Well Am I Doing?" Financial Statement Analysis

LEARNING OBJECTIVES

After studying Chapter 17, you should be able to:

LO1 Prepare and interpret financial statements in comparative and common-size form.

LO2 Compute and interpret financial ratios that would be useful to a common stockholder.

LO3 Compute and interpret financial ratios that would be useful to a short-term creditor.

LO4 Compute and interpret financial ratios that would be useful to a long-term creditor.

Getting Paid on Time

BUSINESS FOCUS

Rick Burrock, the managing director of a Minneapolis-based accounting firm, advises his small business clients to keep a tight rein on credit extended to customers. "You need to convey to your customers, right from the beginning, that you will work very hard to satisfy them and that, in return, you expect to be paid on time. Start by investigating all new customers. A credit report helps, but with a business customer you can find out even more by requesting financial statements . . . Using the balance sheet, divide current assets by current liabilities to calculate the current ratio. If a company's current ratio is below 1.00, it will be paying out more than it expects to collect; you may want to reconsider doing business with that company or insist on stricter credit terms." ■

Source: Jill Andresky Fraser, © 2004 Gruner + Jahr USA Publishing. First published in Inc. Magazine. Reprinted with permission.

All financial statements are historical documents. They tell what *has happened* during a particular period. However, most users of financial statements are concerned with what *will happen* in the future. For example, stockholders are concerned with future earnings and dividends and creditors are concerned with the company's future ability to repay its debts. While financial statements are historical in nature, they can still provide valuable insights to users regarding financial matters. These users rely on *financial statement analysis,* which involves examining trends in key financial data, comparing financial data across companies, and analyzing financial ratios to assess the financial health and future prospects of a company. In this chapter, we focus our attention on the most important ratios and other analytical tools that financial analysts use.

In addition to stockholders and creditors, managers are also vitally concerned with the financial ratios discussed in this chapter. First, the ratios provide indicators of how well the company and its business units are performing. Some of these ratios might be used in a balanced scorecard approach as discussed in Chapter 10. The specific ratios selected depend on the company's strategy. For example, a company that wants to emphasize responsiveness to customers may closely monitor the inventory turnover ratio discussed later in this chapter. Second, since managers must report to stockholders and may wish to raise funds from external sources, managers must pay attention to the financial ratios used by external investors to evaluate the company's investment potential and creditworthiness.

Limitations of Financial Statement Analysis

Although financial statement analysis is a useful tool, it has two limitations that we must mention before proceeding any further. These two limitations involve the comparability of financial data between companies and the need to look beyond ratios.

Comparison of Financial Data

Comparisons of one company with another can provide valuable clues about the financial health of an organization. Unfortunately, differences in accounting methods between companies sometimes make it difficult to compare their financial data. For example, if one company values its inventories by the LIFO method and another company by the average cost method, then direct comparisons of their financial data such as inventory valuations and cost of goods sold may be misleading. Sometimes enough data are presented in footnotes to the financial statements to restate data to a comparable basis. Otherwise, the analyst should keep in mind the lack of comparability before drawing definite conclusions. Even with this limitation in mind, comparisons of key ratios with other companies and with industry averages often suggest avenues for further investigation.

The Need to Look beyond Ratios

Ratios should not be viewed as an end, but rather as a *starting point.* They raise many questions and point to opportunities for further analysis, but they rarely answer any questions by themselves. In addition to ratios, other sources of data should be analyzed in order to make judgments about the future of an organization. For example, the analyst should evaluate industry trends, technological changes, changes in consumer tastes, changes in broad economic factors, and changes within the company itself. A recent change in a key management position, for example, might provide a basis for optimism about the future, even though the past performance of the company may have been mediocre.

Statements in Comparative and Common-Size Form

LEARNING OBJECTIVE 1
Prepare and interpret financial statements in comparative and common-size form.

An item on a balance sheet or income statement has little meaning by itself. Suppose a company's sales for a year were $250 million. In isolation, that is not particularly useful information. How does that stack up against last year's sales? How do the sales relate to the cost of goods sold? In making these kinds of comparisons, three analytical techniques are widely used:

1. Dollar and percentage changes on statements (*horizontal analysis*).
2. Common-size statements (*vertical analysis*).
3. Ratios.

The first and second techniques are discussed in this section; the third technique is discussed in the remainder of the chapter. Throughout the chapter, we will illustrate these analytical techniques using the financial statements of Brickey Electronics, a producer of specialized electronic components.

Dollar and Percentage Changes on Statements

Horizontal analysis (also known as **trend analysis**) involves analyzing financial data over time. This can involve nothing more complicated than showing year-to-year changes in each financial statement item in both dollar and percentage terms. Exhibits 17–1 and 17–2 show Brickey Electronics' financial statements in this *comparative form.* The dollar changes serve to highlight the changes that are the most important economically; the percentage changes serve to highlight the changes that are the most unusual.

Horizontal analysis can be even more useful when data from a number of years are used to compute *trend percentages.* To compute **trend percentages,** a base year is selected and the data for all years are stated in terms of a percentage of that base year. To illustrate, consider the sales and net income of McDonald's Corporation, the world's largest food service retailer, with more than 31,000 restaurants worldwide:

17–1

	2002	2001	2000	1999	1998	1997	1996	1995	1994	1993
Sales (millions)	$15,406	$14,870	$14,243	$13,259	$12,421	$11,409	$10,687	$9,795	$8,321	$7,408
Net income (millions) . .	$894	$1,637	$1,977	$1,948	$1,550	$1,642	$1,573	$1,427	$1,224	$1,083

Be careful to note that the above data have been arranged with the most recent year on the left. This may be the opposite of what you are used to, but it is the way financial data are commonly displayed in annual reports and other sources. By simply looking at these data, one can see that sales increased every year, but the net income has not. However, recasting these data into trend percentages aids interpretation:

	2002	2001	2000	1999	1998	1997	1996	1995	1994	1993
Sales (millions)	208%	201%	192%	179%	168%	154%	144%	132%	112%	100%
Net income (millions) . . .	83%	151%	183%	180%	143%	152%	145%	132%	113%	100%

In the above table, both sales and net income have been put into percentage terms, using 1993 as the base year. For example, the 2002 sales of $15,406 are 208% of the 1993 sales of $7,408. This trend analysis is particularly striking when the data are plotted as in Exhibit 17–3. McDonald's sales growth was impressive throughout the entire 10-year period and was closely tracked by net income for the first part of this period, but net income faltered in 1998 and then plummeted in 2001 and 2002.

Common-Size Statements

Horizontal analysis, which was discussed in the previous section, examines changes in a financial statement item over time. **Vertical analysis** focuses on the relations among

EXHIBIT 17–1

BRICKEY ELECTRONICS
Comparative Balance Sheet
December 31, 2005 and 2004
(dollars in thousands)

			Increase (Decrease)	
	2005	2004	Amount	Percent
Assets				
Current assets:				
Cash	$ 1,200	$ 2,350	$(1,150)	(48.9)%*
Accounts receivable, net	6,000	4,000	2,000	50.0%
Inventory	8,000	10,000	(2,000)	(20.0)%
Prepaid expenses	300	120	180	150.0%
Total current assets	15,500	16,470	(970)	(5.9)%
Property and equipment:				
Land	4,000	4,000	0	0%
Buildings and equipment, net	12,000	8,500	3,500	41.2%
Total property and equipment	16,000	12,500	3,500	28.0%
Total assets	$31,500	$28,970	$ 2,530	8.7%
Liabilities and Stockholders' Equity				
Current liabilities:				
Accounts payable	$ 5,800	$ 4,000	$ 1,800	45.0%
Accrued payables	900	400	500	125.0%
Notes payable, short term	300	600	(300)	(50.0)%
Total current liabilities	7,000	5,000	2,000	40.0%
Long-term liabilities:				
Bonds payable, 8%	7,500	8,000	(500)	(6.3)%
Total liabilities	14,500	13,000	1,500	11.5%
Stockholders' equity:				
Preferred stock, $100 par, 6%	2,000	2,000	0	0%
Common stock, $12 par	6,000	6,000	0	0%
Additional paid-in capital	1,000	1,000	0	0%
Total paid-in capital	9,000	9,000	0	0%
Retained earnings	8,000	6,970	1,030	14.8%
Total stockholders' equity	17,000	15,970	1,030	6.4%
Total liabilities and stockholders' equity	$31,500	$28,970	$ 2,530	8.7%

*Since we are measuring the amount of change between 2004 and 2005, the dollar amounts for 2004 become the base figures for expressing these changes in percentage form. For example, Cash decreased by $1,150 between 2004 and 2005. This decrease expressed in percentage form is computed as follows: $1,150 ÷ $2,350 = 48.9%. Other percentage figures in this exhibit and Exhibit 17–2 are computed in the same way.

financial statement items at a given point in time. A **common-size financial statement** is a vertical analysis in which each financial statement item is expressed as a percentage. In income statements, all items are usually expressed as a percentage of sales. In balance sheets, all items are usually expressed as a percentage of total assets. Exhibit 17–4 (page 792) contains a common-size balance sheet for Brickey Electronics and Exhibit 17–5 (page 793) contains a common-size income statement for the company.

Notice from Exhibit 17–4 that placing all assets in common-size form clearly shows the relative importance of the current assets as compared to the noncurrent assets. It also shows that significant changes have taken place in the composition of the current assets

EXHIBIT 17–2

BRICKEY ELECTRONICS
Comparative Income Statement and Reconciliation of Retained Earnings
For the Years Ended December 31, 2005 and 2004
(dollars in thousands)

			Increase (Decrease)	
	2005	2004	Amount	Percent
Sales	$52,000	$48,000	$4,000	8.3%
Cost of goods sold	36,000	31,500	4,500	14.3%
Gross margin	16,000	16,500	(500)	(3.0)%
Operating expenses:				
Selling expenses	7,000	6,500	500	7.7%
Administrative expenses	5,860	6,100	(240)	(3.9)%
Total operating expenses	12,860	12,600	260	2.1%
Net operating income	3,140	3,900	(760)	(19.5)%
Interest expense	640	700	(60)	(8.6)%
Net income before taxes	2,500	3,200	(700)	(21.9)%
Less income taxes (30%)	750	960	(210)	(21.9)%
Net income	1,750	2,240	$ (490)	(21.9)%
Dividends to preferred stockholders, $6 per share (see Exhibit 17–1)	120	120		
Net income remaining for common stockholders	1,630	2,120		
Dividends to common stockholders, $1.20 per share	600	600		
Net income added to retained earnings	1,030	1,520		
Retained earnings, beginning of year	6,970	5,450		
Retained earnings, end of year	$ 8,000	$ 6,970		

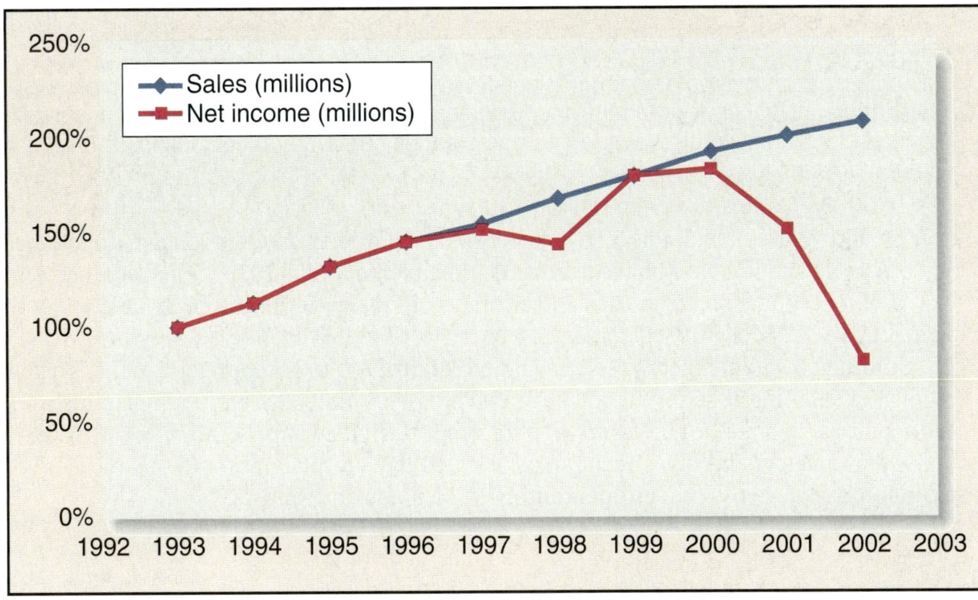

EXHIBIT 17–3
McDonald's Corporation: Trend Analysis of Sales and Net Income

EXHIBIT 17–4

BRICKEY ELECTRONICS
Common-Size Comparative Balance Sheet
December 31, 2005 and 2004
(dollars in thousands)

			Common-Size Percentages	
	2005	2004	2005	2004
Assets				
Current assets:				
Cash	$ 1,200	$ 2,350	3.8%*	8.1%
Accounts receivable, net	6,000	4,000	19.0%	13.8%
Inventory	8,000	10,000	25.4%	34.5%
Prepaid expenses	300	120	1.0%	0.4%
Total current assets	15,500	16,470	49.2%	56.9%
Property and equipment:				
Land	4,000	4,000	12.7%	13.8%
Buildings and equipment, net	12,000	8,500	38.1%	29.3%
Total property and equipment	16,000	12,500	50.8%	43.1%
Total assets	$31,500	$28,970	100.0%	100.0%
Liabilities and Stockholders' Equity				
Current liabilities:				
Accounts payable	$ 5,800	$ 4,000	18.4%	13.8%
Accrued payables	900	400	2.9%	1.4%
Notes payable, short term	300	600	1.0%	2.1%
Total current liabilities	7,000	5,000	22.2%	17.3%
Long-term liabilities:				
Bonds payable, 8%	7,500	8,000	23.8%	27.6%
Total liabilities	14,500	13,000	46.0%	44.9%
Stockholders' equity:				
Preferred stock, $100, 6%	2,000	2,000	6.3%	6.9%
Common stock, $12 par	6,000	6,000	19.0%	20.7%
Additional paid-in capital	1,000	1,000	3.2%	3.5%
Total paid-in capital	9,000	9,000	28.6%	31.1%
Retained earnings	8,000	6,970	25.4%	24.1%
Total stockholders' equity	17,000	15,970	54.0%	55.1%
Total liabilities and stockholders' equity	$31,500	$28,970	100.0%	100.0%

*Each asset account on a common-size statement is expressed in terms of total assets, and each liability and equity account is expressed in terms of total liabilities and stockholders' equity. For example, the percentage figure above for Cash in 2005 is computed as follows: $1,200 ÷ $31,500 = 3.8%.

over the last year. For example, accounts receivable have increased in relative importance and both cash and inventory have declined in relative importance. Judging from the sharp increase in accounts receivable, the deterioration in the cash position may be a result of an inability to collect from customers.

Shifting now to the income statement, in Exhibit 17–5 the cost of goods sold as a percentage of sales increased from 65.6% in 2004 to 69.2% in 2005. Or looking at this from a different viewpoint, the *gross margin percentage* declined from 34.4% in 2004 to 30.8% in 2005. Managers and investment analysts often pay close attention to this measure of profitability. The **gross margin percentage** is computed as follows:

$$\text{Gross margin percentage} = \frac{\text{Gross margin}}{\text{Sales}}$$

EXHIBIT 17–5

BRICKEY ELECTRONICS
Common-Size Comparative Income Statement
For the Years Ended December 31, 2005 and 2004
(dollars in thousands)

			Common-Size Percentages	
	2005	2004	2005	2004
Sales	$52,000	$48,000	100.0%	100.0%
Cost of goods sold	36,000	31,500	69.2%	65.6%
Gross margin	16,000	16,500	30.8%	34.4%
Operating expenses:				
Selling expenses	7,000	6,500	13.5%	13.5%
Administrative expenses	5,860	6,100	11.3%	12.7%
Total operating expenses	12,860	12,600	24.7%	26.3%
Net operating income	3,140	3,900	6.0%	8.1%
Interest expense	640	700	1.2%	1.5%
Net income before taxes	2,500	3,200	4.8%	6.7%
Income taxes (30%)	750	960	1.4%	2.0%
Net income	$ 1,750	$ 2,240	3.4%	4.7%

*Note that the percentage figures for each year are expressed in terms of total sales for the year. For example, the percentage figure for cost of goods sold in 2005 is computed as follows:
$36,000 ÷ $52,000 = 69.2%

The gross margin percentage should be more stable for retailing companies than for other companies since the cost of goods sold in retailing excludes fixed costs. When fixed costs are included in the cost of goods sold, the gross margin percentage should increase and decrease with sales volume. With increases in sales volume, the fixed costs are spread across more units and the gross margin percentage improves.

Common-size statements are particularly useful when comparing data from different companies. For example, in 2002, Wendy's net income was $219 million, whereas McDonald's was $893 million. This comparison is somewhat misleading because of the dramatically different sizes of the two companies. To put this in better perspective, net income can be expressed as a percentage of the sales revenues of each company. Since Wendy's sales revenues were $2,730 million and McDonald's were $15,406 million, Wendy's net income as a percentage of sales was about 8.0% and McDonald's was about 5.8%. In this light, McDonald's performance does not compare favorably with Wendy's performance.

IN BUSINESS

GROSS MARGINS CAN MAKE THE DIFFERENCE

After announcing a 42% increase in quarterly profits, Dell Computer Corp.'s shares fell over 6%. Why? According to *The Wall Street Journal*, investors focused on the company's eroding profit margins. "Analysts . . . said that a decline in gross margins was larger than they had expected and indicated a difficult pricing environment. Gross margins fell nearly a full percentage point to 21.5% of sales, from 22.4%." Dell had cut its prices to increase its market share, which worked, but at the cost of lowered profitability.

Source: Gary McWilliams, "Dell Net Rises, but Margins Spur Worries," *The Wall Street Journal*, May 19, 1999, p. A3.

Ratio Analysis—The Common Stockholder

LEARNING OBJECTIVE 2
Compute and interpret financial ratios that would be useful to a common stockholder.

Topic Tackler PLUS 17–2

A number of financial ratios are used to assess how well a company is doing from the standpoint of its stockholders. These ratios naturally focus on net income, dividends, and stockholders' equity.

Earnings per Share

An investor buys a share of stock in the hope of realizing a return in the form of either dividends or future increases in the value of the stock. Since earnings form the basis for dividend payments, as well as the basis for future increases in the value of shares, investors are always interested in a company's reported *earnings per share.* Probably no single statistic is more widely quoted or relied on by investors than earnings per share, although it has some inherent limitations, as discussed below.

Earnings per share is computed by dividing net income available for common stockholders by the average number of common shares outstanding during the year. "Net income available for common stockholders" is net income less dividends paid to the owners of the company's preferred stock.[1]

$$\text{Earnings per share} = \frac{\text{Net income} - \text{Preferred dividends}}{\text{Average number of common shares outstanding}}$$

Using the data in Exhibits 17–1 and 17–2, we see that the earnings per share for Brickey Electronics for 2005 would be computed as follows:

$$\frac{\$1{,}750{,}000 - \$120{,}000}{(500{,}000 \text{ shares}^* + 500{,}000 \text{ shares})/2} = \$3.26 \text{ per share}$$

*$6,000,000 ÷ 12 = 500,000 shares.

Price-Earnings Ratio

The relationship between the market price of a share of stock and the stock's current earnings per share is often stated in terms of a **price-earnings ratio.** If we assume that the current market price for Brickey Electronics' stock is $40 per share, the company's price-earnings ratio would be computed as follows:

$$\text{Price-earnings ratio} = \frac{\text{Market price per share}}{\text{Earnings per share}}$$

$$= \frac{\$40 \text{ per share}}{\$3.26 \text{ per share}} = 12.3$$

The price-earnings ratio is 12.3; that is, the stock is selling for about 12.3 times its current earnings per share.

The price-earnings ratio is widely used by investors. A high price-earnings ratio means that investors are willing to pay a premium for the company's stock—presumably because the company is expected to have higher than average future earnings growth. Conversely, if investors believe a company's future earnings growth prospects are limited, the company's price-earnings ratio would be relatively low. In the late 1990s, the stock

[1] Another complication can arise when a company has issued securities such as executive stock options or warrants that can be converted into shares of common stock. If these conversions were to take place, the same earnings would have to be distributed among a greater number of common shares. Therefore, a supplemental earnings per share figure, called diluted earnings per share, may have to be computed. Refer to a current intermediate financial accounting text for details.

prices of some dot.com companies—particularly those with little or no earnings—were selling at levels that resulted in unprecedented price-earnings ratios. Many commentators cautioned that these price-earnings ratios were unsustainable in the long run—and they were right. The stock prices of almost all dot.com companies subsequently crashed.

Dividend Payout and Yield Ratios

Investors in a company's stock make money in two ways—increases in the market value of the stock and dividends. In general, earnings should be retained in a company and not paid out in dividends as long as the rate of return on funds invested inside the company exceeds the rate of return that stockholders could earn on alternative investments outside the company. Therefore, companies with excellent prospects of profitable growth often pay little or no dividend. Companies with little opportunity for profitable growth, but with steady, dependable earnings, tend to pay out a higher percentage of their earnings as dividends.

The Dividend Payout Ratio

The **dividend payout ratio** gauges the portion of current earnings being paid out in dividends. Investors who seek market price growth would like this ratio to be small, whereas investors who seek dividends prefer it to be large. This ratio is computed by relating dividends per share to earnings per share for common stock:

$$\text{Dividend payout ratio} = \frac{\text{Dividends per share}}{\text{Earnings per share}}$$

For Brickey Electronics, the dividend payout ratio for 2005 is computed as follows:

$$\frac{\$1.20 \text{ per share (see Exhibit 17–2)}}{\$3.26 \text{ per share}} = 36.8\%$$

There is no such thing as a "right" dividend payout ratio, even though it should be noted that the ratio tends to be similar for companies within a particular industry. As noted above, companies with ample opportunities for growth at high rates of return on assets tend to have low payout ratios, whereas companies with limited reinvestment opportunities tend to have higher payout ratios.

The Dividend Yield Ratio

The **dividend yield ratio** is obtained by dividing the current dividends per share by the current market price per share:

$$\text{Dividend yield ratio} = \frac{\text{Dividends per share}}{\text{Market price per share}}$$

The market price for Brickey Electronics' stock is \$40 per share so the dividend yield is computed as follows:

$$\frac{\$1.20 \text{ per share}}{\$40 \text{ per share}} = 3.0\%$$

The dividend yield ratio measures the rate of return (in the form of cash dividends only) that would be earned by an investor who buys common stock at the current market price. A low dividend yield ratio is neither bad nor good by itself.

Return on Total Assets

The **return on total assets** is a measure of operating performance. It is defined as follows:

$$\text{Return on total assets} = \frac{\text{Net income} + [\text{Interest expense} \times (1 - \text{Tax rate})]}{\text{Average total assets}}$$

Adding interest expense back to net income results in an adjusted earnings figure that shows what earnings would have been if the company had no debt. With this adjustment, the return on total assets can be compared for companies with differing amounts of debt or over time for a single company that has changed its mix of debt and equity. Notice that the interest expense is placed on an after-tax basis by multiplying it by the factor (1 − Tax rate).

The return on total assets for Brickey Electronics for 2005 would be computed as follows (from Exhibits 17–1 and 17–2):

Net income	$ 1,750,000
Add back interest expense: $640,000 × (1 − 0.30)	448,000
Total (a)	$ 2,198,000
Assets, beginning of year	$28,970,000
Assets, end of year	31,500,000
Total	$60,470,000
Average total assets: $60,470,000 ÷ 2 (b)	$30,235,000
Return on total assets, (a) ÷ (b)	7.3%

Brickey Electronics has earned a return of 7.3% on average total assets employed over the last year.

Return on Common Stockholders' Equity

The **return on common stockholders' equity** is based on the book value of common stockholders' equity. It is computed as follows:

$$\text{Return on common stockholders' equity} = \frac{\text{Net income} - \text{Preferred dividends}}{\text{Average common stockholders' equity}}$$

where

$$\text{Average common stockholders' equity} = \text{Average total stockholders' equity} - \text{Average preferred stock}$$

For Brickey Electronics, the return on common stockholders' equity is 11.3% for 2005 as shown below:

Net income	$ 1,750,000
Deduct preferred dividends	120,000
Net income remaining for common stockholders (a)	$ 1,630,000
Average stockholders' equity	$16,485,000*
Deduct average preferred stock	2,000,000†
Average common stockholders' equity (b)	$14,485,000
Return on common stockholders' equity, (a) ÷ (b)	11.3%

*$15,970,000 + $17,000,000 = $32,970,000; $32,970,000 ÷ 2 = $16,485,000.
†$2,000,000 + $2,000,000 = $4,000,000; $4,000,000 ÷ 2 = $2,000,000.

Compare the return on common stockholders' equity above (11.3%) with the return on total assets computed in the preceding section (7.3%). Why is the return on common stockholders' equity so much higher? The answer lies in *financial leverage.*

Financial Leverage

Financial leverage results from the difference between the rate of return the company earns on investments in its own assets and the rate of return that the company must pay its creditors. If the rate of return on the company's assets exceeds the rate of return the company

IN BUSINESS

COMPARING BANKS

Deutsche Bank, the German banking giant, fares poorly in comparisons with its global rivals. Its net-income-to-assets ratio (i.e., return on assets) is only 0.26%, while its peers such as Citigroup and Credit Suisse have ratios of up to 0.92%. Its return on equity is only 10%, whereas the return on equity of almost all its peers is in the 14% to 16% range. One reason for Deutsche Bank's anemic performance is the bank's bloated and expensive payroll. Deutsche Bank's earnings average about $23,000 per employee. At HSBC (Hong Kong and Shanghai Banking Corporation) the figure is $32,000 per employee and at Credit Suisse it is $34,000.

Source: Justin Doebele, "Best Bank Bargain?" *Forbes*, August 9, 1999, pp. 89–90.

pays its creditors, *financial leverage is positive.* If the rate of return on the company's assets is less than the rate of return the company pays its creditors, *financial leverage is negative.*

For example, suppose that CBS's after-tax return on total assets is 12%. If the company can borrow from creditors at an after-tax cost of 7%, then financial leverage is positive. The difference of 5% (12% − 7%) will go to the common stockholders.

We can see financial leverage in operation in the case of Brickey Electronics. Notice from Exhibit 17–1 that the company pays 8% interest on its bonds payable. The after-tax interest cost of these bonds is only 5.6% [8% interest rate × (1 − 0.30) = 5.6%]. As shown earlier, the company's after-tax return on total assets is 7.3%. Since the return on total assets of 7.3% is greater than the 5.6% after-tax interest cost of the bonds, leverage is positive, and the difference goes to the common stockholders. This explains in part why the return on common stockholders' equity of 11.3% is greater than the return on total assets of 7.3%. If financial leverage is positive, having some debt in the capital structure can substantially benefit the common stockholder. For this reason, many companies try to maintain a level of debt that is considered to be normal within their industry.

Unfortunately, leverage is a two-edged sword. If assets do not earn a high enough return to cover the interest costs of debt and preferred stock dividends, then the common stockholder suffers. In that case, financial leverage is negative.

Book Value per Share

Book value per share measures the amount that would be distributed to holders of each share of common stock if all assets were sold at their balance sheet carrying amounts (i.e., book values) and if all creditors were paid off. Book value per share is based entirely on historical costs. The formula for computing it is:

$$\text{Book value per share} = \frac{\text{Common stockholders' equity (Total stockholders' equity} - \text{Preferred stock)}}{\text{Number of common shares outstanding}}$$

Total stockholders' equity (see Exhibit 17–1)	$17,000,000
Deduct preferred stock (see Exhibit 17–1)	2,000,000
Common stockholders' equity	$15,000,000

The book value per share of Brickey Electronics' common stock is computed as follows:

$$\frac{\$15{,}000{,}000}{500{,}000 \text{ shares}} = \$30 \text{ per share}$$

If this book value is compared with the $40 market value of Brickey Electronics' stock, then the stock appears to be somewhat overpriced. However, as we discussed earlier, market prices reflect expectations about future earnings and dividends, whereas book value largely reflects the results of events that have occurred in the past. Ordinarily, the market value of a stock exceeds its book value. For example, in one year, Microsoft's common stock often traded at over 4 times its book value, and Coca-Cola's market value was over 17 times its book value.

Ratio Analysis—The Short-Term Creditor

LEARNING OBJECTIVE 3
Compute and interpret financial ratios that would be useful to a short-term creditor.

Short-term creditors, such as suppliers, want to be repaid on time. Therefore, they focus on the company's cash flows and on its working capital since these are the company's primary sources of cash in the short run.

Working Capital

The excess of current assets over current liabilities is known as **working capital.** The working capital for Brickey Electronics is computed below:

$$\text{Working capital} = \text{Current assets} - \text{Current liabilities}$$

	2005	2004
Current assets	$15,500,000	$16,470,000
Current liabilities	7,000,000	5,000,000
Working capital	$ 8,500,000	$11,470,000

Ample working capital provides some assurance to short-term creditors that they will be paid by the company. However, maintaining large amounts of working capital isn't free. Working capital must be financed with long-term debt and equity—both of which are expensive. Therefore, managers often want to minimize working capital.

A large and growing working capital balance may not be a good sign. For example, it could be the result of unwarranted growth in inventories. To put the working capital figure into proper perspective, it should be supplemented with other analytical work. The following four ratios (the current ratio, the acid-test ratio, the accounts receivable turnover, and the inventory turnover) should all be used in connection with an analysis of working capital.

Current Ratio

The elements involved in the computation of working capital are frequently expressed in ratio form. A company's current assets divided by its current liabilities is known as the **current ratio:**

$$\text{Current ratio} = \frac{\text{Current assets}}{\text{Current liabilities}}$$

For Brickey Electronics, the current ratios for 2004 and 2005 would be computed as follows:

2005	**2004**
$\frac{\$15,500,000}{\$7,000,000} = 2.21$	$\frac{\$16,470,000}{\$5,000,000} = 3.29$

Although widely regarded as a measure of short-term debt-paying ability, the current ratio must be interpreted with great care. A *declining* ratio, as above, might be a sign of a deteriorating financial condition. On the other hand, it might be the result of eliminating obsolete inventories or other stagnant current assets. An *improving* ratio might be the result of stockpiling inventory, or it might indicate an improving financial situation. In short, the current ratio is useful, but tricky to interpret. To avoid a blunder, the analyst must take a hard look at the individual assets and liabilities involved.

The general rule of thumb calls for a current ratio of 2. However, many companies successfully operate with a current ratio below 2. The adequacy of a current ratio depends heavily on the *composition* of the assets. For example, as we see in the table below, both Worthington Corporation and Greystone, Inc., have current ratios of 2. However, they are not in comparable financial condition. Greystone is likely to have difficulty meeting its current financial obligations, since almost all of its current assets consist of inventory rather than more liquid assets such as cash and accounts receivable.

	Worthington Corporation	Greystone, Inc.
Current assets:		
Cash	$ 25,000	$ 2,000
Accounts receivable, net	60,000	8,000
Inventory	85,000	160,000
Prepaid expenses	5,000	5,000
Total current assets (a)	$175,000	$175,000
Current liabilities (b)	$ 87,500	$ 87,500
Current ratio, (a) ÷ (b)	2	2

Acid-Test (Quick) Ratio

The **acid-test (quick) ratio** is a much more rigorous test of a company's ability to meet its short-term debts than the current ratio. Inventories and prepaid expenses are excluded from total current assets, leaving only the more liquid (or "quick") assets to be divided by current liabilities.

$$\text{Acid-test ratio} = \frac{\text{Cash} + \text{Marketable securities} + \text{Current receivables*}}{\text{Current liabilities}}$$

*Current receivables include both accounts receivable and any short-term notes receivable.

The acid-test ratio is designed to measure how well a company can meet its obligations without having to liquidate or depend too heavily on its inventory. Ideally, each dollar of liabilities should be backed by at least $1 of quick assets. However, acid-test ratios as low as 0.3 are common.

The acid-test ratios for Brickey Electronics for 2004 and 2005 are computed below:

	2005	2004
Cash (see Exhibit 17–1)	$1,200,000	$2,350,000
Accounts receivable (see Exhibit 17–1)	6,000,000	4,000,000
Total quick assets (a)	$7,200,000	$6,350,000
Current liabilities (see Exhibit 17–1) (b)	$7,000,000	$5,000,000
Acid-test ratio, (a) ÷ (b)	1.03	1.27

Although Brickey Electronics has an acid-test ratio for 2005 that is within the acceptable range, an analyst might be concerned about several trends revealed in the company's balance sheet. Notice in Exhibit 17–1 that short-term debts are rising, while the cash position seems to be deteriorating. Perhaps the weakened cash position is a result of the increase in accounts receivable. One wonders why the accounts receivable have increased so rapidly within one year.

In short, as with the current ratio, the acid-test ratio should be interpreted with one eye on its basic components.

IN BUSINESS

TOO MUCH CASH?

Microsoft has accumulated an unprecedented hoard of cash and cash equivalents—over $49 billion at the end of fiscal year 2003 and this cash hoard is growing at the rate of about $1 billion per month. This cash hoard is large enough to give every household in the U.S. a check for $471. What does Microsoft need all this money for? Why doesn't it pay more dividends? Microsoft executives say the cash is needed for antitrust lawsuits. Critics of the company's power, including some of its competitors, claim that the cash gives the company a huge competitive advantage. Because of this huge reserve of cash, the company can afford to lose money to enter risky new markets like the Xbox game console.

Sources: Jay Greene, "Microsoft's $49 Billion 'Problem,'" *BusinessWeek*, August 11, 2003, p. 36 and the Microsoft Annual Report for the year 2003.

Accounts Receivable Turnover

The *accounts receivable turnover* and *average collection period* ratios are used to measure how quickly credit sales are converted into cash. The **accounts receivable turnover** is computed by dividing sales on account (i.e., credit sales) by the average accounts receivable balance for the year:

$$\text{Accounts receivable turnover} = \frac{\text{Sales on account}}{\text{Average accounts receivable balance}}$$

Assuming that all sales for the year were on account, the accounts receivable turnover for Brickey Electronics for 2005 would be computed as follows:

$$\frac{\text{Sales on account}}{\text{Average accounts receivable balance}} = \frac{\$52{,}000{,}000}{\$5{,}000{,}000^*} = 10.4$$

*$4,000,000 + $6,000,000 = $10,000,000; $10,000,000 ÷ 2 = $5,000,000 average.

The turnover figure can then be divided into 365 days to determine the average number of days required to collect an account (known as the **average collection period**).

$$\text{Average collection period} = \frac{365 \text{ days}}{\text{Accounts receivable turnover}}$$

The average collection period for Brickey Electronics for 2005 is computed as follows:

$$\frac{365 \text{ days}}{10.4} = 35 \text{ days}$$

This means that on average it takes 35 days to collect a credit sale. Whether this is good or bad depends on the credit terms Brickey Electronics is offering its customers. Most customers will tend to withhold payment for as long as the credit terms allow. If the credit terms are 30 days, then a 35-day average collection period would usually be viewed as very good. On the other hand, if the company's credit terms are 10 days, then a 35-day average collection period is worrisome. A long collection period may result from too many old uncollectible accounts, failure to bill promptly or follow up on late accounts, lax credit checks, and so on. In practice, average collection periods ranging all the way from 10 days to 180 days are common, depending on the industry.

Inventory Turnover

The **inventory turnover ratio** measures how many times a company's inventory has been sold and replaced during the year. It is computed by dividing the cost of goods sold by the average level of inventory on hand:

$$\text{Inventory turnover} = \frac{\text{Cost of goods sold}}{\text{Average inventory balance}}$$

The average inventory figure is the average of the beginning and ending inventory balances. Since Brickey Electronics has a beginning inventory of $10,000,000 and an ending inventory of $8,000,000, its average inventory for the year would be $9,000,000. The company's inventory turnover for 2005 would be computed as follows:

$$\frac{\text{Cost of goods sold}}{\text{Average inventory balance}} = \frac{\$36,000,000}{\$9,000,000} = 4$$

The number of days being taken on average to sell the entire inventory (called the **average sale period**) can be computed by dividing 365 by the inventory turnover figure:

$$\text{Average sale period} = \frac{\text{365 days}}{\text{Inventory turnover}}$$

$$= \frac{\text{365 days}}{\text{4 times}} = 91\tfrac{1}{4}\text{ days}$$

The average sale period varies from industry to industry. Grocery stores, with significant perishable stocks, tend to turn their inventory over very quickly. On the other hand, jewelry stores tend to turn their inventory over very slowly. In practice, average sales periods of 10 days to 90 days are common, depending on the industry.

A company whose inventory turnover ratio is much slower than the average for its industry may have too much inventory or the wrong sorts of inventory. Some managers argue that they must buy in large quantities to take advantage of quantity discounts. But these discounts must be carefully weighed against the added costs of insurance, taxes, financing, and risks of obsolescence and deterioration that result from carrying added inventories.

Inventory turnover should increase in companies that adopt Just-In-Time (JIT) methods. If properly implemented, JIT should result in both a decrease in inventories and an increase in sales due to better customer service.

Ratio Analysis—The Long-Term Creditor

LEARNING OBJECTIVE 4
Compute and interpret financial ratios that would be useful to a long-term creditor.

Long-term creditors are concerned with a company's ability to repay its loans over the long run. For example, if a company were to pay out all of its retained earnings in the form of dividends, then nothing would be left to pay back creditors. Consequently, creditors often seek protection by requiring that borrowers agree to various restrictive covenants, or rules. These restrictive covenants typically include restrictions on payment of dividends as well as rules stating that the company must maintain certain financial ratios at specified levels. Although restrictive covenants are widely used, they do not ensure that creditors will be paid when loans come due. The company still must generate sufficient earnings to cover payments.

Times Interest Earned Ratio

The most common measure of the ability of a company's operations to provide protection to long-term creditors is the **times interest earned ratio.** It is computed by dividing earnings *before* interest expense and income taxes (i.e., net operating income) by interest expense:

$$\text{Times interest earned} = \frac{\text{Earnings before interest expense and income taxes}}{\text{Interest expense}}$$

For Brickey Electronics, the times interest earned ratio for 2005 would be computed as follows:

$$\frac{\$3,140,000}{\$640,000} = 4.9$$

The times interest earned ratio is based on earnings before interest expense and income taxes because that is the amount of earnings that is available for making interest payments. Interest expenses are deducted *before* income taxes are determined; creditors have first claim on the earnings before taxes are paid.

Clearly, a times interest earned ratio of less than 1 would be inadequate. In that case, interest expenses would exceed the earnings that are available for paying interest. In contrast, an interest earned ratio of 2 or more may be considered sufficient to protect long-term creditors.

Debt-to-Equity Ratio

Long-term creditors are also concerned with a company's ability to keep a reasonable balance between its debt and equity. This balance is measured by the **debt-to-equity ratio:**

$$\text{Debt-to-equity ratio} = \frac{\text{Total liabilities}}{\text{Stockholders' equity}}$$

	2005	2004
Total liabilities (a)	$14,500,000	$13,000,000
Stockholders' equity (b)	$17,000,000	$15,970,000
Debt-to-equity ratio, (a) ÷ (b)	0.85	0.81

The debt-to-equity ratio indicates the relative proportions of debt and equity on the company's balance sheet. In 2005, creditors of Brickey Electronics were providing 85 cents for each $1 being provided by stockholders.

Creditors and stockholders have different views about the optimal level of the debt-to-equity ratio. Ordinarily, stockholders would like a lot of debt to take advantage of positive financial leverage. On the other hand, because equity represents the excess of total assets over total liabilities and hence a buffer of protection for the creditors, creditors would like to see less debt and more equity.

In practice, debt-to-equity ratios from 0.0 (no debt) to 3.0 are common. Generally speaking, in industries with little financial risk, creditors tolerate high debt-to-equity ratios. In industries with more financial risk, creditors demand lower debt-to-equity ratios.

Summary of Ratios and Sources of Comparative Ratio Data

Exhibit 17–6 (page 803) contains a summary of the ratios discussed in this chapter. The formula for each ratio and a summary comment on each ratio's significance are included in the exhibit.

Exhibit 17–7 (page 804) contains a listing of published sources that provide comparative ratio data organized by industry. These sources are used extensively by managers, investors, and analysts in doing comparative analyses and in attempting to assess the well-being of companies. The World Wide Web also contains a wealth of financial and other data. A search engine such as Google can be used to track down information on individual companies. Many companies have their own websites on which they post their latest financial reports and news of interest to potential investors. The EDGAR database listed in Exhibit 17–7 is a particularly rich source of data. It contains copies of all reports filed by companies with the SEC since about 1995—including annual reports filed as Form 10-K.

EXHIBIT 17–6
Summary of Ratios

Ratio	Formula	Significance
Gross margin percentage	Gross margin ÷ Sales	A broad measure of profitability
Earnings per share (of common stock)	(Net income − Preferred dividends) ÷ Average number of common shares outstanding	Tends to have an effect on the market price per share, as reflected in the price-earnings ratio
Price-earnings ratio	Market price per share ÷ Earnings per share	An index of whether a stock is relatively cheap or relatively expensive in relation to current earnings
Dividend payout ratio	Dividends per share ÷ Earnings per share	An index showing whether a company pays out most of its earnings in dividends or reinvests the earnings internally
Dividend yield ratio	Dividends per share ÷ Market price per share	Shows the return in terms of cash dividends being provided by a stock
Return on total assets	{Net income + [Interest expense × (1 − Tax rate)]} ÷ Average total assets	Measure of how well assets have been employed by management
Return on common stockholders' equity	(Net income − Preferred dividends) ÷ Average common stockholders' equity (Average total stockholders' equity − Average preferred stock)	When compared to the return on total assets, measures the extent to which financial leverage is working for or against common stockholders
Book value per share	Common stockholders' equity (Total stockholders' equity − Preferred stock) ÷ Number of common shares outstanding	Measures the amount that would be distributed to common stockholders if all assets were sold at their balance sheet carrying amounts and if all creditors were paid off
Working capital	Current assets − Current liabilities	Measures the company's ability to repay current liabilities using only current assets
Current ratio	Current assets ÷ Current liabilities	Test of short-term debt-paying ability
Acid-test (quick) ratio	(Cash + Marketable securities + Current receivables) ÷ Current liabilities	Test of short-term debt-paying ability without having to rely on inventory
Accounts receivable turnover	Sales on account ÷ Average accounts receivable balance	A rough measure of how many times a company's accounts receivable have been turned into cash during the year
Average collection period (age of receivables)	365 days ÷ Accounts receivable turnover	Measure of the average number of days taken to collect an account receivable
Inventory turnover ratio	Cost of goods sold ÷ Average inventory balance	Measure of how many times a company's inventory has been sold during the year
Average sale period (turnover in days)	365 days ÷ Inventory turnover	Measure of the average number of days taken to sell the inventory one time
Times interest earned	Earnings before interest expense and income taxes ÷ Interest expense	Measure of the company's ability to make interest payments
Debt-to-equity ratio	Total liabilities ÷ Stockholders' equity	Measure of the amount of assets being provided by creditors for each dollar of assets being provided by the stockholders

EXHIBIT 17–7
Sources of Financial Ratios

Source	Content
Almanac of Business and Industrial Financial Ratios, Aspen Publishers; published annually	An exhaustive source that contains common-size income statements and financial ratios by industry and by the size of companies within each industry.
AMA Annual Statement Studies, Risk Management Association; published annually.	A widely used publication that contains common-size statements and financial ratios on individual companies; the companies are arranged by industry.
EDGAR, Securities and Exchange Commission; website that is continually updated www.sec.gov	An exhaustive database accessible on the World Wide Web that contains reports filed by companies with the SEC; these reports can be downloaded.
FreeEdgar, EDGAR Online, Inc.; website that is continually updated; www.freeedgar.com	A site that allows you to search SEC filings; financial information can be downloaded directly into Excel worksheets.
Hoover's Online, Hoovers, Inc.; website that is continually updated; www.hoovers.com	A site that provides capsule profiles for 10,000 U.S. companies with links to company websites, annual reports, stock charts, news articles, and industry information.
Industry Norms & Key Business Ratios, Dun & Bradstreet; published annually	Fourteen commonly used financial ratios are computed for over 800 major industry groupings.
Mergent Industrial Manual and Mergent Bank and Finance Manual; published annually	An exhaustive source that contains financial ratios on all companies listed on the New York Stock Exchange, the American Stock Exchange, and regional American exchanges.
Standard & Poor's Industry Survey, Standard & Poor's; published annually	Various statistics, including some financial ratios, are given by industry and for leading companies within each industry grouping.

Summary

The data contained in financial statements represent a quantitative summary of a company's operations and activities. Someone who is skillful at analyzing these statements can learn much about a company's strengths, weaknesses, emerging problems, operating efficiency, profitability, and so forth.

Many techniques are available to analyze financial statements and to assess the direction and importance of trends and changes. In this chapter, we have discussed three such analytical techniques—dollar and percentage changes in statements, common-size statements, and ratio analysis. Refer to Exhibit 17–6 for a detailed listing of the ratios.

Review Problem: Selected Ratios and Financial Leverage

Starbucks Coffee Company is the leading retailer and roaster of specialty coffee in North America with over 1,000 stores offering freshly brewed coffee, pastries, and coffee beans. Data (slightly modified) from the company's financial statements are given below:

STARBUCKS COFFEE COMPANY
Comparative Balance Sheet
(dollars in millions)

	End of Year	Beginning of Year
Assets		
Current assets:		
Cash	$ 113	$ 71
Marketable securities	107	61
Accounts receivable	90	76
Inventories	221	202
Other current assets	63	48
Total current assets	594	458
Property and equipment, net	1,136	931
Other assets	121	103
Total assets	$1,851	$1,492
Liabilities and Stockholders' Equity		
Current liabilities:		
Accounts payable	$128	$74
Short-term bank loans	62	56
Accrued payables	245	174
Other current liabilities	10	8
Total current liabilities	445	312
Long-term liabilities	30	32
Total liabilities	475	344
Stockholders' equity:		
Preferred stock	0	0
Common stock and additional paid-in capital	792	751
Retained earnings	584	397
Total stockholders' equity	1,376	1,148
Total liabilities and stockholders' equity	$1,851	$1,492

STARBUCKS COFFEE COMPANY
Income Statement
(dollars in millions)

	Current Year
Revenue	$2,678
Cost of goods sold	1,113
Gross margin	1,565
Operating expenses:	
Store operating expenses	875
Other operating expenses	93
Depreciation and amortization	164
General and administrative expenses	151
Total operating expenses	1,283
Net operating income	282
Less internet investment losses	3
Plus interest income	11
Less interest expense	0
Net income before taxes	290
Less income taxes (about 37%)	108
Net income	$ 182

Required:

For the current year:

1. Compute the return on total assets.
2. Compute the return on common stockholders' equity.
3. Is Starbucks' financial leverage positive or negative? Explain.
4. Compute the current ratio.
5. Compute the acid-test (quick) ratio.
6. Compute the inventory turnover.
7. Compute the average sale period.
8. Compute the debt-to-equity ratio.

Solution to Review Problem

1. Return on total assets:

$$\text{Return on total assets} = \frac{\text{Net income} + [\text{Interest expense} \times (1 - \text{Tax rate})]}{\text{Average total assets}}$$

$$= \frac{\$182 + [\$0 \times (1 - 0.37)]}{(\$1{,}851 + \$1{,}492)/2} = 10.9\% \text{ (rounded)}$$

2. Return on common stockholders' equity:

$$\text{Return on common stockholders' equity} = \frac{\text{Net income} - \text{Preferred dividends}}{\text{Average common stockholders' equity}}$$

$$= \frac{\$182 - \$0}{(\$1{,}376 + \$1{,}148)/2} = 14.4\% \text{ (rounded)}$$

3. The company has positive financial leverage, since the return on common stockholders' equity of 14.4% is greater than the return on total assets of 10.9%. The positive financial leverage was obtained from current and long-term liabilities.
4. Current ratio:

$$\text{Current ratio} = \frac{\text{Current assets}}{\text{Current liabilities}}$$

$$= \frac{\$594}{\$445} = 1.33 \text{ (rounded)}$$

5. Acid-test (quick) ratio:

$$\text{Acid-test ratio} = \frac{\text{Cash} + \text{Marketable securities} + \text{Current receivables}}{\text{Current liabilities}}$$

$$= \frac{\$113 + \$107 + \$90}{\$445} = 0.70 \text{ (rounded)}$$

6. Inventory turnover:

$$\text{Inventory turnover} = \frac{\text{Cost of goods sold}}{\text{Average inventory balance}}$$

$$= \frac{\$1{,}113}{(\$221 + \$202)/2} = 5.26 \text{ (rounded)}$$

7. Average sale period:

$$\text{Average sale period} = \frac{365 \text{ days}}{\text{Inventory turnover}}$$

$$= \frac{365 \text{ days}}{5.26} = 69 \text{ days (rounded)}$$

8. Debt-to-equity ratio:

$$\text{Debt-to-equity ratio} = \frac{\text{Total liabilities}}{\text{Stockholders' equity}}$$

$$= \frac{\$445 + \$30}{\$1{,}376} = 0.35 \text{ (rounded)}$$

Glossary

(Note: Definitions and formulas for all financial ratios are shown in Exhibit 17–7. These definitions and formulas are not repeated here.)

Common-size financial statements A statement that shows the items appearing on it in percentage form as well as in dollar form. On the income statement, the percentages are based on total sales revenue; on the balance sheet, the percentages are based on total assets. (p. 790)

Financial leverage A difference between the rate of return on assets and the rate paid to creditors. (p. 796)

Horizontal analysis A side-by-side comparison of two or more years' financial statements. (p. 789)

Trend analysis See *Horizontal analysis.* (p. 789)

Trend percentages Several years of financial data expressed as a percentage of performance in a base year. (p. 789)

Vertical analysis The presentation of a company's financial statements in common-size form. (p. 789)

Questions

17–1 Distinguish between horizontal and vertical analysis of financial statement data.

17–2 What is the basic purpose for examining trends in a company's financial ratios and other data? What other kinds of comparisons might an analyst make?

17–3 Assume that two companies in the same industry have equal earnings. Why might these companies have different price-earnings ratios? If a company has a price-earnings ratio of 20 and reports earnings per share for the current year of $4, at what price would you expect to find the stock selling on the market?

17–4 Would you expect a company in a rapidly growing technological industry to have a high or low dividend payout ratio?

17–5 What is meant by the dividend yield on a common stock investment?

17–6 What is meant by the term *financial leverage?*

17–7 The president of a medium-size plastics company was quoted in a business journal as stating, "We haven't had a dollar of interest-paying debt in over 10 years. Not many companies can say that." As a stockholder in this company, how would you feel about its policy of not taking on interest-paying debt?

17–8 If a stock's market value exceeds its book value, then the stock is overpriced. Do you agree? Explain.

17–9 A company seeking a line of credit at a bank was turned down. Among other things, the bank stated that the company's 2 to 1 current ratio was not adequate. Give reasons why a 2 to 1 current ratio might not be adequate.

Exercises

EXERCISE 17–1 Common-Size Income Statement [LO1]

A comparative income statement is given below for McKenzie Sales, Ltd., of Toronto:

MCKENZIE SALES, LTD.
Comparative Income Statement

	This Year	Last Year
Sales	$8,000,000	$6,000,000
Less cost of goods sold	4,984,000	3,516,000
Gross margin	3,016,000	2,484,000
Less operating expenses:		
Selling expenses	1,480,000	1,092,000
Administrative expenses	712,000	618,000
Total expenses	2,192,000	1,710,000
Net operating income	824,000	774,000
Less interest expense	96,000	84,000
Net income before taxes	$ 728,000	$ 690,000

Members of the company's board of directors are surprised to see that net income increased by only $38,000 when sales increased by two million dollars.

Required:

1. Express each year's income statement in common-size percentages. Carry computations to one decimal place.
2. Comment briefly on the changes between the two years.

EXERCISE 17–2 Financial Ratios for Common Stockholders [LO2]

Comparative financial statements for Weller Corporation for the fiscal year ending December 31 appear below. The company did not issue any new common or preferred stock during the year. A total of 800,000 shares of common stock were outstanding. The interest rate on the bond payable was 12%, the income tax rate was 40%, and the dividend per share of common stock was $0.25. The market value of the company's common stock at the end of the year was $18. All of the company's sales are on account.

WELLER CORPORATION
Comparative Balance Sheet
(dollars in thousands)

	This Year	Last Year
Assets		
Current assets:		
Cash	$ 1,280	$ 1,560
Accounts receivable, net	12,300	9,100
Inventory	9,700	8,200
Prepaid expenses	1,800	2,100
Total current assets	25,080	20,960
Property and equipment:		
Land	6,000	6,000
Buildings and equipment, net	19,200	19,000
Total property and equipment	25,200	25,000
Total assets	$50,280	$45,960
Liabilities and Stockholders' Equity		
Current liabilities:		
Accounts payable	$ 9,500	$ 8,300
Accrued payables	600	700
Notes payable, short term	300	300
Total current liabilities	10,400	9,300
Long-term liabilities:		
Bonds payable	5,000	5,000
Total liabilities	15,400	14,300

continued

Stockholders' equity:		
Preferred stock	2,000	2,000
Common stock	800	800
Additional paid-in capital	2,200	2,200
Total paid-in capital	5,000	5,000
Retained earnings	29,880	26,660
Total stockholders' equity	34,880	31,660
Total liabilities and stockholders' equity	$50,280	$45,960

WELLER CORPORATION
Comparative Income Statement and Reconciliation
(dollars in thousands)

	This Year	Last Year
Sales	$79,000	$74,000
Cost of goods sold	52,000	48,000
Gross margin	27,000	26,000
Operating expenses:		
Selling expenses	8,500	8,000
Administrative expenses	12,000	11,000
Total operating expenses	20,500	19,000
Net operating income	6,500	7,000
Interest expense	600	600
Net income before taxes	5,900	6,400
Less income taxes	2,360	2,560
Net income	3,540	3,840
Dividends to preferred stockholders	120	400
Net income remaining for common stockholders	3,420	3,440
Dividends to common stockholders	200	200
Net income added to retained earnings	3,220	3,240
Retained earnings, beginning of year	26,660	23,420
Retained earnings, end of year	$29,880	$26,660

Required:
Compute the following financial ratios for common stockholders for this year:
1. Gross margin percentage.
2. Earnings per share of common stock.
3. Price-earnings ratio.
4. Dividend payout ratio.
5. Dividend yield ratio.
6. Return on total assets.
7. Return on common stockholders' equity.
8. Book value per share.

EXERCISE 17–3 Financial Ratios for Short-Term Creditors [LO3]
Refer to the data in Exercise 17–2 for Weller Corporation.

Required:
Compute the following financial data for short-term creditors for this year:
1. Working capital.
2. Current ratio.
3. Acid-test ratio.
4. Accounts receivable turnover. (Assume that all sales are on account.)
5. Average collection period.
6. Inventory turnover.
7. Average sale period.

EXERCISE 17–4 Financial Ratios for Long-Term Creditors [LO4]

Refer to the data in Exercise 17–2 for Weller Corporation.

Required:

Compute the following financial ratios for long-term creditors for this year:

1. Times interest earned ratio.
2. Debt-to-equity ratio.

EXERCISE 17–5 Selected Financial Ratios for Common Stockholders [LO2]

Selected financial data from the June 30 year-end statements of Safford Company are given below:

Total assets	$3,600,000
Long-term debt (12% interest rate)	$500,000
Preferred stock, $100 par, 8%	$900,000
Total stockholders' equity	$2,400,000
Interest paid on long-term debt	$60,000
Net income	$280,000

Total assets at the beginning of the year were $3,000,000; total stockholders' equity was $2,200,000. There has been no change in preferred stock during the year. The company's tax rate is 30%.

Required:

1. Compute the return on total assets.
2. Compute the return on common stockholders' equity.
3. Is financial leverage positive or negative? Explain.

EXERCISE 17–6 Selected Financial Measures for Short-Term Creditors [LO3]

Norsk Optronics, ALS, of Bergen, Norway, had a current ratio of 2.5 on June 30 of the current year. On that date, the company's assets were:

Cash	Kr 90,000
Accounts receivable, net	260,000
Inventory	490,000
Prepaid expenses	10,000
Plant and equipment, net	800,000
Total assets	Kr1,650,000

The Norwegian currency is the krone, denoted here by the symbol Kr.

Required:

1. What was the company's working capital on June 30?
2. What was the company's acid-test (quick) ratio on June 30?
3. The company paid an account payable of Kr40,000 immediately after June 30.
   a. What effect did this transaction have on working capital? Show computations.
   b. What effect did this transaction have on the current ratio? Show computations.

EXERCISE 17–7 Trend Percentages [LO1]

Rotorua Products, Ltd., of New Zealand markets agricultural products for the burgeoning Asian consumer market. The company's current assets, current liabilities, and sales have been reported as follows over the last five years (Year 5 is the most recent year):

	Year 5	Year 4	Year 3	Year 2	Year 1
Sales	$NZ2,250,000	$NZ2,160,000	$NZ2,070,000	$NZ1,980,000	$NZ1,800,000
Cash	$NZ 30,000	$NZ 40,000	$NZ 48,000	$NZ 65,000	$NZ 50,000
Accounts receivable, net	570,000	510,000	405,000	345,000	300,000
Inventory	750,000	720,000	690,000	660,000	600,000
Total current assets	$NZ1,350,000	$NZ1,270,000	$NZ1,143,000	$NZ1,070,000	$NZ 950,000
Current liabilities	$NZ 640,000	$NZ 580,000	$NZ 520,000	$NZ 440,000	$NZ 400,000

$NZ stands for New Zealand dollars.

Required:

1. Express all of the asset, liability, and sales data in trend percentages. (Show percentages for each item.) Use Year 1 as the base year and carry computations to one decimal place.
2. Comment on the results of your analysis.

EXERCISE 17–8 Selected Financial Ratios [LO3, LO4]

The financial statements for Castile Products, Inc., are given below:

CASTILE PRODUCTS, INC.
Balance Sheet
December 31

Assets		
Current assets:		
Cash		$ 6,500
Accounts receivable, net		35,000
Merchandise inventory		70,000
Prepaid expenses		3,500
Total current assets		115,000
Property and equipment, net		185,000
Total assets		$300,000
Liabilities and Stockholders' Equity		
Liabilities:		
Current liabilities		$ 50,000
Bonds payable, 10%		80,000
Total liabilities		130,000
Stockholders' equity:		
Common stock, $5 per value	$ 30,000	
Retained earnings	140,000	
Total stockholders' equity		170,000
Total liabilities and equity		$300,000

CASTILE PRODUCTS, INC.
Income Statement
For the Year Ended December 31

Sales	$420,000
Less cost of goods sold	292,500
Gross margin	127,500
Less operating expenses	89,500
Net operating income	38,000
Interest expense	8,000
Net income before taxes	30,000
Income taxes (30%)	9,000
Net income	$ 21,000

Account balances at the beginning of the year were: accounts receivable, $25,000; and inventory, $60,000. All sales were on account.

Required:

Compute financial ratios as follows:

1. Gross margin percentage.
2. Current ratio.
3. Acid-test (quick) ratio.
4. Debt-to-equity ratio.
5. Average collection period.
6. Average sale period.
7. Times interest earned.
8. Book value per share.

EXERCISE 17–9 Selected Financial Ratios for Common Stockholders [LO2]

Refer to the financial statements for Castile Products, Inc., in Exercise 17–8. In addition to the data in these statements, assume that Castile Products, Inc., paid dividends of $2.10 per share during the year. Also assume that the company's common stock had a market price of $42 at the end of the year and there was no change in the number of outstanding shares of common stock during the year.

Required:

Compute financial ratios as follows:

1. Earnings per share.
2. Dividend payout ratio.
3. Dividend yield ratio.
4. Price-earnings ratio.

EXERCISE 17–10 Selected Financial Ratios for Common Stockholders [LO2]

Refer to the financial statements for Castile Products, Inc., in Exercise 17–8. Assets at the beginning of the year totaled $280,000, and the stockholders' equity totaled $161,600.

Required:

Compute the following:

1. Return on total assets.
2. Return on common stockholders' equity.
3. Was financial leverage positive or negative for the year? Explain.

Problems

PROBLEM 17–11 Effects of Transactions on Various Ratios [LO3]

Denna Company's working capital accounts at the beginning of the year are given below:

Microsoft Excel - Problem 17-11 screen c...

	A	B
1	Cash	$50,000
2	Marketable Securities	$30,000
3	Accounts Receivable, net	$200,000
4	Inventory	$210,000
5	Prepaid Expenses	$10,000
6	Accounts Payable	$150,000
7	Notes Due Within One Year	$30,000
8	Accrued Liabilities	$20,000
9		

During the year, Denna Company completed the following transactions:

x. Paid a cash dividend previously declared, $12,000.
a. Issued additional shares of common stock for cash, $100,000.
b. Sold inventory costing $50,000 for $80,000, on account.
c. Wrote off uncollectible accounts in the amount of $10,000, reducing the accounts receivable balance accordingly.
d. Declared a cash dividend, $15,000.
e. Paid accounts payable, $50,000.
f. Borrowed cash on a short-term note with the bank, $35,000.
g. Sold inventory costing $15,000 for $10,000 cash.
h. Purchased inventory on account, $60,000.

i. Paid off all short-term notes due, $30,000.
j. Purchased equipment for cash, $15,000.
k. Sold marketable securities costing $18,000 for cash, $15,000.
l. Collected cash on accounts receivable, $80,000.

Required:

1. Compute the following amounts and ratios as of the beginning of the year:
   a. Working capital.
   b. Current ratio.
   c. Acid-test (quick) ratio.
2. Indicate the effect of each of the transactions given above on working capital, the current ratio, and the acid-test (quick) ratio. Give the effect in terms of increase, decrease, or none. Item (x) is given below as an example of the format to use:

	The Effect on		
Transaction	Working Capital	Current Ratio	Acid-Test Ratio
(x) Paid a cash dividend previously declared	None	Increase	Increase

PROBLEM 17–12 Common-Size Statements and Financial Ratios for Creditors [LO1, LO3, LO4]

Paul Sabin organized Sabin Electronics 10 years ago to produce and sell several electronic devices on which he had secured patents. Although the company has been fairly profitable, it is now experiencing a severe cash shortage. For this reason, it is requesting a $500,000 long-term loan from Gulfport State Bank, $100,000 of which will be used to bolster the Cash account and $400,000 of which will be used to modernize equipment. The company's financial statements for the two most recent years follow:

SABIN ELECTRONICS
Comparative Balance Sheet

	This Year	Last Year
Assets		
Current assets:		
Cash	$ 70,000	$ 150,000
Marketable securities	0	18,000
Accounts receivable, net	480,000	300,000
Inventory	950,000	600,000
Prepaid expenses	20,000	22,000
Total current assets	1,520,000	1,090,000
Plant and equipment, net	1,480,000	1,370,000
Total assets	$3,000,000	$2,460,000
Liabilities and Stockholders' Equity		
Liabilities:		
Current liabilities	$ 800,000	$ 430,000
Bonds payable, 12%	600,000	600,000
Total liabilities	1,400,000	1,030,000
Stockholders' equity:		
Preferred stock, $25 par, 8%	250,000	250,000
Common stock, $10 par	500,000	500,000
Retained earnings	850,000	680,000
Total stockholders' equity	1,600,000	1,430,000
Total liabilities and equity	$3,000,000	$2,460,000

SABIN ELECTRONICS
Comparative Income Statement and Reconciliation

	This Year	Last Year
Sales	$5,000,000	$4,350,000
Less cost of goods sold	3,875,000	3,450,000
Gross margin	1,125,000	900,000
Less operating expenses	653,000	548,000
Net operating income	472,000	352,000
Less interest expense	72,000	72,000
Net income before taxes	400,000	280,000
Less income taxes (30%)	120,000	84,000
Net income	280,000	196,000
Dividends paid:		
Preferred dividends	20,000	20,000
Common dividends	90,000	75,000
Total dividends paid	110,000	95,000
Net income retained	170,000	101,000
Retained earnings, beginning of year	680,000	579,000
Retained earnings, end of year	$ 850,000	$ 680,000

During the past year, the company introduced several new product lines and raised the selling prices on a number of old product lines in order to improve its profit margin. The company also hired a new sales manager, who has expanded sales into several new territories. Sales terms are 2/10, n/30. All sales are on account. Assume that the following ratios are typical of companies in the electronics industry:

Current ratio	2.5
Acid-test (quick) ratio	1.3
Average collection period	18 days
Average sale period	60 days
Debt-to-equity ratio	0.90
Times interest earned	6.0
Return on total assets	13%
Price-earnings ratio	12

Required:

1. To assist the Gulfport State Bank in making a decision about the loan, compute the following ratios for both this year and last year:
   a. The amount of working capital.
   b. The current ratio.
   c. The acid-test (quick) ratio.
   d. The average collection period. (The accounts receivable at the beginning of last year totaled $250,000.)
   e. The average sale period. (The inventory at the beginning of last year totaled $500,000.)
   f. The debt-to-equity ratio.
   g. The times interest earned ratio.
2. For both this year and last year:
   a. Present the balance sheet in common-size format.
   b. Present the income statement in common-size format down through net income.
3. Comment on the results of your analysis in (1) and (2) above and make a recommendation as to whether or not the loan should be approved.

PROBLEM 17–13 Financial Ratios for Common Stockholders [LO2]

Refer to the financial statements and other data in Problem 17–12. Assume that you are an account executive for a large brokerage house and that one of your clients has asked for a recommendation about the possible purchase of Sabin Electronics' stock. You are not acquainted with the stock and for this reason wish to do some analytical work before making a recommendation.

Required:

1. You decide first to assess the well-being of the common stockholders. For both this year and last year, compute:
   a. The earnings per share. There has been no change in preferred or common stock over the last two years.
   b. The dividend yield ratio for common stock. The company's stock is currently selling for $40 per share; last year it sold for $36 per share.
   c. The dividend payout ratio for common stock.
   d. The price-earnings ratio. How do investors regard Sabin Electronics as compared to other companies in the industry? Explain.
   e. The book value per share of common stock. Does the difference between market value and book value suggest that the stock is overpriced? Explain.
2. You decide next to assess the company's rate of return. Compute the following for both this year and last year:
   a. The return on total assets. (Total assets at the beginning of last year were $2,300,000.)
   b. The return on common stockholders' equity. (Stockholders' equity at the beginning of last year was $1,329,000.)
   c. Is the company's financial leverage positive or negative? Explain.
3. Would you recommend that your client purchase shares of Sabin Electronics' stock? Explain.

PROBLEM 17–14 Comprehensive Ratio Analysis [LO2, LO3, LO4]

You have just been hired as a loan officer at Slippery Rock State Bank. Your supervisor has given you a file containing a request from Lydex Company, a manufacturer of safety helmets, for a $3,000,000, five-year loan. Financial statement data on the company for the last two years follow:

LYDEX COMPANY
Comparative Balance Sheet

	This Year	Last Year
Assets		
Current assets:		
Cash	$ 960,000	$ 1,260,000
Marketable securities	0	300,000
Accounts receivable, net	2,700,000	1,800,000
Inventory	3,900,000	2,400,000
Prepaid expenses	240,000	180,000
Total current assets	7,800,000	5,940,000
Plant and equipment, net	9,300,000	8,940,000
Total assets	$17,100,000	$14,880,000
Liabilities and Stockholders' Equity		
Liabilities:		
Current liabilities	$ 3,900,000	$ 2,760,000
Note payable, 10%	3,600,000	3,000,000
Total liabilities	7,500,000	5,760,000
Stockholders' equity:		
Preferred stock, 8%, $30 par value	1,800,000	1,800,000
Common stock, $80 par value	6,000,000	6,000,000
Retained earnings	1,800,000	1,320,000
Total stockholders' equity	9,600,000	9,120,000
Total liabilities and stockholders' equity	$17,100,000	$14,880,000

LYDEX COMPANY
Comparative Income Statement and Reconciliation

	This Year	Last Year
Sales (all on account)	$15,750,000	$12,480,000
Less cost of goods sold	12,600,000	9,900,000
Gross margin	3,150,000	2,580,000
Less operating expenses	1,590,000	1,560,000
Net operating income	1,560,000	1,020,000
Less interest expense	360,000	300,000
Net income before taxes	1,200,000	720,000
Less income taxes (30%)	360,000	216,000
Net income	840,000	504,000
Dividends paid:		
Preferred dividends	144,000	144,000
Common dividends	216,000	108,000
Total dividends paid	360,000	252,000
Net income retained	480,000	252,000
Retained earnings, beginning of year	1,320,000	1,068,000
Retained earnings, end of year	$ 1,800,000	$ 1,320,000

Helen McGuire, who just a year ago was appointed president of Lydex Company, argues that although the company has had a "spotty" record in the past, it has "turned the corner," as evidenced by a 25% jump in sales and by a greatly improved earnings picture between last year and this year. McGuire also points out that investors generally have recognized the improving situation at Lydex, as shown by the increase in market value of the company's common stock, which is currently selling for $72 per share (up from $40 per share last year). McGuire feels that with her leadership and with the modernized equipment that the $3,000,000 loan will permit the company to buy, profits will be even stronger in the future. McGuire has a reputation in the industry for being a good manager who runs a "tight" ship.

Not wanting to botch your first assignment, you decide to generate all the information that you can about the company. You determine that the following ratios are typical of companies in Lydex Company's industry:

Current ratio	2.3
Acid-test (quick) ratio	1.2
Average collection period	30 days
Average sale period	60 days
Return on assets	9.5%
Debt-to-equity ratio	0.65
Times interest earned	5.7
Price-earnings ratio	10

Required:

1. You decide first to assess the rate of return that the company is generating. Compute the following for both this year and last year:
   a. The return on total assets. (Total assets at the beginning of last year were $12,960,000.)
   b. The return on common stockholders' equity. (Stockholders' equity at the beginning of last year totaled $9,048,000. There has been no change in preferred or common stock over the last two years.)
   c. Is the company's financial leverage positive or negative? Explain.
2. You decide next to assess the well-being of the common stockholders. For both this year and last year, compute:
   a. The earnings per share.
   b. The dividend yield ratio for common stock.
   c. The dividend payout ratio for common stock.
   d. The price-earnings ratio. How do investors regard Lydex Company as compared to other companies in the industry? Explain.

   e. The book value per share of common stock. Does the difference between market value per share and book value per share suggest that the stock at its current price is a bargain? Explain.
   f. The gross margin percentage.
3. You decide, finally, to assess creditor ratios to determine both short-term and long-term debt-paying ability. For both this year and last year, compute:
   a. Working capital.
   b. The current ratio.
   c. The acid-test ratio.
   d. The average collection period. (The accounts receivable at the beginning of last year totaled $1,560,000.)
   e. The inventory turnover. (The inventory at the beginning of last year totaled $1,920,000.) Also compute the average sale period.
   f. The debt-to-equity ratio.
   g. The times interest earned ratio.
4. Make a recommendation to your supervisor as to whether the loan should be approved.

PROBLEM 17–15 Common-Size Financial Statements [LO1]

Refer to the financial statement data for Lydex Company given in Problem 17–14.

Required:

For both this year and last year:
1. Present the balance sheet in common-size format.
2. Present the income statement in common-size format down through net income.
3. Comment on the results of your analysis.

PROBLEM 17–16 Interpretation of Financial Ratios [LO2, LO3]

Paul Ward is interested in the stock of Pecunious Products, Inc. Before purchasing the stock, Mr. Ward would like your help in analyzing the data that are available to him as shown below:

	Year 3	Year 2	Year 1
Sales trend	128.0	115.0	100.0
Current ratio	2.5	2.3	2.2
Acid-test (quick) ratio	0.8	0.9	1.1
Accounts receivable turnover	9.4	10.6	12.5
Inventory turnover	6.5	7.2	8.0
Dividend yield	7.1%	6.5%	5.8%
Dividend payout ratio	40%	50%	60%
Return on total assets	12.5%	11.0%	9.5%
Return on common stockholders' equity	14.0%	10.0%	7.8%
Dividends paid per share*	$1.50	$1.50	$1.50

*There have been no changes in common stock outstanding over the three-year period.

Mr. Ward would like answers to a number of questions about the trend of events in Pecunious Products, Inc., over the last three years. His questions are:

a. Is it becoming easier for the company to pay its bills as they come due?
b. Are customers paying their accounts at least as fast now as they were in Year 1?
c. Is the total of the accounts receivable increasing, decreasing, or remaining constant?
d. Is the level of inventory increasing, decreasing, or remaining constant?
e. Is the market price of the company's stock going up or down?
f. Is the earnings per share increasing or decreasing?
g. Is the price-earning ratio going up or down?
h. Is the company employing financial leverage to the advantage of the common stockholders?

Required:

Answer each of Mr. Ward's questions and explain how you arrived at your answers.

PROBLEM 17–17 Effects of Transactions on Various Financial Ratios [LO2, LO3, LO4]

In the right-hand column below, certain financial ratios are listed. To the left of each ratio is a business transaction or event relating to the operating activities of Delta Company.

Business Transaction or Event	Ratio
1. Declared a cash dividend.	Current ratio
2. Sold inventory on account at cost.	Acid-test (quick) ratio
3. Issued bonds with an interest rate of 8%. The company's return on assets is 10%.	Return on common stockholders' equity
4. Net income decreased by 10% between last year and this year. Long-term debt remained unchanged.	Times interest earned
5. Paid a previously declared cash dividend.	Current ratio
6. The market price of the company's common stock dropped from 24½ to 20. The dividend paid per share remained unchanged.	Dividend payout ratio
7. Obsolete inventory totaling $100,000 was written off as a loss.	Inventory turnover ratio
8. Sold inventory for cash at a profit.	Debt-to-equity ratio
9. Changed customer credit terms from 2/10, n/30 to 2/15, n/30 to comply with a change in industry practice.	Accounts receivable turnover ratio
10. Issued a dividend to common stockholders.	Book value per share
11. The market price of the company's common stock increased from 24½ to 30.	Book value per share
12. Paid $40,000 on accounts payable.	Working capital
13. Issued a common stock dividend to common stockholders.	Earnings per share
14. Paid accounts payable	Debt-to-equity ratio
15. Purchased inventory on account.	Acid-test (quick) ratio
16. Wrote off an uncollectible account against the Allowance for Bad Debts.	Current ratio
17. The market price of the company's common stock increased from 24½ to 30. Earnings per share remained unchanged.	Price-earnings ratio
18. The market price of the company's common stock increased from 24½ to 30. The dividend paid per share remained unchanged.	Dividend yield ratio

Required:
Indicate the effect that each business transaction or event would have on the ratio listed opposite to it. State the effect in terms of increase, decrease, or no effect on the ratio involved, and give the reason for your answer. In all cases, assume that the current assets exceed the current liabilities both before and after the event or transaction. Use the following format for your answers:

	Effect on Ratio	Reason for Increase, Decrease, or No Effect
1.		
Etc.		

PROBLEM 17–18 Ethics and the Manager [LO3]
Venice InLine, Inc., was founded by Russ Perez to produce a specialized in-line skate he had designed for doing aerial tricks. Up to this point, Russ has financed the company with his own savings and with cash generated by his business. However, Russ now faces a cash crisis. In the year just ended, an acute shortage of high-impact roller bearings developed just as the company was beginning production for the Christmas season. Russ had been assured by his suppliers that the roller bearings would be delivered in time to make Christmas shipments, but the suppliers had been unable to fully deliver on this promise. As a consequence, Venice InLine had large stocks of unfinished skates at the end of the year and had been unable to fill all of the orders that had come in from retailers for the Christmas season. Consequently, sales were below expectations for the year, and Russ does not have enough cash to pay his creditors.

Well before the accounts payable were due, Russ visited a local bank and inquired about obtaining a loan. The loan officer at the bank assured Russ that there should not be any problem getting a loan to pay off his accounts payable—providing that on his most recent financial statements the current ratio was above 2.0, the acid-test ratio was above 1.0, and net operating income was at least four times the interest on the proposed loan. Russ promised to return later with a copy of his financial statements.

Russ would like to apply for a $80,000 six-month loan bearing an interest rate of 10% per year.

The unaudited financial reports of the company appear below:

VENICE INLINE, INC.
Comparative Balance Sheet
As of December 31
(dollars in thousands)

	This Year	Last Year
Assets		
Current assets:		
Cash	$ 70	$150
Accounts receivable, net	50	40
Inventory	160	100
Prepaid expenses	10	12
Total current assets	290	302
Property and equipment	270	180
Total assets	$560	$482
Liabilities and Stockholders' Equity		
Current liabilities:		
Accounts payable	$154	$ 90
Accrued payables	10	10
Total current liabilities	164	100
Long-term liabilities	—	—
Total liabilities	164	100
Stockholders' equity:		
Common stock and additional paid-in capital	100	100
Retained earnings	296	282
Total stockholders' equity	396	382
Total liabilities and stockholders' equity	$560	$482

VENICE INLINE, INC.
Income Statement
For the Year Ended December 31
(dollars in thousands)

	This Year
Sales (all on account)	$420
Cost of goods sold	290
Gross margin	130
Operating expenses:	
Selling expenses	42
Administrative expenses	68
Total operating expenses	110
Net operating income	20
Interest expense	—
Net income before taxes	20
Less income taxes (30%)	6
Net income	$ 14

Required:

1. Based on the above unaudited financial statements and the statement made by the loan officer, would the company qualify for the loan?
2. Last year Russ purchased and installed new, more efficient equipment to replace an older plastic injection molding machine. Russ had originally planned to sell the old machine but found that it is still needed whenever the plastic injection molding process is a bottleneck. When

Russ discussed his cash flow problems with his brother-in-law, he suggested to Russ that the old machine be sold or at least reclassified as inventory on the balance sheet since it could be readily sold. At present, the machine is carried in the Property and Equipment account and could be sold for its net book value of $45,000. The bank does not require audited financial statements. What advice would you give to Russ concerning the machine?

PROBLEM 17–19 Incomplete Statements; Analysis of Ratios [LO2, LO3, LO4]
Incomplete financial statements for Pepper Industries follow:

PEPPER INDUSTRIES
Balance Sheet
March 31

Current assets:	
Cash	$?
Accounts receivable, net	?
Inventory	?
Total current assets	?
Plant and equipment, net	?
Total assets	$?
Liabilities:	
Current liabilities	$ 320,000
Bonds payable, 10%	?
Total liabilities	?
Stockholders' equity:	
Common stock, $5 par value	?
Retained earnings	?
Total stockholders' equity	?
Total liabilities and stockholders equity	$?

PEPPER INDUSTRIES
Income Statement
For the Year Ended March 31

Sales	$4,200,000
Less cost of goods sold	?
Gross margin	?
Less operating expenses	?
Net operating income	?
Less interest expense	80,000
Net income before taxes	?
Less income taxes (30%)	?
Net income	$?

The following additional information is available about the company:

a. All sales during the year were on account.
b. There was no change in the number of shares of common stock outstanding during the year.
c. The interest expense on the income statement relates to the bonds payable; the amount of bonds outstanding did not change during the year.
d. Selected balances at the *beginning* of the current year were:

Accounts receivable	$270,000
Inventory	$360,000
Total assets	$1,800,000

e. Selected financial ratios computed from the statements above for the current year are:

Earnings per share	$2.30
Debt-to-equity ratio	0.875
Accounts receivable turnover	14.0
Current ratio	2.75
Return on total assets	18.0%
Times interest earned	6.75
Acid-test (quick) ratio	1.25
Inventory turnover	6.5

Required:
Compute the missing amounts on the company's financial statements. (Hint: What's the difference between the acid-test ratio and the current ratio?)

PROBLEM 17–20 Comprehensive Problem—Part I: Financial Ratios for Common Stockholders [LO2]

(Problems 17–21 and 17–22 delve more deeply into the data presented below. Each problem is independent.) Empire Labs, Inc., was organized several years ago to produce and market several new "miracle drugs." The company is small but growing, and you are considering the purchase of some of its common stock as an investment. The following data on the company are available for the past two years:

EMPIRE LABS, INC.
Comparative Income Statement
For the Years Ended December 31

	This Year	Last Year
Sales	$20,000,000	$15,000,000
Less cost of goods sold	13,000,000	9,000,000
Gross margin	7,000,000	6,000,000
Less operating expenses	5,260,000	4,560,000
Net operating income	1,740,000	1,440,000
Less interest expense	240,000	240,000
Net income before taxes	1,500,000	1,200,000
Less income taxes (30%)	450,000	360,000
Net income	$ 1,050,000	$ 840,000

EMPIRE LABS, INC.
Comparative Retained Earnings Statement
For the Years Ended December 31

	This Year	Last Year
Retained earnings, January 1	$2,400,000	$1,960,000
Add net income (above)	1,050,000	840,000
Total	3,450,000	2,800,000
Deduct cash dividends paid:		
Preferred dividends	120,000	120,000
Common dividends	360,000	280,000
Total dividends paid	480,000	400,000
Retained earnings, December 31	$2,970,000	$2,400,000

EMPIRE LABS, INC.
Comparative Balance Sheet
December 31

	This Year	Last Year
Assets		
Current assets:		
Cash	$ 200,000	$ 400,000
Accounts receivable, net	1,500,000	800,000
Inventory	3,000,000	1,200,000
Prepaid expenses	100,000	100,000
Total current assets	4,800,000	2,500,000
Plant and equipment, net	5,170,000	5,400,000
Total assets	$9,970,000	$7,900,000
Liabilities and Stockholders' Equity		
Liabilities:		
Current liabilities	$2,500,000	$1,000,000
Bonds payable, 12%	2,000,000	2,000,000
Total liabilities	4,500,000	3,000,000
Stockholders' equity:		
Preferred stock, 8%, $10 par	1,500,000	1,500,000
Common stock, $5 par	1,000,000	1,000,000
Retained earnings	2,970,000	2,400,000
Total stockholders' equity	5,470,000	4,900,000
Total liabilities and stockholders' equity	$9,970,000	$7,900,000

After some research, you have determined that the following ratios are typical of companies in the pharmaceutical industry:

Dividend yield ratio	3%
Dividend payout ratio	40%
Price-earnings ratio	16
Return on total assets	13.5%
Return on common stockholders' equity	20%

The company's common stock is currently selling for $60 per share. Last year the stock sold for $45 per share.

There has been no change in the preferred or common stock outstanding over the last three years.

Required:

1. In analyzing the company, you decide first to compute the following ratios for both last year and this year:
   a. The earnings per share.
   b. The dividend yield ratio.
   c. The dividend payout ratio.
   d. The price-earnings ratio.
   e. The book value per share of common stock.
   f. The gross margin percentage.
2. Next, you decide to determine the rate of return that the company is generating by computing the following ratios for last year and this year:
   a. The return on total assets. (Total assets were $6,500,000 at the beginning of last year.)
   b. The return on common stockholders' equity. (Common stockholders' equity was $2,900,000 at the beginning of last year.)
   c. Is financial leverage positive or negative? Explain.
3. Based on your work in (1) and (2) above, does the company's common stock seem to be an attractive investment? Explain.

PROBLEM 17–21 Comprehensive Problem—Part II: Creditor Ratios [LO3, LO4]

Refer to the data in Problem 17–20. Although Empire Labs, Inc., has been very profitable since it was organized several years ago, the company is beginning to experience some difficulty in paying its bills as they come due. Management has approached Security National Bank requesting a two-year, $500,000 loan to bolster the cash account.

Security National Bank has assigned you to evaluate the loan request. You have gathered the following data relating to companies in the pharmaceutical industry:

Current ratio	2.4
Acid-test (quick) ratio	1.2
Average collection period	16 days
Average sale period	40 days
Times interest earned	7
Debt-to-equity ratio	0.70

The following additional information is available on Empire Labs, Inc.:

a. All sales are on account.
b. At the beginning of last year, the accounts receivable balance was $600,000 and the inventory balance was $1,000,000.

Required:

1. Compute the following amounts and ratios for both last year and this year:
   a. The working capital.
   b. The current ratio.
   c. The acid-test (quick) ratio.
   d. The average collection period.
   e. The average sale period.
   f. The times interest earned.
   g. The debt-to-equity ratio.
2. Comment on the results of your analysis in (1) above.
3. Would you recommend that the loan be approved? Explain.

PROBLEM 17–22 Comprehensive Problem—Part III: Common-Size Statements [LO1]

Refer to the data in Problem 17–20. The president of Empire Labs, Inc., is deeply concerned. Sales increased by $5 million from last year to this year, yet the company's net income increased by only a small amount. Also, the company's operating expenses went up this year, even though a major effort was launched during the year to cut costs.

Required:

1. For both last year and this year, prepare an income statement and a balance sheet in common-size format. Round computations to one decimal place.
2. From your work in (1) above, explain to the president why the increase in profits was so small this year. Were any benefits realized from the company's cost-cutting efforts? Explain.

Appendix A

Pricing Products and Services

LEARNING OBJECTIVES

After studying this appendix, you should be able to:

LO1 Compute the profit-maximizing price of a product or service using the price elasticity of demand and variable cost.

LO2 Compute the selling price of a product using the absorption costing approach.

LO3 Compute the target cost for a new product or service.

Introduction

Some businesses have no pricing problems. They make a product or provide a service that is in competition with other, identical products or services for which a market price already exists. Customers will not pay more than this price, and there is no reason to charge less. Under these circumstances, the company simply charges the prevailing market price. Markets for basic raw materials such as farm products and minerals follow this pattern.

In this appendix, we are concerned with the more common situation in which a business is faced with the problem of setting its own prices. Clearly, the pricing decision can be critical. If the price is set too high, customers won't buy the company's products. If the price is set too low, the company's costs won't be covered.

The usual approach in pricing is to *mark up* cost.[1] A product's **markup** is the difference between its selling price and its cost and is usually expressed as a percentage of cost.

$$\text{Selling price} = \text{Cost} + (\text{Markup percentage} \times \text{Cost})$$

For example, a company that uses a markup of 50% adds 50% to the costs of its products to determine selling prices. If a product costs $10, then the company would charge $15 for the product. This approach is called **cost-plus pricing** because the predetermined markup percentage is applied to the cost base to determine the selling price.

Two key issues must be addressed with the cost-plus approach to pricing. First, what cost should be used? Second, how should the markup be determined? Several alternative approaches are considered in this appendix, starting with the approach generally favored by economists.

IN BUSINESS

DO CONSUMERS REALLY RESPOND TO PRICES? YOU BET THEY DO

Jess Stonestreet Jackson is the founder of Kendall-Jackson (K-J) winery, which specializes in making popular wines that are good enough to command a premium price. Jackson, who is now a billionaire, prices his wines a few dollars higher than other mainstream wines. For example, if a Clos du Bois chardonnay costs $9 at retail, Jackson will charge $11 for his chardonnay. When chardonnay became the rage in the late 1990s, Jackson tried pushing up his prices by another few dollars over the competition. But unit sales dropped by 18%. Jackson rolled back his prices and the volume recovered.

Source: Tim W. Ferguson, "Harvest Time," *Forbes*, October 16, 2000, pp. 112–118.

The Economists' Approach to Pricing

LEARNING OBJECTIVE 1
Compute the profit-maximizing price of a product or service using the price elasticity of demand and variable cost.

If a company raises the price of a product, unit sales ordinarily fall. Because of this, pricing is a delicate balancing act in which the benefits of higher revenues per unit are traded off against the lower volume that results from charging a higher price. The sensitivity of unit sales to changes in price is called the *price elasticity of demand.*

[1] There are some legal restrictions on prices. Antitrust laws prohibit "predatory" prices, which are generally interpreted by the courts to mean a price below average variable cost. "Price discrimination"—charging different prices to customers in the same market for the same product or service—is also prohibited by the law.

IN BUSINESS

BRINGING IN SKIERS

Mike Shirley, the president and general manager of the Bogus Basin ski area in southern Idaho, started a price revolution in the ski resort industry by slashing the price of an adult season ticket from $500 to less than $200. Eight times as many season passes were sold as the previous year. Under the old price, a season pass holder skied on average 23 days. Under the new discounted price, the average dropped to only nine days. The reason? Lapsed skiers who don't ski all that much were buying the cheaper season passes. That year, the total skier visits jumped from 191,000 to over 303,000, but the average revenue per visit dropped by less than a dollar, from $24.84 to $23.89. Shirley notes, "When you have a huge increase in volume and you're collecting as much per skier as before, you're making out like a bandit." In ski resorts, almost all of the costs are fixed with respect to how many skiers are on the hill. Consequently, the increased revenue dropped almost directly to the bottom line as increased profits.

Source: Greg Trinker, "It's the Price, Stupid," *SKI*, October 1999, pp. 33–34.

Elasticity of Demand

A product's price elasticity should be a key element in setting its price. The **price elasticity of demand** measures the degree to which the unit sales of a product or service are affected by a change in price. Demand for a product is said to be *inelastic* if a change in price has little effect on the number of units sold. The demand for designer perfumes sold by trained personnel at cosmetic counters in department stores is relatively inelastic. Raising or lowering prices on these luxury goods has little effect on unit sales. On the other hand, demand for a product is said to be *elastic* if a change in price has a substantial effect on the volume of units sold. An example of a product whose demand is elastic is gasoline. If a gas station raises its price for gasoline, unit sales will drop as customers seek lower prices elsewhere.

IN BUSINESS

ELASTICITY DEPENDS ON THE PRODUCT

The demand for water is much more elastic than the demand for cigarettes. When cities raise the price of water by 10%, water usage goes down by as much as 12%. When the price of agricultural water goes up 10%, usage drops by about 20%. Agricultural users of water are much more sensitive to price than city dwellers, but both are much more sensitive to price than smokers. When the price of cigarettes increases by 10%, consumption of cigarettes drops by only 3% to 5%.

Sources: Terry L. Anderson and Clay J. Landry, "Trickle-Down Economics," *The Wall Street Journal*, August 23, 1999, p. A14; Gene Koretz, "Still Hooked on the Evil Weed," *BusinessWeek*, July 5, 1999, p. 18.

Price elasticity is very important in determining prices. Managers should set higher markups over cost when customers are relatively insensitive to price (i.e., demand is inelastic) and lower markups when customers are relatively sensitive to price (i.e., demand is elastic). This principle is followed in department stores. Merchandise sold in the bargain basement has a much lower markup than merchandise sold elsewhere in the store because customers who shop in the bargain basement are much more sensitive to price (i.e., demand is elastic).

The price elasticity of demand for a product or service, ϵ_d, can be estimated using the following formula.[2,3]

$$\epsilon_d = \frac{\ln(1 + \%\text{ change in quantity sold})}{\ln(1 + \%\text{ change in price})}$$

For example, suppose that the managers of Nature's Garden believe that every 10% increase in the selling price of their apple-almond shampoo will result in a 15% decrease in the number of bottles of shampoo sold.[4] The price elasticity of demand for this product would be computed as follows:

$$\epsilon_d = \frac{\ln(1 + (-0.15))}{\ln(1 + (0.10))} = \frac{\ln(0.85)}{\ln(1.10)} = -1.71$$

For comparison purposes, the managers of Nature's Garden believe that another product, strawberry glycerin soap, will experience a 20% drop in unit sales if its price is increased by 10%. (Purchasers of this product are more sensitive to price than the purchasers of the apple-almond shampoo.) The price elasticity of demand for the strawberry glycerin soap is:

$$\epsilon_d = \frac{\ln(1 + (-0.20))}{\ln(1 + (0.10))} = \frac{\ln(0.80)}{\ln(1.10)} = -2.34$$

Both of these products, like other normal products, have a price elasticity that is less than -1.

Note that the price elasticity of demand for the strawberry glycerin soap is larger (in absolute value) than the price elasticity of demand for the apple-almond shampoo. This indicates that the demand for strawberry glycerin soap is more elastic than the demand for apple-almond shampoo.

In the next subsection, the price elasticity of demand will be used to compute the selling price that maximizes the profits of the company.

The Profit-Maximizing Price

Under certain conditions, the profit-maximizing price can be determined by marking up *variable cost* using the following formula:[5]

$$\text{Profit-maximizing markup on variable cost} = \left(\frac{\epsilon_d}{1 + \epsilon_d}\right) - 1$$

Using the above markup is equivalent to setting the selling price using this formula:

$$\text{Profit-maximizing price} = \left(\frac{\epsilon_d}{1 + \epsilon_d}\right)\text{Variable cost per unit}$$

---

[2] The term "ln( )" is the natural log function. You can compute the natural log of any number using the LN or ln$x$ key on your calculator. For example, $\ln(0.85) = -0.1625$.

[3] This formula assumes that the price elasticity of demand is constant. This occurs when the relation between the selling price, p, and the unit sales, q, can be expressed in the following form: $\ln(q) = a + \epsilon_d \ln(p)$. Even if this is not precisely true, the formula provides a useful way to estimate a product's price elasticity.

[4] The estimated change in unit sales should take into account competitors' responses to a price change.

[5] The formula assumes that (a) the price elasticity of demand is constant; (b) Total cost = Total fixed cost + Variable cost per unit × Quantity sold; and (c) the price of the product has no effect on the sales or costs of any other product. The formula can be derived using calculus.

IN BUSINESS

WHAT DID THAT SALMON DISH COST?

Restaurants mark up food costs by an average of 300% to cover their overhead and generate a profit, but the markup is not the same for all items on the menu. Some ingredients—especially prime cuts of beef and exotic seafood such as fresh scallops—are so costly that diners would not tolerate a 300% markup. So restaurants make it up on the cheap stuff—vegetables, pasta, and salmon. Why salmon? The farmed variety is only $2.50 per pound wholesale, much cheaper than prime restaurant-quality beef. At the Docks restaurant in New York City, a 10-ounce salmon dinner garnished with potatoes and coleslaw is $19.50. The actual cost of the ingredients is only $1.90.

To take another example, the ingredients of the best-selling Angus beef tenderloin at the Sunset Grill in Nashville, Tennessee, costs the restaurant $8.42. Applying the average 300% markup, the price of the meal would be $33.68. But few diners would order the meal at that price. So instead the restaurant charges just $25. In contrast, the restaurant charges $9 for its Grill vegetable plate—whose ingredients cost only $1.55.

Source: Eileen Daspin, "Entrée Economics," *The Wall Street Journal*, March 10, 2000, pp. W1 and W4.

The profit-maximizing prices for the two Nature's Garden products are computed below using these formulas:

	Apple-Almond Shampoo	Strawberry Glycerin Soap
Price elasticity of demand (ϵ_d)	−1.71	−2.34
Profit-maximizing markup on variable cost (a)	$\left(\frac{-1.71}{-1.71 + 1}\right) - 1$	$\left(\frac{-2.34}{-2.34 + 1}\right) - 1$
	= 2.41 − 1 = 1.41 or 141%	= 1.75 − 1 = 0.75 or 75%
Variable cost per unit—given (b)	$2.00	$0.40
Markup, (a) × (b)	2.82	0.30
Profit-maximizing price	$4.82	$0.70

Note that the 75% markup for the strawberry glycerin soap is lower than the 141% markup for the apple-almond shampoo. The reason for this is that the purchasers of strawberry glycerin soap are more sensitive to price than the purchasers of apple-almond shampoo. Strawberry glycerin soap is a relatively common product with close substitutes available in nearly every grocery store.

Exhibit A–1 shows how the profit-maximizing markup is generally affected by how sensitive unit sales are to price. For example, if a 10% increase in price leads to a 20% decrease in unit sales, then the optimal markup on variable cost according to the exhibit is 75%—the figure computed above for the strawberry glycerin soap. Note that the optimal markup drops as unit sales become more sensitive to price.

Caution is advised when using these formulas to establish a selling price. The formulas rely on simplifying assumptions and the estimate of the percentage change in unit sales that would result from a given percentage change in price is likely to be inexact. Nevertheless, the formulas can provide valuable clues regarding whether prices should be increased or decreased. Suppose, for example, that the strawberry glycerin soap is currently being sold for $0.60 per bar. The formula indicates that the profit-maximizing price is $0.70 per bar. Rather than increasing the price by $0.10, it would be prudent to increase the price by a more modest amount to observe what happens to unit sales and to profits.

The formula for the profit-maximizing price conveys a very important lesson. If the total fixed costs are the same whether the company charges $0.60 or $0.70, they cannot be relevant in the decision of which price to charge for the soap. The optimal selling price should depend on two factors—the variable cost per unit and how sensitive unit sales are to changes in price. Fixed costs play no role in setting the optimal price. Fixed costs are

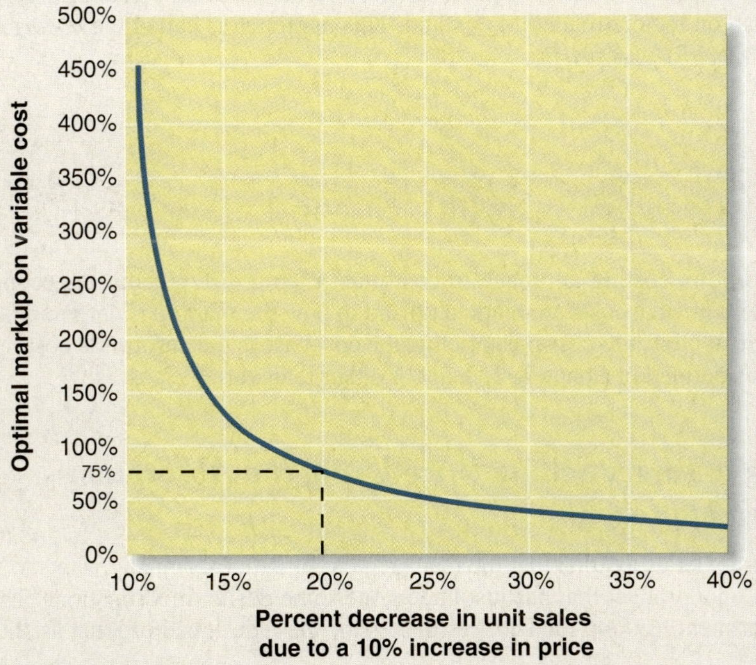

EXHIBIT A–1
The Optimal Markup on Variable Cost as a Function of the Sensitivity of Unit Sales to Price

relevant when deciding whether to offer a product but are not relevant when deciding how much to charge for the product.

We can directly verify that an increase in selling price for the strawberry glycerin soap from the current price of $0.60 per bar is warranted, based just on the forecast that a 10% increase in selling price would lead to a 20% decrease in unit sales. Suppose, for example, that Nature's Garden is currently selling 200,000 bars of the soap per year at the price of $0.60 a bar. If the change in price has no effect on the company's fixed costs or on other products, the effect on profits of increasing the price by 10% can be computed as follows:

	Present Price	Higher Price
Selling price	$0.60	$0.60 + (0.10 × $0.60) = $0.66
Unit sales	200,000	200,000 − (0.20 × 200,000) = 160,000
Sales	$120,000	$105,600
Variable cost ($0.40 per unit)	80,000	64,000
Contribution margin	$ 40,000	$ 41,600

Despite the apparent optimality of prices based on marking up variable costs according to the price elasticity of demand, surveys consistently reveal that most managers approach the pricing problem from a completely different perspective.[6] They prefer to mark

[6] One study found that 83% of the 504 large manufacturing companies surveyed used some form of full cost (either absorption cost or absorption cost plus selling, general, and administrative expenses) as a basis for pricing. The remaining 17% used only variable costs as a basis for pricing decisions. See V. Govindarajan and Robert N. Anthony, "How Firms Use Cost Data in Pricing Decisions," *Management Accounting,* July 1983, pp. 30–36. A more recent, but less extensive, survey by Eunsup Shim and Ephraim F. Sudit, "How Manufacturers Price Products," *Management Accounting,* February 1995, pp. 37–39, found similar results.

On the other hand, a survey of small-company executives summarized in *Inc.,* November 1996, p. 84, revealed that only 41% set prices based on cost. The others charge what they think customers are willing to pay or what the market demands.

up some version of full, not variable, costs, and the markup is based on desired profits rather than on factors related to demand. This approach is called the *absorption costing approach to cost-plus pricing.*

The Absorption Costing Approach to Cost-Plus Pricing

LEARNING OBJECTIVE 2
Compute the selling price of a product using the absorption costing approach.

The absorption costing approach to cost-plus pricing differs from the economists' approach both in what costs are marked up and in how the markup is determined. Under the absorption approach to cost-plus pricing, the cost base is the absorption costing unit product cost as defined in Chapters 2, 3, and 4 rather than variable cost.

Setting a Target Selling Price Using the Absorption Costing Approach

To illustrate, let us assume that the management of Ritter Company wants to set the selling price on a product that has just undergone some design modifications. The Accounting Department has provided cost estimates for the redesigned product as shown below:

	Per Unit	Total
Direct materials	$6	
Direct labor	$4	
Variable manufacturing overhead	$3	
Fixed manufacturing overhead		$70,000
Variable selling, general, and administrative expenses	$2	
Fixed selling, general, and administrative expenses		$60,000

The first step in the absorption costing approach to cost-plus pricing is to compute the unit product cost. For Ritter Company, this amounts to $20 per unit at a volume of 10,000 units, as computed below:

Direct materials	$ 6
Direct labor	4
Variable manufacturing overhead	3
Fixed manufacturing overhead ($70,000 ÷ 10,000 units)	7
Unit product cost	$20

Ritter Company has a general policy of marking up unit product costs by 50%. A price quotation sheet for the company prepared using the absorption approach is presented in Exhibit A–2. Note that selling, general, and administrative (SG&A) expenses are not included in the cost base. Instead, the markup is supposed to cover these expenses. Let us see how some companies determine these markup percentages.

EXHIBIT A–2
Price Quotation Sheet—Absorption Basis (10,000 Units)

Direct materials	$ 6
Direct labor	4
Variable manufacturing overhead	3
Fixed manufacturing overhead (based on 10,000 units)	7
Unit product cost	20
Markup to cover selling, general, and administrative expenses and desired profit—50% of unit manufacturing cost	10
Target selling price	$30

Determining the Markup Percentage

Ritter Company's markup percentage of 50% could be a widely used rule of thumb in the industry or just a company tradition that seems to work. The markup percentage may also be the result of an explicit computation. As we have discussed, the markup over cost ideally should be largely determined by market conditions. However, many companies base their markup on cost and desired profit. The reasoning goes like this. The markup must be large enough to cover SG&A expenses and provide an adequate return on investment (ROI). Given the forecasted unit sales, the markup can be computed as follows:

$$\text{Markup percentage on absorption cost} = \frac{(\text{Required ROI} \times \text{Investment}) + \text{SG\&A expenses}}{\text{Unit sales} \times \text{Unit product cost}}$$

To show how the formula above is applied, assume Ritter Company must invest \$100,000 in operating assets such as equipment to produce and market 10,000 units of the product each year. If Ritter Company requires a 20% ROI, then the markup for the product would be determined as follows:

$$\text{Markup percentage on absorption cost} = \frac{(20\% \times \$100{,}000) + (\$2 \times 10{,}000 + \$60{,}000)}{10{,}000 \times \$20}$$

$$= \frac{(\$20{,}000) + (\$80{,}000)}{\$200{,}000} = 50\%$$

As shown earlier, this markup of 50% leads to a target selling price of \$30 for Ritter Company. As verified in Exhibit A–3, *if the company actually sells 10,000 units* of the product at this price, the company's ROI on this product will indeed be 20%. If it turns out that more than 10,000 units are sold at this price, the ROI will be greater than 20%. If less than 10,000 units are sold, the ROI will be less than 20%. *The required ROI will be attained only if the forecasted unit sales volume is attained.*

EXHIBIT A–3
Income Statement and ROI Analysis—Ritter Company Actual Unit Sales = 10,000 Units; Selling Price = \$30

Direct materials	\$ 6
Direct labor	4
Variable manufacturing overhead	3
Fixed manufacturing overhead (\$70,000 ÷ 10,000 units)	7
Unit product cost	\$20

RITTER COMPANY
Absorption Costing Income Statement

Sales (\$30 per unit × 10,000 units)	\$300,000
Less cost of goods sold (\$20 per unit × 10,000 units)	200,000
Gross margin	100,000
Less selling, general, and administration expenses (\$2 per unit × 10,000 units + \$60,000)	80,000
Net operating income	\$ 20,000

ROI

$$\text{ROI} = \frac{\text{Net operating income}}{\text{Average operating assets}}$$

$$= \frac{\$20{,}000}{\$100{,}000}$$

$$= 20\%$$

IN BUSINESS

COST-BASED OR MARKET-BASED PRICES?

Jerry Bernstein, the director of Emerson Electric Co.'s price improvement team, says that setting prices used to be easy: "You developed a product, looked at the costs, and said, 'I need to make *X*,' and you marked it up accordingly—and people would buy it." Now the company charges based on what customers are willing to pay rather than its own costs. For example, a new compact sensor for factories that measures the flow of fluids would have been priced at $2,650 based on its cost. However, careful analysis revealed that customers would be willing to pay 20% more for the sensors than the company had planned to charge. The company settled on a price of $3,150.

Source: Timothy Aeppel, "Survival Strategies: After Cost Cutting, Companies Turn Toward Price Rises," *The Wall Street Journal,* September 18, 2002, pp. A1 & A12.

Problems with the Absorption Costing Approach

Using the absorption costing approach, the pricing problem looks deceptively simple. All a company needs to do is compute its unit product cost, decide how much profit it wants, and then set its price. It appears that a company can ignore demand and arrive at a price that will safely yield whatever profit it wants. However, as noted above, the absorption costing approach relies on a forecast of unit sales. Neither the markup nor the unit product cost can be computed without such a forecast.

The absorption costing approach essentially assumes that customers *need* the forecasted unit sales and will pay whatever price the company decides to charge. However, customers have a choice. If the price is too high, they can buy from a competitor or they may choose not to buy at all. Suppose, for example, that when Ritter Company sets its price at $30, it sells only 7,000 units rather than the 10,000 units forecasted. As shown in Exhibit A–4, the company would then have a loss of $25,000 on the product instead

EXHIBIT A–4
Income Statement and ROI Analysis—Ritter Company Actual Unit Sales = 7,000 Units; Selling Price = $30

Direct materials	$ 6
Direct labor	4
Variable manufacturing overhead	3
Fixed manufacturing overhead ($70,000 ÷ 7,000 units)	10
Unit product cost	$23

RITTER COMPANY
Absorption Costing Income Statement

Sales ($30 per unit × 7,000 units)	$210,000
Less cost of goods sold ($23 per unit × 7,000 units)	161,000
Gross margin	49,000
Less selling, general, and administration expenses ($2 per unit × 7,000 units + $60,000)	74,000
Net operating income	$ (25,000)

ROI

$$\text{ROI} = \frac{\text{Net operating income}}{\text{Average operating assets}}$$

$$= \frac{-\$25,000}{\$100,000}$$

$$= -25\%$$

of a profit of $20,000.[7] Some managers believe that the absorption costing approach to pricing is safe. This is an illusion. The absorption costing approach is safe only if customers choose to buy at least as many units as managers forecasted they would buy.

Target Costing

LEARNING OBJECTIVE 3
Compute the target cost for a new product or service.

Our discussion thus far has presumed that a product has already been developed, has been costed, and is ready to be marketed as soon as a price is set. In many cases, the sequence of events is just the reverse. That is, the company already *knows* what price should be charged, and the problem is to *develop* a product that can be marketed profitably at the desired price. Even in this situation, where the normal sequence of events is reversed, cost is still a crucial factor. The company can use an approach called *target costing.* **Target costing** is the process of determining the maximum allowable cost for a new product and then developing a prototype that can be profitably made for that maximum target cost figure. A number of companies use target costing, including Compaq, Culp, Cummins Engine, Daihatsu Motors, DaimlerChrysler, Ford, Isuzu Motors, ITT Automotive, Komatsu, Matsushita Electric, Mitsubishi Kasei, NEC, Nippodenso, Nissan, Olympus, Sharp, Texas Instruments, and Toyota.

The target cost for a product is computed by starting with the product's anticipated selling price and then deducting the desired profit, as follows:

Target cost = Anticipated selling price − Desired profit

The product development team is then given the responsibility of designing the product so that it can be made for no more than the target cost.

IN BUSINESS

TARGET COSTING—AN ITERATIVE PROCESS

Target costing is widely used in Japan. In the automobile industry, the target cost for a new model is decomposed into target costs for each of the elements of the car—down to a target cost for each of the individual parts. The designers draft a trial blueprint, and a check is made to see if the estimated cost of the car is within reasonable distance of the target cost. If not, design changes are made, and a new trial blueprint is drawn up. This process continues until there is sufficient confidence in the design to make a prototype car according to the trial blueprint. If there is still a gap between the target cost and estimated cost, the design of the car will be further modified.

After repeating this process a number of times, the final blueprint is drawn up and turned over to the production department. In the first several months of production, the target costs ordinarily will not be achieved due to problems in getting a new model into production. However, after that initial period, target costs are compared to actual costs and discrepancies between the two are investigated with the aim of eliminating them and achieving target costs.

Source: Yasuhiro Monden and Kazuki Hamada, "Target Costing and Kaizen Costing in Japanese Automobile Companies," *Journal of Management Accounting Research* 3, pp. 16–34.

Reasons for Using Target Costing

The target costing approach was developed in recognition of two important characteristics of markets and costs. The first is that many companies have less control over price than they would like to think. The market (i.e., supply and demand) really determines price, and a company that attempts to ignore this does so at its peril. Therefore, the anticipated

[7] It may be *impossible* to break even using an absorption costing approach when the company has more than one product—even when it would be possible to make substantial profits using the economists' approach to pricing. For details, see Eric Noreen and David Burgstahler, "Full Cost Pricing and the Illusion of Satisficing," *Journal of Management Accounting Research,* 9 (1997).

market price is taken as a given in target costing. The second observation is that most of the cost of a product is determined in the design stage. Once a product has been designed and has gone into production, not much can be done to significantly reduce its cost. Most of the opportunities to reduce cost come from designing the product so that it is simple to make, uses inexpensive parts, and is robust and reliable. If the company has little control over market price and little control over cost once the product has gone into production, then it follows that the major opportunities for affecting profit come in the design stage where valuable features that customers are willing to pay for can be added and where most of the costs are really determined. So that is where the effort is concentrated—in designing and developing the product. The difference between target costing and other approaches to product development is profound. Instead of designing the product and then finding out how much it costs, the target cost is set first and then the product is designed so that the target cost is attained.

An Example of Target Costing

To provide a simple example of target costing, assume the following situation: Handy Appliance Company feels that there is a market niche for a hand mixer with certain new features. Surveying the features and prices of hand mixers already on the market, the Marketing Department believes that a price of $30 would be about right for the new mixer. At that price, Marketing estimates that 40,000 of the new mixers could be sold annually. To design, develop, and produce these new mixers, an investment of $2,000,000 would be required. The company desires a 15% ROI. Given these data, the target cost to manufacture, sell, distribute, and service one mixer is $22.50 as shown below.

Projected sales (40,000 mixers × $30 per mixer)	$1,200,000
Less desired profit (15% × $2,000,000)	300,000
Target cost for 40,000 mixers	$ 900,000
Target cost per mixer ($900,000 ÷ 40,000 mixers)	$22.50

This $22.50 target cost would be broken down into target costs for the various functions: manufacturing, marketing, distribution, after-sales service, and so on. Each functional area would be responsible for keeping its actual costs within target.

Summary

Pricing involves a delicate balancing act. Higher prices result in more revenue per unit but drive down unit sales. Exactly where to set prices to maximize profit is a difficult problem, but, in general, the markup over cost should be highest for those products where customers are least sensitive to price. The demand for such products is said to be price inelastic.

Managers often rely on cost-plus formulas to set target prices. From the economists' point of view, the cost base for the markup should be variable cost. In contrast, in the absorption costing approach the cost base is the absorption costing unit product cost and the markup is computed to cover both nonmanufacturing costs and to provide an adequate return on investment. With the absorption approach, costs will not be covered and return on investment will not be adequate unless the unit sales forecast used in the cost-plus formula is accurate. If applying the cost-plus formula results in a price that is too high, the unit sales forecast will not be attained.

Some companies take a different approach to pricing. Instead of starting with costs and then determining prices, they start with prices and then determine allowable costs. Companies that use target costing estimate what a new product's market price is likely to be based on its anticipated features and prices of products already on the market. They subtract desired profit from the estimated market price to arrive at the product's target cost. The design and development team is then given the responsibility of ensuring that the actual cost of the new product does not exceed the target cost.

Glossary

Cost-plus pricing A pricing method in which a predetermined markup is applied to a cost base to determine the target selling price. (p. 825)

Markup The difference between the selling price of a product or service and its cost. The markup is usually expressed as a percentage of cost. (p. 825)

Price elasticity of demand A measure of the degree to which the volume of unit sales for a product or service is affected by a change in price. (p. 826)

Target costing The process of determining the maximum allowable cost for a new product and then developing a prototype that can be profitably manufactured and distributed for that maximum target cost figure. (p. 833)

Questions

A–1 What is meant by cost-plus pricing?

A–2 What does the price elasticity of demand measure? What is meant by inelastic demand? What is meant by elastic demand?

A–3 According to the economists' approach to setting prices, the profit-maximizing price should depend on what two factors?

A–4 Which product should have a larger markup over variable cost, a product whose demand is elastic or a product whose demand is inelastic?

A–5 When the absorption costing approach to cost-plus pricing is used, what is the markup supposed to cover?

A–6 What assumption does the absorption costing approach make about how consumers react to prices?

A–7 Discuss the following statement: "Full cost can be viewed as a floor of protection. If a company always sets its prices above full cost, it will never have to worry about operating at a loss."

A–8 What is target costing? How do target costs enter into the pricing decision?

Exercises

EXERCISE A–1 The Economists' Approach to Pricing [LO1]

Maria Lorenzi owns an ice cream stand that she operates during the summer months in West Yellowstone, Montana. Her store caters primarily to tourists passing through town on their way to Yellowstone National Park.

Maria is unsure of how she should price her ice cream cones and has experimented with two prices in successive weeks during the busy August season. The number of people who entered the store was roughly the same each week. During the first week, she priced the cones at $1.89 and 1,500 cones were sold. During the second week, she priced the cones at $1.49 and 2,340 cones were sold. The variable cost of a cone is $0.43 and consists solely of the costs of the ice cream and of the cone itself. The fixed expenses of the ice cream stand are $675 per week.

Required:

1. Did Maria make more money selling the cones for $1.89 or for $1.49?
2. Estimate the price elasticity of demand for the ice cream cones.
3. Estimate the profit-maximizing price for ice cream cones.

EXERCISE A–2 Absorption Costing Approach to Setting a Selling Price [LO2]

Martin Company is considering the introduction of a new product. To determine a selling price, the company has gathered the following information:

Number of units to be produced and sold each year	14,000
Unit product cost	$25
Projected annual selling, general, and administrative expenses	$50,000
Estimated investment required by the company	$750,000
Desired return on investment (ROI)	12%

Required:

The company uses the absorption costing approach to cost-plus pricing.

1. Compute the markup required to achieve the desired ROI.
2. Compute the selling price per unit.

EXERCISE A–3 Target Costing [LO3]

Shimada Products Corporation of Japan is anxious to enter the electronic calculator market. Management believes that in order to be competitive in world markets, the price of the electronic calculator that the company is developing cannot exceed $15. Shimada's required rate of return is 12% on all investments. An investment of $5,000,000 would be required to purchase the equipment needed to produce the 300,000 calculators that management believes can be sold each year at the $15 price.

Required:

Compute the target cost of one calculator.

Problems

PROBLEM A–4 The Economists' Approach to Pricing [LO1]

The postal service of St. Vincent, an island in the West Indies, obtains a significant portion of its revenues from sales of special souvenir sheets to stamp collectors. The souvenir sheets usually contain several high-value St. Vincent stamps depicting a common theme, such as the life of Princess Diana. The souvenir sheets are designed and printed for the postal service by Imperial Printing, a stamp agency service company in the United Kingdom. The souvenir sheets cost the postal service $0.80 each. (The currency in St. Vincent is the East Caribbean dollar.) St. Vincent has been selling these souvenir sheets for $7.00 each and ordinarily sells about 100,000 units. To test the market, the postal service recently priced a new souvenir sheet at $8.00 and sales dropped to 85,000 units.

Required:

1. Does the postal service of St. Vincent make more money selling souvenir sheets for $7.00 each or $8.00 each?
2. Estimate the price elasticity of demand for the souvenir sheets.
3. Estimate the profit-maximizing price for souvenir sheets.
4. If Imperial Printing increases the price it charges to the St. Vincent postal service for souvenir sheets to $1.00 each, how much should the St. Vincent postal service charge its customers for the souvenir sheets?

PROBLEM A–5 Standard Costs; Absorption Costing Approach to Setting Prices [LO2]

Wilderness Products, Inc., has designed a self-inflating sleeping pad for use by backpackers and campers. The following information is available about the new product:

a. An investment of $1,350,000 will be necessary to carry inventories and accounts receivable and to purchase some new equipment needed in the manufacturing process. The company's required rate of return is 24% on all investments.
b. A standard cost card has been prepared for the sleeping pad, as shown below:

	Standard Quantity or Hours	Standard Price or Rate	Standard Cost
Direct materials	4.0 yards	$2.70 per yard	$10.80
Direct labor	2.4 hours	$8.00 per hour	19.20
Manufacturing overhead (⅕ variable)	2.4 hours	$12.50 per hour	30.0
Total standard cost per pad			$60.00

c. The only variable selling, general, and administrative expense will be a sales commission of $9 per pad. Fixed selling, general, and administrative expenses will be (per year):

Salaries	$ 82,000
Warehouse rent	50,000
Advertising and other	600,000
Total	$732,000

d. Since the company manufactures many products, no more than 38,400 direct labor-hours per year can be devoted to production of the new sleeping pads.
e. Manufacturing overhead costs are allocated to products on the basis of direct labor-hours.

Required:

1. Assume that the company uses the absorption approach to cost-plus pricing.
   a. Compute the markup that the company needs on the pads to achieve a 24% return on investment (ROI) if it sells all of the pads it can produce.
   b. Using the markup you have computed, prepare a price quotation sheet for a single sleeping pad.
   c. Assume that the company is able to sell all of the pads that it can produce. Prepare an income statement for the first year of activity and compute the company's ROI for the year on the pads.
2. After marketing the sleeping pads for several years, the company is experiencing a falloff in demand due to an economic recession. A large retail outlet will make a bulk purchase of pads if its label is sewn in and if an acceptable price can be worked out. What is the minimum acceptable price for this special order?

PROBLEM A–6 Target Costing [LO3]

National Restaurant Supply, Inc., sells restaurant equipment and supplies throughout most of the United States. Management is considering adding a machine that makes sorbet to its line of ice cream making machines. Management will negotiate the price of the sorbet machine with its Swedish manufacturer.

Management of National Restaurant Supply believes the sorbet machine can be sold to its customers in the United States for $4,950. At that price, annual sales of the sorbet machine should be 100 units. If the sorbet machine is added to National Restaurant Supply's product lines, the company will have to invest $600,000 in inventories and special warehouse fixtures. The variable cost of selling the sorbet machines would be $650 per machine.

Required:

1. If National Restaurant Supply requires a 15% return on investment (ROI), what is the maximum amount the company would be willing to pay the Swedish manufacturer for the sorbet machines?
2. The manager who is flying to Sweden to negotiate the purchase price of the machines would like to know how the purchase price of the machines would affect National Restaurant Supply's ROI. Construct a chart that shows National Restaurant Supply's ROI as a function of the purchase price of the sorbet machine. Put the purchase price on the *X*-axis and the resulting ROI on the *Y*-axis. Plot the ROI for purchase prices between $3,000 and $4,000 per machine.
3. After many hours of negotiations, management has concluded that the Swedish manufacturer is unwilling to sell the sorbet machine at a low enough price so that National Restaurant Supply is able to earn its 15% required ROI. Apart from simply giving up on the idea of adding the sorbet machine to National Restaurant Supply's product lines, what could management do?

PROBLEM A–7 The Economists' Approach to Pricing; Absorption Costing Approach to Cost-Plus Pricing [LO1, LO2]

Software Solutions, Inc., was started by two young software engineers to market SpamBlocker, a software application they had written that screens incoming e-mail messages and eliminates unsolicited mass mailings. Sales of the software have been good at 50,000 units a month, but the company has been losing money as shown below:

Sales (50,000 units × $25 per unit)	$1,250,000
Variable cost (50,000 units × $6 per unit)	300,000
Contribution margin	950,000
Fixed expenses	960,000
Net operating income (loss)	$ (10,000)

The company's only variable cost is the $6 fee it pays to another company to reproduce the software on floppy diskettes, print manuals, and package the result in an attractive box for sale to consumers. Monthly fixed selling, general, and administrative expenses are $960,000.

The company's marketing manager has been arguing for some time that the software is priced too high. She estimates that every 5% decrease in price will yield an 8% increase in unit sales. The marketing manager would like your help in preparing a presentation to the company's owners concerning the pricing issue.

Required:

1. To help the marketing manager prepare for her presentation, she has asked you to fill in the blanks in the following table. The selling prices in the table were computed by successively decreasing the selling price by 5%. The estimated unit sales were computed by successively increasing the unit sales by 8%. For example, $23.75 is 5% less than $25.00 and 54,000 units is 8% more than 50,000 units.

Selling Price	Estimated Unit Sales	Sales	Variable Cost	Fixed Expenses	Net Operating Income
$25.00	50,000	$1,250,000	$300,000	$960,000	$(10,000)
$23.75	54,000	$1,282,500	$324,000	$960,000	$ (1,500)
$22.56	58,320	?	?	?	?
$21.43	62,986	?	?	?	?
$20.36	68,025	?	?	?	?
$19.34	73,467	?	?	?	?
$18.37	79,344	?	?	?	?
$17.45	85,692	?	?	?	?
$16.58	92,547	?	?	?	?
$15.75	99,951	?	?	?	?

2. Using the data from the table, construct a chart that shows the net operating income as a function of the selling price. Put the selling price on the *X*-axis and the net operating income on the *Y*-axis. Using the chart, determine the approximate selling price at which net operating income is maximized.
3. Compute the price elasticity of demand for the SpamBlocker software. Based on this calculation, what is the profit-maximizing price?
4. The owners have invested $2,000,000 in the company and feel that they should be earning at least 2% per month on these funds. If the absorption costing approach to pricing were used, what would be the target selling price based on the current sales of 50,000 units? What do you think would happen to the net operating income of the company if this price were charged?
5. If the owners of the company are dissatisfied with the net operating income and return on investment at the selling price you computed in (3) above, should they increase the selling price? Explain.

Check Figure
(2b) Selling price: $150

PROBLEM A-8 Missing Data; Markup Computations: Return on Investment (ROI); Pricing [LO2]

South Seas Products, Inc., has designed a new surfboard to replace its old surfboard line. Because of the unique design of the new surfboard, the company anticipates that it will be able to sell all the boards that it can produce. On this basis, the following incomplete budgeted income statement for the first year of activity is available:

Sales (? boards at ? per board)	$?
Less cost of goods sold (? boards at ? per board)	1,600,000
Gross margin	?
Less selling, general, and administrative expenses	1,130,000
Net operating income	$?

Additional information on the new surfboard follows:

a. An investment of $1,500,000 will be necessary to carry inventories and accounts receivable and to purchase some new equipment. The company's required rate of return is 18% on all investments.

b. A partially completed standard cost card for the new surfboard follows:

	Standard Quantity or Hours	Standard Price or Rate	Standard Cost
Direct materials	6 feet	$4.50 per foot	$27
Direct labor	2 hours	? per hour	?
Manufacturing overhead	?	? per hour	?
Total standard cost per surfboard			$?

c. The company will employ 20 workers to make the new surfboards. Each will work a 40-hour week, 50 weeks a year.

d. Other information relating to production and costs follows:

Variable manufacturing overhead cost (per board)	$5
Variable selling expense (per board)	$10
Fixed manufacturing overhead cost (total)	$600,000
Fixed selling, general, and administrative expense (total)	?
Number of boards produced and sold (per year)	?

e. Overhead costs are allocated to production on the basis of direct labor-hours.

Required:

1. Complete the standard cost card for a single surfboard.
2. Assume that the company uses the absorption costing approach to cost-plus pricing.
   a. Compute the markup that the company needs on the surfboards to achieve an 18% return on investment (ROI).
   b. Using the markup you have computed, prepare a price quotation sheet for a single surfboard.
   c. Assume, as stated, that the company is able to sell all of the surfboards that it can produce. Complete the income statement for the first year of activity, and then compute the company's ROI for the year.
3. Assuming that direct labor is a variable cost, how many units would the company have to sell at the price you computed in (2) above to achieve the 18% ROI? How many units would have to be sold to just break even?

Appendix

B

Profitability Analysis

LEARNING OBJECTIVES

After studying this appendix, you should be able to:

LO1 Compute the profitability index and use it to select from among segments.

LO2 Compute and use the profitability index in volume trade-off decisions.

LO3 Compute and use the profitability index in other business decisions.

Introduction

Perhaps more than any other information, managers would like to know the profitability of their products, customers, and other business segments. They want this information so that they know what segments to drop and add and which to emphasize. This appendix provides a coherent framework for measuring profitability, bringing together relevant materials from several chapters. After studying this appendix you should have a firm grasp of the principles underlying profitability analysis.

The first step is to distinguish between absolute profitability and relative profitability.

IN BUSINESS

TRIMMING THE PRODUCT LINE

A large pharmaceutical company eliminated 20% of its products, despite protests from the marketing department. This resulted in a 5% reduction in sales, but a 60% increase in net profits. Why? The products that were dropped were *absolutely* unprofitable. The company was better off simply dropping them.

Source: Tim Allen, "Are Your Products Profitable?" *Strategic Finance*, March 2002, pp. 33–37.

Absolute Profitability

Absolute profitability measures the impact on the organization's overall profits of adding or dropping a particular segment such as a product or customer—without making any other changes. For example, if Coca-Cola were considering closing down its operations in the African country of Zimbabwe, managers would be interested in the absolute profitability of those operations. Measuring the absolute profitability of an existing segment is conceptually straightforward—compare the revenues that would be lost from dropping the segment to the costs that would be avoided. When considering a new potential segment, compare the additional revenues from adding the segment to the additional costs that would be incurred. In each case, include only the additional costs that would actually be avoided or incurred. All other costs are irrelevant and should be ignored.

In practice, figuring out what costs would change and what costs would not change if a segment were dropped (or added) can be very difficult. Activity-based costing can help in identifying such costs, but the analyst must still examine all costs very carefully to determine whether they would really change. For example, an activity-based costing study of Coca-Cola's Zimbabwe operations might include charges for staff support provided to the Zimbabwe operations by Coca-Cola's corporate headquarters in Atlanta. However, if eliminating the Zimbabwe operations would have no impact on actual costs in Atlanta, then these costs are not relevant and should be excluded when measuring the absolute profitability of the Zimbabwe operations.

For examples of the measurement of absolute profitability see the sections "Decentralization and Segment Reporting" in Chapter 12 and "Adding and Dropping Product Lines and Other Segments" in Chapter 13.

IN BUSINESS

SHIFTING THE EMPHASIS

Ford has decided to reduce its market share in the rental-car market and increase its productive capacity and sales efforts in the police-car market. Why? Ford believes that the police-car business is *relatively* more profitable than the rental-car business.

Source: Russ Barnham, "The Right Price," *CFO*, October 2003, pp. 66–72.

Relative Profitability

Even when every segment is *absolutely* profitable, managers often want to know which segments are most and least profitable. **Relative profitability** is concerned with ranking products, customers, and other business segments to determine which should be emphasized.

LEARNING OBJECTIVE 1
Compute the profitability index and use it to select from among segments.

Why are managers interested in ranking segments or determining the relative profitability of segments? The answer to this deceptively simple question provides the key to measuring relative profitability. The only reason to rank segments is if something forces you to make trade-offs among them. If trade-offs are not necessary, the solution is simple—keep every segment that is absolutely profitable. What would force a manager to make trade-offs among profitable segments? There is only one answer—a *constraint* (also called a *bottleneck*). In the absence of a constraint, all segments that are absolutely profitable should be pursued. On the other hand, if a constraint is present, then by definition the company cannot pursue every profitable opportunity. Choices have to be made. Thus, measuring relative profitability makes sense only when a constraint exists that forces trade-offs. This point cannot be overemphasized; constraints are fundamental to understanding and measuring relative profitability.

How should relative profitability be measured? Start with each segment's measure of absolute profitability, which is the incremental profit from that segment. Then, divide this amount by the amount of the constraint required by the segment. For example, refer to the data below for two of many segments within a company:

	Segment A	Segment B
Incremental profit	$100,000	$200,000
Amount of constrained resource required	100 hours	400 hours

Segment B may seem more attractive than Segment A since its incremental profit is twice as large, but it requires four times as much of the constrained resource. In fact, Segment B would not be the best use of the constrained resource. This is because Segment B generates only $500 of incremental profit per hour ($200,000 ÷ 400 hours), whereas Segment A generates $1,000 of incremental profit per hour ($100,000 ÷ 100 hours). Another way to look at this is to suppose that 400 hours of the constrained resource are available. Would you rather use the hours on four segments like Segment A, generating a total incremental profit of $400,000, or on one segment like Segment B, which generates $200,000 in incremental profit?

In general, the relative profitability of segments should be measured by the **profitability index** as defined below:

$$\text{Profitability index} = \frac{\text{Incremental profit from the segment}}{\text{Amount of the constrained resource required by the segment}}$$

The profitability index is computed below for the two segments in the example:

	Segment A	Segment B
Incremental profit (a)	$100,000	$200,000
Amount of constrained resource required (b)	100 hours	400 hours
Profitability index (a) ÷ (b)	$1,000 per hour	$500 per hour

We have already encountered several examples of the profitability index in previous chapters. For example, in Chapter 14 the project profitability index was defined as:

$$\text{Project profitability index} = \frac{\text{Net present value of the project}}{\text{Amount of investment required by the project}}$$

The project profitability index is used when a company has more long-term projects with positive net present values than it can fund. In this case, the incremental profit from the segment is the net present value of the project. And since the investment funds are the constraint, the amount of the constrained resource required by the segment is the amount of investment required by the project.

As an example of the use of the profitability index, consider the case of Quality Kitchen Design, a small company specializing in designing kitchens for upscale homes. Management is considering the 10 short-term projects listed in Panel A of Exhibit B–1.

EXHIBIT B–1
Ranking Segments Based on the Profitability Index

Panel A: Computation of the Profitability Index

	Incremental Profit (A)	Amount of the Constrained Resource Required (B)	Profitability Index (A) ÷ (B)
Project A	$9,180	17 hours	$540 per hour
Project B	$7,200	9 hours	$800 per hour
Project C	$7,040	16 hours	$440 per hour
Project D	$5,680	8 hours	$710 per hour
Project E	$5,330	13 hours	$410 per hour
Project F	$4,280	4 hours	$1,070 per hour
Project G	$4,160	13 hours	$320 per hour
Project H	$3,720	12 hours	$310 per hour
Project I	$3,650	5 hours	$730 per hour
Project J	$2,940	3 hours	$980 per hour
		100 hours	

Panel B: Ranking Based on the Profitability Index

	Profitability Index	Amount of the Constrained Resource Required	Cumulative Amount of the Constrained Resource Used
Project F	$1,070 per hour	4 hours	4 hours
Project J	$980 per hour	3 hours	7 hours
Project B	$800 per hour	9 hours	16 hours
Project I	$730 per hour	5 hours	21 hours
Project D	$710 per hour	8 hours	29 hours
Project A	$540 per hour	17 hours	46 hours
Project C	$440 per hour	16 hours	62 hours
Project E	$410 per hour	13 hours	75 hours
Project G	$320 per hour	13 hours	88 hours
Project H	$310 per hour	12 hours	100 hours

Panel C: The Optimal Plan

	Incremental Profit
Project F	$ 4,280
Project J	2,940
Project B	7,200
Project I	3,650
Project D	5,680
Project A	9,180
	$32,930

The incremental profit from each project is listed in the second column. For example, the incremental profit from Project A is $9,180. This incremental profit consists of the revenues from the project less any costs that would be incurred by the company as a consequence of accepting the project. The company's constraint is the lead designer's time. Project A would require 17 hours of the lead designer's time. If all of the projects were accepted, they would require a total of 100 hours. Unfortunately, only 46 hours are available. Consequently, management will have to turn down some projects. The profitability index will be used in deciding which projects to accept and which to turn down. The profitability index for a project is computed by dividing its incremental profit by the amount of the lead designer's time required for the project. In the case of Project A, the profitability index is $540 per hour.

The projects are ranked in order of the profitability index in Panel B of Exhibit B–1. The last column in that panel shows the cumulative amount of the constrained resource (i.e., lead designer's time) required to do the projects at that point in the list and higher. For example, the 7 hours listed to the right of Project J in the cumulative column represents the sum of the 4 hours required for Project F plus the 3 hours required for Project J.

To find the best combination of projects within the limits of the constrained resource, go down the list in Panel B to the point where all of the available constrained resource is used. In this case, since 46 hours of lead designer time are available, that would be the point above the solid line drawn in Panel B of Exhibit B–1. Projects F, J, B, I, D, and A lie above that line and would require a total of exactly 46 hours of lead designer time. The optimal plan consists of accepting these six projects and turning down the others. The total incremental profit from accepting these projects would be $32,930 as shown in Panel C of Exhibit B–1. No other feasible combination of projects would yield a higher total incremental profit.[1]

We should reinforce a very important point that may be forgotten in the midst of these details. The profitability index is based on *incremental* profit. When computing the incremental profit for a segment such as a product, customer, or project, only the *incremental* costs of the segment should be included. Those are the costs that could be avoided—whether fixed or variable—if the segment is eliminated. All other costs are not relevant and should be ignored—including allocations of common costs.

Volume Trade-Off Decisions

LEARNING OBJECTIVE 2
Compute and use the profitability index in volume trade-off decisions.

Earlier we stated that you have already encountered several examples of the profitability index in this book. One was the project profitability index of Chapter 14. The other example of the profitability index is in the section "Utilization of a Constrained Resource" in Chapter 13. That section deals with the situation in which a company does not have enough capacity to satisfy demand for all of its products. In that situation, the company must produce less than the market demands of some products. This is called a volume trade-off decision because the decision, at the margin, consists of trading off units of one product for units of another. Fixed costs are typically unaffected by such decisions—capacity will be fully utilized, it is just a question of how it will be utilized. In volume trade-off decisions where fixed costs are irrelevant, the profitability index takes the special form:

$$\frac{\text{Profitability index for a}}{\text{volume trade-off decision}} = \frac{\text{Unit contribution margin}}{\text{Amount of the constrained resource required by one unit}}$$

This profitability index is identical to the "contribution margin per unit of the constrained resource" that was used in Chapter 13 to decide which products should be emphasized. An example of a volume trade-off decision is presented in Exhibit B–2. In this example, the company makes three products that use the constrained resource—a machine that is available 2,200 minutes per week. As shown in Panel B of Exhibit B–2, producing all three products up to demand would require 2,700 minutes per week—500 more minutes than are available. Consequently, the company cannot fully satisfy demand for these three products and some product or products must be cut back.

The profitability index for this decision is computed in Panel C of Exhibit B–2. For example, the profitability index for product RX200 is $3 per minute. The comparable figure

[1] In this example, the top projects exactly consumed all of the available constrained resource. That won't always happen. For example, assume that only 45 hours of lead designer time are available. This small change complicates matters considerably. Because of the "lumpiness" of the projects, the optimal plan isn't necessarily to do projects F, J, B, I, and D—stopping at Project D on the list and a cumulative requirement of 29 hours. That would leave 16 hours of unused lead designer time. The best use of this time may be Project C, which has an incremental profit of $7,040. However, other possibilities exist too. Finding and evaluating all of the most likely possibilities can take a lot of time and ingenuity. When the constrained resource is not completely exhausted by the top projects on the list, some tinkering with the solution may be necessary. For this reason, the list generated by ranking based on the profitability index should be viewed as a starting point rather than as a definitive solution when the projects are "lumpy" and take big chunks of the constrained resource.

EXHIBIT B–2
Using the Profitability Index in a Volume Trade-Off Decision

Panel A: Product Data

	RX200	VB30	SQ500
Unit contribution margin	$15 per unit	$10 per unit	$16 per unit
Demand per week	300 units	400 units	100 units
Amount of the constrained resource required	5 minutes per unit	2 minutes per unit	4 minutes per unit

Panel B: Total Demand on the Constrained Resource

	RX200	VB30	SQ500	Total
Demand per week (a)	300 units	400 units	100 units	
Amount of the constrained resource required (b)	5 minutes per unit	2 minutes per unit	4 minutes per unit	
Total amount of the constraint required per week to meet demand (a) × (b)	1,500 minutes	800 minutes	400 minutes	2,700 minutes

Panel C: Computation of the Profitability Index

	RX200	VB30	SQ500
Unit contribution margin (a)	$15 per unit	$10 per unit	$16 per unit
Amount of the constrained resource required (b)	5 minutes per unit	2 minutes per unit	4 minutes per unit
Profitability index (contribution margin per unit of the constrained resource) (a) ÷ (b)	$3 per minute	$5 per minute	$4 per minute

Panel D: The Optimal Plan

Amount of constrained resource available	2,200 minutes
Less: Constrained resource required for production of 400 units of VB30	800 minutes
Remaining constrained resource available	1,400 minutes
Less: Constrained resource required for production of 100 units of SQ500	400 minutes
Remaining constrained resource available	1,000 minutes
Less: Constrained resource required for production of 200 units of RX200*	1,000 minutes
Remaining constrained resource available	0 minutes

*1,000 minutes available ÷ 5 minutes per unit of RX200 = 200 units of RX200.

Panel E: The Total Contribution Margin under the Optimal Plan

	RX200	VB30	SQ500	Total
Unit contribution margin (a)	$15 per unit	$10 per unit	$16 per unit	
Optimal production plan (b)	200 units	400 units	100 units	
Contribution margin (a) × (b)	$3,000	$4,000	$1,600	$8,600

for product VB30 is $5 per minute and for product SQ500 is $4 per minute. Consequently, the correct ranking of the products is VB30 followed by SQ500, then followed by RX200.

The optimal production plan is laid out in Panel D of Exhibit B–2. The most profitable products, VB30 and SQ500, are produced up to demand and the remaining time on the constraint is used to make 200 units of RX200 (1,000 available minutes ÷ 5 minutes per unit).

The total contribution margin from following this plan is computed in Panel E of Exhibit B–2. The total contribution margin of $8,600 is higher than the contribution margin that could be realized from following any other plan that fully utilizes the constrained resource. Assuming that fixed costs are not affected by the decision of which products to emphasize, this plan will also yield a higher total profit than any other plan that fully utilizes the constrained resource.

Managerial Implications

LEARNING OBJECTIVE 3
Compute and use the profitability index in other business decisions.

In addition to the add-or-drop and volume trade-off decisions discussed above, the profitability index can be used in other ways. For example, which products would you rather have your salespersons emphasize—those with a low profitability index or those with a high profitability index? The answer is, of course, that salespersons should be encouraged to emphasize sales of the products with the highest profitability indexes. However, if salespersons are paid commissions based on sales, what products will they try to sell? The selling prices of products RX200, VB30, and SQ500 appear below:

	Products		
	RX200	VB30	SQ500
Unit selling price	$40	$30	$35

If salespersons are paid a commission based on gross sales, they will prefer to sell product RX200, which has the highest selling price. But that is the *least* profitable product given the current constraint. It has a profitability index of only $3 per minute compared to $5 per minute for VB30 and $4 per minute for SQ500.

This suggests that salespersons should be paid commissions based on the profitability index and the amount of constraint time sold rather than on sales revenue. This would encourage them to sell the most profitable products, rather than the products with the highest selling prices. How would such a compensation system work? Prior to making a sales call, a salesperson would receive an up-to-date report indicating how much of the constrained resource is currently available and a listing of all products showing the amount of the constraint each requires and the profitability index. Such a report is presented below:

Marketing Data Report

	Products		
	RX200	VB30	SQ500
Unit selling price	$40	$30	$35
Unit variable cost	25	20	19
Unit contribution margin (a)	$15	$10	$16
Amount of the constrained resource required (b)	5 minutes per unit	2 minutes per unit	4 minutes per unit
Profitability index (a) ÷ (b)	$3 per minute	$5 per minute	$4 per minute

Total available time on the constrained resource: 100 minutes

The key here is to realize that the salesperson is really selling time on the constraint. A salesperson who is paid based on the profitability index will prefer to sell product VB30 since the salesperson would get credit for sales of $500 if all 100 minutes are used on product VB30 ($5 per minute × 100 minutes), whereas the credit would be only $300 for product RX200 or $400 for product SQ500.[2]

The profitability index also has implications for pricing new products. Suppose that the company has designed a new product, WR6000, whose variable cost is $30 per unit and that requires 6 minutes of the constrained resource per unit. What is the minimum price that should be charged for this new product? The answer is the price of the new

[2] Equivalent incentives would be provided by commissions based on total contribution margin. If all 100 available minutes are used to make product VB30, 50 units could be produced (100 minutes ÷ 2 minutes per unit), for which the total contribution margin would be $500 ($10 per unit × 50 units). Likewise, the total contribution margin for product RX200 would be $300, and the total contribution margin would be $400 for product SQ500 if all available minutes were used to make just those products.

product should *at least cover* both the $30 variable cost of producing it *plus* the opportunity cost of displacing the production of existing products to make it. Since the company is currently using all of its capacity, the new product would necessarily displace production of existing products. If the new product is launched, production of RX200 should be cut first since its profitability index of $3 per minute is less than the other two existing products. We call RX200 the *marginal product* because at the margin it is the product that would be cut back. The opportunity cost of using the constrained resource is thus $3 per minute, the profitability index of the marginal product RX200. The price of the new product should *at least cover* both the variable cost of producing that product *plus* the opportunity cost of making it:[3]

$$\begin{array}{c}\text{Selling price of}\\\text{new product}\end{array} \geq \begin{array}{c}\text{Variable cost of}\\\text{the new product}\end{array} + \left(\begin{array}{c}\text{Opportunity}\\\text{cost per unit of}\\\text{the constrained}\\\text{resource}\end{array} \times \begin{array}{c}\text{Amount of the}\\\text{constrained resource}\\\text{required by a unit of}\\\text{the new product}\end{array}\right)$$

In the case of the new product WR6000, the calculations would be:

$$\begin{array}{c}\text{Selling price of}\\\text{WR6000}\end{array} \geq \$30 + (\$3 \text{ per minute} \times 6 \text{ minutes}) = \$30 + \$18 = \$48$$

WR6000 should sell for at least $48 or the company would be better off continuing to use the available capacity to produce RX200.[4]

IN BUSINESS

DEALING WITH UNPROFITABLE CUSTOMERS

One retailer discovered that many of the biggest spending customers in their "loyalty" program were unprofitable because they bought only sale items and returned lots of items. The company stopped sending these customers notices of upcoming "private" sales.

Source: Larry Selden and Geoffrey Colvin, "Will this Customer Sink Your Stock?" *Fortune*, September 30, 2002 pp. 127–132.

Summary

A strong distinction should be made between absolute profitability and relative profitability. A segment is considered profitable in an absolute sense if dropping it would result in lower overall profits. Absolute profitability is measured by the segment's incremental profit, which is the difference between the revenues from the segment and the costs that could be avoided by dropping the segment.

A relative profitability measure is used to rank segments. Such rankings are necessary only if a constraint forces the organization to make trade-offs among segments. To appropriately measure relative profitability, three things must be known. First, the constraint must be identified. Second, the incremental profit associated with each segment must be computed. Third, the amount of the constrained resource required by each segment must be determined. Relative profitability is determined by the profitability index, which is the incremental profit from the segment divided by the amount of the constrained resource required by the segment. The profitability index can be used in a variety of situations, including selections of projects and volume trade-off decisions.

3 In addition, the selling price of a new product should cover any avoidable fixed costs of the product. This is easier said than done, however, since achieving this goal involves estimating how many units will be sold—which in turn depends on the selling price.

4 If production of WR6000 eventually completely displaces production of RX200, the opportunity cost would change. It would increase to $4 per minute, the profitability index of the next product in line to be cut back.

Glossary

Absolute profitability The impact on the organization's overall profits of adding or dropping a particular segment such as a product or customer—without making any other changes. (p. 841)

Profitability index The measure of relative profitability, which is computed by dividing the incremental profit from a segment by the amount of the constrained resource required by the segment. (p. 842)

Relative profitability A ranking of products, customers, or other business segments for purposes of making trade-offs among segments. This is necessary when a constraint exists. (p. 841)

Questions

B–1 What is meant by *absolute* profitability?

B–2 What is meant by *relative* profitability?

B–3 A successful owner of a small business stated: "We have the best technology, the best products, and the best people in the world. We have no constraints." Do you agree?

B–4 What information is needed to measure the *absolute* profitability of a segment?

B–5 What information is needed to measure the *relative* profitability of a product?

B–6 How should the relative profitability of products be determined in a volume trade-off decision?

B–7 What costs should be covered by the selling price of a new product?

Exercises

EXERCISE B–1 Ranking Projects Based on the Profitability Index [LO1]

MidWest Amusements is in the process of reviewing 10 proposals for new rides at its theme parks in cities scattered throughout the American heartland. The company's only experienced safety engineer must carefully review plans and monitor the construction of all new rides. However, she is only available to work on new rides for 1,590 hours during the year. The net present values and the amount of safety engineer time required for the proposed rides are listed below:

Proposed Ride	Net Present Value	Safety Engineer Time Required (hours)
Ride 1	$1,268,200	340
Ride 2	1,152,000	360
Ride 3	649,600	320
Ride 4	644,100	190
Ride 5	540,000	250
Ride 6	539,200	160
Ride 7	462,000	110
Ride 8	457,200	360
Ride 9	403,200	180
Ride 10	387,500	250
Total	$6,503,000	2,520

Required:

1. Which of the proposed rides should the company build this year? (Note: The incremental profit of a long-term project such as constructing a new ride is its net present value.)
2. What would be the total net present value of the rides built under your plan?

EXERCISE B–2 Volume Trade-Off Decision [LO2]

Heritage Watercraft makes reproductions of classic wooden boats. The bottleneck in the production process is fitting wooden planks to build up the curved sections of the hull. This process requires the attention of the shop's most experienced craftsman. A total of 1,800 hours is available per year in this bottleneck operation. Data concerning the company's four products appear below:

	Adirondack	Lake Huron	Oysterman	Voyageur
Unit contribution margin	$485	$268	$385	$600
Annual demand (units)	80	120	100	140
Hours required in the bottleneck operation per unit	5	4	7	8

No fixed costs could be avoided by modifying how many units are produced of any product or even by dropping any one of the products.

Required:

1. Is there sufficient capacity in the bottleneck operation to satisfy demand for all products?
2. What is the optimal production plan for the year?
3. What would be the total contribution margin for the optimal production plan you have proposed?

EXERCISE B–3 Pricing a New Product [LO3]

Seattle's Top Coffee owns and operates a chain of popular coffee stands that serve over 30 different coffee-based beverages. The constraint at the coffee stands is the amount of time required to fill an order, which can be considerable for the more complex beverages. Sales are often lost because customers leave after seeing a long waiting line to place an order. Careful analysis of the company's existing products has revealed that the opportunity cost of order filling time is $2.70 per minute.

The company is considering introducing a new product, praline cappuccino, to be made with pecan extract and molasses. The variable cost of the standard size praline cappuccino would be $0.30 and the time required to fill an order for the beverage would be 40 seconds.

Required:

What is the minimum acceptable selling price for the new praline cappuccino product?

Problems

PROBLEM B–4 Customer Profitability and Managerial Decisions [LO1, LO3]

Advanced Pharmaceuticals, Inc., is a wholesale distributor of prescription drugs to independent retail and hospital-based pharmacies. Management believes that top-notch customer representatives are the key factor in determining whether the company will be successful in the future. Customer representatives serve as the company's liaison with customers—helping pharmacies monitor their stocks, delivering drugs when customer stocks run low, and providing up-to-date information on drugs from many different companies. Customer representatives must be ultra-reliable and are highly trained. Good customer representatives are hard to come by and are not easily replaced.

Customer representatives routinely record the amount of time they spend serving each pharmacy. This time includes travel time to and from the company's central warehouse as well as time spent replenishing stocks, dealing with complaints, answering questions about drugs, informing pharmacists of the latest developments and newest products, reviewing bills, explaining procedures, and so on. Some pharmacies require more hand-holding and attention than others and consequently they consume more of the representatives' time.

Recently, customer representatives have made more frequent complaints that it is impossible to do their jobs without working excessive overtime hours. This has led to an alarming increase in the number of customer representatives quitting for jobs in other organizations. As a consequence, management is considering dropping some customers to reduce the workload on customer representatives. Data concerning a representative sample of the company's customers appears below:

	Leafcrest Pharmacy	Providence Hospital Pharmacy	Madison Clinic Pharmacy	Jenkins Pharmacy
Total revenues	$272,650	$2,948,720	$1,454,880	$155,280
Cost of drugs sold	$211,470	$2,234,480	$1,119,440	$115,920
Customer service costs	$10,640	$74,400	$42,000	$4,480
Customer representative time	190	1,240	560	80

Customer service costs include all of the costs—other than the costs of the drugs themselves—that could be avoided by dropping the customer. These costs include the hourly wages of the customer representatives, their sales commissions, the mileage-related costs of the customer representatives' company-provided vehicles, and so on.

Required:
1. Rank the four customers in terms of their profitability.
2. Customer representatives are currently paid $25 per hour plus a commission of 1% of sales revenues. If these four pharmacies are indeed representative of the company's customers, could the company afford to pay its customer representatives more in order to retain them?

PROBLEM B–5 Volume Trade-Off Decision; Managing the Constraint [LO2, LO3]
Sammamish Brick, Inc., manufactures bricks using clay deposits on the company's property. Raw clays are blended and then extruded into molds to form unfired bricks. The unfired bricks are then stacked onto movable metal platforms and rolled into the kiln where they are fired until dry. The dried bricks are then packaged and shipped to retail outlets and contractors. The bottleneck in the production process is the kiln, which is available for 2,000 hours per year. Data concerning the company's four main products appear below. Products are sold by the pallet.

	Traditional Brick	Textured Facing	Cinder Block	Roman Brick
Gross revenue per pallet	$756	$1,356	$589	$857
Contribution margin per pallet	$472	$632	$376	$440
Annual demand (pallets)	90	110	100	120
Hours required in the kiln per pallet	8	8	4	5

No fixed costs could be avoided by modifying how much is produced of any product.

Required:
1. Is there sufficient capacity in the kiln to satisfy demand for all products?
2. What is the production plan for the year that would maximize the company's profit?
3. What would be the total contribution margin for the production plan you have proposed?
4. The kiln could be operated for more than 2,000 hours per year by running it after normal working hours. Up to how much per hour should the company be willing to pay in overtime wages, energy costs, and other incremental costs to operate the kiln additional hours?
5. The company is considering introducing a new product, glazed Venetian bricks, whose variable cost would be $820 per pallet and that would require 10 hours in the kiln per pallet. What is the minimum acceptable selling price for this new product?
6. Salespersons are currently paid a commission of 5% of gross revenues. Will this motivate the salespersons to make the right choices concerning which products to sell most aggressively?

PROBLEM B–6 Ranking Alternatives and Managing with a Constraint [LO1, LO3]
Luxus Baking Company has developed a reputation for producing superb, one-of-a-kind wedding cakes in addition to its normal fare of breads and pastries. While the wedding cake business is a major moneymaker, it creates some problems for the bakery's owner, Kari Therau, particularly in June. The company's reputation for wedding cakes is largely based on the skills of Regina Yesterman, who decorates all of the cakes. Unfortunately, last year the company accepted too many cake orders for some June weekends, with the result that Regina was worked to a frazzle and almost quit. To prevent a recurrence, Kari has promised Regina that she will not have to work more than 27 hours in any week to prepare the wedding cakes for the upcoming weekend. (Regina also has other duties at the bakery, so even with the 27-hour limitation, she would be working more than full-time in June.)

A number of reservations for wedding cakes for the first weekend in June had already been received from customers by early May. When a customer makes a reservation, Ms. Therau gets enough information concerning the size of the wedding party and the desires of the customer to determine the cake's price, the cost to make it, and the amount of time that Regina will need to spend decorating it. The reservations for the first weekend in June are listed below:

Customer	Incremental Profit	Regina's Time Required (hours)
Afonso	$ 195	5
Carloni	259	7
Cullins	105	3
Frese	170	5
Gerst	117	3
Jelovich	124	4
Klarr	192	6
Melby	144	4
Rideau	150	5
Towner	256	8
Total	$1,712	50

For example, the Afonso cake would require 5 hours of Regina's time and would generate a profit of $195 for the bakery. Following industry practice, pricing for the cakes is based on their size and standard formulas and does not reflect how much decorating would be required.

Required:

1. Ms. Therau feels that she must cancel enough cake reservations to reduce Regina's workload to the promised level. She knows that customers whose reservations have been cancelled will be disappointed, but she intends to refer all of those customers to an excellent bakery across town. If the sole objective is to maximize the company's total profit, which reservations should be cancelled?
2. What would be the total profit if your recommendation in part (1) above is followed?
3. Assume that for competitive reasons it would not be practical for Luxus Bakery to change the pricing of its wedding cakes. What recommendations would you make to Ms. Therau concerning taking reservations in the future?
4. Assume that Luxus Bakery could change the way it prices its wedding cakes. What recommendations would you make to Ms. Therau concerning how she should set the prices of wedding cakes in the future?
5. What might Ms. Therau be able to do to keep both Regina and her customers happy while increasing her profits? Be creative. (Hint: Review the section on managing constraints in Chapter 13.)

PROBLEM B–7 Interpreting Practice [LO1]

In practice, many organizations measure the relative profitability of their segments by dividing the segments' margins by their revenues. The segment margin for this purpose is the segment's revenue less its fully allocated costs—including allocations of fixed common costs. For example, a hospital might compute the relative profitability of its major segments as follows:

ST. IGNATIUS HOSPITAL
Profitability Report
(in thousands of dollars)

	Emergency Room	Surgery	Acute Care	Total
Revenue	$10,630	$21,470	$18,840	$50,940
Fully allocated cost	10,060	21,090	18,550	49,700
Margin	$ 570	$ 380	$ 290	$ 1,240
Profitability (Margin ÷ Revenue)	5.4%	1.8%	1.5%	2.4%

The hospital's net operating income for this period was $1,240,000.

Required:

1. Evaluate the use of the margin, as defined above, in the numerator of the profitability measure.
2. Evaluate the use of revenue in the denominator of the profitability measure.

Cases

CASE B–8 Redirecting Effort [LO2]

Vectra Corporation recently suffered its fourth straight decline in quarterly earnings—despite a modest increase in sales. Unfortunately, Vectra's industry is highly competitive, so the company is reluctant to increase its prices. However, management believes that profits would improve if the efforts of its sales force were redirected toward the company's most profitable products.

Several years ago Vectra decided that its core competencies were strategy, design, and marketing and that production should be outsourced. Consequently, Vectra subcontracts all of its production.

Vectra's salespersons are paid salaries and commissions. All of the company's salespersons sell the company's full line of products. The commissions are 5% of the revenue generated by a salesperson and average about 60% of a salesperson's total compensation. There has been some discussion of increasing the size of the sales force, but management would rather redirect the efforts of salespersons towards the more profitable products. While management is reluctant to tinker with the sales compensation scheme, revenue targets for the various products will be set for the regional sales managers based on the products that management wants to push most aggressively. The regional sales managers will be paid a bonus if the sales targets are met.

The company computes product margins for all of its products using the following formula:

Selling price
Less: Sales commissions
Less: Cost of sales
Less: Operating expenses
Product margin

The cost of sales in the product margin formula is the amount Vectra pays to its production subcontractors. The operating expenses represent fixed costs. Each product is charged a fair share of those costs, calculated this year as 34.6% of the product's selling price.

Management is convinced that the best way to improve overall profits is to redirect the efforts of the company's salespersons. There are no plans to add or drop any products.

Required:

How would you measure the relative profitability of the company's products in this situation? Assume that it is not feasible to change the way salespersons are compensated. Also assume that the only data you have available are the selling price, the sales commissions, the cost of sales, the operating expenses, and the product margin for each product.

Photo Credits

page 4 © Farina Christopher/CORBIS SYGMA
page 15 © Mark Richards/PhotoEdit
page 18 © Ryan McVay/Getty Images
page 24 © Brett Coomer/Getty Images
page 35 © Cindy Charles/PhotoEdit
page 39 AP/Wide World Photos
page 47 © Image 100/Royalty-Free/CORBIS
page 87 Paramount/The Kobal Collection
page 93 © Thinkstock/Getty Images
page 113 © Ryan McVay/Getty Images
page 145 © Richard Hutchings
page 147 © Bruce Ayers/Getty Images
page 183 Copyright, Knight Ridder/Tribune Media Services. Reprinted with permission.
page 186 © Rob Melnychuk/Getty Images
page 189 Courtesy of Sandee Noreen
page 197 Courtesy of Sandee Noreen
page 229 Courtesy of Joie de Vivre Hospitality
page 243 Martin A. Levick
page 245 AP/Wide World Photos
page 250 © Brownie Harris/CORBIS
page 275 © Brooks Kraft/CORBIS
page 287 AP/Wide World Photos
page 291 © Sacha Orlov/Getty Images
page 313 © Bob Daemmrich/PhotoEdit
page 315 © Gabriel M. Covian/Getty Images
page 321 © Christie's Images/CORBIS
page 336 © Chris Whitehead/Getty Images
page 377 Walt Disney Productions/PHOTOFEST
page 380 © Tony Freeman/PhotoEdit
page 384 © Rob Melnychuk/Getty Images
page 396 Courtesy of BNSF
page 427 Universal Pictures/Getty Images
page 428 © Cleve Bryant/PhotoEdit
page 441 © Rita Maas/Getty Images
page 454 © Tom Stewart/CORBIS
page 491 © Digital Vision/Getty Images
page 497 Courtesy of Peter F. Drucker
page 502 © Don Farrall/Getty Images
page 539 © Bruce Ayres/Getty Images
page 551 Courtesy of Great Harvest Franchising, Inc.
page 555 © Photodisc/Getty Images/Royalty-Free
page 560 © Tony Freeman/PhotoEdit
page 601 © Ryan McVay/Getty Images
page 612 AP/Wide World Photos
page 616 Courtesy of Eric Noreen
page 653 © Justin Sullivan/Getty Images
page 655 Courtesy of Eric Noreen
page 672 Courtesy of Rocky Mountain Institute
page 717 © Helen King/CORBIS
page 720 AP/Wide World Photos
page 731 © Image 100/Royalty-Free/CORBIS
page 749 © Ronnie Kaufman/CORBIS
page 756 © Photodisc Blue/Getty Images
page 765 © Ryan McVay/Getty Images
page 787 © Jack Hollingsworth/Getty Images

Index

Aanonsen/Hodges, Jill, 189
ABC. *See* Activity-based costing (ABC)
Abdallah, Wagdy M., 574
ABM, 335–336
Absolute profitability, 841
Absorption costing, 88
basic idea, 276, 277
changes in production, 284–288
cross-country comparison, 291
CVP analysis, 289–290
decision making, 290
external reporting, 290, 291
fixed manufacturing overhead cost deferred in inventory, 278
income, 278–280, 280–284
income statement, 279
JIT, 292
manager, impact on, 288–289
unit cost computations, 277–278
Absorption costing approach to cost-plus pricing, 830–833
Accenture, 36
Account analysis, 196
Accounts receivable turnover, 800, 803
Acid-test ratio, 799, 803
Action analysis report, 342–348
Activity, 317
Activity base, 185
Activity-based costing (ABC), 96, 312–375
action analysis report, 342–348
activity, defined, 317
assign costs to activity cost pools, 324–326
assign costs to cost objects, 328–330
basic principles, 315
calculate activity rates, 327–328
defined, 314
departmental overhead rate, 316–317
external reporting, 337
first-stage allocation, 325
flexible budget, 502
identity activities/activity cost pools, 320–323
idle capacity, 317
implementation, 320
limitations, 338
management reports, 330
manufacturing costs, 315–317
nonmanufacturing costs, 315
plantwide overhead rate, 315–316
process improvements, 335–336
public sector, 314
relevant costs, 625
second-stage allocation, 328
Activity-based costing (ABC)–*Cont.*
segmented reporting, 548–549
trace overhead costs, 323–324
traditional cost system, compared, 330–333
variations in practice, 314
Activity-based management (ABM), 335–336
Activity cost pool, 322
Activity measure, 322
Adding/dropping product lines, 609–613
Adelphia Communications, 20
Administrative costs, 38
Advanced Micro Devices (AMD), 448
Aeppel, Timothy, 832
After-tax benefit, 692
After-tax cost, 691
Alcoa, 3
Alger, Mike, 620
Allied Signal, 15, 452
Allocation base, 93
Allstate Insurance Company, 448, 718
Almanac of Business and Industrial Financial Ratios, 804
AMA Annual Statement Studies, 804
Amazon.com, 654, 752
AMD, 448
American Airlines, 20
American Express, 16, 314
Analog Devices, 448
Analysis of financial statements. *See* Financial statement analysis
Andersen Windows, 113
Anderson, Terry L., 826
Annuity, 683
Anthony, Robert N., 829
Antitrust laws, 825n
Apple Computer, 448
Appraisal costs, 61
Arizona Diamondbacks, 247
Arkes, Hal, 53
Armstrong Holdings, 564
Arnold, Glen C., 677
art.com, 321
Arthur Andersen, 20
Association of Neurological Surgeons, 314
AT&T, 16, 48, 448, 564
AT&T Power Systems, 554
Auto service centers, 430
Average collection period, 800, 803
Average sale period, 801, 803
Avery Dennison, 621
Avoidable cost, 602, 603
Baan, 19
Bailes, Jack, 676
Balachandran, Bala V., 337
Balance sheet, 41, 400, 401
Balance sheet equation, 751
Balanced scorecard, 448–458
characteristics, 450–452
compensation, and, 454
corporate strategy, 453–454
defined, 449
France, 449n
performance measures, 451, 456–458
ROI, 560–561
timely/graphic feedback, 454–455
Baldwin Technology, 564
Ban Boredom, 454
Bandyopadhyay, P. K., 66
Banham, Russ, 11, 402
Bank of America, 4, 313
Bank of Montreal, 448
Bar code technology, 112–113
Barnett, Donald F., 184
Barnham, Russ, 841
Basic equation for inventory accounts, 42
Batch, 89
Batch-level activities, 321
Batman, 87
Bausch & Lomb, 562
Baxendale, Sidney J., 333
Baxter International, 18
Beach, Cynthia, 11
Bear Sterns, 757
Bechtel International, 89, 555
Bell, Jim, 380
Benchmarking, 16
Bernasek, Anna, 186
Berner, Robert, 653
Bernstein, Jerry, 832
Bertch Cabinet Mfg., 338
Best Buy, 562
Bethlehem Steel, 621
Beverage Can Americas Co., 456
Big Dig project (Boston), 555
Bill of materials, 90, 433
Binney & Smith, 621
Black and Decker, 15
Blocher, Edward, 315
Blockbuster Video, 49
BMW, 452
Body Shop, 450
Boeing, 89, 344n, 492, 548, 621, 717
Böer, Germain, 37n, 316n, 608
Boesen, Thomas, 385
Bogus Basin, 826

Boise-Cascade, 562
Bombardier, 655
Book value per share, 797–798, 803
Borealis, 385
Borg-Warner, 15
Bose, 15
Bossidy, Larry, 452
Boston Consulting Group, 40
Boston Lyric Opera, 448
Bottleneck, 17, 619, 842
Bowen, Robert M., 290n
Brackner, James W., 92, 554
Bradford Soap Works, 93
Brady, Diane, 542
Brandenhausen, Kurt, 671
Brannigan, Martha, 287
Brannigan, Martin, 606
Break-even computations, 239–241, 248–250
Break-even point, 232
Brethauer, Cindy, 657
Brewer, Peter, 549
Bridgeport Hospital and Healthcare Services, 448
Briley, Steve, 551
Brimelow, Peter, 38
Brooker, Katrina, 387
Brown, Herbert E., 13n
Brown, Mark Graham, 452
Brust, Robert, 248
Budget, 5, 378
Budget committee, 384
Budget padding, 382
Budget period, 380
Budget variance, 506–507
Budgetary control, 378
Budgeted balance sheet, 400, 401
Budgeted income statement, 399, 400
Budgeting, 376–425
- advantages, 378–379
- automating the process, 402
- basic framework, 378–385
- budget committee, 384
- budget padding, 382
- budget period, 380
- budgeted balance sheet, 400, 401
- budgeted income statement, 399, 400
- cash budget, 386, 396–399
- continuous budget, 380
- direct labor budget, 393–394
- direct materials budget, 391–393
- ending finished goods inventory budget, 395
- flexible budget. *See* Flexible budget
- human factors, 382–383, 384
- international aspects, 402
- manufacturing overhead budget, 394–395
- master budget, 378, 385
- master budget interrelationships, 386
- merchandise purchases budget, 391

Budgeting—*Cont.*
- politics of, 385
- production budget, 390–391
- sales budget, 385–386, 389–390
- sales forecast, 386–387
- self-imposed budget, 381–382
- selling and administrative expense budget, 395–396
- static budget, 492–494
- zero-based budgeting, 383–384

Buena Vista Visual Effects, 427
Bugs, 64
Burd, Steven, 653
Burgstahler, David, 833n
Burlinghan, Bo, 428
Burlington Northern Santa Fe (BNSF), 396
Burrock, Rick, 787
Burton-Houle, Tracey, 18
Business environment, 12–20
Business process, 16
Byrne, John A., 25

Cadillac Motor Car, 16
Caggiano, Christopher, 191
Calabro, Lori, 454n
Cambridge Hospital Community Health Network, 314
Campbell, Dennis, 454
Campbell Soup, 50
Canon, 14
Capital budgeting, 654
Capital budgeting decisions, 652–714
- future value tables, 687–688
- income taxes, 691–695
- incremental-cost approach, 665–666
- inflation, 684–686
- internal rate of return method, 661–663, 669
- least-cost decisions, 666–667
- net present value method, 655–660, 663, 670
- payback method, 671–674
- postaudit, 676–677
- postponement of investment, 668–669
- preference decisions, 669–670
- present value, 681–684
- present value tables, 689–690
- project profitability index, 670
- real options analysis, 669
- simple rate of return method, 674–676
- time value of money, 654–655
- total-cost approach, 663–665
- types, 654
- uncertain cash flows, 667–669

Carey, Susan, 245
Carley, William M., 59
Carmona, Salvador, 433
Carrier Corporation, 314
Carter, Larry, 3
Casey, Robert W., 61
Cash budget, 386, 396–399
Cash equivalents, 750
Cash flow statement. *See* Statement of cash flows
Castellano, Joseph R., 441
Caterpillar, Inc., 502
Center for Financial Research & Analysis, 757
CEO, 9
Certified management accountant (CMA), 27
CFO, 11
Chaffman, Beth M., 539
Chain of command, 9
Chambers, John, 3
Champion International, 621
Chaplin, Heather, 183
Charan, Ram, 452
Chief executive officer (CEO), 9
Chief financial officer (CFO), 11
Chrysler, 15
Cigarettes, 826
CIGNA Corporation, 448
Cisco Systems, 3
Citigroup, 797
City of Charlotte, 449
City of Indianapolis, 314
Clearing account, 101
CM ratio, 235
CMA, 27
Coburn, Steve, 336
Coca-Cola, 4, 88, 562, 798, 841
Code of conduct
- company, 24–25
- IMA, 22–23
- international level, 26

Colangelo, Jerry, 247
Columbia Pictures, 112
Colvin, Geoffrey, 21, 847
Committed fixed costs, 190–191, 193
Common cost, 51
Common fixed costs, 548, 550, 554–555
Common-size financial statement, 789–793
Company codes of conduct, 24–25
Compaq Computer, 37, 833
Comparative financial statements, 789
Competence, 22
Compound interest, 681
Conair-Franklin, 448
Confidentiality, 22
Conley, Chip, 229
Connelly, Jed, 289
Constrained resource, 618–621
Constraint, 17, 618, 842
Consumer Reports, 667
Continental Airlines, 552
Continuous budget, 380
Contribution approach, 206, 291
Contribution format income statement, 206–207, 291
Contribution margin, 207, 231–233

Contribution margin method, 240–241
Contribution margin ratio (CM ratio), 235
Control, 5, 378
Controller, 5
Controlling, 5–6
Conversion cost, 37, 153
Cooper, Robin, 314, 316n, 317, 551
Copeland, Tom, 665
Coppertone, 146
Corning, 16
Corporate Angel Network, 52
Corvette, 452
Cost
  administrative, 38
  appraisal, 61
  avoidable, 602
  committed fixed, 190–191
  common, 51
  common fixed, 548
  conversion, 37
  curvilinear, 188
  decremental, 51
  differential, 51, 603
  direct, 50
  discretionary fixed, 191
  failure, 62
  fixed, 49–50, 188–194
  incremental, 51
  indirect, 50
  inspection, 61
  inventoriable, 39
  joint, 622
  labor, 37, 58–59
  manufacturing, 36–38
  marginal, 51
  marketing or selling, 38
  nonmanufacturing, 38
  opportunity, 52–53, 615–616
  period, 39
  prevention, 60–61
  prime, 38
  product, 38–39
  quality, 59–63
  relevant, 602, 603
  SG&A, 38
  step-variable, 188
  sunk, 53, 603
  traceable fixed, 548
  value-added, 37
  variable, 48–49, 184–188
Cost behavior, 48
Cost behavior: analysis and use, 182–227
  account analysis, 196
  contribution format income statement, 206–207
  engineering approach, 196
  fixed costs, 188–194
  high-low method, 201–204
  Japanese manufacturing companies, 195
Cost behavior: analysis and use—*Cont.*
  least-squares regression method, 204–206, 210–212
  linear cost behavior, 200
  mixed costs, 194
  multiple regression analysis, 206
  quick-and-dirty method, 198–201
  relevant range, 188
  scattergraph plot, 198–201
  variable costs, 184–188
Cost center, 541, 543
Cost classifications, 47
Cost driver, 96, 185
Cost object, 50
Cost of capital, 659
Cost of goods manufactured, 43
Cost of goods sold, 43
Cost of quality, 59–63
Cost-plus pricing, 825
Cost reconciliation, 156–157
Cost reduction decisions, 654
Cost (price) standards, 429
Cost structure, 184, 244–245
Cost-volume-profit (CVP) analysis, 228–273
  absorption costing, 289–290
  assumptions, 250–251
  break-even computations, 239–241, 248–250
  CM ratio, 235
  contribution margin, 231–233
  contribution margin method, 240–241
  cost structure, 244–245
  CVP graph, 233–234
  equation method, 239–240
  fixed cost, sales price, sales volume, 237–238
  fixed costs/sales volume, 236–237
  margin of safety, 242–243
  operating leverage, 246–247
  regular sales price, 239
  sales commissions, 247–248
  sales mix, 248–250
  target profit analysis, 241–242
  variable cost, fixed cost, sales volume, 238
  variable cost/sales volume, 237
Cost-volume-profit (CVP) graph, 233–234
Cox, Jeff, 443n
Crandall, Robert W., 184
Credit Suisse First Boston, 562, 797
Cruise ship operators, 606
Culp, 833
Cummins Engine, 833
Current ratio, 798–799, 803
Curtin, Margaret, 608
Curvilinear cost, 188, 189
Customer-level activities, 322
CVP analysis. *See* Cost-volume-profit (CVP) analysis
CVP graph, 233–234
Cycle time, 14
D'Agostino, Mary, 456
Daihatsu Motors, 833
DaimlerChrysler, 654, 833
Dana Corporation, 314
Darling, Bruce L., 324
Daspin, Eileen, 828
Davis, Tim R. V., 324
Debt-to-equity ratio, 802, 803
Decentralization, 9
Decentralized organization, 540–541
Decision making
  adding/dropping product lines, 609–613
  investment decisions. *See* Capital budgeting decisions
  make or buy decision, 613–615
  opportunity cost, 615–616
  relevant *vs.* irrelevant costs, 602–608
  sell or process further decisions, 622–625
  special order, 616–617
  utilization of constrained resource, 618–621
  volume trade-off decisions, 844–845
Decremental cost, 51
Degree of operating leverage, 246
Delivery cycle time, 456
Dell Computer, 429, 793
Delta Airlines, 750
Demand software, 390
DeMeyer, A., 37n
Deming, W. Edwards, 66
DenDanto, Deirdra, 25
Denominator activity, 503–504
Department production report, 147. *See also* Production report
Departmental overhead rate, 316–317
Dependent variable, 198
Depreciation tax shield, 692
Desheh, Eyal, 572
Deutsche Bank, 797
Dialysis Clinic, 314
Diamond Courier, 319
Diamond Transportation Group, Inc., 319
Differential cost, 51, 603
Differential revenue, 51
Dillon, Karen, 229
Diluted earnings per share, 794n
Direct cost, 50
Direct costing, 276. *See also* Variable costing
Direct exchange transactions, 759
Direct labor, 37
Direct labor budget, 393–394
Direct labor-hours (DLH), 93
Direct labor standards, 433–434
Direct labor variances, 441–443, 463
Direct materials, 36–37
Direct materials budget, 391–393
Direct materials standards, 432–433
Direct materials variances, 436–441, 462–463

Direct method, 720–721, 758, 771–772
Directing and motivating, 5
Discount rate, 662, 683
Discounted cash flows
  internal rate of return method, 661–663
  net present value method, 655–660, 663
Discounted value, 681
Discounting, 683
Discretionary fixed costs, 191, 192
Disney Company, 36, 377, 548, 750
Disney World, 492, 548
Disposing of old equipment, 657
Dividend payout ratio, 795, 803
Dividend yield ratio, 795, 803
Divisional autonomy, 573
DLH, 93
Docks Restaurant, 828
Doebele, Justin, 797
Donnelly, George, 185, 749
Dornbusch, Victoria, 333
Dropping product lines, 609–613
Drucker, Peter F., 193, 497, 546
Duke Children's Hospital, 448
Dun & Bradstreet, 16, 562
Dunlap, "Chainsaw" Al, 25, 287
DuPont, 36, 37, 557
Duration driver, 322
Dutta, Soumitra, 428n
Dynergy, Inc., 765

E-commerce, 19–20
Earnings per share, 794, 803
Ease of adjustment code, 344, 346
Economic value added (EVA), 562–564
EDGAR, 802, 804
EDI, 112
Efficiency variance
  labor, 442–443
  variable overhead, 444, 500–501
E.I. du Pont de Nemours and Company, 557
Elasticity of demand, 826–827
Electronic data interchange (EDI), 112
Elevating the constraint, 620
Elf Atochem, 448
Eli Lilly, 562
Emergency room (Cook County General Hospital), 197
Emerson Electric, 832
Emore, James R., 555n
Employee health benefits, 613
Employee time ticket, 92
Ending finished goods inventory budget, 395
Engel, Ross, 87
Engineering approach, 197
Enron, 20, 21, 765
Enthoven, Adolf J. H., 291
Environmental costs, 608
Environmental Protection Agency (EPA), 657
Epstein, Marc, 449
Equation method, 239–240
Equipment replacement decisions, 654
Equipment selection decisions, 654
Equivalent units, 152
Equivalent units of production
  FIFO method, 163, 164
  weighted-average method, 152
Ericsson, 16
Ethics. *See* Professional ethics
eToys, 242
Euclid Engineering, 317
EVA, 562–564
Excel, 210–212
Expansion decisions, 654
External failure costs, 62
External reporting
  ABC, 337
  absorption costing, 290, 291
  international trends, 291
  segmented financial information, 552
Exxon, 146
Ezzamel, Mahmoud, 433

Factory burden, 37
Factory overhead, 37
Failure costs, 62
Fast-food outlets, 430
Federated Mogul, 562
FedEx (Federal Express), 16, 335, 429
Feedback, 5
Feil, David, 719
Ferguson, Tim W., 191, 825
FIFO method, 162–168
  equivalent units, 163, 164
  production report, 165–167
  weighted-average method, compared, 163–165, 167–168
Filterfresh, 186
Financial accounting, 4, 6–9
Financial leverage, 796–797, 803
Financial ratios, 794–804. *See also* Ratio analysis
Financial statement analysis, 786–823
  common-size statements, 789–793
  gross margin percentage, 792–793
  horizontal analysis, 789
  limitations, 788
  ratio analysis, 794–804. *See also* Ratio analysis
  trend percentages, 789
  vertical analysis, 789–790
Financial statements
  balance sheet, 41, 400, 401
  common-size, 789–793
  comparative, 789
  income statement. *See* Income statement
  statement of cash flows. *See* Statement of cash flows
Financing activities, 757, 764
Finished goods, 13, 41
Fink, Ronald, 383
Firestone, 430
1st Choice Bank, 657
First National Bank of Chicago, 16
First-stage allocation, 325
Fixed cost, 49–50
Fixed manufacturing overhead cost deferred in inventory, 278
Fixed manufacturing overhead cost released from inventory, 284
Fixed overhead analysis, 502–509
Fixed overhead budget variance, 506–507
Fixed overhead variances, 505–508
Fixed overhead volume variance, 506, 507–508
Flexible budget
  ABC, 502
  defined, 492
  how it works, 494–495
  overhead budget, 498
  overhead rates, 502–505
  performance evaluation, 495–496
Flexible budget performance report, 496
Florida Power and Light, 16, 186
FMC, 448
Focused factory, 14
Ford, Henry, 84
Ford Motor Company, 15, 36, 186, 621, 833, 841
Forecasts, 382–387
Foreign Corrupt Practices Act, 26
Forest product companies, 676
Foroohar, Kambiz, 335n
Forrest Gump, 87
France, Necia, 731
Francis, Graham, 731
Fraser, Jill Andresky, 787
FreeEdgar, 804
Freeman, Julian, 335n
French, Rick, 464
Frequent flier program, 618
Fringe benefits, 59
Fujitsu, 402
Fukami, Cynthia, 336
Full cost, 88, 276. *See also* Absorption costing
Future value tables, 687–688

GAAP, 9
Gallagher, Leigh, 615
Gap, Inc., 36
GE Medical Systems, 314
General cost classification, 36–38
General Electric (GE), 16, 20, 59
General ledger entries, 462–463
General Mills, 16, 146
General Motors (GM), 15, 250, 542, 548, 621
Generally accepted accounting principles (GAAP), 9
Georgia-Pacific, 562

Georgia Tech, 720
Getty Images, 767
Ghosh, K. K., 66
Gibbs, Helen, 52
Gillette, 275, 387
Gilmartin, Raymond, 11
Global aspects. *See* International aspects
Global competition, 18–19
Global Crossing, 20
Gogoi, Pallavi, 16n, 560
Golding, Catie, 32
Goldratt, Eliyahu M., 443n
Goldsmith, Stephen, 314
Goodness of fit, 205
Goodyear, 15
Gordon, Stephen, 183
Gourville, John, 53
Govindarajan, V., 829
Granlund, Markus, 19
Grant, James, 752
Great Harvest, 551
Greco, Susan, 319
Greed, 26
Greene, Jay, 800
Griffin, Tom, 612
Groom, Winston, 87
Gross cost, 556
Gross margin percentage, 792–793
Group Health Cooperative of Puget Sound, 722
Grove, Hugh, 336
GTE Directories, 16
Guidant Corporation, 562
Guideline on Ethics for Professional Accountants, 26
Gutiérrez, Fernando, 433

H & R Block, 192
Haedicke, Jack, 719
Hallmark, 89, 314
Hamada, Kazuki, 833
Harper Ferry Company, 664
Harris, Franco, 324
Harris, Megan, 145
Harris Corporation, 549
Hart, Christopher W. L., 59n
Harvard, 671
Harvard Medical School Hospital, 196
Hassan, Nabil, 13n
Hatzopoulus, Panos D., 677
HealthSouth, 20
Henaxi, John J., 113
Hershey Foods, 562
Heskett, James L., 59n
Hewlett-Packard (HP), 718
High-low method, 201–204
Hilsenrath, Jon E., 40
Hodges, David, 189
Holmes, Neil, 32
Holstein, William J., 14
Hoover's Online, 804
Hopkins, Michael, 551
Horizontal analysis, 789
Hospice of Central Kentucky (HCK), 333
Hospital Corporation of America, 16
House of Fabrics, 185
Housing Authority of Fiji, 448
Hoyt, Louis, 608
HP, 718
HSBC, 797
HTML, 112
Hughes Aircraft, 15, 719
Hunstman Corp., 380
Hunt, Tom, 396
Hurdle rate, 662
Husky Injection Molding, 562
Hyatt Hotel, 540
Hyperinflation, 402

Ibex Outdoor Clothing, 756
IBM, 16
Ideal standards, 431
Idle capacity, 317
Idle time, 58
Ikawa, Bruce, 87
Income statement, 42
  absorption costing, 279
  budgeted, 399, 400
  segmented, 543–547
  variable costing, 279
Income tax, 691–695
Income tax code, 691
Incremental analysis, 237
Incremental cost, 51, 603
Incremental-cost approach, 665–666
Indalex Aluminum Solutions Group, 620
Independent variable, 198
Indirect cost, 50
Indirect labor, 37
Indirect manufacturing cost, 37
Indirect materials, 37
Indirect method, 758
Industrie Natuzzi SpA, 434
Industry Norms & Key Business Ratios, 804
Inflation, 402, 684–686
Innes, John, 339
Inoue, Shin'ichi, 447n
Inspection costs, 61
Inspection time, 456
Integrity, 20, 22
Intel, 15
Interdepartmental services, 719
Interest, 681
Intermediate product, 622
Intermountain Healthcare, 16
Internal failure costs, 62
Internal rate of return, 661
Internal rate of return method, 661–663, 669
International aspects
  absorption costing, 291
  budgeting, 402
  codes of conduct, 26
  quality, 66–67
  transfer pricing, 571–572
International competition, 18–19
Inventoriable costs, 39, 45–46
Inventory, 13
Inventory turnover, 800–801, 803
Investing activities, 757, 764
Investment center, 542, 543
Investment decisions. *See* Capital budgeting decisions
Ipswitch, Inc., 676
ISO 9000 standards, 67
Isuzu Motors, 833
ITT Automotive, 314, 621, 833
Iverson, Kenneth, 184

J.C. Penney, 562
J. K. Gill, 187
Jackson, Jess Stonestreet, 825
Jackson Hole Llamas, 189
Jaguar, 452, 453
Japanese manufacturing companies, 195
Jensen, Michael C., 16n, 384
Jenson, Richard L., 92, 554
JetBlue, 245
Jeter, Debra, 37n
JIT, 12–15, 61, 292, 560
Job, 89
Job cost sheet, 91, 95
Job-order costing, 86–142
  allocation base for overhead cost, 96
  application of manufacturing overhead, 101–102
  cost of goods manufactured, 103
  cost of goods sold, 103–104
  direct labor cost, 91–93
  direct materials cost, 90–91
  flow of costs, 98–104, 111
  flow of documents, 97
  job cost sheet, 91
  labor cost, 99–100
  manufacturing overhead, 93–95
  manufacturing overhead costs, 100–101
  multiple predetermined overhead rates, 110–111
  nonmanufacturing costs, 102–103
  overhead application, 104–111
  overview, 89–96
  predetermined overhead rate and capacity, 117–118
  process costing, compared, 146–147
  purchase/issue of materials, 98–99
  service companies, 111
  under/overapplied overhead, 104–110
  unit costs, 96
John Deere, 15
Johnsen, David, 430

Johnson & Johnson, 16
Joie de Vivre Hospitality, 229
Joint cost, 622
Joint product, 622
Jones, Lou F., 502
Jorgensen, Bjorn, 385
Joseph, Yau Shiu Wing, 280
JP Morgan Chase, 448
Judge, Paul C., 313
Jurassic Park, 427
Just-in-time (JIT), 12–15, 61, 292, 560

Kafka, Peter, 240
Kahn, Jeremy, 24
Kansas City Power & Light, 562
Kaplan, Robert S., 314, 316n, 317, 449, 454, 456, 458, 551, 572
Karafil, Brad and Carole, 197, 616, 655
Karpoff, Jonathan, 21
Kelleher, Herb, 192
Keller, Steven, 615
Keller Design, 615
Kellner, Larry, 552
Kellogg, 146
Kelly, Erin, 242
Kelson, Richard, 3
Kendall-Jackson (K-J) winery, 825
Kentucky Fried Chicken, 36
Keough, Don, 24
Kilts, Jim, 387
King, Alfred, 344n
King, Jeanne, 542
Kinney, Michael R., 560
Klammer, Thomas, 113n
KLM Royal Dutch Airlines, 16
Knight, Joe, 428
Kodak, 248
Kohli, Farooq C., 337
Komatsu, 833
Koretz, Gene, 826
Koumoutzis, Nick, 13n
Kozlowski, Dennis, 542
KPMG, 448
Kroger, 192, 548
Kroll, Karen N., 676
Kublank, David R., 321

L. L. Bean, 654
Labbett, John, 185
Labor costs, 37, 58–59, 192
Labor efficiency variance, 442–443
Labor fringe benefits, 59
Labor rate variance, 441–442
Labor Ready, 32
Landry, Clay J., 826
Lau, Gloria, 191
Lawrence, Stewart, 731
Lawton, Stephen, 676
Lease or buy decisions, 654
Least-cost decisions, 666–667
Least-squares regression method, 204–206, 210–212
Lebas, Michel, 449
Lee, John Y., 722
Leibs, Scott, 456, 561
Leverage, 796–797
Lewent, Judy C., 11
Lilo & Stitch, 377
Line position, 10
Linear cost behavior, 200
Linear programming, 621
Loan applications, 458
London Life Insurance Co., 448
Lovins, Amory, 672
LSG SkyChefs, 89
LTV, 16
Lukka, Kari, 19

MacArthur, John B., 338
MacDonald, Elizabeth, 767
Machine-hours (MH), 93
Machine-hours efficiency variance, 501
Macintosh, Norman B., 19
Mackey, James T., 18, 622
Mahalingam, Maha S., 337
Make or buy decision, 613–615
Making decisions. *See* Decision making
Makris, Philip G., 321
Managed fixed costs, 191
Management by exception, 429, 445–446
Managerial accounting, 4
  certification, 27
  code of conduct, 22–23
  compensation, 27
  financial accounting, compared, 6–9
Managerial activities, 5–6
Manufacturing cell, 14
Manufacturing cycle efficiency (MCE), 457–458
Manufacturing cycle time, 456
Manufacturing overhead, 37
Manufacturing overhead budget, 394–395
Manufacturing overhead standards, 434
Manufacturing overhead variances, 443–444
Manzoni, Jean-François, 428n, 449
Margin, 557
Margin of safety, 242–243
Marginal cost, 51
Marginal costing, 276. *See also* Variable costing
Marginal revenue, 51
Market price, 573
Marketing or selling costs, 38
Markup, 825
Massachusetts Special Olympics, 448
Master budget, 378, 385
Master budget interrelationships, 386
Matching principle, 38
Material requirements planning (MRP), 391
Materials price variance, 438–440
Materials quantity variance, 440–441
Materials requisition form, 90
Matlack, Carol, 560
Matsushita Electric, 833
Maxwell, Jill Hecht, 657
Maxwell Appliance Controls, 314
Mayo Clinic, 49
MBA degree, 671
McCaffrey, Roger, 52
McCormack, Scott, 52
McCuddy, Michael K., 24n
McDonald's, 430, 789, 791, 793
McDonald's France, 560
MCE, 457–458
McKendrick, Joseph, 330
McKinsey, 36
McKittrick, Christopher, 315
McNair, C. J., 113n
McWilliams, Gary, 793
Megan's Classic Cream Soda, 145
Merchandise inventory, 41
Merchandise purchases budget, 391
Merck & Co., 11, 654
Mergent Industrial Manual and Mergent Bank and Finance Manual, 804
Meridien Research, 330
MH, 93
Michelin, 718
Microsoft, 492, 798, 800
Microsoft Excel, 210–212
Milani, Ken, 720
Miller, J., 37n
Milliken & Company, 16
Mission Controls, 191
Mitchell, Falconer, 339
Mitsubishi, 718
Mitsubishi Kasei, 833
Monden, Yasuhiro, 833
Money-losing firms, 87
Monitor Group, 665
Monster Cable, 621
Morais, Richard C., 434
Morrow, Michael, 385
Motorola, 15, 16
Move time, 456
MRP, 391
Mt. Sinai Hospital, 718
Multiple constraints, 621
Multiple predetermined overhead rate, 110–111
Multiple regression, 206
Murphy, James E., III, 720
Myers, Randy, 396

Nagar, Venky, 65
Nakane, J., 37n
National Semiconductor Corp., 402, 621
Nationwide Financial Services, 402

Natuzzi, Pasquale, 434
NEC, 447, 833
Nefcy, Pauline, 722
Ness, Joseph A., 555n
Net book value, 556
Net cash provided by operating activities, 758
Net operating income, 556
Net present value, 655
Net present value method, 655–660, 663, 670
Net profit participation contracts, 87
Nicol, Ron, 40
Nielsen, James, 676
Nippodenso, 833
Nippon Electronics Company (NEC), 447, 833
Nissan, 833
Nissan North America, 289
Non-value-added activities, 16
Nonmanufacturing costs, 38
Nordstrom, 36, 753–755, 762–766
Noreen, Eric W., 18, 290n, 622, 833n
Normal cost system, 94
Nortel Networks (Northern Telecom), 16, 402
Norton, David, 449, 454, 458
Nucor Steel, 184
Nyberg, Alix, 564

Objectivity, 23
Office Depot, 112
O'Hanlon, John, 562n
Ohio State, 671
Olin, 562
Olympus, 833
OMG Center for Collaborative Learning, 504
Onsale, 185
Operating activities, 756–757, 764
Operating assets, 556
Operating department, 718, 727
Operating leverage, 246–247
Operation costing, 159
Opportunity cost, 52–53, 615–616
Oracle, 19
Order-getting and order-filling costs, 38
O'Reilly Auto Parts, 390
Organization chart, 9, 10
Organization-sustaining activities, 322
Organizational structure, 9–12
Ortega, William R., 717
Orwall, Bruce, 377
Oscar Meyer, 88
Out-of-pocket costs, 660
Overapplied overhead, 104–110, 509
Overhead analysis, 492
- actual *vs.* standard hours, 498
- budget variance, 506–507
- denominator activity, 503–504
- fixed overhead analysis, 502–509

Overhead analysis—*Cont.*
- fixed overhead variances, 505–508
- flexible budget, 498, 502–505
- predetermined overhead rate, 504
- under-/overapplied overhead, 509
- variable overhead variances, 443–445, 463, 498–502
- volume variance, 506, 507–508

Overhead application, 94, 117
Overhead efficiency variance, 444, 500–501
Overhead flexible budget, 498
Overhead performance report, 507
Overhead spending variance, 443–444, 500
Overtime premium, 58
Owens & Minor, 336
Owens Corning, 402

Paramount, 36
Parker Brass, 430
Parker Hannifin Corporation, 430
Parsons Brinckerhoff, 555
Participative budget, 381
Pathology lab, 731
Payback method, 671–674
Payback period, 671
Peace Corps, 4
Peasnell, Ken, 562n
Pendergast, Paul, 382
PeopleSoft, 19
PepsiCo., 548
Performance measures, 451, 456–458
Performance report, 6
Period costs, 39
Perpetual budget, 380
Personal budget, 378
Petersen, Steve, 428
Phillips, 16
Pilla, George, 749
Pillsbury, 314
Pizza Hut, 36, 197
Planning, 5, 378
Planning and control cycle, 6, 7
Plantwide overhead rate, 110, 315–316
Porsche, 13
Port, Otis, 64
Post, Claudia, 319
Postaudit, 676–677
Powder-based painting system, 608
Power consumption, 205
Power shortages, 621
Practical standards, 431
Pratt and Whitney Canada, 621
Predatory prices, 825n
Predetermined manufacturing overhead rate, 44
Predetermined overhead rate, 94, 117, 503, 504
Preference decisions, 654, 669–670
Present value, 681–684
Present value tables, 689–690
Prevention cost, 60–61
Price discrimination, 825n
Price-earnings ratio, 794–795, 803
Price elasticity of demand, 826
Price standards, 429
Price variance, 435, 436, 438–440
Pricing, 824–840
- absorption costing approach to cost-plus pricing, 830–833
- antitrust laws, 825n
- cost-plus pricing, 825
- elasticity of demand, 826–827
- markup, 825
- profit-maximizing price, 827–830
- target costing, 833–834

Prime cost, 38
Princess Cruises, 606
Process costing, 88, 144–181
- FIFO method, 162–168
- job-order costing, compared, 146–147
- materials, labor, overhead costs, 148–150
- processing department, 147–148
- weighted-average method, 152–158

Process reengineering, 16–17
Process time, 456
Processing department, 147–148
Product cost flows, 45–47
Product costs, 38–39
Product-level activities, 321–322
Production budget, 390–391
Production order, 90
Production report, 147
- FIFO method, 165–167
- weighted-average method, 153–158

Professional ethics, 20
- company codes of conduct, 24–25
- IMA code of conduct, 22–23

Profit center, 541–542, 543
Profit-maximizing price, 827–830
Profit planning, 378. *See also* Budgeting
Profitability analysis, 841–852
- absolute profitability, 841
- managerial implications, 846–847
- relative profitability, 841–844
- volume trade-off decisions, 844–845

Profitability index, 842
Project profitability index, 670, 842

Quad/Graphics, 613
Quaker Oats, 562
Quality circle, 60
Quality control guidelines, 67
Quality cost, 59–63
Quality cost information, 66
Quality cost report, 63–66
Quality of conformance, 59
Quantity schedule, 155–156
- FIFO method, 165
- weighted-average method, 155–156

Quantity standards, 429
Quantity variance, 435, 437, 440–441
Queue time, 456
Quick-and-dirty method (scattergraph plot), 198–201
Quick ratio, 799

R^2, 205
Rain Man, 87
Rajan, Madhav, 65
Range of acceptable transfer price, 568–569
Ranking decisions, 669
Ratio analysis, 794–804
  common stockholder, 794–798
  long-term creditor, 801–802
  short-term creditor, 798–801
  sources of information, 804
  summary of ratios, 803
Rationing decisions, 669
Raw materials, 13, 41
Raytheon Electronics Systems, 64
Real options, 669
Reason, Tim, 380, 552
Reciprocal method, 722–723
Reciprocal services, 719
Reconciliation method, 758
Red Cross, 4
Reebok, 50
Regression line, 204
Regulatory burden, 193
Reichardt, Karl E., 24n, 27
Reichhold, Inc., 315
Relative profitability, 841–844
Relaxing (elevating) the constraint, 620
Relevant cost, 602, 603, 625
Relevant range, 49, 188, 189, 193
Required rate of return, 662
Residual income, 561–564
Responsibility accounting, 379, 541–543
Responsibility center, 541
Restaurants, 828
Restoration Hardware, 183
Return on common stockholders' equity, 796, 803
Return on investment (ROI), 555–561
  balanced scorecard, 560–561
  criticism of, 561
  defined (formula), 556
  DuPont perspective, 556–557
  JIT, 560
Return on total assets, 795–796, 803
Revell, Janice, 250
Revenue center, 541n
Rexam Pic, 456
Reynolds Aluminum, 88, 146
Richard, Bill, 564
Richtermeyer, Sandra B., 12
Rite Aid, 20
Ritz Carlton Hotel, 16
Robinson, Alan, 61
Rockwater, 448
Rocky Mountain Institute, 672
Roehm, Harper A., 441
ROI, 555–561. *See also* Return on investment (ROI)
Rolling forecasts, 385
Royal Dutch/Shell, 669
Ryan, Glenn P., 677
Ryan, Patricia A., 677

Sacks, Sydney, 731
Safeway, 192, 548, 618, 653
Sales budget, 385–386, 389–390
Sales commissions, 247–248
Sales forecast, 386–387
Sales mix, 248–250
Sanders, Paula M., 13n
Sansoni, Silva, 243
SAP, 19
Sarbanes-Oxley Act, 24
Sasser, W. Earl, Jr., 59n
Scalice, Ray, 427
Scattergraph method of cost analysis, 198–201
Schedule of cost of goods manufactured, 43–44
Schiff, Michael, 290n
Schoenberger, Chana R., 390
Schroeder, David, 24n, 27
Schumacher, Thomas S., 377
Scott Paper, 146
Screening decisions, 654
Sears, 430
Seattle Seahawks, 612
Second-stage allocation, 328
Security measures, 186
Seglin, Jeffrey L., 25
Segment, 8, 543
Segment margin, 550–551
Segmented income statement, 543–547
Segmented reporting, 543–555
  ABC, 548–549
  common fixed costs, 548, 550, 554–555
  omission of costs, 553
  problem areas, 553–555
  segment margin, 550–551
  segmented income statement, 543–547
  traceable fixed costs, 548–550, 554
Selden, Larry, 847
Self-imposed budget, 381–382
Sell or process further decisions, 622–625
Selling, general, and administrative (SG&A) costs, 38
Selling and administrative expense budget, 395–396
Sender, Henny, 765
Senser, Robert A., 92
Service department, 718
Service department costing, 716–746
  actual *vs.* budgeted costs, 724
  allocation base, 718–719, 731–732
Service department costing—*Cont.*
  basic allocation techniques, 725–727
  cautionary notes, 729–732
  cost allocation guidelines, 725
  direct method, 720–721
  example, 728–729
  fixed costs, 723–724, 729–731
  interdepartmental services, 719
  operating departments, 727
  reciprocal method, 722–723
  revenue producing departments, 723
  step method, 721–722
  variable costs, 723
Services companies, job-order costing, 111
Setpoint, 428
Setup, 14
7-Eleven, 4, 36
SG&A costs, 38
Shanghai Bund Steel Works (SBSW), 280
Shank, John K., 61
Sharp, 833
Shell Oil, 429
Shields, Todd, 336
Shim, Eunsup, 829
Shingo, Shigeo, 61
Shirley, Mike, 826
Siegel, Gary, 8, 12
Silicon Valley Bank, 562
Simple rate of return, 674–676
Sinclair, Donald, 339
Skippers restaurant chain, 187
Skousen, Clifford R., 92, 554
Smith, Debra, 18, 622
Smith, Geoffrey, 542
Software bugs, 64
Soman, Dilip, 53
Sony, 429
Sopariwala, Parvez, 430
Sorensen, James E., 12
Southern Gardens Citrus Processing, 448
Southwest Airlines, 192, 429
Spanish Royal Tobacco Factory, 433
Special order, 616–617
Spending variance, 443–444, 500
Split-off point, 622
Springfield Manufacturing, 387
Sprint, 402, 562
Stack, Jack, 387
Staff position, 10
Standard, 429
Standard & Poor's Industry Survey, 804
Standard cost card, 431, 435
Standard cost per unit, 434
Standard cost system, 429
  advantages, 447
  cost flows, 463, 464
  direct labor standards, 433–434
  direct materials standards, 432–433
  ideal *vs.* practical standards, 431
  management by exception, 429

Standard cost system—*Cont.*
manufacturing overhead standards, 434
overhead application, 505
potential problems, 448
standards *vs.* budgets, 435
variable manufacturing overhead standards, 434
variances. *See* Variance analysis
Standard hours allowed, 436, 498
Standard hours per unit, 433
Standard price per unit, 432
Standard quantity allowed, 435–436
Standard quantity per unit, 432
Standard rate per hour, 433
Standards of Ethical Conduct for Practitioners of Management Accounting and Financial Management, 22–23
Statement of cash flows, 748–784
cash, defined, 750
defined, 750
depreciation, depletion, amortization, 766
direct exchange transactions, 759
direct *vs.* indirect method, 758–759, 771–772
financing activities, 757, 764
gross *vs.* net cash flows, 758, 762–763
interpretation of, 765–766
investing activities, 757, 764
noncash balance sheet accounts, 751–753
operating activities, 756–757, 764
simplified statement, 753–755
steps/preparation of statement, 759–760
worksheet, 761–762
Statement of financial position, 41
Static budget, 492–494
Static budget performance report, 494
Statistical control chart, 446
Statistical process control, 61
Steele, William H., 275
Step method, 721–722
Step-variable cost, 188, 194
Stern, Stewart & Co., 562n
Stewart, Thomas A., 3
Stipp, David, 672
Stolle Corporation, 13
Store24, 454
Storyboard, 427
Strupeck, C. David, 720
Suboptimization, 568, 573
Sudit, Ephraim F., 829
Summers, Mary, 247
Sunbeam Corp., 287
Sunk cost, 53, 603
Sunk cost trap, 53
Sunset Grill, 828
Super Bakery, Inc., 324
Surowiecki, James, 20
Sutter Health, 336
Swenson, Dan, 335n
Syfert, Pam, 449
Symonds, William C., 275, 542
System design
job-order costing, 86–142
process costing, 144–181

Tableau de Bord, 449n
Taco Bell, 36, 54
Talbott, John, 539
Tampa Electric Company, 314
Target, 615
Target costing, 833–834
Target profit analysis, 241–242
Tarzan, 377
Tata Consultancy Services (TCS), 337
Tata Iron and Steel Company, 205, 621
Tax code, 691
Taxable cash receipts, 692
Taylor, Alex, III, 289
Technology Recycling LLC, 657
Tektronix, 15
Tempest, Nicole, 456
Tenneco, 448
Teva Pharmaceutical Industries Ltd., 572
Texaco, 402
Texas Eastman Company, 551
Texas Instruments, 16, 36, 833
Theory of constraints (TOC), 17–18, 292
3COM, 448
3M, 16
Throughput time, 14, 456
Time-adjusted rate of return method, 655, 661–663
Time ticket, 92
Time value of money, 654–655
Times interest earned, 801–802, 803
TOC, 292
Total-cost approach, 663–665
Total Quality Management (TQM), 15–16
Touch labor, 37
Tower Records, 36
Towers Perrin, 383
Toyota, 15, 429, 452, 833
Toys R Us, 562
TQM, 15–16
Traceable fixed costs, 548–550, 554
Tracy, Robert, 752
Transaction driver, 322
Transfer price, 568
Transfer pricing, 568–574
ABC-based transfer prices, 572
divisional autonomy, 573
international aspects, 573–574
negotiated transfer price, 568–572
transfers at cost to selling divisions, 572
transfers at market price, 573
Transferred-in costs, 148
Trend analysis, 789
Trend percentages, 789
Tri-Con Global Restaurants, 654
Trinker, Greg, 826
True variable costs, 187, 188
Tuition, 38
Tupperware, 562
Turnover, 557
Tyco International, 20, 542

Underapplied overhead, 104–110, 509
Unit-level activities, 321
United Airlines, 245, 618
United Artists, 36
United Colors of Benetton, 39
United Electric Controls, 92, 621
United States Air Force Logistics Command, 621
U.S. Immigration and Naturalization Service (INS), 314
U.S. income tax code, 691
U.S. Marine Corps, 335
United States Navy Transportation Corps, 621
United States Postal Service, 314, 562
U.S. Veterans Affairs Department, 314
United Way of Southeastern New England, 448
University of Illinois, 4
Upbin, Bruce, 248
US WEST, 335
Utilization of constrained resource, 618–621

Value-added cost, 37
Value chain, 553, 613
Vardi, Nathan, 555
Variable cost, 48–49, 184–188
Variable costing
advantages, 291–292
basic ideas, 276, 277
changes in production, 284–285
external reporting, 290
income, 278–280, 280–284
income statement, 279
JIT, 292
manager, impact on, 288–289
TOC, 292
unit cost computations, 277–278
Variable manufacturing overhead standards, 434
Variable manufacturing overhead variances, 443–445, 463
Variable overhead efficiency variance, 444, 500–501
Variable overhead performance report, 499, 501
Variable overhead spending variance, 443–444, 500
Variable overhead variances, 443–445, 463, 498–502
Variance, 435

Variance analysis
 defined, 435
 direct labor variances, 441–443, 463
 direct materials variances, 436–441, 462–463
 general ledger entries, 462–463
 labor efficiency variance, 442–443
 labor rate variance, 441–442
 management by exception, 445–446
 materials price variance, 438–440
 materials quantity variance, 440–441
 overhead variances. *See* Overhead analysis
 variable manufacturing overhead variances, 443–445, 463
 variable overhead efficiency variance, 444, 500–501
 variable overhead spending variance, 443–444, 500
Variance analysis cycle, 430
Verizon Communications, 448
Verschoor, Curtis C., 47
Vertical analysis, 789–790
Vertical integration, 613
Vesey, Greg, 402
Virtual bakery (Super Bakery), 324
Visual effects, 427
Volume trade-off decisions, 844–845
Volume variance, 506, 507–508
Volvo, 452

W.W. Grainger, 113
W3C, 113
Waikato Hospital, 731
Wal-Mart, 20, 36, 187
Wallace, James S., 564
Walt Disney Company, 36, 377, 548, 750
Water, 826
Weighted-average method, 152–158
 cost reconciliation, 156–157
 costs per equivalent unit, 156
 equivalent units of production, 152
 FIFO method, compared, 163–165, 167–168
 production report, 153–158
 quantity schedule, 155–156
Weisman, Dennis L., 601
Weiss, Dan, 572
Weisul, Kimberly, 613
Wells Fargo, 20
Wells Fargo Online Financial Services, 456
Wempe, William F., 560
Wendy's, 750, 793
Wessel, David, 26
Western Textile Products, 622
Westinghouse, 15
Westinghouse Electric, 16
Weyerhauser, 88
Whistle blowers, 24
White Grizzly Adventures, 197, 616, 655
Who Framed Roger Rabbit?, 87
Wiedeking, Wendelin, 13
Williams, Jerry, 330
Wilson, Ron, 16n
Wing, Kennard T., 504
Woellert, Lorraine, 542
Wong, Betty, 315
Woodruff, David, 13
Woolley, Scott, 50
Work in process, 13, 41
Working capital, 657, 798, 803
World Wide Consortium (W3C), 113
WorldCom, 20
Wright, Bill, 336
Wruck, Karen Hopper, 16n

Xerox, 15, 16
Xilink, 402
XML, 112, 113

Yamada Electric, 61

Zeien, Alfred M., 275
Zeller, Thomas L., 321
Zellner, Wendy, 618
Zero-based budgeting, 383–384
Zero defects, 15
Zhu Rongji, 92
Zion, David, 757